WORLD ERAS

VOLUME 4

MEDIEVAL EUROPE
814 - 1350

WORLD ERAS

VOLUME 4

MEDIEVAL EUROPE
814 - 1350

JEREMIAH HACKETT

A MANLY, INC. BOOK

GALE GROUP

THOMSON LEARNING

Detroit • New York • San Diego • San Francisco
Boston • New Haven, Conn. • Waterville, Maine
London • Munich

WORLD ERAS VOL. 4
MEDIEVAL EUROPE
814-1350

Matthew J. Bruccoli and Richard Layman, *Editorial Directors*

Anthony J. Scotti Jr., *Series Editor*

Library Of Congress Cataloging-in-Publication Data
World Eras vol. 4: Medieval Europe, 814-1350/
    edited by Jeremiah Hackett.
        p. cm.— (World eras; v. 4)
    "A Manly, Inc. book."
    Includes bibliographical references and index.
    ISBN 0-7876-1709-1 (alk. paper)
    1. Europe—History—476–1492.
    2. Middle Ages. 3. Civilization, Medieval. I. Hackett, Jeremiah.
    II. Series.

D102.M38 2001
940.1'4—dc21   2001040737

10 9 8 7 6 5 4 3 2 1

ADVISORY BOARD

For Lilla Hoefer

CONTENTS

CHAPTER 6: POLITICS, LAW, AND THE MILITARY

CHAPTER 7: LEISURE, RECREATION, AND DAILY LIFE

Significant People

Documentary Sources 303

CHAPTER 8: THE FAMILY AND SOCIAL TRENDS

Topics in the Family and Social Trends

ABOUT THE SERIES

PROJECT DESCRIPTION

Patterned after the well-received *American Decades* and *American Eras* series, *World Eras* is a cross-disciplinary reference series. It comprises volumes examining major civilizations that have flourished from antiquity to modern times, with a global perspective and a strong emphasis on daily life and social history. Each volume provides in-depth coverage of one era, focusing on a specific cultural group and its interaction with other peoples of the world. The *World Eras* series is geared toward the needs of high-school students studying subjects in the humanities. Its purpose is to provide students—and general reference users as well—a reliable, engaging reference resource that stimulates their interest, encourages research, and prompts comparison of the lives people led in different parts of the world, in different cultures, and at different times.

The goal of *World Eras* volumes is to enrich the traditional historical study of "kings and battles" with a resource that promotes understanding of daily life and the cultural institutions that affect people's beliefs and behavior.

What kind of work did people in a certain culture perform?

What did they eat?

How did they fight their battles?

What laws did they have and how did they punish criminals?

What were their religious practices?

What did they know of science and medicine?

What kind of art, music, and literature did they enjoy?

These are the types of questions *World Eras* volumes seek to answer.

VOLUME DESIGN

World Eras is designed to facilitate comparative study. Thus volumes employ a consistent ten-chapter structure so that teachers and students can readily access standard topics in various volumes. The chapters in each *World Eras* volume are:

1. World Events
2. Geography

3. The Arts
4. Communication, Transportation, and Exploration
5. Social Class System and the Economy
6. Politics, Law, and the Military
7. Leisure, Recreation, and Daily Life
8. The Family and Social Trends
9. Religion and Philosophy
10. Science, Technology, and Health

World Eras volumes begin with two chapters designed to provide a broad view of the world against which a specific culture can be measured. Chapter 1 provides students today with a means to understand where a certain people stood within our concept of world history. Chapter 2 describes the world from the perspective of the people being studied—what did they know of geography and how did geography and climate affect their lives? The following eight chapters address major aspects of people's lives to provide a sense of what defined their culture. The ten chapters in *World Eras* will remain constant in each volume. Teachers and students seeking to compare religious beliefs in Roman and Greek cultures, for example, can easily locate the information they require by consulting chapter 9 in the appropriate volumes, tapping a rich source for class assignments and research topics. Volume-specific glossaries and a checklist of general references provide students assistance in studying unfamiliar cultures.

CHAPTER CONTENTS

Each chapter in *World Eras* volumes also follows a uniform structure designed to provide users quick access to the information they need. Chapters are arranged into five types of material:

- **Chronology** provides an historical outline of significant events in the subject of the chapter in timeline form.

- **Overview** provides a narrative overview of the chapter topic during the period and discusses the material of the chapter in a global context.

- **Topical Entries** provide focused information in easy-to-read articles about people, places, events, institutions, and matters of general concern to the people of the time. A references rubric includes sources for further study.

- **Biographical Entries** profiles people of enduring significance regarding the subject of the chapter.
- **Documentary Sources** is an annotated checklist of documentary sources from the historical period that are the basis for the information presented in the chapter.

Chapters are supplemented throughout with primary-text sidebars that include interesting short documentary excerpts or anecdotes chosen to illuminate the subject of the chapter: recipes, letters, daily-life accounts, and excerpts from important documents. Each *World Eras* volume includes about 150 illustrations, maps, diagrams, and line drawings linked directly to material discussed in the text. Illustrations are chosen with particular emphasis on daily life.

INDEXING

A general two-level subject index for each volume includes significant terms, subjects, theories, practices, people, organizations, publications, and so forth, mentioned in the text. Index citations with many page references are broken down by subtopic. Illustrations are indicated both in the general index, by use of italicized page numbers, and in a separate illustrations index, which provides a description of each item.

EDITORS AND CONTRIBUTORS

An advisory board of history teachers and librarians has provided valuable advice about the rationale for this series. They have reviewed both series plans and individual volume plans. Each *World Eras* volume is edited by a distinguished specialist in the subject of his or her volume. The editor is responsible for enlisting other scholar-specialists to write each of the chapters in the volume and of assuring the quality of their work. The editorial staff at Manly, Inc., rigorously checks factual information, line edits the manuscript, works with the editor to select illustrations, and produces the books in the series, in cooperation with Gale Group editors.

The *World Eras* series is for students of all ages who seek to enrich their study of world history by examining the many aspects of people's lives in different places during different eras. This series continues Gale's tradition of publishing comprehensive, accurate, and stimulating historical reference works that promote the study of history and culture.

The following timeline, included in every volume of *World Eras*, is provided as a convenience to users seeking a ready chronological context.

TIMELINE

This timeline, compiled by editors at Manly, Inc., is provided as a convenience for students seeking a broad global and historical context for the materials in this volume of World Eras. *It is not intended as a self-contained resource. Students who require a comprehensive chronology of world history should consult sources such as William L. Langer, comp. and ed.,* The New Illustrated Encyclopedia of World History, *2 volumes (New York: Harry N. Abrams, 1975).*

CIRCA 4 MILLION TO 1 MILLION B.C.E.
Era of *Australopithecus,* the first hominid

CIRCA 1.5 MILLION TO 200,000 B.C.E.
Era of *Homo erectus,* "upright-walking human"

CIRCA 1,000,000-10,000 B.C.E.
Paleothic Age: hunters and gatherers make use of stone tools in Eurasia

CIRCA 250,000 B.C.E.
Early evolution of *Homo sapiens,* "consciously thinking humans"

CIRCA 40,000 B.C.E.
Migrations from Siberia to Alaska lead to the first human inhabitation of North and South America

CIRCA 8000 B.C.E.
Neolithic Age: settled agrarian culture begins to develop in Eurasia

5000 B.C.E.
The world population is between 5 million and 20 million

CIRCA 4000-3500 B.C.E.
Earliest Sumerian cities: artificial irrigation leads to increased food supplies and populations in Mesopotamia

CIRCA 3000 B.C.E.
Bronze Age begins in Mesopotamia and Egypt, where bronze is primarily used for making weapons; invention of writing

CIRCA 2900-1150 B.C.E.
Minoan society on Crete: lavish palaces and commercial activity

CIRCA 2700-2200 B.C.E.
Egypt: Old Kingdom and the building of the pyramids

CIRCA 2080-1640 B.C.E.
Egypt: Middle Kingdom plagued by internal strife and invasion by the Hyksos

CIRCA 2000-1200 B.C.E.
Hittites build a powerful empire based in Anatolia (present-day Turkey) by using horse-drawn war chariots

CIRCA 1792-1760 B.C.E.
Old Babylonian Kingdom; one of the oldest extant legal codes is compiled

CIRCA 1766-1122 B.C.E.
Shang Dynasty in China: military expansion, large cities, written language, and introduction of bronze metallurgy

CIRCA 1570-1075 B.C.E.
Egypt: New Kingdom and territorial expansion into Palestine, Lebanon, and Syria

CIRCA 1500 B.C.E.
The Aryans, an Indo-European people from the steppes of present-day Ukraine and southern Russia, expand into northern India

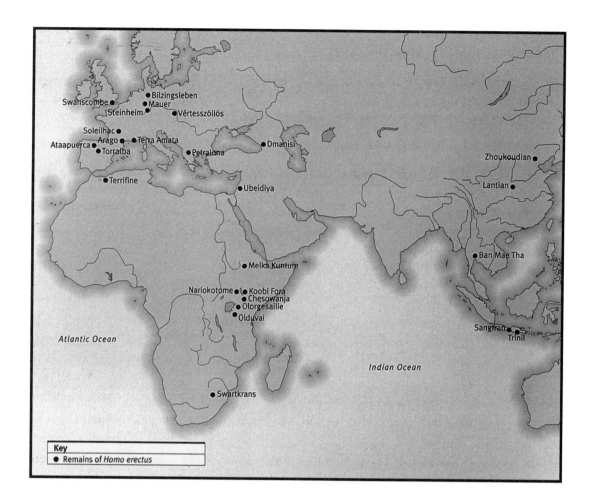

Key
● Remains of *Homo erectus*

CIRCA 1500 B.C.E.
Phoenicians create the first alphabet

CIRCA 1400-1200 B.C.E.
Hittites develop the technology of iron-smelting, improving weaponry and agricultural implements, as well as stimulating trade

CIRCA 1200-800 B.C.E.
Phoenicians establish colonies throughout the Mediterranean

CIRCA 1122- 221 B.C.E.
Zhou Dynasty in China: military conquests, nomadic invasions, and introduction of iron metallurgy

CIRCA 1100-750 B.C.E.
Greek Dark Ages: foreign invasions, civil disturbances, decrease in agricultural production, and population decline

1020-587 B.C.E.
Israelite monarchies consolidate their power in Palestine

CIRCA 1000-612 B.C.E.
Assyrians create an empire encompassing Mesopotamia, Syria, Palestine, and most of Anatolia and Egypt; they deport populations to various regions of the realm

1000 B.C.E.
The world population is approximately 50 million

CIRCA 814-146 B.C.E.
The city-state of Carthage is a powerful commercial and military power in the western Mediterranean

753 B.C.E.
Traditional date of the founding of Rome

CIRCA 750-700 B.C.E.
Rise of the polis, or city-state, in Greece

558-330 B.C.E.
Achaemenid Dynasty establishes the Persian Empire (present-day Iran, Turkey, Afghanistan, and Iraq); satraps rule the various provinces

509 B.C.E.
Roman Republic is established

500 B.C.E.
The world population is approximately 100 million

The ROMAN EMPIRE
before the Barbarian Invasions

CIRCA 400 B.C.E.
Spread of Buddhism in India

338-323 B.C.E.
Macedon, a kingdom in the central Balkan peninsula, conquers the Persian Empire

323-301 B.C.E.
Ptolemaic Kingdom (Egypt), Seleucid Kingdom (Syria), and Antigonid Dynasty (Macedon) are founded

247 B.C.E.-224 C.E.
Parthian Empire (Parthia, Persia, and Babylonia): clan leaders build independent power bases in their satrapies, or provinces

215-168 B.C.E.
Rome establishes hegemony over the Hellenistic world

206 B.C.E. TO 220 C.E.
Han Dynasty in China: imperial expansion into central Asia, centralized government, economic prosperity, and population growth

CIRCA 100 B.C.E.
Tribesmen on the Asian steppes develop the stirrup, which eventually revolutionizes warfare

1 C.E.
The world population is approximately 200 million

CIRCA 100 C.E.
Invention of paper in China

224-651 C.E.
Sasanid Empire (Parthia, Persia, and Babylonia): improved government system, founding of new cities, increased trade, and the introduction of rice and cotton cultivation

340 C.E.
Constantinople becomes the capital of the Eastern Roman, or Byzantine, Empire

CIRCA 320-550 C.E.
Gupta Dynasty in India: Golden Age of Hindu civilization marked by stability and prosperity throughout the subcontinent

395 C.E.
Christianity becomes the official religion of the Roman Empire

CIRCA 400 C.E.
The first unified Japanese state arises and is centered at Yamato on the island of Honshu; Buddhism arrives in Japan by way of Korea

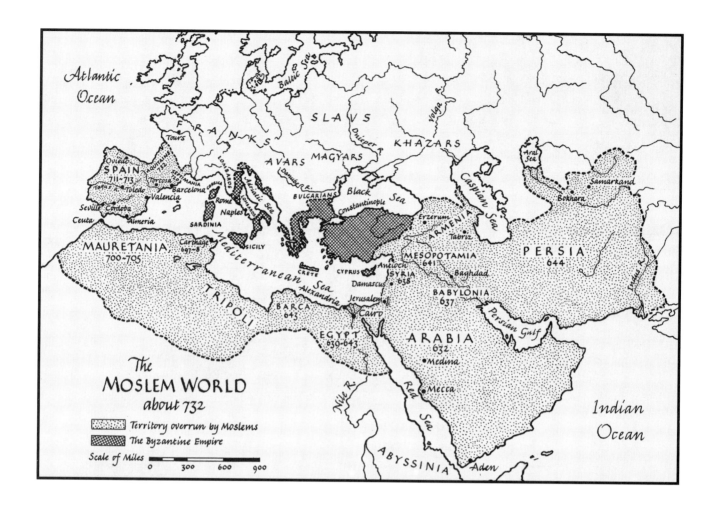

The MOSLEM WORLD about 732

Territory overrun by Moslems
The Byzantine Empire

Scale of Miles
0   300   600   900

CIRCA 400 C.E.
The nomadic Huns begin a westward migration from central Asia, causing disruption in the Roman Empire

CIRCA 400 C.E.
The Mayan Empire in Mesoamerica evolves into city-states

476 C.E.
Rome falls to barbarian hordes and the Western Roman Empire collapses

CIRCA 500-1500 C.E.
Middle Ages, or medieval period, in Europe: gradual recovery from political disruption and increase in agricultural productivity and population

618-907 C.E.
Tang Dynasty in China: territorial expansion, government bureaucracy, agricultural improvements, and transportation and communication networks

632-733 C.E.
Muslim expansion and conquests in Arabia, Syria, Palestine, Mesopotamia, Egypt, North Africa, Persia, northwestern India, and Iberia

CIRCA 700 C.E.
Origins of feudalism, a political and social organization that dominates Europe until the fifteenth century; based on the relationship between lords and vassals

CIRCA 900 C.E.
Introduction of the horseshoe in Europe and black powder in China

960-1279 C.E.
Song Dynasty in China: civil administration, industry, education, and the arts

962-1806 C.E.
Holy Roman Empire of western and central Europe, created in an attempt to revive the old Roman Empire

1000 C.E.
The world population is approximately 300 million

1096-1291 C.E.
Western Christians undertake the Crusades, a series of religiously inspired military campaigns, to recapture the Holy Land from the Muslims

1200 TO 1400 C.E.
The Mali empire in Africa dominates the trans-Saharan trade network of camel caravans

1220-1335 C.E.
The Mongols, nomadic horsemen from the high steppes of eastern central Asia, build an empire that includes China, Persia, and Russia

CIRCA 1250 C.E.
Inca Empire develops in Peru: Civil administration, road networks, and sun worshipping

1299-1919 C.E.
Ottoman Empire, created by nomadic Turks and Christian converts to Islam, encompasses Asia Minor, the Balkans, Greece, Egypt, North Africa, and the Middle East

1300 C.E.
The world population is approximately 396 million

1337-1453 C.E.
Hundred Years' War, a series of intermittent military campaigns between England and France over control of continental lands claimed by both countries

1347-1350 C.E.
Black Death, or the bubonic plague, kills one-quarter of the European population

1368-1644 C.E.
Ming Dynasty in China: political, economic, and cultural revival; the Great Wall is built

1375-1527 C.E.
The Renaissance in Western Europe, a revival in the arts and learning

1428-1519 C.E.
The Aztecs expand in central Mexico, developing trade routes and a system of tribute payments

1450 C.E.
Invention of the printing press

1453 C.E.
Constantinople falls to the Ottoman Turks, ending the Byzantine Empire

1464-1591 C.E.
Songhay Empire in Africa: military expansion, prosperous cities, control of the trans-Saharan trade

1492 C.E.
Discovery of America; European exploration and colonization of the Western Hemisphere begins

LATIN AMERICAN STATES after the REVOLUTIONS
0   500   1000   1500
Scale of Miles

CIRCA 1500-1867 C.E.
Transatlantic slave trade results in the forced migration of between 12 million and 16 million Africans to the Western Hemisphere

1500 C.E.
The world population is approximately 480 million

1517 C.E.
Beginning of the Protestant Reformation, a religious movement that ends the spiritual unity of western Christendom

1523-1763 C.E.
Mughal Empire in India: military conquests, productive agricultural economy, and population growth

1600-1867 C.E.
Tokugawa Shogunate in Japan: shoguns (military governors) turn Edo, or Tokyo, into the political, economic, and cultural center of the nation

1618-1648 C.E.
Thirty Years' War in Europe between Catholic and Protestant states

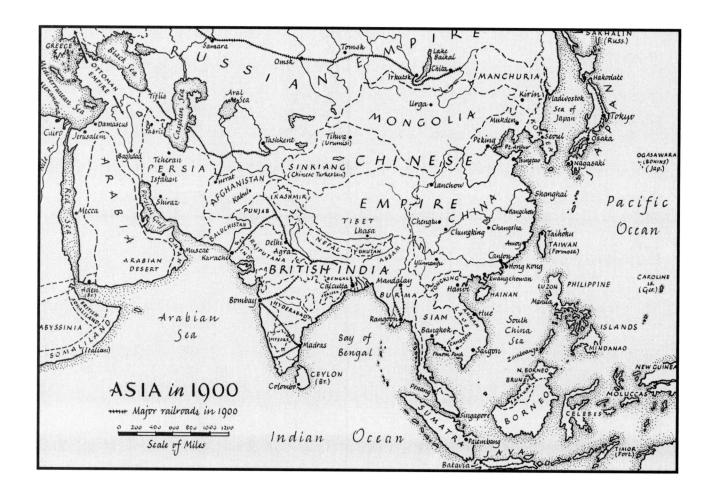

ASIA in 1900

＋＋＋＋ Major railroads in 1900

Scale of Miles

0   200   400   600   800   1000 1200

1644-1911 C.E.
Qing Dynasty in China: military expansion and scholar-bureaucrats

1700 C.E.
The world population is approximately 640 million

CIRCA 1750 C.E.
Beginning of the Enlightenment, a philosophical movement marked by an emphasis on rationalism and scientific inquiry

1756-1763 C.E.
Seven Years' War: England and Prussia versus Austria, France, Russia, Saxony, Spain, and Sweden

CIRCA 1760-1850 C.E.
Industrial Revolution in Britain is marked by mass production through the division of labor, mechanization, a great increase in the supply of iron, and the use of the steam engine

1775-1783 C.E.
American War of Independence; the United States becomes an independent republic

1789 C.E.
French Revolution topples the monarchy and leads to a period of political unrest followed by a dictatorship

1793-1815 C.E.
Napoleonic Wars: Austria, England, Prussia, and Russia versus France and its satellite states

1794-1824 C.E.
Latin American states conduct wars of independence against Spain

1900 C.E.
The world population is approximately 1.65 billion

1914-1918 C.E.
World War I, or the Great War: the Allies (England, France, Russia, and the United States) versus Central Powers (Austria-Hungary, Germany, and the Ottoman Empire)

1917-1921 C.E.
Russian Revolution: a group of Communists known as the Bolsheviks seize control of the country following a civil war

1939-1945 C.E.
World War II: the Allies (China, England, France, the Soviet Union, and the United States) versus the Axis (Germany, Italy, and Japan)

1945 C.E.
Successful test of the first atomic weapon; beginning of the Cold War, a period of rivalry, mistrust, and, occasionally, open hostility between the capitalist West and communist East

1947-1975 C.E.
Decolonization occurs in Africa and Asia as European powers relinquish control of colonies in those regions

1948
Israel becomes the first independent Jewish state in nearly two thousand years

1949
Communists seize control of China

1950-1951
Korean War: the United States attempts to stop Communist expansion in the Korean peninsula

1957 C.E.
The Soviet Union launches *Sputnik* ("fellow traveler of earth"), the first man-made satellite; the Space Age begins

1965-1973
Vietnam War: the United States attempts to thwart the spread of Communism in Vietnam

1989 C.E.
East European Communist regimes begin to falter and multiparty elections are held

1991 C.E.
Soviet Union is dissolved and replaced by the Commonwealth of Independent States

2000 C.E.
The world population is 6 billion

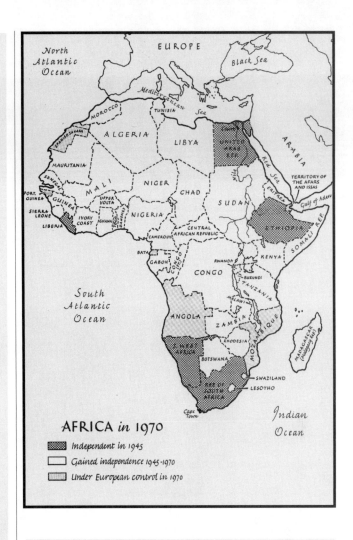

AFRICA *in* 1970

- Independent in 1945
- Gained independence 1945-1970
- Under European control in 1970

INTRODUCTION

Naming an Era. Europeans who lived during the period between the death of Charlemagne in 814 and the spread of the Black Death throughout their continent in 1350 did not think of themselves as living in the "Middle Ages." Indeed, many had a strong apocalyptic awareness. As devout Christians, they looked forward to the imminent end of human history and the judgment of God. They were also conscious of the ancient roots of their civilization and saw themselves as living in a period of cultural and political decline from the glory of the Roman Empire. Living after the collapse of that empire in the West, they saw themselves as the heirs of Rome and sought to re-create its civilization in their own. Indeed, they looked to the pagan classical philosophers and the early Christian Church Fathers as the foundation for all learning and saw themselves as inferior to those thinkers even in the face of medieval advances on their knowledge. A comment John of Salisbury made about one of the great teachers of the twelfth century summarizes the attitude of scholars throughout the Middle Ages: "Bernard of Chartres used to compare us to dwarfs perched on the shoulders of giants. He pointed out that we see more and farther than our predecessors, not because we have keener vision or greater height, but because we are lifted aloft on their gigantic stature."

Dating an Era. The date traditionally assigned to the beginning of the Middle Ages is 476, the year in which Rome was sacked by one of the so-called barbarian tribes that had been gradually settling within the borders of the empire for nearly a century. The end date, 1500, is roughly the time at which Renaissance humanists responsible for the classical revival of the fifteenth century looked back over the ten centuries between them and the days of ancient Rome and disparagingly named them the "Middle Ages" to suggest nothing of cultural or scientific significance had taken place in that long interval between two great civilizations. Twentieth-century scholars, however, have found much evidence to negate this perception. Though much ancient learning was lost after the Roman Empire ceased to exist in the West, even in the period once called the "Dark Ages" (476–1000)—now called the Early Middle Ages—there were significant attempts to preserve the knowledge of earlier times. One extremely important

influence on the period covered in this volume is the Carolingian Renaissance, a revival of learning, government, and piety that began as early as 768, when Charlemagne assumed the throne of France. The revival was well underway by 800, when Pope Leo III crowned Charlemagne ruler of the new Holy Roman Empire—so named to signal the foundation of a second, Christian Roman Empire in western Europe, with its center not in the city of Rome, south of the Alps, but north of the Alps in the city of Aachen (in what is now western Germany).

Perceptions of the Era. For centuries people, even scholars, tended not only to deprecate but also to romanticize the Middle Ages, as some continue to do today in tales of knights and dragons. Beginning in the mid nineteenth century, however, scholars began studying the many surviving manuscripts, archeological evidence, and monumental remains and revising older romantic historical accounts. Because of this new approach scholars began to offer more reliable and thorough interpretations of medieval events.

Church and State. Prior to the Middle Ages the Pope was simply the bishop of Rome, revered as the successor to St. Peter but nominally the equal of any other bishop. With the collapse of the Roman Empire, the advent of the barbarian invasions, and the development of new kingdoms, the bishop of Rome, and indeed all Christian bishops in the territory of the old Roman Empire, were forced by necessity of famine, starvation, and war to take on secular functions of government.

The Development of Law. With the coronation of Charlemagne as Holy Roman Emperor in 800, the Bishop of Rome took on a new role, that of guaranteeing the succession to the imperial throne. Since Christian monarchs were involved in secular and church conflicts, they often sought legal recourse by appealing to the body of bishops and finally to the Pope. With the increasing complexity of urban life and the growth of the Europe in the period 1100–1350, Europe became more and more a society of laws, and the Church of Rome came to be the final appeals court. This situation led to the development of ecclesiastical canon law alongside governmental laws of secular states. As Walter Ullmann has demonstrated, the rebirth of Roman civil law during the Investiture Crisis (1075–

1122)—during which a succession of Popes and Holy Roman Emperors argued over who had the right to appoint bishops within the empire—led to the development of new notions of state sovereignty and in time to a secularization of state government. Perhaps the most important outcome of instituting systems of laws was the limitation of imperial and kingly power in the form of *parlements* (parliaments). The rationale for the U.S. Congress has its roots in the separation of governmental powers during the medieval period. The signing of the Magna Carta at Runnymede in 1215 led in time to a broad limitation of absolutist royal power.

The Crusades and the Spread of Learning. After the expansion of the Islamic Empire across North Africa and into the Iberian Peninsula during the seventh and early eighth centuries, Europe was no longer in control of the Mediterranean Sea. The movement to regain control of the holy sites in Jerusalem from Muslim hegemony is often criticized by modern scholars for its one-sided depiction of "Saracen infidels." Yet, despite such stereotyping, much cultural exchange occurred after Pope Urban II called for troops to wage the First Crusade. From about 1120 to 1290, the existence of Christian communities in the Near East opened up new possibilities for military adventure, trade, travel, and exchange for medieval Europeans. Traders from Genoa and Venice especially were able to introduce new spices, foods, and silks to Europe. Returning Crusaders brought back new military and architectural skills. In brief, interaction among Christians, Muslims, and Jews broadened the outlook of those Europeans who traveled to the East.

Traveling Scholars. Among those who traveled not only to the East but also to Muslim Spain were European scholars who discovered Greek and Arabic manuscripts for classical works that had been lost to the West after the fall of Rome, as well as Arab commentaries on the works and important Arab writings on science and mathematics. These scholars translated into Latin many great philosophical and scientific treatises, such as Aristotle's works and Euclid's *Geometry*. They also encouraged the use of Arabic numerals and mathematics.

Universities. The arrival in western Europe of this great body of translated learning coincided with the creation in the late twelfth century of a new institution in medieval Europe: the university. Prior to the existence of the university as an institution, there were cathedral or municipal schools that provided rudimentary educations. By the thirteenth and fourteenth centuries the universities of Salerno, Bologna, Paris, and Oxford had matured as educational institutions. Some of these universities specialized in a particular subject; others did not. For example, Salerno developed as a medical school while Bologna became the most prominent law university. The University of Paris specialized in the arts and theology, but it also had faculties in law and medicine. The University of Oxford focused on logic, natural science, and mathematics.

An Age of Faith? It has commonly been taught that the Middle Ages were an age of faith. Though all European countries were Christian in name and in practice, however, there were secular areas in education, law, or politics. As Toby E. Huff has shown in *The Rise of Early Modern Science* (1993), the existence in western Europe of secular legal systems distinct from canon law, ensured that universities were also governed by their own sets of laws. As a result a separation of secular and divine learning became institutionalized. At the University of Paris around 1260–1280 theologians taught that a Christian had two basic goals: the exercise of virtue in the present political and moral life and the achievement of eternal salvation. The separation of these two dimensions is apparent in the thought and poetry of Dante Alighieri. In his *De monarchia* (circa 1308) Dante developed the Aristotelian-Thomist doctrine of separate temporal and spiritual dimensions. Indeed, Dante called for a secular imperial power to check the power of the Church, as asserted by Pope Boniface VIII, who in his bull *Unam Sanctam* claimed that the Church had universal hegemony in temporal matters. As modern nation-states emerged by the Late Middle Ages (1300–1500), so too did a general belief that *Rex in regno suo Imperator* (the king was lord in his own domain). People looked to ancient Rome rather than to medieval monarchy for newer forms of city and republican government.

Language and Literacy. Latin was a kind of universal language in western Europe, but by 1300 claims were made for the primacy of the vernacular tongues that evolved into modern European languages during the medieval period. Latin eventually became a technical language used in church, school, government, and medicine. Though it is true that many people in medieval Europe could not read, literacy did increase during the the period. During this age before the advent of printing, one of the most prized possessions for the well-to-do was a manuscript book, especially the Latin Bible. As literacy increased, vernacular literary works that had been handed down orally—including the Celtic epics, *Beowulf*, and the Norse sagas—were written down for the first time.

World Eras. The World Eras series offers cross-disciplinary overviews of world history from a global perspective with a strong emphasis on social and cultural history. This volume on medieval Europe will be useful for students in traditional Western civilization courses as well as history courses on the period. The series provides students with the factual information necessary for comparative study of cultures and cultural interactions. The structure was in part dictated by the World Eras series, but chapter lengths have been adjusted to accommodate the amount of information pertinent to the European Middle Ages. Each chapter includes alphabetically arranged topical entries that focus on events, ideas, developments, material conditions, and personalities.

Acknowledgments. The task of bringing a multi-authored volume to successful completion carries many pitfalls. Thankfully, the authors provided good chapters and were cooperative as the volume went through the editorial process. They attempted to provide up-to-date and accurate accounts that counter the many misconceptions about the Middle Ages that still exist in history books. I want to thank the chapter authors for their great patience and efforts: Kelly DeVries, Kathryn A. Edwards, Mary Beth Farrell, Bert S. Hall, Jacqueline Murray, Betsey B. Price, Karen L. Rood, Giulio Silano, and Steven A. Walton. I also thank my colleagues in the Department of Philosophy, University of South Carolina, for encouragement and interest. I am grateful to my family and friends who encouraged me on the way. In particular, my wife, Lilla, was most supportive of the time and work that went into this book. The volume is dedicated to her. I am also grateful to two mentors who carried out much original research on medieval topics and who understood that the goal of the research is the widening of historical horizons so that truth can appear in a new manner. They are the late Professor F. X. Martin, University College Dublin, and the late Professor L. E. Boyle, University of Toronto.

Jeremiah Hackett

University of South Carolina

Columbia, S.C.

ACKNOWLEDGMENTS

This book was produced by Manly, Inc. Karen L. Rood is senior editor and Anthony J. Scotti Jr. is series editor. James F. Tidd Jr. was the assistant in-house editor.

Production manager is Philip B. Dematteis.

Administrative support was provided by Ann M. Cheschi, Amber L. Coker, and Angi Pleasant.

Accountant is Ann-Marie Holland.

Copyediting supervisor is Sally R. Evans. The copyediting staff includes Phyllis A. Avant, Brenda Carol Blanton, Melissa D. Hinton, Worthy B. Evans, Charles Loughlin, William Tobias Mathes, Rebecca Mayo, Nancy E. Smith, and Elizabeth Jo Ann Sumner.

Editorial associates are Michael S. Allen, Michael S. Martin, and Pamela A. Warren.

Database manager is José A. Juarez.

Layout and graphics supervisor is Janet E. Hill. The graphics staff includes Karla Corley Brown and Zoe R. Cook.

Office manager is Kathy Lawler Merlette.

Photography supervisor is Paul Talbot. Photography editor is Scott Nemzek.

Permissions editors are Ann-Marie Holland and Kathy Lawler Merlette.

Digital photographic copy work was performed by Joseph M. Bruccoli.

The SGML staff includes Frank Graham, Linda Dalton Mullinax, Jason Paddock, and Alex Snead.

Systems manager is Marie L. Parker.

Typesetting supervisor is Kathleen M. Flanagan. The typesetting staff includes Jaime All, Patricia Marie Flanagan, Mark J. McEwan, and Pamela D. Norton.

Walter W. Ross supervised library research. He was assisted by Steven Gross and the following librarians at the Thomas Cooper Library of the University of South Carolina: circulation department head Tucker Taylor; reference department head Virginia W. Weathers; Brette Barclay, Marilee Birchfield, Paul Cammarata, Gary Geer, Michael Macan, Tom Marcil, Rose Marshall, and Sharon Verba; interlibrary loan department head John Brunswick; and interlibrary loan staff Robert Arndt, Hayden Battle, Barry Bull, Jo Cottingham, Marna Hostetler, Marieum McClary, Erika Peake, and Nelson Rivera.

Karen Rood wrote the essay on the Church and State (Religion and Philosophy). Anthony Scotti wrote the following entries: The Mongol Myth (Geography); The Battlefield, Frederick I, Holy Roman Empire, Louis IX, Magna Carta, Mongols, Richard I, and William I (all in Politics, Law, and the Military). Michael Allen wrote the following entries: Music (The Arts); Erik the Red and Leif Eriksson (Geography); Eleanor of Aquitaine and Heloise (Family and Social Trends); The Crusades, East-West Schism, and Thomas Aquinas (Religion and Philosophy).

WORLD ERAS

VOLUME 4

MEDIEVAL EUROPE
814 - 1350

WORLD EVENTS:
SELECTED OCCURRENCES OUTSIDE EUROPE

by MARY BETH FARRELL and KAREN L. ROOD

814*	• Chinese alchemists have discovered how to make gunpowder.
814	• Al-Ma'mūn (Mamūn the Great), whose reign began in 813, is the seventh 'Abbāsid caliph of the Muslim Empire and is known for the House of Knowledge he established in Baghdad. During his twenty-year reign and that of his successor, al-Mu'tasim (833–842), scholars there translate Greek, Syriac, Persian, and Sanskrit works of philosophy, science, and literature, as well as making significant discoveries in fields such as astronomy, mathematics, and medicine.
833	• Al-Mu'tasim becomes caliph of the Muslim Empire. He enlists non-Muslim mercenaries in his personal army, initiating the decline of the 'Abbāsid dynasty. Though they convert to Islam, these troops—which include Berbers, Slavs, and especially Turks—are personally loyal to their officers, not the caliph.
837	• Byzantine forces invade the Muslim Empire of 'Abbāsid caliph al-Mu'tasim in a war that continues until 842 and intermittently thereafter.
838	• Muslim forces take Amorium, birthplace of the Byzantine dynasty, and prepare to lay siege to Constantinople, but their fleet is destroyed in a storm.
842	• 'Abbāsid caliph al-Mu'tasim dies and is succeeded by his son al-Wāthig, who continues his father's policy of enlisting non-Muslims, particularly Turks, further weakening the power of the caliph and making him subject to the demands of his officers.

* DENOTES CIRCA DATE

847

- Arabs sack Rome.

- 'Abbāsid caliph al-Wāthig dies and is succeeded by his brother al-Mutawakkil, who seeks to re-establish the traditional Muslim faith by persecuting Christians and Jews, as well as the unorthodox Muslim Shiites. During his fourteen-year reign Byzantium takes the cities of Damietta in Egypt and Cilicia in Armenia.

849

- An Arab fleet is defeated off Ostia, Italy, by the forces of an alliance formed by Pope Leo IV.

850*

- The Arabs invent the astrolabe, which allows mariners to use celestial navigation to determine latitude.

- Under Vijayalaya, who reigns until 870, the prosperous Hindu Cola (or Chola) dynasty of Tamil kings begins its territorial expansion in southern India.

858

- Fujiwara Yoshifusa, father-in-law of the emperor of Japan, becomes the first commoner to serve as regent when his nine-year-old grandson, Seiwa, takes the throne.

860*

- Norse (Viking) explorers discover Iceland.

860

- 'Abbāsid caliph al-Mutawakkil is assassinated by his Turkish guard and succeeded by his eldest son, al-Muntasir.

862

- After a reign of only six months al-Muntasir is deposed by his Turkish guard and is succeeded by his first cousin al-Mustaʿīn.

866*

- The 'Abbāsid caliphs begin to lose the eastern provinces of their empire as Yaʿqūb ebn Leys as-Saffār, a man of lower-class origins, seizes control of his native province of Sistan in eastern Iran, establishing the Saffarid dynasty of rulers.

866

- Forced to abdicate, 'Abbāsid caliph al-Mustaʿīn is then murdered by a killer sent by his successor, al-Muʿtazz. During his brief reign, Egypt, under Ahmed ibn Tulun (founder of the Tulunid dynasty), becomes virtually independent of the Muslim Empire.

- Emperor Seiwa of Japan achieves his majority, but his grandfather continues to serve as regent, inaugurating a period of clan dominance known as the Fujiwara period (866–1160).

* DENOTES CIRCA DATE

869
- 'Abbāsid caliph al-Mu'tazz is murdered by mutinous troops and is succeeded by al-Wathiq's son al-Muhtadī.

- Ya'qūb ebn Leys as-Saffār has extended his empire to include most of modern-day Iran and parts of Afghanistan and Pakistan.

870*
- Al-Kindī dies. A prominent scholar in Iraq, he has been the first Islamic thinker to attempt to reconcile Greek philosophy with Muslim beliefs.

870
- 'Abbāsid caliph al-Muhtadī is forced to abdicate by his Turkish troops, who choose al-Mu'tamid, son of al-Mutawakkil, as the next caliph. During al-Mu'tamid's twenty-two-year reign and those of his two successors (892–908), the 'Abbāsids manage to keep control over the power-hungry Turkish guard.

874
- Ingólfr Arnarson becomes the first permanent Norse settler of Iceland.

876
- Saffarid ruler Ya'qūb ebn Leys as-Saffār attempts to capture Baghdad, but he is defeated by Al-Muwaffaq, brother of 'Abbāsid caliph al-Mu'tamid.

879
- 'Abbāsid caliph al-Mu'tamid recognizes 'Amr ebn Leys, brother and successor of Ya'qūb ebn Leys as-Saffār, as governor of the eastern provinces of the Muslim Empire.

880
- Fujiwara Mototsune becomes the first kampaku (civil dictator), the defacto ruler of Japan. With one exception, until 1160 a member of the Fujiwara clan serves as kampaku during the reign of adult emperor or as regent when a minor is on the throne.

891
- Fujiwara Mototsune dies and Emperor Uda, whose mother is not a Fujiwara, refuses to appoint a new kampaku. Having ascended the Japanese throne in 887, Uda rules independently of the Fujiwaras until his death in 897. He is supported in his efforts by the powerful scholar-poet-politician Sugawara Michizane (later deified as Tenjin).

894
- Emperor Uda appoints Sugawara Michizane Japanese envoy to the T'ang dynasty of China, but Sugawara convinces the emperor that contact with the Chinese is undesirable because of growing influence from the Near East and that China no longer has anything to teach Japan. Although unofficial contact between the two countries continues, this break in diplomatic relations marks the end of some three centuries of Chinese influence on Japanese culture.

* DENOTES CIRCA DATE

900*

- The Chimú kingdom arises in the Moche Valley of Peru, beginning to fill a vacuum left by the collapse of the Huaris.

- Bantu-speaking peoples establish city-states on the east coast of Africa.

- Rulers of the powerful Ghanian Empire in west Africa adopt Islam.

- The classic period of Mayan civilization in present-day Guatemala, Honduras, southern Mexico, Belize, and El Salvador comes to an end. At its height the Mayan Empire consisted of some forty cities and had a total population of about two million people. While the lowland cities are abandoned after 900, the cities in the highlands of the Yucatán peninsula continue to flourish for several more centuries.

- By this time the last inhabitants of Teotihuacán, near present-day Mexico City, have abandoned what is left of their once-great city, devastated by fire some 150 years earlier. They have been driven away by the arrival of warlike peoples such as the Toltecs.

900

- Though the Saffarid dynasty maintains its position in Sistan into the sixteenth century, its empire collapses after ʿAmr ebn Lys fails to take Transoxiana (present-day Uzbekistan and parts of Turkmenistan, and Kazakstan) from the Sāmānids, who also rule the vast territory of Khorasan (northeastern Iran, southern Turkmenistan, and northern Afghanistan.

902

- ʿAbbāsid caliph al-Muʿtamid dies and is succeeded by al-Muqtafī, who during his six-year reign brings Egypt back under direct control of the caliph and repulses an invasion attempt by the Byzantines.

903

- Qarmatians, a branch of the Shiite Muslim sect called the Ishmaelites, rise up against the ʿAbbāsid caliphate in Syria and Iraq in an insurrection that continues through 906.

907

- The Tʾang dynasty, which has ruled China since 618, falls because of internal rebellions and Turkish invasions, ending a golden age of Chinese culture and beginning the breakup of China into separate kingdoms.

- Khitan Mongol leader A-pao-chi proclaims himself ruler of the Khitan nation, and by 916 he has created a Chinese-style dynasty to rule a nation that includes Mongolia and much of Manchuria.

908

- ʿAbbāsid caliph al-Muqtafī dies and is succeeded by his brother al-Muqtadir. During his twenty-four-year reign, the power of the caliph is significantly weakened.

909

- Al-Mahdī proclaims himself caliph of Tunis, establishing the Fātimid dynasty. Refusing to recognize the sovereignty of the ʿAbbāsid caliphs, he begins his family's gradual conquest of all North Africa from the Muslim Empire. The Fātimids are a branch of Ishmaelites who claim descent from Fatimah, daughter of the Prophet Muhammad.

* DENOTES CIRCA DATE

910
- As the result of a Berber-Arab invasion from North Africa that began in 711, the Muslim Umayyad dynasty now rules all but the northwest corner of Spain.

926
- In return for helping the Juchens of Manchuria to conquer northern China, A-pao-chi is given the northeast corner of China, which includes the city of Beijing.

927
- Mardāvīj ibn Ziyār seizes control of northern Iran from the Sāmānids, soon expanding his domain and establishing the Zeharid dynasty.

930
- Qarmatians from Bahrain sack Mecca and take the sacred Black Stone from the Ka'bah (a small shrine in the Great Mosque). They hold it ransom for about two decades.
- The Persian Shiite Būyid dynasty—founded by the three sons of Buyeh: Ali, Hasan, and Ahmad—begins its rise to power when Mardāvīj ibn Ziyār appoints Ali governor of Karaj. The three brothers spend the rest of the decade conquering most of modern-day Iran and Iraq.

932
- 'Abbāsid caliph al-Muqtadir is succeeded by al-Qāhir.

934
- 'Abbāsid caliph al-Qāhir is succeeded by al-Rādi.

935
- Though they rule as independent sovereigns until 1024, the Zeyarid dynasty suffers a loss of power after the murder of its founder, Mardāvīj ibn Ziyār.

939
- Vietnam gains its independence from China.

940
- 'Abbāsid caliph al-Rādi is succeeded by al-Muttaqī.

944
- 'Abbāsid caliph al-Muttaqī is succeeded by al-Mustakfi.

945
- Būyid brother Ahmad occupies Baghdad, capital of the Muslim Empire, forcing caliph al-Mustaqfi to name him *amir-al-umara* (prince of princes, or commander in chief). Though the 'Abbāsid dynasty continues into the thirteenth century, the caliphs become the puppets of the amir.

* DENOTES CIRCA DATE

| 947 | • The Khitans of northeastern China proclaim the Liao dynasty, which rules that portion of their empire until 1125. |

| 950* | • The warlike Toltecs build their capital city, Tula, about fifty miles north of present-day Mexico City. |

| 960 | • Chao K'uang-yin stages a coup in China and proclaims himself Emperor T'ai-tsu, establishing the Sung dynasty, which remains in power until 1279. During the Sung period Chinese trade goods such as porcelain and steel become world famous. During his reign, which lasts until 976, T'ai-tsu begins the reunification of the Chinese empire. |

| 969 | • The Fātimids conquer Egypt, which they rule for the next two hundred years, founding the city of Cairo and making it—rather than Baghdad—the center of Islamic culture. |

| 972 | • The Chinese begin printing with movable type. |

| 975 | • Fātimid caliph al-Mu'izz dies and is succeeded by his son al-Aziz. During his twenty-one-year reign, he conquers Syria and part of Mesopotamia, extending the Fātimid Empire from the Atlantic in the West to the Euphrates River in the East. |

| 976 | • During his reign, which lasts until 997, T'ai-tsung, brother and successor of T'ai-tsu, completes the reunification of the Chinese empire. |

| 977 | • The Turk Sebüktigin, a former slave who has married the daughter of the governor of the town of Ghazna (modern-day Ghazni, Afghanistan), is recognized as his father-in-law's successor by the ruling Iranian Sāmānid dynasty. Over the next twenty years Sebüktigin rejects Sāmānid control and establishes the Ghaznavid dynasty, extending his territory east to the Indian border. |

| 980* | • By this time Arabs and Persians have settled along the east coast of Africa, where they found cities such as Mogadishu (tenth century) in present-day Somalia, and Manda (ninth century) and Mombasa (eleventh century) in present-day Kenya. They trade with Africans in the interior for ivory, gold, and slaves for sale in India and the Arabian peninsula. |

| 982 | • Banished from Iceland for manslaughter, Norseman Erik the Red settles the island he later calls Greenland. |

* DENOTES CIRCA DATE

985
- Returning to Iceland, Erik the Red recruits settlers for Greenland, choosing the name to make the island seem more attractive than Iceland.

986
- Icelanders led by Erik the Red establish two main settlements in Greenland.
- Blown off course during a storm, Icelander Bjarni Herjulfsson and his crew make the first recorded European sighting of the North American continent.

995
- Fujiwara Michinaga becomes head of his clan and de facto ruler of Japan, fostering a Japanese literary renaissance while struggling to suppress rebellions by warrior families that resent the Fujiwaras' centralized control of the nation.

996
- Fātimid caliph al-Aziz dies and is succeeded by his son al-Hākim. Known as the "Mad Caliph," he declares himself an emanation of deity and attempts to make Shiite Islam the established religion of Egypt, persecuting Jews and Christians. (The cult of Hākim still exists among the present-day Druses of Syria.)

997
- Ghaznavid ruler Sebüktigin dies, leaving his domain to his younger son Ismā'īl.

998
- Backed by much of the nobility, Sebüktigin's eldest son, Mahmud, seizes the Ghaznavid throne from his brother Ismā'īl. Over his thirty-two-year reign he becomes known as the Great Mahmud of Ghazna, extending his empire to include Khorasan (in northeastern Iran), Afghanistan, and northern India and making Ghazna an important cultural center. Under Mahmud, the Ghaznavids abandon their Turkic pagan beliefs for Sunnite Islam.

999*
- Influenced by the success of Christian missionaries sent by Olaf I Tryggvason, king of Norway, the Althing, or Icelandic assembly, decides that all Icelanders must abandon the old Norse religion in favor of Christianity.

1000*
- Over the past three thousand years, people speaking the Bantu family of languages have spread out from western Africa and now dominate the cultures of most of sub-Saharan Africa, diffusing their knowledge of ironwork and agriculture.
- The West African city-state of Benin emerges in what is now Nigeria, becoming renowned for its metalwork. By the late fifteenth century, when Portuguese explorers visit it for the first time, it has become a large, powerful, and prosperous walled city.
- Seljuq Turks, originally from Central Asia, become Sunnite Muslims and begin their westward expansion.

* DENOTES CIRCA DATE

1000* (CONT'D)

- Iranian scientist Avicenna (Abū ʿAlī al-Husayn ibn ʿAbd Allāh ibn Sīnā) becomes court physician to Būyid prince Shams ad-Dawlah of Hamadan (in west-central Iran), where Avicenna writes his *al-Qanun fi at-tibb* (The Canon of Medicine), which is widely considered the best-known single book in the history of medicine, and other important studies of science and philosophy.

- The Incan civilization begins to develop in South America. In the fifteenth century it will begin a period of expansion that leads to its domination of the Andean region.

- Struggles between rival religious groups begin to weaken the Toltec state of central Mexico.

- Ghana emerges as the most powerful empire in West Africa, with gold-rich territory between the Sahara Desert and the headwaters of the Niger and Senegal Rivers (an area that is now part of Mali and southeast Mauritania, not the republic of Ghana).

- Among the Eastern Woodlands peoples in present-day New York State the introduction of corn sparks the development of the Owasco culture, the foundation of the groups Europeans later call the Five Iroquois Nations: the Mohawks, Senecas, Onondagas, Oneidas, and Cayugas. Once they begin practicing horticulture, their population grows, and competition for land increases, leading eventually to the construction of fortified hilltop towns.

- Navajo and Apache peoples from the far north in Canada arrive in the American Southwest, where they encounter Pueblo Indians, including the Zuni and Hopi, who have been in the region for thousands of years. The Navajo learn agriculture, weaving, and artistic styles from the Pueblo tribes, but the Apache remain mostly hunter-gatherers. Only a few groups of their people supplement their diet by growing maize and other vegetables.

- At Cahokia, near present-day East St. Louis, Illinois, members of the group archaeologists call Mississippians begin building the largest earthen structures in pre-Columbian North America. Following a tradition begun around 2300 B.C. these Mound Builders place structures such as the council house, chiefs' houses, and the temple on their mounds. Situation on land well suited for agriculture and strategically located for trade, Cahokia becomes a prosperous and influential city, with a population that eventually reaches about twelve thousand people. Its political and religious rituals, symbols, and costumes spread throughout the Southeast.

1000

- Leif Eriksson, son of Erik the Red, is converted to Christianity during a visit to Norway.

1001

- Leif Eriksson and his crew sail to places they call Vinland, Helluland, and Markland, possibly Nova Scotia, Labrador, and Newfoundland.

- The troops of Mahmud of Ghazna launch the first of many raids into India, continuing until 1026 and spreading Islam into the region.

1002*

- Leif Eriksson and his party return to Greenland, where he proselytizes for the Christian religion, converting his mother, who builds the first Christian church on the island.

* DENOTES CIRCA DATE

1004
- Thorfinn Karlsefni and his wife, Gudrid, lead an expedition of about 130 people from Greenland to the North American continent, landing possibly at Baffin Island, traveling south, and settling along what was probably the Gulf of St. Lawrence. After three years they abandon the settlement they call Vinland and return to Greenland. Thorfinn and Gudrid's son, Snorri (born circa 1005), may be the first European born in mainland North America.

1005
- By this date the Sāmānid Empire has been divided between the Ghaznavids in the east and the Qarakhanids in the west.

1014
- Rajendra becomes king of a Cola empire that includes southern India, the Laccadive and Maldive Islands, and northern Ceylon (Sri Lanka). During his thirty-year reign, he extends the northern boundaries of his kingdom, completes the invasion of Ceylon, and conquers portions of the Malay Peninsula and Archipelago.

1021
- Fātimid caliph al-Hākim dies and is succeeded by az-Zāhir. During his fifteen-year reign, the empire goes into decline.

1023
- Avicenna goes to the court of 'Alā' ad-Dawah in Esfahan (about 250 miles south of Tehran), where he spends the last twenty-two years of his life writing such important works as the first Persian-language work on Aristotelean philosophy, a personal work on the mystic's spiritual journey to God, and a major, unfinished philological work on the Arabic language.

1028
- The death of Fujiwara Michinaga begins the decline of his family's control in Japan, as other clans begin to usurp power in the countryside.

1036
- Al-Mustansir becomes caliph of the Fātimid Empire. During his twenty-eight-year reign, he loses much of the empire, including most of North Africa and the eastern provinces.

1040
- Mas'ūd I, son of Mahmud of Ghazna, suffers a major defeat at the Battle of Dandanqan, losing all Ghaznavid territories in Iran and central Asia to the Seljuqs. The Ghaznavids remain in control of their lands in eastern Afghanistan and northern India.

1047
- Mecca and Medina declare their independence from the Fātimid Empire.

1050*
* DENOTES CIRCA DATE
- Over the next 250 years the Pueblo peoples of the American Southwest build their cliff houses at Mesa Verde and apartment-like housing at Chaco Canyon and other sites.

1055
- Seljuq Turks enter Bagdad, seizing control of the decaying ʿAbbāsid Empire from the Būyid amir Abū Nasr al-Malik ar-Rahim. ʿAbbāsid caliph al-Mustansir recognizes Seljuq Toghrïl Beg, as sultan, or chieftain.

1056
- A bishop's seat is established in Iceland.

1061
- The Almoravids, a militant Berber dynasty, begin their conquest of Morocco and western Algeria.

1064
- Seljuq Turks ravage the Byzantine province of Armenia.

1071
- At the Battle of Manzikert, the Seljuq Turks seize most of Asia Minor from the Byzantine Empire.

1073
- At the invitation of Fātimid caliph al-Mustansir, Badr al-Jamalī seizes power in Cairo, executing leading officials and military officers. As commander of the army, head of the religious establishment, and vizier, Badr al-Jamālī essentially rules the Fatmid Empire. He is succeeded by his son and a series of autocrats, reducing the caliphs to puppets.

1074
- The Seljuqs conclude a treaty with Byzantine emperor Michael II, who has enlisted their aid because his uncle has established himself as a pretender to the throne. In return, however, the Seljuqs establish themselves throughout Anatolia (the Asia portion of present-day Turkey).

1075
- The Seljuqs begin their conquest of Syria from the Fātimids, taking Damascus in 1076.

1076
- The Almoravids pillage the Ghanian capital of Kumbi (about two hundred miles north of the modern city of Bamako in Mali), precipitating the gradual breakup of its empire and years of warfare among successor states. The rulers of the Mandigo kingdom of Kangaba (on the east) and the Songhai kingdom of Gao (on the west) are soon converted to Islam.

1078
- The Seljuqs support the uprising in Anatolia of troops led by Nicephorus Botaniates, who forces the abdication of Michael VII and places himself on the Byzantine throne. As a result the Seljuqs control nearly all of Anatolia.

1089
- The Almoravids begin their conquest of Spain.

* DENOTES CIRCA DATE

1090*	• Ishmaelite leader Hassan-e Sabbah founds the secret society known as the Assassins.
1092	• Seljuq vizier Nizām al-Mulk is murdered by the Assassins, paving the way for Byzantine reconquest of parts of Anatolia.
1094	• On the death of Fātimid caliph al-Mustansir, civil war breaks out as his two sons vie to succeed him. Backed by Badr al-Jamālī's son and successor al-Afdal, the victor reigns over the shrinking empire until 1101 as al-Mustadi. Hassān-e Sabbah, leader of the Assassins, calls the new caliph a usurper and refuses to accept the authority of al-Mustadī and his descendants.
1095	• Under threat from the Seljuqs, Byzantine emperor Alexius I calls on Pope Urban II for assistance.
1096	• Responding to Alexius I, Pope Urban II launches the First Crusade to save the Holy Land from the Muslims.
1097	• The Seljuq capital at Nicaea falls to the Crusaders.
1098	• Antioch is captured by the Crusaders.
1099	• The Fātimids lose Jerusalem to the Crusaders, who establish Christian kingdoms there and in Edessa, Antioch, and Tripoli. The Byzantine Empire recovers most of the western coast of Anatolia.
1100*	• Inuits from North America settle in northern Greenland.
1106	• A second bishop's seat is established in Iceland. • The Almoravids from North Africa have taken control of nearly all Muslim Spain.
1110	• The Seljuqs invade Byzantine Anatolia, initiating a war that lasts until 1117.
1114	• The Juchen tribes of Manchuria rise up against the Kitchin empire.

* DENOTES CIRCA DATE

1117
- Following a decisive victory by the Byzantines at the Battle of Philomelion in 1116, the Seljuqs cede the entire Anatolian coastline and all of the interior west of a line from Ankara southwest to Philomelion (modern-day Aksehir).

1118
- John II Commenus becomes Byzantine emperor and begins a campaign to bring the Christian states in Syria under control of the empire.

1121
- The Seljuqs lose southwestern Anatolia to Byzantine forces.

1123
- The Juchen conquer the Liao dynasty lands in northern China and proclaim the Chin dynasty, which rules until 1234.

1126
- The Juchen conquer the northern portion of the Sung empire in China.
- A bishop's seat is established in Greenland.

1127
- Sung prince Kao-tsung escapes from Juchen invaders and rules the portion of the empire that lies south of the Yangtze River.

1130
- Fātimid caliph al-Amir, who has reigned since 1101, is murdered by the Assassins.

1137
- Byzantine troops complete a three-year campaign to conquer Cilician (Little) Armenian, which has been under the control of the Christian state of Antioch. Raymond of Antioch is forced to do homage to the Byzantine Empire.

1144
- Muslims recapture Edessa, sparking the Second Crusade.

1145
- The Almohads dynasty of North Africa conquers Muslim Spain.

1147
- European troops arrive in the Holy Land for the Second Crusade, which ends in 1149, after their poorly co-ordinated offensive accomplishes little of importance.

1149
- Ghaznavid ruler Bāhram Shah poisons a local Ghurid leader, Qutb-ud-Din, sparking a feud that results in the sacking of Ghazna by Ghurid chief 'Alā'-ud-Din Husayn, founder of the Ghurid dynasty. Although they end Ghaznavid rule in the region, the Muslim Ghurids cannot hold Ghazna, which ends up in the hands of the Oguz Turkmen nomads.

* DENOTES CIRCA DATE

1156
- Civil war breaks out in Japan as retired emperor Sutoku attempts unsuccessfully to regain power from his brother, reigning emperor Go-Shirakawa. The emperor is backed by warriors led by Taira Kiyomori and by the Fujiwaras, who—despite their support of the winning side—continue to lose influence, as the Taira family begins its ascent.

1160
- Minamoto Yoshitomo and Fujiwara Nobuyori, who were allied with Taira forces in 1156, are defeated in a coup attempt against the Taira family, ending the Fujiwara period in Japan and leaving Taira Kiyomori in control of the entire country.

1161
- To secure his borders with the Byzantines while expanding his territory in other directions, Seljuq sultan Qïlïj Arslan II of Rum (eastern Anatolia) makes peace with the Byzantines, acknowledging the primacy of the emperor.

1167
- Kurdish general Shīrkūh, in the service of Emir Nureddin of Damascus, enters Egypt to help protect the Fātimid state from falling to the rulers of the Christian kingdoms in the region.

1169
- On the death of his uncle Shīrkūh, Saladin (Salāh ad-dīn) becomes commander of Syrian troops in Egypt, orders the assassination of Fātimid vizier Shawar, and is appointed to replace him by al-Adid, the last Fāimid caliph.
- Averroës (Ibn Rushd), an Islamic philosopher in Cordoba, Spain, completes the first of his many influential commentaries on the writings of Aristotle.

1171
- On the death of Al-Adid, Saladin abolishes the Shiite Fātimid caliphate and proclaims himself the ruler of a new Sunnite Muslim state in Egypt, establishing the Ayyubid dynasty.

1172
- Saladin conquers the Christian state of Tripoli.

1173
- Ghiyās-ud-Din and Mu'izz-ud-Din, nephews of Ghurid chief 'Alā'-ud-Din Husayn, retake the city of Ghazna. Over the next thirty years they conquer most of Afghanistan, eastern Iran, present-day Turkmenistan, and northern India.

1174
- Saladin enters Syria, beginning a twelve-year campaign to unite—by diplomacy and military force—the Muslim territories of Egypt, Syria, Palestine, and northern Mesopotamia under his rule.
- The Toltec Empire of central Mexico falls after internal chaos and invasions by less-civilized nomads.

* DENOTES CIRCA DATE

1176
- Qïlïch Arslan II invades Byzantine Anatolia, achieving victory at the Battle of Myrio-cephalon and ending Byzantine hopes of regaining all of Anatolia, despite their victory at Bithynia in 1177.

1180
- Taira Kyomori places his two-year-old grandson on the throne of Japan as Emperor Antoku, provoking a rebellion led by Minamoto Yoritomo, whose father Kyomori had executed after his coup attempt in 1160.

1185
- The Minamoto clan defeats the Tairas and establishes the Kamakura shogunate. During this period of feudalism, which lasts until 1333, emperors are ceremonial figureheads, and powerful military governors known as shoguns are the real rulers of Japan.

1186
- Lahore falls to the Ghurids, who gain control of the remaining lands of the Ghaznavids.

1187
- Saladin captures the Christian kingdom of Jerusalem, leading to the Third Crusade.

1189
- During the Third Crusade, which lasts until 1192, Saladin successfully protects his territory against Christian forces.

1191
- Acre, in the kingdom of Jerusalem, falls to forces led by Richard the Lionhearted of England and Philip II Augustus of France. The inhabitants are slaughtered.

1192
- After Christian forces fail to retake Jerusalem, the Third Crusade ends with a three-year truce in which Saladin allows the Crusaders to retain a small strip of land on the Levantine coast and gives them access to Jerusalem.
- Defeated by Indian troops at Taraori 1191, Muslim Ghurid leader Mu'izz-ud-Din returns to win a great victory that marks the destruction of Buddhism in India and opens the way for his subordinates to establish Ghurid control over northern India.

1193
- Saladin dies in Damascus. His dynasty continues to rule in Egypt and neighboring lands until 1250.

1200*
- The Ghanian empire begins to collapse because of invasions by desert nomads, paving the way for the powerful successor state of Mali.

* DENOTES CIRCA DATE

1200*
(CONT'D)

- The Chimú kingdom builds an impressive capital at Chan Chan in the Moche Valley of Peru. Basing its wealth on llamas and agricultural products, the kingdom begins a period of expansion around 1370, becoming the most powerful pre-Incan civilization of the region.

- The major city-state of Great Zimbabwe takes shape in southern Africa, founded by the Shona, one of the Bantu-speaking peoples who have come to dominate the region. Its rulers dominate the trade in gold, slaves, and ivory between the inland regions and the Indian Ocean coast.

- The Chinese invention of gunpowder becomes known in Europe, probably brought there by the Mongols.

1202

- During the Fourth Crusade, which lasts until 1204, Christian knights launch an attack on Constantinople, acting in part because of the wish of Pope Innocent III to reunite the Greek (Orthodox) church of the Byzantines with the Latin church of western Europe and in part because of longstanding trade disputes between the Venetians and the Byzantines.

1203

- Sumanguru, ruler of the Susu kingdom of Kaniaga (in the southwestern part of present-day Mali), plunders the Ghanian capital of Kumbi.

1204

- The Crusaders capture and sack Constantinople with such brutality that the Pope and the crusade movement are discredited. The Crusaders establish a Latin kingdom that controls Constantinople until 1261. The Byzantine Empire never fully recovers from this onslaught.

1206

- Temüjin, a Mongol warrior, is proclaimed Genghis Khan (Emperor within the Seas), uniting the Mongol tribes into a single nation and forging them into a powerful fighting force.

- Muslim invaders establish the Sultanate of Delhi in northwestern India, establishing a dynasty that rules until 1266. It depends on Hindu soldiers and civil servants to maintain the kingdom.

1211

- Led by Genghis Khan, the Mongols begin their invasion of the Chin state in northern China.

1215

- The Ghurid Empire falls to the Khwarezm-shah dynasty, which has come to dominate Central Asia and Iran.

- Genghis Khan's Mongol troops take Beijing.

* DENOTES CIRCA DATE

1216
- The Cola empire of southern India begins to break up.

1218
- The Fifth Crusade begins, with efforts concentrated on Egypt.

1219
- Crusaders capture Damietta in Egypt and, expecting the arrival of more troops, refuse the offer of the sultan to trade the city for Jerusalem.
- Control of the Kamakura shogunate in Japan passes from the Minamoto family to the Hojo family.

1220
- Genghis Khan completes his conquest of Persia, ordering a massacre of Persians to avenge an insult from Persian shah Khwarezmia Muhammad II.

1221
- After advancing on and failing to capture Cairo, Crusaders sign an eight-year truce with the Egyptians.

1223
- The Mongols defeat the Russian and Cuman forces at the Battle of the Kalka River in southern Russia but then return to Asia rather than continuing the invasion.

1224
- Sumanguru conquers the Mandingo (or Mande) peoples of Kangaba (near the modern border of Mali and Guinea) and makes their kingdom part of his West African empire.

1227
- Genghis Khan dies. His kingdom is divided among his sons, with Ögödei, the eldest, as Great Khan, or overlord.

1228
- Against the wishes of the Pope, Emperor Frederick II of the Holy Roman Empire launches the Sixth Crusade to pursue his claim to the throne of the Christian kingdom of Jerusalem.

1229
- The Sixth Crusade ends when Sultan al-Kāmil of Egypt negotiates a treaty that grants the kingdom of Jerusalem the cities of Jerusalem and Bethlehem and a corridor to the sea.

1230
- The Khwarezm-shah Empire in Central Asia and Iran falls to the Mongols.
- Sundiata begins the expansion of the Malian Empire.

* DENOTES CIRCA DATE

1231
- Mongol troops occupy Korea.

1234
- The Mongols annex the Chin empire of northern China.

1235
- Sundiata, Mandingo king of Kangaba, defeats Sumanguru at the Battle of Kirina (near the modern city of Koulikoro in Mali), re-establishing the independence of his kingdom and beginning the expansion of the powerful empire of Mali.

1237
- Mongol armies under Batu, grandson of Genghis Khan, renew their invasion of Russia.

1240
- Mongol troops take Kiev, ending their conquest of southern and central Russia. The western part of the Mongol Empire becomes known as the Golden Horde.
- Sundiata destroys Kumbi, former capital of Ghana, annexing Ghana and taking control of its gold-trade routes.

1241
- Mongol armies menace eastern Europe, successfully invading Poland and Hungary and reaching the Adriatic Sea. Great Khan Ögödei dies, and his wife becomes regent for his son Güyük.

1242
- The Mongol threat to Europe ends when Batu withdraws his troops to conquered Russian territory and establishes the capital of the western part of the empire at Sarai on the lower Volga River.

1244
- Supported by Egypt, Khwarzemian Turks capture and sack Jerusalem, sparking the Seventh Crusade.

1246
- Granada is the only remaining Muslim stronghold in Spain. Its fall in 1492 completes the reconquest of Spain by Christian forces.

1248
- Led by Louis IX of France, Crusaders arrive in Cyprus, preparing for their successful reconquest of Damietta early the next year.
- Great Khan Güyük dies. He is succeeded by his nephew Möngke.

1250*
- The city of Cahokia is in a decline that may have been triggered by factors such as climate changes, a breakdown of its economy, or internal and external strife. Though its society disappears, however, the political and religious influence continues.

* DENOTES CIRCA DATE

1250
- The Crusaders defeat Egyptian troops a few miles outside Cairo but are then forced to retreat back to Damietta, which the Egyptians forced them to surrender, ending the Seventh Crusade.
- Mamluks, members of slave corps in the army, seize control of Egypt and Syria, from the Ayyubid dynasty, ruling the state until its occupation by the Ottoman Empire in 1517.

1255
- Sundiata dies, after having extended borders of the Malian empire north to the Sahara, west to the Senegal River, south to the gold fields of Wangara, and east to present-day Sudan.

1258
- Mongol invaders led by Hülegü, brother of Great Khan Möngke, take Baghdad and kill the last ʿAbbāsid caliph, al-Mustaʿsim, ending the rule of the Seljuqs. Hülegü founds the Il-Khanid dynasty to rule Persia as part of the Mongol empire.

1259
- Great Khan Möngke dies while leading his army in China and is succeeded by his brother Kublai.

1261
- The Latin Kingdom established in Constantinople is conquered by Michael VIII of Nicaea, the successor to the Byzantine emperors.
- Having previously been self-governing, the people of Greenland and Iceland swear allegiance to the king of Norway, who has sought to unite all Norwegian Viking settlements under his reign. Iceland is ruled separately from Norway and continues to hold its Athling, though now mainly to settle legal disputes.

1270
- The Eighth, and last, Crusade is launched by Louis IX of France and Edward I of England; Louis dies in Tunis.

1271
- The Eighth Crusade ends, having accomplished nothing.
- Kublai Khan proclaims the Yüan dynasty in China, establishing his capital at Ta-Tu (present-day Beijing). He rules until 1294, promoting cultural life and religious tolerance while oppressing all opponents of Mongol rule.
- Marco Polo leaves Venice to travel to China.

1274
- Kublai Khan's fleet is virtually destroyed in an attempt to invade Japan.

1275
- Marco Polo arrives at the court of Kublai Khan and lives in his domains for the next seventeen years.

* DENOTES CIRCA DATE

1279
- Kublai Khan completes his conquest of the Sung kingdom in southern China, reunifying all of China under Mongol rule.
- The last king of the Indian Cola dynasty dies.

1281
- Mongol hopes of conquering Japan are dashed when a typhoon ("kamikaze") destroys Kublai Khan's great invasion fleet.

1291
- Acre, the Last Christian stronghold in the Near East, falls to the Mamluks.

1292
- Marco Polo leaves China and reaches Venice three years later. Soon thereafter, he is taken prisoner during a sea battle and is imprisoned in Genoa, where he begins dictating the story of his travels to a fellow prisoner.

1293
- Turkish leader Osman, for whom the Ottoman Empire is named, emerges as the prince of a border principality in northeastern Anatolia, and begins to seize Byzantine territory.
- As the Inuit culture expands in Greenland, Norse settlements begin to decline, dying out by the fifteenth century.
- Perhaps because of prolonged drought in the thirteenth century and conflicts with Navajo and Apache peoples, the Pueblo peoples abandon their cliff dwellings, moving southward and eastward and establishing new, large villages. Designs on the pottery of this so-called Regressive Pueblo period are naturalistic representations of animals and people rather than the geometric patterns of earlier periods.

1295
- Il-Khan Mahmud Ghazan, who has renounced Buddhism for Islam, becomes ruler of Persia. During his reign, which lasts until 1304, his dynasty loses touch with the Mongols of China.

1299
- Il-Khan Ghazan of Persia begins an unsuccessful four-year campaign to invade Syria.

1307
- Mansa Musa, the grandson or grandnephew of Sundiata, becomes the emperor of the Malian empire. He is renowned worldwide for his wealth, his devotion to Islam, and his patronage of the arts.

1317
- During the reign of Il-Khan Abu Sa'id, which lasts until 1335, Mongol rule in Persia begins to collapse because of factional struggles among the Mongol ruling class, economic troubles, and the decline of the ruling family.

* DENOTES CIRCA DATE

1324
- Mansa Musa makes a pilgrimage to Mecca, stopping in Cairo with a retinue that is said to include one hundred camels, each carrying three hundred pounds of gold.

1325*
- Ibn Battūtah leaves Tangiers for some thirty years of travel that provide the basis for his writings about Asia and Africa, major sources of information about those continents for Westerners.
- The Mexica (Aztecs) build their great capital city of Tenochtitlán on the site of present-day Mexico City.

1325
- Mansa Musa annexes the Songhai kingdom of Gao (in the western part of modern Mali), making it part of the empire of Mali.

1330*
- The Bubonic plague, or Black Death, begins to kill huge numbers of people in northeastern China. The epidemic is carried westward by traders, travelers, and nomadic peoples.

1332*
- Mansa Musa, emperor of Mali, dies, having made the cities of Niano, Tombocktu, and Gao into important religious and cultural centers with mosques, libraries, and Islamic schools. He leaves his empire strong and prosperous, but by the end of the century quarrels over royal succession divide Mali and leave it vulnerable to invasion.

1333
- Emperor Go-Daigo of Japan successfully overthrows the Kamakura shogunate, but his subsequent actions provoke civil war.
- Togon-temür becomes the last Yüan (Mongol) emperor of China. During his reign his anti-Chinese policies provoke frequent rebellions, and in 1368 he is forced to flee to the steppes of inner Asia, clearing the way for Ming dynasty rule of China (1368–1644).

1335
- The Sultanate of Delhi now dominates most of the Indian subcontinent.
- After the death of Il-Khan Abu Sa'id of Persia, his dynasty's empire breaks into separate kingdoms ruled by Il-Khanid princes until 1353.

1336
- Ashikaga Takauji, who has proclaimed himself shogun, drives Emperor Go-Daigo of Japan from the capital and places Kogon on the throne, establishing the Ashikaga shogunate, under which Japanese feudalism enters its golden age. During the Ashikaga period, which lasts until 1568, aristocrats depend on armed retainers (samurai), who follow a strict code of conduct (bushido).

1345
- The Ottoman Turks extend their conquest of Byzantine territory into Europe.

* Denotes Circa Date

1346	• Bubonic plague reaches the Golden Horde, beginning the disintegration of Mongol rule in Russia.
1347	• Bubonic plague reaches Sicily.
1348	• Bubonic plague reaches North Africa, mainland Italy, Spain, England, and France.
1349	• Bubonic plague reaches Austria, Hungary, Switzerland, Germany, and the Low Countries.
1350	• Bubonic plague reaches Scandinavia and the Baltic lands.

* DENOTES CIRCA DATE

Saladin taking the Holy Cross from King Guy of Jerusalem during the Muslim defeat of Christian forces at the Battle of Hattin on 4 July 1187; illumination from a manuscript by Matthew Paris (Corpus Christi College, Cambridge)

A mid-thirteenth-century map of the world, with Jerusalem at its center (British Library, London)

CHAPTER TWO

GEOGRAPHY

by KELLY DEVRIES, KATHRYN A. EDWARDS, and JEREMIAH HACKETT

CONTENTS

Sidebars and tables are listed in italics.

| 814 | • T-O maps have circulated throughout Europe since the eighth century. These maps depict a world with a vast ocean surrounding three continents—Africa, Asia, and Europe; two large rivers in the shape of a "T" divide the land masses. |

814

• T-O maps have circulated throughout Europe since the eighth century. These maps depict a world with a vast ocean surrounding three continents—Africa, Asia, and Europe; two large rivers in the shape of a "T" divide the land masses.

874

• Vikings discover Iceland and begin to colonize the island.

922

• An Arabi embassy is sent to visit and report on the Rus (Viking) gatherings along the Volga River. A member of the expedition, Ahmad Ibn Fadlan, records his journeys in *Risala*.

949

• The Lombard prelate Liutprand (Liudprand) of Cremona is sent as an ambassador to the Byzantine Emperor, Constantine VII (Porphyrogenitus).

982

• Erik Thorvaldson (Erik the Red) is exiled from Iceland and in 986 founds the first European colony in Greenland.

986*

• Bjarni Herjulfsson, traveling from Iceland to Greenland, is blown off course and sights North America.

1000*

• Leif Eriksson, the son of Erik the Red, travels west from Greenland and explores the Canadian coast. By the end of the century, Norsemen establish a colony at present-day L'Anse aux Meadows in Nova Scotia.

1050*

• Seljuk Turks begin their conquest of the Holy Land.

1206

• Temuchin receives the title *Ghenghis Khan* (Mightiest King) of the Mongol tribes.

1211-1234

• Mongol armies attack and conquer China.

1222

• The Mongols begin to attack Europe.

* DENOTES CIRCA DATE

1236-1241	• Mongol armies under Subotai and Batu sack several Russian towns including Kiev.
1241	• The Mongols attack Germany, Poland, and Hungary.
1245	• Pope Innocent IV sends Giovanni di Plano Carpini and Lawrence of Portugal on a mission to the Mongol court. They are among the first Europeans to travel to China.
1254-1255	• The Franciscan friar William of Ruysbroeck travels to the Mongol empire and later writes of his adventures.
1256-1260	• Mongol armies attack the Middle East, conquering Baghdad and Damascus.
1262-1269	• Two Venetian brothers, Niccolo and Maffeo Polo, travel east to trade with China.
1271-1272	• Marco Polo accompanies his father (Niccolo) and uncle (Maffeo) to China, remaining there until 1292.
1289	• John of Monte Corvino is sent on a mission to China by Pope Boniface VIII and becomes the first Archbishop of Peking in 1307.
1321	• Four Franciscan missionaries are killed in India.

* **DENOTES CIRCA DATE**

OVERVIEW

Modern Misconception. Most people assume that medieval Europeans had little knowledge of the world outside the boundaries of their homes. That was not the case. From the onset of the Middle Ages, Europeans of all classes and educations were interested in the world beyond their own specific locales. They knew about Byzantium and Russia, considered taking pilgrimages to Italy, Spain, and the Holy Land, pondered the religious problems of the Middle East, and dreamed of and often enjoyed the riches of the Indies and China. Only the most ignorant did not know that the earth was round, although most thought that it was much smaller than Ferdinand Magellan and his crew would prove it to be in 1519–1522. Of course, the center-point of this earthly globe was Jerusalem, but that came from a religious rationale.

Curiosity. Despite this interest in the world outside of their own neighborhoods, only a few brave and wealthy souls made any lengthy journeys. Some of those who could afford it did venture out in groups to distant, but known, lands on pilgrimages or crusades, but their numbers were never large. Meanwhile, other individuals, even fewer in number, decided to take on the adventure of discovery themselves.

Romans. Much of what medieval Europeans knew of the world came from the ancient Romans. For the Romans, the world centered on the Mediterranean Sea, the *Nostrum Mare* (Our Lake) of their empire. However, it was not this "lake" which defined the empire's boundaries. The Roman imperial boundaries, at their height, extended to Spain in the West, Asia Minor in the East, the Sahara Desert in the South, and Scotland in the North. The Rhine and Danube Rivers provided a fairly defensible line in Europe, and the Sahara Desert did the same in North Africa, while elsewhere a large series of impressive fortifications defended the empire; the most memorable of these was undoubtedly Hadrian's Wall, which separated the northern part of Great Britain (populated by Picts) from the southern Roman-controlled section.

Permeable Boundaries. However, for the Romans themselves, these boundaries were largely artificial, defenses meant to keep other people out rather than keep Romans in. Naturally, this situation was evident in the mil-itary excursions of certain emperors who seemed to be able to cross the Rhine, Danube, and Sahara with ease in order to put down a "barbarian" military threat. Indeed, for over a century the Romans even occupied Dacia, a large province in present-day Romania, where rich deposits of tin made it worth the extra military strength needed to secure the region from raids.

Mercantile Activity. Yet, the army was not the most important Roman institution that passed through the imperial borders. The many merchants and traders who left the security of the empire were probably a far more significant force. Archaeological and other evidence has shown that Roman trade extended well beyond the Mediterranean region. Caches of Roman coins and other archaeological remains have been found in Scandinavia, India, China, and Africa, while goods from all of those regions are recorded to have found their way into Roman market stalls. Indeed, the insatiable appetite of wealthy Roman citizens for exotic possessions may have been what fueled this distant trading urgency. By the first century, trading voyages into the Red Sea and Indian Ocean and along the east coast of Africa were commonplace.

Ptolemy. The outside world also interested many Roman geographers and scientists. Building on earlier Greek and Middle Eastern precedents, Roman writers penned many theoretical works of geography. The most famous of these undoubtedly was the second-century Alexandrian, Claudius Ptolemy, who wrote two important treatises, one on astronomy and one on geography. Ptolemy's *Geography* provided not only confirmation of the round earth theories propounded by his Greek predecessors, Aristotle, Eratosthenes, and Hipparchus, but also provided a gazetteer of all known places in the world, including many places in Asia, Africa, along the Atlantic coast, and Scandinavia. His calculations were often wrong, errors which later maps made from Ptolemy's *Geography* duplicated (it is unknown whether Ptolemy's original treatise was accompanied by maps), but the influence of this work extended well beyond the fall of the empire, and even the destruction of the Ptolemaic library in Alexandria.

Barbarians. During the third and fourth centuries, the Roman imperial boundaries began to weaken. Scores of barbarians, as foreigners were called, began to flood into what they perceived were these wealthier lands of the Romans. Of course, the characteristic of these barbarian invasions, coming from outside of the Roman borders, brought an enhanced awareness to Roman civilization. These barbarians brought new customs, some of which were forced upon the Romans. On the other hand, because of the disruption of normal Roman policing activities, and the insecurity that naturally followed this disruption, as well as the decline in citizen wealth, trade with distant lands, even those lands that had fathered the barbarians who invaded the Empire, virtually ceased. Thus, while it may have seemed to the majority of Romans that their contact with other cultures was increasing, in fact it may have decreased, with goods from lands on the continents of Asia, Africa, and even Europe becoming insignificant during the early Middle Ages.

Greek Studies. Yet, intellectual awareness of these lands continued to be active. However, before too long, the decline in the knowledge of Greek among the Latins of Western Europe began to significantly limit study in the earlier texts. Therefore, Ptolemy's *Geography,* which remained an important text among Byzantine scholars in the East, was available in the West only in summaries and abbreviated versions by the fifth century. Frequently, geographical fables replaced the most scientific findings of Ptolemy and his Greek-writing students. Not until the sixth century, did an Alexandrian monk, Cosmas, write *Christian Topography;* later, in the eighth century, the anonymous *Cosmography* appeared, the first new works on geography since Ptolemy. While the former purported to be a worldview based on the Bible, the latter claimed to be a translation of an earlier account of the travels of Aethicus Ister. Both were filled with errors. Cosmas portrayed the earth as an oblong, with the skies a vaulted canopy supported on walls; a second "earth," separated by water from that inhabited by the Europeans, held Paradise and was also encompassed by an ocean. *Cosmography* filled its pages not only with geographical knowledge but also with marvelous creatures: Amazons, an island inhabited by dog-headed men, large, bellicose ants, and so forth. Its European, Asian, and African land masses, too, were surrounded by water. Nevertheless, the *Cosmography* proved to be extremely successful and influential; Cosmas's *Christian Topography* was less so.

Brendan. Other early medieval writings described fantastic travels. Irish monks seemed to have been especially prolific in the writing of these accounts. Undoubtedly, the most famous of these was the *Navigatio Brendani* (The Voyage of Brendan, circa 578). This work describes the westward voyages of a group of monks, led by Brendan, in a sewn-leather boat. They traveled from island to island, with each new island visit forming an even more marvelous adventure for the monastic voyagers. While long thought to be fictional, the *Navigatio Brendani* inspired many of the fourteenth-century and fifteenth-century explorers; these leather-ship voyages were also successfully imitated in the 1970s.

Byzantines. The Byzantines were far more active geographically than their Western European counterparts. For much of the early Middle Ages, trade with India, Africa, and China remained active, although the rise of the war-like Sassanian Persians and the Ethiopian Kingdom of Axum midway through the period made it increasingly difficult to smoothly trade with the first lands. However, Chinese goods remained valuable in Constantinople and elsewhere throughout the Byzantine Empire. Byzantine emperors even sent military envoys east to ask for advice and assistance against the Arabs; missionaries were sent to convert the "pagans" of Asia and Africa.

Pilgrimages. Yet, surprisingly during this period, there was little contact between Byzantium and Western Europe. Only rarely were there interactions on a diplomatic level between the European kingdoms and the Byzantine empire, and often when these did occur, such as the tenth-century ambassadorial voyage of Luitprand of Cremona to Constantinople, the result was an even icier relationship than before. Still, there was constant pilgrimage traffic to the Holy Land, which passed through Constantinople. This traffic increased especially after the triumph of Catholicism in Merovingian and Carolingian Gaul and, later, once Charlemagne had conquered it, in Italy. Even when the Islamic armies captured Jerusalem, Bethlehem, and other holy Christian sites from the Byzantines in the seventh century, pilgrimages did not end, for the Arab masters of the Holy Land seemed every bit as keen on the "tourist" income of the pilgrims as had the Byzantines. The pilgrimage route was so important to the Arab leaders of the Holy Land in the eighth to tenth centuries that they sent legates to the Western European leaders, complete with gifts, including an elephant, which graced Charlemagne's court in Aachen for many years, and established hostels and hospitals to serve the Latin pilgrims while they visited their sacred locations.

TOPICS IN GEOGRAPHY

ASIAN EXPERIENCES: LATE MIDDLE AGES

Continuing Interest. In the Late Middle Ages (1300–1500) there was a decided Western European interest in the Far East, in particular in China. Trade, although frequently dangerous and sometimes hindered by wars and local political struggles, continued along the Silk Road without abatement. Also continuing were Christian missionary efforts. While not significant, there was a European Catholic presence in Asia throughout the period as well.

John of Monte Corvino. This presence began in earnest in 1289 when Pope Boniface VIII sent Franciscan John of Monte Corvino on a mission to China. Monte Corvino traveled overland, following the Silk Road and preaching along the way, and reached Peking in late 1293 or early 1294. Once in China, and perhaps because of the recent death of Kublai Khan, he surmised that his efforts would be better spent in the Chinese region of Ongut (or Tenduc), which had a sizeable population of Nestorian Christians. There he was so successful that he even converted the local governor, Korgis (or George), the son-in-law of the Great Khan, who also gave him land to build a church. In 1298, following the death of Korgis in a dispute with another Mongol khan, John of Monte Corvino transferred his activities to Peking.

Proselytizing Efforts. Monte Corvino's life and proselytizing activities in China were not easy. In 1305 he wrote a letter detailing his loneliness, lack of a spiritual confidant, need for materials for use in worship and teaching, and lack of news about his order and the papacy. He also noted the hostility that others had toward him, especially the Nestorian Christians active in the Far East. However, he also reported the construction of a church in Peking with a tower and three bells and the baptism of six thousand converts. In addition, he had acquired a knowledge of the Mongol language and had translated the New Testament and Psalms into it. Later, in another letter, Monte Corvino added that he had built a second church, near to the palace of the Great Khan from whom he had always received the most friendly welcome and treatment.

Archbishop of Peking. Impressed by these achievements, in 1307 Pope Clement V appointed Monte Corvino as the first Catholic Archbishop of Peking. At the same time, six other Franciscans were appointed as bishops to assist the new archbishop in his office, although only three were ever to reach China, and then not until 1313. By this time, Monte Corvino's ministry had spread beyond Peking to Zayton (Ch'uan Chow), an important seaport along the southern coast of China.

Impact. John of Monte Corvino died between 1328 and 1330. However, the death of such an impressive and diligent religious man did not mean the end of Catholicism in China. He was succeeded as archbishop by one of his bishops, Andrew of Perugia, and from then until at least the middle of the fifteenth century, a small community of Christians thrived in Peking and Zayton. The work continued to be difficult, bringing Christianity to those who had no background for it, but, if reports of these missionaries can be believed, there seems always to have been a consistent rate of conversions. The spiritual isolation for men used to being surrounded by their fellow friars–all early missionaries to Asia were Franciscans–and their loneliness in being so far from home, without the prospect of ever seeing it again, frequently brought despair and frustration. The only welcome breaks in this tedium were the infrequent visits of Western merchants and travelers who brought news from Europe.

Catholic Communities. By the third decade of the fourteenth century both the Franciscans and Dominicans had set up special vicariates for ministry in Asia. While China continued to flourish, Catholic missionary efforts in India and elsewhere in Asia were not so successful. Some missionary friars even met a martyr's death. For example, in India in 1321, four Franciscans allegedly committed blasphemy against Mohammad and were burned to death. Later, others were also killed when they encountered primarily anti-Christian Muslim rulers and inhabitants. (Not having the friendly relationship of a political leader such as the Great Khan in China continually thwarted these missionary activities elsewhere in Asia.) Despite these setbacks, a community of Catholics, although never large, continued also in India into the fifteenth century, led by their devoted and hardworking European ecclesiastics.

Sources:
Eliyahu Ashtor, *The Levant Trade in the Later Middle Ages* (Princeton, N.J.: Princeton University Press, 1983).

Arthur P. Newton, *Travel and Travelers of the Middle Ages* (New York: Knopf, 1926).

J. R. S. Phillips, *The Medieval Expansion of Europe* (Oxford: Clarendon Press, 1998).

ASIAN EXPERIENCES: MARCO POLO AND THE SILK ROAD

Far East. Some Westerners accompanied the Mongols when they traveled to their recently conquered lands in China, thus becoming the first Europeans to visit that Far Eastern land in more than a millenium. When the first of these trips was made is not known. However, by the second half of the thirteenth century, judging from the appearance of Asian products in European markets, most notably in Italy, a trade connection with at least parts of China had been achieved. This development corresponds with the travels of the most famous merchant family to journey to China, the Polos.

Polo Brothers. Between 1262 and 1269 two Venetian brothers, Niccolo and Maffeo Polo, almost by accident made their first trip to China. Cut off from their normal trade route by war, the Polos were forced to travel east with the Mongols whom they had befriended. What they found there was a society certainly different from their own, but one which seemed as equally interested in what trade articles the Europeans had to offer them as the Europeans were to acquire their goods. Of course, only a few could afford these items, and the travel was not only long and tedious but also risky. Still, the Polos, and others like them, seemed to believe that the profit from this trade must have been worth it. (Additionally, there was the adventure of it all, a reason for traveling to the East that should not be discounted.)

Mercantile Family. By the time Niccolo and Maffeo made their first Chinese journey, the Polos were a well-established family of merchants who dealt in luxury goods acquired in far-off locales. One of their other brothers even owned a house in Sudak, a Venetian colony on the Crimean peninsula, which they visited before setting off across Asia. When Niccolo's son and Maffeo's nephew, Marco, came of age to learn the merchant's trade, he also traveled with them to China. Marco also recorded his experiences in the East.

Observations. According to Marco Polo, his father and uncle had returned to the West in 1269 bearing diplomatic messages and a request for Christian missionaries to the Pope from Kublai Khan. But Pope Gregory X was suspicious of these messages and refused to send the large number of men requested to accompany the Polos on a return journey to China. As a result, only Marco Polo accompanied his family members when they returned to the Far East. Traveling from Venice to Armenia by sea in 1271 or 1272, the Polos then made their way across the lands of Asia Minor and Iran into Inner Asia. The journey was not easy. Marco Polo described the water as "brackish and green" and "so bitter that no one could bear to drink it." Diarrhea became commonplace for the European travelers. Although their exact route is hard to follow from Polo's descriptions, it was long; they passed over large plains, great deserts, and high mountains. He was struck by the beauty of the landscape, although at other times he was frightened by the nature he encountered. He also found the air pure and fresh. The travelers journeyed past the city of Balkh, left in ruins by Genghis Khan in 1220. Yet, whatever negative spirit such a display of Mongol violence

Village in Afghanistan near the Silk Road

Thirteenth-century illumination of Kublai Khan handing the golden seal of the Mongol empire to the Polo brothers (from Felix Barker, *The Search Begins,* 1971)

might have had on the young man was soon changed when he first encountered the Mongols and found them to "live by trade and industry." They had orchards and vineyards; they grew cotton, flax, and hemp. Many of their products were completely unattainable in the West. For a Venetian merchant, even a young one, the prospects were exciting.

Kublai Khan. After three and one-half years, Niccolo, Maffeo, and Marco Polo arrived in China, at Shangtu, the summer palace of Kublai Khan. For the next sixteen or seventeen years, Marco Polo would live among the Chinese, staying near Kublai Khan either at Shangtu or at the Great Khan's main imperial palace in Peking. However, exactly what role he played with Kublai Khan in these palaces is uncertain. According to his own writings, he assisted in the governance of the Khan's empire, including the assistance of successful military adventures against some of Kublai Khan's enemies. He claimed even to have been the governor of the large city of Yangchow. However, some scholars dispute these claims, asserting instead that without corroborative evidence these were probably nothing more than Marco Polo's later delusions. (Polo did not dictate these adventures until years after he had returned to Venice.) Other scholars support Marco's tales, noting a certain Po-Lo who appears in Chinese records and is given governmental offices; this person, they claim, might be Marco Polo.

Deep Admiration. Yet, no matter what the truth of some of the adventures that Marco Polo assigns himself, there can be no doubt that he had a great love for the Chinese culture and people and that this love was reciprocated by the Great Khan and others. His insights into their traditions and practices, in daily life as well as in business, made engrossing reading. He was clearly given a freedom of

movement among the Mongols and Chinese that greatly aided his later descriptions.

Return Home. Marco Polo left China in 1290 or 1292. Together with his father and uncle, he escorted a Mongolian princess to Iran to marry the governor there. They traveled by sea, in a convoy of fourteen Chinese junks, making their way by means of Indonesia, Ceylon, and India. Polo would describe each of these lands as well, again increasing the knowledge of the world for his many European readers. The heat in these parts was so intense that some of the travelers died. However, they eventually reached their goal, and after attending to their various duties in Iran, which delayed them for several more months, the Polos all returned to Venice, where they arrived in 1295. Neither he nor his father nor his uncle would ever return to Asia.

Important Route. Marco Polo had traveled along what would become known as the Silk Route. The reason for the name, of course, was simple: silk was one of the most prized commodities that came from the Far East to Europe. Should a merchant be able to deliver a cargo of silk, or of pepper or other spices, the profits made him a wealthy man. Yet, it was a long journey, fraught with risks both to those who financed the travel as well as those who undertook it. Still, because it was so profitable, attempts were continually made to find a way of shortening the trip, as well as making it safer. Marco Polo's trip was one of these attempts, and it seemed to have provided a new and relatively improved means of acquiring trade goods from the Far East. Before long, he and others in his century began to travel overland, through peaceful—at least to them—Mongols, who also seemed to respect if not to completely understand the politics and economics of long-distance trade. They seem also to have profited from it themselves, acquiring goods and knowledge from these European traders. Before the Silk Road was established, the only method for Europeans to acquire Far Eastern items was from the Egyptian port of Alexandria. These goods had been brought either overland or by sea by Muslim traders, and thus their availability (and cost) depended on the good will of Muslim merchants toward Christians. Understandably, during times of war, and especially during the late twelfth and thirteenth centuries, when Muslim military successes eventually caused the Christians to abandon the Holy Land, this route of acquiring Eastern Asian goods would be cut off. With the Silk Road, a new route had been discovered, that did not rely on Muslim peace and friendliness to be successful. Once it began to be used, it was profitable to Muslim merchants, as well. Within less than a century after Marco Polo traveled the Silk Road, most of the trade that was being carried on with Asia came via this route; it is also likely that many Eastern innovations adopted by the West in the Late Middle Ages (1300–1500) were also spread by Silk Road travelers.

Sources:

James Muldoon, ed., *The Expansion of Europe: The First Phase* (Philadelphia: University of Pennsylvania Press, 1977).

Arthur P. Newton, *Travel and Travelers of the Middle Ages* (New York: Knopf, 1926).

J. R. S. Phillips, *The Medieval Expansion of Europe* (Oxford: Clarendon Press, 1998).

Marco Polo, *The Travels of Marco Polo* (London: Everyman's Library, 1908).

ASIAN EXPERIENCES: MONGOLS

Prester John. One of the most enduring tales of the Middle Ages was that of Prester John. It told of a Christian kingdom somewhere in Asia (or, later, Africa) that had been converted by and was ruled over by a benevolent theologian-king by the name of Prester John. Where and when the tale originated is not known, although some conjecture that it could have been associated with the legends of Saint Thomas's mission to India. However, soon after the Crusades were under way, the popularity of Prester John increased. The idea was that once the Holy Land was occupied and returned to Christianity, new Crusaders and explorers would be sent to seek out Prester John and unite his kingdom with the rest of Christendom. Later, when the Crusades proved to be unsuccessful, it was believed that Prester John would bring a military force to the Middle East and restore the Holy Land to Christianity. It was even reported in 1145, following the fall of Edessa and the initiation of the Second Crusade (1144–1187), that a letter had been received from Prester John. In this epistle the theologian-king, after telling of his kingdom and its marvels, expressed his desire to visit the Holy Sepulcher after facing and defeating the enemies of Christianity. (Indeed, so convincing was this now lost letter that in 1177 Pope Alexander III wrote a reply to Prester John and sent it off to the East in the care of an envoy, Philip, who traveled to the Holy Land, but thereafter promptly disappeared.) Even as late as 1221, when the Crusading forces, led by King Louis IX (St. Louis) of France, languished at Damietta, there was a rumor of oncoming aid from Prester John or his descendant King David, although again this promise remained unfulfilled.

Eastern Horde. While Prester John's Christian kingdom in Asia was truly fictional, however, there was another group of people in thirteenth-century Asia who did affect medieval Europe and the Crusader Kingdoms: the Mongols. In 1222 the first onslaught of Mongols against those living west of them occurred. The initial target was southern Russia, and Russia would continue to be plagued by Mongol assaults for the next several generations. Yet, that land would not be the only western ambition of the Mongol conquerors, known throughout history as the Mongol Horde.

Motivations. The reason for the Mongols' conquest is not known, as prior to the early thirteenth century they seem to have been largely disunited tribes far more concerned by their agriculturally dominated economy than in military activity. The man who may have changed this situation was born in 1167 as Temuchin, but has become known historically by the name he took as a military and political leader, Ghenghis Khan (Mightiest King). Early in his life his father was murdered, and Temuchin became a fugitive. By surviving he gained a reputation for enterprise and daring that attracted many followers and eventually, in 1206, bolstered him to leadership over not only the Mongol

Thirteenth-century illumination depicting William of Ruysbroeck and a companion before King Louis IX and the two travelers setting out to visit the Mongol capital (Felix Barker, *The Search Begins*, 1971)

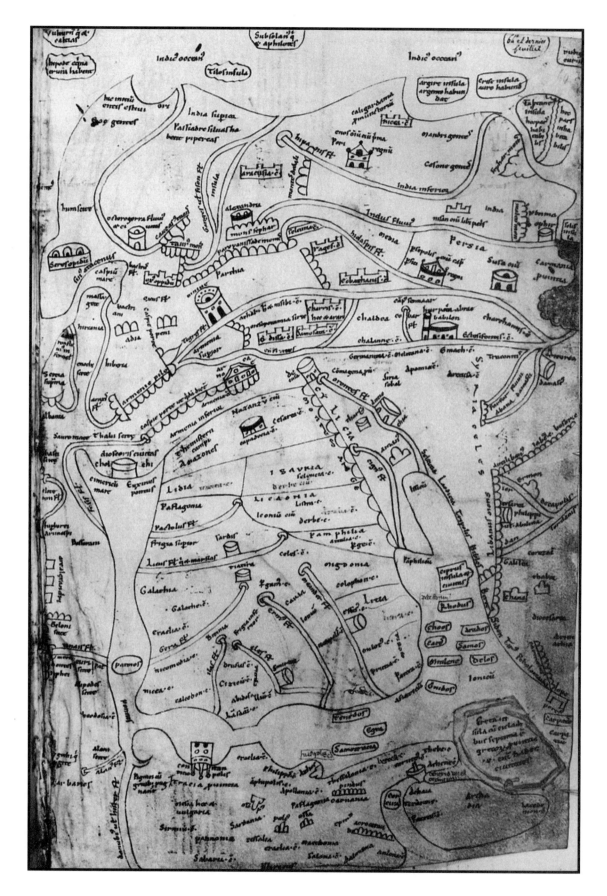

Jerome map of Asia, twelfth century (British Library, London)

tribes, but also over neighboring Tatar, Kerait, Naiman, and Merkit tribes.

Conquest. Genghis Khan's objective as ruler over and military leader of the Mongols was simple: to utilize the horsemanship, which every Mongol male was taught from youth, to make conquests against non-Mongolians. Whether these potential enemies were nearby or far-away did not seem to matter. In 1211 the Mongols attacked China, moving against the Chin Empire, which ruled the northern part of the country, and occupying the capital, Peking, in 1215, although the entire Chin Empire would not fall until 1234, after Genghis's death. In 1218 the Mongols conquered the empire of Kara Khitai in central Asia. In 1222 he attacked the Khwarismian Empire, located in the region between the Aral Sea and Afghanistan. In this conquest, Genghis Khan made his first contact with, and conquest of, a Muslim state.

Successors. In 1227 the Mightiest King died while attempting to besiege Ning-Hsia, capital city of the Tangut kingdom of Hsi-Hsia, which lay between Mongolia and China. However, his dreams of world conquest did not die with Genghis Khan. His immediate successor, Ogotai Khan, made increased territorial gains. Indeed, in the 1230s, while one of his armies set about attacking the Sung empire in China with the conquest of Korea, a second army was attacking the Seljuk Turkish empire of Rum in Asia Minor, and a third army began a conquest of Russia and Eastern Europe.

Devastation in Russia. This latter attack which proved to be the most devastating, and the most brutal, of those that the Mongols made into the west. It was led by the chieftains Subotai and Batu and may have numbered as many as 150,000 (although the entire army never participated in any one military engagement). They set out in 1236, and by the end of 1237 Subotai and Batu had advanced into Russia, capturing and destroying the city of Riazan and killing or enslaving its entire population. They followed this depredation in February 1238 with a similar destruction and slaughter of the towns and people of Vladimir and Suzdal. Two years later, after an unexplained pause in the campaign, the Mongols attacked the impressive city of Kiev, destroying it and nearly wiping out its large population. Indeed, so many were killed that even as long as eight years later the bones of the dead could still be seen lying where the Mongols had left them.

Hungary. Once the Mongols had finished with their attacks on Russia, in early 1241, they turned toward Poland and Hungary. On 9 April 1241 they were met near the borders at Liegnitz by a Western army of Germans, Poles, Teutonic Knights, and Knights Templars. The Western army was devastated, and the Mongols reportedly sent nine sacks of ears from the enemy dead to Karakorum as evidence of their victory. Two days later a Hungarian army was also defeated. Hungary lay open to conquest, which occurred throughout the rest

of 1241, while a contingent of Subotai and Batu's force even rode to the gates of Vienna. It seemed that Germany was to be the next target of this unstoppable Mongol horde, with the rest of Western Europe fearing for its own safety. (The German Emperor, Frederick II, even wrote to King Henry III of England, asking him for assistance against the Mongols.)

New Focus. What Western armies could not do, the death of Ogotai Khan in December 1241 did: the Mongol armies, even those as far away as the borders of Germany, returned to Karakorum for the seating of a new Great Khan, in this case Ogotai's brother, Kuyuk. Yet, Kuyuk's reign was short, and his successor, Mangu Khan, while certainly interested in extending his empire in the West, desired to campaign against Middle Eastern Muslims rather than European Christians. (Although a few Mongol raids were made into Europe in the ensuing years, none came close to the geographical acquisition or brutality of the 1237–1241 attacks.) In 1256, Mangu Khan set upon and completely destroyed the Muslim sect of Assassins, who, living in mountain fortifications in what is now Iran, terrorized all nearby peoples. In 1258 Mangu Khan besieged and captured

A European view of the Mongols as beasts; thirteenth-century illumination (from Felix Barker, *The Search Begins,* 1971)

Baghdad, the intellectual center of Islam and capital of the Abbasid caliphate. In addition he invaded Syria and seized Damascus, but in turn he was defeated by an Egyptian army at the battle of Ain Jalud. By this time, Mangu Khan had died and was succeeded by his brother, Kublai Khan. Kublai had little interest in the West, either in the Middle East or Europe, but was instead engrossed with the Mongol imperial lands of China. In 1259, as soon as he ascended to the throne of his dead brother, he moved the Mongolian capital from Karakorum to Peking, which he renamed Khanbalik. He then, by 1279, completed the conquest of the rest of China, becoming the first Yuan emperor.

Diminishing Threat. With the death of Mangu Khan and Kublai Khan's shift of interest to the Far East, the Mongol military threat to Europe and the Middle East largely vanished. Russia and the Ukraine would continue to be harassed by Mongolian tribes, and, for a while during the early fifteenth century, Eastern Europe, the Byzantine Empire, and the Ottoman Turks were forced to face a new but relatively short-lived Mongolian threat in the Tatar invasion led by Tamerlane. However, on the whole, the time of the attacks of the Mongol horde fell into historical memory.

Missionary Efforts. What did not fall into historical memory, at least to the Christians of Western Europe,

was that many non-Christians lived to the east of them. Proselytizing had not been effective in European Christian relationships with the Muslims of the Middle East, Africa, or Spain, although some missionary endeavors with these people had been attempted and, almost always, failed. However, with the Mongols, especially as they had little discernable religion, at least in the perception of European Christians, missionary efforts might well be successful, and even if not, the Christian missionaries sent among them would be able to serve as diplomats and spies.

Dominicans. The first of these Christian missionaries to the Mongols were Dominican Friars sent by the Hungarian King, Bela IV, in the early part of the thirteenth century. Their target was the Cuman and Bashkir tribes of southern Russia and Siberia. Little is known about this first mission, even whether these missionaries ever encountered their proselytizing subjects, let alone whether they converted any of them. Yet, a later missionary attempt initiated by Bela IV, made by the Dominican priest Julian in 1236–1237, failed to reach the Bashkirs but had discovered plans for the impending Mongol attack that so completely devastated Russia and Eastern Europe.

Franciscans. A second missionary effort followed in 1245 when Pope Innocent IV appointed two Franciscans, Giovanni di Plano Carpini and Lawrence of

Portugal, to travel to the Great Khan himself. Their record, which Carpini regularly wrote, provided the first accurate glimpse into the Mongolian life, which up to that time for Europeans had existed largely of nightmarish myths. Carpini and Lawrence left Lyons bound for Asia in April 1245. In Breslau they were joined by a third Franciscan, Benedict the Pole. Together they arrived at Kiev early in 1246, where the destruction of eight years previously still haunted the region. Certainly this scene was a sorry sight for Christian missionaries to see; yet, undaunted, the missionaries pressed on. By July 1246 they had made contact with the main Mongol army and on 24 August witnessed the crowning of Kuyuk, whose succession had been disputed for several years, as Great Khan. The three Franciscan missionaries were able to acquire a letter from Kuyuk, written to Innocent IV, although its content, which questioned the Christian presumption of "God's Will," did not bode well for either their or future missionary activities among the Mongols.

Growing Interest. Nevertheless, when Carpini returned to Lyon in November 1248 and shortly thereafter published his *History of the Mongols,* despite his detailing all of the depredations of the Mongols, the interest of Europeans for these Eastern marauders was anything but dampened. A veritable flood of Westerners traveled to Karakorum in the following years. By the 1250s the rulers of Russia, Georgia, Hungary, Nicea, and Armenia had either traveled to meet the Great Khan themselves or sent envoys. Merchants, too, journeyed there, from as far away as France and the Low Countries. Also, of course, Christian missionaries continued to try to convert the Mongols, joined in their efforts also by Muslim, Buddhist, Byzantine, and Nestorian Christian missionaries.

Sources:

Christopher Dawson, ed., *Mission to Asia* (Toronto: University of Toronto Press, 1980).

L.N. Gumilev, *Searches for an Imaginary Kingdom: The Legend of the Kingdom of Prester John* (Cambridge: Cambridge University Press, 1987).

Charles J. Halperin, *Russia and the Golden Horde: The Mongol Impact on Medieval Russian History* (Bloomington: Indiana University Press, 1985).

John Mandeville, *The Travels of Sir John Mandeville,* translated by Charles W. R. D. Moseley (Harmondsworth, U.K.: Penguin, 1983).

David Morgan, *The Mongols* (Oxford: Blackwell, 1986).

Arthur C. Moule, *Christians in China Before the Year 1550* (New York & Toronto: Macmillan, 1930).

Igor de Rachewiltz, *Papal Envoys to the Great Khans* (London: Faber & Faber, 1971).

John J. Saunders, *The History of the Mongol Conquests* (London: Routledge & Kegan Paul, 1971).

CARTOGRAPHY

Personal View of the World. Mapmaking and the perception of the world it demonstrates has two distinct aspects in the Middle Ages. The first was theoretical; it constructs an image of the world in keeping with Greco-Roman and Christian authorities and reflects a spiritual perspective on Earth's place in the universe. The second aspect was practical and applicable geographical knowledge that was rarely expressed in permanent maps. The world of medieval Europeans of all social classes was limited to the boundaries of their personal experience. Their grasp of geography was strongly influenced by the people who farmed and the lords who held legal rights to plots of land. In a bill of sale the borders of a property were commonly described by listing the names of the people who held the lands on the borders; if a person reading the document did not know those people or the extent of their lands, it would be almost impossible to draw a picture of the property. This personal knowledge extended into the ways lords, traders, or any other traveler planned his or her movements. These figures relied on local guides at each stage of their journey, as well as information brought to them by others who had previously traveled the route. Changes in this personal knowledge could, however, have the same emotional force that changes in national boundaries have in the modern era. During the 1180s Kings Henry II of England and Philip II Augustus of France frequently fought. The most famous site for negotiating their treaties was under the "elm of Gisors," a large elm tree that according to legend stood on the border between their territories. When the tree was cut down in 1188, it was seen by both sides as a symbol of the impossibility of the two monarchs agreeing.

Geographical Knowledge. If a villager or craftsman was asked to describe the geography where he lived, he would most likely focus on a territory's productive capacity: how the slope of land helped or hindered water retention, how readily wood was available on neighboring hillsides, or how to transport most easily goods to neighboring villages. Knights and nobles might emphasize the defensive attributes of geographical features: vantage points, difficult access, or ready water. When asked to describe the geography of France, Germany, or Italy as a whole, most would probably first need those terms defined. When they thought of a territory, they thought of the lands controlled by their respective overlord or of some province that was only slightly larger: Brittany, Picardy, Artois, Burgundy—all parts of modern France. In describing distant lands, medieval Europeans, scholars and laymen alike, often relied on a mixture of folklore and hearsay interpreted according to a framework that was generally Christian. Scholars, sailors, and others with education or a practical training in geography did, however, know that the world was round, and they had known this fact since before the birth of Christ. Medieval travelers were not afraid of falling off the end of the Earth; they were afraid of getting lost in the vast sea that they believed encircled the globe.

T-O Maps. Although medieval maps are rare, maps do exist that depict this vast, world-encircling ocean.

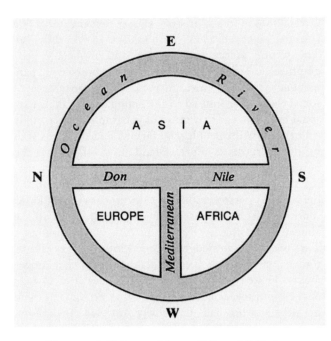

Diagram of a T-O map of the world (from J. B. Harley
and David Woodward, *The History of
Cartography,* 1987)

T-O maps, also known as *mappae mundi* or *mappamundi* (world maps), appeared in Europe during the eighth century. Building on classical knowledge and scholarship, these documents reflected both an awareness of real geographic features and a desire to set them into a Christian, universal framework. One of the most famous and earliest T-O maps is found in Isidore of Seville's *De natura rerum* from the late sixth century to the early seventh century, and it has the basic characteristics of later, more-elaborate versions. In it the world is depicted as a perfect circle with a great ocean around the edges. Two great rivers form the T, one running lengthwise across the globe and the other going down from the middle of the first river to the global ocean on the bottom of the Earth. This pattern divides the land into three continents. The top continent, which covers the top half of the globe, is Asia, and the two smaller continents in the bottom half of the globe are Europe and Africa. Later T-O maps would elaborate considerably on this basic scheme. Frequently Jerusalem would be placed in the center of the Earth; other biblical sites such as the Garden of Eden and Gog and Magog would be situated on the Asian continent; and smaller rivers or principalities would be added depending on the intended audience. By the twelfth and thirteenth centuries when much more detailed maps of the world were being produced, it was often difficult to find the basic T-O framework of the map. World maps such as those from Ebstorf (1234), by Henry of Mainz (circa 1110), and at Hereford Cathedral (circa 1250) were artworks as much as maps. Angels and mythological creatures decorated the borders, legendary buildings and animals denoted geographic locations, and no attempt was made to produce the map according to scale.

Mapping and God. When medieval scholars prepared maps of the world, they thought in holistic terms. In other words, heaven and earth formed a whole; earth and, by inference, human beings could not be separated from the divine geography and the divine plan of which all beings were a part. This logic underlay the inclusion of Asia, Africa, and Europe on the earliest such maps; the division reflected the dispersal of Noah's sons after the Flood. Following logic derived from Greek philosophy, the world was believed to be and sometimes was drawn as a perfect circle. According to medieval theology, as an embodiment of God's power, the Earth is by definition perfect without beginning and without end, just as a circle has no beginning and ending. The T in a T-O map symbolized the cross on which Christ was crucified. By the eleventh and twelfth centuries, maps were increasingly drawn with Jerusalem in the center, thus signifying that the site of Christ's passion, the Holy City, was the spiritual and real center of the world. Produced by monks and churchmen at medieval schools, medieval maps were a vision of how the world should be spiritually rather than how the world was geographically.

Portolan and Other Charts. Although almost all surviving medieval maps emphasized this spiritual depiction of the world, there are examples of other mapmaking traditions, at least during the later Middle Ages. Perhaps not surprisingly they were developed by sailors. Portolan charts were line drawings put into notebooks that captains and navigators would carry with them of the features a sailor could see as he sailed past land. They marked harbors, reefs, sandbars, fresh water, villages, and sometimes stands of wood—all of which were essential knowledge for a medieval sailor. Measuring distance was always a problem, however, given that medieval ways of keeping time were quite imprecise and medieval units of measurement varied greatly depending on the region. For example, time was often measured by how long it took to say a standard prayer such as the Our Father, and measurement was often done based on how long someone could walk in one day or how much land one team could plow in one day, neither of which were particularly effective on a body of water. In the late thirteenth century European sailors adopted the magnetic compass which helped determine direction and curvature in the coastline, but it still did not solve the distance problem. Only in the fifteenth and sixteenth centuries would knowledge be recovered and techniques developed that minimized this problem.

Sources:

Mary B. Campbell, *The Witness and the Other World: Exotic European Travel Writing, 400–1600* (Ithaca, N.Y.: Cornell University Press, 1988).

Evelyn Edson, *Mapping Time and Space: How Medieval Mapmakers Viewed Their World* (London: British Library, 1997).

J. R. S. Philipps, *The Medieval Expansion of Europe* (New York: Clarendon Press, 1988).

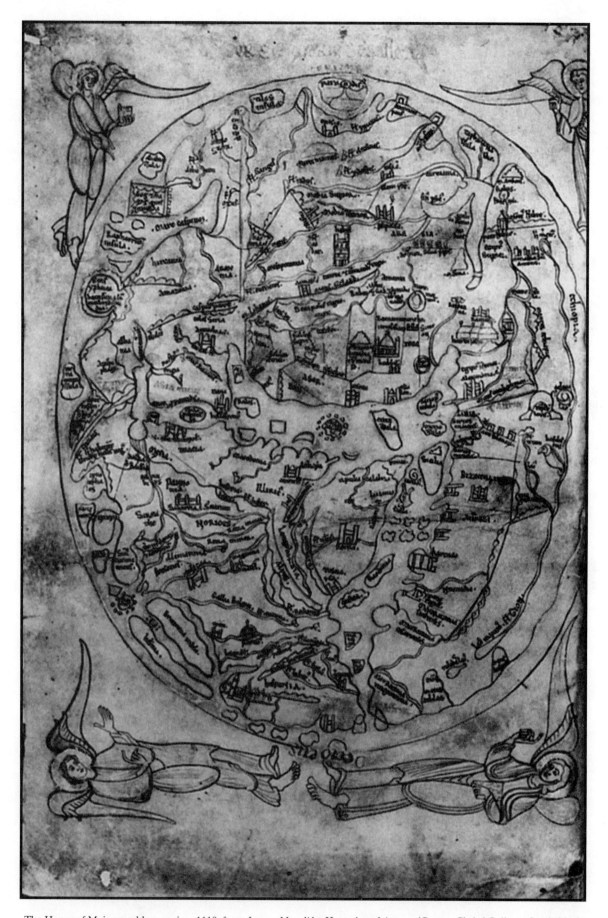

The Henry of Mainz world map, circa 1110, from *Imago Mundi* by Honorius of Autum (Corpus Christi College, Cambridge)

GEOGRAPHICAL KNOWLEDGE: ROGER BACON

Influence. The geographical research of the English philosopher and scientist Roger Bacon in many ways anticipated by one century the new geography of the Renaissance. Although he did not invent map projection, his demand for a new mathematical way for making maps with the use of astronomical instruments certainly contributed to its development. Bacon's account on geography is found in his *Opus Maius* (Major Work, circa 1267) and in the *Opus Tertium* (Third Work, circa 1267). It is based on traditional sources such as Aethicus Ister's *Cosmographia*, Aristotle's *De caelo et mundo* and *Meteorologia*, Sallust's *De bello jugurthino*, Seneca's *Naturales questiones*, Pliny's *Naturalis historia*, Ptolemy's *Almagest*, Saint Jerome's *De situ et nominibus locorum Hebraicorum*, Paulus Orosius's *Historia adversus paganos*, Saint Isidore's *Etymologiae* and *De natura rerum*, the works of Al-Fraganus, Avicenna, and other Islamic writers, and the Bible and biblical commentaries. Bacon saw himself as providing the intelligent reader with a "summary" of the geographic knowledge handed down from antiquity. He omitted discussions of Northwestern Europe and Southern Europe because they were so well known.

Ideological Foundation. Bacon drew much information from the *Travel Account* (1256) of friar William of Ruysbroeck who journeyed in 1253–1255 to the Mongol or Tatar kingdom on behalf of the French King Louis IX. For example, he learned from this work that the Caspian Sea was not an arm of the circular Ocean surrounding the world but was rather a large inland sea. In many respects Bacon's account of world geography may be compared with that of Albertus Magnus; indeed, with the exception of the material taken from William of Ruysbroeck's account, it differs little from what is found in the German scholar's *De natura locorum*. Still, Bacon's account has a definite ideological foundation.

Ultimate Goal. Bacon was interested in geography as far as it could help Christian missionaries. Furthermore, he believed the use of mathematics in geography was important since it led to a greater knowledge of the heavens and the earth. This approach allowed his readers to gain natural knowledge which could serve as a basis for the symbolic knowledge found in sacred scripture. David Woodward and Herbert M. Howe point to Bacon's singular contribution to knowledge of geography in the Middle Ages: "What sets Bacon aside from his contemporaries, however, is his insistence on the need for a systematic, mathematical way of positioning places on the earth for the practical needs of government, both to understand history and to predict from where in the world threats to Christianity are likely to come."

Links with Columbus. One passage from the geography section of the *Opus Maius* has been linked to the voyage of Christopher Columbus in 1492. What is clear is that Columbus owned a copy of the *Imago Mundi* by the French theologian Pierre D'Ailly, and this work contained a long section of Bacon's geographical writing.

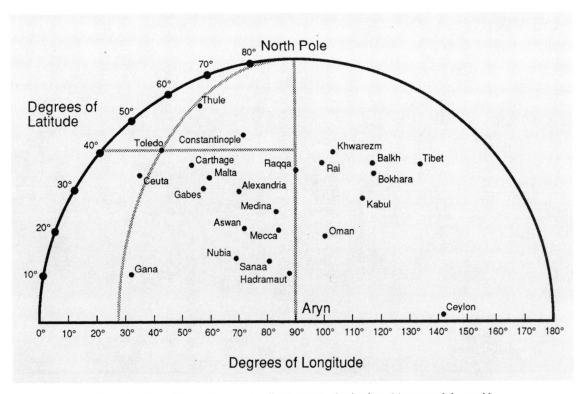

Reconstruction of Roger Bacon's coordinate system plotting key cities around the world
(University of Wisconsin Cartographic Laboratory)

The Inhabitable World. It is in his description of the various latitudinal zones (climates) of the inhabitable world that Bacon offers his most original geographical contribution, "the allusion to a systematic map of the inhabited world." Bacon wrote:

> Since these *climata* and their famous cities cannot well be described by words alone, a map must be used to make them clear to our senses. I shall, therefore, first present a map of our quadrant, and on it I shall label the important cities, each in its own place, with the distance from the equator—what we call the latitude—of the city or the region. I shall also label them according to their distance from east to west, what we call the place's longitude. In my assigning of *climata* and likewise of latitude and longitude, I shall make use of the prestige and experience of the wisest scholars. To locate each city in its proper place [on this map] by its longitude and latitude, which have already been discovered by my authorities, I shall use a method by which their positions may be shown by their distances north and south, east and west. The device is this: parallel to the equator (already drawn on a plane surface), a straight line [i.e. a parallel of latitude] is drawn. This intersects another straight line [a meridian], from the point corresponding to the number of degrees of latitude of the place. This point is also marked on the colure (the quarter of the great circle that passes from the equator to the pole of the universe), and is, in fact, an arc of the colure. This procedure is both easier and better [than anything now in use], and a map drawn in this way is quite capable of representing to the senses the location of any point in the world.

Coordinate System. In this manner, using the "Toledo" or "Alphonsine" Tables, Bacon provided a coordinate system based on parallels and meridians. These tables provided a better estimate of the Mediterranean than those of Ptolemy. Bacon's original map has been lost but it was clearly different from the common medieval *Mappamundi* such as the Hereford Map of circa 1290. Unlike those maps which were focused on the East and Jerusalem, Bacon's map was focused on the North, and used the structural base which only became common in the fifteenth century.

Sources:

Roger Bacon, *Opus Maius*, translated by Robert Belle Burke (Philadelphia: University of Pennsylvania Press, 1928).

Stewart C. Easton, *Roger Bacon and His Search for a Universal Science* (New York: Columbia University Press, 1952).

Paul D. A. Harvey, *Medieval Maps* (London: British Library, 1991).

George H. T. Kimble, *Geography in the Middle Ages* (New York: Russell & Russell, 1968).

David Woodward and Herbert M. Howe, "Roger Bacon on Geography and Cartography," in *Roger Bacon and the Sciences: Commemorative Essays*, edited by Jeremiah Hackett (Leiden & New York: Koln, Brill, 1997), pp. 199–222.

PORTUGUESE INTERESTS IN AFRICA

Land of Mystery. Although quite close geographically, Africa was a continent that was not well known by Europeans during the Middle Ages. Crusading armies at times had tried to enter it, but on each occasion they had been unsuccessful at even getting past the northern coastlines. Merchants and missionaries, too, it seems, were halted from conducting their activities within the continent's borders, stopped as much by Muslim governors as by harsh terrain, and thus they also remained ignorant of what the continent had to offer.

Animals and People. Of course, despite this ignorance, there still remained a European interest in Africa, fueled as it was by constant rumors of strange beasts and peoples. Elephants, lions, and crocodiles were well known in Europe, with several monarchs having menageries or zoos with such creatures displayed, usually sent to them as gifts from Middle Eastern and North African magnates who were seeking to improve political and trade relationships between their two lands. People with black skin were also known in Europe, some of whom may have been brought there as slaves or servants by crusaders or merchants, and others who had traveled there themselves. They were seen as curiosities, with little racial hatred, although being called by the generic name *Moors* reveals a belief that all were of the Muslim religion, whether this belief was true or not. These animals and people, in turn, led the European imagination to assume that other strange beasts and races, and mixtures of the two, existed within the inaccessible continent, as various records and bestiaries from the time have proven. Additionally, once Asia had been crossed and the mythical Prester John had not been found there, it began to be rumored that the great theologian-king dwelled not in Asia but in Africa.

Route to China. By the end of the fourteenth century a new route to China was also sought, one which did not necessarily have to go overland. The protection which merchants had once received from a fairly unified Mongol people had begun to dissolve because of a breakdown in central military authority and the political distance from China. This breakdown led to lawlessness and warfare along the once relatively safe Silk Road.

Reconquista. Before the end of the fourteenth century neither the Portuguese nor the Spanish Kingdoms seemed to have much interest in the non-Iberian geographical world. Having lost this peninsula to Muslim soldiers and their leaders in 711, Spanish and Portuguese Christians fought for more than the next seven hundred years to win it back. So important was the *Reconquista*, as this Crusade became known, that medieval Popes freed those Spaniards and Portuguese warriors involved in it from having to serve in other crusades being fought at the same time, including Crusades to the Holy Land. By the eleventh century, Christian armies had begun to recapture some Muslim-occupied lands, and in 1147, assisted by soldiers on their way to the Second Crusade (1144–1187), they besieged and conquered Lisbon. For the next two centuries, the *Reconquista* was at its strongest, with the kingdoms of Portugal, Castille, and Aragon taking the lead in recovering almost all of the Iberian peninsula. By the beginning of the fifteenth century, only the smallest of holdings was left in Muslim hands, the kingdom of Granada, at the tip of the peninsula and nearest to the African coast.

Prince Henry the Navigator. These military successes gave great confidence to the Spanish and Portuguese and, despite having frequent wars between themselves, the leaders of these Iberian kingdoms began to look abroad for the means to increase their economic and political clout. The Portuguese, and in particular Prince Henry of Portugal, known to history because of his fifteenth-century geographical initiatives as "the Navigator." Before his death in 1460, nearly all of Henry's goals were achieved: the exploration of Africa below Cape Bojador, the furthest south that any European had previously sailed along the western coast; the opening of trade relations with the inhabitants of the region; learning the extent of the Muslim kingdoms; verifying the existence of the legendary Christian kingdom established by Prester John; and spreading Christianity to any nonbelievers whom the Portuguese encountered.

Sources:
Bailey W. Diffie, *Prelude to Empire: Portugal Overseas before Henry the Navigator* (Lincoln: University of Nebraska Press, 1960).

Diffie and G. D. Winius, *The Foundations of the Portuguese Empire, 1415–1580* (Minneapolis: University of Minnesota Press, 1977).

Felipe Fernández-Armesto, *Before Columbus: Exploration and Colonization from the Mediterranean to the Atlantic 1229–1492* (Philadelphia: University of Pennsylvania Press, 1987).

P. E. Russell, *Prince Henry the Navigator: The Rise and Fall of a Culture Hero* (Oxford: Oxford University Press, 1984).

TOPOGRAPHY AND CLIMATE

Landscape and Lifestyle. The economic and social foundations of medieval Europe were based on agriculture. Time was regulated according to seasons for plowing and harvesting, picking fruits, or collecting wood. A drought or flood, hail storm, or wildfire could have disastrous consequences for medieval peasants and, by extension, all those who depended on them for labor and produce: nobles, clergymen, and town dwellers. Moreover, the technology available to medieval Europeans to alter their environment and provide against climatic shifts was limited compared to that with which most modern Westerners are familiar. Dams, dikes, and aqueducts to direct water supplies and drain land fell out of use during the early Middle Ages as Europeans gradually lost the engineering knowledge of the Roman Empire. For earthmoving equipment medieval Europeans had carts and wheelbarrows; to put out fires, they relied on buckets of water or firebreaks prepared with wooden rakes and shovels. For these reasons, geography and climate had a profound effect on the lives of everyone at all social levels during the Middle Ages (814–1350). Soil composition affected the types of crops that could be grown and ultimately the diet of most people living in an area. Buildings were constructed using local materials: stone or wood for walls and different types of grasses for roofs. A temperature shift of only 1-2 degrees during the summer could stunt the growth of basic crops and lead to famine and death for large parts of the population. Because of their profound influence, differences in climate and geography played a key role in forming the many distinct cultures of medieval Europe.

Latitude and the Gulf Stream. A region's latitude is based on its relation to the sun. Latitude is how far north or south a territory is of an imaginary center line drawn around the world from east to west. In this sense, Europe has a high latitude, with southern cities such as Rome being as far north as New York, while cities such as London and Paris are at the same latitude as Newfoundland, Canada. Being this far north would make Europe quite cold, and almost uninhabitable given the technology of medieval Europeans, if it were not for the moderating effects of several other geographical and climatic qualities. Probably the most significant is the Gulf Stream, a current of warm water that travels from the equator across the Atlantic Ocean. It bathes the Atlantic coast of Europe with warm water, which helps keep the temperature of Europe warmer and more consistent than its latitude suggests it would be. In addition, the European continent itself is essentially a peninsula of Asia and is surrounded on three sides by water. The Mediterranean Sea to the south, the Atlantic Ocean to the west and northwest, and the Baltic, North, and Arctic Seas to the north introduce warmer and more humid air to the European continent. The islands that comprise Europe—England, Ireland, and Sicily among others—share this benefit but to a greater degree. Ireland, for example, might expect four to six months a year of snow based purely on its latitude, but it is rare if snow stays on the ground there for a week. Moreover, these islands and the European continent itself include a series of smaller peninsulas jutting into these bodies of water, and these landmasses enjoy even more-balanced climates. Because of the relatively flat plain that stretches from central France through Germany into Eastern Europe and western Russia, the warming effect of the Gulf Stream and bodies of water can be felt hundreds of miles inland.

Climate Zones of Europe. Although water moderates the climate of Europe as a whole, there are six smaller "climate zones" on the European continent. To the south, the Mediterranean Basin enjoys a warm climate with long, dry summers. These summers made droughts and water management an ongoing problem in the Middle Ages, and the relatively loose and sandy soil that existed in many parts of this region molded the types of crops planted and even the plowing technology developed. Just north of the Mediterranean Basin is Alpine Europe, a series of mountains that stretches from the Pyrenees, through southern France and the Alps into the greater Caucasus and Urals in modern Russia. In these regions climate is largely influenced by elevation; with limited potential for cereal growth, animal husbandry often had a greater role in the local economy than in other zones. The third and fourth zones are those of Western-Northwestern Europe and Central Europe. Both of these regions are relatively flat, and an important factor in their climate is the degree to which ocean influences can be felt. In Western-Northwestern Europe, roughly equivalent to modern France, England, Belgium, western Germany, and the Netherlands, which is closer to the Atlantic Ocean and the Gulf Stream, the climate tends to be more humid and moderate with year-round rain, an ideal environment for farming without irrigation. In Central Europe, which corresponds approximately to eastern Germany, Austria, and the western territories of modern Eastern Europe, the winters tend to be longer and colder, although frequent rainfall during the summer helps with crop growth if the rain is not excessive. In the fifth zone, Eastern Europe, the effect of the ocean is much less, and the winters tend to be longer, colder, and dryer while summers are hotter. Compared to the previous two zones, the growing season is shorter, and the living conditions are harsher. The final zone is that of the Scandinavian Mountains. These lands have long winters with heavy snowfall and an extremely short growing season. As in the Alpine regions, animal husbandry and hunting are extremely important in this zone's economy, as is fishing.

Landscape and Commerce. Climate and geography (environment in its broadest sense) were extremely important in determining the basic activities of medieval society; there was no point for Swiss mountaineers to try to grow wheat, which demanded warm, hot summers, while farmers in northern France could more profitably and easily grow grain. Landscape, however, influenced the economy in more-complex ways as well. Bodies of water provided products (fish, salt, and plants) and transportation routes; the Mediterranean Basin had been a commercial zone since at least the second millennium B.C.E. Medieval Europe was crisscrossed with navigable rivers, and in those regions where portage was needed between two bodies of water the medieval Europeans could not frequently rely on roads and other routes developed by the Romans and maintained by local lords, who enjoyed rights to taxes from all who used them. Rivers provided cheaper, quicker, and often safer transportation than overland routes. The Danube, Oder, and Elbe in Central Europe, the Rhine, Thames, Loire, and Seine in western Europe, the Tiber, Guadalquivir, and southern Rhone in Southern Europe were all major trade routes. In addition, the rich soil and ready access to water around these rivers made them valuable agricultural sites as well. As such, it is no surprise that many medieval cities and even smaller villages developed around rivers, streams, lakes, and oceans that could provide water for transportation, drinking, irrigation, technology, and even defense.

Predicting Weather. Despite the benefits medieval Europeans received from the surrounding water and the plans Europeans themselves made, shifts in weather could be both frightening and disastrous. For these reasons, medieval Europeans made attempts to predict and control their climate. Many of their methods may seem magical to modern eyes. Astronomical anomalies foreshadowed hot or cold spells, and prayers and processions were made around the fields to assure their protection and growth. There were attempts, however, to put weather prediction on a less-magical footing. In this area medieval European scholars borrowed from the writings of Muslim philosophers, as they did in many other areas during the twelfth century. Yaqub Ibn Ishaq al-Kindi was a famous ninth-century Muslim philosopher in Baghdad who wrote prolifically on mathematics, physics, astronomy, medicine, geography, logic, philosophy, and even music. During the tenth and eleventh centuries his works were brought into Spain and, from there in the twelfth century, transmitted into France, Italy, and other regions of Europe. Al-Kindi's guides to weather forecasting borrowed from three traditions: native Muslim traditions of predicting weather based on the moon; learned Muslim astrologers who developed ideas found in famous Greek sources such as the writings of Ptolemy; and Muslim, Hebrew, and other physicists indebted to the physics of the famous Greek philosopher, Aristotle. Although al-Kindi's guide was far more mathematical and detailed than the weather forecasting done at the popular level, it was still based on similar premises. Planetary bodies affect climate; climate follows set rules; these rules can be predicted to some extent; and a knowledge of these rules brings a person closer to a greater knowledge of God.

Little Ice Age. From circa 800-1300, Europe enjoyed a relatively warm and benign climate that fostered European agriculture, culture, and society. Around 1300, however, the temperature of Europe appears to have begun to cool, beginning what climatologists have termed the *Little Ice Age*. This Ice Age would last until the middle of the nineteenth century. Modern scholars have no clear sense about why it happened, and medieval people appear to have been just as puzzled. Although Europe's average temperature only appears to have declined about 2 degrees, it had a profound impact on the growing season and, therefore, the amount of crops produced and the number of people who could be fed. The impact of these agricultural shortages would be felt at all levels of society. (As a basis for comparison, modern analyses of global warming are based on temperature changes that are approximately half those of the Little Ice Age.) The 1310s would include a series of long, cold summers, which led

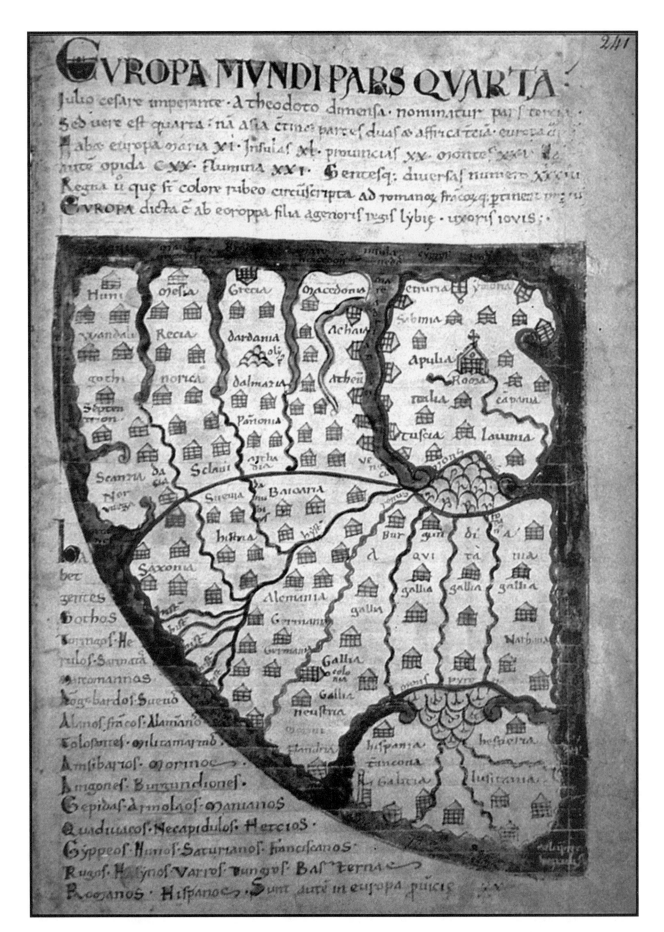

"Europa Mundi Pars Quarta," a map of Europe from *Liber Floridus*, circa 1120 (University Library, Ghent)

to famines and outbreaks of disease unequalled until the Black Death. It is quite possible that the beginning of the Little Ice Age, and its effects on Europe's agriculture, "softened up" Europe's population so that it was more vulnerable to the Black Death when it arrived in Sicily during October 1347. Scandinavian colonies in Greenland and Iceland, which had prospered during the height of the Middle Ages, were abandoned during the early fourteenth century, presumably because of the increased difficulty in growing basic foodstuffs in those regions. Germany's leading scholar of the European witch-hunts, Wolfgang Behringer, has even argued that the social and economic strains caused by the Little Ice Age might have been a key factor in the renewal of interest in witchcraft and its prosecution that began in the fourteenth century.

Tuscan Villages. Corresponding to approximately the northern quarter of the Italian peninsula, the region known as Tuscany had been noted for its geography and climate since the Roman Empire. During the Middle Ages it would continue to be a prosperous region of Europe, supporting many wealthy cities (Florence, Pisa, Siena, Lucca) and enjoying the benefits of its distinct environment. Tuscany was divided into many valleys separated by low mountains and finally the Apennines, even by that time relatively ancient mountains of lower elevation. Villages and cities developed that specialized in grain, wine, and olive oil production. Frequently the villages were built on hillsides, relying on the mountains for protection, and farmers walked down the hill to their fields or vineyards. Different sides of a valley could specialize in different crops, depending on the soil or the amount of sunlight a patch of land received. These microclimates often led farmers to plant the flat lands with grain while covering the hillsides with trees and vineyards, a system that also eased cultivation and harvest. Because the winters were relatively mild compared to much of Europe, the stone farmhouses built from the most available local materials did a satisfactory job of sheltering peasants, unlike in northern Europe, where they would have been too cold and the stone too expensive.

Rhine Valley. Stretching from the English Channel to Switzerland, the Rhine was one of medieval Europe's great rivers, and communities developed along it well before the Christian era. In the Middle Ages the river itself was a major transportation route between north and south, and the plain on its eastern and western banks provided extremely fertile farmland. For these reasons, the Rhine Valley would be one of the earliest and most heavily fortified regions in medieval Europe, with stone keeps and larger castles built by nobles and robber-barons at almost every bend in the river. Traders using the river would be stopped at each of these sites, and a duty was demanded to pass that stretch of river. In spite of these taxes, transportation on the Rhine was still more economical and safer than travel by overland routes. In the thirteenth and fourteenth centuries the Rhine Valley would become one of the regions in Europe that experienced a burst of urbanization, fostered by trade and agricultural prosperity.

Sources:

Wolfgang Behringer, "Weather, Hunger and Fear: The Origins of the European Witch Persecution in Climate, Society and Mentality," *German History* 13 (1995): 1-27.

David L. Clawson and James S. Fisher, *World Regional Geography*, sixth edition (Upper Saddle River, N.J.: Prentice Hall, 1998).

Brian Fagan, *Floods, Families, and Emperors: En Niño and the Fate of Civilization* (New York: BasicBooks, 1999).

Emmanuel Le Roy Ladurie, *Times of Feast, Times of Famine: A History of Climate Since the Year 1000*, translated by Barbara Bray (Garden City, N.Y.: Doubleday, 1971).

THE VIKINGS AS EXPLORERS AND COLONISTS

Northern Invaders. With the invasions of the Vikings, which began in Scotland at the end of the eighth century and followed into Ireland and the continent in the early ninth century, Western Europeans recognized how small their own world was. Here, as had been the case with the third-century and fourth-century barbarian invasions of the Roman Empire, were foreigners who seemed to travel from incredibly long distances simply to make the rather conventional lives of western Europeans extremely difficult. However, it would be wrong to consider the Viking invasions only in their "raid-and-return-to-Scandinavia" context. While it is true that the majority of early Viking raids were just that, before even the ninth century was over several groups of these Northerners had begun to settle on some of their conquered lands and trade with their neighbors. Especially active in this were those Vikings who settled along the eastern rivers that flowed south toward Byzantium. Giving their names, the Rus, to this region, Russia became a stronghold of Scandinavian kings and warriors. While never turning away from a fight when one presented itself, these Vikings seemed to be far more interested in whatever could be had in the markets of Constantinople. Trading furs, cloths, and art objects not often found in Byzantium and the Middle East, these Viking merchants realized goods, principally Islamic silver, that were easily traded in Scandinavia and northern Europe. In fact, so diverse was Viking trade in the East that many different strange and exotic objects have been found among their archeological remains, including an Indian Buddha. At the same time, the Arabs and Byzantines were so curious about these Northerners that they sent emissaries to study them, one of whom was Ibn Fadlan, whose tenth-century report of his encounter with the Vikings is one of the best available for the study of Viking life, including hygiene and funerals. Vikings also served as mercenary soldiers in the armies of the Arabs and Byzantines, forming in the latter the famous Varangian Guard, which fought as a unit in the eastern Mediterranean for more than a century.

THE RISALA OF AHMAD IBN FADLAN

In 921 the caliph of Baghdad sent an embassy to the king of the Bulgars on the Volga, who had expressed interest in learning the Islamic faith. The embassy took a circuitous route from Baghdad, arriving at the Bulgar capital almost eleven months later, on 12 May 922. On the way it encountered a variety of lands and peoples, all of which were described in the account (*Risala*) of Ahmad Ibn Fadlan, a secretary to the embassy. Excerpts of his *Risala* were included in the *Geographical Dictionary* (circa 1200) of the Arab writer Yaqut, as well as in the work of the sixteenth-century Persian geographer Amin Razi. Among the most valuable information in Ibn Fadlan's chronicle is his description of a group of Viking traders the embassy encountered at the Bulgar capital. Though his remarks are not entirely free of prejudice (he refers to them once as "the filthiest of God's creatures"), his work provides a rare and mostly reliable account of the Viking people known as the Rus, and especially of their funeral rituals:

I have seen the Rus as they came on their merchant journeys and encamped by the Atil [*i.e.,* Volga]. I have never seen more perfect physical specimens, tall as date palms, blond and ruddy; they wear neither *qurtaqs* [tunics] nor caftans, but the men wear a garment which covers one side of the body and leaves a hand free.

Each man has an axe, a sword, and a knife and keeps each by him at all times. The swords are broad and grooved, of Frankish sort. Every man is tattooed from finger nails to neck with dark green trees, figures, *etc.* . . . .

When they have come from their land and anchored on, or tied up at the shore of, the Atil, which is a great river, they build big houses of wood on the shore, each holding ten to twenty persons more or less. Each man has a couch on which he sits. With them are pretty slave girls destined for sale to merchants . . .

I had heard that at the deaths of their chief personages they did many things, of which the least was cremation, and I was interested to learn more. At last I was told of the death of one of their outstanding men. They placed him in a grave and put a roof over it for ten days while they cut and sewed garments for him.

If the deceased is a poor man they make a little boat, which they lay him in and burn. If he is rich, they collect his goods and divide them into three parts, one for his family, another to pay for his clothing, and a third for making *nabid,* which they drink until the day when his female slave will kill herself and be burned with her master . . .

The closest relative of the dead man, after they had placed the girl whom they have killed beside her master, came, took a piece of wood which he lighted at a fire, and walked backwards with the back of his head toward the boat and his face turned (toward the people) . . . for the purpose of setting fire to the wood that had been made ready beneath the ship. Then the people came up with tinder and other fire wood, each holding a piece of wood of which he had set fire to an end and which he put into the pile of wood beneath the ship. . .

One of the Rus was at my side and I heard him speak to the interpreter, who was present. I asked the interpreter what he said. He answered, "He said, 'You Arabs are fools.'" "Why?" I asked him. He said, "You take the people who are most dear to you and whom you honor most and you put them in the ground where insects and worms devour them. We burn him in a moment, so that he enters Paradise at once." Then he began to laugh uproariously. When I asked why he laughed, he said, "His lord, for love of him, has sent the wind to bring him away in an hour." And actually an hour had not passed before the ship, the wood, the girl, and her master were nothing but cinders and ashes.

Source: H. M. Smyser, "Ibn Fadlan's Account of the Rus," in *Franciplegius* (New York: New York University Press, 1965), pp. 92-119.

Settlements. The Vikings also began to build settlements in northwestern Europe. In Ireland, Scotland, the Faroes, Orkney and Shetland Islands, and northeastern England, the Vikings mingled and intermarried with the people adopting their languages and customs. In France, a district in the lower Seine River basin was officially granted to them as the duchy of the Northmen (Normandy) in 911. There, too, they assimilated well with the local inhabitants, also adopting their language and many of their customs. Yet, some Vikings were unsatisfied with these settlement plans. Perhaps out of a sense of adventure, or maybe, as in the case of the most famous Viking explorer, Erik Thorvaldson (Erik the Red), out of a sense of outlawry and exile, some Vikings chose to sail farther from their traditional sites of raiding, conquest, and colonization.

Iceland and Greenland. Iceland, an island northwest of the Faroes Islands, had been discovered around 874, with permanent Viking settlement taking place a short time afterward. Despite its name, the island is quite habitable, with significant thermal activity that keeps the climate mild and the land agriculturally viable. However, the same cannot be said for Greenland. Discovered in 982 by Erik the Red, it is surrounded by ice-choked waters and has few habitable farmlands or pastures. Viking colonies survived there into the fifteenth century, when, for some as-yet-unexplained reason, the settlers abandoned them and disappeared.

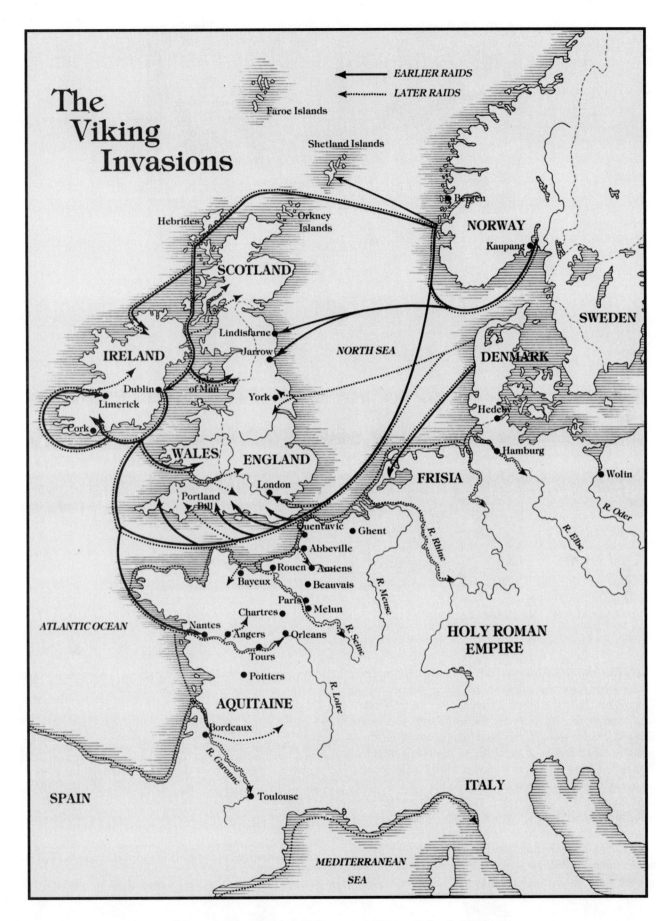

The Viking Invasions

EARLIER RAIDS
LATER RAIDS

Faroe Islands

Shetland Islands

Hebrides

Orkney Islands

NORWAY

Bergen

Kaupang

SCOTLAND

SWEDEN

Lindisfarne

Jarrow

NORTH SEA

DENMARK

IRELAND

Dublin

of Man

York

Hedeby

Limerick

Cork

WALES

ENGLAND

London

FRISIA

Hamburg

Wolin

R. Oder

R. Elbe

Portland Bill

Quentavic

Ghent

R. Rhine

Abbeville

Rouen

Amiens

Bayeux

Beauvais

R. Meuse

Paris

Melun

Chartres

R. Seine

ATLANTIC OCEAN

Nantes

Angers

Orleans

HOLY ROMAN EMPIRE

R. Loire

Tours

Poitiers

AQUITAINE

Bordeaux

R. Garonne

ITALY

SPAIN

Toulouse

MEDITERRANEAN SEA

Map showing the incursions of the Norsemen in Europe during the Middle Ages
(from Anne Savage, *The Anglo-Saxon Chronicles,* 2000)

Illumination of a Viking fleet under Ingvar and Hubba invading England, from *Life, Passion and Miracles of St. Edmund, King and Martyr,* circa 1130 (Pierpont Morgan Library, New York)

North America. In circa 1000 one of Erik the Red's sons, Leif Eriksson, discovered lands westward of Greenland. It is thought that he sailed around Greenland, across the ice floes to Baffin Island, and south along Labrador to Nova Scotia. How far to the south he actually sailed has been debated, as has the location of Vinland, a land supposedly covered with wild grapes. Nonetheless, what is certain is that he and later Vikings continued to travel to North America for cargoes of wood and other goods, with evidence suggesting that these journeys continued until at least the thirteenth century. This theory has been further established by the excavations of a Viking settlement on the north coast of Nova Scotia, L'Anse aux Meadows, which appears to have been a colony that flourished for a time.

Sources:

George Herbert Tinley Kimble, *Geography in the Middle Ages* (New York: Russell & Russell, 1968).

Magnus Magnusson and Herman Pálsson, trans., *The Vinland Sagas: The Norse Discovery of America* (Harmondsworth, U.K.: Penguin, 1965).

Geoffrey Jules Marcus, *The Conquest of the North Atlantic* (Woodbridge, U.K.: Boydell, 1980).

Samuel Eliot Morison, *The European Discovery of America: The Northern Voyages* (New York: Oxford University Press, 1971).

Kirsten A. Seaver, *The Frozen Echo: Greenland and the Exploration of North America, c. 1000–1500* (Stanford, Cal.: Stanford University Press, 1996).

SIGNIFICANT PEOPLE

ERIK THE RED

FLOURISHED TENTH CENTURY
VIKING EXPLORER

Early Life and Exile. Erik Thorvaldson, or Erik the Red, son of Thorvald Asvaldsson, was born into a prominent Norwegian family sometime in the tenth century. When his father was exiled on account of manslaughter, his family moved to Iceland, which had been explored and settled by Vikings around 874. After his father's death, Erik married and moved southward to land owned by his new bride's family in Haukadale. There he prospered, until a violent feud with a neighbor resulted in his own exile from his house and lands. Erik moved once again, but in a little time a new feud arose with a man named Thorgest. True to the epithet he had earned in his youth, the red-haired Erik proved himself to be of a fiery temperament: two of Thorgest's sons were killed, and Erik was banished from Iceland for three years.

Voyage to Greenland. Thorgest and his kinsmen sought revenge, and Erik was forced to go into hiding until he could make preparations for his departure from Iceland. Good land was scarce in those regions, and its ownership often fiercely competitive, so it is not surprising that Erik's attention should have been drawn to rumors of land to the west of Iceland. Sometime earlier Gunnbjorn Ulfsson of Norway had sighted skerries (isolated rocks or small islands) in that direction, and Erik determined to spend his period of exile retracing Ulfsson's course. In 982 he left with his family, and before winter he had reached the icy shores and fjords of a new country. The next three years were spent exploring the new land and preparing it for settlement. Though life was still harsh and farming difficult, there was enough grass for livestock, and a relative abundance of game. Reserving the best stretches of land for himself, Erik decided to return to Iceland at the end of his exile and recruit colonists for the country he had given the intentionally enticing name of Greenland.

Norse Settlements. In 986 Erik set sail from Iceland with a fleet of twenty-five ships and as many as one thousand would-be settlers, though only fourteen of the ships and less than half of the pioneers reached Greenland. The colonists spread throughout the area of the coast Erik had explored, eventually establishing almost two hundred farmsteads and growing in numbers to as many as three thousand. Erik the Red is believed to have died in about 1003, in the winter of a plague that killed many of the early settlers. His life is recorded in several Medieval Icelandic sagas, oral histories first written down in the thirteenth and fourteenth centuries.

Sources:
Gwyn Jones, *A History of the Vikings* (New York: Oxford University Press, 1968).

Farley Mowat, *Westviking: The Ancient Norse in Greenland and North America* (Boston: Little, Brown, 1965).

Frederick J. Pohl, *The Viking Explorers* (New York: Crowell, 1966).

LEIF ERIKSSON

CIRCA 975-CIRCA 1020
VIKING EXPLORER

Iceland, Greenland, Norway. One of three sons of Erik Thorvaldson, or Erik the Red, Leif Eriksson was born in Iceland, but he came of age in the Viking settlement established by his father in Greenland. Resources were scarce in the new territory, and the colonists depended heavily on trade with Scandinavian merchant vessels. In 999 Leif sailed from Greenland to Norway, hoping to convince King Olaf Tryggvason to strengthen trading ties with the Greenlanders. His ship was blown off course, and he was forced to spend the summer in the Hebrides. There Leif fell in love with a woman named Thorgunna, who later bore him a child. In autumn of that year he reached Norway, where Leif converted to Christianity. King Olaf urged him to spread the new faith among his kinsmen and neighbors at home, and accordingly, in 1000, Leif returned to Greenland and encouraged his people to abandon the ways of Norse paganism. With the notable exception of his strong-willed father, Leif's message was well-received by the people, and the early settlement eventually became home to twelve parish churches.

Canadian Coast. According to some medieval Icelandic sources, lands to the south and west of Greenland were first sighted by Leif, whose ship lost its bearings on his return trip from Norway. A variant account is provided in the late fourteenth century *Flatley Book*. According to it, an Icelandic ship led by Bjarni Herjulfsson had set sail for Greenland in 986, just a few months after the departure of Erik the Red's colonial expedition. Bjarni's ship lost its way, and instead of the icy fjords of Greenland the sailors sighted a hilly land covered in forest. They did not land but sailed northeast along the coast, until the ship finally reached the Greenlanders. The *Flatley Book* goes on to explain that the colonists gave little thought to these southern lands until 1002, when Leif Eriksson, who had returned from Norway, set sail on an expedition to explore them and bring back much-needed timber. It is difficult to know which source is more reliable; regardless, all sources agree that Leif was the first to explore the new territory. The first land he sighted was barren and glacial, so he named it Helluland, or "slab-land." Proceeding on, the expedition came to a forested land, and Leif set about to explore what he called Markland, or "wood-land." Finally, his ship came to the third and richest of the lands, called "Vinland" on account of the wild grapes there.

Return to Greenland. On his return voyage Leif, whose eyesight was exceptional, alone among his crew spotted some shipwrecked Norsemen. He brought them home with him on condition that he should take possession of their cargo. Together with the timber he brought back from Vinland, the cargo made Leif wealthy, and he was given the epithet "the Lucky." News of his successful journey inspired other explorers to visit Vinland, but Leif himself seems to have stayed behind. His father, Erik, had died, and Leif inherited both his prominent position in Greenland and his father's farmstead, where he most likely spent the remainder of his life.

Sources:

Gwyn Jones, *A History of the Vikings* (New York: Oxford University Press, 1968).

Farley Mowat, *Westviking: The Ancient Norse in Greenland and North America* (Boston: Little, Brown, 1965).

Frederick J. Pohl, *The Viking Explorers* (New York: Crowell, 1966).

DOCUMENTARY SOURCES

Ahmad Ibn Fadlan, *Risala* (circa 922)—A chronicle written by a secretary to the Muslim ambassador sent to the king of the Bulgars on the Volga River. The author provides rich descriptions of various lands and people, including a group of Vikings known as the Rus.

Flatley Book (circa 1350)—The story of Bjarni Herjulfsson, who left Iceland in 986 and possibly spotted the North American coastline.

Sire Jean de Joinville, *Historie de Saint-Louis* (before 1317)—The author accompanied Louis IX (Saint Louis) of France to Egypt on the Seventh Crusade (1248–1254).

Sir John Mandeville, *The Voyage and Travels of Sir John Mandeville, Knight* (circa 1350)—A travel book written in French by an anonymous author who assumed the pen name *Mandeville*. It provides geographic descriptions of India, the Holy Land, and other Eastern lands. The author borrows heavily from other travel accounts.

Otto of Freising, *Historia de duabus civitatibus* (1143–1146)—A world history by a German bishop who visited the Holy Land. This is the first chronicle to mention Prester John, the legendary Christian ruler of a faraway kingdom.

Marco Polo, *Divisament dou monde* (Description of the World, 1299)—Account of the famed Venetian traveler and his journeys through present-day Turkey, Iraq, Iran, Tajikistan, China, Sumatra, and India.

William of Ruysbroeck, *Travel Account* (circa 1256)—One of the better written medieval Christian travelogues. The author, a Franciscan Friar, was sent by Louis IX (Saint Louis) on a mission to the Mongol empire in 1254–1255.

CHAPTER THREE

THE ARTS

by JEREMIAH HACKETT and KATHRYN A. EDWARDS

CONTENTS

Sidebars and tables are listed in italics.

814*

- By this date the Carolingian Renaissance is under way. Having begun at the court of Charlemagne, it revives literature and learning in Europe and extends into the 860s.

- The Carolingian miniscule, a form of clearly legible handwriting, has been developed by scholars and administrators at the court of Charlemagne and becomes the standard form of handwriting used in documents throughout western and central Europe.

- The Gregorian Chant, named after Pope Gregory I (reigned 590–604), has gradually supplanted other forms of chant sung in the western Christian Church.

814*-1100

- The manuscript decoration of Irish and Anglo-Saxon monks strongly influences manuscript illumination throughout western Europe.

820*-835

- The beautifully illuminated Utrecht Psalter is produced by artists in Rheims.

829*-836

- Einhard, former secretary and adviser to Charlemagne (who died in 814), writes *Vita Caroli Magni* (Life of Charlemagne).

830-840

- Two scribes in a monastery in Fulda write down the Germanic oral folktale *Das Hildebrandslied* (Lay of Hildebrand), a poem about a battle between two warriors. Only a sixty-eight-line fragment survives.

840*-862

- The French Benedictine Lupus, Abbot of Ferrieres, writes eloquent letters and hagiographies (lives of saints).

842

- After defeating the forces of their brother Lothar I at the Battle of Fontenoy (841), Louis II (the German) and Charles II (the Bald) renew their alliance in the Strasbourg Oaths, which are written in language that shows the evolution of modern German and French.

850*

- The first examples of notation in medieval music are developed.

860*

- Irish poet Sedulius Scottus (flourished circa 848–860) writes *De rectoribus Christianis,* a Latin work on the proper behavior for Christian princes.

864-866*

- John Scottus Eriugena—Irish-born educator, poet, and philosopher at the court of Charles the Bald—writes *Periphyseon,* or *De divisione naturae* (About Nature), which attempts to give a Neoplatonic interpretation of God and creation.

* DENOTES CIRCA DATE

871-899
- During his reign, Alfred the Great of England sponsors translations of important classical and early Christian works.

900s
- Many works of vernacular European literatures—Celtic, Old French, Old High German, and Old Norse—are written down for the first time.

910
- The Fianna (or Fenian) Cycle, a collection of fourth-century stories about mythological Celtic warriors, is compiled.

960*-980
- The *Codex Exoniensis* (Exeter Codex) is compiled. Included in the collection are the poems "The Fates of the Apostles" and "Juliana" by the Anglo-Saxon poet Cynewulf, ninety-five riddles by various authors, and such notable Old English poems as "Soul and Body II," "The Seafarer," "The Wanderer," and "Christ."

975*-1025
- *Beowulf,* an Old English epic that has evolved over several centuries, is written down for the first time.

1000*
- The St. Remi church in Rheims, France, is fitted with stained-glass windows, the oldest surviving examples of that art.

1015*
- Elaborate and detailed bronze doors depicting scenes from the Bible are installed in the Church of St. Michael in Hildesheim, Germany.

1025*
- The Italian monk Guido of Arezzo invents the lined staff for musical notation.

1077*
- Work begins on the 230-foot-long, 20-inch-wide Bayeux Tapestry, depicting events leading up to and including the conquest of England by Duke William of Normandy (William the Conqueror) in 1066. Embroidered with wool on linen, it is probably the work of artisans in the south of England and is believed to have been commissioned by Bishop Odo of Bayeux, William's half brother (died 1097).

1088
- The University of Bologna is founded.

* DENOTES CIRCA DATE

1100*
- Troubadour poetry emerges in southern France under the patronage of Duke William IX of Aquitaine and his descendants Eleanor of Aquitaine and Marie of France. Prominent troubador poets include Jaufre Riddle, Bernart de Ventadorn, Bertran de Born, and Beatrice, Countess of Dia.

- The Twelfth-Century Renaissance of education, art, and philosophy begins.

- The French epic poem *La Chanson de Roland* (The Song of Roland) tells the tale of a French warrior killed while defending the rearguard of Charlemagne's troops while returning from Moorish Spain in 788.

1100-1125*
- The German monk Theophilus Presbyter writes *De diversis artibus* (On Diverse Arts), which describes the techniques for many medieval crafts.

1119
- A loose grouping of schools is established at Paris. By 1215 it has become the University of Paris.

1125*
- Latin translations of rediscovered classical Greek works and Arabic writings begin to flood western Europe with scholarship from Islamic lands.

1130*
- French sculptor Gislebertus carves *The Last Judgment* for the west portal of the cathedral of Saint-Lazare in Autun, France.

1135*-1139
- Geoffrey of Monmouth writes *Historia regum Britanniae* (History of the Kings of Britain) and *Vita Merlin* (Life of Merlin).

1140-1144
- The Tree of Jesse, a beautiful and elaborate stained-glass window, is crafted for the Abbey Church of St. Denis.

1150*
- Imported Islamic musical instruments begins to influence western European music.

- German bishop and historian Otto of Freising writes *Gesta Friderici imperatoris* (Deeds of Frederick Barbarossa).

- German Benedictine Heinrich von Melk composes *Von des Tôdes gehugede* (The Remembrance of Death), an attack on the vices of knighthood.

- The Spanish epic poem *Cantar del mio Cid* (Poem of the Cid), recounts the deeds of a hero based on Castilian warrior Rodrigo Díaz de Vivar during warfare to recapture Valencia from the Moors.

* DENOTES CIRCA DATE

1150* CONT.

- German abbess Hildegard of Bingen writes *Symphonia harmoniae caelestium revelationum* (Symphony of Harmony of Heavenly Revelations), a collection of sacred songs.

- Construction of the church of Santiago de Compostela is completed. The supposed burial site of St. James the Apostle, it becomes the third most popular pilgrimage site in Europe.

1160*-1175

- Wandering scholar-poets known as goliards are granted royal protection as they travel throughout Europe, mostly in England and Germany. They include Hugh of Orleans, Walter of Chatillon, and the so-called Archpoet.

1167-1185

- The French philosopher-poet Alain de Lille writes *De planctu naturae* (The Plaint of Nature), a poem about vices, and *Anticlaudianus,* a poem on morals and arts.

1170*

- A large number of scholars have come together in the English town of Oxford.

- Chrétien de Troyes writes Arthurian legends such as *Lancelot.*

1173

- Construction begins on the bell tower that becomes known as the Leaning Tower of Pisa.

1180*

- Middle High German poet Heinrich der Glîchesaere composes the epic poem *Reinecke Fuchs* (Reynard the Fox).

- Marie of France translates Aesop's fables into French.

1190*-1220

- Middle High German poet Wolfram Von Eschenbach composes *Parzifal,* a romantic poem based on the search for the Holy Grail.

1196-1216

- Italian sculptor Benedetto Antelami carves detailed allegorical figures and prophets for the baptistry of the cathedral in Parma.

1200*

- Perotin composes liturgical works for three and four voices.

- Layamon's *Brut* records the legend of the founder of the British race.

1200-1250*

- French poet Guillaume de Loris writes the first part of *Roman de la Rose* (Romance of the Rose).

* DENOTES CIRCA DATE

1209	• Some East Anglian scholars migrate from Oxford to Cambridge.
1220*	• Chartres Cathedral in France, on which construction began in 1120, is essentially completed.
1240*-1260	• Bolognese lyric poet Guido Guinizelli writes vernacular poetry in *la dolce stil novo* (the sweet new style).
1250-1300*	• French poet Jean de Meun completes *Roman de la Rose* (Romance of the Rose).
	• Florentine poet Guido Cavalcanti, a member of the *dolce stil novo* school, produces love poetry and ballads.
1272-1302	• Italian painter Cimabue (Bencivienni di Pepo), the master of Byzantine style, resides in Rome. He is the teacher, and later a rival, of Giotto (Giotto di Bandone).
1285	• Italian painter Duccio di Buoninsegna, a member of the Sienese school, paints *Madonna Rucellai* for the Church of St. Maria Novella in Florence.
1305*	• Florentine painter Giotto paints the frescoes for the Arena Chapel in Padua.
1321	• Shortly before his death Dante completes his *Commedia* (Divine Comedy).
1324-1328	• French miniature painter and illuminator Jean Pucelle produces a Book of Hours, an illuminated prayer book, for Jeanne d' Evreux, Queen of France.
1337	• Giotto dies.
1337-1339	• Italian painter Ambrogio Lorenzetti produces *Good and Bad Government,* a series of frescoes for the Palazzo Pubblico at Siena.

* DENOTES CIRCA DATE

1340* • Italian poet Giovanni Boccaccio arrives in Florence.

1341 • Petrarch (Francesco Petrarca) is named poet laureate of Rome.

1345 • The avid bibliophile Richard Aungerville (Richard de Bury) dies and bequeaths his collection of books to Durham College, Oxford.

1350* • The York Cycle of mystery plays is performed in England on the Feast of Corpus Christi.

***** DENOTES CIRCA DATE

The Puerta de las Platerías (Door of the Silversmiths, 1078–1103) at the Romanesque church of Santiago de Compostela, Spain

OVERVIEW

Defining the Medieval "Arts." During the Middle Ages definitions of the arts were based on assumptions about their value and their production. In general, the arts required specific abilities and training, and ranged from manual crafts (such as carpentry, sculpture, and painting) at the bottom to intellectual or academic labors (such as theology, poetry, and music) at the top. These latter arts were commonly classified as the "liberal arts." The sixth-century scholars Boethius and Cassiodorus developed the standard medieval division of the arts into the *trivium* and the *quadrivium*. The *trivium* became the most basic studies in the medieval schools and universities: grammar, rhetoric, and dialectics (logic). The *quadrivium* was the higher arts: arithmetic, geometry, astronomy, and music. While the "mechanical" arts—including painting, drawing, sculpting, and architecture—were considered inferior, mere crafts in Roman times, by the thirteenth century their status had been elevated in Europe. This chapter discusses subjects that fall within medieval definitions of the both "higher" and "mechanical" arts.

Formative Influences on the Liberal Arts. Medieval perceptions about the arts and the ways they were practiced were founded on the attitudes of several earlier cultures. Probably the most influential was that of the Roman Empire. Its primary language, Latin, survived the fall of the western part of the empire in the fifth century, and Roman architecture, urban design, and sculpture still existed in southern and western Europe, even though increasingly as ruins. Greek culture and its language survived as well, though much of the learning of the ancient Greeks was preserved in the East and did not reach western Europe until later in the Middle Ages. Latin culture and values had been gradually adopted in the third, fourth, and fifth centuries by the tribes who settled on the frontiers of Rome and eventually took over the empire in the West. Of these groups, the Celts were particularly effective in spreading Romanized culture during the early Middle Ages. In the seventh and eighth centuries, missionary voyages by Irish monks contributed greatly to the renewal of classical culture in Europe. Through careful study and copying of ancient texts, they insisted that the philosophical, mythical, and religious heritage of ancient Greece and Rome had

value in a Christian Europe. These views were spread throughout western and central Europe at the monasteries and schools they founded.

The Carolingian Renaissance. In western Europe Charlemagne is generally credited with the first artistic and educational revival after the Roman Empire, the Carolingian Renaissance. His reforms drew on intellectual movements already current in medieval society, but the influence of his court allowed them to thrive and spread through much of western and central Europe. In 794 Charlemagne established a central location for his widespread empire at Aachen (modern Aix-la-Chapelle in eastern France) and made the palace school the center for an educational revival. Under the leadership of Alcuin of York, his school attracted scholars and artists from all over Europe. Charlemagne's early program of reform was thoroughly Christian in inspiration, drawing on expertise honed in the northern monasteries, England, Ireland, and elsewhere outside his Frankish kingdom, but his motivations were primarily pragmatic. The Christian Church remained the primary guardian of literate culture; men who read and wrote, who were exposed to Roman ideas of government, and who had models for strengthening administration looked to the Church for education and their livelihood. Almost all the scholars at Charlemagne's school were clergy; all looked to Charlemagne and his descendants for preferment and offices and brought their expertise into his service, as well as the service of the Church. In other words, Charlemagne and his family, the Carolingians, got quality administrators who made important cultural and bureaucratic contributions. For example, Carolingian scholars and administrators developed a clear form of handwriting, the Carolingian miniscule, which became standard in documents throughout western and central Europe during the Middle Ages. This clear handwriting, on which modern printing is based, assured that administrators could easily read business correspondence and the copies of classical manuscripts that Charlemagne's scholars made by the hundreds. During the ninth century, scholars who were trained according to Carolingian precepts had important roles at monasteries throughout Europe and continued these values and practices at monastic schools, the primary educational and artistic establishments of their era. Charlemagne's orchestrated approach to learning and the practical and intellectual religiosity of his sons were decisive influences to medieval thought.

Changing Patterns. The meaning of classical culture, its value to Christianity, the way it should be taught, and the appropriate methods of expressing it artistically were all debated throughout the Middle Ages. Revisions of these subjects were driving forces behind changes in artistic styles. Celtic Christian culture placed a high value on the word, and the poet (or bard) as interpreter of this word had a key role in tenth- and early eleventh-century literature. Coexisting with this belief was an appreciation given to the other arts—such as metallurgy, jewelry production, calligraphy, and manuscript painting (illumination)—as reflecting the wonders of God's creation. The Roman administrative tradition gradually fused with Celtic values. In many respects, the most significant change in the arts during the ninth and tenth centuries was educational reform designed to build a functional bureaucracy for the State and an educated leadership for the Church. Although the application of this reform was delayed until the eleventh century, the belief in its value persisted. With the reestablishment of the European society and economy after the Viking invasions of the ninth century, major changes in the arts of medieval Europe took place and accelerated after approximately 1100. In the twelfth century the School of Chartres and other cathedral schools sparked a revival education and letters. In the thirteenth century the interaction of Christian scholars and artists with the world of Islam in Spain, Sicily, and the Holy Land opened Western eyes to new kinds of art and knowledge. In the process there was a transfer of scholarship in the form of "translations" of scientific, philosophical, and religious works from both Arabic and Greek into Latin. The result was a renovation of the liberal arts. Moreover, during this period, rapid urbanization and development led to a new respect for what classical society had called the "adulterine" arts, that is, the mechanical arts. To make this development a permanent part of society, it was necessary to rebuild and restructure education at all levels.

Art and the Artist. Medieval attitudes toward the arts also affected their treatment of the artist. Because of the high value placed on products of the liberal arts throughout the Middle Ages, scholars, scribes, and authors of many sorts of works were more likely than mechanical artists to sign their names or to leave clues to their identity in their works. (Yet, authors were generally cautious in how they portrayed themselves.) Even so, the authors of some of the greatest medieval works, such as *The Song of Roland* (circa 1100) or *Beowulf* (first written version, late tenth century), remain unknown, and others are known only because of receipt books that note payments to specific scholars or because of references in other works. For practitioners of the mechanical arts, which were not as prestigious, attribution can be almost impossible. Medieval sculptures, paintings, jewelry, and other crafts were not signed, and it is rarely possible to discover the identities of their creators if they were made before the latter part of the twelfth century, the point from which more-complete records have survived. At about the same time, some artists began leaving clues to their identities in their works—usually with a note such as "Thomas made this" or the inclusion of the artist's face in a painting or sculpture. The practice of "signing" works is far more modern.

Goals. As with modern artists, medieval artists had many goals. They worked to gain recognition and employment, to produce practical goods, to provide brightness or whimsy in their world, or to express their veneration for natural or divine forces. Even the most obscure work, however, generally had some practical purpose. Sculpted pillars supported walls and attested to the power of the person who controlled the building, elaborate jewelry proclaimed the wearer's power and wealth, and illuminated manuscripts provided several ways of learning about God. Art in the service of God might seem esoteric to modern people, but Europeans in the Middle Ages expressed the firm belief that God was present in the world and enjoyed many of the same pleasures as his highest creation, man. Medieval cathedrals and other churches, whatever their style, were lasting monuments to the faith and commitment of the age. They also attest to various medieval visions of God, his creation, and man's place in it all. In brief, the medieval cathedral was a bright, colorful, and living microcosm of God's creation as a whole.

Patronage. Medieval artists did not produce a work with the hope of selling it, as many modern artists do. Even those who wrote histories and theological treatises often wrote with a patron in mind, someone who would express his appreciation of the work through a gift of land, money, or employment. Patrons were key to medieval art. Artists worked on commission and in a variety of tasks; the same person who wrote dramas also acted in them, designed banquets, painted banners, and even performed with a musical instrument. For these services, he (or, rarely, she) would be given a job, such as tax collector in a province, which he would also have to do or find someone to substitute for him. Even when a patron sought out a specific artist for a specific work, such as a painting, the painter had to follow the provisions of a detailed contract. These contracts often included the size of the painting, its subject, the number and placement of the figures in it, the positions they were to assume, the colors that were to be used, and even the texture of certain design elements. A contract also specified a payment plan for the painting and the cost of materials, as well as listing the people involved in the actual creation of the painting; that is, medieval painters often had people working for them who handled various aspects of the painting process. In this sense medieval artists were seen as craftsmen, with many of the creative elements undertaken by their patron. One of the dramatic changes of the Renaissance in the fourteenth through sixteenth centuries was the beginning of the perception that an artist was a creative and autonomous individual.

TOPICS IN THE ARTS

ARCHITECTURE

Practical Structures. Medieval secular architecture—that is, the structures in which peasants, townspeople, and nobles lived their daily lives—was practical. Function determined design. Peasants needed basic structures that were cheap to build and easy to maintain. For this reason, most peasant structures were built from local materials such as wood, grasses, mud, and, in select cases, stone. These one-room buildings could be built by local craftsmen, and they followed standard patterns; only in the thirteenth and fourteenth centuries were specialized design elements, such as stone fireplaces, incorporated. Through most of the Middle Ages many noble homes were only larger versions of peasant structures built with more durable and costly materials, such as stone and large logs, to fit the nobles' wealth and pretensions. They were designed to provide basic protection, shelter dozens of individuals, store several months' supplies, and proclaim a lord's superiority to the surrounding population. Even famous medieval castles were designed with practical purposes in mind: protection and surveillance. Most of their technological and architectural innovations were made to counter medieval military innovations. Only in the later thirteenth and fourteenth centuries did noble houses and castles begin to include decorative and other design elements that suggest aesthetic purposes. At that time stone carvings were added to the private rooms, elaborate mantels began to grace wall fireplaces, and window seats were set next to windows of colored glass. In these cases, however, secular architecture depended greatly on the design and technological innovations already developed in religious buildings.

Romanesque. In 1871 the French architectural historian Arcisse de Caumont described a series of medieval buildings as *Romanesque,* a term meaning "in the Roman manner" and expressing medieval Europeans' indebtedness to Roman architectural principles. This name has since been used to describe many medieval structures built from about 950 until 1060 primarily in France, Italy, and northern Spain—though similar buildings are also scattered through much of western and central Europe. Romanesque structures are characteristically strong and weighty with heavy vaulted ceilings, which required the building of extremely thick walls with strong piers and massive buttresses. Most commonly, churches were built in this style, and they followed a basic cruciform (cross-shaped) ground plan. To provide space within the church, large rounded vaults (barrel vaults) supported the roof and walls. Only a few, small windows could be placed in these structures because the heavy walls were necessary to hold up the building. These windows had the same arched design as the vaults and became increasingly smaller the higher they were on the building. Despite these technological limitations, Romanesque churches could be enormous, well over 150 feet tall, and impressive versions of this style were constructed at Durham in England, Speyer in Germany, and Pisa in Italy. Their massiveness communicated power and permanence, architectural goals that their creators reinforced by modeling their buildings on the ruins of the most powerful and permanent empire of their historical memory: the Roman Empire.

Romanesque Architecture and the Compostela Pilgrimage. By the middle of the eleventh century impressive Romanesque churches could be found in many parts of Europe and had developed distinctive regional characteristics. In southern Germany, Romanesque monastic cloisters showed an Irish influence, while that built at Ripoll in Catalonia was influenced by Arabic design elements. Among the most impressive Romanesque churches were those found along one of the most famous pilgrimage routes in medieval Europe: the roads through France to the shrine of St. James at Santiago de Compostela in northern Spain. Along these three routes, the churches of St. Sernin, St. Pierre, and Ste. Foi in southern France were built in a more-developed form of Romanesque architecture. Large barrel vaults are the primary architectural element in each of these churches, designed to provide space for large numbers of pilgrims. Also, to facilitate visits and impress pilgrims, the churches have wide galleries and aisles. Each of the churches has elaborate sculptural decorations, and in each the entrance and facade are modeled after Roman gates. The church at Santiago de Compostela is more massive than the churches along the pilgrims' route, with a nave (the long section of a cruciform church) around 250 feet long, as befitted the third most-important pilgrimage site of medieval Europe, the supposed burial place of St. James the Apostle. Construction of the church was com-

The Romanesque church of St. Sernin in Toulouse, consecrated in 1096

plete by the mid twelfth century. At that time, the floor plan followed the typical cruciform pattern modeled on St. Peter's in Rome. The aisles and ambulatory were especially wide, and additional altars were placed on the sides of the church to accommodate pilgrims. The elaborate decoration of the church includes examples of various phases in Romanesque art. For example, the west end, also known as the Portico de la Gloria (Gate of Glory), was constructed and carved in 1168–1188, at the end of the Romanesque period, and foreshadows later, more naturalistic Gothic styles, while the south end, the Puerta de las Platerías (Door of the Silversmiths), dating from 1078–1103, is more sparse and rigid in keeping Romanesque design principles.

Byzantine and Moorish Architecture. When Robert of Clari, a French crusader, saw the capital of the Byzantine Empire, Constantinople, in 1204, he was awestruck and wrote, "Not since the world was made was there ever seen or won so great a treasure, or so noble or so rich, nor in the time of Alexander, nor in the time of Charlemagne, nor before, nor after, nor do I think myself that in the forty richest cities of the world had there been so much wealth as was found in Constantinople. For the Greeks say that two-thirds of the wealth of this world is in Constantinople and the other third scattered throughout the world." His reaction to Byzantine style was quite similar to that of his distant ancestors. Left with impressive examples of Byzantine structures in Italian cities such as Ravenna, later medieval rulers and clergy incorporated Byzantine design elements into their structures, hoping thereby to profit from the reflected glory of that powerful Eastern Empire. Charlemagne's churches, particularly at Aachen, included

The Portico de la Gloria (Gate of Glory, 1168–1188), at the Romanesque church of Santiago de Compostela

the elaborate mosaics, octagonal structure, and detailed decoration that typifies western European Byzantine design, and his descendants followed in his footsteps, eventually including some of these elements in the Romanesque style. In the same way, the elaborate sculptural elements of Muslim design influenced architecture in southern Europe, particularly in northern Spain and along the Mediterranean coast. Although neither the Byzantine nor the Moorish styles spread throughout Europe, their pervasive use of complicated geometric patterns, whether sculptural or mosaic, added distinctive aspects to Romanesque and Gothic design in neighboring regions.

Ottonian and Cluniac Styles. In northern and central Europe other styles influenced Romanesque and coexist alongside it. These styles are called Ottonian and Cluniac after the dynasty (Ottonian) and the religious order (Cluny) that promoted them. Inspired by Carolingian and Byzantine architecture, bishoprics such as Mainz, Speyer, and Bamburg, monastic centers at Echternach and Reichenau, and cultural crossroads such as Cologne and Trier began using innovative designs in the middle of the tenth century. Ottonian churches are notable for their monumental scale and spatial experimentation. The Ottonian church most often used as a model was that of Saint Cyriakus (built 961–965). It adapted the basic Carolingian plan but made it more geometrically proportioned to create a more harmonious structure. Churches at Hildesheim and the imperial cathedrals in the Rhineland, particularly at Mainz, improved on these early designs in the twelfth century, reflecting the aspirations of the Ottonian dynasty and the leading churchmen who were its servants. The architects of Cluny in eastern France made similar architectural and technological developments that culminated in the third version of the main church at Cluny, generally known as Cluny III. Its plan featured double transepts, a huge ambulatory (a section parallel to the nave) with radiating chapels, and an impressive portal. This church was dedicated in 1130 and completed under the leadership of the learned Abbot Peter the Venerable. The ordered and measured harmony stressed by its architects greatly influenced Romanesque architecture and buildings throughout eastern France. This harmony was also key to Cluniac spirituality, and this link between spirituality and design was also apparent in the many chapels that radiated out from the main church, allowing for the constant chanting of divine service, an important element in Cluniac religious practice. As such, Ottonian buildings and Cluny III both exemplify the close link between architecture and mind-set throughout the Middle Ages.

The Rise of Gothic Architecture. Gothic architecture is often seen as a distinctively medieval architecture, but its medieval creators developed their style from preexisting architectural forms and placed little emphasis on the "newness" of their work. Italian Renaissance artists and historians in the fifteenth century first named this style "Gothic," using the term in a pejorative sense. For these Renaissance artists, who desired to rediscover classical structures, the architecture of "the Goths" was interpreted as the alien, mutilated work of the northern "barbarians." Such characterization is built on errors. Gothic architecture originated in northern France, not "Gothic" Germany. Its domination of European architecture began in the twelfth century, not during the early medieval barbarian invasions. Moreover, there were various styles of Gothic architecture during this time; it was not as static as Renaissance writers implied. High and light walls, ribbed vaults, pointed arches, and flying buttresses characterize Gothic church architecture. The ability of Gothic architects to solve the problem of thrust and weight enabled them to lighten the massive wall structure of the Romanesque church and to transform God's house into a pillar of light. The Romanesque vault, which was ribbed from side to side and divided the roof into several square bays, gave way to two semicircular ribs joining all four corners of the bay to create a square of ribs (groin vaulting). As it further developed, two diagonal ribs formed a cross between the corners (rib vaulting). This development allowed the triangular section between the ribs to be constructed of lighter stonework. In addition, diagonal ribs broke the round clean lines of the Romanesque vault and rose much higher. From the pillars it was possible to raise the reinforcing arches supporting the pillars to the same height as the diagonal ribs. The architect was also able to transfer structural thrust from the horizontal to the vertical axis. In so doing, the size of supporting columns could be reduced, but the church could still be built higher than Romanesque structures. Cities throughout northern and central France competed to build the tallest and most elaborate Gothic cathedrals, leading to further innovations that allowed even greater height and airiness in these buildings. Flying buttresses allowed architects to spread the weight over the smaller side aisles of the cathedrals, giving essential support to the nave of the church. In the process the walls no longer had to be load bearing and could thus hold large windows that allowed for unprecedented amounts of light. The Abbey of St. Denis, rebuilt under the direction of Abbot Suger around 1135, is generally seen as the earliest example of Gothic architecture and retains many Romanesque aspects. The cathedrals of Notre Dame and Chartres are examples of classic Gothic structures built at the end of the twelfth century and the beginning of the thirteenth, while the cathedral at Beauvais, with its weak tiled foundations and excessive height (157 feet), represents

The west façade of the Gothic cathedral at Chartres, France, completed circa 1220

the limits of Gothic engineering. The nave collapsed in 1284 and was rebuilt with added flying buttresses to support its weight. Although built on a much smaller scale, the Ste. Chapelle that Louis IX of France had built into the royal palace in Paris during the 1240s is often treated as the best representative of a flamboyant, radiant Gothic style.

Theories of Gothic Architecture. Medieval architects and their patrons seldom commented about the inspirations for their structures. One of the earliest Gothic innovators, however, Abbot Suger of St. Denis, left a record of what he and his fellow clergy were trying to achieve. For example, the redesigned portal for St. Denis encorporates design elements of Roman gates and medieval fortifications, suggesting the power of the French king—the defender of the realm—who was crowned in that church. More commonly, however, Suger and his followers stress the importance of light in their spirituality and in the architecture. For the medieval person, a Gothic cathedral was anything but the pale museum-like remnant that remains today. The medieval European was engaged in an act of public worship in a "living City of God." This city in Gothic design created an experience of light and color. With its walls painted with biblical stories and its multicolored stained-glass windows, a Gothic church became a magnificent cinemascopic vision. Another new feature was the attempt by the Gothic artist and architect to give a comprehensive vision and detailed depiction of the universe of nature and of God. An analogy for this vision was the many important summations of theology and philosophy that medieval scholars produced, particularly the *Summa theologiae* of Thomas Aquinas, written in 1265–1273. The intellectual and artistic movements that inspired Gothic architecture—and that Gothic buildings embodied—are frequently described as a mysticism and metaphysics of light.

Gothic Beyond the Frankish Lands. For those who lived in the Middle Ages, the new Gothic style in architecture was called "the work of the French" or "the style of the French" (*opus francigenum*). Although some of the earliest and best-known Gothic structures were built in the Frankish kingdoms, master masons, builders, and architects from all over Europe were trained in this style and took it back to their homes. Gothic masterpieces were constructed at Westminster Abbey in England, the church of St. Francis in Assisi, Italy, and the cathedrals in Burgos and Toledo in Spain. In many ways Gothic architecture replaced local styles in the thirteenth and fourteenth centuries, but regional design elements frequently crept back in. Several examples of these transformations occurred in German Gothic churches. The churches of St. Elizabeth at Marburg (built 1235–1283) and the Wiesenkirche at Soest (built around 1331) have various openings in the arches, spreading diffuse light inside the entire building and making them less dark than the French Gothic cathedrals. As time passed, the Gothic style began to be used for other public buildings, such as city and guild halls. Gothic architecture, however, required technological sophistication, expensive materials, and expert masons and sculptors, so only the wealthiest and most powerful individuals and cities, such as Ypres in Belgium, could afford to have their cloth and town halls built in this style.

Sources:

Robert G. Calkins, *Medieval Architecture in Western Europe: from A.D. 300 to 1500* (New York: Oxford University Press, 1998).

Paul Frankl, *Gothic Architecture*, revised edition (New Haven: Yale University Press, 2000).

Hans Erich Kubach, *Romanesque Architecture* (New York: Electa/Rizzoli, 1988).

Otto Von Simson, *The Gothic Cathedral: Origins of Gothic Architecture and the Medieval Concept of Order*, third edition, enlarged (Princeton: Princeton University Press, 1962).

James Snyder, *Medieval Art: Painting, Sculpture, Architecture, 4th–14th Century* (New York: Abrams / Upper Saddle River, N.J.: Prentice Hall, 1989).

EDUCATION AND THE LIBERAL ARTS

Subjects for Academic Education. During the Middle Ages the word *education* could have several different meanings. Professionals such as artists were most frequently educated through apprenticeship, a system whereby a boy was contracted to work for a craft master for a specified number of years. In return, the master craftsman provided the boy with food, shelter, and sometimes even a small salary and trained the boy in his craft. Women were rarely apprenticed, and a young woman who received this sort of training generally did so because a near male relative took it on himself to train her. Writing, reading, and other basic academic skills were generally taught at home by a member of the household or a private tutor or in a village by a local

STUDENT LIFE IN PARIS

Later a cardinal and patriarch of Jerusalem, Jacques de Vitry (circa 1160–1240) was a student at Paris in the late twelfth century and left an engaging account of student life at that time:

Almost all the students at Paris, foreigners and natives, did absolutely nothing except learn or hear—something new. Some studied merely to acquire knowledge, which is curiosity; others to acquire fame, which is vanity; others still for the sake of gain, which is cupidity and the vice of simony. Very few studied for their own edification, or that of others. They wrangled and disputed not merely about the various sects or about some discussions; but the differences between the countries also caused dissensions, hatreds and virulent animosities among them and they impudently uttered all kinds of affronts and insults against one another.

They affirmed that the English were drunkards and had tails; the sons of France proud, effeminate and carefully adorned like women. They said that the Germans were furious and obscene at their feasts; the Normans, vain and boastful; the Poitevins, traitors and always adventurers. The Burgundians they considered vulgar and stupid. The Bretons were reputed to be fickle and changeable, and were often reproached for the death of Arthur. The Lombards were called avaricious, vicious and cowardly; the Romans, seditious, turbulent and slanderous; the Sicilians, tyrannical and cruel; the inhabitants of Brabant, men of blood, incendiaries, brigands and ravishers; the Flemish, fickle, prodigal, gluttonous, yielding as butter, and slothful. After such insults from words they often came to blows. . . .

Source: *Translations and Reprints from the Original Sources of European History* (Philadelphia: Published for the Department of History of the University of Pennsylvania by the University of Pennsylvania Press, 1894–1907), series 2, volume 3, p. 19.

clergyman. More-advanced academic education focused on subjects deemed important to medieval administration, philosophy, and theology. This teaching increasingly took place at special schools established at courts or monasteries and in major towns. In his *Policratus* (1159), a study of bureaucratic structures and official culture, John of Salisbury summarized the educational assumptions of the High Middle Ages: "All those who are ignorant of the Latin poets, historians, orators, and mathematicians should be called *illiterati* [illiterate or unlettered] even if they know letters." The lower level of academic education focused on the *trivium:* Latin grammar, logic, and rhetoric, three linguistic skills that were deemed essential to further study. More advanced education could then be obtained in the *quadrivium:* arithmetic, geometry, music, and astronomy. Finally, a scholar might specialize in one of the higher disciplines: Roman law, canon law, or theology. The primary language was Latin, and before 1200 the key sources were classical and early Christian. Students were immersed in the writings of authorities on these earlier texts, and only at the highest levels of their training did they read the actual texts.

Continuation of Charlemagne's Schools. The medieval system of higher education built on precedents established during the Carolingian Renaissance at Charlemagne's palace school and at other schools modeled on it. Charlemagne's successors, such as Louis I (the Pious) and Charles II (the Bald), looked to leading scholars of their time, Benedict of Aniane and John Scottus Eriugena, for educational advice. Great efforts were made to collect ancient books, especially those that would establish correct versions of scripture, the Christian liturgy, and the calendar. Their educational reform was guided by the belief that religion was central to the revival of the arts; bad grammar, corrupt texts, and mistaken calculations were "sins," impediments to spiritual renewal. They were also convinced that learning and leadership were essential to the moral reformation of society. For them, the ideal Christian ruler supported secular and religious learning that provided good examples for his subjects. In pursuit of this goal Carolingian courts became havens for scholars from all over Europe, who sparked a Platonic revival in philosophy. Carolingian educational reformers established a basic canon of disciplines and authors based on classical precedents. Their use of Roman grammarians, Roman poets, and commentaries on them reveals a zealous desire to instill classical Latin in students of language. Finally, Carolingian educational reform had an impact on the physical tools of learning as well as on its contents. In many respects, Carolingian education was more about texts and books than about pure intellectualization. From the start of his reforms Charlemagne seems to have regarded the production and collecting of books as an integral part of cultural revival, and his successors built on this model, establishing a court library including works that became central to medieval thought: Augustine's *City of God,* Pliny's *Natural History,* Dionysio-Hadriana (a collection of canon law), the canons of the Council of Nicea, the Rule of St. Benedict, and classical works by authors such as Horace, Cicero, Cato, and Lucan. These texts were put at the disposal of court scholars and monastic scribes alike. Not until Louis IX (reigned 1226–1270) did such a consultative state/kingly library exist again.

Cathedral and Monastic Schools. Faced with the Viking invasions of the ninth and tenth centuries—and the attendant social and economic dislocations—few academic innovations were made; in fact, it was a struggle to keep much formal education alive at all. When schools were reestablished in much of Europe during the later tenth and eleventh centuries, churches led the way. Cathedrals and monasteries founded or expanded schools to train the civil servants necessary for both secular and ecclesiastical government and to foster the study of God's word and his text, nature. Well-known monastic schools, such as that at Bec in Normandy, developed during the eleventh century, and preeminent among these early institutions was the cathedral school of Chartres, under Bernard of Chartres who had become its chancellor (or master) by 1115. The curriculum at Chartres was based on the study of "authoritative" Latin books, which Bernard expected the students to memorize. A student who failed to do so received physical punishment. Bernard also attracted advanced students, who engaged in the *lectio philosophorum,* that is, in the close reading of difficult philosophical texts. Bernard's important students included Gilbert of Poitiers, William of Conches, John of Salisbury, and, perhaps, Adelard of Bath. Bernard had a profound respect for ancient knowledge and skill. As John of Salisbury once remarked, "Bernard of Chartres used to compare us to dwarfs perched on the shoulders of giants. He pointed out that we see more and farther than our predecessors, not because we have keener vision or greater height, but because we are lifted aloft on their gigantic stature." Through his students, Bernard's methods were spread to many of the important schools of western and central Europe.

Translation and Learning. Beginning about 1120 and continuing until about 1280, "new" arts and learning from southern Islamic lands vastly broadened the relatively limited world of earlier medieval Latin culture and education. The first stirrings of this transformation were found when the Henry I of England appointed the converted Jew Pertus Anfusus (Peter Alfonso) to direct education in England. Anfusus's "Letter to the Peripatetics (philosophers) of France" was an exhortation to Western Latin scholars to travel to Spain and to Islamic lands to seek learning especially in the mathematical arts. Significant centers for translating newly discovered texts arose in Toledo, Sicily, Antioch, and Tripoli. Spain experienced a large influx of European scholars, including Robert of Chester, Daniel of Morley, Adelard of Bath, Gerard of Cremona, and Herman of Carinthia. Initially, much of the translation was of mathematical, astrological, and geographical texts. The arrival in northern Spain of Abbot Peter the Venerable from Cluny led to the first translation into Latin of the holy book of Islam, the Koran. In Sicily

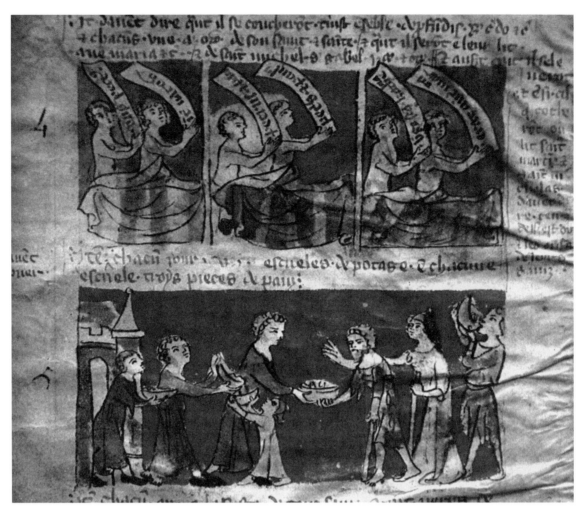

Student life in Paris during the fourteenth century; illumination from the statute book of the College of Hubant, University of Paris (Archives Nationale, Paris)

especially, there were translations of Greek texts into Latin, including Ptolemy's *Almagest*. The reception of these writings in twelfth- and thirteenth-century Europe necessitated a new reorganization of schools and study.

The Rise of the University. In the twelfth and thirteenth centuries a new educational institution arose throughout Europe: the university. Motivated by a need for trained secular and ecclesiastical officials, lords promoted the development of academic communities in their capitals. Reacting to increased demands for their service in various fields of activity and to an influx of new, authoritative texts, the leaders of these establishments fundamentally reorganized the European higher education system. Perhaps, one of the most important aspects of this new institution was its guaranteed juridical status. Because both Church and secular rulers guaranteed academic autonomy, scholarly rights, and free movement of scholars and students, education in the Latin West experienced a qualitative change. Although all universities offered a basic arts curriculum, individual universities gradually specialized in specific subjects, offering advanced degrees in law, medicine, and theology. Students who wanted the best medical education

went to Salerno in Italy and Montpelier in France. Those who wanted to concentrate on Roman and canon law aspired to attend Bologna in northern Italy. The University of Paris was a training center for those seeking secular and ecclesiastical offices, because of its strong emphasis on logic and the arts. By the thirteenth century almost all civil servants, Church leaders, theologians, and philosophers had a higher university education, and many were university lecturers. Leading educational centers such as Bologna, Paris, Oxford, Cambridge, Cologne, and Naples were called *studia generale* (general schools). As such, they could confer the *ius ubique docendi* (literally, the right to teach everywhere), a license to teach at any university. For this reason, some of the greatest medieval theologians and philosophers taught all over Europe. For example, Albertus Magnus taught at Cologne and Paris; Thomas Aquinas taught at Paris, Rome, and Naples; and John Duns Scotus taught at Oxford, Cambridge, Paris, and Cologne.

Educational Goals. Although many of the debates held at medieval universities might seem esoteric to modern eyes, university educators and the lords who patronized universities generally saw themselves as providing practical, almost utilitarian, education as opposed to the less-worldly education of the monastic and cathedral schools. One of the most striking examples of this transformation took place in twelfth-century Paris, where a major struggle between academic disciplines occurred. There the traditional humanistic pursuit of studying classical texts was challenged by a new interest in logic, science, and mathematical studies inspired by a knowledge of Arabic sources. Degrees in medicine and concentrations on rhetoric were often shortcuts to positions in noble households or further university appointments. The study of Roman and canon law became attractive since it often led to better jobs and greater social mobility. The pragmatic side of education became so apparent by the late twelfth century that John of Salisbury, a successful careerist, lamented, "If you are a real scholar you are thrust out in the cold. Unless you are a money-maker, I say, you will be considered a fool, a pauper. The lucrative arts, such as law and medicine, are now in vogue, and only those things are pursued which have a cash value." Medieval thinkers, however, could include theology among the utilitarian subjects they studied because of its role in guiding individuals toward the ultimate eternal goal: salvation. In this way, conservative scholars who attacked the corruptive influences of classical texts furthered the utilitarian bent in medieval university education. Preachers and theologians such as Peter Camestor (circa 1164), Alexander of Villedieu (circa 1200), and Jacques de Vitry (died 1240) fulminated against the study of classical authors as a danger to the morals of the young students. In popular sermons, students were exhorted to pass over from the arts to theology and religion. The meteoric rise of grammatical and logical studies in the twelfth and thirteenth centuries led to the view that logic provided the means by which order and system could be found in the study of nature, humanity, and even divinity. Every subject from grammar to medicine, law, and theology fell under the influence of new semantic and logical methods.

Life at a Medieval University. Life for students at medieval universities varied according to factors such as the location of the university, a student's social class, and his ultimate goals. One of the striking aspects of the medieval university, however, was the similarity in student life at all universities and the ability of scholars who had achieved the *ius ubique docendi* to teach at any European university. Scholars were organized into small "colleges" when they first arrived. These colleges served as residences for groups of up to twenty or thirty and as places where students received basic instruction. Members of the theology faculty lectured in Latin on topics that fell within the general framework of Old Testament or New Testament, while the arts faculty, which also lectured in Latin, could also include pagan authors. Within these categories professors had a great deal of freedom about what subject they covered. Students chose which lectures they attended and paid the professors according to their perception of the value of a professor's instruction. Given this arrangement, it is perhaps not surprising that many professors relied on other sources of income. Student life was relatively informal. There were no set standards governing what academic levels a student was required to pass each year. Examinations in the form of public debates occurred when a student wanted to obtain some university certification or degree. Theoretically, a student could stay at the university all his life, although most students went there hoping to earn degrees and recognition that would get them good jobs. At the well-known universities students came from all over Europe, and there were frequently clashes between different groups, as well as between students and the community at large. Because medieval students were considered clergy (clerics or clerks), they were subject to different laws than the surrounding community, which often resented the fact these laws were less likely to require corporal punishment. Battles between "town and gown"—a distinction based on the academic robes, similar to modern graduation robes, that all students and professors were required to wear—sometimes became so fierce that towns tried to impose curfews, limited the size of knives students could carry, and obliged rich students to support poorer ones so that the poor would not be driven to theft or beggary. Such regulations involved a large number of people; thirteenth-century Paris had a population of twenty-five thousand to fifty thousand, of which university students and professors made up approximately 10 percent.

The Art of Memory. Because medieval books and writing materials were expensive and difficult to come by, students and scholars had to rely on their memories for references that modern academics find in books or on the internet. The result was amazing feats of memory and mental organization. To achieve these ends medieval scholars trained themselves in the *ars memorativa* (the art of memory). Building on the work of classical scholars such as the poet Simonides, any person aspiring to medieval higher education trained his memory to function like a filing system from which to pull information at a moment's notice. A common starting point was a building of some sort. A student would form a somewhat bizarre, and therefore memorable, mental image of the contents of a room and assign a verbal mnemonic device to these contents. For example, a modern medical student could put a Canadian Mountie in a room with a manacled prisoner. That image would then trigger the device, "Some Criminals Have Underestimated Royal Canadian Mounted Police." The first letters of each word— *S, C, H, U, R, C, M,* and *P*— identify the shoulder, arm, and hand bones: scapula, clavicle, humerus, ulna, radius, carpus, metacarpus, and phlanges. This medical student could then build a connecting room for other body parts, working his or her way through the body until all of the bones were treated. Each subject could have its own house, and complicated philosophical or theological topics led to the construction of entire mental villages populated by unusual people and animals. These structures greatly eased the ability of medieval scholars to retrieve items from the storage system of memory and to organize these materials and thoughts into speeches and texts. Thomas Aquinas is one of the best-known examples of a scholar who used this memory system. Aquinas attested to the importance of memory when he wrote, "For things are written down in material books to help the memory." Memory was not an aid to writing, rather writing was an aid to the more important skill, memory. Legends attribute to Aquinas prodigious feats of memory and organization. While it is known that he mentally composed and dictated his multivolume *Summa Theologiae* to scribes, by the thirteenth century it was believed that he "used to dictate in his cell to three secretaries, and even occasionally to four, on different subjects at the same time."

Sources:

T. H. Aston, gen. ed., *The History of the University of Oxford*, volume 1, *The Early Oxford Schools*, edited by J. I. Catto (Oxford & New York: Oxford University Press, 1984).

Mary J. Carruthers, *The Book of Memory: A Study of Memory in Medieval Culture* (Cambridge & New York: Cambridge University Press, 1990).

A. B. Cobban, *The Medieval Universities: Their Development and Organization* (London: Methuen, 1975).

Lowrie J. Daly, *The Medieval University, 1200–1400* (New York: Sheed & Ward, 1961).

Jacques Le Goff, *Intellectuals in the Middle Ages,* translated by Teresa Lavender Fagan (Cambridge, Mass. & Oxford, U.K.: Blackwell, 1993).

LITERATURE: LATIN WRITINGS

Role of Latin in Medieval Culture. With the end of the Roman Empire in the West during the fifth century, Christian scholars trained in Latin culture remained the primary source of literate civil servants for new European lords. The Church and its scholars perpetuated the Greco-Roman culture they found so invaluable and the primary language of the western Roman Empire: Latin. To be learned in the Middle Ages was to know Latin, and intellectuals used it for writing, reading, and speaking. Although Latin altered over the centuries and new vocabulary was added to meet the new needs of the medieval population, reform movements repeatedly worked to maintain an international standard, and evidence suggests that they were largely successful. Moreover, because of the great improvements in education in the twelfth century, literacy, especially in Latin, improved as well. Important later medieval authors, particularly Dante, challenged the primacy of Latin by writing in their own, vernacular languages, and in his work on the nature and primacy of the vernacular, Dante overturned medieval Scholastics' concept of Latin as a "universal language." Yet, even after Dante and other authors challenged the supremacy of Latin, it continued to be the primary language of administrators and the community well beyond the Middle Ages.

Early Models. Classical and early medieval authors greatly influenced their successors. Copying other authors' style, grammar, vocabulary, and even entire sentences was not considered wrong in the Middle Ages. In fact, it was a sign of an individual's learning and skill to have enormous Latin references at hand and to organize them so effectively that they could fit current needs and

POETRY FOR CHARLES THE BALD

The following lines from *Versus Johannis Scotti ad Karolem Regem* (The Poem of John the Irishman for King Charles), written around 860 for Charles II (the Bald) of France, is a good example of one style of courtly writing and the accommodations made for patronage during this period:

The torch of the Sun binds everywhere with golden rays
the concentric circles of the starry court.
Twice does he balance on his scale a night twice equal to the day
And twice he turns himself to the increase that each partakes
So dividing the year by twice two motions
He rules the fourfold universe with fair divide
That universe, encompassed by twelve constellations on its curving vault

The life, the salvation of men, the highest glory of the Heavens:
Grant to our King Charles to whom you have given the sceptres
That he may always live your servant, grant him this with kindly mind.
Grant him happy issues in this passing life
And joys of the heavenly kingdom along with you.

Source: John O'Meara, *Eriugena* (Oxford: Clarendon Press, 1988), pp. 182–187.

debates. Classical writings by Cicero, the Stoics, and the Neoplatonists affected the treatment and presentation of Latin Christian philosophy and rhetoric. Medieval authors also refashioned ancient classics such as the *Aeneid, Iliad,* and *Odyssey* to illustrate Christian and contemporary themes. Virgil, the author of the *Aeneid,* became a key classical figure because of the power of his epic and because his pastoral poetry was seen as foreshadowing the coming of Christ. Writings by early Christian scholars such as Augustine, Jerome, and Isidore of Seville guided later medieval scholars on theology, composition, and argumentative style. Among these late classical works, the *Consolation of Philosophy* (524) by the philosopher Boethius played a foundational role in Latin and vernacular medieval literature down to Dante and Chaucer in the thirteenth and fourteenth centuries. Its theme that Nature—which presides over growth, procreation, and preservation of life—is a creative principle directly guided by the mind of God motivated medieval scholars and authors to study nature for its divine aspects and to express their discoveries in many literary forms. In later centuries scholars from Ireland and Britain also played important roles by bringing many "lost" classical works back to the European continent and by promoting their interpretive and literary methods.

Scriptures and Commentaries. The primary subjects for study at medieval schools were the Christian scriptures. What constituted "scriptural" texts was still being debated, and in the early Middle Ages some works were considered scriptural that no longer have that status. These texts and other authoritative early Christian works inspired the bulk of Latin writing of the Middle Ages. By the ninth century these works had been translated into Latin, and Jerome's fourth-century Vulgate Bible was the primary scriptural text. Medieval scholars devoted their efforts to "commenting" on these scriptures. In fact, the study of commentaries was increasingly the focus of medieval education, especially at the universities. By the twelfth and thirteenth centuries some commentaries had become quite elaborate. A manuscript page often included a small excerpt of scripture surrounded by several layers of theological comments about them, and then comments on the comments. Another form of commentary included a small scriptural quote and a list of all authoritative statements about that passage that had been made since it was written. The commentary tradition was also enshrined in teaching. Students gathered around a teacher who recited a short piece of some set text and then presented all the authoritative commentaries on that text, which the students discussed. A session ended with the teacher explaining the original text himself, after which he moved to the next set passage. Of the hundreds of commentaries produced during the Middle Ages, probably the *Sentences* (circa 1150) by the Italian Peter Lombard had the broadest influence in medieval universities.

Latin Poetry. Particularly in the ninth and tenth centuries, scholars saw poetry as the completion and expression of philosophy, a natural and sometimes preferred way of expressing philosophical and theological truth. This attitude continued, albeit somewhat diminished, throughout much of the Middle Ages, and medieval scholars were also frequently poets. Medieval Latin poems came in many lengths, used many metrical and rhythmic schemes, and had many subjects. Particularly popular among the courts that sponsored poets were epics and histories, generally recounting the brave deeds of ancestors, the current ruler, or some mythical figure. German Emperor Otto I (the Great) (reigned 936–973) tried to make his court a European center for science, art, and literature. Among the poets that he sponsored was the nun Hroswitha of Gandersheim, who composed poems on mythical subjects and two long epic poems in praise of the imperial house. Monks also were enthusiastic poets. Abbot Odo of Cluny wrote poetry against pride and debauchery, which he regarded as the chief vices in world history. During the ninth century, Walafrid Strabo composed his *De visionibus Wettini* (On the Vision of the Wettini), which is often regarded as a precursor to Dante's *Divine Comedy.* Walafrid also composed a detailed poem describing the monastery garden. Poets had many other occupations. For example, one of the best-known ninth-century poets, the Irishman Sedulius Scottus, was also a noteworthy Greek scholar, translator, commentator, grammarian, and philosopher. These pat-

---

THE EXILE OF EL CID

The Poem of El Cid expresses the values of medieval heroic literature, especially the importance of reputation, loyalty, and pride. In the following excerpt, through the treachery of his rivals, the Campeador brothers, El Cid has just incurred the displeasure of King Alfonso of Aragon and has been sent into exile.

When that his host was growing, heard the great Cid of
    Bivar,
Swift he rode forth to meet them, for his fame would spread
    afar.
When they were come before him, he smiled on them
    again.
And one and all drew near him and to kiss his hand were
    fain.
My lord the Cid spake gladly: "Now to our God on high
I make my supplication that ere I come to die I
may repay your service that house and land has cost,
And return unto you double the possession that ye lost."
My lord the Cid was merry that so great his commons grew,
And they that were come to him they all were merry too.
Six days of grace are over, and there are left but three,
Three and no more. The Cid was warned upon his guard to
    be,
For the King said, if thereafter he should find him in the
    land,
Then neither gold nor silver should redeem him from his
    hand.
And now the day was over and night began to fall
His cavaliers unto him he summoned one and all:
"Hearken, my noble gentlemen. And grieve not in your
    care.
Few goods are mine, yet I desire that each should have his
    share.
As good men ought, be prudent. When the cocks crow at
    day,
See that the steeds are saddled, nor tarry nor delay."

Source: *The Lay of the Cid,* translated by R. Selden Rose and Leonard Baccon (Berkeley: University of California Press, 1919), p. 11.

---

terns continued into the literary revival that modern scholars have termed the Twelfth-Century Renaissance. At that time the poets Bernard Silvestris and Alan of Lille argued that poetry was the highest musical expression of wisdom. Although these claims for poetry were contested, Bernard's *De mundi universitate* (On the Universe of the World) and two works by Alan of Lille, *De planctu naturae* (The Lamentation of Nature, 1160–1172) and *Anticlaudianus* (Against Claudius, 1181–1184) outlined an understanding of the medieval cosmos that thinkers such as Dante took up later.

Histories and Biographies. Historical writing had always been an important part of Latin literature, and medieval scholars perpetuated this tradition. Although factual accuracy varied widely, histories were recounted in many Latin literary forms: prose, poetry, musical lyrics, and drama. Poetry continued to be an important medium for historical and mythic writing. The monk Flodoard (circa 1150) composed a legendary account of ecclesiastical history during the first millennium, while other poets wrote about the life of St. Christopher, the Saxon War of Emperor Henry IV, and the Crusades. In the eleventh and twelfth centuries, however, a series of scholars connected historical and autobiographical prose writing and produced books that were so popular that they were read to large audiences as public entertainment. Writers such as Alexander Nequam, Matthew of Paris, and Salimbene provided people with gossip about public matters, church happenings, and general intrigue. Peter Abelard prepared *The History of My Calamities,* a defensive and apologetic autobiography, while the monks Guibert of Nogent (1064–1125) and Othloh of St. Emmeran (1110–1170) wrote about their internal spiritual experiences. Travel writing also blended historical and autobiographical forms. Gerald of Wales's twelfth century *Topographia Hibernica* (The Topography of Ireland) was a strange mixture of geography and observations of foreign practices among the Celtic Irish based on his own travel experiences and reports by others. At this time, also, the legends of King Arthur were set into an historical framework. Building on Celtic poetry, the scholar Geoffrey of Monmouth brought Arthur to a European audience in his *History of the Kings of Britain* and *The Prophecy of Merlin*. These works are both propaganda in service of Geoffrey's ruler and propagandistic history in the service of a new governmental ideal: a united British Isles.

Letter Writing. The writing of letters and certain legal documents, known in the Middle Ages as the *ars dictaminis,* was a valuable skill. Not only did it serve as a means of communication within the European intellectual community and the Christian Church, but the composition of beautiful, learned, and rhetorically adept letters was considered an art form. In order to instruct authors, a series of manuals and collections of exemplary letters were in circulation by the tenth century. These manuals described the five parts of the appropriate letter: the *salutatio, exordium, narratio, petitio,* and *conclusio. Salutatio* (the word from which *salutation* comes) was the sender's introduction of him- or herself to the receiver. Here the sender acknowledged the rank of the receiver (with words such as *Your Majesty* or *Your Eminence*). The contents of the *exordium* (exhortation), *narratio* (narration), and *petitio* (petition) varied according to the sort of letter being written. The *conclusio* (conclusion) followed one of several classical poetic styles and reemphasized the receiver's virtues and the sender's petition. Alberic of Monte Cassino, Hugh of Bologna, and other Italian scholars during the eleventh century composed influential manuals that developed this organizational plan, and northern scholars followed their lead. By the twelfth century, examples of correct letters could be found in books called *formularies,* which were somewhat like modern guides for business correspondence and included letters that a less-skilled writer could copy for almost every possible occasion. The formularies of Peter of Blois, Ulrich of Bramberg, and Berard of Naples not only furnish illustrations of medieval literary style, but because they used examples of actual letters that have since been lost, they also are valuable historical sources.

Saints' Lives and Legends. Medieval saints' lives had a wide impact on medieval society. Saints were viewed as real, historical figures, and a retelling of their lives was a testimony to their holiness and God's blessings, as well as a record of the events in a particular time and place. As with other medieval histories, however, the line between what modern readers would consider fact and fiction is not always clear. Saints were believed to levitate, endure devastating fasts, and cure the sick. In fact, in both the learned and popular literature of the Middle Ages, saints became Christian heroes, exhibiting extraordinary virtues and abilities and inspiring Christians to accomplish much more mundane pious duties. Probably the best-known medieval collection of saints' lives is the *Legenda Aurea* (Golden Legend) by the Dominican Jacobus de Voraigne. Written in 1260, it drew on many other collections and was widely read and quoted in later medieval Europe. Although not regarded as one of the most accurate compilations of saints' lives, it was translated at least once into most of the leading European languages and was recopied repeatedly in Latin. By the fifteenth century, however, the Dominicans had taken it off their list of approved works.

Producing Medieval Books. Medieval books were handmade, and a Bible could take two skilled monastic scribes two years to complete. Books were generally produced in cathedral or monastic *scriptoria* (writing offices), where scribes worked with other book-making specialists. These manuscripts (handwritten documents) were written on parchment. To make parchment, animal skin—preferably sheep or calf—was soaked in lye to remove hair and blemishes, scraped to make it smooth, and dried and stretched on a rack. Once it was dry the skin would be cut to the needed size, which could vary greatly. Some medieval manuscripts are as small as two by three inches, while others are approximately two by three feet. These manuscripts were sometimes quite large and costly to produce; it has been estimated that making some large Bibles required the hides of approximately five hundred sheep. Once a skin was cut to size, faint regular lines were drawn on the skins, and they were bound in booklets of sixteen pages. In the center of each page a scribe copied the basic text using a standard script such as the Carolingian miniscule. Certain words and pairings of letters were often abbreviated using a symbol or a line over another letter. There rarely was punctuation and often words ran into each other. For example, a medieval scribe might write the preceding sentence as "thrarēespunctuā & oftenwordsran into eachothē." The assumption was that the reader would be familiar with the abbreviated word or symbol and could fill in the missing letters. After the text had been written on the parchment, the manuscript was given to an illuminator, who special-

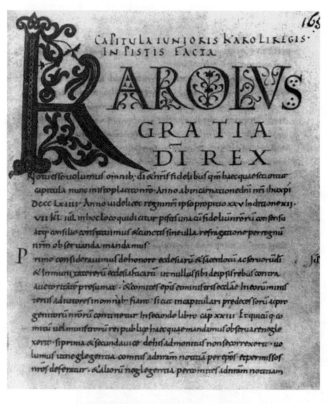

Example of Carolingian miniscule handwriting in the capitularies of Charlemagne, Louis I (the Pious), and Charles II (the Bald), circa 873 (Beinecke Library, Yale University)

ized in painting the highly decorative letters that began many pages and the miniatures that surrounded the text itself. Once all of the booklets and illuminations were complete, the manuscript was bound with thick layers of more parchment compressed together and sewn onto the side of all of the booklets. The result might be a small manuscript for an individual or an elaborate prayer book fit for a king.

Sources:

Marcia L. Colish, *Medieval Foundations of Western Intellectual Tradition, 400–1400* (New Haven: Yale University Press, 1997).

Ernst Robert Curtius, *European Literature and the Latin Middle Ages*, translated by Willard R. Trask (Princeton: Princeton University Press, 1990).

Suzanne Reynolds, *Medieval Reading: Grammar, Rhetoric, and the Classical Text* (Cambridge & New York : Cambridge University Press, 1996).

Gabrielle M. Spiegel, *The Past as Text: The Theory and Practice of Medieval Historiography* (Baltimore: Johns Hopkins University Press, 1997).

LITERATURE: SAGAS AND OTHER EARLY MEDIEVAL WRITINGS

Celtic Literature and Illuminations. Celtic scholars had a great influence on ninth- and tenth-century philosophy and theology. Celtic literature and the decorative techniques used in their manuscripts also influenced European literature, particularly epics and other poetry. Although the stories and themes of this literature were rooted in the pre-Christian era, much of it was written down in the period after 814. In fact, one of the distinguishing characteristics of Celtic literature is its blend of pagan and Christian themes, especially the presence of divinity in nature and a sense of the supernatural. The Celtic hero is often visited by benign and malignant spirits and is susceptible to visions. The voyage across a long, deep sea or to another world is another Celtic motif that had a major influence on later medieval literature. Poems such as the *Tain* (first written down about 900), which recounts the battles and fall of the hero Cuchulain, include themes found in later heroic poetry such as *Beowulf*.

Old Norse and Germanic Legends. Legends from northern Europe also fused pagan and Christian themes, particularly the value of courage and the importance of a warrior ethos. The earliest Old Norse works are the eddas, which were written down in the tenth century, but seem to have been recited beginning in the seventh. In these legends the afterlife includes Valhalla, the upper world presided over by the chief god Odin and his maidens, the Valkyries, and a lower world guarded by the goddess Hel (the origin of the English word *hell*). Other gods include Thor (god of thunder), fertility gods, and gods of nature. One of the more influential eddas is the heroic cycle of the *Volsunga Saga,* which influenced Old English poetry such as *Beowulf* and *Deor's Lament* and in German *Nibelungenlied* (written down circa 1190–1200). The many sagas in Old Norse literature are dramatic retellings of ostensibly historical events whose resolutions offer morals for their listeners. Because of their style and purpose, sagas set in their historical context are important for understanding of Norwegian and Icelandic societies in the early Middle Ages. The story of Sigurd and his relations with the woman warrior Brynhild, the *Volsunga Saga* is like a modern murder movie involving elaborate family relationships, lots of bloodshed, secret meetings, and vicious curses.

Early German Literature. As in Celtic and Old Norse literature, one of the most striking features of early German literature is the fusion of pagan and Christian themes—a sign of the transformations occurring in European society during the early Middle Ages. Indeed, the continued popularity of these works throughout the Middle Ages demonstrates the ongoing influence of pagan, Germanic values in what was ostensibly a Christian, Romanized Europe. Two of the most significant early German works are the epic poems *Hildebrandslied* and *Nibelungenlied,* designed to be chanted over a period of days or weeks as entertainment at large gatherings. The *Hildebrandslied* focuses on the problem of conflicting loyalties, a theme that had particular resonance for medieval nobles who owed feudal dues to several, sometimes opposing, lords. The *Nibelungenlied* has inspired generations of German authors and musicians, in particular the nineteenth-century German composer Richard Wagner. The *Nibelungenlied* was inspired by Old Norse legends such as the *Volsunga Saga,* and much of its plot is derived from that earlier work, with the names changed: Sigurd becomes Siegfried, and Brynhild becomes Brunhild. In the feudalized and Christianized *Nibelungenlied,* Siegfried is a model noble; courageous, determined, and prideful, he dies at the end of a hunt. Brunhild and her supporters are corrupt followers of the old way, the suggestion being that these ways are pagan. Even the Christian examples

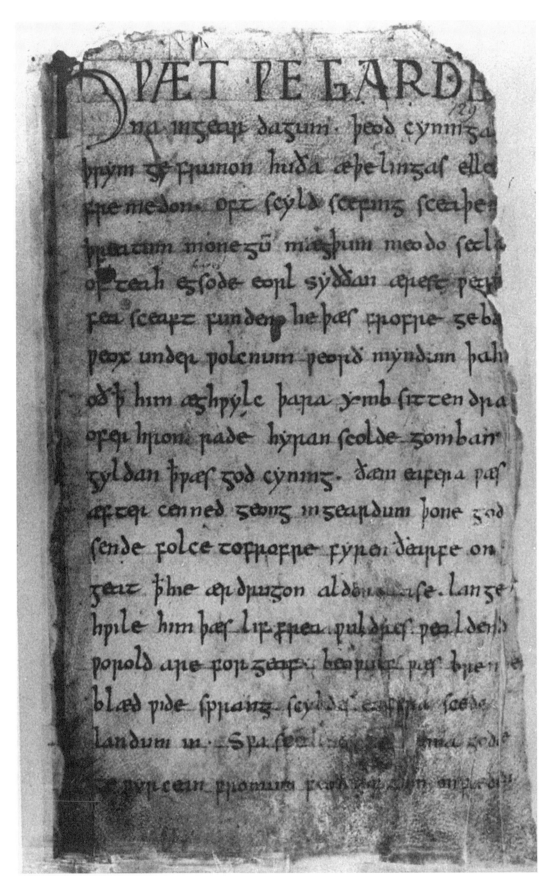

First page of the only manuscript for *Beowulf*, circa 975–1025 (British Library, London)

have mixed cultural messages. Siegfried's love, Kriemhild, is depicted as a devout Christian and a pious benefactor to the abbey of Lorsch. Despite her Christian commitment, however, she has a marked ability to nurse a wrong and to seek revenge, a quality valued highly in pagan Germanic culture.

Beowulf. The best-known Old English epic is *Beowulf.* Scholars remain uncertain about when it was first composed. Many believe that it developed over time, and was first written down at the end of the tenth century—establishing the form in which it came down to modern readers. Like most other northern European works from the early Middle Ages it blends both pre-Christian and Christian themes. The son of kings, Beowulf, as a young man, fights for whatever worthy lord will honor him and give him gifts, a respectable pattern of behavior in early medieval Germanic societies. He learns that the king of the Danes, Hrothgar, is being attacked by an invisible enemy that sneaks into his hall at night and decimates Hrothgar's soldiers. Beowulf promises to kill this monster, Grendel, and a series of dramatic battles ensues, including one under water in which Beowulf eventually kills Grendel and his mother. In many ways Beowulf's society, attitudes, and quest are products of pagan, Germanic ideals. A good king, Hrothgar, is a mighty gift giver rewarding his followers; Beowulf insists on single combat with the monsters in order to prove his courage; and Grendel and his mother are quite similar to other mythical sea monsters in northern literature. Yet, at the same time that Grendel and his mother are Norse sea monsters, they are also set within a Christian framework; both are described as descendants of Cain, the slayer of his brother Abel in the Bible. The second part of *Beowulf* deals with its hero, which occurs at the end of his victory over a fire-breathing dragon, another monster drawn from Norse legends. Although Beowulf is not the gentle and noble king of modern Christian kingship, his attitudes and actions fit medieval ideals of the Christian warrior-king. As such, his epic found favor in aristocratic society, and his behavior provided a model for noble behavior in the Middle Ages.

Epics, Sagas, and Chansons de geste. *Beowulf* is written in a literary form that gained great favor in the Middle Ages: the epic. Epics, sagas, and chansons de geste (songs of heroic deeds) are different names for similar works. All are long poems, in various rhyme schemes, that celebrate the deeds of legendary heroes; generally in medieval literature the terms *epic* and *saga* are commonly applied to northern European works such as Old Norse, German, and English poems of early Middle Ages, while *chanson de geste* is applied to a version of these poems that developed in France and western Germany during the eleventh and twelfth century. These songs (chansons) praised the deeds of secular and ecclesiastical heroes, saints, and soldiers. Examples of them may be found in most medieval European cultures, but probably the best-known medieval chanson de geste in the modern era is *The Song of Roland*, written in approximately 1100. Like other heroic stories, *The Song of Roland* is based on a supposedly historical event and person. In this case, the event was a 788 Muslim attack on Charlemagne's baggage train, in which the leader of Charlemagne's soldiers, Count Roland, was killed.

By 1100 this obscure event had been transformed into an epic battle between thousands of evil Muslims and a small coterie of noble Christians, who are Charlemagne's last defense. Like *Beowulf*, *The Song of Roland* celebrates the military culture of the noble class. Roland and his followers are the perfect nobles: loyal, brave, generous, and determined. *The Song of Roland* is also the product of a male-dominated warrior society. Women almost never appear in the poem, which rarely examines personal hopes, fears, and motivations. Unlike *Beowulf*, however, the poem is clearly Christian. In fact, one of the leading characters, and no mean warrior, is Archbishop Turpin, and Roland and his followers are clearly battling for both Charlemagne and Christianity. *The Song of Roland* was so popular that its characters were depicted in many medieval art forms, including sculpture, glass work, and manuscript illumination.

El Cid. Written slightly after *The Song of Roland*, *The Poem of the Cid* is probably the second most-influential medieval epic, and its title character, El Cid (the Lord, from the Arabic word *sayyid*), became the Spanish national hero, an example of Spanish Christian courage and determination during their reconquest of the Iberian peninsula from the Muslims. Like *The Song of Roland*, *The Poem of the Cid* is based on the supposed deeds of an historical figure. Rodrigo Díaz de Vivar (1043–1099), otherwise known as El Cid, was a mercenary soldier who fought for both Christians and Muslims. He ended his career as a knight and lord in the service of King Alfonso I of Castile, who rewarded El Cid well for his attacks against the same Muslims for whom he once fought. In the poem, El Cid's loyalties are clearer than in real life; yet, his relationships with Muslims and Christians still show the complexity of social relationships in medieval Spain, where religion was not always the primary force in alliance formation. *The Poem of the Cid* exhibits many epic qualities, and in it El Cid is transformed into the model Christian lord, noble, vassal, and father. He is a great military hero, wields a special sword, and is absolutely loyal to his king even after he has been unjustly exiled. Obediently leaving his home and his family, he becomes a great warrior in the lands between the Moors and the Christians. This ability and his unswerving loyalty to his ruler cause Alfonso to forgive and reward him, and at the end of the epic El Cid is recognized as "the Lord," the model nobleman. Yet, he is not the only model in this work. Unlike in *Beowulf* or *The Song of Roland*, in which women almost never appear, *The Poem of the Cid* presents El Cid's wife in heroic terms as well. When El Cid is killed in the assault on Valencia, she dives into the fray and has him propped up on his horse to continue leading his troops even in death, an act that succeeds in frightening the enemy and ensuring a Spanish victory. In this sense El Cid and his family all represent the aspirations of medieval nobility.

Sources:

Carol J. Clover, *The Medieval Saga* (Ithaca, N.Y.: Cornell University Press, 1982).

Marion E. Gibbs and Sidney M. Johnson, *Medieval German Literature: A Companion* (New York: Garland, 1997).

Stephen A. Mitchell, *Heroic Sagas and Ballads* (Ithaca, N.Y.: Cornell University Press, 1991).

LITERATURE: VERNACULAR TRADITIONS

The Significance of Vernacular Literature. The early medieval epics and sagas and the chansons de geste of the eleventh and twelfth centuries are some of the earliest manifestations of a form of literature that grew increasingly prominent and popular throughout the Middle Ages: vernacular literature. The word *vernacular* means "in the vulgar tongue," and when applied to literature it is used to describe literature that is composed or written in the language that the author and his audience speak daily. Although Latin was an international language in medieval Europe and those who knew Latin wrote, read, and spoke it, the majority of Europeans spoke local dialects that eventually evolved into the modern languages now known as French, English, German, Italian, and so on. A medieval author who was interested in gaining an international audience had to write in Latin, but authors who were writing for courts, where many nobles only knew a little Latin at best, or those who were composing for local, popular consumption wrote in the vernacular. Such works were frequently considered "lesser" works than their Latin counterparts, until a significant literary movement in the late Middle Ages asserted the equality of vernacular and Latin compositions. Led by writers such as Dante Alighieri and Geoffrey Chaucer and spurred by increasingly literate urban and noble communities, vernacular literature in the late thirteenth and fourteenth centuries gradually dominated popular entertainment and gained headway in traditionally Latin academic fields such as history, theology, and philosophy.

Troubadours and Minnesänger. In the late eleventh century there emerged a form of poetry that celebrated court culture and emotions and could be performed aloud or even set to music. The authors of these works were known as troubadours in southern France, where they originated, and Minnesänger in Germany, where they had a great influence on court literature. Duke William IX of Aquitaine (1071–1127) is often considered the first troubadour, and he began the patronage of other poets that was continued in the courts of his descendants Eleanor of Aquitaine and Marie of France. These poets covered a variety of themes, from romantic longing for love to a lover's boasts about sexual conquest. Unlike much earlier poetry, troubadour poetry is quite erotic. Even when condemning adulterous love and the foolishness of a lover, the poet Marcabru (active 1130–1150) is far more suggestive than his poetic ancestors. Among the many themes of well-known troubadours such as Jaufre Riddle, Bernart de Ventadorn, Bertran de Born, and Beatrice, Countess of Dia were the daily experience of court life and human emotion. These lines by Castellozza (born circa 1200), the wife of a southern French Crusader, represent common concerns of the troubadours: "Friend, if you had shown consideration, / meekness, candor, and humanity, / I'd have loved you without hesitation, / but you were mean and sly and villainous." The German poets—including Hartmann von Aue

ARTHUR'S TOMB

Gerald of Wales, royal clerk, diplomat, and historian, often wrote accounts of recent events as well. His report of the discovery and excavation of a tomb he and his contemporaries believed to be King Arthur's at Glastonbury, England, circa 1223, suggests the power of the Arthur legend among medieval people.

However, Arthur's body, which the fables allege was like a fantastic thing at the end, and as it were moved by the spirit to far away places, and not subject to death, in our own days was discovered at Glastonbury between two stone pyramids erected in the holy cemetery, hidden deep in the ground by a hollow oak and marked with wonderful signs and marvels, and it was moved into the church with honor and committed properly to a marble tomb. . . . many notable things happened here; truly he had two wives, the second of which was buried together with him, and her bones were discovered with his, but separate however, so that two parts of the sepulcher, toward the head of course, were considered to be containing the bones of the man, and truly the third, toward the feet, contained the woman's bones separately; where a lock of a woman's blond hair was discovered intact with its original color, such that when a certain monk snatched it greedily with his hand and raised it up, at once all of it crumbled into dust.

Most clearly King Henry II of England disclosed to the monks some evidence from his own books of where the body was to be found, some from letters inscribed on the pyramids, although most of it was erased by age, some also through visions and revelations made to good and religious men, just as he had heard from the ancient British bard, how deeply in the earth, 16 feet or more, they would discover the body, and not in the stone tomb but in a hollow oak. . . .

It must also be known that the discovered bones of Arthur were so large that it can be seen to have fulfilled these words of the poet: "And wonder at the giant bones in the opened graves." [Virgil, Georgics, I.497] Truly the shinbone of that man [Arthur] when placed next to the shin of the tallest man there, whom our abbot showed to us; and fixed in the ground next to his foot, greatly extended across the knee of that one by three fingers. Moreover, the skull was spacious and large to the point of being a freak or prodigy, so much so that the space between the eyebrows and the space between the eyes would contain entirely a small handswidth. However, ten wounds or more were apparent on the skull, one of which was greater than all the others, which made a large hole, and which alone seemed to have been fatal; the wounds healed in a solid scar.

Source: Gerald of Wales, *On the Instruction of a Prince (De Instructione Principis)*, circa 1223.

(1180–1210), Wolfram von Eschenbach (circa 1170–1217), and Walter von der Vogelwiede (circa 1170–1230)—also deal with the standard themes of love poetry, such as the longing of the lover and the sadness of unful-

Page from a manuscript for the *Romance of the Rose* produced in France during the second quarter of the fourteenth century; the illumination depicts the narrator as he dreams of the rose tree, while a personification of Danger stands by his bed; then he puts on his clothes, goes outside, and enters a garden (Bodleian Library, Oxford)

filled love, but they also introduced new themes, pointing to the uselessness of court life and arguing that the love between man and woman should be on an even basis.

Courtly Literature and Love. Troubadour poetry is often called the beginning of a new form of vernacular literature dealing with love in all its permutations that arose around 1170 and flourished into the fourteenth century. Known as "courtly literature" because it developed in medieval courts and its audience was based there, courtly literature began in southern France and soon influenced vernacular literature in northern France, Germany, Italy, and Spain. One of its primary themes was "courtly love," a term that is frequently misunderstood. In some of its significant representations, courtly love was the view that love in the context of marriage was impossible and the only true form of love was the adulterous relationship. There were other viewpoints arguing that love inevitably led to unhappiness. Indeed, medieval attitudes toward love tended to be influenced by the variety of responses ranging from approbation to condemnation, found not so much in the Bible as in classical Latin literature. The major writer on love matters in Roman times was Ovid (43 B.C.–18 A.D.), and he greatly influenced some medieval writers. In the view of Ovid, as with many ancient authors, love was a terrifying passion that could separate people from commonsense reason and from daily life. Thus, clerical writers in the Middle Ages who drew on these sources and on biblical themes found a fecund resource for moralistic sermonizing, especially much anti-woman rhetoric. Perhaps the most important of these writers was Andreas Capellanus, who at the end of the twelfth century wrote *Liber de arte honeste amandi* (Book of the Art of Loving Rightly). In the first half of his work, he depicted love as a form of suffering, a strong response to physical beauty. He held that there can be no true love in marriage and that love must be consummated adulterously. Although Andreas recognized that adultery is not acceptable to society, he believed that social stigma could be avoided through discretion and guarding the good name of the woman. Typical of male writers of his time, he was only interested in the positive effects of love on the male lover. He thought that male clerics made the best lovers, while he thought nuns should be banned from love. Prostitutes, peasant women, and promiscuous women were also excluded; youth or old age, blindness, and excessive lust all impeded love. In the second part of his work, Andreas presented a different and quite contradictory picture. He claimed that in part one he was just giving an objective analysis of love so that people could make good judgments. In part two he called for avoiding adulterous love at all costs because it is a sin against oneself and against one's partner, leading to deceit, fear, and an attachment to passing pleasures. Finally, it can have socially disastrous consequences. Moreover, he drew on ancient authorities to claim that women are a major source of vices. The modern reader may well develop the impression that Andreas was taking part in the favorite medieval pastime of presenting opposite points of view for the purpose of conversational entertainment.

The Romance of the Rose. During the first half of the thirteenth century, building on the work of Andreas Capellanus and other medieval poets, Guillaume de Loris began the classic medieval poem in the courtly love tradition, *Roman de la Rose* (Romance of the Rose), which was completed by Jean de Meun later in the same century. Following a common medieval literary conceit, it is a long allegorical poem describing a dream vision in which a lover attempts to gain his beloved. He dreams of a garden surrounded by a wall and containing a rose that symbolizes the female love object. On the wall are ten figures, among them Hate, Felony, Villainy, and Greed, which hinder the lover from attaining the rose. When he finally gets inside, he receives a warning about the treachery of love, but when he sees the rose, he falls in love with the beauty before him. To reach his love, he must become a vassal of Cupid, who embodies a series of paradoxes such as Pride and Humility and Courtesy and Villainy. A new personification, Reason, appears and advises the lover to abandon Cupid. A battle ensues when a series of other figures—a friend of the lover, Venus, Pity, Jealousy, Fear, and Shame—start fighting among themselves about what the lover should do. At this point Guillaume's part of the poem ends. When Jean de Meun wrote his part he offered a different perspective about the relationship between the lover and the beloved. Reason returns but now argues that all earthly love is transitory and advises the lover to seek happiness in eternal goods. The fickle nature of woman is attacked, and the lover's friend reappears to advise on a new strategy based on a woman's nature. The friend argues that the castle (the woman's body) should be stormed and the rose (her virtue and love) should be taken by bribery, hypocrisy, and deceit. More characters appear and join in the argument, which turns into a litany of medieval misogynistic (anti-woman) themes. An old woman advises trickery, infidelity, and frivolity as a means of attaining the rose. For her, love is but the fulfillment of a natural urge. Nature argues that the only true lovers are clerical celibates, and the fact that celibates make the best lovers is enough to free them from their vows. Eventually the lover and his allies take the castle, and the lover is united with the rose. The dream ends, and he awakens. This kind of courtly literature spread through the forms of entertainment for royal houses, and it eventually evolved into popular works of prose and poetry. Rather than elevating a woman's status, as some scholars have asserted, this literary tradition actually popularized and developed as series of medieval beliefs against women.

The Arthur Legends and Romance. Related to the genre of courtly love was another theme in courtly literature which has enjoyed enduring popularity: the Arthurian Romance. The earliest stories about a figure named Artus (Arthur) were old Celtic poems and histories in which he was portrayed as a war leader with a small group of loyal followers, and no Lancelot and Guinevere appear in them. In the hands of French and German poets during the twelfth century, Arthur became the leader of a wealthy and prestigious court that attracted and rewarded virtuous young men from all over Europe. Arthur rarely went on quests; instead, much like the gift-giving kings of earlier epics, he was the person who gave rewards to younger warriors, his favor was the ultimate attainment, and his court the ultimate setting for this idealization of noble culture. Although many authors composed stories, poems, and even musical lyrics on Arthurian themes, probably the most influential early creator of the Arthurian Romance was Chrétien de Troyes (1135–1183), the court writer of Marie de Champagne, daughter of Eleanor of Aquitaine. He explored the contradictions and tensions in human relationships, using Arthur's court as a setting. One of his best-known romances was *Lancelot,* in which Lancelot, a paragon of knightly virtue, loves Arthur's wife, Guinevere, so desperately that he is willing to humiliate himself repeatedly in order to free her from a treacherous knight. This Lancelot character is filled with contradictions: as a knight he should be proud, but he humbles himself by riding in a cart to reach Guinevere; as a vassal, he should honor his lord's wife, not try to sleep with her. The Arthurian Romances also deal with Christian themes, in particular the attempt to establish a truly Christian nobility. In the process, knightly valor is focused on a Christian quest: the attainment of the Holy Grail, the cup from which Christ drank at the Last Supper. This theme reappeared in various poems, particularly Chrétien's last work, *Perceval.* It was also picked up by several German poets: Hartmann von Aue, Gottfried von Strasburg, and in particular Wolfram von Eschenbach. In von Eschenbach's *Parzifal,* the quest for the Holy Grail is turned into a journey of education for the hero. Further, his mission for the Grail is linked to Christian themes and to the gift of the Holy Spirit, uniting Christian and Arthurian values.

Fabliaux and Other Forms of Poetry. Coexisting with courtly and Arthurian literature were other poetic forms, some of which had earlier roots and were performed in both Latin and the vernacular. Probably the most influential of these styles was goliardic poetry. Because of the relatively unstructured style of the medieval university, scholars could wander among them at will, and from the middle of the twelfth century royal and imperial privileges protected many of these traveling scholars. Those who never found permanent appointments continued their wanderings through most of their careers, gaining the name of goliards and a reputation for loose, marginal living. Proud of their Latin learning, they combined this knowledge with vernacular poetry and music that celebrated the joys of wine, women, and song, and goliardic poetry was born. Although respectable figures such as Hugh of Orléans and Walter of Chatillon composed goliardic verse, probably the best known is the German called the Archpoet (died 1165). His *Confessio Goliae* (The Confession of Golias) was a prototype for later goliardic verse. No one was safe from the goliards' critiques; clergymen and nobles, men and women found themselves the butts of goliardic jokes, and parodies

on hymns and prayers provided the framework for their poems. In addition, fables drawing on the Greek author Aesop and on folklore found a place in vernacular literature during the twelfth century. Authors such as Marie de France translated Aesop's fables into French and used his works as a foundation for the creation of new fables. Common themes were love triangles and seduction, as well as revenge, trickery, and deceit. One of the influential legends developed by these writers was the relationship between Aristotle and Phyllis, according to which the philosopher Aristotle married a beautiful young woman, Phyllis, in his old age, thus illustrating how even the most intellectual people could be controlled by love and sex. His subservience is further stressed when Phyllis manages to convince him to put on a bridle so that she can ride him like a horse. This medieval legend of Phyllis and Aristotle was cited long after the Middle Ages as a powerful example of the corruptive nature of women.

Folktales: Robin Hood and Renard the Fox. Other popular fables that arose during the later Middle Ages had few roots in Latin culture. Among the most popular and enduring were the stories that developed around the characters of Robin Hood and Renard the Fox. Although most of the Robin Hood legends were developed during the fifteenth and sixteenth centuries, evidence suggests that popular ballads, poems, and even short plays about him had developed in England by the middle of the fourteenth century. The Robin of these stories is not, however, a displaced noble who steals from the rich and gives to the poor. He is an outlaw and a trickster, who supports nobles over peasants, manipulates anyone who enters his territory, and acts in many ways like a loan shark. In the Renard the Fox legends of medieval France, Renard shares many qualities with this earlier Robin Hood. Pierre St. Cloud was the first known author who wrote about Renard the Fox, Ysengrin the Wolf, and Hersent, Ysengrin's less-than-virtuous wife. Many of the stories revolve around tricks Renard plays on the stupid and greedy Ysengrin, but any other animal in the forest is a potential victim of Renard's somewhat malicious sense of humor. In this sense, Renard, like Robin Hood, is a medieval antihero, parodying the virtuous knights of epic literature but doing so in such a charming and clever fashion that he gains the audience's sympathy. In some cases, the Renard stories explicitly make fun of Arthurian Romances, such as the Grail cycle, and *The Song of Roland.* Renard stories were so popular that by the fifteenth century his name, "Renard," became the French word for fox, replacing the earlier medieval word *goupil.*

Later Medieval Developments. By the thirteenth century most of the major vernacular languages had been established as appropriate vehicles for serious literary and even philosophical compositions. The power of the vernacular was even felt in the religious realm, where the laity increasingly pushed for translations of the scriptures or, at least, of primary spiritual texts. Building on the earlier work of French and German poets and romance writers, Italians in the late thirteenth and

Virgil (right) preparing to lead Dante through Hell; illumination from Canto I of the "Inferno" section in a circa
1345 Sienese manuscript for Dante's *Divine Comedy*
(Biblioteca Laurenziana, Florence)

fourteenth centuries developed a poetic style known as *la
dolce stil nuova* (the sweet, new style) that in turn influenced northern European authors of the fourteenth and
fifteenth centuries. A leading figure in this Italian poetic
movement was the Florentine Dante Alighieri (1265–
1321). A poet, scholar, and civil servant, Dante was
quite familiar with Latin and vernacular literature. In *De
vulgari eloquentia* (On the Vernacular Language, 1308)
he discussed the nature of the vernacular and asserted
primacy over Latin, overturning medieval Scholastic
theory of Latin as a "universal language." His best-
known work, one of the masterpieces of medieval literature, is his *Commedia* (completed in 1321)—known as
the *Divina Commedia* (Divine Comedy) since the sixteenth century. In this three-part epic he traces his travels through Hell and Purgatory with the Roman poet
Virgil as his guide and then to Heaven, where his guide
is his beloved Beatrice, subject of many of his other
poems. Though long and sometimes difficult to understand, the *Divine Comedy* was a contemporary success.
In beautiful Italian, Dante combined the most sophisticated theology and philosophy of his time with rich
poetic traditions, many popular stories, and allusions to
contemporary events, creating an allegorical exposition
of the journey of the human soul toward God.

Sources:
R. Howard Bloch, *Medieval Misogyny and the Invention of Western Romantic
Love* (Chicago: University of Chicago Press, 1991).

Peter Dronke, *The Medieval Poet and His World* (Rome: Edizioni di storia e
letteratura, 1984).

Robert Hollander, *Dante: A Life in Works* (New Haven: Yale University Press,
2001).

Armando Petrucci, *Writers and Readers in Medieval Italy: Studies in the History
of Written Culture,* edited and translated by Charles M. Radding (New
Haven: Yale University Press, 1995).

Francesca Canade Sautman, Diana Conchado, and Giuseppe Carlo di Scipio,
eds., *Telling Tales: Medieval Narratives and the Folk Tradition* (New York:
St. Martin's Press, 1998).

Marcelle Thiebaux, ed. and trans., *The Writings of Medieval Women: An
Anthology,* second edition (New York: Garland, 1994).

MUSIC

Music and Philosophy. The study of music in the Middle Ages embraced much more than the art of composition
and performance. Like the other arts of the *quadrivium*
(arithmetic, geometry, and astronomy), music was considered a science of the cosmos. According to the medieval
theorists, its ultimate object was knowledge of the underlying harmony of the universe. For this reason music was
often held to be the most fundamental of the arts, the one
nearest to philosophy. Just as medieval writers on medicine
gave primacy to speculative medicine over its actual practice, writers on music theory generally believed that the
philosopher of music was the true expert; a musician in the
modern sense of the word would have been considered only
a practitioner of sound.

Boethius's Musical Hierarchy. The emphasis on
music as an intellectual discipline derived in large part
from Boethius (circa 480 – circa 524), whose *De institu-
tio musica* (On Music, circa 503) served as one of the
most authoritative texts on music theory throughout the
Middle Ages and even into the Renaissance. Boethius
divided music into three classes. The highest class is
musica mundana, or the universal structure of things,
often referred to as the "music of the spheres." Next in
the hierarchy is *musica humana,* the harmony of parts in
the human being, namely the rational soul and the irrational body. The final and lowest class of music is *musica
instrumentalis,* which comprises what modern people
think of as music, whether vocal or instrumental.

Symbolic Correspondences. Boethius's hierarchy is
founded on a worldview in which everything in the universe is related to everything else by virtue of an underlying
order or harmony. For Boethius, as for the Pythagoreans—
whose influence is strongly felt in his work—this harmony
is essentially mathematical. Music in the highest sense
meant precisely the study of those proportions that are fundamental to universal harmony. This view of the world and
of the role of music was strengthened in the twelfth century, with the recovery of Platonism at the School of Chartres, where it was taught that music was a key to
understanding the relations between man (the microcosm)
and the world (the macrocosm). This worldview is
expressed in the visual symbol of *homo quadratus,* in which
the physical proportions of man are linked to the four elements and the seven known planets, which are in turn
related to the seven notes of the scale.

The Applications of Music. The philosophical understanding of music led to many applications to other
branches of knowledge and art. Philosopher-theologians
such as Robert Grosseteste and Roger Bacon, for example,
held that scripture could be understood only with the help
of music, which was essential for good theology. Bacon
wrote: "It belongs to music to give the reasons and theories
of (many things in Scripture), although the grammarian
teaches the rules for them." Bacon's argument for the primacy of music over grammar and logic was echoed by
Dante, who claimed that poetry as music was superior to

Among the surviving examples of medieval secular music are songs sung by university students. The following examples express common themes in student songs throughout the Middle Ages.

I, A Wandering Scholar Lad:
I, a wandering scholar lad,
Born for toil and sadness,
Oftentimes am driven by
Poverty to madness.
Literature and knowledge I
Fain would still be earning,
Were it not that want of pelf
Makes me cease from learning.
These torn clothes that cover me
Are too thin and rotten;
Oft I have to suffer cold,
By the warmth forgotten.
Scarce I can attend at church,
Sing God's praises duly;
Mass and vespers both I miss,
Though I love them truly.
Oh, thou pride of N———,
By thy worth I pray thee
Give the suppliant help in need,
Heaven will sure repay thee.
Take a mind unto thee now
Like unto St. Martin;
Clothe the pilgrim's nakedness
Wish him well at parting.
So may God translate your soul
Into peace eternal,
And the bliss of saints be yours
In His realm supernal.

Some Are Gaming:
Some are gaming, some are drinking,
Some are living without thinking;
And of those who make the racket,
Some are stripped of coat and jacket;
Some get clothes of finer feather,
Some are cleaned out altogether;
No one there dreads death's invasion,
But all drink in emulation.

Source: Frederic Austin Ogg, ed., *A Source Book of Mediaeval History: Documents Illustrative of European Life and Institutions from the German Invasions to the Renaissance* (New York: American Book Co., 1907), pp. 352–353, 356–357.

introductory logic and had a truth-revealing capacity. The extension of music to include poetry dates at least to Augustine, who in his *De Musica* (On Music, circa 387–391) deals chiefly with poetic meters. John of Garland, poet-grammarian at the University of Paris in the thirteenth century, equally subscribed to the notion that poetry and music were sister arts, arguing that the rules of musical consonance could be applied to rhyme schemes. Musical concepts were also applied to architecture. The proportions of musical intervals were sometimes incorporated into the building plans of churches, notably the cathedral of Chartres, and the rose windows of the Gothic cathedrals often gave tangible form to the idea of the harmony of the spheres.

Liturgical Music. The use of music in Christian liturgy dates back to apostolic times, when the early church most likely appropriated Jewish melodies for the chanting of psalms. Almost no musical texts exist from the early centuries of Christianity, so it is difficult to trace the evolution of chant in the liturgy. Over time several different systems developed, each bearing the influence of local musical traditions and corresponding to particular liturgical rites. Among these were the Celtic rite of the British isles, the Gallican rite in parts of France, and the Mozarabic rite, which developed in Moorish Spain. These three rites either died out or were suppressed in the name of liturgical uniformity, though a fourth, the Ambrosian rite, has survived even into modern times in the diocese of Milan. The fifth and most important liturgical form was the Roman rite and the musical system that eventually evolved from it, Gregorian chant.

The Origins of Gregorian Chant. The term *Gregorian* refers to Pope Gregory I (reigned 590–604), who according to legend compiled a system of chant to help regularize church music and worship. While Gregory might have played a role in musical reform in Rome, it is unlikely that he was entirely responsible for the vast body of melodies that form Gregorian chant. Once again, however, in the absence of notated musical texts, it is exceedingly difficult to discern a clear historical development. One likely theory is that Gregorian chant emerged as a synthesis of an older Roman form of chant and the local chant of the Franks under the Carolingian Empire. When the Roman liturgy officially supplanted the Gallican rite during the reign (751–768) of Pepin III (the Short), cantors were sent from Rome to teach the Roman form of chant. The pre-existent Frankish style of chant almost undoubtedly exerted an influence on the Roman chant, though to what degree remains uncertain. Regardless, by around 900 the first substantial collections of Gregorian melodies had appeared in notation, and by the beginning of the next century the main body of the chant had more or less been established. This body formed the official chant of the Roman Catholic Church into modern times.

Characteristics of Gregorian Chant. All Gregorian chant, or plainchant as it is sometimes called, falls within eight modes, often referred to as the church modes. Their names are based on the ancient Greek modes, after which they are supposed to be modeled, but in practice the correspondences are at best confused. Each mode is defined by a particular scale, then by dominant, starting, and ending notes within that scale, and finally by characteristic melodic tendencies. As opposed to most Western classical music and even to some secular music of the later Middle Ages,

Musical notation for a Gregorian chant on the four-line staff invented by Guido of Arezzo; from a fourteenth-century missal
(Walters Art Gallery, Baltimore)

the modal development of Gregorian chant avoids dynamism and marked contrast: melodies proceed mostly in what is called stepwise fashion, without large leaps of pitch, and they are performed at a relatively slow tempo. Gregorian chant is purely vocal and entirely monophonic (sung in unison without accompaniment). These characteristics together produce a music of great sobriety, simplicity, and depth.

Sacred Drama. Gregorian chant was used for the entire cycle of liturgical music in the mass and the divine offices for feasts throughout the church year. By the end of the tenth century another forum for sacred music had developed, with the advent of what are referred to as liturgical plays. These musical dramas were typically performed in church, and though never an official part of the services, they immediately followed or preceded them and were sometimes even incorporated into Lauds or Vespers. Such dramas probably began as small dialogues or hymns, expanding in time to full productions including scenery and costumes. Similarly, though on a more-popular level, there

developed what are known as mystery, miracle, and morality plays, dealing respectively with biblical events, miracles of the Virgin Mary or the saints, and allegorical representations of the struggles of the Christian soul. A notable example of the last is the *Ordo Virtutum* (Play of Virtues) of Abbess Hildegard of Bingen (1098–1179), which while based on the Gregorian modes exhibits a remarkable creativity of composition.

Hymns. Religious plays, which were often performed in the vernacular, helped to express the truths of doctrine and liturgy in a form readily grasped by the laity. Another important way in which sacred music was made more accessible was through hymns, simple and expressive religious poems set to music. The Roman liturgy was mostly drawn from scripture; only a limited number of other traditional texts were used, and the Western Church was in general hesitant to accept individually composed hymns into the services. But on the popular level their influence was enormous, and they were gradually incorporated into the divine offices as well. Originally hymns were written in

Latin and based on the melodies of plainchant, but in the course of time vernacular hymns were written, and freer melodic structures were used. Many medieval hymns have survived in usage to modern times, including Christmas carols such as *Puer Natus* (A Son Is Born) and Marian hymns such as *Ave Maris Stella* (Hail, Star of the Sea). The Franciscans, who were known for their emphasis on simple devotion and popular piety, played an especially significant role in hymn writing. Jacopone of Todi (circa 1228 – circa 1306), a Franciscan lay brother, is said to be the author of the beautiful thirteenth-century *Stabat Mater* (At the Cross Her Station Keeping). The work of another Franciscan, Bishop Richard Ledrede (1317 – circa 1361) of Kilkenny, Ireland, is an example of a creative use of hymns at the popular level: the bishop superimposed religious lyrics of his own composition on the popular melodies of drinking songs.

Secular Music and the Troubadours. Virtually nothing is known of the folk music of the early Middle Ages. Vernacular song almost certainly existed among the lower classes, and instrumental and vocal music probably played a sizeable role in village festivals and city street fairs. Even in terms of the literate classes little is known about the early practice of music, though it is likely that some form of musical entertainment was to be found in the great halls of castles. Germany and France were both home to oral traditions of epic poetry composed in the vernacular and performed in a musical context. The French *Chanson de Roland* (Song of Roland) and the Anglo-Saxon *Beowulf*, for example, were probably meant to be recited or sung with the accompaniment of a harp or other instrument, but musical guidelines for the performance of these works were never written down. Documented secular music really begins with the poet-musicians of the south of France, known as the troubadours. The troubadours, writing in Old Occitan (or Provençal), refined vernacular song into an art form. The first known troubadour was Duke William IX of Aquitaine (1071–1127), grandfather of Eleanor. Over the next two centuries troubadours such as Bernart de Ventadorn (circa 1125 – circa 1195) and Bertran de Born (circa 1140 – circa 1215) enjoyed considerable patronage from noble courts. Their love lyrics were in particular well received, contributing greatly to the establishment of the tradition of courtly love.

Troubadour Influences. The music of the southern troubadours gave rise to a similar art form in the north of France. There the trouvères did for Old French poetry what the troubadours did for Old Occitan. The best known among them is Chrétien de Troyes (circa 1140 – circa 1190), the author of several medieval romances. The German equivalents of the troubadours were the Minnesänger, who wrote poems chiefly on the subject of courtly love (*Minne);* though Germany apparently already possessed a rich tradition of poetry in the bards known as scops, written sources for German secular music appeared only with the Minnesänger. In northern Italy the songs of the troubadours were imported directly and imitated; so great was their influence that Dante had considered writing his poetry in Provençal rather than the Tuscan vernacular. A final important influence of the troubadours was on Spanish music. Troubadours traveled freely to Spanish courts, and the earliest songs recorded in medieval Spain were in Old Occitan. By the thirteenth century, however, Galician-Portuguese, the vernacular of the Iberian peninsula, began to be used for the composition of song. This new tradition gave rise to one of the most important compilations of medieval song, the *Cantigas de Santa Maria*. A collection of more than four hundred songs, the collection was compiled at the court of King Alfonso the Wise (1252–1284), a great patron of the arts. The majority of these songs are based on miracles of the Virgin Mary, illustrating an overlap between the lyric tradition of the troubadours, in which an earthly lady is viewed as the supreme object of devotion, and the rise of veneration for the Virgin in the High Middle Ages.

The Introduction of Polyphony. The most important musical development in the Middle Ages, and perhaps in all of Western music history, was the introduction of polyphony. Liturgical music was originally entirely monophonic: the several voices of the choir sang melodies in unison, without harmonies or accompaniment. As early as the ninth century, however, musicians had begun to experiment with polyphony, or the singing of more than one note at once. At first it was used simply as an embellishment to existing Gregorian chants, to set apart particular pieces or feast days. But as the principles of polyphony developed, the new style became more and more prevalent. It also became more and more elaborate, evolving from the primitive use of parallel voices singing at a given interval above or below the melody (a technique known as simple organum) to complicated motets involving several voices singing in melodic and rhythmic independence. The expanded use of polyphony may be traced in part to developments in the twelfth century in the south of France, at the Abbey of St. Martial in Limoges. The next century gave way to the influence of the School of Notre Dame in Paris and its master composers, Leonin and Perotin. Another major source of polyphonic influence was Santiago de Compostela in northwestern Spain, home to a major collection of early polyphonic texts. From centers such as these a new kind of music began to spread throughout western Europe, a kind of music differing from earlier forms both in theory and in sound. The changes often met with resistance by leaders of the Church, who wished to preserve the purity of the traditional chants. As late as 1324 Pope John XXII (reigned 1316–1334) of Avignon issued a decree forbidding the altering of plainchant melodies and allowing only a limited use of polyphony. Nonetheless, by the beginning of the Renaissance in Italy, polyphony had become firmly established as a guiding principle of all new musical activity, whether sacred or secular.

The Problem of Notation. In the early centuries of Western music, melodies were transmitted by oral tradition. Only in the eighth or ninth century did the rudiments of a musical notation emerge, in the form of simple melodic markers, or neumes, written above each line of text in liturgical books. Over the next few centuries a variety of idiosyncratic systems of melodic notation arose throughout Europe. The most significant step toward regularization was the eleventh-century invention of the lined staff, usually attributed to Guido of Arezzo (circa 995–1050). This four-lined staff became the standard form of plainchant notation and in turn served as the basis for the modern five-lined staff. Only later did a corresponding system of rhythmic notation come into being, largely in response to the demands of polyphony. This rhythmic system evolved over the course of several centuries, reaching its final form only in the sixteenth century. Lack of a clearly defined rhythmic notation, together with the absence of indicators of tempo and even orchestration, makes it difficult to know exactly how medieval music sounded, even when its melodies are recorded in manuscripts. Modern research has led to many speculative reconstructions of performance practice in the Middle Ages, especially in the latter part of the twentieth century, when there was a surge of popular interest in medieval or "early" music.

Sources:

Henry Chadwick, *Boethius: The Consolations of Music, Logic, Theology and Philosophy* (Oxford: Clarendon Press, 1981).

Richard L. Crocker, *An Introduction to Gregorian Chant* (New Haven & London: Yale University Press, 2000).

Richard H. Hoppin, *Medieval Music* (New York: Norton, 1978).

PAINTING

Types and Purposes of Medieval Painting. During the period 814–1350, the styles of painting changed dramatically. Using the same terms they apply to the architecture of the period, art historians classify these styles as Romanesque, Ottonian, and Gothic. These categories are, however, modern impositions on medieval styles, and none of the few surviving medieval records describes artists as altering their techniques and topics either suddenly or even over the period of several decades. Medieval authors who discussed paintings focused on their locations, purposes, compositions, and the materials used in creating them. The cost of materials and labor made paintings expensive enough so that they were not generally part of middle- or lower-class households, nor were they usually hung in the private rooms of nobles' homes. Artists rarely painted subjects because of inspiration; instead, a patron contracted for a painting with a specific subject and placement in mind and itemized the size, cost, materials, and composition of the work. Paintings thus commissioned could cover entire walls, be placed over altars, decorate manuscripts, or fit inside lockets. Artists painted on various surfaces other than canvas, including wood, skins, and plaster. They mixed together oils, eggs, and other natural substances to make the pigments with which they painted. In addition, painters were often commissioned to do other types of artwork, such as preparing backdrops for pageants and plays, designing court banquets, and even preparing drawings from which embroiderers or jewelers could pattern cloths

Illumination of Christ in Majesty, surrounded by a prophet and evangelists, in the large manuscript Bible executed for Count Vivian, lay abbot of Tours, 844–851 (Bibliothèque Nationale, Paris)

and jewelry. Expected to be versatile, yet regarded as a mere craftsman, a medieval painter seldom signed his work, and many still-admired works from the Middle Ages continue to be unattributed.

Illuminated Manuscripts. Because of the cost to produce them in a time before the advent of printing presses, books were luxury goods in the Middle Ages. Scholars have estimated that an ordinary medieval manuscript was worth one year's wages for a craftsman, while a work with illuminations painted with precious pigments, and sometimes even crushed jewels, could represent a lifetime's pay. People who bought these expensive works expected their money's worth in elaborate decorations. After the text was completely copied into a manuscript, it was delivered into the hands of artists, generally monks, who specialized in small, detailed paintings in the large letters that typically begin pages and around the edges of the text. These artists were known as illuminators, and their works are some of the most beautiful examples of medieval painting. Medieval Europe drew on a long tradition of illuminating particularly precious texts, such as the Bible. Celtic and English manuscript makers in the ninth century and earlier began producing Bibles in which the art almost dominates the text. One of the most striking of these books is the Book of Kells, written at the beginning of the ninth century. In it the four Gospels inspired entire pages of intricate decoration in the Celtic style. Another important illuminated

During the first quarter of the twelfth century a monk known as Theophilus Presbyter wrote *On Divers Arts*. Although precise information about his identity may never be known, it appears that this German monk had firsthand experience with the technology and philosophy of art. Writing in language that varies from mystical to precise, Theophilus focused artistic production, particularly in areas such as metallurgy, enameling, painting, and sculpture. The following preface to the first part of his work reflects these diverse interests:

Theophilus—humble priest, servant of the servants of God, unworthy of the name and profession of monk—wishes to all, who are willing to avoid and spurn idleness and the shiftlessness of the mind by the useful occupation of their hands and the agreeable contemplation of new things, the recompense of a heavenly reward!

In the account of the creation of the world, we read that man was created in the image and likeness of God and was animated by the Divine breath, breathed into him. By the eminence of such distinction, he was placed above the other living creatures, so that, capable of reason, he acquired participation in the wisdom and skill of the Divine Intelligence, and, endowed with free will, was subject only to the will of his Creator, and revered His sovereignty. Wretchedly deceived by the guile of the Devil, through the sin of disobedience he lost the privilege of immortality, but, however, so far transmitted to later posterity the distinction of wisdom and intelligence, that whoever will contribute both care and concern is able to attain a capacity for all arts and skills, as if by hereditary right.

Human skill sustained this purpose and, in its various activities, pursued profit and pleasure and, finally, with the passage of time transmitted it to the predestined age of Christian religion. So, it has come about that, what God intended to create for the praise and glory of His name, a people devoted to God has restored to His worship. . . .

Wherefore, dearest son,—whom God has made wholly happy in this regard, in so far as those things are offered freely, for which many at the greatest peril of life plough the sea waves compelled to endure hunger and cold, or which others, wearied with long servitude in the schools and not exhausted by the desire of learning, only acquire with intolerable labour—be eager and anxious to look at this little work on the various arts, read it through with a retentive memory, and cherish it with a warm affection. If you will diligently examine it, you will find in it whatever kinds and blends of various colours Greece possesses: whatever Russia knows of workmanship in enamels or variety of niello: whatever Arabia adorns with repoussé or cast work, or engravings in relief: whatever gold embellishments Italy applies to various vessels or to the carving of gems and ivories: whatever France esteems in her precious variety of windows: whatever skilled Germany praises in subtle work in gold, silver, copper, iron, wood and stone.

Source: Theophilus, *The Various Arts*, translated by C. R. Dodwell (London: Nelson, 1961), pp. 14, 16.

manuscript is the Book of Hours (prayer book) created for Jeanne d'Évreux, Queen of France, by the Parisian illuminator Jean Pucelle between 1324 and 1328. Measuring only 3½ by 2½ inches, it is filled with vibrant depictions of the Christmas and Easter stories and the life of St. Louis IX, Jeanne's great-grandfather. In addition to these works, the manuscript is decorated with dozens of marginal illuminations known as drolleries (the amusing figures that frolic on the edges of many Gothic manuscripts), depicting various whimsical and supernatural creations and daily life in medieval Paris.

The Value of Marginalia. Throughout the Middle Ages illuminations covered manuscripts designed for Church use and for presentation at important courts. Theoretically, the pictures were supposed to help the reader understand the meaning of the text (hence the name *illumination*), but in practice the decorations and scenes in illuminated manuscripts were quite fanciful and often seem to have little to do with the text. In addition to illuminations, medieval manuscripts also included notes surrounding the primary text. These pictures and notes, called *marginalia* because of their placement in the margins, have often been considered relatively unimportant parts of medieval books. Recently, however, scholars have argued that marginal illuminations and comments reveal much about medieval attitudes, just as psychologists assert that a person's doodles can reveal much about his or her personality.

Small-Scale Paintings. Although manuscript illuminations are now some of the best-known medieval paintings, medieval painters also created thousands of other small-scale works for churches, castles, and homes. Frequently the subjects of these paintings were religious—including scenes from the lives of Jesus, Mary, or one of the saints; famous episodes from scripture such as the Apocalypse, the Last Judgment, or John the Baptist preaching; or a representation of one of God's attributes, such as Christ in Majesty or the Presentation of the Infant Jesus to the angels. In early and high medieval art, through the twelfth century, the figures were generally quite stylized and stiff, but around 1200 changes in medieval society led to alterations in painting that much later became known as Gothic style. Paintings that decorated the backs of altars, known as altarpieces, became more complex, as can be seen in the altar at Siena or in the Isenheim altarpiece by Matthew

Grunewald in Colmar, France. One significant change came in the depiction of the Virgin and Child and in the figure of Christ. The stylized Virgin and Child of the earlier Middle Ages, strongly influenced by Byzantine art, was replaced by a more human and natural image of the Madonna and Child. Christ was portrayed as nursing, like a normal, human baby, and the Virgin took on more characteristics of a bemused mother rather than the Queen of Heaven.

Wall Paintings. Throughout the Middle Ages, walls were frequently painted, particularly in churches. Romanesque artists incorporated Roman motifs and remains into their works, as in the cathedral of Montreale, Sicily (circa 1172–1189). Later medieval painters and sculptors sometimes integrated strips of glass mosaic—gold, black, and white—into their works. Much medieval decorative work was done on churches, where one of the most frequently chosen subjects was the majesty of Christ, which generally appeared on the half dome of the apse. The fresco on this subject at the Catalan church of San Clemente de Tahull is one of the best preserved and conventional in its depiction of Christ sitting on a rainbow and raising his right hand in blessing. Another common theme, designed as a lesson to parishioners, was the Last Judgment, with the futures awaiting the saved and the damned painted in explicit detail. Images of screeching harpies, devils disemboweling sinners, and the skins of the damned burning off in the flames are often repeated in these works.

Techniques. Wall paintings were executed using several techniques, most commonly fresco or tempura. *Fresco* painting is done on fresh, wet plaster, while paintings done on a dry surface are called *tempura;* often a medieval painter mixed techniques depending on the effect he was trying to achieve. Painters were responsible for all stages in their work: they ground the pigments for colors, prepared the paints and surface to be painted, sketched the composition, and, of course, painted the work itself. In the process they used many tools. Brushes and jars to hold paints were standard equipment. Painters also had various bleaches for preparing surfaces, knives for smoothing them, stilettos to engrave drawings on walls or to vary the texture of the painting, and even small tweezers to inset jewels or other decorative objects. Techniques varied greatly according to the surface to be painted. At an early stage of medieval wall painting, the borders that surrounded the scenes were set in place by dipping strings in paint and then holding them against the wall or by painting or carving lines in the wall. In the fresh plastering typical of the fresco, a drawing was made on paper, transferred onto the plaster, and finally traced over with a tool with a bony or metallic head, leaving a carved outline on the wall. Artists made sure that these sheets stuck to the wall by using a mixture of oil and gum. Once the pattern was placed on the wall, the artist and his assistants began filling in the picture with paint made from a mixture of special soils, oils (including egg yolks), and natural pigments. If the artist was using fresco, he had to work quickly, because the paint had to go on the plaster while it was wet. Otherwise the pigments would soon fade, and the painting itself would crack and flake. An artist's assistants painted routine parts of the work, such as clouds and borders, while the master painter handled facial expressions, clothing, and other areas demanding fine detail. Precious metals such as gold, silver, and lapis lazuli were mixed into pigments to achieve a glowing effect. Painters also used different brushes, varied their brush strokes, and layered paints according to the effect they were trying to achieve.

Painting in Service to the Church. A painter's greatest patrons were generally the leading clergy of their area. The spate of cathedral construction and renovation during the twelfth and thirteenth centuries provided employment for painters as well as other sorts of artists. Painters prepared wall-sized murals, decorated columns with stripes or vegetation, and tinted the features of sculptures in the church. They also provided altarpieces of various sizes for both the side chapels and the high altar. These artworks were first of all instructive. Primarily illiterate, medieval Europeans could learn basic Christian doctrines from the paintings in churches. Second, art reinforced Christian teachings. Sinners looking at graphic depictions of heaven and hell had the benefits of good behavior and the penalties for evil reemphasized before their eyes. Third, art could raise the spirit. A beautifully decorated church illustrated God's majesty and the difference between heaven and earth, thereby providing Christians with a pale reflection of the joys they might experience when saved. Fourth, and most esoterically, the beauty of art and human creativity also supported medieval doctrines about the marvels of God's creation and the potential of God's highest creation, Man.

From Symbol to Nature. Typically, modern observers look at the stiffness and disproportion of the figures in early medieval paintings and think that medieval artists could not draw. That impression is partially false. Medieval artists did not fail to develop the perspective techniques that create the illusion of space because they were ignorant; instead they had goals other than realism for their works. Through approximately the eleventh century, the primary impulse in medieval painting seems to be symbolic. For example, in the Catalan cathedral of San Clemente de Tahull, the Christ in Majesty portrays Jesus in a somewhat unnatural and stiff manner. In the subdued light of the sanctuary, however, it is precisely this totally unrealistic interpretation of the deity that best expresses his all-pervading presence. At Tahull, as in many other Romanesque pictorial works, discarding any reference to the actual appearance of things enabled the artist to achieve the maximum spiritual intensity. The Gothic style of painting that developed in the thirteenth century relied on different images and techniques to convey its messages. Gothic painting layered literal and symbolic meanings, and the figures in these works have realistic and mystical elements. As the Gothic style evolved in the fourteenth and fifteenth centuries, it became known for its attention to natural objects and detail. This International Gothic style also adopted ideas about light, color, and vision known as *perspec-*

Giotto's fresco of Anna meeting Joachim at the Golden Gate to inform him that she is pregnant with the Virgin Mary; painted at the Arena Chapel in Padua, circa 1305

tiva, developed by scholars such as Roger Bacon and John Peckham in the 1260s, 1270s, and 1280s. These developments in Gothic style had a striking effect in Italy, where a series of early fourteenth-century artists pioneered a new, more naturalistic style that still included strong symbolic elements. Painters such as Arnolfo di Cambio (1265–1302), Tino da Camaino (circa 1285–1327), Andrea Pisano (1295–1348), Duccio di Buoninsegna (circa 1255–1318), Ambrogio Lorenzetti (circa 1317–1348), and Bernardo Daddi (circa 1290–1348) were popular in their era and influenced the development of Italian Renaissance art.

Giotto. Undoubtedly the greatest of these late medieval Italian artists was Giotto di Badone (1267–1337). A master of all painting techniques, his Uffizi Madonna and the frescoes at the Bardi and Perruzzi chapels in St. Croce, Florence, were acknowledged masterpieces during his lifetime and inspired artists such as Michelangelo and Leonardo da Vinci. Probably his greatest works were the series of frescoes he painted at the Arena chapel in Padua around 1305. His subjects were quite traditional—scenes from the life of Christ, the Virgin Mary, and Joachim (Mary's father). The challenges he faced in portraying these subjects were extraordinary. The chapel was small and asymmetrical, and in order to carry out his extensive iconographical scheme, he had to balance his work among windows. To frame his main panels, Giotto painted fake marble columns and cornices, a technique that was adopted by later Renaissance painters. Giotto also used illusion to extend the size of the chapel, employing perfect perspective techniques to paint rooms that looked like additions to the chapel. His figures are softer and more voluminous than those of earlier medieval artists. The most important and most dignified figures have a majestic air, an expression of conviction, and a profound, concentrated gaze; yet they are warm and reassuringly human. Some ten years after Giotto's death, the well-known writer Giovanni Boccaccio described Giotto as "the best painter in the world," a judgment later Renaissance artists echoed.

Sources:
Jonathan J. G. Alexander, *Medieval Illuminators and Their Methods of Work* (New Haven: Yale University Press, 1993).

Michael Camille, *Image on the Edge: The Margins of Medieval Art* (Cambridge, Mass.: Harvard University Press, 1992).

Virginia W. Egbert, *The Medieval Artist at Work* (Princeton: Princeton University Press, 1967).

H. W. Janson, *History of Art*, fifth edition, revised (New York: Abrams, 1997).

Luisa Marcucci and Emma Micheletti, *Medieval Painting: A History of European Painting*, translated by H. E. Scott (New York: Viking, 1960).

SCULPTURE

Places and Purposes for Sculpture. Much like painting, sculpture appeared primarily in churches and in the homes of great secular and ecclesiastical lords. It was possible, however, for less-wealthy individuals to enjoy small-scale sculptures, such as the wax models known as ex votos, or to whittle small wood carvings for their personal use. The majority of sculpture commissioned from professional artists had two interrelated purposes: pedagogical and decorative. The sculpture that adorned churches was intended to communicate Christian messages to the illiterate and to reinforce Christian doctrine among the literate and illiterate alike. In addition, stone carvings, metalwork, and other sculptural forms were increasingly used to decorate the houses of the noble and the wealthy during the Middle Ages. Sculpture could serve as an offering to God, a visible testimony of God's favor and a gift of a grateful beneficiary. The twelfth-century leader of the Cistercian order, Bernard of Clairvaux, preferred a simple sculptural style, while Abbot Suger of St. Denis wanted to use all possibilities of stone to speak through art about the divine.

Large-Scale Figures. During the Middle Ages there seems to have been little demand for freestanding, life-size (or larger) sculpture. Medieval sculptors had not lost the ancient techniques that allowed for the production of such works. Instead, large medieval sculptures were generally designed as part of an entire sculptural program, generally decorating an important religious house or cathedral. For example, the entrance to Chartres Cathedral is flanked by larger-than-life sculptures of scriptural characters placed on small platforms carved into the supporting columns of the arches. The churches on the pilgrimage route to Santiago de Compostela employed some of the first medieval workshops that concentrated on monumental sculpture. In fact, it has been argued that the same workshop carved the major sculptures all along the route, traveling from church to church over a period of decades. Initially these Romanesque figures had a distant and almost supernatural appearance, stressing their separation from the common sort. As with painting styles, however, sculptural styles changed during the Middle Ages, and this evolution followed a similar pattern. Beginning in the thirteenth century, large sculptural figures changed from the typical, early medieval stylized forms to more naturalistic, humanistic forms. This move from a more transcendent vision of the divinity and his closest allies to that of an appreciation of the humanity of the human being was also found in the image of Christ. Jesus was no longer depicted as a valiant warrior-hero dressed in kingly attire, but as a youthful bearded man with flowing hair.

Gateways and Portals. The gateways and portals of medieval churches include the greatest surviving concentration of medieval sculpture, generally emerging as part of the sculptural revival of the eleventh century. These gateways were usually composed of three primary scenes that arched over the three entrances on one side of a church (the tympanum) and a series of figures and other decorative motifs that lanked the three main compositions. Churches on pilgrimage routes and major cathedrals all over Europe often had elaborate sculptural gateways. For example, beginning in the 1270s, pilgrims entering the church of St. Sernin on the Compostela pilgrimage route walked through an entrance where Christ in Majesty flanked by his apostles looked down on them. One of the best-known and most-elaborate medieval sculptural programs for a portal was carved at the church in Vézelay. In the tympanum a huge, seated Christ sends energizing rays to his apostles, following a standard way of depicting the descent of the Holy Spirit. The interest in distant lands fostered by events such as the First Crusade (1096–1200) is apparent in the surrounding sculptures, where the reliefs (shallow sculptures carved into architectural structures) illustrate the exotic people and animals that filled medieval travel literature. There are dog-eared men, women in topless gowns, men clothed in leaves, and a child who wraps his enormous ears around himself as a clam does its shell. Almost any theme from medieval literature or Christianity could be carved into portals. Although scenes from the Apocalypse and Last Judgment were quite common, it is also possible to find figures such as King Arthur and Guinevere.

Reliefs and Decorative Carving. Surrounding portals and throughout medieval churches were relief carvings. Reliefs are shallow, smaller carvings that appear to emerge from the architectural elements of the building itself. They could also be carved onto stones that were several inches thick and then set into place, much as a painting is hung. In the thirteenth and fourteenth centuries, as the European economy expanded, reliefs were more and more often carved in elaborate castles and noble residences. The subjects of reliefs were much like those of portals, but small reliefs tended to concentrate on fanciful animals, plants, and scrollwork. The names of artists who executed some of the larger relief compositions have survived. For example, a sculptor named Gilbertus carved his name in one of his reliefs depicting the Flight into Egypt, which he designed and presumably carved in the church of St. Lazare at Autun, France. Apparently Wiligelmo da Modena, Nicolo of Verona, and Benedetto Antelami dominated Italian relief sculpture in the twelfth and early thirteenth centuries. These sculptors also carved other stone structures for their patrons. One of the best-known sculptors of the late thirteenth century, Nicola Pisano, designed and executed a pulpit for the Pisa Baptistry. His work was so innovative that Renaissance artists pointed to it as an inspiration.

Christ and the Apostles sculpted on the tympanum of the church of St. Madeleine at Vézelay, France, after 1120

Woodwork and Altarpieces. Although wood was not as durable as stone and was, therefore, unsuitable for architectural sculpture, the relative ease with which it could be carved and its cheapness when compared to stone or metalwork meant that medieval churches and some prosperous secular homes included many wooden statues. Like stone sculptures, these statues generally depicted religious themes such as the Virgin Mary, Christ in Majesty, a patron saint, or scenes from saints' lives or scriptures. Wood carvings also graced altars in the Middle Ages. At the time the carving was part of a painted altarpiece, a decoration that stood several feet high and was placed upright on the back of the altar. A common form of wood sculpture in eastern France and western Germany was the Black Virgin. Made in the tenth century or earlier out of a local hardwood, these rough statues usually depicted the Virgin Mary as a massive figure sitting on a throne and holding a regal baby Jesus in her lap. These figures were placed in shrines as a focus for worship, and over time the smoke from votive candles and the caresses of the devout darkened the wood, thus giving the statues their name. As focal points for veneration of the Virgin, these statues had great local appeal, and pious individuals donated elaborate and expensive costumes to dress the statue during feast days. By the fourteenth century, it is estimated that the Black Virgin of Dijon had at least a weekly change of clothes, far more than even the wealthiest urban residents.

Metallurgy as Sculpture. Also existing in churches were metal cases and figurines that shared many characteristics with stone and wood sculptures. These caskets often held relics—that is, physical remains of holy figures—so they became known as reliquaries. Because they held such precious contents, reliquaries represent one of the high points in medieval metalcraft. They could be several feet tall, made of gold, silver, or bronze, and embedded with precious stones. Along with the vessels used during religious services, they were some of the most valuable belongings of medieval churches. Metalwork also took other forms reminiscent of the stonework found in the churches. The first known freestanding bronze sculpture made since the fall of the Roman Empire was cast in tenth-century Metz. Approximately two feet tall, it depicted Charlemagne in triumph. Moreover, in the Meuse Valley region of Belgium the Mosan school of metalwork produced one of the earliest medieval bronze masterworks, a baptismal font designed for the church at Liège. Metalworkers and jewelry makers were also patronized by the laity. Belt buckles, clasps, knife sheaths, and other objects could be engraved and inlaid with several kinds of metal. Not only were these works beautiful, they were also quite valuable, and much medieval jewelry has not survived because its owners melted it down when they needed ready cash.

Sources:

Leslie Ross, *Medieval Art: A Topical Dictionary* (Westport, Conn.: Greenwood Press, 1996).

Roberto Salvini, *Medieval Sculpture* (Greenwich, Conn.: New York Graphic Society, 1970).

Veronica Sekules, *Medieval Art* (New York: Oxford University Press, 2001).

James Snyder, *Medieval Art: Painting, Sculpture, Architecture, 4th–14th Century* (New York: Abrams / Upper Saddle River, N.J.: Prentice Hall, 1989).

THEATER AND FESTIVAL

Defining Medieval Theater. Because most early playwrights and performers were wandering minstrels, they were suspect in the eyes of local authorities and the Church. During the eleventh and twelfth centuries, however, these groups began to find powerful patrons, and eventually even cities and the craft guilds in them sponsored performances of plays. Medieval theater took many forms that were quite different from most modern conceptions of drama and staging. In fact, many early plays were essentially chanted poetry or set pieces in which the figures on stage did not move while a narrator explained, in poetic meter, the significance of the scene being portrayed. For example, at Easter a play concentrating on the adoration of the cross might have several individuals kneeling before a cross staring worshipfully at Jesus. (Nativity plays in which the birth of Jesus is illustrated with living figures, who remain silent throughout a reading of the appropriate scriptures, are modern descendants of these performances.) Moreover, the medieval terms used to describe theatrical styles drew on classical definitions that have unusual connotations for modern readers. For the medieval writers, tragedy was a story told in a high style and usually concerned with important people; it began in a happy mood but ended sadly. A comedy was a story that was narrated in an everyday manner about ordinary matters, and it ended happily ever after.

Early Theater and the Church. From its inception, the Christian Church had mistrusted playwrights and performers, and such suspicion was apparently one of the factors that contributed to the decline of theater after the fall of the Roman Empire. Yet, the revival of theater in the Middle Ages was tied to its use in Christian liturgy. Beginning in the ninth century small texts of one to five lines (known as tropes) were inserted in religious services to amplify some passage of the liturgy, particularly at major feasts such as Easter and Pentecost. By the later tenth century, these tropes had started to expand into brief plays. The earliest of these are the *Quem quaeritis* (Whom do you seek?) plays, which consist of lines exchanged between the three Marys as they approached Christ's tomb. These set pieces evolved into short liturgical plays with characters, additional dialogue, props, costumes, and stage directions; church vestments and music were also used. Other brief plays were

THE DAY OF JUDGMENT

The anonymous, early-fourteenth-century play *The Day of Judgment* is a complex medieval drama, with roles for ninety-four characters, and the sole surviving manuscript on which it is recorded is decorated with eighty-nine pictures depicting staging. The following plot summary includes themes that were popular throughout medieval drama.

After an introductory sermon by Le Prescheur [the Preacher] we find Satan and his devils preparing to send one of them, disguised as an elegant youth, to seduce a woman of the tribe of Dan in Babylon. This devil, Angignars, speedily accomplishes his purpose and Antichrist is born of the union. The devils now begin instructing Antichrist in all their arts, and presently he is able to make the blind to see, to cure the leprous, revive the dead, and heap riches upon the poor. He readily wins over the Jews and grows so powerful that even kings and cardinals pay him homage. Only the Pope himself and Enoch and Elijah who have been sent by God to wage war against the enemy are able to resist the magic of Antichrist.

. . . Antichrist is overthrown, Enoch and Elijah who have been killed by his orders are resurrected, and the damned, as in so many poems concerned with the Harrowing of Hell or the Dance of Death, pass in review before us. Here they include an abbess and bishop who have sinned together, a king, bailiff, provost, lawyer, adulterous queen, erring prioress, a usurer, his wife, his servant, and even his small child. Although eight pages of the manuscript are missing, it is obvious that the God of our author was especially condemnatory of all who lived on the fruits of usury and was especially concerned with those who were kind or unkind to the poor. . . . In the final reckoning angels pour out vials of wrath, apostles and saints aid in the task of separating saved from damned, and eventually the just are duly rewarded and the wicked driven to hell by menacing devils. The play ends with a few unique lines of seven syllables spoken by St. Paul, who says that the damned have been taken to hell for eternal torment.

Source: Grace Frank, *The Medieval French Drama* (Oxford: Clarendon Press, 1954), pp. 132–133.

developed for Christmas and Twelfth Night (6 January). These plays were inserted in the liturgy throughout the Middle Ages as a means of teaching the generally illiterate population important doctrines and episodes in Christian history. Medieval religious drama thus had three main functions: to provide religious instruction, to encourage piety, and to establish and support Christian faith. The clergy had some difficulties, however, in enforcing these goals. The plays were quite popular, and eventually the slapstick humor and off-color puns employed to catch the audience's attention led the clergy to remove these plays from the church and even to stage their own instead. In so doing, they increased church attendance so much that the plays had to be moved from the altar to the churchyard and

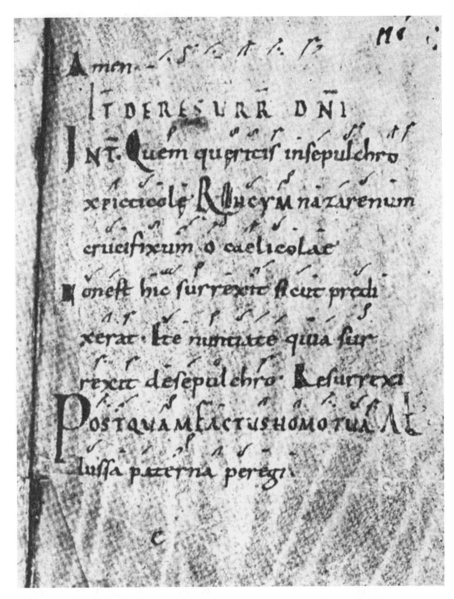

Text, with musical notation, for a *Quem quaeritis* play performed at the monastery church at St. Gall, Switzerland, during the tenth century (from Glynne Wickham, *The Medieval Theatre*, 1974)

eventually to public squares. The further the plays got from the church the less control the clergy had over their contents, even when they supplied some of the actors and the funding. The situation grew so out of hand, from the clergy's perspective at least, that by 1210 a papal edict forbade the clergy to act in churches. The clergy did, however, continue to have some involvement with dramatic productions. From the late eleventh century through the end of the Middle Ages, extended tropes were developed that told the lives of the saints, particularly St. Nicolas, St. Paul, and St. Catherine. Unlike most other tropes, these were performed primarily in monasteries and cathedral schools.

Mystery Plays. One of the favorite styles of medieval theater was the mystery play. The name may come from the claim that it illustrates the "mysteries" of Christianity, or it may be rooted in a guild's responsibilities for the "mastery" (pronounced *mystery*) of its craft; from there the plays guilds produced became known as mystery plays. Whatever the origins of the term, these plays developed from the extended tropes that were part of the medieval liturgy, and they flourished after the clergy distanced itself from public drama in the thirteenth century. The groups responsible for staging these plays became the town guilds, which produced a cycle of plays on feasts and holy days. Guild members filled the major roles, directed the plays, and supplied sets and props for what was an all-day entertainment. For example, early in the morning they might stage a play about the creation of the world or the fall of Satan, then they could continue during the day with plays illustrating various biblical episodes; the Flood, the harrowing of hell, the crucifixion, and Abraham and Isaac were all popular plays. The day would typically end with a depiction of the Apocalypse and the Last Judgment. The production of these mystery plays received a boost in 1264, when the Pope established the Feast of Corpus Christi, which celebrated Christ's redemptive power. Because this feast was not dedicated to a specific saint or event, it gave celebrants great freedom, and by the fourteenth century it became the primary festival where guilds sponsored religious plays that portrayed the history of the world from creation to judgment. These cycles provided the audience with a Christian history that emphasized God's plan and support for all mankind.

The York Cycle. Although most surviving cycles of mystery plays date from the fifteenth century, a few examples of earlier works have survived, especially from medieval England. Of these the Chester cycle (named for the city in which it theoretically originated) is the oldest. The most complete and most influential is the York cycle. The York cycle of plays began in the fourteenth century and was clearly a local affair. The performances were in English, used costumes from everyday life that were designed specifically for the plays, and were staged in the streets, public squares, and town halls by amateur actors affiliated with the guilds, which fronted the cost of the productions. Staging these plays was no minor endeavor; the York cycle grew to include more than three hundred speaking parts. The city and guilds were willing to support these performances because of the wealth and prestige they gave to the city and the professional associations. For example, goldsmiths who provide elaborate props for the Adoration of the Kings play advertised their craftsmanship and artistry to potential buyers. The York plays followed a typical pattern for mystery plays, covering from the creation to doomsday with a series of biblical stories placed in between. In addition, they included some legendary figures, such as the English folk hero St. George.

Farces and Secular Spectacles. At the same time tropes moved from the church to the courtyard, a series of other, more-secular plays were developed and gain, favor in the expanding court society of medieval Europe. These plays took several forms. Common types were morality plays such as *Everyman* that deal with everyday matters and do not include saints or biblical themes. Mimes, dancers, and contortionists could be found in major population centers. Courts sponsored highly staged jousts and tilts, and knights even held mock battles and sieges. In medieval Spain, one form of "dramatic" entertainment had courtiers using oranges as weapons in "sea battles" against fire-breathing dragons and sea monsters. The most widespread of the secular dramas was the farce, a development of the twelfth and thirteenth centuries. Two writers from northern France were particularly important in its growth: Jean Bodel (1165–1202) and Adam de la Halle (died in 1287 or 1288). One of Bodel's best-known works was the play of St. Nicholas, about St. Nicholas of Bari, one of the medieval figures that also provided the basis for later Santa Claus stories. Although Nicholas lived in the fourth century, Bodel set the play in the late Middle Ages in a society where both Christians and Muslims lived. He developed a series of comic scenes in which Nicholas loses his temper, but over the course of the play Nicholas gains control. The play ends with a moral about the virtues of charity and patience. Nearly one hundred of Adam de la Halle's poems, plays, and songs have survived, testifying to his productivity and popularity. Unlike many medieval playwrights, he was willing to address contemporary, and potentially dangerous, topics. He even wrote a farce about the Sicilian Vespers, the famous revolt of the Sicilians orchestrated by Spain against Charles of Anjou, King of Sicily, in 1282.

Staging Medieval Plays. The tropes of the ninth and tenth centuries did not require separate staging; in fact, distinctive staging would have been counterproductive, de-emphasizing the liturgy that the trope was supposed to support and clarify. As plays gained a separate existence, however, their staging techniques evolved as well. The mystery plays of the later Middle Ages demanded more-complex staging. Although evidence from the fourteenth century is scattered, it appears that they were staged around a circular earthworks. Around this circle were scaffolds on which platforms were placed. The sets were quite typical—such as a palace, cottage, or hell's mouth—and were reused year after year. The actors performed on the platforms or at the base of the scaffolding while the audience sat on the earthworks in the center of the scaffolds or in the empty places between the scaffolds. Stage effects could be quite stunning. Actors were lifted up and down by means of pulleys, and clouds that parted to reveal God were standard equipment. There are even records of payments to individuals who hid behind the mouth of hell and kept a fire burning there throughout the play.

Sources:

David Bevington, *Medieval Drama* (Boston: Houghton Mifflin, 1975).

A.C. Cawley, eds., *Everyman, and Medieval Miracle Plays* (Rutland, Vt.: Tuttle, 1993).

Barbara A. Hanawalt and Kathryn L. Reyerson, eds., *City and Spectacle in Medieval Europe* (Minneapolis: University of Minnesota Press, 1994).

Medieval European Drama in Translation home page <http://arts-sciences.cua.edu/engl/drama/index.htm>.

Glyne Wickham, *The Medieval Theater* (London: Weidenfeld & Nicolson, 1974).

SIGNIFICANT PEOPLE

DANTE ALIGHIERI

1265-1321
POET AND POLITICIAN

Political Background. Dante Alighieri, the most important poet of the Middle Ages, was born in Florence in May or June of 1265. His family belonged to the party known as the Guelfs (supporters of the Pope), who were opposed to the Ghibellines (supporters of the Holy Roman Emperor). The bitter feud between the two groups often erupted in open combat, and Dante himself is known to have fought in a battle against the Ghibellines in 1289. In 1266, shortly after Dante's birth, Charles of Anjou had overthrown imperial power in Italy, and by 1269 Florence had become a Guelf city. Political tensions centering around Dante's Florence were to play a major role in the poet's life, for in addition to writing Dante served as an active figure in politics. The conflict between the Guelfs and the Ghibellines, and later between rival factions within the Guelfs, were to become a prominent theme in Dante's most famous work, his allegorical *Commedia*.

Early Years. Little is known about Dante's early life, and much of the chronology is disputed. He went to school in 1277 and in the same year was betrothed to Gemma Donati. His mother died around 1270 and his father in about 1281. Dante is believed to have studied philosophy at the Franciscan and Dominican houses of study in Florence. He must have studied either there or in Paris, since he had acquired a sound knowledge of contemporary philosophy. He may have visited Bologna in 1287. Dante composed his first major poetic work and commentary in the vernacular, the *Vita nuova* (New Life), in about 1292 or 1293. These poems celebrate the influence and inspiration of Beatrice, who seems to have been a real person, a young woman who affected Dante deeply as a young man. The figure of Beatrice haunted Dante's work and in the *Paradiso* became his celestial guide.

White and Black Guelfs. Between 1290 and 1300, a major quarrel occurred between the White and Black Guelfs, who seem to have represented rival families rather than political parties. Dante was a partisan member of the White Guelfs. In 1300 he assumed political power, acting as an ambassador of the White Guelfs to San Gimignano and becoming one of the priors of Florence. Street fighting among the rival factions was common in this period, and the priors had to banish fifteen aristocrats and their families, including Dante's former poet-friend, Guido Cavalcanti. During this period Dante developed a strong dislike for the reigning Pope Boniface VIII, the advocate of absolute papal power. Dante was apparently sent on an embassy to Rome to help negotiate some of Florence's difficulties with this pope. In his absence the papal forces led by Charles of Valois captured Florence, installing the Black Guelfs as its rulers. As a result Dante was sent into exile in late 1301.

***De vulgari eloquentia* and *Convivio*.** From the time of his exile until 1303 Dante joined with White Guelf military forces in the hope of returning to Florence, but he eventually concluded that these efforts were a lost cause. He moved to Verona, where from June 1303 to March 1304 he received the patronage of the Scala family. Sometime between 1304 and 1308 he wrote his *De vulgari eloquentia* (On the Eloquence of the Vernacular) and the *Convivio* (The Banquet). Though unfinished, both works are quite important. The first provides a theoretical justification for the primacy of the vernacular tongue over Latin. The second is a sophisticated work of philosophy and morality, which seems to have been inspired by Boethius's *Consolation of Philosophy*. It is in the *Convivio* that the great Roman poet, Virgil, makes his first appearance in Dante's work.

De Monarchia. The years between 1308 and 1313 are marked by the unexpected coronation of Henry, Count of Luxemburg, as Holy Roman Emperor, followed by his visit to Italy and his death. By the time of Henry's ascendency Dante had begun to express pro-imperial sentiments and had become allied with the Ghibellines. However, the same papacy that had worked for Henry's coronation later turned against the emperor, and Henry failed to capture the city of Florence. He died, probably from malaria, near

Siena on 24 August 1313. Henry's visit, however, had a major influence on Dante's later writings. The work *De monarchia* (On Monarchy) was composed in order to defeat papal claims to temporal power in the empire. While the exact date of its composition is disputed, the work makes direct reference to the period between 1300 and 1308. Although Dante as a Catholic Christian did not challenge the Pope's authority on spiritual matters, he must have touched a raw nerve in the ecclesiastical hierarchy. A cardinal, Bertrand del Poggetto, and a major preacher, the Dominican Guido Vernani, condemned the work as heretical.

The Divine Comedy. From 1314 to 1317 Dante visited Verona for a second time, this time as a guest of Can Grande della Sala, who had been an Imperial Vicar under Henry and who retained the title despite protests and orders for excommunication from the new Pope, John XXII. According to most scholars, much of the *Commedia* was written at Verona in these years. After the victory of the Ghibellines in 1315 at the Battle of Montecatini, Dante expected to be able to return to Florence, but his hopes were let down when the Ghibellines failed to take the city. He spent the last years of his life in Ravenna, where he was reunited with his sons Jacopo and Pietro, and possibly with his daughter, Antonia, who seems to have become a nun, taking the name Beatrice. Dante went on a diplomatic mission to Venice, and he might also have visited Verona and there held a *questio* (medieval lecture-discussion) on the "Question of the Place of the Waters and the Earth" (*Questio de situ aquae et terre*). He died in Ravenna on 13 or 14 September 1321, probably as a result of a fever he may have picked up while in Venice. By that time he had managed to finish his *Commedia,* the last thirteen cantos of which were only discovered after his death. It is fitting that his life should end shortly after the completion of this work, which stands out as one of the greatest literary accomplishments of the Middle Ages.

Sources:

Charles Allen Dinsmore, *Aids to the Study of Dante* (Boston & New York: Houghton, Mifflin, 1903).

Robert Hollander, *Dante: A Life in Works* (New Haven, Conn. & London: Yale University Press, 2001).

GIOTTO DI BONDONE

CIRCA 1267-1337

PAINTER AND ARCHITECT

"The Best Painter in the World." The Italian artist Giotto di Bondone, through his highly skilled and naturalistic interpretation of form, helped change the direction of Western art in the Late Middle Ages. His paintings were innovative in their incorporation of three-dimensional form in a two-dimensional medium, a departure from the Byzantine stylizations that dominated Europe at the time. He also shifted aesthetic emphasis from the divine and ideal to the human and real. Giotto's works therefore mark a stylistic transition to the art of the early Renaissance, and he is sometimes considered the founder of modern painting. Little documentation exists on his life, though it is known that he worked for the Pope at one point in his career. In 1327 he was recorded as a member of the Florentine Painters Guild, the *Arte dei Medici e Speziali.* By the next year he was in Naples, and in 1330 he began work for King Robert of Anjou, one of his many patrons. In 1334 his home city recognized him with the highest artistic office at its disposal, chief architect of the Florence Cathedral. Two years later he was invited by Azzone Visconti to Milan, and the following year he died. Some ten years after Giotto's death, Boccacio wrote in *The Decameron* that he had "that art which had been buried for centuries by the errors of some who painted more to please the eyes of the ignorant than the intellect of the wise," later calling him "the best painter in the world."

Significant Works. Giotto's most well-known works are his paintings, especially his frescoes. His crucifix at the church of Santa Maria in Novella, Florence, painted sometime between 1290 and 1300, is a good early example of his movement toward realism: the impassive and kingly Christ is replaced with the image of a real, suffering human being. Three signed works by Giotto exist: *Coronation of the Virgin* in the Baroncelli Chapel in Florence; *Madonna and Saints,* located in the Bologna Pinacoteca; and *St. Francis Receiving the Stigmata,* which is held in the Louvre, Paris. In 1305 he painted his Madonna in the church of the Ognissanti in Florence. Giotto's *Life of Christ* in the Arena Chapel, Padua, perhaps his most impressive work, was most likely completed the following year. This cycle of thirty-eight frescoes exhibits a remarkable unity of painting and architecture, each detail contributing to the overall harmony; some scholars even contend that Giotto must have designed the chapel himself. As an architect Giotto definitely did design the cathedral bell tower on the cupola of Florence, which remains a striking part of the skyline of that city. There is debate as to whether Giotto is responsible for the fresco cycle of the life of St. Francis of Assisi in the Bardi Chapel, Santa Croce, Florence. Scholars claim that this great work, if it was indeed produced by Giotto, indicates a new direction and maturity in his work. The frescos were painted over with whitewash in the eighteenth century but were uncovered in 1853. A similar fate befell Giotto's last known work, the frescoes of John the Baptist and John the Evangelist in the Peruzzi Chapel, Santa Croce, which were not uncovered until 1841. Both fresco cycles provided immense inspiration for later masters of the Renaissance.

Sources:

Mario Bucci, *Giotto,* translated by Caroline Beamish (New York: Grosset & Dunlap 1968; London: Thames & Hudson, 1968).

John Ruskin, *Giotto and His Works in Padua* (London: 1853-1860).

GUIDO OF AREZZO

CIRCA 995-1050

MUSIC THEORIST AND TEACHER

Life and Writings. Guido of Arezzo was probably educated at the monastery of Pomposa near Ferrara, Italy. He entered the Benedictine order there and served as a choral instructor, but his innovative methods of teaching met with hostility from his fellow monks. Guido left Pomposa for a more favorable environment at the cathedral school in Arezzo, where the bishop of the city, Theobald, appointed him choirmaster. Theobald also commissioned him to write his *Micrologus de disciplina artis musicae* (circa 1025), one of the most important surviving works on music theory in the Middle Ages. At Arezzo, Guido completed an antiphonary (a book of liturgical chant) he had begun in Pomposa, using a new method of notation he had developed. At the request of Pope John XIX, Guido traveled to Rome in about 1028 to explain his new system and display the antiphonary. He was well received by the Pope and was requested to stay in Rome, but ill health prevented him. After a brief return to Pomposa, Guido went back to Arezzo. He died either there or at a Camdolese monastery near Avellano. His authentic works include his *Micrologus,* two prefaces to his antiphonary, both explaining his musical notation, and his *Epistola de ignoto cantu,* an autobiographical letter recounting the initial opposition and final acceptance of his musical ideas by the Church.

Musical Innovations. Prior to Guido of Arezzo, the task of learning liturgical plainchant could take up to ten years. All of the melodies had to be learned by heart from one who had already mastered them. Guido's system of musical notation, which is the basis of modern western staff-notation, greatly facilitated the learning of melodies, allowing one to sing a melody one had never before heard. To Guido of Arezzo is also attributed the invention of solmization, or the use of the simple syllables *ut, re, mi, fa, sol,* and *la* to represent musical pitches. These syllables were taken from the beginning of each of the six lines of a hymn to St. John the Baptist, the melody of which is said to have been composed by Guido. Guido's musical theory was founded on hexachords, or series of six tones used to construct scales. This foundation dominated music for several centuries, until the shift to an octave-based system of seven tones, whence the modern scale: *do (ut), re, mi, fa, sol, la,* and *ti.*

Sources:

Richard H. Hoppin, *Medieval Music* (New York: Norton, 1978).

Claude V. Palisca, editor, *Hucbald, Guido, and John on Music: Three Medieval Treatises* (New Haven, Conn. & London: Yale University Press, 1978).

SUGER OF ST. DENIS

1081-1151

ABBOT

Royal Favorite. Suger, abbot of one of the most influential monasteries in France and close adviser to two kings, came from a humble background. When he was about nine or ten years old, his parents dedicated him to the monastery of St. Denis. There he had for a friend and fellow-student, the future King Louis VI (Louis the Fat). In 1106 he became secretary to Adam, the abbot of St. Denis. Adam sent him to a monastery near Fontrevault, Normandy for further education. Later he attended the Council of Poitiers as the abbot's representative. Suger was subsequently given charge of a defunct monastery in Normandy, where he succeeded in restoring the estates of the monastery. In 1109 he was sent to Touryen Beauce near Chartres, and he also managed to restore this domain to prosperity. He remained the close friend and adviser of Louis VI, acting as a mediator for the king in his wars with his vassals. Louis VI entrusted Suger with several diplomatic missions, in the course of which he met Popes Paschal II, Gelasius II, and Calixtus II. On return from Rome he learned that he had been chosen to succeed Abbot Adam as head of St. Denis.

Advent of Gothic Architecture. A highly capable administrator, Suger was very successful in rebuilding the fortunes of St. Denis. He recorded his activities in *Liber de rebus in administration sua gestis* (Book on the Things Accomplished during his Administration). In 1127 he set about reforming the abbey and the lives of its monks, who had acquired a reputation for worldliness under Suger's predecessor. The most visible and lasting result of his energetic reforms was the restoration, under his supervision, of the abbey church. The existing church had been erected about four hundred years earlier and had fallen into disrepair. The restored church would become a model for all of Europe and for the new architectural style, Gothic. It featured innovations like ribbed vaults, the predominance of pointed arches, and the use of rose windows and other instances of stained glass; some of these innovations are attributed to Suger himself. The restoration involved a lengthy three-stage process. In 1144 the final stage was completed, and the choir was dedicated to St. Denis. In contrast to the darker, less-open churches of Romanesque style, the choir magnificently exhibits the potentials of glass and light. In his *Liber de rebus in adminsratione sua gestis* Suger records the inscription on the doors of the church, typical of the symbolism of the new Gothic style, with an aesthetic based on Dionysian Neoplatonic theory: "The noble work is bright, but being nobly bright it should brighten the mind, allowing it to travel from [earthly] light to the true light, where Christ is the true door."

Regency and Death. When Louis VI was succeeded by his son Louis VII, Suger continued in his role of royal adviser. He was so trusted that when the new king left for the Second Crusade (1144–1187) in 1147 he was appointed regent in the king's absence. Despite internal strife within France, Suger managed to keep the country together, and even improved on some of the existing laws. Louis VII was duly impressed with Suger's administrative accomplishments, and on his return to France he honored him as the "father of his country." In addition to his career as abbot and royal advisor, Suger was a minor historian, composing biographies of Louis VI and Louis VII. He died at the age of seventy on 13 January 1151.

Sources:

Paula Lieber Gerson, editor, *Abbot Suger and Saint-Denis* (New York: Metropolitan Museum of Art, 1986).

Erwin Panofsky, *Abbot Suger* (Princeton: Princeton University Press, 1979).

A troubadour and a dancer painted on a wood box, circa 1180 (Cathedral Treasury, Vannes, France)

DOCUMENTARY SOURCES

Andreas Capellanus (André le Chapelain), *De amore et amoris remedio* (On Love and the Remedy for Love, 1170–1180)—An important text on the proper use of courtly love. It discusses many aspects of love, including the notion that love in an arranged marriage is impossible. This observation leads to the view that the only true love is an adulterous love affair while being married.

Anonymous, *The Poem of the Cid* (circa 1140)—This poem celebrates the faithful service of the Knight Rodrigo Díaz de Vivar (1043–1109) for King Alfonso VI of Castile. He faithfully obeyed his king and departed the kingdom. He then fought as an independent knight on the borders between Islamic Spain and Christian Spain. He died at the siege of Valencia.

Constituciones Universitatis Cantebrigiensis (Constitutions of the University of Cambridge, mid-thirteenth century)—Provides a list of the rules governing academic behavior, teaching, and dress at the University of Cambridge.

Dante Alighieri, *Commedia* (Divine Comedy, 1321)—This poem is structured around the journey of the poet into Hell; the many experiences of people sent there because of their vices; and his move to Purgatory, led there by the Roman poet, Virgil (70–19 B.C.E.), and then higher still by Beatrice, who becomes his new guide. It then follows his journey to Heaven and fulfillment. The poem is a running commentary on all aspects of human life, public and private. Written in rhyme, it exploits all the abilities of the Provençal, Sicilian, and Northern Italian poetic traditions.

Einhard, *Vita Caroli Magni* (Life of Charlemagne, circa 829–836)—A biography (hagiography) of the first Holy Roman Emperor of the Middle Ages.

John Scottus Eriugena, *Periphyseon*, or *De divisione naturae* (The Division of Nature, 862–866)—The first major work in philosophy since Augustine (died 430) and Boethius (died 524), it is a combination of Eastern Christian Neoplatonism—influenced by Pseudo-Dionysius (circa 500), Proclus (410–485), and Gregory of Nyssa (circa 335–circa 394)—with the Western Latin tradition coming from Augustine and Boethius. This work had a significant influence down to 1215, when the book was burned by ecclesiastical authorities in Paris on the suspicion of its alleged pantheism.

Geoffrey of Monmouth, *Historia regum Britanniae* (History of the Kings of Britain, circa 1135–1139)—Use of Celtic myths in an attempt to construct a legend of a unitary kingdom of Britain; includes the "Prophecy of Merlin" (Book Seven).

Gerald de Barri (Gerald of Wales), *Expugnatio Hibernica* (The Invasion of Ireland, circa 1189)—A propagandistic and justificatory account of the Norman invasion of Ireland. A good example of the skillful use of rhetoric to make historical claims. The work provided a foundation for English Renaissance historians who wrote chronicles and histories of Ireland. A good example of the art involved in a complex work of history in the Middle Ages.

Guillaume de Loris and Jean de Meun, *Roman de la Rose* (Romance of the Rose, circa 1240–1305)—The most important French poem of the Middle Ages dealing with the virtues and vices involved in the pursuit of the love object.

Hildegard of Bingen, *Symphonia harmoniae caelestium revelationum* (Symphony of Harmony of Heavenly Revelations, circa 1150)—A collection of seventy-seven of her sacred musical compositions.

Marie de France, *Lais* (circa 1170)—Twelve narrative poems in French covering the romantic role of knights.

Robert de Courçon, Statutes for the University of Paris (1215)—The early rules that governed the living conditions and habits of scholars at the University of Paris.

Bernard Silvestris, *Cosmographia* (1150)—This poem expresses the complex Neoplatonic views of the greater world (macrocosm) and lesser world (microcosm) or human being. It exhibits the teachings and interests of the School of Chartres.

Stephen Tempier, *Articuli Condempnati a Stephano Episcopo Parisiensi Anno 1277* (The Articles Condemned by the Bishop of Paris in 1277)—One of the most celebrated documents in the life of the teaching of the Liberal Arts at the University of Paris. The Bishop condemned 219 propositions taken from the teachings and books of some teachers such as Boethius of Dacia (flourishing 1270), Siger de Brabant (circa 1240–1284), and Thomas Aquinas (1225–1274).

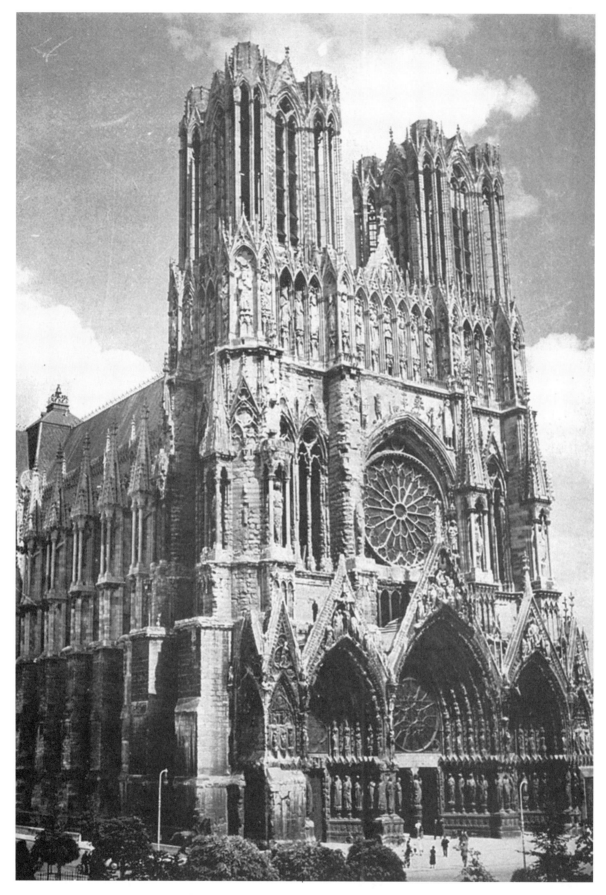

Rheims Cathedral, begun in 1210 and completed circa 1290

CHAPTER FOUR

COMMUNICATION, TRANSPORTATION, AND EXPLORATION

by BETSEY B. PRICE

CONTENTS

Sidebars and tables are listed in italics.

814
- The Carolingian emperors use a system of imperial messengers to achieve greater administrative control of their lands.

842
- At the city of Strasbourg, Charles the Bald and Ludwig or Louis the German, fraternal grandsons of Charlemagne, swear oaths to wage war against their brother Lothar. While Charles the Bald makes his declaration in *lingua romana* (Old French), Ludwig the German makes his in *lingua teudisca* (Old German).

862
- Cyril and Methodius work as Christian missionaries in the newly founded Slavic state of Moravia. Cyril adapts the Greek alphabet to the Slavic tongue, and it becomes known as the Cyrillic alphabet.

874
- Vikings from Norway discover Iceland; by 900 there are twenty-five thousand settlers there.

911-912
- Danish Vikings settle at the mouth of the Seine River, under their chief Rollo.

950*
- The reign of the Abbasid ruler Caliph Harun al Rashid inspires the popular stories of *Thousand and One Arabian Nights* in present-day Iraq and Iran.

982
- The Norwegian navigator Erik Thorvaldson (Erik the Red) leaves Iceland and spends the next three years exploring the coast of what he calls "Greenland." In 986 he establishes a colony near present-day Julianehåb.

1000*
- Leif Eriksson, the son of Erik the Red, sails west from Greenland and visits Helluland, Markland, and Vinland, which may be present-day Labrador, Newfoundland, and Nova Scotia, respectively.

1026
- In Italy, Guido d'Arezzo begins the teaching of singing using the musical scale "ut, re, mi, fa, sol, la."

1096
- Followers of Robert of Arbrissel, an itinerant preacher appointed by the pope, settle at Angers in western France; by 1100 they establish the abbey at Fontevrault.

* DENOTES CIRCA DATE

1148
- Pilgrims on their way to Jerusalem consult various guidebooks, including *Description of the Holy Land* by Rorgo Fretellus of Nazareth. (A similar work by the same title is written by Burchard of Mt. Sion in the thirteenth century.)

1202
- Arabic numerals are introduced into Europe and replace the clumsy Roman numerals still in use.

1250*
- The goose-feather quill is introduced as a pen, becoming the only technological improvement the medieval book-copying process enjoys.

1260
- Written musical notes start to have time values to show how long each is to be held.

1298
- There are twelve bookshops in Paris selling volumes written in Latin as well as the vernacular.

1299
- Rustichello of Pisa, a prisoner with Marco Polo in a Genoese jail, recounts the travels of his cellmate and his father and uncle in *Divisament dou monde* (Description of the World). He vividly describes Song and Mongol China and the vast riches found there: ginger, paper money, postal service, street oil-lamps, and gunpowder.

1300*
- A map of England called *Hereford Mappa Mundi* is drawn; it includes Eden, an unknown land east of the British Isles.

1325
- The Arab world's most renowned explorer, ibn Battuta, goes on a hajj (pilgrimage) to Mecca and begins a twenty-seven-year odyssey that takes him to Russia, India, China, and the Maldive Islands of Sri Lanka.

1338
- The University of Paris library has 1,722 volumes, making it the largest university library to date.

1350*
- Wagon-makers in the town of Kocs in Hungary begin to construct the first carriage, or coach. It is equipped with a suspension system (deriving its name from the town soon to be renowned for its excellence in carriage-making).
- Universities throughout Europe employ runners to act as messengers.

* DENOTES CIRCA DATE

OVERVIEW

The Times. In the early ninth century the Carolingian king Charlemagne formally expressed his wish to divide his realm among his sons after his death. His will was respected, and the first strong medieval European monarchy dissolved. During the six centuries that followed, the nations of modern Europe gradually emerged from the multitude of medieval feudal states that grew up. Succession in the Carolingian Empire followed the Salic Law of equal division among male heirs, hastening the emergence of the multiplicity on political, religious, and linguistic fronts that spelled subsequent disunity, if not disharmony, in medieval European interactions. By 842, as witnessed in the different languages of the Oaths of Strasbourg among two of Charlemagne's sons, Frankish territory itself was already linguistically divided, and Rome was no longer the sole arbiter of authority. In the context of the fluid and heterogeneous collection of governed entities within medieval Europe, most contacts among peoples were determined by similarities of language or religion. Elements of cultural identity increasingly became the significant medieval signs of a people's being united.

Medieval World. The shape of the medieval world changed relatively little at the local level. The focal point shifted only slightly from the family to that of the community. The way space was organized in medieval concentrations of population, the familiar appearance and habits of those who lived and worked close by, and increasing collective decision-making encouraged the formation of strong bonds among households. These bonds led to the creation of villages, towns, and even cities linked by churches, schools, and commerce. Upon the basic skills of interaction—talking and walking—medieval people thus built multiple spheres of communication and mobility.

Interactions. Two main means of human interaction existed during the medieval period: direct face-to-face contact and communication by reading and writing. These means implied both avenues and barriers to exchange among areas with different languages, political control, and religious persuasions. In the many spheres of interaction, from the home to the court of law, talking was the main means of communication. Verbal communication became the focus of much discussion, especially within Church and court, where both silence and eloquence were revered.

During this era of widespread illiteracy, reading was a praiseworthy activity, and the monastic environment specifically sanctioned reading aloud. Speech and the written word were, however, not the only important ways medieval people communicated. Gestures had a dramatic role to play particularly in how emotional messages were conveyed. The medieval "language of signs" is understood to have included everything from tears shed in private to whole ceremonies of the Christian Eucharist or the rituals leading up to and through a knight's dubbing. Even within many crafted objects, symbolic meaning served as a form of shorthand communication, telling at times whole stories, such as in the Bayeux Tapestry with its account of William of Normandy's conquest of Britain in 1066. Over the course of the Middle Ages, growing literacy, vernacular languages, and even the use of money would, however, alter virtually every sphere of communication.

Literary Culture. During the Middle Ages there were parallel oral and literary cultures. The spread of literary culture went hand in hand with the rise of schooling. Latin was gradually replaced by local languages, or vernaculars, in written communication. The rise of literary dialects stimulated the shift from pan-European Latin literature to regional writings and led to the creation of distinctive written forms of local artistic expression. It did so because the vernacular fostered local written communication by a wider variety of individuals than just the clergy. Although increased literacy and the rise of local literature spurred demand for reading material, the only notable technological improvement the medieval book-copying process enjoyed was the introduction of the goose-feather quill as the "pen" for writing. By 1250 increased production of handwritten books created the birth of stationers' shops, lay book copyists for hire, and libraries.

Communication Revolutions. The transition from oral to manuscript culture was part of a broad revolution in communication. In the centuries before Johannes Gutenberg designed movable type in the mid fifteenth century, an increasing quantity of potential readers was being created. The birth of western Christian monasteries and their schools; the strength of urban bishops, their cathedral culture, and its schools; and the evolution of a new setting for teaching masters, the university, and contemporary noble courts that placed growing importance on lay literacy in the political realm all generated readers. Religious readers of manuscripts were the first to share an awareness that their counterparts in other parts of Europe were reading the same text, something that was of enough importance to yield a universal Bible and a harmonized liturgy necessitating checks for scribal error. Scribes developed elaborate abbreviations, the origins of modern contractions, in order to speed up the lengthy process of copying. The availability of books changed the role of churchmen and kings. Now all clerics were expected to be literate, if not scholarly, and the scholars among them were authors per force. Their literate students committed their words to writing and studied the newly written word as assiduously as they had listened to the orally delivered commentary. Kings soon found their role in communication replaced by clerks, who were more gifted at writing. Most medieval texts were in Latin, but over the course of the twelfth and thirteenth century, texts were being translated from Latin or originally written in vernacular languages. The sustained importance of the Roman Catholic Church hinged in part on the control it exerted by its ability to circulate religious ideas throughout Europe in a single language, Latin. The communication revolution, which the use of vernacular languages brought about, created a stronger regional consciousness, and local pockets of well-educated individuals were ready to absorb information in every field: science, politics and warfare, agriculture, medicine, law, geography, travel, cookery, husbandry and hunting, herbs and beasts, ethics, grammar, poetry, heroic feats, and history and social mores.

Military Encounters. Medieval people had many types of interactions with other lands, the most sustained being their contact with the Muslim world. Seven hundred years after Charlemagne's reign, the *Reconquista* eliminated the Muslim Arab political presence from the Iberian Peninsula and hence from Western Europe. The encounters of the Christian reconquest took place from the eleventh century to the fifteenth century. The change wrought by the nibbling away of the Muslim states resulted in a shift of mood throughout Christian Europe from one of uneasy coexistence, which had lasted throughout the Middle Ages, to one of domination. Communication, education, and exchange between Christian and Muslim peoples all shrank subsequent to the fifteenth-century conquest of the southernmost holdout, Granada. Interactions with the Muslim conquerors of Spain were for several centuries quite peaceful, since they were far more tolerant and generous than most people in the medieval world. Through conquest the spread of Islam was rapid; through trade, the spread of knowledge about Islamic culture was even quicker. Medieval Europe's decentralized political structure meant, however, that autonomous kingdoms and principalities could only really be brought together for religious reasons, and then only under a strong papacy. Vis-à-vis the Arab world, the Church and its secular representatives fared rather poorly. From the seventh century on, Muslims controlled the original centers of Christianity in the East. The Cru-

sades to drive them out were relatively unsuccessful. As a result of the First Crusade (1095–1099), four Crusader States were temporarily established along the eastern Mediterranean, and with the Fourth Crusade (1198–1202), Western Crusaders dominated Constantinople and set up a Latin empire there until 1261, but the string of military strikes resulted more in communication and technology transfer between East and West than in any sustained western Christian territorial expansion.

Cultural Exchange. In attempting to wrest biblically significant sites from their Muslim overseers, Christian warriors came into contact with people and places in a way they had not as religious observers or pilgrims. Conquest from either side allowed the competition for holy sites and land to extend beyond military expertise. A poignant exchange of cultural differences occurred when Richard the Lion-Hearted of England became seriously ill during the Third Crusade (1189–1192). His chivalrous opponent, Saladin, sent his own personal physician to the Christian camp, as well as some appetizing fruit. Although the Crusaders did not achieve their ultimate goal of retaining the Holy Land permanently in Christian hands, the encounters of Christians and Muslims greatly influenced their perception of one another. As a result of the Crusades almost every feature of medieval life, from trade to health habits, was scrutinized by both sides. By extension, Europeans began to take intellectual and economic interest in non-Westernized parts of the world as far away as the Silk Route and as foreign as Mongolia.

Religious Links. The origins of a shift in regarding the individual as a king's subject to the compatriot of a nation is thought by many historians to be found in the complicated political transformations from feudal noble landholdings as the economic base to monarchies with a perceived connection to the populace. While Charlemagne's admonitions for preserving territorial or "national" unity fell on deaf ears in the ninth century, their spirit was recognized by translators, long-distance traders, missionaries, and pilgrims during the centuries that followed. Each was part of an attempt to convert non-Christians into a religious unity. A multiplicity of languages on the religious and political fronts definitely spelled disunity, if not disharmony, in medieval interactions. Translators were cosmopolitan members of medieval society, but they were also among its finest intellectuals. They saw the dawning of a new era of constraining language barriers. There were many facets of medieval religious activity that made for interaction between the European west and other parts of the world. Marco Polo and his father and uncle, traders who visited among many sites in China, had been asked by the Mongol Khan to bring priests back with them to teach the Khan about Christianity. Pilgrimages, by their nature, often brought western European Christians into contact with other lands.

Languages. Conversion efforts and even book copying are other instances of sustained religious activities that were moving medieval people toward a more expanding, adventuresome, sometimes intellectual approach to the world. Conversion activity saw language as both a means and a barrier to communication. Eastern Christian or Byzantine missionaries were led to convert the Slavs in the ninth century by two brothers, Cyril and Methodius. During their mission they introduced a new alphabet, Cyrillic, to the oral Slavic language. In the case of the conversion of the Vikings, the western missionaries' approach to language differences was far less accommodating. Conversion and learning a new language went together for the Vikings who adopted Christianity. This focus on language had important ramifications in communication, transportation, and exploration. For instance, scholars began to equate communication with the mastery of various languages, not just Latin.

Travel. Slowness, hardship, and uncertainty characterized travel in the Middle Ages. The majority of all travel was on foot, but just how far and fast is a matter of some speculation. The most accomplished walkers were probably foot soldiers, friars, and merchants. Those who did not travel on foot in the Middle Ages likely rode a horse. The medieval use of the horse reflects both the relatively settled aspect of the society and also its values. Medieval chivalry exalted the horse and travel on horseback. In the Islamic world the Arab warrior was just as obsessed with the horse as was the European knight. Frequently, medieval women as well as men rode a horse or mule, simply because it was more comfortable than either walking or riding in a contemporary wheeled vehicle. The need for portable regalia and equipment, as well as a desire for comfort, led to the improvement of wheeled vehicles during the Middle Ages. A horse or mule pack train on an extended trip seems to have averaged a reasonable ten miles a day, but then not every sort of baggage was conducive to pack transport. Carts with two wheels were most commonly used for smaller, lighter loads and four-wheeled wagons for heavier burdens. By the close of the Middle Ages, rich and powerful travelers had elaborate carriages with suspended cabins for comfort. Throughout history, increased mobility has come via navigable water, and the Middle Ages was no exception. Viking ships were able to navigate most rivers. Warships require speed, high maneuverability, and sufficient space for the warriors. Rowing and oaring were two means of moving early medieval vessels, but wind became the main source of navigational power. Effective use of two masts and sails, which became standard in the Mediterranean by 1200, was made possible by the introduction of the lateen sail, capable of catching the wind on either its front or back surface.

Culture of Travel. Written works and translations fostered the cross-cultural exchange of knowledge about foreign places. In literature, one of the most-popular sets of stories from the Arabic world came to the West as *Thousand and One Arabian Nights,* stemming from the reign of the Abbasid ruler Caliph Harun al Rashi in Iraq and Iran around 950. In philosophy, Al-Andalus was famous for the works of its scholars, Averroes and Maimonides. Travel literature written by Europeans found a lay readership among those curious about other places. Accounts written by Christian pilgrims fostered dreams of realizable travels, particularly given their maps and practical advice on dress, money, expenses, and precautions to take. On the other hand, *Divisament dou monde* (1299), even as it perpetuated many myths of the Orient, described so many existing wonders that it seemed to stretch the credibility of its Italian audience. In the steady rise of pilgrimages to the Holy Land through the Crusades of the twelfth century, travel literature about biblical sites found a widening readership. With the loss of Jerusalem in 1187, Europeans eagerly read travel literature about all other significant religious sites, Rome, Canterbury, and Compostella, and heightened their preparedness for wider-ranging trips into unknown lands.

Voyages of Discovery. In addition to the many navigable rivers with which medieval Europe was blessed, there were two spheres of maritime travel in the Middle Ages: the Atlantic Ocean and the Mediterranean Sea. The story of medieval European navigation is one of interaction between technical developments among those traveling the two bodies of water defining Europe. This cross-fertilization had both technological and psychological components. The medieval crusading spirit, quests for economic exchange with the North and East, the scholarly pursuit of scientific knowledge, demographic expansion, innovations in the construction of ships, and improvements in navigational skills and cartography were all factors in the sporadic medieval voyages of exploration and discovery. Antiquity had provided medieval people with a wide range of theories about geography, formidable maps of the world's landmasses, and experiential accounts of travels and discoveries. Technological advances in ship construction and rigging allowed the Vikings to explore from Scandinavia to the east coast of Canada. Such navigational successes led shipbuilders to reconsider the depth-to-freeboard ratio of Mediterranean vessels and thereby created a link between the technologies of the Mediterranean and the Atlantic. Traders began to set out without a specific known port of entry. Far more exciting than new lands for medieval man to contemplate was the possible discovery of new peoples. The developments that came about as a result of that find had profound effects on postmedieval Europe.

TOPICS IN COMMUNICATION, TRANSPORTATION, AND EXPLORATION

COMMUNICATIONS

Motivation. Given the many spheres of interaction during the Middle Ages, from the home to the court of law, it is important to consider just how medieval individuals communicated. There are two important basic aspects to communication: the means and the substance. If there is a means of communicating, a person or groups of persons will receive for understanding a message passed or transmitted from another. If the message has meaning, it will upon receipt convey an idea or information of some sort. The imparting or transmitting of ideas and information from one person to another, and perhaps among persons separated in place and time, is therefore successful communication.

Talking and Telling. Talking was the main means of communication in the Middle Ages. With the rare exceptions of kings, chiefs, and Churchmen, a medieval's words could reach no further than his voice, but it certainly did reach those closest to hand: family members, coworkers, and the village, castle, or neighborhood community. The times of lively conversation were many and, except during the hardest of labors, heartily sustained. At every fair and festival, raucous talk was hardly containable. Speaking before a gathered group was elevated to art with the storytelling of the *jougleur* and the poetry of the *trouvère* and troubadours. Oral storytelling became a literary device used in later medieval works, such as the *Decameron* (1353), to recreate the atmosphere of close exchange among a group of friends such as Boccaccio's grandees gathered in country houses during the Black Death to divert each other with tales.

Moderation. Verbal communication became the focus of much discussion in the Middle Ages. Old people and some women are described as talking incessantly. The indoor setting of women's work in a group—spinning and perhaps weaving—was conducive to running conversation. Women were, however, also thought to use special meetings in pairs to spread the gossip that moved fast from medieval mouth to ear. Evil or idle words, or words that brought laughter, were particularly condemned.

Biblical Caveats. Within Church and court, silence was revered. In the field it was frequently a practical matter that common laborers worked all day without speaking, side-by-side plowing, cutting wood, and digging ditches. Even at the end of the workday, there was often little energy or desire to chatter, as wives made note. In the monasteries, silence was a conscientious practice. Benedict advocated that his monks should follow the Psalmist: "I said, 'I will guard my ways, that I may not sin with my tongue. I have set a guard to my mouth.' I was mute and was humbled, and kept silence even from good things" (Psalms 38:2-3). Permission to speak, he wrote, should rarely be granted, even to perfect disciples, though it be for good, holy, edifying conversation.

Sanctioned Reading Sessions. The monastic environment did, however, sanction reading, specifically reading out loud. According to the Benedictine Rule, the reader's was the only voice to be heard during meals. Otherwise, absolute silence was to be kept, with no whispering allowed. No one should presume to ask questions about the reading or anything else, lest that give occasion for talking. After the oral reading of an edict or secular pronouncement, questions from even a noble or king would be considered taking liberties against the authority of the word.

Rule of Benedict. Reading was in general a praiseworthy activity. On Sundays and daily during Lent, Benedictine monks occupied themselves with reading—if they could. Reading and writing were usually taught separately in the Middle Ages, occasionally by different clerical instructors, with reading being the first, as it was considered essential for studying the Bible and religious literature. Writing, on the other hand, was regarded as an art or a technical skill for certain occupations, such as scribes and court clerics.

Messengers. The most frequently used means of communicating between places or persons at a distance was via

A tenth-century ivory carving of scribes copying manuscripts in a scriptorium (Kunsthistorisches Museum, Vienna)

In some lineages, oral traditions of ancestry dated back as far as two or three centuries.

Writing and Books. The means of communicating between places or persons separated by the greatest distance in time was, however, via the written word. Before Gutenberg's printing press of 1455, the reading of books, let alone the ownership, was largely the preserve of monks and the rich. Churchmen had their works of devotion; a few bibliophiles, thinkers, and students were keen to read the classical authors. Nobody knows how the idea of movable-type printing filtered from Asia to Europe, but until the middle of the fifteenth century all works had to be hand copied by scribes, however slow and costly the process. Thousands of works were indeed produced by hand by literate medieval authors or scribes.

Manuscripts. Despite little technical innovation, the production of handwritten books did increase by the thirteenth century, a fact that, while short on data to support it, can be affirmed by the birth of stationers' shops and lay book copiers. Although there was a distinction between the old ancient and the new medieval works, the interest in written works in general, and hence the degree of communication through them, can best be assessed by the general number of manuscripts produced in any one period. Unfortunately, virtually the only statistic for medieval manuscript production is the seemingly anecdotal one that states that

> The man born in 1453, the year of the fall of Constantinople, could look back from his fiftieth year on a lifetime in which about eight million books had been printed, more perhaps than all the scribes of Europe had produced since Constantine founded his city in A.D. 330.

Thus, the landscape of book production changed dramatically from the point at which Johannes Gutenberg, a goldsmith, realized in the mid fifteenth century his idea of producing small regular blocks of lead alloy with letters on them that, when fitted into frames, inked, and pressed into paper, would produce individual printed pages. It is reckoned that as many books, about nine million, were produced (not to be confused with "written") in the fifty years after Gutenberg's invention as in the one thousand years before. In 1498, eighteen thousand letters of indulgence were printed in Barcelona alone.

Medieval Libraries. Most medieval written works became parts of libraries owned either collectively by a religious community or individually by a religious person or layman. The typical monastery library contained a small number of books kept in one or two book chests in or near the scriptorium, the room in which manuscripts were copied. Most individuals' private libraries contained less than a dozen volumes, but collections ranged in size. In the twelfth century, Churchmen John of Salisbury and Hugh of Puiset bequeathed several dozen of their own books to their cathedral libraries. The private library Robert de Sorbonne gave to the first college of the University of Paris contained 1,017 volumes according to its catalogue of 1289. By 1338 it had grown to 1,722 volumes and was the largest university library at the time. The Sorbonne collec-

messenger. The Carolingian emperors exploited a system of imperial messengers to bring greater administrative control to the land. Centuries later, universities regularly hired from 12 to 160 runners each. Of all technologies to transport ideas and information across long distances, the most basic of these is the written word, a fact well appreciated and exploited by the end of the Middle Ages.

Memory of Women. There was also the critical issue of communication over time. Throughout the Middle Ages, women were the reservoirs of the day-to-day knowledge of one another and the world around. Mothers knew the ages of their children, for example, and frequently guarded the information of actual conception dates, important for casting horoscopes. Based on oral tradition in the female preserve, medieval people were able to plan feasts, use astrology, and maintain the hierarchy within the extended family. "According to my mother's memory," wrote one merchant in 1299, he knew that he had been born in 1254.

Illumination of a messenger receiving a packet from a king, from the *Smithfield Decretals,* circa 1330–1340
(British Library, London)

tion was one of the largest in Europe. In 1306 the astronomer Pierre de Limoges bequeathed his valuable library of some three hundred scientific, mathematical, and theological works to the Sorbonne. Other notable monastery libraries were at Saint Galen in Switzerland, Corbie in France, and Fulda in Germany. In the twelfth century, cathedral libraries grew rapidly, though most suffered huge losses by fire or through the ravages of time and worms. The better-known cathedral libraries in the Middle Ages were those of Canterbury and York in England, Notre Dame and Rouen in France, Bamberg and Hildesheim in Germany, and Toledo and Barcelona in Spain.

Textual Support. Most medieval libraries contained Bibles, chronicles, and devotional literature, but during the later Middle Ages reading interests expanded to include works of science, herbals and bestiaries, politics and warfare, agriculture, medicine, law, geography, travel, husbandry and hunting, ethics, grammar, cooking, poetry, history, and social mores. Natural philosophy, the term for science at the time, was essentially an armchair occupation. Its practitioners were readers of earlier authors (writing originally in Greek or Arabic), observers, and occasionally collectors of natural curiosities. They were not generally doers. Hence, libraries were extremely important to any academic endeavor. Although there were account or tax books, the *Domesday Book* (1085–1086) being perhaps among the most famous, in most cases all books, even those called "manuals," were not intended as practical works. Bound in leather with heavily decorated pages of thick vellum or parchment (animal skin) as the writing surface, the volumes in the library of a rich nobleman were a sign of prestige, not of his hands-on approach to life.

Copying. Medieval booksellers or stationers, known as *libraires* in France or *cartolai* in Italy, also owned written works. Their business is evidence of an independent book trade outside of the monasteries. By 1298 booksellers numbered about twelve in Paris. They stocked single copies of works from authors in the vernacular as well as in

Latin. Although occasionally booksellers had books reproduced for speculative sales, copies of most works were made to order. A stationer would receive a request for the reproduction of one of his stocked works and either send the order to a monastic scriptorium, farm out sections to independent practitioners, most of whom worked otherwise as notarial or chancery scribes, or lend out a portion of the work, called a *pecia*, or piece, to be reproduced by the lender's scribe outside the shop. Stationers provided an important service, particularly in university towns, by making a master or approved copy of a course "textbook" available to students for recopying. Record of an exceptionally large, and late, medieval order stems from a bookseller in the Netherlands in 1437: 200 copies of the Seven Penitential Psalms, 200 copies of Cato's *Disticha* in Flemish, and 400 copies of a small prayer book, at 340 times what it would cost to have had them printed fifty years later. It has been estimated that for approximately every six thousand inhabitants a medieval city might have had one stationer's shop.

Monastic Libraries. Monasteries supported libraries that were open to the monastic community. Not all monks were free to visit these collections, and the existence of libraries in general was not really prized until around the thirteenth century. Most monastic libraries were actually book collections, as were most private libraries later on. Monastic libraries built their early collections primarily through donations from monks traveling abroad and from noble bishops of letters. Illuminated manuscripts circulated among religious institutions both as diplomatic gifts and for the mutual benefit of monks and clerics. Books that served as symbolic gift objects to monasteries and high-ranking clerics, whether service books or manuscripts of scripture, were among the most sumptuously illuminated in the Middle Ages.

First Language. Gestures are perhaps the first language of all human beings, and the medieval people certainly incorporated the "language of signs" into their many spheres of activity. Novitiate monks had to undertake an apprenticeship during which in part they learned how to express themselves by signs during the monastery's periods of silence, such as at the table. While the monks ate and drank, anything needed was to be requested by means of some visible sign rather than by speech. Rich as the medieval language of signs is, it is much broader than executed gestures. It also includes what we know as symbols, and every medium in which they were conveyed: drawing and painting, carving and sculpture, glass and jewelry, clothing, armor, and so on.

Recipients. While knowledge of medieval instances of gestures is limited today to their textual description or graphic representation, the modern interpretation of them is even more restricted. Scholars have a limited pool of medieval examples to help us re-create the vocabulary, and in addition they bring modern interpretation of the meaning of gestures strongly into play. Nonetheless, descriptions and contextual information aid in guiding scholars to understand the powerful language of medieval movement. Gestures are acts that convey meaning. People walk, nod, bend, and shake, but do not always mean something when they do so. Hence, modern analysis of a gesture begins less with whether it was executed than with whether the movement was meant to communicate meaning.

Gestures. For the most part, gestures are intended to convey emotional messages. Close body contact, as in the exchange of hugs and kisses, is perhaps the most timeless and powerful sign. A medieval novitiate monk was bestowed with the kiss of peace upon being adopted into the community of the cloister. Although it is generally thought that medieval husbands and wives were reticent about expressing feelings for each other, the embrace of a man and a woman was evident in the Middle Ages, as today, as a demonstration of affection for another.

The Signs. In the Middle Ages, tears were apparently usually shed in private, at home among relatives and friends, and they were shed by both men and women. A mother's or a father's tears at the sight of a long-lost son were identified as the "overflowing of the purest happiness." There were also tears of repentance, of compassion, and of grief, sometimes elicited by news from afar. Only women cried at funerals, however, where their tears, mixed with the quasi-verbal signs of wailing and moaning, expressed the grief of all. Their tears were obligatory, since not to shed them would have been a sign of an entire lineage's dishonoring the deceased.

Symbolic Perceptions. Many, if not most, medieval gestures conveyed acquiescence to hierarchy. The suppliant pose of one kneeling, elbows bent, hands together and uplifted, was the position of prayer, the ultimate expression of humility before God. The act of removing another's shoes was a gesture of deference. Medieval marriage was both egalitarian and hierarchical. The joining or holding of hands would be an act among equals, but a hand holding up the chin of another was a gesture of the holder's benevolent superiority; both of these cases signify the relationship between a medieval lord and his lady.

Children would have their heads cupped or their hands held in tenderness by an older relative; friends would give the groom a customary fraternal slap on the back. Medieval husbands exerted authority over their wives, even to the point of beating them.

Conveying the Larger Message. Medieval gestures were frequently part of a whole ceremony in which each one conveyed part of a larger meaning. Some were codified practicalities, which came to symbolize good training, not to say breeding. Recognizable today is the notion of proper ceremonial behavior embedded in table etiquette. Bowls, plates, and cups were shared in twos for lack of dishes and cutlery. Social hierarchy dictated that the male or the younger partner of the pair broke the bread, cut the meat, or passed the cup. Symbolic acts, however, distinguished the couth who did not belch or eat and drink with his mouth full, from the uncouth who did both, as well as putting his elbows on the table and leaving his spoon in the dish.

Ceremonies. The most symbolic ceremony of the medieval period was undoubtedly the Eucharist, the part of the mass in which the eating of bread and the drinking of wine by the priest symbolizes a reenactment of Christ's Last Supper. There were, however, many other symbolic ceremonies. A new monk's integration into his brotherhood would, for example, require a ritual of several days, beginning with the placing on the abbey church's altar of his written pledge of commitment, his assuming the monk's cowled robe, his receiving the round of welcoming embraces, and finally his retreat into total remove and quiet for three days amid his fellow monks. The last part of the ritual was to symbolize Christ's three-day withdrawal into the tomb before his resurrection.

Events of the Day. The dubbing of a knight was another ceremonial sequence of symbolic gestures: from the nightlong vigil, to mass at dawn; to the festive breakfast, bath, and dressing in special undergarments; to the dubbing ceremony itself, with the knight assuming his attire and his arms after kissing the hilt of the blessed sword; to the whack on the side of the head; and the swearing of the oath of fidelity. Every element carried part of the meaning of the whole. There were many embellishments to the dubbing ceremony over the course of the Middle Ages, most particularly emphasizing the connection between the knight's secular calling and his religious one.

Physical Symbols. The physical embodiment of messages to be communicated may have been particularly important in the Middle Ages. It was an era when one's word seems to have been doubted, at least occasionally. Witnesses at a wedding, for example, might subsequently have to testify as to the genuineness of the consent of both parties. If, however, in addition to a wedding band, used for the first time in Europe around 1200, many rings were bestowed upon a wealthy bride, their symbolism as especially significant gifts from the groom's family would go a long way toward vouching for the groom's sincerity in welcoming her into the new family that regarded those rings as precious objects.

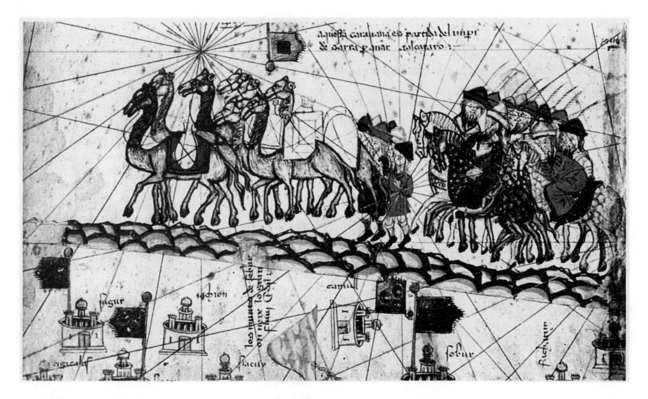

Illumination of a caravan moving from Sarai on the Volga River with a destination of Cathay, or China, from the *Catalan Atlas*, circa 1350 (Bibliothèque Nationale, Paris)

Gifts. Gift giving in general was a highly symbolic part of ceremony and diplomacy in medieval Europe. Gifts were used to secure the allegiance of a ruler's subjects and to solidify ties among high-ranking clergy or between princes. The gift of a bride was not uncommon. Dowries and bride gifts were perhaps the most significant regularly conveyed gifts in monetary terms. The dower was a fixed charge, but it usually became part of the settlement discussions around a marriage. Among the peasantry, the gift a bride brought into the marriage varied from a token to relatively significant amounts of land, chattel, and later money. Among the nobility, the dower was frequently considered in relation to the bride gift. The greater the portion of the estate a groom's family was willing to give to the bride, the larger the obligation on the bride's family to present her with a large dowry. One-third of her husband's lands would be legally hers upon his death, in any case.

Money. Money changed communication as relationships between people became more impersonal and materialistic. Gifts were not always reduced to the crassness of their monetary value. They were a critical feature of "diplomatic" protocol at whatever level of society, demonstrating the donor's goodwill. There were the symbolic traditional gifts at the occasion of a birth and a wedding, but also at a papal or royal ambassador's arrival.

Symbolic Shorthand. Symbolic meaning was crafted in many objects during the Middle Ages and often served as a form of shorthand communication. A maidservant's clothes and hair dressing would immediately prevent her from being mistaken for her mistress. Fully armed knights displayed a symbolic design or coat of arms on their shields or on their surcoat in order to be recognized as from a particular family when in battle. Medieval crusaders wore crosses on their shields and clothing.

Muslim Symbolism. Muslim law forbids the making of pictures or sculptures for religious purposes. Arabic script and its message became the embellishment of choice on the outsides and insides of Islamic architecture. Illustrations in which Muhammad appears are extremely rare. One representation of him from an ancient book shows Muhammad's face hidden by a veil. The prophet's head is crowned with flames, not unlike a halo.

Wordless Storytelling. The most amazing example of wordless—or almost wordless—storytelling to have survived from the Middle Ages is perhaps the Bayeux Tapestry. An embroidered band, it was executed on the orders of Bishop Odo, half brother of William the Conqueror. It is an elongated picture embroidery recording William's Norman conquest of England. In it, as in other such artistic representations, a person becomes recognizable, at least in terms of his walk in life, by virtue of his accoutrements. Bishops or abbots hold the crosier, which might even be used to strike a wicked lord. Kings sport crowns even when bathing or reclining. Among the more amusing elements of medieval artistic shorthand are the representations of adults in varying sizes based on their relative social ranking and the depicting of the simultaneous sharing of an object by all its owners, such as the horse being ridden by its four knights at the same time.

Music. Both educated and uneducated medieval people communicated through the symbolism of music. In the educated sphere, refinements made the expression of musical creativity more and more reproducible. In Italy in 1026 Guido d'Arezzo began the teaching of singing using "ut, re, mi, fa, sol, la". (Now one sings "do, re, mi, fa, so(l), la, ti, do".) By 1260 written musical notes started to have time values to show how long each was to be held. For all its technical limitations, however, most important for the ability of medieval music to communicate was its evocative potential. The intonings of monks, sounds of street hawkers, songs in the fields, dances of many a festivity, and music of the stage or troubadour all had a role in human communication: to create the context for worship, lure buyers to bargains, create solidarity and lighten the tedium of labor, lend rhythm for movement at festive occasions, or carry a narrative along, for example.

Sources:

Norman F. Cantor, *The Civilization of the Middle Ages* (New York: HarperPerennial, 1993).

Carlo M. Cipolla, *Literacy and Development in the West* (Baltimore: Penguin, 1969).

Georges Duby, *A History of Private Life,* translated by Arthur Goldhammer (Cambridge, Mass.: Harvard University Press, 1988).

Lucien Febvre and Henri-Jean Martin, *The Coming of the Book: The Impact of Printing, 1450–1800,* translated by David Gerard (London: N.L.B., 1976).

Francois Garnier, *Le langage de l'Image au Moyen Age,* 2 volumes (Paris: Léopard d'or, 1982–1989).

EXPLORATION

Geography. Having been influenced by traders' successes, especially the exploits of Far Eastern merchants, explorers became the foremost proponents by the end of the Middle Ages of a connection with other lands. Their background as warriors or merchants and their love for adventurous travel formed their belief that exploring would be useful for their lives and their society. To that end they envisioned a new kind of formal outing that would reveal the world's future boundaries. Until 1492, however, what Ptolemy had displayed in his *Geography* (second century C.E.)—a world limited to the Mediterranean basin and its adjacent hinterlands, northern Africa, and parts of Asia— would not be extended. Drawn in about 1300, England's *Hereford Mappa Mundi* included nothing farther away than Eden, at the eastern extreme from Britain.

Roman Legacy. The medieval Christians' ideas departed little from the fundamental geography of the earlier Roman imperial military and intellectual boundaries. In his natural historical work, the Roman Pliny had speculated broadening that conception by adding another patch of land, to balance those already known. Imaging "Paradise," "the island of unknown men," and "Gog and Magog"— places that even they thought might be metaphorical—and employing symmetry as the guide to configuration, mapmakers seemed to base their medieval creations on imagination rather than affirmed information. Their maps could not guide travelers to places in Africa, Antarctica, or to any spot other than the ones classical and biblical education had prepared them to represent, such as the Tanais (Don) River, the Nile, and the Mediterranean

Sea, or the four rivers flowing from Eden. Although mapmakers considered it important to show an earthly and possible location for Paradise, for example, exact coordinate representation was not the organizing focus of their efforts.

Viking Adventurers. With the exception of the fearless Irish monks, the Vikings were the earliest medieval explorers. In the guise of traders and warriors from Scandinavia, they raided and later settled in parts of northern Europe, Iceland, and North America between the ninth and the eleventh centuries. The Vikings' ideas of successful exploration were realized first in 874, when Iceland was discovered; by 900 twenty-five thousand Norwegians had settled there. The new discovery introduced further exploration possibilities: one was via the traditional Viking sea voyage, offering the chance of being blown off course to discover a previously unknown island; the other was the maritime explorer's way in which adventurers would take specific preparatory steps to settle a new land, such as loading supplies for permanent settlement elsewhere, recording sightings of land and sea routes, and taking women along. For the second approach, Snaebjorn, Erik Thorvaldson (known as Erik the Red), and Leif Eriksson formed the core of the Viking explorers, each wanting to find land for new colonies in which they could live and thrive. Snaebjorn saw Greenland, found earlier by his great-grandfather, Gunnbjorn, as an extremely important site to establish a settlement. Later in the tenth century, Erik the Red would lead a voyage of exploration to the west coast of Greenland, once, and then again eventually to settle there.

Transplants. Erik the Red continued his explorations from Greenland. Although he did not become the first Viking to sit on American soil, he planned the expedition of his son Leif, remaining behind only because of a horsefall injury. Having purchased a ship whose owner Bjarni Herjolfsson had originally spotted North America, Leif, as set forth in *Eiriks Saga*, which described the discovery of the New World, happened on "lands which he did not even know existed." The Viking explorations are the favorite example of many historians who seek in the Middle Ages an instance of medieval people venturing into the unknown. But the Vikings were most interested in colonial settlement, each one wanting his to succeed. Intuit presence on the Newfoundland coast overpowered the Vikings' initial settlement attempts, and their colony in Vineland collapsed under the threat of the more numerous local inhabitants whom they called Skraelings. In a few centuries the Vikings were removed as colonists of Vineland and Greenland, but they maintained a presence in Iceland from that era forward. It was not until almost a millennium later that the Vikings' maritime discoveries were affirmed by archaeological findings in North America; in 1968 a Viking settlement was unearthed at L'Anse-aux-Meadows, Newfoundland, one of many Viking archaeological finds that based its searches on some of the Old Norse sagas of the improbable sounding Vikings' maritime explorations.

Marco Polo. In 1271 Marco Polo of Venice began his travels across Asia to China, visiting Hangzhou, the Song

Viking ship from the ninth century, which could accommodate up to thirty men
(from Robert Delort, *Life in the Middle Ages,* 1973)

dynasty's rich second capital of one million merchants, artisans, officials, scholars, servants, and slaves. From 1275 to 1292 he worked for the Mongol ruler Kublai Khan, returning to Venice in 1295. In 1299 Rustichello of Pisa took the idea of the travels of Marco Polo and wrote *Divisament dou monde* (Description of the World), adapting some of the descriptions recounted to him by Marco Polo in jail to give a more exotic and Eastern perspective in this new travelogue. Omissions in the work, such as no reference to the Great Wall of China, have been cautiously explained as elliptical, to shelter the Mongols' world from crudely explicit descriptions. Nevertheless, Rustichello's significant detail has brought much credence to his work. He recounted the splendors of China, including evocative specifics about the seaport Zaiton, the court of Kublai Khan, the sounds of the Gobi Desert, and the mores of Chinese women. Also new were the accounts of Java, Sumatra, polar Russia, East Africa, and Japan. To Marco Polo belonged twin distinctions. He became known for the many exaggerations about his travels, earning the nickname "Mr. Thousands." On the other hand, he respected the distinctiveness of pagan Eastern cultures. Although impracti-

cal and much less concrete than the accounts of John of Plano Carpini (1245–1247), William of Rubruck (1253–1255), and Francesco Balducci de Perlotti (flourished 1340), Marco Polo's description was the broadest and most intriguing. His travels stimulated the explorations later undertaken by Henry the Navigator and Christopher Columbus in the fifteenth century.

Ibn Battuta. About the same time that Marco Polo was writing his last will, ibn Battuta was thinking and talking about new places to see. Born in Morocco and educated in the way of the Maliki legal school, ibn Battuta arrived in Mecca in 1325 and, after consulting a holy man there, proceeded to Russia, India, and China. From ibn Battuta's travel stories ibn Juzayy wrote an elaborately detailed compilation titled *Tuhfat al-nuzzar fi ghara'ib al-amsar wa-'aja'ib al-asfar* (Precious Gift to Those Interested in the Wonders of Cities and the Marvels of Traveling), or *al-Rihla* (The Journey). His "classical" travelogue model was ibn Jubayr's twelfth-century travels to Mecca, Egypt, Iraq, Syria, and Sicily, and his practical orientation was that of a pilgrim traveling to holy sites and Islamic countries. Like Marco Polo's Chinese adventure, this was a rare instance. Ibn Battuta had also advised the Sultan of Delhi in matters of Islamic law and record keeping. Ibn Battuta wrote his notes possibly with the hope that he would be acknowledged as a candidate for *quadi* (adviser) to his own Marinid sultan in Morocco, but he was not eligible until he became a sedentary scholar in 1357. His travels so impressed the sultan Abu 'Inan, however, that he sent ibn Juzayy to compile the notes for ibn Battuta, whom he invited to become *quadi* in a provincial Moroccan town. Ibn Battuta accepted the position. Thus, for the twenty-seven years from 1325, when, under the terms of Islamic law, he went on the hajj (pilgrimage), until five years after becoming *quadi* of Delhi and of the Maldive Islands of Sri Lanka, ibn Battuta traveled to become the Arab world's most renowned explorer.

Sources:

Ross E. Dunn, *The Adventures of Ibn Battuta, a Muslim Traveler of the 14th Century* (Berkeley: University of California Press, 1986).

Felipe Fernandez-Armesto, *Before Columbus: Exploration and Colonization from the Mediterranean to the Atlantic, 1229–1492* (Philadelphia: University of Pennsylvania Press, 1987).

Marcia Kupfer, "Medieval World Maps: Embedded Images, Interpretative Frames," *Word and Image*, 10 (1994): 262–288.

Margaret Wade Labarge, *Medieval Travellers: The Rich and Restless* (London: Hamilton, 1982).

Arthur Percival Newton, ed., *Travel and Travellers of the Middle Ages* (New York: Barnes & Noble, 1968).

J. R. S. Phillips, *The Medieval Expansion of Europe* (Oxford: Oxford University Press, 1988).

Marco Polo, *The Travels*, translated by Ronald Latham (London: Penguin, 1958).

Jonathan Riley-Smith, *The Crusades: A Short History* (London: Athlone Press, 1987).

Marjorie Rowling, *Everyday Life of Medieval Travellers* (London: B. T. Batsford, 1971).

G.V. Scammell, *The World Encompassed: The First European Maritime Empires, c. 800–1650* (Berkeley: University of California Press, 1981).

Kristen A. Seaver, *The Frozen Echo: Greenland and the Exploration of North America ca. AD 1000–1500* (Stanford, Cal.: Stanford University Press, 1996).

Bertold Spuler, *History of the Mongols, Based on Eastern and Western Accounts of the Thirteenth and Fourteenth Centuries*, translated by H. and S. Drummond (London: Routledge, 1972).

EXPLORERS FROM OTHER LANDS

Personal Encounter. Medieval exploration was a personal encounter between two cultures. Both explorer and explored peoples might be changed; rarely was neither affected. Most often in this period and later, explorers, when they brought settlers with them, superimposed their home way of life on the new environment, if not on its people.

Misfits. The Viking society was altered astonishingly little by Atlantic Island exploration. The Viking *Landnamabok* (Book of Settlements), based on a work predating 1189, established the official documentation of colonization in Iceland. Subsequent Viking colonies generally imitated the formal Scandinavian institutions of authority, especially in their social and religious respects, without modifying the system particularly to suit the needs of the colonial economy. In the case of Greenland, native hunting

THE INNKEEPER ON THE ROAD TO COMPOSTELA

The nucleus of this tale appears in various versions, although this one by a Valencian medical doctor is rare in that the innkeeper is explicitly a woman. An important early version is found in the *Codex Calixtinus*, a mid-twelfth-century manuscript compiled of materials relating to Saint James. The codex contains a pilgrim's guidebook to Compostela written around 1130, presumably by a French monk called Aymeric Picaud. Apart from being an invaluable source of information about medieval pilgrimages, it is the first European travel guide to Compostela. In a sermon in Book I, a preacher warns pilgrims about the scams practiced on innocent pilgrims by "evil innkeepers" and tells a version of this tale of the lone pilgrim. From there, the story passes into the *Golden Legend* (thirteenth century), an extremely popular collection of saints' lives by Jacob of Voragine. It is found among the miracles of Saint James and was inserted in the Biblical *Book of Saint James* from the twelfth century. The miracle of the resurrected cock and hen seems to be a fifteenth-century addition to the tale. In commemoration of this event a live cock and hen are kept to this day on display in the cathedral of Santo Domingo de la Calzada.

Following milestones, plains, mountains and low places and crossing rivers, I went on to visit the Holy Corpse of La Calzada, a walled city. A foul and despicable innkeeper with whorish inclinations had staying at that time in her inn a band of pilgrims, old and young. One of them caught her fancy and she asked him to give her pleasure; he declined. The vile [man] put a cup in his baggage and when he went on his way she "discovered" it missing. She had him hung for the theft.

The other pilgrims in his group went on to Compostela and fulfilled their vow. On the way back, they went by just to see him hanging there, a little ways off the great road. He was alive!

He said, "Get me down from here! The Blessed Saint James has held me up."

The dastardly plot was exposed and was given further confirmation, for the pilgrims ran and put their case before the presiding judge. As he was responding to their complaint, right before their eyes, two cooked birds miraculously came back to life and began to crow loudly, both the hen and the cock. The condemned innkeeper was hanged without further ado.

I went on down the road, sometimes pensive, sometimes laughing, and arrived in the west. There I performed my vigil and fulfilled my pilgrim vow.

Source: *Liber Sancti Jacobi, Codex Calixtinus* (Santiago de Compostela, Spain: Consejo Superior de Investigaciones Cientificas, Instituto Padre Sarmiento, de Estudios Gallegos, 1951).

Illumination of a Mediterranean galley, from *Liber ad honorem Augusti,* twelfth century
(Bibliothèque de la Bourgeoisie, Berne)

and fishing exploitation techniques never took hold among the Vikings, however crucial it was to independent survival on the island.

Colonists. Latin Western culture was also transplanted to the Holy Land. Pilgrimages and the Crusades opened up "exploration" to all social classes in the Middle Ages. Almost immediately, however, feudal regulations governing terms of service, seigniorial fees, ages of entry into service, and training and property restrictions were introduced or imported directly into the Crusader States, largely as a result of the shortage of timely help in the form of volunteer armies. In the Crusader colonies, boys could be apprenticed and girls married off. At stable moments females served their husbands under no more undesirable conditions than in Europe and faced the usual threat of mortality in childbirth.

Aggression. Medieval military exploration had, however, a slightly different character about it. Incursions could be undertaken either voluntarily, with a vigorous force choosing its new target, or compulsorily, as arranged by other enemies, circumstances, or internal military unrest.

Mongols' Route. The Mongols' voluntary affront was lengthy and exhaustive but virtually guaranteed them a lasting place in Western history, earned by trade and aggression. They were not enticed to uncover the military secrets of the Song Empire of China or to push further south. Instead they moved West, pursued an advance into Europe, defeated the Christian armies with comparative ease, and turned homeward in 1242. The Westerners, as the explored, met the Mongols on the battlefield, fighting them in Hungary, Poland, eastern Germany, and Austria. Terms could not be negotiated. Since the land in Medieval Europe was poor and backward when measured against China and hard labor was essential to work it, inhabitants were not able to bargain with invaders for more favorable treatment than death. The Europeans' one hope was trade, which would allow the Mongols some form of commercial taxation rights payable in silver.

Military and Political Understandings. The fate of the vanquished in military exploration was well understood. Christian residents in Jerusalem were normally required to serve Saladin as slaves upon surrender in 1187. Fighting in sworn defense of the city, the knight Balian of Ibelin discovered, however, that he could buy freedom from a generous enemy. For some, payment in dinars became the solution to their captivity.

Commodities. Medieval European urban spheres showed many effects of foreign exploration. Medieval commodities fell into different categories determined by their difficulty to procure and prestige to own. Among the easiest to acquire and lowest in terms of ownership status were dietary basics, such as grain, ale, and vegetables; those ranking somewhere in the middle were basic clothing and housewares. At the elite end of the material objects scale were items from foreign lands: precious stones, delicate glassware, spices, or heavily worked manufactured goods, such as complicated silk textiles and carved ivory. The wealthy chose from limited amounts of exotic items. Although some luxuries did come from trained craftsmen in Europe, most were obtained in another land that offered unusual raw materials or different production skills. Gemstones, gold, fine glass, spices, silk, and ivory were treasured.

Rural Impact. In European rural areas the impact of exploration was in some sense much narrower. Rural dwellers did not have the wide variety of specialized goods that the people in cities and large towns enjoyed, but many villages had far more contact with travelers from outside their region than the needs of the community demanded, including pilgrims, missionaries, and itinerant preachers. Furthermore, the connections of the pan-European Christian community meant that most parish priests had to spend some of their time receiving word on doing Rome's new bidding. Their contacts were nonetheless restricted, largely because of illiteracy.

Pilgrimage Accounts. Already by the ninth century literate Christian readers could satisfy their basic curiosity with pilgrimage route maps or one of the pilgrims' guidebooks, many of which included practical advice on dress, money, expenses, and precautions to take. Pilgrims who sought out a mystical experience, in the process of meditating on the example of the venerated person in his or her honored place, sometimes wrote travel narratives in order to help those who meditated without leaving home. For medieval women especially, the mystical accounts of Bridget of Sweden and Margery Kempe on pilgrimage were particularly popular. For men the 1150 travelogue connected with Saint Patrick of the perilous trip into the subterranean passage of Lough Derg by the knight Oengus O'Brien was vicariously exciting. Pilgrims learned of Rome's pagan and Christian wonders from the *Codex Einsidelensis* (late eighth century) and the *Marvels of Rome* (twelfth century). Those on their way to Jerusalem had many guidebooks at their disposal: The *Itinerary from Bordeaux to Jerusalem*, Rorgo Fretellus of Nazareth's *Description of the Holy Land* (1148), and Burchard of Mt. Sion's *Description of the Holy Land* (thirteenth century). Written certificates confirmed a pilgrim's fulfillment of his vow, as did the inscription of a name at the site or the relics and pins that came back from afar. The men and women who went on pilgrimage to the Holy Land often brought back a souvenir of their trip, a palm tree branch, for example, to lay on the altar of their church at home. It was, however, the informal accounts by family members who had traveled that were the greatest testimony to a pilgrimage completed.

Sources:

Ross E. Dunn, *The Adventures of Ibn Battuta, a Muslim Traveler of the 14ᵗʰ Century* (Berkeley: University of California Press, 1986).

Felipe Fernandez-Armesto, *Before Columbus: Exploration and Colonization from the Mediterranean to the Atlantic, 1229–1492* (Philadelphia: University of Pennsylvania Press, 1987).

Marcia Kupfer, "Medieval World Maps: Embedded Images, Interpretative Frames," *Word and Image,* 10 (1994): 262–288.

Margaret Wade Labarge, *Medieval Travellers: The Rich and Restless* (London: Hamilton, 1982).

Arthur Percival Newton, ed., *Travel and Travellers of the Middle Ages* (New York: Barnes & Noble, 1968).

J. R. S. Phillips, *The Medieval Expansion of Europe* (Oxford: Oxford University Press, 1988).

Marco Polo, *The Travels,* translated by Ronald Latham (London: Penguin, 1958).

Jonathan Riley-Smith, *The Crusades: A Short History* (London: Athlone Press, 1987).

Marjorie Rowling, *Everyday Life of Medieval Travellers* (London: B. T. Batsford, 1971).

G.V. Scammell, *The World Encompassed: The First European Maritime Empires, c. 800–1650* (Berkeley: University of California Press, 1981).

Kristen A. Seaver, *The Frozen Echo: Greenland and the Exploration of North America ca. AD 1000–1500* (Stanford, Cal.: Stanford University Press, 1996).

Bertold Spuler, *History of the Mongols, Based on Eastern and Western Accounts of the Thirteenth and Fourteenth Centuries,* translated by H. and S. Drummond (London: Routledge, 1972).

ITINERANT CHRISTIANS

Preachers and Followers. Many heretical religious groups began when preachers traveled to spread the Gospel; over time these groups developed permanent communities where they acquired more followers. One of the first such settlements in medieval Europe began in 1096 at Angers under the leadership of the Canon Regular Robert of Arbrissel, an itinerant preacher papally appointed. Robert of Arbrissel's venture was so successful that by 1100 he and his adepts had established the abbey at Fontevrault, which in turn founded many other priories, including Orsan.

Papal Instruction. The houses of Fontevrault and Prémontré and the abbeys of Savigny and Chaussey with their daughter communities were perhaps the most successful of the medieval apostolic movement. The papacy had recommended to each of the respective founders, Robert of Arbrissel, Norbert of Xanten, Vital de Mortain, and Bernard de Thiron, that they supervise the organization of a community, establish a permanent home for it, and settle its form of government. The first communities lived on alms and were considered by the secular clergy to be careless in their manner of dress, unworthy of a priest or monk.

On the Edge of Orthodoxy. Nevertheless, in the early thirteenth century, Pope Innocent III had the leaders make specific provisions for a religious life for the men and women whom their preaching influenced: "If any men of the world wish to abide in our counsel, we advise that some who are suitable should be selected to exhort and

One of the most important pilgrimage sites in Medieval Europe was Santiago de Compostela in Spain. Below is a list of the distances between the stops along the way.

Town/Village	Interval Distance, miles	Distance Traveled, miles
Saint Jean Pied-du-Port, France	0.0	0.0
Roncesvalles, Spain	15.0	15.0
Zubiri	13.0	28.0
Pamplona	12.0	40.0
Puente la Reina	14.0	54.0
Estrella	12.0	66.0
Los Arcos	11.5	77.5
Logrono	15.0	92.5
Najera	15.0	107.5
Sainto Domingo	12.0	119.5
Belorado	12.5	132.0
San Juan de Ortega	14.5	146.5
Burgos	13.5	160.0
Burgos	13.5	160.0
Hornilles	11.0	171.0
Castrojeriz	11.5	182.5
Fromista	14.0	196.5
Carrion de la Condes	12.0	208.5
Calzadilla	13.5	212.0
Sahagun	12.5	224.5
El Burgo Ranero	16.5	241.0
Mansilla de las mulas	16.5	247.5
Leon	10.5	258.0
Hospital de Orbigo	22.0	280.0
Astorga	9.0	289.0
Rabanal	12.5	291.5
Ponferrada	12.5	304.0
Villafranca del Bierzo	13.0	317.0
Vega del Valcarcel	15.0	322.0
Sarria	15.0	337.0
Barbadalo	10.0	347.0
Portomarin	10.0	357.0
Hospital de Santa Cruz	11.5	368.5
Melide	11.5	380.0
Aruza	9.0	389.0
Sainta Irene	10.5	396.5
Santiago de Compostela	10.5	407.0

Average Miles: 13.5

Total Miles: 407

Source: Arthur Percival Newton, ed., *Travel and Travellers of the Middle Ages* (New York: Barnes & Noble, 1968).

dispute against the heretics, while others dwell together in houses, living religiously and according to rule, dispensing their goods in justice and mercy, laboring with their hands, and paying the tithes, first fruits and offerings due to the Church." In 1212 the Poor Catholics proposed to open a religious house in the Diocese of Elne, but since the converts were so heterogeneous, the monastery would have clerics, laymen, and women. The beginnings of this movement so interfered with the operation of other orders that most of the new orders, particularly the Premonstratensians, retreated toward conformity with monasteries inspired by the Benedictines. In the thirteenth

A wall painting from the church of Saint Nicholas, Tavant, France, of a pilgrim, twelfth century (British Library, London)

Obstacles. The itinerant preachers faced many obstacles in trying to carry out their plans for the Christianization and education of the laity: orthodox supporters were often hard to find; some cities outlawed the presence of preachers; lay nobles resisted; and a fear of preachers' causing unrest slowed acceptance of their ideas. Furthermore, Latin had made it hard for the laity to understand what they were being taught in church and hard for apostolic preachers to instruct them. Perhaps the preachers were naive about what they could accomplish in the radicalizing environment of the twelfth century. Ultimately, the itinerants gathered and educated only a small portion of the lay Christians of the Middle Ages from 1100 on. They were, however, successful in setting precedents, in drawing lay support for vernacular education from influential popes such as Innocent III, and in providing an ideology counter to the one held by orthodox bishops and others opposed to literacy for the laity.

Sources:

Margaret Wade Labarge, *Medieval Travellers: The Rich and Restless* (London: Hamilton, 1982).

Arthur Percival Newton, ed., *Travel and Travellers of the Middle Ages* (New York: Barnes & Noble, 1968).

J. R. S. Phillips, *The Medieval Expansion of Europe* (Oxford: Oxford University Press, 1988).

Jonathan Riley-Smith, *The Crusades: A Short History* (London: Athlone Press, 1987).

Marjorie Rowling, *Everyday Life of Medieval Travellers* (London: B. T. Batsford, 1971).

LANGUAGE AND FOREIGN LANDS

Skepticism. Language was definitely both a means and a barrier to communication between different lands. The activities of political alliance, religion, and schooling each had an important linguistic element. For both trade and war, language was almost an ancillary form of communication. Numeracy was far more important than literacy within the medieval trade sphere. The introduction of Arabic numerals into Europe in 1202 could have afforded much-eased interaction in becoming the *numerus francus* between traders of different lands. The numerals themselves were, however, identified with the translation movement centered in Toledo, Spain, so strongly in fact that they were known as *toletanae figurae* (Toletan numbers), and European regimes interpreted the use of the Arabic import quite hostilely. In Florence an edict was issued in 1299 forbidding bankers from using Arabic numerals instead of the cumbersome Roman numerals they had gladly abandoned.

The Route of War. As for the sphere of war, there is no better means to communicate aggressive intentions than direct action. To exchange ideas or information, however, even between hostile parties of different lands, language worked as well in the Middle Ages as it does today. Examples of the rhetoric of war abound in connection with the Crusades. Stories of Turkish cruelties against pilgrims fueled the anger of Christian Europe. One example of a direct exchange between the two sides illustrates the use of

century, however, the laity dominated itinerant preaching in Europe for the bands of the "apostolic movement," and after the start of the Inquisition, exposed the ordinary course of clerical life. Their continued attempts to maintain lay dominance, in Peter Valdes's Waldensians and the Cathars, for example, failed, partly because orthodox clergy willing to entertain an ideal of the whole Church independent of any distinction of clergy and laity were difficult to find.

language as war propaganda. Two Muslim emissaries queried the patriarch of Jerusalem as Crusaders besieged the town of Caesarea in the thirteenth century: "Why do you tell your people to invade our land and kill us, when your religion says no one must kill anyone made in the image of your God?" The patriarch replied: "Well, this town is not yours. It is Saint Peter's whom your fathers chased away. We want to get back his land, not take your property. As for killing, whoever fights to destroy God's law deserves that. Give up the land, and you can go unharmed with your goods. If not, the sword of the Lord will kill you."

Political and Linguistic Limits. In the context of exchanges among antagonists of different lands in the Middle Ages, one might rightly wonder whether they shared a common language. In the medieval period, the notion of different lands went virtually hand in hand with distinct tongues. In the case of the Carolingian dynasty, fraternal conflicts over one kingdom took on irreparable seriousness as the warriors for the two parties could no longer understand one another in the same Frankish dialect. Among their other lacks, the Carolingians had neither the transportation system nor the administration to govern their empire for long, but it was raw conflict between the grandsons of Charlemagne that led to the partition of his Empire into Western, Middle, and Eastern kingdoms. At the battle of Fontenay in 841 Lothar, one of three brothers, was defeated by the other two. In 842 at the city of Strasbourg Charles the Bald and Ludwig or Louis the German swore oaths in league against Lothar. As recorded by Nithard, grandnephew of Charlemagne and historian of the later Carolingians, the oaths took a parallel form in two vernacular languages: *lingua romana* (Old French) and *lingua teudisca* (Old German). By 870, at the Treaty of Mersen, most of Lothar's Middle Kingdom was split between the Eastern and Western kingdoms, and the future outlines of Germany and France had begun to take shape.

Religious Communication. The same phenomenon seems to have played itself out in the religious sphere as well. Once an acceptable Latin translation of the Bible was completed and Latin became officially adopted as the language of western Christianity, the divisions between the eastern half of Christendom using Greek and the Latin-speaking western half became profound. The ensuing schism of the Western Church from the Eastern turned not in small part on impasses in communication stemming from Christendom's lack of a shared language.

Law. Latin was for much of the Middle Ages the language of pan-European communication. It served as the means for all parts of the Church and the highest levels of government to communicate across regional boundaries. One of the greatest medieval boons to its strength as a universal secular language was the late-eleventh-century rediscovery of the *Corpus Juris Civilis*, a huge compilation and refinement of Roman law, completed five centuries earlier under the direction of the Byzantine emperor Justinian I. Centered on the University of Bologna, established in 1119

OATHS OF STRASBOURG

In 842 in the city of Strasbourg, the grandsons of Charlemagne, Charles the Bald and Ludwig or Louis the German, swore oaths against their brother Lothar. What is interesting about these declarations is that both men spoke in the vernacular language of their respective realms: *lingua romana* of the western Franks (present-day French) for Charles and *lingua teudisca* of the eastern Franks (present-day German) for Ludwig. Since he was the older brother, Ludwig swore first in his brother's language:

Pro deo amur et pro christian poblo et nostro commun salvament, d'ist di in avant, in quant deus savir et podir me dunat, si salvara eio cist meon fradre Karlo et in aiudha et in cadhuna cosa, si cum om per dreit son fradre salvar dist, in o quid il mi altresi fazet, et ab Ludher nul plaid numquam prindrai, qui meon vol, cist meon fradre Karle in damno sit.

When Ludwig had finished, Charles took the same oath in *lingua teudisca*:

In godes minna ind in thes christanes folches ind unser bedhero gehaltnissi, fon thesemo dage frammordes, so fram so mir got geuuizci indi mahd furgibit, so haldih thesan minan bruodher, soso man mit rehtu sinan bruodher scal, in thin thaz er mig so sama duo, indi mit Ludheren in nohheiniu thing ne gegango, the minan uuilon imo ce scadhen uuerdhen.

Literal translation of the *lingua romana*, the *lingua teudisca* being the same with the names changed:

By God's love and by this Christian people and our common salvation, from this day forth, as far as God gives me to know and to have power, I will so aid this my brother Charles in each and every thing as a man ought to aid his brother, in so far as he shall do the same for me; and I will never have any dealings with Lothar that may by my wish injure this my brother Charles.

Source: Nithard, *Histoire des fils de Louis le Pieux*, edited by Ph. Lauer (Paris: Librairie ancienne Honoré Champion, 1926), pp. 101–109.

in northern Italy, generations of law scholars would produce a vast literature in Latin commenting on and expanding Roman civil law, inspiring countries as well as the Church in Rome to refine legal codes.

Language of Learning. Latin was the medieval language of learning. For many centuries it was the language into which many pre-medieval or non-Western works were translated, providing a bridge of understanding to the past and other contemporary cultures. For learning to be reborn again in Europe after the fall of the Roman Empire, people had to begin to read more than the books of their own creation. They had, however, through the upheavals in education and livelihood, lost touch with the

Illumination of Western propaganda against Islam: a Turkish king orders the decapitation of a Christian in front of an idol (Bibliothèque Nationale, Paris)

skills of reading other languages. As books came to be collected from different parts of Europe and the Middle East, they were translated into Latin to allow for them to be understood in medieval Europe. Works translated from Arabic, Hebrew, and Greek were among the most influential in the Middle Ages.

Works of Muslims and Jews. Al-Andalus was famous for its scholars, such as Averroes and Maimonides. Both men were notable practitioners of medicine, a field in which Europe realized it had much to learn from its neighbors. The works of the Islamic expert, Averroes, born Ibn Rushd in Córdoba in 1126, were the result of thirty years of study. They presented a stimulating yet troubling collection to Christian scholars. An educated person from the Middle Ages brought up in the Christian tradition saw the world and humankind as the whole point of Creation; therefore, Averroes's arguments that both the creation of the world by God and personal immortality were impossible were strikingly strident to Latin Europe. Based as they were on his interpretation of Plato and Aristotle, Averroes's ideas served, for the Latins, as an intermediary to Greek

philosophy. The great Jewish thinker Maimonides also was born in Córdoba, although a period of intolerance there forced him first to Morocco and ultimately to Cairo. There he codified Jewish law in his *Mishne Torah* and wrote in Arabic his classic *Guide to/for the Perplexed,* whose linking of religion, philosophy, and science influenced medieval Christian scholarship.

Authors. In literature, the Arabic world gave the West the popular stories from *Thousand and One Arabian Nights,* stemming from the reign of the Abbasid ruler Caliph Harun al Rashid, in Iraq and Iran, around 950. Great literary works, including the poem the *Rubáiyát* by Omar Khayyám, also made their way through translation into the West. Arab poets were earlier than Christians to sing of their loved ones, and their poetry, often set to music, flourished in al-Andalus. Samuel Halevi, later known as Hanagid, typified the many-sided society of Arabic Spain. A Jewish boy of Córdoba of the eleventh century, he was pushed to leave by local violence, even though it was between Arabs and Berbers, not directed against Jews. He made his career in Granada. In 1027 he was named, or named himself, *nagid* (prince or governor) of al-Andalus's Jews. Service to successive Muslim kings led in 1037 to his appointment as grand vizier of Granada and, for most of the years until he died in 1056, leader of troops in battle. He was a poet and a scholar as well. His verse, suffused with his rabbinical learning, drew on both Arabic and Jewish cultures and is one of the gems of Hebrew literature.

Latin and Vernaculars. Through the competition of vernacular languages, politically powerful regional interests, and a lack of secular higher education in Latin, the common language of the Church was slowly becoming less important in the interaction between people from different lands. Translation into the different vernaculars of medieval Europe was definitely on the rise by the middle of the twelfth century. Books collected from different parts of Europe and the Middle East were translated into many vernacular languages, medieval forms of Italian, English, Spanish, and French. Even before the development of the printing press in the mid fifteenth century, religious works and Latin and Greek authors were translated into regional vernaculars. In this way, more and more people could read a work in a tongue closer to their own regional language, which presumably improved communication.

Roger Bacon and Ramon Lull. A few scholars saw in the tendency of letting translators do the linguistic interactive work the dawning of a new era of language barriers. Both Roger Bacon and Ramon Lull lamented not giving language instruction in Greek, Latin, and Arabic an honored place, because lack of linguistic ability reduced access to the ideas of other cultures. An English scholar and scientist, Bacon carried out research into optics, but he was also extremely interested in the acquisition of foreign languages. While his own linguistic skills were not as high as his ideals for others, his curiosity and scientific/alchemical interests led to attributions to him of all kinds of adoptions from manuscripts in Arabic, including the first recipe for gunpowder in 1249. The Spaniard Lull in 1276 founded a monastery on Majorca with the main purpose of training churchmen for interaction with Moorish and Arabic Muslims in the Arabic language.

Translations. Translation was, however, to win out largely over language mastery in the Middle Ages. Boethius's *Consolation of Philosophy,* which, when originally written in Latin in 526, went unmentioned by any of the author's contemporaries, became the most widely copied work of secular literature in Europe from the Carolingian epoch to the end of the Middle Ages. A nonreligious work in monastic libraries, it was a religious work within secular collections where it appeared frequently in translation. The *Consolation of Philosophy* made its way into every one of the strong medieval vernaculars: into Old English by the graces of King Alfred, into Old French by Jean de Meun, and into Middle English by Geoffrey Chaucer. Despite the fact that a popular pastime among students was to gather at taverns to drink and compose vernacular songs, of which the *Carmina Burana* collection has rousing examples, the number of vernacular works written in the Middle Ages was smaller than the number of works that were translated from an ear-

lier language into a medieval vernacular. Throughout the Middle Ages, works were imported from Byzantium, but by the middle of the period every foreign port was seen to be a source of written works to be translated.

Nontranslation. A multiplicity of languages on religious and political fronts definitely spelled disunity, if not disharmony, in medieval interactions between peoples of different lands. Europe was abandoning forever nontranslation, the use of communication in a common language on the level of the continent or large geographic area. In so doing, Europeans were also shifting the space in which translation was not needed out of the geographic sphere and into the intellectual. Only those who did not require translations because they were multilingual, intellectuals in cathedrals, courts, and classrooms across Europe, had occupied translation-free space during the Middle Ages. That rare community would by the thirteenth century become so small as to consist almost exclusively of translators.

Translators. Translators were the more cosmopolitan members of medieval society, but they were also among its finest intellectuals. Translating was by no means an uncreative function. In twelfth-century Spain, John of Seville and Abraham bar Hiyyâ both translated and wrote original scientific works, the latter highly colored by their own efforts in translation. Medieval translation involved the creation in the vernacular and in Latin of virtually a new language, particularly for scientific works, where Arab scientists had vastly enlarged the range of observational data and hence descriptive vocabulary, and incorporated mathematics, particularly algebra. Although various translators from Arabic into Latin worked alone, the usual process was for two scholars to work in tandem, with one scholar translating aloud from the Arabic text into the vernacular and a second translating from the vernacular into Latin. As John of Seville noted on the translation of the *De Anima* of Avicenna (ibn Sîna): "The book . . . was translated from Arabic, myself speaking the vernacular [Castilian or Catalan] word by word, and the archdeacon Dominic converting each into Latin." Thus, ibn Dâwûd worked with Gundisalvo; Abraham bar Hiyya probably with Plato of Tivoli; and Gerard of Cremona with a Mozarab named Galippus." Some intermediary translations into the vernacular were committed to writing, particularly in the period of Alfonso the Wise of Castile, who in the late thirteenth century assigned an additional scribe to translating sessions to write down the Castilian draft as well. There was a welcome place for Jews in this translation practice, since many were trilingual, knowing Hebrew, Arabic, and a Romance language.

Missionaries. Medieval conversion activity also illustrates that language was both a means and a barrier to communication in the interaction between peoples of different lands. If the interaction was from the East, the converted land was subsequently connected to the Greek linguistic sphere. If, however, the missionaries had derived from the West, subsequent interaction between the Christian groups would be in Latin. Initially, however, the missionaries had

Illumination of a Christian and a Muslim playing chess, circa 1284 (Escorial Monastery, Madrid)

to learn the converts' vernacular languages, to explain the great truths in them and to deal day by day with the fierce Slav or the high-spirited Celt. Frequently, religious works were translated into the vernacular. The earliest samples of Anglo-Saxon literature are nearly all ecclesiastical. The oldest long piece in Old German is the *Heliand,* or paraphrase of the Gospel. The only preserved work in the old Gothic tongue, the foundation of German philology, is the translation of the Latin Vulgate Bible by Bishop Ulfilas or the communiqués of Saint Columbanus and his Irish missionary companions to convert the Arian Goths of Lombardy. The first Irish missionaries in Germany, Saint Gall and Saint Kilian (both died in the seventh century) spoke to the people both in Latin and in German, and it is believed that they compiled the first German dictionary to help with daily interaction and preaching.

Cyril the Missionary. Eastern Christian or Byzantine missionaries were led in the ninth century by two brothers sent to convert the Slavs. In 862 Cyril and Methodius worked as Christian missionaries in the newly founded Slavic state of Moravia (830). While they learned the language of the Slavs, the missionaries found its lack of a written form an impediment to furthering Christian education. Cyril therefore adapted the Greek alphabet to the Slavic tongue; it became known as the Cyrillic alpha-

bet after its adapter. In 990–992 Poles and other western Slavs converted from the Eastern to the Western (Roman Catholic) Church, while the remaining Slavs stayed within the Eastern (Greek Orthodox) Church. In 1035 Poland became a fief, or subject state, of the Holy Roman Empire. In 1278 Bohemia and Moravia became estates of the Holy Roman Emperor.

Viking Converts. In the case of the conversion of the Vikings, Western missionaries' approach to the language difference was far less accommodating than that of Cyril in the East. During the reign of King Canute of Denmark, who ruled an empire covering Denmark, England, and part of Sweden and Norway from 1018 until 1035, English missionaries converted the Danes to Christianity. Although it is clear that the Vikings incorporated pictures symbolic of Christian belief into their stone carving, it also seems that any knowledge the missionaries had of the Viking tongue, which did have a written form in runic letters, was not transmitted into the dominating Latin linguistic culture. Rune stones have been found decorated with both Christian symbols and runes, the Viking letters, but no Runic Bible is known to have been produced.

Norman Christians. Conversion and new language acquisition also went together for the group of Vikings who settled on the continent. By the early tenth century the

Danish Vikings who had attacked Paris in 895 had settled at the mouth of the Seine River, under their chief Rollo. The Frankish king, Charles the Simple, had given him and his followers Rouen and its surrounding land on condition that he swore the king allegiance, defended the land from other Viking invaders, and became a Christian. With Rollo and his men's willingness to adopt Christianity, the Archbishop of Rouen baptized them, and Rollo was made Duke over Normandy, known in Latin as *terra Normanorum*, the land of the Northmen/Norsemen. Their shared religion and close proximity to the *lingua romana* of the western Franks led these Northmen to learn both Latin and French. This linguistic shift would accompany them across the English Channel in 1066, when their local duke, William, led them to claim the English crown. Although it was clearly a land grab, that foreign invasion was not bad for educational standards and linguistic fertilization. The soldiery, which brought the Norman French tongue to England, was followed soon by a flood of Latin scholars and documents. Among the resident Angles and Saxons, whose land the Normans had come to exploit, there was a slow increase in the number who read and wrote Latin while speaking Anglo-Norman. They had new access to interaction with all corners of the European continent.

Means of Interaction. Upon the basic skills of interaction, talking and walking, the medieval people built multiple spheres of communication and mobility. While communities defined themselves predominantly through social exchanges and activities close to home, war, political alliances, trade, travel, and schooling brought contact between different peoples of different lands. Religion was undoubtedly the major catalyst to interaction among people in the Middle Ages. The Latin of the Church and ecclesiastical translations into vernacular languages provided an initial formal dimension to both spoken and written medieval languages. Travelers and explorers also pushed the bounds of the Roman Christian legacy, spreading active modes of expression and empirical appreciation of the world.

Sources:

Philippe Aries, *Centuries of Childhood,* translated by Robert Baldick (London: Cape, 1962).

Charles Burnett, "The Translating Activity in Medieval Spain," in *The Legacy of Muslim Spain,* edited by Salma Khadra Jayyusi (Leiden & New York: E. J. Brill, 1992), pp. 1036–1058.

Norman F. Cantor, *The Civilization of the Middle Ages* (New York: HarperPerennial, 1993).

Carlo M. Cipolla, *Literacy and Development in the West* (Baltimore: Penguin, 1969).

Georges Duby, *A History of Private Life,* translated by Arthur Goldhammer (Cambridge, Mass.: Harvard University Press, 1988).

Lucien Febvre and Henri-Jean Martin, *The Coming of the Book: The Impact of Printing, 1450–1800,* translated by David Gerard (London: N.L.B., 1976).

Daniel A. Frankforter, *The Medieval Millennium: An Introduction* (Upper Saddle River, N.J.: Prentice Hall, 1999).

Francois Garnier, *Le langage de l'Image au Moyen Age,* 2 volumes (Paris: Léopard d'or, 1982–1989).

LANGUAGE AS A MEANS OF AND A BARRIER TO COMMUNICATION

Reading and Writing. The inability of most medieval people to read and write was more of an impediment than it appeared to be at the time. Indeed, society depended much more on oral than on written communication, and information certainly circulated by word of mouth in public announcements, sermons, and performances. Most medieval children were not schooled enough to read or write. Both were expensive activities: books were scarce; writing surfaces were costly; and to write one had to be equipped with basic writing tools, if not quills and ink. For most people, especially those of the laity, neither reading nor writing was seen to be a necessary part of life. Some females from noble families learned to write, but for most, writing was not deemed as useful as spinning. Writing, especially in the Latin shorthands that developed regionally, was, however, a useful skill for employment, and when taught, it was to boys, although exceptions to this pattern did exist. Kings' courts and religious houses taught reading and writing to both sexes, as did nobles' tutors.

Literacy. General reading and writing literacy rates for the Middle Ages are hard to estimate, since they varied widely according to place, socio-economic status, gender, religious or lay calling, and occupation. Towns had a higher number of literates than rural areas, and professional and wealthy people were generally more literate than poorer people. At no time in the Middle Ages did any laws require children to be taught to read. This situation, combined with the dearth of schools, made the population of the Middle Ages predominantly illiterate. While the literacy rate increased dramatically in certain areas and religious groups during the later Middle Ages, it did not reach the levels achieved during the Renaissance.

Dhouda. It is, however, extremely difficult to create firm generalizations for the Middle Ages, as the example of Dhouda, the laywoman who wrote during the ninth century, should help illustrate. Fully literate in Latin, she wrote *Liber Manualis,* a book she intended to give to her son William. In this manual Dhouda gives her son advice on how he should conduct his life. She says that he should obey and respect authority, worship God, and read. Dhouda stresses the importance of reading, suggesting that it should be like a game. The reader should study the work until he understands everything about it. In the initial epigram the first letters of the lines spell out in Latin the message, "Dhouda Greets Her Dear Son William. Read."

Translation Necessity. Medieval literacy, no more than literacy today, did not give the reader access to all written works. A perceived need in the Middle Ages for translation was a clear indication that language then as now is both a means and a barrier to communication. Language, in the case of translations, is, on the one hand, the means of communication between peoples of different tongues; on the other hand, since it is the difference in languages that creates the need for translation at all, the lack of a lingua franca or shared language is in fact a barrier to communica-

Charter of King Canute I, written in Latin and signed by witnesses, granting land to the monk Aefic, circa 1020
(British Library, London)

tion. For the most part, nonetheless, translation, or the ability to transfer meaning through languages from one to another people, is a means to greater communication. There are, however, two instances in which the move toward translation might be seen to be more of a catalyst to impeding communication than enhancing it. The first is that brief interval during which languages are beginning to evolve away from one another when, with effort and goodwill, it might still be possible to speak with one tongue rather than emphasize the lack of ability of parties to exchange in a shared language.

Adherence to One Tongue. The Oaths of Strasbourg of 842, as they came to be called, occurred just after such a transition point. Ludwig the German and Charles the Bald, both kings in the Carolingian dynasty, swore one oath in two languages in the presence of their troops, promising to unite their interests. The text of the Oaths is widely considered the first document in Old French and certainly the first in both Old French and Teutonic, or Old German. Each leader took the oath and communicated it to his soldiers in the language of the followers of the other—Ludwig the German in *lingua romana* and Charles the Bald in *lingua teudisca*—each presumably spoke both languages. The two languages have been considered a sure sign that some of the brothers' troops did not understand both tongues. They reveal a moment of contact when the differences between the Frankish tongues of their subjects had evolved so far as to become unintelligible to the rank and file of the opposing sides. The warriors in the field might not have participated in the pact had they understood it. The evolution of the two languages as apparently mutually exclusive in the two portions of the empire, the Germany of Ludwig the German and the France of Charles the Bald, respectively, suggests that a fairly advanced stage of differentiation between the German and the French parts of the former Carolingian Empire had already been reached and that only for the brother kings would the use of two languages represent a means for communication rather than a barrier.

Yielding to Translation. The other instance in which the move toward translation might be seen to be an impediment to communication is when translation becomes a crutch for those who might otherwise learn to speak or at least read the language of the other land. During the Middle Ages there were repeated situations in which people who spoke different languages dealt with their communication problems. The first instance occurred long before the ninth century, but its legacy lived throughout the whole of the medieval period: the loss of a command of the Greek language. Greek, Aramaic, and Hebrew were the earliest languages of the Christian faith, but Greek and its unique alphabet became the official language of the first unilingual versions of the Bible. It was the first religious language of pan-Christendom. The completion of an acceptable Latin Biblical translation went, however, hand in hand with a different tongue's becoming officially adopted as the language of Western Christianity.

With the Latin Bible as the language textbook of medieval rudimentary education, the study of Greek was virtually abandoned in Western Europe. The linguistic isolation of the West was profound, and the ensuing schism of the Western Church from the Eastern turned not in small part on their impasse in communication.

New Mind-Set. As translation was to reveal, Latin was the next universal tongue to be neglected in the medieval period. The process was a slow one, however, and Latin enjoyed being the language into which most works were translated throughout the Middle Ages. Nonetheless, the lingua franca of the Church was slowly being excluded as a potentially common language. Translations of works into vernacular languages tended to impose the dialect of a translation on wider areas than its oral use encompassed. Hence, the dialects of London, Paris, and Florence began to impose themselves on England, France, and Italy, respectively. Linguistic standards were also being set through the models of vernacular language in writing.

Limited Contact. The few scholars who fought to preserve language instruction were among the most highly educated in the Middle Ages. They, perhaps more than anyone, reflected on the extent to which ignorance of a language could be a barrier to communication. Direct understanding of Muslim culture and religion, for example, was impossible for those who did not read Arabic. The Muslims had founded great universities, especially in Egypt, Baghdad, and Spain. They had built many libraries and schools for the study of Islam. They had brought the use of zero and Arabic numerals, a notation adopted from India, to their empire and made advances in algebra and geometry. Their astronomers had kept lengthy records of the heavens. Arabic scientists had studied the properties of light. They had used chemicals to make medicines, had begun performing delicate surgeries, and had written medical textbooks, including the famous *Book of Healing* and the *Canon of Medicine*, two of more than two hundred works on diseases by the early-eleventh-century scholar Avicenna.

Science in Arabic. Translation into Latin was, however, the way in which most Arabic works were appreciated in western medieval Europe. Two Muslim studies on the eye were translated and remained in use as reference works until the eighteenth century. Due to the innovative content of many of the works, Latin words did not exist to convey accurate meaning. Arabic names therefore were often transliterated into Latin. Names of many stars, visible to the naked eye, and technical terms for astronomical configuration points, such as zenith and nadir, are examples. By 1202 Arabic numerals were adopted in Europe, whereupon despite some setbacks they slowly replaced the clumsy Roman numerals in use then.

Communicating between People. Despite what people today regard as a tremendous lack of technology, medieval people had the means to communicate and much substance to convey. While it may be misleading to speak of manuscripts in terms of books, since the medieval practice was to bind more than one work within a single volume and call that a book, libraries held books for the literate, and oral communication flourished in Church, countryside, and town. The unspoken languages of gestures, rituals, symbols, gifts, and artistic representations also provided many avenues of communication in the Middle Ages. It is, perhaps, the efforts of medieval Europeans to communicate that gave the greatest color to their culture in terms of written works, art, and music. Communication certainly was the catalyst to much of their local travel and even to some of their greatest explorations.

Sources:

Norman F. Cantor, *The Civilization of the Middle Ages* (New York: HarperPerennial, 1993).

Carlo M. Cipolla, *Literacy and Development in the West* (Baltimore: Penguin, 1969).

Georges Duby, *A History of Private Life*, translated by Arthur Goldhammer (Cambridge, Mass.: Harvard University Press, 1988).

Lucien Febvre and Henri-Jean Martin, *The Coming of the Book: The Impact of Printing, 1450–1800*, translated by David Gerard (London: N.L.B., 1976).

Francois Garnier, *Le langage de l'Image au Moyen Age*, 2 volumes (Paris: Léopard d'or, 1982–1989).

ROAD TRAVEL

Impact of Roads. Any overland travel presumes that roads or ways, at least, were passable, which was certainly not always the case. The crux of the problem of land transportation during the Middle Ages was the extent to which the Roman road system had survived in Europe. Where the Empire's roads still existed, they formed a ready-made grid for the movement of any type of traveler, but most of the European portion of them fell into grave disrepair in the early Middle Ages. There was a lack of an overriding political authority in Europe and often an inability or, perhaps, desire to maintain transportation routes. Stretches of road in good condition tended to be a reflection of private maintenance, whether by a lord as part of his domain or by the citizens of a town. The Castilian king Alfonso the Wise stated that as a general rule citizens of towns were under obligation to maintain "the pavements of the great highways and of the other roads which are public."

Roman Roads. In certain areas, maintenance and continued use of Roman roads were reinforced by military or economic stimuli. In 1066 Harold II had traveled over the old but well-maintained Roman road between Londinium (London) and Eboracium (York). Trade between the Mediterranean coast of Spain and France and trans-Pyrenean or -Alpine Europe took place along the Roman system. In the eleventh and twelfth centuries, when commerce revived, it was often oriented on routes dictated by the surviving Roman roads and bridges. The land travel of traders is not easy to generalize, but a couple of examples might serve briefly to illustrate the range of their overland activities. Before 1300 few peasants ever traveled more than a few miles from home, but by then peasant women were known to sell eggs and produce in market towns as far as 12 miles away from their village. Between 1296 and 1346 English merchants sold grain from manors in Wiltshire in local markets within a 10.5-mile radius. Nonetheless, in 1326–1327 a reeve in Kent sent an expedition more than 180 miles away to Gloucestershire to buy horses, and continental overland merchants traveled from town to town, the length of trade routes stretching from Flanders to Italy.

Effect of Pilgrimages. The demands of travelers and commerce connected with pilgrimages in Christian Europe had, however, a different effect on transportation. Originally the route of these journeys was determined outside the framework of trade or military use, although occasionally the three coincided, as in the case for reaching the site of Rome via the existing *iter romanum*, *via Francigena*, or *chemin romeret*. Initially within the pilgrim's context of good and pious works, there was much to encourage the organization of road-building or maintenance projects. At first Church orders were established to seek the minimum improvements in bridge building, road construction in mountain passes, and other forms of construction to facilitate religious travel along Roman roads or even older routes where possible.

Route Improvements. When the pilgrimage to Santiago de Compostela became popular, it created enthusiasm for nine passable land routes and for alterations to beaten ways. In the early eleventh century King Sancho the Great of Navarre, for example, changed a section of the road to Santiago de Compostela to make it safer. There were routes from the east coast of Spain and two roads through Portugal. The Camino de Campostela (also known as the Camino Frances) crossed the Pyrenees from France, following routes from Paris, Vezelay, Le Puy, or Arles to meet the Roman *via Traiana* running about four hundred miles in northern Spain to Astorga. Following the old Roman silver road from Huelva in the south, the Camino Mozarabe was the approximately four-hundred-mile route taken by pilgrims from southern Spain leading north, either through Braganza, or in a more or less straight line from Seville to join the Camino Frances in Astorga, or through Verfn and Ourense and straight from there to Santiago.

Via Nova. Medieval centers of habitation not on Roman roads were more isolated and, as population increased and settlement became denser, documents begin to mention the *via nova*, starting out perhaps as no more than a foot or riding path. New roads helped lords link their holdings together more efficiently. Sheep ways (*cañadas*) developed for the seasonal movement of flocks provided an increasingly viable new road grid for the traveler on foot in southern France or Spain. The Romans had known how to design a road of good quality: straight, with no steep inclines, and without marshes. In the Middle Ages bad weather and illness combined with the often poor roads to slow medieval travel. Stiff climbs could easily lengthen good travel time by a quarter or more.

Stone relief of a pilgrim outside of the Shrine of Santiago de Compostela, Spain, circa twelfth century

fields, through vineyards, and to cut across boundaries in order to traverse the way with cart, horse, or pack mules." By custom, towns had the right to demand that their citizens spend a specified time in corvée work on roads and bridges. Even so, instances of roads washed out due to neglected ditches or road pits so deep that they caused accidents were not unusual.

Need for Infrastructure. Users of wheeled vehicles saw the greatest practicality in improving the surface, alignment, and grade of roads so that people and goods could be moved safer and more quickly. By the end of the Middle Ages there was a diverse and highly specialized choice of vehicles that transported passenger as well as freight. At the close of the Middle Ages, France, which had the largest national population, the most powerful army, and the most advanced economy, became the first country to plan and execute a national system of roads.

Sources:

Margaret Wade Labarge, *Medieval Travellers: The Rich and Restless* (London: Hamilton, 1982).

Arthur Percival Newton, ed., *Travel and Travellers of the Middle Ages* (New York: Barnes & Noble, 1968).

J. R. S. Phillips, *The Medieval Expansion of Europe* (Oxford: Oxford University Press, 1988).

Marco Polo, *The Travels*, translated by Ronald Latham (London: Penguin, 1958).

Jonathan Riley-Smith, *The Crusades: A Short History* (London: Athlone Press, 1987).

Marjorie Rowling, *Everyday Life of Medieval Travellers* (London: B. T. Batsford, 1971).

SEA TRAVEL

Antiquity's Secret. Throughout history, increased mobility has come via navigable water, and the Middle Ages was no exception. The two main uses for water travel in the Middle Ages were for military action and trade. Though initially warships and cargo vessels were different shapes and used different propulsion systems, over time they came to resemble each other in shape and mobility.

Specialization. Warships require speed, high maneuverability, and sufficient space for the warriors. Long and narrow ships became the standard design for early medieval naval fighting vessels. In contrast, trading ships seek to carry the maximum tonnage of cargo with as few crew members as possible. The bulbous medieval merchant vessel was in effect a navigable bowl designed with as much freeboard as possible. Freeboard, the height between the waterline and open deck level, would determine whether a ship's cargo would be swamped in the high swell of an angry sea.

Human Power vs. Wind Power. Rowing (propulsion forward by the pulling action of an oarsman) and oaring (propulsion forward by a pushing action) were two means of moving early medieval vessels. With the need for increased freeboard on cargo ships, oars either had to be longer or placed well below the top deck. Both solutions posed difficulties. Oars became awkward with

Legal Matter. Medieval road conditions generally did not favor the use of wheeled vehicles. Pack mules continued to play an important role in land transport. Only a few roads were as wide as twenty feet, necessary for the comfortable transportation of goods other than by packhorse or draft horse pulling a load attached by poles. The ill state of repair of most old roads and the limited width of newer roads made passage for vehicles difficult, if not impossible. A Castilian document of 972 allows the monks of Cardeña to drive "a cart through whatever place it might go; if there is no direct route, we give license to go through woodlands, through cultivated

Painting of a boatload of Vikings, circa 1300 (from Felix Barker, *The Search Begins*, 1971)

increased length, and since the number, strength, and synchronization of the crew mainly determine the speed of a rowed ship, poor conditions for work below deck reduced the efficiency of the oarsmen. Harnessing the wind with mast and sail presented a welcome supplementary source of propulsion in medieval vessels, both military and cargo. To allow ships to maneuver, sails and rigging had to undergo technical improvement. The simple large square canvas suspended from a single yard was joined by the lateen, or "triangular" sail, and rigging which allowed a sail to pivot on the mast to catch the force of the wind from any direction.

Surface Area and Maneuverability. Canvas area is the main factor in a sailing vessel's speed. The larger and more numerous the sails the greater the canvas area. Hence, to gain speed medieval ships added more masts to carry more sails. Vessels rigged with the square sail had to have clear decks in an arc around the mast equal to the movement of the sail on the boom from which it was suspended. This situation meant that a single sail hanging amid ships monopolized much of the early ships' decks.

Lateen Sail. Effective use of two masts and sails, which became standard in the Mediterranean by 1200, was made possible by the introduction of the lateen sail, a fore-and-aft sail (capable of catching the wind on either its front or back surface). With a ratio of length to breadth of about three to one, the lateen sail was fixed to a long yard in the longitudinal axis of the ship. A combination of square and lateen sails was used in many vessels, the main mast often carrying a square sail.

Independent Evolution. In addition to the many navigable rivers with which medieval Europe was blessed, there were two spheres of maritime travel by Europeans in the Middle Ages: the Atlantic Ocean and the Mediterranean Sea. For Atlantic and northern European river travel, ships were built in clinker fashion: ship-length planks fitted one over another from a center axis upward to form a hull. An internal skeleton, if there was one, was mounted within the strong yet flexible hull. Five types of clinker-built vessels plied the northern waters during the Middle Ages: the flat-bottomed cog of the southern North and Baltic seas; the molded-plank hulk of river and North Sea travel; the flat-bottomed, straight-sided punt of river ports; the fishing buss of the Netherlands; and the keeled Viking vessels–the longships and the cargo ships, such as the large *knarr*. Mediterranean navigation had specialized crafts as to need, yielding the galley, a rowed fighting ship, and a sail-propelled trading vessel. The basic Mediterranean vessel was a flush-plank Venetian form of the cog, which went by the name *buss,* a full-bodied, high-floating two-masted lateen sailing ship, and in its later guise, the Mediterranean car rack, ultimately a larger three-masted cargo ship.

Speed. The Viking warships could cover roughly 100 miles a day, but a replica of the tenth-century Gokstad longboat logged its greatest distance sailed in 24 hours at about 250 miles. Although Viking cargo ships were undoubtedly slower, supply voyage times to and from Iceland by the Norse indicate expected speeds in favorable weather of from 100 to 150 miles in 24 hours. Most medieval cargo ships, whether under sail exclusively or oar-and-sail-equipped, seem on extended trips to have averaged only about 20 miles every 24 hours; nonetheless, a river barge or raft apparently averaged only 7 miles a day.

Cross-Maritime Interchange. The story of medieval European navigation is one of interaction between technical developments in the two bodies of water defining Europe. The rise of oceanic navigation began when the cog passed through the Straits of Gibraltar carrying crusaders from England and the Netherlands. During the reign of Richard I of England (1189–1199), the cog made its way northward again, now transformed into the Venetian buss with castles or enclosed deckhouses at the bow and stern, and a bellied bow for increased cargo capacity. Sailors from Bayonne in southwestern France were thought to have introduced the Mediterranean carrack into northern European waters in the fourteenth century.

Technology and Psychology. This cross-fertilization had both technological and psychological components. The art of medieval navigation was improving, aided by the use of sails and a rudder instead of steering oars. A single large steering oar was first attached to the "steer-board" (starboard) side of the boat, being opposite from the port, or docking, side of the vessel. A straight post rudder was then adopted and firmly attached to the stern for greatest effect. By 1252 the port books of Damme in Flanders distinguished ships with side rudders from those with stern rudders. While the compass was known in Europe at the end of the twelfth century, it was not until two centuries later that the magnetic properties of the lodestone began to be used consistently in navigation and that serious, long-distance travel was mounted with its aid. Crusader voyages introduced northern Europeans to forays longer than the coasting and North Sea navigation they had previously undertaken. Also, the technical modifications to familiar northern ships were considered to offer greater security for ocean travel for the Atlantic-facing regions of France, Spain, and Portugal. In 1418 the Portuguese reached Madeira and in 1427, the Azores, about a third of the way to the Americas. Ferdinand Magellan's circumnavigation of Earth followed within the century, as did Christopher Columbus's voyage to the Caribbean.

Sources:

Felipe Fernández-Armesto, *Before Columbus: Exploration and Colonization from the Mediterranean to the Atlantic, 1229–1492* (Philadelphia: University of Pennsylvania Press, 1987).

Marcia Kupfer, "Medieval World Maps: Embedded Images, Interpretative Frames," *Word and Image*, 10 (1994): 262–288.

Arthur Percival Newton, ed., *Travel and Travellers of the Middle Ages* (New York: Barnes & Noble, 1968).

J. R. S. Phillips, *The Medieval Expansion of Europe* (Oxford: Oxford University Press, 1988).

G. V. Scammell, *The World Encompassed: The First European Maritime Empires, c. 800–1650* (Berkeley: University of California Press, 1981).

Kristen A. Seaver, *The Frozen Echo: Greenland and the Exploration of North America ca. AD 1000–1500* (Stanford, Cal.: Stanford University Press, 1996).

TRANSPORTATION: MEANS OF CONVEYANCE

Travel on Horseback. Travelers who did not make their way on foot in the Middle Ages likely rode a horse. The actual speed would depend on the type of horse, the weight the horse was carrying, its feed and forage, and the rest breaks for both man and mount. Sources differ, but it seems that the distance one could cover riding a horse on an extended trip, such as from Venice to Bruges, ranged from 20 to 30 miles a day depending on the weather, with a courier being expected to cover as much as 60 miles every 24 hours. A horse can easily carry a rider 40 miles in a day and even 50 miles without duress, but the lower figure of 20 miles is probably a more realistic average. In the tenth century it is recorded to have taken one week to travel from Algeciras to Córdoba, a distance of 150 miles.

Walking vs. Horseback Riding. Pushing a horse to achieve 60 miles daily would certainly cause it to founder sooner rather than later. On a pilgrimage a rider might average five to seven miles an hour, and medieval travelers accustomed to walking found travel on foot faster. A horse fatigues long before a man and recovers more slowly. Italian merchant families hired runners who would travel 55 miles a day for a week's stretch and then rest for a week instead of messengers on horseback.

Suitable Horses. Medieval chivalric values exalted the horse and travel on horseback. Once it became possible to mount a soldier bearing heavy armor and weapons, medieval warfare in Europe was dominated by the cavalryman until well after the Middle Ages. The destrier, or heavy warhorse, could carry some 250 to 300 pounds and, weighing twice as much as a conventional riding horse, could give greater force to the impact of the knight's lance. Off duty or perhaps on the round of visits a lord financed for his eldest son and other new knights immediately after their dubbing, knights rode the palfrey, a short-legged, long-bodied horse, which had a gentle ambling gait. While the destrier and palfrey excelled others in power and comfort, they were not fast horses.

Muslim Provisioning. In the Islamic world, the Arab warrior was just as obsessed with the horse as was the European knight. In al-Andalus, Muslim warriors stayed aloft and did not deign to fight on foot. Huge stables maintained by the eleventh-century Caliph at his palace Madînat al-Zahrâ, five miles west of Cordoba, testified not only to the Andalusian use of horses but also to the careful breeding of them. European Latin and Arabic cultures alike prized horses of Turkish or Arabian blood. Within Latin Europe, the need for a fast carrier of messages between armies or kingdoms gave rise to the courser, a strong, lean horse. Neapolitans, of the kingdom of Naples, were the major suppliers of this breed, a hybrid of the Turkish/Arabic and European stocks. In one of the many tales about him, Robin Hood was said to have given both a courser and a palfrey to a downtrodden knight:

In 1389 in Montpellier, "a good 450 miles from Paris," the King of France and his brother, the duke of Touraine, turned to talking about how good it would be to be in Paris with their wives and families. They worked themselves into a challenge as to who could reach Paris first, each one starting at the same time on the same morning accompanied by only one other person. A bet of five thousand francs was riding on the outcome. The following is an extract of the account of this episode by the chronicler Jean Froissart.

Those four keen young men continued riding night and day or had themselves taken on in carriages to give themselves a rest, when they felt like it. Of course they made several changes of horses. . . .

Think of the discomforts those two rich lords endured through sheer youthful spirits, for they had left all their household establishments behind. The King took four-and-a-half days to reach Paris, and the Duke of Touraine only four-and-a-third; they were as close together as that. The Duke won the bet because the King rested for about eight hours one night at Troyes, while the Duke went down the Seine by boat as far as Melun, and from there to Paris by horseback. . . .

The ladies treated the whole thing as a joke, but they did realize that it was a great feat of endurance, such as only the young in body and heart would have attempted. I should add that the Duke insisted on being paid in hard cash.

Source: Jean Froissart, *Chronicles*, translated and edited by Geoffrey Brereton (Baltimore: Penguin, 1968).

"Take him a grey courser," said Robin,

"And a saddle new;

He is Our Lady's messenger;

God grant that he be true."

"And a good palfrey," said little Much,

"To maintain him in his right";

"And a pair of boots," said Scarlock,

"For he is a gentle knight."

Question of Comfort. Frequently, medieval women as well as men rode a horse or mule, simply because it was more comfortable than either walking or riding in a contemporary wheeled vehicle. The smooth ride afforded by the palfrey made it a suitable horse for the majority of medieval travelers on horseback who might have been less skilled at mounting and riding the heavier destrier or faster courser. For medieval women, riding horseback was, nonetheless, no mean feat. Until the sidesaddle was devised, probably in the Middle East as early as the twelfth century but not arriving west until the fourteenth century, both men and women rode astride. This would have been particularly uncomfortable for women given the elaborate dress of the time.

Determining Horse Use. The medieval use of the horse reflects the relatively settled society required to support it. Cultivation of oats, integrated use of the stirrup, saddle, and horseshoe, and the breeding of a range of horses from the destrier to the palfrey and courser all led to an increased adoption of the horse into medieval travel. The saddle became so important that if merchants and other people were traveling partly by sea and partly by land, they would take their own saddle along to place upon a hired horse or mule when the overland portion of the trip began. Horses were expensive to buy, and compared to oxen and donkeys who were foragers, expensive to keep. With the development of the rigid horse collar, the Middle Ages saw the horse used on a large scale in agriculture for the first time in history.

Vehicular Transportation. During the Middle Ages several different wheeled vehicles were in use in Europe. One notable boon to medieval transportation technology was advancement in the harnessing of horses as draft animals to the wheeled vehicle. One or more shafts extending from the vehicle and attaching to a band around the horse's breast allowed its chest to serve to pull the weight behind. Where shafts could not be used, a special form of the rigid horse collar was devised. A significant addition to these changes was the widespread integration of a pivoting front axle, already known for centuries among the Celts and the Chinese.

Horses and Carts. The need for portable regalia and equipment may have driven some of the improvement in carts. Medieval armies and monarchs traveled extensively. Some of the German kings and Holy Roman Emperors traveled as much as two thousand miles a year, so there was a constant need for the transportation of baggage, if not personnel. The real problem for any medieval military relocation was not just in moving individuals, but also supplies. In Harold II's famous rapid march, physical and logistical strengths both came into play. There was also the matter of booty, which carts made much easier to transport. For booty alone a victor in Spain had thirty carts made. In the Arabic world, transport by camel was more economical than by horse and cart by a factor of 20 percent.

Need for a Wagon. A horse or mule pack train on an extended trip seems to have averaged ten miles a day, but then not every sort of baggage was conducive to pack transport. Iron or wood chests and waterproofed leather boxes, the luggage containers of choice for the nobility, demanded wheeled vehicles. During the early Middle Ages, heavy wagons of the sort known for centuries were still in use, although the improved harnessing did allow for the use of a single animal instead of two as before.

Wagon Speeds. Carts with two wheels were most commonly used for smaller, lighter loads and four-wheeled wagons for heavier burdens. A mule- or horse-drawn wagon covered an average distance of twenty miles a day, compared to the ten to twelve miles a day of an oxen-drawn one. If road conditions were good, the speed for wagons could reasonably have been between fifteen to twenty-five

Viking wagon, ninth century (Viking Ship Museum, Oslo)

miles in a day's time, with rest stops about every ten miles. Pilgrimages, like any organized medieval travel practice, contributed in the long run to the effort to improve wheeled vehicles. As the movement of pilgrims increased, larger wagons and carts were designed to carry groups.

Four-wheeled Vehicles. There was considerable momentum for change in human travel by four-wheeled vehicle. The ordinary wagon was terribly rough and uncomfortable. Women in particular, if they chose not to ride on horseback, suffered in being packed into rough carts called litters, which consisted of little more than a few boards and wheels haphazardly assembled. Significant advances in transportation technology became possible from the Carolingian era forward. The Magyars or Hungarians, who after threatening Europe settled into the former Roman province of Pannonia in the ninth century, possessed high competence in the use of wheeled vehicles. During the Middle Ages, Europe was poised for considerable transport advances.

Coach of Kocs. By the close of the Middle Ages, rich and powerful travelers had quite elaborate carriages that provided more comfort. What distinguished the carriage or coach (derived from the name of Kocs, a town in Hungary that became renowned for its excellence in carriage making around 1350) from the wagon was a suspension system. In the Middle Ages, leather straps, instead of the more complex later device of iron springs, were used to suspend the passenger compartment above the axle and thus to dampen the jolts that characterized the rigidly built wagon body. The swaying of suspended compartments might have led to motion sickness, but it reduced the number of passengers with broken bones or severe bruises. Improved suspension in four-wheeled vehicles made traveling behind a horse instead of on one increasingly more comfortable. What remained to be accomplished was an increase in speed. The poor condition of medieval roads made it impossible for any vehicles to make better speed than a good walker could achieve, at most some eighteen to twenty miles a day. With improvements in the harnessing of horses in tandem, one behind another, speeds could be somewhat increased.

Sources:
Ross E. Dunn, *The Adventures of Ibn Battuta, a Muslim Traveler of the 14th Century* (Berkeley: University of California Press, 1986).

Margaret Wade Labarge, *Medieval Travellers: The Rich and Restless* (London: Hamilton, 1982).

Arthur Percival Newton, ed., *Travel and Travellers of the Middle Ages* (New York: Barnes & Noble, 1968).

J. R. S. Phillips, *The Medieval Expansion of Europe* (Oxford: Oxford University Press, 1988).

Marco Polo, *The Travels*, translated by Ronald Latham (London: Penguin, 1958).

Marjorie Rowling, *Everyday Life of Medieval Travellers* (London: B. T. Batsford, 1971).

TRAVEL

Impact. All of medieval communication over distance required travel. Most travel took place by walking, but horse and cart, cog, and carrack all played an important role in medieval mobility. Even if undertaken by traders, some long-distance journeys could rightly be thought of as exploration. While the longer-term effect was frequently economic, the initial impact of exploration and explorers themselves was more often cultural and linguistic.

Characteristics. Travel in the Middle Ages was characterized by slowness, effort, and uncertainty. By whatever means, it was seasonal. Travelers walked, and if unaccompanied by animals, carried or dragged any luggage or wares. Farmers walked to their fields and back. Shepherds also walked at least a stretch each day to move livestock to pasture. On a daily basis, medieval craftsmen moved about only within town. Medieval urban dwellers usually resided directly above or next to their shops. In virtually every respect medieval nobles had the greatest mobility.

Hearth and Home. Farming and husbandry were the most-common concerns of the populace, and travel on foot to accomplish these tasks was definitely reduced in winter in the Middle Ages. Crops presented few cares, however, except for root vegetables to be dug as needed. Livestock was in the close or low pastures, and otherwise animals were tended to in the farmyard, including the slaughtering and curing of them, as feed dwindled. For the peasantry, winter was the season to stay out of the weather, a time to sit by the fire and spin, sew, carve, or cane. In winter almost no peasant traveled.

Time Equals Distance. In spring, as soon as the ground could be broken, fields for sowing had to be plowed. Except within a short range, medieval distances were measured in terms of time rather than distance. In this agricultural context of walking and prodding draft animals, however, "travel time" was equated to "travel distance." The early, and slower, draft animals' pace, that of yoked oxen, determined the field measure of an acre. The area that a yoke of oxen could plow in a day originally defined the "acre," an Old English word meaning a field. Virtually every medieval vernacular language had a name for the same area of land. A *joch* (from the same word in German for yoke) amounted to a somewhat larger area, about 1.4 acres. The *journal*, from the French word for day, *journée*, varied from region to region, amounting at most to 1.1 acres (or one-third of a hectare).

Agricultural Standards. Horses and mules were the other medieval draft animals. Their pace, a good deal faster than that of oxen, gave another agricultural "travel distance." By at least the year 1200, a medieval acre came to mean the area of a field of standardized dimensions: one furlong (40 rods or 10 chains) in length by 4 rods (or 1 chain) in width. The rod was equal to a full step, or the length of two strides (*gressus*), anywhere from 10 to 16 feet long. By about the twelfth century it became standardized at 16.5 feet and was also known as a *perche*, or perch. The word *furlong*, from the Old English *fuhrlang*, was originally defined by the length of the furrow (or plowed line) made on a square field of 10 acres, hence a field of 40 rods (one furlong or 100 chains) by 40 rods. It has also been suggested that the length of a furlong and hence of both the common square and rectangular fields was determined by the distance a horse could pull a plow in a straight line before needing to stop for a rest (approximately one-eighth of a mile). This medieval emphasis on distance in the agricultural sphere makes it possible to estimate the average travel of a plowman and his drover to about two miles per day.

Seasons. To the European peasantry, summer between planting and harvesting left some free time, depending on the locale and climate. Warmer weather was usually more conducive for a visit to relatives, perhaps as far away as a neighboring village. By June those with herds to graze moved to higher elevations. The herdsmen of the medieval transhumance, the annual migration of sheep flocks in southern France and Spain, were true travelers, walking as much as 250 to 400 miles into the hills and back. Since they would not go home for long stretches, their families might also make the trip to be among the shepherds for the late spring shearing or to relocate them to their temporary summer quarters by helping them build their *orri*, tiny, round stone huts. The herds' return trip in October coincided with the fall harvest season and imminent winter, for all a period of activity again close to home.

Travels of the Nobility. Town dwellers were the least traveled of medieval society. Their pattern of relatively little movement was virtually the same all year around. The nobility, however, varied its travel patterns seasonally, depending upon what type and how much land they held and who populated the lands. Nobles frequently summered at one property and wintered at another, checking on their villages, fields, or the farming peasantry.

Footsteps. The majority of all travel in the Middle Ages was on foot, but just how far and fast an average person on a trip walked is a matter of some speculation. It has been said that the ordinary medieval person walked ten to twenty or more miles per day, depending on the quality of the road. Just as today, there is clearly a difference in what someone who is used to walking can accomplish and the average achievement. It has been recorded that a highly trained walker can complete seventy miles in a twenty-four-hour period.

Foot Soldiers. In the Middle Ages, the most accomplished walkers were probably foot soldiers and merchants. The whereabouts of the infantry and their speed are critical issues to any army, and ever since the Persians and Romans, the capabilities of trained foot soldiers have worked their way into distance calculations and military strategy. The Romans adopted the ancient Celtic unit of the league, which was intended to represent roughly the distance a person could walk in an hour.

Map by Matthew Paris of the road to Rome, circa 1250 (British Library, London)

Its length seems to have varied from one and one-half to three miles. The Persian *parasang,* equal to an hour of march, was roughly 4 miles in length and subsequently divided into 3 *milia* in Roman times.

Harold's Lightning March. Although foot soldiers rarely played a major role during most of the Middle Ages and not much time was spent drilling them in fighting or presumably in marching efficiently, there is one instance of superior achievement of a medieval infantry. Just before the Battle of Stamford Bridge (1066), Harold II of England marched some seven thousand men from London to York. The army moved even faster than news of its approach, in a feat still known as "Harold's Lightning March." The rate of the march was about thirty miles a day, which means that those medieval foot soldiers were marching at the same rate as fourteen Roman infantry cohorts at a long league an hour for ten hours a day, or a Persian armies' at a *parasang* an hour for a seven-and-a-half-hour day. For the period, a sustained rate of thirty miles per day for seven days was in most circumstances unheard of. A sustained twenty miles per day would have been considered extraordinary.

Rise to Eminence. The Muslims hired mercenaries to be their foot soldiers, and in the Douro Valley of Spain free peasants were becoming foot soldiers in the late tenth century. By the eleventh century the rewards were often great enough to elevate infantrymen to nobility and knighthood, as is reflected in the *Poema de mio Çid,* where the hero, El Cid, makes knights of those who had fought on foot and gives them land in Valencia. The peasantry is described as trudging along in quilted battle coats to fight on foot with pikes and pole axes. Still in the fourteenth century the speed and ability for surprise attack of the foot soldier made him a valuable military asset.

Pilgrimage. Religion motivated many travelers. Christians wished to visit places associated with the life of Jesus Christ or the early martyrs; Muslims were obliged, as they are today, to make the Hajj, the pilgrimage to Mecca, once in a lifetime. These journeys in search of physical or spiritual succor were undertaken by all who could be mobile. For Christians, seeking grants of indulgence for the remission of sins was an added late medieval stimulus to travel. The act of moving around or between holy sites was a common one for pilgrims, and direct contact in the form of a touch or kiss of the object of veneration at a pilgrimage site was the goal. Pilgrimage landmarks also became associated with sites of local religious importance en route to the ultimate destination. As the movement of pilgrims increased, religious foundations provided shelter and food at punctuated intervals along the way.

Labor Itineris. The travel of pilgrims on foot was undeniably hard, but its discomfort was welcomed as a kind of penance (*labor itineris*). Some pilgrims went to the extreme of going barefoot. The purest of pilgrims plodded on foot, girded with the staff and shoulder sash they were given by a churchman upon departure, even if

they could afford a horse, wagon, cart, or carriage. For some, riding on horseback was thought to invalidate the medieval pilgrimage. Abu al-Husayn ibn Jubayr, who went to Mecca from Spain in 1184, reflected on how popular the Hajj was at the time. "Pilgrims were arriving from various countries, so many that only God could count them. Mecca lies in a valley a bow shot wide. It expands miraculously to hold them all–like the womb for the fetus, as scholars say."

Pilgrims' Gait. For a sense of how far and how quickly common people traveled on foot in the Middle Ages, the experiences of medieval pilgrims are a good indicator. Although their travel in groups could have moved along to the cadence of prayers or songs, pilgrims do not seem to have traveled as steadily as the foot soldier. The progress of walkers depended heavily on their pace, stamina, and desire to have some rest days. Given the distances between the overnight refuges provided near a monastery, parish, or town hall, it seems that the average rate for an extended pilgrimage was about twelve to fifteen miles per day, based, for example, on a thirty-five-day trip along the Camino de Santiago in Spain. The long gaps between places of accommodation on the Camino de Seville, however, indicates that its pilgrims had to be able to walk longer distances on a regular basis, upward of twenty miles a day. While a few pilgrims, such as Bertrand, a French knight who was on permanent pilgrimage as punishment for murdering his lord, never stopped anywhere for long, many early medieval pilgrims, especially those traveling to Rome, saw their journey as a one-way trip, intending to spend the rest of their lives near the holy site they had reached.

Pilgrims and Shrines. Although shrines to local saints and holy persons were known only within a narrow region, there were several internationally known pilgrimage destinations within medieval Europe: the shrine of Saint Thomas Becket in England, the city of Rome itself, and the tomb of Saint James of Compostela in Spain. The pilgrimage site connected with Archbishop Thomas Becket was the Cathedral of Canterbury where he was martyred on 29 December 1170. It comprised five different stations within the cathedral, four of which commemorated phases of his murder and burial. With miracles immediately credited to the archbishop, by 1179 King Louis VII of France traveled to Canterbury to pray for a cure for his son. Lothar de Segni, the future Pope Innocent III, went north as an Italian student in Paris.

The Eternal City. Of the 414 churches of medieval Rome, pilgrims went mainly to visit the early basilicas of Saint Peter's, Saint Paul Outside the Walls, Saint Mary Major, Saint John Lateran, and the churches making up the Forty Stations. Pilgrimages to Rome grew and waned depending on the stability of the papacy and on the possibility of visiting the sites of the Holy Land. As a pilgrimage goal, Rome lost in popularity with the Crusaders' capture of Jerusalem in 1099, but it regained its

Illumination from the Bible of Saint Sulpice of a traveler, twelfth century (Bibliothèque municipale, Bourges)

prestige by the thirteenth century as travel to the Holy Land became ever more precarious under the Muslim Turkish presence. It is estimated that around two million pilgrims visited Rome for the first Jubilee, called by Boniface VIII in February 1300.

Santiago de Compostela. Routes from France and from Portugal and southern Spain all guided pilgrims to Santiago de Compostela. There is evidence that a tradition of some form of pilgrimage through northern Spain may have had roots in Roman or even prehistoric times, because instead of stopping at Santiago de Compostela, many pilgrims continued due west some fifty miles more to Finisterre, or "the End of the Earth," a point with mythical or mystical connotations. The end of the medieval Christian pilgrim's route was, however, the Cathedral of Santiago (Saint James) de Compostela (from Latin *compostum,* meaning burial place), the site where the body of Jesus' disciple, James (the Great) was buried. In Spain, James was the most popular of all saints. One of the several legends that evolved among his cult told how he came to be buried in Galicia in the northwestern corner of the Iberian Peninsula, where he had preached the Gospel before returning to Palestine where he suffered a martyr's death in around 44. Another legend recounted how in the ninth century a hermit called Pelagius received a vision of miraculous starlight (hence, possibly Compostela from *campus stellae,* or star field), which revealed to him the forgotten burial place of Saint James. Saint Francis of Assisi and Saint Bridget of Sweden were among the medieval thousands to make the pilgrimage of about four hundred miles from the Pyrenees to Santiago.

Sources:

Ross E. Dunn, *The Adventures of Ibn Battuta, a Muslim Traveler of the 14th Century* (Berkeley: University of California Press, 1986).

Felipe Fernandez-Armesto, *Before Columbus: Exploration and Colonization from the Mediterranean to the Atlantic, 1229–1492* (Philadelphia: University of Pennsylvania Press, 1987).

Marcia Kupfer, "Medieval World Maps: Embedded Images, Interpretative Frames," *Word and Image,* 10 (1994): 262–288.

Margaret Wade Labarge, *Medieval Travellers: The Rich and Restless* (London: Hamilton, 1982).

Arthur Percival Newton, ed., *Travel and Travellers of the Middle Ages* (New York: Barnes & Noble, 1968).

J. R. S. Phillips, *The Medieval Expansion of Europe* (Oxford: Oxford University Press, 1988).

Marco Polo, *The Travels,* translated by Ronald Latham (London: Penguin, 1958).

Jonathan Riley-Smith, *The Crusades: A Short History* (London: Athlone Press, 1987).

Marjorie Rowling, *Everyday Life of Medieval Travellers* (London: B. T. Batsford, 1971).

G.V. Scammell, *The World Encompassed: The First European Maritime Empires, c. 800–1650* (Berkeley: University of California Press, 1981).

Kristen A. Seaver, *The Frozen Echo: Greenland and the Exploration of North America ca. AD 1000–1500* (Stanford, Cal.: Stanford University Press, 1996).

Bertold Spuler, *History of the Mongols, Based on Eastern and Western Accounts of the Thirteenth and Fourteenth Centuries,* translated by H. and S. Drummond (London: Routledge, 1972).

Vernacular Language

Choice of Language. What was spoken at home, in the field, street, and shop, and at most public gatherings was the language of medieval everyday life. It was the native language of a locality, known as its vernacular language. Until well after the first millennium, the common language of a medieval region had little or no expression in writing. The first and most widespread written language of Europe was its literary language, Latin. It was used throughout the Christian realm, especially for all official documents, particularly those of a religious nature. The use of spoken Latin in Church and in some government meetings and courts of law was an exception to the general use of the vernacular in verbal exchanges.

Literary Horizons. Over the course of the later Middle Ages, many vernaculars developed a written form and came to be used in poems, tragic tales, comedies and some public documents. There were, for example, many romantic stories about the British king, Arthur, his court at Camelot, and the knights of the Round Table inspired by an early Latin chronicle that told of a leader named Arthur who led the British against Saxon invaders in the 800s. Frequent repetition of the Arthurian legends, due especially to their spread in the vernacular, led to their being received with great credence in the Middle Ages.

Lingua Franca. The relatively small area over which the local dialect could be understood was inevitably a barrier to wider communication. Throughout the Middle Ages the Church attempted to maintain Latin as a pan-European or common language (lingua franca). It was intended to unite and to maintain the unity of Christendom, the "land" of all Christians. In Latin, messages, religious promulgations, and books could circulate over broad areas unified only by religion. The more medieval people depended on vernacular language to the exclusion of Latin, the less Europeans from one area to the next were able to understand each other or the pronouncements of the Church. Over time, although Christian artists, lawgivers, and writers struggled along in Latin, few of their countrymen could read their work, and vernacular texts, essential for the non-Latin literate, became almost as prevalent as the Latin Bible in the homes of medieval nobles.

Sources:

Philippe Aries, *Centuries of Childhood,* translated by Robert Baldick (London: Cape, 1962).

Charles Burnett, "The Translating Activity in Medieval Spain," in *The Legacy of Muslim Spain,* edited by Salma Khadra Jayyusi (Leiden & New York: E. J. Brill, 1992), pp.1036–1058.

Daniel A. Frankforter, *The Medieval Millennium: An Introduction* (Upper Saddle River, N.J.: Prentice Hall, 1999).

SIGNIFICANT PEOPLE

CANUTE I (CANUTE THE GREAT)

DIED 1035

KING OF DENMARK

Respect. Canute or Cnut I (Canute the Great) was the king of England from 1016–1035 and king of Denmark from 1018–1035. (At the time the kingdom of Denmark comprised present-day Norway and parts of Sweden, Germany, and England, as well as Denmark.) A powerful political figure of the eleventh century, Canute I was respected by both the Holy Roman emperor and the pope.

England. In 1013 Canute I accompanied his father, Danish king Sweyn I Forkbeard, on his invasion of England. When he assumed the English crown, Canute I began to rule over a Christian maritime kingdom. Canute I did not create the Viking interest in extended territory, but his ruthlessness encouraged his people, and through a series of battles at Penselwood (Somerset), Sherston (Wiltshire), Brentford (Middlesex), Otford (Kent), and Assandun (Ashington), they conquered the British Isles.

Motives. A mixture of military and economic motives are evident in many of Canute I's undertakings. Contemporary stories about him emphasize his personal piety and fascination with the idea of penance, as well. Several chroniclers offer hints at the motivations behind his conquest of England. The *Encomium Emmae Reginae,* written in praise of Canute I's wife Queen Emma by *Jomsviking Saga,* a monk of Saint Omer, and the account of Adam of Bremen, a monk with the diocese of Hamberg-Bremen, recount his rise to power and emphasize the king's expansionist visions. They suggest a basic medieval formula of conquering and strengthening Christianity, but they also claim that the strongest motive was Canute I's aspiration of fulfilling the goals of his father without sustained hostility.

Commercial Gain. Modern historians debate the degree to which Viking travels were motivated by attempts to combat the local inhabitants and make inroads for settlement, but virtually all concede that the Vikings had economic aspirations. Canute I maintained a prosperous trade relationship within his empire and some degree of commercial pressure over territories encountered by his merchants. He used a pilgrimage to Rome (1027) to secure easier trading conditions for merchants of his realm in northern Italy. Unlike royal patrons of trading ventures, Canute I was not interested in claiming vast amounts of wealth for himself. He focused instead on the strategic and pragmatic guarantees of trade at major ports and across key water routes. Church chroniclers from the era provide functional records of Canute I's fleets that link his vessels to the feats of tenth-century explorers.

Impact. Canute I has been credited with establishing a northern maritime empire and transforming the city of Lund in southwestern Sweden into a capital the equal of London. Contemporary chroniclers certainly contributed to his reputation, as did evidence of prosperous ports. Recent assessments suggest a complex man who was given more credit in his own time for his religious gestures than any other accomplishments. Canute I did not, however, establish Christianity in England, and there is no evidence that he held any unique theological understanding of that faith. He certainly did not lead a Christian expedition in conquering England, something a man of his status could have done were his soldiers not pagans. His support of pilgrims in Rome and churches in England were more likely motivated by the value of trade and real estate in secure hands than in an idealistic expression of religious fervor. After his death, the English church continued to benefit from the stability of the *pax Cnutonis* (the peace of Canute I's reign), though church authorities remained unwilling to elevate his status beyond "Canute the Great."

Sources:

M. K. Lawson, *Cnut: The Danes in England in the Early Eleventh Century* (London & New York: Longman, 1993).

John D. Niles and Mark Amodio, ed., *Anglo-Scandinavian England: Norse-English Relations in the Period before the Conquest* (Lanham, Md.: University Press of America, 1989).

Alexander Rumble, ed., *The Reign of Cnut: King of England, Denmark and Norway* (London: Leicester University Press, 1994).

RAMON LULL

1235-1316
MISSIONARY

Family and Personality. Ramon Lull, a lay brother from Majorca, did not begin his life as a zealous missionary. During his early years he had married (1257), had two children, and was surrounded by lively company. As seneschal or chief steward in the household of the king of Aragon, he supervised the royal feasts and ceremonies, and, as he later wrote, even enjoyed the pleasures of "sinful companionship." However, after several visions of Christ dying on the Cross in July 1266, Lull abruptly ended his career as seneschal. He turned to the life of a mendicant preacher and by October 1266 had sold all of his property because of his new convictions. Lull's stubborn adherence to his calling prompted some contemporaries to concur with his description of himself as "Ramon the fool."

Enterprise of Conversion. Lull believed that he had a sacred duty to convert the Muslims of North Africa and the Near East. He had planned his conversion enterprise for many years and had made pleas to princes, kings, and popes. Popes Nicholas IV, Boniface VIII, and Clement V brushed him aside, as did some royalty such as King Henry de Lusignan II of Cyprus and Frederick III of Sicily. James II, king of Aragon, had, however, sufficient confidence in Lull to recommend him to King Abu Hafs Omar I of Tunis, to give Lull permission to proselytize to the Moors of Aragon, and to respond to Lull's proposals for a crusade. At one point James II exercised his influence purportedly to request of the king of Bejaia that Lull be released from prison there.

Travels. Lull traveled as far north as Paris and west to Barcelona. More remarkably, however, he also journeyed as far east as Armenia, a territory allied with the Knights Templar whose Master Jacques de Molay obtained permission for Lull to visit, before perhaps heading south to Jerusalem. He also made three trips to North Africa.

Franciscans. It is likely that Lull had at one point hoped to be accompanied by follow Franciscans on his voyages, particularly after the founding of his monastery in 1276 at Miramar on Majorca to prepare brethren for missionary activity. He was well known for persistence in his own ideas. This trait did not lead him to form a stable link with contemporary Franciscans or Dominicans, but it did seem to work well in his relationship with his patrons.

Missionary versus Scholar. Contrary to a popularized image, Lull did not share the millenarian doctrines of the Spiritual Franciscans. Although none of the alchemical writings traditionally attributed to Lull can be plausibly ascribed to him, in the Renaissance, alchemists made Lull their guiding leader. He appears to have educated himself, like his contemporary Franciscans and Dominicans, in the ideas of Aristotle, Augustine, Anselm, and mendicant scholars. The Dominican and Franciscan Orders each approved of his goals, but the views he expressed in his first major work, *Ars magna*, or *Ars compediosa inveniendi veritatem*, were not shared by the Dominicans, who ultimately rejected the treatise by 1292.

Writer. Having spent his young adulthood in a royal setting, Lull had had the opportunity to learn the poetic techniques of the court troubadours. He also knew firsthand about the Moorish culture of Aragon during the reign of James II. In many of his over 250 works, Lull revealed his familiarity with Arabic culture, poetry, logic, and mathematics. He may also have been heavily influenced by Al-Khwarzimi's *Kitab Surat-al-Ard* on geography and proposed therefore that there was another continent on the opposite side of the Atlantic Ocean.

Legacy. Lull transformed himself from a self-interested, well-placed courtier into a traveling Christian missionary. He certainly was not the first Christian to travel to North Africa after the eighth-century arrival of Islam, but he was among the first to train others to become missionaries and to use Arabic in their travels. The record shows his energetic enthusiasm for conversion missions. Circumspection also reveals a man of questionably effective approaches, whose perseverance produced a good deal of animosity. Lull and his contemporaries viewed Islam in one of two ways, either as a religion that could be fully assimilated by the expansion of Christianity or as one that had to be eradicated through the militant techniques of the Crusaders' assaults begun years earlier. Lull's intellectual version of the second approach helped turn his hapless quest for the conversion of North Africa and the Near East into a contribution that changed the way missionaries undertook their task. Historians may never agree on Lull's scholarly intentions and the merits of his writings, but they continue to recognize the fact that he has forced the reconsideration of how Christians might inform themselves about the world's disparate religions and how the significant roots of modern mathematics might lie in the inspiration he derived from Arabic thinkers. Lull's legacy lies in the convergence of the Christian's quest for more believers and the ever-growing appreciation of the fruits of Muslim culture.

Sources:

J. N. Hillgarth, *Ramon Lull and Lullism in Fourteenth-Century France* (Oxford: Clarendon Press, 1971).

Mark D. Johnston, *The Spiritual Logic of Ramon Lull* (Oxford: Clarendon Press, 1987).

Ramon Lull, *The Book of the Lover and the Beloved* (New York: Paulist, 1978).

Richard W. Southern, *Western Views of Islam in the Middle Ages* (Cambridge, Mass.: Harvard University Press, 1962).

Frances A. Yates, *Lull and Bruno* (London: Routledge & Kegan Paul, 1982).

MARCO POLO

1254-1324
MERCHANT TRAVELER

Travels to the East. Marco Polo, a young Venetian traveling with his merchant father and uncle, is credited as being the first European to have spent a lengthy time in southeastern China. In reality his voyage was not the first one to reach the winter court of the Mongolian khan in present-day Beijing. The variety of land and sea routes that he successfully traveled and the experiences he had in the Middle East and Asia are, however, striking. While on the 7,500-mile route to China starting in 1271 or 1272, Polo had at least two brushes with death from disease and caravan robbers, but after about three and one-half years, uncle, father, and son did reach Khanbalic (Beijing), the khan's winter residence, and Shang-tu, the khan's summer palace. Later Marco went on to Hangchow, his favorite city, on the east coast of China. Nicolo and Maffeo Polo, Marco's father and uncle, had already completed a similar journey by 1269 and thus became the first Europeans actually to make their way across Asia. Marco's mother had died in Nicolo's absence, having given birth to his son, who was already fifteen years old when his father returned to Venice. The subsequent twenty-four-year journey of the three Polos is recounted in the work which bears Marco's name as author: *Divisament dou monde* (Description of the World). It became the key account for future travelers and explorers who would subsequently direct themselves by Marco's story of routes to the wondrous East.

Personal Experience. Marco Polo's name is well known today, but to his Italian contemporaries he was relatively unknown. Like those of many other Venetian merchants, his foreign contacts cannot, however, be overlooked. In fact, the account of his journey, written in a Gallo-Italian dialect by a Pisan, was recorded in a Genoese prison where Marco was being held. Marco traveled to China with his father and uncle, known traders, but his own personal skills as linguist and royal administrator were developed acting for the Mongol khan. He had been introduced to Kublai Khan as his servant and ultimately served him as a regional ambassador. Prior to becoming a favored bureaucrat, Marco distinguished himself as a messenger to the khan. During most of the period the khan ruled all of China, between 1279 and 1294, Marco served as his trusted set of eyes and ears. He went on an expedition from the Yellow River to the Indian border in northwestern China. He wrote that around 1269 Nicolo and Maffeo had helped in the Mongol conquest of a city in southern China by designing catapults for its siege and recounted the Mongolian general's accepting the surrender of the last representatives of imperial China in the Sung capital city of Hangchow. He continued to travel and serve the khan until 1292, when, a little more than a year before the khan's death in 1294, he and his father and uncle were given permission to escort a Mongol princess, Kokachin, to Persia (to be given in marriage to Arghun, the widower of a Persian queen, a fate she avoided by her death before her arrival) and to return to Europe.

Kublai Khan's Request. Kublai Khan solicited the support of Nicolo and Maffeo in contacting the Catholic Church. The logic behind the brothers' first return to Italy from China in 1269 was based on their seeking "as many as a hundred wise men" to teach about Christianity to the Mongol khan. Like the Polos, who had successfully judged the interests of the Mongols, earlier missionaries such as

John of Plano Carpini and William of Ruysbroeck had actually whetted their curiosity about Christianity. When the brothers returned to China, they were also requested to bring back oil from the lamp at Jesus' tomb in Jerusalem. The taking of Jerusalem by Saladin's Muslim forces (1187) had caused the Crusader kingdom of Jerusalem to move to Acre on the Mediterranean coast, a port whence the three Venetians started their land travel east. The Polos obtained the oil, but found almost no interest among Churchmen in continuing the journey with them. The dangers of long routes and Mongol tribesmen were known, so it was impossible to persuade even two friars to travel north as far as Turkey. Nicolo and Maffeo considered that the request of Kublai Khan for Holy Oil was a sign of the sincerity of his profession to hold Christ in veneration and to consider him as the true God, and thus made every effort to please him accordingly.

Eyewitness Account. Rusticello of Pisa, a writer of vernacular romances, wrote the descriptive chronicle of Marco's journey that included a perspective appreciative of the Eastern wonders that were so hard to reach. After leaving Acre on the Mediterranean, the Polos traveled for more than three years without secure escorts. Marco describes some of the more difficult moments of their journey. While the Polos liked the idea of taking the known sea route from the Persian Gulf to China, the primitive construction of the ships at Hormuz (Minab) dissuaded them because they feared that the vessels, whose planks were lashed rather than nailed together, could actually be "a great danger to sail in." This change of course added more than eight hundred miles and thirty-five days of riding to their trip. En route through Iran, most members of a caravan the Polos had joined "were taken and sold, and some were killed." Like his father and uncle, Marco learned how to diminish his foreignness in part by learning four Eastern languages and acquiring great respect for what must initially have been a strange environment for him. Once within the khan's domain, over the course of twenty years, Marco saw all of the land in northern and southern China conquered by the Mongols. He detailed towns and cities, religious and cultural practices, local professions, Mongol military prowess, appetites, and aesthetics, because other messengers had bored the khan with dry factual accounts. "After having

held for seventeen years various offices in the imperial administration in lands subject to the conqueror, attaining one after another the ascending grades of the courtly and bureaucratic hierarchy, Marco, like many other foreigners residing in China, considered himself an adoptive son of this new country and a faithful servant of its sovereign, in spite of some feelings of nostalgia for his homeland."

Significance. Marco Polo opened the world of readers to the Khanate of the Mongols and the culture of China in the late thirteenth century. The phrase "It's a Marco Polo" still bears, however, the connotation of an overly embellished account. No actual journal has survived for his journey and from Rusticello's literary account of the adventures Marco acquired the nickname "Il Milione," or "one who exaggerates a thousands of times over." His contemporaries were unable to suspend the disbelief that intruded upon their ability to appreciate this remarkable "description of the world." Nonetheless, less than a century after Marco's journey, Abraham Cresques incorporated some of the work's information into the Catalan world map of 1375, and thereafter his account intrigued Prince Henry the Navigator of Portugal and Christopher Columbus, who sought routes East. The actual veracity of the Polos' itineraries remained a great mystery until the nineteenth century, when many of Marco's details of the routes and stops from Acre to Hangshow were corroborated. Marco Polo's travels to the East have played a crucial step in medieval understanding of Eastern buildings, races, languages, governments, manufactured products, plants, animals, minerals, and the terrain itself. "I believe," Marco concluded, "that it was God's will that we should return, in order that people might learn about the things that the world contains, since, as we have said in the first chapter of this book, no other man, Christian or Saracen, Mongol or pagan, has explored so much of the world as Messer Marco, son of Messer Nicolo Polo, great and noble citizen of the city of Venice."

Sources:

Richard Humble, *Marco Polo* (New York: Putnam, 1975).

Leonardo Olschki, *Marco Polo's Asia: An Introduction to His* Description of the World *Called* Il Milione, translated by John A. Scott (Berkeley: University of California Press, 1960).

Chris Twist, *Marco Polo: Overland to Medieval China* (Austin, Tx.: Raintre Steck-Vaughn, 1994).

Frances Wood, *Did Marco Polo Go to China?* (Boulder, Colo.: Westview Press, 1996).

Documentary Sources

Avicenna, *Book of Healing* (early eleventh century)—A vast philosophical and scientific encyclopedia that owes its influence to Aristotle. Probably the largest work of its kind ever written by one man, it has entries on logic, the natural sciences, mathematics, astronomy, metaphysics, and music.

Avicenna, *Canon of Medicine* (early eleventh century)—One of the most famous books in the history of medicine in both the East and the West. It provides a systematic analysis of the achievements of ancient Greeks, Romans, and Arab physicians.

Eiriks Saga (Saga of Erik, circa 1000)—A commemorative history of Erik the Red's Norse settlement on Greenland.

Jean Froissart, *Chronicles* (fourteenth century)—A detailed history of feudal times and an important exposition of chivalric and courtly ideals.

Ibn Juzayy, *Tuhfat al-nuzzar fi ghara'ib al-amsar wa-'aja'ib al-asfar* (Precious Gift to Those Interested in the Wonders of Cities and the Marvels of Traveling, early fourteenth century)—Also known as *al-Rihla* (The Journey). The travel account of the Arab diplomat ibn Battuta who journeyed throughout North Africa, Eastern Europe, the Middle East, India, and China.

Landnamabok (Book of Settlements, circa 1189)—An Icelandic genealogical record probably compiled by Ari Thorgilsson the Learned. It lists the names of the four hundred original Viking settlers of Iceland and their descendants.

Marco Polo, *Divisament dou monde* (Description of the World, 1299)—Later known as the *Il Milione*. The story of Marco Polo's travels in the Far East; it was dictated to a fellow prisoner while both men were in the custody of the Genoese.

Thousand and One Arabian Nights (circa 950)—A collection of Eastern fairy tales, romances, legends, fables, parables, anecdotes, and exotic adventures of uncertain authorship. Some of the stories, such as Aladdin, Ali Baba, and Sinbad the Sailor, have become part of Western folklore.

Jacobus de Voragine, *Legenda Aurea* (Golden Legend, thirteenth century)—A collection of saints' lives, accounts of events in the lives of Jesus and Mary, and information about holy days and seasons arranged as *legenda* (readings) for the church year. A popular book, it was eventually translated into all Western European languages.

CHAPTER FIVE

SOCIAL CLASS SYSTEM
AND THE ECONOMY

by BETSEY B. PRICE

CONTENTS

Sidebars and tables are listed in italics.

900*

- A technological breakthrough occurs with the introduction of the horseshoe in Europe. Along with the collar harness (circa 800), it makes it easier for peasants to produce crops and to sustain themselves.

910

- Duke William the Good of Aquitaine donates land directly to the Papacy in Rome to found the Cluniac Order at Cluny in Burgundy, France. Exemplifying the agriculturally self-sufficient medieval monastery, Cluny counters the contemporary lack of religious independence from local ecclesiastical and lay secular authority.

1000*

- The European population is estimated at forty million people, only about 5 percent of whom live in towns.

- The ratio of seed to grain yield is consistently poor throughout the period of the High Middle Ages (1000–1300). About two bushels of seed are required to produce six to ten bushels of grain in good times.

- Guilds, associations of craftsmen or merchants established for mutual aid and protection and for the furtherance of their professional interests, begin to flourish throughout Europe.

1050*

- Rich silver mines are discovered in Saxony. Other mines soon open in the Alps and Tuscany.

1085-1086

- King William I (William the Conqueror) has the *Domesday Book* compiled to include all the information the king needs to determine the taxable capacity of his kingdom.

1100*

- The basic silver coin in circulation is the denarius (penny). Twelve denarii make one *solidus* (shilling) and twenty *solidii* equal one *libra* (pound).

- The Italian city of Milan has a workforce of sixty thousand, allowing it to start fine-cloth production and to flourish as the first prominent fine-textile production center in southern Europe. There are generally more than enough workers than needed to farm the land, so the rural peasant of whatever station can hope to escape his tie to land and lord with manumission, a grant of freedom and sometimes land ownership, or with an escape to a town where he could turn his talents or skills to a craft.

- The first Champagne Fairs, a series of markets in the French region of Champagne, occur. These fairs allow northern and southern European merchants to meet and conduct business in regulated and safe settings.

1115

- The Knights Templar, a religious military order, is founded. Aside from protecting pilgrims in the Holy Land, these knights also become bankers and money brokers because their honesty is considered to be above reproach. The brotherhood holds estates throughout Europe, and these heavily guarded sites act as clearinghouses for transactions between different provinces and states.

***DENOTES CIRCA DATE**

1140
- Doctors in France have to have a license to practice, although their guilds are yet to have the same authority as those for practitioners less highly ranked in the medical order of social status: the surgeon, the apothecary, and the barber.

1159
- King Henry II of England officially introduces scutage, a shield tax in lieu of military service. Monetarized vassalage, the rendering of a vassal's obligation by paying money instead of fighting in wars, becomes an enormously successful military fund-raising tactic for the nobility.

1166
- The first personal property taxes are imposed in England.

1200*
- The European population is estimated at sixty million people.

- In England, the silver *grossus denarius* (groat) is introduced and is worth several pennies. Meanwhile, in Germany the first silver *mark* is struck and is worth thirteen *soldii* and four denarii.

- Apprentices throughout Europe learn their respective trades by serving anywhere from two to twelve years with master craftsmen. Some of the shorter apprenticeships are baker and ropemaker, both at four years, while a goldsmith and cooper are each ten years.

1212
- Mines in England produce five hundred tons of tin; within twenty-five years, this figure rises to seven hundred tons.

1214
- Louis IX ascends to the French throne and reigns until 1270. During his rule, he issues a decree that the Paris pound is accepted currency throughout his dominions. Nevertheless, regional coins remain in circulation for another one hundred years.

1215
- The Great Council is established in England by the Magna Carta. Medieval kings and nobles begin to share administration with the new merchant class.

1227
- The German princes are victorious against the Danes at Bornhöven, opening the way for south-coast Baltic merchants to dominate northern trade.

1250
- The Hanseatic League is founded by cities on the Baltic and North Seas. This *hanse,* or commercial trade association, promotes commerce in the region and protects shipping against pirate attack. Its membership eventually rises to eighty cities, including Bremen, Cologne, Danzig, Hamburg, Lübeck, Lüneberg, Magdeburg, Reval, Riga, and Rostock. Similar organizations soon develop in northern France and the Netherlands (Hanse of the Seventeen Cities) and in England (Hanse of London).

* DENOTES CIRCA DATE

1252

- The first gold coin, known as a florin, is struck in Florence.

1272

- Edward I ascends to the English throne and rules until 1307. During his reign, London carpenters make an average daily wage of three to five *denarii*.

1300*

- The European population rises to seventy-three million people.

- There are only fifteen German towns of more than ten thousand inhabitants each. London has a population of thirty-five thousand people and is the largest English city.

- Most European households farm less than eight acres of land.

- Two successive bad harvests in France reduce the city population of Ypres by one-tenth.

- Pork is a major source of protein for peasant families. Pig herds in southern France, northern Spain, and England range in size from fifty to one thousand head.

- The average workday is from fourteen to fifteen hours in the summer and around eight hours in the winter. Most tradesmen are not allowed to work on Sundays and all high-church holy days and festivals (around one hundred a year).

- A shortage of silver leads to a corresponding dearth of coinage throughout Europe.

1303

- The *Carta Mercatoria* is issued in England. It allows merchants full freedom of trade and safe conduct as well as imposes a new schedule of customs duties.

1312

- A council of bishops in France determines the punishment of excommunication for those who take interest on transactions, as well as for rulers who allow anyone in their jurisdiction to do so.

1313

- The French city of Ypres produces 92,500 pieces of cloth annually.

1317

- In France, appeal to Salic Law officially bans women from inheriting the throne, in accordance with the general sentiment that a woman's duty is simply to offer love, patience, and obedience to her husband.

1328

- Philip VI ascends to the French throne. During his twenty-two-year reign, he undermines his nation's economy by repeatedly debasing the currency in order to help finance his war with England. Debts are paid with "black coins," then the currency is "revalued" so that income from taxes is paid in "good" money.

* Denotes Circa Date

1336-1338	• There are more than two hundred wool shops in Florence producing seventy- to eighty-thousand pieces of cloth worth 1.2 million florins.
1337	• The first English dukedom is created.
1340	• Paris has a population of approximately eighty thousand people.
1349	• The Black Death (1347–1351) and accompanying decrease in population disrupts production and exerts an upward pressure on wages and prices throughout Europe. In England, Edward III issues a proclamation concerning the laborers of his realm. This ordinance imposes wage and price ceilings as well as defines the terms of service for various workers.
1350	• Bruges, in present-day Belgium, spreads well outside its early walled jurisdiction, with an estimated population of forty-six thousand and a huge cloth market to which foreign traders crowd.

* DENOTES CIRCA DATE

A Crusader galley being loaded; illumination from a fourteenth-century manuscript (Bibliothèque Nationale, Paris)

OVERVIEW

Emerging Stability. In Europe several centuries of unsettled conditions and regress followed closely upon the collapse of the Roman Imperial civilization (476) in the Mediterranean basin. The so-called Dark Ages (500–850) were a time of tribal migrations into central and western Europe. Over the course of the ensuing period between 814 and 1350, no one social class system or economic form developed that could be used to describe Europe as a whole. Despite the perspective of Adam Smith and others of the eighteenth century who saw in "the disorders" of the medieval period obstacles to progress toward national prosperity, the Middle Ages as a whole laid the foundation for the rise of Europe to its later economic predominance in the world. Admittedly, since the economy of medieval Europe did not become fully urban, its actual progress was slow, but some major transformations were taking place with the shift in European economic activity from the south to the north and from the east to the west.

Causes of Change. The foremost example of a new socioeconomic system with far-reaching consequences was European medieval feudalism. What available evidence there is of its impact consists of archaeological finds of technical transformations in medieval agriculture and military practice, and a written collection of heterogeneous documents. The feudal system has become the foremost example of an interrelationship between a social class system and an economy and was, perhaps along with urban growth, the single most important factor for all aspects of the economic development of medieval Europe. Most economic historians of the Middle Ages would consider it amiss, however, not to note as a contributing cause the "rise" of a European merchant class, that is, enough traders to influence contemporary political and fiscal entities.

Rural Production. At first, earning a living during the Middle Ages was limited to "those who worked" (peasants) and "those who fought" (knights). The overwhelming majority of the medieval population lived directly from the countryside, and to earn their livelihood, peasants simply worked from sunrise to sunset, fueling economic growth through society's dependence on agricultural products. Between 814 and 1350 a gradual improvement in farming technology took place, with a new horse collar, rigid yet padded so the animal would not strangle itself when pull-ing with force, and a plow heavy enough to turn the soils of northern Europe. Food production became easily the largest and most productive sector of the economy.

Land Distribution. Agricultural production was shaped by the feudal system of land ownership and distribution and a general lack of interest of the nobility in the technical aspects of planting and harvesting. In much of Europe the main system of land ownership was seigneurialism, wherein a lord, or seigneur, formally owned the land, which peasants had the responsibility of working. The economic viability of the lord-peasant social stratification depended, however, upon land distribution originating in grants of usufruct, or "land-use" made by a most powerful lord to his loyal military supporters, who became his vassals. The lord-vassal relationship was elaborated and adapted in many ways. For example, by the eleventh century, some vassals subdivided their lands and acquired the military services of their subvassals. Through an economic relationship with a vassal, serfs farmed the lord's land in exchange for his protection and some return from farming for themselves.

Rural Economic Prosperity. Often those of the lesser nobility, most notably mere knights, never became full-fledged landowners like their lords, the princes, or dukes but remained their lord's vassals for most of their lives. Nonetheless, throughout much of the Middle Ages, the knight was commonly also a "lord," as "resident user" of land, whose agricultural return gave him the means to meet his military obligations to his lord. The vassal controlled the peasants as serfs bound to the land through his management. Once agricultural surplus came into existence, lord and vassal turned to the marketing of agricultural products. As for the peasant only if he or she were to surpass the expectations of his or her servile status and obtain full or partial freedom, or manumission, from the lord would he or she gain any amount of control over personal economic prosperity. One indication of this is found in medieval peasants' clothing, which, unlike that of the urban dwellers, varied little throughout the whole of the Middle Ages and gave the peasantry a characteristic appearance.

Typology of the Merchant Economy. Two types of economies came into being and developed over the course of the medieval period, the emerging merchant economy and the feudal one. Though much smaller in terms of numbers involved, mercantile exchange was by far the more conspicuous area of economic activity, if only because the general attitude of medieval merchants toward their trade seems to have been their eagerness to practice it. Mercantile activity involved a livelihood dependent upon having a product to sell and a buyer to purchase. Towns took advantage of their concentrations of population to provide ready markets and their achievement of self-government to offer secure fairs. The medieval fair was a wholesalers' gathering organized at a specially determined market area along a major trade route, with trading in specific goods permitted and protected for a fixed number of days. In a fair cycle each participating town would, during its period, attract buyers and sellers from all over Europe.

Urban Socioeconomic Environment. The most important sociopolitical achievement of the medieval period was the creation of communes, urban environments comparatively free of domination by the rural nobility. Like all land in the Middle Ages, most towns were part of the feudal system, and their location and inhabitants were originally controlled by kings or nobles. With their land freed from noble ownership, town or city dwellers became part of a new social organization and began defining themselves as Europe's middle class. By 1100 peasants could escape to urban communes and, in living there for a year and a day, obtain freedom as any other citizen or burgher from land and lord. Free urbanites were to have a tremendous influence on European history.

Political Limitations. The political fragmentation of medieval society into independent entities of varying sizes no doubt is a partial explanation for the slowness of economic change throughout the countryside and town. Political divisiveness created problems for the medieval trader. Few strong political and fiscal entities existed to facilitate trade. Traders of any era preferred to use money—whether in selling or buying—since exchanges with money are generally less cumbersome than those in which both parties bring goods to the transaction. Few coins in the Middle Ages, however, had consistent metal content and were therefore not acceptable as a standard of value outside the territory of their minting authority.

Merchants' Responses. There were medieval regions that failed to become politically united and thus fostered little economic growth. Medieval merchants thought unifying different lands and peoples under a central political authority was the best way to establish the necessary pan-European infrastructure for trade. Sensing that adherence to law might well be a precondition to the growth of trade, merchants favored a political power that could set up a code of laws for everyone in the land, the larger in size the better. Some groups of merchants simply took matters of creating a hospitable environment for trade within different lands into their own hands, creating merchant guilds and trading leagues.

Methods of Economic Investment. If economic survival was the medieval trader's basic purpose, gathering wealth was his next priority. One important principle was asking a just price in relation to the demand and need for the available goods. Another feature of the merchant's economy was the contract that generally afforded financial support to a trading venture. For example, the *columna* contract of eleventh-century southern Italy created a partnership between merchants, seamen, and shipowners, whereby a venture's final gains and losses would be shared according to the value of each partner's initial contribution. Yet, other practices were to flourish both as a result of the increase in trade and medieval money use: moneylending and currency exchange.

Transactions Based on Production. Medieval commercial trading came about before commercial production, but the latter was not far behind. Two economic transactions dominated the medieval production sphere: the selling of produced goods and services and the procuring of the raw materials used to produce those goods. Selling services based on one's training was also a viable way to make a living in the Middle Ages. One archetypal medieval situation that derived from the payment-for-service-rendered relationship was that of the medieval artisan whose work was made possible by patronage.

Guilds. The guilds of merchants and tradesmen were established to preserve the strength, proficiency, and dedication of the merchant or craftsman to his demanding tasks. As well as their attention to set hours, conditions, and standards of work, guild rules reflect a further moral perspective: recognition that as a guild member one was part of a community of like merchants or craftsmen. An artisan who sold his goods at a higher-than-allowed price was fined and publicly humiliated. In keeping the number of artisans and the number of products available for purchase artificially low at times, however, guilds caused prices to rise and frequently to remain far higher for longer than otherwise would have been the case. It was obvious sometimes that neither the guild collective nor the individual artisan was acting out of a desire to live up to high ideals of requisite remuneration for work of excellent quality. Thus, over time, urban artisans came under criticism for the economically sheltered life they could lead as members of guilds, which seemed to place wealth and power ahead of production quality and commercial leadership.

Social Limits on Economic Change. In the Middle Ages social stratification played as much a part in determining the economics of the time as being determined by it. In the case of the clergy of the monasteries, the notion of social stratification itself was an anathema, but as the organization of the church grew during the Middle Ages, so too did the stratification of its clergy. Medieval social stratification derived initially directly from the earliest means of survival of European medieval peoples, migratory warfare, when most of the land's resources were the rewards of fighting. Among the laity, gender continued to play a large part in social stratification, and only occasionally were even noblewomen raised for power and subsequently allowed to assume it. In some parts of Europe, the peasant who wanted to innovate ended up being more constrained by fellow peasants than by the landlord.

Collective Work. The peasants' labor was fundamentally physical and hard, but some agricultural innovations, such as crop-rotation techniques, helped to shape a collective approach to work in the fields. The medieval peasant lived within a cluster of small houses in a village, often with its own church, blacksmith's shop, and mill (all of which were owned by the lord of the land), and village traditions determined when and how all the fields would be planted and the work divvied up. The life of the monk in a monastery differed little from that of the peasant farmer in the activities by which he maintained his livelihood. Since, however, monks prayed as well as worked together in their monasteries, the daily schedule of the monk was much more ordered than that of the village peasant. This fact is perhaps one of the reasons that monastic farms were considered to have been the best in medieval Europe.

Urban Social Stratification. The urban environment with its many social organizations reflected blatant social stratification. Apprentices held a low position in the craft social hierarchy because of their age and lack of training. Only upon completion of his training as an apprentice would a medieval craftsman become a worker who was paid by the day (*journée* in French), a journeyman. Of all the medieval service professions, medicine was among the most lucrative and for a physician with good fortune and presumed skill, the best of employers, a lord. Traveling from town to town along specific trade routes was characteristic of many medieval traders, but in the social hierarchy of merchants, the highest place was held by the rich and powerful sedentary urban "middlemen" exchanging across or through the Mediterranean or Baltic Seas, east and west, north and south.

Christian Society and Economy. The economic life of the Middle Ages was connected to the institution of the Christian Church in many subtle ways that became almost completely exposed by the end of the era. Throughout the Middle Ages, both the monastic and the secular clerical Church institutions differentiated themselves markedly from the rest of medieval social structure. Without a prominent urban economic base, however, the Church preserved its early rural and feudal economic practices; in this respect it has retained the characteristics of the early medieval feudal period throughout its economic history. In addition to "those who worked" and "those who fought," the changing medieval economy nonetheless continued to envelope "those who prayed." In the early Middle Ages (814–1150) most economic transactions could be carried out without heavy monetary investment, and although the monastic economic ideal was agricultural self-sufficiency, early medieval parish clerics obtained a subsistence benefice from the church through donations from lay believers. In time, however, the urban environment with its administrative loci and a centralizing religious life demanded a more advanced

fiscal economy beyond the scope of earlier theological interpretations of work, profit, risk, and usury. The Franciscans and the Dominicans, medieval fraternal orders new in the thirteenth century, served as models for an entirely different urban economic existence. Mendicancy represented a church at no time, perhaps, more critical of the economic life of the artisan and merchant than during the Middle Ages.

Modern Model. Economists today do not think twice about arguing that all modern social relations have an economic base. It is not difficult to apply this assertion to the medieval period as well. Most medieval economic relations were in some sense contractual. One party was the landowner, craftsman, or merchant; the other was the vassal, peasant, or apprentice. In a quick review of the type of social organizations that medieval culture enveloped, one might, however, ask if the economic relationships between individuals are all they represented.

Feudal Economic Determinism. The establishment of a new order of monks at Cluny in Burgundy, France, in 910 exemplified the agriculturally self-sufficient medieval monastery. Indeed, the new agricultural commune liberated the monastery from the secular church, allowing it to become a sustained source of austerity. It strengthened the monastic rule by de-emphasizing wealth, property ownership, and economic transactions—characteristics that had come to be recognized as distractions to the Benedictines' pursuit of the religious life. Yet, was maintenance of a community of strict celibates an important economic goal when manpower was limited and work hard? King Henry II of England's official introduction of scutage in 1159 monetarized vassalage with the rendering of a vassal's obligation for service by paying money instead of fighting in wars. Although feudalism continued to entail the necessity for knights to provide offensive and defensive military service, with the monetarization of the medieval economy, the means to pay mercenaries rather than the personal participation of vassals was to be the key to a king's organizing an army. Nevertheless, why, from an economic point of view, would a knight of the feudal manorial system prefer to pass on the possible further returns of war, not to mention the glories of battle?

Urban Economic Determinism. By 1100 peasants could escape to the urban communes and, in living there for a year and a day, obtain freedom from land and lord. The new urban commune was based, however, on artisan rather than agricultural production, on activities that would bring artisans into professions of manufacture and commerce, through undertakings increasingly other than the ones life among the peasantry had prepared them for, such as stained-glass making, barbering, and goldsmithing. Was a year and a day the time it took for a peasant to acquire economic stability in the new urban environment? Why have the economic aspects of the Magna Carta, or Great Charter, which King John was forced by the nobles and high clergy of England to sign in 1215, which deal with transformations of the taxation powers of the English monarch become overshadowed by its seeds of democratic political principles? As early as the mid twelfth century, medieval craftsmen had to create a masterpiece to become members of their professional guilds, but was it exclusively economic criteria that hailed a pinner's one thousand pins a masterpiece; or a shoemaker's pair of boots, three pairs of shoes, and a pair of slippers; or a butcher's dressing of the carcasses of a cow, a calf, a sheep, and a pig?

Political Economic Determinism. In 1250 the cities along the Baltic and North Seas formed the Hanseatic League to protect against pirates and strengthen trade, but why over time did the leadership of their alliance in trade pass from merchants to lawyers? In 1312 a council of bishops in France determined the punishment of excommunication for those who took interest on transactions, as well as for rulers who allowed anyone in their jurisdiction to do so, but why was the medieval church concerned about interest-bearing exchange in the first place? In 1085–1086 King William the Conqueror of England had the *Domesday Book* compiled, and while it seemed to be intended to

include all the information the king needed to determine the taxable capacity of his kingdom, the 109,000 Anglo-Norman *villains*, those who owned a pair of oxen and thirty to fifty acres of land, were grouped not only with the 90,000 *cotters* and *bordars*, the peasants who had no plow team and only a cottage and garden and perhaps five acres or so of land, but most surprisingly as well with bondsmen or slaves numbering 25,000 thousand!

Explanations. Medieval social structure was clearly not the simple product of medieval economic values or practices. It was, however, the beneficiary and often the catalyst. The amount of new land brought into cultivation was significant enough to allow for the population to double, if not triple, and, as did their general economic condition, their absolute numbers increased. A food supply was available to feed town populations. Whether in agriculture, trade, or commercial production, all people were the players who from 1000 and 1300 enjoyed together a spurt of economic growth and prosperity.

TOPICS IN SOCIAL CLASS SYSTEM AND THE ECONOMY

CLERGY

Regular Clergy. The life of the monk in a monastery differed little from that of the peasant farmer in the activities by which he maintained his livelihood. Both worked hard in the fields, clearing land and farming. The monk's religious vocation meant, however, that the same tasks were seen to be directed to a particular end or purpose, the service of God. Unlike the aphysical ascetic lifestyle that eastern monks took on, western monks stressed the spiritual value of physical work. Western monks or "regular" clergy followed a set of regulations known as the Rule, a pragmatic articulation of the habits that would keep monastic communities alive.

Daily Schedule. The daily schedule of the monk was much more ordered than that of the village peasant, one of the reasons perhaps that monastic farms were considered to have been the best in medieval Europe. Benedict of Nursia had set up life in his own monastery at Monte Cassino according to a Rule whereby the monks could devote their lives to both work and prayer. The Benedictine Rule provided, in the twenty-four-hour day, for eight hours of

work, eight hours of sleep, and eight hours of devotion, reading, meditation and meals. According to the Rule, monks were to be educated so they could help themselves in their Christian studies, and each day began with collective prayer and study at dawn. In the morning the monks were found in prayer, at a general meeting, and at work for the two hours before midday. The strict schedule continued into the afternoon with lunch, study, work, and prayer until dinner at dusk. One evening hour was reserved for further prayer with bedtime following dusk by only two and a half hours.

Austerity. Benedictines thus worked and prayed together in their monasteries. For nuns the schedule was similar to that for monks of the same order, dedicated to prayer, study, and the exercise of sustenance skills, including spinning. However grueling the awakening at around 3:00 A.M. for nocturnes and again for prime at around 6:00 A.M., six unequal hours before noon, those acts, like virtually every one of the monk's and nun's schedule, repeated daily, became almost automatic. Monks had two meals a day in the monastery, and neither the food nor utensils

Dominican monks in an attitude of contemplation before a bleeding crucifix; illumination from *De Novem Modis Orandi,* Codex Rossianus, circa 1300 (Vatican Library)

were luxurious. Eggs, fish or fowl, bread, vegetables, and a little fruit made up their main diet. There was no red meat. Their clothing consisted of long loose robes of coarse material, with hoods to cover their heads.

Monastery. A monastery, the home of the monks, was a collection of specialized buildings. There was the dormitory where the monks slept on hard cots, special separate cells where they studied and thought, the refectory where they ate, and the chapter house where they discussed monastery business. Other buildings that comprised the monastery included a kitchen, bakery, brewery, workshops, storehouses, and a hospital. Posterity has been fortunate to have had preserved the actual plan of an ideal monastery, dating from the ninth century. The plan, ostensibly drawn up for the rebuilding of the monastery of Saint-Gall, consists of a series of architectural drawings to scale with explanatory legends, which did indeed guide the construction of numerous monasteries of the period, most notably Corbie, which in 852 housed 150 monks, fed another 150 widows, and gave lodging to 300 guests daily.

Secular Clergy. The local priest was not really a common member of the rural community until after 1000, when Western Europe was divided into parishes with defined territories and local churches were a part of the rural landscape. His role was to represent the church at the local religious center, the parish church or chapel, where he administered the sacraments and blessings of the Christian calendar. Probably of peasant origin and poorly educated, the local priest took his part alongside the peasantry in

some farming tasks. In his role as priest, however, he daily said mass and had prayer several times, all in Latin. He usually preached in the vernacular; however, he taught the local parishioners to memorize the Lord's Prayer and the Nicene or Apostles' Creed in Latin. The remuneration that allowed him to pursue his usual tasks was the percentage of tithes, compulsory donations to the church, which was permitted to stay with him locally, and the fees which were charged for special services such as baptisms.

Sources:

Marc Bloch, *Feudal Society* (Chicago: University of Chicago Press, 1961).

G. G. Coulton, *Medieval Village, Manor, and Monastery* (New York: Harper, 1960).

Georges Duby, *The Three Orders: Feudal Society Imagined,* translated by Arthur Goldhammer (Chicago: University of Chicago Press, 1980).

M. M. Postan, E. E. Rich, and Edward Miller, eds., *The Cambridge Economic History of Europe* (Cambridge: Cambridge University Press, 1965).

COMMERCIAL PRODUCTION: INTERACTION AMONG PEOPLES

Vikings. In the early Middle Ages, when the agricultural sphere was dominated by the manor system, there was little chance for local producers to have contact with people outside their village. There were, nonetheless, examples of fine craftsmanship both within and without the European rural economy. The Vikings provide perhaps the best example of early European medieval craftsmanship. They made many beautiful objects from gold, silver, and stone, such as bracelets, sword hilts, and even ship decorations. Not until the Vikings became the sedentary peoples of

Britain, Normandy, and part of present-day Russia, however, were these products more than fleetingly glimpsed by the continental peoples.

Non-European Goods. Of course, foreign-trade goods made their way into the growing trade centers of medieval Europe. Despite their efforts, the guilds were frequently not well enough integrated to place total limits on the sale of foreign goods. Thus, local markets were a site where craftsmen might encounter the products of other peoples and lands. Undoubtedly, during the week of the fair when the city would attract the attendance of buyers and sellers from all over Europe, such exposure could hardly be avoided.

Traveling Journeyman. In yet another way, however, the impact of different craft practices filtered into medieval Europe. Once a young worker had served an apprenticeship under a craft master, he became a journeyman. Of all artisans, the journeyman had the greatest opportunity to interact with peoples from different regions. Frequently, he moved through a series of different "household" settings, working in each under the master there. During this time a journeyman was to master the craft completely. Journeymen and the few other craftsmen who traveled were among the relative few of local medieval craft societies who came into stimulating contact with people and ideas of different regions.

Crossroads. Throughout the Middle Ages, trading and commercial production went together. Goods produced in one area were in demand in another, which meant that the existence of production in one location frequently amounted to the amassing of much wealth for that town or city by artisans, merchants, and urban dwellers alike. During the 1100s and 1200s the community of merchants made the business, which grew of the new contacts between Europe and the Middle East, no accident. Slowly by land, sea, and rivers, merchants began creating a long-distance demand for products of the new economy of the West. Trade fostered wine production in France, timber and iron-ore extraction in Germany, and hunting and fur-procuring in Scandinavia. Florentine merchants built such a trade around Florentine cloth manufacturers that together they made of Florence on the Arno River, not even on the sea, a worldwide cloth-manufacturing and marketing center, as well as one of the first banking centers in medieval Europe. As merchants represented Florentine wares in many lands in and beyond Europe, Florence became rich and powerful, benefiting particularly in the middle of the fourteenth century from the doubling of prices and craft wages.

Importance of Craftsmen. The importance of craftsmen to Europe's economic and social development was immense. The variety of natural and human-created conditions for the craft environment in Europe, combined with the prevalence of villages and towns deriving from agriculture and trade, made the Middle Ages a highly active period for craft production. In the towns the peasants' skills of weaving and other jobs helped build commerce. The growth of trade and industry led to the rise of the new merchant and artisan classes from the 1100s to the 1400s. With city administrators, such as Siena's city council, offering tax and other incentives to attract newcomers,

Charter of Richard I for the burgesses of Exeter, granting merchants freedom from tolls in Rouen, 24 March 1190 (Exeter City Archives)

many people left the farms and manors and moved to the cities to find new work. The number of skilled crafts workers living in the cities grew steadily, and the few workers left farming the land could demand wages of the large landowners who needed their labor. Craftsmen, like merchants, never fit into the feudal system, the predominant economic system of the early Middle Ages. Thus, when European medieval society entered a time of difficulty about 1300 and was already undergoing monetarization, commercial craft production initially through the strength of its guild institutions was to thrive on the gradual changes away from the feudal economy. As the late Middle Ages drew to a close, the guild declined in power and influence, but craftsmen were nonetheless able effectively to survive and increase based alone on their production of goods and providing of services.

Sources:
Prosper Boissonade, *Life and Work in Medieval Europe* (New York: Harper & Row, 1964).

Steven A. Epstein, *Wage Labor and Guilds in Medieval Europe* (Chapel Hill: University of North Carolina Press, 1991).

Joseph Gies and Frances Gies, *Life in a Medieval City* (New York: Harper & Row, 1981).

O. F. Hamouda and B. B. Price, "The Justice of the Just Price," *European Journal of the History of Economic Thought*, 4 (1997): 191–216.

Robert S. Lopez, *The Commercial Revolution of the Middle Ages, 900–1350* (Englewood Cliffs, N.J.: Prentice-Hall, 1971).

First Fruits. As it is in modern society, production activity in the Middle Ages was directed to the end of creating a product. It was not, however, always the case that a produced item would be sold. Most of the medieval population, the massive peasantry, never did acquire skills for commercial production purposes. Homemade goods were in the earlier Middle Ages most frequently produced for home use and not for commercial transactions. Production was undertaken simply as part of one's social position both within and without the family. Since, however, medieval society depended more on local than long-distance exchange, any goods that were surplus to a household, modest or wealthy, did circulate, if not strictly speaking for commerce, by barter, gifting, or in payment of taxes or debts. Given the inherent shortages in the medieval economy, virtually any item produced could, if its owner desired, make its way into the market.

Production. Commercial production was, however, a part of the medieval economy as well and, just as mercantile exchange, an activity by which one earned part or the whole of one's livelihood. Medieval farmers, for example, who came to town and exchanged their goods with those of the townsmen, were engaged in part in earning a living from the commercial production of agricultural products. The medieval peasant carpenter or spinner might also have lived in part by farming, in part by practicing his or her skilled trade. Most urban medieval craftsmen, however, lived almost exclusively by selling manufactured goods for barter or money. The rural blacksmith or the fine-metal smiths who settled in the medieval towns would be examples of those who lived by trading goods they had produced, goods whose manufacture requires a specific skill or "art," such as horseshoes and broaches.

Trading. Commercial trading came about before commercial production. The former was necessary for the few goods, such as salt and iron, which had to be secured outside the village. Many of those who traded exclusively for a living, especially those whose livelihood derived from rare goods, came into towns at fair time and were not a constant presence in the local region. Local producers were the main, regular traders in a town. While producers in the urban environment traded from the front of their shops, the earliest and busiest of urban trading places was the market. Part of the normal routine of a town, the market was the highlight of the week. Most towns had market days once or twice weekly, which is when the farmers would come to town and exchange their goods with those of the townsmen. Farmers usually sold their surplus at the most local markets, but by 1300 peasant women were bringing eggs and produce to market towns as much as twelve miles away from their villages.

Economic Transactions. Two economic transactions dominated the medieval production sphere: the selling of produced goods and services, and the procuring of the raw materials used to produce those goods. The trade component to commercial production was what first made it a viable medieval activity. Predominantly providing self-employment, a craftsman was both artisan and shopkeeper, living and working in the same building. Although a craftsman's house could range in height from two to sometimes six stories, the ground floor at street level was of the greatest economic importance. It was where artisans sold directly to their customers with the help perhaps of the artisan's wife

A coin die from England, circa 915 (York Archaeological Trust)

and maybe a relative to attract the buyer. In this setting for the economic transaction of a sale of goods, the producer's role differed superficially little from any merchant's.

Selling Services. Selling services based on one's training was also a viable way to make a living in the Middle Ages. Although many of the service providers were professionals, as, for example, notaries, advocates, or doctors, the model for their method of economic survival was the craftsman. The sale of a commercially produced item had originally borne much greater resemblance to the rendering of a service than to the sale of a good. In an example from the tenth century, a weaver received wool from a textile merchant, and when the cloth was woven, it was supplied to the merchant in return for a wage. This type of economic transaction, which allowed for those who were providing a service to survive in the Middle Ages, was quite different from the standard exchange involving the purchase and sale of produced goods. In the case of a service rendered, one of three possible things was actually being remunerated: a duty's having been carried out or a task performed such that a product was realized and supplied; the expertise of the individual supplying the service; or the time/labor of the one providing the service.

Patronage. One archetypal medieval situation that derived from the payment-for-service-rendered relationship was that of the medieval artisan whose work was made possible by patronage. Rich people who wanted to beautify their homes and churches supported financially the artists, sculptors, and painters of the day. With this backing, these craftsmen could devote all their time to artistic endeavors. The same relationship existed in the Middle Ages between teachers, writers, and master builders or architects, and their supporters. Patronage is prominently linked to the artistic production of the Renaissance era, but kings and queens, wealthy merchants, Italian patricians, and rich noble families of the Middle Ages became important patrons of the arts. King Louis IX of France gave so much financial encouragement to learning, arts, and architecture that his reign has been called "the Golden Age" of medieval France.

Guild Regulations. In an age when economic laws were few and thieves plentiful, many an honest artisan had reason to bless the power of the guild and its regulations for assuring him a welcome at the town market or on his speciality's street, where he could find respect for his wares, a guaranteed return, and safety from theft and exploitation. The craft masters, the actual guild members, were all highly skilled in their trades. Therefore, as long as the guild could be assured of the sustained quality of their production, it felt it could also regulate the prices for the goods they sold and/or the wages they were paid for services rendered. Thus, guilds set standards of work and checked their artisans' products to make sure they were of a high quality. An artisan who sold goods of poor quality would be fined and forced to spend time in the stocks at the marketplace.

Guild Manipulation. Although an artisan who sold his goods at a higher-than-allowed price would also be fined and publicly humiliated, it was obvious sometimes that neither the guild collective nor the individual artisan was acting out of a desire to live up to high ideals of requisite remuneration for work of excellent quality. Guilds saw as one of their main goals to protect the price of their goods and their commerce in the towns. Guilds regulated the numbers of individuals who could be engaged in any trade. Of course, guilds were simply manipulating the economic principle of supply and demand in price determination. The price of manufactures was dependent on the number of products available for purchase, and hence on the number of craftsmen producing them.

Price Determination. In keeping the number of artisans and the number of products available for purchase artificially low at times, guilds caused prices to rise and frequently to remain far higher for longer than otherwise would have been the case. Whenever, during the Middle Ages, the production of goods decreased, such as during the Black Death (1347–1351), when population dropped generally and many craftsmen died, prices rose. They rose markedly, if at the same time, trade into the same markets also declined, since goods that might have substituted for the missing production were also not available. A guild, by holding effectively a monopoly, in the name of the quality of its artisans could reap major economic advantages for its members. Guilds, which functioned by their own rules, frequently found themselves, however, in the position of having to resolve disputes, some of which derived from their placing limits on foreign artisans and products.

Independence of Guilds. Thus, over time, urban artisans came under criticism for the economically sheltered life they could lead as members of guilds, which seemed to place wealth and power ahead of production quality and commercial leadership. Guilds afforded them this luxury in that they established their own rules and judgments to handle internal guild disputes and turned to the town courts to settle commercial disagreements, some of which derived from the merchants responsible for supplying raw materials to artisans or for buying their wares for resale. For most of the Middle Ages guilds played an important role in organizing the new economic and social life of the medieval townsman, but the increasing importance of money changed the guild system. The old personal relationship of a master with his craftsmen-in-training, the journeyman and apprentice, often gave way to a relationship based on cash wages. After the period of the Black Death, the shortage of workers in towns led to a definitive appeal to substantial craft wages. Free peasants moved openly to the towns, where wages were high; serfs fled there secretly. Guilds had less power as production grew in scale and at the hands of wage laborers.

Church and Artisan. The church played a critical role in the commercial life of the artisan. Artisan and customer sold and bought in a single transaction together, which according to church law had to follow a set of moral regulations summed up in the "just price." The necessary steps to transforming a good from a raw to a processed form were thought by medieval intellectuals to make the end product justifiably more expensive: wine, for example, had invested labor in it that grapes themselves did not; raw materials had a cost; and craftspeople had to purchase tools to create end products. On the other hand, a producer ought not price his product so high that his would-be customer could not afford the item and thus not have his need for it met. Purchases for most people in the Middle Ages meant stretching one's means as best one could and, with the prices of medieval manufactures dependent on the number of craftsmen and traders in any locale, when prices rose markedly, one simply had to go without. Of course, the laws of supply and demand, however artificially manipulated, could not be completely counteracted by church teaching, and the "just price" remained more of an intellectual exercise for medieval scholastics than a practiced method of economic exchange.

Wealth. Nonetheless, few craftsmen ever figured among the rich of the Middle Ages. Most were of modest means, from their dwellings with oilcloth-covered shuttered windows to their small back gardens that supplemented their craft incomes with garden produce and pigs and chickens. The earliest medieval measure of wealth was land, usually cultivated land, followed by forest land, villages, swamps, and finally wasteland. In the thirteenth century most medieval nobles would still have put landholdings at the top of their assets list. Money, precious metal currency, was, however, becoming more popular as a sign of wealth, especially as the development of trade, commerce, and town life continued and money was needed to buy goods and even to pay workers.

Copper Coinage. Towns became increasingly dependent upon money, not only gold or silver coinage but also copper. The latter metal was less valuable because it is easier to find, yet its lesser value was precisely the reason why tradespeople desired copper coins. They could serve as a medium of exchange for less expensive items. The average daily wage of most later medieval craft professions was quite modest: for example, for agricultural tasks in thirteenth-century Italy, about 2 denarii (silver penny = 1/240 of a pound) in the winter, 3 denarii during the summer for men and half that for women; for carpentry in England at the beginning of the fourteenth century, from 3 denarii to 5 denarii depending on the time of the year; and for wet-nurse services in thirteenth century Italy, 1/4 denarii per baby. Thus, the currency which represented a fraction of the denarius, black (copper) money, proved useful to commercial producers and their customers.

Moneylender. One artisan in particular was to flourish as a result of the increase in medieval money use: the moneylender. Fluctuation in a coinage's value was one reason for moneylending's having become a popular medieval occupation, especially if a bank treasurer or precious-metal storehouse holder could play to his advantage the fact that the apparent value of the coinage was usually ostensibly stronger than the actual value behind it. Another reason for the strength of the moneylender's occupation was that in the

interface between trade and commerce, it offered many different ways of making a profit. The symbiosis of trading and commercial production was obvious when money lent toward the nurturing of production led to favorable prices for the lender once goods were produced. In this scenario the lender would gain from the end purchaser of the product, not from the producer himself, so merchant and producer effectively worked together. One example might be Italian merchants lending to English sheep farmers in return for favorable delivery terms. A more common scenario had town moneylenders being the source of funds for landowners who needed help to get money for goods and wage payments.

Money Wages. From kings, noblemen and women, merchants, and peasants, money began to circulate into the hands of artisans in the form of payment for goods or as wages for service. The increase in the number of large-scale industries after 1200 was a sure indication that money use was on the rise in the Middle Ages in the artisans' sphere. Both large-scale commercial production and the long-distance trade that fostered it required large amounts of capital investment. Textile production and ore mining are two examples of large-scale commercial production with some characteristics of capital intensity, if only in their wage bills. The Italian city of Milan had a workforce of sixty thousand when it started fine-cloth production around 1100, although it was the only prominent fine-textile production center in southern Europe until the next century. Between 1212 and 1237 tin mining in England rose from five hundred to seven hundred long tons. In the thirteenth century, twelve textile cities and towns, among them Ypres, were a part of the sought-after production of Flanders (present-day Belgium); and by 1313 Ypres alone was producing 92,500 pieces of cloth annually, a total rivaling that of Florence with its workforce of thirty thousand.

Sources:
John W. Baldwin, *The Medieval Theories of the Just Price* (Philadelphia: American Philosophical Society, 1959).

Robert H. Bautier, *The Economic Development of Medieval Europe* (London: Thames & Hudson, 1971).

Thomas N. Bisson, *Conservation of Coinage: Monetary Exploitation and its Restraint in France, Catalonia, and Aragon, c.A.D.1000–c.1225* (Oxford: Clarendon Press, 1979).

Robert S. Lopez, *The Shape of Medieval Monetary History* (London: Variorum, 1986).

Norman J. G. Pounds, *An Economic History of Medieval Europe* (London & New York: Longman, 1974).

COMMERCIAL PRODUCTION: OCCUPATIONS AND WORK HABITS

Marketing. During the Middle Ages, trade and commercial production were usually undertaken by different people, except at the outset of the period. Marketed produce of agricultural origin was the first sign of either economic activity, since the sale of the surplus in essentials for survival first jump-started the medieval exchange economy. Subsequently, production of goods and rendering of skilled services became the bases of most medieval occupations, known collectively as crafts or artisan activities. A general profile of the medieval artisan is difficult to establish, however, for while his contacts outside Europe were relatively limited, the possible variations in his way of life were still broad depending on the type of craft, the location and concentration of his population group, his socioeconomic status, gender, and age.

Historiography. Just to enumerate the myriad walks of life of those involved in production in the Middle Ages is not an easy task. One way scholars attempt to determine typical production occupations of the Middle Ages is by examining medieval pictorial documents for representations of an activity that led to the manufacture, or the making, usually by hand, of a product, versus an activity pursued without apparent production goals. If someone could not write, he probably left no account of his work life, but sometimes with a picture, most often a manuscript illustration, its story has been told, at least in brief and despite the fact that most production techniques have changed dramatically since the Middle Ages. Nothing guarantees, however, that the medieval working person was accurately represented, since illustration, most commonly undertaken as an embellishment of the written word, was a particular medieval skill in itself, usually perfected by a member of the clergy or the nobility. Nonetheless, a person depicted at his task would probably have borne some resemblance to the contemporary depiction, and although he might not have had any part in its representation, in knowing how to go about his craft, he at least presented an accurate model to the artist of the painting.

Visual Images. One might expect the illustrations of medieval craftsmen to be less than obvious as to the trade, since of the crafts with a commercial component, only farriery or blacksmithing from the rural sphere and prostitution and beggary in the urban areas are still conducted as they were in the Middle Ages. Nonetheless, candle makers, saddle makers, or shoemakers at work would presumably still be recognizable as such. Glassblowing, masonry, and sculpture were also clearly illustrated medieval artisan activities. Often grouped together in a single image, various crafts were connected to medieval textile production: spinning, weaving, dyeing, sewing, tailoring, millinery work, and embroidery. Of course, there were also the undisguisable public hairdressers, the first opening for business in Spain in 840.

Products. Yet another detective route to posit the variety of medieval producers has been to enumerate the known products of the time. Who raised the British wool, wove the Flemish and Italian textiles, smithed the prized armor, jewelry, and religious metal objects for the churches and cathedrals? This approach is also a potentially informative method for deriving the multitude of services that medieval artisans provided. Medieval learning and art were the products of teachers and artists. The self-employed teacher conducted classes in front of groups of students; the court painter executed frescoes or decorative wooden panels. A slow and ultimately expensive process, the copying of certain manuscripts was painstakingly and efficiently carried out by scribes for hire in booksellers' shops, particularly in university towns and cities. In the early fourteenth century, nine doctors, for example, lived and practiced in Carcassone, along with sixty-three notaries and fifteen advocates; in Florence, there were sixty doctors and eighty moneychangers. Although the back-garden pig remained the most effective town garbage collector, a human undertaker of the task also existed in the Middle Ages. Through his services, town litter and refuse, which were usually just dumped into the street, were cleaned up as often as once a week.

Rural and Urban Producers. Given its variety, medieval craft activity necessarily split into different ways of life, at least into that of the rural craftsman and that of the urban artisan. The rural peasantry emphasized crop and animal production that entailed hard physical labor. A boost in their standard of living came to them through work of the land and permission from their rich or generous lords to sell their surplus goods. The early medieval agricultural economy was not designed to allow for the agricultural surpluses of individual peasant families to be sold directly by them, but over time so many lords gave that right to their peasantry, often in return for rent or monetary payments for land use, that for the last centuries of the Middle Ages, agricultural surplus was effectively being sold by all order of peasants: serfs, villains, aldus, tenant farmers, and anyone licensed to sell produce at a local market. What had begun as the landowner's acknowledgment to a peasant, that his obligations could be fulfilled through his labor and a portion of his own yield less than his own surplus, led to farm produce being regularly for sale. This development was a welcome sign to any town or city dweller who procured it. With carpenters and blacksmiths as the main exceptions, the medieval population, the massive peasantry, never did acquire a skill for commercial purposes, but once surpluses could be sold publicly, this lack was not as much of an impediment then as it would be today. Piers the Plowman lamented he could not be Piers the Businessman, for had he the crop, he would have brought new "corn" to market and there bought pullets, geese, and piglets.

Occupations. In urban areas craftsmen of all sorts were well represented: shoemakers, tailors, candle makers, carpenters, blacksmiths, goldsmiths, glassmakers, and so forth. Their absolute numbers were higher in urban than in rural areas. Those individuals dedicated to earning a living by their craft tended to settle in towns, each with his whole household, and to sell goods and/or skills for barter or money. Studies show that approximately four-fifths of the inhabitants of most towns and cities were involved in the production of goods and other services by the fourteenth century, with, in northern Europe and Italy, the highest percentage in textile production. The increase in urban populations along the Northern and Italian coasts was, however, more rapid than in the balance of Europe, and the reason for this is largely what is reflected in the overwhelming number of workers dedicated to a single area of production.

WAGE LABOR

The following is a list of the wages that London carpenters could earn during the reign of Edward I (1272–1307):

Time of Year	Wage
St. Michael-St. Martin (29 September–11 November)	4d. or 1-1/2d. and table
St. Martin-Candlemas (11 November–2 February)	3d. or 1d. and table
Candlemas-Easter (2 February–Easter)	4d. or 1-1/2d. and table
Easter-St. Michael (Easter–29 September)	5d. or 2-1/2d and table

Source: Steven A. Epstein, *Wage Labor and Guilds in Medieval Europe* (Chapel Hill: University of North Carolina Press, 1991).

Enhancement to Family Income. Since through sales and payment for service, medieval craftwork was initially an enhancement to a family's income, it is not surprising that artisan activity continued to be more attractive among the lower social classes than it was among the wealthy. The noble male with his preoccupying acquisition of the skills of knighthood, horsemanship, and weaponry is somewhat of an exception to this generalization, representing another form of commercial "production" in the Middle Ages, the rendering of a service with accomplished skills. The females of wealthier families who learned artisan skills, most notably spinning and weaving, exemplify better the distinction between the craft involvement of the wealthy and those of lesser means, since wealthy women rarely deemed either "distaff" skill to be perfected to a business end. Free but poorer women and men availed themselves of access to virtually all types of day-labor employment. Those people who made it through the lower ranks of training in any variety of craft guilds could remain in someone else's steady employ throughout their lives, even if they could not save enough money to establish their own business.

Women and Artisanal Work. Although when they did commercial work, women as well as men were the artisans, the variation in type and scale of production throughout Europe predominantly based on the area and its local raw materials, which affected the role of specific genders in a craft. Most craft associations or guilds did not allow women to join, and in any case they could choose only among limited options for training. They might be apprenticed in another household to learn domestic skills, but some did receive employment training in the hairdressing trade or a textile craft. Where the making of thread and cloth were undertaken primarily for personal use, such as in Britain, women were most frequently the spinners and weavers. In Flanders, where for several centuries weaving cloth from the surplus of British raw wool production had been a commercial enterprise, men, however, became the expert textile workers. Nonetheless, true to Geoffrey Chau-

cer's characterization that "deceit, weeping and spinning" were traditional women's skills, in late medieval England many women were also commercial textile workers. In the fourteenth century, a city such as Florence had thirty thousand workers, male and female, in its two hundred textile shops.

Children's Work. Children as well as adults were skilled craft workers, although many towns did have laws that disallowed children from working in certain crafts. For peasant children, learning a skill other than farming was not necessary nor even permitted for their future livelihood. Occupational choices were quite narrowly defined in rural areas, as they did not have the wide need of the specialized crafts of cities and larger towns, but only of those that supplied the agricultural community, such as farming, blacksmithing, and carpentry. The demands of the medieval rural economy and society meant that most children had to spend much of their time farming or helping with farm tasks. For rural children, craft training took place in the home. Boys learned agricultural skills from their fathers, and girls learned housewifery from their mothers.

Distinct Characteristic. Although the type of craft, the location and concentration of a population group, socio-economic status, gender, and age caused great variation among craftsmen, one unifying characteristic of the urban artisan was his house, not perhaps in terms of building materials but in layout. Given the craftsman's means of livelihood, urban shops and homes were often not separate. As artisan and shopkeeper, the medieval craftsman lived, worked at his craft, and sold his goods or services in his home. Virtually all town dwellings and shops were, like rural houses, built of whatever materials were handy, such as stone, brick, or little more than mud. At first, town houses were two—sometimes three—stories high. As the urban population grew, however, and as land became in short supply, they often stretched up to five or six stories, with the upper floors built seemingly precariously out over the street.

House of the Urban Artisan. A craftsman's home consisted of a living-refectory-dormitory area, where the artisan and his family lived, ate, and slept. This domicile part of the building was small, possibly containing separate bedrooms but often simply a single undivided living-sleeping room. Until the end of the Middle Ages, glass was too expensive for use in any but public buildings or the homes of the rich, so the windows of artisans' homes had shutters, with oilcloth coverings. Often there was a garden or court at the rear of an individual craftsman's house. Once again, however, as the pressure for land became intense, gardens gave way to new buildings.

Master Artisan's Shop. The house contained special rooms where the artisan worked at his craft, and in the front at street level, an area where the public could see and purchase his wares. Like craftsmen tended to settle together in the same quarter, and city streets often derived their names from artisan activities located there. The craftsman presented the "best" side of his house to the street. Its sign and largest opening, doubling as a door to the workroom and business area, defined by a pair of shutters, presented the artisan as ready for business. It has been noted that a striking feature of medieval cities was their paucity of public buildings and spaces, and indeed in addition to the many craftsmen's shops, most other urban buildings were part of town commercial life, including the bakery, tavern, perhaps a brewery, storehouses, and even a hospital.

Lifestyle. To a rough-and-ready society, medieval artisans presented a vibrant example of a productive and well-ordered life. As unsheltered as they were from the world, artisans frequently nonetheless lived lives of quiet industry. Undoubtedly the guilds, which by the eleventh century crafts workers began forming, afforded them this

Laborers in a vineyard: hired at the market (top); tilling the fields (middle); and receiving wages (bottom); illumination from an eleventh-century manuscript (Germanisches National-Museum, Nurnberg)

luxury. By the twelfth century, virtually every town had its guilds, fraternities, or associations, representing each type of commercial or manufacturing enterprise: baking, butchering, weaving, dyeing, and so forth. The lives of artisans were controlled to a large extent by their membership in a guild, in that the guilds set the standards for skilled work. In effect they did their best to identify the practices that they felt ought to be almost automatic to the best guild artisans. Most of these were craft dependent, as for example that the bead maker must reject any beads that are not perfectly round; that the alewife use no ingredients other than grain, hops, and water to make ale; and that the butcher not mix tallow with lard.

Discipline. Guild rules seem to have fought against two possible characteristics of the life of an artisan. Their strategies for countering the first, that the craftsman's life was comprised largely of exhausting toil, will be discussed here. Guilds stressed the value of physical work, recognizing that craftsmen had to work hard in their ateliers. The blacksmith raised and lowered his hammers, even the light ones weighing up to five pounds, continuously. The weaver firmly beat his newly placed weft thread into place with every pass of the shuttle. The back-and-forth motion of the carpenter's saw had to be repeated until the wood was cut.

Conditions of Work. Guilds wanted to preserve the strength, proficiency, and dedication of the craftsman to his demanding tasks. Largely to this end, guild rules set hours as well as conditions and standards of work, among them the provision that craftsmen should work only during daylight. This situation led to seasonal schedules even for year-round crafts, such as blacksmithing or weaving. The workday varied from fourteen to fifteen hours in the summer season to from dawn to dusk, or as little as eight hours in the winter season. Enforcement was, however, apparently extremely strict only for the noisy crafts, such as smithing, because work could disturb the neighborhood's sleep. Craftsmen of most trades were obliged not to work on Sundays and on all high-church festivities, particular those in connection with Christmas and Easter. The longest work-year estimates run three hundred days, with the church requiring sexual abstinence and fasting for at least one hundred days annually to honor holy days and seasons.

Workday. Although most details about a craftsman's workday date from the fifteenth century, certain allowances in the work schedule, reflecting the need for meals and occasional rest intervals, would have figured already in the earlier period. With work beginning at dawn, quarter-hour rest periods would have broken up the morning, perhaps as often as twice. Midmorning breakfast and midday lunch breaks would have counted anywhere from half an hour to an hour and a half depending on the time of year. Artisans had two meals "on the job" supplied by the employer if the craftsman were working for "wage and table"; neither the food nor utensils were lavish. Beans, dough cakes or bread, soup, vegetables, and as much meat as was affordable made up their main diet. There was beer and wine for festive meals.

Guild's Moral Perspective. As well as their attentions to set hours, conditions, and standards of work, guild rules reflect a further moral perspective: recognition that as an artisan one was part of a community of like craftsmen. The guilds provided many special services to their members. At guild schools, often established for the offspring of their members, children in the cities and towns of the mid twelfth century could meet their basic educational needs. Guilds did much to care for their poor and sick members, providing them with food, clothing, and medical attention, as well as for traveling artisans from like guilds, providing them with hospitality in the form of rest places and food. When a guild member fell sick or became too old to work, he was moved into the care of other guild members with fraternal artisans serving as the next of kin.

Guild Association. Generally guild brethren continued to care for the widows and children of members who died, although the bonds of guilds were stretched to the limit during the years of the Black Death (1347–1351), when members looked after their craft brothers, however dreaded the disease. As described by a chronicler in Flanders, town dwellers would visit a sick man, "do business with him, or even carry him to the grave," although inevitably they would "quickly follow him there." This highly developed sense of corporate responsibility led public authorities to spread the duties of policing and creating civic ceremonies across a city's guilds. Both the guild's cohesion and power and the tactics of the urban nobles worked toward the entry of middle and lower social classes into political life. Some municipal guilds created such tight administrative communities that in many places kings and nobles sold charters to them, allowing them collectively to rule their city.

Sources:

Prosper Boissonade, *Life and Work in Medieval Europe* (New York: Harper & Row, 1964).

Steven A. Epstein, *Wage Labor and Guilds in Medieval Europe* (Chapel Hill: University of North Carolina Press, 1991).

Joseph and Frances Gies, *Life in a Medieval City* (New York: Harper & Row, 1981).

O. F. Hamouda and B. B. Price, "The Justice of the Just Price," *European Journal of the History of Economic Thought*, 4 (1997): 191–216.

Robert S. Lopez, *The Commercial Revolution of the Middle Ages, 900–1350* (Englewood Cliffs, N.J.: Prentice-Hall, 1971).

FEUDAL SOCIETY

Definition. The term *feudalism* refers to an economic, political, and social system that prevailed in Europe from about the ninth century to the fifteenth century. With the chronic absence of effective centralized government during the Middle Ages, kings and local rulers granted land and provided protection to lesser nobles known as vassals. In return, these vassals swore oaths of loyalty and military service to their lords. Peasants known as serfs were bound to the land and were subject to the will of their lords.

European Medieval Feudalism. European medieval feudalism has become the foremost example of an interrelationship between a social class system and an economy. Having been influenced, however, by previous cultures and their economies, especially those that combined agricultural and exchange bases, the medieval economic environment cannot be understood through exclusive examination of the feudal system. The backdrop of Greek and Roman civilization and the fundamental need for survival formed the foundation for a far more heterogeneous medieval economic culture, useful for sustenance and for social organization. To these two ends, traders, artisans, peasants, churchmen, and the nobility created an economy that enveloped Europe's contemporary medieval population. It was comprised of many different elements: trade alliances; exchange methods, both interest bearing and interest free; a manorial system combined with a monetarized vassalage (nobles avoiding military service by paying their overlords); professional guilds; agriculturally self-sufficient monasteries; urban communes; and tax-based kingdoms, some of which were transformed into representational fiscal monarchies. The composite European medieval economy, derived from these many diverse elements, departed radically from economies of earlier Western cultures.

General Characteristics. No one social class system or economic form was realized for Europe over the course of the whole Middle Ages. A postmedieval new economy, often identified as capitalism, was merely in formation and would not be considered all-enveloping for centuries to come. Undeniably, one element of the medieval world was the traditional economy of land and military service, leading to a feudal-based social-class system; the other was an urban society where merchants and artisans undertook trade and commerce in an economy based on money, or capital. For the urban environment, merchants, artisans, and customers formed the core of the society because towns served as centers for the individuals who lived and worked there. They saw manufacture as the most important endeavor, to provide goods for sale and purchase in the local mercantile economy. Furthermore, local manufacture was to have an impact in other areas, such as regional fairs, port cities, and eventually long-distance trade destinations.

Urban Economy. During the Middle Ages, the economy did not become fully urban. As medieval towns grew into cities and frequently dominated the abutting countryside, the agricultural economy kept itself at an independent distance, was rarely stimulated by market supply and demand, and remained relatively ignorant of means of economic progress. The late medieval nobility complained that changes in the workforce had violated its source of livelihood, virtual free labor assumed since the beginnings of the feudal economy, and set forth in many feudal codes of law which had fixed the purpose of the peasantry. The rural economy continued nonetheless to be the safer source of sustenance for many people, who saw in its connection to the soil the chance for the family to survive in good and bad years. The fact that the vast majority of the medieval population was rural overpowered some towns' premature bid for communal independence, and the urban environment was vulnerable to the vagaries of agricultural provisioning. In the later fourteenth century the peasantry was recast as a

An eleventh-century illumination depicting the notion that society consists of three mutually supporting orders: those who pray; those who fight; and those who work (British Library, London)

political force but remained fundamentally an economic tool as it had been for the whole of the Middle Ages.

Christian Church. During the same period as feudalism and urban growth, the Christian Church was expanding and exploring new forms of social and economic expression. Established in Rome in the first century of the Christian era, the Christian faith had arrived in Europe during the Roman Empire and was spread throughout Western Europe during the first millennium, as missionaries traveled to and beyond the present-day British Isles, Germany, France, and Spain. Medieval clergymen wrote many works, among them some in which they discussed two sets of economic and social ideals, occasionally offering guidance as to how to achieve them. The ascetic approach was for men and women planning to be monks and nuns, but it was also for young women, widows, and the devoted. The more worldly approach was for men and women leading integrated, secular lives.

Modern Study. In 1776 Adam Smith took the idea for the viability of a nation and wrote "an elementary treatise on that very extensive and difficult science," political economy, presenting his ideas in the *Inquiry into the Nature and Causes of the Wealth of Nations* to explain how "those [obstacles to the progress of national prosperity] which arose from the disorders of the feudal ages, tended directly to disturb the internal arrangements of society." Part of his pioneering work, such as that devoted to "what the circumstances are, which, in modern Europe, have contributed . . . to encourage the industry of towns, at the expence of that of the country," has received less attention in more-recent times. Nevertheless, his work is still considered so significant as to have defined the beginnings of the science of economics. To this perspective have since been added, however, studies focused specifically on the economy of the Middle Ages: trade, commercial production and services, economic structure, and social organizations. Though older and less well documented than the eighteenth century of Smith, the Middle Ages offers equal opportunity for comprehensive, innovative, and perhaps unanticipated analyses of its economy and social class system.

Sources:

Georges Duby, *The Three Orders: Feudal Society Imagined* (Chicago: University of Chicago Press, 1980).

Paul Halsall, ed., *Internet Medieval Source Book*, <http://www.fordham.edu/halsall/sbook.html>.

John Hicks, *A Theory of Economic History* (Oxford: Oxford University Press, 1969).

R. H. Hilton, *English and French Towns in Feudal Society: A Comparative Study* (Cambridge & New York: Oxford University Press, 1992).

M. M. Postan, E. E. Rich, and Edward Miller, eds., *The Cambridge Economic History of Europe* (Cambridge: Cambridge University Press, 1965).

Susan Reynolds, *Fiefs and Vassals: The Medieval Evidence Reinterpreted* (New York: Oxford University Press, 1994).

Dugald Stewart, "Account of the Life and Writings of Adam Smith LL.D.," *Transactions of the Royal Society of Edinburgh,* 21 January and 18 March 1793.

George Unwin, *Studies in Economic History* (London: Macmillan, 1927).

MODES OF ECONOMIC EXISTENCE

Feudal System. The economic expression of the lord-vassal-peasant social stratification was in grants of land coming from the most powerful warrior to his loyal military supporters. As a result of one military enterprise alone in 732, the Frankish leader Charles Martel usurped from the medieval church, the only vulnerable source at the time, a large portion of its landholdings in Frankish territory. After his defensive defeat of the Muslims who were attacking Frankish lands from the south, he needed land to give to his followers as an adequate source of revenue to allow them to continue to equip themselves as knights with the costly horses and armor required. Martel's strategy of compensating his loyal followers led to what would come to be identified as the medieval feudal system with its economic ingredient, land grants, its military service based on fealty, and its social component, collective protection. The combination of the economic and military character of the lord-vassal relationship was cast cynically in poetry in the eleventh century by the Andalusian Jew Hanagid:

Why did he hire you, your master, then?

So you could work, while he earned.

You're just his tongs. When the fire gets hot,

You'll be the one that gets burned.

Vassalage. The lord-vassal relationship was elaborated and adapted in many ways such that by the eleventh century it encompassed the initial subdivision of the land that a vassal had been granted directly—among individuals who received smaller plots of land and in turn became his vassals. Before subdividing, in the eleventh century, for exam-

ple, a great baron in England was known to have held 793 farms in more than twenty counties, and in Italy, a noble had one hundred thousand acres. This intricate system was only economically effective, however, if even at the lowest level of vassalage the land a knight received, perhaps just one small village or manor with a few dozen peasant inhabitants, could provide himself and his community with an adequate livelihood. Most of the medieval social hierarchy was being supported directly by farming. Not in a position or disposition to work the land because of their military obligations, vassals turned to the peasantry to do it for them.

Serfdom. Through an economic relationship with a vassal, partly identified as serfdom, peasants farmed the vassal's land. About one third of the land a village tilled was reserved for the lord. The village serfs and free men and women had a way of life dependent on the days of labor they could devote to it. The vassal's peasants, or serfs, were obliged to give the lord specific workdays, and especially at harvest time they had to spend much time on the lord's land. The peasant was also obliged to grind his grain into flour, for a price, at the mill owned by his landlord. In return for their labor, peasants were granted personal use of some portion of the vassal's farmland. Each villager also received the right to use village lands, as well as some of the lord's woodland, meadows, and pastures, to procure wood and to pasture livestock, likely pigs and cows. There was yet another benefit that accrued to the peasantry for its labor, the expectation of being protected by the lord in the case of a warring noble's attack on the village.

Raising Revenue. The expenditures for war could not in principle exceed the income a lord's vassals could collectively derive from their granted lands, nor could the number of knights required from each immediate vassal be more than the size his fief lands could support. The strongest medieval lords did, however, apparently frequently miscalculate their vassals' viable burden and found many remaining obligations falling to themselves. Continually squeezed for financing, they usually demanded in addition to service certain rents, dues, and taxes of their vassals, which they in turn passed along to their peasants. By the year 1100 the most-powerful lords devised an enormously successful military fund-raising tactic: scutage, a shield tax in lieu of military service. Since a vassal's obligation of service was usually limited to forty days of the year (one plow season), to many lords scutage was preferable to this limited military presence; the payment could be used to obtain hired soldiers, who would be available for longer campaigns.

Standing Armies. In the mid twelfth century the original military base of the feudal system, the rough illiterate strongman whose job was mainly to fight, ceased to be as important as he once was. The king's decision to introduce scutage incorporated a needed economic change in the relationship between lord and vassal. Scutage brought in enough for kings to consider establishing a standing army and extending periods of battle. With sufficient vassals for their own armies raised from their new resources, nobles received all the encouragement they needed to expand, and they started looking for more territory. The most obvious prize was a neighbor's land, which when targeted by a noble with a large band of knights destroyed many acres of good farmland. Still other sites were the Saxons' territories in the east, the Muslim caliphates in the Iberian Peninsula, or the lands of the Scots and the Welsh.

Land for Crusaders. Another source of wealth was, however, offered by Pope Urban II, who promised knight-crusaders part of the Holy Land. Hoping to inspire Latin Christians to capture the Holy Land, the Pope appealed to different motives—faith, ambition, and love of adventure—but among them also greed. He promised to suspend taxes and cancel debts for those who joined the Holy Pilgrimage and identified economic conditions and incentives as pushing western Christian nobles to fight one another:

> This land which you inhabit is too narrow for your large population; nor does it abound in wealth, and it furnishes scarcely food enough for its civilization. Hence it is that you kill and devour one another, that you wage war. . . . Enter upon the road to the Holy Sepulchre. . . . That land which, as the Scripture says, "floweth with milk and honey" . . . is fruitful above others . . . may you deem it a beautiful thing to die for Christ in that city in which He died for us. . . . The possessions of the enemy, too, will be yours, since you will make spoil of their treasures. . . .

Ephemeral Gains of the Crusades. Many ambitious knights and barons went seeking new land, riches, opportunities, and power in the East. European accounts of the capture of Jerusalem in 1099 show something of the Crusaders' priorities: "Our men . . . rushed through the city, seizing gold and silver, horses and mules, gods of all sorts. Then they went rejoicing and weeping for gladness to worship at the sepulchre of our Savior." The gains of the First Crusade, the lands around Nicea, Antioch, Tripoli, and Jerusalem were, as touted, divided up among the followers of the victorious Frankish, Flemish, and Norman leaders. However, with Jerusalem lost by the end of the twelfth century, medieval vassals, and now kings, found themselves reconfronted with the land limitations of European territory and caught within its rapidly changing economy. Their livelihood remained with the land rather than with long-distance trade and craft production. Only in Italy were medieval landowners really ever assimilated into the environment of the new urban economy. The rest of Europe's landowners and vassals still lived on the demesne, but the general monetarization of the economy and the transformation of the agricultural workforce from the peasantry in serfdom to a group of hired wage earners would link the formerly independent entity of the manor willy-nilly to the economic sphere of the town and city.

Social Status of the Clergy. The medieval economy played an important role in the social status of the clergy. The parish priest was very much one of the manor's villagers or at the least, in the case of the common private churches, one of the lord's serfs. Often he was a vassal's appointee; frequently he survived by farming small plots like the local peasantry or at the most by receiving a portion of the fees the local lord had instituted for church services and some of the tithes. Bishops, however, were usually of noble families and carried their landed wealth with them into their episcopal vocation. They survived economically as would any lord from the return of their lands and frequently had knights or vassals and serfs under their secular authority. The Investiture Controversy, which the Concordat of Worms brought into quiescence, turned as much on the question of a bishop's appointment given his role as a secular lord as it did on his spiritual authority.

Regular Clergy. There were several transformations of the regular clergy which can perhaps best be understood in an economic light. Early medieval monks, while in a world apart, were akin economically to the peasantry itself. In short they also survived from the agricultural production of their lands. The initial foundation would include land around the monastery for gardens, orchards, and the monastery's own farm. If the land had derived from a donation, the patron might also give the monks rights to build a mill, to catch fish in nearby rivers, and to receive gifts of food and produce from people who lived in nearby villages and towns.

Self-Sufficiency. Although Benedict of Nursia founded monasticism, leaders of many different orders were his successors, most of whom represented a renewed desire to return to serious adherence to the Benedictine Rule. By 814 clerical writings had defined and distinguished the western monastic lifestyle (from its eastern counterparts) by characteristics, such as moderate asceticism, communal property ownership, *labore et ore* (the combined tasks of work and prayer), and economic self-sufficiency. Monks of the early Middle Ages were described in the thirteenth century as having been "as a glowing coal in charity. . . . They were a garment of mercy, clothing the naked and feeding the famished. . . ." More important, however, for what was to follow, they were also recognized to have been "princely in their poverty, for they were subject to none but God."

Monasteries and Secular Authority. Monastic independence from secular authority was, however, not to be sustained for two reasons: medieval monasteries accepted donations from lay believers, and monasteries, with their increasing wealth, were subject to pillaging and in need of protection. One particular story captures both those elements of monastic economic life. The targeting of monasteries for pillage had begun as far back as the monasteries of the sixth century. Around Monte Cassino, the site of Benedict of Nursia's first monastery, the barbarian Visigoth Zalla was determined to take everything he could find from the local farmers. One farmer admitted under torture that he had given gold to Benedict. Zalla tied the farmer to his horse and rode to the monastery, where he found Benedict reading a book. As Zalla demanded the gold, the rope that tied

A monk-craftsman using a chisel and a mallet; wood-carving from a thirteenth-century choir stall (Niedersächsisches Landmuseum, Hanover, Germany)

had an additional workforce to help maintain their granges, farms, and ever-expanding flocks of fine fleece sheep.

Franciscans and Dominicans. Subsequent fraternal orders, the Franciscans and the Dominicans, served as models for an entirely different monastic economic existence within the church. Attached to collective dwellings and schools in various urban centers, these two groups of friars carried out their holy work as teachers and preachers. Their means of economic survival was not, however, charging for professional service, but rather mendicancy, or beggary. They survived by receiving the charity that theretofore monastic orders were renowned for giving. They had in effect, however, adopted the same financial means of livelihood from which, in the form of compulsory tithes and donations, the secular arm of the church, its priests, bishops, and even the papacy, had been living for many centuries.

Feudal Society. The feudal society and its tiered agricultural economy represented a departure from the previous nomadic warrior societies of premedieval Europe, but it lasted really only for the Middle Ages, with the most representative years from 1050 to 1250. Growth in prosperity through the twelfth and thirteenth centuries was to be the key success of the period. Some of the inspiration for the overall rise in the standard of living was the rapid expansion of trade and commerce and the growth of towns. This change had had in turn its own catalyst, feudalism. The feudal system had brought increased law and order, and improvements in agricultural methods, which, along with the fact that crops and flocks were no longer being destroyed by invaders or warring nobles, had increased farm production beyond the needs of the rural inhabitants. The towns and cities that the agricultural surplus allowed to grow could not, however, fit into the feudal system and function properly as trading centers at the same time. A merchant could not carry on his business satisfactorily if he might be summoned to serve as a knight when his lord went to war. An artisan could hardly live by the same rules and regulations that were acceptable for the village peasant. By the end of the medieval period, a complex economy open to the importance of cities and their ruling bodies that often disputed royal, noble, or churchly power, the growing number of freemen, and the use of money and of paid soldiers and laborers would all help to contribute to the decline of its initial, far more simple feudal economic structure.

Sources:

Marc Bloch, *Feudal Society* (Chicago: University of Chicago Press, 1961).

G. G. Coulton, *Medieval Village, Manor, and Monastery* (New York: Harper, 1960).

Georges Duby, *Rural Economy and Country Life in the Medieval West* (Columbia: University of South Carolina Press, 1968).

M. M. Postan, E. E. Rich, and Edward Miller, eds., *The Cambridge Economic History of Europe* (Cambridge: Cambridge University Press, 1965).

the farmer to the horse fell away. Apparently Zalla was so amazed that he leaped from his horse and threw himself at Benedict's feet.

Monastic Patronage. However inviolate Monte Cassino remained, in many instances the vulnerability of the monasteries brought them under the control of local strongmen, especially during the era of the Viking and Muslim invasions. Feudal kings and nobles thus came to dominate protectively specific monastic houses, regarding them, however, like their own realms as pieces of property to be used to increase their own wealth and power rather than as centers of religious life. In 910 Duke William the Good of Aquitaine offered the possibility of a new start. A wealthy noble, he donated land directly to the Papacy in Rome to start a new order of monks, the Cluniacs in Burgundy, thus giving them economic and other liberties from the start, from local ecclesiastical and lay authority. A new order following the Cluniacs, the Cistercians, returned with even greater rigor to combining work and prayer, and with such efficient results as to become the best, most prosperous farmers in medieval Europe. With their introduction of *conversi*, the third order of lay brothers, they

Chivalric Knight. In addition to "those who worked" (peasants) and "those who prayed" (clergymen), the medieval economy enveloped also "those who fought." The mental and moral disposition of the medieval knight has become perhaps his most striking characteristic. The rules to guide his behavior formed the code of chivalry, the name of which is derived from the French *chevalier,* meaning horseman. During the early Middle Ages, chivalry was a simple code that existed between fighting men to govern their relations with one another. In its later guise, however, the knight was expected to be loyal to his lord and devoted to the church, which supported its ideals. The medieval knight was thus expected not only to possess a host of manly and military qualities (to be utterly courageous, to fight fairly, and never to seek victory through trickery and cunning), but also to be true to his word, pure, temperate, courteous, charitable and kind to the poor and defenseless, and respectful to women and ever ready to protect them. He was to be unwaveringly brave before an enemy, yet treat him with gallantry in defeat.

Feudal Fighting. In many respects the chivalry of the later medieval period was unreal. The typical early medieval knight was a rough, illiterate strongman whose main job was to fight. Already by the twelfth century, however, the feudal knight had ceased to be as important as he once was on the battlefield. Feudal fighting became a kind of game, as the nobility tried to display its fighting skills by staging elaborate tournaments. By 1130 the tournament had already undergone a transformation from being a war game designed to keep the knight at the ready and peak of his fighting efficiency to an elaborate, violent pageant. In the later tournaments, nobles worked desperately to impress one another and to amuse their admiring ladies, whose colors they wore. Compared with earlier events where large bands of knights engaged in bloody mock battles, Matthew Paris notes French tournaments, *conflictus Gallicus,* before 1259 in his *Chronica Majora,* and English royal accounts record a tournament at Windsor Park in 1278. By 1300 the common tournament format was a series of jousts, contests between two knights encased in heavy armor and using blunted lances, swords, or axes.

Knight as Lord. Throughout much of the Middle Ages, the knight was commonly also a lord, or at least a "resident user" of land, whose agricultural return gave him the means to meet his military obligations to his lord. His livelihood derived directly from having others work the land he owned or received from a noble lord, his fief, or manor. A manor might have one village and the land around it, or two or three villages and their surrounding lands. The whole fief of a knight was made up of two unequal parts: his demesne, or personal landholding, and the holdings of the peasants.

Duties of a Knight. In return for his fief the knight had to perform many duties. The main one was to give military aid to his lord: to serve personally whenever his lord summoned him to war and to provide a certain number of fully

A knight paying homage to King Henry III of England; illumination from a circa 1250 manuscript (British Library, London)

equipped mounted knights. The way of life of the land-exploiting knight was different from that of the merchant, artisan, monk, or peasant. Knights spent much of their time either at war or in training for war. The knight's military obligations were those for which he was so well trained in horsemanship that the skill, as well as the chivalric mindset that accompanied it, were almost automatically put into action. Nonetheless, if the noble lived to be much over forty, he was fortunate to have enjoyed an exciting short life, even if it was not easy. There was always the hope of victory in battle leading to the booty of plundering and pillaging, but it was no less true, as contemporary Bertrand de Born realized, that there was "no real war without fire and blood."

Training. At an early age young nobles, called squires, trained to become knights. A noble child might start out as a helper to a lord. By the mid eleventh century he was learning, at fourteen or fifteen years of age, to ride a horse and to use weapons. Once, during his period of apprenticeship or training, a squire had learned the further skills and duties of the knight, he became a soldier for a lord and was given occasion to prove his ability in real battle. When he finished his training and passed the test on the battlefield, he would be knighted in the ceremony of adoubement, in which he received arms and armor. Before being invested, with spurs and a sword, for example, the knight swore to uphold the true Christian faith.

Military Service. The military service a knight supplied was usually limited to one-ninth of the year, but presenting himself and his knights ready to fulfill their warrior responsibilities was by no means a light obligation. The provision of each one knight reflects his characteristic appearance. It included not only the man himself but also his mount, the expensive weapons and armor, and perhaps a change of horses, servants to look after the knight and his equipment, and food to feed both men and animals for forty days. Several aspects of the medieval knight's attire made it particularly distinctive. During the twelfth century, a coat of arms, or the design that a knight displayed on his shield or surcoat to identify himself in battle, became the symbol, and property, of a particular family, launching the system known as heraldry. The increasing weight of the armor of the knight and his horse was also legendary: by the sixteenth century a German knight's armor could weigh as much as fifty-six pounds, while that of his horse was ninety-two pounds.

Sources:

Marc Bloch, *Feudal Society* (Chicago: University of Chicago Press, 1961).

G. G. Coulton, *Medieval Village, Manor, and Monastery* (New York: Harper, 1960).

Georges Duby, *Rural Economy and Country Life in the Medieval West* (Columbia: University of South Carolina Press, 1968).

Duby, *The Three Orders: Feudal Society Imagined,* translated by Arthur Goldhammer (Chicago: University of Chicago Press, 1980).

Kate Mertes, *The English Noble Household 1250–1600* (Oxford & New York: Blackwell, 1988).

M. M. Postan, E. E. Rich, and Edward Miller, eds., *The Cambridge Economic History of Europe* (Cambridge: Cambridge University Press, 1965).

PEASANTRY

Survival. The Middle Ages (earlier known as the Dark Ages) refers in Europe to a period that started with the precarious survival of enough men and women to reproduce themselves. The feat to keep its numbers up against malnutrition, poor hygiene, parasitic infections, and disease in order to cultivate the land and support a new generation so that they could carry on the societal groups and reproduce themselves was, as late as 1000, hard for the medieval populace. The natural hostilities of climate made many a poor infant defenseless with a mortality rate of several hundred per thousand. Many adults' lives were brought to an end in their thirties by death from war or disease. Yet, medieval Europeans were not wiped out because after 814 there was a remarkable economic growth that was to make Western Europe a rich and powerful part of the world.

Earning a Living. At first, earning a living during the Middle Ages was limited to "those who worked" and "those who fought." The Christian Church, however, rapidly interposed its institutions within this context, making

"those who prayed," particularly in the monastic setting, a part of the medieval economy of the ninth century.

Farming. To earn their livelihood, medieval peasants simply worked from sunrise to sunset. Peasant life followed the seasons and most of the already time-honored practices of cultivating fields: preparing the land, sowing, cutting, and stocking the grain, and usually threshing and winnowing it, since they grew predominantly wheat-type grains for food. In spring the peasants raked and planted seed for grain. From summer into early fall was weeding, haying, and harvest time for fathers, mothers, sons, and daughters, on their land and the lord's, cutting the crop with scythes and turning it with rakes. Sheep were left to graze on fallow areas. For women there was the milking of the cows and the feeding of the chickens at home. Some women made ale to quench the thirst of the field laborers. During the winter, peasants stayed indoors. They made candles, wove cloth, and did other tasks.

Technological Transformations. Two technological transformations in medieval agriculture by about 800—a new horse collar, rigid yet padded such that the animal would not strangle itself as soon as it began to pull with significant force, and the integration of the heavy plow—altered somewhat the previously habitual routines. The heavy plow added plowing to the spring tasks and led in particular to the arduous task of bringing more land under cultivation. The peasantry cut down forests and removed bushes and briars to clear vast new areas of land for farming. A slowly integrated technique of dividing all the land of a single estate into communally worked fields also had an impact on peasant livelihood. Eventually across Europe, each community of peasants worked two or three large fields in rotation. One would be planted with wheat or rye in the fall and a second left uncultivated to lie fallow; a third was sown with oats, barley, or legumes in the spring.

Husbandry. Work in the fields was fundamentally physical and hard. Some aspects of the exhausting toil of the medieval peasant were diminished by the exploitation of both water- and windpower to raise water and grind grain, as well as to drive trip-hammers and saws. By 1300, with agricultural surpluses available, a part of the peasantry specialized in sheep and pig raising. In southern France, northern Spain, and in England in the Cotswolds and East Anglia, herds ranged in size from fifty to a thousand head. In most regions an amount more than a thousand head was so large that the sheep or pig herders needed to move them from one foraging area to another, beginning in some areas the seasonal practice of transhumance.

Peasant Home. The medieval peasant lived within a cluster of small houses in a village, often with its own church, blacksmith's shop, and mill, all of which was owned by the lord of the land. Each house was a simple single-room, single-story, high-roofed structure. At the center of the room was an open-hearth fire on the packed-earth floor; it vented through a hole in the roof. The term *hut* is often used to describe the peasant home, perhaps to evoke the fragility of its construction from

A French peasant sharpening his scythe; stone relief from the façade of the Cathedral of Notre Dame of Amiens, circa 1270

tage, or porridge—peasant fare, which was hardly lavish, consisted of oatcakes, cheeses, and perhaps the odd chicken. The bread, a dark loaf of four or more pounds weight, was made of *maslin,* a coarse wheat-rye or barley-rye flour mixture. The vegetables a peasant grew would be available in a variety in spring and summer: cabbage, onions, lettuce, leeks, spinach, and parsley. There was also the seasonal fruit from his trees: apples, pears, and cherries. Peas, beans, eggs, and the occasional fish supplied the only protein. There was meat only rarely, since the livestock that was raised was most often used to pay rent and other obligations. Animals that were not needed for breeding were killed every winter, since over the winter there was little spare hay from the meadow left to feed other animals after giving the plow team of four to eight oxen its daily rations. Animals that survived the winter by remaining on the common pasture were apparently not the most appetizing. One medieval observer declared that if he had to choose between the meat and the hide, he would eat the hide.

Clothing. Their clothing, which varied little throughout the whole of the Middle Ages, unlike that of the urban dwellers, which changed with fashion, gave the peasantry a characteristic appearance. It consisted, for women, of long loose gowns of rough material, belted at the waist, with wimples to cover the head. For men, the attire was a short tunic and either short, below-the-knee stockings or long hose, which fastened to the waist belt. A hood or cloth cap covered the male head. The peasant man also would have had coarse gloves or mittens and heavy leather shoes, while his wife might well have had neither. This discrepancy in protective clothing ought not perhaps be surprising, for Peter Lombard, a twelfth-century theologian, had to remind Christians that, while God had indeed made Eve from Adam's rib and not his head, he had also not created her from Adam's foot, as a slave. Women of every station were obliged, once married, to look after the home, "cooking, sweeping, cleaning pans"; peasant women had, however, the additional challenge of helping their husbands look after the land.

Written Documentation. Accounts of peasants who spoke for or about themselves are virtually nonexistent. To thirteenth-century contemporaries who did write of the peasantry from a certain distance, several dispositions are echoed as if characteristic. From the description of one author, medieval peasants were frequently overwhelmed by the conditions of life: "Her cake is burning on the [hearth] stone, and her calf is licking up the milk. The pot is boiling over into the fire, and the churl her husband is scolding." At the same time, peasants were also described as dealing with their lot in life with great equanimity: when the bread was of common grain or of beans, and their drink, of the spring, when cheese and milk were their only feast, with their garments of sober gray, "the world of such folk [was] well ordered in its estate." Perhaps the most realistic general description stems from a clergyman who did not push beyond his scorn for the dissipations of the peasantry to analyze their difficult home life or their stamina to face it.

readily available, often highly flammable materials, including a thatched straw roof, unsupported by roof trussing until the thirteenth century. Most peasant houses had to be rebuilt by every new generation. At the back of their house many peasants had a rudely constructed shed or lean-to. Behind the house and shed was a stretch of enclosed piece of ground. This was usually broken up and planted with vegetables. Both at the immediate back and in the rough grass beyond, there would be a few fruit trees. At the bottom of the garden there might be a pigsty or pecking space for a few fowl. The fortunate peasant might have a cow tethered at the base of the garden grazing on the naturally growing grasses.

Food Consumption. Peasants ate at least two meals a day, using wooden or earthenware bowls and wooden spoons. In addition to the staples of the diet—bread, pot-

In simply condemning their enjoyment of "idle play and japes, carolings, making of fool countenances, . . . [giving] gifts to jongleurs to hear idle tales, . . . smiting, wrestling, in other doings of strength," he did more than he realized perhaps to evoke their need for such pleasures.

Sources:

Marc Bloch, *Feudal Society* (Chicago: University of Chicago Press, 1961).

G. G. Coulton, *Medieval Village, Manor, and Monastery* (New York: Harper, 1960).

Georges Duby, *Rural Economy and Country Life in the Medieval West* (Columbia: University of South Carolina Press, 1968).

Duby, *The Three Orders: Feudal Society Imagined,* translated by Arthur Goldhammer (Chicago: University of Chicago Press, 1980).

Barbara A. Hanawalt, *The Ties that Bound: Peasant Families in Medieval England* (New York: Oxford University Press, 1986).

David Herlihy, *Medieval Households* (Cambridge, Mass.: Harvard University Press, 1985).

M. M. Postan, E. E. Rich, and Edward Miller, eds., *The Cambridge Economic History of Europe* (Cambridge: Cambridge University Press, 1965).

Shulamith Shahar, *The Fourth Estate: A History of Women in the Middle Ages* (London & New York: Methuen, 1983).

SOCIAL HIERARCHY

Rewards of Fighting. Medieval social stratification derived initially directly from the earliest means of survival of European medieval peoples—migratory warfare—when most of the land's resources were the rewards of fighting. The warrior most fearsome in battle, frequently identified as the king, was as well the most powerful in peacetime. It was he to whom the winnings of battle were attributed and from whom any redistribution of them would come. The victorious Frank Charles Martel was ostensibly the first to create the relationship of vassalage whereby fighters loyal to a leader in past battles were bound by oath and a benefice or gift to provide future services in the same leader's wars. To his action can also be attributed the giving of a new social authority to the warrior class.

Warrior-Vassal System. Beginning in the mid eighth century the warrior-vassal system brought a specific societal order to Europe, based as it were on "employment." Warriors in service of a landowning lord in the highest social position, his vassals, were deemed of next highest social rank. The peasants were considered of lesser station because they worked for the vassals who were off fighting. A hierarchy of nobility established itself, those commanding very large territories assuming the more prestigious titles of count or duke. A second rank of nobles, those subinfeudated to a vassal, having medium-sized or small properties as their fiefs, were far more numerous.

Crusades. In 1096 the First Crusade set forth, with the armies of Frankish, Flemish, and Norman knights, to capture Nicaea in 1097, Antioch in 1098, and Jerusalem in 1099 and to establish on the conquered land what would become the four Christian kingdoms of Jerusalem, Antioch, Edessa, and Tripoli. As successful as the Crusades had been, by 1187 the Muslims had recaptured Jerusalem—a city the Christians never reclaimed—and it was apparent that they had truly dealt a devastating blow to the nobility of the time. Before the Crusades, weak kings could not require the local nobility to stay in check, but with the death of so many nobles in the battles of the Crusades, kings gained enough power to place themselves securely at the top of the social strata.

Position of Power. Medieval nobility had more than small successes, nonetheless, in keeping high social rank even with a king heading feudal society. In France, although a king united the country into a monarchy, a host of greater and lesser nobles flourished beneath him, ranging from dukes to counts to viscounts and barons. As a precautionary measure, however, most kings remained wary of the nobility, and some sent out their most loyal vassals to prevent feudal nobles from building castles to use as

Land grant from 1085; the recipient, Roger, son of Walter, is obliged to provide the bishop of Hereford with the services of two knights (Public Record Office, London)

strongholds to increase their power at the expense of the king.

Noble Trends. In a larger sense, most nobles held onto their feudal rights and the medieval monarchy failed to assert itself fully. The knightly calling and military prowess had not fallen out of favor with the noble class, and the code of chivalry became even more complicated and rarefied from the twelfth century on. Recruitment into knightly ranks changed little; from 1065 on, young European noblemen were quite generally being taught horsemanship and chivalry. Later, medieval nobility sensed enough of the shift in power to be uneasy in the new autocratic environment but also to realize that they did not choose to be assimilated into the new urban social configuration of merchants, artisans, and free townsmen. After the establishment in England of the Great Council by the Magna Carta of 1215 and the French king's excessive taxation of the Champagne fairs that destroyed their importance, medieval kings and nobles nonetheless spent most of their time sharing administration with the new merchant class. Although the best trained and most noble among the knightly class continued to play a part in political and military leadership, during the fourteenth century the increasing use of hired soldiers and the introduction of gunpowder decreased the demand for them in their classic feudal role.

Religious Society. Medieval social stratification created a special place for those who had chosen the religious vocation. There was, however, tension between the regular, or monastic, and the secular clergy, such that the life of the monk usually ranked higher in social esteem for its perceived greater holiness. The secular clergy, from bishops to parish priests, while presumed chaste, were perceived to be far less poor, otherworldly, and self-denying and were hence less revered in the eyes of the contemporary public. In fact this was in reverse of the legal organization of the church institution, which determined the secular clergy as the first order, with bishops frequently having administrative authority over monastic houses, and the regular clergy as the second. A group of laity, though far below the two other ranks of this social stratification, became identified as a third religious order, comprised of lay brethren or sisters who worked within the monastic community.

Secular Church. Throughout the Middle Ages, both the regular and the secular clerical church institutions differentiated themselves markedly from the rest of medieval social structure. Secular church hierarchy, which began at the bottom with the parish priest, included most prominently bishops and the Pope. In 800 Pope Leo III appointed the first Holy Roman Emperor. The title was intended to set one king, the one the papacy chose, above all other kings in western Europe, and to offer to the Pope an alliance with an authority of the secular world of almost equal social and political rank to his own. Despite the title, or perhaps because of it, Holy Roman Emperors never succeeded in breaking the power of local lords, even as the feudal system broke down, and it proved to be disappointing in that regard to the papacy's designs for a new Christian

Roman Empire in Europe. Even more challenging to papal authority, however was the rivalry that established itself between the Holy Roman Emperor and the Pope himself, particularly over the appointment of bishops. It took the Concordat of Worms, instituted in 1122, to force the European kings to accept that the rank of emperor had less authority, even temporal authority, than the papacy.

Sources:
Marc Bloch, *Feudal Society* (Chicago: University of Chicago Press, 1961).

G. G. Coulton, *Medieval Village, Manor, and Monastery* (New York: Harper, 1960).

Georges Duby, *Rural Economy and Country Life in the Medieval West* (Columbia: University of South Carolina Press, 1968).

Duby, *The Three Orders: Feudal Society Imagined,* translated by Arthur Goldhammer (Chicago: University of Chicago Press, 1980).

M. M. Postan, E. E. Rich, and Edward Miller, eds., *The Cambridge Economic History of Europe* (Cambridge: Cambridge University Press, 1965).

SOCIAL ORGANIZATIONS: INTERACTION AMONG PEOPLES

Pilgrimages. Popular Christian pilgrimage sites outside Europe included the tomb of Thomas the Apostle in India, the column of Symeon the Stylite in northern Syria, the basilica of Thessaloniki, site of miracles of the martyr Demetrius, and the original tomb of Nicholas of Myra, the patron saint of sailors and travelers, in Asia Minor. Nevertheless, the shrines of Jerusalem, which commemorate the days of Jesus Christ's life, were the most important. Jerusalem also houses sites of religious importance to Islam, such as the rock from which Muslims believe Muhammed ascended into heaven. The Dome of the Rock, which covers the site in Jerusalem, is one of Islam's holiest shrines today. In Jerusalem medieval pilgrims of both faiths could strengthen their beliefs without the intermediary of textual accounts. The different Christian and Islamic religious groups of the medieval period competed, however, with each other in heated conflicts over control, protection, and use of the shrines of Jerusalem. Each group wished to impose its own regulations, revered leaders, and means of preserving the sanctuaries, cities, and treasures.

Expedition to Jerusalem. Throughout the Middle Ages, religious pilgrimages were undertaken by Christians, and if the pilgrim made it to the Holy Land any time after the mid seventh century when the Middle East came under Arab control, he would have encountered Muslim Arabs or Turks. Until the later eleventh century, religious faith was the major requirement for free passage and most of the interactions between Christians and Muslims were peaceful. The first Muslims in the area were open-minded about Christian pilgrims, whom they allowed to travel freely. The situation changed in 1071, when the Byzantines were defeated at Manzikert (Myriokeplalon) by the Seljuk Turks who then took over a lot of territory in Asia Minor (Turkey), and then further in 1076, when the Fatamids were overcome in the Holy Land, and most especially in 1085, when the Fatamids relinquished to the Seljuks the city of Jerusalem. As militant Muslims, the Turks were less tolerant than the previous rulers of the Holy Land and not open-minded about Christian pilgrims. Thus, in 1095 Pope Urban II called for a crusade or holy war against the Muslims who were persecuting Christian pilgrims.

Tourism. Of course, every Crusader became a traveler to a different land. Medieval men, women, and even children came together with a collection of European "foreigners," to set off on foot and/or by ship only to encounter cultures even more strange, at least in terms of religion. In addition to Jerusalem, the successful First Crusaders saw Anatolia, Syria, and Palestine and the cities of Nicaea and Antioch. Those of the Fourth Crusade marveled at Constantinople. While most returned to Europe, those who stayed on to live in the new Christian Crusaders' lands obviously had the most intense contact with local culture.

Crusader Trade. During the eleventh century the Crusades stimulated the development of trade. This meant some mercantile travel to and from the Near and Middle East, especially for the Italian traders who played a leading role in supplying the ships and equipment for the Crusading armies. Venice, Pisa, and Genoa, clearly having an eye on the advantages that would come when the Crusaders captured eastern cities, prepared for the possibility by breaking Muslim control of the eastern Mediterranean waterways. With Crusader victories, the way was indeed opened for much greater trade between the eastern Mediterranean and Europe, and the ensuing commercial development continued well into the thirteenth century.

Cultural Exchanges. There was also a cultural side to the commercial contacts. Crusader galleys loaded with cargo plied the Mediterranean. The eastern cities had already developed a trade along caravan routes with China, but now with Crusader ships bringing back silks, sugar, spices, and other luxuries from the Middle East, Chinese goods were to be seen in the courts and castles of medieval kings and nobles. Even after the Crusades, oriental goods came into Europe by way of Venice, Genoa, and other ports, in quantities unknown since the days of imperial Rome. Perfumes, rugs, and glass were brought to Europe from the Middle East. European ladies now used glass mirrors from the East instead of polished metal disks. All these goods improved life in Europe. The spices, for example, made food taste better. Ideas as well as products from eastern cultures also filtered in, such as bathing from the Islamic world.

Missionaries. Religious fervor was often displayed by those who traveled extensively within Europe itself. For those whose purpose of religious travel was not specifically to visit pilgrimage sites, it was probably to carry out the missionary journey Jesus admonished his followers to assume. The experience of the wandering preachers, canonical and dissident alike, was not to see, but to be seen and heard, truly to interact with peoples of different regions. Although their itineraries are nowhere near as well known as those of the Crusaders, examples of these gyratory evangelists abound. In the late eleventh century Robert of Arbrissel traveled barefoot and in rags through central France, coming to a stop to establish a sanctioned order

A fourteenth-century pilgrim badge of Thomas Becket, Archbishop of Canterbury (London Museum)

and nunnery at Fontevrault. Valdes, founder of the preaching Valdenisians, prepared his followers for their travels barefoot in southern France and northern Italy with the instructions: "Ask for someone trustworthy and stay with him until you leave." The Cathar leaders traveled throughout southern Europe to preach and debate with orthodox Christians.

Medieval Academics. Medieval academics were a third subgroup of travelers. Their experience was almost completely akin to that of the craft journeyman, except that most students from one region rarely found themselves singly representing their land of origin. A student from England might well travel to Paris only to find himself surrounded by many other English students as well as peers from Spain, Italy, and France. The impact of students, possibly as many as two to three thousand of different "nations" coming together to study a group of ideas was certainly felt in medieval Europe. However much the university gave young men the greatest opportunity to interact with peoples from different regions, the end product of the intermingling was more a distinct intellectual synthesis at each university, whether Paris, Orleans, Angers, Oxford, Cambridge, and so forth than an encounter with the particular university's regional culture. Frequently, a student studied in more than one university setting, working in each under the renowned master there. During this time of exposure to different mentors a student who was to become an academic found himself also seeking out a new home. Students who traveled away to the university and became teaching masters rarely came home. While it was common in the era of the cathedral schools for teaching masters to adopt the name of their school, such as Thierry of Chartres (Cathedral), the names of some of the greatest medieval scholars reflect their origins as being far from the universities where they eventually taught; Thomas Aquinas, Giles of Rome (Roman Italy), Gregory of Rimini, and Henry of Friemar all became professors at the University of Paris.

Legal Statutes. Specific legal statutes, those of the monastery, manor, guild, and city, institutionalized most of the standard relationships within these various medieval social organizations. The *jus palae,* or "spade right," created the right of inheritance lease (*erbpachten*) to the *hörigen,* or serfs, of the German peasantry. The rules of the tailors' guild of Bologna stipulated the length of apprenticeships, at five years for "a little apprentice less than ten years of age" and three years for one above ten. The Grand Ordinance of King Jean II of February 1351 established notions of the just price in French markets with its ceiling limits, such as 6d for a pint of the best white wine. Most stipulations were the reflection of the general medieval social order with its hierarchical moral and occupational rankings.

Modifications. The regulations of medieval social organizations occasionally did more, however, than just reflect established roles. In many instances they also modified or ignored existing legal stipulations and altered formal institutional strictures to suit the needs of the current economic situation. The broad sweeping changes have long since been identified. Education and acculturation, undertaken by priests and monastic clergy within the monasteries of the early Middle Ages, became the task of universities throughout later medieval Europe. The keeping of records of births, deaths, and the sale of lands, universally maintained by the medieval clergy, was taken over by the early humanists, soon to be the learned men of the Renaissance, in the cities of northern Italy.

Social Regulations. Some modifications of social organization have had, however, a more defined moment of demarcation. In 1317 France officially banned inheriting the throne for women, at times crucial to smooth succession in France and England, under appeal to Frankish Salic Law. Specific periods of labor shortage, such as the one brought on by the Black Death (1347–1351), have been perhaps the most dramatic medieval cause of punctuated transformations in laws, statutes, and contracts. Regulations governing terms of service, entry fees for guild members, ages of entry into service, training, and property use restrictions were loosened or ignored altogether at such times. Serfs who would normally be required to serve a lord until death were allowed in hard labor times for landowners to increase their holdings and even build up a surplus with which they could buy their freedom. The lump sum "savings of a lifetime" came in handy to their lord who needed to pay for help to sow and harvest. Some landlords would

offer serfs their freedom if they would agree to leave their village and to *assart,* or clear new land, for the lord to claim as his new territory. The ultimate indicator of flexibility in the structure of medieval social organizations was the generally recognized right of a serf, if he could escape and live for a year and a day in a town, to obtain thereby his freedom under protection of the town administrators.

Sources:

Christopher Brooke, *The Structure of Medieval Society* (New York: McGraw-Hill, 1971).

Lester K. Little, *Religious Poverty and the Profit Economy in Medieval Europe* (Ithaca, N.Y.: Cornell University Press, 1978).

Joseph H. Lynch, *The Medieval Church, A Brief History* (London & New York: Longman, 1992).

John H. Mundy and Peter Riesenberg, *The Medieval Town* (Princeton, N.J.: Van Nostrand, 1958).

SOCIAL ORGANIZATIONS: OCCUPATIONS AND WORK HABITS

Divisions of Medieval Society. There are many different ways in which medieval society was divided. The most striking division was that between the clergy and laity, those who had adopted a fully religious lifestyle and those who, although believers, went about their economic and social lives immersed in the world around them. The subdivisions of each of these groups give greater nuance to their character. The clergy was divided into the secular or worldly clergy and the regular or monastic clergy. Divisions of lay believers could be made with regard to their proximity to the clerical vocation with third order brothers and sister ranking the closest. Social class structure might also follow the most usual outlines of the economic categories of peasant, artisan, merchant, and noble. Even specific subdivisions of medieval society played a significant part in distinguishing the lives of some medievals, as a group, from others: certain monastic orders, *conversi,* Crusaders, religious dissidents, subgroups of the peasantry, the castle society, the middle class, and students.

The Church. Of all medieval social organizations those of the Church were the most universally known. There were principally the three official orders: the secular clergy, the regular clergy, and the believing laity. While the secular clergy strove to maintain the image of a shared union, the regular clergy could not sustain any real illusion of a single communal association. The Middle Ages had many different monastic orders: Benedictines, Cluniacs, Cistercians, Franciscans, and Dominicans, among others. There were three other groups connected with the church community that should rightly be identified as distinctly organized groups: *conversi,* Crusaders, and religious dissenters.

Religion in Daily Life. Religion played such a crucial part in medieval people's daily lives that it called many believers to dedicate themselves fully to it. Men could become either priests or monks within the church. If they became priests, they joined the secular clergy. In canon law, the secular clergy were considered to be in a separate social class by virtue of their ordination to the priesthood, their knowledge, their behavior, and their legal status. From the

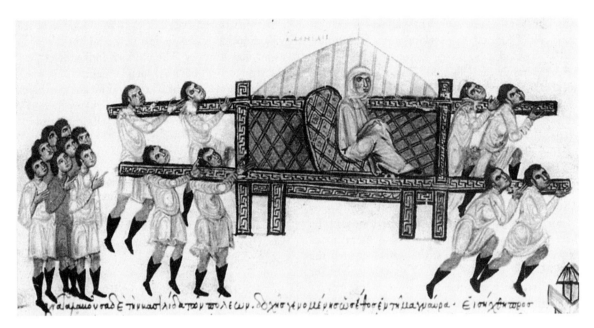

A noblewoman being carried by her slaves while she inspects her lands; illumination from a thirteenth-century manuscript (Biblioteca Nacional, Madrid)

lay believers' point of view, the tenets of their moral behavior were what most obviously set them apart. They were to remain celibate and were forbidden to live with women except for the closest of female relatives. They were not to accept employment and if rich, not to loan money at interest. While they lived in the secular world, they were to forswear the aspects of it, such as taverns, which were connected to immoral behavior.

Vocation in the Regular Clergy. Dedication of one's life to service in the medieval regular church meant taking on an even more strictly regulated life, becoming a monk if a male believer, or a nun if a female. Belonging was either voluntary, with an adult choosing his or her monastic home and accepting not being allowed to leave the community except on the most urgent matters, or compulsory, as arranged for children (*oblati)* and female relatives given by parents, guardians, or church officials to a monastery. Acceptance of entry in a monastery was a binding obligation. The act of joining the monastery was undertaken by Christian believers to save their own soul or that of a loved one. To work, study, and attend to religion, these were places where people could live apart from the distractions of the world. Parents and relatives who gave a child, spouse, widowed sister, and so forth to a monastery disinherited them, so that the newly encloistered person would not be tempted to return to the tainted world.

Monastic Rule. The responsibilities of the child, monk, or nun of any specific community group were spelled out in the particular monastery's Rule. The Benedictines with their Rule of St. Benedict were the first most widely spread medieval order. For all Benedictines, who lived communally with their abbots, behavior was measured by adherence to the three basic vows: poverty, chastity or purity, and obedience to the head of the monastic community, the abbot. Their training was spiritual and occupational;

learned by example and participation, it virtually guaranteed the entrant all necessities for life. Not only was idleness considered by Benedict of Nursia "an enemy of the soul," but since the community as a whole provided for each of its members, Benedictines were obliged to work and to turn their labor to serving others, by building schools, churches, and libraries, and by feeding the poor. In addition to *ora* (prayer), *labora* (the tasks of work) figured so prominently that the Benedictine monk wore a billhook or pruning hook in his girdle as a sign of his habitual involvement in manual labor.

Monastic Lifestyle. Virtually every monastic order asserted that a monk or nun should live a life of unencumbered purity. He or she could neither marry nor be unchaste, nor appear immodestly without a headcovering. The monastery, for its part, fed, clothed, and lodged monks or nuns and instructed them in reading and writing. The role of education in the lifestyle of monks and nuns was not uniform throughout the Middle Ages, and the early Benedictine order was not particularly concerned about the formal education of its members. It was, however, quite strict about property ownership: a regular could not own anything as an individual, with permission granted to possess only two pieces of clothing consisting of a cowl and a long robe. The color of the robe would be a defining feature in distinguishing one order from another.

Early Monastic Orders. Well before the seventh century, there were many monasteries for monks and some convents for nuns, but the Benedictine community was by far the most dominant. The relaxation by the order of certain terms of the Benedictine Rule led, however, to the establishment of different monastic orders after the ninth century. A new order of Cluniac monks was the first established in an attempt to bring reform to the Benedictine monastic movement. Since many monasteries had come to be founded or overseen by a great landowner, who had become not only its patron but also its administrator, they ceased to adhere closely to many of the tenets of the Benedictine Rule. The founding of the Cluniac abbey at Cluny in Burgundy, France, in 910 was to counter that lack of religious independence from secular authority. Since gifts of rich or generous medieval families continued to be forthcoming, the Cluniac movement spread rapidly from around 950 to 1100. As time passed, the Cluniac monasteries became great landowners in their own right, and their agricultural prosperity led them to lose much of their desire for reform. They succumbed to the evils of wealth, good food, tournaments, hunting, and politics.

Cistercian Order. The next major monastic society to establish itself was the Cistercian Order. Founded at Citeaux in France in 1098, it was another influential reform group. The Cistercians, called white monks because of their white robes, wanted a simple way of life away from worldly distractions. The greatest spokesman for the order was Bernard of Clairvaux, a Cistercian monk who bitterly attacked the wealth of the church. He said, "The Church gilds its stones and leaves its children naked. With the silver of the wretched it charms the eyes of the rich." The Cistercians represent the great age of the monasteries that was the twelfth century.

Decline. By the end of the century the popularity of the Cistercians was in decline. Their hard work, particularly at sheep raising, had been extremely lucrative, and the order had allowed itself to accumulate virtually every form of riches. Although the Cistercians had eschewed the town environment and its wealth, they had not maintained the simple rural life. The Rules of both the Cluniacs and the Cistercians were written in the hope that monks would become spiritual and economic models in their rural cloisters. Both were, however, in fact so successful in economic terms as to become repulsive in spiritual terms. When the Cistercians were named in the thirteenth century to head the attempt to bring Christianity's wayward believers back into the fold, they were virtually ineffective.

New Religious Orders. The next new religious orders would test the possibility of living simply and religiously within the wealthy urban setting previous orders had avoided. The Franciscans, recognized in 1210, and the Dominicans, in 1215, were the most renowned of those orders based in towns. Francis of Assisi, the founder of the Franciscans, was the son of a prosperous Italian merchant. He gave up the commercial life he deemed sinful for its attachment to riches to live in poverty. He wandered barefoot from town to town, caring for the sick, begging from the rich, giving to the poor, and preaching the love of God. The followers of Francis and Dominic were called mendicant friars and, as their leaders had, lived on alms or donations. The roles they assumed were slightly different ones for the regular clergy: they preached and they taught. In respect to preaching, they became in effect the parish priests of the towns and cities. As for their role in teaching, they set up their own urban schools and became among the

most prominent educators within the universities that were forming in the thirteenth century. Long before the idea took hold in the West that extending education to the masses was a responsibility of the state, the church had come to see it as part of its mission. The Benedictine monasteries had been the main early focus for education and culture. The bishops' schools of important towns gradually saw secular priests assuming the role of teacher, and ultimately the Dominican and Franciscan friars would number among those most concerned with education in the later Middle Ages.

Attraction of the Monastic Life. Both rural and urban monastic orders presented an attraction to individuals who because of social or economic ties could not devote themselves completely to the monastic lifestyle. Allowance was made for their worldly attachment and a new, third, official monastic lay order came about to embrace them. In the rural areas they proved extremely useful in a practical way. However self-sufficient in terms of natural resources, the monks of the different rural orders often found themselves shorthanded. In the urban context, the third order believers were the best defense of the church against the attraction of contemporary heretical beliefs and institutions.

Integrating the Laity. The most systematic rural response to integrating the laity was by the Cistercians, who instituted a suborder, the *conversi* (from the same etymological root as "convert"). Their role was to aid in the hardest of the agricultural work. They lived and worked on monastic land in farms called granges. The *conversi* played a full economic part in the monastic community but had fewer religious obligations and less political participation. They were extremely important to numerous Cistercian houses, numbering on average fifty, although in one setting in Flanders, at the monastery of Les Dunes, they outnumbered the 180 regular monks by almost two to one.

Franciscan Third Order. In the urban setting, the Franciscans gave a different role to lay adherents. It was clearly the rigor of the religious life that appealed to these lay people. The Franciscans saw therefore that they observed as closely as any monk or friar all the practical aspects of the religious vocation: fasting, penance, prayer, seeking spiritual guidance, and so on. The Franciscan third order, unlike the *conversi*, did not change their source of livelihood nor abandon their spouses or children. Nonetheless, frequently their lives were spent quite dislocated from the walk into which they were born, with their spending much time ministering "among humble despised folk, among the poor and weak, sick, lepers, beggars."

Crusaders. The Crusaders were yet a different group of dedicated lay believers, a public religious society. Pilgrims at heart who desired to know they could come and go freely in the land where Jesus had lived and preached, the Holy Land, became soldiers "enlisted" by Pope Urban II to carry out a crusade or holy war against the Muslim Seljuk Turks who had taken to persecuting Christian visitors. The Pope warned that "Even now the Turks are torturing Christians, binding them and filling them with arrows, or making them kneel. . . ." All the rhetoric that was fomented to encourage a Crusader corps created a fervor that continued for almost two hundred years, between 1095 and 1291, when the last Christian stronghold at Acre in Palestine fell to the Muslims. Christians were ranked by the Pope in power according to their dedication to the cause, and pressure on the masses was rigidly maintained, especially by the upper clergy, who demanded impassioned and expensive involvement in ways similar to the secular obligation of the call to arms.

Career Crusaders. The thousands of people who took part in the Crusades were an eclectic group to share a collective endeavor. There were the career Crusaders, those who were members of religious military orders. The Hospitalers and the Teutonic Knights, or the Knights Templar, founded in Germany around 1190, were among the most feared of Christian warriors during the Crusades. The Hospitalers at first helped sick pilgrims and maintained a hospital in Jerusalem, while the Templars were originally a group of humble knights who protected pilgrims. Both chose to serve God by fighting rather than through prayer. The Teutonic Knights were also used in eastern Europe to gain converts between 1226 and 1283, during which time the Holy Roman Emperor Frederick II sent them to convert the Prussians to Christianity. Some noble knights were equally dedicated to the Crusades. Richard I (the Lionheart), favorite son of Eleanor of Aquitaine from her marriage to Henry II of England, spent much of his ten-year reign as king fighting in the Crusades, most notably in the Third Crusade of 1189–1192. Among the Crusaders, however, there were also serfs who were running away from rural hardship and nobles, from impecunious circumstances, in addition to those who were truly religious and hoping to free the Holy Land.

Series of Crusades. Between 1095 and 1099 there were different waves of Crusaders all attached to the First Crusade. The first military expedition was made up of French, Flemish, and Norman knights. They fought their way overland to Jerusalem, surviving attacks by the Turks, blistering heat, and shortages of food and water. Between 1202 and 1204 the Crusaders were the puppets of greedy Italian merchants who launched and financed the Fourth Crusade. It was not directed against the Muslims but against Constantinople, the great trade rival of the Italian cities. The Crusaders were led to sacking, burning, and stealing in the wealthy city of Constantinople, at the time one of the greatest cities in the world, with magnificent palaces, churches, schools, and public gardens. The Venetians, who had often been to Constantinople as traders, were able to seize the most valuable treasures. The victorious Crusaders set up a short-lived Latin empire there between 1204 and 1258–1261, when a Greek emperor was restored. In 1212 some fifty thousand children from France and Germany joined the Children's Crusade, or Crusade of Innocents, intended to regain the original spirit of the Crusades lost in the Fourth Crusade's attack on Constantinople. None of them reached the Holy Land, as many died of hunger, dis-

ease, or drowning. Some were sold as slaves. The Crusaders of the Sixth Crusade, however military, were forced to surrender and pay a heavy ransom after being surrounded by Turks in the city of Damietta, which they had just captured.

Crusader Settlements. While the Crusaders were for the most part dedicated to liberating the Holy Land, most of them were not committed to living there. Four Western-European-style feudal regimes were established, collectively known as *Outremer*. The knightly Crusaders settled in to build huge stone castles at the most strategic places within their kingdoms, particularly along the routes used by trading caravans. Although colonists were needed to hold the territory, having survived a crusade few Crusaders of less than noble birth stayed in the east. So if there is one feature that was shared by most of the Crusaders it was that while they made pilgrimages to the Holy Land, few of them remained there.

Religious Dissidents. Medieval Christian dissidents would not usually be recognized along with the *conversi* and Crusaders as a social grouping that enveloped some of the most devout believers of the period. Undoubtedly however, each one of those now remembered as unorthodox, the odd wandering preacher or hermit who acquired a following reflected a high degree of dedication to considering and weighing Christian ideas and practices, while admittedly attempting to revise the canonical position. Most dissident groups were a response to the Church's own open emphasis, at least in the twelfth and thirteenth centuries, on a minimalist lifestyle and preaching. Christian dissidents quite universally adopted the life of poverty, if rich to start, by giving away all their riches, if of lesser means, by making their lacks a virtue. It was, however, their social fervor as much as their religious revisionism that made them perhaps uneasy neighbors for the orthodox clergy. Most dissident, if not heretical, groups advocated a transformation of the whole social order hand-in-hand with their religious convictions.

Peasantry. Social organizations were also to be found outside the medieval religious sphere. There were at least four different categories of peasant: the free peasant, half-free peasants, serfs, and slaves. Free peasants were those who had personal liberties of mobility and were free to cultivate land that they might hold outright or by payment of a rent. The half-free peasant also had personal freedom, but frequently without land to his name, and had such extremely onerous constraints on his possibility to earn a living that at the very least his freedom of mobility was fully compromised. There were then the serfs who, although they were not technically the property of a lord as was a slave, had every condition of their lives dictated by the lord in return for a guaranteed livelihood from working the land. A serf could be sent to another manor, traded for another serf, denied the right to marriage or forced to marry, and so on. Not until there were more than enough workers than were needed to farm the land, which occurred by 1100, could the rural peasant of whatever station hope to escape his tie to land and lord with manumission, a grant of freedom and sometimes land ownership, or with an escape to a town where he could turn his talents or skills to a craft.

Castle. The life of the castle community of medieval nobles was not nearly as glamorous as some Romantic literature suggests. It created, however, a world unto itself, a world centered on the castle. Early medieval fortifications were little more than timber forts, protected by ditches, moats, and drawbridges. Later, stone castles were built with high towers and thick walls. The most powerful feudal lords lived in magnificent castles. A castle's living quarters did not, however, provide a comfortable home. Although early writings could be found in the libraries of the rich, the castles themselves were cold, damp, and dark, unwelcoming to quiet intellectual activity. Open fireplaces provided what heat there was, and in the absence of chimneys, introduced for the first time in Europe around 1100, it was probably just as well that the windows lacked glass.

Living Nobly. The medieval castle was erected to protect the lord, his lady, his family, and his serfs from attack. Indeed it protected the whole castle community, even in terms of provisions. Vegetables were grown and animals were kept all within the castle walls. The confines of the castle were tight for the quarters of all who needed protection. As people of the medieval castle community needed more room and began to spill outside of the walls, for the wealthy the castles themselves were to become country houses, more like their scattered manor homes.

Castle Fare. It is small wonder that in good weather the noble spent little time indoors, greatly preferring to hunt or fight. The nobility had a plentiful diet, if not otherwise greatly distinct from that of the peasantry. The main foods were meat and fish, cheese, peas, beans, carrots, and turnips. Either wine or beer was the main beverage. Fruit was seasonal, and sugar and spices were available only to the rich. The fare of the noble is often described as uninteresting, which perhaps explains why most accounts of medieval dining also speak of the nobility being diverted while eating by entertainment, players, singers, and so forth. Jesters were employed by European royalty by 1202. Table etiquette was unknown. A knife was the only utensil used, and each guest brought his own. There were no rugs to be soiled, and when filth reached unacceptable limits—not often—the straw covering the floor was easily replaced.

Feudal Towns. Like all land, most towns were part of the feudal system, and their land and inhabitants were originally controlled by kings or nobles. What the townsman needed to come out from under the economic yoke of feudalism was freedom: freedom to work, to own and to sell personal property, to establish courts to settle the problems that came up in trade and commerce, and to move about as desired. Virtually every group of medieval town dwellers struggled to be free and to secure personal freedom for everyone among them. Some towns, particularly in Italy, were strong enough to revolt and become independent city-states. In most places, however, the townsmen bought a charter from the king or lord.

Self-Government. With the freedom of their land from noble ownership, town or city dwellers became part of a new social organization. Several terms were used to identify that organization—the *commune*, *freiburgh*, or *fribourg*—the last two terms simply meaning free town. Since the town or city itself had not changed in acquiring its new status, more evocative of the new phenomenon of the medieval free town were terms that identified the community association, the newly unified group of urban inhabitants. City dwellers were no longer either nobles or serfs but of a class in between, a middle class. Members of this middle class were called by different names in the different medieval vernacular languages. In the Netherlands they were called burghers; in France, the bourgeoisie. In England they were known as factors. Later on, the buildings the English factors used as sites both for employing wage laborers to make goods and for storing raw materials and finished goods were called factories.

A writ ordering compulsory knighthood, 1256 (Public Record Office, London)

Urban Middle Class. This urban middle class was to have a tremendous influence on European history. The same town charter that declared that the residents of a town were personally free also permitted a town to develop its own form of government. By and large it could regulate its own affairs. The governing body in most towns was a council, made up largely of the wealthier merchants or of nobles who had moved to the city. Often there were serious conflicts within the town between rival groups as they fought to control the council: nobles, whose power had derived from their high social and economic station within the feudal system, and merchants, who had much to gain by determining civil government and law. Sometimes the struggles were between the wealthy, who governed, and the poor, who had little voice in government. Over the coming centuries it was to be the middle class who pressed the nobility and the kings to share power with them, not just in the cities, but also in the country at large.

University Population. The last urban societal subgroup to note is the medieval university population. Medieval universities grew out of associations of students and teachers, the journeymen and teaching masters of the guild of scholars, who organized themselves respectively into groups that would set up whole institutions of higher education. Students began to gather in Oxford by 1100, and their organization would by the thirteenth century yield Oxford, England's first university. At about the same time, Paris was also becoming a center for study with independent teachers. By 1231 the collective body of "the masters and students of Paris" was granted a papal charter to establish the University of Paris, its "constitutions and ordinances regulating the manner and time of lectures and disputations, the costume to be worn, the burial of the dead; and also concerning the bachelors, who are to lecture and at what hours, and on what they are to lecture; and concerning the prices of the lodgings or the interdiction of the same; and concerning a fit punishment for those who violate your constitutions or ordinances, by exclusion from your society." Not only did such a charter acknowledge the difference between the *universitas* of the scholars and other like associations of the town or city, it also became the source of a new rivalry, the *universitas* of the gown and the *universitas* of the town.

Sources:

Christopher Brooke, *The Structure of Medieval Society* (New York: McGraw-Hill, 1971).

Lester K. Little, *Religious Poverty and the Profit Economy in Medieval Europe* (Ithaca, N.Y.: Cornell University Press, 1978).

Joseph H. Lynch, *The Medieval Church, A Brief History* (London & New York: Longman, 1992).

John H. Mundy and Peter Riesenberg, *The Medieval Town* (Princeton, N.J.: Van Nostrand, 1958).

SOCIAL ORGANIZATIONS: STRATIFICATION

Secular Church Hierarchy. As the organization of the church grew during the Middle Ages, so too did the social stratification of the secular clergy. Parishes were established and priests appointed to take care of these tiniest jurisdic-

Seal of Raimon de Mondragon from Provence, depicting a vassal kneeling before his lord in an act of homage, twelfth century (Bibliothèque Nationale, Paris)

tions. The bishop, the next rank up in the secular church echelon, ruled over many parishes. The independence and political aggressivity of medieval bishops often made them ineffective in functioning as part of the larger church. At certain intervals the position of archbishop was established to group bishops into provinces under more direct supervision than that of the Pope. After all, the Pope in Rome was the leader of the whole Christian Church, and while he was in charge of all the bishops, he could not have his entire attention diverted to overseeing an obstreperous bishop or two.

Hierarchy in the Regular Clergy. In the case of the regular clergy, the notion of social stratification itself was an anathema. Monasteries were to be the site of social equalization as all entrants stood in their terrestrial communities as they would before God. Involuntary entrants, or oblates, were no less worthy members of the community than those who had joined voluntarily. Nonetheless, there was a social bias of sorts: monks received more attention than nuns. Emphasis on education for monks and nuns was not uniform throughout the Middle Ages. The early Benedictine order was not particularly concerned about the formal education of its members in general, but many of the most educated men of the early church were to come from its monasteries. Granting a few exceptions, not until the mid twelfth century would nuns, such as Heloise and Hildegard of Bingen, be able to be recognized as well educated and learned, in nunneries, which were allowed to function for women as important centers of learning.

Lay Marriage. Among the laity, gender also played a part in social stratification. While the role of the male noble was initially primarily to fight, at the highest echelons of the nobility, men also were trained to govern.

LENGTH OF SELECT APPRENTICESHIPS IN THE THIRTEENTH CENTURY

The following apprenticeships were the more common ones found in medieval cities such as Paris and Genoa.

Apprenticeship	Years
Baker, Carpenter, Draper, Ropemaker, Spinner	4
Barber, Cloth worker (wool), Cobbler, Hatter (fur hats), Mason	5
Coppersmith, Cutler, Dyer, Tailor	6
Blacksmith, Carder, Hatter (felt hats), Turner	7
Butcher, Cloth worker (silk and linen), Locksmith, Painter of saddles, Religious artifacts maker (bone), Tanner	8
Bookbinder, Harness maker, Religious artifacts maker (beads and buttons)	9
Armorer, Cooper, Religious artifacts maker (amber), Saddler, Silversmith, Tapestry maker	10
Chestmaker	11
Lapidary, Religious artifacts maker (coral)	12

Source: Steven A. Epstein, *Wage Labor and Guilds in Medieval Europe* (Chapel Hill: University of North Carolina Press, 1991).

Noblewomen were raised for the most part to be chaste wives to the nobility. Marriage made for love was not unknown in the Middle Ages. Geoffrey Chaucer celebrates it in "The Franklin's Tale," a hymn to equality and love in marriage. Yet, by and large, a woman of the landed classes was a commodity to be traded by parents with calculating care, for territorial or commercial advantage, status, power, or influence. Some marriages brought the English kings the great lands of Aquitaine, Anjou, Gascony, and Brittany. Love, it was thought, might grow out of marriage, but there was no need to take love into it. Most daughters of the nobility were "sold into marriage," such as an English noble child, in around 1200, who at age eleven was married for the third time for a payment in cash.

Noblewomen. Only occasionally were noblewomen raised for power and subsequently allowed to assume it. For example, Mathilda, though queen of England, was never crowned. In the civil war between herself and a contender, Stephen (1139–1148), she was defeated. Nonetheless, her son, Henry of Anjou, recognized by the victorious Stephen as heir to the throne, did rule England (including Northumbria, Cumbria, and Westmoreland by 1157, and Ireland by 1171) and France, as Henry II (1154–1189). Duke William of Aquitaine was the exceptional medieval father in raising his daughter, Eleanor, to rule his land in central and southwestern France in the twelfth century. Upon her marriage to King Louis VII of France, Eleanor brought more territory to the kingdom than he had. Her chance to rule came, however, only in her second marriage, when her son by Henry II of England, King Richard I (the Lion-Heart), was away on crusade. By 1317 in France,

appeal to the Salic Law officially banned women from inheriting the throne, in accordance with the general sentiment, frequently expressed as in 1200 by an elderly Parisian man to his new fifteen-year-old wife, that a woman's duty was simply to offer love, patience, and obedience to her husband.

Urban Strata. The urban environment with its many social organizations also reflected blatant social stratification. As noted earlier, the cities were filled with craftsmen of all sorts. Trades for males fell into different categories of difficulty and prestige. Among the easier trades to learn and the lowest in terms of status were shoemaking, tailoring, and candle making. Those ranking somewhere in the middle were carpenters and blacksmiths. At the elite end of the artisan scale, and the most expensive in which to be trained, were trades such as goldsmithing and glassmaking. Females faced the social stratification for religious and noblewomen. In the craft sphere, women chose among limited options.

Apprentices. The lowest strata in the urban community belonged to the apprentices of whatever craft. Within the European commercial production community, master workers ran their own shops. These craft masters frequently hired young people to serve under them. An apprentice was usually a boy of seven or eight who wanted to learn a trade. His work was where the master's household was; therefore the apprentice usually lived in his master's house, receiving there a room, food, and some clothing. He was not given any payment, however. An apprentice was bound to his master, studying under him to learn the trade and business for anywhere from two to twelve years.

Allegory of the Dominican Order, depicting the temporal and spiritual hierarchy of powers; fresco
by Andrea da Firenze in the Spanish chapel Santa Maria Novella in Florence, circa 1350

Education. Apprentices' low position in the craft social hierarchy was because of their age and lack of training. Children and adolescents, still in need of sheltering from the world, were nonetheless part of the employment work ladder, receiving training in a craft or skill and often at the same time learning the basics of reading, writing, and sometimes ciphering. However low the station, it was an important one particularly for children of the poor who usually had only one other means of survival. They could be sent to a monastery or at least to a religious school set up by the monks or priests for the purpose of teaching children. That route would more probably lead to a life in the church, rather than to the potential riches of a craft profession. Apprenticeships ideally offered a dual education: training in a skill as well as the rudiments of education, both of which became increasingly important in the medieval urban economy. In this way apprenticeship was an important vehicle for educating medieval children in an era when formal education was neither required nor the time to indulge in it readily available.

Gaining Master Status. Upon completion of his training as an apprentice, a would-be medieval craftsman became a journeyman, a worker who was paid by the day (*journée* in French). If he remained within his master's household, rather than traveling to learn different techniques under other masters, he would work there for wages

for the first time. His greater training gave him a position higher in the stratification of the craft world than that of the apprentice. A journeyman was indeed the second and last rank before becoming a craft master. The journeyman would devote part of his work time to the crafting of an exemplar of his skill worthy of a master, a "masterpiece." If his masterpiece were acceptable to masters of the guild he hoped to join, the former journeyman would then be permitted to open his own shop as a craft master, the highest rank in the craft world, and maybe teach his sons the trade.

Medical Service. Of all the medieval service professions, medicine was among the most lucrative. Then as now, satirists jeered at the exorbitant salaries of doctors. Although from as early as 1140 in France, doctors had to have a license to practice, the guilds that did the licensing were yet to have the same authority as those for practitioners less highly ranked in the medical order of social status: the surgeon, the apothecary, and the barber. Then as now, patients sued their doctors for malpractice, winning in some cases substantial awards, such as the recorded more than twice a day laborer's maximum annual wages. These penalties provided some means of hitting the unqualified, incompetent, or downright fraudulent physicians, if not of lowering the outright cost of seeing a doctor. By the fourteenth century, some physicians were trying to protect themselves by bringing a patient's relatives before the civic authorities to sign consent documents before any treatments were rendered, yet a course of treatment might still cost a patient almost half of a day laborer's annual wages!

Doctors. A physician with good fortune and presumed skill, since the penalties for misdiagnoses or bad treatments could be far harsher than fines, could work for a lord. In one year alone he could earn five or more times the pay of a common laborer. On top of his salary he would receive costly gifts as well. Doctors in the service of royalty did even better. The English king paid his favorite court physicians a yearly salary of up to three or more times what a lord might make and showered them with honors and gifts, even bestowing sizable estates on them.

Sources:

Christopher Brooke, *The Structure of Medieval Society* (New York: McGraw-Hill, 1971).

Lester K. Little, *Religious Poverty and the Profit Economy in Medieval Europe* (Ithaca, N.Y.: Cornell University Press, 1978).

Joseph H. Lynch, *The Medieval Church, A Brief History* (London & New York: Longman, 1992).

John H. Mundy and Peter Riesenberg, *The Medieval Town* (Princeton, N.J.: Van Nostrand, 1958).

TRADE: INTERACTION AMONG PEOPLES

Contact. There certainly was contact by medieval traders with peoples of different lands. By the late ninth century the Vikings met Inuits in Greenland and North America, Celts in Ireland, and Angles and Saxons in Mercia, Northumbria, and East Anglia. Traders from the cities of Genoa and Pisa had met the Muslims in violent clashes at sea by the year 1000. The German princes' victory over the Danes at Bornhöven (1227) opened the way for south-coast Baltic merchants to dominate trade in Scandinavia. In the late thirteenth century the Venetians Marco Polo, his father, Niccolo, and his uncle Maffeo reached Mongolian China and became personally acquainted with one of the emperors, Kublai Khan.

Muslims. The Muslims, believers of the prophet Muhammed's religion, carried on trade in Europe as well as in Africa, China, and Central Russia, especially from 750 until 1055, under the family of caliphs called the Abbasids. The Arabs were traditionally traders who crossed the deserts in caravans or large groups. When the people of the North African highlands, the Berbers, became Muslims, they too became part of the great network of Islamic merchants. Using copper ingots and cowry shells as currency, Berbers traded for ivory, skins, slaves, salt, and gold, which made their way into the Islamic Spanish markets. Arab culture encouraged agriculture and manufacturing, especially of silk and linen cloth, pottery, enamels, and fine metalwork; and Muslim cities, including those in Spain from the 700s onward, were filled with fine trade goods: cloth, rugs, leather goods, and many others.

European Encounters. In a practical sense medieval traders encountered different peoples and different lands within close range of one another and perhaps of their own homes. The cities of medieval England, France, and Germany have been described as isolated islands of urban life amid the great rural sea of villages, manors, forests, swamps, and wasteland. Indeed, many a city in the Middle Ages was so different from the surrounding countryside as to be a different land, if not a distinct landmass. In addition to the urban-rural differences, regional geographic ones were marked. Northern Europe was different from southern Europe, and again, when by 1300 ships were coming from the Mediterranean to reach North Sea port cities, such as Bruges, one could speak of "new lands" being opened beyond "old borders." Suitability for the extraction or production of some goods in one area alone made it distinctive from the merchant's perspective, since its goods could be sold as special in other areas not suited to their production. Flourishing trade between two geographical areas, such as Britain and Flanders, exporting and importing raw wool respectively, almost defined their being different lands. Merchants' calls for tariffs, or taxes placed on imported goods, reinforced this perception, since the premise behind tariffs is that the goods that are being sold for less have arrived for trade from "other lands" and that a limit on them through taxation would help the manufacturers and traders of "this land."

Differences. The reality of the differences among lands and peoples was for the medieval trader a double-edged sword. On the positive side, the revival of trade in Europe provided an exciting, lucrative outlet for adventurous merchants. There were always some who wanted to learn more than the skills of trade; they also wanted to understand the world in which they lived. Aside, however, from the personal pleasure some merchants derived from travel to exotic places, learning of new goods to be bought from afar was the principle, stimulating reward of new contacts, as, for example, for European traders in visiting the Middle East or the Polos' discovering the extensive inland-waterway mercantile activity of thirteenth-century China. To European merchants, the riches of Byzantium were ample suggestion that exchanges over ever longer distances worked well and that traders should establish more connections in the disparate lands of the Far East. For some traders, such as those of Venice, interaction among peoples from different lands was a foregone eventuality. Since their coastal city had no land, the Venetians were forced to make their living on the sea. Gradually, Venetian sailors began to trade all along the Mediterranean coasts. Indeed, the first important European trading cities, Venice, Genoa, Pisa, and Florence, along with London, Paris, and Marseilles, all expanded largely because their traders sought out novel and rare goods from lands separated by water. Northern Italian merchants had rendered Eastern silks, sugar, and spices (pepper, ginger, cloves, and cinnamon) luxury items by the eleventh century, and although these products were more common by the thirteenth century, they still brought in enormous profits. The exploits of the Swedish Vikings, also called Varangians, represent another trading success story. The Vikings were traders, warriors, and farmers in Scandinavia who left their homes and traveled widely between the ninth and the eleventh centuries. Travel along the Russian rivers that led them to settle among the Slavs and along Russia's Baltic coast made them part of the fruitful long-distance trade between the diverse spheres of the Baltic Sea and the Islamic world.

Black Death. As positive as were the sellable goods distant lands afforded, they also offered a "hidden" export or two. The worst of the Middle Ages came in the winter of 1347–1348, when a Genoese ship returned to Italy from the east, via the Crimea, to the southern Italian port of Messina. The cargo that came ashore brought with it rats carrying a terrible disease known as the Black Death. It was the bubonic plague, a type of plague carried by the fleas living on black rats, likely transported over trade caravan routes from China. When the ship returned to Genoa, it permitted the disease to spread to other Italian cities. Other ships brought the plague to Marseilles in southern France. Many medieval towns and especially the burgeoning cities saw their populations cut by one-third to one-half by this new trade import. It killed, at low estimates, between one-fifth and one-third (about twenty million) of Europe's population by 1351.

Ship Travel. The other part of the relationship between disparate peoples and lands was, however, of a more sustained nature. Different lands were separated by distance, and distance between buyer and seller in any medieval exchange entailed risk. Wrecks of ships sailing to reach far-off ports caused great losses frequently enough to slow acceptance of the idea of investment in maritime trade. Until the thirteenth century, ship construction without watertight bulkheads or stern-post rudders made it a challenge to persuade investors they would receive their goods. Until the later Middle Ages the Viking ships were perhaps the safest and most versatile. Designed for both sailing and rowing, the low and narrow long-ships, or warships, were shallow enough to be rowed up rivers. Their cargo ships were higher and wider, designed to carry up to thirty-eight tons of cargo. Both types of boats could be dragged over the snow between rivers if necessary. By the year 1000, the cities of Genoa and Pisa had nonetheless built strong fleets of galleys, made the Mediterranean safe for their commerce, and reduced considerably the military dangers of maritime distance travel. By 1300, ships were successfully coming from the Mediterranean to reach northern European port cities.

Instability. A lack of political centrality also created problems for the medieval trader. People under different political regimes tended in the Middle Ages, and earlier, to fight rather than to trade peacefully. Political decentralization in Europe from invading tribes and wars had brought the destruction of Roman imperial commercial life. Trade had not surprisingly almost completely disappeared during the turmoil, but the road system that had been so beneficial to it also virtually disappeared. From the point when Charlemagne's son, Louis the Pious, shared his inheritance of 814 with his three sons, Europe was to be made up of a patchwork of small kingdoms or other political entities, ruled by kings, princes, or dukes. Even in the East, constant warfare imposed a heavy strain on Byzantium's ability to remain a rich trading power.

Impact. Medieval merchants thought unifying different lands and peoples under a few strong political and fiscal entities was the best way to establish the necessary pan-European infrastructure for trade. In early medieval France each kingdom was supposed to take care of its own roads and bridges, but local princes or nobles to whom the responsibility fell rarely did. Short-term movement was so limited by bad roads and transport that merchants began to need much better forms of transportation. Roads and bridge maintenance continued throughout the Middle Ages to be a matter of different approaches, adapted to local conditions, but general improvement in the forms of merchants' transportation was essentially seen as a matter for a central authority to oversee. Medieval merchants also wanted marine and land armed forces they could count on to protect them and their property as well as the general purchasing citizenry, wherever they traveled. To simplify their lives and save their profits, merchants sought to avoid exchanging the currencies of many different regions at the hands of the money changers by encouraging monarchs to centralize the minting of money and to punish those who made counterfeit coinage. They also wanted the harmonizing of the merchant taxes of the many different lands they passed through.

Codes in Law. Sensing that adherence to law might well be a precondition to the growth of trade, merchants also favored a political power that could bring back the rule of law and set up a code of laws for everyone in the land, the larger in size the better. Once the Viking kings established firm control of their lands, trade flourished there, as did agriculture. It was obvious to medieval merchants, whose travel gave them many points of comparison, that local princes or nobles applied local rules in a sporadic and often capricious way. Both arbitrary and narrow customary ways of coping regionally were seen to be ill suited to growth in trade and expansion of towns. Merchants favored the eventual administration by an enlightened noble of ever greater swatches of territory and the establishment of some sort of pan-European administration. Although nothing close to a central government ever materialized again in the Middle Ages after ninth-century Carolingian France, rules inspired by the rediscovery of Roman law in the late eleventh century spread throughout Europe. A rather common stock of procedures and concepts emerged, the *jus commune* as it came to be known, which gave continental Europe a strong sense of legal unity and merchants their own section of "international" law.

Hanseatic League. Some groups of merchants simply took matters of creating a hospitable environment for trade within different lands into their own hands. Initially in order to protect themselves from attacks by pirates, sea merchants of several young and vigorous commercial cities along the Baltic and North Seas formed the Hanseatic League (1250–1669). To strengthen their safety in trading, this group of cities banded together for their mutual pro-

Venetian merchants exchanging cloth for oriental produce; illumination from an
early-fourteenth-century manuscript (Bibliothèque Nationale, Paris)

tection and set up trading associations, called *hanse*. The league of about eighty cities, including Hamburg, Bremen, Cologne, Danzig, and Lübeck as its center, in northern Germany, went on to draw up rules for internal cooperation. The League built permanent warehouses in such cities as London and maintained its own armed forces. Once the League was tightly formed, merchants could safely and profitably ship their goods. By keeping warships for protection, it got rid of the pirates in the North Sea, and by the late Middle Ages its maritime army, strong enough to protect its members, was also powerful enough, under threat of war, to force other cities, feudal nobles, and even kings to grant League traders favorable treatment. Birger Jarl of Sweden, for example, gave trading privileges to the League upon his conquest of Finland. In fact, so dominated was Baltic and North Sea trade by the Hanseatic League that Lübeck could prosper alone from shipping continental goods across the Baltic Sea to Scandinavia. As the Hanseatic cities came to dominate northern Europe, the trade route from Italy to the north moved east. This situation meant not only that the League came to watch over the land routes now between Germany and Italy, but also that the Duchy of Champagne was no longer on the main north-south trade route, which spelled one of the reasons for the end of the Champagne Fair cycle.

Importance of Trade. Observing also that peace was a precondition to the growth of trade, merchants in the Middle Ages favored it as well. Although later medieval merchants were not historians and were probably mainly concerned about the safer passage and consistent markets that peace between different peoples and lands made possi-

ble, indeed it was, in the early Middle Ages, local stability that had brought agricultural productivity, which in turn had brought the surplus of goods requisite for trade to flourish. Following the devastating fall of Rome, farmers no longer produced enough food to sell. Their villages were simply local communities trying desperately to provide the necessities for their inhabitants. With more peaceful local conditions, however, by around 900, buying and selling slowly began to develop with lords' selling their new agricultural surplus at a profit. With market sites fostered by feudal nobles, it was natural for old towns to begin to grow again and new ones to form, all to become centers of trade from which many a medieval merchant would profit.

Facilitation of Trade. As the work of Marco Polo reflects in its descriptions of the improbable wonders of China, most buyers were blissfully naive about what the merchant could accomplish in the difficult trade environment of the Middle Ages. That traders at the end of the Middle Ages were incomparably richer than their counterparts at its beginning is proof positive, however, that they more than met the challenges of distance and political instability that different lands and different peoples presented. Medieval cities became the homes of men of great wealth or capital who had made their fortunes in trade. Long before the Middle Ages had ended, merchants and former merchants, the bankers, of the medieval towns rivaled feudal nobles, princes, and even kings in wealth. Not all the credit for their successes can be given to medieval traders alone, however. By the late Middle Ages the civil society of the Christian Church and the increased power of the European kings had helped Europe recover markedly from centuries of invasions, lawlessness, and economic breakdown. Increasing law and order had encouraged new economic activity, which had made Europe prosperous and strong, and experiences such as the Crusades had taught Christians that it was safer and more profitable to trade with those of another place and faith than to fight with them. Nonetheless, if the nobility had done much to create an economically viable world of the Middle Ages out of the wreckage of the Roman world, the merchant had done his part to begin shaping the modern world out of the Middle Ages.

Sources:

G. G. Coulton, comp., *Social Life in Britain from the Conquest to the Reformation* (Cambridge: Cambridge University Press, 1918).

Odd Langholm, *Economics in the Medieval Schools. Wealth, Exchange, Value, Money and Usury according to the Paris Theological Tradition, 1200–1350* (Leiden & New York: E. J. Brill, 1992).

Robert S. Lopez and Irving W. Raymond, *Medieval Trade in the Mediterranean World: Illustrative Documents Translated with Introductions and Notes* (New York: Columbia University Press, 1955).

Henri Pirenne, *Medieval Cities: Their Origins and the Revival of Trade*, translated by Frank D. Halsey (Princeton: Princeton University Press, 1969).

Susan Reynolds, *Kingdoms and Communities in Western Europe, 900–1300* (Oxford: Clarendon Press, 1984).

TRADE: METHODS OF EXCHANGE

Barter. The earliest medieval method of economic exchange for trader and nontrader alike was barter. The markets for the early trader were largely the feudal village and the manor household. Their internal economy was based on service and duties, not on payments of money. Goods that had to be secured outside the village or manor were few in number, and they could usually be procured in direct exchange for agricultural products. Even trade for some of the most prized items, salt and iron, occurred most widely by barter throughout the Middle Ages. Indeed, without money as the medium of an exchange, serving as a standard of value for whether an item had sold for more than it was purchased, it was perhaps more difficult for a medieval trader to determine whether he had gained in a single transaction. Relatively sedentary merchants could, however, barter goods purchased for goods they needed personally, valuing them as any buyer would for their esteemed value. Even the more mobile merchants of the Middle Ages could, where they developed regular trade, establish consistency in the relative values of bartered items. For example, a merchant might set the value of a pair of shoes consistently at a certain number of hen's eggs, or a thrashing tool at a bushel of oats.

Monetization. In addition to barter, which continued throughout the Middle Ages to be a part of local trade, another main method of economic exchange entered the mercantile realm: coinage, or money, as the medium. Already in the ninth century, coins were coming into increasing use in medieval Europe. The first step in the establishment of money as the main basis of all value was the acceptance of gold and other precious metals as barter payments for goods. Most monetary transactions would involve the use of metals of known quality, determined initially by weight, hardness, and so on. Confirmation of the consensual value of gold in the Middle Ages took many forms.

Gold and Silver. Gold and silver were highly sought-after commodities of trade. Throughout the Middle Ages, Berber traders exchanged horses, copper, and tools for gold mined in the Saharan desert, much of which would become a medium of European exchange. Gold and silver were also material rewards of battle. As the most prized booty of the Vikings, these precious metals became the substance of their renowned bracelets, sword hilts, and even their decorative shipboard weather vanes. Traders' carrying gold and silver presented a worthwhile incentive for road robbery.

Advantages. The major advantage to traders of exchanges with money—whether in selling or buying—was that they were less cumbersome than those in which both parties brought goods to the transaction. The loss of the distance trade of Roman times in Europe meant there was less need for money in the early Middle Ages. By the twelfth and thirteenth centuries, however, exchanging goods for goods proved restrictive to longer-range trade. Although its potential advantages were obvious, coinage, weighed pieces of precious metal usually stamped symbolically by a minting authority, only slowly took the place of validated gold or silver ingots. Most medieval coins were unrecognized beyond the region of their minting and hence served predominantly in local transactions of all sorts, as, for example, in the measure of what a noble owed his king, or even a peasant, his lord, in terms of service and duties.

Coin Metals and Weights. A few coins did become, outside the territory of their minting authority, respected for being of consistent metal content and therefore acceptable as a standard of value in long-distance trade. By the ninth century, silver had become the preeminent metal in medieval coins, used for the especially dominant *denarius* (penny) that formed the pivotal surviving part of the Carolingian monetary system, comprised of the *abolis* (half-penny), *solidus* (equal to 12 pennies), and the *libra*, or pound (equal to 240 pennies). The hefty quantity of silver in an Italian coin, the *grosso* of Venice and Genoa, from 1200 on set the course for the silver minting of the *gigliato* in southern Italy, the larger *gros tournois* in France, the still larger groat in England, and the *groschen* in the German kingdom. Two gold coins became important in the later Middle Ages, the florin of Florence and the ducat of Venice. Although of the same complete purity and equal weight, just exceeding 3.5 grams, the florin dominated over the *genovino* of Genoa and all other coins as the trading currency of Western Europe as far north as the North Sea. Merchants gave the ducat, of the same standard as the florin, more influence in Mediterranean trade, to the point that it usurped the earlier spread in that sphere of Byzantine and Islamic gold coins.

Markets. The regular market, and at intervals the cyclical fair, were the medieval traders' main loci for exchange. The highlight of town life was the market. Markets took

A late-thirteenth-century illumination of women at a fair shopping for Eastern silk, rugs, leather, and jewelry (Escorial Monastery, Madrid)

place on market days, once or twice a week in most towns or cities, which welcomed mercantile activity. Concentrations of people and trade proved mutually reinforcing in the Middle Ages. The towns and cities that eventually grew into the most prosperous trading locations had often sprung from sites where people had originally gathered to trade, at perhaps a fortification or a prominent church. Since life was safer and easier near the castles of the nobles or the possible sanctuary of the church, people settled where they were most protected from wars and other dangers. As the more secure of these trade towns grew from little more than colonies within walled fortresses, many people had to reside outside the original walls, creating a newly inhabited area. An actual marketplace often became the center of a town's new quarter, and eventually the center of the entire town as it expanded even more. Bruges, in present-day Belgium, for example, which grew from a small fortress site in the mid ninth century into a fortified settlement for various merchants and craftsmen by the eleventh century, had long since exceeded its walled jurisdiction by 1350, with an estimated population of 46,000

and a huge cloth market to which foreign traders crowded. By the fourteenth century, formerly small walled towns had many merchants in residence. For example, Carcassone, with a population of about 9,500, counted 42 merchants, and the much larger Florence had 1,500.

Fairs. The medieval fair was similar to a wholesalers gathering organized by an area's local nobility on a specially determined market area along a major trade route to permit and protect trading in specific goods for a fixed number of days. Until about 1250, cyclical international fairs flourished in Europe as the traders' most important point of exchange. Many medieval merchants would move from fair to fair during the good traveling months, carrying their products north to England, Sweden, Flanders, and Germany, south through France to Italy, and east to the Middle East. As the Duchy of Champagne in France was on the main trade route between Flanders and Italy, it hosted the most prominent medieval fairs, near Chalons-sur-Marne, Troyes, Provins, Lagny-sur-Marne, and Bar-sur-Aube. Each Champagne fair was actually a sequence of specialized fairs.

Fair Cycle. During its period in the fair cycle, each participating town would attract in turn the attendance of buyers and sellers from all over Europe. Stalls and booths would be set up, and at the Fair of Cloth, for example, textile merchants would display British wool, Asian silks, and Flemish and Italian cloth. The Fair of Fabricated Items would attract traders of armor, jewelry, and religious objects for churches and cathedrals. At the Fair of Weight, spice merchants would be present. The stalls and booths came down when the fair was over. Before setting off, merchants changed the many coins of varying denominations with which they had been paid for coinage of immediate future use or more stable value. They then went on to the next fair on the international route or to one closer to or at home, and the town settled down to its normal routine, returning to the local market for procuring goods.

Currencies. As inextricably linked as coinage with methods of economic exchange in trade were the currencies the merchants created for their own circumstances. These currencies all took the form of a written contract and hence reflected the same confidence in the guarantee behind a piece of writing that was essential to the later adoption of paper money in Europe. Medieval people learned of monetary notes by the later thirteenth century at least, from the accounts of the Venetian trader Marco Polo who, in writing of his hospitable stay in China under Emperor Kublai Khan, told of the Mongolians' use of many important inventions, including paper money. The various written "notes" of medieval merchants were not, strictly speaking, methods of exchange as it has been understood thus far, but rather methods that created contractual obligations among specific parties. Nonetheless, each one fostered the procuring and sale of goods to other traders or end users, and some bore particularly close similarity to instruments of exchange.

Contracts. Medieval merchant contracts generally afforded financial support to a trading venture. Some were mere financial testimonials, letters of credit; others, such as bills of exchange, were statements of fund transfers, backed by credit, across different currencies. Significantly, neither type required the changing hands of goods or money before the culmination of the venture itself, which is the main reason medieval trading and what would actually pass today for banking transactions went together. Where actual financing was required, such a contractual voucher would serve as the guarantee for promissory notes presented to those offering the materiel for travel. When a trader could front his own venture, two different types of delayed compensation contracts could come into play: the *emptio*, a purchase contract, obliging a buyer to pay, usually at a predetermined price, for goods when delivered, and/or the *venditio*, a sale contract committing a seller to deliver goods once available at the agreed-upon price. The existence of these two contracts, each representing distinctly a buy or a sell, lends great credence to their role as actual methods of exchange.

Lending. The *columna* contract of eleventh-century southern Italy created a partnership between merchants, seamen, and shipowners, whereby a venture's final gains and losses would be shared according to the value of each partner's initial contribution. The *commenda*, known as well by other names including the *collegantia*, of Venice allowed for one party to finance a trade venture and the other to execute it with no financial commitment. At the conclusion of the expedition, both partners would share in the return at an agreed-upon percentage, with the financial partner shouldering any eventual losses. Outright loans, with no apparent vested expectation of gain from a maritime trading venture, carried over from the Roman period into the Middle Ages. They highlighted, however, one of the reasons the reputation of medieval merchants was often so besmirched, in that such loans, usually from one wealthy merchant to a colleague, often entailed a payment of interest on the principal investment, frequently in the guise of currency exchanges. Demands for repayment of more than an initial loan amount were interpreted as contrary to church teaching and hence to Christian faith, and all parties to such contracts were anathematized.

Sources:

G. G. Coulton, comp., *Social Life in Britain from the Conquest to the Reformation* (Cambridge: Cambridge University Press, 1918).

Odd Langholm, *Economics in the Medieval Schools. Wealth, Exchange, Value, Money and Usury according to the Paris Theological Tradition, 1200–1350* (Leiden & New York: E. J. Brill, 1992).

Robert S. Lopez and Irving W. Raymond, *Medieval Trade in the Mediterranean World: Illustrative Documents Translated with Introductions and Notes* (New York: Columbia University Press, 1955).

TRADE: OCCUPATIONS AND WORK HABITS

Economic Endeavor. Medieval trade was primarily an economic, rather than a social, endeavor, dedicated to buying and selling transactions in local and distant market settings. Sedentary or peripatetic, its principal participants were the medieval merchants or traders whose livelihood depended upon their purchasing goods cheaply and selling them dear. The life of bringing goods to market was never an easy one in the Middle Ages; the merchant was made the target of church doctrine and the golden egg of regional nobility. Exchange did, however, have its potential for lavish compensation, and despite the difficult environment of risky transport conditions, political decentralization, and fiscal disharmony, the key mercantile figures of the Champagne Fairs, the Flemish textile trade, or the Hanseatic League all made a good living. As a collective, medieval merchants were to leave a legacy of having fostered new tools of investment and exchange and having brought respectful contact through goods among disparate contemporary peoples.

Characteristics of Traders. Medieval traders bought and sold or exchanged goods in trade. Except for the fact that commerce was their immediate undertaking, it is difficult to establish other essential features of medieval traders as a group and thereby to identify the main aspects of their occupation as buyers and sellers. First, medieval traders were both a settled and a highly mobile group. Many a

THE LIFE OF A MEDIEVAL MERCHANT

Reginald of Durham, devoted disciple and biographer of Godric of Finchale, wrote one of the few surviving accounts of the life of a medieval merchant, telling of the Englishman Godric's early life as scavenger, peddler, businessman, and sailor and of his later path as a hermit attracting visitors such as Reginald himself to the Finchale forest near Durham. The following is an extract from the biography of Godric, who was born at Walpole, Norfolk, circa 1065 and died in Finchale, Durham, on 21 May, circa 1170.

When the boy had passed his childish years quietly at home; then, as he began to grow to manhood, he began to follow more prudent ways of life, and to learn carefully and persistently the teaching of worldly forethought. Wherefore he chose not to follow the life of a husbandman, but rather to study, learn and exercise the rudiment of more subtle conceptions. For this reason, aspiring to the merchant's trade, he began to follow the chapman's way of life, first learning how to gain in small bargains and things of insignificant price; and thence, while yet a youth, his mind advanced little by little to buy and sell and gain from things of greater expense. For, in his beginnings, he was wont to wander with small wares around the villages and farmsteads of his own neighborhood; but, in process of time, he gradually associated himself by compact with city merchants. Hence, within a brief space of time, the youth who had trudged for so many weary hours from village to village, from farm to farm, did so profit by his increase of age and wisdom as to travel with associates of his own age through towns and boroughs, fortresses and cities, to fairs and to all the various booths of the market-place, in pursuit of his public chaffer. He went along the high-way, neither puffed up by the good testimony of his conscience nor downcast in the nobler part of his soul by the reproach of poverty.

Source: Reginald of Durham, "Life of St. Godric," in G. G. Coulton, comp., *Social Life in Britain from the Conquest to the Reformation* (Cambridge: Cambridge University Press, 1918).

medieval merchant resided, with his whole household, in a town and lived by selling wares in the local area. For a significant number of the earlier medieval traders, the sedentary way of life was, however, not seen to be the merchant's ultimate vocation.

Travels. Traveling from town to town along specific trade routes was characteristic of many medieval traders, but the culminating goal of the profession seems to have been to become a rich and powerful "middleman" of exchanges across or through the Mediterranean or Baltic Seas, east and west, north and south. Undoubtedly not entirely representative even of fellow traders, since at the peak of his sixteen-year career he turned to the life of a hermit, the Englishman Godric of Finchale is nonetheless an interesting illustration of a twelfth-century medieval merchant. Once an adult, he became first a chapman or peddler for four years in Lincolnshire, then a merchant traveling on

foot north to Scotland and south to Rome, and finally a maritime trader with loci or interests in two merchant ships, which sailed frequently to Denmark and Flanders. Thus, although he began his mercantile career living at his family home and peddling goods at nearby villages and farms, in time his mobility became ever greater and the sphere in which he sold goods ever wider. By the thirteenth century, a sedentary lifestyle for the middleman returned to become in fact the most esteemed, especially in Italy, where it reflected one's mercantile expertise that goods ordered could arrive safely, unaccompanied by any peripatetic trader.

Merchants' Exchange. Second, characterizing further the occupation of the medieval trader poses another difficulty arising from the contemporary methods of economic exchange. Medieval merchants are usually identified as such because they sold goods for money. Whether money was a part of a medieval exchange has little to do with identifying any partner in the transaction as a merchant. The far more important element of the situation would be the consideration as to whether any party to the exchange saw transactions per se as his sole source of livelihood. The medieval merchant was the one whose principal endeavor was to survive by buying and reselling, and thus necessarily he was the one selling for more what he had acquired for less, to be able to live on the difference. If a medieval man could live from the return on his "outside affairs," such that he could keep a household and a wife to provide him with "fresh stockings . . . good food and drink . . . white sheets . . . and privies about which I am silent," he was worthy of the title *merchant*.

Wealth Gathering. If economic survival from exchanges was the medieval trader's basic purpose, gathering much wealth was his next priority. This task required creating the greatest spread possible between the purchase cost of an item to the trader and its end sale price. Two economic "verities" already existed in the Middle Ages: the rarer the item the greater its value, and the greater the value of an item the greater its "markup" potential, the realizable difference between its purchase and sale price. Thus, trade in luxury goods, particularly items rare at any one point in time or region, offered the greatest opportunity for high return in exchanges. This type of trade would explain in large part the reason long-distance travel to bring luxury goods from their source to a market far away where they were considered rare was seen to be the pinnacle of a medieval merchant's undertakings.

Transport. Sea voyages, overland transits, and the transporting of the goods in whatever circumstances were all part and parcel of the activities by which medieval merchants earned a good living. These mercantile efforts were not without cost. In the earlier Middle Ages all travelers confronted the dearth of roads. For merchants carrying any obvious prize for preying bandits, safe passage of goods and self were often hard to secure. At sea, pirates obstructed the use of coastal routes in some areas and political enemies resisted port entry. Given the vagaries of weather, maraud-

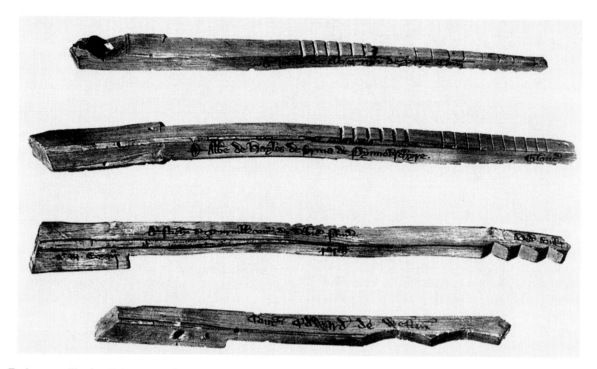

Exchequer tallies (credit instruments) with the amounts payable indicated by the size of the notches on the sticks and the sources of the payments written on them, thirteenth century (Public Record Office, London)

ers, and wars, medieval transportation conditions were never so consistent as to become automatic to the trader. The only sure aspect of the job was that a market somewhere had to be reached to make the sale of goods purchased.

Profit Motive. The aspect of the general attitude of medieval merchants to their trade most striking to their contemporaries seems to have been their eagerness to practice it. When described by nonmerchants in a positive light, this zeal was seen to be the driving force behind boldness in travel and attention to "subtle conceptions." More often, however, the enthusiasm with which medieval merchants sold goods was painted, again by nonmerchants, in a negative light. It was seen as greed or cupidity, which drove merchants to be deceitful in tampering with merchandise or measurement of its quantity, or even to sell more or at a higher price than needed for their own necessities. They were portrayed as weak to the temptations of fraudulent transactions and unmindful of the main tenet of exchange that no profit should accrue to him who simply buys and sells and adds no value to the goods themselves.

Accounts. There are few surviving documents in which medieval traders characterize themselves. Late medieval manuals written by merchants as collections of pertinent trade information are one such source. In their collection of advice on the quality of specific goods, routes, and markets and their practical data on regional weights, measures, and currencies, traders reflect the intense interest in their business invariably attributed to them by others. They also let the reader imagine that they recognized their heavy dependence on experience and reflected on their own and that of others. The merchant was a self-consciously free man whose hard work, or luck, could bring him fame and fortune. Godric of Finchale had, for example, trained first in "how to gain in small bargains and things of insignificant price" and only then "advanced little by little to buy and sell and gain from things of greater expense."

Social Group. Although widely disdained in the Middle Ages, merchants could not be identified by any detectable characteristic appearance. They came from all regions and parentage. The description of Godric, the seafaring merchant, is interesting because it is so detailed, but his broad shoulders, deep chest, middle stature, long face, piercingly clear gray eyes, bushy brows, broad forehead, long, open nostrils, comely curved nose, and pointed chin would have been his even had he become a husbandman like his father. Clearly, however, traders were recognizable to one another, and lively camaraderie was an important part of medieval merchant culture. Godric could not wait "to travel with associates . . . in pursuit of his public chaffer."

Sources:
G. G. Coulton, comp., *Social Life in Britain from the Conquest to the Reformation* (Cambridge: Cambridge University Press, 1918).

Odd Langholm, *Economics in the Medieval Schools. Wealth, Exchange, Value, Money and Usury according to the Paris Theological Tradition, 1200–1350* (Leiden & New York: E. J. Brill, 1992).

Robert S. Lopez and Irving W. Raymond, *Medieval Trade in the Mediterranean World: Illustrative Documents Translated with Introductions and Notes* (New York: Columbia University Press, 1955).

SIGNIFICANT PEOPLE

JOHN II

1319-1364

KING OF FRANCE

Famous Family. One of the greatest royal families of the French Middle Ages was the Valois dynasty. In the course of the fourteenth, fifteenth, and sixteenth centuries, the Valois became dukes and countesses (for example, Louis, Duke of Orleans, and Jeanne, Countess of Bar), empresses and queens (for example, Catherine of Constantinople and Madeleine of Scotland), archbishops and abbesses (for example, Michel de Bucy and Madeleine of Orleans), and after 1328 the kings of France when the Capetian Charles IV died leaving no sons. The Valois had in fact started out as nobles—their rise to power stemmed from their having created a lineage from Charles, Count of Valois, the brother of King Philip IV the Fair of France. Hardly a pivotal figure in the rise to power of the Valois, the renown of John II in particular would rest in part on his role in creating a more modern system of French coinage.

Political Connections. The reign of John II (1350–1364) was determined by his father, Philip VI, who became the first Valois king in the early fourteenth century to give continuity to the French crown under succession claims from the English king, Edward III. The threat from English royalty was to play an important part in the early Valois' strength. Under Philip VI, the French royal council became the dynasty's strongest supporters against King Edward III. Philip's son, John, also became thereby the most powerful representative of the French throne, despite his inability to exert the necessary political influence over a reform-minded nobility, a power-hungry bourgeoisie, and his own opportunistic courtiers. In 1356 day-to-day control of the kingdom fell to his son, heir apparent Charles V, who took charge of trying to raise the ransom sum of twelve and one-half tons of gold, three millions ecus, to free his father from English imprisonment stemming from his capture at the Battle of Poitiers. The English crown freed King John II in 1360 on four conditions: the signing of the Treaty of Brétigny-Calais; the relinquishing by France of about half its continental territory; the paying of a king's ransom; and the retention of surrogate hostages.

Branching Effects. The fortunes of the French economy had been growing all the more precarious under the Valois's reign. A series of monetary debasements were instituted from 1337 with the beginning of the Hundred Years' War (1337–1453) between France and England. Unlike the English royalty of the fourteenth century, which had extremely circumscribed taxation rights, historically each of the French kings had been granted a great deal of autonomy in levying. As war began, however, to take a larger share of their tax revenues, only devaluation seemed to insulate them against the losses in real terms. King John II instituted several economic reforms upon his release from English captivity. A new system was introduced to prevent a full-blown monetary crisis from bringing down the French economy: the *Pied de Monnaie* system denoted with one number the intrinsic worth of a coin with respect to its weight and fineness, with reference to the sound money of 1329. New taxes were ordered, the most unpopular being the gabelle (tax on salt).

Ruler of His Destiny. As monetarists, the Valois were enabled to pay about one-third of King John's ransom, with, in addition, three of his fourteen children playing a major role in his release, as surrogate hostages. John's primary activities once at liberty were aimed at his indebtedness to the English crown, and he was able to find support by unusual means through economic maneuvers, making himself ruler of France again in everything but power. Through connections with a rich duke in Milan, Galeas Visconti, John managed to have his daughter Isabelle, age twelve, sold into marriage for more than another one-third of his English ransom amount. Indeed, France was so buoyed at his liberation that the royal mint marked the event by releasing a new gold coin. This first commemorative French coin backfired in spirit, however. When one of the king's sons, Louis of Anjou, was reported in 1364 to have escaped from his prison in Calais ostensibly to go on crusade, the king himself returned to England as hostage to restore the family honor. Until his death in April of that year in London, the king's imprisonment set the tone for a return to regency in France.

Patron of Knights. John's rule not only influenced the distribution of economic power in France and England, but it also affected medieval chivalric life. He promoted the military pursuits of knights through the foundation of a new chivalric order, the Order of the Star. He was particularly active in military encounters himself in the Hundred Years' War. The Order of the Star became his centerpiece military entourage. John supported a new knights' order to instill bravery through oaths of steadfastness in battle. His ideals came under challenge in the Battle of Poitiers, where he saw most of the Order's members killed. The Order of the Star, started in 1351, nonetheless set the standard for a national chivalric order. Its attire, the red cloak bearing a huge black star of eight points, and motto, "They show the way to kings by the star," guaranteed the predominance of the king's military order. In his own prowess on horseback and as patron of knights, John sustained a chivalric code of military conduct that would not persist for long with his successors.

Image Concerns. John's interest in coinage was partly prompted by his worries about how his captivity had affected his royal/knightly image. The Order of the Star, for example, had not survived his years as a prisoner in London. The king became strongly attached to minted symbolic representations also as a counterpoint to the stresses on the economy. On the first coin he issued, the *Franc à Cheval*, at 3.764 grams of pure gold, he made sure there was a worthy representation: the king in full armor on horseback holding his sword in his left hand. He also, however, took special pains at humility, complementing an obverse caption, "John, King of the Franks, by God's grace," with a reverse motif of a cross bedecked with flowers surrounded by the caption "May Christ conquer, rule and reign." With his release from captivity, the king chose to create his own sense of freedom through the newly "franchised" (hence the word *franc*) coinage.

Collapse of Royal Strength. French royal strength began seriously to falter with John's first imprisonment in 1356. Even before being captured, the Valois had focused more on his image and patronage roles than on sound rule. Charles V became, however, an active behind-the-scenes ruler of France and a major support to his father during his captivity. He forged per force administrative ties with the leading merchants of Paris who under the leadership of Etienne Marcel, in league with John's cousin, Charles "the Bad," King of Navarre, had arisen in revolt. Even as the political alliances in Paris were collapsing in 1356, two years later, the standing of Charles V's economic strength in his own county of Dauphiné could no longer depend on the resources of the peasantry. Royal demands for contributions in labor and money to aid in the king's ransom were met by a peasant rebellion, the Jacquerie.

Impact. With the imprisonment of King John II, Charles V had to step in to take the lead in political and economic rule. Charles V was in the long run to prove to be a much more competent administrator. His greater prominence earned him the title of Charles "the Wise," as opposed to his father's John "Bon Homme" (Good Fellow). Nevertheless, the close relationship between father and son and the kingdom was to remain a defining feature of the early generations of the Valois dynasty. While Louis of Anjou, too, would acquire royal power as King of Naples, Sicily, and Jerusalem in 1382, after having become the adopted son of Jeanne I, Queen of Naples, much of his father's positive legacy would stem from his act to cleanse the "blemished honor to the lineage," which his son's escape had caused.

Sources:
Anne Denieul-Cormier, *Wise and Foolish Kings: The First House of Valois, 1328–1498* (Garden City, N.Y.: Doubleday, 1980).

John Bell Henneman, *Royal Taxation in Fourteenth-Century France: The Captivity and Ransom of John II, 1356–1370* (Philadelphia: American Philosophical Society, 1976).

Henneman, *Royal Taxation in Fourteenth-Century France: The Development of War Financing, 1322–1356* (Princeton: Princeton University Press, 1971).

MATTHEW PARIS

CIRCA 1200-1259
ENGLISH MONK AND HISTORIAN

Obscure Origins. Matthew Paris was a monk of the Benedictine Order at the Abbey of St. Albans in England in the first half of the thirteenth century. The exact date of his birth is not known, nor are the details of his early life, but his activities become somewhat easier to follow once he became a monk on 21 January 1217 and subsequently expressed himself in many writings.

Monk of the Monastery. It is quite common to associate monks of the Middle Ages with remote monasteries, because generally only monastic monks had the privilege of engaging in a relatively pure religious life, especially important to contemporary notions of spirituality, such as isolation and economic independence of the community. A religious site was founded at St. Albans in Hertfordshire, England, around 793 and developed with construction of the renowned abbey church in 1077, leading to greater wealth and importance for the shrine of the first martyr for Christianity in Roman-held Britain, the pagan Alban. The abbey church generated so much attention to the story and remains of Alban that the invading Danish kings, wishing both to protect and control the relics, took them back to Denmark. For much of the Middle Ages, St. Albans was nonetheless a market town, a Roman outpost transformed into a medieval center of exchange. The secular residents of St. Albans were, however, to feel the sometimes overpowering presence of the abbey. The town seemed to hold a particular attraction during the early thirteenth century, in return for which the townspeople paid a heavy price in disruptions: in 1213 a council was held at the Abbey at which both barons and churchmen discussed their grievances in what was to become the first step toward the Magna Carta of 1215; in 1217, after the Magna Carta was ignored by

King John and the barons invited the French to help them depose him, the dauphin of France, Louis, initially occupied the town for a while, then later that same year returned to despoil it after it had been sacked by the king's mercenary leader, Faulkes de Bréauté. As monk at the Abbey, and as a traveler to London and other English cities as well as to Norway, Paris had a front-row seat to observe the town, as well as the kingdom, in some disarray throughout an important period of English history.

Accounts. Paris's writings, which could only be carried out in the duly privileged environment of monastery or court, start with his original accounts beginning in 1235 in his great work, the *Chronica Majora* (Great Chronicle). The first task of the chronicler, as medieval writers of history were called, was to observe and record events, either from direct experience or from local sources. Paris conceived of his project as a large-scale enterprise: a single chronicle might encompass several thousand years in one continuous account. Generally, a medieval chronicler did not re-create originally every part of an account from biblical Creation to his present day, but rather re-edited an earlier author that he chose to use up to a certain date, as Paris had Roger of Wendover's *Flowers of History*. Once, however, Paris reached the date of 1235, the content of his *Chronica Majora* is his own and is presented accordingly as a first-hand account and/or critical commentary. Some of Paris's works are written in his own hand in either a weighty "book" handwriting, or a cursive "court" or "charter" script. Although there seems no evidence to corroborate an inference from his name that Paris was directly connected with the city of Paris either by birth or education, it is thought by some that before he entered the Abbey of St. Albans, Matthew may have studied in Paris and acquired there a curiously secular character to his handwriting. The lack of a consistent, finished, and technical quality to Matthew's penmanship suggests, however, that he was not actually trained as a scribe. Perhaps writing en route, Paris may have devised a rapid script as an expedient solution carefully contrived to meet the urgent need to write prodigiously, but with elegant authority. Once back at the abbey, his hand could become more deliberate on the piece of vellum and further embellished with telling little drawings in the margins or his various maps and plans which were unsurpassed in European medieval geography, before the rise of *portolani*, or nautical charts. His works, *Chronica Majora, Historia Minor* (Smaller History), *Historia Anglorum* (The History of the Angles), and *History of St. Albans* (perhaps as well a *Life of Stephen Langton* also attributed to him), made for fascinating reading for many of his contemporaries within and outside England who sought to supplement their libraries with current history. Such chronicles were often within collections of otherwise strictly religious works.

Observations. Paris traveled about freely, to London and the English royal court. During the reign of Louis IX of France, he went to Norway with letters of the king of France inviting the Norwegian king, Haakon IV, to join his crusade. As he traveled, Paris seems to have visited locals, observed, then reflected and commented upon what he saw, readying his thoughts to be contemplated by others. If possible, he encapsulated his observations and feelings together to persuade the reader, who could in turn, of course, reject his opinions (and observations). Without doubt, Paris was, as he has been described by historians of our day, "a man of strong views" whose "sympathies and prejudices color every line he wrote." Foreigners, the king, churchmen, and mendicant friars are all repeatedly criticized throughout his works, while the honor of St. Albans and associated English people is always preserved. Much of the evidence in Paris's own writings supports the assertion that he was on intimate terms with the French king Louis IX; the English king Henry III and his brother Richard, Earl of Cornwall; and perhaps with many members of both French and English royal families.

Stereotypes. However much exposure Paris's ideas might have had when forming the most recent component of his various histories, his readers still faced the age-old difficulty of all readers when it comes to another's account. In the thirteenth century many religious writers were playing out their side of a rivalry between monks and friars, between the older religious orders, like the Benedictines, and the newly established ones, like the Franciscans and Dominicans. Paris, like some other contemporary authors, accepted at face value the many different epithets applied to the other side: "hypocrites," "false preachers," or "vagabonds." When, however, he turns to the subject of the economic lifestyle of the friars, it does appear that Paris has his own accounts to settle. He questions, as others do, the ability of a community of Dominicans at Dunstable to be able to pay for the building of a comfortable house, while professing voluntary poverty. The number of indulgences, the need for accounting, the possibilities for spiritual wrangles made theirs a business as highly specialized as the sale of sheep on the wool market. Yet, it was so highly lucrative, with revenues regularly augmented by other forms of mendicancy, that they could not help but become wealthy men.

Personal Affairs. Paris wrote his series of chronicles from a specific perspective, which historians of today have described as "a gathering behind walls." On the other side he encountered Dominicans and Franciscans, whose contemplative "cell is the whole earth" and whose "cloister is the ocean." While he had waited as much as thirty-five years to join the abbey at St. Albans and had since tasted much of life outside the cloister, he still could not refrain from exhorting other brethren to keep well to themselves so they might not "usurp to themselves the functions of the clergy or the scholar." Paris remained at home in St. Albans until his death in 1259, sustaining what might be called the historical school or institute of the monastery of St. Albans, then the chief center of English narrative history or chronicle. With a slightly different evolution for his abbey, it might have become the nucleus of a great university, and like few among the regular orders, he might have found himself a colleague of the friars he so criticized.

Sources:

Patrick J. Geary, ed., *Authors of the Middle Ages: Historical and Religious Writers of the Latin West* (Brookfield, Vt.: Variorum, 1995).

Richard Vaughan, *Matthew Paris* (Cambridge: Cambridge University Press, 1958).

SOCIAL CLASS SYSTEM AND THE ECONOMY

ROBERT OF ARBRISSEL

CIRCA 1047–CIRCA 1117
ITINERANT PREACHER

Marginal People. There are few records of the people who have lived on the margins of society, because most could not themselves read or write nor were they amid others who could write or cared to read or write about them. The only times the lives of marginal people were recorded in the Middle Ages were when they ran into trouble with religious or secular law or were needed to bring others out of trouble. Tribulations and trials were undoubtedly a part of the account. Only under major changes in circumstances do the lives of such figures, as even Robert of Arbrissel, and particularly his followers, come to light.

Background. At the time of Robert's connection with marginalized Christians in 1096 at the monastery of Saint Mary of La Roë, he was already about age fifty, having been born at Arbrissel (now Arbressec) in Brittany, circa 1047. Robert had, just three years before, been archpriest (vicar general) to Bishop Sylvester de la Guerche in his native Diocese of Rennes, a calling which, though assumed at the invitation of the bishop, became dangerous upon Sylvester's death. Robert's enemies forced him, becuase of his overly zealous efforts to suppress simony (the buying or selling of a church office), lay investiture, clerical concubinage, irregular marriages, and feuding, to disassociate himself from the diocese, so threatening had been the bishop's desires to reform his flock. Without benefice or connections, Robert went to Angers, commencing there the severe ascetic lifestyle of a hermit in the forest of Craon. Although not from the region, he attracted followers impressed by his piety, eloquence, and strong personality. After keeping itinerant company with Bernard, subsequent founder of the Congregation of Tiron, Vitalis, later the founder of the Abbey of Savigny, and other aesthetes of considerable note, Robert founded the monastery of Canons Regular of La Roë, becoming its first abbot. Robert had done some preaching of "the word of God in villages, at castles, and in the cities" between leaving Rennes and establishing La Roë, although he was never officially upbraided for taking such liberties. In his fiftieth year he was, however, summoned to meet the Pope, who was traveling in France. So impressed was Urban II with a sermon he heard by Robert that he gave him the firm prospect of future security: Robert became a "preacher" (*semini verbus*) answerable only to the Pope "with orders to travel everywhere in the performance of this duty."

Naked Poor. Although little is known of his missionary journeys over the whole of Western France in the last two decades of his life, with the exception of his last year recounted in the *Vita Andreæ*, Robert did in fact realize his commitment to preaching. When Robert died at around seventy years old, he had left La Roë and had founded the double monastery at Fontevrault which in seventeen years had grown to house three thousand nuns. It is not clear what role Robert intended to play upon his resignation as archpriest, but he ended, like several contemporary preachers, as an example of destitute poverty. For Robert, poverty was crafted as "nakedness," "as Christ naked upon the Cross"; generally his sermons were given to the indigent population, whom he would have known only as the "poor of Christ." By 1097 Robert's disciples were of every age and condition, including even lepers and reformed prostitutes. Canons of the La Roë community, once "outsiders" themselves, who had now embraced the monastic state under Robert's leadership, objected to the number and diversity of the postulants. That fact did not stop the poor from coming, however, and in 1099 Robert embraced the many whom La Roë could not accommodate by founding the double-gender Benedictine monastery of Fontevrault. The same situation of overflow capacity was repeated several times, with one Fontevrault priory, or dependent house, being founded by the penitent Bertrade at Hautebruyère and another at Orsan, where Robert duly came to his final rest. After years of traveling from town to town preaching the theme of the abandonment of the world and the adoption of poverty, Robert had undoubtedly been exposed to another sermon subject: the Crusades of Urban II. Some historians assert that Robert did indeed preach the Crusades at Nantes, and although not a military man, Robert was portrayed iconographically wearing a coat of mail next to his skin, enjoying a vision of the crucified Christ, Virgin Mary, and Saint John. His own orientation engaged him, however, rather in the other necessary, if less honorable, battle: "This man preached the Gospel to the poor, he called the poor, he gathered the poor together." Women with unsavory pasts were a marginal group of relatively recent concern to the twelfth-century itinerant preachers, redefining the practice of encompassing sinful womankind and rescuing the lowest among them with religious communities. Robert became a savior of women, then their protector. Since the governance of the double abbey of Fontevrault was in the hands of its female population, Robert became known for his respect and vote of confidence for the Fontevrist nuns, who were reciprocally staunch supporters of Robert and all his foibles. His second biographer, Andrea tells how Robert at the approach of death assembled the canons of Fontevrault around him to say: "Know that whatever I have wrought in this world I have wrought as a help to nuns."

Odd Rules. Robert continued throughout the latter decades of his life to wander "barefooted in various sections of France," with ever more followers forthcoming. He and his friends Bernard and Vitalis reacted to the demand by creating the monastic communities of Fontevrault, Tiron and Savigny, which were copies of Benedictine Order houses, either in a new setting or, where possible, with new conditions for the double abbey. The Benedictine Rule adapted for Fontevrault enjoined the utmost simplicity in the materials of the black-and-white habit, a strict observance of silence, in food—abstinence from meat even for the sick—and rigorous enclosure. In the first Rule of Fontevrault, the topics of silence, good works, food, and clothing were taken on especially, as well as the issue of the succession of an abbess. At first a new abbess was not to be chosen from among those who had been brought up at Fontevrault; she should be someone who brought to her position experience of the world (*de conversis sororibus*) and who could perhaps thereby submit wayward monks to ask her pardon to regain the fellowship of the brethren. As a less conventional side for the male community of an abbey, the subjection of its monks to the abbess and nuns was marked. The monks "shall lead a common conventual life with no property of their own, content with what the nuns shall confer upon them." The scraps from the monks' table were to be "carried to the nuns' door and there given to the poor." On the more traditional side of religious gender relations and the superior sacramental authority of men, the separation of the nuns from the monks was carried to such a point that a sick nun had be brought into the church to receive the last sacraments from the male priest. Over the course of its initial twenty years, Fontevrault established itself solidly under its first two abbesses, Hersende of Champagne and Petronilla of Chemillé, testifying to the fact that among the nuns Robert had confidently found women endowed with high qualities and in every way fitted for governance.

Trials. After twenty years of scraping by on the margins of orthodoxy without attracting much attention from Church authorities, Robert of Arbrissel was, upon his death, throroughly scrutinized, having been denounced as extremely indiscreet in his choice of exceptional ascetic practices by Geoffrey of Vendôme and Marbodius of Rennes. There was no clear evidence to support their claims, but they placed Robert under a cloud of suspicion. The normal procedure of consideration for canonization would have gone forward from the time of Robert's death after a fairly lengthy period of investigation. Unfortunately for him, the suspicions came at a moment when official and popular concern for double abbeys and aberrant ascetic practices was building, so instead of receiving Robert's somewhat unusual, but theologically informed behavior (from his training at the Parisian schools of Nôtre-Dame or Ste-Geneviève), his accomplishments and devotion as itinerant preacher became snagged in controversy. Robert, sensing his approaching death, took steps in 1116 to ensure the permanence of the monastery at Fontevrault: he imposed a vow of stability on his monks and summoned a monastic Chapter meeting to settle the form of government and the house Rule. His preparedness led to the survival of the double abbey for many generations of abbesses, who did everything in their power to discredit the attacks on their founder. Other evidence of eccentric actions on Robert's part and scandals among his mixed followers may have helped to give credence to negative rumors. Since male and female cohabitation in the same monastery had been abused by earlier generations, double abbeys had generally died out by the eleventh century. With memory of them freshly revived by Robert of Abrissel's monastery at Fontevrault, it is not surprising to find that such institutions were still an object of solicitude and strict legislation at the hands of ecclesiastical authority. Further, three characteristics of Robert's own life—his severe penance, his strikingly ascetic appearance, and his metaphorical "nakedness" in following Christ—made him personally a target. Horrified by sexual impropriety, however, Robert supported the papal legates at the Council of Poitiers in 1100 in excommunicating King Philip I of France on account of his immoral union with Bertrade de Montfort. Certainly there were other testimonials to Robert's spiritual sincerity and purity, but the twelfth-century tone was that of the least respectable impressions expressed by his contemporaries, with the resounding exception of his biographies, especially the *Vita Andreae,* written by Robert's chaplain Andrew, a loyal subject and witness to his death. Although never formally beatified, Robert is nonetheless usually given the title of "Blessed." A letter of exhortation to Countesse Ermengarde of Brittany is all that remains of Robert's own hand, hence the poor, "naked" scholar-priest-hermit-preacher-abbot, representing the spiritual needs of the marginalized, can no longer speak in his own defense.

Sources:

Rosalind B. Brooke, *The Coming of the Friars* (London: Allen & Unwin, 1975).

Jacqueline Smith, "Robert of Arbrissel, Procurator Mulierum" in *Medieval Women*, edited by Derek Baker (Oxford: Blackwell, 1978).

URBAN II

CIRCA 1042-1099
POPE

Family Business. The characteristic activity of the second son of virtually any large medieval family was as a member of the Church. This type of activity was carried out to the fullest by Eudes or Odo of Lagery, after his able "apprenticeship" with Bruno, head of the Cathedral School of Reims; Hugh, abbot of Cluny; and Pope Gregory VII. Scholars know about his life from his own writings and administrative papers as Canon and Archdeacon at Reims, Prior at Cluny, Cardinal Bishop of Ostia, Papal Legate in France and Germany, and Pope Urban II, as well as from the accounts of many others writing of events between 1065 and 1099. Eudes was from a family of established noble knights in service to the counts of Semur, and his earliest education at the Cathedral School in Reims was almost certainly arranged by his pious parents.

Three Essential Skills. Generations of medieval families had sought education for their sons in the hopes each would become pope, and Eudes too was set on the path of training for the same occupation as a matter of the ultimate course. As a boy, he learned the three essential skills for high religious life—reading, writing, and resilience, probably including compliance—spending eight to ten years at the feet of Bruno, the re-established head of the episcopal school. By about the age of twenty-eight, Eudes had completed his education in Reims, as well as a period there as canon and archdeacon. With his family based in Chatillon-sur-Marne in Champagne, Eudes next maintained a pious presence at Cluny, the famous Cistercian monastery in central Burgundy, where he followed a strict spiritual life under the great abbot Hugh and came to hold the office of prior. The standard product of Cluny at the time was a reform-minded monk. As one of a group of monks sent to provide assistance as bishops for Pope Gregory VII in the difficult task of reforming the Church, Eudes ended up continuing to spend much of his time outside Rome, either in Ostia, or traveling in papal convoy as legate in France and Germany. Within ten years he had become so firmly established as a resourceful papal strategist that he himself was nominated and elected pope of Rome.

Pope and Partners. From the time of his election in 1088, Eudes of Lagery, now Urban II, became Gregory VII's confident successor (once removed) in policy and image. He was then forty-six years old and had received sound training as canon, monk, and resilient politician. His first job was to supervise Rome: to enter the city itself, make it safe for others, and create peace between the political factions along its borders, including reconciling Norman princes and making sure the Holy Roman Emperor could not support an antipope in the Eternal City. He arranged for Emperor Henry IV and Antipope Guibert of Ravenna to be excommunicated and sought restitution from Guibert in a three-day encounter between papal and antipapal troops. In addition to subduing imperial and antipapal forces, Urban II also gathered seventy bishops, as well as other Church officials, to a synod at Melfi in 1089. Their agenda was, however, in Urban II's hands, and, if he were to have had difficulty obtaining collective decrees against simony and clerical marriage, he would have simply sent for the bishops of the sees in Saxony that he had filled in 1084–1085 with men faithful to Gregory. Urban II acted initially as a stand-in for the emperor's son Conrad, and Matilda, Countess of Tuscany and Welf V, heir to Bavaria and Este in these important initial moments of his papacy, vis-à-vis the Holy Roman Emperor, Henry IV. The Lombard League cities—Milan, Lodi, Piacenza, and Cremona—came finally to welcome Conrad, and he was crowned king in Milan, the center of the imperial power in Italy. It is clear from Urban II's correspondence that he consulted bishops and abbots on both German and French soil on financial matters and issues of judgment. The French abbot, Gregory of Vendôme, hearing of Urban II's plight on the outskirts of Rome against Antipope Guibert, thought of a "business activity" to provide for a papal residence, so "that he might become a sharer of his [the Pope's] sufferings and labour and relieve his want": with the money Gregory obtained by selling certain possessions of his monastery, the Pope was able to purchase the Lateran palace on payment of a large sum of money. In his letters, the papal and quasi-personal news of Urban II are

mingled with rhetorical flourish and firm evocations of events, such as Urban II's entering the Lateran in time for the Paschal solemnity of 1094 and his sitting for the first time on the papal throne six years after his election. Urban II signed his name, "Urban, by the permission of God chief bishop and prelate over the whole world" or "Urban, bishop, servant of the servants of God, to all the faithful, both princes and subjects . . . ; greeting, apostolic grace, and blessing." Thus, although the contents of the Pope's missives were often filled with advice, it was always conveyed with his deference as servant of God and leader of the faithful.

Piety and Work Ethic. Reform and peace were both priorities for Urban II, who infused his own piety into all activities. He thanked God for the successes in Rome and began to use Church councils, loaded with supportive bishops, for the continued well-being of the Church institutions in Rome and the spirituality of its followers throughout Christendom. He believed that God would reward marital fidelity, not the dynastic goals of contemporary royalty, and although the subject reached into the courts of both Henry IV, King of the Germans and King Philip I of France to restrain them from what they considered their purview, Urban II had his next council at Piacenza address the matter and summon both kings to the council. At this council Urban II was also able to broach the subject of the Crusades for the first time. As the Seljuk Turks continued seriously to menace the Empire of Constantinople, a worried Eastern Emperor, Alexius I, turned to the Pope asking for help. In a following council at Clermont in 1095, Urban II used his wonderful gifts of eloquence to the utmost, to depict the captivity of the Sacred City where Christ had suffered and died and encourage the faithful to rescue it from harm: "Let them [Christian knights] turn their weapons dripping with the blood of their brothers against the enemy of the Christian Faith. Let them—oppressors of orphans and widows, murderers and violaters of churches, robbers of the property of others, vultures drawn by the scent of battle—let them hasten, if they love their souls, under their captain Christ to the rescue of Sion."

Sense of Accomplishment. Pope Urban II's successes, and those of his ambassadors, gave him an enviable position of power. Urban II had never liked the life of tension, however. Its one advantage, he believed, was that hard work of any kind (military, constructional, and so forth) keeps one from the temptations caused by human vices. It was by God's great mercy, he felt, however, that he had become the spiritual leader rather than the knightly leader of the First Crusade (1095–1099), which role fell to Ademar, the Bishop of Le Puy. Urban II also disliked being on the road all the time, constantly faced with difficult local decisions. By 1098 he was able to enjoy a brief period of repose after a life of incessant activity and fierce strife, which had brought exile and want. With the presence of well-disciplined troops, under the most distinguished knights of Christendom, returning from the Crusade through Rome, Urban II finally acquired the military resources to strike terror into the wild partisans of any lingering antipope. In October 1098 the Pope held a council at Bari with 180 bishops in attendance with the intent of reconciling the Greek and Latin Churches on the doctrinal issue of the relation of the "Son" to the Father in the Holy Trinity. The Pope then returned to Rome to the more settled life of a pontif secure in the Papal States. He died nine months later, having lived just long enough to hold his last council in Rome in April, 1099 at which he once more raised his eloquent voice on behalf of the Crusades. Although Urban II would not live to hear of the Crusaders' victory in Jerusalem, with new response in April to his call for more Crusaders, Urban II undoubtedly died with some sense of accomplishment in Western Christianity's defense of the Holy Land. On virtually every other front, without Urban II's persistent work, most of the reform efforts of his predecessor Gregory VII would probably have been extremely ephemeral.

Sources:

Alfons Becker, *Papst Urban II (1088–1099)* (Stuttgart: A. Hiersemann, 1964–1988).

Charles Morris, *The Western Church from 1050 to 1250* (Oxford: Oxford University Press, 1989).

DOCUMENTARY SOURCES

Thomas Aquinas, *Summa Theologica* (1266–1273)—Includes a section on the sin of usury, or charging interest on loans.

Baldric or Baudry of Dol (Baldricus Dolensis), *Vita Beati Roberti de Arbrissello* or *Vita Baldrici* (Life of Blessed Robert of Arbrissel, circa 1117)—The more expansive of two biographies of the itinerant preacher and founder of Fontevrault, Robert of Abrissel. Commissioned by the second abbess of Fontevrault, Petronilla, it followed the standard hagiographic conventions of the time period as an account of a saintly person's life designed to influence readers to be guided by and model themselves after the behavior of the "saint." Its author, a celebrated poet and archbishop, attempted as well to provide a rhetorically powerful portrait glorifying Robert, which, it was hoped by the nuns of Fontevrault, would persuade the church establishment that Robert, recently deceased, was worthy of sainthood.

Barcelona Navigation Act (1227)—Barcelona was one of the leading ports of medieval Europe, and as such, James I of Aragon granted it a monopoly in the carrying trade.

Abbot Bernard of Reichenau, *Plan of St. Gall* (circa 815)—the schematic of an ideal monastery, this work is the earliest known "plan" drawing in European architectural history. It was apparently designed both to convey a monastery's lay-out in accordance with the Benedictine Rule as interpreted by Charlemagne and to account for all structures required for the secluded life of the monk: cloister, church, refectory and dormitory, pilgrims' hospice and an almshouse, school, workshops for craftsmen, and so forth.

Capitulary for the Jews (814)—Charlemagne's ordinance limiting the trading activities of Jews in his kingdom.

Chartularium Universitatis Parisiensis (1200–1454)—A massive and detailed collection of the documentary history of the University of Paris. The volumes include letters and virtually every other type of text written in connection with the organization, the professors and students, the academic life, the relations with popes and kings, and the controversies of the University, during the period when Paris was the chief center of theological learning.

Chroniques des Comtes d'Anjou (Chronicle of the Counts of Anjou, circa 1100)—Probably compiled by a monk. It is a mythical account of the rise of the nobles in this western region of France from the tenth century to the late eleventh century.

Clericis laicos (1296)—a bull that forbade secular rulers to levy taxes on the clergy without papal consent.

Decree on Sale of Unfree Christians (922)—An edict passed by the Council of Koblenz. Anyone "who led away a Christian man and then sold him" was guilty of homicide.

Dialogue of the Exchequer (circa 1181)—Written by an official of the exchequer, a department of state in medieval England charged with the collection and management of the royal revenue. The dialogue is between a student and a high official concerning the office's many rules and regulations.

The Domesday Book (1085–1086)—A survey of English lands ordered by William I following his conquest of

England in 1066. The title is from the Norse word *dome*, which means "reckoning" (and from which the modern word *doom* is derived). It was one of the most comprehensive censuses ever undertaken in medieval Europe. Every English settlement, no matter how small, was listed and described. The result was a detailed assessment of the realm, which allowed William I to tax it accordingly.

Edict of Pistes (864)—One of the most complete documents on Carolingian coinage. Issued by Charles the Bald, this decree reduced the number of places in France that had the right to mint coins from nine to three. It also regulated the punishment for counterfeiting.

Grant of Market, Coinage, and Taxation Privileges to Bishopric of Osnabrück (952)—Decreed by Otto the Great as a favor to the Church.

An Inquiry into the Tolls of Raffelstettin (circa 905)—A statement on what tolls were customarily levied on the eastern frontier of the kingdom of King Louis the Child of Germany. Staple articles of exchange included livestock, salt, and serfs.

Leges Edwardis Confessoris (Laws of Edward the Confessor, 1115)—Includes Tithable Products of the Land, a list of taxable agricultural goods.

Leges Henrici Primi (Laws of Henry I, circa 1109–1118)—Includes the Law of Partnerships, a statute that reflects Saxon views of business arrangements and their dissolution. It called for a fair division of all property in the presence of witnesses.

Modus Faciendi Homagium & Fidelitatem (The Manner of Doing Homage and Fealty, circa 1275)—A set of instructions on the proper words and ceremonies for a tenant swearing allegiance to his lord. By the mid 1300s more than half of all common law statute books had these instructions.

Munimenta Gildhallae Londoniensis, Volume III, *Liber Horn* (circa 1325)—A municipal record dealing mostly with trade in the city of London.

St. Omer Inheritance Law (1128)—Legal conditions by which an heir might lay claim to an inheritance in Alsace.

Matthew Paris, *Chronica Majora* (Great Chronicle, 1235–1259)—A world history in the form of a composite of annals, chronologies of the events of each significant year. Written in Latin, it was intended to serve as a summary of the important religious and political occurrences from the Creation until 1259. The chronicle records Matthew Paris's own observations on current issues, institutions, ideas, customs, and even individuals from 1235 to 1259. Matthew Paris's chronicle and his other works derivative from it, *Historia Minor* (Smaller History), *Historia Anglorum* (The History of the Angles), and *History of St. Albans,* present his contemporaries and later historians with so much rationalized detail that the images he formulated, such as the hostile one of the English king John, became a standard basis of "fact," copied by historians until recent times.

Reginald of Durham, *Life of St. Godric* (circa 1175)—The biography that popularized the image of the wealthy merchant.

Roll-Book of the Arte Della Seta (1225)—A record of the guilds and their members associated with silk manufacturing in Florence.

Giovanni Scriba, *Cartolario* (1155–1164)—The Genoese version of a financial diary of the era: a commercial account book. In its pages were preserved documents of business venture contacts. It offered a glimpse of the parties and their witnesses in the export trade out of Genoa. Venetian merchants produced an earlier extant version of the trade contract, but none forms part of a whole account record like Scriba's text. Investors from the highest merchant nobles of Venice to artisan tanners are recorded in contemporary contracts.

Walter of Henley, *Husbandry* (circa 1275)—A professional bailiff or manager of estates probably in the south of England, Walter uses the "how to" format to present his ideas on the successful management of the direct farming of medium to large estates. The work is divided into short sections on topics principally aimed at improving the return from the land and its chattels: surveying, management of servants and laborers, proper plowing and sowing techniques, the use of manure, keys to sound ox, pig and sheep breeding, exploitation of draft and milk animals, buying and selling in season, and keeping estate accounts.

POLITICS, LAW, AND THE MILITARY

by KELLY DEVRIES and NORMAN J. WILSON

CONTENTS

Sidebars and tables are listed in italics.

814

- Charlemagne, the king of the Franks, dies on 28 January and is succeeded by his son, Louis I (the Pious).

814* - 915*

- The Muslims raid along the Mediterranean seacoast of Europe.

817

- Louis the Pious divides his kingdom into three portions and gives one piece each to his sons, Lothar I (Italy), Pepin I (Aquitaine and Burgundy), and Louis the German (Bavaria), but the three men are not to take control of their portions until their father's death.

- The Umayyid Moorish ruler al-Hakam I puts down a revolt in Córdoba and expels the rebels.

827

- Muslims from North Africa invade the southern coast of Sicily. They make Palermo their capital in 831 but do not completely quell local resistance until the 960s.

830

- Louis the Pious's sons try to overthrow him but fail; another attempt three years later also proves unsuccessful.

- Danish raiders sail up the Thames River in England.

837

- A revolt of Christians in Spain against the Moors is put down by Abd ar-Rahman II of Córdoba.

838

- Louis the Pious's son by his second wife, Judith of Bavaria, Charles II (the Bald), is given Neustria (modern northwestern France); he is later given Aquitaine after his brother Pepin's death.

840

- Louis the Pious dies. Lothar I attempts to gain control of his father's kingdom.

840*

- The Vikings (Norsemen) found the towns of Dublin and Limerick on the Irish coast as bases for trade with their homeland.

*Denotes Circa Date

841
- Lothar I is defeated by his brothers, Louis the German and Charles the Bald, at the Battle of Fontenoy.
- Normandy is invaded by Vikings (Scandinavians). By 843 they have made it all the way to the shores of the Mediterranean Sea.

843
- The Treaty of Verdun gives Lothar I control of northern Italy and Lorraine; Louis the German receives the lands east of the Rhine River; Charles the Bald becomes the king of the West Franks (modern-day France).
- Genoa becomes a republic.

845
- The Vikings sack Paris.

849
- A combined fleet and army of a league of united Italian seaport cities, aided by bad weather, defeats a Muslim force at the Battle of Ostia.

855
- Lothar I dies. His lands are divided among his three sons: Louis II gains Italy; Charles gets Provence; and Lothar II obtains Lotharingia.

862
- Charles the Bald grants Flanders to his son-in-law, Baldwin I (Iron Arm).

865
- Louis the German divides his kingdom among his three sons: Carloman (Bavaria and Carinthia), Charles the Fat (Swabia); and Louis the Younger (Franconia, Thuringia, and Saxony).
- Robert the Strong, a vassal of Charles the Bald, defeats a Viking incursion into France at Neustria and receives that land to rule. He is killed in battle the following year.

866
- The Danish "Great Army" of close to three thousand men attacks England and captures Northumbria; the Danes then begin to build settlements.

869
- Lothar II dies and his lands are split between Louis the German and Charles the Bald.

*Denotes Circa Date

870*
- Vikings begin to settle Iceland.

871
- The Vikings raid London.

875
- Louis II dies; Charles the Bald invades Italy and is crowned the Holy Roman Emperor.
- Byzantine forces capture Bari in southern Italy. They later take Tarentum and Calabria.

876
- Charles the Bald attempts, but fails, to capture his brother's territory in Germany. On 8 October, Louis the German's son, Louis the Younger, defeats his uncle Charles at the Battle of Andernach.

877
- Charles the Bald dies.

878
- The Vikings, led by the Danish king Guthrum, are defeated by the King of Wessex, Alfred (the Great), at the Battle of Edington in Wiltshire. The peace of Wedmore is established, and Guthrum accepts Christianity.
- The Muslims capture Sicily (Syracuse), forcing many of the former inhabitants to flee to Byzantine–held regions in southern Italy.

880
- Carloman dies.
- The Treaty of Ribémont gives Louis the Younger western Lotharingia.

882
- Louis the Younger dies; Charles the Fat gains Saxony.

884
- Charles the Fat gains the West Frankish lands.

885-886
- The Vikings lay siege to Paris, but the city is defended by Count Eudes (Odo). Charles the Fat fails in his attempt to aid Eudes.

*Denotes Circa Date

887
- Arnulf, the illegitimate son of Carloman, becomes king of Germany after his uncle Charles the Fat is deposed by the German magnates. Charles dies in 888.

891
- The Vikings are defeated at the Battle of the Dyle (in present-day Belgium) by Arnulf.

- Arnulf attacks the Moravians, who are making incursions into Germany, then invades Italy, capturing Rome in 896. With his victory he is crowned Holy Roman Emperor by Pope Formosus.

893
- Charles III (the Simple) becomes king of France, instead of Eudes, and rules from Laon.

899
- Arnulf dies.
- Alfred I dies and is replaced as king of the English by his son, Edward (the Elder).

899-955
- The Magyars conduct raids into Central Europe.

905
- Edward the Elder defeats an internal struggle for his throne in England, initiated by his cousin Aethelwald, who had Danish support.

911
- The Duchy of Northmen (Normandy) is ceded to Rollo (Robert) by Charles the Simple.
- The last Carolingian king of the East Franks, Louis III (the Child), who assumed the throne as a seven-year-old child in 893, dies. Germany splinters into many smaller principalities.
- Conrad I, the duke of Franconia, is elected king of Germany but has to fight challenges from Swabia and Bavaria and gives up the throne in 919.

912
- 'Abd ar-Rahman III an-Nasir begins his reign as emir of the Umayyids. He consolidates control over the Iberian Peninsula and captures Seville in 913.
- Danes in East Anglia are forced to submit to the authority of Edward the Elder.

*DENOTES CIRCA DATE

919
- Henry I (the Fowler), the duke of Saxony and the strongest opponent of Conrad I, is elected king of Germany. The Swabian and Bavarian dukes are brought to heel, and Henry forms an alliance with Charles the Simple. He is forced to pay tribute to the Magyars, though it is only a temporary measure while he builds an army and fortifies the territory.

923
- Charles the Simple defeats Robert, Count of Paris, at Soissons, only to be captured by Hebert, Count of Vermandois, in whose custody Charles dies.

924
- Edward the Elder dies and is succeeded by his son, Aethelstan, who annexes Northumbria in 926 on his way to controlling most of England.

927
- Henry the Fowler launches an attack on, and defeats, the Heveller, a Slavic tribe that has a strong fortress on the Havel River that was thought to be invincible.

933
- Cisjurane and Transjurane Burgundy are united into the Second Kingdom of Burgundy.
- Henry, after refusing to pay any more tribute, defeats the Magyars at Riade on the Unstrut River. The Huns, who invade with a force of nearly one hundred thousand men, are crushed by two German armies.

936
- Henry dies and is replaced on the German and Holy Roman thrones by his son, Otto I (the Great).

937
- Aethelstan's forces defeat the armies of the Scottish king Constantine, Owain of Strathclyde, and Olaf Guthfrithson at the Battle of Brunanburh, which helps to unify the Anglo-Saxon kingdom.

941
- Russian ruler Igor, the duke of Kiev, attacks Byzantium, but his fleet is defeated by the Greeks.

951
- Otto the Great invades Italy, largely to open the passages through the mountains.

*Denotes Circa Date

955

- The Magyars attempt another invasion of Germany, but they are defeated at the Battle of the Lechfeld by Otto the Great and driven back into Hungary, where they establish a permanent kingdom.

- The independence of Leon and Navarre are secured in a treaty between Ordono III and 'Abd ar-Rahman III an-Nasir.

962

- After invading Italy for the second time, Otto the Great obtains an imperial coronation from the Pope.

967

- Otto the Great forces Pope John XIII to crown his son, Otto II, as joint emperor.

973

- Otto II becomes the Holy Roman Emperor upon the death of his father.

978

- A revolt by Henry II of Bavaria is put down by Otto II.

- Aethelred II (the Unready) rules in England, but he faces new Danish attacks.

982

- Otto II's troops are defeated by the Muslims near Stilo in southern Italy.

983

- Otto II's son, Otto III, who is only three years old, becomes the Holy Roman Emperor upon his father's death. His mother, Theophano, rules as regent alongside his grandmother.

987

- Last Carolingian king of the West Franks, Louis V, dies and is succeeded by Hugh Capet, the first Capetian king of France.

994

- The Danes, led by Sweyn I Forkbeard, invade England and impose tribute.

1000

- The Danes, led by Sweyn I, defeat the forces of Olaf Tryggvason of Norway.

1002

- Otto III dies. Henry II becomes the king of Germany, but he will not be crowned Holy Roman Emperor until 1014.

- Danish settlers are massacred in England, prompting the Danish king to send regular raiding parties to the island for the next twelve years.

*DENOTES CIRCA DATE

1005

- Malcolm II Mackenneth becomes the king of Scotland and rules until 1034.

1013-1014

- Danish king Sweyn I campaigns in England and is acknowledged the ruler of the country; Aethelred the Unready flees to France. Sweyn's victory is short-lived, as he dies in Gainsborough.

1014

- Brian, the king of Munster since 976 and of Ireland since 1002, defeats the Norsemen at Clontarf, four miles north of Dublin, on 23 April, forcing many of the Vikings back aboard their ships in Dublin Bay. This action ends Viking control of Ireland, although many of the northern settlers stay in the region.

1016-1018

- Canute I (the Great), son of Sweyn I, becomes the king of England and Denmark. He defeats the army of Edmund II Ironside at Assandun in 1016 but does not conquer the whole country until after the death of Edmund. Canute rules England until his death in 1035.

1018

- Lombard and Norman forces led by the nobleman Melus invade Italy and are defeated at Cannae by a Byzantium army, which is aided by a Viking unit (the Varangian Guard) provided by Emperor Basil II. Melus escapes to the protection of Henry II but dies two years later.

1024

- Conrad II becomes the king of Germany; in 1027 he is made the Holy Roman Emperor. He is regularly challenged by revolts in Italy and Germany, but he manages to suppress them and rules until 1039.

1026

- The Danes defeat an attempt by the Swedes and Norwegians to conquer their country. Canute the Great turns the victory into an opportunity to become king of Norway in 1028.

1028

- Hardecanute, son of Canute the Great, is made the king of Denmark by his father.

1030-1031

- Conrad II of Germany leads two expeditions, against the Hungarians and the Poles. The former fails, while the latter forces the Poles to pay homage.

1034

- Malcolm II of Scotland dies and is replaced on the throne by Duncan I. His reign lasts only to 1040, when he is killed by his cousin Macbeth during a battle near Elgin.

*Denotes Circa Date

1035
- Harold I (Harefoot), the illegitimate son of Canute, becomes regent of England and seizes the throne outright in 1037.

- William II becomes the duke of Normandy.

1039
- Conrad II dies and is replaced on the German throne by Henry III (the Black). During his reign, which lasts until 1056, he controls Poland, Bohemia, and Saxony.

1040
- Hardecanute invades England and unseats his half brother Harold from the throne.

1042
- Edward (the Confessor), son of Aethelred the Unready, takes the throne of England upon the death of his half brother Hardecanute; Edward rules England until 1066.

1047*
- The Norman Robert Guiscard leads troops into Italy; the Normans are invited by the Pope to aid in pushing the Byzantines out of the region. Robert attacks Sicily in 1060 and conquers the island (1071–1076), although the last strongholds do not fall until the 1090s. Rome is taken in 1084.

1051
- William II of Normandy defeats Geoffrey Martel and captures Anjou.

1053
- Guiscard's troops defeat an army of Pope Leo IX at the Battle of Civitate and capture the pontiff, who had been trying to reign in the power of the Normans.

1056
- Six-year-old Henry IV takes the German throne, although his mother Agnes serves as regent for nine years. He rules until 1106.

1057
- Macbeth of Scotland is killed by Malcolm III MacDuncan, the son of Duncan I. Malcolm rules Scotland until his death in 1093.

1066
- Harold Godwinsson becomes king of England upon the death of Edward the Confessor. He defeats an invading army led by King Harald Hardrada of Norway at the Battle of Stamford Bridge (25 September) in Yorkshire. Meanwhile, Norman troops under William the Conqueror land on the southern coast of England; Harold Godwinsson's weary army marches south to meet them, but is defeated at the Battle of Hastings (14 October). Harold Godwinsson is killed, ending Saxon rule of England. William the Conqueror becomes king of England on Christmas Day and rules until 1087.

*DENOTES CIRCA DATE

1071

- The Seljuk Turks defeat the Byzantines (whose army is made up largely of mercenaries) at the Battle of Manzikert. The power of the Byzantine state is broken.

1072

- The Scots are forced to pay homage to William the Conqueror.

1080

- Rudolf of Swabia, who led a revolt of nobles in Germany, is defeated and killed by Henry IV.

- Henry V becomes king of Germany. He conducts many military incursions into Flanders, Hungary, Bohemia, and Italy during his reign, which lasts until 1125.

1085-1086

- The Domesday survey in England is carried out; information collected on local resources is compiled in the *Domesday Book* for administrative and tax purposes.

1087

- William the Conqueror is fatally wounded in a fall from a horse during warfare with Philip I of France. He is replaced on the English throne by his son, William II (William Rufus), who rules until 1100.

1088

- Byzantine emperor Alexius I Comnenus appeals to Pope Urban II for assistance against the Turks.

- William II puts down a revolt against his rule in Normandy.

1094

- The Spanish military leader Rodrigo Diaz de Vivar, known as El Cid (the lord or master), takes control of Valencia. After his death five years later El Cid becomes the national hero of Castile and the subject of many legends.

1095

- At the Council of Clermont, Pope Urban II gives a sermon calling for a crusade to liberate the Holy Land (Jerusalem) from the Muslims.

1095-1096

- The Peasant's Crusade is led by Peter the Hermit. A twenty-thousand-strong army marches on Asia Minor, where, after some successes against the local population, they are routed by the Turks and either killed or sold into slavery. A second contingent of crusaders, marching through Germany, attacks and massacres the Jewish population of Worms and elsewhere.

*DENOTES CIRCA DATE

1097
- Norman-French Crusaders, possibly as many as thirty thousand, reach Constantinople. Nicea falls to a combined Greek and Crusader army.

1098
- Antioch falls to the Crusaders after a successful siege.

1099
- Soldiers of the First Crusade capture Jerusalem and establish a feudal kingdom, as well as three other "Crusader Kingdoms" in Antioch, Tripoli, and Edessa.

1100
- William II is killed while hunting. Henry I (Henry Beauclerc) becomes king and rules until 1135. He restores the laws (*Coronation Charter*) of Edward the Confessor, extends the jurisdiction of royal courts and expands the authority of the state. He also transforms the Court of the Exchequer into a body that handles financial matters.

1104
- Alfonso I (the Battler) becomes king of Aragon and Navarre, which he rules until 1134.

1106
- An army of Henry I defeats the troops of his brother, Robert II (Curthose), the duke of Normandy, on 28 September at the Battle of Tinchebrai, a city in northwest France. Robert is imprisoned.

1112*
- The first military and religious order, called the Knights of St. John (Hospitalers), is formed; the order started as a hospital organization (probably established in the 1090s) that was run by monks. One of many groups dedicated to protecting pilgrims to the Holy Lands, this order attracts the patronage of knights; it eventually becomes the Knights of Malta.

1118
- Alfonso the Battler defeats the Moorish defenders of Saragossa, a province in northeast Spain. The Moors had held the territory for nearly four hundred years.

1125
- Lothar II is elected the king of Germany.

1130
- The kingdom of Sicily is formed.

*Denotes Circa Date

1135
- On the death of Henry I, Stephen, the grandson of William the Conqueror, claims the English throne. He had been forced by Henry to recognize Matilda of Germany as the rightful heir to the throne, but decided to take the crown himself. A civil war breaks out between the forces of Stephen and Matilda. Stephen is captured, but released, in 1141.

1137
- Louis VII (the Young), son of Louis VI, becomes king of France.

1138
- Conrad III becomes the king of Germany. He loses Saxony to Bavaria but expands German control in the Scandinavian areas.

1144
- The kingdom of Edessa falls to Moslems from Syria, an action that initiates the Second Crusade, which is preached by Bernard of Clairvaux (St. Bernard).

1147-1149
- A two-pronged army of Crusaders, with Conrad III and Louis VII leading separate German and French armies, moves out of Europe toward Constantinople. The armies are severely ravaged by Turkish attacks and fail to capture Damascus. The failure of this crusade causes a backlash in Europe against such endeavors.

1152
- Frederick I (Barbarossa) becomes king of Germany and is elected the Holy Roman Emperor upon the death of his uncle Conrad III. An aggressive ruler, he leads six expeditions into Italy, as well as a crusade to the Middle East.

1153
- Stephen recognizes Matilda's son, Henry of Anjou (Henry II), as his heir.

1154
- Henry II assumes the English throne upon the death of Stephen. He increases royal control over the baronies and institutes new financial and judicial reforms, including placing men who are selected by the royalty as sheriffs.

1156
- Austria is formed out of the duchy of Bavaria.

1157
- Valdemar I (the Great) becomes king of Denmark and rules until 1182. He greatly improves the military capabilities of his country and ends Wend power.

1166*
- A system of traveling judges, who rule on serious crimes such as murder and robbery, is established in England. Their rulings help develop a body of common law.

* DENOTES CIRCA DATE

1176
- The Lombard League defeats the army of Frederick I at the Battle of Legnano. A truce is brokered between the two sides in 1183 with the Peace of Constance.

1178
- A permanent central court of five judges is established by Henry II in England.

1179
- Philip II (Augustus) is crowned king of France. He reigns until 1223.

1182
- Canute VI becomes king of Denmark upon the death of his father, Valdemar the Great. During his reign, which lasts until 1202, Canute expands the influence of the Danes to Pomerania, Holstein, and Mecklenburg.

1187
- The sultan Saladin defeats the Christians of Palestine at the Battle of Hattin and conquers Jerusalem. Pope Gregory VIII calls for a crusade to recapture the area.

1188*
- English jurist Ranulf de Glanville writes *Tractatus de legibus et consuetudinibus regni Angliae* (Treatise on the Laws and Customs of the Kingdom of England), one of the first compendiums of English common law.

1189
- Richard I (the Lionhearted), eldest son of Henry II, becomes king of England upon his father's death. With Frederick Barbarossa and Philip Augustus, he leads the Third Crusade.

1190
- Frederick Barbarossa drowns in Cilicia; Henry VI is crowned king of Germany and Holy Roman Emperor.

1191–1192
- Acre and Jaffa are captured by the Crusaders, but otherwise the Third Crusade is a failure.

1194
- Richard the Lionhearted, who is captured in Austria by King Leopold, is ransomed to England. After his release he begins a war against France.

1198
- Pope Innocent III calls for another crusade. His plan is for the army to gather at Venice for transportation by sea to the Middle East. There is little enthusiasm for the endeavor, however, and few nobles initially join the cause.

* DENOTES CIRCA DATE

1199

- Richard the Lionhearted is mortally wounded while making war against Philip II in France. His successor is John (Lackland), son of Henry II, who rules until 1216. He continues the war against France but loses English-held territories on the mainland.

1201

- Count Theobald takes leadership of the Fourth Crusade, but he dies before the troops can be gathered. Crusaders continue to arrive in Venice, but there are delays over transportation because of financial problems.

1202-1241

- Much of the Baltic region comes under the control of the Danes during the reign of Valdemar II.

1202

- The Fourth Crusade begins when a fleet leaves Venice, sailing first to capture Zara (a Christian town) on the Dalmatian coast. After wintering in Zara, the Crusade continues on to Constantinople.

1202-1204

- Philip Augustus captures Normandy and other French provinces from the English.

1203-1204

- French and Venetian Crusaders attack Constantinople in an effort to overthrow the Byzantine ruler Alexius III Angelus Comnenus. The Greeks, with English and Danish mercenaries, block the French advance, but the Venetians break into the city. Alexius III Comnenus flees and Alexius IV Comnenus is placed on the throne. Anti-western sentiment, however, rises in the city and a challenger, Alexius V (Murtzuphlus), gains support and murders Alexius IV Comnenus. The Crusaders conquer and loot the city (13 April 1204). The Fourth Crusade ends here, with many knights returning to Europe with their plunder.

1209-1229

- Several Albigensian crusades, called by Pope Innocent III, are carried out against religious heretics in southern France.

1212

- Frederick II becomes king of Germany and Holy Roman Emperor.
- Inspired by the preaching of a shepherd boy, Stephen, people in France join a Crusade. They sail to Egypt where many of them are captured and sold into slavery. Another group responds to the call of a young man in Germany for a similar crusade. Many die of starvation and exposure as they march through the Alps into Italy, where they are stopped from continuing to the Middle East.
- Duke Leopold VI (the Glorious) of Austria joins a crusade against the Moors of Spain.

*DENOTES CIRCA DATE

1214
- The army of Philip Augustus defeats a combined army of John of England and Holy Roman Emperor Otto IV at the Battle of Bouvines.

1215
- John of England is forced by barons meeting at Runnymede to sign the Magna Carta (15 June), a feudal charter that includes reforms in the responsibilities and concessions given to the barons; a system of uniform weights and measures; limitations on the seizure of private property and the protection of personal liberties; consent to be gained prior to the levy of taxes; and no penalties to be made without a proper trial by one's peers.

1216
- Nine-year-old Henry III, the son of John, becomes king of England. William Marshal, Earl of Pembroke, serves as his regent until 1219. Henry does not assume personal control of the throne until 1227.

1217-1221
- King Andrew II of Hungary, John of Briene, and Leopold the Glorious begin the Fifth Crusade, called by Pope Honorius III, to Palestine and Egypt. Held up by late arriving soldiers and winter weather, the Crusade actually starts in April 1218 when ships leave for Acre and then proceed to Egypt. Despite early successes, the Crusade fails.

1220-1231
- The first invasions of Mongols into Eurasia occur. By midcentury they will control Iran, Syria, Russia, and the Ukraine.

1226
- Louis IX (Saint Louis) becomes king of France and rules for forty-four years.

1228-1229
- Frederick II leads the Sixth Crusade, captures Jerusalem, Bethlehem, and Nazareth, and is named the king of Jerusalem.

1231
- Frederick II captures Sicily.

1240*
- The Great Council of England begins to be called "Parliament." Mostly an administrative body, it slowly takes on legislative duties.

1244
- Jerusalem is recaptured by the Turks.

*DENOTES CIRCA DATE

1248
- Pope Innocent IV calls for the Seventh Crusade; Louis IX answers the call. The Crusaders capture Damietta but by 1250 are forced to withdraw after being defeated in Egypt.

1250
- Conrad IV becomes king of Germany upon the death of Frederick II, who is buried in Palermo.

1258
- A committee is seated to reform English government, resulting in the *Provisions of Oxford*, which establishes baronial veto over decisions made by the king. The chancellor and treasurer are selected by the baron's council. Henry III reneges on his oath to support the provisions in 1161 and puts his supporters on the committee, which leads to the outbreak of civil war, known as the Baron's War.

1261
- Byzantine emperor Michael VIII Palaeologus recaptures Constantinople.

1263
- Haakon V Haakonsson, king of Norway, dies. During his reign, which began in 1217, he leads the Norse capture of Iceland and Greenland, although he fails in an attempt to capture Scotland.

1264
- Henry III is captured by his brother-in-law, Simon de Montfort, Earl of Leicester, at the Battle of Lewes (14 May). Simon forces Henry to renew his pledge to the reforms of 1258 in the *Mise of Lewes*. Two knights from each shire and two burgesses from each borough are called to attend a parliament.

1265
- Edward I, with the help of troops from the Welsh borderlands, comes to the aid of his father, Henry III, and defeats and kills Montfort at the Battle of Evesham (4 August). The barons therefore are unable to establish their control of the king. Although Henry returns to the throne, it is Edward who has the power.

1266
- The army of Neapolitan and Sicilian king Charles I (Charles of Anjou), who was given his lands, defeats the forces of his rival, Manfred, at the Battle of Benevento.

1268
- Conradin, who also claims Sicily, is captured by Charles of Anjou and beheaded in Naples.

*DENOTES CIRCA DATE

1270

- French, English, and Italian Crusaders attack Tunisia.

1272

- Henry III dies. Called back from a crusade, Edward I assumes the throne in 1274 and rules until 1307. During his reign three common-law courts are established: Court of the King's Bench (for criminal and royal cases), Court of the Exchequer (financial cases), and Court of Common Pleas (cases between subjects).

1278

- Knighthood requirements are extended in England to insure that there is a large-enough pool of militia under royal control.

1282

- Edward I marches an army into Wales to put down a revolt led by Llywelyn ap Gruffudd, who had supported the barons in their fight against Henry III and had refused to do homage to Edward. Despite being once subjugated (1277), Llywelyn rebels again and is killed near Builth. Llywelyn's brother David is executed in 1283.
- Erik V (Glipping), the king of Denmark from 1259 to 1286, is forced to grant the nobles a constitution, which recognizes a national assembly and puts the king under its authority.

1285

- The Second *Statute of Westminster* reorganizes the militia of England.
- Philip IV (the Fair) becomes the king of France.

1291

- The fall of Acre signals the end of the Crusader Kingdoms in the Middle East.

1292

- John Balliol is awarded the kingship of Scotland by Edward I, after the death of Alexander III (1286). Balliol and the Scots are soon angered by Edward I's machinations and look for help from France.

1295

- Edward I calls the Model Parliament, with the broadest representation to date, including clergy, knights, burgesses, and aristocrats, as well as representatives of shires, towns, and parishes.

1296

- Edward I invades Scotland with around thirty thousand infantrymen and five thousand cavalry. His army destroys Berwick and massacres the inhabitants, and then it defeats the forces of Balliol at the Battle of Dunbar. Edward I captures a sacred stone, removes it to Westminster Abbey, and forces Scotland to swear allegiance to England.

*DENOTES CIRCA DATE

1297
- William Wallace, a Scottish noble whose men are engaged in attacking English outposts, gathers an army and defeats the English at Stirling Bridge.
- The Confirmation of Charters further limits the levies the Crown can make without parliamentary approval.

1298
- Wallace's men attack border settlements. Edward I sends another army against the Scots, who are defeated at the Battle of Falkirk. Wallace escapes, but in 1305 he is captured, found guilty of treason, then hanged, drawn, and quartered.

1302
- Flemish burghers defeat an army of French knights at the Battle of Courtrai (Battle of the Golden Spurs).
- Philip IV calls the first Estates-General, the French national representative body, which had members from the clergy, nobility, and common people.

1306
- Robert I (the Bruce) murders his rival John Comyn and assumes the Scottish throne.

1307-1313
- The Order of Templars is suppressed in France.

1314
- Robert the Bruce defeats an English army at the Battle of Bannockburn.

1326
- Ottoman Turks begin to invade the Byzantine Empire.

1327
- Edward III becomes the king of England and rules until 1377. His reign is marked with constant conflict with France.

1328
- Scotland is recognized as independent by Edward III in the Treaty of Northampton.

1333
- The English, who support Edward de Baliol, defeat a Scottish army at Halidon Hill.

1337
- The Hundred Years' War, a conflict between the French and English over Continental lands, begins; it ends in 1453.

*DENOTES CIRCA DATE

1340
- Edward III claims the French throne.
- The English navy defeats a combined French-Spanish-Genoese fleet at the Battle of Sluys on 23 June.

1346
- Edward III invades Normandy and defeats the French on 26 August at the Battle of Crécy. The power of the longbow and discipline gave the English an advantage over their enemy.

1347
- The Black Death, or bubonic plague, ravages Europe until 1351. It spreads out of China, carried by traders traveling along the Silk Road, and kills more than 25 percent of the European population.

1350
- The French king, Philip VI, dies.

*DENOTES CIRCA DATE

Aerial view of the ruins of Krak de Montreal, a castle southeast of the Dead Sea, built by King Baldwin I of Jerusalem in 1115 to maintain the Crusaders' control over the roads from Syria, Egypt, and Arabia

POLITICS, LAW, AND THE MILITARY

OVERVIEW

Clarification. Most historians interpret the fall of the Roman Empire in 476 as the date for the beginning of the formation of the Middle Ages, and they see the discovery of America in 1492 as the end of the Middle Ages. Although the time frame for this book begins in 814, historically, this date would involve the omission of the early Middle Ages, the age of the barbarian kingdoms and the formation of the Carolingian Empire. Moreover, it is commonly accepted that the following three institutions survived the fall of Rome, and they are fundamental for an understanding of the beginning of the Middle Ages: the Eastern Roman Empire at Constantinople; the Christian Church at Rome with its bishop as the successor of St. Peter; and the continuity of Roman law. Roman law continued in the East, where under the Emperor Justinian was completed the Codification of Roman law, the *Corpus Juris Civilis* (Codex and Digest of Civil Law). A body of law had begun to be assembled in the Church of Rome and it would develop by the thirteenth century into what is known as canon, or ecclesiastical law. Roman law would continue to be practiced in what remained of the towns of the old Western Roman Empire. This situation would in time help to provide West European society, especially after the twelfth century foundation of the Legal University at Bologna, with an extremely sophisticated body of law, which would have major influence on the construction of daily life. Because the student may not be aware of the fate of the world after the Fall of Rome, it is necessary to preface the period 814–1350 with an account of how the Middle Ages in the West came to be formed out of the confluence of the Frankish Kingdoms and the needs of the Roman Church.

Fall of Rome. Historians have provided many explanations for the fall of Rome. Some seem to be solidly based on scholarship; others sound more like moralizing. Among the first are: the failure of the emperors to deal with crises or to alter government to meet crises; the various civil wars, which sucked manpower from the outer defenses of the Empire; the radical difference between rich and poor; class struggle, which led to apathy toward imperial institutions; plague; and the introduction in 212 C.E. under Caracalla of "universal citizenship," which meant that males did not have to obey the required military draft and service. Exam-ples of the more moralistic explanations are: lead poisoning because of the use of lead pipes and lead utensils; too much "bread" (prosperity); too many "circuses" (amusements); venereal disease; God punished the Romans; and finally, Christianity weakened the uprightness of the Roman order. Yet, whatever the correct explanations, it is well known who were the ones who brought about the end of the Roman Empire. They were the so-called non-imperial barbarian tribes who lived outside of the Roman Empire, across the Rhine and Danube Rivers and beyond the deserts of Mesopotamia. The descendants of these tribes mixed with the descendants of Rome, who by 800 C.E. re-established a new kind of "Holy Roman Empire" based on the hegemony of the Franks.

Causes. Perhaps, however, four different phenomena between 235 and 600 led to the birth of the political, legal, and military situation of the Middle Ages. The first was the sharing of power of the office of emperor. This situation lead to much civil war among the Roman leaders. The final outcome was the victory of the Emperor Constantine at Milvian Bridge on 29 October 312. He attributed his victory to Jesus Christ, his soldiers having painted the *Chi/Rho* (X and P) monogram of Christ on their shields. The second phenomena was the emergence of Christianity under Constantine and his successors as the official religion of the empire. The third was the foundation by Constantine of the new city, Constantinople, as the center of the Eastern Roman Empire. The fourth was the attempt by Justinian in the 500s to reconquer the Western Roman Empire.

Legacy of Justinian. Nevertheless, despite this failure, Justinian passed on to the Latin Middle Ages an institution that in a sense prolonged the life of the Roman Empire, that is, the *Corpus Juris Civilis*. This massive codification of all of Roman Law would become the foundation of later medieval legal practice. Further, even in the cities and small towns of the West, Roman traditions of law and education did not die out. They co-existed with a barbarian hinterland, and gradually the barbarian tribes took on the trappings of Roman legal usage. Such a continuity in law and education proved to be more long lasting than the stones and mortar of Roman aqueducts, theaters, and coliseums.

Barbarian Kingdoms. Various names are given to the barbarian tribes: Alans, Suevi, Ostrogoths, Gepids, Vandals, Alemanni, Lombards, Thuringians, Burgundians, Saxons, Franks, Frisians, Angles, and Jutes. (Notice how many of these correspond to present-day areas in Europe.) These tribes took on Christianity, and since they were generally looking for settled conditions in order to feed their big populations, they settled down in the conquered lands. For example, by the late fifth century, the Ostrogoths settled in Northern Italy. They performed their soldierly duties while the Romans such as Boethius and his colleagues continued to run the legal aspects of Roman municipal life. Their practices of landholding and family settlement would, however, have an influence on the Middle Ages. Whereas in the Roman Empire, land and property were passed on from father to son (even to adopted and sometimes illegitimate sons), the barbarian Germanic tribes practiced a form of communal "partible inheritance" (the property was divided evenly among all the male heirs). This situation could, of course, lead to much family strife. In addition, it would cause instability among all barbarian kingdoms throughout the early Middle Ages.

Loyalty. A second major change brought about by these tribes was in the nature of recruitment and advancement of the military. No one in Germanic society was more respected than a warrior, nor was anyone deemed worth more in the *wergild* (legal codes). Military service was not a problem; loyalty was the crucial issue. Distinguished soldiers generally sold their services to the highest bidder. The Franks solved this problem by procuring permanent service through the awarding of lands and titles. This system provided a permanent bank of a ready and trained militia, but it also brought economic duties. The lands had to be developed and the farmworkers had to be organized. Failure to provide military service would immediately result in the loss of tenure.

Franks. By the seventh century the Lombards controlled Italy, the Visigoths Spain, the Anglo-Saxons England, and the Franks Gaul. Of these, the most powerful undoubtedly were the Franks, and unlike other barbarian tribes, they were not Christians. This situation changed, however, in the late fifth century, when Clovis accepted Christianity. Unlike the other barbarians, who were normally Arian Christians, the Franks took on Catholic Christianity.

Merovingian Period. The period from 511 to 740 was a time of much instability. Yet, out of the Merovingian period emerged people who would chart the future medieval kingdom of the Franks. These individuals were nonroyal holders of power in the office of the *major domus* (Mayor of the Palace). The three important ones were those of Austrasia, Neustria, and Burgundy. Pepin I and Peppin II were able to consolidate these, and in 714, Pepin II's illegitimate son, Charles Martel, got control of all three mayorships.

Tours. Charles Martel (Charles the Hammer) was faced with an entirely new phenomenon: the invasion of the lands of the Franks by the expanding Muslim kingdoms in the Mediterranean and in Spain. These powerful armies reached as far north as Poitiers, just south of modern Paris. He would defeat these Muslim forces in 732 at Tours and gradually he pushed them back into Spain.

Carolingians. This development gave enormous force to a cavalry carrying lances when confronted with a cavalry who rode without stirrups. In 751 his son Pepin III took over the kingship of the Franks and established the Carolingian dynasty, which was named after his father. It would be the first and emblematic medieval kingdom in the full sense of the word.

Oath of Fealty. Charlemagne (Charles the Great) began his reign in 768, and by the time of his death in 814 he had doubled the size of his kingdom: it encompassed modern France, Belgium, Holland, Switzerland, most of Germany, a large part of Italy, northern Spain, and Austria. The reason for this expansion was simple: he was the most successful of all medieval military leaders. In 800 his great success was rewarded by his being crowned Holy Roman Emperor in Rome by the Pope. He had wiped out the Avars, subdued the Saxons through brutal military action, and pacified Italy. He, like his father, realized the power of a diverse, professional force equipped with expensive arms and armor. He required all property owners to be part of the war effort. Further, all soldiers were required to take an oath of fealty to Charlemagne. It was the first time since the Fall of Rome that such an oath was required. It helped guarantee a loyalty that earlier leaders had not been able to realize. He brought overwhelming power to battle, heavy cavalry, siege equipment, and long and plentiful baggage trains. He built large fortifications along his borders and sought alliances with border tribes. His only defeat was by the Basques as he sought to enter France from Spain at Roncesvalles.

Division. Unfortunately, the consolidation of Charlemagne's kingdom did not last: in 843 the kingdom was divided among his grandsons Lothar I, Louis the German, and Charles the Bald. These kingdoms were pressed hard on three sides: the Muslim forces in Sicily and Spain harassed the South; the Magyars threatened the East; and the Vikings descended from the North.

Vikings. It is important to understand the Vikings not simply as destructive marauders. From their appearance in Northern England in the late eighth century and for the next three hundred years, they would alter the landscape and structure of medieval Europe.

Why these invasions took place and in such numbers has baffled historians. The size and structure of the Viking boats enabled them to navigate into the interiors of most European countries. The first populations to feel the force of these invaders were the small church settlements in Scotland, England, and Ireland. Here, the Viking raiders pillaged and plundered the monastic settlements, taking away gold and silver objects as war treasures. They succeeded in attacking Atlantic Europe down to Spain and raided Muslim lands. After 911 Viking activity seems to have slowed. The Vikings had founded settled communities in Ireland, Scotland, England, Russia, Normandy, the Faroe and Shetland Islands, Iceland, and Greenland. Ireland provides a good example of their influence. Prior to the Viking settlements there were no cities. Viking river camps developed into trading centers and later became the cities of Limerick, Waterford, Wexford, and Dublin.

Lesser Threats. In the East the Magyars constantly threatened the Frankish kingdoms until finally in 955 they were defeated by King Otto the Great at the battle of Lechfeld. In the South, Muslim raids continued, although they were never able to overcome stiff resistance.

Assimilation. The Vikings who settled in Normandy, France, assimilated to French ways. They paid homage to the French king, fought in his battles against new Viking invaders, and took on Christian religious practices. Descendants of these Vikings emerged in the eleventh century. Robert Guiscard and his brothers conquered Sicily, and this kingdom would play a major role in the political, legal, and military situation in southern Europe. William, Duke of Normandy, the Conqueror, overcame the Saxons in England. His defeat of King Harold Godwinsson at the Battle of Hastings in 1066 altered the course of English and European history. England quickly developed into a Norman kingdom; the language of the court was French. Meanwhile, efforts were made all over Europe to impose a new kind of peace, "The Peace of God." This effort was an attempt to restrain group violence.

Expansion of Islam. Ever since its appearance in the seventh century, Islam as a military-political operation developed with great speed. Within one hundred years of the Prophet Muhammad, the Mediterranean had changed from being a Roman to being an Islamic sea. This massive military expansion was driven by the Koranic religious doctrine of the religious war for Islam, the jihad. After 750, Muslim armies were not able to penetrate into Gaul. From the late eighth century to the eleventh century there was little military activity between the Europeans and the Muslims except in southern Italy. In the early eleventh century the Christian kings of northwest Spain, lands that had never succumbed to Muslim conquest, began a *reconquista*, a reconquest of the Iberian Peninsula, a fight that was to be long in duration, lasting until 1492, but which ultimately would free all of Spain and Portugal from Muslim control.

Crusades. The defeat of the Byzantine army by the Seljuk Turks at Manzikert in 1071 sent a wave of crisis through Western Europe. The Eastern Roman Emperor Alexius I Comnenus appealed to the Pope in Rome for help. Pope Urban II in turn advocated a crusade, the first in a series of religiously inspired military efforts to free the Holy Land of the infidels. The First Crusade was launched on 27 November 1095 at the Council of Clermont. In 1096 many of the noble houses of France organized an army. This Norman army took Antioch in 1098 and Jerusalem on 15 July 1099.

A new Kingdom of Jerusalem was set up under the leadership of Godfrey of Bouillon. By 1124 most of modern Syria and Israel were controlled by Crusader castles, although a second crusade ended in failure.

Muslim Counterattacks. However, the hinterland was firmly in the control of Muslim forces, first under Nur-al-Din and later Saladin. Muslim forces retook Jerusalem on 2 October 1187, an event that caused amazement in Europe. In the Third Crusade the leading royalty of Europe, including Richard I or the Lionhearted (England), Philip II or Philip Augustus (France), and Frederick I or Frederick Barbarossa (Holy Roman Empire), set out to reconquer the Holy Land. While the Europeans conquered Jaffa and Acre, they failed to take Jerusalem. A fourth crusade in 1198 ended in the Crusaders attacking the city of Constantinople and setting up the Latin Kingdom of Constantinople. By the mid thirteenth century the military situation in the Near East was complex: a new force appeared, the Mongols. The fall of Baghdad in 1256 to the Mongols sent fear throughout the Middle East. However, the period from 1265 to 1292 was to be one of gradual loss of control of the Holy Land and the Near East by the Western Europeans.

Internal European Strife. In the period from the eleventh century to the fourteenth century many difficult internal struggles took place in Germany and Sicily for the control of the Holy Roman Empire. In the 1260s, and especially with the papacy of the Frenchman, Guy le Gros de Foullques (Pope Clement IV), French power began to dominate Italy. In particular, the brother of the king of France, Charles of Anjou, would engage in a massive military action in southern Italy and Sicily against the German Hohenstaufen leaders of the Holy Roman Empire. Hegemony in Europe moved toward France and away from Germany. The battles of Benevento, Tagliacozzo, and Lucera in the 1260s brought the end of Hohenstaufen control in southern Italy. However, the kingdom ruled by Charles of Anjou did not last, and it fell in the Sicilian Vespers in the late thirteenth century, thereby leading Spain to gain hegemony in southern Italy.

Hundred Years' War. By the end of the century the first contours of a distinctly national, centrally organized state emerged in the figure of Philip the Fair of France. He would directly challenge the territorial ambitions of the papacy. Tensions, however, began to arise between the French and the English over the English claims to territories in France. In 1337 the first battles of the Hundred Years' War took place, and despite greatly outnumbering the English, the French were eventually defeated in 1453. The English military expansion was halted by an event that is commonly seen by historians as an historical watershed: the Black Death. The spread of the plague by vermin led to a massive loss of life all over Europe. More than one-third of the population was destroyed. This devastation led naturally to a great decrease in the size of armies. As a result, a new form of warfare developed: the *chevauchee*, or quick cavalry raid.

TOPICS IN POLITICS, LAW, AND THE MILITARY

THE BATTLEFIELD: TACTICS AND WEAPONS

Dominant Arm. As the individual most representative of medieval warfare, the mounted knight became the dominant arm on the battlefield, while the infantryman was held in contempt for his social inferiority. The infantry, armed mostly with sword, battle-ax, spear, javelin, and short bow, usually acted in a supportive role, while opposing cavalry clashed with sword, mace, and lance. The tactic of the day was to close with the enemy as quickly as possible and to decide the contest with hand-to-hand combat. Poorly equipped and organized, most medieval infantry could not withstand the shock of a full-scale cavalry charge, although at Bouvines in 1214, the infantry of Boulogne repelled several assaults made by French horsemen before succumbing. When geographic conditions dictated, knights would fight on foot, such as occurred at the Battle of Tinchebrai in 1106.

Armor. During this period most knights wore chain-mail armor, with plate armor restricted to helmets. However, with the increasing effectiveness of infantry missile weapons, knights began to don more and more plate armor because of the protection it afforded; by the fifteenth century this type of armor predominated. Two weapons in particular accelerated the trend toward greater armor protection: the crossbow and the longbow.

Crossbow. A medieval form of the ancient ballista, the crossbow was small enough to be operated by a single soldier. Made with an iron bow and a wooden stock, the crossbow was cocked with either a foot stirrup or a wind-

Viking axe-heads and spearheads (circa tenth century) found at London Bridge (London Museum)

lass. Its projectile, the bolt or quarrel, could penetrate chain mail up to fifty yards and was deadly to unarmored men at twice that range. At the instigation of the nobility, the Second Lateran Council in 1139 attempted to ban the use of this weapon between Christian opponents. Although greatly feared (a crossbow bolt mortally wounded Richard I in 1199), the crossbow did have a major disadvantage: its slow rate of fire meant that the operator was vulnerable to enemy attack.

Longbow. A more devastating and ultimately decisive weapon on the battlefield of the Middle Ages was the longbow. Originally a hunting weapon, the longbow was the preferred weapon of the English yeomanry, a class of peasant freeholders. Six feet in length, the longbow was usually made of yew, elm, hazel, or basil wood. A skilled archer could accurately fire a "broadcloth" (a unit of measurement equal to thirty-seven inches) arrow up to three hundred yards. The longbow had a greater rate of fire than the crossbow (up to six arrows per minute), but like the crossbowman, the longbowman was vulnerable to enemy forces if they could get close enough. The English victories at Crécy (1346) and Poitiers (1356) can in part be attributed to archers armed with longbows.

Swiss. A mountainous and isolated country, Switzerland never developed a powerful noble class for its military and instead relied heavily on a citizenry armed with pole arms such as pikes and halberds. The basic Swiss formation was a company of 250 pikemen arrayed in a square of sixteen ranks with 50 halberdiers and crossbowmen in support. The strength of such a tactical formation made the Swiss into formidable foes, and by the 1400s foreign rulers sought to hire them as mercenaries.

Siege Artillery. The construction of stone castles and walled cities during the High Middle Ages (1000–1300) increased the difficultly of armies to lay siege to them. In response to this predicament, medieval armies used the catapult, a siege weapon of antiquity, and a new device, the trebuchet or mangonel. While the catapult used tension or torsion for its propelling force, the trebuchet used a counterweight for kinetic energy. A trebuchet with a fifty-foot-long arm and a ten-ton counterweight could hurl a three-hundred-pound stone three hundred yards. Several of these weapons firing at a stone wall could eventually reduce it to rubble.

Naval Engagements. Medieval states did not maintain war fleets as nations do today. Many times their war vessels were actually converted merchantmen (warships were too expensive to build and to maintain in peacetime). Naval tactics and weapons during the era were the same as the ones used on land: the melee with edged weapons. Warships were basically floating castles in which wooden structures were erected on the bows and sterns to shelter archers while men-at-arms waited in the waist (middle) of the ship. Ships would close with each other, firing projectiles until they could grapple together. Boarding parties then decided the issue by hand-to-hand fighting, as occurred at

Emperor Henry VI preparing his fleet and army for the invasion of Sicily in the 1190s; his troops include foot soldiers, Bohemian archers, and Bavarian crossbowmen; illumination from a twelfth-century manuscript (Burgerbibliotek, Bern).

the Battle of Sluys (1340). Sometimes, innovations could help tip the balance. At the Battle of Dover (1217) thirty-six English warships defeated a French force of eighty vessels. The English sailed downwind, their sailors firing crossbows and throwing lime to blind the enemy.

Sources:
John Beeler, *Warfare in Feudal Europe, 730–1200* (Ithaca, N.Y.: Cornell University Press, 1971).

Jim Bradbury, *The Medieval Siege* (Woodbridge, U.K. & Rochester, N.Y.: Boydell Press, 1992).

Philippe Contamine, *War in the Middle Ages,* translated by Michael Jones (Oxford, U.K.: Blackwell, 1984).

Kelly DeVries, *Medieval Military Technology* (Peterborough, Canada: Broadview Press, 1992).

Nicholas Hooper and Matthew Bennett, *The Cambridge Illustrated Atlas of Warfare: The Middle Ages* (New York: Cambridge University Press, 1996).

Maurice Keen, ed., *Medieval Warfare: A History* (Oxford & New York: Oxford University Press, 1999).

David Nicolle, *Medieval Warfare Source Book,* volume one, *Warfare in Western Christendom* (London: Arms & Armour, 1995).

Nicolle, *Medieval Warfare Source Book,* volume two, *Christian Europe and its Neighbors* (London: Arms & Armour, 1995).

Michael Prestwich, *Armies and Warfare in the Middle Ages: The English Experience* (New Haven: Yale University Press, 1996).

Malcolm Vale, *War and Chivalry: Warfare and Aristocratic Culture in England, France, and Burgundy at the End of the Middle Ages* (Athens: University of Georgia Press, 1981; London: Duckworth, 1981).

J. F. Verbruggen, *The Art of Warfare in Western Europe During the Middle Ages: From the Eighth Century to 1340,* translated by Sumner Willard and R. W. Southern (Woodbridge, U.K. & Rochester, N.Y.: Boydell Press, 1997).

CAROLINGIAN MILITARY MACHINE

Legacy of Charlemagne. Charlemagne (Charles the Great) ruled the Carolingian kingdom from 768 to 814. By the end of his life that kingdom had taken on a completely different shape, having more than doubled in size. At that time it encompassed modern France, Belgium, Holland, and Switzerland, most of Germany, and a large part of Italy, northern Spain, and Austria. The reason for this growth was simple: of all medieval leaders none was so militarily successful as Charlemagne. He summoned his armies to fight in nearly every one of his forty-six years on the Frankish throne. All of these campaigns were used to extend the borders of the Carolingian kingdom, and, because each campaign was against a non-Catholic foe, all of his wars were waged with the blessing and for the benefit of the Church. As such, Charlemagne defeated the Avars in the East, the Lombards in Italy, the Saxons (several times) in the northeast, and the Muslims in northern Spain. In fact, on only one occasion was even a small part of his army defeated, when his booty-laden rearguard led by Roland was ambushed coming out of Spain at Roncesvalles in 778.

Professional Army. The Carolingian army led by Charlemagne and his successors was a diverse, professional force equipped with expensive arms and armor. Many of these soldiers also had to be mounted on equally expensive warhorses. Because such a force needed to be quite large, the Carolingian kings required all the property holders of the realm to participate in military service, either with their own service in the army or by their outfitting and paying for a suitable replacement. The nature of this obligation is laid out in a law (known as a capitulary) dated 808:

Every free man who has four mansi (a measurement of land) of his own property, or as a benefice from anyone, shall equip himself and go to the army, either with his lord, if the lord goes, or with his count. He who has three mansi shall be joined to a man who has one mansus, and shall aid him so that he may serve for both. He who has only two mansi of his own property shall be joined to another who likewise has two mansi, and one of them, with the aid of the other, shall go to the army. He who has only one mansus of his own shall be joined to one of three who have the same and shall aid him, the latter shall go alone; the three who have aided him shall stay home.

Even subject peoples were required to fill the ranks of the Carolingian army. However, they were always commanded by Frankish nobles.

Horsemen. The cavalry was supplied by the more wealthy noble class, who could afford the expensive armaments and horses. They were required to muster for any long campaign and lost their lands and titles if they failed to come in support of the king. When not required to fight in a campaign, they were put in command of a garrison along the borders of Spain or Saxony.

Oath of Fealty. All soldiers were required to take an oath of fealty or allegiance to the king. This was the first time since the Fall of Rome that such an oath was required. In doing so, the Carolingian kings secured a viable, legal means from which military service could be obtained from men who were previously not required to serve them. The kings also guaranteed a loyalty that earlier leaders had not been able to realize.

Weapons. All soldiers had to be well armed and protected. The cavalry was to be equipped with a lance, a shield, a long sword, and a short sword. They were also required to be outfitted with a bow and arrows. The infantry was also well equipped, either with a bow (complete with two bowstrings and twelve arrows) or a spear. Most cavalry and infantry soldiers had a chain-mail coat, a shield, and a helmet for protection. These Carolingian mail coats were so important that one of Charlemagne's capitularies forbade the sale of any mail coat to a non-Frank or even to a merchant; the punishment for doing so was death. The cost of this

Carolingian light cavalry carrying lances and riding without stirrups; illumination from the *Utrecht Psalter,* 820–830
(Bibliotheek der Rijksuniversiteit, Utrecht)

equipment was to be shouldered by the property owners themselves or, if a soldier served in a noble's retinue, by those nobles under whom he served.

Invincibility. Once in battle the Carolingian army was almost invulnerable. Its overwhelming power was wisely utilized by a tactical system of advances that allowed the heavy cavalry troops to be used to the extent of their capability, even against lighter, swifter armies. Sieges were also well planned and executed. At the sieges of Pavia in 773 and Barcelona in 802, Charlemagne's army was provided with heavy siege equipment and massive baggage trains for supplies.

Fortified Positions. However, the Carolingians also knew the value of a wise defense. They built several large fortifications along the borders of their kingdoms and established a good signaling system to call for reinforcements anywhere in the large empire. They also bribed certain enemy chieftains, most notably the Danes, to remain at peace with the empire. The Danes themselves seem to have feared the Carolingians, as they constructed their own large and extensive fortification, the Danewerk, to wall off their kingdoms from that of Charlemagne.

Sources:

Bernard S. Bachrach, *Early Carolingian Warfare: Prelude to Empire* (Philadelphia: University of Pennsylvania Press, 2001).

Heinrich Fichtenau, *The Carolingian Empire: The Age of Charlemagne*, translated by Peter Munz (New York: Barnes & Noble, 1963).

François Louis Ganshof, *Frankish Institutions Under Charlemagne*, translated by Bryce and Mary Lyon (Providence, R.I.: Brown University Press, 1968).

Rosamund McKitterick, *The Frankish Kingdoms under the Carolingians, 751-987* (London & New York: Longman, 1983).

ENGLISH COMMON LAW

Henry II. Although there had been various legal codes in Anglo-Saxon England, they had all been declared moot by the conquest of William the Conqueror in 1066. For the next century of English history the Norman and early Angevin kings did not issue a code of laws, nor were many legislative acts made. Only during the reign of Henry II (1154–1189) were new laws, the assizes, regularly issued. Some of these laws abolished older traditions and statutes, while others established new legislation. Also during this reign the first English account of legal proceedings, *De legibus et consuetudinibus regni Angliae* (Concerning the Laws and Customs of

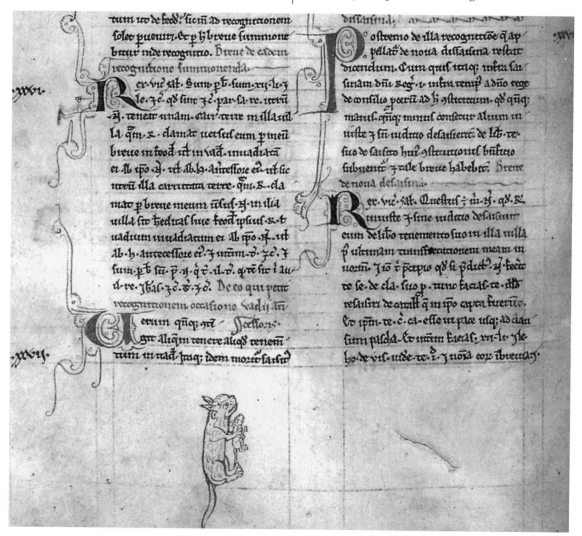

Part of a page from a manuscript for Ranulf de Glanville's *Treatise on the Laws and Customs of England* (circa 1188), the first authoritative text on English common law (Balliol College, Oxford)

the Kingdom of England) was published, probably written by the king's chief legalist, Ranulf de Glanvill. Finally, by the end of Henry II's reign, royal clerks were taking notes of the decisions made in the king's court and the opinions uttered in support of them.

Documentation. From this time forward in England, law books, assizes, and law collections (both of common and canon law) began being written, especially by private lawyers seeking to exhibit their expertise. These statutes concerned both the administration of justice and judicial procedure. They discussed the specificity of the powers and duties of judges, sheriffs, and other lawgivers and law enforcers. They also established the procedures of bringing and carrying out lawsuits, of which there were many during this and later medieval periods. Finally, the ethics of law were emphasized: all legal actions were to be carried out with expertise and experience.

General Eyres. Of the practicalities that English common law established, one of the most important procedures was that of the "general eyres." The general eyres were regular, kingdom-wide visitations made by royal judges to each and every county in England. These judges would visit local centers of importance, stay for at least a week and sometimes for several weeks, hear any cases within their royal jurisdiction, make their decisions, and then move on to a neighboring locale. The jurisdiction of these judges was widespread: they could decide cases that dealt with pleas to the Crown; pleas initiated by royal writs, tenancies, wardships, and marriage rights; criminal cases; payments for the king's ransom; rebellions against the crown; the sale of wine against regulations; cases regarding ownership of land below a certain value; the election of coroners; a tallage (tax) of the royal demense (manorial land); the loans of Jews; and the exactions of royal officials. These circuit judges, combined with the Court of Common Pleas (or the Bench), the central royal court, heard any civil cases put forth by all common men, regardless of rank. They were the first legal body to do so in the western world and established a precedent upon which all judicial bodies in England and English colonial lands were built. Undoubtedly, English common law also led to the further establishment of other freedoms of governance for common men in England and elsewhere.

Sources:

John Hudson, *The Formation of the English Common Law: Law and Society in England from the Norman Conquest to the Magna Carta* (London & New York: Longman, 1996).

George Williams Keeton, *The Norman Conquest and the Common Law* (London: Benn, 1996; New York: Barnes & Noble, 1996).

S. F. C. Milsom, *Historical Foundations of the Common Law* (London: Butterworth, 1969).

FIRST CRUSADE (1095–1099)

Holy Land. The Muslims who controlled the Holy Land (Palestine) were more often than not friendly to visiting European pilgrims who, after all, were good for the local economy. The Muslims even allowed the existence of monasteries of every Christian denomination in the region. In fact, between the late eighth century and early eleventh

IMPERISHABLE GLORY OF GOD

In a sermon at the Council of Clermont on 26 November 1095, Pope Urban II painted a gruesome image of the Muslim occupation of Jerusalem and promised remission of sins for all those who would go on a crusade to liberate the Holy Land. Thousands of knights responded to this call to arms, and the result was the First Crusade (1095–1099).

From the confines of Jerusalem and the city of Constantinople a horrible tale has gone forth and very frequently has been brought to our ears, namely, that a race from the kingdom of the Persians [that is, the Seljuk Turks], an accursed race, a race utterly alienated from God, a generation forsooth which has not directed its heart and has not entrusted its spirit to God, has invaded the lands of those Christians and has depopulated them by the sword, pillage and fire; it has led away a part of the captives into its own country, and a part it has destroyed by cruel tortures; it has either entirely destroyed the churches of God or appropriated them for the rites of its own religion. They destroy the altars, after having defiled them with their uncleanness. They circumcise the Christians, and the blood of the circumcision they either spread upon the altars or pour into the vases of the baptismal font. When they wish to torture people by a base death, they perforate their navels, and dragging forth the extremity of the intestines, bind it to a stake; then with flogging they lead the victim around until the viscera having gushed forth the victim falls prostrate upon the ground. Others they will bind to a post and pierce with arrows. Others they compel to extend their necks and then, attacking them with naked swords, attempt to cut through the neck with a single blow. What shall I say of the abominable rape of the women? The kingdom of the Greeks is now dismembered by them and deprived of territory so vast in extent that it cannot be traversed in a march of two months. On whom therefore is the labor of avenging these wrongs and of recovering this territory incumbent, if not upon you?...

Jerusalem is the navel of the world; the land is fruitful above others, like another paradise of delights. This the Redeemer of the human race has made illustrious by His advent, has beautified by residence, has consecrated by suffering, has redeemed by death, has glorified by burial. This royal city, therefore, situated at the center of the world, is now held captive by His enemies, and is in subjection to those who do not know God, to the worship of the heathens. She seeks therefore and desires to be liberated, and does not cease to implore you to come to her aid. From you especially she asks succor, because, as we have already said, God has conferred upon you above all nations great glory in arms. Accordingly undertake this journey for the remission of your sins, with the assurance of the imperishable glory of the kingdom of heaven.

Source: *Original Sources of European History*, volume 1 (Philadelphia: Department of History, University of Pennsylvania, 1910), pp. 5–7.

Aerial view of the medieval citadel at Jerusalem

century, trade and educational ideas flowed between the Christians and Muslims with little disruption.

Seljuk Turks. However, all of that peaceful interaction was to cease in the 1050s with the rise of a powerful, united Muslim group, known as the Seljuk Turks, who came south into the Middle East from an area that is today Afghanistan. The Seljuk Turks did not hold the same tolerance for Christians that those who controlled the Holy Land, the Fatamid Egyptians, did. Their view became especially evident in 1064–1065 when they massacred a large group of German pilgrims in Syria. Yet, what may have been even more stunning to those European Christian powers, who for so long had counted on peaceful relations between themselves and the Muslims, was the defeat of a large Byzantine army by the Seljuk Turks at the battle of Manzikert in 1071, a defeat that forced the Byzantine Empire to surrender almost all of Asia Minor to Muslim control. In response to this grave setback the Byzantine emperor, Alexius I Comnenus, made an appeal to the Roman pope, Urban II, that he summon an army from the western political leaders to aid the Byzantines in regaining their lost territories.

Call to Arms. This papal summons was, it seems, not only a solution that might aid the Byzantines but also a solution to the problem that had plagued Europe for almost two centuries. By sending the soldiers of Europe to the Holy Land, the amount of intra-European violence and warfare would obviously diminish. On 26 November 1095, at the Council of Clermont, attended by many ecclesiastic and lay leaders, Urban II made an emotional plea for the First Crusade by painting a savage picture of supposed Muslim depredations.

Two Armies. Just how many Urban II expected would answer this call to arms is not known. Certainly, the Byzantine emperor did not expect the large turnout that formed the First Crusade, as he was completely unprepared for the onslaught of those willing to serve the church by "taking up the cross" (the Crusaders affixed a crucifix to their tunics and shields) and fighting against the Muslims in the Middle East. For no sooner had Urban II called for the Crusade before bishops and priests began preaching it throughout Europe. Itinerant preachers, such as Peter the Hermit and Walter the Penniless, who mostly served the poor, also began to take the message of the Crusade to their congregations. Soon two armies of European Christians were making their way overland toward the Byzantine Empire. One, which assembled on Urban II's declared day, Assumption 1096, included many knights of renown: Raymond, Count of Toulouse; Hugh of Vermandois, brother to Philip I, the French king; Robert, Count of Flanders; Stephen, Count of Blois and son-in-law of William the Conqueror; Robert, Duke of Normandy and son of Wil-

The Battle of Dorylaeum (1097) in Asia Minor at which Godfrey of Bouillon defeated the Seljuk Sultan Kilij Arslan; illumination from a late-eleventh-century manuscript (Bibliothèque Nationale, Paris)

liam the Conqueror; Godfrey of Bouillon, Duke of Lower Lorraine, and his brother, Baldwin; and Bohemond Guiscard, the son of Robert Guiscard, and his nephew, Tancred. Absent were any kings of Western Europe, but those who were sent in their place were certainly the finest military leaders the West could offer. However, the second army was not so well known or well led. It was filled with many unarmed peasants, including women and children who had also answered the call, expecting that their faith alone would defeat the enemies of God. Together the two groups may have numbered more than one hundred thousand. In charge of both armies, at least in name, was Adhemar, the bishop of Le Puy; he traveled with the soldiers.

Struck with Awe. By the beginning of 1097 these armies by separate routes had reached Constantinople. Their numbers struck Alexius I Comnenus with awe, especially those in the peasants' army, who arrived at the city first. This situation was not at all what he wanted or expected. He fed the peasants and ferried them across the Bosporus Strait, where they quickly met their end at the

hands of a Muslim force. Nor did Alexius expect the large numbers of Western soldiers when they arrived; it is thought that he was hoping at best for a couple thousand soldiers to serve as a division in his army, not an army itself. He gave the troops no warm welcome, nor would he allow them to proceed across the Bosporus until they had taken an oath of fealty to him and had promised that any lands that they regained from the Muslims would be returned to him. The Crusaders reluctantly agreed, although to most of them this oath and promise meant nothing.

Difficult March. The march across Asia Minor brought many difficulties. Although it began with a victory over the Turks outside the walls of Nicea, a city that was dutifully given back to the Byzantines, it soon became apparent that the Crusaders had made a gross misjudgment in the distance of the march and their ability to live off the land. There was almost perpetual famine and lack of water. Many of the more prominent nobles gave up and returned home. Yet, most kept on marching, and every time they encountered a Muslim force they defeated it, which brought them great confidence in their endeavor despite its hardships.

Antioch. Finally, early in 1098 they reached the first large Muslim city. Antioch was a powerfully built, entirely walled city with a large citadel that towered over the rest of the city. Although the Crusaders were weakened by starvation, they were a determined group, and, besides, their only means of escape was back across Asia Minor, a journey that no one wanted to make again. Ultimately, they were able to gain access to the city, but not the citadel, when they bribed one of the defenders of a city gate. Immediately, they began to engorge themselves on the fresh fruits and victuals that the city had to offer, which quickly led to dysentery throughout the army. In that condition they became besieged by a large Turkish relief army. The starvation that ensued because of this siege actually cleared up their dysentery. On 28 June 1098, after being inspired by one of their accompanying priests who claimed to have found the lance of Longinus (the lance that pierced Christ's side on the cross), the location of which he said he saw in a dream, and spurred on by further sightings of St. George and other military saints, they sallied out of the city and defeated a much larger, but extremely surprised, Muslim force.

Jerusalem. The Crusaders were helped at Antioch and elsewhere on this first Crusade by the fact that the Seljuk Turks and Fatamid Egyptians had been fighting their own war for a few years prior to the Europeans' appearance in the Holy Land. The Seljuks had captured Jerusalem in 1070, but early in 1099, when the Crusaders were marching from Antioch toward the holy city, the Fatamids had regained it. Thus when the Crusaders, now possibly numbering no more than 10,000 to 20,000, reached their primary target, Jerusalem was a weakened shell of its earlier military strength. Nevertheless, Jerusalem still held out until 15 July 1099 when a major assault of the walls using siege towers and catapults finally allowed the Westerners to capture it. In response to their hard task, and impelled by rumors of great treasures hidden by the city's residents, the Crusaders butchered all of the inhabitants and searched their entrails for precious stones they may have swallowed.

Sources:

John France, *Victory in the East: A Military History of the First Crusade* (Cambridge & New York: Cambridge University Press, 1994).

Hans Eberhard Mayer, *The Crusades,* translated by John Gillingham (London: Oxford University Press, 1972).

Jean Richard, *The Crusades, c.1071–c.1291,* translated by Jean Birrell (Cambridge & New York: Cambridge University Press, 1999).

Jonathan Riley-Smith, *The Crusades: A Short History* (New Haven: Yale University Press, 1987).

SECOND CRUSADE (1144-1187)

Crusader States. After the fall of Jerusalem in 1099 the Crusaders began their control over the various lands and cities that they had captured. Refusing to give these territorial gains either to the Byzantine emperor or to make them papal fiefs as desired by Pope Urban II, the Crusaders set up their own kingdoms: Bohemond Guiscard took Antioch and the area around it; Baldwin of Bouillon captured

Edessa to the northeast; Raymond of St. Gilles established a kingdom in Tripoli (although its seat of power was elsewhere until Tripoli fell in 1109); and Godfrey of Bouillon, who had become the leader of the Crusaders after many other nobles had returned to Europe, became the king of Jerusalem. Yet, most of the Crusaders wanted to return home. They had been traveling under the harshest conditions for more than three years, and most had little desire to remain in the Holy Land with these newly self-appointed lords. As a result, the Crusaders who remained behind faced severe hardships. By the turn of the twelfth century, the Kingdom of Jerusalem was left with only three hundred soldiers to defend it, and other kingdoms had even smaller contingents.

New Conquests. Initially, this development created few problems for the resident Crusaders, especially as they periodically received reinforcements from Europe, younger warriors who wanted to make their names and fortunes in the Holy Land. In addition, neither the Seljuk Turks nor the Fatamid Egyptians were in any state to try and regain their lost lands. At least through the early years of the twelfth century the lack of enemy resistance led to further conquests by the Crusaders. Caesarea fell to them in 1101, Tartous in 1102, Acre and Jubail in 1104, Tripoli in 1109, Beirut and Sidon in 1110, and Tyre in 1124. Furthermore, the resident Crusaders undertook to build large fortifications, stone castles the likes of which had never been seen in Europe, large enough to sustain a garrison for five years in some cases, or, it was hoped, at least as long as it would take to receive relief from Europe. Finally, to make up for the loss of military manpower, three military monastic orders were established in the Holy Land: the Knights Hospitalers, Knights Templars, and Teutonic Knights. These "monks of war" proved at least to be stable fighting elements that could be counted on to vigorously defend all of the conquests that the first Crusaders had made in the Holy Land.

Maintaining the Peace. Yet, even with the addition of the strong fortifications and the monastic military orders, the only clear means of preserving the Crusader Kingdoms was to make peace with neighboring Muslims as well as employing non–Christians to keep internal dissatisfactions from developing into rebellions, to govern the native populations, and to collect taxes. Invariably, such relationships brought criticisms from anyone newly arriving from Europe to serve in the Holy Land, especially as the rhetoric in Europe was so anti–Muslim. Nonetheless, they also soon saw the necessity for it.

New Threat. In 1144 the city and kingdom of Edessa fell to a new Seljuk Turkish army. Edessa was not a well-protected Crusader State, being quite a distance from the other kingdoms and with no natural defenses guarding it. Also, a recent inheritance crisis over the kingship there had left the Crusaders divided and easy targets for reconquest, especially as the army that did the reconquesting was led by a young general named Nār-ad-Din. Although Nār-ad-Din would direct his army around the remaining Crusader

Kingdoms toward Egypt, the Crusaders had no means of knowing that this was his plan, and they immediately put out a call for a second Crusade to travel to the Holy Land.

St. Bernard of Clairvaux. The Second Crusade was spurred on by preachers such as St. Bernard of Clairvaux, whose call to arms is exemplified in this passage from one of his sermons:

> The earth trembles and is shaken because the King of Heaven has lost his land, the land where he once walked. . . . The great eye of Providence observes these acts in silence; it wishes to see if anyone who seeks God, who suffers with him in sorrow, will render him his heritage. . . . I tell you, the Lord is testing you.

Quarrelsome Leaders. Among the Crusaders to "take the cross" this time were two kings, Conrad III of Germany and Louis VII of France. However, unlike their first crusading counterparts, these leaders had absolutely no success at all. First, they quarreled with the resident Crusaders whose dealings with the Muslims they felt were treasonous; in turn, the resident Crusaders resented these new arrivals, no matter what their rank or status, for interfering with their own military leadership. The plan of the resident Crusaders was simple: they wished to take this second Crusade army north to Aleppo, a city controlled by one of Nār-ad-Din's lieutenants. However, the Second Crusaders saw a closer target, Damascus, a city controlled by the Muslims, although allies to the Crusaders and enemies of Nār-ad-Din. Despite this fact being made clear, on 24 June 1148 the Second Crusaders decided to advance on the allied Damascus. Their attack failed, largely because of the bickering of the two kings. Met with this defeat, Conrad III immediately set out for home. Louis VII lingered a bit longer, but in the summer of 1149 he, too, returned to Europe without attempting further military action.

Saladin. With the Second Crusade a defeat for the Christians, Nār-ad-Din began to extend his power in the region. Damascus, weakened by the Crusaders' attack, fell in 1154, and Egypt fell in 1168. Nār-ad-Din died in 1174, but he was succeeded by an even greater general, his nephew Saladin. Fervent in jihad zeal, while at the same time patient and chivalrous, Saladin inherited control of all of the territory surrounding the Crusader States. His next moves seem to have been clear, and the resident Crusaders quickly sued for peace with the Turkish leader. As the strongest military figure they had ever faced, the Crusaders clearly needed time to regroup and build their defenses before Saladin's threat to them became realized. Perhaps, too, they could gain more reinforcements from Europe.

Fall of Jerusalem. Instead of cooperating, the Crusaders began to bicker over their defense plans. What the regent over the kingdom of Jerusalem, Count Raymond III of Tripoli, wanted the Master of the Templars, Gerard of Ridfort, did not, and vice versa. Peace broke down finally in 1185 when the child king of Jerusalem, Baldwin the Leper, died. Because there were no heirs, an election was held to replace the king. Raymond of Tripoli, who had served as regent for the king since 1174, felt that he

deserved this most important kingship, but the other barons chose Guy of Lusignan instead. Raymond immediately made a separate alliance with Saladin against the other Crusaders, the first result of which was the annihilation of 130 Templars in an accidental battle against a large part of Saladin's army. Saladin then laid siege to the Crusader city of Tiberias. The Crusaders tried to relieve the city, but were surrounded by Saladin's force at the Horns of Hattin on 4 July 1187, where they were defeated. Following this victory, Saladin moved against the now largely undefended city of Jerusalem, which he conquered on 2 October 1187. Remembering the outrageous massacre of all the town's inhabitants by the First Crusaders nearly a century before, Saladin allowed all Christians there to be ransomed to safety.

Sources:

Hans Eberhard Mayer, *The Crusades,* translated by John Gillingham (London: Oxford University Press, 1972).

Jean Richard, *The Crusades, c.1071–c.1291,* translated by Jean Birrell (Cambridge & New York: Cambridge University Press, 1999).

Jonathan Riley-Smith, *The Crusades: A Short History* (New Haven: Yale University Press, 1987).

Riley-Smith, ed., *The Oxford Illustrated History of the Crusades* (Oxford & New York: Oxford University Press, 1995).

Steven Runciman, *A History of the Crusades,* three volumes (Cambridge: Cambridge University Press, 1951–1954).

R. C. Smail, *Crusading Warfare, 1097–1193* (Cambridge: Cambridge University Press, 1956).

THIRD CRUSADE (1189-1192)

Three Kings. The loss of Jerusalem to Saladin in 1187 came as quite a shock to all Christians in Europe. Immediately, a new Crusade was called. The Third Crusade attracted not only a large army, but also three kings: Frederick I (Frederick Barbarossa) of Germany, Philip II (Philip Augustus) of France, and Richard I (the Lionhearted) of England. Frederick left in 1189 via an overland route, but his force, decimated by disease, never reached the Holy Land. (The aged Frederick himself died when he fell off his horse into the Salaph River in Asia Minor and drowned.) The other two kings traveled by ship and arrived safely, but, once having arrived, they began to quarrel over their respective roles in the fighting.

Lack of Unity. Although they did succeed in retaking Acre and Jaffa in 1191, moving within sight of Jerusalem, Richard I and Philip II could never achieve the unified attack that was necessary to recapture that city. Finally, in October 1191, Philip II returned to France and began attacking Richard I's territory there. A year later, in October 1192, Richard I also returned to Europe, but on his route home he was captured, imprisoned, and held for ransom by Leopold, the duke of Austria, whose banners he had insulted at the siege of Acre. The Third Crusade failed to accomplish almost everything it set out to do, although it included the best and brightest that the warrior class of Europe could provide.

Tenuous Hold. The failure of the Third Crusade sounded the death knell for the remaining Crusader States.

Frederick Barbarossa and his sons en route to the Holy Land; illumination from a German manuscript, circa 1185 (Burgerbibliotek, Bern)

The resident Crusaders there still held onto these kingdoms, but their hold was tenuous at best. The arguments between Philip II and Richard I had caused quite a scandal in Europe, where the populace had become quite cynical of further crusading efforts. Although the rhetoric continued, in reality the Crusades were dead. Trade with the Muslims resumed, and those who were able to take advantage of that trade, most notably the Genoese and Pisans, profited greatly from it. The papacy, too, had lost face. Unable to deliver a victory in more than one hundred years, in 1197 papal control over the Crusades even became threatened by the Holy Roman Emperor, Henry VI, who prepared to lead an army to the Holy Land on his own without permission of the pope, Celestine III, and to declare all that he gained there as his own kingdom. However, he died suddenly before he was able to undertake the journey.

Sources:

Hans Eberhard Mayer, *The Crusades,* translated by John Gillingham (London: Oxford University Press, 1972).

Jean Richard, *The Crusades, c.1071–c.1291,* translated by Jean Birrell (Cambridge & New York: Cambridge University Press, 1999).

Jonathan Riley-Smith, *The Crusades: A Short History* (New Haven: Yale University Press, 1987).

Riley-Smith, ed., *The Oxford Illustrated History of the Crusades* (Oxford & New York: Oxford University Press, 1995).

Steven Runciman, *A History of the Crusades,* three volumes (Cambridge: Cambridge University Press, 1951–1954).

R. C. Smail, *Crusading Warfare, 1097–1193* (Cambridge: Cambridge University Press, 1956).

FOURTH CRUSADE (1198–1202)

Doomed from the Start. A new, stronger pope, Innocent III, was elected at the death of Celestine in 1198, and he immediately called for the Fourth Crusade. This effort seemed doomed from the start. Although again a large army assembled, it never seemed to matter what their goals were, for they were destined not even to reach the Holy Land. Trying to arrange passage by sea from the Venetians, they were first compelled by them to attack a Hungarian city, Zara, which despite being Christian, threatened the Adriatic trading monopolies of Venice. Then they proceeded to Constantinople, where in 1202 they were forced to besiege that Byzantine city because it had recently signed a trading pact with the Genoese, rivals to the Venetians. Under the guise of asking for money and supplies to proceed to the Holy Land, the Crusaders became impatient with the city's inhabitants and took the city by storm. The Latin Kingdom of Constantinople, which they established there, lasted until 1261, when an attack from the exiled Byzantine emperor, Michael VIII Palaeologus, acting in concert with the Genoese, restored its capital city to the rest of the Byzantine Empire.

Sources:

Donald E. Queller, *The Fourth Crusade: The Conquest of Constantinople, 1201–1204* (Philadelphia: University of Pennsylvania Press, 1977).

Jean Richard, *The Crusades, c.1071–c.1291,* translated by Jean Birrell (Cambridge & New York: Cambridge University Press, 1999).

Jonathan Riley-Smith, *The Crusades: A Short History* (New Haven: Yale University Press, 1987).

Riley-Smith, ed., *The Oxford Illustrated History of the Crusades* (Oxford & New York: Oxford University Press, 1995).

Steven Runciman, *A History of the Crusades,* three volumes (Cambridge: Cambridge University Press, 1951–1954).

LATER CRUSADES

Children's Crusade. With the embarrassment of the Fourth Crusade (1198–1202), all remaining crusading fervor seems to have left European warriors. There were a few thirteenth-century crusades, but these were also almost always embarrassments, such as in the case of the Children's Crusade of 1212 when a large number of adolescents thought that they could simply defeat the Muslims with their childlike faith. (It was wisely stopped by the Pope and its leaders were put to death, although some of the children did make it to Egypt, where they were sold into slavery.) That is not to state, however, that those who strived to participate in the Holy Land during that century were not earnest in their endeavors, such as the crusaders who went with Andrew II, the king of Hungary, and Leopold VI, the duke of Austria, in 1217–1219, or with Emperor Frederick II in 1227 or 1228, or with Louis IX in 1248–1250 and 1254, but these Crusades were almost always poorly planned and even more poorly executed. There were some victories, such as the capture of the Egyptian city of Dami-

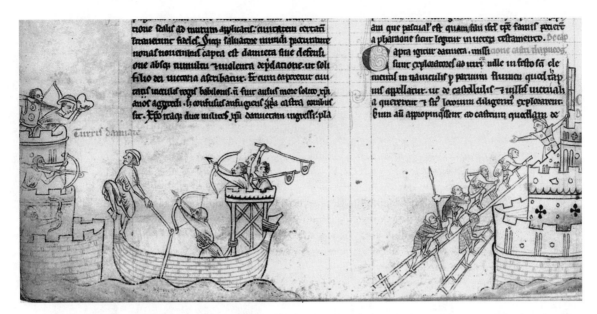

The siege of Damietta, Egypt, between May 1218 and November 1219; illumination from a thirteenth-century manuscript
(Corpus Christi College, Cambridge)

etta by Leopold VI in 1219 and its recapture by Louis IX in 1248 (in between those two conquests, it had been retaken by the Egyptians in 1221) or the recapture of Jerusalem by Frederick II in 1228 (it was lost again in 1244), but even those could not outweigh the large number of defeats that these Crusaders suffered. Indeed, on one occasion, in 1250, King Louis IX and his entire army were taken prisoner by the Egyptians, necessitating the payment of a huge ransom for their freedom.

Demise of the Crusader States. Not even the onslaught of the Mongols against the Muslims in the Holy Land in the middle of the century allowed the Christians to take advantage of the situation. (The Mongols conquered all of Turkey, Persia, and Syria, destroying Aleppo, Damascus, and Baghdad, but withdrew from the Holy Land because of Ghengis Khan's death in 1227 before encountering any of the Crusader holdings there.) By the end of the thirteenth century the remaining Crusader Kingdoms began to fall: in 1265 Caesarea, Haifa, and Arsuf were taken; in 1268 Antioch fell; in 1289 Tripoli was captured; and, finally, in 1291 the last vestige of the Crusader Kingdoms disappeared when Acre fell to the Egyptians.

Albigensian and Northern Crusades. During the thirteenth century a shift occurred in priorities when Crusades began to be called not to the Holy Land but to places in Europe. Two of these are the most famous, the first a successful Crusade against the Albigensians, a heretical Christian sect living in southern France, which took place between 1209 and 1229, and the second against the people of Prussia and Livonia, the inhabitants of which had never accepted Christianity. To fight this latter Crusade, the Teutonic Knights shifted their emphasis from the Holy Land to northeastern Europe. Begun in 1226, this Northern Crusade never really ended before the Reformation and early sixteenth-century Ger-

man nationalism reduced the political role of that monastic military order to almost nothing.

Royal Duty. There would be continual calls for Crusades into the Holy Lands well into the early modern era. It almost became the duty of every late medieval king to agree to participate in one, only to readily and quickly break the promise. Moreover, by the middle of the fourteenth century a new and far more violent Islamic foe would appear in the Middle East: the Ottoman Turks. Their presence in the eastern Mediterranean quickly altered the balance of power there and throughout southeastern Europe. Even before the fourteenth century was over they had occupied not only the Holy Land and Asia Minor but had also soundly defeated a large Anglo-Franco-Burgundian-Hungarian force at the battle of Nicopolis in 1396.

Sources:
Eric Christiansen, *The Northern Crusades* (London & New York: Penguin, 1997).

Norman Housley, *The Later Crusades, 1274–1580: From Lyons to Alcazar* (New York: Oxford University Press, 1992).

Jonathan Riley-Smith, *The Crusades: A Short History* (New Haven: Yale University Press, 1987).

Riley-Smith, ed., *The Oxford Illustrated History of the Crusades* (Oxford & New York: Oxford University Press, 1995).

Steven Runciman, *A History of the Crusades*, three volumes (Cambridge: Cambridge University Press, 1951–1954).

Jonathan Sumption, *The Albigensian Crusade* (London & Boston: Faber & Faber, 1978).

HIGH MIDDLE AGES: POLITICAL DEVELOPMENTS

Selection of Kings. Much of the security and many of the problems faced by the largest and most populous kingdoms of the post–Carolingian Middle Ages can be traced to the ways they chose their kings and how they viewed those monarchs once they had been selected. In the case of Germany and France, the new era began when the last

Carolingian king was replaced by a non–Carolingian ruler; for England it started with the succession to the monarchy after the death of William the Conqueror. (Scandinavian, Spanish, and eastern European kingdoms are not be considered here both because of their size and their frequent lack of stability.)

Election Method. Arnulf, the king of the East Franks and victor over the Vikings at the battle of the Dyle in 891, was succeeded by his young son, appropriately named Ludwig III the Child, who died without an heir in 911. With his death the eastern branch of the Carolingian dynasty perished. The East Frankish nobles thus became the first to have to choose a non-Carolingian king, and they did so by the election method. In other words, when a king died, his successor would not necessarily be his son. Instead, the more powerful nobles of the realm, serving as electors, would meet and decide, generally among themselves, who would succeed the deceased king. From a twenty-first-century viewpoint this system might seem more democratic and therefore present more of a consensus and fewer disagreements, and the first election certainly seemed to verify this view, as Conrad I, the duke of Franconia, was easily elected and reigned from 911 to 918. (Franconia was Germany's second most powerful duchy, but as Henry, the duke of the most powerful duchy, Saxony, was quite old and expected to die soon, the electors passed him by.) However, such a system was fraught with potential and eventual problems. For one thing, if there were two (or more) strong candidates who vied for the kingship that obviously only one of them could hold, the loser and his supporters generally became bitter and dissatisfied with the selection, sometimes even waging civil war against the new king. This rivalry was exemplified in the election of 1125 when, after the death of King Henry V, the electors in Germany chose the duke of Saxony, Lothar of Supplinburg, over the nearest relative to childless Henry, Frederick the One-Eyed, Duke of Swabia. Immediately, a struggle between the two, Lothar, of the Guelf house, and Frederick, of the Ghibelline house, ensued. Eventually, this struggle would develop into a civil war that would spread throughout Germany and Italy and last until the beginning of the fourteenth century.

Frederick Barbarossa. A second disputed election occurred in 1152 when Frederick Barbarossa, the duke of Swabia, won the throne over Henry the Lion, Duke of Saxony. For most of his reign Frederick was forced to fight for control of the kingdom against Henry and his supporters, a fight that even took him by various expeditions into Italy, against the many city-states that did not support his kingship. Ultimately, it made him one of the strongest kings of medieval Germany; it was, however, a reputation that was gained only on the blood of large numbers of Germans and Italians.

Voice of the Pope. Another problem that came with the election system of naming a new king was that these German rulers were to be, by tradition, the descendants of Charlemagne's title, Holy Roman Emperor. Yet, this came about only if the pope at the time of his election deemed

Holy Crown of Hungary (1074–1077), a gift to King Geza I from Emperor Michael VII Ducas (Magyar Nemzeti Muzeum, Budapest)

that king worthy of being named as Holy Roman Emperor. Thus, the voice of the pope also played a role in the election of a new emperor, although to be historically accurate only rarely did the will of the papacy matter to the German electors. What resulted, however, was several German kings who were not named as Holy Roman Emperor. Moreover, when there was a politically aggressive pope on the throne, he would sometimes go to great lengths, even to excommunication, to try and remove a German king from the throne whom he particularly disliked. Thus, Pope Gregory VII not only excommunicated King Henry IV twice but also tried to provoke a rebellion against him among the other German nobles. (Henry's response was to march to Rome, imprison the pope, and name an "anti-pope," Clement III, in his stead, Clement then naming the king as Holy Roman Emperor.) While Pope Innocent III, who had supported a candidate he named as emperor, Otto IV, excommunicated the elected king Frederick II no fewer than three times, once for simply planning a Crusade without the pope's permission. (Frederick's response was to simply ignore the pontiff, who after all had limited political and military powers.) So, while on the surface the electoral system seemed more democratic and reliable, it must be blamed for the political chaos and civil war that was evident throughout much of the history of the

HOLY ROMAN EMPIRE

The *Heiliges Römisches Reich* or *Sacrum Romanum Imperium* (Holy Roman Empire) was a political entity created by the papacy. Ruled first by the Frankish kings and then by the German kings, it existed for ten centuries and included what is now Germany, Austria, the Czech Republic, Switzerland, eastern France, the Low Countries, and northern and central Italy. Pope Leo III first conferred the title of *king of the Romans* on Charlemagne in 800. (The term *Holy Roman Emperor* was actually never used; it is a convention adopted by modern historians.)

Originally an instrument of the papacy, the Holy Roman Empire developed into a rival. Between the mid eleventh century and mid thirteenth century the empire and the papacy vied for control of Christian Europe. By the early 1400s the imperial title became virtually hereditary in the Austrian house of Habsburg. Following the Thirty Years' War (1618–1648), the empire devolved into a loose collection of semi-autonomous states, causing the French philosopher Voltaire to observe that it was "neither holy, nor Roman, nor an empire." Napoleon Bonaparte officially dissolved the empire in 1806.

Source: Giorgio Falco, *The Holy Roman Empire: A Historic Profile of the Middle Ages*, translated by K. V. Kent (London: Allen & Unwin, 1964).

German kingdom (including Italy) from the twelfth century until the end of the Middle Ages.

Hugh Capet. The French, who named their first non–Carolingian king later than the Germans, would not repeat their neighbors' problems. Instead, at the death of their last Carolingian king, Louis V, in 987, the power to select a new king was held completely by the duke of the Franks (whose power base lay in the lands around Paris), Hugh the Great, and his son, Hugh Capet. At the death of the childless Louis, Hugh Capet immediately and without opposition named himself king. In addition, he brought into this enterprise the archbishop of Reims, the most revered ecclesiastical leader in France, who signed on to this exchange of power when he crowned Hugh as king by declaring that he was receiving the crown "by divine right." God had determined that he was to be king. This declaration, while seemingly only a disposable addition to the naming of this new king, set a precedent in France that was tied to the kingships of no other European kings: God wanted Hugh Capet and his successors to be kings, and, therefore, anyone opposing them would be opposing God. Cynically, one would think that such a belief would not have affected any baronial opposition to the French king, and yet, despite the presence of often far more powerful lords than the kings they served under, such as the dukes of Normandy, the counts of Aquitaine, and the counts of Flanders, few rebel-lions against the Capetian dynasty are recorded during their uninterrupted rule from 987 to 1328.

Henry I. If the French succession system proved to increase the power and security of its kings and the German system proved to weaken and endanger its kings, the English system might be said to have fallen in between. William the Conqueror's victory at the Battle of Hastings (1066) gave him a military legitimacy over the English kingdom, which he quickly parlayed into an absolute kingship. Lords in England were set up by him from those who had distinguished themselves in the conquest. They were his companions, faithful to him as their leader and devoted to him for their titles and land. However, when William died in 1087, there became some confusion over which one of his three sons should rule over England and Normandy. Before he died, William had named his eldest son, Robert, as duke of Normandy and his second son, William Rufus, as king of England. Why did he split his holdings? And why had he given the duchy of Normandy to his eldest son, but the kingdom of England, certainly more independent from the French crown, if not more important overall, to his middle son? Was it possible that he saw in William Rufus a stronger leader? Actually, the latter point became moot when within a few years it proved that the strongest of all three of William's sons was neither of those who inherited their father's territories at his death but the youngest son, Henry. First, Henry took over the English throne when William Rufus was killed in a hunting accident, and then he rose against Robert, defeated him at the Battle of Tinchebrai in 1109, and took over the duchy of Normandy as well. Later, he also proved his military abilities and claim to his father's territories by defeating his nephew, Robert's son, William of Clito, at the battle of Bremûle, despite the presence of the French king, Louis VI, in support of William of Clito. He also put down an uprising among his English nobles at the battle of Northallerton in 1138 (also known as the Battle of the Standard).

Strife among the Successors. The concept of "divine right" to rule might have saved Henry I in the latter conflict, as it had so often kept the French king from baronial uprisings, but such had never been declared in England. Nor would it be declared, and this situation meant that almost every king who sat on the throne there had to contend with noble uprisings and civil war. The most egregious of these would come at the death of Henry I when a dispute arose over who would succeed him as king. Henry's named heir, his nephew Stephen, was quickly opposed by Henry's daughter, Mathilda, who had her own English supporters. What resulted was a devastating civil war that lasted from 1139 to 1153. A second example of this type of baronial chaos occurred during the reign of King John, when in 1215 the lords of England forced their monarch to sign the Magna Carta, which gave them certain powers over the king, a move provoked by John's loss of most of the English lands in France. A third example of baronial infighting can be seen during the reign of John's son, Henry III, for despite weathering an earnest

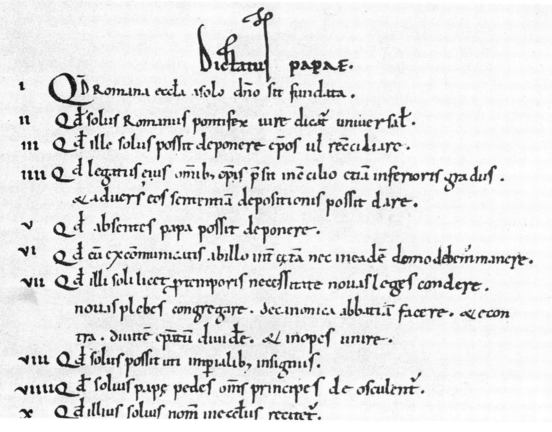

Beginning of *Dictatus Papae* (1075), a compilation of twenty-seven dictations written by Pope Gregory VII setting out the authority of the pope over secular states (Archivio Segreto, Vatican)

effort to unseat him by one of his barons, Simon de Montfort, he was constantly forced to sign away more of his powers to the nobles in amended versions of the Magna Carta; eventually, this included the establishment of the first English Parliament. Put simply, without the "divine right" to rule provision of the French crown, the English kings were forced to prove their military leadership. Should they be strong military leaders, such as Henry I, Henry II, and Edward I, they had peace at home and conquest abroad; should they be weak military leaders, like Stephen, John, Henry III, or Edward II, they suffered internal uprisings and, generally, also suffered military losses to foreign powers.

Dual Kingdoms. Because of the protection of the English Channel, when these losses to foreign powers came, they came largely at the expense of English holdings in France. A curious thing occurred when William the Conqueror became king of England. This development meant that the king of England was also, as duke of Normandy, obligated to do homage to the king of France. Perhaps this is the reason why William separated the two holdings between his eldest sons at his death. However, because of Henry I's dissatisfaction with this inheritance, the two lands once again became joined only a short time after the death of William. Furthermore, with the succession of Henry II to the English throne after the death of Stephen (the irony of this situation was that Henry II was Mathilda's son, Stephen's foe throughout almost his entire

reign), the county of Anjou in France was also added to the English royal holdings, and with Henry II's marriage to Eleanor of Aquitaine, so too was her inheritance, the duchies of Aquitaine and Gascony and the counties of Ponthieu and Poitou. As a result, when their son, Richard I (the Lionhearted), succeeded to the kingship of England, he held much more land in France than all of the other nobles combined, and certainly more than the king of France, Philip II (Philip Augustus). Of course, this situation led to the difficulties between those two kings on the Third Crusade (1189–1192) and to Philip's attacks of these lands after he had returned from the Holy Land. Richard I, in returning from the Crusades and from his imprisonment by the duke of Austria, spent the rest of his life trying to defend those same French holdings; he would die after being shot by a crossbow during one of these wars. Ultimately, Philip II would defeat the armies of the Holy Roman Empire, England, and thier allies at the Battle of Bouvines in 1214. Philip II's impressive victory there led to the confiscation of all of the other English lands in France except for Gascony. Yet, this was not to be the last English-French war, as the Hundred Years' War (1337–1453) would prove.

Basis of Power. All of these royal selection systems produced powerful nobles. Because the early medieval tradition and policy of military obligation, once called by the generic title "feudalism," had not changed with the selection of post–Carolingian kings, and in fact had been imported by William the Conqueror into England with his conquest, there was always a large political level of nobility that wielded power in their kingdoms. Furthermore, as can be seen, for example, in the problems that occurred between the English and French kingdoms; sometimes these nobles exceeded the wealth and power of the king himself. What must be recognized is that these nobles, too, based their power on their own military strength. To improve this strength these nobles practiced their military skills in tournaments and other displays, and to show their worth above those of the lower classes they practiced chivalry and built large stone castles.

Internal Threat. As no king anywhere in Europe before the fourteenth century possessed a "national" standing army, they were reliant upon the noble retinues to provide them with armies. This dependence produced two problems: first, it meant that any time a king wished to carry out a military expedition, either against an internal or a foreign foe, he was forced to rely on his nobles, some of whom simply did not reply to his requests; second, it also meant that any potentially rebellious noble had at least the kernel of an army that he could lead against the king in his own retinue. For any European king to begin to form a state in the early modern or modern ideal, he had first to remove this kind of power from his nobles. This development would not come until the last century of the Middle Ages.

Sources:
Christopher Brooke, *Europe in the Central Middle Ages, 962–1154,* third edition (Harlow, U.K. & New York: Longman, 2000).

R. H. C. Davis, *A History of Medieval Europe: From Constantine to Saint Louis* (London & New York: Longmans, Green, 1957).

John H. Mundy, *Europe in the High Middle Ages, 1150–1300,* third edition (Harlow, U.K. & New York: Longman, 2000).

Brian Tierney and Sidney Painter, *Western Europe in the Middle Ages, 300–1475,* sixth edition (Boston: McGraw-Hill, 1998).

HUNDRED YEARS' WAR

Continual Warfare. During the last two centuries of the Middle Ages, there was almost continual warfare throughout all of Europe. The most famous, and longest, of these conflicts exemplifies all of the various wars of the late medieval period. Known erroneously as the Hundred Years' War (1337–1453), it began over disputed Continental lands.

England versus France. English king Edward III launched his attack on the French, seemingly in an attempt to recover his crown as king of France. In his view the crown had been "stolen" from him in 1328 when, despite being the closest heir to the dead king, Charles IV, he was declared ineligible because his royal descent was gained through a woman. The throne instead was given to a cousin, Philip of Valois, who was crowned as King Philip VI of France.

French Military Might. At the time Edward's move was thought to be foolhardy; France had a strong and renowned military. During the thirteenth century, under able warrior kings such as Philip II (Philip Augustus) and Philip IV the Fair, it had won many wars, strengthening the borders against the Spanish kingdoms, Italy, and the Holy Roman Empire, while at the same time restoring almost all of the English lands in France. Rebellious lords and heretical sects had also felt the strength of France's military might, ending up in prisons or, more often, in death. Indeed, Philip IV felt so confident in his military might that in 1307 he even challenged the Knights Templars, the largest military monastic order, declaring this crusading relic to be heretical and confiscating its treasures and lands. There were some defeats, it is true, most notably by King Louis IX on crusade in Egypt and North Africa and by noble-led French armies against the Flemings at the battles of Courtrai in 1302 and Arques in 1303, but these were quickly forgotten and whatever setbacks had resulted were quickly reclaimed.

Sluys. The first major engagement of the Hundred Years' War was fought aboard ships in the harbor at Sluys on 24 June 1340. By the end of the day, Edward III's navy, ably assisted by their allies, Flemings from Sluys and nearby Bruges who watched the fight from the shore and kept any French sailors from escaping to land, had won the battle. In doing so, they had almost completely annihilated the French navy. Edward III followed this victory with a siege of Tournai, the largest northern town that had declared its allegiance for the French king. Yet, it was there that he momentarily lost his momentum. Despite destroying many French–allied lands and villages near Tournai, and though it seemed that the town was on the verge of surrendering, Edward III lost his alliance through bickering and saw his own parliament hold up needed funds for him to carry on the war. He was forced to retreat to England and sign the truce of Espléchin with the French.

Crécy. What appeared to be a victory for the French quickly proved, however, to be nothing more than a short recess before even greater defeats. Edward III used the time to remove those elements in his representative government that opposed war with France, and then he planned his return. According to the truce of Espléchin, Edward III could not "legally" wage war against France for five years. However, before that time elapsed, a civil war broke out in Brittany between two heirs to the vacant ducal throne. Edward III used this excuse to reenter conflict with France, supporting one candidate in his claim, with France supporting the rival candidate. Four years later, in 1346, after the truce of Espléchin had expired, Edward III wasted little time in attacking the French kingdom. Landing in Normandy with a large army, probably as many as fifteen thousand troops, Edward III marched toward the Low Countries. However, he surprisingly stopped at Crécy, in the county of Ponthieu. The French army, still under the leadership of Philip VI, who was following the English decided this time to give him a battle, and, on 26 August 1346, the first great land battle of the Hundred Years' War was fought. Establishing a repeated pattern throughout the next century, the French soldiers greatly outnumbered their opponents but lost. Philip VI was able to escape the carnage, departing to Paris under the cover of darkness, but

The French historian Jean Froissart's account of the great English victory at Crécy (1346) is both colorful and stirring. Although Froissart felt that a historian had a duty to recite the valorous deeds of knightly heroes, he nevertheless carefully based his writings on information obtained from firsthand experience or from interviews with participants.

There is no man, unless he had been present, that can imagine or describe truly the confusion of that day, especially the bad management and disorder of the French, whose troops were out of number. . . . The English, who . . . were drawn up in three divisions, and seated on the ground, on seeing their enemies advance, rose up undauntedly and fell into their ranks. . . .

You must know that the French troops did not advance in any regular order, and that as soon as their king came in sight of the English his blood began to boil, and he cried out to his marshals, "Order the Genoese forward and begin the battle in the name of God and St. Denis." There were about 15,000 Genoese crossbow men; but they were quite fatigued, having marched on foot that day six leagues, completely armed and carrying their crossbows, and accordingly they told the constable they were not in a condition to do any great thing in battle. The earl of Alençon hearing this, said, "This is what one gets by employing such scoundrels, who fall off when there is any need for them." During this time a heavy rain fell, accompanied by thunder and a very terrible eclipse of the sun; and, before this rain, a great flight of crows hovered in the air over all the battalions, making a loud noise; shortly afterward it cleared up, and the sun shone very bright; but the French had it in their faces, and the English on their backs. When the Genoese were somewhat in order they approached the English and set up a loud shout, in order to frighten them; but the

English remained quite quiet and did not seem to attend to it. They then set up a second shout, and advanced a little forward; the English never moved. Still they hooted a third time, advancing with their crossbows presented, and began to shoot. The English archers then advanced one step forward, and shot their arrows with such force and quickness that it seemed as if it snowed. When the Genoese felt these arrows, which pierced through their armor, some of them cut the strings of their crossbows, others flung them to the ground, and all turned about and retreated quite discomfited.

The French had a large body of men-at-arms on horseback to support the Genoese, and the king, seeing them thus fall back, cried out, "Kill me those scoundrels, for they stop up our road without any reason." The English continued shooting, and some of their arrows falling among the horsemen, drove them upon the Genoese, so that they were in such confusion they could never rally again.

In the English army there were some Cornish and Welsh men on foot, who had armed themselves with large knives; these advancing through the ranks of the men-at-arms and archers, who made way for them, came upon the French when they were in this danger, and falling upon earls, barons, knights, and squires, slew many, at which the king of England was exasperated. . . .

This battle . . . was murderous and cruel; and many gallant deeds of arms were performed that were never known; toward evening, many knights and squires of the French had lost their masters, and, wandering up and down the plain, attacked the English in small parties; but they were soon destroyed, for the English had determined that day to give no quarter, nor hear of ransom from anyone. . . .

Source: John Froissart, *Chronicles of England, France, Spain and the Adjoining Countries*, volume 1, translated by Thomas Johnes (New York: Colonial Press, 1901), pp. 36–45.

many of his lords and captains were killed. Edward moved victoriously to the town of Calais, and after a yearlong siege, again with the French king camping idly by, the townspeople could no longer withstand their forced hunger and the town fell. The English would use Calais as their Continental "beachhead" for the next two centuries.

Black Death. The Black Death, as it became known to contemporaries, began to spread throughout Europe in 1347 and effectively halted the military progress of Edward III and the English. The effects this plague had on the fighting of the Hundred Years' War, on the manpower, leadership, finances, or strategy and tactics, were major. Not only was there a cessation of hostilities for nearly a decade, but when they did begin anew, in 1355–1356, the sizes of armies could be seen to have dramatically decreased. There was also a new tactic of warfare that the English began to adopt and that for the

rest of the war they would practice with regularity and proficiency: the *chevauchée*, a quick cavalry raid through the countryside with the intention of pillaging unfortified villages and towns, destroying crops and houses, stealing livestock, and generally disrupting and terrorizing rural society.

Poitiers. On one of these *chevauchées* in 1356, Edward's son, Edward the Black Prince, was raiding through the north-central regions of France. Outside of the town of Poitiers he encountered the new king of France, John II the Good (Philip VI had died in 1350). Another French defeat ensued, but this time the king was unable to flee from the battlefield; instead, John II was captured and imprisoned in the Tower of London. The French were forced to the negotiation table, and the Treaty of Brétigny was signed in 1360. The French promised the English a ransom of 3,000,000 golden crowns for John's return and the surrendering of the duchies of Aquitaine and Ponthieu and the town of Calais. Edward III, in turn, promised to renounce his claim to the French throne.

Charles V. The imprisonment of King John II in London may have been the best thing that could have happened to the French. John II's ransom was long in coming to London—indeed, it was never completely raised—and he lingered in his English jail. In the meantime, John's son and heir, the later Charles V, was forced to defend his kingdom's shrinking borders, not only against the English, but also against the Navarrese and against roving bands of hungry soldiers left without employment by the Treaty of Brétigny but carrying on their own war by plundering the countryside. In this the dauphin Charles was aided ably by a rising French military superstar, Bertrand du Guesclin. Du Guesclin fought in several impressive engagements. In some he was dreadfully overmatched and unsuccessful. In fact, he found himself a prisoner after his defeats both at Auray, in 1364, and at Nájera, in Castile, in 1367. At the latter conflict, du Guesclin had taken the side of Henry of Trastamara in his Castilian succession struggles with his half brother, Pedro the Cruel, who was supported by the Black Prince. However, in most of the engagements that du Guesclin fought he was victorious.

Regaining Strength. With these victories and others, Charles V—for he had assumed the throne in 1364 on the death of his father in London—saw his military fortunes begin to rise, and slowly he began to regain his kingdom. By 1369 he had taken back Aquitaine; by 1371 he had made peace with Charles of Navarre; that same year he again began to exert authority in Brittany; in 1372 his allies, the Castilians, defeated the English fleet off the coast of La Rochelle; and by 1377 he had outlived both of his chief enemies when Edward the Black Prince died (in June 1376 of a disease that he had acquired during his campaign in Spain), followed less than a year later by Edward III. These deaths left a child, Richard II, untrained in the warfare of his father or grandfather, as king of England, a situation that Charles V, and after his death in 1380, his son, Charles VI, took full advantage of, pushing the English back until they could only barely hold onto Calais and Gascony.

French Divisions. In 1396 Richard II signed a truce in Paris, dependent on the marriage of the still-young English monarch to Isabella, one of Charles VI's daughters, and a coequal Anglo-French attendance on a Crusade to the east against the Ottoman Turks. France and England themselves did not exchange blows during the period between the Treaty of Paris and 1415, when Henry V launched his attack of France. Nevertheless, the war did continue. Although English troops stayed away, in France during this period the military situation was far more demanding and far less resolved. Charles VI's mental illness had left an unstable government with several nobles vying for power. Quickly, two of these came forward and faced one other in what just as quickly became solid opposition to one other. The dukes of Burgundy and Orléans both were cousins to

the king, which of course made them cousins to one other. However, their family ties did not bring them to an accord, and for almost the rest of the Hundred Years' War, these two factions, typically known as the Burgundians and Armagnacs, utilized every means of warfare, from actual combat to assassination, to fight against one other. It was quite simply a civil war, one that would infect the French and weaken them to such a point that when Henry V did invade the geographical kingdom, he found instead a divided realm, with one side, the Burgundians, willing either to collaborate with his invasion or to ignore it, and the other side, the Armagnacs, unwilling to decide whether it wished more to fight against the English or the Burgundians. Still, there had been little more than words between the two parties before 20 November 1407, when Louis of Orléans was assassinated in Paris. John the Fearless was quickly implicated, and the kingdom of France became divided between the two sides.

Duke of Burgundy. There seems little doubt among historians that John the Fearless planned this assassination with the idea of taking advantage of the then weakened Armagnacs to extend his own lands and political power. His involvement put many of the other French nobles against him. Yet, the duke of Burgundy did not become discouraged and he became resolved to reinforce his position by military means. Simply put, he began to wage war against all who opposed him. He used his large army, well supplied with perhaps the largest, most diverse gunpowder artillery train in Europe, to attack his French enemies, and by 1419 he had gained a large part of France, including Paris.

Agincourt. In March 1413 Henry V came to the throne of England. Henry immediately set out to attack France, and on 14 August 1415 Henry V's invasion force landed in the mouth of the Seine and began to besiege the nearby town of Harfleur. It was not a large army, probably numbering no more than 8,000-9,000 soldiers, only one-fourth of whom were men-at-arms. However, the French seem to have been completely unprepared for this attack, and six weeks later, on 22 September, the town surrendered. In early October, Henry V began a march to Calais, hoping, it is argued, not to encounter the French army but willing, it seems from the result, to engage this army in a battle should they catch him. On 25 October 1415, the French finally caught the English outside of the village of Agincourt. As at Crécy (and elsewhere throughout the Hundred Years' War), the French army should have easily defeated their English foes, if for no other reason than that they outnumbered them by almost 5 to 1 (25,000 to just over 5,000), with most of the French soldiers, knights, and men-at-arms. Yet, they did not. In what was certainly one of the greatest and most immortalized victories won during the entire Middle Ages, the English severely defeated their opponents. At the end of the day, more than 10,000 French soldiers lay dead, including the commanding general, the constable of France, the admiral of France, 3 dukes, 7 counts, and more than 90 other lords and 1,560

Mid-fourteenth century illumination of Edward III's troops sacking Crécy in 1346 (Bibliothèque Nationale, Paris)

knights. Other important French lords had been taken prisoners. On the English side the casualties were light, with only a few hundred killed, including only 2 nobles.

Aftermath. There was little English military action immediately following the battle of Agincourt, with Henry V back in London raising more money and troops for a larger invasion of France. Henry V returned to France late in 1417 intending to capture more of that kingdom. By 1420 he had taken Normandy. This gave him complete control of the northeast and southwest of France (the English, of course, still held Gascony), with his allies, the Burgundians and Bretons, holding onto the northwest and east of France, including Paris, as well as the Low Countries. On 21 May 1420, the Treaty of Troyes was signed between Henry V, Philip the Good (the duke of Burgundy after his father's murder in 1419), and Charles VI. This treaty in all its intricacy can be reduced to one single provision: it made Henry V heir to the throne of France. Charles VI was still recognized as king, but should he die, and he was ailing almost all of the time, then Henry V would assume his throne. Charles's own son, the dauphin Charles, was effectively disowned. In addition, Henry V would marry Charles VI's youngest daughter, Catherine, with their eldest son then being heir to both the French and the English kingdoms.

Death of Henry V. Had someone suggested to Henry at the signing of the Treaty of Troyes that he might die before the frail Charles VI, he probably would have been laughed at. However, that is precisely what happened. During the siege of Meaux in 1422, Henry V contracted what was probably an intestinal illness, perhaps dysentery. He died a few weeks later on 31 August. Charles VI was still alive, although he would follow Henry to the grave later that same year. Also in 1422, Catherine, Charles's daughter and Henry's wife, gave birth to a son, named after his father. That baby was, almost from the moment he was born, Henry VI, king of France and England. However, he was not destined to rule France without the disinherited dauphin, Charles, to voice his and his supporters' objections. And one of these supporters was a young peasant girl named Joan of Arc.

Joan of Arc. Joan of Arc arose in 1429. In between the death of Henry V and her rise to leadership, the English had been able to push further into Armagnac territory, reaching as far as the Loire River and attacking the region's capital, Orléans. This site became Joan's first target. Having gained recognition and leadership in the army, Joan arrived at Orléans. The English had been besieging the city for five months and, despite having too few soldiers even to surround the town, seemed on the verge of capturing it. Joan refused to allow this, however, and after capturing several of her opponents' field fortifications, as well as the Tourelles, the stone bridgehead in which they were headquartered, the English were forced to withdraw. The next month, and again by direct assaults on their positions, Joan removed the English from the rest of their Loire holdings and then participated in the battle of Patay, which was fought against these retreating troops. Following a relatively uneventful march from the Loire through Burgundian-held territory to Reims, on 17 July 1429, Joan's patron, Charles the Dauphin, was crowned King Charles VII. Joan then set out to capture Paris. Here, she met her first defeat; unsupported by the new king and several of his counselors, and after suffering a debilitating wound, Joan was forced to retreat from the French capital after only one day of assaulting the walls. After her defeat at Paris and a few uneventful engagements in the southern Loire River area, the following spring Joan moved to support the French town of Compiègne against a large Burgundian army. On 23 May 1430, leading a sortie out of Compiègne, Joan was separated from the main body of her force, captured by the Burgundians, and eventually sold to the English. A little more than a year later, on 30 May 1431, Joan of Arc was burned to death as a heretic in the marketplace of Rouen.

Impact. Joan's influence had been great. Not only had she crowned the dauphin as King Charles VII, after her death there would be no sustained retreating by Charles and the French. More important, within six years a peace conference would be held at Arras, which, while failing to make peace between the English and the French, did force the Burgundian duke, now Philip the Good, to reassess his alliance with England and to effectively switch sides, pulling away from an active support of England if not completely allying himself with Charles VII. This decision was a difficult one for Philip. However, it was more difficult for the English. England would never recover. It would take another seventeen years, but eventually the English would lose all of their lands in France (except for Calais): first Maine in 1449, then Normandy in 1450, and finally Gascony in 1453, a part of France that had been in English hands since Eleanor of Aquitaine had passed it to her royal English sons, Richard the Lionhearted and John, in the twelfth century.

Sources:

Christopher Allmand, *The Hundred Years' War: England and France at War c. 1300–c. 1450* (Cambridge & New York: Cambridge University Press, 1988).

Matthew Bennett, *Agincourt 1415: Triumph Against the Odds* (London: Osprey, 1991).

Alfred H. Burne, *The Agincourt War: A Military History of the Latter Part of the Hundred Years' War from 1369 to 1453* (London: Eyre & Spottiswoode, 1956).

Burne, *The Crécy War: A Military History of the Hundred Years' War from 1337 to the Peace of Bretigny, 1360* (London: Eyre & Spottiswoode, 1955).

Kelly DeVries, *Joan of Arc: A Military Leader* (Stroud, U.K.: Sutton, 1999).

DeVries, *The Military Campaigns of the Hundred Years' War* (Stroud, U.K.: Sutton, 2002).

Joycelyne Gledhill Dickinson, *The Congress of Arras, 1435: A Study in Medieval Diplomacy* (Oxford: Clarendon Press, 1955).

Kenneth Fowler, *The Age of the Plantagenet and the Valois: The Struggle for Supremacy, 1328–1498* (London: Elek, 1967; New York: Putnam, 1967).

H. J. Hewitt, *The Black Prince's Expedition of 1355–1357* (Manchester, U.K.: Manchester University Press, 1958).

Hewitt, *The Organization of War Under Edward III, 1338–62* (Manchester, U.K.: Manchester University Press; New York: Barnes & Noble, 1966).

Richard Ager Newhall, *The English Conquest of Normandy, 1416–1424: A Study in Fifteenth Century Warfare* (New Haven: Yale University Press, 1924).

Edouard Perroy, *The Hundred Years' War,* translated by W. B. Wells (London: Eyre & Spottiswoode, 1951; New York: Oxford University Press, 1951).

A. J. Pollard, *John Talbot and the War in France* (London: Royal Historical Society, 1983).

Jonathan Sumption, *The Hundred Years' War,* two volumes (London: Faber & Faber, 1990).

Malcolm Vale, *War and Chivalry: Warfare and Aristocratic Culture in England, France, and Burgundy at the End of the Middle Ages* (Athens: University of Georgia Press, 1981; London: Duckworth, 1981).

Richard Vaughan, *Valois Burgundy* (London: John Lane, 1975; Hamden, Conn.: Archon, 1975).

LATIN LAW IN THE CRUSADER STATES

Necessity. Once the First Crusaders were able to conquer the Holy Land and establish their kingdoms there in 1099, they were faced with the necessity of ruling a disparate population, most of whom had never been governed by European laws or customs. Furthermore, it quickly became apparent, with the return of many of these Crusaders to their homes in Europe, that the majority of administrative and judicial officials needed to govern the newly conquered population would also be subject peoples, probably Jews and Muslims. These officials, while they might function based on their own laws and traditions, would have to be controlled from above by the Resident Crusaders, based on a European legal system.

Dual Offices. Local officials collected taxes and sent them to their *Secretes,* Resident Crusader revenue offices, and from there to the *Grant Secrete,* the kingdom's central treasury. Courts, too, functioned in this two-tradition manner. The *Cour des Bourgeois* was established to deal with violations of maritime and merchant laws and with claims involving large amounts of money, while the *Cours des Syriens* was founded to rule on matters concerning the violations of Muslim and Jewish customs and laws. However, if a jurisdictional dispute between the two courts occurred, it was always the *Cour des Bourgeois* that was awarded the right to decide the legal matter. Additionally, all cases involving "High Justice," the ability to impose the death penalty, and all cases concerning property held by Resident Crusaders were decided in the *Cour des Bourgeois* alone. With this type of administrative flexibility, as Usamah Ibn-Munquidh and other witnesses testify, the Resident

Krak des Chevaliers, Syria, a castle built in the late twelfth century by the
Hospitalers to guard the coastal regions of the Holy Land

Crusaders were able to rule over a subject population with justice and peace.

Sources:

Hans Eberhard Mayer, *The Crusades*, translated by John Gillingham (London: Oxford University Press, 1972).

Jean Richard, *The Crusades, c.1071–c.1291*, translated by Jean Birrell (Cambridge & New York: Cambridge University Press, 1999).

Jonathan Riley-Smith, *The Crusades: A Short History* (New Haven: Yale University Press, 1987).

LEGAL PROCEDURES, CRIME, AND PUNISHMENT

Origins. *Beowulf,* an Anglo-Saxon epic poem written just before 800, is a story of bravery, vengeance, and justice that reveals much about legal procedures, crime, and punishment in early medieval Europe. The monster Grendel slays Hrothgar's warriors until the hero Beowulf arrives. Beowulf kills Grendel and peace is briefly restored, but Grendel's mother soon appears seeking blood vengeance. Eventually, Beowulf slays Grendel's mother, and the feud ends because Grendel has no living relatives.

Kinship. The control of crime in Europe became a question of kinship after the fall of the Roman Empire. The unwritten code of the blood feud demanded vengeance whenever kin or a knightly retainer was killed. Crimes were viewed as attacks on entire families, and thus families were expected to pursue justice. Merchants, peasants, and others who lacked large and powerful families were forced to seek protection from local overlords. One who was wronged turned to real or artificial kinship for help. The resulting blood-feud system of vengeance was not without rules, however. Women, small children, and older males were excluded from the actual feuds, although they were responsible for soliciting support from male relatives if they were aggrieved. Furthermore, a kinship group both supported its aggrieved members and policed other members of the family. Kinship groups prohibited indiscriminate killing because such actions could force the entire kindred group to fight. During the post-Roman era, vengeance and revenge contributed to vicious cycles of families fighting families.

***Wergild* and Oaths.** Blood feuds ended when one side was eliminated or when a killer paid *wergild* or *wergeld,* or the price of a man, to the family of the victim. The amount of *wergild* was contingent on the status or dignity of the victim. The money served as an example that the dead man's kin had acted correctly by defending him. The use of *wergild* was an early step in the transition from blood feud to the modern court system. Once territorial lords amassed sufficient power to legislate kinship vengeance, deliberations over *wergild* evolved into crude court cases based on oaths. Oaths were public statements made with the support of kin, and early decisions involved elaborate forms of communal oaths. An accused man would gather "oath-helpers" to stand beside him as he made a profession of innocence. Rulers and feudal overlords also demanded oaths of their vassals and subjects. Oaths therefore played an important role in the early administration of justice and in the creation of centralized lawgivers such as King Alfred the Great of Wessex. In 886 King Alfred demanded an oath of allegiance from all West Saxons and Mercians in his struggle against the Vikings. King Alfred later issued a law code that stressed the importance of keeping oaths, remaining loyal to a lord, and settling feuds without undue bloodshed. The shift from actual blood feuds to the battle of oaths included a strong Christian component: oaths were sacred and it was believed that God would intervene and determine the guilt or innocence of the accused.

Trial by Ordeal. The ordeal was a natural development of the blood-feud mentality of Beowulf's age: Beowulf fought three main battles, or ordeals, during which he proved that God was on his side by killing his opponent. The ordeal was a simple way to test whether an oath-taker was telling the truth. Trial by ordeal tested the credibility of the accused in situations where witnesses were unable to settle a case. An accused person would offer an oath and then submit to physical testing, usually with water or hot irons, to ascertain the veracity of the testimony. Water was commonly used to test those of lower social standing and hot iron was used for those of higher social standing, but the ritual itself was fairly similar. In the presence of a priest, the accused made an oath and then either placed one hand and forearm into boiling water or carried a red-hot iron a certain distance. The arm was then bandaged for three days. There was certain ambiguity in most cases as to whether the hand was sufficiently scathed. The decision of guilt or innocence was ultimately made by the assembled community, not by the priest or judge. The criterion for determining guilt or innocence thus varied from community to community. Cold water could also be used for an ordeal. The accused was lowered into water and judgment was made as to whether or not the person floated. The assembled community also rendered the ultimate decision in ordeals by cold water. Verdict by ordeal was based on the belief that God would intervene to determine guilt or innocence. Priests would celebrate mass before the ordeal and admonish the accused as to the severity of divine judgment.

Rise of Juries. Powerful overlords opposed blood feuds and insisted on court cases involving oaths and witnesses. Rulers redefined crimes as attacks on the state instead of mere attacks on the individual. These changes contributed to the distinction between criminal cases and civil cases. Individuals could still pursue civil cases, but the state became responsible for criminal cases. Twelfth-century changes in the notion of crime influenced the way that criminals were judged and punished. The shift from accusatory justice to inquisitorial justice did not happen at the same time across Europe, and some areas never adopted inquisitorial trials. However, the rise of juries in accusatory systems, such as in England, corresponded with the rise of inquisition processes in areas that combined Roman and canon law traditions.

End of the Ordeals. The Fourth Lateran Council (1215) of the Roman Church prohibited priests from participating in ordeals. Ordeals were useless without the religious component and thus the council's elimination of ordeals from church courts also effectively eliminated them from secular courts. One remnant of the ordeal was the belief that torture was an acceptable form of extracting a confession. The ordeal was, after all, a form of torture meant to persuade the guilty to confess. The elimination of the ordeal as a viable judicial process forced rulers across Europe to develop suitable replacements. The methods tended to develop along two lines: accusatory justice with trials in England, and inquisitorial trials based on a mixture of Roman and canon law for the rest of Europe. Continental Europe tended to follow a Roman-canon law system that employed inquisitorial trials quite distinct from the open jury trials of the English accusatory model. This tradition evolved out of efforts at the Fourth Lateran Council to reform the church and society. The Council attempted to control the beliefs and actions of the laity, reform the clergy, stifle heresy, deal with non-Christian minorities within society, and to institutionalize a process of church inquisition. The first four goals combined to provide a new impetus for the creation of inquisitional practices. In order to monitor belief and stop false beliefs, known as heresy, the church needed a severe legal system that could sniff out and destroy heresy. Since heresy was the equivalent of treason against God, it was punished by death. The Roman-canon law tradition allowed the church and the state to progress through inquisition trials. The authorities could initiate legal procedures without actual accusations. Courts took the initiative and began investigations by collecting evidence and arresting suspects. The authorities ceased to be bystanders at trials and became the force of the trial. Communal self-regulation based on communal deliberations was replaced with a system of prosecution exerted from above. Moreover, the inquisitorial model called for two eyewitnesses or a confession; hence, torture became an accepted method of extracting confessions. Vengeance became a burden of the state.

Inquisition. In 1231 Pope Gregory IX gave a convent of Dominicans the right to form an inquisitorial tribunal. This right came directly from the Pope and was part of the rise of Inquisitions within the Roman Catholic Church. The inquisition was not one uniform movement; rather, it was a series of court proceedings aimed at destroying heresy. The Church was especially severe with heretics who remained obstinate in their beliefs. Relapsed and unrepentant heretics were turned over to the state for actual punishment or execution. The church thus avoided pollution of the clergy by the shedding of blood. Condemned heretics were occasionally burned alive by secular authorities, thereby exterminating forever any memory of the shameful person or purifying the community of evil. Ultimately, the community would avoid God's wrath by destroying all memory of the heretic's deeds. The *auto-de-fe* originated as a religious act of penitence and justice, but it evolved into a public spectacle. Bernard de Gui held a number of famous *auto-de-fe* in early fourteenth-century France.

Procedures and Incarceration. Inquisitorial tribunals were lengthy affairs that contributed to the development of prisons since accused heretics were incarcerated throughout the process. Inquisitors would arrive in an area and announce a grace period where all could confess sins. Males over age fourteen and females over age twelve were required to offer personal confessions and to report any indiscretions in the community. The resulting atmosphere of suspicion would continue as the grace period was recalculated. Inquisitors then incarcerated potential heretics without offering explicit charges and without explaining who the accusers were and what they had said. Heretics were presumed guilty until proven innocent and thus lost all rights including control over their own property. If heretics did not confess, then the inquisitors would show them the tools of torture and explain what would happen if they did not confess. Ecclesiastical inquisitors viewed heretics as the worst possible threat to society and thus they altered procedures in significant ways: names and testimonies of witnesses were withheld; the defendant's access to counsel was limited; testimony from questionable witnesses was accepted; and the accused was offered false promises of leniency in attempts to win confessions. These changes were significant because government courts turned to the Inquisition as a model for actions. As a result, torture became a standard procedure in most of Europe.

Torture. The Roman-canon legal tradition called for two eyewitnesses or a confession. With the shift to *ex officio* cases, where the state brought charges against an individual, it was frequently difficult to find two eyewitnesses. Torture was not a means of proof, but rather of obtaining a confession that could stand in court. If the court decided that a confession could be obtained, then the accused was given religious encouragement to confess. This was followed by a display of the instruments of torture in order to encourage confession. Judges turned to torture as a last recourse in the pursuit of truth. Authorities frowned on innovations in torture and insisted that no blood be shed and that no permanent injury be inflicted. Common forms of torture included physical stretching such as the rack, sleep deprivation, and fire torture. The strappado, a pulley system whereby the hands of the accused were tied behind the back and a rope was placed through a pulley or over a beam, was used to repeatedly lift the victim into the air. Children, women, and everyone charged with less severe crimes would simply have their hands tied tightly, then released and tied again. Water torture involved restraining the accused and forcing the person's mouth open. A piece of linen was placed in the mouth to conduct water down into the throat. The accused had trouble breathing and could die if blood vessels in the neck ruptured.

Proceedings. Suspected criminals were taken to criminal courts of the local city or territory. They were placed in jails that served both as places of detention and physical suffering. Suspects were interrogated and encouraged to confess immediately. Those who did not confess were tortured. Not surprisingly, most suspects confessed under torture. These events occurred without recourse to a defense attorney. The pursuit of justice had become the concern of local authorities, but sentencing was public and thus differed from community to community. Two main factors contributed to the sentencing: the deterrence of future crime and the appearance of merciful courts. Courts were eager to show the mercy of a judgment and they forced the guilty to swear "oaths of truce" stating that the guilty would not seek revenge for the decision. Those sentenced to death were given three days to prepare for death. Those not sentenced to death were usually punished in the part of the body that committed the offense, or they were banished from the community. Mutilations, branding, and flogging were the most common forms of bodily punishment and they were frequently combined with social disgrace such as the pillory. Fines and church punishments involving penance were also issued. Death, the most severe punishment, was always a ritualized ceremony. Executions by burning, drowning, and burying alive were common ways to purify the community because they destroyed all traces of the evil person. Corpses of those executed in this manner could not be buried in a churchyard and thus, from the community's perspective, the corpse no longer existed. Executions were public affairs that sent a message to the community. The community also participated by witnessing the execution and thereby showing communal consent. Residents who lacked strong social connections were treated more harshly because they lacked public support at the sentencing stage of trials. Punishments were public events that inflicted pain and shame on the guilty.

Punishment. Medieval imprisonment was usually employed in order to extract a ransom from relatives and not to exercise judicial punishment. Canon law, on the other hand, sought penitential punishment, and thus monks and secular clergy were the earliest inmates in institutionalized disciplinary systems. Monks fell under canon law as well as monastic regulations that could be quite severe. The Rule of Saint Benedict does not mention imprisonment, but most monasteries had a place for penitential imprisonment. By the twelfth century, monasteries were expected to contain some sort of prison. Monastic imprisonment included beating with rods and dietary restrictions, but imprisonment was rare and generally not excessive. Monastic imprisonments represent early examples of confinement for specific durations based on the notion of moral correction.

Leper Colonies and Forced Labor. Other medieval forms of imprisonment included leper and other communities, places of forced labor, and hospitals. Unlike the modern hospital where disease is cured, the medieval hospital was a place to house the terminally sick. In the eleventh through thirteenth centuries, European rulers systematically confined certain residents without actually imprisoning them. Lepers were forced to live in separate communities apart from the towns and cities, whereas Jewish residents were confined to clearly defined residential quarters within cities. The galleys were a common form of forced labor in the Mediterranean area, and across Europe forced labor was used on public building projects, such as fortifications and city walls. Simple banishment was more widespread than imprisonment in the Middle Ages.

England. The Norman invasions (1066) contributed to the birth of the modern prison system in England. After the Norman conquest of England, William I or William the Conqueror (ruled 1066–1087) built the Tower of London in order to imprison his enemies. The Tower of London has long been revered as the ultimate medieval place of imprisonment. Its unique location, partly inside and partly outside of the city walls, gave it a daunting stature to all who traveled to London. The tower is best known as a prison for famous aristocrats. In the thirteenth and early fourteenth centuries it was also used to house ordinary felons, but it usually was vacant except for the occasional important prisoner. Also in London, the Fleet was an early royal prison that housed prisoners of war and hostages. Newgate, on the other hand, was built after Henry II's 1188 order to purchase land and construct a jail for London. Newgate was reconstructed in 1236 at the direction of Henry III. The jail and dungeons underneath housed the worst criminals in the city of London until the construction of Ludgate Jail at the end of the fourteenth century.

Jails and Jailors. In the eleventh century, royal officials known as sheriffs became responsible for the safe custody of suspected criminals. Offenders were housed in dungeons of castles, manors, and gatehouses. The 1166 Assize of Clarendon instituted the use of juries and decreed that all counties needed to provide sheriffs with buildings to house suspected criminals. Theoretically, the king owned the county jails, but they were controlled locally with no funding from the Crown. Jailors were usually unpaid, or poorly paid, entrepreneurs who made their living through bribery, fees, and even rents. Rooms in the jail ranged from squalid quarters on the "common side" to beautiful apartments on the "master's side." Beyond this financial segregation, criminals were usually kept separate from debtors. Male and female inmates, on the other hand, could mingle. Separate facilities known as Bishops' Prisons were used to imprison members of the Church who fell under Episcopal jurisdiction instead of royal jurisdiction. The *Tuns* were a third type of facility that was used for the overnight incarceration of vagabonds and suspicious people.

Continental Prisons. Continental rulers began constructing prisons and jails in the thirteenth century. The Châtelet was a fortress in Paris that was converted into the prison of the provost early in the thirteenth century. A tower in the fortress housed prisoners in a wide range of rooms based, as in England, on the status of the prisoner. Prisoners tended to be citizens awaiting decisions of the provost's court, which was also in the Châtelet, although a small number were imprisoned for punitive sentences. Outside of Paris, portions of royal castles were occasionally used for prisoners. Rulers in Castile faced the same problems as the French kings in attempting to impose centralized law and authority. The 1265 "Collection in Seven Parts" issued by King Alfonso X outlines prison regulations, but historians know little about actual prisons or implementation of the regulations. Italy was the center of legal study and the home of one of the most famous early public prisons. In 1297 the city of Florence began construction of a public prison called Le Stinche. The name *Le Stinche* became so well known as a prison that citizens of other cities, such as Siena and Pistoia, used *Le Stinche* as a slang term for their prisons. Florence, Bologna, and other northern Italian city-states were the earliest areas on the continent to use punitive imprisonment. Those same cities also housed influential universities that attracted law students from across Europe. Le Stinche and the Italian model had a profound influence on incarceration and justice in late medieval Europe.

Sources:

R.I. Moore, *The Formation of a Persecuting Society* (Oxford: Blackwell, 1987).

Norval Morris and David J. Rothman, eds., *The Oxford History of the Prison* (Oxford: Oxford University Press, 1995).

Edward Peters, *Torture* (Oxford: Blackwell, 1985).

Petrus Spierenburg, *The Spectacle of Suffering: Executions and the Evolution of Repression, from a Preindustrial Metropolis to the European Experience* (Cambridge: Cambridge University Press, 1984).

Ikins Stern, *The Criminal Law System of Medieval and Renaissance Florence* (Baltimore: Johns Hopkins University Press, 1994).

MAGNA CARTA

Richard I. Richard I (the Lionhearted) ruled England mostly as an absentee monarch from 1189 to 1199. Perpetually fighting abroad, he lost touch with his nobles, especially in matters pertaining to the enhancement of royal authority. He imposed burdensome taxes in order to support foreign Crusades and a war with France. When returning home from the Third Crusade (1189–1192), the Duke of Austria, Henry VI, captured and imprisoned him and demanded a high ransom for his

THE ARTICLES OF THE BARONS

The English nobility placed restraints on the monarchy by making King John I affix his seal to the Articles of the Barons (more commonly known as the Magna Carta or Great Charter) at Runnymede in Surrey on 15 June 1215.

A free man shall not be fined for a small offense, except in proportion to the gravity of the offense; and for the great offense he shall be fined in proportion to the magnitude of the offense, saving his freehold [property]; and a merchant in the same way, saving his merchandise; and the villein [a free serf, bound only to his lord] shall be fined in the same way, saving his wainage [wagon], if he shall be at [the king's] mercy. And none of the above fines shall be imposed except by the oaths of honest men of the neighborhood. . . .

No constable or other bailiff of [the king] shall take anyone's grain or other chattels without immediately paying for them in money, unless he is able to obtain a postponement at the good will of the seller.

No constable shall require any knight to give money in place of his ward of a castle [i.e., standing guard], if he is willing to furnish that ward in his own person, or through another honest man, if he himself is not able to do it for a reasonable cause; and if we shall lead or send him into the army, he shall be free from ward in proportion to the amount of time which he has been in the army through us.

No sheriff or bailiff of [the king], or any one else, shall take horses or wagons of any free man, for carrying purposes, except on the permission of that free man.

Neither we nor our bailiffs will take the wood of another man for castles, or for anything else which we are doing, except by the permission of him to whom the wood belongs. . . .

No free man shall be taken, or imprisoned, or dispossessed, or outlawed, or banished, or in any way injured, nor will we go upon him, except by the legal judgment of his peers, or by the law of the land.

To no one will we sell, to no one will we deny or delay, right or justice.

Source: James Harvey Robinson, ed., *Readings in European History*, volume I (Boston: Athenaeum, 1904), pp. 236–237.

Magna Carta, 1215 (British Library, London)

release. Upon Richard I's death, his brother John I came to the throne and continued his fiscal policies.

John I. Aside from taxes, John I antagonized the English nobility in other ways as well. He seized the revenues the nobles received from the growing towns in their fiefdoms. After being excommunicated by Pope Innocent III in 1209 for disputing the papal choice of the archbishop of Canterbury, John I made the humiliating concession of declaring his country a fief of the Pope. Following a defeat at the hands of the French at Bouvines in 1214, the English barons, supported by the clergy and townsmen, openly revolted against the king. On 15 June 1215 they forced John I to sign the Articles of the Barons, or what is more commonly known as the Magna Carta (Great Charter).

Clear Statement. Earlier kings of England, such as Henry I and Henry II, had issued charters making concessions to their nobles. However, the Magna Carta was different because it was exacted from, not willingly granted by, the king. It also clearly delineated English liberties, something that previous decrees had failed to do. It allowed for the participation of the nobility and clergy in high office and ensured an equitable system of justice and taxation. In essence, the Magna Carta created a limited monarchy, although the monarchy was still strong.

Provisions. The Magna Carta consisted of a preamble and sixty-three clauses that addressed such issues as church rights, landholding, tenancy, towns, trade, mer-

chants, royal forests, the behavior of royal officials, and legal reform. The final clauses provided for a council of twenty-five barons to monitor all future kings' adherence to the charter.

Impact. The decree was reissued with alterations in 1216, 1217, 1225, and 1264. Over time it became more of a sourcebook of legal precedents rather than a statement of current law. Nevertheless, the Magna Carta is a cornerstone of modern English law. The Petition of Right (1628), Habeas Corpus Act (1679), and U.S. Constitution (1789) are all based on principles expressed in the Magna Carta. There are four extant copies of the original 1215 charter: one each at Lincoln Cathedral and Salisbury Cathedral and two at the British Museum.

Sources:
A. E. Dick, *Magna Carta: Text and Commentary* (Charlottesville: University Press of Virginia, 1994).

James Clarke Holt, *Magna Carta* (Cambridge: Cambridge University Press, 1965).

Anne Pallister, *Magna Carta: The Heritage of Liberty* (Oxford: Clarendon Press, 1971).

William Finley Swindler, *Magna Carta: Legend and Legacy* (Indianapolis: Bobbs-Merrill, 1965).

MONGOLS

Ghenghis Khan. The Mongols, or Tatars, represented the premier military force in the thirteenth century. A pastoral people of Mongolia, they first conquered northern China and Korea before moving across Siberia to invade Persia and Eastern Europe. The organizer of this powerful

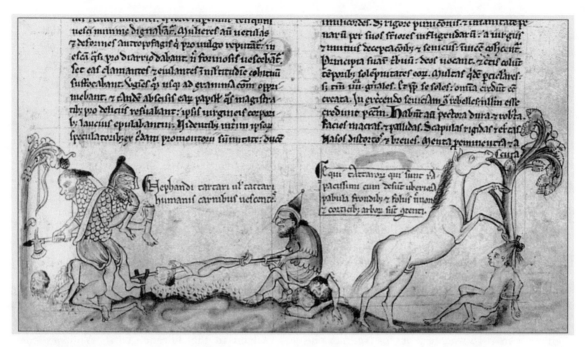

Mongol warriors eating human flesh; illumination from a thirteenth-century manuscript (Corpus Christi College, Cambridge)

military machine was Temuchin, who took the title of *Ghenghis Khan* (Mightiest King) in 1206. By the time of his death twenty-one years later he had created the largest contiguous land empire ever seen.

Poland and Hungary. In 1237 Batu, grandson of Ghenghis, raided Riazan and then began to systematically destroy all settlements in northeast Russia. Meanwhile, a second Mongol army under Subotai sacked Kiev and occupied southwest Russia. Subsequent conquests extended Mongol control into Poland and Hungary. In April 1241 a Mongol army of 120,000 men under Subotai inflicted a stunning defeat on a Hungarian army of 90,000 troops under King Bela IV at the Sajo River. (Reportedly, 70,000 Hungarians died in the battle.) Afterward, the invaders sacked the city of Pest.

Golden Horde. The western portion of the vast Mongol Empire became known as the Kipchak Khanate (Golden Horde, a phrase derived from the Tatar words for the color of Batu Khan's tent) and it flourished until the late fourteenth century, when internal dissension developed among the various khans. Between 1360 and 1380 there were no fewer than twenty-five claimants to the Mongol throne. In 1380 a Russian army under Prince Dimitri Ivanovich defeated a Mongol force at the Battle of Kulikovo Field. The Russian ruler Ivan III (the Great) finally threw off the "Tatar yoke" in the late fifteenth century.

Misconception. Contrary to popular belief, sheer numbers do not represent the secret behind Mongol victories; the real reasons include excellent discipline, a military organization based on the *tumen* (a division of ten thousand), and mobility. Archers and lancers mounted on fast horses often proved superior to any Russian or Near Eastern foes. Moreover, Mongol soldiers were a hardy lot, capable of living off of mare's milk and wild game indefinitely.

Sources:
James Chambers, *The Devils' Horsemen: The Mongol Invasion of Europe* (London: Weidenfeld & Nicolson, 1979).

Leo de Hartog, *Genghis Khan, Conqueror of the World* (New York: St. Martin's Press, 1989).

David Morgan, *The Mongols* (Oxford & New York: Blackwell, 1986).

THE NORMAN CONQUESTS

Viking Legacy. It might be said that the Viking raids did not stop when the Scandinavians stopped taking part in them. If it is recognized that the Normans were the descendants of the Vikings, in military characteristics and goals as well as genealogy, then one might recognize their military endeavors against England, France, Sicily, and southern Italy as continuing Viking raids.

Birth of the Normans. It seems quite clear that when Charles the Simple gave the Viking chieftain Rollo the territory surrounding the lower Seine River in 911 there were no pretenses that either he or his followers would become "French." Yet, shortly thereafter that is precisely the direction that they took. They adopted the French language and religion, and they began to intermarry with the local peasantry and nobility. Soon the new dukes of Normandy, as Rollo and his descendants became known, were doing homage to the French king and fighting with him in his battles, obligated it seems with a similar code as the king's other nobles. However, these new religious, linguistic, and familial ties never seemed to have removed their military instincts nor their desire for further conquests and invasions. This situation came to a head in the second half of the eleventh century, when two successful Norman invasions took place. The first was led by a Norman adventurer, Robert Guiscard, and his brothers against Sicily and southern Italy; the second was accomplished by the Norman duke, William, known at the time as "the Bastard" because

The final moments of the Battle of Hastings (1066), when the Norman cavalry charged Harold's bodyguards and killed the Anglo-Saxon king; from the Bayeux Tapestry, circa 1092 (Centre Guillaume le Conquerant, Bayeux)

of his illegitimate birth and later as "the Conqueror" for his subduing of England.

Rumors of Wealth. The Normans first glimpsed Sicily and southern Italy in 1016 when a group of Norman pilgrims returning from the Holy Land hired themselves out as mercenaries in the wars fought there first between the Italians and the Byzantines and later against the Muslim Arabs, who tried to take advantage of those wars to conquer these regions. In doing so, they became quite wealthy, and when news of this easily acquired wealth reached Normandy others traveled to the south as well. Among those new recruits were twelve brothers of the Hauteville family. All of these brothers were warriors of superb quality and skills, but it is one of the youngest, Robert Guiscard, who gets most of the credit for what followed. First, they led their forces against Byzantine-controlled Sicily, and then they turned their sights on southern Italy, which Robert captured between 1057 and 1071. Robert Guiscard seemed to fear nothing, and in 1053 he even captured and imprisoned Pope Leo IX at the battle of Civitate. A later Pope, Nicholas II, would employ him and his forces at different times against the Germans and Byzantines; in 1059, in recognition of this service, Nicholas named Robert as his duke and vassal. From this point until his death in 1085, Robert continued to uphold his position as the king of Sicily—a kingdom that he continued to enlarge—and defender of the Papacy, even defeating the Holy Roman Emperor, Henry IV, in 1084 as he was besieging Rome and Pope Gregory IX.

Duke of Normandy. William the Conqueror, first as duke of Normandy and later as king of England, showed a similar military skill to that of his countrymen fighting in the Mediterranean. Coming to the ducal throne as an illegitimate heir after the untimely death of his father, Robert the Magnificent, William almost immediately had to defend his right to that throne. As such, he may have fought in and lived through more battles than any other medieval military leader. Especially as his Norman opponents were favored and funded by King Henry I of France, William was forced to win victories at Val-ès-Dunes in 1047, at Mortemer in 1054, and at Varaville in 1057.

Later, in 1063, he was also forced to attack and conquer the county of Maine in support of his son's claims there, fighting again against Henry I.

Claim to the Throne. It is William's conquest of England for which he is justifiably the most famous, for although England was of minor significance in 1066, when his invasion took place, William's descendants there would make great political and military impacts throughout the rest of the Middle Ages. There is some dispute as to why William believed that he had a right to England. Legend based on the slimmest of historical evidence has William being named heir to the English throne by its childless king, Edward the Confessor, who had spent some time at the ducal court of Normandy when he was an exiled youth. However, when Edward died on 5 January 1066, the Anglo-Saxon assembly named his chief earl and brother-in-law, Harold Godwinsson, as king. William considered this not only an affront to his claims to the throne but also treason, as, again based on less than credible evidence, Harold was supposed to have promised William that he would support only his right to the throne.

Stamford Bridge and Hastings. William was not alone in believing that the English throne should be his. At least two others, King Harald Hardrada of Norway and King Svein Estridson of Denmark, also claimed the crown of England. Harald Hardrada even went so far as to launch his own invasion of the island kingdom, forcing King Harold to march his army from the southern coast of England, where they awaited the invasion of William, all the way to York in the north of England. At the battle of Stamford Bridge on 25 September 1066 Harold defeated the Norwegians; Harald Hardrada was killed in the fighting. However, King Harold was not able to celebrate this victory, as word quickly reached him that, while he was in the north, William and the Normans had landed in the south. Evidence shows that William anticipated a lengthy campaign, but that would not be necessary. Harold, flushed with recent victory, chose instead to immediately face the Norman invaders in battle. Fighting between the two armies took place on Senlac Hill, north of Hastings, on 14 October 1066. After what one historian has described as an "unusual battle" because of its uncommon length, William's forces prevailed, killing Harold, his brothers, and many of their soldiers. Although there would still be some limited resistance, with this victory William conquered England.

Sources:

Jim Bradbury, *The Battle of Hastings* (Stroud, U.K.: Sutton, 1998).

R. Allen Brown, *The Normans and the Norman Conquest,* second edition (Dover, N.H.: Boydell Press, 1985).

Kelly DeVries, *The Norwegian Invasion of England in 1066* (Woodbridge, U.K. & Rochester, N.Y.: Boydell Press, 1999).

David C. Douglas, *William the Conqueror* (Berkeley: University of California Press, 1964).

Dorothy Whitelock and others, *The Norman Conquest: Its Setting and Impact* (London: Eyre & Spottiswoode, 1966).

THE PEACE OF GOD AND THE TRUCE OF GOD

Outlaws. As the Viking and Magyar raids began to lessen in the tenth century, Europe found itself confronted with a new problem. For so long the people had faced the uncertainty of their safety. In response many of the more capable men had taken up the profession of soldier, their employment secured as a result of the continuing invasions. Yet, with the impending end of the raids, these martial skills became less and less necessary, and soon, it seems, many unemployed soldiers were roaming the countryside. Finding peace a burden and unwilling to return to agricultural work, these men tried to eke out a living by doing exactly what they had been paid to defend against: terrorizing the local inhabitants. They became violent outlaws who thought little about participating in the crimes of theft and murder.

Solution. Something needed to be done, especially since these lawless and unethical men often perpetrated their crimes against the defenseless: the poor, the clergy, and women. As one of the principles of the Catholic Church was to protect the unfortunate and defenseless, the matter became an issue for the ecclesiastical leaders who, in turn, chose to work with the legal authorities, the nobles, to curtail this violence. The answer was to develop the "Peace of God." The Peace of God began to be proclaimed everywhere throughout Europe in the last half of the tenth century. Although varying in detail depending on who was proclaiming it (the ecclesiastic) and who was enforcing it (the noble), the basic tenets of the Peace of God were the protection of those who could not protect themselves, as well as the protection of certain types of material things, such as church buildings, church property, and the means of livelihood for the poor. An example of this type of decree can be seen in the following record of the Peace of God proclaimed in the Synod of Charroux in southern France:

We assembled there in the name of God, made the following decrees:

1. Anathema [an ecclesiastical punishment] against those who break into churches. If anyone breaks into or robs a church, he shall be anathema unless he makes satisfaction.

2. Anathema against those who rob the poor. If anyone robs a peasant or any poor person of a sheep, ox, ass, cow, goat, or pig, he shall be anathema unless he makes satisfaction.

3. Anathema against those who injure clergymen. If anyone attacks, seizes, or beats a priest, deacon, or any other clergyman, who is not bearing arms (shield, sword, coat of mail, or helmet), but is going along peacefully or staying in the house, the sacrilegious person shall be excommunicated and cut off from the church, unless he makes satisfaction, or unless the bishop discovers that the clergyman brought it upon himself by his own fault.

Effectiveness. As no crime statistics remain from this period, it is difficult to know whether the Peace of God was effective. Evidence that it did not bring complete peace, however, comes from the need for the Catholic Church, again in concert with noble lawmakers, to introduce a similar proclamation, known as the "Truce of God," soon afterward. The Truce of God varied from its predecessor in that it focused less on protecting certain peoples and more on the banning of military activity at certain times of the year and the week. Military activity was prohibited during Lent and also from Thursday sunset until Monday sunrise. Generally more detailed and more legalistic than the Peace of God, the Truce of God tried to protect everyone at least some of the time, as an example proclaimed in 1063 in the Bishopric of Terouanne, in the southern Low Countries, shows:

Drogo, the bishop of Terouanne, and Count Baldwin [of Hainault] have established this peace with the cooperation of the clergy and the people of the land.

Dearest brothers in the Lord, these are the conditions which you must observe during the time of the peace which is commonly called the Truce of God, and which begins with sunset on Wednesday and lasts until sunrise on Monday.

1. During those four days and five nights no man shall assault, wound, or slay another, or attack, seize, or destroy a castle, burg, or villa, by craft or by violence.

2. If anyone violates this peace and disobeys these commands of ours, he shall be exiled for thirty years as a penance, and before he leaves the bishopric he shall make compensation for the injury which he committed. Otherwise he shall be excommunicated by the Lord God and excluded from all Christian fellowship . . .

5. In addition, brethren you should observe the peace in regard to lands and animals and all things that can be possessed. If anyone takes from another an animal, a coin, or a garment, during the days of the truce, he shall be excommunicated unless he makes satisfaction. If he desires to make satisfaction for his crime he shall first restore the thing which he stole or its value in money, and shall do penance for seven years within the bishopric . . .

6. During the days of peace, no one shall make a hostile expedition on horseback, except when summoned by the count; and all who go with the count shall take for their support only as much as is necessary for themselves and their horses.

7. All merchants and other men who pass through your territory from other lands shall have peace from you.

8. You shall also keep this peace every day of the week from the beginning of Advent to the octave of Epiphany and from the beginning of Lent to the octave of Easter, and

from the feast of Rogations [the Monday before Ascension Day] to the octave of Pentecost.

9. We command all priests on feast days and Sundays to pray for all who keep the peace, and to curse all who violate it or support its violators.

Failure. Had it ever been fully effective, the Truce of God would have completely eliminated warfare for the rest of the Middle Ages. Of course, it did not do that; nor does it seem to have had much effect on the warriors to whom it was directed. Again, there is no evidence to support this claim—although the fact that Robert Guiscard and William the Conqueror did most of their fighting in the Truce of God period certainly seems to indicate its ineffectiveness—but the notion of bringing peace to Europe would persist, and it was not too long before an ecclesiastical leader came up with a solution that would bring peace to the European people: send all of the warriors on a crusade to the Middle East.

Sources:

Christopher Brooke, *Europe in the Central Middle Ages, 962–1154,* third edition (Harlow, U.K. & New York: Longman, 2000).

R. H. C. Davis, *A History of Medieval Europe: From Constantine to Saint Louis* (London & New York: Longmans, Green, 1957).

Thomas Head and Richard Landes, eds., *The Peace of God: Social Violence and Religious Response in France Around the Year 1000* (Ithaca, N.Y.: Cornell University Press, 1992).

Brian Tierney, ed. and trans., *The Middle Ages,* volume I, *Sources of Medieval History,* fourth edition (New York: Knopf, 1983).

SALIC LAW

Germanic Legal Codes. Of the many Germanic legal codes and traditions that were passed down by the barbarian tribes that invaded the Roman Empire, few had any great significance except to those curious parties who collected them almost purely out of antiquarian interest. The only exception to that case may be the *Lex Salica,* or Laws of the Salian Franks. These statutes are significant not because of what they included as far as legal issues, but because of what they excluded as far as who was fit to rule.

Ancient Customs and Traditions. The first codified version of the *Lex Salica* was probably issued by Clovis at the beginning of the sixth century for use by his Merovingian justices. Although written in Latin at this time, it was undoubtedly formulated from oral transmissions of ancient Frankish customs and traditions. By the time of Charle-

JUSTINIAN AND ROMAN LAW

Once Justinian had secured his throne as emperor of the Byzantine Empire in 527, he turned his attention to the reformation of domestic matters. The principal among these was the codification of the various laws on which the empire's system of justice was built. Roman law, as these laws were generically called, had existed in many forms for many centuries. Emperors and senates had issued legal directions since the earliest days of late antiquity, few of which had been systematically published or catalogued. In addition, judicial opinions had been issued frequently on these laws, many of which were contradictory and inaccessible. When legal collections were attempted—for example, two in the third and fourth centuries—their usefulness was disputed. Finally, earlier imperial attempts at correcting the situation, primarily by Valentinian III in the west and Theodosius II in the east, had only partially succeeded, their commissions smothered under heaps of bureaucracy. In short, by Justinian's time the administration of systematic justice within the Byzantine Empire was practically impossible.

In the first year of his reign Justinian appointed a commission to produce a new imperial legal code that could and would become standard throughout the entire Empire. It was comprised of ten legal experts under the leadership of a *quaestor,* or chief legal officer, and was to take into account all of the preceding col-

lections of laws, as well as new and noncollected laws issued more recently. They were to systemize all of these laws and make them more simple. They worked quickly and after little more than a year produced the *Codex Justinianus.* Following this success, a new commission of sixteen jurists met to collect, coordinate, and codify all of the legal opinions that had existed in the Roman Empire and afterward. Working through more than two thousand works comprising some three million lines of law, this commission in less than three years published the *Digest.* This latter effort was extraordinary, amounting to more than fifty books of "definitive" legal opinion.

The *Codex* and the *Digest* would be supplemented and reworked throughout the entire reign of Justinian. Initially, these legal texts were written in Latin, but quickly Greek translations were made, and as quickly they were sent throughout the Empire and carried by conquering Byzantine armies. Before too long, Roman law had been established once again throughout the old Roman Empire. Despite the changes in boundaries that would come in the years following the death of Justinian in 565, the Roman law of his *Codex* and *Digest* would remain in force throughout the medieval period and into the early modern and modern eras. Indeed, it is upon these early codifications of law and legal opinion that much modern law is based.

Source: J. A. S. Evans, *The Age of Justinian: The Circumstances of Imperial Power* (New York: Routledge, 1996).

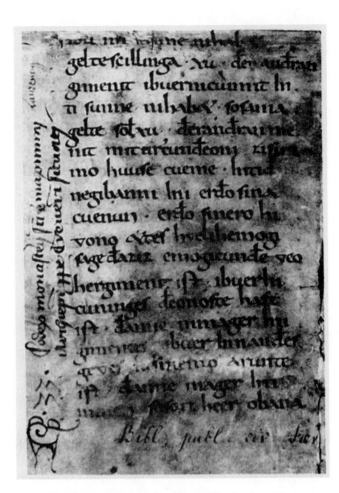

Page from a manuscript for a Frankish legal code written
in Old High German, circa 1000 (Stadtbibliothek, Trier)

Sources:

Katherine Fischer Drew, trans., *The Laws of the Salian Franks* (Philadelphia: University of Pennsylvania Press, 1991).

Theodore John Rivers, trans., *Laws of the Salian and Ripuarian Franks* (New York: AMS Press, 1986).

THE VIKINGS AND MAGYARS

Disintegration. The empire created by Charlemagne did not survive long after his death in 814. Only one of his three sons, Louis the Pious, outlived him, and after his death in 840 Louis was succeeded in 843 by his three feuding sons, Charles the Bald, Lothar I, and Louis the German. Their division of the kingdom would form the geographical basis of modern France, the Low Countries, Italy, and Germany, but it also ushered in the eventual end of the Carolingian dynasty. Even if they had not practiced partible inheritance, however, Charlemagne's grandsons and their descendants would have probably found it extremely difficult to put up an effective defense against all the raiders on all of the sides of the kingdom. Spanish Muslim armies continued to harass the borders of the empire across the Pyrenees mountains, while other Muslim forces had begun to attack Sicily and southern Italy; they were joined by new and more-determined threats from the Vikings in the north and west and the Magyars in the east.

Greatest Threat. Of these, the greatest threat was the Vikings. As of yet, no historian has been able to offer a satisfactory reason for the sudden outburst of Viking raiders from Scandinavia in the late eighth century, although the destruction of the Frisian fleet by Charlemagne at about the same time certainly left no effective deterrents to their sea travel and may have been a factor in the launching of their invasions. Still, this fact alone cannot be sufficient cause to explain the large number of voyages that were launched from Sweden, Norway, and Denmark between 789 and 1066 and extended along the coasts of continental Europe, England, Ireland, the Baltic region, east to Russia, south to Byzantium, Italy, and North Africa, and west to the Faroe and Shetland Islands, Iceland, Greenland, and North America.

Initial Contact. The first recorded attack of the Vikings was made in 789 on the southeastern coast of England. Four years later they again appeared off the coast of England, and this time their violent purposes became clear. The *Anglo-Saxon Chronicle* recorded the incident:

> 793. Here, terrible portents were come over the Northumbrian land, which miserably frightened the people; there were huge flashes of lightning, and fiery dragons were seen flying in the air. Much hunger soon followed these signs, and a little after that in the same year, on January 8, the raiding of heathen men miserably destroyed God's church on Lindisfarne Island by looting and the killing of men.

Plunder. For a while after the attack on Lindisfarne Abbey these Scandinavian raiders, carried onto the English, Irish, and northern European shores in their dragon-prowed ships, were content to feast on the easy monastic and small urban pickings that were spread throughout the countryside. These were fairly rich loca-

magne it was considered obsolete, kept and studied only for its antiquarian interest.

Rebirth. However, in 1328 the Salic Law was remembered once again, and its provisions created a situation that may ultimately have caused the Hundred Years' War (1337–1453). The part of the Salic Law that was called into use was its Law of Succession, which suggested that women could not inherit property or succeed to the throne; nor could inheritance be transmitted through a woman. When Charles IV died in 1328, he was the last direct heir to the throne of his grandfather, King Philip III of France. The only grandson left was the King of England, Edward III, heir to the French throne through his mother, Isabella, daughter of King Philip IV and sister of Charles IV. However, instead of granting this throne to Edward, the French nobles instead chose his cousin Philip VI of Valois as the new king. They determined by consulting Salic Law that because Edward's inheritance was through a woman, Philip VI, the son of Philip IV's brother, had more right to the French throne. In 1337, when Edward III initiated a military conflict with France, the main reason he suggested for fighting the war was to regain the crown that he felt had been unjustly stolen from him.

Viking head carved on a wagon, circa 850
(Universitetets Oldsaksamling, Oslo)

tions waiting, it seems, for someone to attack them. The fact that they were filled with unarmed ecclesiastics and farmers meant nothing to the raiders, whose plunder and booty would be returned to their homelands, giving purpose to their journeys away from families and fields, while at the same time inspiring new Viking raiding voyages. Eventually, the Scandinavians even wintered in England and France, establishing base camps from which they could raid longer and farther inland than ever before.

Rich Targets. Early on, Ireland, Scotland, and northern England provided the richest targets; attacking lands filled with monasteries but without many fortifications or militias, there was little opposition to the violent raids of the Vikings. But by around 834 the ancient Irish civilization had been virtually destroyed and the countrysides of Scotland and northern England also had been almost completely despoiled of their ecclesiastic targets. The Vikings were forced to turn elsewhere for their booty, toward the continent. Without the military strength of a Charlemagne there was little to stop these attacks. Their targets, too, had become larger. By 840 the Vikings had raided the Low Country towns of Noir-

moutier, Rhé, Duurstede (sacked no fewer than four times), Utrecht, and Antwerp. In 843 they wintered for the first time in Gaul, capturing Nantes, ravaging the valleys of the Loire and Garonne Rivers, and even, on their way home to Scandinavia, threatening the Muslim cities of Lisbon and Cadiz. Moreover, in 845 a Viking force of more than 120 ships sailed up the Seine River and sacked Paris.

River Routes. The many rivers on the continent provided them with conduits to a large number of inland sites, and in the following thirty years, the Vikings raided up the Rhine, Meuse, Scheldt, Somme, Seine, Marne, Loire, Charente, Dordogne, Lot, and Garonne Rivers. No town, village, or monastery even remotely close to a waterway was immune from attack. Nor were any coastal European sites seemingly too far from Scandinavia to warrant concern, for as the century progressed the Vikings became bolder. One expedition from 859 to 862 even sailed through the Straits of Gibraltar and raided Nekur in Morocco, the Murcian coast of Spain, the Balearic Islands, and Roussillon. After wintering on the Rhone delta, it raided upstream to Valence and sacked Pisa and then Luna (which the Vikings apparently thought was Rome) before sailing back past Gibraltar and north to their base in Brittany.

Alfred the Great. In 866 a main force of the Vikings, the Danish "Great Army," attacked southern England, quickly overrunning East Anglia, Northumbria, and Mercia, but met bitter resistance a few years into their conquest from the West Saxons under their king, Alfred the Great. Alfred defeated the Vikings in battles fought at Englefield and Ashdown. Following these engagements, in 878 he won a major victory against the Danes at Edington. Alfred also devised a system of fortifications, earth-and-wood ramparts known as *burhs*, that surrounded many of the larger and previously unfortified towns in his kingdom. All of this resistance led to peace treaties being signed, a diminishing of Viking activity, and Alfred's assumption of the kingship over the entirety of England.

Continental Raids. Once again the Scandinavians turned to the Continent and the weaker Carolingian rulers there. They attacked Ghent (879), Courtrai, and several sites in Saxony (880), Elsloo and Aachen (881), where they even sacked Charlemagne's palace, Condé (882), Amiens (883), and Louvain (884). In 885–886 a large Viking army again attacked Paris with a force said to have numbered seven hundred ships and forty thousand men (undoubtedly an exaggeration); they did not sack the city, however, but were bought off by King Louis the Fat who paid them £700 of silver and gave them permission to spend the summer raiding Burgundy, a land that he did not own. In 891 the Vikings were back in the Low Countries, where they were defeated by Arnulf, the king of the East Franks, at the battle of the Dyle. Yet, they were still powerful enough to establish a district in the lower Seine river basin, which in 911 was officially ceded to them as the duchy of the Northmen (Normandy).

Colonization. After 911, Viking activity seems to have slowed. Colonization in the conquered territories had been taking place for some time during the raids, and by the beginning of the tenth century Scandinavians had founded communities in Ireland, Scotland, England, Russia, Normandy, the Faroe Islands, the Shetland Islands, Iceland, Greenland, and, shortly thereafter, North America. Trading with these communities and others had become more of a practice than raiding, especially with the discovery of cheap Islamic silver that could be obtained and taken back to Scandinavia for enormous profits. At the end of the tenth century, perhaps because of the drying up of the Islamic silver market, Viking raids again started to take place, especially against England. From 991 on, a succession of Scandinavian leaders attacked England, and in 1014 one of them, Sweyn I Forkbeard, conquered it and ruled for a short time as king, being succeeded by his son, Canute I (the Great). An English king, Edward the Confessor, regained the throne in 1042, but it was not until later invasions in 1066 and 1085 were turned back that the Viking threat to Europe had finally ended.

Raiders from the East. Far less famous than the Viking invasions, but equally devastating to post–Carolingian Europe, were the Magyar raids. Originating in the late ninth century and lasting until the middle of the tenth century, raiding Magyar horsemen made their presence felt especially in the areas of central Europe near their Hungarian homelands. Oddly enough, these warriors may first have glimpsed what they would later view as easy targets, the riches of the West, when they became employed in 892 by Arnulf, the king of the East Franks, in an attack against the Slavs in Moravia. Seven years later they returned to the West on an expedition of their own. They first advanced south to Pavia, which they sacked, and then wintered in Lombardy. The next year, 900, they raided Bavaria, and the year after that Carinthia. After a five-year period of peace the Magyars returned in 906 when they rode into Saxony; in 907 they rode again into Bavaria, in 908 into Saxony and Thuringia, and in 909 into Swabia. Civil wars in their homelands prohibited further raids for eight years, but when those raids again resumed, the Magyars returned to the West with great violence. From 917 until 926 these renewed raids were much more destructive than previous raids, and they stretched farther, to Basle, Alsace, Burgundy, Lombardy, and Provence. However, after 926, and for reasons not completely explained by historical sources, Magyar power began to decline, although the raiders remained a threat to those German lands within close proximity. Finally, in 955 the Magyars were defeated and driven back to Hungary by King Otto the Great at the battle of Lechfeld.

Rationale. While the reasons behind the Muslim raids in the Mediterranean regions during this period

The Gjermundbu Helmet, the only complete Viking helmet ever found, tenth century (Gjermundbu, Buskerud, Norway)

appear to have been religious in nature, those for the Viking and Magyar attacks cannot be fully understood. They do not seem to have been conquests, like those invasions that the Germanic tribes had made into the Roman Empire half a millennium before. Even in the Vikings' case, actual colonization did not take place until late in their raiding chronology. At the conclusion of their individual raids, most Vikings and Magyars returned to their homelands. They returned laden with booty, and it must be concluded that the success of the early raids promoted their continuation.

Disunity. There is also little doubt that the disunity and military weaknesses of the post–Carolingian kingdoms of continental Europe and the Anglo-Saxon kingdoms of England encouraged the success of these raids. Since the death of Charlemagne few militias had been recruited and few fortifications had been built. Thus, there was not much to stand in the way of the raiders. (In fact, Charles the Bald was so concerned about the possibility of rebellions against his rule that just as the Vikings were beginning to spread their invasions to his lands he was disarming the people and tearing down their fortifications.) Nor were new defensive endeavors undertaken during the time of these invasions. Even when a leader could raise an army of sufficient strength to oppose the raiders, neither the Vikings nor the Magyars generally allowed themselves to be forced to fight in a pitched battle. This approach seemed logical to both the Vikings and Magyars since they usually lost such engagements.

Attrition. By the time the raids had ended, the Vikings had been invading Europe for almost three centuries and the Magyars had been invading for more than fifty years. So, why did they finally end? There may be several plausible answers. First, there was undoubtedly an attrition factor. The Vikings and Magyars simply could not continue to participate in raids on Europe for much longer than they did, as the number of viable targets seems to have dwindled considerably by the later raids. This reason may explain why the Magyars spread their final raids out farther from their homeland and why the Vikings began to attack larger and more-fortified places.

Guardians of Settlements. Second, at least for the Vikings, colonization certainly played a role in diminishing and finally ending the invasions. As Vikings began to settle in lands that had previously been targets of their raids, these lands became no longer suitable for further raids. In other words, the Scandinavian presence in the lands necessarily forbade future raids. Indeed, the Vikings who participated in these raids were never a unified political entity, and they seem to have shown little concern whether they were attacking lands that were controlled by Scandinavian colonists or by other Europeans. However, the Vikings who had settled on these lands seem to have been much more formidable opponents to those raiders than the land's former inhabitants. That is why Charles the Simple had settled Vikings in Normandy: they provided a buffer against further invasions. (When Vikings were not available to provide a defense against further raids, sometimes other strong military leaders could be found to do so, as in the case of naming Baldwin the Iron Arm as count of Flanders and Reiner with the Long Neck as duke of Brabant in the ninth century; after their ascension neither area was further threatened by Viking raids.)

Other Occupations. A third reason for the ending of these raids was that several former raiders found it safer and more profitable to become traders or merchants or to find other occupations. Sailors of skill were always needed, as were warriors, and Scandinavians soon became desired throughout Europe and the Middle East for their expertise on the sea and in war. The Byzantine emperors, for example, employed a large number of Vikings in their special bodyguard unit, the Varangian Guard.

Conversion to Christianity. Fourth, by the end of the ninth and beginning of the tenth centuries most Scandinavians began to convert to Christianity. While not affecting the end of the Magyar raids—their conversion to Christianity would come later—the desire of Vikings to raid monasteries and other Christian sites obviously was diminished by these conversions.

National Leaders. Finally, by the eleventh century the loose confederations of Vikings and Magyars that had long participated in invasions were becoming unified into states in their homelands. Norway, Sweden, Denmark, and Hungary all had kings by this time, and these "national" leaders frequently needed whatever soldiers they could find, including all who in previous generations would have gone on raids. In fact, all of the so-called eleventh-century invasions undertaken by Vikings against England were in actuality attempted conquests by Danish and Norwegian kings: those of Sweyn I Forkbeard and Canute I were successful; those of Harald Hardrada and Olaf III were not.

Sources:
R. H. C. Davis, *A History of Medieval Europe: From Constantine to Saint Louis* (London & New York: Longmans, Green, 1957).

Peter G. Foote and David M. Wilson, *The Viking Achievement: The Society and Culture of Early Medieval Scandinavia* (London: Sidgwick & Jackson, 1970).

Gwyn Jones, *A History of the Vikings* (London & New York: Oxford University Press, 1968).

F. Donald Logan, *The Vikings in History,* second edition (London & New York: HarperCollins Academic, 1991).

C. A. Macartney, *The Magyars in the Ninth Century* (Cambridge: Cambridge University Press, 1968).

Peter Sawyer, *The Age of the Vikings* (New York: St. Martin's Press, 1962).

Sawyer, *Kings and Vikings: Scandinavia and Europe, A.D. 700–1100* (London & New York: Methuen, 1982).

SIGNIFICANT PEOPLE

FREDERICK I (FREDERICK BARBAROSSA)

CIRCA 1123-1190
HOLY ROMAN EMPEROR

Consolidation of Power. The son of Frederick II, duke of Swabia, Frederick I (Frederick Barbarossa or Frederick the Red Beard) of the Hohenstaufen dynasty was elected Holy Roman Emperor on 4 March 1152. As the king of Germany (1152–1190) and later the king of Italy (1155–1190), Frederick I constantly struggled for the predominance of the Empire over the various European monarchies and the papacy. His adoption of the term *Holy Empire* to describe his kingdom and steadfast opposition to the Pope made him a symbol of German unity for later generations.

Lombardy. The key to Frederick I's plan to dominate Europe was the rich region of Lombardy in northern Italy. By integrating Lombardy with his German holdings, the emperor would have the financial resources to control his German princes and build a powerful state. Eventually, Frederick I conducted six military campaigns in Italy in a futile effort to accomplish this goal.

Opposition. In 1155 he restored Pope Adrian IV to power and received as his reward a coveted papal coronation. Although an imperial diet or general assembly officially sanctioned his Italian claims, Milan and the Norman Kingdom of Sicily resisted his extension of authority. Alexander III, the new pope as of 1159, also voiced his opposition. In 1176 Italian forces soundly defeated Frederick I's army at Legnano, and in the subsequent Peace of Constance (1183) Frederick I recognized the autonomy of the Lombard cities.

Providing for the Future. After the Peace of Constance Frederick I seems to have come to the realization that the Holy Roman Empire would never be more than a fragmented entity. Nevertheless, he attempted to ensure a new territorial base for future emperors by permitting his son, the future Henry VI, to marry Constance, heiress to the Kingdom of Sicily, in 1186. Unfortunately, such political machinations only alienated the papacy even further.

Third Crusade. In 1189 Frederick I answered the call to participate in the Third Crusade (1189–1192) to free Jerusalem from the Muslims under Saladin. Before departing, he attempted to appease the Pope by returning lands in Tuscany to the control of the papacy. While fording the Saleph River in present-day southern Turkey in 1190, Frederick I fell from his horse and drowned.

Sources:

Peter Munz, *Frederick Barbarossa: A Study in Medieval Politics* (Ithaca, N.Y.: Cornell University Press, 1969).

Marcel Pacaut, *Frederick Barbarossa* (New York: Scribners, 1970).

Brian Tierney and Sidney Painter, *Western Europe in the Middle Ages, 300–1475,* sixth edition (Boston: McGraw-Hill, 1998).

LOUIS IX (SAINT LOUIS)

1214-1270
KING OF FRANCE

Perfect Ruler. Louis IX or Saint Louis of the Capetian dynasty ruled France from 1226 to 1270 and embodied the medieval view of a perfect ruler. The grandson of Philip II Augustus and son of Louis VIII, he inherited a stable kingdom. Louis IX was endowed with a piety and moral character that surpassed that of other kings and even popes. His domestic reforms helped instill a strong sense of national feeling throughout his realm.

Foreign Policy. Part of Louis IX's success as king was his ability to steer a neutral course through the delicate waters of medieval international relations. For example, in the Treaty of Paris (1259) Louis IX allowed the English monarch, Henry III, to keep substantial territorial possessions on the Continent, although the French king clearly had the upper hand. He received many papal favors by remaining out of the prolonged struggle between the German Hohenstaufens and Rome.

Domestic Policy. Domestic reform represented Louis IX's greatest achievement as king. He dispatched *enquêteurs* (royal commissioners) to monitor local governmental administration and provided for the judicial right of appeal from local to higher courts. Moreover, he devised a tax system, which by medieval standards was quite equitable.

Canonization. Louis IX patronized the arts and literature. During his reign some of the greatest intellectuals in Europe, such as Saint Thomas Aquinas and Saint Bonaventure, flocked to Paris. Something of a religious fanatic, he sponsored the French Inquisition and personally led two crusades against the Muslims. The first military expedition (1248–1254) resulted in his capture in Egypt and eventual ransom for one million marks. In 1270 he embarked on a second equally disastrous mission. He landed in present-day Tunisia, where he quickly succumbed to the plague. His body was brought back to France via Italy, and crowds gathered to witness the procession. In 1297 Pope Boniface VIII canonized Louis IX, the only French king ever to receive a sainthood.

Sources:

H. E. J. Cowdrey, *Popes, Monks, and Crusades* (London: Hambledon, 1984).

William C. Jordan, *Louis IX and the Challenge of the Crusade: A Study in Rulership* (Princeton: Princeton University Press, 1979).

Jean Richard, *Saint Louis* (Cambridge & New York: Cambridge University Press, 1992).

RICHARD I (RICHARD THE LION-HEART)

1157-1199
KING OF ENGLAND

Absentee Monarch. Richard I (Richard the Lion-Heart) was the third son of Henry II and Eleanor of Aquitaine. He inherited the English throne from his father in 1189; from that date until his death in 1199, he spent only five months in his island kingdom. The rest of the time, Richard I spent either administering his French territories (Aquitaine, Poitou, Normandy, and Anjou) or fighting the Muslims in the Holy Land. Despite Richard I's reputed brave leadership, from which he acquired the sobriquet *Lion-Heart,* both of these endeavors turned out less than successful, in part because of his impetuous nature and cruelty.

Third Crusade. In 1187 Saladin, the sultan of Egypt and Syria, took the city of Jerusalem, which caused the papacy to call for the Third Crusade (1189–1192). Richard I quickly diminished his royal coffers by purchasing arms and ships and assembling a large army to defeat the Islamic menace. His forces participated in the siege of Acre (which

fell in July 1191) and won a brilliant victory over Saladin at Arsuf on 7 September 1191. However, the recapture of the holy city of Jerusalem eluded him. The French, German, and English contingents of the Crusaders' army distrusted each other. The hot-tempered Richard I argued with Philip II Augustus of France and on one occasion he insulted Leopold V, duke of Austria, by tearing down his royal banner.

Imprisonment. In September 1192 Richard I signed a three-year truce with Saladin and sailed for home via the Adriatic Sea in order to avoid traveling through France. Driven ashore by a storm, he landed in Venice and quickly donned a disguise in order to avoid discovery by Duke Leopold. Unfortunately, his identity was soon revealed and the duke imprisoned him in a castle at Dürnstein on the Danube River. Leopold eventually turned his English prisoner over to the Holy Roman Emperor Henry VI who demanded a hefty ransom from Richard I: 150,000 marks.

Return Home. By early 1194 most of the ransom had been paid and Richard I returned to England. After being crowned for a second time, he departed for Normandy to wage war on the French king. He rashly attacked the Vicomte of Limoges's castle after hearing rumors of local peasants discovering gold and hoarding it there. A bolt fired from an enemy crossbow wounded the English monarch, who died shortly thereafter of an infection.

Sources:

James A. Brundage, *Richard, Lion Heart* (New York: Scribners, 1974).

John Gillingham, *Richard the Lionheart* (London: Weidenfeld & Nicolson, 1978).

Geoffrey Regan, *Lionhearts: Saladin, Richard I, and the Era of the Third Crusade* (New York: Walker, 1998).

James Reston, *Warriors of God: Richard the Lionheart and Saladin in the Third Crusade* (New York: Doubleday, 2001).

WILLIAM I (WILLIAM THE CONQUEROR)

CIRCA 1028-1087
DUKE OF NORMANDY AND KING OF ENGLAND

Establishing Authority. William I (William the Conqueror or William the Bastard) was the son of Robert I, duke of Normandy, and his concubine Herleva, a peasant girl. This illegitimacy did not, however, keep him from becoming one of the most important military and political leaders of the Middle Ages. As a youth he developed an intelligence and shrewdness that served him well as an adult. Succeeding his father as duke in 1035, William I began to put down rebel elements of the duchy who questioned his right to rule, a process not completed until 1060, when he defeated a combined army sent against him by King Henry I of France and Count Geoffrey Martel of Anjou. He then conquered the county of Maine in 1063.

Across the Channel. When Edward the Confessor died in 1066, William I made a hereditary claim to the Anglo-Saxon throne (Edward's mother was a Norman) and invaded the island kingdom. He won a brilliant victory at Hastings that same year and on Christmas Day he was crowned king of England in Westminster Abbey. Nonetheless, opposition to his rule was not effectively crushed for another twenty years. In fact, the intermittent civil strife gave William I a distaste for his newly acquired kingdom, and he decided to rule it from Normandy.

Maintaining Control. William I organized his new territory across the Channel carefully: he established a strong monarchy by making every landholder a direct vassal of the Crown and not some territorial prince; he allowed the Anglo-Saxons to keep most of their own statutes and courts; and he preserved the quasi-democratic tradition of "parleying" (the frequent holding of conferences between the king and the nobles). Between 1085 and 1086 William I commissioned a county-by-county assessment of his English realm. This detailed census became known as the *Domesday Book* (from the Old English word *dome*, meaning "reckoning") for its thoroughness and finality.

Continental Threats. Meanwhile, political intrigue on the Continent mounted as William I's enemies there (Philip I of France and Canute IV of Denmark) became more powerful and threatened the frontiers of Normandy, primarily Maine and the Vexin on the Seine. In 1077 Philip I seized three key towns in the eastern part of the Vexin—Chaumont, Mantes, and Pontoise. Ten years later when William I entered Mantes by surprise, he suffered a severe injury while the town burned. He lingered for five weeks, during which time he divided his territorial possessions among his two oldest sons: Robert Curthose received Normandy and Maine while William Rufus took control of England. William I died on 9 September 1087.

Sources:
Frank Barlow, *The Feudal Kingdom of England, 1042–1216* (London & New York: Longmans, Green, 1955).

Barlow, *William I and the Norman Conquest* (London: English Universities Press, 1965).

David C. Douglas, *William the Conqueror: The Norman Impact Upon England* (Berkeley: University of California Press, 1964).

C. Warren Hollister, ed., *The Impact of the Norman Conquest* (New York: Wiley, 1969).

David Armine Howarth, *1066: The Year of the Conquest* (London: Collins, 1977).

Dorothy Whitelock and others, *The Norman Conquest: Its Setting and Impact* (London: Eyre & Spottiswoode, 1966).

DOCUMENTARY SOURCES

Anglo-Saxon Chronicle (circa 871–1154)—Manuscript records that were compiled into a chronological account of Anglo-Saxon and Norman England; only seven of the manuscripts are extant.

Bayeux Tapestry (circa 1092)—An embroidery measuring 231 feet in length and 19.5 inches in width. It depicts more than seventy scenes from the Norman Conquest of England in 1066. The tapestry is an important source of medieval history, especially in regard to military equipment and tactics. The French antiquarian and scholar Bernard de Montfaucon credited Matilda, the wife of William I (the Conqueror), with making the tapestry, although there is no evidence to sustain this theory.

Cantar del mio Cid (The Poem of the Cid, circa 1150)—A poem about the Castilian hero Rodrigo Diaz de Vivar, known as El Cid (the lord or master), who captured the rich Muslim kingdom of Valencia and defeated the Almoravides, a warlike people from North Africa.

Munimenta Gildhallae Londoniensis, volume II, *Liber Custumarum* (circa 1320)—A compilation of London customary laws in the time of King Edward II (1307–1327), a work that was consulted by the mayors of London and other towns seeking constitutional guidance.

Domesday Book (1085–1086)—A comprehensive census of England undertaken after the Norman conquest of 1066.

Ekkehard of Aura, *Hierosolymita* (circa 1101)—A painstaking and rather objective account of the First Crusade (1095–1099) by a German monk and historian.

De legibus et consuetudinibus regni Angliae (Concerning the Laws and Customs of the Kingdom of England, circa 1154–1189)—The first authoritative text on English common law, possibly written by Ranulf de Glanvill, Henry II's chief legal adviser.

Magna Carta (Great Charter, 1215)—A charter of English liberties granted by King John I under threat of civil war. It reaffirmed traditional rights and personal liberties that are the basis of current English law.

Bartolo of Sassoferrato, *Treatise on City Government* (circa 1330)—A commentary on tyranny in Italian city governments.

Giovanni Villani, *Florentine Chronicle* (circa 1300)—A history of a leading Italian city-state and a vivid picture of medieval life. The author was a prominent merchant and politician of Florence who died in 1348, presumably from the Black Death.

Geoffrey de Villehardouin, *Memoirs* or *Chronicle of the Fourth Crusade and the Conquest of Constantinople* (circa 1202).

Knight taking communion; thirteenth-century stone relief from the Rheims Cathedral

CHAPTER SEVEN

LEISURE, RECREATION, AND DAILY LIFE

by KATHRYN A. EDWARDS

CONTENTS

814*

- Prepared during the early decades of the ninth century, the Plan of St. Gall diagrams all the facilities that should be a part of an ideal monastery.

- Having conducted raids on Great Britain for several decades in the late eighth century, the various Scandinavian peoples known collectively as the Vikings begin to raid the European continent, disrupting European society and economy for approximately the next one hundred years.

900*

- Over the next century the spread of the heavy moldboard plow and effective harnessing for horses allows farmers to increase crop yields from the heavy soil of northern Europe.

- Hops is used in brewing beer—stabilizing and preserving the beverage so that it can be shipped more easily and stored for longer periods; by the fourteenth century the use of hops has spread throughout Europe.

980

- The first stone castles are built in Germany and France.

1070*

- To commemorate the Norman Conquest of England in 1066, Bishop Odo, brother of William the Conqueror, commissions the Bayeux tapestry, one of the greatest surviving examples of the medieval weaver's art and an excellent source of information about military equipment in the eleventh century.

1085

- King Alfonso VI of Castile captures the Muslim city of Toledo in Spain, beginning an acceleration of the Christian reconquest of Muslim territories in Spain and Portugal and the transmission of Islamic manuscripts, including ancient Greek and Roman writings, to the Christian West.

1100*

- A new rural landscape emerges in Europe with extensive land clearance and the establishment of many new villages.

- Towns and cities become increasingly important in the European economy, especially in the most urbanized areas, such as the Mediterranean basin, the Rhineland corridor, southwestern Germany, and the Low Countries.

- Reading and listening to romances becomes fashionable in the courts of western and central Europe.

- The mechanized horizontal loom is developed, allowing for more efficient and precise weaving of cloth, contributing to the rise of the professional weaver, and gradually removing from the medieval household the task of weaving cloth for family use.

1103

- Strong winds and hail damage crops throughout the center of England, resulting in famine.

* DENOTES CIRCA DATE

1144
- Abbot Suger's renovations of St. Denis outside of Paris begin the development of the Gothic style in cathedral architecture.

1150*
- Fitted clothing becomes fashionable among the nobility, and later in the decade multicolored hose comes into style.

1180*
- Glass mirrors with lead backing come into use.

1182
- King Philip Augustus of France expels the Jews from all of the territory he controls. Similar expulsions occur throughout much of Europe at various times in the Middle Ages.

1190*
- Philip Augustus of France passes a series of regulations designed to make Paris a fit capital for a king. His plans include rebuilding the fortifications and paving the main thoroughfares.

1191
- An eclipse of the sun is seen in England and interpreted as foreshadowing great trials that King Richard the Lionheart will face.

1200*
- Specialized agriculture has been established in various regions throughout Europe. Burgundy and Bordeaux concentrate on wine, while the area around Toulouse in southern France focuses on cloth dye. Northern England is known for its sheep and wool, while northern Germany develops a reputation for its cattle.
- During the early part of this century wall fireplaces with chimneys come into use for heating German houses.

1250*
- Coats of plate armor, known as brigandines, are developed to be worn over mail; this armor protects knights against cuts and crushing injuries better than mail, but it is less flexible.

1285
- Eyeglasses are developed in Florence, Italy. They have convex lenses to help farsighted people; lenses for correcting nearsightedness are not invented until the sixteenth century.

1315
- Over the next three years famine spreads throughout most of central and western Europe. Recurrent famines and outbreaks of disease mark the first half of the fourteenth century.

* DENOTES CIRCA DATE

1330*

- The term *fashion of the young* is used to describe the costumes in style at the court of Philip of Valois, King of France. Their short tunics distinguish young nobles from the elderly, commoners, and women, who wear long, less-stylish tunics.

1347

- The first cases of the Black Death appear in Sicily; by 1350 it has spread all over Europe.

* **Denotes Circa Date**

An abandoned medieval peasant village in Northumberland, England, with the outlines of buildings and the ridges and furrows of surrounding fields still apparent from the air

OVERVIEW

A Society of Orders. In the eleventh century Bishop Adalbero of Laon wrote a poem to King Robert of France that included the following lines: "Triple then is the house of God which is thought to be one: on Earth, some pray, others fight, still others work; which three are joined together and may not be torn asunder." These lines express an ideal view of society that became a commonplace among medieval intellectuals. While this three-part system may have had little to do with reality—and had less and less as time passed—it suggests how medieval Europeans of all social classes tried to create order in their world. The three orders, as Adalbero's schema was later called, may seem rigid to modern eyes, but many medieval people equated stability and structure with security. Medieval Europeans did not reject change, but they preferred it to occur within established frameworks and relatively predictable patterns. Such assumptions and values also underlay the daily practices and material culture of medieval Europeans. Festivals, sports, individual combat, and banquets provided outlets for tensions while affirming the established order. Clothing, residences, furniture, and livestock were both necessary commodities and statements of an individual's or a household's status within a precisely defined community. Property, appearance, and behavior were expected to reinforce an orderly and stable society.

Society and Disorder. People of all social classes in medieval Europe had good reasons for valuing stability and peace. Through most of western and central Europe, the ninth century began with Viking raids, and they recurred for more than a century. With the breakdown of governmental institutions came increased lawlessness, and a peasant never knew what would happen when he saw a group of horsemen rounding a bend. Chronicles from the ninth, tenth, and eleventh centuries are filled with accounts of bands of soldiers who plundered for their livelihoods. Attempts were made to curtail these activities: lords increased their fortifications and garrisons, and the clergy proposed the Peace and Truce of God, which penalized soldiers if they fought at certain days and times. Such measures were largely ineffective. Warfare was not the only random threat to the daily lives of medieval Europeans. Farmers' dependence on the climate meant that famine was an ongoing possibility during much of this time period. In

a bad decade it could occur every three years, while during good times peasants might expect to face a bad harvest every five to ten years. With famine generally came disease, as the body's resistance was lowered because of poor nutrition. Epidemics and more-common medical conditions made the lives of peasants and nobles, men and women, hazardous and unpredictable. Kings died of salmonella from eating undercooked pork, peasant women from infections after childbirth, and monks from influenza after exposure to cold during their prayers. Order was valued precisely because the world seemed so disordered.

The Ideal and the Real. The ideal of the "three orders" thus had a place in medieval European society. In reality, however, this classification was simplistic even by the standards of the eleventh century. Under the category of those who work fell the landed and the landless, craftsmen and beggars, bankers and manual laborers. Members of this third order fully appreciated the distinctions among the social groups within their order and expressed them through their property and practices. The three orders omitted townspeople, who by the thirteenth century had become the most dynamic and innovative members of medieval society. If townspeople are added as an unofficial fourth order, however, this structure can be quite useful in describing the daily lives of medieval people. It suggests the varied environments in which they lived, the ways their lives were organized, and the expectations they could have—as well as the distinctions in their clothing, food, and shelter and their work and fun.

A Medieval Renaissance. Beginning in the mid eleventh century, medieval European society gave clear signs that it had recovered or would soon recover from the disorder of the previous centuries. The years circa 1050–1250 are often called the High Middle Ages because of the growth and innovations that occurred in this period. The dramatic developments in governmental centralization, education, philosophy, religion, and literature had parallels in the daily lives of many Europeans. Expanded tax bases and international trade allowed nobles and members of the higher clergy to improve their castles, clear more land, enjoy more luxury materials, and experiment with a more diversified diet. Through noble patronage, cities grew throughout western and central Europe and played a key role in fostering the expanding medieval economy. Innovations in many basic crafts—farming, weaving, and metallurgy, to name a few—added further impetus to economic expansion. For the first time in centuries, Europeans from many social groups (notably nobles, clergy, and merchants) were exposed to non-Europeans when they fought in the series of Crusades to the Holy Lands that began in 1096 and when they went on missions and trading voyages as far east as China. Although the average peasant was unaware of such travels, he benefited from the economic growth they sparked. Depending on local conditions, peasants had opportunities to diversify into additional crafts, to contract with a lord to pioneer new territory, or to move to a city, where after a year and a day he or she would gain freedom from serfdom.

The Crisis of the Fourteenth Century. By the last quarter of the thirteenth century, evidence suggests, the medieval economy was slowing. Given its limited capacity for economic growth, it appears that medieval society was nearing the peak population it could support. Future prospects for the young at all social levels became grim; there were only so many times a peasant holding or a lordship could be subdivided. Cities continued to need influxes of people from the countryside to maintain their populations, but migration to a city was no guarantee of success and comfort. In France the Hundred Years War, which began in 1337, left companies of unemployed soldiers searching for food, shelter, and plunder during the many breaks in the fighting, and in the Holy Roman Empire the weakness of the emperor resulted in its many lords fighting for territories and status. A series of bad winters and damp summers led to harvest failures throughout the second decade of the fourteenth century, and the ensuing famine swept across all of Europe. With this famine came various plagues: typhoid, cholera, malaria, influenza, and many that cannot be identified. At the same time several of the leading banks in Europe collapsed, which shocked international trade. The 1320s and 1330s were difficult decades in many parts of Europe as everyone from peasants to nobles faced uncertain harvests and wobbly economic foundations. Finally, in 1347 Europeans faced the most dramatic crisis yet: the Black Death. Indiscriminately striking rich and poor, leaving some villages untouched while wiping out others, the Black Death seemed like the wrath of a vengeful God punishing all mankind for its sins. The reconstruction of Europe as the first wave of the Black Death began to pass in 1350 set the stage for innovations in material culture and daily life that would become the Renaissance.

TOPICS IN LEISURE, RECREATION, AND DAILY LIFE

FARMERS AND PEASANTS: BUILDING PEASANT COMMUNITIES

The Appearance of Medieval Europe. European society in the Middle Ages was essentially rural, and most of its population made its living through agriculture. Beginning in the tenth century, as the worst of the Viking raids tapered off and the European population and economy began to rebound, medieval people started to clear land at a rate that had not been matched for centuries. The extent of these clearances has led some historians to talk about a "new rural landscape" developing in Europe by 1100. Villages—communities with populations of fifty to four hundred people—expanded all over Europe, even into areas that had not previously been populated. Despite these clearances, however, much of Europe was still unsettled. Peasants lived close to forests that could be mysterious and dangerous, and, when the sun set, darkness settled everywhere. With unknown threats surrounding them, many people spent most of their lives within a twenty-mile radius of where they were born. In this sense, then, the village in which the peasant lived and the manor of which it was a part were the basic social units of medieval Europe.

Manors and Communities. Approximately 90–95 percent of the medieval European population lived in the countryside, and many of these people lived in villages. The size of a village depended on many conditions, including its age, location, prosperity, and level of health. Villagers were essentially farmers, and they distributed neighboring lands and cultivated them in different ways depending on where in Europe they were located. As a general rule, the land-distribution system known as open field was practiced on the plain of northern Europe and in a large band of land stretching through England. In woodlands distribution,

Reconstruction of a medieval peasant house at Singleton Open Air Museum in Sussex, England

country pasture and arable lands were intermixed; the areas where this distribution was practical included Brittany, Normandy, and patches of the west, northwest, and southeast of England. In southern Europe, in particular, some villages were located on hills overlooking the lands the villagers cultivated. The judicial and administrative unit of the manor overlay these villages; it is sometimes useful to think of the village as a piece of paper with the basic outline of a picture on it, and the manor as another transparent piece of paper that is put on top of the village and, when combined with the village, adds depth to the picture. The manor was the basic source of revenue for medieval lords and nobles. While a manor was usually about the size of a village and its lands, some villages were divided between manors, and other manors controlled several villages. In general the manors and their lords controlled 35–40 percent of a village's land, although at times this figure could be as high as 75–80 percent. The populations of villages—and the people whom manors controlled—were often quite small when seen village by village. For example, there were approximately two dozen households and 125–150 people living in the English village of Cuxham during the thirteenth century. Even within this small community, however, there were distinctions in wealth and status that every member of the community appreciated. At the top of the village hierarchy were the village priest, two free tenants, a miller, and the reeve (the lord's representative and all-purpose judge). Next came the approximately fourteen unfree tenants who had their own land, some of whom were women. Below them in the community came the approximately

eight unfree cottagers, that is, people without their own land to cultivate.

Village Organization in Northern Europe. Although villages did vary region by region, successful villages shared some common patterns. Villages in much of northern Europe were either organized around a village square that often had the church and churchyard in the center or around a main street or junction with the church or manor house at a crossroads. This second pattern is often the sign of a planned village with layout and lots determined by a representative of the villagers' lord. Most European villages did not have fortifications nearby, and the church frequently served as the village stronghold. The roads and paths between houses were dirt, and in a well-located site a stream was nearby to supply water for the community. Village houses did not share walls, as increasingly happened in cities. The houses were built on long, not quite rectangular lots (known in English as *tofts*), which the tenant either leased or in rare cases owned. On a toft would be a garden, a cesspit, and whatever outbuildings the peasant could afford. Chickens, goats, and other small livestock would be kept on this property, and their produce—along with that of the garden—would supplement the peasant's harvest from the fields. At the center of the village might be a village green on which cattle and other livestock could graze and wander. This green or the village churchyard also served as a meeting place where villagers might have community councils, determine the allocation of fields, or even hold a festival. Here, too, would be the location of a market, if a village had permission from its lord to hold one, and sometimes the market stalls would spread into the cemetery that was part of the churchyard. The living and the dead existed near each other in the medieval village.

Village Organization in Southern Europe. While villages in southern Europe had many of the same components as their northern counterparts, they could be organized quite differently, depending on the environment. In hilly or mountainous regions villages tended to be on a hillside with the village lands spreading down the hillside or in flatter spaces. Such a village also had a village square and individual peasant homes with small lots. In general, however, the houses were far closer together—sometimes even touching—than in northern Europe; the lots were also much smaller, and the population density was much higher. Many such villages were built along one or two primary streets and almost looked as if they were part of the hillside. Although there is no set explanation for why the appearance of southern European villages evolved so differently from that of the north, it has been suggested that they were built in these locations for protection and convenience. These large villages proved more difficult to conquer, and in them it was easier to obtain help from a neighbor.

Peasant Residences. While peasant houses were not the size of some modern homes, they were not the tiny hovels that popular imagination often makes them out to be. It has been repeatedly shown that in England, France, and Germany medieval peasant homes were rectangular, about 49–75 feet long by 13–20 feet wide—that is 637 to 1,500 square feet, the size of an average apartment or a two-to-three-bedroom house. Particularly in northern Europe, these buildings were divided into two parts, one for the humans and another for the animals; in southern Europe, where the climate was milder, a peasant might be able to afford a separate small stable or lean-to for his animals. There was typically a single door for the human residents and perhaps another for the animals' side and the storage areas. A wooden bar was placed across a door to lock it at night; only the rich used keys and generally only for chests and secure storage. Because windows let heat out and glass was expensive, the residence typically had only one window, which had no glass and was covered with shutters at night for security and warmth. The floor was dirt, but a wealthier household might strew some rushes or straw on it. In a peasant house that had been in place for several decades the floor level was often slightly lower than the ground outside because of years of sweeping and packing down the earth by walking. The fire was generally located in the center of the residence in an open pit. There was a small hole in the roof that was supposed to let out the smoke, but the room would often remain smoky. For peasants, wall fireplaces and enclosed stoves were generally later developments. Only in early thirteenth-century Germany did wall fireplaces with chimneys appear, but even at that time they were uncommon because of the difficulty and expense of construction.

Building a Peasant Home: Foundations and Walls. Houses were constructed in various ways, depending on the wealth of the peasant and the available building materials. The most basic houses had foundations that were just support posts driven into holes in the ground. Other foundations were posts set in trenches, while a third type had posts set in the ground on top of relatively flat stones, and the spaces around the posts were filled with a mixture of stones and dirt. The third type was the most labor intensive and expensive, but it made the foundation last longer because it did not have as much direct contact with dirt and moisture, which rotted the wood. The most expensive and elaborate constructions had stone foundations, but only in areas of predominantly stone construction would peasants be likely to have houses built with such supports. In most parts of Europe wood was the basic building material for the walls of peasant houses. Compared to stone, wood was relatively easy to obtain, move, and shape, and wooden walls kept the interior of the house warmer than stone walls. Wood walls, however, needed more frequent maintenance and rebuilding than stone. The most common wall-building method was to interlace tree branches to form the basic support and then to coat them with a clay and straw mixture, a process generally known as wattle-and-daub construction. While this method minimized drafts between the branches, it required continuous maintenance, but it was work that a relatively unskilled peasant could perform. More-elaborate peasant structures in northern European areas, such as Germany, were built with wooden planks linked together, but such construction was extremely expensive and became even more costly as wood became scarcer. Though stone was the most durable material, the costs of quarrying it, the skill needed to work it, and the time involved in building with it made stone peasant houses rare. Of course, there were exceptions. In certain areas of Scotland and Ireland wood was a precious commodity, and stone was the most plentiful building material available. Moreover, in the twelfth and thirteenth centuries villages of predominantly stone arose, especially in southern Europe, but they were also in regions where wood was considered too valuable for building and stone was easy to obtain.

Roofs and Materials. Roofing a peasant house was a problem. A roof needed almost the same amount of wood as the walls, which made construction expensive. Moreover, finding roofing materials to put over the wooden framing could be difficult. The most common roofing material was of some form of straw; wheat, rye, or various wild grasses were used, depending on the region. Groups of trained men wove the straw and then layered it to a thickness of approximately 1–2 feet. They performed this work on the wooden roof framework, which had to be built at a 40–55 degree angle to allow for water runoff. While the materials were relatively inexpensive and easy to obtain, there were drawbacks to such a roof, commonly called a thatched roof. It was quite flammable and provided a home for mice, wasps, spiders, and other small pests. Wooden roof shingles were also used in areas where wood was relatively plentiful, such as medieval England and Scandinavia.

Stone and turf were other possible roofing materials, but they were available in only a few areas or were too expensive for common use in villages. Tiles and slates were generally luxury materials and, as such, might be found only on the roof of the village church or the local manor house. Even when only the least expensive and most basic materials were used, a peasant house was still a substantial investment. An excavation of a Neolithic house that was built by construction methods almost exactly like those used in medieval France provides a telling example of the materials and effort involved in building a house. The tools used to build were an ax, sickle, and spade. The roof required 200 wooden poles about 1½–2½ inches in diameter; 80 of these poles were 13 feet long, and 120 were 8 feet long. A total of 1½ tons of reeds were also used for the roof. To tie the poles and reeds together the builders used three miles of vegetable material, such as hemp. The walls needed 6,000 flexible sticks of ⅜ to ¾ inches in diameter and 4 feet long. The walls also required 15 tons of clay soil and 440 pounds of chopped straw mixed with around 1,000 gallons of water to form the daub that filled in the spaces in the walls between sticks. All these materials were used in a building 18 feet wide and 39 feet long, in other words a relatively small house.

Sources:

Jean Chapelot and Robert Fossier, *The Village and House in the Middle Ages,* translated by Henry Cleere (London: Batsford, 1985).

Christopher Dyer, "English Peasant Buildings in the Later Middle Ages (1200–1500)," *Medieval Archaeology,* 20 (1986): 19–45.

John Hunt, *Lordship and the Landscape: A Documentary and Archaeological Study of the Honor of Dudley c. 1066-1322* (Oxford: BAR, 1997).

Norman J. G. Pounds, *Hearth and Home: A History of Material Culture* (Bloomington: Indiana University Press, 1989).

Pierre Riché, *Daily Life in the World of Charlemagne,* translated by Jo Ann McNamara (Philadelphia: University of Pennsylvania Press, 1978).

FARMERS AND PEASANTS: FOOD AND THE HARVEST

Reclaiming Land. The available technology limited the size of the village. All the land its residents worked had to be within close enough walking distance for the peasant to be able walk back and forth to his field and do a full day's work within twelve to fourteen hours. In other words, most of the land that peasants farmed was within a one-hour walk from the village, and much of it was closer. These limitations meant that a medieval village could quickly become pressed for land as its population grew, and some techniques were developed to extend a village's arable land or at least to make it more fertile. Large-scale land reclamation in the form of dikes and other drainage projects did not occur in Europe until the eighteenth and nineteenth centuries, but certain areas, such as Flanders and the Netherlands, took steps in that direction in the later Middle Ages. It is possible to drain land by plowing in a direction that facilitates runoff, such as on top of a ridge, and there are examples of peasants in England and France using this technique when planning fields. Ways to increase the fertility of the soil were employed more widely than such attempts at land reclamation. The traditional and least

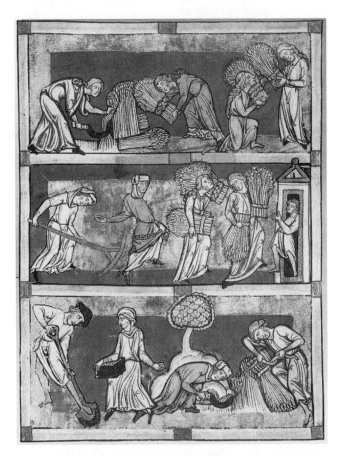

Peasants harvesting grain; illumination in a twelfth-century manuscript for *A Mirror for Maidens,* an advice book for novice nuns (Rheinisches Landesmuseum, Bonn)

labor-intensive method was to leave a field alone for a season, that is, to let it lie fallow. Depending on their resources, peasants also amended the soil. In parts of England marl was spread on fields; marl is a clay soil containing a carbonate of lime, and lime increases nitrogen in the soil, accelerating plant growth. Manure mixed with straw (compost) could also be spread on fields. Yet, often neither marl nor compost was available in a quantity necessary for it to be effective. In other words, peasant resources for improving or expanding arable land were limited.

Crops and Land. Peasants used much of the arable land they controlled, beyond that around their residences, for growing grain. The type of grain and the method they used to plow and plant varied greatly depending on climate and tradition. The staple grain was whichever variety grew best in the region: rye in the mountains; wheat in lowlands; barley, oats, vetch, and others throughout Europe. By the tenth and eleventh centuries in most parts of central and western Europe, these grains were grown in rotation to maximize productivity. For example, wheat and rye were traditionally sown (planted) in the fall, while barley, oats, vetch, and peas were sown in the early spring. Crop rotation could occur two or three times a year depending on the period and the region, but generally every second or third year a field was left fallow to recover some fertility. By the twelfth and thirteenth centuries, as the European economy grew, certain regions began to specialize. For example, Burgundy and Bordeaux produced wine, while around Toulouse in southern France the peasants concentrated on growing the plants from which blue and yellow dyes were made. Northern England was known for its sheep, while northern Germany specialized in cattle. In order to support such varied styles of agriculture, the ways peasants distributed village lands were also different. In some parts of Europe a peasant's landholdings formed a solid block of property, but the common pattern in France, England, and western Germany was for all the village lands to be divided into strips. Each landholding peasant had rights to a certain number of strips, and they were scattered all over the village lands. This method ensured that no single peasant household monopolized all the best land.

Plowing and Planting. One of the great technological revolutions of the Middle Ages was the development of the moldboard plow, which allowed a farmer to plow the land more deeply than he could using an older, traditional plow, thus making his land more arable. In the areas where the traditional plow continued to be used—and there were many—the general procedures were similar. Depending on climate, around the beginning of October a farmer began to break up the soil in his fields so that it would be ready for planting. He and his son, a male relative, another farmer, or even a female family member hitched a team of horses or oxen to the plow. While one person guided the team, the other guided the plow, and they would begin making long, straight furrows up and down their narrow strips of land. After the furrows had been made, the farmer placed his seed in a basket or bag draped across his chest and scattered the seed on the field. After all the seed had been spread, he brought the team of horses or oxen out again and attached them to a harrow, a rectangular or square metal frame with downward-facing metal spikes that raked the fields as it was pulled, leveling the furrows and covering the seed. Finally each household in the village was responsible for planting or maintaining a certain length of hedge or border around the field so that village animals could not eat the crop. All this work needed to be completed within a month, and it was repeated again in the spring, when a new crop was sown. While grown men normally did the plowing and planting because of the strength that was needed to use a moldboard plow, boys as young as seven could remove stones from the fields and chase away birds and other animals that might eat seeds or damage the crop. When they were needed, women also worked in the fields.

The Harvest. One of the peasants' most backbreaking and important chores was harvesting their crops. At harvest time in particular all members of the village turned out to lend a hand. Women and children worked alongside husbands, fathers, and brothers to bring in the crop on which they depended; a mother with an infant would put it in a carrier that was hung from a low limb so that animals could not injure or eat the child. Those villagers who did not have sufficient land for their needs or who had no land at all

worked as laborers for other villagers. Harvesters worked their way down a field using sickles to cut off the grain near its base. This grain was left to dry and turned with pitchforks, usually for a few days, depending on the climate. A sudden downpour could mean famine for a village. Once the grain was dry enough so that it would not rot while stored, it was gathered into bundles (sheaves) and brought back to buildings where it would be kept. The poorest peasants might end up carrying these bundles on their backs, but normally several wagons owned by the most prosperous peasants in the village were hired out to carry the grain. Once the harvest had been gathered, peasants opened the barriers around the fields, and cattle and other livestock were allowed to graze on the stubble (chaff).

Gathering Food. Peasants had other sources of food besides the grain they grew in their fields. In their tofts they grew garden vegetables appropriate to their climate, including radishes, celery, carrots, cabbage, onions, lettuce, and spinach. They also might have a few fruit and nut

AN OXHERD'S JOB

A medieval lord prepared lists of customary rents and services that he was owed and generally bound them together in a book known in England as a custumal. The following excerpt is from the Bleadon Custumal, prepared in Bleadon in southwestern England during the early thirteenth century. It describes the duties of an oxherd who worked on the manors of St. Swithin's Priory in Winchester.

[An oxherd] is ordained by office to keep oxen: He feedeth and nourisheth oxen, and bringeth them to leas [pasture] and home again; and bindeth their feet with landhaldes and spanells [types of hobbles] and nighteth and cloggeth them while they be in pasture and leas, and yoketh and maketh them draw at the plough; and pricketh the slow with a goad and maketh them draw even. And pleaseth them with whistling and with song, to make them bear the yoke with the better will for the liking of melody of the voice. And this herd[er] driveth and ruleth them not only to eat, but also to tread and to thresh. And they lead them about upon corn to break the straw in threshing and treading the flour. And when the travail is done, then they unyoke them and bring them to the stall, and feed them thereat. . . . when he fastens the cattle of the lord in the byre in winter, he must watch over them and get the hay and straw which they must eat, and he will carry it into the byre, and he will have what is left before two oxen, which is called orte, for the whole time the oxen of the lord are standing in the byre; and he will have his own ox fastened between two oxen of the lord from Christmas Eve to noon on Ascension Day; and he will watch over the oxen and cows and the other beasts of the lord in the byre day and night and he will give them to eat and will water them when it is needful.

Source: George C. Homans, *English Villagers of the Thirteenth Century* (New York: Norton, 1941), p. 47.

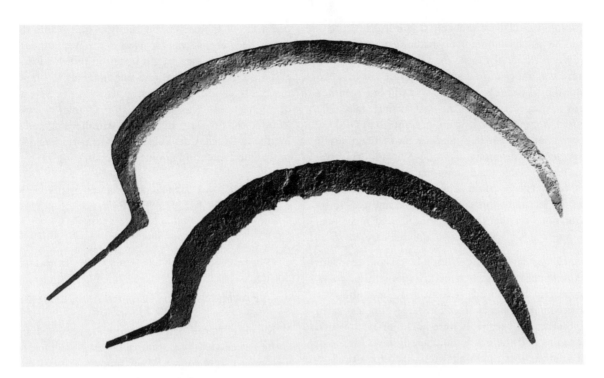

Medieval sickles, found at Caerlaverock, Dumfriesshire, in Scotland

trees; apple, pear, cherry, plum, chestnut, walnut, and almond trees are frequently mentioned in medieval documents. Peasants also brewed beer or made wine from their grain or grapes. Beer in northern Europe and wine in southern Europe were staple foods. Moreover, peasants had the right to gather food in the forest, which made available to them various herbs, fruits, and nuts, as well as wild mushrooms. Peasants were, however, prohibited to hunt and often not allowed to fish, and the penalties for violating these laws could be quite severe. Such regulations meant that peasant foods, especially for poorer peasants, were mostly limited to vegetables and fruits.

Storing and Preserving Food. It is estimated that an adult man in the Middle Ages needed at least 4,500 calories a day to support his activities, a figure that is almost twice the recommended caloric intake for an average modern man. With such needs it is not surprising that the bulk of a peasant's time was devoted to gathering and preserving food. Moreover, much of a medieval peasant's food supply was available only seasonally. Fruits and nuts were harvested when they were ripe, and certain seasons were known by what fruits appeared then. Some of whatever food was gathered needed to be kept for times of hardship, so preservation was a central problem and an important chore. Although cereals could be stored year-round in sheds, bins, or even in the rafters, there was always a chance that they would spoil or that rodents would get into them. When cereals were made into flour, they had a longer shelf life. Because beans and peas could be dried for use year-round, they were staples in a peasant diet. Peasants also preserved cow and goat milk by making it into butter and cheese; butter was packed in salt, and the reduced water content of cheese made it keep better. When meat was

available, it was salted and dried, and before it was used it had to be soaked in water several times. Meat was also a seasonal commodity because of the expense of keeping livestock through winter. November was known as butchering month, when elderly and excess livestock was killed, and meat was salted. As a result of their methods of obtaining food and their means of storing it, peasants had an extremely uneven diet, with feasts and famines occurring within months of one another.

Daily Meals. Although peasants had access to various foodstuffs, basic peasant food was quite simple. Generally meals were cooked over the fire in a pot into which had been put water, grains, and peas or beans. The mixture could be made more appetizing by adding herbs, other vegetables, fat, oil, or even a pinch of salt—depending on their availability and a peasant's wealth. Medieval peasants generally did not eat breakfast. Normally, the first meal was eaten between 10 A.M. and noon—after a morning's work had been accomplished. Supper was eaten in the early evening. The first meal was usually the largest, and if extra foodstuffs such as meat were available, they would appear on the table then. When meat was to be served, it was roasted beside the fire, and a wooden platter or container was placed under it to catch the drippings. This fat was useful in cooking and as grease for other household uses, such as softening chapped hands and oiling shoes. Beer and wine were another source of vitamins and calories for peasants, with the choice of beverage depending on region. The production of beer and wine for household use was most frequently women's work, although by the thirteenth century wine production had become more commercialized. It is estimated that a medieval European drank approximately a gallon of ale or a half-gallon of wine a day, although many peasants would have probably drunk less because of the cost. The alcohol content of medieval wine and ale, however, was substantially lower than their modern equivalents. Bread was another product that became less of a luxury during the Middle Ages, but it was still less common than grain porridge because of the cost in time, materials, and expertise to produce it. Because peasant homes did not contain ovens or did not have ready ways of maintaining the consistent heat necessary to produce bread, bread was often baked at a village bake house, and only a fairly large and prosperous village could support one. Moreover, the danger of fire led many lords and village committees to set strict regulations on the kinds of fires allowed in peasant homes and how hearths should be maintained and used.

Livestock. Aside from a peasant's house and land, his greatest investment was in livestock. Cattle, sheep, goats, pigs, and poultry were expensive to maintain and often the first sacrificed in times of famine. The largest domesticated animals peasants used regularly were horses or oxen, which were needed to pull the heavy moldboard plow. Although medieval treatises about plowing often called for a team of eight horses or oxen, it seems that most peasants worked with four animals. Oxen were cheaper to obtain and could tolerate coarser feed, but horses did not require any more feed and did half again as much work, making horses preferred draft animals. Given the costs of such animals, peasants combined their resources to buy a team or rent one from a prosperous neighbor. One reason that horses or oxen were expensive to support was that medieval peasants rarely cultivated hay just to feed their animals. Farmers relied on that natural hay that grew near rivers and streams, or in other low, wet places, and mowed these areas when they could. It was also common to allow cattle and horses into harvested fields to eat the chaff left after harvesting, a practice that had the advantage of scattering manure—that is, fertilizer—on the fields. A town bull was allowed to run loose in the town to impregnate cows. While the ownership of this bull and rights to a percentage of its calves' value was originally a noble's privilege, by the thirteenth century the village priest or a village committee also seems to have had this right. Medieval documents do not mention a town stallion, so it is not entirely clear how medieval villagers bred their horses.

Small Animals. Peasants often owned livestock such as pigs, goats, and poultry. Women generally tended these animals, as well as dairy cattle, and processed many of the animals' products. They clipped hair from sheep and goats to make cloth. They milked cows and churned the milk to produce butter and eggs. They collected eggs from chickens, which laid them all around the chicken yard and sometimes pecked at the egg gatherers. While many animals were kept in the farmyard around the peasant residence, others grazed on common lands, and some escaped from their enclosures. For example, pigs and other smaller livestock ran half wild. Many villages and even cities had individuals whose job it was to turn the villagers' livestock into the woods in the morning so that pigs and other animals could fatten themselves on the nuts and plants there. At times the livestock was gathered in the evening, but certain animals, such as pigs, might be left in the woods for weeks at a time. Peasants identified their animals by brands or by marks carved into the animal. Cats and dogs were also part of a village, more as working animals than as pets. Dogs guarded the property and helped with herding and managing the livestock. Cats killed the rodents that tended to live in thatched roofs and got into the grain supply.

Sources:

Robert Fossier, *Peasant Life in the Medieval West,* translated by Juliet Vale (Oxford & New York: Blackwell, 1988).

George C. Homans, *English Villagers of the Thirteenth Century* (New York: Norton, 1941).

Del Sweeney, ed., *Agriculture in the Middle Ages: Technology, Practice, and Representation* (Philadelphia: University of Pennsylvania Press, 1995).

FARMERS AND PEASANTS: CLOTHES AND HYGIENE

Keeping Warm. The fire pit in the center of a peasant house served as the sole source of heat, the cook fire, and the primary light source. Maintaining it was crucial and an ongoing chore. If the fire died out, it had to be restarted either by using embers borrowed from a neighbor or with a flint and steel, a relatively valuable tool. In the fire pit the peasant built a small pile of highly flammable objects, including materials such as dry grasses, tiny pieces of wood, or old scraps of cloth. When a spark flew off into these objects, the peasant coaxed it into flame by blowing on it and gradually feeding slightly larger kindling to the flame until a usable fire was achieved. Wood, however, was an exhaustible resource, and peasants were generally entitled only to windfall wood—branches or trees blown down in storms. The thin sticks that a peasant gathered were frequently bundled together to make something approximating a log and, therefore, a more consistent and durable fire. Although fire was essential for peasants, it was also a danger. Medieval records are filled with stories about people, especially young children, falling into a fire and being critically burned. To minimize such hazards, the fire was allowed to die down into embers during the evening and at night, so that the house cooled significantly while people were sleeping. Mornings were long and chilly, because reheating the house usually took hours. The fire had to be stoked; new wood and other supplies had to be gathered; and the heat had to radiate from the fire. Perhaps it is not surprising that peasants generally went immediately to the fields in the morning and returned to their homes only a few hours later for the main meal. The difficulties in heating peasant residences help to account for peasant clothing.

Medieval Clothes. Clothing in medieval Europe, even among peasants, had several functions. It kept a person warm, covered nakedness (which was considered shameful), and marked a person's status. For example, while medieval men and women sometimes stripped down to their shirts when doing heavy labor, both sexes considered public nakedness exceptionally embarrassing once one was no longer a child. In fact, a common part of medieval punishments

Peasants wearing braies that they have shortened with
ties hooked to their belts; illumination from the
Maciejowski Bible, Paris, circa 1250–1255
(Pierpont Morgan Library, New York)

involved stripping the guilty person and making him or her face his sentence naked. Clothes were thus an important investment, and an expensive one. Medieval peasants rarely, if ever, bought new clothes. They made their own basic garments or purchased secondhand ones from a merchant who specialized in selling used goods. Moreover, a peasant generally owned only a few pieces of clothing: two of each undergarment, one outer garment, a hat, a belt, and a pair of shoes. A person usually had only one article to wear while the rest were being washed. Men's and women's clothes differed to some extent. The first piece of clothing a man put on was a pair of half trousers made of linen or another thin material; known in English as *braies,* they resembled modern boxer shorts but went down to about mid calf. Elastic and zippers are modern inventions, and buttons were expensive decorations for a wealthy person's clothing, so braies were held up by rolling the top over at the waist several times and cinching it in place with a belt. Sometimes braies had ties at the bottom of each leg. They could be run through this belt to shorten the braies when one was working in the heat. Next a peasant pulled on a pair of woolen hose that ran from waist to foot and was attached to the braies by several leather thongs. Although medieval pictures depict hose as formfitting, the lack of elastic probably meant that it fit close to the body but not snugly. In many ways hose resembled loose modern stirrup pants. Over the braies and hose was put a linen shirt, which reached at least to the thighs and was slit up the side for mobility. Over all of these layers came a tunic, which for laborers probably reached no further than the knee, so that it did not get in the way while the peasant

worked. Tunics could have sleeves or be sleeveless, and they usually had a large head opening, which might have laces so that the material could be gathered close to the neck for warmth. Medieval women did not wear braies; instead, their first piece of clothing was a shirt that was a longer version of the man's shirt. When a woman wore hose, it generally went only to the knees. Her tunic was also like a man's, but it always went to the floor. Over their tunics both men and women wore narrow belts around their waists, and they could attach various objects to their belts, money pouches and knives being among the most common. In cold weather a peasant wore a wool mantle, a simple half circle of fabric with a center slit through which a person could put his or her head. Peasants might decorate any of these articles, but such work took time away from their extremely busy lives. There is almost no mention in medieval documents of specialized underwear or special clothes for sleeping. Normally peasants slept in the nude. If it was cold, a peasant might remove only his outer layer of clothes before he went to sleep.

Making Cloth and Clothing. One of a medieval woman's most time-consuming and onerous activities was making thread (spinning) and weaving it into cloth. Girls in the Middle Ages began helping with this task by at least the age of seven and did not stop until they died or their hands were so crippled from arthritis (or other diseases or injuries) that they were unable to manipulate the tools. In the early Middle Ages, when weaving was done on an upright loom, it could be a source of supplemental income for peasant families. By the twelfth and thirteenth centuries weaving for trade had become more of an urban craft, and most peasant weaving was done for private consumption. Producing clothes in medieval Europe began with the basics: gathering the raw materials. Flax plants (for linen) or wool from sheep was generally the base for thread, although many kinds of hair and fibers could be spun. First, the material was cleaned and combed to remove all dirt, and unusable fibers were removed to make the remaining fibers run parallel, which made it easier to spin and led to better cloth. The spinner attached one end of a fiber to the top of a spindle, a stick about one foot long with a weight at the bottom. Then she started spinning the spindle, which twisted the fibers together, and the weight pulled them into thread. Later in the Middle Ages a fairly prosperous peasant might have a spinning wheel, which allowed more thread to be spun with less effort, but it was always a luxury item. Once the thread was spun, it was made into cloth on a loom. After it was woven, fabric had to be finished, with the process varying depending on the type of fabric. If the cloth were dyed, and that worn by most medieval peasants was not, the dyes were based on natural materials. These dyes faded in the sun, so even dyed peasant clothes often looked washed out. Only the richest people could afford to redye their clothing. Once the cloth itself was produced, it had to be made into clothes. The tools used in this process involved a substantial investment: shears, needles, and some form of pin or fastener to hold pieces of cloth together. Metal needles were valuable goods. In many cases peasant clothing was designed to require little sewing, but darning and other repairs were needed during the long lifetime of a garment. Clothes were too valuable to be discarded just because they were torn.

Hats. In medieval society a hat was a necessary piece of clothing. It helped retain warmth, protected farmers from the heat and sun, and marked a villager's wealth and status. The most basic hat worn by men, particularly workers and farmers, was called a coif. It was a linen cap that covered the head and tied under the chin. It kept a man's head warm and his hair clean while he worked. Women's head coverings were also made of linen, but theirs were generally triangular. Rather than wrapping fully around a woman's head like a man's coif, a pointed part of the cloth draped off the back of the head and dropped down to the nape of the neck. Sometimes in the summer men and women wore straw hats, particularly while working the fields, to protect themselves from the sun. Hoods made of wool or even leather might be worn in cold weather for additional warmth or protection from rain or snow. While fur linings were the best way to keep warm, fur was generally a luxury and might only appear in or on a peasant's hat if it had been passed down from a wealthier owner.

Shoes and Other Apparel. Shoes provided important protection and warmth. Because making them required specialized skills and because they were made of leather, shoes were expensive, and they could wear out quickly. For these reasons, although medieval manuscripts generally depict farmers wearing something on their feet, it is unlikely that all peasants always wore shoes. When peasant men and women did wear shoes, they favored a low, leather boot, which probably lasted six months at most. By the twelfth century, shoes were held on a person's feet by leather thongs, which were laced around the ankle; examples from the next century also show these lacings going up the side of the ankle. There was no heel, and, when the sole wore through, another piece of leather was sewn on top of the existing sole. To make shoes somewhat watertight, people greased them with animal fat from slaughtered livestock. Attachments were also available to make shoes more functional. For example, wooden platforms could be laced onto regular leather shoes so that the wearer could avoid getting his or her shoes muddy.

Washing Clothes and Bodies. When the fabric was thought to be washable, it appears that peasants washed their clothing every week at most. Linen was one fabric that was washed in water using lye; then it was laid in the sun on a rock or the grass to dry. (Clothespins are another modern invention.) Wool was, however, probably the most common medieval fabric, and it was normally brushed rather than washed to remove dirt. In the rare cases that medieval peasants cared about wrinkles, a heated stone was run over the cloth. Laundry and bathing were both extremely laborious processes. Peasants generally washed their clothing in nearby streams and needed to carry it there. If hot water was used for washing, it had to be carried from the village water supply to a cauldron—itself a valuable commodity that not every peasant owned—and enough firewood had to be gathered to heat the water to an acceptable temperature. The effort and expense of generating hot water helps to explain the medieval reluctance to take full-immersion baths and even the insistence in some treatises that such baths cause sickness. Imagine taking a bath in a river when the water is near freezing, when it is 30–40 degrees outside, and the house is barely heated. Medieval people did wash parts of their bodies with some regularity, but peasants were often criticized for excessive odors. Hair was washed using a solution like that used for clothes. It also appears that medieval Europeans tried to clean their teeth; at least there are reports of people using woolen cloths and hazel twigs for this purpose. Shaving was also difficult because of the lack of hot water, mirrors, and skin softeners. It was a weekly occurrence at most and done with the all-purpose, long knife that most peasant men carried. Some peasants just settled for beards, and being clean shaven was often a mark of status.

Human Waste. Because they had no running water, there was no such thing as a flush toilet. Generally the most sophisticated plumbing facility available to a peasant was an outhouse built over a cesspit. Those living more comfortably might have a chamber pot in the house to use in the evening and be emptied into the cesspit in the morning. After defecating, people used hay, straw, grass, or some other vegetation to wipe themselves. Because of a relative lack of privacy for grooming or attending to basic bodily needs, medieval Europeans seem to have had a higher threshold of embarrassment than modern people about bodily fluids. According to Jeffrey L. Singman, "Medieval people were not very squeamish about urine: not only was it an essential element in tanning leather and fulling cloth, but the medieval physician's analysis of a patient's urine was expected to take into account taste as well as appearance."

Sources:

Hans-Werner Goetz, *Life in the Middle Ages: From the Seventh to the Thirteenth Century*, translated by Albert Wimmer, edited by Steven Rowan (Notre Dame, Ind.: University of Notre Dame Press, 1993).

H. E. Hallem, *Rural England, 1066–1348* (London: Fontana, 1981).

Jeffrey L. Singman, *Daily Life in Medieval Europe* (Westport, Conn.: Greenwood Press, 1999).

John Storck and Walter Dorwin Teague, *Flour for Man's Bread: A History of Milling* (Minneapolis: University of Minnesota Press, 1952).

FARMERS AND PEASANTS: HOUSEHOLD GOODS

Lighting a Peasant House. Because medieval residences had few windows, peasant homes were often so dark that it took one's eyes a few seconds to adjust when a person entered, even in daylight. Candles were a medieval invention. They could be made of wax from the honeycombs of bees or fashioned from tallow, which was made from sheep fat. Such candles, though, were often beyond the means of the ordinary peasant. When they had artificial lighting at all, most peasants made do with rushlights, which were lengths of rush, a variety of grass, dipped in fat. When lit, they offered little light and more smoke. Sometimes, particularly in southern Europe, peasants also used oil lamps, made according to a technology that went back to the Greeks and Romans. Each of these solutions cost precious

Interior of a medieval peasant house, with an open hearth on right, at the Singleton Open Air Museum in Sussex

resources, however, and many peasants just made do with natural light and whatever illumination they got from their fire. Soon after sunset, the day's activities ended because there was no longer enough light to work. At times several families congregated during the evenings in one residence to share light while socializing or working.

Basic Utensils. A peasant's basic goods were quite limited and varied greatly depending on whether the peasant was male or female, a landholder or landless; the descriptions in this article focus on what a peasant family comprising a husband, wife, and young child might have owned if they had a middle level of wealth. Farm implements were stored in the home and included a wooden shovel (preferably metal shod around the end), a small axe, sickles (one that could be held in one hand and a large one that had to be used with two hands), and a knife for each adult. If the peasant had his own plow team, there would be a harness to attach animals to the plow, a goad to move the animals along, and the plow itself. For furniture, there was a table and a bench. Chairs required specialized carpentry, so they were more expensive and much rarer than benches. At least one metal pot was suspended from a metal pole that could swing over and away from the fire pit. There was also at least one wooden spoon for stirring the food in the pot, and there might

also be a pot that could be used to roast meat or vegetables in the coals. Various baskets and pots were used to carry water or food. They were most often made of wicker or leather because making good pottery required access to the right type of clay and a kiln. A few wooden bowls held meals, and the basic eating utensils well into the end of the Middle Ages were a knife and fingers. Soup was drunk like water or eaten with fingers, and the same bowls were also used for beer or wine. Linens were a mark of status, and a peasant took pride in being able to cover his table with a cloth. In the same way bedding was a major expense in a peasant household. Beds were generally thick fabric stuffed with materials such as dried grasses, wool, and old clothing scraps. Woolen blankets, leather hides, and fur, when available, were layered on top of them. There is some evidence that by the thirteenth and fourteenth centuries a prosperous peasant might have had a raised bedframe, which made the bed substantially warmer and more comfortable. A few rushlights or oil lamps might lighten the night, and a few barrels might be off to the side holding beer or wine. A medieval peasant lived with such basic supplies.

Carpentry. Many of the goods in medieval houses were made of wood, and carpentry was an essential skill. While many peasants might be able to effect basic repairs and whittle basic tools, a carpenter was called in to produce objects that needed firm joinery or specialized attachments. For example, a plow required various pieces of wood to be cut to size and assembled in such a way that it could take repeated heavy use. Moreover, making plows demanded that a carpenter know how to attach metal parts to wooden frames. Although not every village needed a resident who concentrated on carpentry, a peasant with a solid knowledge of carpentry had a valuable source of supplementary income. Carpentry skills were also useful when building or repairing houses, but, prior to a series of innovations in building during the late thirteenth century, most villages did not need specialized building craftsmen.

Village Fairs. Village fairs were the source of goods that peasants could not produce or buy in smaller villages. Most small villages in settled areas were located within half a day's walk of a larger one, which hosted markets where its residents and those of neighboring villages offered their goods for sale. These markets occurred at regular intervals: every seven or ten days. From a small village peasants started out early in the morning with carts of goods or what could be carried on their backs. They then spent the morning selling what they had and buying what they needed. Market days were also times for negotiating contracts, paying taxes, and holding celebrations. Later in the day they walked back to their villages.

Sources:

Frances Gies and Joseph Gies, *Marriage and Family in the Middle Ages* (New York: Harper & Row, 1987).

Hans-Werner Goetz, *Life in the Middle Ages from the Seventh to the Thirteenth Centuries,* translated by Albert Wimmer, edited by Steven Rowan (Notre Dame, Ind.: University of Notre Dame Press, 1993).

Cecil Alec Hewett, *English Historic Carpentry* (London: Phillimore, 1980).

FARMERS AND PEASANTS: VILLAGE FIGHTS AND FESTIVALS

Village Tensions. Villagers lived in close proximity to their neighbors, and fights were bound to occur. The records of village meetings and manorial courts provide lists of troubles that happened in these communities, particularly when land, tools, and crops were shared. As Frances and Joseph Gies have noted, the charges included "trampling another tenant's grain; cutting hay in the meadow without waiting for lots to be drawn; allowing one's cows, pigs, or geese to damage another's crops, 'stealing plow furrows,' that is, plowing part of a neighbor's land." Village bylaws and rules often stated that

> "able-bodied" people should not be allowed to do the relatively easy work of gleaning reserved for "the young, the old, and those who are decrepit and unable to work," but should be employed to their capacity in reaping. Peas and beans, especially valuable in a protein-short diet, could be picked only at specified times when all villagers were present and could watch each other. All kinds of precautions were taken to prevent the theft of sheaves. Rules restricted carting and carrying to daylight hours, via specified entries and exits to the fields.

Those who violated village procedures suffered various penalties. If they offended against a lord's rights, the lord could extract payment or, in serious cases, even replace one tenant with another. Within the community, a villager could be ostracized. Unless he was quite prosperous and therefore able to manage his land on his own, this sentence carried serious economic consequences for his entire household because he would have no one to help him lead a plow team or bring in his crop. Honor was also important to medieval people, and shaming was another way to punish transgressors. A man whose wife cheated on him might be made to wear horns, as a sign that he had been cuckolded.

Village Time. The position of the sun in the sky determined time during the day, and the chores that needed to be done distinguished the months. The annual calendar did not really begin in a particular month, and peasants often lost track of what year it was. January was the month of cold; February was the time of digging or cleaning the fields; and March and April were devoted to chores such as taking livestock out to the fields, trimming grapevines, or cutting posts. Medieval calendars linking chores and climate to months of the year appeared in books from the ninth to the fourteenth centuries and continued to be a common artistic pattern well after the Middle Ages. A peasant generally headed to the fields at daylight, ate the main meal when the sun was at its highest point, and returned home when the sun began to set. Given this schedule, the workday was longer in the summer than in the winter, and the days were of a more consistent length in southern Europe than northern Europe. Holidays were tied

SUNDAY CHORES

In 789 a statement of Church policy for both clergy and laity was issued under Charlemagne's name. Known as the *admonitio generalis*, it mentions the chores that peasants were likely to do on a Sunday despite regulations against such work. Although it is from a slightly earlier era than the period covered in this book, it suggests ongoing difficulties in enforcing "sacred" time on a day when the only permissible chores were carting services for the purpose of supplying vital goods during times of war or, occasionally, for a funeral.

We also order that . . . no servants' chores be performed on Sundays . . . that men not perform farm chores, that they refrain from cultivating the vineyards, from plowing the fields, from mowing, from cutting hay or building fences, constructing houses, or working in the garden. By the same token, women are not to manufacture cloth on Sundays, make patterns for clothes, sew, or embroider, card wool, scutch flax, wash clothes in public, or shear sheep.

Source: Hans-Werner Goetz, *Life in the Middle Ages from the Seventh to the Thirteenth Centuries,* translated by Albert Wimmer, edited by Steven Rowan (Notre Dame, Ind.: University of Notre Dame Press, 1993), p. 151.

to the religious calendar. For peasants, Sunday was supposed to be a day of rest, although harvest or other jobs could encroach on this time. In the same way other holy days or market days could also be holidays. It is estimated that medieval peasants had around 200–240 working days a year, that is, close to those of modern people. These estimates, however, cannot show if peasants actually took off the days that were supposed to be holidays.

Amusements and Festivals. Medieval people, including peasants, amused themselves in various ways. Toys such as dolls, hobbyhorses, carts, whistles, tops, balls, and swings were generally made out of wood, fabric scraps, and other easily accessible materials. Children mimicked adults by playing at harvesting, cooking, and building. Men and women went for walks, had meals together, and gossiped. Certain days of the year were especially festive, and among the most popular was May first, May Day. One of the earliest descriptions of May Day celebrations comes from Bishop Robert Grosseteste (circa 1168–1253), who wrote to complain about the festivities. According to his description, priests and commoners alike joined in a series of kissing and drinking games "which they call the bringing-in of May." These games apparently included dancing around a large pole set up in the village. When the village could afford them, streamers were tied to the pole. Young women each took one end of a streamer and danced around the pole while inviting the young men in the village to join them. Flutes, drums, and singers provided the music. In the evening villagers made a large bonfire and continued their celebrations by firelight. Even though reforming clergymen frequently condemned such festivities, particularly the participation of some clergymen in them, these celebrations endured into the early twentieth century in some regions.

Sources:
Frances Gies and Joseph Gies, *Life in a Medieval Village* (New York: Harper & Row, 1990).

Ronald Hutton, *The Stations of the Sun: A History of the Ritual Year in Britain* (New York: Oxford University Press, 1990).

Theresa McLean, *The English at Play in the Middle Ages* (Windsor Forest, U.K.: Kensal Press, 1983).

Jeffrey L. Singman, *Daily Life in Medieval Europe* (Westport, Conn.: Greenwood Press, 1999).

LORDS AND LADIES: BUILDING CASTLES

Castles as Fortresses and Homes. The noble class and the people who worked immediately for them (their retainers) were only a small percentage of the medieval European population, at most 3–5 percent. Yet, this small community had a disproportionate influence on many aspects of European society and culture. One of the most striking artifacts of their power is the medieval castle, and many modern assumptions about castle structure and noble life are based on anachronistic, romantic perceptions. Castles were frequently the homes of only a small garrison, which might include one or two knights, mercenary soldiers, and civilian-soldiers who owed military service. Even in massive structures built by kings and princes the actual number of people living within the castle walls

A MEDIEVAL CASTLE

In their discussion of castle life Frances and Joseph Gies drew on the twelfth-century *History of the Counts of Guines,* by Lambert of Ardres. The castle Lambert described is generally assumed to be the castle of Bouquehault in northeastern France. It was controlled by the Montgardin family, related to the counts of Guines. No ruins survive.

The castle Lambert of Ardres describes . . . was not one of the newer masonry structures but the old motte-and-bailey timber fort of the tenth century. It had its hall and attendant service rooms (larders, pantry, and buttery) on the second floor, above the ground-level storerooms with their boxes and barrels and utensils. Adjoining the hall were "the great chamber in which the lord and lady slept" and "the dormitory of the ladies-in-waiting and children," in other words, the nursery. The attic, designed mainly for the adolescents, was divided into two sections, evidently outfitted with pallets. On one side the sons of the lord stayed "when they so desired," and sometimes the watchmen and servants; on the other the daughters "because they were obliged"—where they could be watched over until they were suitably married. There was only one "great chamber"; the castle was not designed for more than one married couple. The heir could not marry until his father died, unless he found an heiress and won a house and bedchamber of his own.

Source: Frances Gies and Joseph Gies, *Marriage and Family in the Middle Ages* (New York: Harper & Row, 1987), p. 143.

was not large: around forty to fifty when the lord was in residence, perhaps twenty when he was not. Many medieval lords were essentially itinerant. A lord might have a primary residence or even two, but it was rare that he would spend more than several months of the year there. Only in the thirteenth and fourteenth centuries, near the end of the Middle Ages, did court protocol and lifestyles begin to approach the modern conception of them. Even then only a few courts established in castles were so stylized, and some of the most elaborate were led by an ecclesiastical lord, such as the papal court in Avignon.

What Was a Castle? A castle was essentially a structure built to fortify and maintain control over an area. Medieval castles were built according to many designs using many different materials, and some were more defensible than others. Few had the elaborate architecture and furnishings that modern people associate with them. Particularly in the tenth and eleventh centuries, castles were built solely as fortifications and not designed as luxury accommodations. Life in castles could be isolated and harsh, though comfortable by comparison to the lives of the peasants surrounding them. Many of the comforts associated with noble and castle life did not begin to emerge until the thirteenth century, and they were often a development of the fourteenth century and the Renaissance.

Mottes and Baileys. The earliest medieval castles were mottes and baileys. In essence a *motte* (French for mound or hill) was a pile of dirt. It could be an actual hill or an artificial mound about 15–20 feet high and large enough to support a square tower at least three stories tall and 50 feet long per side. In some cases people built wooden walls around the edges of the motte and in the process formed a ring-work fort; this sort of protective structure was in use as late as the twelfth century in places such as England, and they formed the basis for many town walls well into the thirteenth and fourteenth centuries. A motte-and-bailey structure included an enclosed courtyard, called the bailey, generally on a lower level than the motte. The motte was the most defensible area, while the bailey was the area in which most of the basic activities of castle life took place. The bailey often contained at least one primary structure, generally known as the keep, and a larger fortification often enclosed several additional buildings for storage and housing of soldiers and livestock. Cisterns were also included so that residents did not need to obtain water from outside the castle during a siege. Every region had its variations, depending on geography, custom, or personal preference. Sometimes mottes had several baileys or none at all. At other times mottes had ditches around them that could be filled with water (moats), but in some instances they had no moats, and water could be difficult to obtain.

Stone Castles. Archaeological evidence suggests that stone castles began to appear a little before 1000 A.D., while historical records of stone castles emerged a bit later. The period from the eleventh through the thirteenth centuries was the great age of medieval castle construction, as stone castles replaced mottes and baileys as the preferred fortifications. At the same time, castles were relocated from lowlands near villages to hills and mountaintops. By the twelfth century, castles were frequently separate from the communities they were ostensibly protecting. The walls were built in straight lines, but the enclosure they surrounded could be shaped in many ways, with the most common being a sort of oblong; round walls were a later invention. While towers were not constructed at every bend in the walls, there were often several on a side or at least one on each corner. Inside the walls, there was one tower, several stories tall, called the keep. Though medieval castles housed few people, living space within the castle enclosure (the yard) was at a premium. Much of the structure was composed of walls with various outbuildings built into them or attached to their sides. These structures could include offices, stables, barns, personnel quarters, and a kitchen, and smaller castles often just had one or two structures that combined all these functions. Many medieval castles were built or modernized because of pressing military needs, and some of the largest were constructed quite quickly, within a year or at most five. The only medieval structures of comparable size, cathedrals, frequently took decades to build. For this reason castle construction required an incredible concentration of resources. Workmen from miles around were pulled from other tasks and

The keep at Dover Castle, built by Henry II of England, circa 1180–1190

crammed together in the castle yard to work at levering stone, mortaring walls, and framing the keep. The costs were equally impressive. For example, Château-Gaillard in Normandy, the key fortification of Richard the Lionhearted, was built in just over a year at a cost of £21,203, the equivalent of one year's pay for approximately eleven-thousand foot soldiers.

Castle Walls. The walls of medieval castles were massive, designed to present formidable obstacles to invasion and to repulse any objects catapulted at them. To fulfill these functions, they often were at least seven feet thick and more than thirty feet high. In great castles the walls could measure up to twenty feet thick. Sometimes walls that were especially vulnerable or strategic could have an even higher secondary wall behind them. Because tunneling and setting explosives under a wall was a real danger, ditches were sometimes dug around the walls. These walls, however, were more than just obstacles. They were platforms from which a garrison could fight during a siege. Towers were generally built on the walls at intervals every two hundred to three hundred feet, and they furnished high points for maximum visibility and protection from rain. Built with walls as thick as those of the castle walls themselves, towers were often keys to castle defense. Gates were necessary, but they were frequently the weak points in castle defenses, and extra precautions were taken to strengthen them. Towers flanked the two sides of the gate, and in the most technologically advanced castles those

Caernarvon Castle in Wales, begun by Edward I of England in 1283 and completed in 1330

entering the gate would first have to go through a barbican, a small fortification right before the gatehouse. Inside the barbican there was a ninety-degree turn in the path, which allowed anyone already inside the castle to ambush an unwelcome visitor.

The Keep. Near the center of most medieval castles was the keep, which served as the main storehouse and residence and the tower of last resort. Generally the tallest structure by several stories, the formidable keep had walls that were frequently twelve to fifteen feet thick. Its multistory structure also accommodated its varied functions. The cellar, located half underground, was the storage area for all the basic supplies, including a portion of the water for the castle. Like the cellar, the next floor was entered through an external staircase. This floor consisted of two great rooms with smaller side rooms, service areas, and even a bedchamber or two. In Dover Castle, one of the largest and strongest castles in thirteenth-century England, the entrance to this story led into a rectangular hall approximately twenty to twenty-five feet wide and forty feet long. In the middle of one wall was a doorway that led to another such hall, which was only slightly narrower than the first. Off the first hall were privies, a guard room, a chapel, a service area, and possibly a kitchen, while off the second hall were two bedchambers and another privy. The largest hall served as a banquet and meeting room, and the smaller one

housed more-private assemblies and served as a sleeping chamber for soldiers and servants. Only the highest-ranking visitors to the castle were given separate bedchambers, and even then their closest servants probably slept in the same room. The keep of a major castle, such as Dover, had another floor above the second one, and a third floor that was in many cases a duplicate of the one below it. Finally, the top of the keep itself was a lookout post and could serve as sleeping quarters on hot summer nights. By the thirteenth and fourteenth centuries, great lords often decided that the facilities of earlier keeps were too stark and primitive, and alongside the castle walls they built additional halls that followed the design of manor houses. Even in these cases personal space was at a premium.

Caernarvon Castle. One of the most impressive series of castles was built or begun during the last quarter of the thirteenth century by King Edward I of England to control the territory of Wales, which he had recently conquered. Among Edward's many Welsh castles Caernarvon (or Caernarfon in Welsh) had a special purpose: to serve as a governmental seat and a symbol of English domination over the Welsh. It took the builders of Caernarvon Castle more than forty years of construction to achieve these goals, with a first period of building in 1283–1292 and a second in 1294–1330. The total cost was more than £25,000, and the result was a castle designed to hold the household of the king's eldest son, Edward, Prince of Wales (later Edward II), and his council. The king's choice of site was not original. Caernarvon Castle was built next to the town named Caernarvon on the Welsh coast and on the site of a Roman fort and a Norman motte-and-bailey castle. Timber was brought from various sites in western England, and building stone came from the moat that was dug for the new castle. In constructing the walls, towers, and gates, the builders used the latest in medieval military technology. The walls contained arrow slits, crenelations for protection of the defenders, and murder holes (small openings in the walls from which defenders poured pitch or other materials to disable attackers). Towers flanked each of the main gates, and the gates had a drawbridge and other fortifications. The walls were up to twenty feet thick, designed to withstand attacks from the strongest siege engines devised at that time. The seven towers at Caernarvon were at least five stories tall, and the four largest contained some living accommodations and private chapels on each story. The great hall was inside the castle walls near to the middle of the enclosure. As in other castles, this hall served as an eating area, reception room, and council chamber. To further strengthen the defense of the castle, a wall more than a half mile long and up to twenty feet thick surrounded the city itself. Caernarvon Castle withstood battles and sieges throughout the Middle Ages and was not surrendered to opposing forces until 1646, when it fell to Parliamentary forces during the first English Civil War.

Sources:
Hugh Kennedy, *Crusader Castles* (Cambridge & New York: Cambridge University Press, 1994).

John R. Kenyon, *Medieval Fortifications, The Archaeology of Medieval Britain* (London: Leicester University Press, 1990).

Robin S. Oggins, *Castles and Fortresses* (New York: Metrobooks, 1975).

A. J. Taylor, *Caernarvon Castle and Town Walls* (London: HMSO, 1975).

LORDS AND LADIES: CASTLE FURNISHINGS AND MANAGEMENT

Privacy. The medieval keep did not allow much personal privacy. Most of the rooms were multifunctional, and the keep was the primary living space in the castle. Soldiers, servants, and even lords- and ladies-in-waiting were expected to sleep in groups segregated by sex. For example, the women may have slept in the bedchambers while the male servants, courtiers, and soldiers slept in the great hall. Even the lords and ladies of castles, when they were in residence, often shared a room with a servant or conducted some business in the same rooms in which they slept. Since the staff of a major castle could include at least two dozen household officials, another dozen knights, and other aristocrats, several dozen foot soldiers, and assorted servants and spouses, the keep could also become quite crowded. The castle was not a place to seek privacy.

Furniture. The furnishings of a medieval castle varied depending on who was in residence. Many medieval lords lived itinerant lives, and when they moved they brought their favorite and most valuable furnishings with them. The baggage trains involved could be enormous; for exam-

MANAGING A LORDSHIP

The *Capitulare de villis* is a ninth-century manuscript that describes the appropriate management of the properties belonging to the king of the Franks. This excerpt from section sixty-two lists some of the duties of a medieval steward.

Every official is to report annually on our total yield: how much profit he made with the oxen in the service of our cowherds, how much he made off the manses to provide plowing, how much from pig tax and other [property] taxes he collected, how much he has received in fines and how much for keeping the peace, how much for game caught without our permission in our forests, how much from fines, [fees] from mills, forests, pastures, how much toll from bridges or ships, how much rent from freemen and tithing areas on cultivated lands belonging to the crown, the income from markets, vineyards and from the wine tax, how much hay was harvested, how much wood and how many torches, shingles and various other lumber, how much was harvested from abandoned fields, the amount of vegetables, millet, wool, flax and hemp, fruit, and nuts, how much was harvested from grafted trees and gardens, in beet fields and in fish ponds, how many skins, pelts, horns were collected and how much honey, wax, fat, tallow and soap, how much profit was made from blackberry wine, spiced wine, mead, vinegar, beer, cider and old wine, old and new harvest, chickens, eggs, geese, how much was taken in by fishermen, smiths, shieldmakers and shoemakers, how much money was made with kneading-troughs, chests or shrines, how much turners and saddlers took in, how much profit was made by ore and lead mines, how much was collected from other people who had tax obligations, how many stallions and breeding mares they had; all this is to be presented to us by Christmas in the form of a detailed, exact and clear list, so that we will know what and how much of each we own.

Source: Hans-Werner Goetz, *Life in the Middle Ages from the Seventh to the Thirteenth Centuries*, translated by Albert Wimmer, edited by Steven Rowan (Notre Dame, Ind.: University of Notre Dame Press, 1993), p. 116.

ple, when the countess of Leicester decided to stay at Dover Castle in 1265, she arrived with a baggage train that required more than 140 horses to transport it, and more goods were sent later. Among the most valuable and important furnishings were those for the bedchamber. A wooden bedstead with cords woven across it provided a base for several layers of mattresses. The first was likely of straw, the second of wool, and the third of goose down—essentially going from hardest to softest. Linen sheets, wool blankets, quilts, and furs were laid on top of these mattresses. A long pillow called a bolster stretched the width of the bed, and a feather pillow or two was set on top of it. Then heavy curtains were hung all around the bed for decoration and warmth. Probably the most common form of medieval furniture was the chest. Almost all household goods were placed in chests for storage or moving, includ-

The great hall at Hedingham Castle, England, built circa 1140

smoky. By the twelfth and thirteenth centuries, however, stone wall fireplaces were increasingly coming into use, and even a bedchamber might have its own fireplace. Although these fireplaces increased the warmth and light in a room, they were far from perfect heat sources; fires were still allowed to die down at night for safety, and by the morning rooms were quite cold. Probably the first sound that many medieval lords and ladies heard in the morning was a servant stoking the fire.

Decoration. Although the gray, stone walls of surviving medieval castles make them appear bleak and dreary today, in the Middle Ages the rooms were more colorful. Medieval people took some care when decorating a keep. The cloths that covered walls to minimize drafts and retain heat were dyed festive colors and embroidered with elaborate scenes, either by the lady of the castle and her ladies or later, increasingly, by professional embroiderers. (Tapestries are a late-medieval invention.) Moreover, the great halls and the bedchambers were generally plastered and whitewashed. On top of this whitewash were various colors of paint; red, green, yellow, and blue were considered most appropriate for the inside of a castle. As the medieval economy improved, especially in the fourteenth century, prosperous castle lords might commission a painter to decorate their chambers with moralizing, mythical, or recreational scenes such as hunts and picnics. One of the most striking examples of medieval architectural painting is the Sainte-Chapelle built onto the palace of King Louis IX of France in the 1240s; the entire chapel was painted dark blue and gold with stars and fleurs-de-lis, the heraldic device of Louis's dynasty. The wooden framing of a castle ceiling could also be gilded or painted. Coats of arms, animals, and fantastic figures seem to have been popular designs. Floors were not often decorated. A layer of rushes on top of the wood provided basic insulation and could be discarded when it became too dirty. By the fourteenth century, however, there is some evidence that the most prosperous and stylish members of the aristocracy were installing tiled floors in their castles, and these tiles came in many colors and patterns.

The Soldier's Life. Although the life of a soldier in a castle garrison was not harsh compared to that of a medieval peasant, it was still far from easy by modern standards. Generally, soldiers were either professionals or men who were required to serve at a castle for a set number of days a year. The professionals could be in permanent residence, while the others stayed at the castle for a month at a time. Among the soldiers there were hierarchies. The knight was at the highest level and enjoyed the greatest privileges as the commander of the whole garrison or of a part of it. Only a great castle had more than one or two knights in residence. The knights were either housed together in a separate chamber, or, if they were placed in the hall with the rest of the soldiers, they were in an area curtained off from the common fighters. Moreover, a knight had one or more servants attending him. During ordinary times a knight was responsible for keeping the castle in a state of

ing clothes, documents, pots, and pans. When a lord arrived in a castle, his servants took the clothes out of the chests and hung them from wooden rods suspended from the walls. Each of the great chambers included tables, but in many cases they were probably only boards on top of trestles; this structure allowed them to be stored when the room was used for something else and made them easier to move when the lord relocated. Wooden stools and benches were the most common seats. Chairs were a mark of status. Generally, most furniture was made out of wood, which could be carved, gilded, or otherwise decorated. Metal was used to reinforce corners, for decorative handles, and for locks. Leather could be made into seats but was more often used as strapping or for ties.

Warmth. Warmth was an ongoing problem for stone castles, even in southern Europe. While stone was the best material for building fortifications, it retains the cold, and even in Italy or on the Mediterranean coast winter can be bitter. Furthermore, fire was a hazard in medieval castles. The framing for the roofs was wood, and the construction of many outbuildings was just a slightly more sophisticated version of that used for wooden peasant huts. Thatch and wood were always flammable. Like peasant residences, early castles often relied on central fire pits for warmth and light, which left the side chambers cold and the main hall

A lady directing a servant in a castle kitchen; illumination from a medieval English manuscript (Trinity College, Cambridge)

readiness and making sure that the soldiers stayed disciplined and skillful. The ordinary soldier's primary duties were to take a daily tour of guard duty, to make sure his weapons were maintained, and to keep himself fit. Soldiers ate and slept together, generally in the great hall or in quarters built along the inside of the walls. It appears that boredom was the greatest problem regularly faced by a soldier in a castle garrison.

The Servant's Life. Servants were the backbone of medieval castles. No lord expected to clean his rooms, prepare his food, or care for his horse. Castles were equipped with a staff ranging from skilled craftsmen to scullery maids and men responsible for cleaning garbage dumps and cesspits. Clearly their standards of living varied greatly, with the craftspeople generally enjoying the greatest privileges. Artisans working at the castle earned a daily or annual wage, bonuses for certain projects, and their clothing, food, and shelter. The food was more varied and contained more meat than the typical peasant menu, and the shelter was probably in a building next to the artisan's place of work. People at the highest levels of staff may have even been prosperous enough to support families of their own. Although castle servants could expect better pay than the average villager, they worked long hours. Always available at the lord's whim, a servant could have a working day that lasted from before daylight to well past sundown. There was always a trade-off in service jobs, too; although it might be possible to have a more regular schedule or more time off in a job more distant from the lord, those who directly served the lord or lady were most likely to get special preferment and bonuses, so positions such as a serving maid or chamberlain (the lord's personal servant) were among the most desired.

Managing a Castle: The Lady. Noblewomen in medieval Europe had many roles. A few fought alongside their husbands, as did Gaita, wife of a Norman prince, and Duchess Agnes of Burgundy. Even when they did not fight, others accompanied their husbands to war and, thereby, stood in real peril, as did Eleanor of Aquitaine when her first husband, King Louis VII of France, went on crusade. More common, however, were noblewomen with important managerial roles, both of individual castles and of a family's estates more generally. Such responsibilities increased in wartime, when men were away fighting. A noblewoman's day began at daybreak. After she dressed and heard mass, she went to the great chamber. After a bite to eat, she began the series of tasks that filled her day. Her work included hearing messengers, resolving disputes in the castle and neighboring territories, and reviewing the castle and manorial accounts. She bought provisions for the castle and negotiated with other lords and merchants for any men or materials she or her husband might need. She had to hear reports from important servants in the castle, such as the garrison commander and the steward, and respond as she felt necessary. She also needed to pay her respects to any visitors that might be taking shelter in the castle. Inns were rare and generally considered inappropriate accommodations for upper-class travelers, so a noble gave temporary housing to traveling aristocrats or important clerics. In addition, a noblewoman was responsible for supervising the care of her children, if not actually doing all the work herself. Essentially, she was like the manager of a business.

Managing a Castle: A Steward's Day. Nobles did not always live in their castles, or, even when they did, they might need extra help in managing them. For that assistance, they turned to a steward, a highly trusted servant, who was generally a freeman raised in status by the lord. A steward's tasks were essentially those described for a noblewoman, although he did not have direct responsibility for his lord's children except in unusual circumstances. In many respects, the steward was a lord's right-hand man. He was completely dependent on the lord for his wealth and status, and this dependency was seen as a way of insuring a steward's loyalty and best efforts. A steward often had the privilege of being given separate quarters inside the castle walls, although they were nowhere near as luxurious as those reserved for the lord's family. He was supplied with money, food, and clothing; in fact, he might receive the lord's hand-me-down clothing, which was of far higher quality than that worn by most servants. As the lord's representative, the steward did not need his own servants; all the lord's servants were answerable to him. Like the lord's family, then, stewards rarely had to perform menial tasks such as drawing water, sewing, and cooking. It was, however, their responsibility if other servants performed these tasks poorly.

Sources:
Sally Crawford, *Childhood in Anglo-Saxon England* (Phoenix Mill, U.K.: Sutton, 1999).

Georges Duby, ed., *A History of Private Life: Revelations of the Medieval World* (Cambridge, Mass.: Harvard University Press, 1989).

Penelope Eames, *Furniture in England, France and the Netherlands from the Twelfth to the Fifteenth Century* (London: Furniture History Society, 1977).

Joseph Gies and Frances Gies, *Life in a Medieval Castle* (New York: Crowell, 1974).

David Herlihy, *Opera Muliebria: Women and Work in Medieval Europe* (New York: McGraw-Hill, 1990).

Eric Mercer, *Furniture, 700–1700* (New York: Meredith Press, 1969).

LORDS AND LADIES: CASTLES UNDER SIEGE

Castle Storage. The large cellar at the base of the castle keep contained everything necessary to supply a fortified village under siege, including grain, dried foodstuffs, military supplies, and cloth. Because it was half underground, the cellar provided cool storage that helped to preserve foodstuffs. Since access to the cellar was by the same external stairwell that provided access to the next floor of the keep, the castle had to be in grave danger before the supplies in the cellar became unavailable to defenders, and by that time, anyway, the supplies would probably be close to, if not totally, exhausted. Later in the Middle Ages, goods were also stored in structures all around the castle yard, next to where they were most needed. Hay was kept near the stables, weapons caches were at the towers, and iron and other metals were stored beside the smithy.

Water Supply. Water supply was a problem for medieval castles, especially when they were under siege. Few were built alongside streams. From the standpoint of defensive strategy, the preferred castle sites were on coastlines and mountain tops, and potable water was often a good distance away. One of the first tasks in castle construction was to build a well in the castle yard; at times it was even made part of the keep. Water might be hundreds of feet below ground, and drilling a well was dangerous work. After a well was constructed, water had to be pulled up by a chain and pulley mechanism and poured into the castle cisterns. In some castles, the cisterns were located at a high elevation in the castle complex, which allowed lead pipes to be connected to the cistern so there could be running water in various rooms in the castle, but such a luxury was rare. Water cisterns to collect rainwater were also built within the castle walls; in the case of Dover Castle, these cisterns were in a building attached to and in front of the keep. Pipes carried rainwater from the roof into the cisterns, and it was also possible to get water from a well by using a bucket on a chain. Even when a castle had a moat with water in it—and such moats were rare—the moat was not a source of drinking water except in desperation because privies and household wastewater were generally emptied into the moat.

Breaking Down the Walls. Although the most common way of taking a castle was to surround it and wait until the residents ran out of food and water, medieval people also designed weapons that could threaten these enormous structures. Sometimes besiegers provided cover for a team of men who dug under the castle walls and weakened its foundations. Sometimes explosives were planted in these tunnels. Medieval armies also used battering rams to strike

Soldiers attempting to undermine castle walls as defenders throw rocks and pour boiling water from above; illumination from a fourteenth-century manuscript (British Library, London)

trained to deal with the stresses of battle, and medieval warriors repeatedly used it. Threats to destroy farms or injure loved ones were all weapons that an attacking army used to unnerve villager-soldiers. In sieges such threats gained real immediacy because the defenders were trapped inside the castle walls and unable to ascertain what was happening in their village. Besiegers even practiced a form of germ warfare. As Philippe Contamine has pointed out, "In 1332 when besieging the castle of Schwanau [in modern Germany], the men of Strasbourg captured 60 prisoners, of whom they massacred 48, including three carpenters, whose bodies they placed in barrels, together with all kinds of rubbish, which they then catapulted into the castle." Medieval sieges were brutal, and any technique that assured victory was considered legitimate—a fact that gives the lie to the modern image of medieval warfare as chivalrous single combat.

Sources:

Jim Bradbury, *The Medieval Siege* (Rochester, N.Y.: Boydell Press, 1992).

Philippe Contamine, *War in the Middle Ages,* translated by Michael Jones (Oxford & New York: Blackwell, 1984).

David Nicolle, *Medieval Warfare Source Book,* 2 volumes (New York: Sterling, 1995, 1996).

LORDS AND LADIES: COURT CULTURE AND FASHION

Castles Are Transformed. The castles of the highest nobility during the ninth, tenth, and eleventh centuries became increasingly luxurious, and, by the thirteenth and fourteenth centuries, noble culture was becoming increasingly formal and complex. As the seats of noble courts, the largest castles were becoming more elaborate as well. More outbuildings were constructed in castle yards to supply more goods and services, and the number of castle servants was increasing. At the same time nobles became less itinerant, and powerful lords increasingly divided their time among only a few residences, except when they were needed elsewhere for political considerations. These changes affected only the greatest castles and their lords; yet, the development of this noble, court culture was a distinctive feature of the later Middle Ages.

Clothing the Lord and Lady. Basic clothing for aristocrats was based on the same patterns as that of villagers and craftsmen, but it was made of more valuable materials and had more intricate detailing and decoration. Silks, velvets, and other luxury fabrics were staples of nobles' wardrobes, although nobles might have their everyday clothes made from wool or linen. Even when they were woolen, however, cloaks and other clothes were lined with luxurious furs for warmth; ermine and sable were two of the most prestigious furs. Nobles were able to afford more elaborate dyes, and there is some evidence that their clothing was more colorful and that the colors lasted longer than those in peasants' clothes. When a piece of clothing faded, nobles had it re-dyed or gave it to an underling and commissioned a new garment. At the beginning of the Middle Ages, even court clothing followed patterns similar to peasant clothes; yet, by the twelfth century fitted clothing had come into style

at castle walls and gates. These rams were made of wood—generally a tree trunk—with handles attached to them and the front sheathed in metal. Hammering a ram into a gate or wall was a dangerous business, however, because the defenders shot arrows and threw stones, garbage, burning oil, or boiling water at the attackers. Because of these dangers, medieval craftsmen developed ways of damaging walls that kept their soldiers at a greater distance. One of the most fearsome developments of the thirteenth century was the trebuchet, a catapult that could throw stones weighing hundreds of pounds. These boulders demolished structures, crushed people, and acted somewhat like mortars, fragmenting, maiming, or killing people just with splinters of stone. By the fourteenth century, the trebuchet was being praised as a technological marvel and condemned as a demoniacal weapon. It also caused serious damage to all but the most powerful medieval fortifications.

Breaking Down the People. Much of the staff of a medieval castle was made up of residents from neighboring villages; these same people provided most of the foot soldiers defending the castle in times of siege. Psychological warfare could have a great impact on individuals not

Ivory carving of a lord and lady playing chess, circa
1330 (The Louvre, Paris)

clergyman might have the story of Christ's life embroidered on them, court robes for nobles could be decorated with hunting scenes or heraldic devices. The threads and materials used varied greatly. In the earlier Middle Ages much embroidery thread was made and dyed with local materials; by the eleventh century embroiderers used costly imported materials. Silk, silver, and gold threads were regularly used, and jewels were sometimes sewn into the patterns. Quilting and fringes could also be worked into the cloth to provide added decoration. Because of the time and craft needed to produce it embroidered clothing was usually worn by only nobles and the clergy, and the materials and techniques used in embroidered goods reflected the wealth and status of the wearer.

Fashion. Although fashions changed much more slowly in the Middle Ages than in modern times, nobles were concerned with being fashionable. Fashion in medieval Europe was reflected in the tailoring of a gown or mantle, the decoration of a hat, or the length of toes on shoes. Men as well as women were condemned for fashion excesses. In southern Europe during the twelfth century a new fashion developed that remained part of a stylish man's wardrobe for centuries: colored and patterned woolen hose. Like peasants' hose, they were generally woven of wool—though hose made for festivals might be of heavy silk or some other luxurious fabric—and were designed to fit much like stirrup pants. A stylish young man had his hose sewn close to his body and tightened it even further by lacings at the hips, a style that some clerics condemned as obscene. A noble might also have one side of his hose woven one color and another side a different one; for example, red on one side and yellow on the other. Tunics could be dyed the same way. These two styles continued throughout the rest of medieval Europe and well into the Renaissance; only the preferred colors and patterns changed as time went on. Eventually stripes and checks of varied colors were mixed in vibrant patterns that commentators condemned for their vanity. Nor were hose the only medieval fashion statement that made clerics or more-conservative laymen cringe. In late-twelfth-century Germany another aristocratic style was to cut the bottom of a tunic into strips that resembled fringe, and these strips could be decorated with embroidery or other material. Some hairstyles called for a woman's hair to hang "wantonly" down, while the points of shoes at times were made so long that the wearer had to tie them to his waist or thighs in order to walk. When it came to clothing, noblemen were just as, if not more, likely to follow the whims and extremes of fashion as noblewomen.

for the aristocracy. Some nobles, men and women, went so far as to have themselves pinned into pieces of their garments to make them as close-fitting as possible. Lacings were also used to make clothing fit more closely to the body. In the early fourteenth century buttons were employed as both decoration and fasteners, which allowed for a tailored fit. At the highest levels of society and during royal or ecclesiastical ceremonies, clothing might even be encrusted with jewels or embroidered with precious metals. Clothing was particularly important to a noble because of the value placed on display. Tailored clothes of the finest material and with the most costly decorations shouted a noble's status and aspirations, and men and women alike had an extensive knowledge of the quality and cost of various kinds of cloth.

Embroidery. One way of decorating clothing in the Middle Ages was to embroider it. Embroidery was considered an appropriate occupation for noblewomen throughout the era, and embroideries produced by the wives and daughters of high-ranking men could have powerful symbolic value when presented as gifts. For example, in the eleventh century when King Canute of England presented altar cloths embroidered by his wife to the abbeys of Croyland and Romsey, clergymen and nobles throughout his kingdom saw it as a sign of royal favor for those abbeys. To supply the demand for ornate clothes and linens professional embroiderers increased in number during the course of the Middle Ages. By the thirteenth and fourteenth centuries embroidered wall hangings and bedclothes were important marks of noble status. This idea carried over into noble clothing. Embroidery decorated capes, hats, money pouches, and even shoes. The designs could be quite elaborate and specific to a profession as well; while robes for a

Jewelry. Noblemen and women both wore jewelry of many kinds, and it had practical uses. Cloaks and mantles needed clasps; swords needed scabbards; and belts needed fasteners. A medieval lord wore a signet ring, generally made of gold and engraved with his coat of arms or some other identifying mark or saying. These rings could be used as seals or for stamping documents to authenticate them. They could also be sent with a courier to testify to his legitimacy. Jewelry was often made of precious metals and gemstones. The jewels came from Europe, Africa, and Asia, testimony to the extent of medieval trade. Goldsmiths also used Roman cameos and classical coins in medieval jewelry. The technique of faceting jewels was not known in the Middle Ages. Instead, jewels were rubbed and shaped to enhance their luster. Gold and silver were often enhanced with elaborate engraving or formed into unusual shapes; pendants and pins were frequently larger than most of their modern counterparts. Large pieces became family heirlooms, and because medieval money was based on gold and silver, having jewelry made from these metals was like having cash in hand. It also represented a substantial investment, and, if necessary, it could be melted down to supply cash.

Other Clothes. Gloves, shoes, and hats were other basic parts of a noble's wardrobe. Gloves were made of thick leather to protect a knight's hands while riding or fighting, or of thinner and more-delicate materials, such as doeskin, linen, or silk when worn as a fashion accessory. They could be dyed or embroidered and might be held tightly around the wrist with delicate lacings or, in the fourteenth century, with buttons. Like those of the peasant, nobles' shoes were leather and generally flat bottomed. Men's clothing styles left shoes exposed, so they became fashion statements. Jeweled, beribboned, and dyed, the shoes of a court dandy could be almost useless for walking. Much more practical and widely used were heavy leather riding boots with wooden heels. There were both practical and fashionable hats as well. Although linen caps might suit men or women of the minor nobility while they were outdoors supervising their manors, the upper nobility wore hats made of the same expensive materials as their other clothing, and they could be quite ungainly. An aristocratic woman generally wore a veil on top of her hair that draped down the back of her head. In the twelfth century various stylish ways of securing the veil were developed. One, called a barbette, was a strap attached to the veil that went under the chin and back around to tie at the top of the head. A second, the wimple, was another piece of fabric attached to the veil; it wrapped under the chin and covered the entire front of the neck. The elaborate pointed hats and veils in many modern depictions of medieval life were later medieval developments.

Hair and Cosmetics. Aristocratic women and, infrequently, men used cosmetics. Some of them, such as creams and balms, had medicinal value. During cold European winters they prevented the skin from chapping and cracking, which could lead to infections. Other forms of cosmetics were just for aesthetic purposes. White powders made the skin appear fairer; charcoal enhanced eyes; and plant dyes hid gray hair. Although aristocratic women also frequently wore hats, certain styles demanded that their hair be visible. For example, in twelfth-century France and England one style for women was to wear the hair in two braids going down the back or wrapped in ribbons or fabric. As the Middle Ages went on, however, it was increasingly regarded as immodest for an adult woman to wear her hair unbound and her head uncovered; in fact, wrapping hair and covering it with some form of veil or hat was one ritual in a girl's coming of age.

Sources:
Q. W. Cunnington and P. Cunnington, *Handbook of English Medieval Costume* (London: Faber & Faber, 1952).

Françoise Piponnier and Perrine Mane, *Dress in the Middle Ages,* translated by Caroline Beamish (New Haven: Yale University Press, 1997).

Kay Staniland, *Medieval Craftsmen: Embroiderers* (Toronto: University of Toronto Press, 1991).

Naomi Tarrant, *The Development of Costume* (New York: Routledge, 1994).

LORDS AND LADIES: KITCHENS FOR CASTLES

Theories behind Aristocratic Food. Aristocratic diet was far more diverse than that of the medieval peasant, and several factors affected it: religious prohibitions, a product's availability, and medical theories. Wednesdays, Fridays, and Saturdays were officially fast days, when meat and eggs were prohibited; the same fasting rules applied to evenings before major religious holidays and to Lent, the forty days before Easter. Like the medieval peasant diet, aristocratic menus were tied to the growing season. Yet,

THIRTEENTH-CENTURY TABLE MANNERS

The following advice about table manners comes from thirteenth-century France. The original was written in rhyming lines, so the rules would be easy to remember.

No one should take food before the blessing has been made,

Nor should he take a place other than that assigned to him by the one in charge of the meal.

Refrain from eating until the dishes have been placed before you,

And let your fingers be clean, and your fingernails well-groomed.

Once a morsel has been touched, let it not be returned to the plate.

Do not touch your ears or nose with your bare hands.

Do not clean your teeth with a sharp iron while eating.

The salt is not to be touched with the food where it sits in the salt dish.

If you can, I ask again, refrain from belching at the table.

Know that it is forbidden to put your elbow on the table.

It is ordered by regulation that you should not put a dish to your mouth.

He who wishes to drink must first finish what is in his mouth,

And let his lip be wiped first.

Nor can I avoid mentioning that he should not gnaw a bone with his teeth. . . .

Once the table is cleared, wash your hands, and have a drink.

Source: Jeffrey L. Singman, *Daily Life in Medieval Europe* (Westport, Conn.: Greenwood Press, 1999), p. 133.

while certain foods were not available at some times of the year, a member of the upper nobility had the resources to take advantage of whatever distribution facilities might be available. Medical theories at both popular and learned levels helped guide food choices and preparation. The proper diet was considered essential to maintaining a healthy balance of the four humors in the body and the mind. Texture was important in medieval food for medical reasons as well. Many ingredients were chopped, ground, or filtered through cloth mesh—sometimes because of the consumers' teeth, but in most cases because of medical theories that, by the thirteenth century, seem to have been known to cooks for nobles, monks, and wealthy town residents. Not just the preparation, but the food itself, could have serious consequences for the eater. For example, Sally Crawford quotes an Anglo-Saxon warning about the consequences of improper diet for a pregnant woman: "if the pregnant woman is four or five months gone, and she frequently eats nuts or acorns or any fresh fruits, then it sometimes happens that the child is silly. Again, there is another matter, if she eats bull's meat, or ram's or buck's, or boar's or cock's or gander's flesh or that of any begetting

animal, then it sometimes happens that the child is humpbacked and ruptured."

Aristocratic Food. Despite such prohibitions and fears, medieval nobles ate with gusto. On fast days fish and cheese were still permitted, in addition to grains, fruit, vegetables, and other dairy products. A wide variety of fish—including trout, perch, halibut, sardines, and bass—was available. Sometimes it came from neighboring waters, but fish was also farmed in ponds or salted and brought from elsewhere by merchants. On the other days meat was a dietary staple, seasoned with expensive spices imported from Asia and the Near East. Because of medieval cooking tools, it was most often boiled or roasted. Bread was commonly served at every meal, and the whiter the bread the better it was believed to be. Alcoholic drinks were consumed by adults and children at every meal. Medieval wine was served young, less than a year old, because storage and sanitation techniques were not adequate to prevent it from spoiling over long periods. It was often mixed with water, spices, or sweeteners. Compared to water, it was purer and had some nutritional value. Milk was rarely drunk and was usually kept to make cheese and butter. Several modern

Workers in a castle kitchen; illuminations from the Luttrell Psalter, produced for Sir Geoffrey Luttrell of Irnham, in Lincolnshire, England, sometime before his death in 1345 (British Library, London)

The kitchen fireplace at Marksburg Castle in Germany, built circa 1100

editions of medieval cookbooks attest to the wide variety of foods that could be made with these ingredients. The aristocrat's diet did have flaws. It appears to have been deficient in vitamins A and C and possibly low in fiber, but the aristocrat at least benefited from a consistent food supply.

Spices. One of the most common modern misapprehensions about medieval cooking is that medieval cooks covered meat with spices to hide spoilage. While this practice might have taken place elsewhere and at other times, a medieval noble who could afford to stock his pantry with expensive, imported spices could certainly afford to replace spoiled meat with fresh cuts. Spices were used for taste and decoration and because they were seen as having medicinal value. Saffron and parsley, for example, were mixed into or spread on foods to give them color. A cook cared about color for its aesthetic value, and the use of rare and expensive spices gave prestige to the cook's employer. Medieval nobles were aware of which spices were the most expensive and, therefore, which gave the most honor to the host. Sometimes a cook could buy spices only from a nearby apothecary, roughly equivalent to a modern pharmacist. According to D. Eleanor Scully and Terence Scully, "Spices (including sugar) were considered to be simply that, varieties of drugs, to be employed only with a full, conscious understanding of their respective strengths and virtues." Probably as late as the thirteenth century sugar was

used only in recipes for the sick; honey was the common sweetener. During the fourteenth and fifteenth centuries, sugar became a common condiment at any prosperous table, in part because of its assumed medicinal qualities. According to humoral theories, sugar was a moderately warm and moist substance, giving it just the characteristics of the ideal human temperament.

Kitchens. In the wealthiest households the kitchen was located in a building separate from the main structure. This arrangement helped to minimize the dangers of fire and the unpleasant cooking odors in the residential areas. Even when the kitchen was attached to the main building, as it usually was in the early Middle Ages and in most castles, it was organized and stocked in much the same way as separate facilities. Generally a kitchen had at least one primary hearth, which could be eight to ten feet long and almost two feet deep. Around this hearth were metal poles for suspending pots over the fire and rotisseries for roasting meat. A top-notch kitchen might include a clay oven for baking bread and other confections. Around the sides of the room and even in the center were rows of tables and chests for storing ingredients and pots. The tables also served as places for preparation, much like modern countertops. For example, a roast was scooped out of the pot in which it was boiling and placed on a wooden platter. That platter was brought to a kitchen table, where the meat might be cut into pieces small enough for two diners and garnished with vegetables, herbs, and spices. For an elaborate banquet, an entire roast pig or other animal could be placed on one of these tables and prepared with great artistry. It might be stuffed with fruit, and other ingredients could be used to make it look almost as if it were still alive. The kitchen also contained a scullery area, where pots, platters, and other tools were washed. Large spoons and knives were hung from racks, and iron pots of various shapes and purposes were stacked in corners. Although daily cooking in an ordinary castle might require a staff of only three or four people, for a large aristocratic banquet dozens of assistants were necessary.

Banquets and Manners. Banquets were the most luxurious medieval meals and had the strictest protocols. Tables were covered with linens, and diners sat on one side of the table so that servants could easily reach them from the other. The table was set with trenchers. Basically a large platter meant to be shared by two people, a trencher appears to have been made of either wood or bread (to sop up sauces) during much of the medieval period, but by the fourteenth century bread trenchers were rare. The host also provided a spoon for each diner, but generally the diner had his or her own knife. Spoons, knives, and fingers were the main utensils, and the fingers were probably used most frequently. Two diners shared a trencher, a salt cellar, and a drinking cup, and many medieval guides to manners focus on the correct protocol for sharing food and servers. For example, diners were urged to rinse their fingers frequently in the finger bowl, so that they remained relatively clean. A diner was also told not to replace food on the tray after taking a bite from it and to finish swallowing food before taking a drink. After each of the courses—and there could be ten of them—a servant offered more wine or beer and more water for washing. At the beginning and the end of the meal a clergyman said grace, and during the meal musicians played, or some other form of entertainment might be devised.

Recipes. Several collections of late medieval recipes have survived, but they can be difficult to adapt to modern cooking terms and practices. Some of the important ingredients in aristocratic dishes, such as almond milk, are rarely available today, and ways of preparing food were based on different technology. For example, when medieval cooks marked time in a recipe, they often did so by noting that something should be done for as long as it took to say a common prayer, such as the Our Father. Such measurements are imprecise by modern standards, and it is clear that most medieval cookery was learned through experience and apprenticeship. Some medieval recipes, however, have modern equivalents. One of the most common aristocratic dishes of the Middle Ages, which was praised for its balanced properties, was blancmange. The following recipe is one of several acceptable modern versions, adapted by D. Eleanor Scully and Terence Scully:

Blancmange

Ingredients:
1 4–5 pound stewing chicken
½ cup ground almonds
3 cups chicken bouillon
2 tbsp. white sugar
1½ tbsp. fresh ground ginger
1 cup long-grain rice
1½ tsp. ground coriander
2 tbsp. toasted almond slices
optional: ¼ cup pomegranate seeds

Cut the chicken into quarters. Cover with water and cook in a saucepan until tender. Save 3 cups of the degreased cooking liquid; add chicken bouillon if there is not enough liquid until you reach 3 cups. Separate white meat; tear the white meat into strips and set aside. Chop the dark meat finely.

In a blender, combine the dark meat, almonds, and 1 cup of bouillon. Add the rest of the bouillon. Blend, then strain.

In a pot, combine the strained mixture, sugar, and ginger; bring to a boil.

Add rice. Reduce heat, cover, and cook about 20 minutes or until the rice is tender. Add more bouillon if necessary. Fold in white meat. Remove to serving platter.

Once the mixture is on the platter, sprinkle it with coriander. Garnish one half of the dish with toasted almonds and the other half with pomegranate seeds. Sprinkle everything with sugar. Serve.

Sources:
M. P. Cosman, *Fabulous Feasts: Medieval Cookery and Ceremony* (New York: Braziller, 1976).

Sally Crawford, *Childhood in Anglo-Saxon England* (Phoenix Mill, U.K.: Sutton, 1999).

Rachel Laudan, "Birth of the Modern Diet," *Scientific American*, 283 (August 2000): 76–81.

Stephen Mennell, *All Manners of Food: Eating and Taste in England and France from the Middle Ages to the Present* (Oxford: Blackwell, 1985).

D. Eleanor Scully and Terence Scully, *Early French Cookery: Sources, History, Original Recipes and Modern Adaptations* (Ann Arbor: University of Michigan Press, 1996).

LORDS AND LADIES: MILITARY TRAINING

The Castle Yard. Medieval soldiers received varying degrees of training. Conscripted villagers were given little, while training a knight could take a decade. For a member of a garrison or a young noble, the training site was the castle yard. In the small, open spaces inside the castle walls, various tools could be set up to aid the apprentice soldier. Archers had targets, and swordsmen had their training ground. One of the most common pieces of equipment was a cloth dummy stuffed with straw and set on a rotating pole at a man's height. This dummy could be used to train a foot soldier with a sword or a horseman with various weapons. Because the dummy was the size of a man, the soldier could learn to aim his strokes instinctively, and because it moved, it could swing around and even hit a soldier who did not place or time his blow correctly. Soldiers also learned swordplay by fencing with each other. Their vulnerable areas were wrapped in padding, and they attacked

Knights in training; illuminations from a fourteenth-century manuscript (Bodleian Library, Oxford)

each other with a wooden sword. While some mock battles followed set procedures, injuries could occur, and broken bones or cuts needing stitches were not uncommon. As long as these injuries were caused unintentionally, a fighter who hurt a fellow trainee was not liable for any penalties, as he would be during individual combat.

Exercise and Education for the Noble Soldier. By the thirteenth century literate soldiers could read a series of treatises about the art of war, some of which were written by people with battle experience. This sort of literature—along with classical examples such as Julius Caesar's *Gallic Wars*—continued to be popular among nobles well into the Renaissance. Yet, much of a medieval nobleman's training was based on experience, repetition, and hard work. Daily training involved hours of individualized practice with various weapons, not group drills as in modern armies. Hours of horseback riding were also expected, as the horse was both an essential tool in noble warfare and the fastest

means of transportation. In the process, a knight who escaped injury could develop impressive strength.

Medieval Armor. Armor became increasingly complicated throughout the Middle Ages. The protective clothing worn by foot soldiers, archers, and even poorer nobles was never as complex or expensive as that worn by members of the upper nobility. In fact, the modern conception of knightly armor and combat in the Middle Ages is based on accounts of "knightly" combat from the fourteenth and fifteenth centuries, just as armor was becoming impractical. The primary components of the medieval armor used in the eleventh and twelfth centuries were wool, highly cured leather, and steel. Wool was the basic fabric for most of medieval soldiers and knights' underclothes. It provided padding in especially vulnerable areas, such as the thighs, or in places where chafing might occur, including around the shoulders. Layers of cured and hardened leather had been the foundation for protective gear since at least the

Jean le Meingre, more commonly known as Boucicaut, was marshal of France and governor of Languedoc and Guyenne in the fourteenth century. A knight, councilor to the king of France, and chamberlain of the king, he was known throughout France and England for his military feats. This contemporary description of his physical abilities illustrates the strength and coordination necessary for a successful medieval soldier.

He executed a somersault fully armed, except for his basinet, [a light steel helmet], and whilst dancing he was armed with a mail coat. Item, he leapt onto a courser without placing his foot in the stirrup, fully armed. Item, with a strong man mounted on a great horse, he leapt from the ground onto his shoulders by taking his sleeve in one hand and without any other hold. Item, placing one hand on the saddle pommel of a great courser and the other near the horse's ears, seizing the mane, he leapt from the ground through his arms and over the horse. Item, if two walls were an arm's length apart and as high as a tower, he could climb to the top without slipping on the ascent or descent, simply using the strength of his arms and legs, without any other assistance. Item, wearing a coat of mail he ascended the under side of a great ladder placed against a wall to the top without using his feet, simply jumping with both hands from rung to rung and, then, taking off this coat, he did this with one hand until he was unable to ascend any higher.

Source: Philippe Contamine, *War in the Middle Ages*, translated by Michael Jones (Oxford & New York: Blackwell, 1984), pp. 216–217.

Roman Empire, and they were the most-common defense in the Middle Ages. The headgear that many fighting men wore was made of layers of hard leather tied onto the head, and chest and leg protection were fabricated from the same material. Such armor was so insubstantial that shocked chroniclers sometimes described these soldiers as going "naked" into battle. Leather had the advantage of being relatively cheap, flexible, and light, at least when compared with the other available material for effective armor: steel. Steel, however, gave far more protection than leather and was the preferred armor for any soldier who could afford it. The most common form of steel protection was mail, which was made of small steel rings laid over each other and welded together. Mail was good protection from sword thrusts, but it could only partially deflect damage from a blow. Although a soldier wore padding under his mail, medieval documents record cases in which mail was driven into a soldier's body and then needed to be cut out. Horses also had armor. Leather, mail, and other steel protectors were placed over a horse's vulnerable areas, such as the chest, the neck, and between the ears. Like the knights who rode them, horses were dressed elaborately on ceremonial occasions. A horse might be draped with an elaborately embroidered cloth featuring the knight's coat of arms or other decorative patterns and colors with symbolic meanings.

Making Armor. Armor and weapons were custommade through much of the Middle Ages. In fact, it was remarkable when, at the beginning of the thirteenth century, the Capetian monarchy of France began creating small stockpiles of crossbows, shields, lances, and armor. Although certain regions, such as Toledo in Spain, were known for the quality of their steel and, therefore, their armor and weapons, the local blacksmith-armorer made much of the arms and armor that medieval nobles used. Customized production also helps account for modern debates about the techniques used in making military essentials, such as mail shirts and leggings. Scholars have discussed for decades how the rings were interwoven and the exact method of attaching them (such as riveting or welding). It appears that there were local variations in how mail was made. Most larger villages, towns, and castles supported a blacksmith. Although a smith could specialize in armor, most often he also supplied all of the metal tools to his community and the villages within market distance. The forge was in a separate building at a good distance from other structures to minimize the danger of fire.

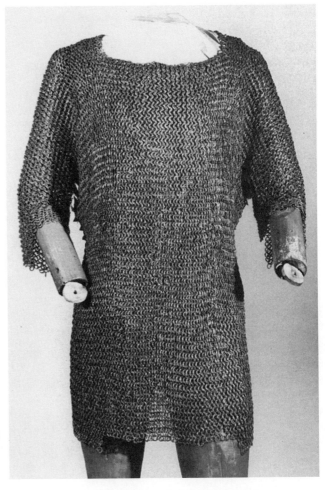

A fourteenth-century mail shirt (The Royal Armories, Tower of London)

Working with steel demanded large, hot fires and sometimes ovens for softening or melting materials. One feature of a medieval armory or smithy was a large, brick fire pit about three feet tall and located at least several feet from a wall. A well-equipped smith had a large bellows with a foot pump angled alongside this fire so that he could regulate the air getting to the fire and, thus, the heat at which it was burning. Water was another essential commodity for a medieval smith. Not only did it cool the metal while it was being worked, it could be used to put out small fires. Leather buckets were as essential to a smith as iron hammers, anvils, bellows, and the various pliers and other tools he used for shaping metal.

Dressing the Noble Soldier. The clothes of the medieval soldier varied greatly according to century and the soldier's social status. The description that follows is based on what a nobleman would have worn in approximately the middle of the thirteenth century. A soldier started by putting on a pair of linen breeches, or braies. Noblemen's braies were generally made of higher-quality cloth than peasants' braies, and slits were cut on both sides of the front near the waistband in order to attach other clothes. A soldier then slipped on a pair of wool hose over his braies and tied them to the braies by threading leather thongs through those slits. A wealthy knight then put on two coverings. The first was a layer of flexible-mail hose known as *chausses*. Chausses even sometimes had feet attached to them, like the pajamas with feet that small children sometimes wear. Further padding, generally stuffed with wool, was placed at the thighs. The layering on the upper body mimicked that found on the hips and thighs, with a shirt, another lightly padded shirt, and a full-mail hauberk (a sleeveless tunic) draped over the two shirts. The head was covered with a padded woolen cap and then a mail hood was set over the cap; sometimes this hood was attached to the hauberk, and other times it was a separate piece of armor. Finally, the mounted soldier wore steel sheet armor that protected his shoulders and torso. Heraldic devices painted on the sheet armor were relatively new at this period and became more common in the later-thirteenth and fourteenth centuries. All these layers were topped by a riveted steel helm with eye slits, holes around the mouth for breathing, and a strong and straight noseguard. One of the most common misconceptions about medieval knights is that these outfits weighed so much a knight was helpless. His armor and weapons weighed between sixty and seventy pounds, about the same weight as the weapons and pack carried by a modern foot soldier. To stand up, a knight had to roll onto his knees.

Sources:

John Clark, ed., *The Medieval Horse and Its Equipment* (London: HMSO, 1995).

David Edge and John Miles Paddock, *Arms and Armour of the Medieval Knight: An Illustrated History of Weaponry in the Middle Ages* (New York: Defoe, 1988).

Maurice Keen, *Nobles, Knights, and Men-at-Arms in the Middle Ages* (London & Rio Grande, Ohio: Hambledon Press, 1996).

David C. Nicolle, *Arms and Armour of the Crusading Era, 1050–1350*, 2 volumes (White Plains, N.Y.: Kraus, 1988).

Matthias Pfaffenbichler, *Medieval Craftsmen: Armourers* (Toronto: University of Toronto Press, 1992).

LORDS AND LADIES: RECREATION

Hawking. A common recreation, hawking also had a practical application: it provided meat for the table. Carried by men and women on their wrists, hawks were useful aids to hunters. Their importance can be gauged by the large number of manuals on hawking that have survived. The best known of these is *The Art of Falconry*, written in the 1240s by Frederick II, who ruled the Holy Roman Empire from 1212 to 1250. Frederick stressed the care and patience every falconer must have while training his falcon, as the trained birds were called. After capturing a wild hawk, the handler first placed a hood over its head, tied leather straps (jesses) to its ankles, attached bells to the jesses, and set the bird on its perch. Over a period of weeks and even months the bird grew accustomed to human noises and contact, even beginning to take food from its handler's hand. When first teaching the bird to hunt and return, the handler tied a long cord (creance) to its leg and threw a piece of meat for the falcon to retrieve. If the falcon picked up the meat and brought it back, the handler rewarded the bird by allowing it to eat a bit of its prize. This process was repeated over increasing distances and with various lures. The telling moment was the first time the hawk was let off its lead to hunt. Birds were sometimes lost at this crucial point in their training.

Gambling and Games. Other common pastimes were gambling and cards. Almost anything could be the subject of a wager, including the number of soldiers in a company, the winner of a mock combat, or the conclusion of a successful hunt. Various dice games, similar to modern craps, could be played on tables or floors, and wagers were frequently made on their outcome. Many board games were also available. Variations on backgammon were played; panquist, tables, and "six, two, and one" were some popular ones. Boards for other types of play have been found as well. Probably the most familiar medieval board game was chess, which was played by rules similar to those in the modern game. One of the best sources for medieval games at court is the *Book of Games*, written in the mid thirteenth century by Alfonso X "the Wise," king of Castile and León from 1252 to 1284.

Reading. Medieval aristocrats could also pass their time reading or having written works read to them. Some medieval nobles were not literate in the sense that they could sit down and read books, but they often had literate courtiers who were required to read to them. Many of the preferred stories were about classical heroes and knightly bravery, including the tales that developed about the English figure known as King Arthur and his mythical court. Arthurian romances were so popular in the high Middle Ages that the figures of Arthur and his queen, Guinevere, were carved on churches as far from England as Italy. Arthurian romances

Men practicing falconry; illumination from a mid-thirteenth-century manuscript for Frederick II's *The Art of Falconry,* written during the 1240s (Vatican Library)

are part of a literary genre known as courtly literature that developed in southern French courts during the eleventh century and spread all over Europe. In the process, each region developed its own "Arthurian" heroes and villains. The works of leading twelfth-century writers such as Marie of France, Andreas Capellanus, and Chrétien de Troyes were recited at courts and inspired generations of nobles well into the Renaissance to mimic the pride and valor of Arthurian heroes.

Music. Music was another common form of courtly entertainment, and the styles and subjects of songs varied widely. Common medieval instruments for the aristocracy included lap harps, flutes, and the ancestors of modern violins and guitars, such as lutes. Their songs included melodies praising the deeds of the Virgin Mary, bemoaning lost love, celebrating bright spring days, or lauding martial accomplishments. Some songs were sung without instrumental accompaniment (a capella), and some included forms of harmony. Other music was purely instrumental. One kind of music practiced in court society was the canticle, in which the "singer" chanted lyrics to an instrumental accompaniment. One of the best-known musical collections of the Middle Ages, *The Cantigas de Santa Maria* (Canticles of Holy Mary) of Alfonso X "the Wise," comprises more than four hundred canticles. Lavishly illustrated, this manuscript is one of the largest collections of medieval solo songs. Alfonso's court is also the source of another valuable compilation of medieval songs with satirical themes, including jabs at lecherous monks, weak knights, ignorant scholars, and other common objects of ridicule in the Middle Ages. While some nobles, and especially noblewomen, might be able to perform these songs alone or with a small group of musicians, at large and wealthy courts such as Alfonso's the performers were

almost certainly professionals, sometimes known as troubadours, minnesingers, and minstrels. They were either kept on retainer or hired for a set number of performances. In a smaller court or castle a professional might also provide entertainment, but there were far fewer musicians, and the songs they sang were generally less complex.

Sources:
Meg Bogin, *The Women Troubadours* (New York: Paddington Press, 1975).

John Cummins, *The Hound and the Hawk: The Art of Medieval Hunting* (New York : St. Martin's Press, 1988).

Maurice Keen, *Chivalry* (New Haven: Yale University Press, 1984).

Theresa McLean, *The English at Play in the Middle Ages* (Windsor Forest, U.K.: Kensal Press, 1983).

MONASTERIES

The Church in Daily Life. As a landlord, institution, and spiritual guide, the Church was an integral part of the daily lives of all people in medieval Europe. Yet, the Church also had its own material culture, which shared aspects of the lives of nobles and peasants but had distinctive characteristics as well. Monasteries were in principle separate from the rest of the community, and their structures and the lives of their residents were designed to be self-contained. In practice, however, medieval monasteries fulfilled many important roles in the daily lives of the entire Christian community. Churches also had a central role in medieval villages and cities, and the construction of the most dramatic structures in medieval Europe—Romanesque and Gothic cathedrals—highlights the value of the church in urban communities and the integration of clergy and laity in medieval life.

Monasteries and Medieval Society. Monasteries were supposed to follow rules that regulated every aspect of their community life. The Rule of St. Benedict was the most influential. Medieval monasteries were much like prosperous lordships and manors, and their monks had the privileges and responsibilities of large landowners. The wealth of monasteries made them attractive to the sons of the nobility, and monks generally came from the upper classes of medieval society. Yet, for all their influence the number of residents in the average medieval monastery—even when residents who had not taken vows were counted—was relatively small. Large and prestigious institutions such as the Benedictine monasteries of Westminster Abbey in England, Monte Cassino in Italy, and St. Gall in Switzerland had approximately eighty to one hundred monks at their peak, and most medieval monasteries were at least half that size. Yet, monks and monastic institutions greatly influenced medieval society even though they were definitely a minority population.

Nunneries. Around 1100 an advocate for women's pursuit of the monastic life wrote the following description of a laywoman's life: "When she comes in the house, the wife hears her child screaming, sees the cat at the bacon, and the dog gnawing her hides; her biscuit is burning on the stone, and her calf is sucking up her milk; the crock is boiling over into the fire, and the husband is scolding." Although such descriptions were clearly polemical, they emphasize that life in a cloister could provide a fulfilling alternative for medieval women. Like monasteries, nunneries came in many sizes, with wide varieties of wealth, and with great social distinctions in their population. From early in the Middle Ages, certain nunneries were reserved to the nobility, and their lifestyle was relatively luxurious. Monastic rules set up different standards and guidelines for male and female religious communities. In general, however, the female abbeys were poorer and smaller than monasteries. Unlike their male counterparts, they did not actively acquire lands, but waited for gifts to come to them. Although their complexes followed the patterns for male monasteries, their buildings were frequently smaller, their outbuildings less numerous, and their community less diverse. For example, in all but the poorest monasteries, the abbot had a detached residence to himself, while in the nunneries abbesses were told to sleep communally, that is, in the same room, with their nuns. Although the abbesses of the great female abbeys could wield significant secular power, most communities had only local influence.

The Complex and Its Residents. In keeping with their purpose of individual contemplation and prayer, many monasteries were initially built in relatively isolated areas and designed to be self-contained; all the facilities available in a prosperous village or castle could normally be found in a monastic complex, including stables, barns, cisterns, latrines, and kitchens. At the heart of this complex were the church and the cloister. Attached to the church structure, the cloister was a square series of buildings with a central, enclosed courtyard in which the monks did most of their daily living. It was rare for a nonmonk to enter this part of the monastery. Medieval monasteries could have residents other than the monks, and lay brothers, individu-

HOW THE SISTERS ARE TO SLEEP

Written in the sixth century by Benedict of Nursia, the Rule of St. Benedict became the most influential guide for monastic life and monasteries in the Middle Ages. In this section Benedict organized the sleeping chamber for female communities that followed his rule.

Let each one sleep in a separate bed. Let them receive bedding suitable to their manner of life, according to the Abbess's directions. If possible let all sleep in one place; but if the number does not allow this, let them take their rest by tens or twenties with the seniors who have charge of them. A candle shall be kept burning in the room until morning. Let them sleep clothed and girded with belts or cords—but not with their knives at their sides, lest they cut themselves in their sleep—and thus be always ready to rise without delay when the signal is given and hasten to be before one another at the Work of God, yet with all gravity and decorum. The younger shall not have beds next to one another, but among those of the older ones. When they rise for the Work of God let them gently encourage one another, that the drowsy may have no excuse.

Source: *The Rule of St. Benedict*, chapter 22, on-line at <www.osb.org/rb/text/toc.html>.

als who had taken less binding vows than the monks, performed many menial tasks around the monastery. They were housed in separate quarters and ate their meals in separate buildings or separate parts of the dining hall (refectory). Not only did monasteries have lay brothers in residence, but they could have noble and prosperous individuals who essentially used the monastery as a retirement home or a place of refuge. The latter was especially common in upper-class nunneries. Finally, as landowners, monasteries and nunneries had peasants and serfs working for them and under their care. Generally all these people had access to some buildings in the monastic complex, including the church. To deal with these demands and preserve the original purpose of monastic life, parts of the church were reserved for the different sorts of people affiliated with the community. Increasingly during the Middle Ages men and women were separated in distinct religious communities for monks and nuns.

The Ideal Monastery: St. Gall. In the early ninth century, a plan was developed for an ideal Benedictine monastery, filling in the many gaps Benedict left in his description of its structures. Because the plan has been in the library of the Swiss monastery of St. Gall, it is known as the Plan of St. Gall although the layout of that monastery has significant differences from the plan. The more than thirty buildings and the several gardens of this ideal plan illustrate the medieval vision of a monastery's spiritual and social roles. Although the church, cloister, and residential buildings for the monks are at the heart of the complex, the Plan of St. Gall describes buildings for services second only to those obtainable in a large city or a

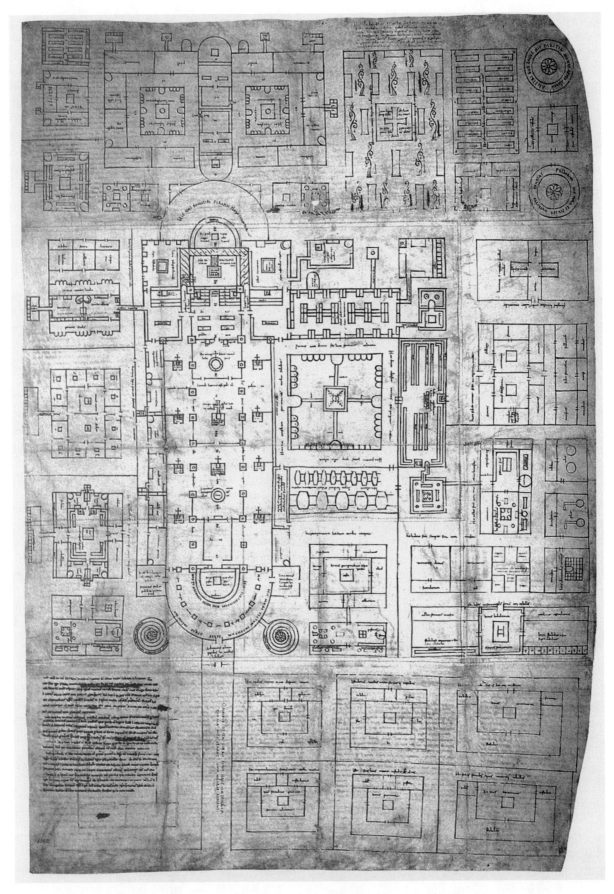

The plan for an ideal Benedictine monastery found in the library of the Swiss monastery of St. Gall (School of Tours, Bibliothèque Municipale, St. Gall)

great castle. There are separate barns for geese, cattle, dairy cows, sheep, goats, pigs, mares, and other horses. The servants caring for these animals also have several buildings as quarters. A brewery, pantry, cellar, bakery, winepress, and several kitchens provide for food preparation. The monastery also needed skilled craftsmen in various fields; tanners, shoemakers, saddlers, turners, goldsmiths, cloth workers, and even sword makers each have a separate workshop. Buildings were designed to hold guests of different social statuses and their retinue. Even public welfare and hygiene were considered. Latrines were placed throughout the complex; there were baths for the monks and others affiliated with the monastery; and there was even a hospital with a separate home for its manager and chief doctor (the infirmarian). A monk living in such a place had little need to leave it to find anything necessary for his livelihood or comfort.

Variations from the Ideal. Although many monastic institutions followed the general organization found in the Plan of St. Gall, they rarely had all the services and separate buildings included there. The church and cloister were always at the center, and kitchens, barns, and various outbuildings were constructed soon after a monastery was established. Because a monastery was intended to be a self-contained complex, it also had storage facilities for food, tools, and raw materials—as well as separate buildings designated for travelers and other visitors. Given the lack of large hotels or other accommodations, large ecclesiastical structures, castles, and manors had a duty to house the retinues of traveling lords. The key differences between the Plan of St. Gall and actual monasteries are found in the number of separate structures, the geographic orientation of the buildings, and the materials with which the buildings were constructed.

Building Monasteries. The ideal monastery was built entirely of stone, and actual monasteries worked to achieve this goal as much as possible. Generally the church, cloister, and other key buildings were stone; workshops and barns were likely to be wooden. The materials used in building monastic structures were predominantly local; in parts of Europe, buildings might be sandstone, in other areas, brick or granite. As such, building techniques took into account local demands and variations. Building methods for wooden structures were much like those for peasant structures, while stone buildings were constructed in the same way as castles and cathedrals. When monasteries were first founded, monks might have worked alongside craftsmen, if craftsmen were even available outside the monastic community. Once the monastery was established, monks generally worked separately from lay craftsmen or brothers, although monks did perform manual labor, and some were skilled artisans.

Plumbing and Water. Medieval monasteries were known throughout Europe for the sophistication of their plumbing systems and their relatively easy access to water. In addition to digging several wells in the com-

plex itself, monastic planners generally established systems of pipes and drains that supplied running water to the monastery. These provisions helped monks enjoy a standard of living about which most medieval Europeans could only dream. For example, Westminster Abbey had a system of pipes that took water to every major building in the monastery. Moreover, Westminster had a series of settling tanks for purifying the water; sediment settled to the bottom and water was taken only from the top. Such provisions contributed to the health of monastery residents and were rare outside of monastic complexes. Latrines were often constructed so that running water washed away the excrement immediately, the closest thing to a flush toilet until the modern era. This access to water made it easier for monks to take baths, although the Benedictine Rule limited full-immersion bathing to four times a year. Baths were considered a worldly luxury, and the rule tried to redirect the monks from worldly to spiritual concerns. For this reason, medieval monks enjoyed the benefits of running water less than aristocrats, who by the thirteenth and fourteenth centuries had apparently incorporated some of this technology into their structures and were enjoying the sanitary benefits.

Decorating Monasteries: Tiles. Monastic structures were decorated by many of the same techniques used in noble castles and cathedrals, but monastery builders were also innovators. It appears that monasteries were among the first medieval buildings to employ tiles extensively as roofing and flooring materials. The manufacture of tiles demanded a supply of the appropriate clay, a large area in which a kiln could be built without endangering other structures, and a group of skilled craftsmen. By the twelfth century glazed, monochrome, and patterned tiles were being used as flooring over wooden supports. Tiles were, of course, custom-made and highly decorative, often covered with floral, animal, and heraldic motifs. Tiles of various colors could be interlaid to form beautiful mosaics, as at Byland Abbey in England. Tiles could also be used on walls almost like paintings and, in the same way, could be used to illustrate stories. Tile decorations brightened medieval monasteries and churches, making them more colorful and vibrant than the sparse structures that modern people frequently imagine.

Sources:

Elizabeth Eames, *Medieval Craftsmen: English Tilers* (Toronto: University of Toronto Press, 1992).

John Fitchen, *Building Construction before Mechanization* (Cambridge, Mass.: MIT Press, 1986).

C. H. Lawrence, *Medieval Monasticism: Forms of Religious Life in Western Europe in the Middle Ages* (London & New York: Longman, 1984).

MONASTERY RELIGIOUS OFFICES AND WORK

Monastic Hours. Medieval monks kept time in the same way that all other people in the Middle Ages did: according to the positions of the sun and the moon. The time from daylight to sunset was divided into twelve equal parts. The twelve hours of the monastic day had more than just an organizational purpose. They structured a series of religious devotions that occurred approximately every three hours during the day and that were central to monastic life. The monastic day began in the middle of the night, around 2:00 or 3:00 A.M., when the monks rose from their beds and recited the prayers known as Matins and Lauds. These prayers lasted for an hour to an hour and a half, unless it was a high holy day when the service might be even more elaborate and longer. The monks then went back to bed until first light, when they rose again to say Prime after they had washed their faces and hands and combed their hair. Between Prime and Tierce (the third hour since sunrise, approximately 9:00 A.M.) a monk had time for prayer or work. After the short service of Tierce, there was morning mass, then a meeting of the monks at which the abbot led discussion and disciplinary matters were handled. Between the end of the meeting and the office of Sext (the sixth hour after daylight, around noon) a monk had time to attend to various personal chores and activities. During this time of the day he was allowed to speak, but for most of his day he was supposed to be silent. After Sext, the main meal was served, and then there was another period for work or reflection, which lasted until None (the ninth hour of the day, around 2:00–3:00 P.M.). At None there was another, brief religious service, which might be followed by a second, light meal. More work or rest took place for another three "hours," until Vespers, which was a longer and more complicated service than most. The evening meal followed, and monks were enjoined to keep silent for the rest of the day. The final service of the day was Compline, which occurred at sunset. After this service, the monks were sprinkled with holy water and went to their dormitory, where they prepared for bed and for the cycle to resume about midnight.

Gregorian Chants. Most of the earliest surviving examples of medieval music were used in religious services, in particular the daily offices. Although there were various forms of church music in the Middle Ages, probably the best known and most widespread were the Gregorian chants. These songs ranged from simple melodies in which each syllable of a word was assigned one note to complex polyphonic (many-voiced) songs with elaborate equations of notes to syllables. Most medieval religious services were chanted, and the number of songs that monks and other clergy might need to learn could be staggering. It has been estimated that by the ninth century almost four thousand chants were part of every church year, and every new feast day meant new songs. In order to make some sense of this huge collection and to ensure that future generations of monks learned the proper chants, the song leaders of medieval churches (cantors) developed one of the first musical notation systems and recorded their songs in huge books. These books were frequently two to three feet tall, almost two feet wide, and at least six inches thick. Although it appears that some monastic communities might have had monks whose vocation was composing new chants, the

EQUIPPING A GOLDSMITH'S SHOP

According to legend, Alexander of Neckham was born the same night as Richard the Lionhearted and became Richard's foster brother. Whatever the truth of these stories, Alexander prospered in his career, becoming Abbot of Cirencester in England. During the late eleventh and early twelfth centuries, Alexander wrote many books on a wide variety of subjects. The following excerpt is from his account of his student days in Paris and describes the tools and materials required by a skilled goldsmith:

The goldsmith should have a furnace with a hole at the top so that the smoke can get out. One hand should govern the bellows with light pressure and with the greatest care so that the air pressed through the nozzle may blow upon the coals and feed the fire. Let him have an anvil of extreme hardness on which the iron or gold may be laid and softened and may take the required form. They can be stretched and pulled with the tongs and the hammer. There should also be a hammer for making gold leaf, as well as sheets of silver, tin, brass, iron, or copper. The goldsmith must have a very sharp chisel with which he can engrave figures of many kinds on amber, hard stone, marble, emerald, sapphire or pearl. He should have a touchstone for testing, and one for distinguishing steel from iron. He must also have a rabbit's foot for smoothing, polishing and wiping the surface of gold and silver. The small particles of metal should be collected in a leather apron. He must have small pottery vessels and cruets, and a toothed saw and file for gold as well as gold and silver wire with which broken objects can be mended or properly constructed. He must also be as skilled in engraving as well as in bas relief, in casting as well as in hammering. His apprentice must have a waxed table, or one covered with clay, for portraying little flowers and drawing in various ways. He must know how to distinguish pure gold from latten and coper, lest he buy latten for pure gold. For it is difficult to escape the wiliness of the fraudulent merchant.

Source: John Cherry, *Medieval Craftsmen: Goldsmiths* (Toronto: University of Toronto Press, 1992), p. 24.

songs of certain individuals circulated widely. One of the most renowned composers of the twelfth century was Hildegard of Bingen, who during her lifetime was also the abbess of Bingen, a mystic, and an author of theological and medical treatises. Her songs were even approved by the Pope.

Vestments. Medieval clergy wore special clothing when celebrating mass and conducting other religious services, and monks were no exception. While the average monk reciting the office remained in his cowl and tunic, the monks officiating at the ceremony often wore elaborately decorated garments called vestments. Vestments followed patterns of other medieval clothing, but the craftsmanship

Examples of medieval goldsmiths' work: a candlestick made for Gloucester Abbey in England at the behest of Abbot Peter, circa 1104–1113, and a chalice made circa 1240 from sardonyx, other precious stones, and metals for Abbot Suger of the Abbey of Saint-Denis in France (left: Victoria and Albert Museum, London; right: Widener Collection, National Gallery, Washington, D.C.)

was infinitely more detailed and the fabrics more valuable than that in the clothing of most laypeople. An important monastery such as Cluny in France, St. Gall, or Westminster had capes for celebrants (called copes) made from thick silks or other luxury fabrics and worked in embroidery that depicted, for example, the life of Christ as a series of fifteen to twenty separate scenes. As with clothing for wealthy nobles, jewels and threads made of precious metals were worked into the fabric. Moreover, the altar cloth and other linens used while serving mass were made of similar fabrics and were also elaborately embroidered. Monks could do such work as part of the labor they were required to perform, but generally these works of art were the product of years of work by professional craftsmen. Sometimes the abbot commissioned them, while at other times they were gifts from wealthy, aristocratic patrons of the monastery. A great religious house that had existed for centuries might have a veritable treasure trove of liturgical clothing. Such clothes were seen as paying honor to God, who was present at the mass, and as testaments to the holiness of the religious services.

Vessels for the Mass. Among the most beautiful examples of the medieval goldsmiths' art are the hundreds of surviving cups, goblets, platters, and other vessels used for mass and other religious offices. Like vestments, these vessels were obtained as gifts, fabricated by professionals, and used to emphasize the sacred nature of the ceremony. A

goldsmith might have his own workshop on the monastery grounds. Such shops were equipped with a large number of specialized metal tools; the money needed to purchase them, as well as a basic stock of raw materials, made the capital outlay for such a shop substantial. Goldsmiths did not just fabricate the basic structure of objects needed for mass. They were responsible for their decoration and, at times, for their design. Thus, the medieval goldsmith needed to be a designer, and many subjects were available to him for decorating objects for religious service. For example, the crosses that decorated the altar table and held relics might be inlaid with jewels, embossed with plants or geometric patterns, and filigreed. At the base, miniature sculptures of saints set inside miniature cathedral doorways might support the cross. Like a noble's jewelry and plate, a monastery's collection of sacred vessels formed its treasury, and if necessary an object could be melted down and converted to ready cash.

Work and Prayer. As the schedule set by the monastic hours suggests, a monk's life was more than just prayer. St. Benedict had directed monks to perform some physical labor during the day as well, arguing against classical and early medieval prejudices when he wrote that God had instituted such work, and it was therefore equally divine. For several hours of the day monks had to perform some sort of "manual" labor. This work could range from supervising the monastic infirmary to working in the gardens,

Monks working in a scriptorum; illumination from the *Moralized Apocalypse*, circa 1226–1234
(Pierpont Morgan Library, New York)

helping in the stables, or instructing novices or lay pupils. During the course of the Middle Ages, monastic reformers had to repeat Benedict's injunction again and again, and the activities considered appropriate for monks were modified over time in response to social pressures. Lay brothers and craftsmen supplied skills that the monks did not have and performed some of the onerous labor, such as harvesting the fields or digging ditches. How much physical labor medieval monks did depended greatly on the religious order to which they belonged, the strictness of their abbot, and personal preference or conviction.

Illumination and Writing. One labor of medieval monks resulted in both beautiful objects of art and the preservation of classical knowledge: writing and illuminating medieval books. A large monastery had a scriptorum, a room reserved for books and for writing them. The preparation of a book began with the gathering of materials: the text that was to be copied, quills and ink of various colors, and the vellum on which it was to be written. Vellum was made of animal hides, preferably sheep, scraped, stretched, and treated so that it could be written on without the ink blurring. Slight imperfections in a hide could make it useless for forming the pages of a book, and it has been estimated that the average medieval Bible took the hides of a hundred sheep. Once the vellum was selected and cut to a uniform, rectangular size, the page was designed. Someone looking closely at a medieval manuscript might see fine, straight lines drawn on the center of the page like the lines in modern binder paper. Generally the text filled only half the page, leaving the margins for decoration. The text was usually written in black ink with the first letter of the page or of a significant word written in different colors and sometimes even designed with a small scene in it. Charlemagne's court developed the standard handwriting used in ecclesiastical documents for centuries—the Carolingian miniscule—but by the thirteenth and fourteenth centuries handwriting had evolved into a distinctive Gothic script with definite regional variations. After the text was written a monk was free to exercise his imagination, at least to some extent. The margins of medieval manuscripts are filled with miniatures depicting not only Bible stories and scenes from saints' lives, but pictures of daily life, elaborate floral patterns, and even fantastic animals. Copying and illuminating a book such as the Bible could take decades and involve a whole workshop of monks. Done by candlelight or the light of a window and in rooms with almost no heat, these manuscripts are testimony to the dedication, piety, and artistry of medieval monks.

Sources:
Patricia Basing, *Trades and Crafts in Medieval Manuscripts* (London: British Library, 1990).

John Cherry, *Medieval Craftsmen: Goldsmiths* (Toronto: University of Toronto Press, 1992).

Christopher De Hamel, *A History of Illuminated Manuscripts* (Boston: Godine, 1986).

Richard H. Hoppin, *Medieval Music* (New York: Norton, 1978).

MONASTIC LIFESTYLES

Communicating in the Monastery. Monks were supposed to be silent during much of the day. Silence not only aided spiritual contemplation, but it helped to prevent disputes and gossip. Monks were not allowed to speak in the church, kitchen, dormitory, and refectory. Even when monks could speak, they were instructed to do so quietly and to speak only about spiritual subjects.

Moreover, monks could not speak with anyone except other monks, even the lay brothers, except in emergencies or if they held office in the monastery. Yet, there were times when communication was essential even if speech was forbidden, and monks developed sign language for use in these periods. Most sign language had to do with basic foodstuffs and activities, but it could become quite elaborate and excessive. Gerald of Wales, who visited Canterbury in the eleventh century, complained about the monks' violation of the spirit, if not the letter, of the Benedictine Rule: "They gesticulated with fingers, hands, and arms, and whistled to each other instead of speaking. . . . It would be more consonant with good order and decency to speak modestly in human speech than to indulge ridiculously in this mute chatter."

Diet. Food had an important place in medieval monasteries for several reasons. First, it was essential to life, and St. Benedict had condemned fasts and other austerities that prevented monks from performing their spiritual duties. Second, as central social and spiritual institutions, monasteries had the responsibility to provide food to travelers and the poor. Finally, food and gluttony were symbols of the worldly preoccupations that monks were supposed to avoid. As such, dietary regulation permeated monastic life. Like other medieval people, monks were subject to meatless fast days as part of their religious observations. On those days fish, vegetables, cheese, and grains formed the basis of their meals. On other days meat was consumed quite frequently, generally at every meal, in all but the strictest religious houses. Bread was served at every meal, and the allotment was often around a pound a day. All leftovers were distributed to the poor. In addition, the number of foods available at each meal was quite diverse. The Benedictine Rule required two cooked dishes to be served at each meal in addition to bread, cheese, seasonal fruit, and beverages. It also provided for dietary supplements and additional dishes, called pittances, on special occasions. By the twelfth and thirteenth century it was common for several pittances to be included with each meal. In the course of the Middle Ages, monastic dietary rules also became increasingly lax. In order to fulfill dietary regulations while appeasing delicate palates, fine distinctions were drawn among kinds of meat. As Barbara Harvey has noted,

> They distinguished between the muscle tissue of animals—"butcher's meat," as we should say—and the offal and entrails, which were not to be regarded as "meat"; and between fresh meat cut from the joint, on the one hand, and salted, pre-cooked, or chopped meat, on the other. A monk, they said, kept the Rule if all that he consumed was a pork fritter, for which the meat was pre-cooked, or "umbles"—sheeps' entrails cooked in ale and breadcrumbs—but he broke it if he ate fresh roast beef.

Monastic Mealtime. Sit-down meals were served in medieval monasteries at least twice a day. With anywhere from twenty to many more than one hundred individuals to be fed in several locations, preparing and serving them could become quite a production. Monks were required to

MONASTIC SIGN LANGUAGE

The reform movement based at Cluny in France was probably the most significant monastic movement of the tenth and eleventh centuries. While a monk there, Udalric composed a book called *The Ancient Customs of the Monastery of Cluny* (circa 1086). Among many other topics, Udalric describes the sign language used by monks when they were not allowed to speak.

For the sign for bread, make a circle with both thumbs and index fingers, since bread is usually round. . . .

For the sign for beans, place the tip of the index finger on top of the first joint of the thumb, and in this way make the thumb stick out. . . .

For a general sign for fish, imitate the motion of the fish's tail in the water with your hand.

For the sign for honey, stick out your tongue just a bit, and apply your fingers to it as if you were going to lick them.

For the sign for garlic or horseradish, open your mouth slightly and extend your finger toward it, on account of the sort of odor that comes from it.

For the sign for water, place all your fingers together, and move them sideways. . . .

For the sign for a dish, hold out your hand flat. . . .

For the sign for the tunic, hold its sleeve with three fingers, the little finger and the two next to it.

For the sign for braies, do the same thing, and at the same time pull your hand up along your thigh like someone who is putting on his braies.

[Sign used by someone asking permission to leave early from a meal:] He rises from the table, comes toward the dais, and with his hand stretched out, draws it away from his chest.

[Sign used by someone wishing to see a priest for confession:] Taking his hand out of his sleeve, he places it on his chest, which is the sign for confession.

Source: Udalric, "Antiquiores Consuedtudines Cluniacensis Monasterii," in *Patrilogia Latina*, edited by J.-P. Migne, 149 (Paris: Garnier, 1882), cols. 703–704, 707, 711.

eat their meals in the refectory unless they were sick or had pressing duties; sick monks ate diets tailored to their illnesses in the infirmary. Monastic complexes generally had separate refectories for the lay brothers and the monks. Moreover, the abbot might take his meals in his own lodgings, particularly if he were entertaining an influential visitor. Serving meals was a chore rotated among the healthy monks, and it qualified as one of their good works, a meritorious duty blessed by God. The meal began with grace and prayers. Then the monk in charge of provisions and the kitchens (the cellarer) sent his assistants into the dining hall to distribute platters of food. The monks were supposed to remain quiet during meals, but one monk might be given the task of reading psalms or biblical verses to the others. Like medieval nobles, monks placed their food on bread trenchers and, by the twelfth and thirteenth centuries, wooden plates. They ate with spoons and knives. Ale, wine, and water were served with each meal. Once a monk was done, he waited at the table until everyone was dismissed.

Clothes. Monastic garments were distinctive, and medieval people could tell to which religious order a monk or friar belonged by the color and cut of his clothes. Among a monk's most dramatic differences from the laity, however, were his hair and the thick cowl that covered his head. When a monk took his preliminary vows, his hair was cut into a tonsure, that is, it was shaved leaving a row of hair around the skull just above the ears. (The size of the area shaved varied somewhat.) Generally made of wool, the cowl was a long, loose, sleeveless garment with a deep hood attached. The hood provided warmth, and, if a monk needed to leave the monastery, it protected him from the outside world by hiding his face from view and blocking the world from his field of vision. Under his cowl, a medieval monk wore clothes similar to the peasant or nobleman's braies, tunic, hose, mantle, and shoes. Over his cowl a monk put a loose gown with long sleeves that usually covered even his hands. Depending on the religious order, the gown came in different, albeit subdued, colors; for example, Benedictines generally wore black, while the Cistercian's gown was of white wool. Depending on a monk's activities additional clothes might be issued to him, such as gloves to protect hands while gardening or sheepskin slippers for ill monks. Although a medieval monk's wardrobe might seem minimal, compared to even many minor nobles he was quite comfortable.

Laundry and Hygiene. Laundry services were available for the monks in the cloister, and there is some evidence that by the later Middle Ages monks also sent their laundry out of the monastery when such services were available. A monk who needed to wash his clothing removed it modestly—generally under his blankets—folded it, and took it to the washing facilities. Laundry was left to soak in the tub during the chapter meeting, and during the afternoon the monk washed out his clothing and hung it out to dry. Any clothes that needed mending were put in a location where they were taken to the monastery's tailor, and any clothes that were beyond basic repairs or were getting threadbare were set aside for distribution to the poor. Running and piped water made laundry easier in a monastery than elsewhere; it also aided shaving, bathing, and other aspects of personal hygiene. Although full-body baths were considered sensuous and, therefore, potentially sinful, monks were expected to wash their hands, feet, faces, and other body parts as needed every day. Based on biblical models, foot washing even became a valuable ritual of humility, and monks washed the feet of other monks and of poor people who came to the monastery. Shaving and barbering appears to have been done weekly, and often the monks took turns caring for each other. In the late Middle Ages some more-lax monasteries might hire a professional barber. These activities were socially segregated. Monks cared for other monks, while the lay brothers helped only other lay brothers. Such segregation was carried out at many levels; at

An abbot preaching to nuns; illumination from a mid-fourteenth-century Flemish manuscript describing the duties of Abbot Gilles li Muisis (Bibliothèque Royale, Brussels)

Westminster Abbey there were even separate latrines for the monks, the monks' officials, the lay brethren, and for common use.

Sleeping. The dormitory where most of the monks slept was often one of the largest buildings in the monastic complex, sometimes measuring more than 150 feet long and 30 feet wide. The monks' beds were arranged in rows down the two long walls, much like those in a military barracks. A monk had no privacy in these dormitories, and only monasteries that deviated from the Benedictine Rule allowed curtains to separate the monks' beds, which were wooden frames lined with straw. A mattress made of canvas and probably filled with straw was put on the frame and covered with a woolen blanket or two. A monk got into bed fully clothed, even with his hood over his head. After he crawled under the covers, he removed the top layers of his clothing, which he placed at the head of his bed so that he could easily reach them when called to Matins. These provisions were designed to protect the monks' modesty and minimize any sexual impulses that a naked body might cause. Luxurious dormitories might provide a small chest for a monk's few clothes and possessions; the chest was supposed to remain unlocked. There were often windows set high on the dormitory walls, and a large dormitory had some sort of fire. Fires and other lights were extinguished once the monks went to bed, so getting up for Matins must have been cold and dreary.

The Infirmary. Most monasteries had at least one monk with medical expertise (the infirmarian) who managed the infirmary. Sometimes infirmarians engaged in the sort of medical practices performed by surgeons or apothecaries—which were looked down on as manual labor and as crafts in the Middle Ages—but infirmarians were generally diagnosticians and left to others the treatment they prescribed. The Benedictine Rule allowed ill and elderly monks additional comforts and dietary privileges, and custom diets were even developed for them. The infirmary surroundings could be relatively luxurious, and a trip to the infirmary could seem like a brief vacation. For example, the infirmary in Westminster Abbey had red and green worsted wall hangings and blue cushions with a pattern of foliage and birds in flight. A sick monk brought his own bedclothes—generally the undergarments he wore every day—but beds, mattresses, and blankets were provided. There were also attempts to make the infirmary more sanitary and comfortable. The thick rushes that covered the floors retained heat, minimized sound, and gave some cushioning underfoot. These rushes were changed at least once a month. Moreover, the infirmary hall, its parlor, and even the individual rooms where the sick were housed had fires. Even though the fires were extinguished at night, the infirmary's rooms were still significantly warmer and less drafty than the dormitory. Most monasteries also treated sick people from the neighboring community, and the infirmarian and his assistants might be called to mix drugs, set bones, and contain contagious diseases.

Sources:

Judith M. Bennett, ed. *Sisters and Workers in the Middle Ages* (Chicago: University of Chicago Press, 1989).

Barbara Harvey, *Living and Dying in England, 1100–1500: The Monastic Experience* (New York: Oxford University Press, 1993).

Berenice M. Kerr, *Religious Life for Women, c.1100–c.1350: Fontevraud in England* (Oxford: Clarendon Press, 1999).

C. H. Lawrence, *Medieval Monasticism: Forms of Religious Life in Western Europe in the Middle Ages* (London & New York: Longman, 1984).

URBAN CHURCHES

Churches and Chapels. Many churches other than monasteries existed, and even monasteries varied widely. A village often had a local church whose priest ministered to that community and sometimes even to neighboring villages. Within towns there could be urban monasteries (generally founded before the town itself), parish churches whose priests acted much like village priests, private chapels, and other ecclesiastical institutions and structures. Like monasteries, most were built of stone, and, like monks, the clergymen who ran them had a higher standard of living and controlled a larger amount of property than most of their neighbors. Like their monastic counterparts, these clergy also had a day that was regulated at least in part by an ecclesiastical calendar and the need to say mass or perform other religious services. Urban churches often had significant differences from their rural counterparts. In particular, the urban church was often identified with the urban community,

---

CONTRACT FOR A PAINTING

In 1308, when Duccio di Buoninsegna, the leading painter in Siena during the late thirteenth and early fourteenth centuries, was hired to paint a *Maestà* (Virgin in Majesty) to replace the old altarpiece in the cathedral of Siena, his contract included the following provisions:

> [He agrees] to make the said panel as even he was able . . . and to work continuously upon it at such times as he was able to work on it, and not to accept or receive any other work to be carried out until the said panel shall have been made and completed. . . . [Duccio is to be paid] sixteen *soldi* of Sienese money for each day that the said Duccio shall work with his own hands on the said panel except that if he should lose any part of the day there should be a deduction from the said salary established in proportion to the time lost . . . .

> In like manner, the said Clerk of the Works . . . promises to supply and to give all those things which shall be necessary for the working of the said panel, so that the said Duccio shall be bound to put nothing into it except his person and his work. . . . Moreover the said Duccio, for greater precaution, swore voluntarily on the Holy Gospels of God, physically touching the book, that he would observe and implement each and everything in good faith and without fraud.

Source: Paul Binski, *Medieval Craftsmen: Painters* (Toronto: University of Toronto Press, 1991), pp. 50–51.

---

and its maintenance and the activities of its residents were seen as reflections on that community. For this reason, among others, urban laity became increasingly involved in the Middle Ages with the administration of their churches and the daily life of their clergy.

Cathedrals and Civic Life. A cathedral was a church that was the seat of a bishop; it was the symbolic center of his authority because it sheltered the episcopal throne that represents his spiritual and temporal authority. The cathedral complex of which it was a part housed the episcopal court and a college of canons, clergymen who assisted the bishop and who administered the cathedral and its properties. Because it was the tallest and largest building, the cathedral came to symbolize the status and aspirations of the city. A city with a cathedral had enormous regional stature and a consistent source of revenue from pilgrims, donors, and other visitors. In addition, the cathedral often provided a dramatic backdrop for key urban events. Not only were religious feast days celebrated most dramatically there, but the square in front of the cathedral and the cathedral cemetery gradually became the largest open spaces in most medieval towns. As such, they were sites for assemblies, elections, marketplaces, and even playing fields. Surrounded by the graves of their ancestors, urban citizens elected their leaders.

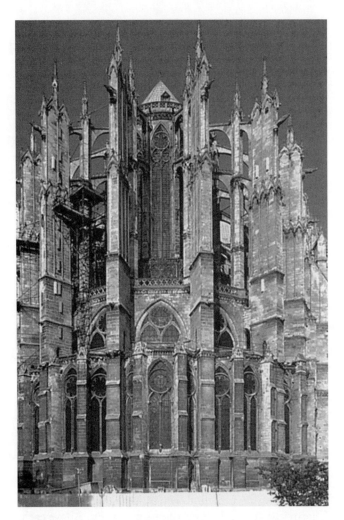

The 157-foot-tall nave of Beauvais Cathedral, reconstructed after it collapsed in 1284, and the flying buttresses that were added to the exterior of the building to support the weight of the rebuilt roof

Cathedrals and Education. Cathedral schools were one of the few ways a young man could receive a literary education. Although most of the pupils were intended for the priesthood, by the twelfth and thirteenth centuries boys of the upper or prosperous classes might receive a year or two of formal schooling from the church or a cathedral school. Some students were admitted on charity. In cathedral schools boys learned to read, write, and add basic figures. Any further education was often dependent on the career a boy's father or guardian chose for him. Boys who were in training to be churchmen might get further schooling, particularly by the twelfth and thirteenth centuries.

Building Cathedrals. Citizens and clergy often cooperated in building enormous and elaborate cathedrals, developing along the way many of the most innovative building techniques and designs of the Middle Ages. From the tenth to the twelfth centuries, churches were built and rebuilt all over Europe in the Romanesque style. At the same time that the Romanesque style was reaching its height, a new architectural style was developed: Gothic design. Led by Abbot Suger of the monastery of St. Denis outside of Paris, Gothic architects attempted to transcend the height limits imposed by heavy stone construction and to convey the light and mysteriousness of God. In the pro-

cess they raised medieval churches to unheard-of heights; for example, the interior of Notre Dame Cathedral in Paris is 107 feet high (approximately ten stories tall) and 493 feet long. Spreading from northern France to Germany, Switzerland, Italy, Spain, and England by the fourteenth century, Gothic architecture became the style most frequently associated with medieval churches. Towering over the towns that surrounded them, Gothic cathedrals were a dramatic statement of the devotion, determination, and prosperity of both the ecclesiastical and secular community. These qualities often led to competition between towns over which could build the highest or most elaborate cathedrals. Such competitions halted in 1284 when the nave at Beauvais in northern France collapsed.

Builders. The figures responsible for developing the innovations that made Gothic cathedrals possible—such as groin and rib vaults and flying buttresses—were the master masons, who also coordinated the hundreds of workmen and dozens of craftsmen employed in constructing cathedrals. Some masons signed their work. Villard de Honnecort is probably the best known because of the survival of his sketchbook. Like other master masons, Villard was proficient in geometry and algebra. Using sketches and models he guided stonemasons, carpenters, and other craftsmen in working with thousands of tons of lumber, stone, and metal. The first stages in building a cathedral involved laying stone foundations and building a timber framework to support the vaults and arches during construction. Stone was lifted into place using a simple hoist or the "Great Wheel," a treadmill-powered hoist mounted in the roof beams that looks like a much larger version of the wheels put in hamster cages. Scaffolding was built next to the structure as it was being constructed; and, as passages and stairways were completed, stairways between layers of the building gave access to outside walls and the roof. While some of the workers were highly skilled craftsmen, other individuals provided brute force and were paid minimal salaries.

Sculptors. Among the important contributors to the beauty of cathedrals were the sculptors, most of whom did not sign their work. Sculpture was used extensively in decorating the insides and outsides of Gothic cathedrals. While gargoyles are probably the best-known medieval sculptures, elaborate traceries and life-size statues were more common. On the columns and pillars inside the church were statues of saints and carvings representing key moments in the lives of Jesus and the saints. Later in the Middle Ages gravestones with relief carvings of the dead were set into the floors, and freestanding tombs with effigies and other decorative motifs were placed between pillars or in side chapels. The doorways of Gothic cathedrals commonly included sculptures designed to convey important messages about Christianity and salvation to all who entered the cathedral. For example, the cathedral of Chartres has three doorways on its west front. Above each doorway in a recessed arch is a carved scene depicting the story of Christ and his redemption. The large panel (tympanum) on the right shows Mary giving birth, presenting Jesus at the temple, and sitting on a throne with the baby Jesus. The left door portrays Christ ascending into heaven; a series of signs pointing to the end of the world and the Last Judgment accompany Christ. Above the center entrance the sculptor displayed Christ in Majesty with the Apostles below him and figures from the Book of Revelation surrounding him. Supporting each of these arches and surrounding the entrances to the Church are twenty-four life-size sculptures of kings and prophets from the Old Testament, Christ's human and spiritual ancestors. The sculptures at the west front of Chartres are representative of the decorative and instructive schemes of Gothic cathedrals.

Other Artisans. Medieval builders and craftsmen decorated Gothic cathedrals using many other techniques besides sculpture. Floors were tiled or inlaid with marble; walls were whitewashed or painted with religious scenes; and architectural features might be highlighted with gilding. The lower tier of windows and the main windows in the front and back of the church were made of stained glass, which set prisms of colors radiating around the church. Parishioners and other devout people presented the cathedral with silver and gold candlesticks, embroidered linens, and devotional paintings. Even poor people could express their piety, leaving little images around altars or other places in the church in remembrance of some favor God had shown them. These images were known as *ex votos* and could take many shapes: dolls, tiny pictures, no-longer-needed crutches. Another sign of devotion was an Agnus Dei (Lamb of God), a small wax statue in the shape of a lamb, about three or four inches high. Especially by the late Middle Ages, a Gothic cathedral was an almost riotous mix of color, image, and texture, not the plain and stately structures that remain.

Painters and Patrons. Devotional pictures played a central role in the medieval church. Not only were they testimonies to the faith of the person who ordered them and had them hung, but they served as lessons for illiterate churchgoers. Cathedrals were frequently decorated with wall paintings, frescoes (paint applied to wet plaster), and canvases commissioned by major corporations or powerful clans. The contracts for such work show the important role of the patron in medieval art. The painter was regarded as a skilled craftsman, not as an inspired artist. The client often determined the subject and composition of the painting and specified the materials and colors to be used in creating it. Colors were particularly important because of their symbolic and actual value; certain paints, such as gold and blue, required expensive dyes. The use of such materials testified to the client's willingness to spend a great deal of money to glorify God or the saints depicted in the painting—and gave earthly glory to the client. Because painting cycles could cover entire church walls, whole workshops could work for years on them; for example, in the Arena Chapel in Padua murals by the Italian master Giotto cover the walls entirely from floor to ceiling, and even the ceiling is painted to look like the heavens. Painters often decorated the altars, the pillars, and various freestanding sculptures in the cathedral.

Sources:
Paul Binski, *Medieval Craftsmen: Painters* (Toronto: University of Toronto Press, 1991).

Jean Bony, *French Gothic Architecture of the Twelfth and Thirteenth Centuries* (Berkeley: University of California Press, 1983).

Nicola Coldstream, *Medieval Craftsmen: Masons and Sculptors* (Toronto: University of Toronto Press, 1989).

Frances Gies and Joseph Gies, *Cathedral, Forge, and Waterwheel: Technology and Invention in the Middle Ages* (New York: HarperCollins, 1994).

Hans Erich Kubach, *Romanesque Architecture* (New York: Electa/Rizzoli, 1988).

Elizabeth Bradford Smith and Michael Wolfe, eds., *Technology and Resource Use in Medieval Europe: Cathedrals, Mills, and Mines* (Aldershot, U.K. & Brookfield, Vt.: Ashgate, 1997).

URBAN FORTIFICATIONS AND PUBLIC PLACES

The Scope of Medieval Cities. By the tenth century urbanization in Europe followed two patterns. Almost every city of any substantial size (5,000–10,000 residents or larger) in Christian Europe was located south of the Alps or along the Mediterranean, while those few surviving cities north of the Alps were based around administrative centers or were located in Flanders and along the western Rhine. Scholars have many theories about the reasons for this division; the influence of Roman foundations, traditions of urbanism, and the extent of Viking or other invasions are three of the most convincing. By the fourteenth century, this pattern remained roughly the same, but the number and size of urban centers all over Europe had grown enormously. Spurred by administrative centralization and economic revival throughout Europe, cities such as London and Paris reached 30,000 and 70,000–80,000 residents respectively, and entire regions of northern Europe, such as Flanders and the southwestern Holy Roman Empire, were dotted with cities whose populations ranged from 3,000 to 20,000 people. In southern Europe the cities had grown proportionately larger, and leading cities such as Florence, Milan, and Venice formed city-states (communes) of their own, independent from any noble lord. Although the European population that lived in cities remained only 5–10 percent, medieval city dwellers had a disproportionate impact on European history.

The Appearance of Cities. Medieval law made a technical distinction between a city and a town. A city was the seat of a bishop and contained a cathedral with its dependent population, while a town was an urban center that did not have a bishop. This distinction may be important legally, judicially, and even socially, but from the point of view of how people lived their daily lives it is insignificant, and this discussion applies *city* and *town* according to population. Some cities were based on old Roman establishments, particularly in southern Europe. Often a city grew up around a monastery, cathedral, or castle, while still others were plantations, promoted by lords who wanted to establish a community in a particular region so that its resources could be exploited. Creating a new town was a relatively simple procedure. A lord gave permission for a settlement to develop on his land. Although he leased the land to the settlers as well as exacting labor and other services from them, these taxes of rent and services were generally at reduced rates, and the peasants who settled in a new town also enjoyed legal privileges. Frequently they were granted lucrative rights, such as the ability to hold fairs, and they might even be given permission to collect taxes to build some sort of fortifications to protect their city.

Size. Medieval cities were generally quite small by modern standards and remained so long after 1300. Size depended on the location and the economic and social foundations of the city or town. For example, in thirteenth-century Germany the average city numbered 2,000–3,000 residents, and at most only fifty cities had populations of more than 5,000. Yet, in Italy or Spain more than a dozen cities had populations in excess of 25,000. Because of the differences in population, the geographic sizes of cities varied enormously. A large city such as Cologne, the biggest city in medieval Germany, might have almost 1,000 acres of land within its city walls, but most cities were sub-

stantially smaller. The typical area enclosed by city walls was between 50 and 200 acres. Moreover, much of this area was undeveloped; only in the fourteenth century, and then only in certain towns, was there pressure to build on the open spaces within the walls. In addition, most cities had at least some jurisdictional rights beyond the city walls, and most residents owned or worked land there. For these reasons medieval city dwellers were sometimes uncertain about where the city stopped and its exact size. It depended on what aspect of a city a person was considering.

City Walls. Walls were one of the qualities that distinguished a city from a village. The strength and maintenance of these walls varied enormously from place to place. Many cities were content to rely on old Roman walls or on wooden palisades until the twelfth century. Even then, when town councils around Europe began to rebuild and sometimes extend their walls, their efforts were piecemeal. Wars inspired urban residents to open their coffers for improving, maintaining, and extending fortifications, and in times of peace the structures were frequently neglected. There are even records of walls being propped up by wooden braces or of itinerants digging through the walls at night after they had been denied admission through a gate. When a wealthy and powerful lord decided to fortify a city, however, the results could be impressive. In the late twelfth century, the French king Philip Augustus renovated the walls of Paris and extended them so that they enclosed all the residents on both sides of the river Seine. In this case the appearance of the walls, as well as the money and resources expended on them, might be compared to those of well-fortified castles. The fortifications at Paris had walls six to ten feet thick and up to thirty feet tall. Every two hundred feet a tower was constructed, and six gates were built into the walls on each side of the river. A series

The double-walled town of Carcassonne, France

of castles provided further fortification. As in other medieval cities, groups of citizens patrolled the walls night and day and were led by craft masters or members of the town council. Many regional centers could not afford such elaborate walls, especially since many medieval cities needed to expand their walls at least once to accommodate the population surge of the High Middle Ages.

Markets. Many cities were established to be markets or developed at the site of markets, and market squares remained important locations in every medieval town. Any city had one site designated for general markets at least once a week, and they were often held more frequently. Larger commercial towns such as those in Flanders had several markets open several days a week with each specializing in a particular kind of goods, including cloth, food, and flowers. Frequently craftsmen built their houses around the market where they sold their goods. Although markets began as open squares where a craftsman or farmer displayed his or her goods on the ground or on tables, they rapidly gained set locations and structures, particularly in mercantile centers. A town looking to attract merchants built a covered market hall and rented fixed spaces to traders, assuring consistent attendance even in poor weather by sellers and buyers alike. Moreover, merchants who had shops around the market square opened the fronts of their shops, providing both free access during markets and a secure and convenient shelter for their products. Both methods enhanced trade because consumers could be sure that their shops would be at the market month after month, year after year. In addition, markets attracted less-

prosperous sellers. Peddlers and farmers working from carts were licensed by the town council to sell used goods and produce from their farms. When a city had bridges, they often became important commercial centers for luxury goods; London Bridge had such shops, and the Ponte Vecchio in Florence continues to house elegant jewelry shops. A city of 5,000–10,000 had markets and shops that could supply any goods a resident might need, and large commercial ports sold goods from Africa, Asia, and the Near East at their markets.

Roads. By modern standards, the roads in medieval towns were narrow, dark, crooked, and filthy, a natural outgrowth of the lack of early medieval urban planning. Even cities founded by lords developed in a relatively random way, with maybe only one or two straight streets laid out as part of the original plan. These main roads were dirt and were often only twelve to fifteen feet wide. Most medieval cities expanded gradually and with minimal supervision from town councils or lords. Roads developed to connect markets, churches, and buildings belonging to civic leaders, and they wove around the fronts of established structures and vacant lots. As foot or cart paths, most of these secondary roads needed to be no wider than eight to ten feet wide. Once buildings were constructed alongside these paths, they could not be widened. To get more light inside their structures, medieval masons built each story so that it jutted out a foot or two beyond the level below it. Although this style did not hinder passage in the street, it reduced the amount of light that reached street level. Horses, dogs, and other livestock roamed city streets and left their droppings behind them. A well-planned city might have a drain in the center of the road with water running through it, and city street cleaners infrequently pushed the garbage that collected on the road into the drain, so that it would run into a neighboring stream, river, or lake. Because the roads were dirt, dust was an ongoing problem, and when it rained the roads turned into quagmires. There were no sidewalks. During the Middle Ages some attempts were made to put cobblestones on at least their major thoroughfares, but they were successful only in major cities that had wealthy and powerful patrons. Most regional centers had primarily dirt streets well into the fifteenth century.

Water. Access to water was a problem in most medieval cities. Even though many were founded alongside rivers, lakes, or streams, every river in the more populous parts of Europe was polluted by the Middle Ages. To obtain a supply of pure water, most cities in medieval Europe built wells. They were generally lined with masonry, and some even used animal power to lift the buckets of water. Although digging and maintaining these wells could be a difficult task, most cities were built on low ground and were, therefore, closer to the water table than structures such as castles, which were usually built on hills. Some cities around the Mediterranean enjoyed piped water carried to them on ancient Roman aqueducts, but as in cities elsewhere in Europe this water was generally made available to residents in public wells or fountains. Obtaining clean water was an arduous chore for the residents of most medieval cities.

Sanitation and Cleanliness. As the descriptions of roads and water supplies suggest, sanitation was poor, and cleanliness was difficult to achieve in most medieval towns. Roaming animals did more than just defecate and urinate in the streets; loose pigs and dogs sometimes wandered into houses and were known to attack unsupervised children. Rats, mice, fleas, flies, and lice were common, and medieval guides to household management despaired of eliminating such vermin, concentrating instead on maintaining acceptable levels of them. Although the Black Death of the mid fourteenth century is the most dramatic disease that struck medieval urban concentrations, throughout the Middle Ages cities were susceptible to diseases of various sorts. Malaria, typhoid, influenza, and other sicknesses with names that have not been linked to specific diseases were recurring killers. In fact, cities would have declined in population if rural residents did not regularly move to the city to take advantage of the freedoms and opportunities there. Disposing of industrial waste was also a problem. Crafts such as tanning leather and dyeing cloth demanded large quantities of water, so tanners and dyers located their shops on rivers. Despite repeated injunctions by town councils to locate those shops downstream from the town, there is repeated evidence that their by-products entered the urban water supply. Even if craftsmen obeyed these injunctions, the pollution was in the water supply for all downstream communities. Human waste was also a serious problem. Some cities made feeble attempts to concentrate the waste in one area for ease of removal. For example, medieval London had at least sixteen public latrines, but they were for a population of at least twenty-five thousand. Most medieval houses had their own cesspits in back, where waste was disposed, and the contents gradually seeped into the water table. These cesspits also created an incredible stench. People without yards frequently dumped the contents of their chamber pots out the window into an alley or into a neighboring river. The filth in rivers could reach amazing extremes. In medieval London, jailers complained that the Fleet River, which ran alongside the prison, was "so obstructed by dung" that the river had become almost solid and no longer hindered prisoners from escaping. Under such conditions, it is amazing that some residents of medieval cities lived to ripe old ages.

Families, Rivalries, and City Towers: The Example of Genoa. Although medieval cities might seem small by modern standards, they often intimidated medieval people, and both new and old residents formed smaller communities within the city for support. In urban Italy, these leagues left visible marks on cityscapes: fortified towers. Although these towers were originally wood, stone or brick was preferred and used by the most powerful leagues. Towers were designed so that league members could throw or shoot projectiles at members of rival leagues who were passing below or stationed in neighboring towers during the frequent feuds in medieval Italian cities. City governments did try to stop these feuds. For example, cities such as Pisa passed laws limiting heights of towers and banning private citizens from owning the most deadly weapons of the time. Such laws were frequently ignored, however, and another powerful Italian city, Genoa, was known for its towers. Anyone approaching the city saw the standard urban landmark, the main church, and then a cityscape bristling with towers that surpassed the official city limit of eighty feet. According to Frances and Joseph Gies, these "rugged square towers dominated neighborhoods that were fortified compounds, within which banded together the great aristocratic lineages. The core of each enclave was composed of a few wealthy families claiming relationship, around which were settled a number of lesser families, some of them poor relations, some dependent clients. Houses fronted on a square enclosing market, shops, covered corridors and walkways (loggias), ovens, gardens, bath, and church." The social life of aristocratic Genoese and their urban leagues centered around such complexes, each dominated by its tower. In the thirteenth and fourteenth centuries, urban governments in Italy became strong enough to tear down most of these towers, but remnants can be seen in most Italian cities.

Sources:

M. W. Barley, *European Towns: Their Archaeology and Early History* (New York: Academic Press, 1977).

Maurice Beresford, *New Towns of the Middle Ages* (Wolfboro, N.H.: Sutton, 1988).

Frances Gies and Joseph Gies, *Marriage and Family in the Middle Ages* (New York: Harper & Row, 1987).

Urban Tigner Holmes, *Daily Living in the Twelfth Century, Based on the Observations of Alexander Neckham in London and Paris* (Madison: University of Wisconsin Press, 1952).

Diane Owen Hughes, "Domestic Ideals and Social Behavior: Evidence from Medieval Genoa," in *The Family in History*, edited by Charles E. Rosenberg (Philadelphia: University of Pennsylvania Press, 1975).

David Nicholas, *The Growth of the Medieval City: From Late Antiquity to the Early Fourteenth Century* (London & New York: Longman, 1997).

URBAN LIVING: BURGHERS

Who Was a Burgher? *Burgher* is a synonym for many words used in modern English, including *bourgeoisie, burgess, citizen*, and *urban elite*. Although generally not aristocrats or nobles, medieval burghers enjoyed a special legal and economic status because they were citizens of a particular town. To become a citizen in many medieval towns, a person had to be male or born into a citizen family, reside in the city a certain number of years, be engaged in a respectable business, pay a substantial entry fee, and have other citizens vouch for his character. By no means was every resident of a medieval city a citizen, and the exact percentage varied from place to place. Moreover, although their status might not be documented officially, burghers were often a special class of citizen. Generally the most prosperous, prestigious, and politically influential citizens, urban burghers dominated their towns, becoming almost urban lords. As such, their standard of living was substantially higher than that of their fellow residents.

Burghers' Houses. As in villages, homes in medieval cities were initially laid out with substantial yards. For example, lots of 40 by 80 feet and 50–60 by 100 feet were common in twelfth-century Regensburg, Germany. Burghers often owned buildings scattered throughout the town, and it was not uncommon that a burgher's primary residence was built on several lots. As with medieval castles and peasant homes, construction materials depended on what was available and traditional in a region. Although southern European burghers had stone houses from the early Middle Ages, in northern Europe many burghers' houses were made of wood. The mark of a prosperous burgher became the construction of a stone house, a pattern found throughout Europe by the twelfth century. These houses were frequently long and narrow, to fit on a city lot. They had several stories and, when the water table permitted, a cellar to store household supplies. Business was conducted on the ground floor, while the upper floors were reserved for household members or privileged guests. Styles differed dramatically from region to region. In southern Europe, for example, it was customary to build a stone house around an open central courtyard, continuing the style of the ancient Romans. In medieval northern Europe such a courtyard, with a heavy wooden gate, might be built at the primary entrance, but it was more common for burgher houses to open directly onto the street, with the entire property fenced and entrances to the storage areas opening off back alleys. By the thirteenth century the number of windows in the upper stories had increased, and glass was being used to control drafts. Moreover, by this time increased attention was being paid to the facade facing the busiest street, and wooden trim and sculptural elements were added. The ground floor, however, remained quite stout with no windows and thick wooden doors reinforced with iron—providing some protection in case of an urban riot or a fight between rival clans.

Decoration. In matters of decoration and taste, urban burghers imitated the secular and ecclesiastical lords around them. Painted walls, embroidered wall hangings, and tiled floors all moved in and out of style in the course of the Middle Ages. Only the richest merchants could afford decorations as good or expensive as those of the upper nobility. Prized possessions were silver candlesticks and plates and thick, elaborately decorated linens; inventories made of burghers' possessions after their deaths included the material, ornamentation, and wear of each piece of linen in a household. The rooms in a burgher's house most likely to have extensive embellishments were the public room—where the master of the house received his clients, hosted dinners, and otherwise presented a public facade—and the master's bedroom. The supplies for a kitchen might be costly but they were rarely decorative. The other rooms in a medieval burgher's home had undifferentiated functions, as suggested by furnishings and decorations. In many cases, it was a question of where to use the available resources most productively.

Furnishings. Furnishings also followed the pattern of those in medieval castles, although the number and quality of the pieces were never as great as those of the upper nobility. Chests were the most common objects, while beds were some of the largest and most costly furnishings. Furniture was generally wooden and of local manufacture. Only the wealthiest families could purchase large objects that had to be shipped. Metal objects were especially valuable and listed as such in inventories. Chests could be carved, painted, and gilded, and burghers availed themselves of all these techniques to add color and luxury to their homes. Certain chests, such as the Italian marriage chests known as *cassone,* could have elaborate scenes of nature or true love painted on them. Although burghers often patronized different painters for the decoration of furniture and for wall or canvas paintings, some workshops produced both sorts of decorative objects and others as well.

The Yard. Many households in early medieval cities started with tofts much like those of the medieval peasant. As the population grew and space was at a premium, these lands were sold, and by the fourteenth century generally the only members of the urban lay community who had substantial yards within the city walls were burghers. (Ecclesiastical communities often had their own enclosed compounds inside city walls.) The burgher's yard contained a variety of outbuildings and reflected the close connections many medieval burghers still had with the countryside. There were sheds to store farm tools, brewing vats, and wine presses. Small and large barns housed horses, pigs, and poultry. A garden provided herbs and vegetables for

Notaries of Perugia, Italy, carrying lighted candles in their Candlemas Day procession, 1347; illumination for the *Statuto dell' Arte dei Notari* (Biblioteca Augusta, Perugia)

household consumption, as did several fruit trees. The cesspit was generally placed in the far corner of the yard, and in an especially prosperous and fortunate household, there might even be a private well. Depending on a burgher's needs, other outbuildings might exist as well; for example, a dyer might have a separate dye shop in his yard at some distance from the residence. Stone walls enclosed the burgher's yard to prevent theft.

Food and Guests. A burgher's diet had much in common with that of medieval monks and nobles, although it probably lacked the variety and luxury. Bread was the staple and was supplemented by dairy products, fruits, vegetables, nuts, fish, and beer or wine. Meat was served whenever possible, generally four to five times a week. Burghers made extensive use of spices and subscribed to the same dietary theories and practices as the nobility. Like other medieval people, burghers observed set fast days when meat was prohibited. Burghers also participated in banquets, especially those hosted by craft masters

or their religious confraternity. At such festivities they strove for the level of luxury achieved by the upper nobility and clergy. In general, though, there were fewer courses; the presentation was simpler; and the ingredients were usually local and seasonal.

Dressing Like a Citizen. Burghers had the same basic clothing as medieval peasants and nobles: braies, shirts, hose, tunics, mantles, cloaks, shoes, belts, and knives. Like the noble he imitated, a burgher attempted to wear clothes made with fine tailoring and fabrics. The cloth was generally professionally woven fabrics, and clothes were custom-made for the wearer, unlike those of many other urban residents, who made do with secondhand garments. For daily work, medieval burghers favored woolen tunics and hose in muted colors, but at a festival or banquet they often wore furs and dramatically colored clothing embellished with embroidery. Like many nobles, however, the burgher owned only a few outfits. A typical wardrobe might include several pairs of braies, shirts, and hose, a couple of tunics and cloaks, a basic mantle designed for daily wear, a more elaborate festival mantle, one pair of boots and another of shorter leather slippers, several belts, and a good knife. Women's clothes were also like those of the middle nobility with variations similar to those for men's wardrobes. Jewelry, used as decorations or fasteners, was a sign of the wearer's status and could represent substantial expense. Men and women wore several rings when they could afford them, and belts, scabbards, and clasps had filigree work or jewels set into them. Hats were both practical and fashionable and were made of various materials and with different degrees of decoration. Feathers could be put in a hatband; silver- or gold-thread trim might be added to the rim; and embroidery might embellish the crown. The fashions worn by medieval burghers were a visible statement of their social status and aspirations.

Controlling Style: Sumptuary Legislation. To protect the outward signs of their status, burghers attempted to regulate clothing practices. These ordinances, known as sumptuary laws, limited certain fabrics to certain social classes and limited the value of clothing that could be worn by people in different professions. Only burghers could have jeweled scabbards, and only burgher women might wear velvet hats. Makeup was generally condemned for all social classes. Certain colors were prohibited to particular groups and professions; for example, many sumptuary laws dictated that only town councilmen could wear clothes in the color of the town livery. Fines and confiscations awaited anyone who broke these laws. In fact, an additional point of evidence at a trial could be that someone dressed above his or her station, an act thought to illustrate that the accused was a threat to society. Despite the existence of such laws, the frequency with which they were repeated, particularly in the thirteenth and fourteenth centuries, suggests that medieval urban residents dressed to limits of their ability rather than the limits of the law.

Sources:

Joseph Gies and Frances Gies, *Life in a Medieval City* (New York: Harper & Row, 1981).

David Herlihy, *Medieval Households* (Cambridge, Mass.: Harvard University Press, 1985).

David A. Hinton, "'Clothing' and the Later Middle Ages," *Medieval Archaeology*, 43 (1999): 172–182.

John Schofield, *Medieval London Houses* (New Haven: Yale University Press, 1994).

Claire Sponsler, "Narrating the Social Order: Medieval Clothing Laws," *Clio*, 21 (1992): 265–283.

URBAN LIVING: CRAFTSMEN AND TRADESMEN

Urban Crafts. One of the qualities that distinguished a city from a village or even a market village was the diversity of crafts that could be found in a city. Specialties and subspecialties in almost any area of manufacture could be found in a regional center. Moreover, as the European economy expanded in the twelfth and thirteenth centuries, the demand for diverse artisanal skills also grew. One way in which scholars can track the variety of crafts is through

last names, which were just coming into use at that time. Many craftsmen took names that identified their family with their trade; for example, families working in construction included the Smith, Schmidt, Faber, Tinker, Plumb, Houseman, Mason, Maurer, Thatcher, Glazer, Turner, Carpenter, and Dauber. Craftsmen often dominated urban governments, and certain crafts and their guilds were more prestigious and prosperous than others. The following description of an artisan's household is based on that of a master craftsman in a less-prestigious craft, such as shoemaker or candlemaker.

A Craft Master's Household. The household of a craft master was different than that of a burgher, although it could approach the same size. Craftsmen frequently had smaller families because they married later and had poorer living conditions and nutrition than nobles and burghers, but their households were frequently quite large because they included apprentices and journeymen as well as a servant or two. The size of a craft master's household depended on his ability to support it; a poor craftsman was unable to maintain more than a journeyman and/or an apprentice, while a large, prosperous shop might have several of each.

At Home. While craft masters aspired to houses like those of urban burghers, generally their homes were smaller and less elaborately furnished. A successful craftsman might own his house outright, but some rented them. Moreover, by the thirteenth and fourteenth centuries, urban craftsmen were unlikely to have large yards attached to their homes unless they were in professions that needed space—such as butchers, bakers, and blacksmiths. In some cases their workshops might be on the outskirts of town or in specific, marginal neighborhoods, while their homes and shops were in a different quarter. The average medieval craftsmen lived only slightly better than a prosperous peasant. His house consisted of two rooms, one for general living and a sleeping chamber. Journeymen and apprentices might have their own chambers or might have to sleep in the main room, which at least had the advantage of a hearth. Wooden tables, benches, and chests were the most common furnishings, and cooking was done on an open fire in either the center of the room or, increasingly, against one of the outside walls. An artisan's home followed the same model as that of a burgher, but it was often shorter and narrower and consisted of only two stories. Floors in the downstairs were most likely packed dirt, while the walls were similar to wattle and daub.

Integration of Home and Work. A craft master's household integrated work and family life. The front of the house was often the workshop; sales took place in that room or at a market stall nearby. The bulk of most craftsmen's wealth was in their tools and supplies, which were stored in the workshop or in small cellars or outside sheds. The craftsman's family included not only biological relatives but also those bound to him under long-term work contracts. Generally apprentices paid for their apprenticeship. They received no wages, but they were given training,

REGULATIONS FOR PARIS BAKERS

Beginning in the late twelfth century, the town council of Paris passed a series of regulations for bakers. The following excerpts from twelfth- and thirteenth-century laws show the widespread government concern about certain crafts.

Mastery ceremony: "The new baker . . . shall take a new clay pot and fill it with nuts and wafers; and he shall come to the house of the master of the bakers, and he shall have with him the tax collector, and all the bakers, and the master-journeymen. . . . And this the new baker shall hand his pot and nuts to the master of the bakers, and say, 'Master, I have finished and completed my four year.' And the master shall ask the tax-collector whether this is true. And if he says that it is true, the master shall hand the new baker his pot and nuts, and command that he throw them against the wall, and then the new baker shall throw his pot and nuts and wafers against the outside wall of the house, and then the master, the tax-collector, the new baker, and all the other bakers and journeymen shall enter the master's house, and the master shall provide them with wine and a fire, and each of the bakers, and the new one, and the master-journeymen, all owe a penny to the master of the bakers for their wine and the fire."

Judging breads: "And at the windows where they find bread for sale the master takes the bread and gives it to the jurors, and the jurors examine it to see if it is adequate or not, and if it is adequate, the jurors return it to the window, and if it is not adequate, the jurors put the bread in the hand of the master; and if the master determines that the bread is not adequate, he can confiscate all the rest of it, even that which is in the oven. And if there are several types of bread in a window, the master will have each one assessed. And those which are found to be too small, the master and jurors will have them donated to charity."

Provisions for sales: "The bakers living within the region of Paris can sell their defective bread (that is their rejects, such as damaged bread that rats or mice have gnawed on, excessively hard bread, burnt or scorched bread, overrisen bread, doughy bread, ill-turned or undersized bread, which they are not allowed to sell in the stall) on Sunday in the Halles, at the place where iron is sold in front of the cemetery of Saints-Innocents; or, if they like, they can sell it on Sunday between the portico of Notre-Dame and St.-Christopher. The bakers . . . can carry their bread on Sunday in these places in their baskets or in their panniers, and carry their stall or boards or tables, provided the stalls are no more than 5 feet long."

Source: Jeffrey L. Singman, *Daily Life in Medieval Europe* (Westport, Conn.: Greenwood Press, 1999), pp. 195–196, 198–199.

room, and board. Sometimes their master gave them some small change, but it was not required. Journeymen's contracts provided for salaries, but when cash was tight the craft master was often behind in payments. Wives and daughters were involved in managing the shop and sometimes in producing goods.

Crafts and Neighborhoods. Originally attracted to a location because of its amenities, such as water or good roads, crafts concentrated in specific neighborhoods and along certain roads. Street names in modern Europe perpetuate these medieval patterns; most European cities have a Carpenter, Furrier, or Saddlery Street. Streets were also named after churches and religious communities that existed on them, such as the Road of St. Genevieve or Mary Magdalene, or for activities that occurred in the area, such as the "rue où l'en cuit les oeufs" (the road where they cook eggs) of medieval Paris. These neighborhoods allowed members of a similar craft to band together for mutual protection and at the same time to police each other for violations of craft statutes. These practices are reflected in medieval laws. The laws of many medieval towns and crafts made the person who failed to report a crime just as guilty as the person who committed it and liable to the same penalties.

Money. Cash was a rare commodity in medieval Europe, and much trade in rural communities was conducted through barter and credit. Not until the thirteenth and fourteenth centuries did a cash economy trickle down to the village level. Because of their commercial nature, however, cities had always been much more dependent on coins than villages. The problem facing the development of cities and the medieval economy in general was the variable worth of such coins. In the ninth century many lords had the right to mint their own coins, and it took centuries for kings and major lords to reserve these rights to themselves. Moreover, the worth of a coin was based on its precious metal content, which meant that all but the smallest coins were worth more than most peasants or smaller artisans might earn in a week. For example, a single ounce of silver was generally a week's wages for a skilled worker. Because of this standard, people shaved or otherwise diluted the precious metal content of a coin, and, as long as it still contained the seal attesting to its value, they could make their own money by reminting the metal into additional coins; such counterfeiting occurred and invoked stiff penalties. A merchant in medieval Europe needed to know the value of gold, silver, and copper coins minted by many sovereign states at different periods. Moreover, he or she needed to be able to translate this value into one of the standard units of account used throughout Europe. Given the complexities of such conversions, the development of coins with guaranteed and stable values, such as the Florentine florin and the Venetian ducat, was of inestimable value to European trade.

Wages and Prices. Wages and prices varied according to many factors: the current economy, the size of the local work force, the availability of a product, the quality of the worker or product, and the negotiator's skill. Inflation was far less a factor than in the modern world, and, on average, prices stayed the same for centuries. These averages, however, conceal sizable annual variations—especially in the prices of foodstuffs, which could increase up to ten times their normal cost in several months if the weather had been especially bad and supplies had become short. During these times town councils attempted to fix prices and patrol cellars to prevent hoarding and price gouging, both from a sense of Christian charity and to prevent riots by starving urban residents. Wages also differed. Some workers were paid by the year; some were paid by the number of days they worked; and others were paid by the piece. Pay varied according to the time of the year, in part because the length of the working day varied depending on the hours of daylight. An employee generally received at least one meal a day from his employers, and it was not unheard-of for a worker to earn housing and clothing as well.

The Reseller. Although it was not a prestigious profession, selling used goods was a widespread trade in medieval Europe. Medieval people rarely threw away clothing and other goods. When one person considered something too old or unfashionable, it was sold to someone else. The resellers or used-goods dealers acted as middlemen in these transactions and made provisions to have the goods repaired if necessary. Although a prosperous reseller might have a storefront attached to his house, many operated from a cart or a table near a market square. The regulations for resellers were generally less stringent than those placed on other professions, but a used-goods dealer was not supposed to misrepresent his goods. Women could also work as resellers, and they continued to practice this profession even after they were barred from many others in the later Middle Ages and Renaissance.

The Apothecary. The apothecary's job was a prestigious profession, and some apothecaries became burghers and town councilors in the thirteenth and fourteenth centuries. The coat of arms of one of the wealthiest and most powerful Italian families during the Renaissance, the Medicis of Florence, includes the balls that stand for their ancestor's membership in the apothecary's guild. An apothecary's job carried such status because of the education and training it required, the value of his goods, and its lack of manual labor. Much like modern pharmacists, apothecaries dispensed a wide variety of medicines. For example, St. John's wort, mandrake root, and ground seed pearls were all obtainable at an apothecary shop and had assorted medical uses. The apothecary also dealt in a wide variety of goods, generally small and expensive. He stocked spices and sugar, which were seen as having medicinal properties, as well as lye for making soap or washing clothing, and the dyes and solutions for making ink. Every household of any standing needed to buy goods from an apothecary. Because of the expenses of obtaining these products and their costs to buyers, apothecaries also often had a substantial store of coin, at least according to medieval standards. It was not a large step, therefore, for apothecaries to serve to some extent as community bankers, tendering loans and safeguarding other residents' resources. Because an apothecary's work was rarely dirty, he could dress and carry himself like the prosperous tradesman that he was, an appearance that further affected perceptions in medieval society.

The Baker. Because urban bakers supplied basic foodstuffs, they belonged to one of the largest guilds. It was also one of the most tightly regulated. Master craftsmen working for the town council generally inspected shops and bread weekly, setting the prices for each kind of bread produced. In the early Middle Ages bakers were paid much like millers; residents brought their own flour to the bakeshop, and the baker made it into loaves and baked it, reserving a percentage of the flour as his pay. Increasingly in the Middle Ages the system became less complicated, especially in larger towns whose governors feared grain shortages. There central grain markets or barns were established, and a member of the baker's household went there daily to collect that day's supply of grain. The baker then produced several kinds of loaves, differentiated by weight and grain, and he sold them for set prices. To minimize the danger of fire from their large, hot ovens, bakeshops were concentrated in set locations within the city. Few urban residents could afford private baking ovens and did not have time to watch their fires all day. Because bread was so essential to the medieval urban diet, bakers worked long hours, and the regulations about when they could work were more relaxed than for other professions. For example, bakers were not allowed to bake on Sundays or major holy days, but they were allowed to open their shops for sales. Moreover, many medieval crafts were not allowed to work after dark or before dawn, but bakers could work at any time. Given the hundreds of loaves a medieval bakeshop was expected to produce in a day, it was common for a baker to have at least one assistant from outside the family. His wife and daughters managed the shop, while the baker focused on preparing the dough and watching the oven. Although the size of his household definitely placed the baker in the ranks of prosperous craftsmen, it was rare for a baker to ascend into the higher levels of urban society. For one reason, the baker's craft was manual; he kneaded dough, formed loaves, and pulled them in and out of a hot oven throughout the day. In the process bakers might strip to their shirts and tunics, thereby losing the appearance appropriate to a prosperous burgher. Moreover, although a baker sold many loaves, his profit margin was not high. He might live comfortably, but he was unlikely to have the riches of a goldsmith, cloth dealer, or apothecary. Finally, by the nature of his profession, a baker was unlikely to deal with and, therefore, know the most influential members of urban society; burghers and bankers sent servants to buy their bread.

The Butcher. The butcher inspired mixed reactions in the urban community. In the medieval mind a butcher's profession was necessary but smelly and coarse. Located near a water supply, a butcher's yard contained livestock waiting to be slaughtered, carcasses in the process of being carved, and meat ready to be sold. Puddles of blood seeped into the dirt, offal was piled into baskets, and skins were set aside to be sold to tanners. The smells were strong, and the noise at times was overwhelming. Yet, a butcher's goods were in demand, and their sale could be quite profitable.

Sometimes a butcher might accumulate enough wealth to be admitted to burgher status. This craft was often closely regulated, in part because butchers had ready access to long, sharp knives and cleavers and were believed to be ready to use them as weapons.

Sources:

John Blair and Nigel Ramsay, eds., *English Medieval Industries* (London: Hambledon Press, 1991).

Steven A. Epstein, *Wage Labor and Guilds in Medieval Europe* (Chapel Hill: University of North Carolina Press, 1991).

Barbara Hanawalt, *Growing Up in Medieval London: The Experience of Childhood in History* (New York: Oxford University Press, 1993).

Jacques LeGoff, *Medieval Callings,* translated by Lydia G. Cochrane (Chicago: University of Chicago Press, 1990).

James Masschaele, *Peasants, Merchants, and Markets: Inland Trade in Medieval England, 1150–1350* (New York: St. Martin's Press, 1997).

URBAN LIVING: RECREATION AND RIOT

Processions. Medieval towns were the sites of many festivals, some of which included processions or parades. For example, a city commemorated the holy day of its patron saint or a day on which the town was delivered from plague or siege with a procession. It generally began at a fairly large church and wound its way through the main streets until it arrived at the primary church in the community. All participants were dressed in their finest clothing. If they were members of guilds, they might be required to wear cloaks or mantles that bore their guild crest, and frequently participants carried large candles, relics, and statues relevant to the theme of the procession. Precedence mattered a great deal, and it was not uncommon for groups to fight with each other over their places in the procession. Sometimes these combats set clergy against laity. Prior to a parade, the town government attempted to clean the roads and remove any wandering animals. People who had houses along the street where the procession passed might be required to drape cloth from their windows or to provide some other festive decoration. When the procession was to honor a visiting dignitary, the city might stage small plays on specially built platforms at key sites on the processional route. Often these plays were *tableau vivant,* that is, with actors frozen in place to create living pictures to illustrate major historical, mythological, or allegorical scenes or themes. Some processions included hundreds of participants, but they could also be much smaller. For example, in fourteenth-century Dijon the bodies of dead urban leaders were accompanied to their burial by several representatives of the town council bearing large candles.

Community Sports. Medieval town councilors and other community leaders made many attempts to control youth violence through the development of community sports, generally linked to major religious festivals. Often these activities took the form of mock combats. On a designated day, young men from two opposing factions met in a preassigned area, generally a town square, and the combat began. Free-for-alls, these mock combats involved men in full foot-soldier armor swinging wooden maces at each other until one side yielded the

WAR GAMES IN ITALY

Like many other Italian cities, Siena faced repeated feuds and gang warfare. By the thirteenth and fourteenth centuries its government attempted to control these groups through staged and regulated "civic" battles, which became quite popular.

Faced with an already centuries-old culture of intramural violence, Siena's earliest communal governments sought to condone and control what they could not eliminate by also initiating an annual Sienese version . . . the Game of the Helmet, it was a city-wide group combat, pitting Siena's most populous terziere [neighborhood] against the other two. For generations, thousands of Sienese, participating under their military banners, wielding wooden weapons (maces, swords and spears) and throwing stones, sought to drive their fellow citizens from the Piazza del Campo under the watchful eyes of their elected officials looking on from the windows of the Palazzo Pubblico, the seat of government. Sheer numbers, however, made effective control nearly impossible. When even the intervention of the city's police forces still failed to prevent ten fatalities in 1291, sufficient political will was finally generated to ban the "game" permanently. . . . the Fist Fight, was a favourite pastime in medieval Siena. Wearing cloth caps with protective cheek-pieces tied together under the chin similar to the sparring head-gear of modern boxers, and with their fists wrapped in cloth bindings to protect their knuckles, participants sought to drive their fellow citizens from one of the city's piazzas. Whether arranged in advance or held impromptu between just two neighbourhoods in a nearby piazza, or organized by the communal government . . . , the [fist fight] seemed to satisfy the blood-lust of the Sienese, judging from the participation of 1,200 in a city-wide [fight] in 1324.

Source: Raymond E. Role, "The War Games of Central Italy," *History Today,* 49 (June 1999), on-line at http://www.historytoday.com/article/article.cfm?article_id=1428.

field of battle. In some towns there were separate battles, one for aristocratic youth who fought on horseback and a second for craftsmen or poorer citizens who fought hand to hand on foot. Governments encouraged such ritual battles and provided a "field of honor" marked off by chains and with set entrances. Just because they had community sanction, however, does not mean these "mock" battles were safe. Since these battles took place in a public square, if a combatant fell he hit hard-packed dirt or stone. By this time in medieval European cities, particularly in Italy, the public squares that were large enough for such battles were surrounded by houses of several stories. Partisans from each side watched the battles and were known to throw rocks or other projectiles at members of the opposing factions; bricks, sticks, water, and even the contents of chamber pots were fair game. Moreover, the battles themselves were brutal. A blow to the head from a wooden club

The Bishop of Paris blessing a fair; illumination from a fourteenth-century manuscript for *Pontifical de Sens*
(Bibliothèque Nationale, Paris)

could easily fracture a combatant's skull or do worse damage. By the fourteenth century, with such consequences in mind, many medieval towns were attempting to ban these combats, but similar events occurred in cities such as Venice well into the seventeenth century.

Gangs. Violence was always a problem in medieval towns. Knives were a standard part of male costume, and social standards required both men and women alike to respond promptly and forcefully to any threat to their honor. Moreover, the cities of later medieval Europe had a growing itinerant population that was difficult to police and had few social ties to the city itself. As opportunities for young craftsmen and laborers in general lessened along with population growth during the thirteenth and fourteenth centuries, a restive group of young men emerged. They ranged in age from their late teens to thirties and could not afford to marry and establish households of their own. After work there was little for them to do but to hang out on street corners, to drink, talk, and fight. The judicial records of medieval towns are filled with stories of young men breaking into shops, getting into knife fights, and playing practical jokes. Town councils attempted to curb them by instituting curfews and even legalizing prostitution in specific neighborhoods. Despite these efforts, gangs and youth violence remained a threat in most medieval towns, and people avoided going out after dark.

Rape. With such gangs loitering on medieval streets, it is probably not surprising that rape was a hazard to many young women. Cities attracted rural dwellers of both sexes. Generally the women became servants; if they were particularly lucky they married craftsmen. Because their family was distant, these women had few, if any, protectors and were easy targets for predatory gangs. Young women walking on the streets at night or even at twilight might be accused of being prostitutes, which legitimized rape in the eyes of medieval judges. Sometime gangs of young men even broke into the house of a woman's employer to rape her, if they felt they could argue before the court that the young woman had behaved in a wanton fashion, "inviting" such attentions. Once a young woman was raped, the burden of proof that she had not willingly participated was on her. She had to show that she had fought her attackers, that she had repeatedly cried out for help, that she had a good reputation, and that she had never sought sexual attention in the past. Even if she was able to prove her innocence, and few were able to do so, her reputation was affected, injuring her ability to arrange a marriage or to find other employment if necessary. Thus, it seems that many medieval women tried to hide the information that they had been raped.

Police. Gangs could have a powerful influence on cities after dark because there were no urban police forces. In many cities powerful individuals or their supporters policed their own neighborhoods and anyone who was affiliated with them. The cities did have small staffs of "sergeants," who were usually unwilling or unable to take the initiative in preventing or solving crimes. A sergeant's job was basically to support an urban administrator who might be arresting an offender or collecting back taxes. Most cases that were brought before city courts originated in complaints made by one or more residents; if a person was murdered and had no relatives, or if he was injured and did not wish to prosecute his assailant, there was no case. At night citizen patrols led by town councilors policed sections of the city, but if they were outnumbered, they could do nothing but beat a hasty retreat.

Sources:

Robert Brentano, *Rome before Avignon: A Social History of Thirteenth Century Rome* (Berkeley: University of California Press, 1990).

Vito Fumagalli, *Landscapes of Fear: Perceptions of Nature and the City in the Middle Ages,* translated by Shayne Mitchell (Cambridge, U.K.: Polity Press / Cambridge, Mass.: Blackwell, 1994).

Barbara A. Hanawalt and Kathryn L. Reyerson, eds., *City and Spectacle in Medieval Europe* (Minneapolis: University of Minnesota Press, 1994).

E. Raymond Role, "The War Games of Medieval Italy," *History Today,* 49 (June 1999), on-line at http://www.historytoday.com/article/article.cfm?article_id=1428.

URBAN LIVING: THOSE ON THE MARGINS

The Poor. Medieval cities were home to a large underclass, and it has been estimated that in some late-medieval cities up to 40 percent of the population was too poor to pay taxes. Like cottagers and laborers in the countryside, such people lived a hand-to-mouth existence. If one of these people had shelter, it might be a rented, unheated room in a building where several families were housed. Such residences might be furnished with a cookpot, a thin mattress, a table, and a bench. Their clothes were threadbare wool or linen, and their shoes—when they had them—were patched. Without any savings or resources to sell, the poor were the first to suffer in famine, drought, or plague. Hungry people and beggars were common sights on medieval streets.

Welfare. Medieval people were not insensitive to the needs of the poor and made attempts to help them. Many of these efforts were administered through city churches. Prosperous urban residents often provided in their wills for bread to be distributed to the poor, for dowries to be established for deserving poor girls, and

for the apprenticeship dues of poor orphans to be paid. While distinct relief institutions, such as poorhouses and orphanages, were a later development, the poor could look forward to the distribution of extra food in the afternoons and evenings from the kitchens of the more prosperous. Town councils also took a person's wealth into consideration when assessing various civic dues, and it could eliminate payments by poor families or even contribute to them. Such charity, however, was based on an assessment of the moral and social state of the poor, who were generally classed into two categories: deserving and undeserving. The deserving poor were members of good families fallen on hard times, young widows, orphans, and preachers who lived through begging. The undeserving poor were foreigners, people with bad reputations, and people believed to be able to work. Any welfare distributed in medieval towns was given only to the deserving poor.

"Hospitals." Only cities with populations of several thousand had hospitals, which had more diverse functions than their modern counterparts. When medieval people spoke of "hospitals," they include leper houses, almshouses, hospices for poor travelers and pilgrims, and institutions that cared for the sick poor. These institutions were frequently located on the outskirts of town so as to minimize any threat of infection to the urban community. In some cases, if a person in a hospital was believed to have a contagious disease, he was exiled from the city. In other words, hospitals in the modern sense of the word did not exist. Instead medieval people used the word *hospital* to describe buildings and institutions with various functions. These medieval hospitals were administered by the Church, but they also depended for part of their income on the generosity of urban residents. Women who had taken minor religious vows (sisters) and female servants often provided much of the care of the sick; hospital brothers handled general administration and fulfilled religious functions. The residents of medieval hospitals ate and slept in common halls, wore distinctive clothes, and attended daily mass. When medical care was provided, it was minimal. Medieval doctors and surgeons rarely treated hospital patients, and the cures that were effected often stemmed from bed rest, warmth, cleanliness, and good diet.

Jewish Communities. The Jews of medieval Europe lived primarily in towns. In the ninth and tenth centuries Jewish quarters, where Jews could more easily band together for protection, existed in many communities stretching from Spain to Germany and England. These communities always lived on the sufferance of the town lord. Jews were often taxed more heavily than other urban residents and could be expelled at the lord's whim. For example, the Jewish community of medieval Paris was large and prosperous until King Philip Augustus expelled the Jews from France in 1182. Jewish sections were also a potential source of disorder in towns and, therefore, troubling to town governments. Popular opin-

Medieval lepers using a noise maker to warn people of their approach; illumination from a fourteenth-century manuscript
(Bibliothèque d' Arsenal, Paris)

ion made the Jews scapegoats for many misfortunes, and during times of religious enthusiasm, such as the calling of the First Crusade in 1095, many communities faced waves of anti-Semitic violence. Within their communities the daily life of medieval Jews was similar in many ways to that of the Christian communities. Their houses were built with the same materials and designs, their clothes were made of similar cloth and patterns, and they faced many of the same difficulties, such as finding warmth, light, and supplies. In large cities such as Paris and Venice, Jews had a synagogue. Jews also faced difficulties that were not shared by their Christian neighbors. Most towns limited the professions Jews could practice, excluded them from guilds, and denied them

the ability to own land. Jews began to practice money-lending and long-distance trade because they were among the few occupations open to them in much of Europe. In medieval Europe, where Christianity and community were so closely integrated, Jews always lived on the margins of society even when the Christian majority tolerated them.

Sources:

Jane S. Gerber, *The Jews of Spain: A History of the Sephardic Experience* (New York: Free Press, 1992).

Lindsay Granshaw and Roy Porter, eds., *The Hospital in History* (London & New York: Routledge, 1989).

Michel Mollat, *The Poor in the Middle Ages: An Essay in Social History*, translated by Arthur Goldhammer (New Haven: Yale University Press, 1986).

SIGNIFICANT PEOPLE

HILDEGARD OF BINGEN

1098-1179

POET, HEALER, AND THEOLOGIAN

Entering the Religious Life. Hildegard of Bingen was the tenth and last child of noble, wealthy German parents who were involved in worldly affairs. Despite their worldly preoccupations, they supported Hildegard's early interest in a pious life. As a child, she was made the companion of Jutta, daughter of Count Stephan of Spanheim, who was living a life of religious seclusion in a cell near a neighboring Benedictine monastery. Jutta taught young Hildegard to read and write, and the reputation of these two young women eventually led to the establishment of a convent near the site of Jutta's cell. At fifteen Hildegard took a nun's vows and joined this monastery, where she gained some local renown as a visionary. When Jutta died in 1136, Hildegard took over Jutta's position as head of the convent. In 1150, after disputes with the abbot and monks who supervised the convent, Hildegard founded a new convent near Bingen, which she led until her death in 1179.

Mysticism and Theology. Surviving records suggest that Hildegard lived a rather ordinary life until 1141, when during an illness, she began having a series of visions. In these visions, which recurred for the rest of her life, she heard God tell her to write down what she had learned about scripture, the psalter, and other holy writings. When she doubted her abilities, she fell ill, which she regarded as a sign of God's displeasure. Unlike the writings of many other visionaries, Hildegard's books received the highest earthly approval, being blessed by Pope Eugene III at a synod in 1147. Throughout her life Hildegard wrote books and letters in Latin on a variety of theological and mystical topics, and these writings were apparently widely circulated. In a trilogy written during the 1140s and 1150s Hildegard analyzed a wide range of theological subjects, from the creator and creation to the redemption and the apocalypse. Like many medieval writings, her works could be allegorical, as in this passage from *Know the Ways of God:*

then I saw, as it were, a high round tower entirely built of white stone, having three windows at its summit, from which such brightness shone forth that even the conical roof of the tower appeared very dearly in the brightness of this light. . . . Now the reason why you see a huge round tower . . . is because the sweetness of the Holy Spirit is immense and comprehensively includes all creatures in its grace, so that no corruption in the integrity of the fullness of justice destroys it; since glowing, it points the way and sends forth all rivers of sanctity in the clarity of its strength. . . .

Medicine and Herbs. Beginning in the 1150s, Hildegard also wrote on practical subjects such as medicine and science. Benedictine monasteries had a long tradition of being refuges for the sick, and Hildegard's interest in these subjects may have stemmed from that background. In her scientific writings she analyzed metals, stones, plants, birds, and mammals according to current medical theories of humors and properties. In this sense, her works on nature were closely related to her books on medicine, in which she listed hundreds of medical conditions and a selection of herbal cures. Like many medieval medical treatises, Hildegard's analysis could move quickly from diagnosis to prognostication. For example, she wrote "Those conceived on the thirtieth day of the moon, if male will be poor and if noble will always descend to lower things and will not have happiness; they will easily fail in bodily strength and the flesh but will live quite a long while. Females will be poor . . . and will more willingly live among foreign folk than familiar ones; they will not be very weak in body and will live long enough."

Music and Ministry. In her role as the head of a convent, Hildegard undertook to guide the spiritual life of her fellow nuns. As her renown increased, people from all over Europe also wrote to her for spiritual advice. Hundreds of letters and several lives of saints that she wrote have survived and attest to her concern to spread the insights she gained through her visions. She also believed that music could touch the holy in a way that verbal prayer could not, and she composed more than seventy songs for her convent. Hildegard was also called on to preach publicly, an unusual position for a medieval woman. She went on three preaching tours throughout Germany during the 1160s and

1170s. Hildegard's life demonstrates that women could have active, public lives in medieval Europe.

Sources:

Charles Burnett and Peter Dronke, eds., *Hildegard of Bingen: The Context of her Thought and Art* (London: Warburg Institute, 1998).

Sabina Flanagan, *Hildegard of Bingen, 1098–1179: A Visionary Life* (London & New York: Routledge, 1989).

JOCELIN OF BRAKELOND

CIRCA 1156 – CIRCA 1215
MONK AND CHRONICLER

The only known likeness of Jocelin of Brakelond

Jocelin's Life. Jocelin of Brakelond is well known as a monastic chronicler of medieval Europe, but little is known of his biography beyond what he revealed in his writings. He was born around 1156, probably in the English town of Bury St. Edmunds. The name of Brakelond comes from one of the ancient street names there. By 1173 he had become a novice in the abbey of Bury St. Edmunds, under the care of Samson of Tottington, who was then master of novices. When Samson became abbot of Bury St. Edmunds in 1182, Jocelin became Samson's chaplain and close companion. Throughout his life in the monastery, Jocelin filled monastic offices such as guest master and almoner, and gained a reputation for devotion and determination. A fellow monk described Jocelin as "a man of excellent religious observance, as well as a power both in word and work." Jocelin outlived his mentor Samson by at least several years. Samson died in 1212, and the last record of Jocelin appeared in 1215, when the new abbot consulted him about some of the abbey properties.

Becoming an Author. The date when Jocelin began writing is uncertain, but his purpose is clear: "I have undertaken to write of those things which I have seen and heard, and which have occurred in the church of Saint Edmund, from the year in which the Flemings were taken without the town, in which year also I assumed the religious habit, and in which Prior Hugh was deposed and Robert made prior in his room. And I have related the evil as a warning, and the good for an example." His chronicle covers the years 1173–1202, spanning the government of two abbots and the reigns of several English kings. Like many other medieval chroniclers, Jocelin seldom wrote about himself, except for the time he focused on his failings in a chapter titled "How the author spoke his mind too hastily." Instead, the chronicle dwells on politics within the monastery and between the monastery and secular and other ecclesiastical powers. Central to the chronicle is the figure of Abbot Samson, whom Jocelin depicted as a savior after the well-intentioned mismanagement of the previous abbot. Because of Samson's key role, the chronicle is often called as much a biography of Samson as an account of the history of the monastery.

Personalities in the Monastery. Strong personalities emerge throughout Jocelin's story, and one of the dominant themes is the opposition Abbot Samson faced inside and outside the abbey. The monks schemed over who should become abbot, whispered behind closed doors about Samson's plans, and plotted against him. Jocelin condemned these actions, and the plotters always failed. He also supported Samson's involvement in what modern people might call worldly affairs. Jocelin described Samson as an active and ambitious landlord, fighting for abbey property rights, suppressing rebellious townsmen, and controlling upstart lords. He served as a judge for the region and supported Richard the Lionhearted during his captivity in Austria (1192–1194). Jocelin did not remain separate from the world either; as guest master and almoner he provided for travelers who needed shelter at the monastery and distributed alms to the local needy. Jocelin and his chronicle are testimony to the central place of monks and religious communities in medieval Europe—and the humanity of those communities.

Sources:

Thomas Carlyle, *Jocelin of Brakelond: From Past and Present* (New York: Rudge, 1923).

Jocelin of Brakelond, *The Chronicle of the Abbey of Bury St. Edmunds*, translated by Diana Greenway and Jane Sayers (Oxford & New York: Oxford University Press, 1998).

VILLARD DE HONNECOURT

FLOURISHED 1200–1250
MASON AND ARCHITECT

Early Life and Career. Biographies of Villard de Honnecourt are filled with conjectures, some more romantic and appealing than others. Everyone agrees that he was born in Picardy in northern France near the beginning of the thirteenth century. The only source of information about him from near that time is Villard's sketchbook, which comprises approximately sixty-six pages and two hundred and fifty drawings. According to this source, he had "been in many lands" and "had been sent to the land of Hungary" where he "remained many days." Such a trip would have taken several months and was remarkable for a medieval European of his class. Beyond this basic information, most of the facts of his biography are in dispute. His name does not appear in any surviving contracts, guild registers, payment receipts, or inscriptions—the most common sources of information about medieval masons. He is commonly believed to have been a master mason and architect who compiled his sketchbook while traveling around France looking for work. Where he received his training is unclear, although it has been suggested that he attended a monastic school, a plausible education for a medieval mason. Some have speculated that Villard worked on many of the major monuments depicted in his sketchbook—such as the cathedrals at Rheims, Chartres, Laon, Meaux, and Lausanne—but Villard mentioned only his work at Lausanne. Other scholars have pointed to his drawings of mechanical objects, such as trebuchets, and have called him an inspired inventor and tinkerer. Still others have described him as merely an interested layman with a gift for drawing. Whatever the truth about Villard's life, his travels and the content of his sketchbook challenge modern notions that medieval people lived isolated and insular lives and that they were interested only in theology, not in technology. Villard's interests were wide-ranging and worldly.

The Sketchbook. The objects described and drawn in Villard's sketchbook fall into roughly ten categories: animals, architecture, carpentry, church furnishings, geometry, masonry, mechanical devices, people, recipes or formulas, and surveying. These categories do not do justice to the range of his drawings; his "people," for example, include sketches as diverse as a medieval king, dancers, and "the sepulchre of a Saracen." The accuracy of his drawings varies widely. This inconsistency has caused some scholars to question Villard's status as a master architect and mason and to dispute the nineteenth-century claim that his sketchbook was designed to guide young masons and architects. Instead, the sketchbook is most commonly described as an album or record of his voyages that was intended to serve much the same purpose as a scrapbook or photo album for a modern traveler. Whatever Villard's technical weaknesses, he was a fascinated viewer of medieval technology. When he visited the cathedral of Rheims, which had already been under construction for ten to twenty years, Villard drew examples of buttresses, interior walkways, and windows. He apparently even studied the architectural plans for the building and included excerpts in his notebook. He also included examples of the many small, decorative objects—such as bronze statues, engravings, and sculptures—that were commonly found in cathedrals during the medieval period but since then have in many cases been lost. Alongside a drawing of a portable candleholder, Villard wrote: "See here a sconce that is good for monks in order to carry their burning candles. You are able to make it if you know how to design." How to make one is obvious from the picture.

Sources:
Carl F. Barnes Jr., "Villard de Honnecourt," in *The Dictionary of Art*, edited by Jane Turner, 34 volumes (New York: Grove's Dictionaries, 1996), XXXII: 569–571.

Villard de Honnecourt, *The Sketchbook of Villard de Honnecourt*, edited by Theodore Bowie, second edition, revised (Bloomington: Indiana University Press, 1962).

DOCUMENTARY SOURCES

Peter Abelard and Heloise, *The Letters of Abelard and Heloise* (1120s)—the letters of one of the best-known and most ill-fated couples of medieval Europe; he was castrated by her father, and she took vows as a nun.

Alexander of Neckam, *De nominibus utensilium* (*Daily Life in the Twelfth Century*, 1190s)—a twelfth-century bishop and scholar's observations during his travels in England and France; his descriptions of towns and craftsmen's lives are particularly useful to modern scholars.

Alfonso X the Wise, *Cantigas from the Court of Dom Dinis: devotional, satirical & courtly medieval love songs* (mid 1200s)—one of the best surviving collections of a wide variety of medieval secular songs.

Benedict, *Mirabilia Urbis Romae* (*The Marvels of Rome*, circa 1143)—a guide for pilgrims that lists all the medieval Roman tourist attractions with descriptions of why they are significant.

Chrétien de Troyes, *Lancelot, or the Knight of the Cart* (circa 1170)—one of the best-known poems by a renowned troubadour and creator of medieval Arthurian romances; it provides an interesting contrast to modern ideas about King Arthur's knights.

The Domesday Book (1085–86)—the greatest census of a medieval lordship, commissioned by William the Conqueror so that he could organize and exploit the kingdom he had conquered in England.

Frederick II of Hohenstaufen, *The Art of Falconry* (1240s)—a step-by-step guide for the training of hunting birds and the practical and spiritual significance of such training.

Hildegard of Bingen, *Causae et curae* (*Book of Healing*, 1150s)—a detailed guide to common and uncommon illnesses and how to cure them; the book also includes treatments for common medical conditions, such as pregnancy, and discusses the places of health and sickness in God's plan and natural philosophy.

Jocelin of Brakelond, *The Chronicle of Jocelin of Brakelond* (1173–1202)—a firsthand account of what Jocelin saw and heard while a monk in the abbey of Bury St. Edmunds, one of the oldest and most prestigious monasteries in medieval England, providing a useful picture of the personalities and politics in a medieval monastery.

Villard de Honnecourt, *The Sketchbook of Villard de Honnecourt* (circa 1230–1235)—notes and drawings by a medieval master mason and architect who has been called the "Leonardo da Vinci" of the thirteenth century.

Walter of Henley, *On Husbandry* (1270s)—an English steward's description of the best methods for hands-on estate management.

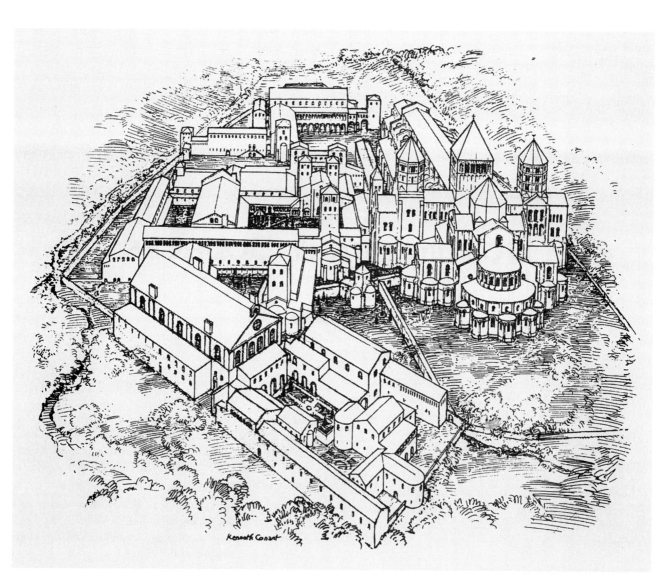

An artist's reconstruction of the Abbey of Cluny, circa 1157 (drawing by Kenneth J. Conant)

THE FAMILY AND SOCIAL TRENDS

by JACQUELINE MURRAY

CONTENTS

814*
- A survey of the area near Marseilles, in southern France, reveals that 35 percent of households comprise as many as five generations of married couples.

820
- A survey conducted by the abbey of Santa Maria di Farfa, near Rome, reveals that the great majority of households on its estate consist of one married couple, with or without children.

839
- A survey made at St. Germain-des-Prés, near Paris, sometime between 809 and this date reveals that 43 percent of households comprise two, occasionally three, generations.

841
- Dhuoda, a Frankish noblewoman, writes a letter advising her sons on proper conduct.

858
- Lothair II, King of Lotharingia (Lorraine), begins divorce proceedings against his childless wife, Theutberga, in order to marry his mistress, Waldrada, to legitimize his children by her and secure an heir to his kingdom. Pope Nicholas I eventually refuses to grant the divorce.

866
- Pope Nicholas I writes a letter to Boris I of Bulgaria summarizing the practices of Christian marriage—such as betrothal, dowry, and the consent of the couple and their parents.

1066
- William I (William the Conqueror), Duke of Normandy, invades England and imposes systematic feudal land tenure; because this system favors those with large holdings, impartible inheritance and male primogeniture become prevalent.

1075*
- Influenced by Gregorian reformers, Church councils prohibit priests from marrying and try unsuccessfully to enforce clerical celibacy.

1084
- Drogo writes a biography of Godelieve of Ghistelle, a woman murdered by her husband and subsequently recognized as a saint.

1092
- Philip I of France repudiates his wife, Bertha of Holland, and marries Bertrade, the wife of Fulk IV (the Surly), Count of Anjou. Two years later, Pope Urban II excommunicates Philip for this act.

* DENOTES CIRCA DATE

1140*
- Italian ecclesiastic and jurist Gratian (Franciscus Gratianus) compiles his *Concordance of Disconcordant Canons* or *Decretum*, which systematizes canon law, including church regulations relating to marriage, and reconciles earlier decisions.

1150*
- Italian theologian Peter Lombard writes *Sententarium libri IV* (The Four Books of Sentences), which includes his interpretation of church dogma on the subject of marriage.

1155*
- Pope Adrian IV asserts that even slaves and serfs have the capacity to choose their marriage partners.

1193
- Philip II (Augustus) of France repudiates his second wife, Ingeborg, on the day after their wedding.

1215
- Pope Innocent III convenes the Fourth Lateran Council, which reforms laws and practices governing marriage.

1234
- Pope Gregory IX consolidates canon laws governing marriage.

1347
- The Black Death reaches Europe, killing one-third to one-half the population by 1350 and leading to changes in marriage and family life.

* Denotes Circa Date

OVERVIEW

Consent in Marriage. By the twelfth century, European civilization had been transformed from a tribal to a feudal system. One profound change during this process, which affected all aspects of society, was the assertion of the rights of the individual as expressed in necessity for "consent" by the parties entering into marriage. In the course of establishing this fundamental norm, the Church found itself in a great struggle with the landed aristocracy, who used arranged marriage and family ties to build alliances and extend power. The development of medieval law, both canon (Church) and civic, played a major part in disciplining medieval practices. New notions of freedom of choice, marital affection, and—above all—personal consent resulted in a new model for marriage, which evolved into a sacrament based on mutual consent between two people, with the community and Church serving as witnesses.

Kinship and Marriage. The rise of feudalism, in which landholdings were an essential part of the struggle for political and economic power, resulted in a move from the Germanic system of bilateral kinship, in which a person traced his or her descent from both the male and the female sides of the family, to a system of patrilineal descent. This revolution was tied to securing land tenure through the male line, consequently reducing the role of women. From this point on a woman could claim only her dowry. Yet, within this social context, the doctrine of individual consent in marriage—in which a woman's freedom to choose a spouse was no less important than a man's—slowly came to be accepted as a moral norm. At the same time, the Church asserted women's conjugal rights in marriage, as may be seen in its upholding the wife's rights in the divorce proceedings brought by Lothar II in 858–865 and in the attempts of Philip I and Philip II (Augustus) of France to repudiate their wives in 1092 and 1193, respectively.

Influences on Marriage Practices. There were three central influences on the development of marriage customs in the Middle Ages: Roman law, Christian theology, and Germanic traditions. In some areas these value systems were in accord; in others they differed and needed to be modified and integrated into a coherent set of beliefs and practices. All three gave priority to the family unit and prohibited incest. They also sought to promote exogamy (marriage outside the immediate family group).

Two areas of divergence from Christian practice included the Germanic practice of polygamy (marriage to more that one mate at the same time) and concubinage (cohabitation with a person to whom one is not legally married). The Romans and the Germanic peoples accorded men greater sexual freedom than women. Both allowed men to dissolve their marriages, but only Roman law allowed women to divorce their husbands. While recognizing the patriarchal authority of fathers and husbands, the Church prohibited all divorce and wanted to restrict sexual activity to married couples. The process by which these three value systems were integrated was slow and involved a growing tension between secular and ecclesiastical values. The needs of the laity, especially in the aristocracy, were frequently at odds with the Church's ideal of matrimony as central to the order of salvation.

Limits on Marriages. One significant change in Church doctrine on marriage came in the eighth century with its extension of the degree of unacceptable consanguinity (relationship by blood or descent from a common ancestor) between husband and wife, increasing the unacceptable distance of kinship from four degrees (first cousins) to seven (fourth cousins by the Roman system used in the eighth century or sixth cousins by the Germanic system the Church began using in the ninth) and encouraging marriage outside family groups. One unexpected result of these new limits was the extent to which members of the aristocracy in particular used consanguinity as grounds for divorcing unwanted spouses, and in 1215 the Church returned to the Roman system and lowered the prohibited degree of consanguinity from seven to four.

Monogamy. In the eighth century the immediate effect of the Church's prohibitions was to force marriage to be more exogamous than under Roman law. At the same time it required a man to look outside his family for a spouse, the Church was also successful at imposing monogamy on the laity. Prior to the eighth century, powerful men often followed the Germanic customs of having multiple wives as well as concubines. This practice had concentrated women among a small elite and left many men without the possibility of finding marriage partners. Exogamy and monogamy helped to distribute women more evenly across society, allowing more men to marry and more households to be established. This process, however, took centuries and was met with great resistance by the aristocracy, who resisted the imposition of monogamy openly in the ninth century and more indirectly, but just as energetically, into the thirteenth.

Secular versus Church Control. Marriage in feudal society was closely tied to the manorial system. Lords had the right to levy fines against servants and tenants who wanted to marry, but the insistence of Pope Adrian IV (circa 1055) that consent of the betrothed was necessary for a valid marriage meant that servants, tenants, and even slaves had the right to select their own marriage partners. Among the elite there was a similar conflict between secular desires to control the selection of marriage partners and the Church's insistence on individual consent. No lord wanted a vassal's child or widow to marry one of his enemies. The nobility also exerted power through the institution of wardship. If a vassal died while his heir was underage, the lord, rather than a relative, had the right to be the child's guardian, supervise the child's estate, and ultimately arrange the ward's marriage. Many kings of England, particularly Henry II (reigned 1154–1189) and his son John (reigned 1199–1216), frequently arranged marriages to reward loyal retainers. As a result of this practice, wards and widows of noblemen were frequently married to men of lesser rank, an abuse of royal privilege known as *disparagement*, which so outraged the aristocracy that a provision to curtail it was included in the Magna Carta (1215). Also, lords frequently sold marriage rights to other nobles as a means of raising ready cash, or they sold a widow a license permitting her to marry a man of her own choosing. Thus, the control of marriage carried significant economic benefits and created a constant tension between the Church's assertion of the individual's right to consent and the aristocracy's efforts to manipulate marriage rights for the purpose of secular power.

Extension of Church Control. In the ninth century a wedding was essentially a secular ceremony that a priest might be invited to bless; by the twelfth century marriage had become one of the seven sacraments and as such was celebrated in church as a public ecclesiastical ritual. An outcome of this change was the doctrine of the indissolubility of marriage. A couple united by God should not be separated for earthly considerations. At the same time the Church regularized the marriage ceremony and required that banns be posted in advance of the ceremony so that possible impediments to the union could be revealed and investigated. The Church also tried unsuccessfully to eliminate secular marriages, but—in accordance with its emphasis on the importance of mutual consent and the indissolubility of the marriage bond—it recognized these unions if there was proof of consent.

Defining Marriage. As the Church was extending its control over marriage, it was also in the process of developing the Christian theory of marriage. Two different views emerged. One emphasized the consensual nature of marriage, while the other focused on the coital aspects. By the

early thirteenth century the Church had come to define marriage as both a spiritual union founded on mutual consent and a physical union based on sexual intercourse.

The Conjugal Debt. The notion of conjugal debt (the requirement that husband and wife engage in sexual intercourse), was also a matter of legal comment. Ancient pagan ascetic traditions argued against the notion of pleasure even in sexual intercourse between husband and wife. Indeed, many churchmen accepted the notion that the male was active and female passive, making the female subordinate to the male. The Church also stressed the importance of marital affection. Emotional estrangement could lead to the breakdown of a marriage.

Sexuality. Many medieval people believed that virginity was a higher state than marriage and procreation, and a celibate lifestyle was adopted by many religious people. Some ongoing ancient traditions condemned sexual pleasure as sinful and sought to regulate it in sexual acts. Above all, the Church taught that procreation—not sexual enjoyment—was the important outcome of the conjugal act and prohibited any sex act that did not fall into that category. Nevertheless, it is apparent that sexual activity outside marriage was common.

Birth Control and Abortion. Throughout the Middle Ages, the clergy condemned contraception, whether coitus interruptus, or potions to bring about sterility, or abortion. There is much evidence, however, that medieval Europeans did attempt to practice birth control. Midwives were often suspected of providing the means of contraception and abortion.

Childbirth and Baptism. Because of limited medical knowledge and unsterile conditions, having a baby was one of the most dangerous times in a medieval woman's life. Midwives assisted in childbirth, drawing on knowledge and experience passed down through generations. By the thirteenth century, midwives were being trained and licensed. If possible an infant was baptized in a formal ceremony about one week after its birth. Often the mother was not present, either because of illness or because she had not yet attended her churching—a religious ceremony held about one month after childbirth at which the new mother presented herself in public to be spiritually cleansed.

Childcare. Much of the surviving information on child rearing and education during this period comes from the pens of clerics. These works are good natured in tone, but in some cases it is difficult to see any signs of paternal and maternal affection. In his treatise *On the Propertie of Things* (circa 1250), Bartholomew the Englishman (also known as Bartholomaeus Anglicus) outlined the natural development of children, described the requirements of child rearing, and showed a sensitivity to the emotional care of the child. During the second half of the same century, Giles of Rome emphasized the importance of the bonds of loving affection. Ecclesiastical authorities urged parish priests to use their weekly sermons as an opportunity to exhort their parishioners about the proper care and feeding of infants.

Education, Apprenticeships, and Servitude. The level of education a child received was a function of its birth. Noble families engaged in fosterage, sending their sons to other noble families for training. During the twelfth century most market towns established schools, many of which were associated with the local cathedral. These schools became a means of social mobility. Other children's training began at an early age as they performed menial chores and errands on the farm or in urban workshops. Formal apprenticeships and service were one way children were educated for work positions, though this process was more common in cities than in rural areas. Girls as well as boys served apprenticeships. Going into service was another way in which a young person might prepare for adult work and responsibilities. A servant was governed by a contract for a fixed period and often married or moved to another household when a contract expired.

Orphans and Widows. Because early and often sudden death was common in the Middle Ages, orphans and widows were found at all levels of society, and there were many second marriages and blended families. While a child of the aristocracy became the ward of a nobleman, orphans from other classes came under the guardianship of relatives or neighbors, or they were housed in institutions such as monasteries or in some cases hospitals that were established for their care. Urban artisans' guilds and neighbors in peasant communities also cared for vulnerable members of society. The medieval widow had important rights, among them the ability to maintain her dower and serve as the executor of an estate. Marriage to a widow was often an attractive option because it brought new economic opportunities.

Old Age. If a medieval European survived birth, infancy, childbearing, and war, there was a good likelihood that he or she would live to a ripe old age and become an elder in the family and community. The burden of caring for the elderly usually fell on their children, placing old people in danger of poverty when younger members of society did not act responsibly. Though the Church and local communities offered charity, elderly people who had neither property nor family to care for them were often reduced to begging, starvation, or death from exposure.

TOPICS IN THE FAMILY AND SOCIAL TRENDS

ANCESTRY AND KINSHIP: HOUSEHOLD STRUCTURES

Defining the Household. During the Middle Ages all people who lived together, including those not related by blood or marriage, were considered a household. A typical household might include not only parents and children but also other relatives, servants, and apprentices. In the upper levels of society, especially in the homes of the medieval aristocracy, guards and other military retainers, along with the large number of servants necessary to run an aristocratic estate, were also included in the household.

Household Cycles. Several different family structures existed across Europe during the Middle Ages, and it is sometimes difficult for modern scholars to describe them exactly or to do a systematic analysis of their growth and development. Because there were no population censuses or tax assessments for most of the period, documentation is haphazard and allows only limited insights into family structures at various times and places. Medieval households appear to have gone through stages of development over time, according to the life cycle of the family. At one point, a household would be a husband and wife, who then had children. When the offspring grew up, they would leave to form new households. As each son married, he might bring his wife to live with his parents, thus creating a household of two or more married couples. When the parents died, this multiple household tended to break into several conjugal units, at which point the cycle began again. Some households may never have reached the multiple stage. Perhaps the father died before the son married, or no sons lived to adulthood; or the family did not have enough land to feed that many people. Households might also have been extended to include various relatives—such as unmarried children, siblings, and stepchildren—as well as various nonrelatives.

Early Records. In 820 the abbey of Santa Maria di Farfa, near Rome, surveyed the holdings of the estate. The resulting document reveals that the great majority of households were simple conjugal families, with or without children. A father remained head of the household until he died. When a widowed father lived with a married son,

A late twelfth-century noble household with men in the main hall, a woman in a side chamber, and children playing in another room; illumination from a manuscript for *Scholastic History* by Peter the Eater (Bibliothèque Nationale, Paris)

Stem Families. Another form of family structure, the stem family, has also been identified as part of the familial life cycle. This complex grouping included the conjugal unit of husband and wife, their children, grandparents, unmarried siblings, and servants. In this system only one child would marry and remain at home to inherit the family farm. The other children would have to remain unmarried while living at home, or marry and move away to start a new household. Thus, a man might cycle through three stages of life: son and heir, head of the household, and a retired parent. While this kind of family structure may have been the ideal among the peasant population, the realities of daily life—including high infant mortality, low life expectancy, and the inability of holdings to support many people—often made it unattainable.

Impartible Inheritance. To maintain the ideal stem family required a system of impartible inheritance. To keep the family holding intact, only one child could inherit it. The other children would be required to forgo inheritance and, consequently, were unlikely to marry. Under partible inheritance—in which the estate is divided, equally or unequally, among some or all of the children—the family holding would have become increasingly smaller as each portion was divided and redivided in succeeding generations; ultimately each portion of land would have become too small to support even a single conjugal family.

A Moral Unit. A focus on household structure and inheritance practices should not obscure the fact that the family was a moral, as well as an economic, unit. Members of the household shared the labor on the family holding and developed a sense of solidarity. For example, when a family made donations for prayers on behalf of relatives, they were usually for a person who was or had been a member of the immediate household. Thus, people remembered mothers, fathers, wives, and sons. Less frequently mentioned were sisters and daughters—women who had left the household when they married and were, in some sense, no longer members of that domestic group.

Sources:

Frances Gies and Joseph Gies, *Marriage and the Family in the Middle Ages* (New York: Harper & Row, 1987).

Jack Goody, *The Development of Family and Marriage in Europe* (Cambridge: Cambridge University Press, 1983).

David Herlihy, *Medieval Households* (Cambridge, Mass.: Harvard University Press, 1985).

the father was still listed as the head of the household. Moreover, it appears that sons who inherited property were already married or widowed when their fathers died. When a son married, he either established his own household or brought his wife into his father's house. Married daughters left their parents' households and did not tend to return when widowed. These findings are quite different from the information provided in a survey made at Saint Germain des Prés, near Paris, sometime between 809 and 839. Here almost half of the households (43 percent) were multiple families; in a few cases, they included three generations. Moreover, this survey lists husbands who were not from the local area. Sometimes the man moved to his wife's home, rather than taking her to live in his father's household. Similarly, an 813–814 survey of the area near Marseilles, in southern France, reveals that 35 percent of households were multiple, some comprising as many as five conjugal couples. This particular structure might have been the result of the need for protection from the Saracens, who were then threatening the area with invasion. While these surveys do not allow firm conclusions about medieval households, they do provide important and rare glimpses into the living arrangements of rural peasants in the ninth century.

ANCESTRY AND KINSHIP: LINEAGE AND INHERITANCE

Bilateral Kinship. Among the Germanic peoples, kinship networks were bilateral in nature—an individual traced his relationships with aunts, uncles, cousins, and other kin through both his father and mother. Relationships of support and obligation, including vengeance, were thus extended through both sides of the family, and a person had many people on whom to rely for support or advice. How distantly one cultivated these relationships varied according to local custom and changed over time. One of the significant features of bilateral kinship is that it is unique to each person. Thus, a parent's kin group will not be identical with his or her child's, and each generation redefined its kinship network. Bilateral kinship tends to focus on the individual, with lines of relationship running from the individual in both directions, through male and female lines alike. How far these lines stretched depended on the system employed. For example, the Romans determined four degrees of kinship (parents, grandparents, uncles and aunts, and first cousins) while the Germanic peoples traced seven degrees in a different way (parents and their siblings, grandparents and first cousins, second cousins, third cousins, fourth cousins, fifth cousins, and sixth cousins).

Naming Practices. One means of tracing the prevalence of bilateral kinship networks is through the conventions that governed the naming of children. In the Saint Germain des Prés survey (circa 809–839), the names of sons and daughters frequently combined elements of the names of both parents. For example, Rainordus and Agenildis named their daughter Ragenildis. Part of a parent's name might also be included in the names of all the siblings: Godelharius, Godelhildis, and Godelberga were all children of Godelhardus. These naming conventions suggest a sense of family cohesiveness stretched across the kinship group.

Direct Lineage. By the ninth century, charters ceding land to monasteries provided evidence that bilateral kinship was increasingly being overshadowed by relationships with kin in the direct line—for example, grandfathers, fathers, brothers, sons, and grandsons. Cousins were beginning to be perceived as more distant relatives. This situation reflects the changing circumstances of the period. Rather than needing to rely on large kinship networks for protection and revenge, people now needed support in maintaining unchallenged possession of land and offices, as well as a secure social position. For this necessity, lineal descent was more important than bilateral kinship. Nevertheless, bilateral kinship did not disappear completely. For example, it continued to be dominant in Flanders throughout the Middle Ages.

Joint Ownership. Evidence suggests that by the tenth century a crisis had developed among the European aristocracy. As a result of partible inheritance, the size of aristocratic holdings was diminishing. The wealth and power of families was decreasing while the number of families was increasing. One attempt to halt this ever-increasing fragmentation was the *frérèche,* a form of joint ownership of property by all the brothers who had a claim to a portion of it. The brothers agreed to keep the patrimony intact, even after one or more of them had married. This practice resulted in a joint-family household structure. A *frérèche* is inherently unstable. At some point, the brothers or their sons would want to divide the property. Gradually, the *frérèche* system was modified into something resembling a stem family, thus keeping the patrimony intact.

Transfers of Land. The problem of ever-diminishing holdings was also exacerbated by individualistic attitudes to

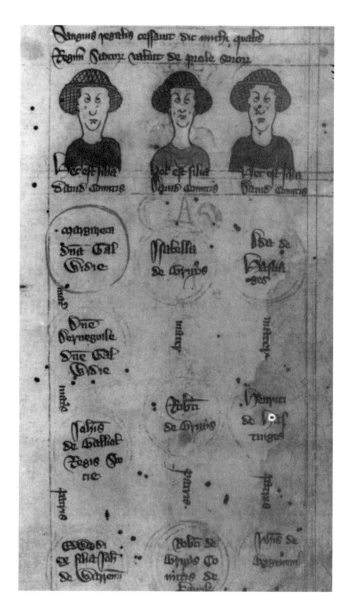

Part of a family tree showing the descent of the main claimants to the throne of Scotland in the late thirteenth century; the three women are daughters of David, Earl of Huntingdon, a younger son of King David I; illumination from an early-fourteenth-century French verse chronicle by Peter of Langtoft (Conway Library, Courtauld Institute, London)

property and inheritance. Because no restrictions were placed on inheritances of land, sons could dispose of the property they inherited as they wished. Similarly, husbands and wives had control of their own estates, which each could sell without consulting the other. The wife also had free control of her dower lands from the outset of the marriage. Consequently, individuals could dispose of portions of their patrimony whenever and however they wished. Some scholars have suggested that during the Middle Ages huge tracts of land were transferred to the Church through outright gifts by the living and bequests in wills. These land transfers were seen as acts of piety and done for the good of the souls of the donors and their families. Land was also transferred to the Church as part of endowing men and women who were entering religious life.

Patrilineage. In the eleventh and twelfth centuries, as aristocratic lineage became increasingly important across Europe, more and more people began to reckon kinship according to a system of patrilineage. This form of determining family connections focuses on male descent groups, stretching forward and backward in time. Women were marginalized within this system: as daughters grew up and were married, they left to become auxiliary members of another man's lineage. A daughter's children would have no part in their maternal grandfather's lineage. Their allegiance was to their father's lineage, not their mother's. A woman could expect little beyond her dowry, as required by the terms of her marriage contract. After marriage a woman would maintain few ties with her natal family.

Stable Lineage. The system of ascertaining patrilineage is, in a sense, backward looking. It traces back through the male line to the ancestor who founded the family. This practice was a significant departure from bilateral kinship. Because membership in the patrilineal system was fixed, kinship relationships were clear, stable, and not subject to change from one generation to the next. This stability allowed the members of the lineage to cultivate a sense of membership and identity based on their common ancestor and their blood relationship.

Strengthening Patrilineage. One of the reasons for the shift from bilateral to patrilineal kinship was the success of the Church in imposing monogamy and suppressing concubinage in the eleventh century. In societies that permit multiple sexual relationships, patrilineal relationships are obscured, making it difficult to establish an organized and closed descent group. A second reason for the change was the decline in resources to support large elite households. In the early Middle Ages the aristocracy lived by pillage, gifts, and rents. From the eleventh century onward, however, the stability that feudal organization brought to Europe strictly limited opportunities for plunder or enrichment. The aristocracy was required to live off its own land, collecting rents and managing its resources. Thus, they had to limit the division of their estates among their many offspring. The introduction of primogeniture, inheritance by the eldest son to the exclusion of daughters and younger sons, was a means of preserving the patrimony intact. A daughter received a portion for her dowry, but neither she nor her children had any claim on the patrimony itself. As a strategy to reunite portions of the original patrimony, the aristocracy also developed a preference for endogamy (marriage between cousins). This practice also strengthened patrilineage.

The _Consorteria_. Patrilineage took various forms in medieval Europe. In areas of northern Italy the _consorteria_ was a common means of avoiding the partition of ancestral family. In a _consorteria_ the members of a descent group banded together in a corporation to own property in common and make decisions about it collectively. This form of kinship organization suited wealthy and powerful merchant families in the urbanized economy of Italy. Sons basically inherited membership in the corporation.

In addition to the land they owned collectively, members of a _consorteria_ own property individually as well. They frequently lived in the same area of town, attended the family church, and were buried in the family crypt. Membership was regulated by contract, usually defining an inner circle of decision makers, which could change each time the contract was renewed. Even after many generations and the development of several collateral lines, these lineage groups frequently had a strong sense of shared identity. The great Italian banks that developed in the course of the thirteenth century are examples of the _consorteria_ at work and show just how successful these large mercantile family corporations could be.

Dynastic Lineage. Another form of patrilineage, dynastic descent is closely connected with the rise of feudalism across northern Europe. Both Germanic and Roman law assumed that inheritances were partible among the heirs. Over time, as fiefs evolved from temporary land grants to heritable and partible holdings, new inheritance rules were introduced that affected the organization of families. Though they were technically owned by a ruler and held by a vassal in return for his loyalty, fiefs came to be similar to land held in absolute ownership, which carried unconditional, permanent, and hereditary title. At the highest levels of society, feudal estates were only rarely divided because they were essential to the stability and defense of the crown. There is evidence of how primogeniture crept into the system. For example, in 877 Charles II (the Bald) declared that if a count should die while his son was serving with the king, then the son should succeed to his father's office, which before that time had not been guaranteed to one's descendants. On the Continent there were a variety of systems. In most areas with impartible inheritance, the eldest son was heir, but in some places different systems developed, such as ultimogeniture, in which the youngest son inherited. In England, where feudal tenure was imposed uniformly in the wake of the Norman invasion (1066), there was a distinct preference for impartible male primogeniture from the beginning, thus enhancing patrilineage.

The Development of Surnames. The success and influence of dynastic patrilineages are reflected in the development of distinct naming patterns. In the course of the eleventh century, surnames began to be used at an increasing rate and tended to be derived from the names of the castle or principal estate of a family. As family names were adopted and regularized, the pool of first names shrank and certain ones were used by different families, frequently appearing in alternating generations. Families began to adopt coats of arms that encorporated symbols of their status and to draw up complex genealogies that stressed the nobility of the family's lineage and its founder. Another indication of patrilineal loyalty is found in the increase, during the eleventh century, in the proportion of family members who appeared as witnesses to deeds and other documents. In the tenth century, blood relatives—brothers, uncles, nephews, and cousins—had rarely appeared as witnesses. Thus, by the end of the eleventh century, roughly at the same time that feudal forms of land tenure were beginning to dominate, aristocratic patrilineage developed and became the dominant family system among European elites, overshadowing the maternal line and bilateral kinship, but not erasing it. When it was expedient, the aristocracy still turned to this wider kinship group for support. Slowly, but surely, some of the values of patrilineage, in particular impartible inheritance and primogeniture, gradually permeated other levels of society.

Conflicting Views. As the patrilineage increased in power it extended its collective control over the individual. This shift is clearly evident in the adoption of impartible inheritance and changes made to the terms governing dowries, both of which prevented property from being divided by individuals. Another area in which patrilineal interests overrode individual desires was in marriage, which represented the future of the patrilineage and needed to be negotiated to benefit the collective lineage group rather than the individual. Marriage was a fundamental method of extending political or economic ties or cementing a truce. Thus, for the aristocracy, marriage was a social institution. The Church, however, had a different view of marriage, which was grounded in the individual's quest for salvation. It was thus inevitable that the needs of society, especially the aristocracy, came into conflict with the laws and theology of marriage that the Church was developing and disseminating at about the same time as the rise of patrilineage.

Sources:

Georges Duby, *Medieval Marriage: Two Models from Twelfth-Century France,* translated by Elborg Forster (Baltimore: Johns Hopkins University Press, 1978).

Jack Goody, *The Development of the Family and Marriage in Europe* (Cambridge: Cambridge University Press, 1983).

David Herlihy, *Medieval Households* (Cambridge, Mass.: Harvard University Press, 1985).

BETROTHAL: EXPENSES

Marriage Agreements. After a man and woman were betrothed, their families typically negotiated a marriage contract. There were many different economic arrangements involved in a marriage contract. Inherited from the ancient practices of the Romans and the Germanic peoples, these compacts evolved and changed over the course of the Middle Ages. In Roman practice the bride's family provided a *dos* (dowry) at the time of her marriage to assist the couple in establishing their household. By the third century the groom's family was providing the bride with a substantial marriage gift, the *donatio propter nuptias* (donation on account of marriage). This gift usually exceeded the amount of the dowry, indicating that wives had become increasingly prized. In an 866 letter to the Boris I, King of the Bulgarians, Pope Nicholas I mentioned that in the marriage ceremony the man conveyed property to the woman through a written agreement. Moreover, there is evidence that throughout the early Middle Ages, the value of this gift was increasing, suggesting that women were in

demand as marriage partners and men were having to pay for the privilege of marrying. This situation has been explained in two ways. Some scholars have suggested that there was a demographic imbalance in the population, with men significantly outnumbering women. Others have pointed out that the practices of polygamy and concubinage made a large proportion of eligible women the wives and mistresses of relatively few elite men; thus, there were fewer women available to marry other men. In either case men would have had to make themselves attractive to prospective partners.

Payments to Brides. Among the Germanic peoples, the ancient bride price that had once been paid to the bride's family had transformed into a payment to the bride herself from the groom. Moreover, this practice was supplemented by the *Morgengabe* (morning gift) made to the bride after her first night with her husband, a recognition that she had surrendered her virginity to the groom and that he had acquired sexual rights to her. Both these payments were originally monetary but, over time, they began to include land grants as well.

Payments to Grooms. Sometime in the early twelfth century, the economic burdens of marriage gradually shifted from the groom and his family to the bride and her family. This shift may be explained in part by another demographic change. During this period religious life was becoming increasing popular, and many new orders were founded. It is possible that the large numbers of men entering religious life, as well as strict enforcement of clerical celibacy, led to a shortage of marriageable men. Consequently, a woman had to make herself an attractive marriage partner by bringing a larger dowry to the union.

Equal Contributions. According to twelfth-century records, lawyers such as the Italian ecclesiastic and jurist Gratian stated that the bride's contribution to the marriage (the dowry) should be at least equal to that of the groom (the dower). Notarial records kept in Genoa from 1155 to 1164 reveal that the contributions of the bride and groom were, in fact, equal, but that equality did not last for long. The *Morgengabe* fell into disuse, and the dower, which had previously been a free gift from husband to wife, was now reduced to lifetime use. At the wife's death the property reverted back to her husband's heirs, and the wife could no longer dispose of it freely in her will. For example, a woman could not bequeath to children of a second marriage land she had received as dower in a first marriage.

Other Marriage Expenses. When a female customary tenant (or serf) wanted to marry, she first had to pay the lord of the manor a fine known as the *merchet*. Long after other customary fines had fallen into disuse, lords still exacted the *merchet*. By the late fourteenth century, establishing whether a mother or sister had paid the *merchet* was one means of determining whether a villager was free or servile. The practice of allowing a woman to buy the right to marry freely became increasingly prominent after the mid ninth century, when the Church asserted the necessity of consent in marriage. Records of manorial courts include many instances in which a woman, or her father, paid a fine to the lord so she could marry freely. Though in such a case a specific man had not yet been chosen as a husband, this practice was essentially the same as paying the *merchet*.

Dowry Inflation. As early as the mid twelfth century, some Italian cities were limiting to one-third the amount of household property a wife could claim upon her husband's death. This practice was also common in French custom and occurred in England as well. Other legislation tried to limit the amount of the man's donation to one-quarter of the value of the woman's dowry. At the same time, however, the wife's dowry was fully incorporated into the family's property, with the result that it could be inherited by her husband and children rather than being left to a person or persons chosen by the wife in her will. By the late Middle Ages the husband's contribution had dwindled to insignificance while the size of the dowry had grown significantly. In fact, dowry inflation was so great that, as Dante commented, the birth of a daughter could strike terror in her father's heart as he contemplated casting his family into poverty in order to provide her with a dowry. In the thirteenth century the problem was so severe that leaving money to provide dowries to poor girls became a favorite form of deathbed charity.

The Declining Status of Women. Other late medieval innovations indicate the declining status of women in marriage. For example, in the thirteenth century, married women in England were no longer allowed to control movable goods. All a woman's land and chattels passed into her husband's control at marriage. Instead of inheriting from her husband outright, a woman only had lifetime use of the land her husband had given her as dower. These changes were likely the result of marriage strategies implemented to consolidate the patrilineage. Families tried to betroth all their daughters, but only their eldest son. Consequently, this practice added to the demographic imbalance as more women than men were actively seeking marriage partners. Thus, women needed large dowries to attract an appropriate husband. At the same time, however, a wife's rights to part of her husband's estate were also curtailed. While these practices helped to conserve and even enhance the husband's property and lineage, they did so at the expense of the woman's father's lineage and interests.

Sources:

Georges Duby, *Medieval Marriage: Two Models from Twelfth-Century France,* translated by Elborg Forster (Baltimore: Johns Hopkins University Press, 1978).

Frances Gies and Joseph Gies, *Marriage and the Family in the Middle Ages* (New York: Harper & Row, 1987).

David Herlihy, *Medieval Households* (Cambridge, Mass.: Harvard University Press, 1985).

BETROTHAL: MARRIAGE AGE

Various Factors. In the absence of records of births and marriages, it is difficult to ascertain the usual age of marriage in the early Middle Ages. Economic structure and social rank influenced when men and women would marry, as did values concerning education, procreation, honor, and

A man giving a woman a ring as a sign of their betrothal; illumination from a twelfth-century manuscript for Gratian's *Decretum* (circa 1140), an authoritative treatise on canon (Church) law (Biblioteca Laurenziana, Florence)

modesty—all of which differed markedly according to social rank and geographic region. For example, Mediterranean attitudes about marriage were different from those of northern Europe.

Rural Marriage Ages. Some of the estate surveys from the ninth century suggest that among the rural peasantry the bride and groom were quite close in age. For example, the Saint Germain-des-Prés survey (circa 809–839) listed 86 widowers and 133 widows. If there had been a large age gap at marriage, there should have been a significantly greater number of widows than widowers in the community. The evidence of the Marseilles survey (813–814) suggests that both peasant men and women were waiting until they were in their late twenties to marry. Moreover, the community appears to have had few widows, suggesting women were not significantly younger than their husbands. Given the high population found on these family farms, it is not surprising that marriage was postponed to lessen the demands put onto a small plot of land.

Youthful Marriages. Among the aristocracy in the early Middle Ages there are occasional references that suggest girls might marry in their mid teens. The legal age for marriage set by canon law was twelve for girls and fourteen for boys. There is no shortage of examples of youths from the highest ranks of the aristocracy or royalty being married at such young ages. In the cities of Italy, the age at which girls married seems to have become progressively younger over this period. One fifteenth-century moralist criticized the young marriage age of his day—fifteen for girls—and looked back to the better days of the twelfth century, when girls were married at twenty-four or twenty-five. Yet, writing in the mid thirteenth century, Philippe de Navarre advised that boys be married at

twenty and girls at fourteen. While most of the information on marriage ages in the upper ranks of society
remains anecdotal, it suggests that girls often married
between the ages of fourteen and eighteen.

Grooms' Ages. Anecdotal evidence relating to marriage
ages of men is problematic because men were more likely to
marry again as widowers, and sources do not always note
the fact that a marriage was the groom's second. Furthermore, most descriptions of marriages do not mention the
age of the groom, even when they note the bride's age.
While eleventh- and twelfth-century evidence suggests that
those men who were slated to marry did so in their teens,
the situation had changed by around 1200. At this time,
men were postponing marriage or refusing to marry. There
are many examples of men who did not marry until they
were in their forties. Fourteenth-century commentators
often said thirty was an appropriate marriage age for men.

Factors Influencing Marriage. Several social factors
could also influence the age at which men and women
married. A man in the feudal aristocracy might delay
marriage until he had come into his title and estate at his
father's death. A younger son might wait until he had
proved himself in war, which might lead to a grant of land
or an opportunity to marry an heiress. If these chances did
not arise, younger sons were doomed to live without the
trappings of full adulthood: a wife, children, and one's
own household. The situation was quite different for aristocratic women. Because of the importance of the patrilineage and the need for legitimate heirs, family honor
came to be increasingly tied to the chastity of wives and
the virginity of daughters. As a result, fathers tried to
marry off their daughters as young as possible, before they
were exposed to sexual temptation or had opportunities to
compromise their virtue.

Elite Italian Marriage. Among the large urban elites of
the Italian peninsula, young men of mercantile families
underwent significant training, often spending time abroad
in order to learn about the economic interests of the family
in various parts of Europe and the Mediterranean. Moreover, these youths generally were not emancipated from
their fathers' control until they were thirty or thirty-five, at
which time they tended to marry. For girls the situation
was quite different and akin to that of their aristocratic sisters in northern Europe. Because of the increasing value
placed on virginity, it was not unusual for girls as young as
fifteen to marry men of thirty-five.

The "European Marriage Pattern." In rural Europe,
and among the urban artisans and laborers, the pattern of
marriage ages differed again. These lower social ranks
tended to follow the so-called European marriage pattern.
According to this model, people usually delayed marriage
until they were in their mid twenties, and a significant proportion of the population did not marry at all. In rural areas
children tended to live at home until they married.
Although there were no prohibitions against early marriage
and the incorporation of a wife into the household of her
father-in-law, marriage tended to be delayed for both men

and women. Evidence suggests that although the married
couple occasionally might be in their mid to late teens, it
was more common for both men and women to be in their
early twenties. In rural society this stage of life was the
standard age of inheritance, but in cities the economic
foundation necessary to start a new household was often
such that neither men nor women could expect to inherit
the means to marry. Consequently, both men and women
tended to work prior to marriage. In this way, a man
learned a craft or had the opportunity to save money, while
a woman saved some of her earnings for her dowry and was
able to bring household goods to the union. Thus, young
people in urban areas, especially those working as servants
or apprentices, tended to marry in their mid to late twenties. Women may have been two or three years younger
than their husbands but, in general, there was not as significant an age difference as there was among the urban elites.

Sources:
Christopher N. L. Brooke, *The Medieval Idea of Marriage* (Oxford & New
    York: Oxford University Press, 1989).

Barbara A. Hanawalt, *The Ties That Bound: Peasant Families in Medieval
    England* (New York: Oxford University Press, 1986).

David Herlihy, *Medieval Households* (Cambridge, Mass.: Harvard Univer-
    sity Press, 1985).

ECONOMIC PARTNERSHIP IN MARRIAGE

Urban Family Units. One of the most significant features of marriage among urban artisan groups was its function as an economic partnership. Marriage was
unencumbered by the demands of lineage and patrimony,
and the extended family exerted little control over the individuals. Households tended to be small. A husband and
wife with their children were the basic family unit. These
people lived and worked together because the household
was also an economic unit. Husbands and wives were also
business partners, working together in the family shop.

Equal Partnership. The result of this economic interdependence was a more companionate view of marriage and a
less hierarchical family structure. Both the husband and
wife contributed to the household economy and the financial well-being of the family. Moreover, before marriage,
during their teens and early twenties, wives had usually
experienced a period of relative autonomy while living away
from parental supervision as servants or workers in other
families' households. Thus, women entered marriage having made decisions, earned money, and spent it independently. Such a woman did not easily accept a husband who
expected to wield absolute patriarchal authority over her
and their children.

Rural Cooperation. Much the same situation pertained
in the countryside. A peasant's holding required the labor
of husband and wife equally, and both contributed to the
financial burden of establishing the household. Wives
could also inherit land, either because there were no sons,
or because they received bequests from relatives, or because
they were widows entering a second marriage. Thus, in
some cases, the family was established on the wife's land
rather than the husband's.

A married couple owning goods in common; illumination from a French manuscript for Justinian's *Digeste*, circa 1280 (Bibliothèque Nationale, Paris)

Gender Roles. Farming tasks tended to be gender specific: men ploughed the fields; women looked after the garden and animals. Each spouse made an essential contribution to the household economy. Though her contribution gave the wife status within the household and family, it did not influence her public role. Women were excluded from village offices and did not serve as jurors or pledges, but they were often fined by the manorial court for a variety of infractions and frequently appeared to pay their own *merchets* (marriage fines) or *legerwites* (fines for being caught fornicating or giving birth to illegitimate children).

Supplemental Income. Part of a rural woman's work brought in supplemental income. Thus, women typically spun cloth or sold eggs, butter, or other produce at the market. They also frequently brewed and sold ale. This activity was particularly well suited to the busy mother with young children. It did not require a significant outlay for equipment because ale could be brewed using standard household items such as pots and spoons. Moreover, small children could help, for example, by stirring the vats. In fact, women with children engaged in brewing more frequently than childless women and widows.

Sources:

Judith M. Bennett, *Women in the Medieval English Countryside. Gender and Household in Brigstock Before the Plague* (New York: Oxford University Press, 1987).

Barbara A. Hanawalt, *The Ties That Bound: Peasant Families in Medieval England* (New York: Oxford University Press, 1986).

David Herlihy, *Medieval Households* (Cambridge, Mass.: Harvard University Press, 1985).

MARRIAGE: CHURCH VIEWS

Marriage as a Means to Salvation. In the course of the ninth century the Church struggled to develop a view of marriage based on the role it played in the order of salvation. From the outset there was an inherent tension between ecclesiastical and secular views of marriage.

The Church considered marriage inextricable from the individual soul's quest for God and was less concerned than secular society in the importance of marriage to the wider family. As far as the Church was concerned, marriage was "the union of two in one flesh" (Gen. 2.24); it joined two souls, not two families, and it should be undertaken, not for political or economic advantage, but for spiritual reasons.

The Marriage Sacrament. From its early days the Church had attributed a mystical element to marriage, drawing an analogy between the marriage of a man and a woman and the union of Christ with the Church. Though this connection gave marriage a special spiritual quality, however, marriage was not firmly instituted as one of seven sacraments until the twelfth century. As a sacrament, marriage was considered an outward and visible sign of an inner, invisible grace. As the theology of marriage developed, this sacrament was believed to be effected by the couple themselves through their exchange of consent. The Church's insistence on the indissolubility of marriage is based on its spiritual and sacramental nature. Those whom God had joined together, no human could separate.

Augustine's Influence. In his important treatise *De bono conugali* (On the Good of Marriage), St. Augustine (354–430) developed what became the Church's fundamental concepts of the nature, meaning, and function of marriage. Augustine argued that God had instituted marriage in the Garden of Eden and that it was the only sacrament established before the Fall from Paradise. Augustine also wrote that there were three goods inherent in marriage: the procreation of children, marital fidelity, and mutual obligation. These ideas were encorporated into all subsequent Church teachings on marriage and became the foundations for the doctrines of monogamy and indissolubility, as well as the

---

A MEDIEVAL WIFE'S STATUS

In his *Sententiarum libri IV* (Four Books of Sentences, 1148–1151), Peter Lombard defined a wife's place in Christian marriage:

1 *Why woman was formed from the side of man.* Now, because she was not given as a servant or mistress, therefore, in the beginning she was neither formed from the highest nor the lowest, but from the side of man on account of the conjugal partnership. If she had been made from the highest, that is from the head, she would seem to have been created for domination. But if from the lowest, that is from the feet, it would seem that she ought to be subjected to servitude. But because she was intended neither as a mistress nor as a servant, she was created from the middle, that is the side, because she was intended for conjugal partnership.

Source: Translation by Jacqueline Murray and Abigail Young, from Peter Lombard, *Sententiae in IV libris distinctae*, third edition (Grottaferrata: Collegii S. Bonaventurae, 1981), III: 435.

prohibition of birth control. By the late twelfth century the Church's theology of marriage was firmly established on the deceptively simple teaching that marriage was one of the seven sacraments and required the consent of the couple alone. The implications of this statement, however, were worked out through the development of a complex canon law that reached its final form in 1234 with the *Decretals* of Pope Gregory IX.

Defining a Valid Marriage. By the twelfth century, having successfully asserted its jurisdiction over marriage, the Church faced the complicated task of refining its theories and practices. One of the most serious and vexing issues was defining exactly when a valid and indissoluble marriage occurred. In other words, it needed to decide which factors or acts were essential for a marriage and which were simply customary—as well as spelling out when a couple could be sure that they were, in fact, married. Most commentators agreed that the mutual consent of the two parties was required. This consensual theory of marriage accorded with both the precepts of Roman law and the teachings of the Church Fathers. There were many questions, however, regarding the nature of this consent, especially in a period when it was expected that children would obey their parents in such matters. Linked to this concern were questions about the role of sexual relations in the formation of the marriage bond.

Gratian's Definition. The great canonist Gratian discussed at length the issues surrounding marriage and consent in his *Concordance of Disconcordant Canons* (circa 1140), a compilation of canon law better known as the *Decretum*. Arguing that marriage was both a spiritual union founded on mutual consent and a physical union based on sexual intercourse, Gratian saw marriage as occurring in two stages. The first was the exchange of mutual consent, indi-

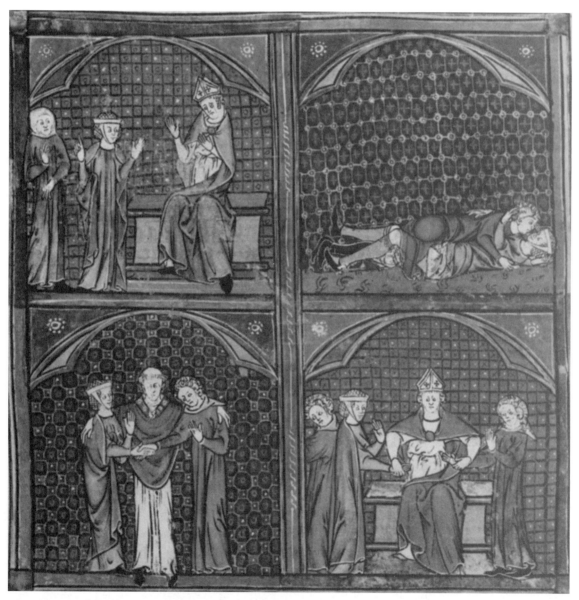

Grounds for annulment: after a couple exchanges consent (bottom left), the husband is unable to consummate their union (top right); and the wife complains to a bishop (top left), who dissolves their union, symbolically disjoining the couple's hands (bottom right); illumination from a thirteenth-century manuscript for Gratian's *Decretum* (Fitzwilliam Museum, Cambridge)

cating the couple agreed to marry one another. This action initiated the marriage, which was subsequently perfected when the couple consummated their union through sexual intercourse. Both stages of the process were necessary to create an indissoluble marriage: neither coitus without consent nor consent with consummation resulted in marriage. For Gratian, consummation, not consent, made marriage a sacrament and henceforth indissoluble. An unconsummated marriage lacked the same force as a consummated one. Thus, after the exchange of consent, but prior to consummation, either spouse could enter religious life without the permission of the other. Moreover, if, for some reason, such as impotence, one spouse was unable to consummate the marriage, the union could be dissolved and the partner who was sexually capable could marry someone else. If the marriage had been consummated, however, even with only one act of intercourse, and the man subsequently became impotent, the union could not be dissolved. Another example of how Gratian believed consummation created a superior bond is the case of bigamy or perceived bigamy. For example, a person who had exchanged consent with someone but had not consummated the union might subsequently marry another person and consummate that relationship. The consummated union would then take precedence over the unconsummated one. Only the second union would be considered a valid marriage.

Clerical Resistence. Gratian's teaching met with resistance from many churchmen, particularly because of the primacy he accorded to sexual relations. Clergy who were suspicious of sexual relations in particular and the pleasures of the flesh in general rejected his views, questioning how an institution as holy as marriage could require an act as base and sinful as sexual intercourse to give it validity. Moreover, according to Gratian's theory, the marriage of Mary and Joseph, which was unconsummated, would not have been a "perfect" marriage, a notion that was absolutely unthinkable to many.

Peter Lombard's Response. The other major twelfth-century theorist of marriage, Italian theologian Peter Lombard, came to quite a different conclusion about the formation of the marriage bond. In his theological compilation, *Sententiarum libri IV* (Four Books of Sentences, 1148–1151), Lombard rejected the necessity of consummation and sought to refine the understanding of consent. He argued that there were two different kinds of consent involved in marriage as it was then practiced. The first was the consent to marry found in betrothal agreements, which, he argued, was too tentative and remote to form a marriage bond. This consent, in *verba de futuro* (words of the future), amounted to no more than a promise to marry. What was needed to form the sacramental marriage bond were *verba de presenti*, words of consent in the present. The marriage ceremony included unambiguous words stating explicitly that the couple agreed they were married to one another from that moment forward; these words made a real, binding marriage. The impact of Lombard's teaching on the consensual theory was dramatic. He gave full force to the

words of the couple: "I take you as my husband"; "I take you as my wife." Nothing else, he said, was necessary for a valid union. The blessing of a priest, the approval of family and friends, and the bestowing of a dowry were all desirable, but in the end they were extraneous.

Consent and Consummation. Subsequent Church leaders, in particular Pope Alexander III, adopted and adapted Lombard's notion of present and future consent. Alexander III refined the consensual theory to allow the bond to be established in two ways. The first way was through the exchange of consent in words of the present tense. The second way pertained to a couple who had exchanged a promise to marry in words of the future tense and subsequently engaged in sexual intercourse. These two acts together, he said, also formed a valid and indissoluble marriage. In the second case, some of the emphasis that Gratian had given to consummation endured. Sexual intercourse served to ratify the future consent and transform a betrothal into a marriage.

Sources:

Christopher N. L. Brooke, *The Medieval Idea of Marriage* (Oxford & New York: Oxford University Press, 1989).

James A. Brundage, *Law, Sex, and Christian Society in Medieval Europe* (Chicago: University of Chicago Press, 1987).

Charles Donahue Jr., "The Policy of Alexander the Third's Consent Theory of Marriage," in *Proceedings of the 4th Congress of Medieval Canon Law*, edited by Stephan Kuttner (Vatican City: Biblioteca Apostolica Vaticana, 1976), pp. 251–281.

Frances Gies and Joseph Gies, *Marriage and the Family in the Middle Ages* (New York: Harper & Row, 1987).

MARRIAGE: IMPEDIMENTS TO CHRISTIAN UNIONS

Invalidating Marriages. The medieval Church identified two types of impediments to marriage. Diriment impediments blocked the creation of the marriage bond. If two people exchanged consent and a diriment impediment were discovered, the couple was required to separate immediately because no valid marriage bond existed—nor could ever exist—between them. The second type was the prohibitive impediment. Though this second impediment forbade a marriage between two individuals, if they married anyway, their union was considered valid and indissoluble.

Consanguinity. Consanguinity, or blood relationship, was the most significant and most ancient reason for prohibiting a union. Most societies throughout history have forbidden marriage between siblings or relatives in the direct line, such as grandfather and granddaughter. In ancient Rome, aunts and uncles could not marry their nieces and nephews, but first cousins were permitted to marry. The Christian Church, however, sought to extend the degrees of relationship that were considered to prevent incestuous marriages. As early as the sixth century, at the Council of Agde (506), the Church extended the prohibitions to marriages between first cousins and between their children (second cousins).

Degrees of Relationship. A far more dramatic extension of prohibited kinship ties occurred in the first half of the

A "Tree of Marriage" diagramming forbidden degrees of affinity (relationship through marriage) according to canon law; illumination from a thirteenth-century manuscript for Gratian's *Decretum* (Fitzwilliam Museum, Cambridge)

eighth century. Until then, the Church had used the Roman system to compute the degrees of relationship between two people. According to this method, every degree of relationship was counted from one member of the couple, through their common ancestor, to the other spouse. According to this system the furthest relationships that were considered to be within the prohibited degrees of consanguinity were first cousins (the fourth degree of kinship). In the year 747, however, the English missionary Boniface convinced the Pope that the prohibited degrees be extended to seven. This change meant that second, third, and fourth cousins were also forbidden to marry.

Germanic Consanguinity. In the early ninth century, another innovation occurred that extended the degrees of consanguinity even further. The Roman method of counting from one person back to the common ancestor, and then forward to the other person was replaced by a method of Germanic origin. In this system of calculation, degrees were counted back to the common ancestor only. Thus, in the Roman system, first cousins were related in the fourth degree; in the Germanic system they were related in the second degree. The result of this change was to extend the prohibited degrees of relationship to a sixth cousin, a

descendant of one's great-great-great-great-great grandparents. This regulation was unenforceable because it was virtually impossible for a medieval European to trace his or her lineage that far back. Furthermore, even if it had been possible, the practical result would have left people in some social ranks, or in geographic areas with small populations, without any permissible marriage partner at all.

Affinity. Affinity, a tie formed through marriage, was another impediment, which was designed to encourage the practice of exogamy. St. Augustine had argued that marriage should expand the circle of relatives to whom one was tied through bonds of affection and charity. Consequently, people were prohibited from marrying their close affines, or in-laws. For example, a widow was forbidden to marry her deceased husband's brother. In the eighth century, as part of his reforms prohibitions relating to degrees of consanguinity, Boniface introduced an innovation that extended the concept of affinity significantly. He argued that an impediment to marriage was created if a man and woman had sexual relations outside of marriage. Such people became affines and were forbidden to marry one another. If one did so, the marriage was considered invalid, and lifelong penance was necessary. This

DEGREES OF RELATIONSHIP

The Romans calculated kinship only to the fourth degree. In the eighth century the Church extended the Roman system to seven degrees, as follows:

Self

1. Father and Mother

2. Brother and Sister, Grandfather and Grandmother

3. Uncle and Aunt

4. First Cousin

5. Second Cousin

6. Third Cousin

7. Fourth Cousin

In the ninth century the Church adopted the Germanic system of determining kinship:

Self

1. Father and Mother, Brother and Sister, Uncle and Aunt

2. Grandfather and Grandmother, First Cousin

3. Second Cousin

4. Third Cousin

5. Fourth Cousin

6. Fifth Cousin

7. Sixth Cousin

impediment had widespread implications. For example, a man who frequented a prostitute would be forbidden to marry the sister of any of her other clients. It was difficult to know that such an impediment existed, but ignorance did not change the situation.

Spiritual Kinship. The prohibition based on spiritual kinship, a bond formed between people through the sacraments of baptism or confirmation, was another innovation of the eighth century. People who had participated together in the sacrament of baptism or confirmation were considered already bound in a familial relationship, so marriage between two such related individuals was inappropriate. Thus, a godparent was forbidden to marry a godchild, and, prior to the imposition of clerical celibacy, a priest could not marry a woman he had baptized or confirmed.

Consent. Several other factors that were considered diriment impediments to marriage centered on a person's ability to render valid and informed consent. If a person had previously taken vows as a monk or nun, he or she was forbidden to contract marriage because the vow of celibacy took precedence. People who were considered to be insane were not permitted to marry because they could not appreciate the nature of consent that spouses exchanged. The

canonists were quick to point out, however, that if a person oscillated between moments of sanity and insanity, consent exchanged while sane created an indissoluble and valid union.

The Age of Majority. For a marriage to be valid both parties had to have reached the age of majority, twelve for girls and fourteen for boys, roughly the onset of puberty. At these ages people were considered sufficiently mature to give informed consent to marry. They were also thought old enough to appreciate the nature of the marriage commitment, to be able to consent to sexual relations, and to have the physical capacity to consummate the marriage. Prior to coming of age, however, children above the age of seven could be betrothed by their families. In such cases, however, the betrothed had to ratify the compact on reaching the age of majority in order for it to remain binding. Either person was able legally to reject a union arranged by their parents, but in practice familial and social pressures made such a decision difficult to implement.

Freedom of Consent. Consent to marry had to be given freely. Consequently, consent that was coerced by threats of death, bodily harm, or other frightening consequences was considered to be invalid. While children were encouraged to accept their elders' advice and to obey their commands, friends, relatives, and lords were not allowed to force an unwilling person to marry someone against his or her will. The spouse who had been coerced into marriage was expected to give outward signs of unwillingness, such as weeping, and to leave the situation as soon as possible.

Consummation. Since marriage was the only legitimate outlet for sexual desire, the inability to consummate a union was also an impediment to the formation of the conjugal bonds. This condition put the Church in the awkward situation of having to pass judgment on the sexual abilities of a married person whose spouse sued for an annulment on the grounds of nonconsummation. Such cases almost always involved a woman alleging that her husband was impotent and seeking an annulment so she could be permitted to marry another man and have children. If sexual disability could be proven, the spouse who had been found impotent was required to remain single while the other spouse was permitted to marry again.

Minor Impediments. A minor impediment to marriage was dictated by the Church calendar. Marriages should not be contracted during Lent, Advent, or other penitential seasons. Similarly, all marriages were forbidden in a region that was under an ecclesiastical interdict. However, if the couple went ahead and exchanged consent, their union was considered to be valid.

Sources:

Christopher N. L. Brooke, *The Medieval Idea of Marriage* (Oxford & New York: Oxford University Press, 1989).

James A. Brundage, *Law, Sex, and Christian Society in Medieval Europe* (Chicago: University of Chicago Press, 1987).

Frances Gies and Joseph Gies, *Marriage and the Family in the Middle Ages* (New York: Harper & Row, 1987).

MARRIAGE: MORAL DUTIES

Sex and Affection. The medieval church recognized that both sexual relations and affection between spouses were necessary to maintain the indissoluble bond of marriage. Husband and wife were charged with the moral responsibility to attend to both aspects in their life together.

Conjugal Duty. The importance of the sexual dimension was highlighted by the apostle Paul in his first letter to the Corinthians, where he wrote: "The husband should give to his wife her conjugal rights, and likewise the wife to her husband. For the wife does not rule over her own body, but the husband does; likewise the husband does not rule over his own body, but the wife does. Do not refuse one another except perhaps by agreement for a season, so that you may devote yourselves to prayer; but then come together again, lest Satan tempt you through lack of self-control. I say this by way of concession, not of command" (1 Corinthians 7.3-6). Thus, Paul argued, coitus was so important in the marriage relationship that neither spouse could deny the other legitimate marital relations. This doctrine came to be known as the conjugal debt. One of the reasons Paul gave so much importance to the conjugal debt was his fear that, without a legitimate outlet for sexual desire, a person would fall into the serious sins of adultery (sexual relations in which one or both participants is married) or fornication (sexual relations between two unmarried participants). He introduced his discussion by saying, "It is well for a man not to touch a woman. But because of the temptation to immorality, each man should have his own wife and each woman her own husband" (1 Corinthians 7.1-2). The medieval Church so feared that people would not be able to control their lust that it rigorously interpreted Paul's teaching, asserting that neither husband nor wife had the right or ability to deny the other sexual access. Each was required to render to the other the conjugal debt whenever and wherever it was sought. To refuse was considered a serious sin because one spouse would be exposing the other to sexual temptation that might prove irresistible. The only exception to this rule was if, by mutual consent, the spouses decided to abstain from marital relations for a definite period of time so that they could concentrate on prayer, fasting, and other religious activities. The important condition was that both spouses should agree, and neither spouse should take unilateral action that would deprive the other of conjugal rights.

Enforcement. Though Paul's advice was straightforward, the canon law related to it created a complicated doctrine with layers of meaning and interpretation. According to canon law, spouses were under a mutual obligation to pay the conjugal debt, so logically there had to be legal mechanisms to enforce it. In general, priests warned married people in sermons and during confession of the serious consequences of not living up to their marital obligations. If the Church became aware of an individual's recalcitrance, it had more coercive means of enforcement. A spouse could ask the ecclesiastical courts to make the other marriage partner pay the conjugal debt. This strategy became particularly useful in forcing a partner who had deserted the family to return home. One could also prosecute a lover or anyone else who interfered with the sexual rights of a spouse.

Clerical Suspicions. Another problem surrounding the doctrine of the conjugal debt was clerical suspicion of the physical pleasure inherent in it. The Church had inherited an ascetic view of life from antiquity. Although no less an authority than Paul had proclaimed conjugal relations the legitimate outlet for human sexual desire, theologians and canonists gradually developed the notion that, since there was always a degree of pleasure inherent in sexual relations, then some aspect of sin inhered in every sex act, even those between married people. In the middle of the twelfth century, Gratian taught that there was a qualitative difference between rendering the conjugal debt and seeking it. He adopted Augustine's view that rendering the debt when it was sought was blameless, but exacting the debt because of lust or sexual incontinence was a venial sin. This clarification was a significant departure from the original teaching of Paul, who had not distinguished between the spouse who sought the debt and the spouse who rendered it.

Sexuality. Some of the subsequent commentators who reinterpreted and refined the notion of the sinful nature of conjugal relations approached the issue from a far more negative perspective than Gratian. For example, the Italian canonist Huguccio (died 1210; also known as Hugh of Pisa) argued that because sin adhered to any sort of sensual pleasure, and every sex act, regardless of motivation, involved pleasure, then even marital relations motivated by a desire for procreation were sinful. The only distinction was the degree of sin involved, depending on the motives for intercourse. Other commentators, however, took the position that only lustful pleasure was sinful, and, therefore, sex for purposes of procreation or rendering the conjugal debt was without sin.

A Reciprocal Obligation. Medieval theologians and canonists considered the obligation of the conjugal debt to pertain equally to husband and wife. Historians have cited this teaching as proof that marital sexuality was one area of medieval life in which women had complete equality with men. While women might be considered subordinate to men in ecclesiastical doctrine, secular law, and daily life practice, in the marital bedroom the husband and wife were on an equal footing. A woman's sexual desires and her right to satisfy them legitimately within marriage were protected by the Church and proclaimed publicly through sermons and in confession. Yet, some historians have questioned if a woman who was subordinate to her husband in daily life and was expected to be obedient in all things, suddenly could assert her sexual rights as an equal. In fact, Thomas Aquinas addressed this issue in the thirteenth century and concluded that "the husband and wife are not equal in marriage, neither is the conjugal act in which what is more noble is due the husband, nor in regard to the administration of the home, in which matter the wife is ruled and the husband rules." Thus, he perceived the wife to be as subordinate to her husband in sexual matters as she was in every other aspect of life.

The Sin of Lust. The prevailing medieval view was that women were by nature sexually passive while men were sexually active. Consequently, it was considered proper and natural that only men would actively seek payment of the conjugal debt. The English moralist Thomas of Chobham (circa 1158 – circa 1233) discussed the problem of a man who constantly sought sexual relations from his wife because he was consumed by lust provoked either by her beauty or by the temptation of other women. Identifying this overexaction of the debt as sinful, Thomas wrote that men motivated by lust alone were guilty of lascivious kisses and filthy embraces and committed serious sin, albeit with their own wives. Despite such views, men were generally considered to have a stronger libido than women and thus a greater need for access to conjugal sex.

Female Sexuality. Prevailing medieval notions of decency would have been affronted by female displays of sexual assertiveness. Moralists seemed aware of the potential double standard inherent in fulfilling the conjugal debt. While medieval Europeans assumed that a man would be forthright about seeking marital relations, they also expected that, given her natural modesty and sexual passivity, a woman might be hesitant to ask her husband for sex. Consequently, a husband was instructed to watch his wife for indirect signs that she might want to have intercourse but was too embarrassed or shy to ask. As Aquinas stated, "The husband is bound to render [the conjugal debt] to his wife when she does not ask." Other moralists offered opinions that, in fact, limited a woman's sexual access to her husband. For example, if her husband had already rendered the debt and was tired, the wife did not have the right to ask for sex again. If she did, she was considered to be behaving like a prostitute. Some scholars have suggested that the doctrine of the conjugal debt deprived a woman of the ability to reject her husband's sexual advances. Thus, women were considered to be sexually available at all times, but the physical limitations that could inhibit male sexual performance were such that a wife might not always be able to exact the debt whenever she wanted. In practice, then, the equality and reciprocity of the conjugal debt may have been illusory.

Marital Affection. As the consensual nature of marriage gained greater recognition, the emotional relationship between spouses gained increasing importance. Marital affection (*affectio maritalis*) was closely linked to the consent to marry and was considered indispensable for the creation of a valid and indissoluble marriage. This legal concept was incorporated into the medieval Church doctrine from Roman law. For the Romans, marital affection was a quality that distinguished the marital relationship from concubinage. Children born from a relationship imbued with marital affection were able to inherit their parents' property. For the Romans as well, it was implicitly understood that when marital affection ceased to exist between spouses the marriage itself ceased to exist. By the

A husband and wife rendering the "conjugal debt," the only sexual outlet approved by the medieval Church; illumination from a manuscript for Aldobrandino of Siena's *Le Regime de Corps,* circa 1285 (British Library, London)

early sixth century the concept of marital affection included an emotional aspect similar to love, as well as implying the intention of the couple to procreate and to live together in a union that would be monogamous and enduring. In other words, where marital affection existed so did the three "goods" of marriage articulated by St. Augustine. Roman law did not establish criteria for judging the presence or absence of marital affection in a relationship. It was necessary to rely on external manifestations of consent and, when it was available, the legal registration of marriages.

Love and Sex. In the middle of the twelfth century, Gratian asserted that marital affection was the essential ingredient that distinguished real marriage from simple cohabitation. Moreover, Gratian argued that marital affection was necessary to form a marriage bond that could be broken only by the death of a spouse. For Gratian, marital affection did not necessarily include the intention to procreate. Perhaps most important, Gratian distinguished between consent to accept a person as spouse and marital affection, which imbued the relationship between the spouses with a specific emotional quality.

Enduring Affection. Marital affection was expected to last throughout the marriage, and spouses were told that they could and should cultivate it actively so that it would grow and develop in the course of their union. Pope Alexander III was so convinced that marital affection could be cultivated that he ordered troubled or separated couples to reunite and behave toward one another with marital affection. He did not seem to consider the potential for obstacles such as hostility, differences in social class, or adultery to impede this process. Similarly,

Alexander exhorted anyone who was married to a leper to care for that spouse with marital affection. While some historians have suggested this charge included rendering the conjugal debt, others have argued that this directive referred only to the kind of mutual care expected of married couples.

Detecting Marital Affection. It was difficult for outsiders to judge the presence or absence of marital affection in a relationship. Frequently inappropriate behavior such as domestic violence was characterized as contrary to the ideals of marital affection; in other cases so was husbands' failures to provide their wives with proper clothing, nourishment, and other necessities. Although ecclesiastical authorities remained unable to articulate or investigate the internal emotional manifestations of marital affection, they nevertheless continued to recognize and assert its centrality to the relationship between spouses.

The Lay Interpretation. The idea of marital affection was not limited to the theoretical discussions of canonists and theologians. Evidence from marriage cases brought before the ecclesiastical courts suggests that marital affection was a meaningful concept among the laity. For example, in one case heard in York, England, in the fourteenth century, a man explained that he wanted to base his marriage on "an affection that holds good," that is, an enduring emotional affection. Many witnesses described marital affection as an ongoing process that began with the initial promises to marry and endured thereafter. It also was frequently mentioned in connection with sharing the marriage bed, although by no means was it limited only to conjugal relations. The substance of marital affection for the laity, however, was connected to the ownership of property. Marital affection was not only an essential ingredient of a marriage but also a requirement for spouses to be able to receive property from one another, just as it had been in Roman law.

Sources:

James A. Brundage, "Sexual Equality and Medieval Canon Law," in *Medieval Women and the Sources of Medieval History*, edited by Joel T. Rosenthal (Athens: University of Georgia Press, 1990), pp. 66–79.

Dyan Elliott, "Bernardino of Siena versus the Marriage Debt," in *Desire and Discipline: Sex and Sexuality in the Premodern West*, edited by Jacqueline Murray and Konrad Eisenbichler (Toronto & Buffalo: University of Toronto Press, 1996), pp. 168–200.

Elizabeth M. Makowski, "The Conjugal Debt and Medieval Canon Law," *Journal of Medieval History*, 3 (1977): 99–114.

John T. Noonan, "Marital Affection in the Canonists," *Studia Gratiana*, 12 (1967): 481–509.

Pierre J. Payer, *The Bridling of Desire: Views of Sex in the Later Middle Ages* (Toronto & Buffalo: University of Toronto Press, 1993).

Frederik Pedersen, "'*Maritalis Affectio*': Marital Affection and Property in Fourteenth-Century York Cause Papers," in *Women, Marriage, and Family in Medieval Christendom: Essays in Memory of Michael M. Sheehan, C.S.B.*, edited by Constance M. Rousseau and Joel T. Rosenthal (Kalamazoo, Mich.: Medieval Institute Publications, 1998), pp. 175–209.

Michael M. Sheehan, "*Maritalis Affectio* Revisited," in *The Olde Daunce. Love, Friendship, Sex, and Marriage in the Medieval World*, edited by Robert R. Edwards and Stephen Spector (Albany: State University of New York Press, 1991), pp. 32–43.

MARRIAGE: SECRET AND CLANDESTINE UNIONS

Informal Unions. Since the only requirement for a valid indissoluble union was the freely given consent of the man and woman, marriage could be contracted at anytime and anywhere. The possibilities and dangers presented by this consensual doctrine were recognized almost immediately. An avalanche of legislation aimed to minimize the impact followed in the wake of Pope Alexander III's adoption of the consensual theory. The problem of clandestinity continued to preoccupy legal commentators and Church councils through the Middle Ages, ending only in the mid sixteenth century when the Council of Trent (1545–1563) prohibited such unions completely.

Legal and Religious Problems. Clandestine unions posed several problems. Secular society needed to know who was married in order to oversee property transfers and inheritance provisions for legal spouses and legitimate children. The Church, concerned with enforcing sexual morality, needed to know if a couple were married in order to enforce laws against fornication and adultery. Moreover, since marriage was a sacrament, the Church needed to know that no impediment barred the couple's exchange of consent and that they appreciated fully the nature of their actions.

Defining Informal Marriages. Two types of unions were included under the category of clandestine marriage. One was a union that occurred informally, without the usual ecclesiastical solemnities and marriage liturgy. At this sort of wedding the couple was not necessarily alone. Clandestine marriages might occur at home, with friends and family gathered round, or even in the local tavern or at other public venues. Secret marriages, on the other hand, occurred without the knowledge and presence of others. Because of the absence of witnesses, these unions were the most difficult to prove in court.

Exchanging Consent. Although a marriage occurred clandestinely, it did not mean that the union was entered into thoughtlessly or casually. The evidence of some court cases reveals that couples used clandestine marriage as a means to evade disapproving parents or avoid arranged marriages. In other cases, however, the parents approved of the exchange of consent or were even involved in it— another indication that clandestine marriages were not always secret. Frequently, they were private unions achieved without formal recourse to the Church and its representatives but with the full participation and blessing of family and friends. There is evidence that couples took some care with their exchange of consent. Sometimes a senior man in the community, perhaps the employer of the bride or groom or an older relative, supervised the exchange of consent to ensure the couple used the correct formula and that the present consent was unambiguous. Court records indicate that a couple might have clasped hands as they repeated the words of consent. The man frequently reported that he had endowed the woman with some sort of small gift or token or placed a ring on her finger. There

An exchange of consent at which a priest is present as a witness but does not perform the marriage ceremony; illumination from a fourteenth-century manuscript for *Artus le Restore* (Bibliothèque Nationale, Paris)

is also an example of the couple kissing through a garland of flowers after they exchanged consent.

False Promises. Secret marriages made women vulnerable to men who sought sexual relations by making false promises of marriage and later denying them. Similarly, if a couple married legitimately in secret, and one subsequently married publicly, the public union, not the secret marriage, would stand. This unhappy situation was the result of the belief that, if an external witness could prove consent had been exchanged, this marriage must take precedence over a secret consent that was unprovable or ambiguous. In such cases, a person married without witnesses was condemned to live in perpetual adultery because the secret union could not be proven.

Avoiding Control. With the option of clandestine marriage, people had a mechanism by which to avoid parental and feudal control and to marry the spouse of their choice. Surviving records for marriage cases brought before the ecclesiastical courts, especially in England, show that people most frequently brought suits to have their marriages declared valid or to have their conjugal rights restored. A significant proportion of the cases involved informal marriages in which present consent was alleged, but there was difficulty proving it had been exchanged.

Reasons for Clandestine Marriages. The consensual doctrine and valid clandestine marriages made the consent of one's parents or lord unnecessary. This innovation was significant in a period when people believed that children should obey their parents and vassals should obey their lords. Furthermore, marriage had not only a sacramental aspect but also a social function. During the Middle Ages, at all levels of society, marriage had significant familial, feudal, and financial ramifications. At the highest levels of society it could also have political and military implications. Consequently, secular authorities considered the personal inclinations of either spouse to be subordinate to the wider considerations of land, lineage, and lord. Another reason for a clandestine marriage was the expense of a religious ceremony. Although the Fourth Lateran Council (1215) forbade priests to charge for performing ecclesiastical services such as marriage, in practice parishioners made voluntary donations for such liturgical functions. Consequently, for some couples, clandestine marriage may have been a more affordable alternative to the formal solemnization of their union.

Unintended Marriages. There was another danger involved in clandestine marriage. If people were joking and playacting, it was conceivable that they could marry one another without intending to do so. For example, one moralist warned that the marriage ceremony should "be decently celebrated, with reverence, not with laughter and ribaldry, not in taverns or at public drinkings and feastings. Let no man place a ring made of rushes or of any worthless or precious material on the hand of a woman in jest that he may more easily gain her favors lest, in thinking to jest, the bonds of marriage be tied. Henceforth let no pledge to contract marriage be given except in the presence of a priest, and of three or four respectable people called together for that purpose." The moralists' warnings notwithstanding, there are many examples of consent being exchanged in all manner of unlikely places including under an ash tree, in bed, in a garden, in a field, in a storeroom, in a blacksmith's shop, and in a kitchen. Obviously, people exchanged consent where and when it was convenient.

Unchecked Practice. Throughout the Middle Ages, the Church sought to strengthen and extend its control over the marriage ceremony. Part of this process was the unsuccessful attempt to eliminate private and secret marriages. Throughout the Middle Ages, however, couples continued to avail themselves of the autonomy offered to them by valid clandestine marriages.

Sources:
Charles Donahue Jr., "The Canon Law on the Formation of Marriage and Social Practice in the Later Middle Ages," *Journal of Family History*, 8 (1983): 144–158.

Donahue, "The Policy of Alexander III's Consent Theory of Marriage," *Proceedings of the 4th Congress of Medieval Canon Law*, edited by Stephan Kuttner (Vatican City: Biblioteca Apostolica Vaticana, 1976), pp. 251–281.

A. J. Finch, "Parental Authority and the Problem of Clandestine Marriage in the Later Middle Ages," *Law and History Review*, 8 (1990): 189–204.

MARRIAGE: SPOUSAL CHOICE

Increased Autonomy. The freedom to choose one's spouse was closely related to the consensual theory of marriage and the principle that clandestine marriages, although illegal, were valid. The impediment of coercion was a logical extension of the doctrine that marriage required only the freely given consent of the couple. Forced consent through threats to kill or injure them or members of their families could hardly be considered free consent to marry. Consequently, the promotion by the Church of consensual marriage gave increased autonomy to individuals who had hitherto been little more than pawns in dynastic, economic, or political negotiations.

An Unwilling Bride. In his *Decretum* (circa 1140), Gratian recorded a case that had been referred to Urban II, who was Pope from 1088 until 1099, for resolution. Jourdain I, the ruler of Capua, had been compelled to give his daughter in marriage to the duke of Gaeta. The daughter, whose name is unknown, was described as "unwilling, weeping, and resisting as much as she was able." The case had little to do with the desires of the daughter, and Urban's decision rested on the father's unwillingness, but Gratian interpreted the ruling to mean that a father could not compel his daughter to marry someone she did not want to wed. In a similar case, Urban had explained that those who would be united in one body ought also to be of one spirit. If they were not, there was a risk of desertion, fornication, or other evils.

Invalidating Forced Marriages. Gratian tended to ignore authorities such as St. Jerome, who argued that

A woman choosing one suitor over another; illumination from a thirteenth-century manuscript for Gratian's *Decretum* (Walters Art Gallery, Baltimore)

every marriage, coerced or not, was binding. Jerome believed that a marriage remained valid even if it had been contracted through violent abduction, paternal coercion, or direct threats. In an 866 letter to Boris I, King of the Bulgarians, Pope Nicholas I instructed that marriage was to be celebrated with the consent of the people to be married and their parents or guardians. Gratian, however, overlooked the stipulation of parental consent and focused only on the consent of the couple. Moreover, Gratian chose to word his opinion so that it highlighted a daughter's freedom to choose a spouse: "no woman should be joined to anyone except by her free will." By focusing on the woman—the person most vulnerable to parental compulsion—he used the strongest example available to ensure there was no interpretive ambiguity in his opinion.

Promoting Free Choice. Gratian's interest in promoting free choice in marriage may have been linked to the gradual extension of the jurisdiction of the Church over marriage. As secular concerns were made subordinate to religious considerations, the individual's power was concomitantly increased, as well, at the expense of secular society. This freedom to choose at the expense of familial and feudal considerations was further reinforced by other marriage regulations. For example, by requiring that children must have reached the age of consent, the Church ensured that people were in a position to make a knowledgeable choice of a spouse.

Secular Pressures. Canon law, however adamant it was in establishing individual freedom of choice in marriage, could not abolish the social or psychological pressure that might be placed on a person to acquiesce to a marriage arranged by a lord or by parents. Since lords and parents were not punished for coercion—the only result of such a claim was the nullification of the marriage—there was little to prevent pressure being brought to bear on vassals or children. Nevertheless, as the Church refined the doctrine of marriage, especially as a sacrament that the couple administered to one another, freedom of choice became an increasingly important component in the process.

Increasing Freedom. Over time the freedom of choice doctrine influenced how medieval people approached marriage. The idea was disseminated from the Church to the laity by means of preaching and confession. Cases from ecclesiastical courts and other evidence suggest that the laity understood the rules of marriage, in particular those governing clandestine marriages and consent. There are several recorded incidents of couples marrying against the wishes of their families and lords and insisting on the validity of their secret marriages despite opposition. Indeed, it can be argued that throughout its legislation on marriage the Church minimized the role of the family. For example, during the reading of the banns, it was the community, not the family, that was consulted about the suitability of the union. Therefore, Church legislation helped the individual move toward a more autonomous view of marriage and choosing a spouse.

Sources:

Jacqueline Murray, "Individualism and Consensual Marriage: Some Evidence from Medieval England," in *Women, Marriage, and Family in Medieval Christendom: Essays in Memory of Michael M. Sheehan, C.S.B.*, edited by Constance M. Rousseau and Joel T. Rosenthal (Kalamazoo, Mich.: Medieval Institute Publications, 1998), pp. 121–151.

John T. Noonan, "Power to Choose," *Viator*, 4 (1973): 419–434.

Michael M. Sheehan, "Choice of Marriage Partner in the Middle Ages: Development and Mode of Application of a Theory of Marriage," *Studies in Medieval and Renaissance History*, 1 (1978): 1–33.

THE MARRIAGE CEREMONY

Religious Rites. The impetus for developing a religious marriage ceremony came from two sources. Christian families, as well as the Church, desired to have a couple's union blessed by a priest or bishop. This practice developed early among people who had recently been converted to Christianity. After the secular marriage rites were complete and the bride had been handed by her parents to her husband, a priest was invited to bless not only the couple but also their bridal chamber and marriage bed. Gradually, this practice was superseded by the Roman liturgy, which was spread across Europe by missionaries, especially in the eighth and ninth centuries, as part of Carolingian church reform. In this liturgy the nuptial blessing was conferred on the couple in the church during mass and prior to communion. The secular rites of marriage took place at home after the church ceremony, and the blessing of the chamber and the bed continued. At the same time, there was growing pressure to have all first marriages blessed by a priest.

Ascertaining Eligibility. The second impetus came from ecclesiastical authorities, who sought to develop means by which to investigate would-be spouses' freedom to marry. As the various impediments to marriage were developed, it became important that the Church develop a way to ascertain that the couple were able to marry and were entering their union by their own free will. Thus, the priest came to function as a kind of judge who decided the

THE WEDDING CEREMONY

P̲ope Nicholas I described the marriage ceremony in an 866 letter to Boris I, King of the Bulgarians.

Our people, both men and women, when they make the marriage contracts do not wear on their heads bands of gold, of silver, or of any metal. After the betrothals, which are a promise of future marriage, with the consent of those who have made them and of those under whose authority they stand, certain agreements are struck. After the groom has betrothed the bride through a ring of fidelity which he puts as a pledge on her finger, and after the groom has given to her the dowry upon which both have agreed together with the written instrument containing the agreement, in the presence of persons invited from both sides, then, immediately or after a suitable interval, lest it be presumed that such an act was done before the legal age, both are brought to the marriage vows. And first the vows are taken in the church of the Lord with offerings, which they ought to offer to God through the hands of the priest. Thus finally they are given the blessing and the celestial veil.

Source: David Herlihy, *Medieval Households* (Cambridge, Mass.: Harvard University Press, 1985), p. 74.

appropriateness of the union. During the Carolingian reforms at the beginning of the ninth century, priests were encouraged to conduct a prenuptial enquiry to ascertain that the couple were not related within the prohibited degrees.

Establishing the Marriage Ritual. One of the earliest descriptions of the rituals surrounding marriage is found in Pope Nicholas I's 866 letter to Boris I, King of the Bulgarians. The Bulgarians had only recently converted to Christianity, and they were at pains to understand how to accommodate their customs and traditions to their new religion. Nicholas's letter provides a summary of how marriage occurred in western Europe in the ninth century. The union was initiated by a betrothal or engagement, which Nicholas described as a promise of future marriage. The second step involved the man giving a pledge by placing a ring on the woman's finger. Then, after completing the negotiations, the groom endowed his future bride with property, in writing and in the presence of witnesses for both man and woman. What is significant about these three steps is that they are essentially secular and familial acts. The events occurred within the family, and the presence of a priest is not mentioned.

Exchanging Vows. There was some indication in Nicholas's letter that the couple might be young, because he called for not only their consent but also that of their parents or guardians. Moreover, he cautioned that the couple not rush from betrothal to marriage in unseemly haste—although, if they were of legal age they could proceed to exchange the marriage vows. Only at the point

Philippe of Artois and Blanche of Brittany exchanging
consent to marry at the church door, 1280
(British Library, London)

when the couple exchanged their vows did Nicholas stress the presence of a priest. The marriage occurred in a church after offerings had been made and has been understood to be in the context of the Eucharistic celebration. The priest blessed the couple and covered their heads with the nuptial veil. The blessings included references to Adam and Eve and their fertility, and to Tobias and his wife, who prayed for three nights before consummating their union. The veil was an indication of the purity of the union, and Nicholas noted that it was not used in second marriages. Finally, the bride and groom donned crowns as they left the church and began their life together as a married couple. Nicholas's letter demonstrates that the foundations of marriage as they would be passed down were already in use during the ninth century. His letter was incorporated into Gratian's *Decretum* (circa 1140) and thus entered into the core of Church teaching on marriage.

Ecclesiastical Ritual. In the early twelfth century the secular rite of marriage and the priest's inquiry and blessings were transformed into an ecclesiastical ritual. While marriage had been a family ritual to which the priest was invited, by this time it had become a public religious ceremony at which the parish priest officiated and in which the wider community participated as witnesses. This type of ceremony came to be known as marriage before the church or in the face of the church (*in facie ecclesie*).

Marriage Rules. The rules governing the proper form of a marriage ceremony were consolidated by the Fourth Lateran Council in 1215, at which Pope Innocent III caused several aspects of marriage to be regularized and developed rules that were to be observed all across Europe. Subsequently, European bishops enforced the new regulations governing marriage and informed the clergy exactly how couples ought to be married.

The Marriage Setting. Because of its sacramental character, marriage was to be performed with dignity and in a religious setting. There is some hint that Church authorities thought that such a setting would preserve the principle of free consent, which was more likely to be lost in the unruliness that could accompany some marriages. Moreover, those entering into informal unions might overlook impediments that could lead to tragic results, including the couple's separation. To help prevent such problems, the new rules separated the betrothal from marriage, required witnesses to the betrothal, and specified that it must occur prior to the reading of the banns.

The Banns. The rules also specified that all marriages should be preceded by the publication of the banns, announcements that a couple intended to marry. This practice appeared in England and northern France in the early thirteenth century before it was adopted by the Fourth Lateran Council and was subsequently applied throughout Christendom. The banns were read aloud in church on three successive Sundays or feast days so that members of the local community could have the opportunity to raise objections to the marriage or inform the local priest about impediments that might prohibit the couple from exchanging consent. If the man and woman were from different parishes, the banns were read in both places.

Establishing Controls. The Church recognized the possibility that people could make false allegations of impediments to the union, and those who did so were punished. The Church took the reading of the banns seriously. A priest who blessed an unpublicized marriage was suspended from his office for three years. If the betrothed were strangers to the parish, they could not be married until letters affirming their eligibility to marry had been received from their previous parish priest. Nevertheless, marriages for which the banns had not been read, while illegal, were valid and indissoluble.

Exchange of Consent. The final stage in the process of getting married was the exchange of consent, which was done solemnly and publicly, and was supervised by the priest in the presence of witnesses. Marriages most likely occurred on Sundays, before noon, as part of the normal Sunday worship and mass. In this way, the whole community participated in the marriage. While the liturgy might vary in details from one diocese to another, the basic outline was similar throughout Europe.

The Marriage Ceremony. The exchange of consent occurred at the door of the church. The priest inquired about the couple's intention and ensured they had not been brought there under compulsion. He also attempted to identify impediments of consanguinity or affinity. The dowry and dower were announced, and then the priest joined the couple's hands and led them through the formal exchange of present consent. The groom said, "I take you [name] as my wedded wife, to have and to hold, from this day forward, for better, for worse, for richer, for poorer, in sickness and in health, until death parts us, if holy church will allow it, and to this I give you my faith." The woman replied, "I take you [name] as my wedded husband, to have and to hold, from this day forward, for better, for worse, for richer, for poorer, in sickness and in health, to be bonny and buxom, in bed and at table, until death parts us, if holy church will allow it, and to this I give you my faith." After he blessed the ring, which symbolized the dowry, the priest handed it to the groom, while he helped him to recite the proper words: "With this ring I you wed and with my body I you honor." The groom then took the ring, slipped it on and off the thumb and second finger of the bride's left hand, and finally placed it on the third finger. This digit was known as the finger of faith because it was popularly believed to hold a vein that ran up to the heart, so it was connected with ideas of love and fidelity. While most of the liturgies were spoken in Latin, the exchange of consent was in the vernacular language of the couple, to ensure that there was no misunderstanding or ambiguity.

The Wedding Liturgy. After the exchange of consent, the priest led the couple into the church to participate in the mass. Immediately before communion, the couple was called forward for the nuptial blessing. Kneeling before the priest, the wedding veil was held over their heads by four men. If the couple had engaged in sexual relations prior to the solemnization of their marriage, their children would join them under the veil and be legitimized by their parents' marriage. This use of the wedding veil was ancient. A final blessing completed the solemn liturgy of marriage.

Marriage Celebrations. Following the ecclesiastical services, family, friends, and the community engaged in secular celebrations with the newly married couple. These occasions were frequently boisterous because the usual times of year to marry were periods associated with celebrating. Marriages tended to occur in January, a month pre-Christian society had associated with ribaldry and fertility rituals, and these connotations had endured in rural Christian Europe. The other popular time of year for weddings was October and November, the months immediately following the harvest. The Church prohibited marriages during Lent, Advent, and other holy seasons.

The Marriage Feast. The community expected that a banquet, as elaborate as the couple's circumstances permitted, would accompany the celebration of marriage. In the records of one manor court, there is a note that a groom was fined because he had not provided the appropriate wedding feast to his fellow villagers. At some point after the couple had left the church, coins might be thrown over their heads in the belief that they might bring the blessing of prosperity to the relationship and new family. Mentions

The nuptial blessing of a couple under a veil, the final stage of the medieval marriage ceremony; illumination from a fourteenth-century manuscript for Gratian's *Decretum* (Bibliothèque Municipale, Dijon)

of this custom have appeared in the account books of the English kings, so it seems to have occurred across the social spectrum. The couple might also set aside a few coins to distribute to the poor.

Blessing the Marriage Bed. After the music, drinking, and revelry was enjoyed, the day ended with the newlyweds being led by jesting friends and relatives to their marriage bed. Sometimes, if he were still present, the parish priest might bless the bed and the couple, and then pray for their fertility. Frequently, grain was scattered on the bed as a folk ritual to enhance fertility. After all, no matter what the economic situation or social status of the couple, children were the desired result of their union.

Sources:
Christopher N. L. Brooke, *The Medieval Idea of Marriage* (Oxford & New York: Oxford University Press, 1989).

David Herlihy, *Medieval Households* (Cambridge, Mass.: Harvard University Press, 1985).

Michael M. Sheehan, "The Bishop of Rome to a Barbarian King on the Rituals of Marriage," in *In iure veritas: Studies in Canon Law in Memory of Schafer Williams,* edited by Steven B. Bowman and Blanche E. Cody (Cincinnati: University of Cincinnati, College of Law, 1991), pp. 187–199.

Sheehan, "Choice of Marriage Partner in the Middle Ages: Development and Mode of Application of a Theory of Marriage," *Studies in Medieval and Renaissance History,* 1 (1989): 1–33.

THE MARRIAGE OF BERTOLF AND GODELIEVE

A Saintly Woman. In 1084 a monk named Drogo wrote the life story of a remarkable Frenchwoman whom the local community had begun spontaneously to venerate as a saint. The story of Godelieve of Ghistelle, who led an unhappy life and experienced horrible betrayal, illustrates the clash between secular values and ecclesiastical teachings about marriage toward the end of the eleventh century.

An Arranged Marriage. A member of the lesser aristocracy, Godelieve's father was a knight and vassal of the count of Boulogne. When Godelieve reached the proper marriage age, her father and mother decided which of her many suitors she would marry, selecting Bertolf, a distinguished officer of the count and, thus, from their social rank. Because she was meek and obedient, Godelieve accepted her parents' decision without question. According to Drogo, they chose Bertolf because he was the wealthiest of the suitors and would bring a sizable dower to the marriage. Instead of courting Godelieve, Bertolf had approached her parents directly. Nor had he sought the advice of his family and friends, a significant departure from custom. His family was quick to criticize his action as hasty and ill-advised.

Scandalous Behavior. Bertolf took his new bride from her parents' home near Boulogne to Ghistelle, near the Flemish coast, where he lived with his mother, who was separated from his father. During the trip to Ghistelle, Bertolf conceived a dislike for his new bride, which was soon strengthened by his mother's disapproval of her daughter-in-law. When the couple arrived at Bertolf's home, they were supposed to participate in a nuptial ceremony to finalize their union. Bertolf, however, refused to participate. Instead his mother stood in for him at the ceremony, which occurred, according to custom, over the course of three days. This behavior was scandalous and was considered a breach of the moral and sexual order of society. Although the hagiographic accounts suggest that Godelieve remained a virgin, the marriage was probably consummated because the Church eventually ruled that her marriage to Bertolf was indissoluble.

Harsh Treatment. After their marriage, Bertolf left Godelieve alone at home, where she spent her time in prayer and works of charity. The townspeople of Ghistelle considered her a model wife: she worked hard, governed her servants well, and fulfilled social expectations that she be modest and obedient. Bertolf, however, grew more and more impatient and wished to be rid of her. He ordered the servants to give her only bread and water to eat; when this regimen did not break her spirit, he halved the size of her rations. Finally, exhausted by this harsh treatment and the impossible situation in which she found herself, Godelieve fled to her parents, flouting the secular and religious teaching that a wife should not leave her husband's house.

A Father's Appeal. Hoping to protect his daughter and defend her rights, Godelieve's father appealed to the count of Flanders, who—despite his secular authority over Bertolf—acknowledged that the Church had jurisdiction over marriages and sent the father to the bishop of Noyon-Tournai. Mindful of the conjugal bonds that linked husband and wife, the bishop could not countenance the separation of Bertolf and Godelieve: there had been no adultery and the marriage had been consum-

mated. So, Bertolf swore an oath to treat his wife appropriately, and Godelieve was sent back with her husband to Ghistelle, where he locked her in the house and deprived her of contact with the outside world. The townspeople, who considered Godelieve a chaste wife and a model of conjugal virtue, were outraged by her treatment and moved by her forbearance.

Murder. Bertolf, however, did not share their admiration and conspired with two of his serfs to murder Godelieve. One night, he arrived home and treated Godelieve with the kindness expected of a husband. He promised her that from then on they would live together in marital harmony and said that the problem in their relationship was that they were strangers and unaccustomed to one another. He asked her to get a potion from a neighborhood wise woman that would ease her fulfillment of the conjugal duty. Godelieve agreed to do as her husband asked. In the middle of the night, she went with the two serfs, who claimed they would guide her secretly to the wise woman. En route, they murdered Godelieve and returned her body to her bed to be discovered in the morning by her servants. Meanwhile, Bertolf had traveled to another town in order to establish an alibi.

Sainthood. The people of Ghistelle considered Godelieve a martyr, and shortly after her death they claimed that miracles were occurring at the site of her grave. Moved by the piety of the community, the Church elevated Godelieve to sainthood. Godelieve's plight demonstrates how completely a medieval woman was the mercy of the her husband. Once a woman left her natal family, their ability to help her was limited. Moreover, Church teachings on wifely subordination and the indissolubility of marriage created a situation in which representatives of the Church were unable or unwilling to protect a woman from an abusive husband.

Sources:
Georges Duby, *The Knight, the Lady and the Priest: The Making of Modern Marriage in Medieval France,* translated by Barbara Bray (New York: Pantheon, 1983), pp. 130–135.

Jacqueline Murray, *Love, Marriage, and the Family in the Middle Ages* (Peterborough, Ont.: Broadview Press, 2001).

Renée Nip, "Godelieve of Gistel and Ida of Boulogne," in *Sanctity and Motherhood: Essays on Holy Mothers in the Middle Ages,* edited by Anneke B. Mulder-Bakker (New York: Garland, 1995), pp. 191–223.

THE MARRIAGE OF LOTHAR AND THEUTBERGA

A Necessary Divorce? One of the best-known cases of a contested marriage in the early Middle Ages—involving Lothar II, King of Lotharingia (Lorraine), and his wife, Theutberga—illustrates the tensions between the secular and ecclesiastical visions of marriage and the issues that were at stake on both sides. In 858 Lothar sought to divorce Theutberga because she had not borne him children. He wanted to marry his concubine, Waldrada, so that he could legitimize the children he had had by her and thus secure the inheritance of his kingdom. This practice had been common among the European aristocracy, who needed to assure an heir in order to avoid civil war and

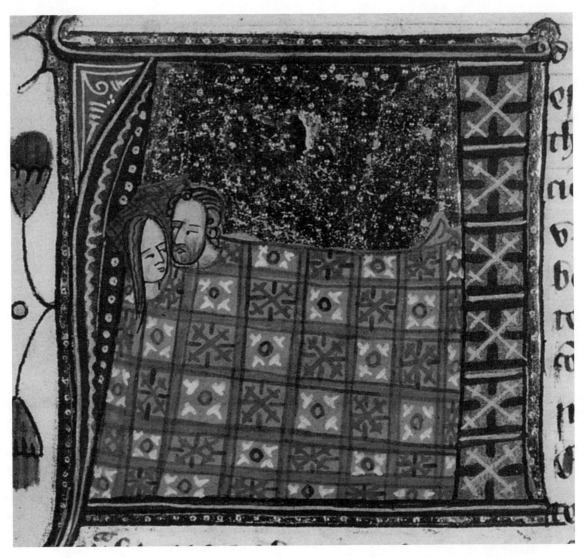
Illumination in the entry on adultery in a fourteenth-century manuscript for James le Palmer's *Omne Bonum*
(British Library, London)

unrest on a leader's death. In Lothar's case his uncles were prepared to split Lorraine between them if their nephew remained without a legitimate heir.

Grounds for the Divorce. In order to make sure that he received his divorce, Lothar leveled several charges, including premarital sexual activity and incest, against Theutberga. Lothar claimed that before their marriage, Theutberga had had sexual relations with her brother, Hubert. Lothar acknowledged that he had waited more than two years to make his allegations. He also admitted that he had given Theutberga her *Morgengabe* (morning gift), an act by which a husband recognized that his wife had come to him a virgin, but explained that Hubert and Theutberga had engaged in anal intercourse, so she had technically been a virgin when she married. Moreover, despite the impossibility of becoming pregnant through anal intercourse, Lothar went so far as to accuse Theutberga of having conceived her brother's child and then having had an abortion. There is no clear explanation for why Lothar felt it necessary to make this outrageous charge.

Trial and Appeals. Theutberga proclaimed her innocence and sought to be exonerated by one kind of trial by ordeal, in which a knight chosen to be her champion fought another surrogate chosen by Lothar. Her champion won, thus affirming her innocence. Lothar, however, did not accept the verdict and imprisoned his wife. Under the stress and coercion of imprisonment, Theutberga gave a confession to the king's chaplain. When the written version of this confession was presented at a synod held in Aachen in 860, however, Theutberga refused to repeat her confession publicly. Acting under Lothar's influence, the bishops at this synod ordered her to retire to a convent to await the annulment of her marriage. At this point, Lothar began to live with Waldrada. When another synod met later that year, Theutberga was threatened with torture and consequently confessed to the charges against her in front of the assembled bishops. She then sought refuge at the court of one of Lothar's uncles, Charles II (the Bald), King of France. The bishops suddenly became hesitant about acting on Lothar's charges, and instead of authorizing his marriage to Waldrada, they appealed to Archbishop Hincmar of Reims, one of the leading canon lawyers of the day, for his legal opinion and advice.

Treatise on Divorce. After examining the evidence in the case between Lothar and Theutberga, Hincmar, who had been a supporter of Charles the Bald for many years, wrote *De divortio Lotharii et Teutbergae* (On the Divorce of King Lothar and Queen Theutberga, 860), a treatise that became one of the foundations of the canon law on marriage. In his treatise Hincmar affirmed the legitimacy of trial by ordeal and dealt in a straightforward fashion with the impossibility of a virgin conceiving a child through anal intercourse and then aborting the fetus. Providing a detailed explanation of how conception occurred, he demonstrated that this fanciful allegation had no basis in fact. He also argued forcefully that adultery, if proven publicly and by witnesses, was only grounds for separation; it was invalid grounds for divorce. So, even if Lothar's accusations were true, this guilt would only allow him to put Theutberga in a nunnery; it would not be grounds for annulling the marriage so that he could marry another woman while Theutberga was alive. Moreover, Hincmar argued, the bishops were too lenient toward Lothar, because they tolerated his living with Waldrada prior to his being granted a divorce. Lothar was, therefore, guilty of adultery, for which the bishops should have censured him.

Competing Jurisdictions. Another area that Hincmar explored was the competing religious and secular jurisdictions over marriage. He said that secular society had the power to regulate the social aspects of marriage, such as the transfer of property, and the right to concern itself the political implications of a union. The Church, on the other hand, had jurisdiction over the moral and sacramental aspects. Thus, Hincmar advised that the proper procedure was for Lothar to accuse his wife in secular court. If she were found guilty, and accordingly sentenced to death, she could appeal to the ecclesiastical court. This court would certainly commute the sentence and enjoin a penance, which normally would involve ten years of penance and perpetual chastity. Her marriage to Lothar, however, would still be valid. It was, therefore, indissoluble, and the king could not dismiss his wife and marry Waldrada.

A New Strategy. Lothar continued to press his case for another two years, but he did not go so far as to marry Waldrada in the face of Hincmar's decision. He called another synod, at which he complained that his sexual needs were not being met and asserted that, if Theutberga had not polluted the marital bed by her incest, he would gladly have reconciled with her. This synod declared the marriage null on the grounds of incest; Lothar married Waldrada, and she was crowned queen. Nevertheless, he was still unsure of the legal standing of this marriage. In 863 he convened a synod at Metz and offered completely new grounds for confirming his second marriage, alleging that he had actually been married to Waldrada all along, and Theutberga's brother had bullied him into marrying Theutberga.

Papal Intercession. At this point Theutberga appealed to Pope Nicholas I, alleging she had been coerced to make her original confession. Pope Nicholas sent a team of clerics to investigate, instructing them to examine Lothar's allegation that he had married Waldrada before Theutberga and to dis-

cover whether he had, in fact, married Waldrada, with a dowry and witnesses, according to the rituals of the Church; whether they had been publicly accepted as husband and wife; and, if so, why Lothar had repudiated Waldrada so he could marry Theutberga. If this early marriage to Waldrada had not occurred, said the Pope, Lothar must be reconciled with Theutberga if she were again found innocent of the various allegations that had been made against her.

The Pope's Ruling. The Pope's representatives found Theutberga innocent of Lothar's allegations. Consequently, Nicholas called his own synod, canceled the findings of the Metz synod, and removed from office those who had participated in it. Finally, he ordered Lothar to reconcile with Theutberga. In 865 Theutberga was again formally recognized as queen of Lorraine, and twelve of Lothar's chief noblemen were required to take oaths guaranteeing that she would be well treated. One observer of the reconciliation, Bishop Adventius of Metz, reported that Lothar and Theutberga attended mass, ate together, and then, according to rumor, went to bed to discharge their conjugal duties.

New Appeals and Resolutions. This optimistic report did not close the case. Within months of the reconciliation with Theutberga, Lothar was again sleeping with Waldrada. In 866 he brought force to bear on Theutberga, making her appeal to Pope Nicholas for a divorce on the grounds of sterility and the alleged prior marriage of Lothar and Waldrada. She also requested permission to enter a convent. Nicholas remained unmoved, however, replying that sterility was not grounds for divorce. Moreover, he said, Theutberga's sterility was not caused by her body, but rather by Lothar's iniquity. Finally, even if she took religious vows, the Pope said, Lothar would not be free to marry again. A year later, when it was rumored that Lothar intended to murder Theutberga so he could marry Waldrada, Nicholas declared that even if his wife were dead, Lothar could never marry Waldrada because he had committed adultery with her. The following year Theutberga went to Rome to appeal to a new pope, Adrian II, for freedom from her unhappy marriage. She is reported to have said that she preferred fleeing to the pagans over seeing Lothar again. Ultimately, both Theutberga and Waldrada entered religious life, and Lothar sought absolution from Pope Adrian. In 869 Lothar died without a legitimate heir.

Defining Church Jurisdiction. The divorce case of Lothar and Theutberga established some important points concerning Church jurisdiction over marriage. Hincmar's treatise and the various papal judgments categorically rejected several grounds for divorce that secular society considered valid. Thus, they confirmed and strengthened the religious principle that a marriage was indissoluble.

Sources:

Jane Bishop, "Bishops as Marital Advisors in the Ninth Century," in *Women of the Medieval World: Essays in Honor of John H. Mundy,* edited by Julius Kirshner and Suzanne F. Wemple (Oxford & New York: Blackwell, 1985), pp. 53–84.

James A. Brundage, *Law, Sex, and Christian Society in Medieval Europe* (Chicago: University of Chicago Press, 1987).

Frances Gies and Joseph Gies, *Marriage and the Family in the Middle Ages* (New York: Harper & Row, 1987).

THE MARRIAGE OF PHILIP I AND BERTHA

Divorce. More than two hundred years after Hincmar of Reims and Pope Nicholas I pronounced that a valid marriage was indissoluble, another notorious divorce case demonstrated that the Church was still having difficulty promoting the principle that marriage was indissoluble. The marriage of Philip I, King of France (reigned 1059–1108) to Bertha was arranged in 1072 as part of a reconciliation between Philip and the count of Flanders, Bertha's stepfather. After nine childless years of marriage, Bertha gave birth to a son, Louis. Three daughters followed. Then, in 1092 Philip repudiated Bertha, shut her up in a castle that was part of her dower, and married Bertrade, the wife of Fulk IV, Count of Anjou. Whether the count consented to this marriage is uncertain. Some sources suggest that love and passion caused Philip's action, but others suggest that he may have been motivated by a fear for the succession to the kingdom. He had only one legitimate son in an age with a high mortality rate, and Bertha was by then past childbearing age. Philip may well have considered the succession to his crown precarious and wanted to father more heirs to the kingdom, who needed to be the legitimate offspring of a valid marriage.

Church versus State. To lend validity to his second marriage, Philip assembled the clergy of France to bless the union. Ivo, Bishop of Chartres, was one of the few clerics who refused to condone Philip's behavior, telling the king, "You will not see me in Paris, with your wife of whom I know not if she may be your wife." These words foreshadowed the development of the consensual theory of marriage; that is, Ivo acknowledged that by virtue of their consent to be wed and their subsequent acts of sexual intercourse Philip and Bertrade were already married and that the blessing of the clergy was only the celebration and solemnization of something that had already occurred. Ivo was unsure, however, whether it was possible for Philip and Bertrade to be wed. Calling for a church council to examine the validity of Philip's divorce from Bertha and to decide if he and Bertrade were eligible to marry legitimately, Ivo referred the situation to Pope Urban II, who forbade the French bishops to crown Bertrade queen. Bertha's death in 1094 could have resolved the situation, but neither Ivo nor the pope were willing to let that happen. When Philip again convened a council to affirm his marriage to Bertrade, the Pope excommunicated him. The king continued to occupy the throne under excommunication, and then went through the motions of acceding to the Pope's judgment. Dressed in penitential garb, Philip and Bertrade swore to abjure one another's company. In fact, however, they continued to live together and raised three children. Their union gained some measure of public recognition and ended only with Philip's death in 1108.

Defining Marriage. This case illustrates several important points about marriage as it was understood at the beginning of the twelfth century. First, while betrothal followed by sexual union might form a marriage even without a religious ceremony, the laity agreed that the participation

THE IMPEDIMENT OF CONSANGUINITY

At the Fourth Lateran Council (1215), the clergy reduced from seven to four the prohibited degrees of consanguinity allowed in a valid marriage, doing away with a loophole in canon law that many aristocrat couples had exploited in order to obtain a divorce:

> Since therefore the prohibitions about contracting marriage in the second or third degree of affinity and about uniting the offspring of a second marriage to the kindred of the first husband frequently lead to difficulty and sometimes endanger souls, we . . . revoke with the approval of the holy council decrees published on this subject and by the present constitution decree that contracting parties connected in these ways may in future be freely united. Also the prohibition of marriage shall not in future exceed the fourth degree of the consanguinity and affinity, since in grades beyond that such prohibitions cannot now be generally complied with without grave harm.

Source: Harry Rothwell, ed. *English Historical Documents 1189–1327*, volume 3 (London: Eyre & Spottiswood, 1975).

of the Church in the solemnization of the union was not only desirable but necessary. On the other hand, however, the Church still faced significant opposition from secular society about its vision of marriage as indissoluble. Kings, nobles, and the laity in general continued to believe that a husband could and should be able to divorce his wife. Moreover, Philip's case illustrates a change in the position of the Church in society—it was one of the first instances in which the Church demonstrated the extent of its power and influence by excommunicating a king who refused to obey a Pope in a matrimonial case. The Church was set not only to extend, but also to exercise effectively and aggressively, its jurisdiction over marriage. The case also, however, had some unintended consequences that had considerable influence on marriage for years to come.

Consanguinity and Affinity. One of the greatest canon lawyers in the eleventh century, Ivo of Chartres brought his considerable acumen to bear on the case and in the process introduced a new consideration to the question of divorce. He was less concerned about whether Philip and Bertrade's marriage was bigamous or adulterous than with the issue of affinity. He had discovered that Philip and Bertrade's first husband shared a distant relative and thus argued that Philip and Bertrade were barred from marrying through too close a relationship of affinity. He thus opened a new loophole: if a person seeking a divorce could discover a shared relative, either by blood (consanguinity) or by marriage (affinity), the marriage could be declared invalid and, since a bond had never been formed, the couple would be free to separate and remarry. With this decision, invoking the impediments of consanguinity and affinity became widely used by the European aristocracy, who had been deprived of the ability to repudiate a spouse by the successful imposition by the Church of the

A couple who commit adultery (left) and marry after the birth of their child (right); illumination from a fourteenth-century manuscript for Gratian's *Decretum* (Biblioteca Nazionale Marciana, Venice)

doctrine of the indissolubility of marriage. For example, in 1152, after fifteen years of marriage to King Louis VII of France, Eleanor, Duchess of Aquitaine, used this strategy to obtain a divorce on the grounds that she and Louis were related in the fourth and fifth degrees of consanguinity. The Fourth Lateran Council in 1215 finally put an end to the use and abuse of consanguinity and affinity to obtain de facto divorces.

Sources:

James A. Brundage, *Law, Sex, and Christian Society in Medieval Europe* (Chicago: University of Chicago Press, 1987).

Georges Duby, *The Knight, the Lady and the Priest: The Making of Modern Marriage in Medieval France,* translated by Barbara Bray (New York: Pantheon, 1983).

Duby, *Medieval Marriage: Two Models from Twelfth-Century France,* translated by Elborg Forster (Baltimore: Johns Hopkins University Press, 1978).

Constance M. Rousseau and Joel T. Rosenthal, eds., *Women, Marriage, and Family in Medieval Christendom: Essays in Memory of Michael M. Sheehan, C.S.B.* (Kalamazoo: Western Michigan University, 1998).

THE MARRIAGE OF PHILIP AUGUSTUS AND INGEBORG

Consanguinity and Affinity. The case that stimulated the Church to revise its method of computing degrees of kinship and limit the number of prohibited degrees of consanguinity and affinity was that of Philip II (Augustus), King of France, who reigned from 1180 until 1223. In 1180, when his father, Louis VII, was close to death, Philip Augustus, who was fifteen, was married to nine-year-old Isabella of Hainaut. Philip's maternal uncles had considered breaking the betrothal because it interfered with their family strategies, but the marriage was performed and consummated when Isabella reached the legal marriage age of twelve. The couple had one son before Isabella died in 1190. In 1193 Philip, who had but one rather frail son to inherit his kingdom, married Ingeborg, the sister of King Canute VI of Denmark. The day after the wedding, how-

ever, before Ingeborg could be crowned queen, Philip dismissed his wife. The true reasons for his startling behavior are not known, but he made allegations seeming to suggest that she had cast evil spells and made him unable to consummate the union.

Resisting Divorce. Philip's need for additional legitimate heirs had not lessened, however, and he was determined to contract another marriage. Consequently, he sought a legal divorce invoking the usual pretext of the impediment of relationship. Fifteen senior clergy and members of the aristocracy swore an oath that Ingeborg was related to Isabella of Hainaut in the fourth degree, thus rendering a union with Philip impossible on the grounds of affinity. What distinguishes this case from so many other contemporary divorces because of consanguinity or affinity is that Ingeborg objected to the divorce and would not cooperate. Moreover, her brother, Canute VI of Denmark, appealed directly to the papacy on her behalf. Declaring that the degrees of kinship were inaccurately computed and that the oaths affirming them were false, he produced alternate genealogies to prove his case. In the meantime, Philip had found another bride, Agnes, daughter of the duke of Méran, whom he married and made his queen in 1196. Canute increased his pressure on the papacy, demanding that Philip be excommunicated for bigamy.

Papal Interdict. The papacy did not react until Innocent III became Pope in 1198 and ordered Philip to abjure his third wife, Agnes, and return to Ingeborg. He argued that Philip's marriage to Agnes was going to be dissolved in any case because Agnes's sister had already been married to the king's nephew, placing Philip and Agnes within the prohibited degrees of affinity. He did not excommunicate them, but in 1200 he placed France under interdict because of the king's marital irregularities. The interdict proved ineffective, however, because the French bishops were firmly controlled by the Crown. They required only that Philip promise not to separate from Ingeborg until the matter was settled. In other words, they would have been content if the king had simply agreed to recognize ecclesiastical jurisdiction in the matter.

Reconciliation. In 1202 a hearing was convened at Soissons to assess the situation. After two weeks of arguments, Philip suddenly departed, taking Ingeborg with him. Agnes died shortly thereafter, and the Pope continued to refuse to allow Philip to divorce Ingeborg. The king kept pressing for freedom from Ingeborg, explaining that since he was denied the right to marry legitimately, he was being forced into illegitimate unions. He reminded the Pope that King John of England and Emperor Frederick I (Barbarossa) of the Holy Roman Empire had both been permitted to separate from their wives, but the common knowledge that the genealogies in Philip's case were false inhibited a resolution of the stalemate. Gradually, however, a new cause for annulment was developed: nonconsummation of the union. Although she alleged the contrary, Philip had, from the beginning, steadfastly denied he had had sexual relations with Ingeborg. In 1213, however, Philip announced he would reconcile with Ingeborg, just as suddenly as he had rejected her in 1193. In the intervening years, Philip's son, Louis, had matured and had fathered a son of his own, making the line of succession reasonably secure and lessening Philip's need to produce more legitimate heirs.

Redefining Limits. Partly in response to the struggle involving Philip, Ingeborg, and the papacy, the Fourth Lateran Council (1215) reduced the prohibited degrees of consanguinity from seven to a more-manageable four and recognized only two degrees of affinity—a spouse's siblings and cousins—as impediments to marriage. With this decision the possibilities of incestuous unions were significantly reduced, and the abuse of impediments through the compilation of false genealogies was abolished, strengthening the Church's ability to control marriage and make it monogamous and indissoluble.

Sources:
Jim Bradbury, *Philip Augustus: King of France, 1180–1223* (London & New York: Longman, 1998).

Marie-Bernadette Bruguière, "Le mariage de Philippe Auguste et d'Isambour de Danemark: aspects canoniques et politiques," in *Mélanges offerts à Jean Dauvillier* (Toulouse: Centre d'Histoire Juridique Méridionale, 1979), pp. 135–156.

Georges Duby, *The Knight, the Lady and the Priest: The Making of Modern Marriage in Medieval France,* translated by Barbara Bray (New York: Pantheon, 1983).

THE MARRIAGE RELATIONSHIP: SEXUALITY AND THE CHURCH

Marital Relations. Married people were confronted with a bewildering array of teachings and prohibitions controlling and restricting marital sexuality. First and foremost was the notion that sexual intercourse rendered the participants unclean. As a result, the Church tried to restrict when, where, and how married people could have sex. Intricate regulations prohibited sex during the holy seasons of Advent, Lent, and Whitsuntide; on Sundays, Wednesdays, Fridays, and Saturdays; and on other holy days. Intercourse was also forbidden during menstruation, pregnancy, and lactation. Moreover, newlyweds were expected to wait three nights to consummate their union and couples who had sexual relations were advised not to receive communion the next day. Related to these notions of pollution were prohibitions against sex in a church, cemetery, or other holy place. While these restrictions may sound unrealistic and even unnecessary, there was little privacy in medieval houses, so an empty church or deserted cemetery might, in fact, have provided a couple with the privacy they could not find elsewhere. It remains uncertain to what extent any of these regulations influenced actual sexual behavior.

Roots. These rules were developed in the sixth century, primarily in the teachings of the penitentials. Much of the worldview that the early Church Fathers absorbed into Christian theology came from the ancient Stoics, who had praised abstinence and chastity, even within marriage, and taught that sex was only permitted for purposes of procreation. Christianity also incorporated many of the teachings of Judaism, especially those pertaining to ritual purity and blood taboos. Finally, the ancient Gnostics, who denigrated the physical world and promoted complete abstinence, influenced Christian attitudes toward the body, reproduction, and sexuality. Throughout the Middle Ages, the Church associated sex with the loss of reason and rational control of the senses. Gradually, sex came to be viewed as the primary source of sin. Although Jesus had not spoken about sexuality, and St. Paul had indicated that marriage had been instituted to provide a legitimate outlet for sexual desire, the medieval church was preoccupied with examining, evaluating, and controlling marital, as much as extramarital, sexual activity. The rigid views of the Church gradually overshadowed the relationship between sexual activity and love and affection.

Abstinence versus Marriage. For the Church Fathers, such as St. Jerome (circa 347–419), virginity was preferable to marriage. He wrote that married people would be rewarded in heaven thirtyfold, widows sixtyfold, and virgins a hundredfold. For Jerome, every sex act was shameful and sinful, and he likened a man who loved his wife too much to an adulterer. His contemporary St. Augustine, however, believed that marriage and the capacity for procreation had been granted to Adam and Eve in the Garden of Eden, before the Fall. If Adam and Eve had engaged in sexual intercourse in Paradise, Augustine argued, it would have been totally blameless and devoid of lust and irrationality. Consequently, marriage and sexuality were inherently good, but were tainted by Original Sin. He preached that intercourse within marriage and for the purpose of procreation was blameless, and that marital relations motivated by lust were only a minor sin. (Sexual acts outside marriage, however, were always sinful.) Although Augustine's milder evaluation of human sexuality prevailed during the Middle Ages, always lurking behind the clergy's rigid condemnations of lasciviousness was Jerome's uncompromising harshness.

Sex and Conception. The idea that the conception of children excused sex acts of their sinfulness posed a problem for canonists and theologians. If a child were conceived, presumably the act was blameless. While some writers continued to teach that the couple received some taint of sin, a small minority, such as the French theologian Anselm of Laon (died 1117), believed that the love between married people gave even childless unions some merit and excused the sexual relations of a couple who could not have children. Procreation still remained paramount for churchmen, who censured couples for any kind of contraceptive behavior, including practicing unusual sexual positions.

Regulation of Sexuality. By the mid twelfth century, canonists such as Gratian reduced the number of prohibited days and de-emphasized sexual abstinence for married people, but from that time through the mid fourteenth century, the Church was preoccupied with the canon law pertaining to the regulation of sexuality. Fornication came to be considered a crime, and ecclesiastical courts established new procedures to enforce its moral code. Moralists began lamenting the frequency of fornication among the laity and reminded them in sermons and during confession that fornication was a mortal sin. Couples who were rumored to be fornicators were called before the court and required to account for their behavior. They might be sentenced to some form of public penance, such as being whipped around the church on three successive Sundays. Fornicators who habitually consorted with one another might be required to abjure further sexual relations on penalty of marriage (*sub pena nubendi*). Such a couple would make a conditional promise of marriage in the future that would be ratified if they engaged in sexual relations again.

Degrees of Sinfulness. Sexual sins were ranked according to their degree of sinfulness. This hierarchy was established originally by Augustine, who believed that fornication was the least sinful offense. Adultery was more sinful than fornication, and incest was even worse. The worst sins were those sex acts considered "unnatural," an elastic category that ultimately encompassed any sexual activity that was not between married people for purposes of procreation and not performed in the "missionary position." Any other sexual position was proscribed. In the thirteenth century, definitions of sex acts that were contrary to nature (*contra naturam*) were clarified and included under the broad rubric of *sodomy*. This list included not only "unnatural" heterosexual positions, but also masturbation, homosexual acts, and, worst of all, bestiality. While bestiality and homosexual acts could lead to prosecution by secular as well as ecclesiastical authorities, the other sexual crimes were generally dealt with in confession and were assigned appropriate penances. Consequently, it is impossible to know what, if any, effect such prohibitions had on how people, married or single, actually behaved and the extent to which the moral code of the Church might have influenced private sexual behavior.

Sources:

James A. Brundage, *Law, Sex, and Christian Society in Medieval Europe* (Chicago: University of Chicago Press, 1987).

Brundage, "Playing by the Rules: Sexual Behaviour and Legal Norms In Medieval Europe," in *Desire and Discipline: Sex and Sexuality in the Premodern West*, edited by Jacqueline Murray and Konrad Eisenbichler (Toronto & Buffalo: University of Toronto Press, 1996), pp. 23–41.

Brundage, *Sex, Law and Marriage in the Middle Ages* (Aldershot, Hampshire, U.K. & Brookfield, Vt.: Variorum, 1993).

THE MARRIAGE RELATIONSHIP: SEXUALITY AND MEDICINE

Ancient Medical Teachings. Some medieval ideas and values about human sexuality were inherited from ancient medicine. Because ancient medicine had developed prior to Christian morality and had remained for the most part independent of it, medical learning and conventional Christian morality were often at odds. Yet, throughout the Middle Ages the two went through a process of mutual influence and accommodation. The medical knowledge of the ancients had been preserved in the eastern Roman Empire and was incorporated into Arabic learning with the spread of Islam. In the tenth century, Constantine the African translated many ancient medical texts from Arabic

King David in bed with concubines; illumination from a fourteenth-century manuscript on canon law (Cambridge University Library)

into Latin, thus making available to Europe a sophisticated body of medical knowledge.

Galen on Sexuality. The understanding of the human body and sexuality presented in medieval medical texts was based primarily on the teaching of the great second-century Greek physician, Galen. According to Galen, a woman's body was composed of the same organs as a man's, including the genitalia. The only difference was that a woman's sex organs were inverted and inside her body, rather than external like a man's organs: the ovaries were like testicles, and the vagina and uterus were like an inverted penis. As a result, Galen considered women to be basically the same as men, but somewhat inferior because their genitalia were internalized.

The Humors and Sexuality. The "one-sex" theory of the human body greatly influenced how physicians understood human sexuality and reproduction—as did Galen's theory of the bodily humors—blood, phlegm, yellow bile, and black bile—and their corresponding qualities—hot, cold, wet, and dry. According to this theory men and women had different sexual complexions because women were cold and wet, while men were hot and dry. The humors were thought to build up in a person and become unbalanced, so they needed to be released and balanced by such means as sweating, urination, and bloodletting. Women had a natural outlet for harmful humors through their monthly menses, while men expelled humors through the ejaculation of semen. Thus, from a medical point of view, some moderate sexual activity was a requirement for good health—a view that ran counter to the Church's promotion of celibacy—but too much could potentially be dangerous. According to another medical theory, the conception of children required both the father and mother to ejaculate seed, preferably simultaneously, so both the man and the woman needed to experience sexual pleasure and orgasm in order to conceive. At the same time the Church urged married couples to restrain their desires and preached that too much sexual pleasure could lead to illness and might even prove fatal. Early medical treatises discussed these issues objectively and dispassionately without considering the moral implications of their advice.

Opposing Views. As the Church taught that sexual pleasure should be avoided as much as possible—while accepting the fact that without orgasm conception could not occur—medical writers of the Middle Ages gradually began to be influenced by moral considerations. Thus, by the thirteenth century, some writers were reporting what earlier medical authorities had advised but adding caveats about how this advice should be modified to correspond with the moral teaching of the Church. For example, rather than prescribing sexual intercourse as a treatment for an illness, these later authors prescribed marriage. This solution met the necessities of morality, while presumably resulting in intercourse, the appropriate cure. Theological and moral discussions of married life gradually incorporated the two-seed understanding of conception. Therefore, confessors were sometimes instructed to advise husbands to ensure their wife was sexually satisfied in order to promote procreation. On the other hand, clerical writers held out as examples to be emulated cases in which a holy person refused the medically advised treatment for an illness, preferring death to immoral activities. While, from the eleventh through thirteenth centuries, moral considerations were given increasing prominence in medical texts, religious and medical thought continued to coexist quite separately throughout the Middle Ages, influencing one another but remaining distinct in their understanding of the role of human sexuality.

Sources:

Joan Cadden, *Meanings of Sex Difference in the Middle Ages. Medicine. Science, and Culture* (Cambridge: Cambridge University Press, 1993).

Danielle Jacquart and Claude Thomasset, *Sexuality and Medicine in the Middle Ages,* translated by Matthew Adamson (Princeton: Princeton University Press, 1988).

Jacqueline Murray, "Sexuality and Spirituality: The Intersection of Medieval Theology and Medicine," *Fides et Historia,* 23 (1991): 20–36.

THE MARRIAGE RELATIONSHIP: SEXUALITY AND SOCIETY

Records of Sexual Behavior. One of the few ways in which historians track the actual sexual practices of medieval people is by studying the cases of sexual transgressions that were documented in the records of secular and ecclesiastical courts. There are many extant records of cases of unmarried couples having to swear to cease having sexual relations on pain of marriage (*sub pena nubendi*). Records from both ecclesiastical and local manor courts reveal that villagers and the Church differed quite markedly in their views of sexual behavior. Occasionally, comparisons of the records show that people who were convicted of fornication (premarital sex) by Church courts were often found innocent by manor courts. Sometimes the manor jurors

appeared uncertain exactly what fornication involved. Many people who were joined in informal or clandestine marriages were considered married by the local community but not by the Church.

The *Legerwite*. Another sort of case found in the records of manorial courts also helps to identify the incidence of fornication. In England customary laws allowed lords to fine villein women who were caught fornicating or who gave birth to illegitimate children. Called the *legerwite* (literally, a fine for lying down), this fine can be dated to the Anglo-Saxon period. The *legerwite* was one of the few fines, along with the *merchet,* that did not fall into disuse in the course of the twelfth century. Thirteenth- and fourteenth-century manor records indicate that the *legerwite* was frequently levied, although the reason why was not always recorded. In some cases, it appears that the woman was first found guilty of fornication by the Church and was then was fined the *legerwite* by the manor court. This practice may have been the result of economic considerations rather than morality. If the woman had paid a fine to the Church rather than submit to corporal punishment, she would have probably have sold goods theoretically belonging to the lord, who then sought to recover the value of his property by levying the *legerwite*.

Visible Transgressions. Because the clergy who supervised morality in local communities were unpopular among the villagers, neighbors were unlikely to inform on each other. Authorities most often became aware of unmarried women's sexual transgressions if they became pregnant. In the court records the *legerwite* was more frequently associated with pregnancy, sure proof of fornication, rather than with fornication alone. The amount of the fine varied with the nature of the transgression and the woman's status. The manor court reduced the size of the fine for poor women, but a woman who had fornicated with more than one man or a cleric paid a higher fine. The *legerwite* disappeared in the mid fourteenth century, in the wake of the Black Death, along with the last vestiges of customary dues and services. Communities developed other means by which to supervise the morality and control the sexual conduct of its members.

Illegitimate Children. The presence of illegitimate children, at all levels of society, throughout the Middle Ages, is another indication that sexual practice deviated from the moral code. Unfortunately for historians, the lack of birth and marriage records prevents an estimate of the number of premarital pregnancies or illegitimate births. Ecclesiastical and secular law placed many restrictions on illegitimate children, who were nevertheless a part of everyday life. Secular society valued legitimate heirs to perpetuate the family's lineage, but noble fathers did not hesitate to recognize and grant property to their illegitimate children. The Church forbade the ordination of illegitimate men, but it regularly granted dispensations so that such men—frequently the sons of clerics—could enter service of the Church. Official sanctions existed throughout the medieval period. For example, in 1234 Pope Gregory IX instituted legislation that barred illegitimate children from inheriting property unless they had been legitimated by their parents' subsequent marriage. Yet, it has been suggested that in some rural areas premarital conception was a precondition to marriage. Children were so central to the household economy that a couple did not want to risk marrying and then discover they were infertile.

Rural Sex. Some sources suggest that people in rural areas engaged quite freely in sexual activity outside the bonds of marriage. The *fabliaux,* bawdy popular stories from rural France, tell of sexual adventures and improprieties whose participants express little regret or guilt. Another form of evidence comes from the records of the Inquisition, which interrogated suspected heretics in the village of Montaillou during the early fourteenth century. In the process the inquisitors recorded information about many aspects of daily life, including concubinage and other informal sexual liaisons, which occurred across the lines of social class and religious status. For example, the widow of the lord's local representative, Beatrice de Planissoles, maintained a sexual relationship with two brothers. One of these men, Pierre Clergue, was the parish priest. Not only were these relationships fornication, but they were also incestuous because they involved brothers and sacrilegious because one of the men was a cleric. Moreover, Pierre instructed Beatrice in contraceptive techniques, including the use of certain herbs, and the couple engaged in intercourse in the church and on holy days, such as Christmas Eve. This one example shows how far popular practice could deviate from conventional morality. It must also be remembered, however, that many of those involved in these activities were Cathar heretics, who explicitly rejected the teachings of the Catholic Church.

Sources:
Barbara A. Hannawalt, *The Ties That Bound: Peasant Families in Medieval England* (New York: Oxford University Press, 1986).

Emmanuel Le Roy Ladurie, *Montaillou, the Promised Land of Error,* translated by Barbara Bray (New York: Braziller, 1978).

Tim North, "Legerwite in the Thirteenth and Fourteenth Centuries," *Past and Present,* 111 (1986): 3–16.

MARRIED LIFE: BIRTH CONTROL

The Duty of Procreation. The medieval church taught that birth control was not only sinful but could actually impede the goals of marriage, one of which was the procreation of children. Consequently, a valid marriage could not be contracted if one of the spouses made it conditional on avoiding the conception of offspring. In the 1230s Pope Gregory IX decreed that if one spouse had never intended to have children and had planned to avoid conception, the conjugal bond was not formed, and no marriage existed between the couple. There is no dearth of evidence, however, suggesting that contraception was practiced throughout the Middle Ages, sometimes more, sometimes less, effectively.

Coitus Interruptus. Perhaps the most common and oldest means of avoiding conception was coitus interruptus. According to the Church, this practice was not only sinful but had a "polluting" effect, because it involved the spilling of semen "outside the appropriate vessel." Nevertheless, it was the easiest form of birth control available in medieval society. Some medieval writers linked the practice of coitus interruptus with poverty and the inability of a family to support additional offspring. By the early fourteenth century, moralists and preachers were condemning coitus interruptus with such regularity that historians have concluded it was practiced throughout Europe.

Birth-Control Potions. Another common method of birth control, which was condemned by moralists from the fifth century onward, involved using potions to induce sterility. Medieval society inherited many prescriptions for such potions from ancient learned medical treatises and through the folk medicine passed on by oral tradition, primarily among women. Potions intended to prevent conception were closely related or identical to abortifacients and potions to bring on retained menses or afterbirths. Consequently, even though they were officially condemned by the Church, the recipes for contraceptives and abortifacients circulated under the rubrics of more acceptable medical procedures.

Midwifery and Birth Control. Midwives, with their specialized knowledge of gynecological and obstetrical matters, were believed to have information on potions and charms to counteract sterility and encourage conception as well as to prevent conception and procure a miscarriage. They were most certainly learned about herbal remedies. Indeed, modern research has validated the contraceptive effects of many herbs that were recommended by folk medicine or tradition. Along with herbs, incantations and other less-effective means of contraception might have been recommended by medieval midwives. These means were closely linked to attempts to manipulate nature by magic, and they are one reason that moralists frequently criticized midwives as purveyors of superstition. Some historians have argued that the perception that midwives could bring about fertility or sterility and abortion led to their condemnation and, ultimately, their persecution in the witch hunts of the fifteenth century.

Controlling Abortions. A woman who concealed a pregnancy and birth and subsequently claimed she had miscarried or had a stillborn child was routinely suspected of abortion. Midwives were given strict instructions to report all births to the parish priest in order to avoid accusations of abortion or infanticide. Indeed, midwives were frequently accused not only of aiding women to procure abortions but also of helping them to conceal a pregnancy, disposing of a newborn child, or switching a live child for one who was stillborn.

Penalties. Moralists and authors of penitentials tended to consider contraception a less serious sin than abortion, which was frequently equated with homicide because they believed the soul had already entered the fetus. Contraception, on the other hand, was merely sinful and linked to wantonness. One penitential advised that a woman

Depiction of a good marriage as a prolific union; illumination from a thirteenth-century Latin Bible (Orléans Library)

who procured an abortion within forty days of conception should do one year of penance. However, if she did so after the child had quickened or taken on life, she should do the far-more-serious penance for homicide. The author made another important distinction that indicates something about the social circumstances that could attend efforts at birth control. He noted that the woman's personal situation made a great difference in the seriousness of the crime. If the woman were poor and unable to support a child, she should not be judged as harshly as a wealthy woman or a wanton woman who was trying to conceal her immorality. Other motives attributed to women who tried to avoid conception included fear of childbirth and wanting to avoid its pain, as well as the desire to preserve their beauty. Despite the repeated condemnations of moralists, however, there is overwhelming evidence that the laity practiced various forms of birth control throughout the medieval period.

Sources:

Clarissa W. Atkinson, *The Oldest Vocation: Christian Motherhood in the Middle Ages* (Ithaca, N.Y.: Cornell University Press, 1991).

Peter Biller, "Birth-Control in the West in the Thirteenth and Early Fourteenth Centuries," *Past and Present*, 94 (1982): 3–26.

John M. Riddle, *Contraception and Abortion from the Ancient World to the Renaissance* (Cambridge, Mass.: Harvard University Press, 1992).

MARRIED LIFE: CHILDBIRTH AND BAPTISM

Childbirth as Punishment. Childbirth was one of the most significant and dangerous experiences that faced a medieval woman. Medieval ideas about childbirth may be traced back to ancient Hebrew and Christian beliefs. The theologians taught that a woman's pain in childbirth was part of the punishment God inflicted on Eve for her role in the Fall from Paradise. Genesis records that God said to Eve, "I will greatly multiply your pain in childbearing; in pain you shall bring forth children" (Genesis 3.16). The Virgin Mary, however, was considered to have liberated women somewhat from the anguish of childbirth, hence women called on her for assistance during labor.

Heavenly Intercession. Childbirth was particularly dangerous in the Middle Ages. The Virgin Mary and St. Margaret were the patrons of women in childbirth. Female children were often named Mary or Margaret after the saints who aided in their delivery. The cult of St. Margaret, an especially old one, was promoted by women, particularly midwives. Women in labor often sought the intercession of local saints as well. In the period 1301–1417 more than 3 percent of the miracles reported in canonization processes pertained to cures for sterility or assistance in difficult childbirths.

Masculine Views. Many male ecclesiastical writers described pregnancy and childbirth with evident distaste. They focused on the physiological changes in a pregnant woman's body, including the discomfort associated with an enlarged uterus pressing on other organs, aches and pains throughout the body, the swelling of the woman's breasts, and nausea. They described labor as filled with torment, with little means of relief. Around 1250 Bartholomew the Englishman described pregnancy and delivery, commenting: "Mothers have nausea and vomiting and are heavy and cannot work. In labor, they are compelled to cry and are easily killed, especially young women with small and narrow members. The more woe and sorrow a woman has in childbirth, the more she loves the child when he is born." Unlike Bartholomew, most male writers had little personal experience with the process of birth.

Woman's Sphere. Childbirth was one area of life that was distinctly female; men, including the baby's father, were generally excluded from the birthing chamber. Childbirth was presided over by the local midwife or wise woman, who cared for all the gynecological and obstetrical needs of medieval women. Female friends, neighbors, and relatives provided the mother with pre- and post-natal care, assisted in the delivery, and cared for the newborn. Limited medical intervention and the inability to provide a sterile environment meant that if the birth had complications there was a high likelihood that it would end in the death of mother or baby or both.

Midwives. Midwives or wise women were found both in small villages and larger cities. Their training tended to be through apprenticeship; younger women learned as they assisted older and more experienced midwives. While their knowledge was primarily practical rather than theoretical, as was usual among university-educated male physicians, this deficiency did not detract from the women's expertise. The hands-on experience of midwives gave them a broad knowledge of all areas pertaining to pregnancy and childbirth, including how to assist women in labor and how to cope with difficult and dangerous births. Their intervention was important because it was considered immodest and threatening to the prevailing moral code for a woman to be given a physical examination by a male physician. Medical treatises from the thirteenth and fourteenth centuries make clear that midwives were trained and, in many locales, licensed. Untrained women who tried to perform the functions of midwives were widely criticized because they lacked the requisite expertise and knowledge.

Oral Traditions. Midwives' techniques of their profession were handed down through oral tradition, so few of their specific techniques and prescriptions have survived. Generally, historians have had to rely on occasional references made by critical male practitioners or information in court cases prosecuting midwives for malpractice. While it was conventional to denounce midwives for superstition or ignorance, no pregnant woman would have wanted to face labor and childbirth without the aid of a trusted midwife from her community.

Advice for Midwives. Medical treatises provide some information on what a midwife might do to assist women in labor. Such books prescribed baths to relieve labor pains and walking to hasten the birth. Midwives were expected to reposition the child manually in the womb should it not be in the correct position to be born. One source, attributed to an eleventh-century Salernitan author known as Trotula, includes specific information on the midwife's therapies and shows how religious and medical considerations intersected: Above all things when there is difficulty in childbirth one must have recourse to God. Descending then to lower means, it is helpful to the woman in difficult labor to be bathed in water in which has been cooked mallow, chick peas, flaxseed, and barley. Let her sides, abdomen, hips, and flanks be rubbed with oil of roses or oil of violets. . . . Let sneezing be provoked. . . . Let the woman be led at a slow pace through the house." Abbess Hildegard of Bingen said that during childbirth a woman's body felt as though it were being turned inside out.

Medical Remedies. Medicines were also recommended to help to prevent miscarriages, and prescriptions were available for potions to help expel a fetus that died in the womb, so that it would not kill the mother because it could not be delivered. Medical authorities did not advise that the mother's life be sacrificed to try to save the child. One anonymous fourteenth-century treatise observed, "When the woman is feeble and the child cannot come out, then it is better that the child be slain than the mother of the child also die." Treatises also discussed remedies to ensure that the mother could expel the afterbirth. The same herbal remedies tended to be recommended to hasten a slow birth, expel a dead fetus, and expel a retained afterbirth.

Folk Medicine. There were several folk remedies and spiritual aids designed to help women in labor. Herbal remedies could be drunk or mixed into salves to anoint the body, especially the stomach or vaginal areas. Special prayers and incantations would be said over the woman.

PRAYERS FOR WOMEN IN CHILDBIRTH

A mass performed in honor of the Virgin Mary for pregnant women or women laboring in childbirth included the following prayers:

To your assistance, oh Mary, poor women in labor flee. I entreat you not to despise them in their necessity, but, virgin ever blessed, free them from every danger. . . .

Oh, Mary, handmaid of Christ, mother of God, hear a poor sinner truly sighing unto you, lest infants be in danger in their mother's womb.

Who, not being baptized, ensnared in the net of original sin, descend together into limbo, which is part of hell.

And so, Mary, succor the wretched little children, who, on account of the heavy cloud [of sin] of Adam, the first man, are there forever deprived of the vision of God.

Oh the abyss of God's many judgements, who although they perish without guilt, however, do not perish without cause.

How pernicious, therefore, was Eve's bite of the forbidden fruit, by which death was thus established on her posterity.

But, oh how happy and joyous, oh Mary, was the dialogue between you and the angel, by which life came forth for the whole world.

But your most blessed childbirth, free from pain, seems to outshine all others,

Through which the curse of Eve was dissolved, and equally a blessing was bestowed on all women.

To whom, therefore, other than to you, consoler of all women, shall desperate pregnant women, groaning with tears, flee?

Hear them, immaculate Virgin, and do not let your only begotten child regard the sins of our parents.

But mercifully hear the wailing of the little ones, lest forever they should be plunged into the fearful punishment of hell.

And then, after they have been regenerated by the water of holy baptism, deem them worthy to lead to eternal joy. . . .

Source: Revised translation by Jacqueline Murray, from *The Sarum Missal in English*, part 2, translated by Frederick E. Warren (London: Moring, 1911), pp. 161–165.

Certain stones and crystals were believed to have a healing effect. Some women sought to have the relics or tokens of saints brought to them to aid in the delivery. For example, in the thirteenth century Eleanor of Provence, wife of King Henry III of England, had the girdle of the Virgin Mary, which was kept at a church in Westminster, brought to her as she went into labor and later credited the power of the girdle for her safe delivery. Along with invoking saints, women engaged in special ritual actions, such as measuring the pregnant woman with a thread that was subsequently used as the wick in a special candle donated to a saint's shrine. Sometimes the woman in labor, or her family,

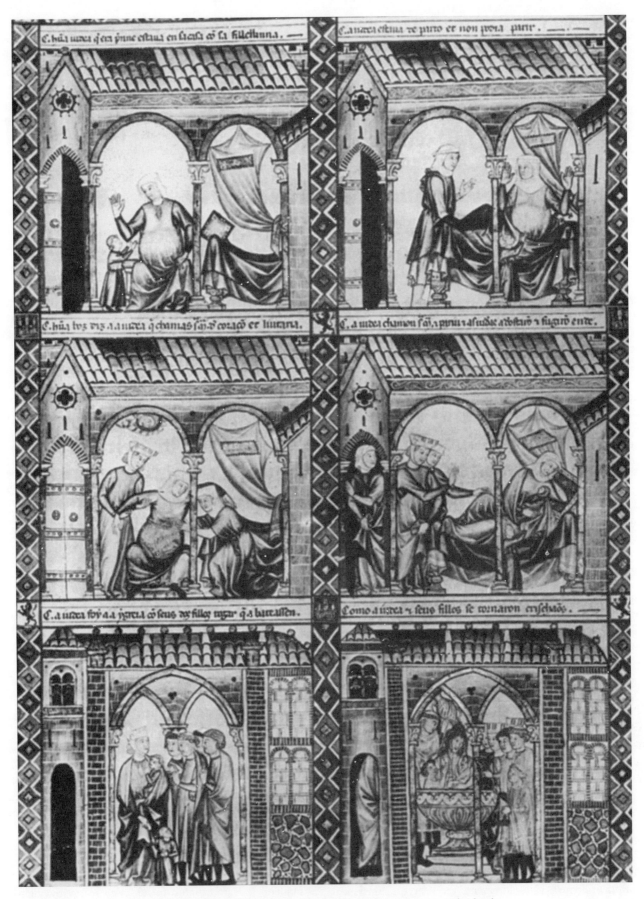

Medieval childbirth; illumination from a thirteenth-century manuscript for the
Contigas of Alphonse the Wise (Escorial Library, Madrid)

promised to visit a saint's tomb or to make a special donation to the shrine.

Hospitals. From about 1100 onward hospitals were founded in cities and towns. Pregnant women, especially poor or single women without friends or family to help them, were able to go to hospitals and receive care throughout the process of giving birth. The baby was then baptized by the hospital chaplain, and the mother received postpartum care. The normal hospital stay was three weeks. If the mother died in childbirth, her child was brought up in the hospital; if the newborn died, it would be buried nearby.

Dangers. The danger of childbirth was widely recognized. Pregnant women were urged to confess their sins before they went into labor. There was a fear that if the birth were difficult, the woman might die without the benefit of a priest to hear her confession. Religious writers urged that water always be present in the birthing chamber and that midwives know the proper formula for baptism. That way, should it appear that the baby might die in childbirth or shortly thereafter, the midwife could baptize it, even in the womb. If the mother died in the process of giving birth, the midwife was expected to perform a Caesarian section immediately, in case the child in the womb was still alive. This practice was documented as early as the beginning of the eleventh century, indicating that knowledge of this medical procedure had endured from antiquity.

Postpartum Purification. The safe delivery of both mother and child was a cause for celebration; for the mother, it took the form of churching, or purification. This practice was a religious ceremony that took place roughly a month after the woman had given birth. The justification for this activity was found in regulations inherited from Jewish practice, which prescribed periods of abstinence prior to ritual cleansing for new mothers. The length of the period depended on the sex of the child born: thirty-three days after a boy and sixty-six after a girl. In the sixth century Pope Gregory I (the Great) taught that this process should be understood allegorically rather than literally. He believed that if a woman got up from her childbed and ran to the church to give thanks, she did nothing wrong. In customary practice, churching was the first time after giving birth that a new mother went to church and had the opportunity to give thanks for a safe delivery. She partook of a liturgical ceremony to purify her of the blood that was believed to have polluted and tainted her in the process of giving birth. A married couple was expected to abstain from sexual relations until at least after the churching, although it was thought preferable to wait until the child was weaned. In medieval society, the social function of churching was more important than its religious rationale. Though churching was not an ecclesiastical requirement, the laity practiced the ritual long after the Church had officially dispensed with it. Among the wealthy the purification ceremony could be an occasion for celebration and excess.

Infant Baptism. If a child did not appear so fragile as to warrant an emergency baptism by the midwife, it was usually baptized when it was about one week old. Infant baptism was inspired by the doctrine of Original Sin and the notion that no one, not even the youngest and most innocent of newborns, was completely free from sin. Consequently, baptism was needed to cleanse the infant and welcome it into the community of believers. Given the high infant mortality of the medieval period, parents quite naturally wanted to ensure their young child would be saved should it die shortly after birth. Until the twelfth century it was commonly believed that unbaptized children would be condemned to Hell. In the course of the twelfth century this belief was replaced by the more moderate one that, although an unbaptized infant could not go to Paradise, it would not suffer in Hell either. Rather, it would remain in limbo for eternity.

Absent Mother. The child's mother was generally not present at her child's baptism, either because she had not completely recovered from giving birth or because she observed the custom of not entering the church prior to her churching. It was common for the godparents and relatives to send the absent mother presents, which might include cakes and sweets, candles, rich fabrics, or elaborately decorated trays celebrating the baby's birth. Female friends and relatives also visited the mother and kept her company during her recuperation.

Baptismal Rituals. When the baptismal party arrived at the church door, the priest asked the godparents for the child's name and their qualifications to be godparents. Naming practices differed in various locales and at various times. The child might be named after its parents, grandparents, godparents, or a special saint, such as one whose intercession had aided in the birth. The priest then performed a variety of rituals designed to banish evil spirits and protect the infant, including the laying on of hands and anointing the child with holy oil. Salt was placed in the child's mouth to symbolize the reception of wisdom and the banishment of evil.

Cleansing the Spirit. The baptismal group then moved into the church to the baptismal font. In the course of the tenth century, there was a gradual transition from the practice of immersing the child's whole body in the baptismal font to pouring water over the baby's head. Full immersion was still being performed as late as the thirteenth century. Infants were baptized naked, despite the threat that this practice represented to their health. The godparents lifted the child from the font after it had been baptized, and the godmother clothed it in a white garment. The godparents promised to teach the child the basic tenets of the Christian faith, answered the priest's questions on behalf of the child, and recited the Creed in its name. This ceremony was fairly time consuming and uncomfortable for the attendees. It was common for children to cry throughout the ceremony, and it was not unknown for an infant to urinate in the baptismal font. Although canon law prohibited it, some priests expected payment for baptizing an infant.

A medieval baptism; illumination from a late-thirteenth-century manuscript for Gratian's *Decretum* (Walters Art Gallery, Baltimore)

Folk Superstitions. Popular beliefs about baptism included the notion that a baptized infant was better able to fight off illness and disease. Moreover, some superstitions suggested that an unbaptized child could be stolen away by fairies or wood spirits and another child substituted for it. Thus, along with baptism, people invoked various incantations and charms to protect their children from dangers. An unbaptized child that died might also be perceived as dangerous to the living. In the eleventh century, Burchard of Worms recorded that the laity would bury an unbaptized infant with a stake through its heart so that the dead child could not leave the grave. This practice was vehemently condemned by the Church.

Conditional Baptism. Baptism was considered a sacrament that should be administered only once in a lifetime. If a child had been abandoned and no one was certain if it had been baptized, the priest would administer a conditional baptism. Similarly, a foundling hospital would baptize infants left at its door, especially if the baby appeared to be only a couple of weeks old.

Godparents. Every baptized child had godparents. Baptism created an important and lifelong familial bond between a godchild and its godparents. Families took care in selecting the godparents because the choice was one means of extending a person's kinship network. Customarily, a female child had two godmothers and one godfather; a male child had two godfathers and one godmother. Godparents were expected to participate in the child's religious education, as well as in its physical and spiritual upbringing. The Church, however, warned against the relationship becoming too intense or intimate and roundly denounced the sexual abuse of children by their godparents. The importance of the spiritual relationship seemed to vary according to age. Godchildren do not figure largely in the wills of young adults who had their own families. Older people, however, tended to include their godchildren quite frequently in the list of beneficiaries in their wills. Godparents could also act as patrons and help their godchildren find their way in the world, either through providing financial aid, helping them finding jobs, or standing surety in court. Thus, although the exact nature of the relationship varied with the individuals involved, there were some social expectations about godparents' responsibilities and the kind of support they should provide.

Sources:

Danièle Alexandre-Bidon and Didier Lett, *Children in the Middle Ages: Fifth-Fifteenth Centuries,* translated by Jody Gladding (Notre Dame, Ind.: University of Notre Dame Press, 1999).

Clarissa W. Atkinson, *The Oldest Vocation: Christian Motherhood in the Middle Ages* (Ithaca, N.Y.: Cornell University Press, 1991).

Peter Biller, "Childbirth in the Middle Ages," *History Today,* 36 (August 1986): 42–49.

Barbara A. Hanawalt, *Growing Up in Medieval London: The Experience of Childhood in History* (New York: Oxford University Press, 1993).

Bernhard Jussen, *Spiritual Kinship as Social Practice: Godparenthood and Adoption in the Early Middle Ages,* translated by Pamela Selwyn, revised edition (Newark: University of Delaware Press, 2000).

Shulamith Shahar, *Childhood in the Middle Ages* (London & New York: Routledge, 1990).

Fiona Harris Stoertz, "Suffering and Survival in Medieval English Childbirth," *Medieval Family Roles: A Book of Essays,* edited by Cathy Jorgensen Itnyre (New York: Garland, 1996), pp. 101–120.

MARRIED LIFE: CHILD REARING AND PARENTAL AFFECTION

Infant Care. In general, newborns and infants were recognized as especially vulnerable and in need of loving care. Writing around 1250, Bartholomew the Englishman said that if it is too hot or too cold when a baby comes from the womb into the air, the baby becomes miserable and cries. Following the advice of medical writers, he suggested that to cleanse the infant's limbs of their stickiness, they should be washed in rose petals pounded with salt and that the midwife should rub the child's gums and the roof of its mouth with honey to cleanse and soothe its mouth and stimulate the baby's appetite. He also advised that the infant should be bathed frequently and anointed all over with the soothing oil of myrtle or roses, and he warned that the newborn should lie in a dim room because too bright a light would hurt its young eyes. Other writers recommended that the newborn be wrapped in warm wool or cotton and placed in its mother's arms to ease its transition from its mother's womb and minimize the trauma of birth as much as possible.

Nursing of Infants. Mothers were told to nurse their children for eighteen months to two years. Moralists frequently denounced women who sent their newborns to wet nurses, interpreting the act as motivated by a mother's selfish desire to restore her looks and resume sexual relations, which lactating mothers were supposed to avoid. Furthermore, beginning with St. Jerome in the fifth century, didactic writers warned against wet nurses who were gossips, or drunken and lascivious. This warning was based on the medical belief that the blood that had nurtured the

A mother watching as women bathe and care for her newborn twins; illumination from a medieval manuscript
(British Library, London)

child in the womb transformed into breast milk after birth, and that any mental or physical defect of the wet nurse could be transmitted to a child through her milk. If a nursing infant became ill, its mother or wet nurse, not the baby, was given medicine.

Tender Care. The writings of Bartholomew the Englishman provide many glimpses into medieval child rearing, including the practice of swaddling, or wrapping a child tightly with narrow strips of cloth. He argued that young children should be swaddled so their limbs would grow straight, and they would not grow up deformed. He also advised that children need a great deal of sleep because they eat so much and must digest the food: "Therefore, nurses are accustomed to rock children in their cradles, . . . to bring the child gently and pleasantly to sleep. Also, they are accustomed to sing lullabies and other cradle-songs to please the child." A mother, or nurse, tends to be happy if the child is happy and sad if the child is sad: "She picks him up if he falls, and gives him milk if he weeps, and kisses him when he lies down, and gathers him up and holds him tight when he sprawls. She washes and cleans him when he soils himself, and feeds him with her fingers when he refuses to eat."

Overlaying. The clergy encouraged parents to nurture their children. Their sermons also frequently included warnings about overlaying. Priests regularly admonished parents about bringing an infant into their bed, for fear that a sleeping parent might roll on top of the child and smother it by accident. How frequently such deaths occurred is unclear because the records of medieval courts and coroners do not record cases of this sort.

Childhood. Medieval society generally recognized that children went through a variety of stages of life as they grew, matured, and became more independent. Bartholomew the Englishman identified childhood as between the ages of seven and fourteen. During these years children were considered easy to mold and educate. Because young children were impressionable, Bartholomew warned, particular care had to be taken with their food and drink.

Little Boys. Bartholomew described small boys as worried about nothing and caring only about their own enjoyment. Boys did not fear dangerous activities, he said, and were always hungry; they loved apples more than gold and enjoyed games and singing; and they laughed or cried easily. Bartholomew also described how they squirmed and wriggled while their mothers tried to wash their faces and comb their hair, noting that within minutes of their mothers' efforts at grooming, they were dirty and disheveled again.

Little Girls. In contrast to his rather lively and realistic description of little boys, Bartholomew offered only a brief description of little girls. He said they were modest, timid, and liked to wear dainty clothing. Girls walked with small steps and a light gait. Most of his description of girls was based on the works of ancient authorities such as Aristotle and Isidore of Seville. He also made conventional comments about women's weaker and deceitful nature and the absolute necessity for a woman to remain a virgin. Like Bartholomew, many other medieval writers on child rearing and education focused mainly on boys while tending to ignore girls and expect that they would be brought up by their mothers to be chaste daughters and obedient wives.

Parenting Advice. Many of the pedagogical sources on medieval child rearing repeat harsh commonplaces not unlike "spare the rod and spoil the child." Equally familiar were admonitions to children to honor and obey their parents. Yet, some writers urged parents not to be too harsh and alienate their children through overzealous discipline. Ratherius of Verona, who wrote around 950, advised children that if they became financially secure in adulthood they should be sure their parents did not languish in poverty, as happened all too frequently in his view.

A mother with her children; illumination from a medieval manuscript (Bodleian Library, Oxford)

Parental Duties. Medieval writers rarely went into great detail about the child's growth and psychological development because their focus was on the religious education of children. In the thirteenth century, however, Bartholomew and other writers began to discuss the stages of childhood in more depth and to offer age-specific advice on the upbringing of children. For example, John of Wales (died 1285) urged parents to educate their children well and in a manner appropriate to their station in life, so they would have the skills necessary to handle their inheritance. He went beyond formulaic references to biblical teachings to include ancient models of proper education; for example, that of Alexander the Great and the Spartans' training their children to withstand physical hardships such as cold or hunger. While John approved of physical punishment, he warned parents not to discipline their children to excess. If parents did not correct their children's faults, he argued, they would be accountable for their negligence before God, but by the same token, parents should present good examples to their children, avoiding drinking, gambling, and wasting their estates.

Child's Play. Gilbert of Tournai (died 1284) presented a lively account of boyhood, describing how boys trampled corn, stole grapes and apples, and broke the branches of trees. He also mentioned behavior he considered inappropriate and immature in boys, such as revealing their limbs, kissing girls, swearing, truancy, being disrespectful, and doing what they wanted rather than obeying adults. Girls were warned against laughing in church, wearing makeup and perfume, and being overly interested in fashion.

Parental Affection. The stern tone of most medieval moralists and educational writers can leave the impression that medieval children grew up in a harsh and uncaring environment. Part of this impression results from the nature of the evidence that has survived. Learned treatises written by clerics, who did not have children themselves, cannot convey the quality of the emotional bonds between medieval parents and children, and there is little direct evidence of paternal or filial affection because illiteracy was widespread among medi-

eval Europeans and because few personal documents by those who could read and write have survived. One valuable exception to this dearth of historical material is the manual written by the Frankish mother Dhuoda, in 841–843. Written in the form of a long letter to her elder son, who with his infant brother had been taken away from her by their father, Dhuoda's advice reveals her deep parental affection for her children and abiding concern for their upbringing. Mothers were often parted from their children throughout the Middle Ages. The inquisitorial records of Jacques Fournier include a poignant description of a mother leaving behind her child in the fourteenth century, as she fled the Inquisition: "She wanted to see him before going away; seeing him, she embraced him; then the child began to laugh; as she had just begun to leave the room where he was lying, she returned to him again; again the child began to laugh; and so it went, many times over. So it was that she could not bring herself to part with the child."

Familial Love. Giles of Rome, a thirteenth-century writer, considered parental love for children to be stronger than children's love for their parents because it lasted longer. Parents start to love their children before they are even born and are more certain of their relationship with their children. Giles believed that a child was never able to achieve absolute certainty about who its mother and father were and came to love its parents through living with them. This conclusion is an interesting early opinion about the socially constructed nature of familial love.

Maternal and Paternal Affection. The mother's affection for her child was a common motif in religious and popular literature. Hagiography included many stories of mothers who overcame the dangers and difficulties of travel to bring a sick or wounded child to the shrine of a saint. Religious writers frequently compared God's love to a mother's feeling for her child. Nor was this belief merely literary convention. Coroners' records are filled with examples of mothers running into burning houses or fighting with animals in desperate efforts to save their children. Descriptions of fathers taking sick children to saints' shrines or attempting heroic rescues exist as well.

There are many accounts of fathers who died while trying to save their adolescent daughters from rape or abduction.

An Unloving Mother. Not all medieval mothers were naturally warm and caring. In the eleventh century the French theologian and historian Guibert de Nogent recorded how he was raised by his widowed mother and a tutor she had hired. Guibert professed to love his tutor, even though the man beat him frequently, and he was devoted to his mother, although she seems to have been rather remote. When Guibert was about twelve years old, she decided to enter religious life and left Guibert alone in the world to survive by his own devices until he found his way into monastic life. Though he claimed to love his mother and to believe that she loved him, Guibert described her as a "cruel and unnatural mother" for abandoning him, and his memoir presents a picture of a troubled man who never came to terms with the experiences of his childhood.

Sources:
Bartholomew of England, *On the Properties of Things: John of Trevisa's Translation of Bartholomaeus Anglicus* De Proprietatibus Rerum: *A Critical Text,* 3 volumes, edited by M. C. Seymour and others (Oxford: Clarendon Press, 1975–1988).

Guibert de Nogent, *A Monk's Confession: The Memoirs of Guibert of Nogent,* translated by Paul J. Archambault (University Park: Pennsylvania State University Press, 1996).

James Marchand, "The Frankish Mother: Dhuoda," in *Medieval Women Writers,* edited by Katharina M. Wilson (Athens: University of Georgia Press, 1984), pp. 1–29.

Marie Anne Mayeski, *Dhuoda: Ninth Century Mother and Theologian* (Scranton, Pa.: University of Scranton Press, 1995).

Jenny Swanson, "Childhood and Child Rearing in *ad status* Sermons by Later Thirteenth Century Friars," *Journal of Medieval History,* 16 (1990): 309–331.

MARRIED LIFE: CHILDREN AND STEPCHILDREN

Blended Households. Because of the high mortality rate in the medieval period, especially of women in childbirth, it was common for a child to lose a parent. Moreover, given the dependence of the typical household on the labor of two adults, it was equally common for widows and widowers to remarry. At the highest social and political ranks, second marriages served to extend ties and cement alliances just as effectively as first marriages. Consequently, it was not unusual to find children of different parents growing up together in the same household, raised by a natural parent and a stepparent. Indeed, sometimes a medieval household could be quite complex, incorporating children from previous unions of both the husband and wife, along with the children they had together.

Stepmothers. Popular imagination has not been kind to the stepmother. Even in the early Middle Ages, the stepmother was portrayed as wicked, evil, and even cruel. Writers assumed that the stepmother would ignore, or even dislike, the children from her husband's previous marriage because these offspring were in competition with her own natural children for their inheritance and that she would seek ways to promote her own son as heir at the expense of the firstborn child of a first wife.

Bonds of Affection. Such negative experiences, however, may have been unusual. The evidence of wills suggests the bonds of affection among stepparents and stepchildren could be as deep and strong as in conjugal families. Parents frequently divided the family's goods among all the children equally. Court records reveal that stepbrothers and stepsisters turned to each other for help and advice in marriage or to serve as guardians for underage children. Living in the same household was as important as blood relationship for developing bonds of affection.

Sources:
Danièle Alexandre-Bidon and Didier Lett, *Children in the Middle Ages: Fifth-Fifteenth Centuries,* translated by Jody Gladding (Notre Dame, Ind.: University of Notre Dame Press, 1999).

Frances Gies and Joseph Gies, *Marriage and the Family in the Middle Ages* (New York: Harper & Row, 1987).

Mary Martin McLaughlin, "Survivors and Surrogates: Children and Parents from the Ninth to the Thirteenth Centuries," in *The History of Childhood,* edited by Lloyd deMause (New York: Psychohistory Press, 1974), pp. 101–182.

ORPHANS

Unfortunate Children. Orphans were found at all levels of medieval society. Orphans were often among the poorest and most vulnerable members of society and were considered worthy of special protection from secular rulers and the Church. Medieval literary works, biographies, and saints' lives often express profound sympathy for orphans. Generally, provisions were made for the guardianship of an orphan and the administration of his inheritance in his parents' wills. Often, however, parents died without a will, especially if they were in the lower ranks of society or had died young. In such instances, the care of the child was arranged according to law and guided by social conventions.

Aristocratic Orphans. Among the aristocracy, feudal customs decreed that the orphan and heir of a vassal would come under the guardianship of his father's lord or king. Indeed, at this level of society, being orphaned was defined as being without a father; widows were rarely granted guardianship of their own children. The demands of the patrilineage were such that a mother was considered something of an outsider. Moreover, a mother's natal family might demand that she return to them or remarry to the benefit of her family. In this case, a woman was required to leave her children with her husband's relatives. If the lord or king was not in a position to exercise supervision of the child and property personally, he frequently appointed a proxy or sold the right of guardianship to another nobleman. A guardian had the use of the orphan's property during his minority, but the law required a guardian to return it in full and with a complete accounting when the child reached the age of majority. The guardian also had the right to arrange the child's marriage. Such betrothals frequently benefited the guardian more than his ward.

Commoner Orphans. Among the lower ranks of society it was more common for a mother to be guardian of her children and administer their property, either alone or with a co-executor. If the parents had died intestate, the manor court would make provision for the care of the child. Usually his land was given to another tenant to work, and in return that person would feed, clothe, and house the child. When the child came of age, he would then take up his parents' holding. This arrangement was precarious, and manor courts had to be vigilant to ensure that the orphan was being cared for properly.

Urban Orphans. In the towns and cities of Europe, civic governments recognized their responsibility to care for orphans and enacted ordinances to protect their persons and property. The mayor and aldermen supervised the guardianship of the orphans of citizens and required an accounting of the administration of their estates when the child reached adulthood. A father's guild also had an interest in protecting an orphan and would ensure that the child was educated, placed in an apprenticeship, and taught a craft. Urban guardians had many of the same rights and responsibilities as feudal guardians. They could use an orphan's property, as long as they could account for it in the end. Sometimes, they could also arrange a ward's marriage to their own advantage. The abundant records of medieval cities include guardians accounting for their behavior and wards complaining that they were defrauded, coerced into marriage, or abused in some other way. Overall, however, the careful provisions of civic ordinances leave the impression that orphans received a great deal of care and consideration in medieval cities.

Poor Orphans. Orphans who were left no land or property were in the most precarious situation. Without an inheritance to guarantee the interest of a guardian, there was little incentive for anyone to care for a child. In the absence of strong extended family ties, orphans could not depend on relatives to look after their needs. In some villages, the neighbors appear in the records as looking after the orphaned children of the community. Religious houses frequently took in orphans and cared for them as part of their charitable mission, and some hospitals specialized in caring for and educating abandoned children. These children were the "poor and miserable" of society, and their institutionalized and impersonal upbringing could hardly have fulfilled their emotional needs or leave them in a position to make their way in the world successfully.

Peter Damian. Some poor orphans, however, were luckier than others. Italian ecclesiastic Peter Damian, who became one of the leaders of eleventh-century church reform, was born to a poor family with many children. After an older brother reproached his mother for giving birth to yet another hungry mouth, his mother sank into depression and would not nurse or care for her newborn. The infant Peter was saved from certain death by a compassionate neighbor woman, who took him in and eventually shamed Peter's mother into taking her child back and nursing him. Shortly thereafter, however, both Peter's parents died, and he was left to be brought up by one of his older brothers. This brother and his wife looked after Peter grudgingly, fed and clothed him poorly, and set him to work as a swineherd at an early age. Finally, however, Peter was sent to live with another, kinder brother, and found a more comfortable place in that family.

Sources:
Barbara A. Hanawalt, *Growing Up in Medieval London: The Experience of Childhood in History* (New York: Oxford University Press, 1993).

Hanawalt, *The Ties that Bound: Peasant Families in Medieval England* (New York: Oxford University Press, 1986).

Shulamith Shahar, *Childhood in the Middle Ages* (London & New York: Routledge, 1990).

SCHOOLING CHILDREN

Malleable Minds. The education of medieval children began at an early age. For the most part, people considered that young children were malleable and impressionable; therefore, the sooner good habits and knowledge were inculcated the better they would be retained. Children were believed to learn through word and example, so parents and teachers were told to take care in how they behaved and spoke in front of children.

Aristocratic Children. In the late eighth and early ninth centuries Charlemagne sought to have his children thoroughly educated in a manner suitable for the offspring of an emperor. He wanted both his sons and his daughters to be taught to read and be familiar with the liberal arts. Along with this higher education, the children were also instructed in skills associated with their gender roles. Thus, the boys learned to ride horses, use weapons, and hunt, while the girls were taught how to spin and sew.

Training Warriors. Charlemagne's desire that his children learn the liberal arts may have reflected his own thirst for learning. Most aristocratic boys were educated mainly in skills that would serve them in their careers as warriors, military leaders, and defenders of home and realm. This training was concentrated on developing excellent riding skills and expertise with weapons such as swords, axes, and bows. Even boys as young as six were instructed in horseback riding and the use of arms. From a young age they also participated in the hunt, an activity that not only provided food but also honed their skill with weapons. Virtue was also considered important for boys of the warrior class. They were expected to be good leaders and loyal vassals, who would wield their weapons and exercise their authority with prudence and wisdom.

Knights in Training. Throughout the Middle Ages, the aristocracy placed their sons with other families to complete their military training and preparations for knighthood. The families were usually related or united by bonds of loyalty and honor, if not by blood. A boy started out as a page in a noble household, serving his elders but growing up, often side by side, with the lord's son. This period usually lasted from about the age of seven until the boy was ten. While serving in the hall, the boy observed the manners of the knights and learned how to comport himself. By the age of sixteen or seventeen, a boy had usually become an accomplished rider and been well trained in the military arts. Physical games such as wrestling and running races helped to build the strength necessary to wield weapons while wearing full armor. Hardiness was important, and

young boys were trained to be able to sleep in uncomfortable circumstances and endure physical discomforts similar to the conditions of military expeditions.

Knighthood. When a boy had acquired the necessary expertise, experience, and maturity, he was presented with his arms, a rite of passage that initiated him into the responsibilities of his rank. This stage might occur between the ages of thirteen and fifteen. Sometimes the arms were presented by the boy's father, at other times by the man who had supervised the boy's military training. This presentation was a means of consolidating the relationship between the two families. Groups of young knights formed the retinues of kings or lords. These groups helped to foster the honor and loyalty that bound men together. In the early Middle Ages they were joined together as warriors, while in later, more peaceful times, they were united in their loyalty to a lord, wearing his livery and living in his household.

Rural Education. Less is known about how the children of common rural folk were educated, both in religion and in reading and writing. Parish priests, parents, and godparents gave such children a basic religious education, which might be supplemented by the depictions of religious stories that decorated the local church. In the late eighth century Charlemagne ordered the establishment of schools where priests were to teach reading, writing, arithmetic, and singing to local children, both free and serf, at no charge. Similar orders were issued by the Church. For example, at the end of the eighth century, Theodulf, Bishop of Orléans, decreed that "priests have schools in the agricultural areas and the large rural villages, and if the

Blanche of Castile supervising the education of her son Louis IX (center); illumination from a fourteenth-century manuscript for William of St. Panthus's *Life and Miracles of Saint Louis* (Bibliothèque Nationale, Paris)

Schoolboys being disciplined; illumination from a
medieval manuscript (British Library, London)

faithful want to entrust their children to them to learn letters, let them not refuse to receive them." By the eleventh
century, these types of schools had multiplied. There is evidence that the inhabitants of a locale cooperated to hire
and pay a schoolmaster for their children. It is likely, however, that most rural children did not move beyond the
most elementary level of education.

Urban Education. From the thirteenth century onward,
as urbanization increased, schools began to appear at a
rapid rate in cities throughout Europe. For example, it has
been estimated that, by about 1350, there were some eight
thousand to ten thousand children attending schools in
Florence. Merchants and members of the urban elite
tended to give their sons more education than did those
lower on the social scale. The children of merchants and
artisans, both boys and girls, attended neighborhood
schools, where they learned arithmetic, reading, and writing. In the upper ranks of urban society, boys might also
learn Latin and progress on to grammar school. From
there, a career in the Church became a possibility.

Education for Girls. There is less available information
on the education of girls than of boys. In aristocratic circles
a girl was carefully trained for the extensive responsibilities
she would assume as mistress of a large and complex household that incorporated farming, craft, and military functions. Like girls in other social classes, she would learn to
spin, sew, and embroider. Like her brothers, a girl would
also be taught how to ride horses and hunt with falcons.
Aristocratic girls were taught to read so they could read the
psalter and other devotional texts, keep household

accounts, and introduce their children to letters. Their
model in schooling young children was St. Anne, who was
frequently depicted teaching the young Virgin Mary to
read. In fact, mothers of all social ranks were responsible
for teaching their children, boys and girls, the Lord's
Prayer, the Creed, and the Hail Mary. An aristocratic girl
might have a nurse or governess to assist with her education or teach her specific skills. For example, if the girl were
destined to marry and live in a foreign land, she might have
been taught from an early age the language and customs of
the country where she would spend her adult life.

Preparing Girls for Marriage. Girls who lived in a city,
especially if they were from the families of established artisans, were sometimes sent to the local elementary school
along with their brothers. There they would learn to read
the vernacular and perhaps to write and do basic arithmetic. Girls from wealthy families might also be sent to
convents to be educated and taught comportment. A girl's
education, however, ended much earlier than her brother's
because she was not trained for any profession. The most
important qualities for a medieval girl were good comportment, modesty, and chaste behavior—all of which helped
her to attract a husband and be a good wife. Even a daughter of a poor household could enhance her marriageability
with a good upbringing and strong morals. Also, if she
knew how to keep a household and could spin, a woman
had skills that made her a valued wife and partner in the
household economy.

Sources:
Danièle Alexandre-Bidon and Didier Lett, *Children in the Middle Ages:
Fifth-Fifteenth Centuries,* translated by Jody Gladding (Notre Dame,
Ind.: University of Notre Dame Press, 1999).

Jeremy Goldberg, "Girls Growing Up in Later Medieval England," *History Today,* 45 (June 1995): 25–32.

Barbara A. Hanawalt, *The Ties That Bound: Peasant Families in Medieval
England* (New York: Oxford University Press, 1986).

Shulamith Shahar, *Childhood in the Middle Ages* (London & New York:
Routledge, 1990).

TRAINING CHILDREN FOR ADULTHOOD

Home Training. It is difficult to make a distinction
between the education of children and their training for
work. At an early age, children in the countryside accompanied their parents as they worked. Gradually children
were assigned their own tasks in the household or fields.
This work was essential to the well-being of the family, but
at the same time it was part of the process by which children learned the skills they needed as adults. Similarly, the
children of craftsmen learned their trade at their parents'
knees, watching and then helping with simple tasks. Surviving images have shown quite small children helping to
press wine, running alongside a plow, watching their
mother as she feeds animals, and generally getting underfoot as they followed their parents at work. Such times gave
parents opportunities to explain to their children what they
were doing and why.

Chores. As soon as they were able, children were
assigned tasks such as feeding chickens, weeding the gar-

den, collecting firewood, running errands, bringing water from the local well, or carrying meals to workers in the fields. Boys frequently looked after the family's animals, herding the sheep, watching the geese or pigs, or leading the plow horse. In addition to helping in the garden, girls often watched younger children, mended clothes, and helped in the house with cooking and cleaning. Girls, however, also helped in the fields and watched grazing animals. These tasks were considered relatively light and suitable for children, but they were not without their difficulties or dangers. It was generally considered inappropriate for children to take on heavier chores until they had grown firm and strong, at about the age of twelve.

Manorial Duties. In castles and manor houses there were many young children scampering around, combining work and play. The large kitchens necessary to feed a complex household that included a noble and his family, servants, and retainers needed many young helpers. These children, usually boys, turned spits over fires, plucked chickens, swept floors, and carried out the garbage. Occasionally, young children were also musicians and entertainers in the halls. Boys might also serve as stable hands and, in the process, learn the valuable skills of riding and caring for horses. Children sometimes cared for the hunting dogs as well.

City Chores. City children also worked at a young age. They might help in the family's shop or sell wares on the streets, as well as performing small chores in the house, similar to the tasks of country children. When they were between ten and twelve, city children were expect to enter service or apprenticeship and to begin working or learning a trade in a systematic fashion.

Sources:

Danièle Alexandre-Bidon and Didier Lett, *Children in the Middle Ages: Fifth-Fifteenth Centuries,* translated by Jody Gladding (Notre Dame, Ind.: University of Notre Dame Press, 1999).

Barbara A. Hanawalt, *The Ties That Bound: Peasant Families in Medieval England* (New York: Oxford University Press, 1986).

Shulamith Shahar, *Childhood in the Middle Ages* (London & New York: Routledge, 1990).

TRAINING CHILDREN FOR WORK: APPRENTICESHIPS

Leaving Home. Most boys followed in the craft of their fathers—which guaranteed the son membership in the guild—but it was common for a boy to serve his apprenticeship in the household of a master other than his father. Girls could also serve as apprentices, particularly in the various trades associated with the cloth industry. In general, girls were apprenticed to female masters to limit the possibilities of inappropriate conduct or sexual abuse of young girls. An apprenticeship could last from three to ten years, depending on the difficulty of the craft and the regulations of each guild. During this period, an apprentice was integrated into the household of the master and was under his control and guardianship. Young apprentices might begin by

cleaning and sweeping the shop and watching the older apprentices. Gradually, they were introduced to the tools of the trade, shown how to use them, and then given small jobs.

Contracts. Because a large number of apprenticeship contracts from throughout medieval Europe have survived, scholars have been able to examine in detail the conditions and expectations of apprenticeships. An agreement was signed by the master and the parents or guardian of the apprentice and was subject to the supervision of the guild. Contracts stipulated not only the term of apprenticeship and the skills that the apprentice should be taught but also an apprentice's position in a master's household. Masters were responsible for clothing, feeding, and housing apprentices. They might also be required to send an apprentice to school to learn to read and write. Sometimes they might be required to provide the apprentice with the tools of the trade. The apprentice had many responsibilities as well. The contract might specify the starting time of the workday, often at sunrise or earlier in winter. Contracts also protected an apprentice from doing work deemed too heavy and made provisions for what was to be done if the master were absent for a lengthy period and not providing proper instruction.

Female Apprentices. Most crafts were open only to boys, but girls could become apprentices in the cloth industry (the most frequent choice for girls entering a trade)—where women worked as embroiderers, linen makers, and ribbon weavers and also made small cloth articles. Girls could also be apprenticed in the food industry, where women worked as bakers or pastry workers. Occasionally, girls entered more highly skilled and lucrative trades, learning to be scribes, artists, or gold workers. Many girls learned the crafts of their parents and did leave home for formal apprenticeships. Moreover, a girl could inherit her parents' shop, or she might marry a member of her father's guild and assist her husband at the trade she had learned from her father. Thus, for many girls, learning a trade was part of their domestic education, and practicing it continued within the context of the family economy. This system also protected young girls, who were even more vulnerable to the abuse of a cruel or lascivious master than were boys. There is evidence that if a girl served an apprenticeship outside her home, her family continued to take an interest in her well-being and occasionally even sued an abusive master.

Sources:

Danièle Alexandre-Bidon and Didier Lett, *Children in the Middle Ages: Fifth-Fifteenth Centuries,* translated by Jody Gladding (Notre Dame, Ind.: University of Notre Dame Press, 1999).

Jeremy Goldberg, "Girls Growing Up in Later Medieval England," *History Today,* 45 (June 1995): 25–32.

Barbara A. Hanawalt, *Growing Up in Medieval London: The Experience of Childhood in History* (New York: Oxford University Press, 1993).

Shulamith Shahar, *Childhood in the Middle Ages* (London & New York: Routledge, 1990).

A father endowing a monastery where he is placing his son for education and training as a monk; illumination from a twelfth-century manuscript for Gratian's *Decretum* (Bibliothèque Municipale, Douai)

TRAINING CHILDREN FOR WORK: SERVICE

A Stage of Life. Going into service was integrated into the fabric of medieval urban society, especially in England, and was not necessarily indicative of low social status. In many ways service was simply a stage of growing up. A period of service allowed children approaching adulthood to become independent of their parents and natal families. For girls, service generally provided a safe transition from girlhood to marriage in their early twenties.

Contracts. Service was governed by a contract that endured for a fixed period. Most servants would work for an employer for a year or two and then move to another household. Often service was taken up in the household of a relative of the family. Male and female servants were about equally in demand in towns, but women had fewer opportunities than men for service in the countryside.

Women's Work. Female servants performed a variety of tasks for their employers. They helped to supervise the shop, ran errands, drew water, carried food, lit candles, and washed dishes. Some trades, especially in the mercantile, textile, and victualing industries, were more likely to employ female servants than heavy or highly skilled trades. In rural areas, female servants were hired to look after the animals, work in the dairy, shear sheep, care for poultry, and cut hay—all tasks considered to be women's work. In both town and country, women servants also helped with child care, preparing the meals, marketing, and general housework.

Learning Valuable Skills. Service provided an opportunity to learn a great deal about household management, keeping records and accounts, and a variety of other life skills that benefited the child as he or she assumed adult responsibilities. Moreover, service allowed children to learn things their parents did not know, such as new crafts. Service also helped children to move to areas with greater opportunities, such as from countryside to city. Finally, since many tasks were age specific, employers benefited from having streams of servants of different ages cycling through their households and businesses.

Courtship. While they were in service, young women remained single, but they quite frequently began courtships at this point in their lives, often with other servants or apprentices. Because servants had considerable financial autonomy from their families, they also had some freedom of choice in selecting a spouse. Courtship usually began toward the end of a woman's time in service, perhaps as late as her early twenties, and it was common for people to marry in their mid twenties. Once they had agreed to marry, the couple might exchange consent privately in the presence of friends and employers, rather than their natal families, who often lived too far away to be present. For many young women in service, however, the goal of an honorable marriage was unrealizable. In the High Middle Ages there was a general demographic imbalance between the sexes. Large numbers of men were in holy orders, and men of marriageable age were particularly vulnerable to death in wars. These factors, coupled with the economic exigencies of starting a new household, meant that many young women lived out their lives as spinsters.

Sources:

Danièle Alexandre-Bidon and Didier Lett, *Children in the Middle Ages: Fifth-Fifteenth Centuries*, translated by Jody Gladding (Notre Dame, Ind.: University of Notre Dame Press, 1999).

Jeremy Goldberg, "Girls Growing Up in Later Medieval England," *History Today*, 45 (June 1995): 25–32.

Barbara A. Hanawalt, *Growing Up in Medieval London: The Experience of Childhood in History* (New York: Oxford University Press, 1993).

Shulamith Shahar, *Childhood in the Middle Ages* (London & New York: Routledge, 1990).

WIDOWS AND THE ELDERLY

The Independence of Widows. In the High Middle Ages single women were supervised by their fathers, and wives were controlled by their husbands. Widows, however, were able to exercise considerable personal and economic independence—despite changes in inheritance customs, property law, and marriage provisions that had significantly weakened women's economic autonomy. Some widows were poor, and law, morality, and social conventions considered them among the most vulnerable members of society, but many women found widowhood the most pleasant stage of life.

Economic Advantages. On the death of her husband, a widow was given back her dowry, had the use of her dower, and frequently was the executor of her husband's estate and guardian of the children. All these responsibilities were hers by law and by right, without male supervision. In the highest ranks of society a widow might have charge of considerable amounts of land and movable wealth. In fact, a widow frequently had much more wealth and land than a younger woman could bring as a dowry to a marriage. In this light, the feudal lord's desire to control the marriage of his vassal's widow is understandable. Her land and wealth could empower an enemy or turn an ally into a rival. By the same token her remarriage could significantly extend the lord's ties of friendship and loyalty. Medieval records include many cases in which lords tried to arrange marriages for unwilling widows and instances of widows buying their freedom to

remain unmarried. Among the aristocracy, it was not uncommon for a wealthy woman to be widowed two or three times and then—after a series of arranged marriages—to seek to lead a single life by taking a vow of perpetual chastity. This arrangement freed her from marriage but did not require her to live in a religious community.

Widows of Tradesmen and Farmers. In the lower reaches of society, widows also gained economic control of their property, which might include the family farm, craft shop, and tools of a trade. Widows were highly prized as marriage partners because their wealth usually exceeded a single woman's dowry. Marriage to a widow could also provide a propertyless man with the land and family that might otherwise be out of reach. Similarly, it could allow an apprentice or journeyman to become a master and guild member. On a farm widowhood was difficult. Because the household economy was based on the labor of both husband and wife, the death of the husband, especially one whose children were too young to take over his tasks, left the family shorthanded. In such cases, widows who did not remarry had to hire help. Whether in town or country, a widow with young children usually managed better with a new husband to share the burden. If a widow were childless or had adult children, however, remaining single offered a freedom and autonomy she had not hitherto experienced.

The Elderly. The Ten Commandments admonished children to honor their parents. Medieval moralists understood this obligation to be a lifelong commitment, not one that ended when the child reached adulthood. Thus, medieval society expected children to care for their aged parents. There were, however, many opportunities for, and instances of, intergenerational conflict. At most levels of society, in town or country, a child, especially the heir, could not expect to start a new household until he succeeded to his father's estate. Among the aristocracy, a knight could not achieve full manhood, receive his title, and be able to assume the privileges and responsibilities that came with the family's estate until he had inherited it. A rural villager, who stood to inherit much less land than a noble, remained landless and dependent until his father's death. Thus, along with facing physical and perhaps mental decline, the elderly were vulnerable to pressure from their children. As elderly villagers became unable to perform the hard physical labor associated with agricultural work, they faced difficult decisions about how to support themselves.

Vulnerable Dependents. The difficulties that could develop between the generations were amply attested to by preachers, moralists, and writers. Many examples used by preachers to illustrate their sermons featured aged parents who were harshly treated by their adult children. Most frequently, the elderly described by preachers were victims of their children's greed and had been cast out of the house into the cold, left to eat scraps, or to starve outright. The morals of these stories usually involved divine intervention on behalf of the elderly parent. In other examples, an abusive parent was threatened in old age with similar treatment from his own child. Such stories served to highlight how the vulnerability of the elderly and to illustrate the cycle of interdependence that characterized medieval family life.

May-December Relationships. Another point of tension between the generations arose in situations where older men had married younger women. The young men of the community were likely to resent the older man for removing her from the pool of marriageable women. Moreover, if this marriage was the older man's second, he might have adolescent or adult children who feared that the younger wife, as potentially a young widow, might deprive them of their inheritance for years to come. The marriage of a widow might also elicit resentment from young women who saw a potential husband removed from the pool of eligible men.

Retirement Contracts. One way that the elderly could provide for their support in old age and accommodate pressure to pass on their land to children was through retirement contracts. In these contracts an older couple, or a surviving widow or widower, drafted an agreement giving conditional use of the land to a designated person, usually one of their children, but sometimes a more-distant relative, such as a niece or nephew, or even a landless stranger. The Bible warned, "Give not to your son . . . power over yourself while you are alive, and do not give your estate to another" (Ecclesiasticus 33.20). Nevertheless, these agreements were extremely popular in the thirteenth and fourteenth centuries, when the large European population created a great demand for land and little new land was becoming available for cultivation. A retirement agreement allowed an otherwise landless young person the chance to work a plot of land and start a family.

Obligations. In exchange for the right to work the land and inherit it on the death of the owner, the recipient agreed to provide the retiree with food, clothing, shelter, and whatever else the agreement specified. The agreements were frequently detailed, enumerating, for example, the amount of wheat or the number of pairs of shoes to which the retiree was entitled annually. Other agreements carefully partitioned the family house, indicating the entrances, fireplaces, and rooms to which the retiree had access. In other agreements the elderly couple negotiated to have a separate house built for them, stipulating the size and appearance, including the number of windows and doors. Other conditions might include having their laundry done for them, having fuel provided, or even having a horse to ride.

Imposed Agreements. Sometimes these contracts were imposed on aging tenants by a lord or a community after it became clear that the elderly people could no longer work the land. This kind of arrangement was recorded in the manor court and was perceived to be of benefit to all concerned: the lord continued to collect rent; the community provided for its aging members; and a young person was given access to land and the ability to establish a new family. If retirees were not well off, the arrangements might include not only their land and cottage, but also all their household goods, farm implements, and animals, and even their clothing and other moveable goods.

Protective Provisions. To protect the retiree from any abuse of the terms, retirement agreements were usually conditional. If a younger person did not meet all the provisions of the agreement, the land reverted back to the elderly owner. The conditions and reversion of ownership were enforced by the lord, the manor court, and the community in general. It was considered to everyone's benefit for these agreements to be enforced with integrity.

The Destitute Elderly. The most vulnerable of the elderly were those who were without property or family to care for them. Coroners' records provide examples of elderly vagrants who died of exposure. Some of these unfortunates were poor members of a village community, while others may have been dispossessed from their lands or even thrown out by their children. Records indicate the occasional case of an elderly person being forced to beg even though an adult child lived in the village. One sermon included a story about an elderly woman who ceded her property to her son and daughter-in-law in exchange for food and lodging but was then forced from the house and consigned to the life of a beggar. One night, when the young couple was about to sit down to a fine chicken dinner, the old mother came to the door begging for something to eat. The son hid the chicken in a chest while he got rid of the old woman. When he returned to retrieve the chicken, it had been transformed into a snake that wrapped itself around his neck and would not let go. The snake insisted on taking the man's food away, just as he had deprived his mother. These kinds of tales were aimed to keep greedy children from neglecting their dependent parents.

Charity. Medieval society recognized the perilous existence of some of its older members. For example, it was common in village communities to allow the elderly to glean in the fields after the harvest as a means of supplying themselves with grain. Gleaning was difficult work, however, and could be performed by only the relatively able-bodied. The parish clergy and local religious houses were also sources of charity, distributing food and clothing, and occasionally providing shelter and burial.

Bequests. The wills of elderly people who were in relative good financial circumstances provide quite a different picture of old age during the medieval period. Men took care to leave bequests to their wives, children, and sometimes grandchildren. The wills of widows often included bequests to their children, friends, neighbors, distant kin, godchildren, and servants. Many explicitly mentioned servants who had cared for them during illness or their declining years.

Sources:

Elaine Clark, "Some Aspects of Social Security in Medieval England," *Journal of Family History*, 7 (1982): 307–320.

Frances Gies and Joseph Gies, *Marriage and the Family in the Middle Ages* (New York: Harper & Row, 1987).

Barbara A. Hanawalt, *The Ties That Bound: Peasant Families in Medieval England* (New York: Oxford University Press, 1986).

David Herlihy, "Age, Property, and Career in Medieval Society," *Aging and the Aged in Medieval Europe*, edited by Michael M. Sheehan (Toronto: Pontifical Institute of Mediaeval Studies, 1990), pp. 143–158.

SIGNIFICANT PEOPLE

DHUODA

FLOURISHED 824-843
NOBLE MOTHER

A Difficult Life. Dhuoda was the wife of a nobleman, Bernard of Septimania, a retainer and godson of Louis I (the Pious), Holy Roman Emperor and King of France. Bernard was close to Louis and had served as tutor to one of Louis's sons. Bernard's prominent family is frequently mentioned in medieval records; Dhuoda is known only through the survival of a long letter she sent to one of her sons. In it she recorded that she and Bernard were married at the emperor's palace in Aachen on 29 June 824 and that she gave birth to a son, William, on 29 November 826, describing him as her "so longed-for firstborn son." Her marriage was not happy. She suffered from the uprooted- ness of military life, following her husband as he moved around the kingdom. Moreover, in 830 her husband was accused of an adulterous relationship with Louis's wife, Judith, and became caught up in a civil war that wracked the kingdom in subsequent years. Fifteen years after the birth of William, Dhuoda gave birth to a second son. By then she was probably in her late thirties or early forties. Bernard was absent and, while the baby was still so young that he had not yet been baptized, his father ordered that the child be brought to him, probably to protect him from his father's enemies.

A Lonely Woman. Dhuoda was left alone, bereft of the company of her newborn child and her fifteen-year-old son. To fill her lonely hours Dhuoda composed a manual for her sons, to guide them as they grew to manhood, with- out the benefit of their mother's company and advice. The manual, which she sent to William, was written in Latin and filled with quotations from the Bible and other author- ities, indicating that Dhuoda was well educated. Moreover, beyond her conventional advice, citations, and quotations, Dhuoda conveyed her heartfelt maternal affection. She wrote that among her many concerns, "seeing you again one day with my own eyes is the greatest." She warned William to watch over his little brother as they made their way in the world: "When your little brother, whose name I

still do not know, has been baptized in Christ, do not fail to instruct him, to educate him, to love him." Expressing her longing for her children, she lamented, "Most women have the joy of living in this world with their child, and I, Dhuoda, oh my son William, am separated and far from you." Dhuoda's book allows modern readers a rare glimpse of the affection that bound parents and children during the violent upheavals of ninth-century Europe. Nothing is known of Dhuoda's life after 843. Her husband was cap- tured and beheaded by Louis's son Charles the Bald in 844; William died in battle in 850. The fate of her second son, whose father named him Bernard, is uncertain.

Sources:
Dhuoda, *Handbook for her Warrior Son, Liber Manualis,* edited and trans- lated by Marcelle Thiébaux (Cambridge: Cambridge University Press, 1998).

Dhuoda, *Handbook for William: A Carolingian Woman's Counsel for Her Son,* translated by Carol Neel (Lincoln: University of Nebraska Press, 1991).

James Marchand, "The Frankish Mother: Dhuoda," in *Medieval Women Writers,* edited by Katharina M. Wilson (Athens: University of Geor- gia Press, 1984), pp. 1–29.

ELEANOR OF AQUITAINE

1122-1204
QUEEN OF FRANCE AND ENGLAND

Eleanor's Inheritance. The life of Eleanor of Aquitaine illustrates how the clever manipulation of family ties could enhance an aris- tocrat's power in the Middle Ages. Although the several regions of twelfth-century France were nominally bound to the Capetian monarch in Paris, all but a few of the king's vassals ruled their lands indepen- dently. The succession of the dukes of Aquitaine, the largest and most powerful of these regions, was therefore of great importance to the political balance of Western Europe. When William X of Aquitaine died in 1137 without a surviving male heir, his fifteen-year-old daughter, Eleanor, inherited the duchy, thus beginning her career as one of the most politically influential women of the Middle Ages.

Queen of France. On his deathbed Eleanor's father had entrusted her to the protection of King Louis VI, who promptly betrothed her to his son, the future Louis VII. When the elder Louis died in 1137, just a few days after the wedding, the teenaged Eleanor and Louis were crowned monarchs of a newly strengthened French kingdom. The temperament of the quiet and devout new king contrasted with that of his fiery wife, who had spent the last ten years not in a cloister, like her husband, but at the side of her well-traveled and worldly father. Louis VII was deeply impressed with Eleanor's beauty and intelligence, and, since the young and inexperienced king was only a year older than his new queen, it was natural that she was able to exert great influence over him during the early years of his reign.

The Second Crusade. In 1147, responding to a papal bull encouraging France to defend Crusader holdings in the Holy Land, Louis VII traveled east to take part in the largely unsuccessful campaign now known as the Second Crusade. Eleanor, unwilling to be excluded from her husband's affairs, insisted on going with him. The French company was met in Antioch by Eleanor's charismatic uncle, Raymond of Poitiers, and, whether justified or not, rumors began to circulate that Raymond and Eleanor were having an affair. When a dispute between Raymond and Louis broke out, with Louis deciding to press on to Jerusalem rather than defend Antioch, Eleanor demanded that their marriage be annulled. Tensions between the French king and queen had existed even before this crusade, owing in part to the couple's infertility: Eleanor had borne only one child, a daughter, in their first ten years of marriage. Eleanor was doubtless as unhappy as her husband about their lack of a male heir, since controlling a son would have been the surest way for her to secure her political influence. Then there were the temperamental differences between the two; Eleanor is said to have complained, "I married a monk, not a king." Whatever the causes of their strife, by the time the two left for home in 1149—on separate ships—the dissolution of their marriage seemed inevitable. Divorce, of course, was not a canonical possibility, but annulments especially among the aristocracy were quite common in the Middle Ages. It had long been rumored that Eleanor and Louis were connected by distant ancestry, and their kinship in the fourth and fifth degrees was sufficient to allow an annulment on grounds of consanguinity. After an unsuccessful attempt at reconciliation following their return to France, Eleanor and Louis were finally separated in 1152.

Queen of England. After her virtual divorce from Louis VII, Eleanor regained control over her lands. Within two months she had secured a new alliance for Aquitaine with her marriage to Henry Plantagenet, who was not only lord of Normandy and Anjou in France but

heir to the English throne. After the death of King Stephen in 1154, Eleanor and Henry II united their realms, becoming monarchs of the most powerful kingdom in western Christendom. Though her new husband was twelve years younger, Eleanor was not able to control him to the extent she had Louis VII. Eleanor's resentment grew when Henry II began an open affair with the well-known beauty Rosamond, daughter of one of his knights. In early 1168 Eleanor, with her husband's permission, left England and Normandy to establish a court at Poitiers.

Patroness of Art and Love. For at least two generations Eleanor's family had been great patrons of the arts; her grandfather, himself a poet and musician, had been styled William "the Troubadour." Eleanor carried on this tradition at Poitiers, which during these years became a meeting place for many of the greatest writers and troubadours of the twelfth century, including Bernart de Ventadour, Chrétien de Troyes, Bertran de Born, and perhaps even Marie de France. Eleanor's first daughter, by Louis VII, Marie de Champagne—to whom Chrétien dedicated his famous romance of Lancelot—is believed to have come to her mother's court as well, and the two are credited with founding the "courts of love," tribunals in which noble ladies ruled on questions of romantic love and courtly etiquette. The best-known description of courtly love is Andreas Capellanus's *De Arte Honeste Amandi* (The Art of Noble Love, circa 1185), the second book of which was based directly on the rulings of Eleanor and her daughter while at Poitiers.

Unsuccessful Rebellion. In the years before her move to Poitiers, Eleanor had given birth to three daughters and five sons by Henry. All the daughters were eventually wed to powerful kings or nobles from as far abroad as Sicily and Bavaria. Eleanor encouraged their sons to revolt against their father in 1173–1174. After the rebellion was put down, Henry II had Eleanor sent to his castle in Touraine. Unable to move from place to place without his permission, she spent the next sixteen years of her life in confinement at various castles.

Kings Richard and John. By the time of his death in 1189, Henry had been forced to acknowledge his eldest living son, Richard, as heir. The next year, Richard, later dubbed "the Lion-Hearted," left for the Third Crusade, naming his mother as regent. The sixty-eight-year-old queen mother defended her favorite son's lands against his brother John, who was plotting with Richard's former ally Philip of France to depose his elder brother. After Richard's return home from the Crusade in 1194, Eleanor retired for a time to the abbey of Fontevrault but entered politics again at Richard's death in 1199. She helped secure the succession of her youngest son, John, serving as a powerful adviser and diplomat throughout the early years of his reign. Even at her advanced age she traveled throughout Europe preparing treaties and arranging marriages for her remaining relatives. Active to the end, Eleanor of Aquitaine died at Fontevrault in the spring of 1204.

Sources:

Amy Ruth Kelly, *Eleanor of Aquitaine and the Four Kings* (Cambridge, Mass.: Harvard University Press, 1974).

Marion Meade, *Eleanor of Aquitaine: A Biography* (New York: Hawthorn Books, 1977).

Desmond Seward, *Eleanor of Aquitaine* (New York: Times Books, 1979).

HELOISE

CIRCA 1100-1164
WIFE, ABBESS

A Famous Love Affair. Heloise was no more than sixteen years old when she began her studies with the cleric Peter Abelard, the best-known philosopher of his day. She so excelled at her studies in Paris that Peter of Cluny later described her as having "surpassed all women and nearly all men." Yet, Heloise is mostly remembered for her love of Abelard, who—as lover, husband, and correspondent—became the focus of Heloise's life.

Heloise and Abelard. As a child, Heloise was educated at the convent school of Argenteuil in France, and then went to Paris to live with her uncle, the canon Fulbert. In 1116 her uncle accepted the thirty-seven-year-old Abelard into his house to serve as Heloise's tutor. In his autobiographical *Historia Calamitatum* (Account of My Troubles), Abelard admitted that in lodging with Fulbert his intention had been not to teach, but to seduce, the young Heloise. For her part, Fulbert's niece offered little resistance to the advances of her charismatic tutor. Their affair went undiscovered for several months before rumors finally reached Fulbert. Abelard was cast out of the house, but the two continued to meet in secret. When Heloise learned she was pregnant, Abelard encouraged her to flee her uncle's house. She went to stay with Abelard's family in Brittany, where she bore a son she named Astrolabe. Before the child was born, a conscience-stricken Abelard approached Fulbert with an offer to marry Heloise.

Secret Marriage. Marriage was the only way to appease Fulbert's anger and preserve Heloise's honor; nonetheless, Heloise protested vehemently. Her love for Abelard was complete and unselfish, and she wished only to save his reputation. Abelard was a philosopher, a teacher, and a cleric—the lowest rank in the ecclesiastical hierarchy—and though marriage was not forbidden to him by canon law, it would almost certainly have damaged his career. Celibacy and a complete devotion to study were expected of a man in his position, and Abelard understood this fact as well as Heloise. Despite her protests, he visited Fulbert with his proposal, but with the stipulation that the marriage be kept secret. The uncle agreed, and Heloise and Abelard were wed. Before long, however, Fulbert broke his vow and publicized the marriage. Heloise and her new husband denied the marriage and denounced Fulbert, who responded by venting his wrath on his niece. Finding this situation intolerable, Abelard sent Heloise to the convent at Argenteuil. Though Abelard never intended for her to become a nun there, Fulbert believed that Abelard was discarding his wife and set out to take revenge: hired assailants broke into Abelard's lodgings at night and castrated him.

Monastic Life. Abelard fled his shame by retreating to a monastery and taking the vows of a monk. He instructed Heloise to do the same. She felt no calling to such a life, but, out of obedience to her husband and guilt for the suffering he had endured, she accepted the veil without hesitation, becoming a nun and later prioress at Argenteuil. In 1128, nine years after Heloise took religious vows, Abbot Suger of Saint-Denis laid claim to the convent where she was staying and expelled the nuns. Hearing of their misfortune, Abelard offered them the use of some lands he owned in Champagne. The sisters built a new convent there, around a chapel called the Paraclete, or "Comforter." The community of the Paraclete received official recognition from the Pope in 1135, and three years later, under the papacy of Innocent II, Heloise was appointed abbess.

Letters to Abelard. In the early years of her life at the Paraclete, Heloise came across a copy of her husband's recently written *Historia Calamitatum*. She is believed to have begun a correspondence with him soon afterward. In her letters she chided her husband for having so long neglected her; she made it clear that her love for him was as constant as ever; she accused herself of hypocrisy in her outward life of virtue, claiming that she held Abelard more dear than God; and she pleaded with him to write to her.

Death and Influence. In 1142, less than a year after their final correspondence, Abelard died. His body was taken to Heloise's convent, where she saw to it that his tomb was well prepared and that prayers were said for him daily. During the last two decades of her life, Heloise was an admired and capable abbess, earning the regard of popes and fellow monastics. By the time of her death on 16 May 1164 she had overseen, in addition to the affairs of her own convent, the development of six daughter houses of the Paraclete. She was buried beside her beloved Abelard. In 1817 their remains were moved to the cemetery of Père-Lachaise in Paris. The story of Heloise and Abelard, and especially of Heloise's love, first became well known with its inclusion in the second part of the *Roman de la Rose* (Romance of the Rose, circa 1275), in which Jean de Meun concluded his description of Heloise with the couplet, "Upon my soul, I do not believe / another such woman has ever lived."

Sources:

Peter Abelard, *Historia Calamitatum*, translated by Henry Adams Bellows (New York: Macmillan, 1972).

Elizabeth Hamilton, *Héloïse* (London: Hodder & Stoughton, 1966).

The Letters of Abelard and Heloise, translated by C. K. Scott-Moncrieff (New York: Knopf, 1942).

Barbara Newman, "Authority, authenticity, and the repression of Heloise," *Journal of Medieval and Renaissance Studies*, 22 (1992): 121-157.

DOCUMENTARY SOURCES

Bartholomew the Englishman, *On the Properties of Things* (circa 1250)—an encyclopedia that includes summaries of medieval ideas about conception, childbirth, the nature of children, and the roles and responsibilities of family members.

Dhuoda, *Letter to William* (841–843)—a mother's attempt to inculcate in her sons the values necessary to lead a good life, revealing her love for her children and her anguish at being separated from them.

Fourth Lateran Council, *Canons* (1215)—a revision and consolidation of Church rules governing marriage, including the requirements that banns be read and a priest preside at the exchange of consent, an affirmation of the validity of clandestine unions, and a reduction in the degrees of prohibited relationship.

Geoffroy de la Tour-Landry, *The Book of the Knight of La Tour-Landry* (1371–1372)—a treatise written in French by a knight from the province of Anjou for the instruction of his three daughters; widely popular and eventually translated into other languages, it reflects the moral values of the rural gentry pertaining to morality, marriage, and manners.

The Goodman of Paris, Housekeeping Manual (1392–1394)—a manual of household management written by an elderly Parisian merchant for his new, beloved, and much younger wife, whom he addressed as "Dear Sister," concerned that she learn how to supervise her servants and administer an urban household in a worthy and economical fashion so that if she were widowed and subsequently remarried, she would bring honor to him; his manual includes tips on cooking, running a household, and contemporary ideals of marriage.

Guibert de Nogent, *De Vita Sua* (1124)—a memoir by a monk who was neglected and abandoned by his mother and mistreated by an older brother.

Hincmar of Reims, *De divortio Lotharii et Teutbergae* (On the Divorce of King Lothar and Queen Theutberga, 858)—a treatise that helped to establish ecclesiastical jurisdiction over marriage and entrenched the principle that a valid marriage was indissoluble.

Peter Lombard, *Sententiarum libri IV* (Four Books of Sentences, 1148–1151)—a rejection of consummation as a requirement to make a marriage valid and a redefinition of the concept of marital consent.

Pope Nicholas I, Letter to Boris, King of the Bulgarians (866)—a summary of ninth-century practices attending Christian marriage, including the couple's exchange of consent, the consent of their parents, and the conferral of the dower on the bride.

Polyptychs (early ninth century)—documents including the results of surveys of various estates and recording the members of each household, an important resource for historians studying family structures in early medieval rural societies.

Trotula of Salerno, *The Diseases of Women (Trotula Major)* (eleventh century)—treatises about women's health, in particular matters such as menstruation, conception, pregnancy, and childbirth; the treatise reveals a practical and compassionate view of women's bodies, distinguishing it from the more theoretical and judgmental medical works; the treatises attributed to Trotula were translated from Latin into many vernacular languages.

Jesus, Mary, and Joseph; illumination from the *Berthold Missal*, 1212-1232 (Pierpont Morgan Library, New York)

CHAPTER NINE

RELIGION AND PHILOSOPHY

by JEREMIAH HACKETT, KATHRYN A. EDWARDS, and GIULIO SILANO

CONTENTS

814*

- Benedict of Aniane begins his educational reform.

846

- Arab pirates sack the Vatican.

850*

- The "Isidorian Decretals," purportedly ancient precedents for the comprehensive and immediate exercise of papal authority over other churches, are circulated throughout Europe.

- John Scottus Eriugena writes *De Diuinae predestinatione liber* (On Divine Predestination), explaining how man can have free will if God is all-knowing.

863

- Cyril and Methodius of Thessalonica go on a mission to convert the Slavs.

864

- Boris, King of the Bulgars, converts to Eastern Christianity.

865*

- Eriugena writes *Periphyseon* (About Nature), his masterwork on the relationship of God and his Creation.

877

- John Scottus Eriugena dies.

909

- Duke William the Pious of Aquitaine founds a monastery at Cluny.

1000

- King Olaf introduces Christianity to Sweden.

1028

- Bishop Fulbert, who has begun construction of the great Gothic cathedral at Chartres, dies.

1049

- At the Councils of Rheims and Mainz, Pope Leo IX condemns simony, the buying and selling of Church offices or ecclesiastical seniority.

1051

- Ibn Gabirol, a Jewish philosopher and poet in Moorish Spain, dies; his Neoplatonic *The Fountain of Life* influences Christian Scholastic philosophers.

* DENOTES CIRCA DATE

1054
- The Patriarch of Constantinople anathematizes the Roman Church, an act widely regarded as the beginning of the schism between the Roman Catholic and Orthodox Churches.

1070
- William the Conqueror names his trusted adviser Lanfranc, an Italian cleric, archbishop of Canterbury.

1075
- Pope Gregory VII forbids investiture of bishops by laypeople such as kings and lords.

1076
- Pope Gregory VII excommunicates and deposes Holy Roman Emperor Henry IV because of his insistence on reserving for the Church the right of lay investiture, which has created a power struggle between Church and State.
- Anselm of Bec writes *Monologion,* on the attributes of God.

1077
- Henry IV humbles himself before Pope Gregory VII at Canossa, is readmitted to the Church, and thus retains his crown.

1078
- Anselm of Bec writes *Proslogion* (An Address of the Mind of God), his ontological argument for the existence of God.

1093
- William II Rufus, son and successor of William the Conqueror, appoints Anselm of Bec archbishop of Canterbury.

1095
- At the Council of Clermont in France, Pope Urban II preaches a stirring call for troops to take the Holy Land away from Muslim "infidels," beginning the First Crusade.

1099
- The Crusaders take Jerusalem and establish Christian kingdoms there as well as in Edessa, Antioch, and Tripoli.

1112
- Bernard of Clairvaux helps to found the Cistercian abbey at Cîteaux.

1122
- The Concordat of Worms settles the Investiture Controversy between the Holy Roman Empire and the Church. The emperor renounces his power to invest bishops while the Pope acknowledges the right of the emperor to grant bishops fiefs before and after their investiture by the Church.

* DENOTES CIRCA DATE

1125
- James of Venice begins translating the works of Aristotle; over the next twenty-five years scholars in Spain and Sicily translate many of Aristotle's works.

1128
- According to tradition, Bernard of Clairvaux writes the Rule of the Knights Templar.

1130*
- Peter Abelard completes his *Logica ingredientibus* (The Greater Glosses on Logic).

1140*
- Gratian writes his *Decretum*, which marks the beginning of an autonomous canon (Church) law.

1142*
- Peter Abelard completes *Dialogus inter philosophum, Judaeum et Christianum* (Dialogue of a Philosopher with a Jew and a Christian).
- Spanish Jewish philosopher Judah ha-Levi dies.
- Peter Abelard completes his *Ethica* (Ethics).

1142
- Peter Abelard dies.
- English scientist-philosopher Adelard of Bath dies.

1147
- European troops reach the Holy Land for the Second Crusade, which lasts for three years and is characterized by a lack of military co-operation among Christian forces.

1150*
- Peter Lombard writes his *Sentinarium* (Sentences), marking the beginning of an autonomous science of theology.

1151
- The Spanish philosopher Domingo Gundisalvo (Dominicus Gundissalinus), an important translator who was instrumental in introducing Neoplatonism to western European scholars, dies.

1153
- Bernard of Clairvaux dies.

1159
- English cleric John of Salisbury writes *Policraticus*, criticizing the growth of bureaucratic specialization in government.

* DENOTES CIRCA DATE

- John of Salisbury writes his *Metalogicon*.

1170
- Archbishop Thomas Becket is murdered at Canterbury Cathedral because of his resistance to King Henry II's demands for greater royal control over the Church.

1173
- Valdes (also known as Waldo) founds the Waldensian movement, advocating a more evangelical Church that embraces poverty.

1189
- European troops on the Third Crusade, which lasts until 1192, are unsuccessful at retaking Jerusalem from Saladin, who had invaded the Christian-held city in 1187.

1190*
- Spanish Islamic philosopher Averroës (Ibn Rushd) completes his commentaries on Aristotle.

1190
- Moses Maimonides (Moshs ben Maimon), a Spanish Jew living in Cairo, writes *Dalalat al-Ha'irin* (Guide for the Perplexed)—Hebrew title *Moreh Nebukim*—his chief work of religious philosophy.

1198
- Innocent III becomes Pope; the exercise of papal authority over secular rulers reaches its height during his pontificate.
- Averroës dies.

1202
- French theologian and poet Alain de Lille, who sought to combine mysticism with the rationalism of the Scholastics, dies.
- During the Fourth Crusade, which lasts until 1204, Crusaders capture the Byzantine capital of Constantinople, an event often said to mark the definitive schism between Eastern and Western Christianity.

1204
- Maimonides dies.

1209
- An internal European Crusade is launched against the Albigensian heretics in southern France.

1210
- Pope Innocent III gives oral approval for the founding of the Franciscan Order of Friars Minor.
- French officials forbid the teaching of Aristotle's *Physics* and *Metaphysics* at the University of Paris.

* DENOTES CIRCA DATE

1215

- Pope Innocent III calls the Fourth Lateran Council, which sets out fundamental rules of Christian practice and belief, clerical decency, and prosecution of heretics.

- Papal legate Robert of Courçon writes the statutes for the University of Paris, marking its formal establishment as an institution of learning. The statutes renew the ban on teaching Aristotle's *Physics* and *Metaphysics*.

1216

- Pope Innocent III approves the founding of the Dominican Order.

1218

- The Fifth Crusade begins in Egypt, accomplishing little and ending in 1221 with an eight-year truce between the Crusaders and the Saracens in Egypt.

1220

- William of Auxerre writes his *Summa aurea* (Golden Compendium).

- Over the next decade Scotsman Michael Scot translates Arabic manuscripts of Aristotle and commentaries on Aristotle by Averroës.

1221

- Dominic (Domingo de Guzman), founder of the Dominican Order of friars, dies.

1225*

- Robert Grosseteste writes his *Commentarius in Posterium Analyticorum Libros* (Commentary on [Aristotle's] Posterior Analytics).

1226

- St. Francis of Assisi dies.

1228

- Emperor Frederick II of the Holy Roman Empire launches the Sixth Crusade, which ends the following year with a treaty granting the Crusader kingdom of Jerusalem the cities of Jerusalem and Bethlehem and a corridor to the sea.

1231

- Pope Gregory IX appoints a group of theologians to "correct" the works of Aristotle and bans the teaching of his natural philosophy and metaphysics.

1236

- Philip the Chancellor, of the University of Paris, dies.

1244

- Turkish troops capture and sack Jerusalem.

* DENOTES CIRCA DATE

1245

- English theologian Alexander of Hales, who attempted to synthesize the teachings of Augustine with elements of Aristotelianism, dies.

1248

- Hoping to retake Jerusalem, Louis IX of France leads the Seventh Crusade to the Holy Land.

1249

- Philosopher and theologian William of Auvergne, Archbishop of Paris, dies.

1250

- Louis IX is captured by Egyptian troops, ending the Seventh Crusade with Jerusalem still in Muslim hands.

1253

- Robert Grosseteste dies.

- Friar William of Rubruck begins a three-year journey to visit the Great Khan Güyük, ruler of the Mongol Empire, learning much about Buddhist, Islamic, Greek Christian, and pagan religions and writing an account of his journey.

1263

- Pope Urban III renews the 1231 condemnation of Aristotle, but since midcentury, scholars have been lecturing in Paris on all the known works of Aristotle.

1267*

- Roger Bacon writes his *Opus maius* (The Great Work) on the academic situation of his time, philosophy and theology, language, applications of mathematics, optics, experimental science, and moral philosophy.

1268

- French Dominican William of Moerbecke translates Proclus's Neoplatonic *Elements of Theology* from Greek into Latin.

1269

- Siger of Brabant writes *Quaestiones in Tertium De Anima* (Questions on the Third Book of [Aristotle's] On the Soul).

1270*

- Albertus Magnus (Albert the Great) writes *De XV Prolematibus* (On the Fifteen Problems).

- Thomas Aquinas writes *De Unitate Intellectus contra Averroistas* (On the Unity of the Intellect against the Averroists).

* DENOTES CIRCA DATE

RELIGION AND PHILOSOPHY

1270
- Bishop Stephen Tempier of Paris condemns some philosophical positions arising from the teachings of Averroës.
- Louis IX of France and Edward I of England launch the Eighth— and final—Crusade. Louis dies in Tunis.

1271
- The Eighth Crusade ends, having accomplished nothing.
- The Church canonizes Louis IX.

1273
- Thomas Aquinas completes his *Summa theologiae* (Comprehensive Theology).

1274
- The leading thinkers of their age, Thomas Aquinas and Bonaventure, die.
- Siger of Brabant writes *Quaestiones Morales* (Moral Questions).

1277
- Bishop Stephen Tempier of Paris and Archbishop Robert Kilwardby of Canterbury condemn 219 Aristotelian propositions by scholars such as Siger of Brabant, Boethius of Dacia, Thomas Aquinas, and Giles of Rome.

1280
- Albertus Magnus dies.
- Roger Bacon edits *Secretum secretorum* (The Secret of Secrets), a pseudo-Aristotelian work on the education of a prince.

1282*
- Giles of Rome writes *De regimine principium* (On the Rule of Princes).

1286
- William of Moerbecke dies.

1290
- Edward I expels the Jews from England.

1291
- Acre, the last Christian stronghold in the Holy Land, falls to Muslim troops.

1292
- Roger Bacon writes his *Compendium Studii Philosophiae* (Summary of the Study of Theology).

* DENOTES CIRCA DATE

1294
- Meister Eckhart begins his *Book of Spiritual Counsels*, completing it in 1298.

1296
- Over the next decade Dietrich of Freiberg writes his most important philosophical works.

1301
- Giles of Rome writes *De Ecclesiastica Potestate* (On Ecclesiastical Power), completing it in 1302.

1302
- Over the next two years John Duns Scotus (whose name means "John from Scotland"), delivers his Paris lectures, collected as *Reportata Parisiensia* (Parisian Commentary of Sentences).
- Meister Eckhart occupies a professorship at Paris.

1303
- Pope Boniface VIII enters into a dispute with Philip IV (the Fair) of France, who has his agents kidnap the Pope. Boniface dies later this year.

1306
- Philosopher and theologian John of Paris dies.

1308
- John Duns Scotus dies.

1313*
- Dante writes *De monarchia* (On Monarchy), asserting that the Pope has no jurisdiction over secular governments defending the idea of universal monarchy.

1320
- Jean Buridan of Paris writes his *Summa Logicae* (Comprehensive Logic).

1322
- William of Ockham writes his *Summa Logicae* (Comprehensive Logic).

1326
- Meister Eckhart writes *Von Abgeschiedenheit* (On Detachment).

1328
- Meister Eckhart dies.

1329
- Spanish Jew Gersonides (Levi ben Gerson) completes *Sefer Milhamot Ha-Shem* (The Wars of the Lord).

* DENOTES CIRCA DATE

1335
- Barlaam of Seminara writes *Works against the Hesychasts*.

1339
- The first Anti-Ockhamist statutes are published at Paris.

1344
- Thomas Bradwardine writes *Summa de Causa Dei* (On the Cause of God).

1347
- The Black Death arrives in Europe.

- Gregory of Rimini completes his *Lectura super Primum et Secundum Librum Sentientiarum* (Lectures on the First and Second Books of the Sentences).

- William of Ockham dies.

* **DENOTES CIRCA DATE**

The subordination of kingship to the papacy; illumination from a twelfth-century manuscript for Gratian's *Decretum*
(Staatsbibliothek Preussischer Kulturbesitz)

OVERVIEW

The Roots of Medieval Religion and Philosophy. Traditionally, medieval Christianity is said to have begun in about the year 313, when Roman Emperor Constantine I extended legal tolerance to the Christian Church. From this beginning, the Christian religious tradition grew to inspire and permeate all aspects of medieval European culture, including its philosophy and religion, by the ninth century. Although the Eastern and Western Christian Churches had essentially separated by this time, all Christians in western Europe were theoretically united in devotion to one Church, and by the tenth century this Church had spread into northern and central Europe. Indeed, medieval European civilization may be described as the most complete and coherent attempt in history to realize a Christian society. For much of the Middle Ages this western Church was relatively unconcerned with complex doctrinal questions. Instead it focused on proclaiming that, in Christ, a new way of relating to other human beings had been revealed and on developing a ritual system that supported this claim. In the process of spreading these ideas, the Church contributed greatly to fusing the Germanic and Romanized populations of Europe into the European nations that still exist.

Religious and Philosophical Authorities. From its origins Christianity was both syncretic and eclectic. It was syncretic because it believed that all knowledge and all things contained some divine spark; it was up to the learned Christian to synthesize this knowledge to understand God truly and to best structure God's Church on earth. It was eclectic because it felt able to choose from among classical, pagan philosophies those ideas that were best suited for inclusion in Christian thought. For example, the Church took some ideas from Plato and Aristotle while excluding others. Based on this eclecticism, from its establishment the Church was profoundly influenced by the societies in which it developed and those it encountered. After the fall of Rome in the fifth century, Christianity served as a mediator between the conquerors and the conquered, channeling the energies of the invading Germanic tribes to the effort to restore elements of Roman civilization in the radically new conditions of Europe. From the key figures of early Christianity (the Church Fathers) the medieval Church held the belief that

the Hebrew Old Testament continued to be relevant after Christ's coming. From the Church Fathers also came the conviction that classical culture was important and useful because it contained seeds of truth that illuminated the historical Christian mission. Of particular importance for Christian theology and doctrines were the Greek and Roman philosophers, especially Plato and Aristotle, but also the Stoics and the followers of Plato known as the Neoplatonists. This attitude underlay the medieval interest in classical texts and made clerics and monks the agents of their survival and, indeed, of their continued centrality in Western thought and education. In addition, medieval Christianity incorporated philosophical thought from Celtic realms such as Ireland and the spiritual interpretations of Jews and Muslims, particularly in the twelfth and thirteenth centuries when many classical works were transmitted into Christian Europe through Jewish and Muslim intermediaries.

Defining Christianity. Defining appropriate Christian belief and behavior was a continual process throughout the Middle Ages. In these definitions, medieval theologians built on classical foundations. Once the Christian Church became legal and influential in the fourth century, it became essential for Christians to have a clear statement of their fundamental beliefs. In 325 Church leaders met, under pressure from Emperor Constantine, and developed the Nicean Creed, which lists the basic tenets of Christianity: the Trinity, the resurrection, the central role of Christ, and the return of Christ in judgment. As a brief statement, however, the Nicean Creed left many areas open to interpretation, especially how to instruct Christians in these beliefs and what behavior showed that an individual held them. The medieval Church passed hundreds of decrees and held dozens of councils trying to grapple with these questions. In the process of defining Christianity, the medieval Christian Church also defined the sources of spiritual authority for all Christians. These authorities are often summarized as *scripture* and *tradition*, terms that are more complicated than they appear. Scripture was the Bible, not yet in its modern form, and a series of other authoritative writings by early Christians. Councils worked to reach a consensus on the "truest" Christian writings, almost all of which were composed at least forty to fifty years after Christ's death. This text became known as Jerome's Vulgate Bible. It was known as the "vulgate," because it was written in the vulgar, or vernacular, language of the time—Latin—the language that became the common language of all activities in the medieval Church. Although it was considered a fundamental source of revelation, the Bible was not the sole source of Christian belief and practice. Tradition was the common practices and interpretations of the early Christian Church handed on to later generations. Interpretations by early Christians, such as Augustine, Gregory, and Isidore of Seville, fundamentally influenced medieval Christianity—and the modern Church. In addition, tradition in the form of legal documents and ritual practice also helped to define Christianity, as it did medieval law. This method was based on the idea that God's will was made manifest in worldly events and objects and that he would not let his people (Christians) live in ignorance. These beliefs help to explain the key role of the Church and its rituals in medieval Christianity. For most medieval Christians whose views survive, there was no salvation outside the Church and hardly any distinction to be drawn between the institutional Church and the body of Christ. Medieval religion was as much in the organizational features of the Church as in those experiences and doctrines that other ages might more readily regard as religious.

The Church as an Institution. Christian leaders in the fourth and fifth centuries turned to the administrative model with which they were most familiar when they made provisions for organizing Christian communities. That model was the bureaucracy of the most successful institution of their age: the Roman Empire. With the fall of the Roman Empire in the West, the Christian Church became the sole community that transcended tribal boundaries, and it continued to be the largest and most comprehensive European bureaucracy throughout the Middle Ages. This institution was not developed because the medieval Church was greedy and power hungry—common modern misconceptions. Certainly some clergy abused the system, but in general the medieval Church took this form because the majority of clergy believed that only through such an institution could the Church fulfill its responsibilities to the Christian community. To them, anything other than hierarchy and structure meant anarchy, a view shared by the medieval laity. Although the effectiveness of its administration varied greatly depending on local circumstances, churchmen by the twelfth century had formulated an ideal Church structure that various churchmen attempted to put into effect. It was hierarchical with the Pope and his court (the curia) at the summit; they were followed by archbishops, bishops, priests, canons, and a series of other clergy charged with the "cure of souls"; that is, the responsibility of administering the basic rites that marked the stages of a Christian's progress toward salvation. These rites, known as sacraments, were key aspects of medieval Christianity, and much of the bureaucracy of the medieval Church developed because of the need to clarify what they were and

why they mattered, to teach clergy and laity about them, to administer them to all Christians, and to censure those who avoided participating in them. In addition there were a variety of other clergy—such as monks, nuns, and friars—who prayed for the benefit of all Christians. Given the many and diverse demands on the Church, it is perhaps not surprising that approximately 10 percent of the medieval population were Church officials of some sort.

Bishops and Parishes. The institutional Church most frequently affected the life of an ordinary Christian at the level of his or her bishopric and parish. During the third and fourth centuries, the leading figure of a Christian congregation was the bishop, but his responsibilities were expanded in later centuries to include entire cities and provinces. Well into the tenth century, the bishop embodied the Church in a region; he was regarded as a touchstone of orthodoxy, the guardian of the true faith, and the carrier of the correct traditions that were inherited from the Apostles and held in common with other Christian communities throughout the world. The term *diocese* was applied to the whole territory over which a bishop's supervisory and legal authority stretched. Over time, dioceses came to be grouped into provinces, in which one bishop was given pre-eminence, if not legal authority, over the others; he became known as an archbishop. As Christianity spread, bishops began to subdivide their district into parishes assigned to priests, also known as curates. Because the bishop could not administer to the spiritual needs of all Christians in his territories he delegated certain tasks to these priests, such as the administration of baptism and absolution of sinners after repentance. By the eleventh century, a parish tended to correspond in territory to a rural village. The faithful were supposed to attend and pay tithes to their own parish church and no other; the priest was given a monopoly over the spiritual direction of his parishioners, and his church was responsible for an annual payment to the bishop. The priest remained under the direct authority of the bishop of the diocese, who in turn owed obedience to the ultimate bishop: the bishop of Rome, otherwise known as the Pope. Clergymen trained to this structure and these ideologies also became some of the most effective civil servants for secular lords, setting the stage for the conflict between the Church and states that would punctuate medieval history.

Communicating Belief and Thought. One of the primary challenges facing early Christian missionaries was communicating a religion that had grown increasingly literate and Romanized to a frequently illiterate, Germanic population. These challenges continued well into the Middle Ages, with territories such as Scandinavia not being converted to western Christianity until approximately 1000. Missionaries built on existing religious beliefs and rituals and transformed some into Christian rites. For example, pagan societies had celebrated the twenty-fourth of June as marking the summer solstice, and Christian missionaries equated it with the Feast of St. John the Baptist. Christians symbolically interpreted the solstice bonfires as Christ's light and warmth burning away the darkness of sin. Paintings, sculptures, sermons, and stories about holy figures were all part of a Christian education for the learned and the illiterate alike. The sacraments demanded active, thoughtful participation by all Christians, and the performance of the various stages of these rituals was thought to bring the participant to a closer understanding of God. In the Eucharist, the ultimate moment of the main Christian religious service (the mass), this understanding was even portrayed as a physical incorporation through the symbolic partaking of Christ's actual body. The general population also made contributions to a creative and evolving Christianity. They influenced the creation of saints, chose figures and doctrines that they preferred to patronize, demanded a say in selecting their preachers and ministers, and helped to stage religious plays on feast days. In other words, medieval Christian piety and thought were vibrant and creative; they were not beliefs imposed by repressive authorities on a passive and ignorant population.

Opposing Orthodox Patterns. Despite the flexibility found in medieval Christian doctrines and practices, the Church still insisted on a general conformity to established beliefs and piety (orthodoxy), and not all medieval people supported these beliefs. Among the Christian community, there were small groups who felt that the Church, or at least the local authorities who embodied it, had fallen away from the true Christian faith. Probably the best known of these groups were the Cathars (or Albigensians) and the Waldensians. Like many medieval heretics, they maintained that they were Christians and that everyone else defied God's teachings. Opposition to orthodoxy could also occur at academic levels. Medieval universities included scholars who espoused doctrines that the Church condemned. Instruction and punishment of those who challenged orthodoxy was an ongoing problem for the medieval Church, in part because its own doctrines and practices were not yet clearly defined in some of the areas that were being questioned. Before the thirteenth century, examination of opponents was done at a local level: by committees at the universities or by lawyers at a bishop's court. While the procedures in these courts varied depending on the time and place, the Church courts were often more lenient and fairer by modern standards than most secular courts of that time. Certainly the clergy benefited; if a clergyman was found guilty of any crime, the Church courts set his punishment, and considering that their penalties were often gentler, the laity frequently resented this system. In the early thirteenth century, Pope Innocent III set a precedent when he established an independent court to try the Cathars of southern France. Known as the Inquisition, this court existed only when needed during the Middle Ages, and many modern conceptions of it are tied to the events and propaganda of the sixteenth and seventeenth centuries. Also subject to suspicion, and sometimes trial in these courts, were the communities of Jews and Muslims that existed in Europe. Medieval Spain, in particular, was a Muslim center, and the conquest of the Muslim territories by Christians, which began in the eleventh cen-

tury, exposed Christians to diverse spiritual and philosophical perspectives. Generally, Muslims were either made to convert or existed as a subject population, much as the Jews did throughout medieval Christian territories, and just as Jews and Christians were allowed to live as subject populations in Muslim lands. Muslim philosophy, however, especially translations of and commentaries on classical Greek and Roman texts, greatly influenced later medieval philosophy and theology.

Philosophy versus Spirituality. With the collapse of the schools of the late Roman Empire, the preservation of classical culture in the western part of the old empire was entrusted to Christian thinkers, such as Augustine of Hippo, Boethius, and Pseudo-Dionysius. These figures and others like them developed systems of thought that integrated Christian, Hebrew, Platonic, Aristotelian, Neoplatonic, and Stoic thought. In so doing, they established a medieval philosophy founded on Christian principles, a philosophy that would not be effectively challenged until the seventeenth and eighteenth centuries. Philosophy as a rigorous study of logic and linguistics was seen as the handmaiden to Christian spirituality, allowing the true philosopher a closer glimpse of the source and subject of all philosophy: God. Although medieval philosophers examined questions that seemed to have little spiritual relevance, even such academic figures as Roger Bacon examined nature because of spiritual goals, as well as intellectual curiosity. This medieval insistence that all objects of study and philosophy were related to the divine was also fostered by those early Christians who transmitted classical learning and methodology to the medieval West. More than 113 books and treatises, 200 letters, and 500 sermons by Augustine of Hippo have survived, and Boethius wrote on mathematics, astronomy, and music, while also translating and commenting on Aristotle's early works on logic. With the establishment of cathedral schools, universities, and the Scholastic method by the twelfth century, a rigorous, and sometimes formulaic, process was applied to all fields of knowledge.

Scholasticism and the Medieval University. Until the eleventh century, monasteries and cathedral schools were the primary centers of medieval learning. In the twelfth and thirteenth centuries there was a development of specific communities dedicated to the clarification, elaboration, and instruction of law, medicine, philosophy, and theology: universities. Part of the impetus for this institutionalization of learning was the flood of Latin translations of Greek and Arabic philosophical and scientific books that western European scholars had discovered in Spain and the Near East—and the desire to integrate these bodies of thought into Christian philosophy and theology. By the early thirteenth century there were major universities in England (Cambridge and Oxford), France (Paris and Montpelier), and Italy (Salerno, Padua, and Bologna), and other regions of Europe soon had their educational centers as well. Universities and houses of study established by religious orders—rather than the rural monasteries that had been the repositories of learning in the early medieval period—became the sites for the practice of philosophy and theology during the years 1200–1350. Members of these universities fundamentally influenced medieval philosophy and the medieval Church. Building on the work of previous scholars, the twelfth-century philosopher Peter Abelard moved theology away from "divine meditation" to the pure rational analysis of language and logic. One of his major works, *Sic et Non* (Yes and No, written circa 1117–1128), helped to develop this methodology by collecting opposing or conflicting statements and developing a process by which opposing claims could be harmonized or correctly synthesized. It also provided the student with material for logical exercises. This approach to learning became known as the Scholastic Method, and the scholars and theologians who employed it, such as Thomas Aquinas, became known as Scholastics or Schoolmen. Though Scholasticism is sometimes described as a philosophical school, the Scholastics were not necessarily united by a common philosophy; instead they shared a common set of scholarly techniques, which remained influential throughout the rest of the Middle Ages and beyond.

The End of Medieval Religion and Philosophy. Historians disagree about when the medieval form of Christianity came to an end. Perhaps that is because so much of it still exists. Yet, something changed with the great social and economic crises of the fourteenth century. Decades of famine and sickness culminated in the Black Death, which destroyed 15 to 20 percent of the European population and recurred at regular intervals until the early eighteenth century. Years of medieval attempts to reform the clergy seemed mocked by the Great Schism (1378–1415), which gave Europe the spectacle of two popes and two Churches, each of which claimed the other was false. Faced with these facts, Christians in the latter half of the fourteenth century began to doubt the possibility of entirely fulfilling the great aspirations of the medieval Church. During the fourteenth and fifteenth centuries the growth of the secular conviction that one may act for social or political reasons that are unconnected to religious belief may be taken as a sign of the end of the Church's authority and influence over all aspects of European culture.

TOPICS IN RELIGION AND PHILOSOPHY

THE ASCENT OF THE ROMAN CHURCH

Early Christian Roots. Throughout the early Christian era, the Church of Rome grew in importance within the Church at large. Because the apostle Peter had been martyred in Rome, the bishops of Rome, or popes, were seen as his successors. Even though the bishop of Rome was nominally the equal of any other bishop, a belief in the primacy of the bishop of Rome began to develop as early as the third century, when the North African Church Father Tertullian wrote of "Rome, from which there comes . . . the very authority of the apostles themselves." Pope Leo I (reigned 440–461) became the first systematizer of papal primacy, interpreting older statements about the papal role in the Church by means of the principles of Roman law, according to which all the rights and duties of the deceased were transferred to the heir. Thus, the Pope was the heir to all St. Peter's powers, but he did not receive the merits that came to Peter by his personal acknowledgment of Christ as the Son of God. Leo, who was also known as the Great, expressed this principle in a phrase that designated the

Pope the "unworthy heir of St. Peter." Leo's views were accepted with great rapidity in the West; on 17 July 445 the western Roman emperor, Valentinian III (reigned 425–455), acknowledged and gave imperial sanction to the jurisdictional primacy of the Pope, asserting that "nothing is to be done against or without the authority of the Roman Church." In 451 the Council of Chalcedon resolved a theological dispute by accepting a formula proposed by Leo and declaring "St Peter has spoken through Leo!" Another Pope who earned the soubriquet "the Great" was Gregory I (reigned 590–604), who asserted the primacy of the papacy over the entire Church (including the East) and established the independence of the Roman Church from both the Byzantine Empire and the Germanic tribes that had conquered Italy.

The Church and the Empire. During the ninth and tenth centuries the power of the papacy was in decline. Having created the Holy Roman Empire and placed the papacy under its protection when he crowned Charlemagne emperor in 800, Pope Leo III (reigned 795–816) estab-

Pope Innocent III; from a thirteenth-century fresco in the monastery of Sacro Speco, Subiaco, Italy

lished a rival institution that sought, often successfully, to exert its power over the papacy. For example, both Otto I (reigned 912–973) and his grandson Otto III (reigned 983–1002) appointed and removed popes and presided over Church synods.

The Isidoran Decretals. Around 850 a collection of forged documents that were purported to be decrees by Popes and Church councils during the first seven centuries of Christianity began to circulate throughout Europe. By the end of the tenth century this collection, which was wrongly attributed to a scholar known as Isidore of Seville,

had served to reinforce the authority of the Pope. Some twelfth-century critics began to question the authenticity of this collection, but the Isidoran Decretals were not fully discredited until the seventeenth century.

Expanding Church Authority. With Pope Leo IX (reigned 1049–1054) the papacy began to assert and widen its power. Leo made lengthy visits to Europe beyond the Alps, held regular synods to pass degrees on matters of disciple and doctrine, and began the practice of sending papal legates throughout Christendom to assure that his rulings were heeded and followed. He also began appointing non-Romans to posts in the papal administration (the curia). Pope Nicholas II (reigned 1059–1061) made another important contribution to papal independence when he decreed in 1059 that seven cardinal (pre-eminent) bishops were solely responsible for electing a new Pope, thus eliminating—in theory—the emperor or any other secular ruler from the selection process. His victory was short-lived. Two years later the German bishops, who were loyal to the emperor, declared the decree void, deposed Nicholas, and elected Pope Alexander II (reigned 1061–1073). Yet, Nicholas's decree established the important precedent of reserving power within the Church to the ecclesiastical hierarchy.

Church Reform. Known for his attempts to rid the Church of simony (the buying and selling of ecclesiastical offices and influence) and married clergymen and for his long battle to end lay investiture of bishops and abbots, Pope Gregory VII (reigned 1073–1085) brought to the papacy a crusader's zeal to spread Christianity, and with it papal authority, throughout the world. Gregory centralized the Church, claiming for the Pope such rights as direct control over bishops, canonical elections, synods, the publication of canon laws, and the issuing of manifestos. His reformist principles lived on after his death, influencing a new generation of bishops, who proved far more obedient to papal authority than their predecessors. Gregory indelibly impressed on his successors the idea that in his quest for establishing the ideal Christian empire the Pope ought to involve himself in secular as well as spiritual matters and assert his supremacy over secular rulers.

Papal Leadership. In 1095 Pope Urban II (reigned 1088–1099) demonstrated the growing power and prestige of the papacy in his ability to mobilize a large army of volunteers to wage a sacred—and ultimately unsuccessful—war to rid the Holy Land of Muslim "infidels." He was the first Pope to head such a large European endeavor. During the twelfth and thirteenth centuries local churches looked more and more to the papacy for leadership. One result was the increase of the Pope's judicial and legislative authority. Since every important Pope from 1159 until 1303 was a lawyer, the body of canon (ecclesiastical) law grew rapidly. After earlier unofficial attempts to collect and rationalize this huge number of degrees and rulings, Pope Gregory IX (reigned 1227–1241) produced the first official compilation of canon law in 1234.

The Zenith of the Medieval Papacy. Under Innocent III (reigned 1198–1216), the papacy reached the height of its prestige and power. He took advantage of an ongoing dispute over the election of a successor to Henry VI, king of Germany and Holy Roman emperor (reigned 1190–1197), to assert the principle of papal authority over the emperor and ultimately to place his own choice of successor on the throne. His zeal to extend Roman Christianity resulted in his calling the Fourth Crusade (1202–1204). Though he did not plan the Crusaders' sack of Constantinople in 1204 and the establishment of the Roman Church in that center of Eastern Christianity, he nonetheless welcomed this forced (and relatively brief) union of the two Christian Churches. He also instituted a crusade against the so-called Albigensian heretics, or Cathars (1209). Yet, at the same time he declared all-out war on these enemies of the Church, he gave his official approval to the monastic orders founded by Francis of Assisi (1210) and Dominic (1216), who had been mistrusted for their espousal of poverty and self-sacrifice in imitation of Jesus. Innocent also called the Fourth Lateran Council (1215), which established the dogma of transubstantiation (the belief that in Communion the bread and wine become the body and blood of Christ), and established fundamental rules of Christian practice and belief that are still followed today. The council included representatives from all regions to which Christianity had stretched, reinforcing the notion that the Church of Rome was indeed the Church Universal.

New Challenges. The seeds for a decline in papal prestige, however, may be seen in Innocent's triumphs. By the middle of the thirteenth century, as several heretical movements denied basic tenets of Church theology, a new generation of reformers were criticizing the corruption of Church officeholders and calling for a return to the poverty and piety of the Franciscans and Dominicans. Furthermore, the involvement of Innocent's successors in secular politics weakened the papacy. In 1303 Pope Boniface VIII attempted to end a war between France and the Holy Roman Empire through an agreement that restated the Pope's supremacy to all secular rulers and made the emperor overlord to all the kings of Europe. Philip IV (the Fair) of France (reigned 1285–1314)—who had been at odds with the Pope before—retaliated by launching a mission to undermine the papacy in Italy. Demonstrating the relative hollowness of the Pope's claim to secular supremacy, one of Philip's councillors and a member of a powerful Italian family kidnapped Boniface, physically abused him, and held him captive for two days. Boniface died soon after, and the prestige of the papacy was severely damaged.

The Avignon Papacy. In 1309 Pope Clement V (reigned 1305–1314), who was English by birth but brought up in France, sought to assuage the anger of Philip IV, who was calling for the posthumous trial of Boniface on charges that included heresy and fornication, by moving the papal seat to Avignon in France. From that time until Pope Gregory XI (reigned 1370–1378) moved the papacy back to Rome in 1377, all seven new Popes and 111 of 134 new cardinals were French, and the power exerted by Philip and his successors served to limit the temporal power of the papacy—as well as increasing French power within the Church of Rome.

Attacks on the Papacy. During this time the papacy also came under fire from intellectuals within and without religious orders. In *Il convivio* (The Banquet, circa 1304–1307) and *De monarchia* (On Monarchy, circa 1313) Dante blamed political chaos in Italy on papal interference in secular government and argued that the Pope should confine his interest to spiritual matters. A few years later his fellow

Italian, philosopher Marsilius of Padua, completed his *Defensor Pacis* (Defender of the Peace, 1324) in which he contended that the Pope had no authority in secular affairs and that his spiritual authority must be subordinated to that of temporal rulers. In his three-part *Dialogus de Potestate Papae* (Dialogue on the Power of the Pope, 1332–1346) and other works, William of Ockham, a member of the Franciscan order, questioned the doctrine of papal infallibility in religious as well as secular matters.

The Religion of the Common People. While politicians and intellectuals attacked the papacy, however, most medieval Christians remained firm in their devotion to the Church and its leaders throughout the first half of the fourteenth century. A large number of parish churches were built during this period, and many popular prayers, hymns, and carols also date to this time. Moreover, the Church earned the loyalty of its communicants by reforming and reorganizing its administration, cracking down on clerical excesses, and founding many almshouses and hospitals. It also expanded its missionary activities, sending representatives as far away as China. Despite these positive achievements, however, the removal of the papacy to Avignon and criticism of its claims to supremacy in all secular and ecclesiastical affairs damaged the prestige of the papacy and lay the groundwork for the division of the Church during the sixteenth century.

Sources:

Adriaan H. Bredero, *Christendom and Christianity in the Middle Ages: The Relations Between Religion, Church, and Society*, translated by Reinder Bruinsma (Grand Rapids, Mich.: Eerdmans, 1994).

F. Donald Logan, ed., *A History of the Medieval Church: An Introduction* (London & New York: Routledge, 1999).

R. W. Southern, *Western Society and the Church in the Middle Ages* (Harmondsworth, U.K.: Penguin, 1970).

Walter Ullmann, *The Growth of Papal Government in the Middle Ages. A Study in the Ideological Relation of Clerical to Lay Power* (London: Methuen, 1955).

Ullmann, *A Short History of the Papacy in the Middle Ages* (London: Methuen, 1972).

CANON LAW

Defining "Canon Law." Beginning in the second century and particularly after Christianity became legal in the Roman Empire (313), Christian leaders strove to define what it meant to be a Christian (theology and doctrine), how Christianity should be practiced (piety), and how Christians should think and behave (morality). The result was the production of a large number of provisions, or canons, by synods and Popes whose intentions were to resolve emerging difficulties in defining and living a Christian life. The body of documents and precedents that evolved became known as *canon law,* a term that did not come into use until the beginning of the twelfth century, when effective attempts were made to develop a clear collection of these laws. Medieval canon law was an evolving series of texts incorporating Greek, Germanic, and Roman legal principles. Canon law has been systematized since the Middle Ages, and it remains the law code of the Roman Catholic Church.

Canon Law and Eleventh-Century Reform. For centuries in the Middle Ages, little attempt was made to extract the general principles underlying canon law or to regularize the laws currently in effect. Decrees from ancient and medieval Church councils, papal letters, and episcopal statutes were collected so they could be consulted for guidance when similar situations recurred. By the eleventh century, however, the number of texts had grown unwieldy, and there was a need for a clear set of directives. Reformers of that time, such as Pope Gregory VII and his followers, faced an heterogeneous mass of precedents as they tried to deal with fundamental questions about the structuring of Christian society and the discipline that was to be observed within the Church. One of their pressing tasks was to increase this mass of precedents, so as to have at their disposal all possible solutions to the problems that faced them and to try to discern coherence among them. At the same time, the University of Bologna had just revived the study of Roman law, which was far more structured than Church law because of Emperor Justinian's sixth-century systematization, the *Corpus juris civilis.* Roman law provided an example of what could be done, and circumstances in the eleventh and twelfth centuries provided the necessity for doing it.

Gratian's *Decretum*. Gratian was a Benedictine monk who taught canon law at the University of Bologna in the 1130s. Apparently frustrated by the lack of a synthetic reference for canon law, he set out to compile one himself. The result was the *Concordia Discordantium Canonum* (The Harmonizing of Discordant Canons), which became commonly known as Gratian's *Decretum* (Decrees), published around 1140. The *Decretum* was designed to be a general treatise on canon law with insertions of authoritative texts relevant to various topics. From the mass of earlier canons, he selected only those then in force, ignoring those that were no longer commonly used, had been revoked, or were not generally applicable. He also expanded on the principles underlying the law. Although it was not an official compilation, it was for all practical purposes accepted as the fundamental text of Church law and taught as such in the universities throughout the Middle Ages. There were several reasons for its appeal and influence. While the *Decretum* was incomplete, it was far more systematic than any preceding collection. It provided a starting point for the generations of canon lawyers who later developed more comprehensive and better organized codes. Finally, Gratian's work made plausible the view that there was, in Christian society, a supreme court to which everyone might appeal for justice. This court, of course, was the papacy, a view that supported the claims of twelfth- and thirteenth-century Church leaders.

Building on Gratian: Later Canonists. The papacy took up with enthusiasm the function that Gratian and other canonists outlined for it. From the 1160s to the end of the Middle Ages and beyond, the papal court functioned as the supreme court of Christendom and, in doing so, provided the most influential model of what came to be regarded as

A monk presenting Pope Gregory IX the completed manuscript for his compilation of canon law; illumination from a thirteenth-century copy of Gregory's *Decretals* (Universitatsbibliothek, Salzburg)

the rule of law. In its efforts to Christianize all aspects of society, the papacy also produced the bulk of what is still European family, testamentary, and corporation law. Later influential additions were made by St. Raymond of Pennafort and promulgated by Pope Gregory IX in 1234 as the *Liber Extravagantium* (Book of Outside or Additional Materials), more commonly known as Gregory's *Decretals*. Although Gregory did not wish to supplant Gratian, his *Decretals* eventually did. According to *The Catholic Encyclopedia*, the *Decretals* were "composed in great part of specific decisions, represented in fact a more advanced state of law; furthermore, the collection was sufficiently extensive to touch almost every matter, and could serve as a basis for a complete course of instruction."

The Fourth Lateran Council. Probably the most influential Church council during the Middle Ages was the Fourth Lateran Council, called by Pope Innocent III in November 1215. In canon law texts the council is known simply as "the Great Council," suggesting its influence on medieval canon law. The Fourth Lateran passed eighty decrees (canons) clarifying and codifying key aspects of theology, Church management, and Church reform. Its ordinances on marriage continue to guide some Christian churches.

Other Decretals. Most medieval popes after Gregory published updates of the *Decretals*, and Boniface VIII in 1298 and John XXII in 1317 produced other collections of

canon law. In 1500 canonist John Chapuis edited the previous collections and added to them subsequent papal decretals. These works together are what came to be called the *Corpus Juris Canonici* or Body of Canon Law.

Methods of Interpretation (Commentaries). Medieval scholars working with canon law relied on precedents that they analyzed following a set system. The written product of these analyses were books known as *commentaries*. Essentially commentaries are notes between the lines or in the margins of texts. These notes cite the responses of other authorities to the claims made in the text. Sometimes medieval scholars produced commentaries on commentaries, with the actual text taking perhaps a quarter of the page and the layers of commentaries filling the remaining space. By the thirteenth century, canon law was divided into a series of categories—for example, universal law, particular law, common law, and special law. Each law in each of the many categories was analyzed according to a triple method of exposition: historical, philosophical, and practical. The historical commentary focused on the source and evolution of customs suggested by the law; the philosophical interpretation explained the law in light of its legal and theological principles; and the practical analysis considered the ways the law could be applied. Through development of codes of canon law, especially the commentaries on them, canon law became a subject of study that could take decades to master.

THE FOURTH LATERAN COUNCIL

The breadth of the topics covered at the Fourth Lateran Council in 1215 is suggested in the following summary of some of the canons it issued:

Canon 1: Statement of the basic doctrines of the Catholic faith and the dogma of Transubstantiation.

Canon 3: Procedures and penalties to be used against heretics and their protectors.

Canon 5: Proclamation of papal primacy as recognized since antiquity. The order of primacy after the Pope is the bishops of Constantinople, Alexandria, Antioch, and Jerusalem.

Canon 8: Procedures to be used in accusations against churchmen.

Canons 14-17: Legislation against inappropriate behavior of the clergy.

Canon 21: Requirement that every parishioner make a yearly confession to his or her parish priest.

Canons 23–30: Regulation of ecclesiastical elections and the provision of benefices and other ecclesiastical properties.

Canons 78-79: Requirements that Jews and Moslems wear a special dress to distinguish themselves from Christians and that Christian princes must take strict measures to prevent blasphemies against Jesus Christ.

Universities and Canon Law. Because years of training were necessary to comprehend canon law and the elaborate methods of interpreting it, the growth of canon law and the medieval universities toward the end of the twelfth century went hand in hand. In the fledgling universities, the faculty of canon law was to become an important fixture and shaped itself around the study of Gratian and Gregory's works. This process produced the new figure of the canon lawyer, who made it his task to define the procedures and legal doctrines by which the bishops' and papal courts were to operate and become a model for the ubiquitous ecclesiastical tribunals that were called into being across Europe. The canon lawyer's job was to train people in the necessary grammatical, logical, and juridical techniques to resolve contradictions in sources and to isolate general principles that, after imposing a certain coherence on the records of past legislative activity in the Church, also set out the conditions under which such an activity might occur henceforth. Universities such as Paris and Bologna gained reputations for their canon law faculties that endured long after the Middle Ages.

Sources:

Harold J. Berman, *Law and Revolution: The Formation of the Western Legal Tradition* (Cambridge, Mass.: Harvard University Press, 1983).

Stephan Kuttner, *Studies in the History of Medieval Canon Law* (Brookfield, Vt.: Variorum, 1990).

Richard W. Southern, *Scholastic Humanism and the Unification of Europe*, volume 1: *Foundations* (Oxford & Cambridge, Mass.: Blackwell, 1995).

Brian Tierney, *Religion, Law, and the Growth of Constitutional Thought, 1150–1650* (New York: Cambridge University Press, 1982).

CHURCH AND STATE: ALLIES OR OPPONENTS?

Feudal Overlords. During the Middle Ages, the Church fought to establish and maintain its autonomy, while secular rulers wanted to treat Church officials in the same way as members of the nobility. Since the Church had substantial holdings in western Europe, the income from them was a considerable fortune for whomever had control over them. Nobles held their lands and titles at the pleasure of the king, who could take both away if a liege lord displeased him. Thus, kings maintained that they, not the Church, should be able to appoint bishops and abbots and to determine what land should be allotted to them.

The Role of the Holy Roman Empire. By the ninth century the Holy Roman emperors had established themselves as the "protectors" of the Church, a role that gave them extraordinary power over both the bishops of the empire and the papacy itself. In 1046, in fact, Emperor Henry III (reigned 1039–1056) had resolved a dispute over papal succession by deposing three rival claimants and placing his own choice, Clement III, on the papal throne. Later in the century, however, Pope Leo IX (reigned 1049–1054) began a campaign to establish papal autonomy, and in 1059 Pope Nicholas II (reigned 1059–1061) asserted the right of the pope, not the emperor, to elect cardinals.

The Investiture Controversy. When the great church reformer Hildebrand became Pope Gregory VII in 1073, he began a crusade to free the Church from secular control, but he underestimated the power of the emperor and the German bishops he controlled. His prohibition of simony (the buying and selling of Church offices) and clerical marriages in 1074 had already angered German bishops and priests when Gregory decreed at the Lenten Synod of 1075 that no lay person should henceforth have the right of ecclesiastical investiture (conferring a Church office). When Emperor Henry IV (reigned 1056–1106) ignored Gregory's order and continued to appoint German and Italian bishops, Gregory threatened him with excommunication and the loss of his throne in December 1075. Instead of backing down, Henry staged a show of strength. In January 1076 twenty-six bishops gathered at the Diet of Worms in Germany and deposed Gregory from the papacy on the grounds of supposed irregularities in his election. Gregory then excommunicated Henry and freed his subjects from their oath of allegiance to him, effectively deposing him as emperor. By October support for Henry had eroded, and the princes of the empire gave him an ultimatum: apologize to the Pope or lose the crown.

The Investiture Controversy: (top) Pope Gregory VII (right) being driven from Rome by a soldier of Holy Roman Emperor Henry IV (left), who appointed Clement III (center) as antipope; (bottom) Gregory's exile and death in Salerno; illumination from a twelfth-century manuscript for Otto of Freising's account of the controversy (Üniversitats Bibliothek, Jena)

Henry's Penance. In January 1077 Henry surprised everyone by arriving at the Castle of Canossa, where Gregory was staying, and standing for three days in the snow barefoot and dressed in penitential garb. (Despite romanticized depictions of this event, the idea that he stood shoeless in the snow for three days is an exaggeration.) Impressed by Henry's humbling himself, Gregory lifted his excommunication. Henry, however, had made no concessions on the investiture issue and the battle of wills continued.

The Antipope. Gregory's German supporters decided to ignore the so-called reconciliation between emperor and Pope, and in March 1077 they elected a new emperor, Rudolf of Rheinland, sparking a civil war. In 1080 Henry told Gregory that unless he excommunicated Rudolf, Henry would depose him and replace him with an antipope. Gregory responded by excommunicating and deposing Henry for a second time and repeating his ban on lay investiture. Many of the Pope's supporters, however, felt this excommunication was unjustified, and the balance of power shifted decisively in Henry's favor. At the Synod of Brixen in June 1080, the bishops who supported Henry deposed and excommunicated Gregory, as well as electing Guilbert, Archbishop of Ravenna, Pope Clement III. After Rudolf was slain in battle the following October, Henry was free to follow through on his threat to install an antipope in Rome. Beginning in 1081 he attacked Rome four times, finally taking control of the city in 1084 and making Clement pope. Gregory fled the city and died in exile the following year. Gregory's supporters rallied and managed to elect a new Pope, Victor III (reigned 1086–1087), who

was too weak to force a resolution to the investiture controversy between the empire and the papacy.

The Conflict in England. At roughly the same time as Gregory was trying to impose his will on Henry, similar issues were causing contention in England. After William I (the Conqueror) invaded England in 1066, he set out to take charge of the English Church and lessen the influence of the Pope among his subjects. In 1070 William appointed one of his trusted advisers, the Italian prelate Lanfranc, to the powerful post of archbishop of Canterbury and proclaimed that he owned no fealty to the Pope. When Gregory objected, William decreed that England would recognize no pope without the king's consent and that no English noble or royal official could be excommunicated. Together Lanfranc and William instituted major reforms in the English Church, but they incurred the displeasure of Rome by doing so without direction or sanction from the Pope. After Lanfranc died in 1089, the Conqueror's son, William II (Rufus), did not appoint a successor for several years, during which he appropriated the revenues of archbishopric lands for crown use. In 1093 he named Anselm of Bec, in Normandy, archbishop of Canterbury, expecting that Anselm, like his fellow Norman, Lanfranc, would support the crown in opposition to the Pope. Anselm, however, did homage to William for the temporal aspects of the office but insisted on investiture from Pope Urban II (reigned 1088–1099). He also demanded that William recognize Urban as rightful Pope against the antipope Clement III. William reluctantly agreed, and over the next few years relations between the king and archbishop worsened until 1097, when Anselm went into exile in France. He

The dispute between Henry II of England and Thomas Becket, Archbishop of Canterbury; illumination from a medieval manuscript for *Fragments d'une vie de St. Thomas* (Librarie de Firmin, Didot, Paris)

returned to England when Henry I took the throne in 1100 but fled into exile almost immediately after Henry insisted that he, not the Pope, should invest Anselm as archbishop. The dispute was settled at the Synod of Westminster in 1107, when Henry gave up the right of investiture in return for the right to supervise the election of the archbishop and to receive homage for the secular aspects of the office before the investiture could take place.

The Conflict in France. In France Philip I (reigned 1059–1108) openly sold Church offices and invested bishops and abbots, but Urban II gained an advantage in France, and his successor Paschal II (reigned 1099–1118) was able to bring about a resolution. In 1094, after Philip repudiated his first wife and married the wife of a vassal, Urban excommunicated Philip. When Philip's son, who became King Louis VI in 1108, took over the administration of the kingdom in 1104, he and Paschal negotiated a reconciliation that included an agreement that French kings would no longer appoint or invest bishops and abbots but would have the right to ratify their appointments and to exact an oath of temporal fealty from them.

The Empire Strikes Back. Despite its successes in France and England, the papacy remained at odds with the Holy Roman Empire. Under Urban, the Church gradually eroded support for the antipope, and when Clement died in 1100 Henry IV seemed ready to recognize Urban's successor, Paschal II. When Henry refused once again to renounce the right of investiture, however, Paschal renewed his excommunication—and when the emperor's successor to the throne of Germany, Henry V (reigned 1106–1125), continued to assert the right of investiture, Paschal excommunicated him in 1108. Three years later, as Henry led a strong army toward Rome, Paschal offered a compromise in which the German clergy would give up all their lands and privileges to the crown if Henry would

renounce investiture. Henry agreed at first, but after a storm of protest from the German prices, he insisted that Paschal not only restore his right of investiture but also crown him Holy Roman Emperor. When Paschal refused, Henry kidnapped and imprisoned him and thirteen cardinals. After two months of imprisonment, Paschal agreed to Henry's demands. The following year, however, he renewed the ban on lay investiture, leading to more conflict and excommunication. In 1119 Henry even tried appointing another antipope but had less success than his father garnering the bishops' support. Finally in 1122 Henry and Pope Calistus (reigned 1119–1124) agreed to the Concordat of Worms, which was modeled on the agreement reached between the Pope and Henry I of England at the Synod of Westminster in 1107.

Henry II and Thomas Becket. The resolution of the investiture controversy did not end all conflict between the Church and secular rulers. Kings continued to involve themselves in ecclesiastical affairs and tried in other ways to exert control over Church property and officials. The best-known medieval example of such attempts is probably the quarrel that arose between Henry II of England (reigned 1154–1189) and his one-time friend Thomas Becket. In 1162 Henry was able to have Becket, who had served the king ably and loyally as chancellor since 1155, elected archbishop of Canterbury. Henry hoped that he and Becket would run the English Church as William I and Lanfranc had done in their day, but once Becket became archbishop, he placed loyalty to the Pope over loyalty to his king in regard to the rights of the Church while acknowledging the king's sovereignty in temporal matters.

The "Criminous Clerks" Issue. The tension between the two friends reached crisis point in 1163, when Henry sought to redress the unequal punishment of clerics who broke civil laws. In western Europe these "criminous clerks" were by tradition tried in Church, rather than secular, courts and were generally given punishments far less severe than laymen were given for similar crimes. He demanded that once a cleric was found guilty in a Church court, he should be sent to a royal court for sentencing. Becket took the position of the papacy, which asserted that only the Church had the right to try and punish clerks in major orders. The following January Henry included his position in the Constitutions of Clarendon, which also banned the excommunication of royal officials, forbade clerics from appealing to the Pope without the king's permission, and gave the king the right to revenues from vacant sees—all provisions that were contrary to Church law. Becket verbally agreed to the constitutions but later revoked it and appealed to Pope Alexander III (reigned 1159–1181).

Exile and Return. Henry responded by summoning Becket to trial on the charge that he had misused royal funds while chancellor, and the archbishop fled to France. After six years of exile, Becket and Henry were reconciled without resolving any of the issues that had divided them. Once back in England, Becket continued to anger Henry by taking the side of the Church and suspending bishops

THE DEATH OF THOMAS BECKET

Accounts of Becket's death circulated throughout Europe soon after his murder in 1170. Writing a generation later, clergyman-historian William of Newburgh offered a more balanced treatment of Becket and Henry II than any of their contemporaries.

The bishops . . . being suspended, at the insistence of the venerable Thomas, from all episcopal functions, by the authority if the apostolic see, the king was exasperated by the complaints of some of them, and grew angry and indignant beyond measure, and losing the mastery of himself, in the heat of his exuberant passion, from the abundance of his perturbed spirit, poured forth the language of indiscretion. On which, four of the bystanders, men of noble race and renowned in arms, wrought themselves up to the commission of iniquity through zeal for their earthly master; and leaving the royal presence, and crossing the sea, with as much haste as if posting to a solemn banquet, and urged on by the fury they had imbibed, they arrived at Canterbury on the fifth day after Christmas, where they found the venerable archbishop occupied in the celebration of that holy festival with religious joy. Proceeding to him just as he had dined, and was sitting with certain honourable personages, omitting even to salute him, and holding forth the terror of the king's name, they commanded (rather than asked, or admonished him) forthwith to remit the suspension of the prelates who had obeyed the king's pleasure, to whose contempt and disgrace this act redounded. On his replying that the sentence of a higher power was not to be abrogated by an inferior one, and that it was not his concern to pardon persons suspended not by himself, but by the Roman pontiff, they had recourse to violent threats. Undismayed at these words, though uttered by men raging and extremely exasperated, he spoke with singular freedom and confidence. In consequence, becoming more enraged than before, they hastily retired, and bringing their arms, (for they had entered without them,) they prepared themselves, with loud clamour and indignation, for the commission of a most atrocious crime. The venerable prelate was persuaded by his friends to avoid the madness of these furious savages, by retiring into the holy church. When, from his determination to brave every danger, he did not acquiesce, on the forcible and tumultuous approach of his enemies, he was at length dragged by the friendly violence of his associates to the protection of the holy church. The monks were solemnly chanting vespers to Almighty God, as he entered the sacred temple of Christ, shortly to become an evening sacrifice. The servants of Satan pursued, having neither respect as Christians to his holy order, nor to the sacred place, or season; but attacking the dignified prelate as he stood in prayer before the holy altar, even during the festival of Christmas, these truly nefarious Christians most inhumanly murdered him. Having done the deed, and retiring as if triumphant, they departed with unhallowed joy. Recollecting, however, that perhaps the transaction might displease the person in whose behalf they had been so zealous, they retired to the northern parts of England, waiting until they could fully discover the disposition of their monarch towards them.

Source: William of Newburgh, *History, Book II* (circa 1200), quoted in *The Church Historians of England*, volume 4, part 2, translated by Joseph Stevenson (London: Seeley, 1856), pp. 478–481.

who disagreed with him. Finally, Henry made an angry statement that was misconstrued by four knights. Thinking to please the king, they murdered Becket in Canterbury Cathedral on 29 December 1170.

Sainthood and Resolution. Almost immediately, people began making pilgrimages to Becket's grave, and Alexander III canonized him in 1173. To make amends with the Pope, Henry accepted a compromise that allowed royal courts to try clerics on violations of forestry laws and gave Church courts jurisdiction over all their other crimes, but he did not back down on any of the other provisions of the Constitutions of Clarendon. Finally, after he did penance at Canterbury and allowed the monks there to scourge him, Henry received absolution. While medieval Christians tended to consider Thomas a martyr and Henry the villain, some modern historians have praised Henry's attempts at reforming the English legal system and accused Becket of fanaticism.

Sources:

Uta-Renate Blumenthal, *The Investiture Controversy: Church and Monarchy from the Ninth to the Twelfth Century* (Philadelphia: University of Pennsylvania Press, 1988).

David Knowles, *Thomas Becket* (Stanford: Stanford University Press, 1971).

Colin Morris, *The Papal Monarchy: The Western Church from 1050 to 1250* (New York: Oxford University Press, 1989).

Ian S. Robinson, *The Papacy, 1073–1198: Continuity and Innovation* (Cambridge & New York: Cambridge University Press, 1990).

Jane E. Sayers, *Innocent III: Leader of Europe, 1198–1216* (London & New York: Longman, 1994).

Walter Ullmann, *A Short History of the Papacy in the Middle Ages* (London: Methuen, 1972).

CHURCH REFORM

A Corrupt Medieval Church? One of the most common modern clichés about the medieval Church is that it was corrupt and that its unwillingness to institute reforms resulted in the division of Christendom into separate Christian Churches during the sixteenth century. There are many historical weaknesses with this argument. It is based on the idea that the Church had the power to control the behavior of every bishop, cleric, and monk throughout Christendom, and it overlooks the many reform movements that punctuated medieval Church history. Certainly medieval clergymen felt at various times that the Church was not living up to its mission or aspirations, but one of the primary reasons why reformers had such a difficult time instituting reform were the demands that the laity placed on clergy and the ways the laity expressed their religious devotion. Ideally the Church was a spiritual body, but it inhabited the temporal world. Secular rulers often exercised more control over bishops and abbots than the Pope was able to exert. Clergymen were dependent on their parishioners for food, and communities demanded relief, care, and protection by the clerical institutions in their midst. Given the close interaction of the clergy and the laity on the local level, it would have been impossible for the medieval Church to escape the influence of worldly concerns.

Francis of Assisi presenting the rule for the new Franciscan order to Pope Innocent III; from a fresco attributed to Giotto in the Upper Church of Assisi

Bishops and Rulers. While the medieval bishop enjoyed relative independence from his often-distant ecclesiastical superiors, the same could not be said of his relationship to his secular lord. Charlemagne in the eighth and ninth centuries, and the German rulers thereafter relied on clergymen to supply their leading civil servants. In fact, Henry the Fowler, the duke-king of Saxony (912–936) agreed to lead a federation of German nobles only if he was given control over the Church throughout Germany. He was granted his request. Such broad powers led to the creation in Germany of "prince-bishops," churchmen who combined the responsibilities and prerogatives of a bishop and a prince of the Holy Roman Empire and who were always of the highest noble blood. Although the empire was the most

extreme example, similar demands and compromises occurred throughout Europe. A bishop usually was a trusted subject of his sovereign and a member of the nobility. Because of their interest in appointing churchmen with the greatest administrative skills (who were not necessarily the most pious individuals), lords in Spain, France, England, and elsewhere were tempted to intervene in Church affairs. In fact, by the beginning of the eleventh century, it was extremely unusual for someone to become bishop against the will of his secular ruler. Indeed, his appointment was frequently dictated by political rather than spiritual merits. Although many of the bishops so selected were worthy and spiritual men, reform-minded clergy thought that these bishops were compromised by the method of their selection; it was easy to level against them the accusation that they had been chosen by favoritism or had purchased their offices outright.

Church Autonomy. By the late tenth century, it was obvious to many that the Church could not effectively retain its spiritual dimension if it continued to be so closely involved in temporal affairs. Reformers pointed to widespread simony (the purchase or sale of Church offices or preferments), clerical marriage, and clerical concubinage and connected these abuses to Church involvement in temporal affairs and the excessive meddling of the laity in Church business. Critical reflection on the experience of the Roman Empire led to a sustained effort to reform the Church or, as reformers such as Cardinal Hildebrand (later Pope Gregory VII) put it, to recover its liberty. Although the reformers who gathered around Pope Gregory VII and others like him were considered extreme, the desire to reform, or free, the Church colored many aspects of European life from the eleventh century onward. By the eleventh century, the struggle for the liberty and renewal of the Church had brought together the papacy and the mass of Christians. The first was interested particularly in freeing the Church from the domination of lay lords, while the laity was more interested in a fitter clergy. Their agendas had enough in common to ensure some popular support for the fight that the papacy was waging. When the papacy became more and more involved in attempts to control secular political events, however, its alliance with the lay population ended and even became hostile. Popular sentiment increasingly focused on ethical and mystical concerns that challenged a political papacy.

Problems with Church Offices. By the year 1000, it seemed clear to many that the personal unworthiness of many clerics had reached a crisis point and that the Church had reached an even more serious institutional crisis. Theoretically, the Church hierarchy was divided into degrees, each subordinate to the other; the Pope supervised archbishops, who supervised bishops, who supervised clerics. In effect, however, autonomy had become the rule, and the practice of subordination had been lost. In practice, a bishop within his diocese had no one to supervise him and check his actions. His decisions might eventually be appealed to the archbishop, but that could be done only at meetings of all the bishops, which, in the best of cases, only took place once a year. The process was extremely cumbersome, and appeals—if they were heard—could go on for years. Even more difficult to combat was the method by which many clergymen were appointed to their offices. As Christianity had expanded throughout Europe in the early Middle Ages, it had relied on secular lords to provide land and the other goods necessary to support parishes, monasteries, and eventually bishoprics. Pious laity were willing to endow these institutions but often on the condition that they have some say in running them. These "family churches" essentially became the private property of a noble house, which reserved lucrative appointments for family members. Attempts at reform ran directly into the legiti-

mate legal rights of such families, and even pious secular lords were often hesitant to abandon rights and privileges that might prove vital to their descendants. Moreover, bishops and abbots of larger monasteries often were required to supply fighting men to the secular lords of the region, and sometimes even the clergy acted as warriors, such as Bishop Turpin in the eleventh-century *Song of Roland.* If reform were to take place in these establishments, it would require a redefinition of the clergy's role in society, and that change was resisted in part by clergy and laity alike.

Reform in Bishoprics and Monasteries. Many of the reform movements that began in Christendom at large during the eleventh century had their roots in monastic reform movements that arose during the tenth century. Particularly influential in this regard was the monastery at Cluny in eastern France. Monastic movements had several key components that reformers attempted to apply to the Church as a whole. The first was the belief that the monastic life of contemplation and distance from worldly concerns was the most perfect Christian life; because clergymen needed to divorce themselves from secular preoccupations, sex and personal attachments, such as wives and concubines, were seen as especially dangerous. The second was the conviction that the Church, as Christ's representative on earth, is superior to any secular power. As such, no clergyman—bishop, abbot, pope, or priest—should be controlled by a lay lord, because all clergymen were superior to all laity by dint of their sacred vows and the ability to transmit divine grace through the sacraments. Finally, the example of monastic reform demonstrated that changes are most effectively and quickly made through regulation from above. In the case of monastic reform, it led to greater centralization in the new religious orders such as the Cluniacs and Cistercians, and in the case of clerical reform in general it meant that the Pope should be the source of guidance and authority. Although these ideas remained principles instead of explicitly formulated doctrine, they guided reform movements throughout the rest of the Middle Ages and into the sixteenth and seventeenth centuries.

Reforming the Ministry. At the same time that some clergymen moved to separate the Church from secular governments, the medieval laity also called for increased attention to the needs of individual Christians. By the twelfth century there were more and more strident complaints about poor clerical behavior. Lay people criticized clerical drunkenness, avarice, sexual insatiability, ignorance of Christian teachings, and unwillingness or inability to perform the sacraments or even preach. Responding to these complaints and acting on their religious beliefs, Church leaders called for reform in the daily lives of the clergy. The Fourth Lateran Council (1215), in particular, passed wide-ranging decrees on these subjects. The council drew up guidelines on the degree of literacy required of a priest; it made plans for how frequently he had to preach and administer the sacraments; and it made regulations on how he should conduct himself in public and private. It even passed decrees about what sort of housekeeper a priest could have. One difficulty facing all Church reformers, however, was the lack of a strong infrastructure to put these decrees into effect; they relied on an individual reforming bishop or abbot for most effective change. These authorities conducted visitations, surveys of the churches, monasteries, and parishes for which they were responsible. Visiting an entire bishopric could be a lengthy process, and a diligent bishop examined institutions and individuals in detail. A bishop was commended for his zeal if he were able to visit most major establishments in his dioceses every two years, a timetable suggesting that even the most reform-minded bishop had difficulty in implementing far-reaching changes.

The Mendicants. One of the most influential reform movements of the Middle Ages was the mendicant reform led by Saints Dominic and Francis. The word *mendicant* means beggar, and the mendicant friars initially insisted on living from the proceeds of begging and owning no property, so that they could avoid the entanglements created when other orders became dependent on secular rulers for lands and income. In addition, mendicant orders responded to the increased need for an active ministry, particularly in growing market towns. St. Francis of Assisi (1181–1226) represents this active aspect of the mendicant movement. The son of a rich merchant, he renounced all his worldly goods in order to care for the sick, repair churches, and preach where he could. Once he received approval from Pope Innocent III in 1210, he began to organize his followers into a group of "friars" (from the Latin word *fratres,* which means brothers). Francis's first guidelines (known as a Rule) for his order stressed poverty, simplicity, preaching, and service, but in 1223 he rewrote the Rule somewhat to provide a more-structured training and hierarchy for the extraordinary influx of new members. An important spiritual thinker, St. Francis also stressed the importance of education for his followers, especially as they were to preach and minister to the poor. By the thirteenth century some of Europe's greatest thinkers—including Bonaventure, John Peckham, and Roger Bacon—were Franciscans. Like other reform movements, however, the Franciscans had troubles of their own, many of which stemmed from the issue of property. Despite his earliest vows, even during his lifetime St. Francis had to accept some property for his friars. Like other religious orders, the Franciscans were granted land, buildings, pensions, and other worldly goods to support their ministry. By the middle of the thirteenth century Popes had to intervene in disputes within the Franciscans over these properties. These disagreements eventually led to a split within the order by the end of the century.

Poverty and Reform. In fact, the issue of property was at the heart of medieval Church reform. The clergy needed some property so that they could survive and effectively minister to their congregations. These needs were always in a precarious balance with the corruptive influence of prop-

REFORMING THE CLERGY

The following decrees from the Fourth Lateran Council (1215) suggest the sort of problems that faced Church reformers during the Middle Ages:

All clerics shall carefully abstain from drunkenness. Wherefore, let them accommodate the wine to themselves, and themselves to the wine. Nor shall anyone be encouraged to drink, for drunkenness banishes reason and incites to lust. We decree, therefore, that that abuse be absolutely abolished by which in some localities the drinkers bind themselves . . . to an equal portion of drink and he in their judgment is the hero of the day who outdrinks the others. Should anyone be culpable in this matter, unless he heeds the warning of the superior and makes suitable satisfaction, let him be suspended from his benefice or office.

We forbid hunting and fowling to all clerics; wherefore, let them not presume to keep dogs and birds for these purposes. . . .

Clerics shall not hold secular offices or engage in secular and, above all, dishonest pursuits. They shall not attend the performances of mimics and buffoons, or theatrical representations. They shall not visit taverns except in case of necessity, namely, when on a journey. They are forbidden to play games of chance or be present at them. They must have a becoming crown and tonsure and apply themselves diligently to the study of the divine offices and other useful subjects. Their garments must be worn clasped at the top and neither too short nor too long. They are not to use red or green garments or curiously sewed together gloves, or beak-shaped shoes or gilded bridles, saddles, pectoral ornaments (for horses), spurs, or anything else indicative of superfluity. At the divine office in the church they are not to wear *cappas* [capes with hoods] with long sleeves, and priests and dignitaries may not wear them elsewhere except in case of danger when circumstances should require a change of outer garments. Buckles may under no condition be worn, nor sashes having ornaments of gold or silver, nor rings, unless it be in keeping with the dignity of their office. All bishops must use in public and in the church outer garments made of linen, except those who are monks, in which case they must wear the habit of their order; in public they must not appear with open mantles, but these must be clasped either on the back of the neck or on the bosom.

Source: H. J. Schroeder, *Disciplinary Decrees of the General Councils: Text, Translation and Commentary* (St. Louis: Herder, 1937), canons 15 and 16; from the Internet Medieval Sourcebook <http://www.fordham.edu/halsall/source/lat4-select.html>.

erty, particularly the danger that the clergy might focus too much on worldly concerns. For this reason, many medieval reform movements attempted to distance themselves from property ownership. Their stress on poverty, however, placed them in an ambiguous relationship with the rest of society. Medieval society distinguished between the worthy and unworthy poor. Those who chose poverty for spiritual reasons were classified with the worthy and thus deserved aid from the rest of the Christian community. Yet, medieval society also tended to classify people on the basis of outward appearance. Kings and clergy did not wear luxurious fabrics just because they wanted to and could afford them; their subjects and congregations expected these displays. Moreover, assisting pious individuals was considered a good deed that could help assure a donor's place in heaven. For this reason successful reformers who practiced extreme poverty could find themselves deluged with gifts. Finally, by challenging the legitimacy of the Church holding property and by demanding clerical poverty, reformers threatened the entire infrastructure of the medieval Church and risked alienating many of their more materialistic colleagues. It is not surprising that some of the more-radical groups that insisted on extreme poverty, such as the Fratecelli, were excommunicated and prosecuted.

Sources:

Michael Frassetto, ed., *Medieval Purity and Piety: Essays on Medieval Clerical Celibacy and Religious Reform* (New York: Garland, 1998).

C. H. Lawrence, *The Friars: The Impact of the Early Mendicant Movement on Western Society* (London & New York: Longman, 1994).

Karl F. Morrison, *Tradition and Authority in the Western Church, 300–1140* (Princeton: Princeton University Press, 1969).

THE CRUSADES

The Religious Impetus. While political and economic motivations undeniably entered into the Crusades of the Middle Ages, they were motivated by religious ideals. The successive campaigns launched to recover the Holy Land of Jerusalem and the surrounding territories were viewed as holy wars against the Muslim "infidels" and fought for the glory of God and the good of all Christendom. The name "Crusader" refers to the emblem of the cross presented to Crusaders by papal legates, a badge signifying that its bearer was not a soldier of any earthly king, but of Christ. "God wills it," those present at the Council of Clermont in

Peter the Hermit leading troops on the First Crusade;
illumination from a fourteenth-century manuscript
for *Histoire Universelle* (British Library, London)

URBAN II CALLS FOR THE TROOPS

At the Council of Clermont in 1095, Pope Urban II gave a stirring speech designed to rouse Christian knights for a holy war against Muslim "infidels." Five versions of his speech survive. The following excerpt is from the version recorded by a monk called Fulcher of Chartres:

All who die by the way, whether by land or by sea, or in battle against the pagans, shall have immediate remission of sins. This I grant them through the power of God with which I am invested. O what a disgrace if such a despised and base race, which worships demons, should conquer a people which has the faith of omnipotent God and is made glorious with the name of Christ! With what reproaches will the Lord overwhelm us if you do not aid those who, with us, profess the Christian religion! Let those who have been accustomed unjustly to wage private warfare against the faithful now go against the infidels and end with victory this war which should have been begun long ago. Let those who for a long time, have been robbers, now become knights. Let those who have been fighting against their brothers and relatives now fight in a proper way against the barbarians. Let those who have been serving as mercenaries for small pay now obtain the eternal reward. Let those who have been wearing themselves out in both body and soul now work for a double honor. Behold! on this side will be the sorrowful and poor, on that, the rich; on this side, the enemies of the Lord, on that, his friends. Let those who go not put off the journey, but rent their lands and collect money for their expenses; and as soon as winter is over and spring comes, let hem eagerly set out on the way with God as their guide.

Source: Oliver J. Thatcher and Edgar Holmes McNeal, eds., *A Source Book for Medieval History* (New York: Scribners, 1905), pp. 516–517.

France declared in 1095, shortly before the First Crusade. This declaration, which became the Crusaders' battle cry, summarizes the medieval view of the Crusades as a divine undertaking.

The Islamic Threat. More than four hundred years before the First Crusade, the Muslims had begun a series of jihads, or holy wars, with the aim of spreading Islam to the entire world. In less than a century North Africa, Arabia, Persia, Sicily, and most of Spain had become part of the Islamic world. Europeans felt threatened by Islamic expansion, and Christian rhetoric portrayed the new invaders in unfavorable terms such as *pagans, infidels,* and *barbarians.* Europeans felt the Islamic threat even more keenly with the eleventh-century rise of the Seljuk Turks, who began to press westward into the Christian Byzantine Empire and who were less tolerant of Christian pilgrims to the Holy Land than their predecessors. When the Byzantine Emperor Alexius Comnenus sent an envoy to Pope Urban II requesting military aid against the Turks, the Pope did not hesitate to respond. Answering the emperor's call would help stop Islamic expansion, would place the holy

Anna Comnena (1083 – post-1148) was the daughter of the Byzantine Emperor Alexius I. Her account of the First Crusade and the Crusaders provides a realistic and unflattering account of the Crusader's motives.

Before he [Alexius I] had enjoyed even a short rest, he heard a report of the approach of innumerable Frankish armies. Now he dreaded their arrival for he knew their irresistible manner of attack, their unstable and mobile character and all the peculiar natural and concomitant characteristics which the Frank retains throughout; and he also knew that they were always agape for money, and seemed to disregard their truces readily for any reason that cropped up. For he had always heard this reported of them, and found it very true. However, he did not lose heart, but prepared himself in every way so that, when the occasion called, he would be ready for battle. And indeed the actual facts were far greater and more terrible than rumour made them. For the whole of the West and all the barbarian tribes which dwell between the further side of the Adriatic and the pillars of Heracles, had all migrated in a body and were marching into Asia through the intervening Europe, and were making the journey with all their household. The reason of this upheaval was more or less the following. A certain Frank, Peter by name, nicknamed Cucupeter [Peter of the Cowl], had gone to worship at the Holy Sepulchre and after suffering many things at the hands of the Turks and Saracens who were ravaging Asia, he got back to his own country with difficulty. But he was angry at having failed in his object, and wanted to undertake the same journey again. However, he saw that he ought not to make the journey to the Holy Sepulchre alone again, lest worse things befall him, so he worked out a cunning plan. This was to preach in all the Latin countries that "the voice of God bids me announce to all the Counts in France that they should all leave their homes and set out to worship at the Holy Sepul-

chre, and to endeavour wholeheartedly with hand and mind to deliver Jerusalem from the hand of the Hagarenes." And he really succeeded. For after inspiring the souls of all with this quasi-divine command he contrived to assemble the Franks from all sides, one after the other, with arms, horses and all the other paraphernalia of war. And they were all so zealous and eager that every highroad was full of them. And those Frankish soldiers were accompanied by an unarmed host more numerous than the sand or the stars, carrying palms and crosses on their shoulders; women and children, too, came away from their countries. And the sight of them was like many rivers streaming from all sides, and they were advancing towards us through Dacia generally with all their hosts. Now the coming of these many peoples was preceded by a locust which did not touch the wheat, but made a terrible attack on the vines. This was really a presage as the diviners of the time interpreted it, and meant that this enormous Frankish army would, when it came, refrain from interference in Christian affairs, but fall very heavily upon the barbarian Ishmaelites who were slaves to drunkenness, wine, and Dionysus. For this race is under the sway of Dionysus and Eros, rushes headlong into all kind of sexual intercourse, and is not circumcised either in the flesh or in their passions. It is nothing but a slave, nay triply enslaved, to the ills wrought by Aphrodite. For this reason they worship and adore Astarte and Ashtaroth too and value above all the image of the moon, and the golden figure of Hobar in their country. Now in these symbols Christianity was taken to be the corn because of its wineless and very nutritive qualities; in this manner the diviners interpreted the vines and the wheat. However let the matter of the prophecy rest.

Source: Anna Comnena, *The Alexiad,* edited and translated by Elizabeth A. Dawes (London: Kegan Paul, Trench, Trübner, 1928), pp. 248–249.

sites of Jerusalem back in Christian hands, and would perhaps heal the breach between the eastern and western Churches, which had separated in 1054. Urban II made a stirring speech on the subject at the Council of Clermont in 1095, and within a year the first Crusaders had arrived in the Holy Land.

Preaching the Crusades. Charismatic preachers and religious leaders traveled throughout Europe stirring up support for the eight Crusades, which continued intermittently until 1271, among nobles and peasants alike. Urban II's eloquent urging at Clermont, five versions of which were recorded by medieval historians, was the first example of such preaching. Urban commissioned many other preachers of the Crusade, notably the revered Peter the Hermit, who personally recruited and led one of the first eastward marches. Likewise, Pope Innocent III commissioned a popular priest named Foulques of Neuilly to preach the cause of the Fourth Crusade. The most influen-

tial preacher of any Crusade was St. Bernard, Abbot of Clairvaux, who through a series of fiery orations and tracts almost singlehandedly launched the Second Crusade. The German Emperor Conrad III, on hearing one of St. Bernard's sermons, was said to have wept and declared that Bernard's words came directly from God.

Personal Religious Motives. In addition to furthering the general good of Christendom, the Crusades provided an opportunity to individual believers seeking to express their devotion or to be purified of their sins. Pilgrimage to the Holy Land was a tradition dating back to the first centuries of the Christian faith, and many Crusaders took vows of pilgrimage along with their military vows. Indeed, one reason for the failure of the Second Crusade may have been the pious Louis VII's personal goal of pilgrimage. Against the wishes of his Crusader allies in Antioch he decided to press on to Jerusalem rather than fight in Asia Minor. Another personal motive for some Crusaders was the indulgence repeatedly promised by Popes. Urban II had declared that "all who die by the way, whether by land or by sea, or in battle against the pagans, shall have immediate remission of sins," and Innocent III extended the promise of indulgence to everyone assisting the Crusades, without the requirement of martyrdom.

Military Orders. Final evidence of the religious aspect of the Crusades is to be found in the military monastic orders that flourished in the Holy Land in the eleventh and twelfth centuries. One of the best known of these orders was the Knights Templar, founded in 1115. The group was dedicated to the protection of pilgrims and the Holy Land in general, and its members were required to take religious vows and follow a monastic rule laid out for them by Bernard of Clairvaux. Other significant orders were the Knights Hospitaler, or the Knights of St. John, who survived into later centuries as the modern Knights of Malta, and the Teutonic Knights of Germany. These crusading orders inspired similar movements in western Europe, such as the Knights of Santiago de Compostela, a Christian brotherhood dedicated to the reconquest of Moorish Spain.

Sources:

Francesco Gabrieli, ed., *Arab Historians of the Crusades,* translated by E. J. Costello (New York: Routledge, 1969).

C. Warren Hollister, *Medieval Europe: A Short History,* eighth edition (New York: McGraw-Hill, 1998).

Angus Konstam, *Atlas of Medieval Europe* (New York: Checkmark Books, 2000).

Jonathan Riley-Smith, ed., *The Oxford History of the Crusades* (New York: Oxford University Press, 1999).

Steven Runciman, *A History of the Crusades,* 3 volumes (Cambridge: Cambridge University Press, 1951–1954).

R. W. Southern, *Western Society and the Church in the Middle Ages* (Harmondsworth, U.K.: Penguin, 1970).

EARLY MEDIEVAL PHILOSOPHY: ANCIENT AND EARLY CHRISTIAN ROOTS

Ancient Roots. Textbooks and histories have often called the Early Middle Ages an age of Platonism. Yet, from the Carolingian Renaissance of the ninth century through the School of Chartres in the twelfth, other philosophical traditions—including Stoicism and Aristotelianism—were influential as well. For these reasons it is best to consider early medieval philosophy as a continuation of Greek and Roman philosophy.

Platonism. Not many of Plato's writings were known in the Middle Ages. In fact, the only Platonic dialogues available to western European scholars were the *Meno,* the *Phaedo,* and a part of the *Timaeus,* and they became available only in the twelfth century. While the *Meno* and the *Phaedo* were known in Paris, they do not seem to have been widely used. The *Timaeus* was studied with the aid of a commentary by the fourth-century Christian scholar Calcidius.

Neoplatonism. The teachings of Plato came to the medieval scholars of Western Europe largely through two diverse traditions of interpretation: the Neoplatonism of the Latin tradition in the thought of Augustine, Boethius, Cicero, and other Roman writers, and the Neoplatonism of the Greek tradition in the writings of the anonymous author known as Pseudo-Dionysius, who lived in Syria during the late fifth and early sixth centuries, as well as in the thought of the Greek Church Fathers Gregory of Nyssa (fourth century) and Maximus the Confessor (circa 580–662). The Greek tradition goes back to the fifth-century Greek Neoplatonist Proclus, while the Latin tradition has its roots in the third-century Neoplatonists Plotinus and Porphyry, who were part of an important intellectual circle in Rome. These two traditions came together in the thought of the Irish philosopher John Scottus Eriugena (circa 810 – circa 877). In the Neoplatonic system, the world and human life are part of a vast hierarchical structure. At the apex of the triangle is the super-transcendent One. Below the One is Intellect, from which the spirit, the mind, and all realities emanate down to particular material objects. This system involves a graded order of reality. For example, an animal has a lower degree of reality than a human. Capable of rising above base materiality by a process of purification and contemplation, a human can achieve a kind of union with pure thought and can contemplate, but not know, the One.

Stoicism. The Stoics divided philosophy into logic (including language study), physics (the study of natural things, including divinity), and ethics. Stoicism came directly to the medieval scholars of western Europe through Roman writers, especially Seneca and Cicero, as well as indirectly through early Christian writers, such as the Greek Church Fathers Clement of Alexandria and Origen in the late first and early second centuries and Gregory of Nyssa and Nemesius in the fourth century and the Latin Fathers Tertullian (third century), Lactantius (early fourth century), Jerome (late fourth century), Ambrose (late fourth century), and Augustine (early fifth century). The Roman Stoics were especially influential later, in the thirteenth century. Peter Abelard and Roger Bacon considered Seneca the greatest of all moralists, and both Seneca and Cicero had a deep influence on Thomas Aquinas. The teaching at the School of Chartres included elements of Stoicism as well as Platonism. Platonism and Christianity both held that the basic structure of reality was spiritual. That is, the human soul and God were spiritual substances and, as such, higher forms of reality than matter. Stoicism, however, held that the highest principle or world soul is corporeal. Yet, despite this major disparity between Stoicism and Christianity, medieval Christian thinkers managed to incorporate much of Stoic thought into their philosophical systems. Perhaps this synthesis was made possible because Plotinus had "spiritualized" certain forms of Stoicism and because late Stoicism included a recognition of some form of moral spirituality. It is amazing, however, that the Church never condemned Stoicism as a pagan philosophy and religion—as it did certain aspects of medieval Aristotelianism. Stoicism was absorbed into Christian thought slowly, over six hundred years, while

The earliest known depiction of St. Augustine,
in a fresco painted in the Lateran,
Rome, circa 600

most of Aristotelianism appeared virtually all at once between 1140 and 1260.

Assimilation of Stoic Thought. Stoicism has features that allowed it to be assimilated into medieval Christian thought. It preached internal liberation; what happened to one's physical being was relatively unimportant so long as one's mind was free to rise above misfortune and devote itself to knowledge and virtue. For this reason the Stoics taught that all human beings—male or female, aristocrat or slave—are fundamentally equal. The Stoics also believed that the entire development of the world was determined by a built-in Reason, and they had a doctrine of seminal reasons to explain the development of organisms from initial seeds. Much of this teaching was taken up in both pagan and Christian Neoplatonism. The main impact of Stoicism was in ethics and the debate over determinism and free will. The Stoics preached rational,

moral self-control through the exercise of right or correct reason and promulgated the doctrine that the primary precepts or norms of a moral natural law are implanted in every human being. That is, while positive laws vary from one country to another and from one people to another, basic human values and rights are the same for all humans because they share a common humanity. These ideas were attractive to medieval Christian thinkers and had a major influence on medieval ethical and political theory.

Aristotelianism. Though most of the works of Aristotle did not become available in western Europe until after 1120 and did not become widely influential until the thirteenth century, some of Aristotle's writings on logic (*Categories, On Interpretation, Prior Analytics,* and *Topics)* were known in the early Middle Ages through translations by Boethius and were a respected part of the philosophical method and heritage. Philosophers such as Eriugena in the ninth century and Anselm of Bec and Canterbury in the eleventh used Aristotelian logic to explain theological doctrine.

Augustine. The early Church Father who most influenced western philosophy was Aurelius Augustinus (354–430), who lived most of his life in North Africa during the final days of the Roman Empire. Though not strictly speaking a "philosopher," he was deeply concerned with the philosophical quest from the time he was a teenager and read Cicero's *Hortensius,* a now-lost introduction to the philosophic life. His *Confessiones* (Confessions, written 397–401) document his intense quest for wisdom. His search led him first to the Manichaeans, a Gnostic sect whose views Augustine later rejected. Around the time he converted to Christianity in 386, he discovered the works of the Neoplatonists Plotinus and Porphyry, as well as those of Christian Neoplatonists such as Marius Victorinus.

Augustine's City of God. Augustine's writings synthesized many Neoplatonic, and Platonic, doctrines with Christian teachings and had a major influence on medieval philosophical and religious thought. One of his most influential works during the Middle Ages was *De civitate Dei* (The City of God, written 412–425). It includes an account of the Christian religion and its superiority to pagan beliefs, a general history of western philosophy, a description of the doctrine of creation, a theory of society that allows for separation and integration of the secular and the sacred, and an account or theory of beauty.

Augustine's Contributions to Education. In addition to his contributions to religious and philosophical thought, Augustine, who started out as a professor of rhetoric, contributed to the Latin West a basic theory of signs (what is now called semiotic), a theory of the liberal arts, an account of how to interpret a text, and a general philosophy of education. He also helped to pass on the works of Virgil and other Roman authors to the Middle Ages. While he did not have a thorough knowledge of the Greek language, he did master and transmit to the Middle Ages significant elements of ancient thought, including basic

Aristotelian and Stoic semantics, Neoplatonic philosophy and aesthetics, some elements of ancient Skepticism, and aspects of Pythagorean and Epicurean thought. Throughout the Middle Ages the Christian scholars of western Europe looked to Augustine's thought as the basis for philosophical speculation and the yardstick against which to measure the validity of their ideas.

Boethius and the Consolation of Philosophy. Another philosopher who was widely read in medieval Europe was Anicius Manlius Severinus Boethius (circa 480 – circa 524), who was born into the Roman nobility at about the time of the fall of the Roman Empire in the late fifth century. Boethius was interested in both Greek philosophy and Christian theology, especially that of Augustine. His best-known work, today as in the Middle Ages, is *De Consolatione Philosophiae* (On the Consolation of Philosophy, written circa 524), which includes significant elements of Neoplatonism and Stoicism. The impetus for writing *De Consolatione Philosophiae* came when Boethius, who was master of offices for the Ostrogoth king Theodoric, fell out of favor with Theodoric and was condemned to death for conspiracy and treason. During the year he spent in prison before his execution he wrote his most magnificent literary and philosophical achievement, which is still studied in the twentieth century. Every educated person in the Middle Ages and Renaissance had a knowledge of this work, particularly those who were being prepared for positions of leadership in society. (Queen Elizabeth I of England made her own English translation.) Written in prose and verse, the book asks why the evil prosper while the innocent suffer and concludes—in an argument that echoes Plato, Aristotle, the Neoplatonists, and the Stoics—that the only sure source of human happiness is in the life of the mind; that is, if one renounces the lures of wealth and power and seeks knowledge and virtue, one finds the "consolation of philosophy." Because Boethius drew heavily on Greek poetry and philosophy for this work and made few references to the Christian and Jewish scriptures, Samuel Johnson commented to his biographer James Boswell in the eighteenth century that Boethius showed himself more a philosopher than a Christian. Recent scholarship, however, has noted references to scripture and to Augustine in this work. Moreover, he exhibited his religious faith in works such as *De Fide Catholica* (On the Catholic Faith) and *De Trinitate* (On the Trinity), both written circa 521. In another philosophical-theological work from the same period, *Quomodo Substantiae in Eo Quod Sint Bonae Sint cum Non Sint Substantialia Bona* (Whether Everything That Exists Is Good Just Because It Exists), he introduced medieval philosophers to the basic Platonic doctrine of transcendental notions such as Being, Good, Unity, and Truth, identifying God as both the First Good and the First Being in which all finite beings strive to participate.

Boethius's Contributions to Medieval Learning. Boethius's major scholarly project was an attempt to reconcile the differences in the philosophical systems of Plato and Aristotle and to translate their works into Latin. He never completed this monumental task, but he did succeed in translating and writing commentaries on Aristotle's *Categories, On Interpretation,* and *Prior Analytics and Topics.* These works introduced Aristotle's basic logic and semantics to early medieval scholars in western Europe. Boethius made his own contributions to logic in *De Syllogismo Categorico* (On Categorical Syllogisms, written circa 505–506), *Liber de Divisione* (On Division, written circa 508), and *De Syllogismis Hypotheticis* (On Hypothetical Syllogisms, written after 516). In his polemical work *Contra Euthycen et Nestorium* (Against Eutyches and Nestorius, written circa 512) he fashioned a Latin vocabulary to interpret the Greek philosophical concepts of *person* and *nature.* Indeed, he set out the technical vocabulary of medieval Latin philosophy, including *essence, substance, nature, subsistence,* and *reason.* He made significant contributions to the mathematical arts in his *De Institutione Arithmetica* (On the Institution of Arithmetic) and *De Institutione Music* (On the Institution of Music), both written around 503.

Pseudo-Dionysius. With Augustine and Boethius, the anonymous scholar now known as Pseudo-Dionysius, was the most important influence from late antiquity on the Early Middle Ages. Indeed, his influence lasted into the Renaissance. Nothing is known about his life other than the facts that he lived in Syria around the year 500 and that his works were used in public debates in the Eastern Christian Church during the rule of the Roman Emperor Justinian I (reigned 527–565).

A Case of Mistaken Identity. Modern scholars have suggested that he was a monk trying to bring about the resolution of doctrinal disputes plaguing the early Church. To lend authority to his theological arguments, however, this monk identified himself as "Dionysius the Areopagite," who is mentioned in the Acts of the Apostles as a Greek that Paul converted to Christianity when he preached at the Areopagus (Hill of Ares) in Athens at some time before the year 60. Medieval scholars believed this story and accorded him almost full "Apostolic" authority, but Renaissance literary scholars such as Lorenzo Valla and Erasmus of Rotterdam cast doubt on the authenticity of the works of Dionysius, providing evidence that the language in which they are written is not New Testament Greek. Another clue to the author's misidentification is his reference to the martyrdom of Ignatius of Antioch, which occurred in 107. Thus, the sixth-century "forger" now known as Pseudo-Dionysius was either planting a clue to his hoax, or he wanted his readers to believe that he had an extremely long life. Modern scholars have demonstrated that portions of his writings were excerpted from the writings of the pagan Neoplatonic philosophers Proclus (circa 410–485) and Damascius (480–circa 550).

Pseudo-Dionysius's Theology. It is difficult to underestimate the fundamental importance of Pseudo-Dionysius's *De Divinis Nominibus* (The Divine Names) and *De Mystica Theologia* (The Mystical Theology) to medieval

Christian theology. He provided the manner of speaking about God that was employed by all the major western theologians, including John Scottus Eriugena, Anselm of Bec and Canterbury, Robert Grosseteste, Albertus Magnus, Bonaventure, Thomas Aquinas, Meister Eckhart, and Nicholas of Cusa. In Pseudo-Dionysius's language about God, positive and negative terms must be mutually related. Positive theology, called *kataphatic,* involves attributing to God those good attributes of earthly creatures that may be applied to him. Since God is unlimited and transcendent, however, it is necessary to guard those qualities by means of a careful use of language. That is, to avoid the simple-minded view that God is good in exactly the same sense that a human is good, it is necessary to state that God is super-good. Negative theology, called *apophatic,* states that God is not good in the limited human sense of good. For example, humans are changeable, but God is not; thus, God is ultimately unknowable and indescribable. This manner of speaking has a prehistory in Greek thought and in the first-century Jewish philosopher Philo of Alexandria. Furthermore, the idea that God is unknowable has its predecessor in Plato's Good "beyond being," and his "One which is not." Thus, the ultimate mystical experience is beyond light and darkness: it is utter silence. Dionysius's *Mystical Theology* provided the basis for much of medieval mysticism, especially among philosophers of the first rank such as Grosseteste, Albertus Magnus, Bonaventure, Aquinas, Eckhart, and Nicholas of Cusa—for whom the way to God is a journey through stages of purification, illumination, and perfection.

Church Hierarchy. Pseudo-Dionysius's *De Ecclesiastica Hierarchia* (The Ecclesiastical Hierarchy) provided the Middle Ages and Renaissance with their notion of cosmic and human order. He based his notion of hierarchy on the fundamental notion of holiness, especially the superior holiness of the divinity. He coined the word *hierarchia* (hierarchy) from *hierarch,* the Greek word for high priest or bishop. Ultimately, it refers to the ordering of all reality under a transcendent unity. Thus, all religious representatives in the Middle Ages were seen as having a definite place in a strict hierarchical order, and religious rites were initiations into sacred mysteries that had to be performed by the appropriate *hierarch.* Aspects of this hierarchy may be seen in some branches of modern Christianity, most notably the Greek and Russian Orthodox Churches, the Roman Catholic Church, and the Anglican Church.

Cosmology. In Pseudo-Dionysius's *De caelesti hierarchia* (The Celestial Hierarchy) he described different levels of heavenly reality from the unseen spiritual divinity, through levels of angelic powers, down to the human being. These angelic powers are the "intelligences" that move the spheres in Dante's *Commedia* (The Divine Comedy, completed 1321). This hierarchical system is based on an ordered outpouring from the One and a return to the One. In this way the varieties of things in the universe emerge from unity and return to unity.

Sources:

Peter Brown, *Augustine of Hippo: A Biography* (London: Faber & Faber, 1967).

Henry Chadwick, *Boethius: The Consolations of Music, Logic, Theology and Philosophy* (New York: Oxford University Press, 1981).

Peter Dronke, *A History of Twelfth-Century Philosophy* (Cambridge: Cambridge UniversityPress, 1988), pp. 21–150.

Stephen E. Gersh, *From Iamblicus to Eriugena* (Leiden: Brill, 1978).

J. C. Marler, Entry on Pseudo-Dionysius, in *Dictionary of Literary Biography,* volume 115: *Medieval Philosophers,* edited by Jeremiah Hackett (Detroit & London: Gale Research, 1992), pp. 325–333.

Ralph McInerny, Entry on Boethius, in *Dictionary of Literary Biography,* volume 115, pp. 110–117.

Renee Roques, *L'Univers dionysien: Structures hierarchique du monde selon le pseudo-Denys* (Aubier: Montaigne, 1955).

Frederick Van Fleteren, Entry on Augustine, in *Dictionary of Literary Biography,* volume 115, pp. 53–67.

Gerard Verbeke, *The Presence of Stoicism in Medieval Thought* (Washington, D.C.: Catholic University of America Press, 1983).

Garry Wills, *Saint Augustine* (New York: Viking, 1999).

EARLY MEDIEVAL PHILOSOPHY: EMERGING FROM THE DARK AGES

Eriugena's Greek-Latin-Christian Synthesis. The years 500–1066, sometimes called the Dark Ages, were indeed something of a desert for western European culture. In fact, F. C. Copleston has noted that there was only one major western philosopher between 500 and 1090: John Scottus Eriugena (circa 810–circa 877). Eriugena derived his Neoplatonism not only from Latin sources, such as Augustine, but also through his translations of Greek sources, such as Pseudo-Dionysius and Maximus Confessor. Thus, he discovered the Neoplatonic doctrines of Proclus, whereas earlier western scholars had been exposed mainly to the Neoplatonic ideas of Plotinus that they found in Augustine. Eriugena's most important work, *Periphyseon* (About Nature, circa 864–866), is an original synthesis of these Latin and Greek sources, in which he created a complete philosophical system to describe the nature of the universe. Eriugena divided Nature (by which he meant all reality, including God and his creatures) into four aspects: that which creates and is not created (God to creator); that which is created but which also creates (the primordial causes, which emanate from God); that which is created and does not create (material universe that flows from the primordial causes, including man); and that which is neither created nor creates (God as the End of the cosmic process, when God will be all in all). This synthetic vision depicts the emergence of all things in their diversity and their dynamic return from multiplicity to unity as the world is actively refashioned in the *officina* (workshop) of human life. That is, as the workshop of nature, human creativity is the place for the recuperation and re-visioning of nature. Human thought and work re-create nature, but it does not create the world from scratch. Furthermore, Eriugena divided Being into "that which is" and "that which is not," exhibiting a vision of nature at once in change and at rest. The language of Eriugena's system is indebted not only to the positive and negative theologies of Pseudo-Dionysius and Maximus the Confessor but also to *Categories* of Aristotle. Indeed, Eriugena's synthetic reason and acute rational analysis are his greatest assets as a philosopher. He gives reason its rightful place in the interpretation of all myth, story, and belief—asserting the capacity of reason, to figure out the ambiguities of difficult texts, the possible meanings of myths and oracles, and the human meaningfulness of religious mystery, and thus restoring reason to the central place it was accorded in Greek philosophy. Eriugena's writings were read into the thirteenth century, but after Amaury of Bène and David of Dinant used them in arguments for their pantheistic theologies, the theologians of Paris convinced Pope Honorius II to condemn Eriugena's *Periphyseon* as heretical in 1225, and many copies of *Periphyseon* were burned. Nonetheless, Eriugena found congenial readers in Meister Eckhart (circa 1260 – 1328) and Nicholas of Cusa (1401–1464), and his writings were rediscovered by the German Idealists during the first part of the nineteenth century.

Anselm's Proof of God. Anselm of Bec and Canterbury (1033–1109) took up traditional Latin sources, especially Augustine and Boethius, and developed them to their logical conclusions. He is well known among modern students of philosophy for his so-called ontological argument for the existence of God (that is, an argument based on the meaning of the word *God*). In fact, he was the first western scholar to attempt such a proof. In his *Monologion* (Monologue, 1076) he gave many reasons for the existence of God, but the monks at the monastery of Bec in Normandy asked him for one comprehensive proof instead. He obliged them with the ontological argument in *Proslogion* (An Address to the Mind of God, 1077–1078), in which he answers the fool in Psalms 14 and 53 who "hath said in his heart, There is no God." Writing as a theologian and one who firmly believed according to Christian faith, Anselm exercised the task of faith seeking understanding. Addressing God, he stated, "I desire to understand in some measure thy truth, which my heart already believes. . . . And indeed I do believe it, for unless I believe I shall not understand." Thus, Anselm was not trying to provide a simple-minded proof of God's existence by "reason alone"; rather, he was seeking to draw out the implications of his existing religious belief by using his reason to make it explicit that the meaning of the word *God* includes the fact of God's existence. In other words, the first premise of the argument—the meaning of the word *God*—is provided by faith; the further steps of the argument are provided by reason. When reason is carefully applied to the definition of *God,* the word exhibits implications not found in everyday language usage. Technically, Anselm's argument is an indirect or "reduction to absurdity" proof. It proceeds as follows: first, state a premise that contains truth (in this case God is "that than which nothing greater can be thought"); second, assume for the sake of argument that such a being does not exist; third, if from this assumption the argument ends in a logical contradiction, then it follows that the first premise is true.

Anselm of Bec and Canterbury; illumination from
a late twelfth-century manuscript
(Bodleian Library, Oxford)

The Structure of Anselm's Argument. Paul Vincent Spade has provided a succinct account of the logical structure of Anselm's argument that can be paraphrased as follows: (1) By *God* we mean "that than which nothing greater can be thought" (a premise known to be true by faith). (2) Assume for the sake of argument that "that than which nothing greater can be thought" does not exist in reality. (3) Nevertheless, it can be *thought* of as existing in reality. (This premise is obviously true, since most people—at Anselm's time, virtually all people—think of God as existing in reality.) (4) Now, "that than which nothing greater can be thought" is greater if it really exists than if it does not (Anselm takes it as self-evident that it is "greater"—that is, better—to exist in reality than just to be a figment of someone's imagination). Hence, (5) from premises (3) and (4), it is possible to think of something greater than "that than which nothing greater can be thought." Since (5) is self-contradictory, the supposition made in premise (2) is false; so by reduction to absurdity, (6) "that than which nothing greater can be thought"— that is, God—must exist. As Spade notes, "The premises of this argument are (1), (3), and (4). (3) seems innocuous enough, and (1) is simply a definition that does express a unique property of, even if it does not exhaust, what we normally mean by 'God.' The real work of the argument is done by step (4)." Anselm's argument has often been used with a different "ontological argument" that was put forth by the seventeenth-century French philosopher René Descartes and by others.

Gaunilo's Response. A monk, Gaunilo of Marmoutier, was the first to attack Anselm's proof, writing a "Reply on Behalf of the Fool." Gaunilo, of course, believed in the existence of God as much as Anselm did; but he did not think that Anselm's argument was adequate to prove what it purported to establish. Gaunilo had two main objections to Anselm's proof. First, he argued, the proof rested on the notion that one could have an adequate idea of the nature of God in one's mind; but God, as an infinite and totally perfect being, transcends any conception that human beings can have of him. Second, Gaunilo said, if Anselm's reasoning was valid in the case of God, it would also apply in other cases: for example, if one thought about the most beautiful island that one could conceive, one had to assert that such an island must exist. There would be no need to go out and look for it; the mere idea of it would be sufficient to establish its reality. But such a claim would obviously be absurd. Therefore, if the ontological argument is not valid in the case of the most beautiful island, it is not valid in the case of God, either.

Anselm's Rejoinder. Anselm replied that Gaunilo was mistaken on both counts. First, the ontological argument does not require human beings to possess an adequate conception of God; all it requires is an understanding of the phrase "that than which nothing greater can be thought," and such an understanding is within the grasp even of the fool. Second, the reasoning involved in the argument does not apply to islands or any other finite thing but only to God.

The School of Chartres. All the great cathedrals in Christian Europe had schools associated with them, but none approached Chartres in its twelfth-century revival of classical learning in a curriculum that focused on the language arts and mathematics. All the great thinkers associated with this school—Gilbert of Poitiers, William of Conches, Thierry of Chartres, and John of Salisbury—were indebted to Bernard of Chartres (circa 1060–1124), who in the years 1114–1124 was first head and then chancellor of the school. Bernard taught his students to revere the ancient authors. According to John of Salisbury, "Bernard of Chartres used to compare us to dwarfs perched on the shoulders of giants. He pointed out that we see more and farther than our predecessors, not because we have keener vision or greater height, but because we are lifted aloft on their gigantic stature."

The *Lectio philosophorum*. The major achievement of the School of Chartres was its teaching on the *lectio philosophorum* (the reading of philosophy). Bernard of Chartres and his colleagues perfected a new methodology of close, careful reading of difficult philosophical and grammatical texts that combined the older form of glossing on a text with that of careful commentary. Glosses (explanatory notes written in the margins or between lines of a text) were usually brief, unsystematic notes related to grammar and word origins and did not concern the larger signifi-

ANSELM'S ONTOLOGICAL ARGUMENT

Anselm's proof of the existence of God is an excellent representation of the religious philosophy of his time:

Well, then, Lord, You who give understanding to faith, grant me that I may understand, as much as You see fit, that You exist as we believe You to exist, and that You are what we believe You to be. Now we believe that You are *something than which nothing greater can be thought*. Or can it be that a thing of such a nature does not exist, since "the Fool has said in his heart, there is no God"? [Psalm 14.1] But surely, when this same Fool hears what I am speaking about, namely, "something-than-which-nothing greater-can-be-thought," he understands what he hears, and what he understands is in his mind, even if he does not understand that it actually exists. For it is one thing for an object to exist in the mind, and another thing to understand that an object actually exists. Thus, when a painter plans beforehand what he is going to execute, he has it [the picture] in his mind, but he does not yet think that it actually exists because he has not yet executed it. However, when he has actually painted it, then, he both has it in his mind and understands that it exists because he has now made it. Even the Fool, then, is forced to agree that something-than-which-nothing-greater-can-be-thought exists in the mind, since he understands this when he hears it, and whatever is understood is in the mind. And surely that-than-which-a greater cannot-be thought cannot exist in the mind alone. For if it exists solely in the mind even, it can be thought to exist in reality also, which is greater. If then that-than-which-a-greater-cannot be-thought exists in the mind alone, this same that-than-which-a-greater-*cannot*-be-thought is that-than-which-a-greater-*can*-be-thought. But this is obviously impossible. Therefore there is absolutely no doubt that something-than-which-a-greater-cannot-be-thought exists both in the mind and in reality.

Source: *St. Anselm's Proslogion*, translated by M. J. Charlesworth (Notre Dame, Ind. & London: University of Notre Dame Press, 1979), p. 117.

cance of the work. Bernard taught his students to write commentaries that considered the overall meaning of the work while also considering details and specific points. According to John of Salisbury, Bernard said there were three kinds of intellectuals: one flies, ignoring the specifics; one crawls and is unable to grasp higher meanings; and one takes the middle way, walking, and is capable of taking into account both specific details and overall meanings. Bernard's method takes the middle way.

Commenting on the Ancients. The books available to Bernard and the students were the same Latin texts that had been available in western Europe for three hundred years. The main texts studied at Chartres were works by the Roman grammarian Priscian, Macrobius's *The Dream of Scipio*, Porphyry's *Isagoge*, Boethius's philosophical and theological writings, and a part of the *Timaeus* of Plato. The chief example of Bernard's method is his *Glosae super*

Platonem (Glosses on Plato, written circa 1100–1115), a commentary on the Timaeus for which Bernard and his colleagues relied to some extent on a commentary by the fourth-century Christian scholar Calcidius. In his Christian interpretation of Plato, Bernard established a hierarchy in which God was the creator of both the primordial matter from which all corporal beings and things derive and the Ideas, the essences of beings or things (ideals or universals) that according to Plato are separate from and more real than specific beings or things. Like Plato (and unlike Aristotle) Bernard held that Ideas are eternal and completely separate from the changing and corruptible things of concrete existence. He also maintained that the Ideas are separate from God. Though they come from him, they are not identical with him. Furthermore, to explain how concrete beings and objects are formed in imitation of Ideas if the two principles are completely separate, Bernard introduced the idea of the "native form" which mediated between Ideas and the concrete by entering into primordial matter to beget the material world. Overall, by means of its commentary on the *Timaeus* and related subject matter, the school introduced Plato to western European philosophers of the later Middle Ages.

Poet-Philosophers. One major feature of philosophy in both the Carolingian era and in the period 1066–1200 is the fact that major philosophers such as Eriugena, members of the School of Chartres, and Peter Abelard were not only logicians and philosophers but also poets. That is, the aim of the grammatical expert, the logician, and the philosopher was to combine eloquence with wisdom and to find pure linguistic expression in the poetic word. This combination did not continue after 1200. The necessity of producing bureaucrats led to a much more utilitarian demand for logical and mathematical competence. The pursuit of literary culture in the arts was sacrificed in the curriculum at the University of Paris though literary studies were still included at Toulouse.

Sources:

Werner Beierwaltes, *Eriugena* (Frankfurt am Main: Klostermann, 1994).

Mary Brennan, *A Guide to Eriugenian Studies (1930–1987)*, Vestigia 5 (Freibourg, Switzerland: Editions universitaires / Paris: Editions du Cerf, 1989).

Frederick C. Copleston, *A History of Philosophy*, volume 2, parts 1 and 2: *Mediaeval Philosophy* (Westminster, Md.: Newman Press, 1950).

Copleston, *Mediaeval Philosophy* (London: Methuen, 1952).

Peter Dronke, ed., *A History of Twelfth-Century Philosophy* (Cambridge: Cambridge University Press, 1988).

Charles Hartshorne, *Anselm's Discovery* (La Salle, Ill.: Open Court, 1965).

Paul Henry, *The De grammatico of St. Anselm* (Notre Dame, Ind.: Notre Dame University Press, 1964).

Henry, *The Logic of St. Anselm* (Oxford: Clarendon Press, 1967).

Edouard Jeauneau, *Etudes Eriugéniennes* (Paris: Etudes Augustiniennes, 1987).

Jeauneau, *"Lectio philosophorum," Recherches sur L'Ecole de Chartres* (Amsterdam: Hakkert, 1973).

John Marenbon, *Early Medieval Philosophy* (London: Routledge, 1983).

Dermot Moran, *The Philosophy of John Scottus Eriugena: a Study of Idealism in the Middle Ages* (Cambridge & New York: Cambridge University Press, 1989).

John J. O'Meara, *Eriugena* (Oxford: Clarendon Press, 1988).

Alvin Plantinga, "A Valid Ontological Argument?" in *The Ontological Argument*, edited by Plantinga (Garden City, N.Y.: Doubleday, 1965), pp. 160–171.

R. W. Southern, *Saint Anselm: A Portrait in a Landscape* (Cambridge & New York: Cambridge University Press, 1990).

Paul Vincent Spade, "Medieval Philosophy," in *The Oxford History of Western Philosophy*, edited by Anthony Kenny (Oxford & New York: Oxford University Press, 1994).

THE EAST-WEST SCHISM

Christendom East and West. In the early centuries of Christianity the Church was governed by local bishops. Each community over which a bishop presided was jurisdictionally independent from the rest, but they were all regarded as part of a single, united body of Christ. The five most important episcopal sees were in Rome, Constantinople, Alexandria, Antioch, and Jerusalem, with the bishops of these cities taking on the title of patriarch. After the spread of Islam in the eighth century the balance of ecclesiastical power was upset: the churches of North Africa and the Middle East lost much of their influence, and only the patriarchates of Rome and Constantinople remained as great centers of Christendom. When Charlemagne was crowned Holy Roman Emperor in 800 the situation became more polarized. Not only were there two religious centers within the Christian world, but two rival empires as well. The political tension between eastern and western Christendom emerged from this polarity.

Dogmatic and Liturgical Divergences. Over the centuries the predominantly Greek-speaking Eastern Church and the Latin-speaking Western Church had developed different canonical and liturgical practices. In the West, for example, unleavened wafers called "azymes" were used for the celebration of the Eucharist, while in the East only leavened bread was used. Priests under the jurisdiction of Rome were under strict requirements of celibacy, while in the East married laymen could be ordained. The beginning of Lent was observed on Ash Wednesday in the West, while for the Greek Church it began two days earlier, on Monday. In addition to these lesser differences, there were two important dogmatic divergences. First, there was the increasingly widespread insertion of the word *filioque* (and from the Son) into the Nicene Creed in the West. In that context the word signifies that the Holy Spirit proceeds not only from the Father, but from the Son as well. The Eastern Church vehemently opposed this addition, which had serious implications for the central Christian doctrine of the Trinity. Then there was the question of papal authority. By at least the late sixth century the patriarchs, or Popes, of Rome had begun to claim that as successors of the Apostle Peter they should have authority over all other bishops and patriarchs. The Eastern Church rejected this notion.

The First Signs of Schism. The divergences between the two Churches led to direct conflict in the ninth century, when missionaries from both Rome and Constantinople found themselves working against each other in their efforts to convert Bulgaria. Each side wanted to convert the Bulgarians not only to Christianity, but to their own particular practices and dogmas. This situation prompted Photius, the Patriarch of Constantinople, to convene a council in 867 at which Pope Nicholas I was excommunicated and the Western Church was declared heretical for its divergent practices, especially for its use of the word *filioque*. The question of Bulgaria was eventually settled in favor of the Byzantines, and the breach sometimes referred to as the "Photian Schism" was healed. Rome and Constantinople were once again in communion, but tensions between them remained.

The Schism of 1054. A new controversy arose in the early eleventh century, when the Normans of southern Italy began forcing the Byzantine churches there to adopt Latin practices. The Patriarch of Constantinople, Michael Cerularius, responded by demanding that the Latin-rite churches of Constantinople should conform to local usage. When the Latin churches refused, the Patriarch ordered them closed, leading the Roman Pope to dispatch legates to settle the controversy. The attempt at reconciliation was a failure; in the end the leader of the papal legates, Humbert of Silva Candida, placed a bull of excommunication on the high altar of the cathedral of Hagia Sophia in Constantinople, prompting the Greek Patriarch to respond with excommunications directed at the West. This event is sometimes referred to as the Great Schism, and the year 1054 is traditionally taken to mark the separation of the Eastern and Western Churches. Irreparable animosity between the two did not arise, however, until the western crusade against Constantinople one-and-a-half centuries later.

The Fourth Crusade. The Crusades to the Holy Land began after the Byzantine emperor Alexius Comnenus appealed for western aid against the Turks in 1095, but instead of repairing the rift between East and West these so-called holy wars eventually led to enduring hostilities between Byzantium and Rome. In 1201 Pope Innocent III mustered support for the Fourth Crusade against the Muslims in the Holy Land, but in this case the Crusaders never reached their destination. Rival claims to the Byzantine throne had arisen in Constantinople, and the son of the defeated claimant, Isaac Angelus, had fled westward in hopes of finding support among the Crusaders. He promised them not only military aid in their eastward mission, but also great wealth and the reunion of the two Churches on Roman terms. The Crusaders succeeded in overthrowing the usurper, Alexius III, and installing Isaac Angelus and his son Alexius IV, on the throne. Shortly thereafter, Isaac Angelus died and Alexius IV was murdered. Frustrated and undisciplined Crusaders decided to claim the city and elect a new emperor from their own ranks. In 1204 they seized and looted Constantinople, killing many of its Christian inhabitants. Indeed, according to local reports the Crusaders were far less respectful to the altars and holy vessels of the churches than the Muslims had been. Baldwin, Count of Flanders, was placed on the throne at Constantinople, and the empire was then divided among him, other leaders of the Cru-

Crusaders attacking Constantinople in 1204, during the Fourth Crusade; illumination from a mid-thirteenth-century manuscript for William of Tyre's unfinished history of the Crusades (Bibliothèque Nationale, Paris)

sade, and the Venetians. When Innocent III first heard of the Crusaders' outrageous actions he was appalled, but he later pardoned them, believing that this forced reunion of East and West would bring "great blessings" to Christendom. The Churches were nominally united under Rome until 1261, when the Byzantines overthrew the Latin regime, which was never popularly accepted in the East. Though attempts at ecclesiastical reunification were later made, none was successful, and the sack of Constantinople may be taken to mark the definitive schism between the Eastern and the Western Church.

Sources:

C. Warren Hollister, *Medieval Europe: A Short History,* eighth edition (New York: McGraw-Hill, 1998).

Philip Sherrard, *Church, Papacy, and Schism* (London: SPCK, 1978).

R. W. Southern, *Western Society and the Church in the Middle Ages* (Harmondsworth, U.K.: Penguin, 1970).

Timothy Ware, *The Orthodox Church* (Harmondsworth, U.K.: Penguin, 1997).

HERESY

What is Heresy? Heresy is a series of religious beliefs and practices that the established (orthodox) Church deems false, and heretics are the people who support these unorthodox beliefs and practices. Heresy is therefore a firm commitment of the will and not just belief. As these definitions suggest, defining heresy is always subjective. What is heresy to one group of believers may be orthodoxy to another, and people who are labeled heretics can establish orthodoxies of their own and call others heretics. In medieval Christendom defining a heretic was ostensibly simple because everyone—except small enclaves of

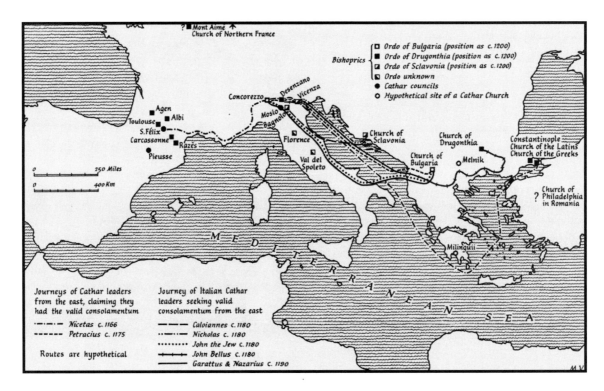

Map of the routes by which dualist heresies spread from the East to Italy and southern France
(from Malcolm Lambert, *Medieval Heresy*, 1977)

Jews or Muslims—was Christian as defined by the one Christian Church. Even within Christianity, however, there were differences between Eastern and Western Christianity and the definition of orthodox Christianity and its appropriate practices was still evolving during the Middle Ages. For this reason, what was considered heretical also changed with time. By the twelfth century—as orthodoxy was becoming more clearly defined—the strongest and most widespread heretical movements of the medieval period emerged in Europe. Many of these movements had similar characteristics: an urge to flee from worldly concerns, a stress on purity, and a revulsion for material objects, human flesh, and human desires. Many of them also condemned the medieval clergy for insufficient care of lay pastoral needs.

Early Christian Heresies and Medieval Christianity. Medieval theologians tended to write about heresies in light of standard classifications handed down from the early Christian centuries. From the first century of Christianity there had been disagreements about the nature of the Trinity, the nature of Jesus, the nature of the Christian Church, and a wide variety of collateral topics. Often medieval churchmen cited classical heresies such as Donatism, Nestorianism, and Pelagianism when condemning challenges to contemporary orthodoxy. Among the most enduring classical heresies were Arianism and Gnosticism. Arians opposed the idea of the Trinity, arguing that it was impossible for God the Son (Christ) to be at the same level as God the Father; thus, they asserted, Christ was a man just like other men. Arianism appealed to the "common sense" of many Christians, especially given the patriarchal nature of classical society and the Germanic

tribes into which Christianity spread. Gnosticism was the idea that the world and all physical things in it are corrupt and that salvation, therefore, is purely internal. The Gnostics believed that the goal of a true Christian should be to reject all things of this world, which is at best a battleground between the forces of good (God) and evil (Satan). Gnosticism and Manichaeism, to which it was closely related, flourished in various forms throughout the Middle Ages, one of the most dramatic was found in southern France during the early thirteenth century.

Cathars. Although there were also heretical movements during the ninth, tenth, and eleventh centuries, in the twelfth century organized heretical movements seemed to sprout throughout Europe. One of the most influential and dramatic appeared in southern France during the late twelfth century: the Cathars, also known as the Albigensians. There were various Cathar strongholds in medieval Europe—northern Italy and southern France around the city of Albi in particular—and each group had some common beliefs. The Cathars believed in two universal principles (dualism): good, which was equated with God and the spirit, and evil, which was linked to Satan and this world. In this schema all natural phenomena, from germination to earthquakes, are caused by the Devil, who governs this world, which is also the only hell human souls will ever know. For orthodox Christianity evil is the absences of good, and dualists seemed to set up the Devil as nearly a second god. For Cathars the goal of man was to free his spirit from everything of this world, including the prison of human flesh, and attain communion with God. In order to achieve this goal, celibacy was considered best, but for those who found themselves unable to give up the pleasures

Carcasonne was one of the strongholds of the Cathar heresy, and the city suffered greatly during the Albigensian Crusade. The following excerpt from a Dominican manual used by inquisitors there in 1248–1249 gives the methods that should be employed when questioning individuals suspected of heresy.

Thereafter, the person is diligently questioned about whether he saw a heretic or Waldensian, where and when, how often and with whom, about others who were present; whether he listed to their preaching or exhortation and whether he gave them lodging or arranged shelter for them; whether he conducted them from place to place or otherwise consorted with them or arranged for them to be guided or escorted; whether he ate or drank with them or ate bread blessed by them; whether he gave or sent anything to them; whether he acted as their financial agent or messenger or assistant; whether he held any deposit or anything else of theirs; whether he received the Peace from their book, mouth, shoulder, or elbow; whether he adored a heretic or bowed his head or genuflected and said "Bless us" before heretics or whether he was present at their baptisms or confessions; whether he was present at a Waldensian Lord's Supper, confessed his sins to them, accepted penance or learned anything from them; whether he was otherwise on familiar terms with or associated with heretics or Waldenses in any way; whether he made an agreement,

heeded requests, or received gifts in return for not telling the truth about himself or others; whether he advised or persuaded anyone or cause anyone to be persuaded to do any of the foregoing; whether he knows any other man or woman to have done any of the foregoing; whether he believed in the heretics or their errors.

Finally, after that which he has confessed about himself or testified about other persons on all of these matters—and sometimes on others about which he was questioned, but not without good reason—has been written down, in the presence of one or both of us [the inquisitors], with at least two other persons qualified for careful discharge of this task associated with us, he verifies everything which he caused to be recorded. In this way we authenticate the records of the Inquisition as to confessions and depositions, whether they are prepared by the notary or by another scribe.

And when a region is widely infected we make general inquisition of all persons in the manner just described, entering the names of all of them in the record, even of those who insist that they know nothing about others and have themselves committed no crime, so that if they have lied or if subsequently they commit an offense, as is often found true of a number of persons, it is on record that they have abjured and have been interrogated in detail.

Source: Edward Peters, ed., *Heresy and Authority in Medieval Europe* (Philadelphia: University of Pennsylvania Press, 1980), pp. 200–201.

of the flesh, concubinage was preferable to marriage because having a mistress was impermanent. The Cathars also commended abstention from all animal food, except fish. Cathars leaders, called *perfecti*, traveled the countryside in groups of two or three preaching Cathar doctrines and following—with varying degrees of success—Cathar behavioral standards, including celibacy. The highest good a Cathar could obtain on this earth was the *endura*, a ritual fast in which a person starved him- or herself to death, thereby showing complete rejection of worldly concerns. Although Cathar doctrines were heretical, most people did not consider them truly dangerous until the Cathars were linked to movements for political independence by southern French nobles. For this reason, when Pope Innocent III called for a crusade against them in 1207–1208 he found ready allies among impoverished northern French nobles. This Albigensian Crusade, which began in 1209, was notoriously bloody. Although the well-known saying of "Slay them all; God will know his own," which was attributed to crusaders at the siege of Béziers, is apocryphal, there were incidents of massacres involving six thousand people, including women and children. Despite the viciousness of the Albigensian Crusade and the establishment of inquisitorial Church courts in southern France to root out and punish the remaining heretics, Cathars continued to be a strong minority in this region throughout the Middle Ages.

Waldensians. Waldensianism was less a system of belief than a way of life that stressed apostolic poverty and the ministry. Early Waldensians were known for their personal simplicity and poverty, their care for the unfortunate, and their preaching (generally unauthorized). Because of their rejection of many aspects of the institutional Church, including its wealth and worldly possessions, they have often been confused with the Cathars, who were more distinctly dualist than the Waldensians. The Waldensians' roots can be found in the life of Valdes, a rich businessman in Lyons, France, who in the mid 1170s gave up his family and—after assuring that his wife and children had places in monasteries—donated all his wealth to the poor. Admired by the general population for his exceptional sacrifices and holiness and mistrusted by the clergy because of his rejection of Church control over preaching and the sacraments, Valdes soon attracted a group of followers. Thus far, Valdes's career sounds much like that of St. Francis, but there were some fundamental differences. Waldensian leaders argued that the vernacular scripture, rather than the Latin version used by the Church, should be the foundation text for all Christians. They also called for the elimination of key aspects of medieval piety such as religious images, pilgrimages, and the belief in purgatory. In this sense, they challenged foundations of medieval Christianity and the right of the Church to legislate for all Christians. For this reason, the Church attempted to curtail Valdes's

Marguerite Porete exemplifies the learning and personal spirituality that was possible in some Beguine communities. Her book *Mirror of Simple Souls* is proof of her extensive scriptural knowledge and her familiarity with the work of thinkers such as Bernard of Clairvaux. Her fate and that of her book also reveal the tensions within medieval Christianity. Though the Church feared women who stepped beyond the bounds of traditional piety, at least some of the mysticism in her book found popular acceptance. As Malcolm Lambert has explained, around 1306–1308,

Marguerite Porete of Hainault, one of whose books had already been burnt by the bishop of Cambrai, was arrested for spreading heresy "among simple people and beghards" through another book, and was sent to Paris. There she refused to respond to interrogation, and was convicted of heresy on the strength of some extracts taken from this book, submitted for judgement to a commission of theologians. Her earlier conviction meant that she was guilty of relapse, and she was burnt in Paris in 1310.

The charge was again heretical mysticism, but in this instance we have the heretic's own work with which to check the veracity of the accusations made against her. By chance, the treatise which caused her conviction and burning, the *Mirror of Simple Souls*, survived, to circulate anonymously in monasteries and nunneries, in the original and in translation, from the fourteenth century to the present. So little obvious was the heresy in it that hardly any of its readers over the centuries questioned its orthodoxy. . . .

Marguerite was aware of the dangers . . . and remarked that "simple minds might misunderstand them at their peril." She was treating of esoteric matters, and it was not a book for the many, although obviously designed for reading aloud in the vernacular. Two factors seem to have weighed in her condemnation: her pertinacy, shown in the repeated dissemination of her views and her refusal to respond to interrogation, and the alleged publicity given to the *Mirror* among simple people. What might have been possible in an established nunnery, without publicity, appeared not to be allowed to a beguine who wanted to propagate her work. Her views were not fairly represented.

Source: Malcolm Lambert, *Medieval Heresy: Popular Movements from the Gregorian Reform to the Reformation*, second edition (Oxford, U.K. & Cambridge, Mass.: Blackwell, 1992), pp. 184–185.

preaching, and by 1184, after Valdes's death, Waldensianism had been declared heretical. Compared to Catharism, however, Waldensian doctrines were closer to the primary doctrines of Christianity. The Waldensians outlasted the thirteenth-century persecutions, mainly in remote parts of Europe and in the lower social classes.

Combating Heresy: Dominicans and Education. The Dominican Order of friars was founded in response to the Albigensian heresy and had a key role in combating the heretical movements of the thirteenth century. In 1206 Dominic Guzman (1170–1221) joined a papal mission against the Albigensians and entered into discussions with their leaders. Near the end of the Albigensian Crusade, around 1215, Dominic founded a religious community with a mission to study in order to preach and teach. In fact, preaching is so central to the Dominican Order that its proper name is the "Order of Preachers." Dominic and his follows traveled throughout Italy, Spain, and France as well as visiting major cities in other parts of Europe. Because of their emphasis on preaching, Dominicans had to be ordained clergymen and generally had years of university education. Although they took vows of poverty, it was never as central an issue for them as it was for the other great mendicant order: the Franciscans. For the same reason Dominicans put far less emphasis on living a cloistered, or enclosed, life than most medieval monks. Dominicans and Dominican theology had a strong influence at European universities, and some of the greatest thinkers of medieval Europe were Dominicans, including St. Thomas Aquinas.

Combating Heresy: The Medieval Inquisition. The Dominicans' emphasis on education, particularly in canon law, made them naturals to staff the new courts that were developed to deal with heretics, and their prevalence in these courts gave them the nickname "hounds of the Lord," based on a Latin pun on their name: Domini (of the Lord), Canes (hound). The courts they staffed are the most misunderstood institutions in the medieval Church: the Inquisition. Even calling these courts "the" Inquisition is a misnomer because there was no single Inquisition supervised by Rome. Instead, the Inquisition of medieval Europe was a series of courts, staffed by papal delegates, and the name refers to a particular method of legal *inquiry*, thus the term *inquisition* used in secular and ecclesiastical courts. There was nothing particularly diabolical about it by medieval standards. In fact, in many cases the medieval inquisitorial courts were more lenient and fair by modern standards than many secular courts. Yet, inquisitorial courts had common procedures that might be surprising. Inquisitors were generally free from episcopal control, and they could proceed against a suspected heretic even if he or she had not been formally accused. According to James B. Given, people called before the inquisitors were forced to testify against themselves or face prosecution for contumacy (contempt of court) or perjury. All court sessions were held in secrecy, and the accused were usually denied legal representation. Moreover, they were rarely told the names of people who testified against them, and inquisitors accepted depositions from people whom canon law barred from testifying—including children, convicted criminals, accomplices, and heretics. Among the best-known medieval inquisitors is Jacques Fournier, Bishop of Palmiers, who conducted an extensive campaign against the Cathars of his region from 1318 to 1325. Some of the books recording the testimonies of witnesses and the accused have survived and are valuable sources of information about Catharism and medieval inquisitorial courts.

The Movement of the Free Spirit. Although Catharism and Waldensianism are probably the best-known medieval heresies, they are not the only ones that spread hundreds of miles. Beginning in the late thirteenth century and throughout the fourteenth, a powerful heretical movement emerged in western Germany (the Rhineland) and in the Low Countries. This movement, known as the heresy of the Free Spirit, stressed the believers' freedom from not just the institutional Church but from all religious authorities. Basing their argument on the writings of St. Paul, members of the Free Spirit stated that all morally just people were "sons of God." For this reason, they did not need the sacraments of the Christian Church, including baptism and the eucharist; they had truly free spirits. All who followed this movement believed that everyone in the community of the Free Spirit was morally just and everyone outside the community was not. Because they rejected the sacramental structure of the Church, but especially because they saw themselves as free to make independent moral decisions without the guidelines of the established Church, the Free Spirits were accused of heresy for denying God's moral laws.

Women and Heresy: The Beguines. Although the medieval Church offered women outlets for their piety—they could become nuns and practice the same sacraments as most men—the Church was influenced by the patriarchal society of which it was a part. In general, female spirituality was more suspect than men's and fewer opportunities for social and intellectual advancement were open to churchwomen than to churchmen. Given this situation, it is probably not surprising that many heretical movements found a disproportionate share of their support among women. One of the best-known heresies emerged within communities of Beghards (men) and Beguines (women). The Beghards and Beguines were lay people who did not want to join religious orders but who wished to live a life following basic scriptural tenets and Christian ideals, such as poverty and chastity. They found strong support in the Low Countries, and many towns in modern Belgium and Holland still have buildings that were used by this movement. The Beguines, in particular, faced strong legal obstacles. In medieval society it was rare for a woman to be legally independent; generally, she went from the legal authority of her father to that of her husband and eventually her son. If a woman wanted to be a Beguine, people asked, who would supervise her? The religious orders, such as the Benedictines, were suspicious of Beguines because they were not responsible to canon law or any Rule authorized by a bishop or Pope. Moreover, in regions such as Germany and Holland, Beghards actually preached, and Beguines ministered to the poor and sick and published religious treatises. All these activities were traditionally clerical responsibilities and sources of income for the clergy. Because of their ambiguous legal position and their challenge to the social structures and gender roles of late medieval society, by the late thirteenth and fourteenth centuries prosecution of Beguines and Beghards was widespread, and they ended as an organized movement by 1400.

Sources:

Malcolm Barber, *The Cathars: Dualist Heretics in Languedoc in the High Middle Ages* (Harlow, U.K. & New York: Longman, 2000).

James B. Given, *Inquisition and Medieval Society: Power, Discipline, and Resistance in Languedoc* (Ithaca, N.Y.: Cornell University Press, 1997).

Malcolm Lambert, *The Cathars* (Malden, Mass.: Blackwell, 1998).

Lambert, *Medieval Heresy: Popular Movements from the Gregorian Reform to the Reformation*, second edition (Oxford, U.K. & Cambridge, Mass.: Blackwell, 1992).

JEWS AND MUSLIMS

Multiculturalism in the Medieval West. Traditionally, historians have treated medieval western and central Europe as "Christendom," reflecting a unified ideal supported by medieval philosophers and theologians. Europe was, however, far more-divided than such a concept implies, and European religion was no exception. Although Europe was ostensibly Christian, most cities

Jews and Muslims playing games in a garden in Seville, Spain; illumination from a manuscript for *Libro de ajedrez, dados, y tablas*, 1283 (Escorial Library, Madrid)

The expulsion of the Jews from England, 1290; illumination from an early-fourteenth-century manuscript for *Flores Historiarum* (British Library, London)

had Jewish enclaves, particularly if they were near trade routes or royal or noble courts. Spain was even more diverse with large communities of Muslims, Jews, and Christians who lived and worked together and even intermarried. In the process it developed a distinctive culture and can truly be described as multicultural.

The Establishment of a "Muslim" Spain. In 710 Muslims from North Africa invaded Spain and began a conquest that ended with their defeat in 753 in central France. Retreating back to Spain, Muslim leaders established a series of small kingdoms ostensibly answerable to a caliph (ruler) based in the city of Cordoba. The Muslim kingdoms were anything but the homogeneous culture that such a name implies. Political necessity caused Muslims to intermarry with Christian families, and the children of such unions were raised as Muslims. Islamic thought argued for relative tolerance to Christians and Jews as fellow "people of the book." The Muslim society of medieval Spain had an urban orientation, leaving room for Christian nobles and peasants, who were traditionally more rural, and for Jewish communities, which often concentrated in cities. Involved in trade and cultural exchange with a Muslim community that stretched from West Africa to modern Afghanistan, the Muslim kingdoms of medieval Spain prospered during the ninth, tenth, and early eleventh centuries.

Accomplishments of European Muslim Culture. At a time when Christians living to the north and east of Spain had dirt roads, little or no plumbing, no police, and regular invasions by Vikings or other marauders, Muslims in medieval Spanish cities enjoyed cobblestone roads, running water, policed streets, and peace. Christian travelers visiting Cordoba commented on its cleanliness, splendor, and artistry. Involved in a truly transcontinental commerce, medieval Spaniards had access to products from Africa, the Near East, and Asia. Medieval Muslims traveled, in part because

of the requirement for all Muslims to make a pilgrimage once in their lifetime to Mecca in modern Saudi Arabia. There were also active Muslim schools whose scholars collected and commented on classical authors. During the twelfth and thirteenth centuries, as connections between Muslim Spain and Christian Europe increased, these Muslim commentaries were incorporated into medieval Christian philosophy.

Christian Attitudes toward the "Moors." The name "Moor" was given to the Muslims of medieval Spain by Christians who increasingly saw all Muslims as the same. Although the Christians of medieval Spain paid homage to and cooperated with Muslim rulers, there was some sense of a fundamental distinction between the two communities. The eleventh-century French epic poem *The Song of Roland* depicts the common attitude of Christians north of Spain: Muslims provide a treacherous, vicious, and "base" foil for the Frankish hero Roland and his peerless ruler, Charlemagne. In the later eleventh and twelfth centuries, as relations between Christians and Muslims in Spain became more strained, that attitude became increasingly prevalent. The Muslims against whom Crusaders fought in the Near East were condemned in even stronger language. In 1095 Pope Urban II, for example, called them a "race so base, so despised, an instrument of demons." Despite the growing distrust of Muslims by Christian Europeans, Christian Spaniards still cooperated with them. One of the national heroes of Spain is Rodrigo Díaz de Viviar, known as El Cid, who in the twelfth-century *Poem of El Cid* makes alliances with both Muslim and Christian nobles. Although there are unprincipled and treacherous Muslims among his enemies, there are treacherous Christians as well, and other Muslims are portrayed as valiant and effective warriors.

One of the earliest recorded accusations of ritual murder against the Jews was written by Thomas of Monmouth around 1173. This story about the 1140 murder of William, an English boy of Norwich, includes charges that were commonly leveled against Jews throughout the Middle Ages.

Then the boy, like an innocent lamb, was led to the slaughter. He was treated kindly by the Jews at first, and, ignorant of what was being prepared for him, he was kept till the morrow. But on the next day [Tuesday, 21 March 1140], which in that year was the Passover for them, after the singing of the hymns appointed for the day in the synagogue, the chiefs of the Jews. . . . suddenly seized hold of the boy William as he was having his dinner and in no fear of any treachery, and ill-treated him in various horrible ways. For while some of them held him behind, others opened his mouth and introduced an instrument of torture which is called a teazle [a wooden gag] and, fixing it by straps through both jaws to the back of his neck, they fastened it with a knot as tightly as it could be drawn.

After that, taking a short piece of rope of about the thickness of one's little finger and tying three knots in it at certain distances marked out, they bound round that innocent head with it from the forehead to the back, forcing the middle knot into his forehead and the two others into his temples, the two ends of the rope being most tightly stretched at the back of his head and fastened in a very tight knot. The ends of the rope were then passed round his neck and carried round his throat under his chin, and there they finished off this dreadful engine of torture in a fifth knot.

But not even yet could the cruelty of the torturers be satisfied without adding even more severe pains. Having shaved his head, they stabbed it with countless thorn-points, and made the blood come horribly from the wounds they made. [Jesus worn a crown of thorns.] And so cruel were they and so eager to inflict pain that it was difficult to say whether they were more cruel or more ingenious in their tortures. For their skill in torturing kept up the strength of their cruelty and ministered arms thereto.

And thus, while these enemies of the Christian name were rioting in the spirit of malignity around the boy, some of those present judged him to be fixed to a cross in mockery of the Lord's Passion, as though they would say: "even as we condemned the Christ to a shameful death, so let us also condemn the Christian, so that, uniting the lord and his servant in a like punishment, we may retort upon themselves the pain of that reproach which they impute to us." . . .

And we, after enquiring into the matter very diligently, did both find the house, and discovered some most certain marks in it of what had been done there. [This house was supposed to be the home of a rich Jew, Eleazar, who was later murdered by order of his debtor, Sir Simon de Novers.] For report goes that there was there instead of a cross a post set up between two other posts, and a beam stretched across the midmost post and attached to the other on either side. And as we afterwards discovered, from the marks of the wounds and of the bands, the right hand and foot had been tightly bound and fastened with cords, but the left hand and foot were pierced with two nails. Now the deed was done in this way, lest it should be discovered, from the presence of nail-marks in both hands and both feet, that the murderers were Jews and not Christians, if eventually the body were found. [That is, both hands and feet were not nailed lest it look like a crucifixion.] . . . And since many streams of blood were running down from all parts of his body, then, to stop the blood and to wash and close the wounds, they poured boiling water over him.

Thus then the glorious boy and martyr of Christ, William, dying the death of time in reproach of the Lord's death, but crowned with the blood of a glorious martyrdom, entered into the kingdom of glory on high to live for ever. . . .

As a proof of the truth and credibility of the matter we now adduce something which we have heard from the lips of Theobald, who was once a Jew, and afterwards a monk. He verily told us that in the ancient writings of his fathers it was written that the Jews, without the shedding of human blood, could neither obtain their freedom, nor could they ever return to their fatherland. [There is no such statement in Jewish law or literature.] Hence it was laid down by them in ancient times that every year they must sacrifice a Christian in some part of the world to the Most High God in scorn and contempt of Christ, that so they might avenge their sufferings on Him; inasmuch as it was because of Christ's death that they had been shut out from their own country, and were in exile as slaves in a foreign land.

Source: Jacob Marcus, *The Jew in the Medieval World: A Sourcebook, 315–1791* (Cincinnati: Union of American Hebrew Congregations, 1938), pp. 121–127.

The Reconquista. In the eleventh century Christian nobles took advantage of the disintegration of the Cordoba caliphate to begin the Reconquista, a reconquest of the Iberian peninsula. Under the well-known king Alfonso I (reigned 1065–1109), Christians captured the Muslim stronghold and commercial city of Toledo, which is located in the geographic center of the peninsula. During the twelfth and early thirteenth centuries Christian lords gradually pushed south until, by around 1250, the only Muslim kingdom left in the peninsula was the small territory of Granada in the far south. Granada existed as a Muslim enclave until it was conquered in 1492. Although territories changed hands, it took years for life to change fundamentally in the reconquered lands. Muslim populations still supplied necessary labor and taxes to their Christian rulers, who had no intention of destroying their best tax base, and there is some evidence that a disproportionate amount of craft and trade work was done by Muslims. By the fourteenth century, however, Muslims increasingly found themselves under suspicion. Along with the Jews, they were blamed for the outbreaks of famine and plague that punctuated the first half of the fourteenth century. Under such pressures and for various economic and social advantages, Muslims converted to Christianity. These converted Muslims continued to have a strong economic and social presence in later medieval Spain although the derogatory nickname of "conversos" (the converted ones), which was applied to Jewish and Muslim converts, shows the suspicion to which they were still subjected.

Life in a Jewish Enclave. Jews existed in small enclaves in most major commercial and governmental centers in medieval northern Europe as well as throughout the urban population in medieval Spain. These small communities developed for religious purposes—medieval Jews defined themselves as a "community of the chosen" while those who were not Jews were by definition not chosen—and for protection. Within these enclaves Jews lived much like other medieval Europeans. There were rich and poor Jews; the stereotypical idea that all Jews were wealthy money-lenders is completely false. Although Jews, like other medieval Europeans, attempted to obtain land, because they tended to live in cities they generally practiced craft and mercantile professions rather than farming. In some cases they were allowed trade with Christians, while in others their market was confined to other Jews or to export. Outside of the doctrinal and ritual differences between Christianity and Judaism, the primary difference between Jewish and Christian life in the Middle Ages was the constant insecurity that Jews faced. Their lack of attendance at the religious rituals that were so fundamental to many medieval Europeans automatically put them outside the community at large and made them seem suspicious. For this reason, communities generally knew who the Jewish residents were. The situation for Jews worsened in 1215, when the Fourth Lateran Council decreed that the Jews had to wear distinctive robes or marks on their clothing. Although it was possible to obtain waivers, these documents were expensive. For protection Jews relied on Christian secular and religious leaders, who did so mainly when they found aiding Jews advantageous.

Establishing Jewish Communities and Authority. Before they settled in an area, most Jewish communities received charters from their Christian lords. One clause that frequently reappears in these charters is the right of self-government within the Jewish community. Medieval Jews were led by a council of male elders who governed Jewish behavior, religious practices, and commercial dealings. These councils also acted as liaisons with Christian rulers and could be quite effective. In the middle of the fourteenth century the Jewish leaders of various communities in Aragon (a Spanish kingdom) met and were able have made into law a detailed ordinance that protected Jewish rights and properties. Often these councils were led by the community rabbi, their religious and intellectual

leader, who had spent many years studying the Torah, Talmud, and other sacred writings.

Jewish Employment and Medieval Lords. Always a minority religious group, Jews relied on medieval lords for protection, paying hefty taxes and making many "gifts" in return. Nevertheless, medieval lords did frequently expel Jews from their cities and even their kingdoms. For example, the French king Philip II Augustus (reigned 1180–1223) expelled the Jews from his kingdom in 1182, gaining the goodwill of the Church and profiting from confiscated Jewish wealth. In 1198, however, he readmitted the Jews but regulated one of the Jewish community's most lucrative professions, banking, as well as other Jewish commercial ventures, in such a way that he reserved large profits to himself. In medieval Spain the situation was far better for Jews. Jews held high offices in Muslim kingdoms, becoming diplomats and court physicians. In tenth-century Cordoba there was even a Jewish school (a yeshiva) with an international reputation, and Jews emigrated from all over the Mediterranean to live in Spain. It has been suggested that by about 1100, 90 percent of the Jews in the world lived in medieval Iberia. Even after the reconquest had begun, Spanish Christian rulers seem to have shown greater tolerance than their northern counterparts. Jews in many Spanish Christian kingdoms were put under the protection of the rulers, who until the later fourteenth and fifteenth centuries, seemed more willing to enforce their guardianship than other Christian lords. Christian kings in northern Spain used Jews as physicians, scientists, tax collectors, diplomats, judges, and public officials, and in the thirteenth century King James of Aragon encouraged Jews from North Africa and France to settle in his kingdom through property grants and tax exemptions.

Attitudes toward One Another—Jews and Christians. The attitudes of Christians and Jews toward one another were complex to say the least. At their most extreme Christians viewed the Jews as Christ killers and heretics, while Jews saw Christians as a fallen, impure people. In general, however, in medieval Spain the communities coexisted, and the attitudes varied depending on the individuals involved. Outside the Iberian peninsula, attitudes were more extreme. Jews saw Christians as treacherous and cruel, ready to renege on promises and legal contracts at a moment's notice. The general population of Christians tended to view the Jewish enclaves as a potential subversive community in their midst, dangerous precisely because their rituals and meetings were held "secretly" and must, therefore, be conspiracies. Christian theologians saw Jews as deliberately rejecting Christ's message and, for this reason, as not much different from heretics. A theologian and letter writer of the late twelfth century, Peter of Blois, expressed these attitudes in a treatise "Against the Perfidy of the Jews": "For the Jew is always inconstant and shifty. Now he says Yes, anon he says No, at one time he quibbles about the literal meaning, at another he refers all to the times of his own Messiah, i.e. of the Antichrist, and after the manner of his father the devil often changes into monstrous shapes."

Cases of Ritual Murder. Some medieval Christians believed that Jews seized children and tortured them to death as part of the rites for Passover. The need for blood—particularly innocent, young, children's blood—formed a key part of accusations that Jews performed ritual murders and of general suspicion of Jews in much of Christian Europe well into the seventeenth century. The first complete version of this myth appeared in the writings of Thomas of Monmouth, who recorded around 1173 the supposed ritual murder of a boy named William in the English town of Norwich during 1144. As the economy of Europe worsened in the late thirteenth century and as famines and plagues struck during the first half of the fourteenth century, Jews were increasingly accused of poisoning wells, causing crop failures, killing livestock, and performing magical ceremonies that led to plagues.

Sources:

Jon Irving Bloomberg, *The Jewish World in the Middle Ages* (New York: KTAV Publishing House, 2000).

Gilbert Dahan, *The Christian Polemic against the Jews in the Middle Ages*, translated by Jody Gladding (Notre Dame, Ind.: University of Notre Dame Press, 1998).

Salomon Grayzel, *The Church and the Jews in the Thirteenth Century*, 2 volumes (New York, Hermon Press, 1989).

Hugh N. Kennedy, *Muslim Spain and Portugal: A Political History of Al-Andalus* (London & New York : Longman, 1996).

JEWS AND MUSLIMS: DISCOVERING NON-CHRISTIAN PHILOSOPHIES

Traveling Scholars. During the early twelfth century Western Christian scholars began traveling to cities in Spain, Sicily, Antioch and Tripoli , where they came into

A scientist teaching with an astrolabe, an Arab invention for observing and calculating the position of celestial bodies; illumination from a 1348 Barcelona manuscript for Moses Maimonides' *Guide for the Perplexed* (Royal Library, Copenhagen)

contact with the works of non-Christian philosophers and began translating them into Latin. The arrival of Peter the Venerable in Spain in 1142 led to the first translation of the Koran, the Muslim holy book, into Latin. In the 1240s *Dalalat al-Ha'irin* (Guide for the Perplexed, written 1190) by the great Jewish legal thinker and philosopher Moses Maimonides (1138–1204) of Cordoba, Spain, was translated from Arabic into Latin and discussed in Christian schools, especially at the University of Naples, where Master Peter of Ireland, the teacher of Thomas Aquinas, placed great emphasis on this work, which influenced not only Aquinas but also Meister Eckhart and other medieval thinkers. Scholar-travelers also discovered and brought home works by Arabic philosophers, especially Avicenna (Abū 'Alī al-Husayn ibn 'Abd Allāh ibn Sīnā, 980–1037), from northern Persia (Iran) and Averroës (Ibn Rushd, 1126–1198) of Cordoba. Avicenna's works became a staple of university reading and commentary, and his metaphysics influenced every western philosopher from the twelfth century up to and including René Descartes in the seventeenth. After 1230 all medieval philosophers read Aristotle in conjunction with Averroës commentaries. In fact, he became known as "The Commentator" and Aristotle was called "The Philosopher."

Moses Maimonides. As Colette Sirat has written, "The whole history of Jewish medieval thought revolves about the personality of Maimonides . . . he is the term of reference as Thomas Aquinas is for scholasticism, and it is no accident but rather the mark of a profound affinity that the latter so often cites Rabbi Moses." Keenly aware that prophecy cannot be expressed by natural science, Maimonides acknowledged the limitations of human reason when speaking about the Divinity. Yet, he firmly believed that there is no necessary conflict between natural philosophy and knowledge of the Divine. Indeed, accurate natural knowledge can serve as preparation for the quest to understand the Divine. Like Thomas Aquinas, Maimonides held Aristotle in high regard. Indeed, following Aristotle, he showed that while one can expect rigor in mathematics, it is less possible in morality and religious understanding; yet, they do not lack foundation. Maimonides was concerned with precision in speaking about God. He took issue with thinkers who used anthropomorphic language to describe God because God does not have the human form or attributes those words imply. Instead he stressed that the best way for humankind to understand God was to determine what God is not—that is, how he differs from human beings. His theology is one of reverential silence in the face of divine mystery.

Averroës. In North Africa in 1168–1169 Averroës began a series of commentaries on the works of Aristotle, some of which—including Averroës work on Aristotle's *Poetics*—were translated into Latin in the thirteenth century. His coherent explanations of Aristotle's difficult and elliptical texts were a great benefit for the medieval philosophers of western Europe. Regardless of their disagreement with Averroës on the interpretation of Aristotle's doctrines on some philosophical and theological issues they welcomed his clarification of Aristotle. The Averroës that influenced western European scholars was Averroës the philosopher. They do not seem to have known about his Islamic religious and legal writings. The western European followers of Averroës' philosophy were commonly called "Latin Averroists" and included Siger of Brabant and Boethius of Dacia. Even if they disagreed with Averroës on significant issues, most medieval philosophers made use of his commentaries on Aristotle.

Avicenna. Some medieval scholars considered Avicenna the most important philosopher next to Augustine. Roger Bacon calls Avicenna the "Leader of the Philosophers." That is, Bacon believed that he was the leading interpreter of Aristotle, more important even than the Commentator on Aristotle, Averroës. Avicenna was a medical expert, a logician, a philosopher, a poet, and a government adviser. The most important of his works for the Christian West was *Al-Shifa'* (Healing, written 1020–1027), a philosophical synthesis of logic, physics, and metaphysics. In the influential metaphysics part of this work, which deals with the basic structure of reality, Avicenna made an important distinction between essence (what a thing is; the definition of the thing) and existence (that a thing is). In only one being are essence and existence identical: that being is God. Therefore, God exists necessarily; his existence is part of his very nature or definition. Every other being—whether angel, human, animal, plant, celestial body, or inanimate terrestrial object—is a composite of essence and existence. Therefore, anything else is only a possible, not a necessary, being, and if it is to exist, it must be brought into and preserved in existence by some cause external to itself. Avicenna also made an important distinction between a spiritual soul and a living body, and he helped focus attention on the fact that the human being is made up of a "plurality of forms" (or essential structures, including mineral, vegetative, animal, and rational).

Sources:

H. A. Davidson, *Alfarabi, Avicenna and Averroës on Intellect: Their Cosmologies, Theories of the Active Intellect, and Theories of Human Intellect* (New York: Oxford University Press, 1992).

Idit Dobbs-Weinstein, Entry on Moses Maimonides, in *Dictionary of Literary Biography*, volume 115: *Medieval Philosophers*, edited by Jeremiah Hackett (Detroit & London: Gale Research, 1992), pp. 263–280.

Oliver Leaman, *Averroës and His Philosophy* (Oxford: Clarendon Press / New York : Oxford University Press, 1988).

Leaman, *Introduction to Medieval Islamic Philosophy* (Cambridge & New York: Cambridge University Press, 1990).

Colette Sirat, *History of Jewish Philosophy in the Middle Ages* (Cambridge & New York: Cambridge University Press / Paris: Editions de la Maison des Sciences de l'Homme, 1985).

MONASTICISM

The Monastic Movement in Christianity. Monasticism developed between the fourth and fifth centuries, as the Christian Church was increasingly integrated into the world around it. The Desert Fathers such as Anthony of Egypt, the Celtic monks and missionaries such as St. Columban, and the developers of monastic guidelines such as St. Benedict of Nursia were among the early monastics who influenced the medieval tradition. During the early Middle Ages there arose a distinction between hermitical monasticism, where monks lived solitary lives, and cenobitic monasticism, where monks lived in common with other monks. Cenobitic monasticism was particularly influential in the medieval West from the ninth century, while the Greek East continued to have a strong hermetic tradition. Behind cenobitic monasticism was the idea that the act of living together might be an instrument of perfection, even as it allowed for mutual assistance, both spiritually and mentally.

A Monk's Role. In the West a conception of the monastery's role in a Christian society was developed by the sixth century and continued throughout the Middle Ages. This ideal saw the monastery as a spiritual citadel, a refuge for silence, prayer, and work. When a monk entered this fortress, he abandoned all worldly ties. Frequently, monasteries required that monks who went outside the monastery were not to speak of what they saw when they returned, and monastic clothing was designed to keep a monk's face from prying eyes—and to make it difficult for a monk to see other than straight ahead. Such distance from the world was not viewed as selfish, however. An ideal monk was seen as a spiritual warrior, devoted to prayer and good works that earned divine benefits for all Christians. In this sense the monk was a soldier of Christ who battled the corruptions of the world. In his battle for Christian souls, the monk was chiefly concerned with the opus Dei (work of God), which consisted primarily of common prayer at set times throughout the day. But the monastery was also meant to be a self-sufficient community, in which the monk might work manually in order to provide for his needs and those of his brethren; his work might also be intellectual and, if he were able, he might have copied books that served as the cultural and spiritual formation of the community. The abbot governed the monastic community following a strictly paternal model and was assisted by monks holding various offices. Despite these spiritual roles, monks also had great influence in secular society. Monks became the developers of advanced agrarian techniques, carried out the conversion of the rural population to Christianity, and served as the chief agents of preservation of ancient culture through their copying of ancient manuscripts.

Monastic Rules. Monastic communities were organized following rules developed by the ostensible founders of their community. Throughout the Middle Ages, especially through the tenth century, the most influential of these monastic rules was that formulated by St. Benedict of Nursia: the Benedictine Rule. He composed the rule for his monastic community at Monte Cassino in Italy between 530 and 560; over the next several centuries his rule was adopted in the vast majority of western monasteries and influenced many nonmonastic religious communities as well. Reform movements in medieval monasteries often started with the Benedictine Rule as a model and altered it

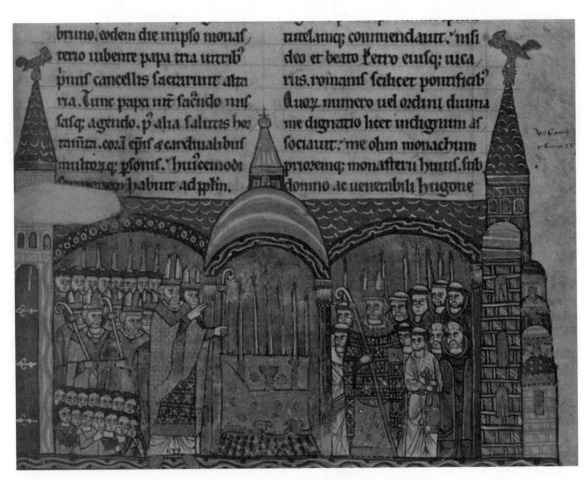

The consecration of the Abbey of Cluny, 1131; illumination from a twelfth-century manuscript for *Chronicle of the Abbey of Cluny* (Bibliothèque Nationale, Paris)

to suit their needs. There were other important rules as well. The rule attributed to St. Augustine was extremely influential in the later Middle Ages, and modifications of the Benedictine Rule, such as the Carta Caritatis (the charter of charity) of the Cistercians, gained powerful lives of their own in the twelfth and thirteenth centuries. Both St. Francis and St. Clare of Assisi wrote rules for their communities as soon as the Pope approved their formation. These rules were important not only because they regulated, in great detail, how the monks lived, but also because they expressed a vision of the monks' roles in society and in Christian spirituality.

Monks and Property. As with other Church institutions, monasteries had a complicated relationship to property and material goods. In the vows a man took when becoming a monk were oaths of poverty, chastity, and obedience. Often, in their pursuit of solitude, monks were pioneers moving into uninhabited or sparsely inhabited parts of Europe to establish their communities. In other cases, however, pious laity awarded the monks plots of land. Possession of land in medieval Europe came with a series of responsibilities that monks could not in good conscience ignore. Whether peasants came with these land grants or peasants settled in areas the monks had pioneered, monasteries were soon saddled with the burdens of medieval lordship, such as gathering taxes, supervising workers, enforcing laws in the communities surrounding them, and providing religious services. Given the structures of medieval society, it was impossible to ignore these demands and morally reprehensible to abandon peasant communities to marauding bands. Monasteries, thus, frequently took on the same duties as medieval lordships, including hospitality for travelers, military protection, and law enforcement. Yet, monasteries also enjoyed the profits that came from their lands. Individual monks were supposed to be poor, and many were, but monasteries were frequently enormously rich. Not all medieval Europeans were bothered by this situation either. Nobles frequently endowed monastic communities with the provision that members of their families would become abbots or abbesses, and some monasteries demanded initiation fees that were affordable only for nobles. One such place was the French "royal abbey" at Fontevrault that sheltered such figures as Eleanor of Aquitaine, Queen of England and Duchess of Aquitaine. Faced with the contradiction between ideals and practice, monastic reformers frequently grappled with the question of poverty, and by the later Middle Ages popular opinion gradually turned against the older, wealthy monastic communities. At the same time, however, medieval Europeans still tried to get their sons and daughters places in these abbeys.

Monks and Government. Monastic relations with property were further complicated because of the important roles certain medieval monks played in governmental administration. At the time of Charlemagne's death in 814 the best-known monk in western Europe was St. Benedict of Aniane, a friend and councilor of Louis I, Charlemagne's successor. Benedict's role represents one career opportunity available to medieval monks: government official. Such activity required a dispensation, an exemption from some parts of the monastic vows provided by the head of the order or the Pope. Medieval lords were quite eager to enlist qualified monks into their service. Monks, particularly those who had been abbots at major monasteries, had years of education and experience at running complicated bureaucracies. They knew how to develop long- and short-term strategies, were familiar with the major political players in a region, brought some of their own alliances, and could conduct themselves appropriately in noble society. Moreover, a monk might have family members that he wanted to help, but he was rarely interested in establishing a dynasty in the way that secular lords would. For these reasons, medieval rulers turned to monks such as Abbots Suger of St. Denis, Lanfranc of Canterbury, and Anselm of Canterbury to serve as their chief ministers.

The Cluniac Reform. Beginning in the tenth century, several new monastic foundations were established. The best known of these foundations was Cluny, founded by William the Pious, Duke of Aquitaine, in 910. Although a Benedictine community, the charters for Cluny made several important changes to the Benedictine Rule, especially in the centralization of its monastic government. Monasteries who followed the Cluniac reform and monasteries founded by Cluniac monks remained under the sovereignty of the abbot of Cluny; their abbots and monks had to be approved by Cluny, and every monk had to spend some years at Cluny. Cluniac monasticism stressed individual simplicity among its monks, but liturgical and ritual complexity among the monastic community as a whole. Additional devotional exercises were added to the six a day already required by the Benedictine Rule. Cluny became known for its wealth and the beauty and complexity of its religious services. By the twelfth century, on some of the important feasts days of the Church year—such as that of St. Peter, to whom the abbey of Cluny was dedicated—the monks were required to pray from sunset to dawn of the next day without interruption. Even on ordinary days, much of the Cluniac monk's day was taken up by prayer, without leaving much time for reading or other activities. These activities took place in an abbey church that was the largest in Christendom when it was consecrated in 1131. The impressiveness of the monk's public prayer helped make its support a good investment in the eyes of contemporaries and extended the influence of Cluny throughout Europe. In addition, Cluny was fortunate to have a series of brilliant and influential abbots during its first two hundred years. For example, the eighth abbot of Cluny, Peter the Venerable (1092–1156), instituted reforms in the order,

sheltered Peter Abelard, defended the Jews, and refused to have anything to do with the Second Crusade, arguing that the Muslims should be met with rational scholars instead of armies. He served as a papal envoy throughout Europe and wrote hymns, religious tracts, and many letters, more than two hundred of which still survive.

Reactions to Cluny. In its early years other monasteries often asked Cluny to send monks to show them how things were done in the Cluniac style. By the end of the tenth century, Cluny began to exert its influence in a more formal manner. In traditional Benedictine monasticism, each monastery was autonomous, ruled by its own abbot. Cluny decided to found or accept monasteries that were not independent; each of these communities was intended to be directly subject to the abbot of Cluny. After the mid eleventh century, the abbot of Cluny was formally the ruler of more than nine hundred monasteries, largely in France and Switzerland, but also in Britain, Spain, and Italy. It is interesting that the ideal of independence from secular interference in monastic life characterized Cluny from the moment of its foundation. Duke William of Aquitaine, in establishing the house and dedicating it to St. Peter, renounced his right, as founder, to elect the abbot of the new monastery; he asked his own kinsmen, the king of France, bishops, and the Pope to refrain from interfering in any way in the life of the abbey. He placed it under the protection of Saints Peter and Paul and the popes, who were asked to excommunicate anyone who interfered with the liberties of the monastery. Before the end of the tenth century the popes had accepted the duke's request and even declared Cluny independent of the supervision of the local bishop. Cluny became one of the seed houses of reform and of resistance to traditional involvement of lay people in electing abbots. This independence was one of the sources of the agenda of the eleventh-century reformers, who, in effect, attempted to make the autonomy of Cluny the norm for all sorts of ecclesiastical institutions and bishoprics themselves. Also, they said, papal control over the rest of the Church should essentially mirror the control of the abbot of Cluny over the daughter houses. This kind of control was regarded as the necessary safeguard against contamination of the Church's function to ensure the authenticity of the religious experience of the faithful.

The Cistercians and Bernard of Clairvaux. Despite Cluny's great influence, by the early eleventh century there were reactions against Cluny that led to the formation of new monastic communities, such as the Carthusians. Probably the most influential medieval reaction against Cluny occurred in 1098 with the foundation of the Cistercians by Robert of Molesmes. Among the early members was the best-known medieval Cistercian, Bernard of Clairvaux (1090–1153). At the age of twenty-seven Bernard was sent with other young monks to form the fourth Cistercian monastery at Cîteaux in what is now eastern France. Clairvaux and the community Bernard led became the models for Cistercian reform. Like the Cluniac Rule, the Cistercian Rule called for centralization and accountability to the head of the Cistercian order. The Cistercians were, in fact, the first to use the term *order* to describe all those who followed their rule. Unlike the Cluniacs, Cistercians placed a far higher priority on poverty and physical mortification, a difference that led to an exchange of letters between Bernard and Peter the Venerable. Although most Cistercians distanced themselves from worldly concerns, Bernard was pulled into them because of his reputation for personal piety. One of the most influential clergymen of his generation, Bernard inspired reform in bishoprics and monasteries throughout Europe, and he sent groups of Cistercians to establish monasteries in Germany, Sweden, Scotland, Portugal, and Italy. He disputed with Peter Abelard and raised troops for the Second Crusade. His activity at the Council of Troyes, called to resolve disputes within the French church, led one cardinal to complain, "It is not fitting that noisy and troublesome frogs should come out of their marshes to trouble the Holy See and the cardinals." Bernard the frog and the Cistercians, however, had far more supporters than detractors.

Nuns. Just as male religious communities had been part of the earliest Christian communities, so too were communities of women. In fact, early medieval monasteries sometimes included male and female communities that had separate sleeping quarters but shared the monastery church and other facilities. It was even possible in the ninth and tenth centuries for a female abbess to rule over both monks and nuns, although it was exceptional, and the abbess was generally of noble descent. Eleventh- and twelfth-century reform movements gradually led to the complete separation of male and female monastic communities. Women entered monastic communities for much the same reason as men: personal piety, social security, and family pressure. Monasteries provided nuns with a sure livelihood and families with an individual who would certainly pray for them—an inside track to God. Although nuns tended to be less involved in intellectual pursuits than their male counterparts, some—such as Heloise, Hildegard of Bingen, and Mechtild of Hackeborn—made valuable contributions to medieval thought and piety. One important difference between male monasteries and female nunneries was that women's communities tended on the average to be poorer, not attracting the type of lucrative or consistent donations that their male counterparts did.

Sources:

H. E. J. Cowdrey, *The Cluniacs and the Gregorian Reform* (Oxford: Clarendon Press, 1970).

G. R. Evans, *Bernard of Clairvaux* (New York: Oxford University Press, 2000).

C. H. Lawrence, *Medieval Monasticism: Forms of Religious Life in Western Europe in the Middle Ages,* second edition (London & New York: Longman, 1989).

Ludo J. R. Milis, *Angelic Monks and Earthly Men: Monasticism and Its Meaning to Medieval Society* (Rochester, N.Y.: Boydell Press, 1992).

MYSTICISM

The Place of Mysticism in Medieval Christianity. Although the medieval Church stressed the importance of good works to salvation, a strong mystical streak existed alongside this practical Christianity. Mysticism emphasizes individual and immediate communion with God through means beyond rational understanding. It may be manifested through dreams, raptures, and visions. Mystics spent days fasting, received signs of divine favor, and made prophesies. The medieval Church had an ambivalent attitude toward such mystics. On the one hand, the Church had no doubt that God could choose to communicate directly with Christians, and its theology stressed the importance of personal experience of the divine and how that experience would transcend all forms of worldly experience. On the other hand, how could they be sure these visions were from God? Satan was by definition the prince of deceivers, and sending false visions was something he would do to thwart Christians. For these reasons, many medieval mystics and their spiritual guides were often torn when they began having visions and other mystical experiences, and the Church generally regarded mystical movements quite closely and with great skepticism.

Revelation and Apocalypse. Religious life in the Middle Ages appears to have been lived in perennial expectation of the end of the world. Basing their belief on the Book of Revelations, medieval clergy and laity had a clear vision of this final battle between the forces of good and evil. Images of the Apocalypse (the final battle) adorned medieval churches, and descriptions of its terrors fill medieval manuscripts. Figures from the Apocalypse also provided a rhetoric of evil used long after the Middle Ages; to call an opponent the Antichrist (the opposite of Christ and the leader of the evil force in the final, 1,000-year battle) remained the ultimate condemnation in Christian society during the sixteenth and seventeenth centuries. Although much has been written about the supposed "terrors of the year 1000," the expectation that the end of the world was near was a major feature of the whole medieval age rather than something people discovered only at the millennium. Yet, the coming of Christ in judgment was not only a fearful prospect but also a joyful one. One strand in the millenarian tradition that was already very much present as early as the tenth century is the belief that a time of justice and joy will be enjoyed between the Second Coming of Christ and the end of time. Although emphasized less frequently than the terrors of battle and judgment, this expectation of a better age to follow the end of present decadence and injustice was an important part of medieval beliefs about the Apocalypse.

Orthodox Mysticism: Christ and Female Mysticism. A particularly enduring expression of mystical trends may be found in the experience of unity with the suffering Christ, which was experienced by a host of women mystics. In the high Middle Ages, this tradition of female mysticism included Hroswitha of Gandersheim (circa 1000) and Hildegard of Bingen (1109–1179), and it came to a fuller and more striking maturity with women who were linked to the Mendicant movement, such as Clare of Assisi (died 1253), Catherine of Siena (died 1380), Bridget of Sweden

Hildegard of Bingen having a mystical vision of man's nature and his place in the cosmos; illumination from an early-thirteenth-century manuscript for her *Liber divinorum operum* (Biblioteca Governativa, Lucca)

self in public debate. His case gained such international recognition that he pleaded it before the papal court. Censured for his sermons, in particular his focus on direct individual communion with God over the sacraments of the Christian Church, Eckhart retreated from preaching. In the fifteenth century, however, he became a model for people seeking more personalized religious expression.

Suspect Mysticism: Joachim of Fiore. One of the most influential mystics on marginal religious groups in the Middle Ages was the Italian Joachim of Fiore (1132–

(died 1373), and many others. Their mystical experiences had an intense visual quality; from their descriptions it is possible to draw detailed pictures of Christ's crucifixion, of a spiritual marriage ceremony with Christ, and of Christ's lifting them spiritually and physically. Although the themes of their piety were not radically different from those of their male counterparts, these women were often more identified with the Christ-like bearing of suffering. The description of mystical experience as a bridal relationship with Christ crucified also acquires a particular power with these women, as does their expression of desire for union with Christ in the eucharist. Through them these themes and approaches became characteristic of medieval, and of much modern, Christian piety.

Academic Mysticism: Meister Eckhart. Eckhart (circa 1260–1328) was a German Dominican who was trained in theology at Paris and Cologne, two of the leading universities of his time. It has been argued that while in Paris he saw the heresy trial of the mystic Marguerite Porete and was influenced by her courage. Certainly, he was exposed to the Movement of the Free Spirit in the Rhineland, and he preached in German to Beghard and Beguine groups. They wrote down his sermons and their interpretations of them, which could vary greatly from the content of Eckhart's original. In 1325–1326 he was accused of heresy by the archbishop of Cologne and attempted to defend him-

SPIRITUAL POVERTY

Meister Eckhart was known for the mysticism of his sermons, and his style affected the preaching of other German scholars. For this reason some thirteenth-century sermons that are attributed to Eckhart, including the excerpt below, may well have been written and delivered by others. Spiritual poverty was a common topic among medieval mystics and often aroused the suspicions of the Church about the preacher's orthodoxy.

The poor in spirit go out of themselves and all creatures: they are nothing, they have nothing, they do nothing, and these poor are not save that by grace they are God with God: which they are not aware of. St Augustine says, all things are God. St. Dionysius says, things are not God. St. Augustine says, God is all of them. But St. Dionysius: God is nothing we can say or think, yet God is the hope of all the saints, their intuition of him wherein he is himself. He [Dionysius] finds him more in naught; God is naught, he says. In naught all is suspended. All that has being is in suspension in naught, this naught being itself an incomprehensible aught that all minds in heaven and on earth cannot either fathom or conceive. Hence it remains unknown to creatures. When the soul attains to the perfection of hanging to (being suspended from) naught she will find herself without sin. This is due to the freedom she is poised in. Then on coming to the body and awareness of herself, and again finding sin as before, she becomes bound and then she returns into herself and bethinks her of what she has found yonder. Thus she raises herself up above herself and crosses over to the seat of all her happiness and all her satisfaction. St Bernard says the soul knows very well that her beloved cannot come to her till everything is out of her. St Augustine says, Well and truly loves the man who loves where he well knows he is not loved; that is the best of all loving. St Paul, we know right well that all things work together for good to them that love God. And Christ said, Blessed are the poor in spirit, God's kingdom is theirs. They tell of various kinds of poverty of spirit. There are four. What he refers to here is the first poverty of spirit the soul knows when, illumined by the spirit of truth, things that are not God weigh with her not a jot; as St Paul tells us, "All things are dung to me." In this indigence she finds all creatures irksome.

Source: Franz Pfeiffer, ed., *Meister Eckhart*, 2 volumes, translated by C. De B. Evans (London: Watkins, 1924, 1931), quoted on-line at <http://www.geocities.com/hckarlso/eckhart.htm>

1202). Beginning as a courtier with the Norman kings of Sicily, he turned from worldly concerns after viewing a great calamity; later writings suggest that this event might have been an outbreak of disease, but there is no clear evidence. By the time he was twenty-seven he was preaching, without any theological training, without joining any religious order, and without becoming a priest. When the clergy objected to his activities, he took monastic vows. He spent the rest of his life moving from monastery to monastery in Italy, where many saw him as a prophet. Although Joachim disavowed this claim, his interpretations of the Apocalypse and the doctrine of the third age of the spirit, which he developed, influenced generations of mystics. According to Joachim, history could be divided into three ages, which correspond to the three persons of the Trinity. God the Father ruled the first age, the age of the Old Testament, while God the Son ruled the second age and its New Testament revelations. The third age, ruled by the Holy Spirit, will be an age of universal love that will transcend the Gospel, and in it disciplinary institutions will be unnecessary. For Joachim the second age was coming to an end, and the third age would begin around 1260, after some disaster. Although some of his teachings were condemned at the Fourth Lateran Council (1215), the idea of the ages was not suspect until the middle of the thirteenth century. By this time a group of radical followers, calling themselves Joachimists or Joachimites, had arisen in the Franciscans. The Joachimites argued that around 1200 the New and Old Testaments had lost their force and that the new age was at hand, prefigured by the persecutions of true believers (the Joachimites). Even more radical forms of Joachimites evolved. Joachim's relatively harmless idea of an angelic pope, come to cleanse the Church, became a female pope, who—working with cardinals who were all women—would convert the Jews and write new scriptures guided by the Holy Spirit.

Sources:

Norman Cohn, *The Pursuit of the Millennium: Revolutionary Millenarians and Mystical Anarchists of the Middle Ages*, revised edition (New York: Oxford University Press, 1970).

Amy Hollywood, *The Soul as Virgin Wife: Mechthild of Magdeburg, Marguerite Porete, and Meister Eckhart* (Notre Dame: University of Notre Dame Press, 1995).

Bernard McGinn, *Visions of the End: Apocalyptic Traditions in the Middle Ages*, expanded edition (New York: Columbia University Press, 1998).

Marjorie Reeves, *Joachim of Fiore and the Prophetic Future* (New York: Harper & Row, 1977).

Ulrike Wiethaus, ed., *Maps of Flesh and Light: The Religious Experience of Medieval Women Mystics* (Syracuse: Syracuse University Press, 1993).

PIETY

Defining Piety. Piety is the outward expression of that form of belief usually called *spirituality*. The medieval Church recognized that a person's actions were relatively easy to ascertain and, thus, placed great emphasis on good deeds. At the same time it recognized the difficulty in supervising a person's spirituality, and it focused much of its Church policy on developing correct piety, hoping that this outward expression would correlate to an equally correct spirituality. The piety of the medieval Europeans also reflected the synthetic elements in medieval Christianity. By the ninth century most European peoples had been nominally Christian for centuries; a few, especially the Scandinavians, were converted only around the year 1000. Little evidence has survived about the extent of the religious instruction that most laypeople received, but it is known that many old pagan superstitions survived. Furthermore, the elements of Christianity that had most in common with a people's pagan beliefs and practices were those that most firmly gripped the illiterate converts in early days. The old Germanic religion, for example, had high gods and a host of lesser spirits, who were especially attached to specific physical places and objects. Christianity too had its high God and welcomed devotion to many saints, all of whom had their favorite local habitations that were closely associated with their physical remains. Equally alive were the evil spirits, or devils, who took over many of the activities of the underworld that could not be attributed to God and his saints. There is, however, a danger in putting too much emphasis on a supposed continuity from paganism to Christianity. While historians know little about the beliefs of common people in the Christian period, they know even less of the paganism that these beliefs replaced.

The Foundations of Salvation. By the thirteenth century the Christian Church in the West had developed a theory and system of salvation designed to facilitate the movement of all Christians into heaven, a passage that Christ had opened to Christians by his sacrifice on the cross. Based on the premise that all humans were born sinful, the Church designed a series of steps to mark a Christian soul's progress. These steps were called sacraments, and by the thirteenth century a general sacramental system was in place. The seven sacraments were, in the order a Christian might receive them: baptism, confession, eucharist, confirmation, marriage, holy orders, and last rites. Holy orders, which marks the reception of an individual into the priesthood, was the only sacrament not experienced by the majority of Christians. The appropriate performance of these rites was one of the many good works Christians were expected to perform in order to prepare themselves for salvation. In addition, there were many other activities in which Christians could be involved to express their piety and to ease their salvation, including providing dowries for poor girls, giving land or buildings to the clergy, contributing to poor relief, and aiding the sick.

Liturgy. Holding a divine service was one of the most powerful ways medieval Christians expressed their piety. Modeled on the Last Supper, the mass of the medieval Christian Church combined prayers, chants, Gospel readings, and even sermons. The service culminated in the offering of the eucharist, a wafer that had been transformed into the actual body of Christ, to members of the congregation that had prepared themselves spiritually through fasting, a confession of their sins, and true repentance for them. These masses took various forms in the Middle

Henry II of England carrying a relic of the Holy Blood from St. Paul's Cathedral to Westminster Abbey on St. Edward's day (13 October) in 1247; illumination from a thirteenth-century manuscript by Matthew Paris (Corpus Christi College, Cambridge)

Ages, depending on whether communion was offered to the congregation at large or the priest alone took it as the mediator between the laity and God. They also differed depending on the degree of ritual, and the masses held to commemorate the highest holy days of the year, such as Easter (Christ's death and resurrection) and Pentecost (Christ returning to the disciples after his resurrection) were the most elaborate of the year. There were also a series of secondary services held throughout the year. A medieval church frequently had one main, central altar and a series of smaller altars on the sides of the building, so a church often echoed with the sound of chants, prayers, and other services throughout the day and well into the evening. Moreover, it was not uncommon for medieval Christians to attend these services as often as they were available, and medieval rulers, clergy, and other laity were praised for hearing mass daily.

Churches and Their Furnishings. The sites for these liturgical practices were churches, and during the period between the tenth and twelfth centuries great effort and wealth were expended in building them. Impressive buildings arose everywhere, from the cathedrals of France and England to the royal chapels of Sicily. These buildings reveal the generosity of the patrons who provided the bulk of the construction funds. The donors' motives were often secular as well as religious. Some of these patrons hoped not only to win heaven but also renown; the Normans of England may have been partly motivated to build such impressive buildings to impress the conquered English. Even religious motives might have been mixed, according to the simplicity or sophistication of the religious thought of the patron. A church was the house of God: his image looked down in majesty from somewhere in all these buildings. The drama of Christ's passion was reenacted daily, at mass. After God, the patron saint of the specific church

could be regarded as the chief living presence. A saint was thought to have a special interest in a church dedicated to him or her, and an overwhelming interest in the church that housed his or her mortal remains. After the saint, the most important occupants of the greater churches were the bishop or abbot and the community of monks and canons. Priests performed the sacrifice of the mass, whose growing importance in general piety is also demonstrated by the increasing number of side chapels that appeared in churches during the Middle Ages, each with an altar at which celebrations of the mass might take place. In churches large and small, cycles of paintings and stained glass instructed the illiterate laity. The artistic efforts expended in church building were clearly meant to be primarily pedagogical, rather than decorative. A council of Arras, as early as 1025, put it this way: "the simple and the illiterate cannot see in the Scriptures Christ in the humble state in which he willed to suffer and die for us; let them therefore contemplate this by means of paintings." In addition, pious individuals paid for paintings, sculptures, and small offerings to be placed throughout the church. Although medieval churches strike modern viewers as having a stark majesty, during the thirteenth century they were riots of color. Walls were painted; sculpted tombs were set in walls and floors; families hung banners near their personal altars; and small wax images called *ex votos* were left at key locations in a church to thank God, Mary, or a saint for a blessing or favor.

Preaching. Because, at most, 5 percent of the medieval European population was in any way literate, communicating Christian doctrine and correct pious practices was a challenge for the medieval Church. Modern scholars often suggest that one method the Church used was preaching. Unfortunately, not much evidence of preaching survives from before the thirteenth century. Much earlier preaching that appears to have been "learned," in the sense that it consisted in reading translations or summaries of the homilies of the Fathers of the Church. Examples do exist, however, of twelfth-century sermons by preachers such as Bernard of Clairvaux, who could sway large lay audiences. With the friars in the late twelfth century the sermon became an important means of Christian instruction and entertainment. It is hard to minimize the effect that the revival of urban life, which began in the eleventh century, also had over religious practices. The urban environment provided a concentration of Christians, a disproportionate number of whom had some education and were literate, as an audience for the friars' sermons. These sermons in turn apparently inspired medieval city dwellers to a closer examination of the Gospels and increased their hunger for additional sermons. This medieval urban piety, inspired by a succession of famous preachers, fostered reform movements well into the sixteenth century.

Intercession and Saints. Given humanity's innately sinful condition and the difficulties of attaining heavenly perfection, much less just the difficulties of life on earth, Christians turned to conspicuously holy figures for guidance and support. By the ninth century some regulation had been given to these beliefs, and by the late twelfth century a system of recognition of these figures, known as saints, was in place. Key to this system was their role in interceding on behalf of less-blessed Christians. It was regarded as shocking in the Middle Ages that the average Christian should pray directly to God; instead, saints were advocated as appropriate go-betweens or intercessors between mortals and God. Considered more approachable and less preoccupied with universal matters, saints were perceived as having special interests not only in particular places but also in specific sorts of people. In addition to places where they had lived or churches where pieces of their earthly bodies were kept, they were often believed to protect their namesakes and people in specific professions. For example, St. Sebastian was the patron saint of archers because he was shot to death with arrows, and St. Francis was the patron saint of animals because he preached to them. Collections of miracles, such as the popular thirteenth-century *Golden Legend* of Jacobus de Voraigne, are full of stories of how a saint cured the sick who came to his tomb, saved from harm those who prayed to him, or destroyed those who were rash enough to attack his property or molest his faithful. Whatever modern views of miracles may be, it is clear that, in the Middle Ages, many people expected the supernatural to impinge on daily life. God and his saints were active in their world.

Pilgrimage and Relics. Among the laity, pilgrimages most commonly took the form of trips to visit relics of holy figures and saints. Physical objects associated with a saint, relics, were generally a saint's bones. Relics could be quite personal; among the relics on display in the Middle Ages were the milk of the Virgin and the foreskin of Jesus. More than a reminder of the saint, a relic was seen as a sign of the actual presence of that figure at the site where his or her

A POSSESSED WOMAN

Like stories of the saints' blessings, stories of how the Devil and his servants caused human misfortune were prevalent in the Middle Ages. The following story comes from Caesar of Heisterbach's well-known thirteenth-century collection of miracles, which was used extensively in medieval sermons. As in most accounts of the Devil's work, he is eventually defeated by the Church and saints.

When our abbot was celebrating mass last year on the Mount of the Holy Saviour near Aachen, a possessed woman was brought to him after the mass. When he had read the gospel lesson concerning the Ascension over her head and at these words, "They shall lay hands on the sick and they shall recover," had placed his hand upon her head, the devil gave such a terrible roar that we were all terrified. Adjured to depart, he [the Devil] replied, "The Most High does not wish it yet." When asked in what manner he entered, he did not reply nor did he permit the woman to reply. Afterward she confessed that when her husband in anger said, "Go to the devil" she felt the latter enter through her ear. Moreover that woman was from the province of Aachen and very well known.

Source: Caesar of Heisterbach, *Caesarii Heisterbacensis monachi ordinis cisterciensis dialogue miraculorum*, 2 volumes, edited by Joseph Strange (Cologne: Published for H. Lempertz by J. M. Heberle, 1851), I: 291.

relic was housed; thus, their importance and the value of visits to them. Promises to go on pilgrimage were a common part of medieval repentance. Most pilgrimages were to sites within two or three days' travel from a pilgrim's primary residence. Certain pilgrimages, however, were regarded as especially meritorious and adventurous, once in a lifetime trips. Among these were travels to Rome to visit the tombs of the apostles and the martyrs. St. Martin at Tours in France, St. Patrick's purgatory in Ireland, and St. Michael in southern Italy were popular throughout the Middle Ages. St. James of Compostela in Spain became increasingly attractive in the course of the Christian reconquest of Muslim Spain; the image of St. James as Moor slayer was long a favorite. Dramatic events of the Middle Ages gave rise to new shrines. Such was the case when the dispute between King Henry II of England and Thomas à Becket, archbishop of Canterbury, led to the murder of the archbishop in 1170. Thomas's tomb at Canterbury almost immediately became an important pilgrimage center and remained so until it was torn down during the Reformation. For the truly pious, or the truly foolhardy, the Tomb of Christ in Jerusalem remained the ultimate pilgrimage destination. Jerusalem drew the faithful because of its close association with the life, death, and resurrection of Christ. The holy voyage to Jerusalem became the archetypal pilgrimage, joining the ascetic practice of an arduous and risky journey and satisfying the duty to do penance for sin in order to truly renew oneself. At the end of the trip bathing in the Jordan River at the same place where Jesus had been baptized was a dramatic sign of rebirth. In fact, one of the most enduring forms of pilgrimage in the second half of the Middle Ages was the Crusade.

Images of Christ. Christ always had an important role in religious art and contemplation in the Middle Ages, but the way Christ was approached and visualized varied over time. In the eleventh and twelfth centuries Christ was frequently depicted in majesty, which emphasized his divinity, and in judgment, which stressed reward of virtue and the penalties of sin. The crucifixion was also represented, although not as frequently as the majesty, and even on the cross Christ was usually depicted as triumphant over death and was frequently shown crowned with the crown of royalty. Toward the end of the eleventh century artists began to depict the suffering Christ. In the thirteenth century a greater emphasis on Christ's humanity was related to the more personal spirituality of that period. Christ was depicted helping his mother, as a real infant, or interacting with his disciples as a fellow man. Medieval mystics took this personal emphasis and visualized Christ, using traditional Christian rhetoric, as a bridegroom, waiting for the repentant and faithful Christian just as a benevolent groom waits for a reluctant and embarrassed bride.

The Virgin Mary. By the thirteenth century, with the emphasis on Christ's humanity, came a stress on the person of his mother. Veneration of the Virgin Mary spread to people at large. In the late Middle Ages the Virgin Mary became a kind of ultimate saint, the mother of all mankind, who was interested in everything having to do with her Christian children. As a benign but strict mother, she filled an intermediate position between the sinful Christian and God the Father, who seemed to be increasingly distant and patriarchal. Focus on the Virgin's tender care for Christians was a key element in mendicant piety, and quickly spread throughout Europe through Franciscan and Dominican preaching. In fact, the veneration of the Virgin Mary is an important exception to the localness of most devotion to saints and its vast spread, from the eleventh century onward, operated as a powerful element of spiritual unification of the entire West.

Criticisms of Medieval Piety. The concentration of effort, the excitement, and the sense of dedication in the building of so many churches might lead one to believe that everyone in medieval Europe must have supported the efforts. These elaborate and expensive efforts were considered symbols of man's devotion to God, but some people took a different view. They saw the gold, silver, and precious stones that adorned sacred objects as symbols of worldly riches and pride in a society where most people were poor. These objects were also called proof that the Church was the Church of the powerful and the privileged. The most extreme critics argued that sacred images were perhaps idolatrous. St. Bernard of Clairvaux said of the great building efforts of the monks of Cluny: "I put aside the vast height of their churches, the excessive length, the empty spaces, the rich finish, the curious paintings. We will

look rather at the sumptuous ornaments encrusted with gems and gold, put there so that money may breed money and pilgrims may give to the monks alms that should be bestowed upon the true poor. . . . Just Heaven! Even if they are not choked by their impropriety, they might at least hesitate at the cost."

Sources:

Caroline Walker Bynum, *Jesus as Mother: Studies in the Spirituality of the High Middle Ages* (Berkeley: University of California Press, 1982).

Bernard Hamilton, *Religion in the Medieval West* (London & Baltimore: Edward Arnold, 1986).

Jeffrey Burton Russell, *Lucifer, The Devil in the Middle Ages* (Ithaca, N.Y.: Cornell University Press, 1984).

André Vauchez, *The Laity in the Middle Ages: Religious Beliefs and Devotional Practices,* edited by by Daniel E. Bornstein. translated by Margery J. Schneider (Notre Dame, Ind.: University of Notre Dame Press, 1993).

Diana Webb, *Pilgrims and Pilgrimage in Medieval Europe* (New York: Tauris, 1999).

THE PROBLEM OF EVIL: AUGUSTINE AND AQUINAS

Definitions of Evil. Medieval theologians' responses to the problem of evil were influenced by two related but different religious and philosophical systems. A movement that can be called medieval Manichaeism offered a dualist explanation of evil, which differed considerably from that proposed by the Christian Platonism of Augustine in the fifth century and the Christian Aristotelian Platonism of Thomas Aquinas in the thirteenth. For the Manichaeans, the human body as material was evil. Human reason was a good. Thus, their philosophical and religious life consisted in a purification of the body so that the true "rational" self-purification could be achieved. Manichaeans believed that since God is perfectly good he could not have created the physical world, which is evil, and, thus, there must exist another purely evil principle in opposition to God. Plotinus, however, taught that evil was a privation, not an actual force. Thus, Augustine wrote that God created the world as wholly good and that evil is an absence of good that occurs through man's exercise of free will.

Rejecting Manichaeanism. Augustine also inherited the Christian tradition of respect for the human body. Early in his life Augustine had been a committed Manichaean for more than a decade. As he matured, he rejected not only their definition of evil but also their dualistic view that soul and body were two entirely unrelated and antagonistic substances, and converted from Manichaeanism to Catholic Christianity. For Augustine, as for the Neoplatonic philosophers, being is essentially good, and evil is a privation, not an actual positive force in nature.

Aquinas and Aristotle. Thomas Aquinas inherited both the theological tradition of Augustine, including his definition of evil, and the philosophical-theological tradition of Aristotle. By the time Aquinas earned his doctorate from the University of Paris in 1256, the philosophy faculty had already made Aristotle "the Philosopher" (*Philosophus*). Just as the Apostle Paul was the "Scriptural" authority, Aristotle was the "Philosophical" authority. Thinkers still read Platonic texts, but Aristotle had provided them with explicit logical methods for the analysis of arguments, and with significant new ideas in physics, metaphysics, theory of knowledge, ethics, and philosophy of mind. Aquinas attempted to correlate the new Aristotelianism with traditional Stoic and Neoplatonic teachings. Like Augustine, Aquinas was fundamentally optimistic even in a time of great military and geopolitical turmoil. His family in the Kingdom of Naples had suffered much during the war between the Holy Roman Emperor and the papacy, including the murder of his brother, but Aquinas adopted a positive and serene attitude to life. For him, as for Augustine, the human body was not something to be despised. Because he held that matter was a positive good, he saw reason and the human body as existing in a positive relationship to one another.

Sources:

J. A. Aertsen, *Nature and Creature: Thomas Aquina's Way of Thought*, translated by Herbert Donald Morton (New York & London: Brill, 1988);

John M. Rist, *Augustine: Ancient Thought Baptized* (Cambridge: Cambridge University Press, 1994);

Edward A. Synam, Entry on Thomas Aquinas, in *Dictionary of Literary Biography*, volume 115: *Medieval Philosophers*, edited by Jeremiah Hackett (Detroit & London: Gale Research, 1992) pp. 35–53.

Frederick Van Fleteren, Entry on Augustine, in *Dictionary of Literary Biography*, volume 115, pp. 53–67.

THE PROBLEMS OF UNIVERSALS AND INDIVIDUATION

Roots in Boethius. Through his commentaries (written circa 504–509) on Porphyry's *Isagoge*, Boethius introduced a philosophical concern that became a major topic of discussion in the eleventh and twelfth centuries and re-emerged in the late thirteenth and early fourteenth centuries: the problem of universals, which has its roots in a fundamental disagreement in metaphysics between Plato and Aristotle. Plato believed that the essence of a thing—that which makes the thing the kind of a thing it is—has a separate and more real existence than the thing of which it is the essence. He called these essences *eidos*, a Greek word that means "kind" or "type" but in relation to Plato's philosophy is usually translated as "Form" or "Idea." For example, all dogs are dogs because they share or "participate in" the Form of Dog. The Forms are perfect, immaterial, and universal, whereas the things that participate in them are imperfect, material, and individual. Aristotle, on the other hand, said that a universal essence, or form, is combined with matter to constitute an individual thing, which he called *ousia* or substance. The form can be thought of in separation from the individual substance of which it is the form, but it has no actual existence independent of the thing. Thus, all dogs are dogs (rather than, say, cats) because they possess the form of dog; but there is no Form of Dog that exists in another world over and above the individual canines.

A Mediating Concept. In his *Glosae super Platonem* (Glosses on Plato, written circa 1100–1115), a commentary on Plato's *Timaeus*, Bernard of Chartres, a Platonist, introduced the concept of "native forms" as a mediator between the completely separate universal Forms and individual things. These native forms, he said, are images of the Forms that interact with matter to create individual objects that imperfectly imitate the Forms. Bernard and many of his contemporaries considered the hypothesis of native forms a way to resolve the differences between the two ancient philosophers, but John of Salisbury remarked that it was a pointless exercise to try to reconcile the philosophies of two dead Greeks who had never agreed while they lived.

Realism versus Nominalism. In the later Middle Ages the two main sides in regard to the problem of universals were Realism and Nominalism. Realism was the claim that universals are real; Nominalism was the contention that they are merely names. Despite their difference of opinion as to whether universals exist apart from individuals, Plato and Aristotle would both be considered Realists in the medieval context because of their insistence that universals do exist. Some medieval Realists, such as Bernard of Chartres in the twelfth century, agreed with Plato that they exist independently, while others, such as Thomas Aquinas in the thirteenth century, were Aristotelian Realists. The Nominalists, whether in the twelfth century or the fourteenth, went one giant step further than Aristotle and said that universals do not exist at all, either separately from individual things (Plato) or combined with matter to form individual things (Aristotle). Only the individual things exist; there are no universal structures that they share. Instead, people recognize similarities among various individuals and use a common word, such as *human* or *dog,* to refer to all individuals of that kind. But "human" and "dog" are not names of universals in the same way as "Socrates" is the name of an individual. Perhaps the person who most skillfully defended the notion that all reality is individual is the English logician William of Ockham (circa 1285–1347).

Implications of Nominalism. The implications of the Nominalists' position are far-reaching. If only individual things are real, then a word such as *human* is a mere sound (in Latin, *flatus vocis*) without a reference, and there is no common human nature in which all people share. This metaphysical position raises theological problems. If there is no common human essence, how are all later generations affected by original sin as a result of Adam's transgression? Furthermore, if there are only individual realities, it follows that the individual persons of the Trinity do not share a "common divine nature," and therefore there are three gods.

The Necessity of Universals. Humans need to use "universal" or "general" terms in language. In the twelfth century Peter Abelard, who rejected the argument of his teacher Roscelin de Compiègne that a universal is just a word, said that "humanity" is not a thing but a "state" or "condition" and that this condition could serve as the basis for universality without there being any need to argue for the existence of a universal reality. This position is known as Moderate Realism. Despite his rejection of his teacher's Nominalist views, Abelard was influenced

John Duns Scotus; illumination from a fourteenth-century manuscript (Biblioteca dell'academia dei Concordi, Rovigo, Italy)

by Roscelin and has been called a Nominalist as well as a Moderate Realist.

Abelard versus William of Champeaux. In addition to asserting his moderate views against extreme Nominalism, Abelard became involved in a dispute with another of his teachers, William of Champeaux, an Ultra-Realist. William held that one single universal essence is present in every individual of a given kind, and that the differences among individuals are merely accidental. In other words, there is only one "humanity"; Socrates and Plato are modifications of that essence. Abelard responded by saying that if Socrates and Plato were really the same substance, then when Socrates was in one town and Plato in another, Socrates must have been in two places at once. (While this retort may be amusing, scholars such as Frederick C. Copleston have pointed out that in William's theory Socrates was not in two places at once because the word *Socrates* refers to accidental modifications of the universal substance, not to the substance itself. It is reasonable, however, to say that the same substance, with different accidents or qualities, was in two places at the same time.) William then changed his mind and said that members of a species are the same not essentially but "indifferently," by which he seems to have meant they are not the same but only similar. This vague formulation, which Abelard treated as a verbal subterfuge, amounts to an abandonment of Ultra-Realism and a victory for Abelard.

Thomas Aquinas and Roger Bacon. In the thirteenth century Thomas Aquinas offered another Moderate Realist solution. Following Aristotle, he said that universals or essences may be abstracted by the mind from material things or substances, but that they have no being apart from substances. As part of a substance, however, the essence does have objective reality. For Aquinas, as for Aristotle and his other followers, abstracted essences are the means by which one can know individual objects. Like Aquinas, Roger Bacon explained human knowledge of the world by means of a sensible species (image), which represents the material thing itself. The species exists itself and is an image of that thing. Following the Arab philosophers Alhazen (Abu 'Ali al-Hazen ibn al-Haytham) and Avicenna, Bacon argued that the image is processed by the brain through common sense, imagination, fantasy, and memory. He also said that all animals have an internal sense of danger and usefulness. Even brute animals are capable of a kind of intelligence, and the human being has a cogitative sense that connects with rationality to produce human rationality and language. How a sensible image guarantees certain knowledge about an external object is the basic problem of knowledge (epistemology). For example, since people can experience afterimages, optical illusions, and delusions as well as seemingly true direct perceptions of objects in the world, how can people be sure that they are seeing a real, extramental object and not an internal impression, or to put it another way: how can one know if a sensible image provides necessary and certain knowledge of an individual thing in the world?

The Problem of Individuation. In the early fourteenth century John Duns Scotus took a new approach to the problem of species and individual. He argued that individuation, what makes a thing unique, is more important than any sort of general essence or species. He asserted that there must be a special principle of individuation, which he called *haecaeity* or "thisness." Whereas for Plato, Aristotle, and Aquinas, knowledge could be only of universals, in Duns Scotus's view the mind has a direct perception or intuition of the "thisness" of the individual being. The mind does use universals as a means of understanding, and the totality of these universal concepts does objectively represent the world. But such generalizations represent both existent and nonexistent objects; intuitive knowledge of *haecaeity* alone provides certain knowledge of the existence of objects. The important question for Duns Scotus is not "What is a universal?" but, rather, "What is it that makes an individual an individual?" How, for example, does common human nature become individuated in different people? Duns Scotus rejected Aquinas's position that matter, which is inherently unknowable, individuates (that is, that Socrates is Socrates and Plato is Plato because their common human essence takes up different parcels of matter); he also rejected the view that various "accidental" features individuate. He held that only what is determinate and distinct in itself, "thisness," can individuate. The "thisness" of Socrates makes the human nature in him particular to him, even though human nature is found in all other human beings. Duns Scotus was not a Nominalist; he thought that mental abstractions and common nouns are grounded in a fundamental objective reality.

Ockham's Response. William of Ockham responded to Duns Scotus's Moderate Realism with a theory that is purely Nominalist. According to Ockham, everything that exists in the natural world is utterly singular or individual. Thus, there are only individual humans; there is no common "humanity" in which they all share. In Ockham's radical individualism all traces of objective universality are rejected. There is no need for a special principle of individuation, such as Duns Scotus's "thisness," because God created a world of individuals. The mind does construct general or universal concepts; but they exist only within the mind, where they serve as signs that recall images of individuals. In his words: "No universal exists outside the mind of the knower." In Ockham's fictive (*fictum*) theory of general ideas one intuits (perceives) real individual things and then abstractively constructs general concepts.

Sources:

Frederick C. Copleston, *Mediaeval Philosophy* (London: Methuen, 1952).

Armand A. Maurer, *The Philosophy of William of Ockham in the Light of Its Principles* (Toronto: Pontifical Institute of Mediaeval Studies, 1999).

Marilyn McCord Adams, *William Ockham*, 2 volumes (Notre Dame: University of Notre Dame Press, 1989).

Paul Vincent Spade, ed., *The Cambridge Companion to Ockham* (Cambridge & New York: Cambridge University Press, 1999).

Katherine H. Tachau, *Vision and Certitude in the Age of Ockham: Optics, Epistemology and the Foundations of Semantics* (Leiden & New York: Brill, 1988).

RECOVERING ANCIENT TEXTS

Arab Preservation of Learning. One of the positive outcomes of the Crusades was the new cultural interaction among the worlds of Judaism, Islam, and Christianity. Because most educated Romans read Greek as well as Latin, many ancient Greek philosophical works were never translated into Latin, and in the chaos that followed the fall of Rome many Greek texts were lost to the Latin West. They survived in the East, however, and many were translated into Arabic. Beginning in the early twelfth century, through exchanges with Jewish and Islamic scholars, western Christian scholars in Spain, Sicily, Antioch, and Tripoli came to know about all the works of Aristotle, which had survived in Arabic-language translations, and they discovered manuscripts in the original Greek as well. Furthermore, they discovered ancient scientific texts, such as Claudius Ptolemy's first-century *Almagest* (Great Mathematical Synthesis, a name acquired from the Arabic versions) in the Kingdom of Sicily. Other texts, in both Arabic and Greek, were also found and examined.

Translators. As scholars began the task of translating these works into Latin, they launched a major revival of learning in western Europe. Early translators, such as the Englishman Robert of Chester and Herman of Carinthia (in modern Austria and Slovenia), dealt with texts in astrology. In the Spanish city of Toledo many Muslim, Jewish, and Christian scholars interacted. One of the significant translators working in Spain was John of Seville and Limia, who translated Arabic works on mathematics, astronomy, meterology, medicine, and occasionally philosophy. The major translators of philosophical works include the Italians Gerard of Cremona and James of Venice, Michael the Scot, Herman the German, and especially in the thirteenth century, the Belgian William of Moerbecke who translated Aristotle from Greek directly into Latin.

New Books for Scholars. Between 1120 and 1280 all the known works of Aristotle were made available in Latin to students in the schools of western Europe. Many scientific works—including Ptolemy's *Almagest* and *Optics*, Euclid's *Optics*, and other works of astronomy—were translated. Many English scholars went to Spain in the early twelfth century, including Adelard of Bath, Daniel of Morley, and Robert of Chester. These scholars brought books back to England, where Robert Grosseteste established a school of translators in Lincoln, which prepared a new version of the works of Pseudo-Dionysius as well as other Latin versions of Greek philosophical works. By 1249 Grosseteste had achieved a major breakthrough: he had translated a major work of Western ethics, Aristotle's *Nicomachean Ethics*.

The Rise of European Universities. The massive influx of works from the Arab world partially motivated a reor-

Part of a leaf from an eleventh-century Arabic translation of the works of Galen, with notations from
Avicenna in the margins (Bibliothèque Nationale, Paris)

ganization of the educational curriculum and institutions. After the foundation of the medieval universities toward the end of the twelfth century and prior to 1255 some schools specialized in individual subjects, philosophers, or movements. For example, the University of Bologna became the center for the study of Roman law. The schools at Salerno and at Montpelier became centers for the study of medicine. Oxford and Cambridge emphasized training in logic and natural philosophy. In the thirteenth century the University of Paris became the main graduate university for theology students, but in the fourteenth century the Oxford theology curriculum gained in prestige, and European scholars began to travel to England for theological study.

Sources:

A. B. Cobban, *The Medieval Universities: Their Development and Organization* (London: Methuen, 1975).

Jacques Verger, *Les universités en Moyen Age* (Paris: Presses Universitaire de France, 1973).

RESPONDING TO ARISTOTLE

With the translation of all Aristotle's known works from Greek and Arabic into Latin during the twelfth and thirteenth centuries, western Europeans had access to a "complete system" of philosophy. That is, logic, epistemology, metaphysics, natural philosophy, philosophy of mind, and ethics were presented in what looked like systematic order. Medieval philosophers responded to this new body of knowledge by attempting to integrate it with previously established philosophical systems, constructing their own syntheses by combining elements of Neoplatonism, Stoicism, Aristotelianism, and Christianity.

Aristotle's Major Contributions. First, Aristotle provided a logical method for analyzing arguments, the syllogism, a form of argument that includes a major premise, a minor premise, and a conclusion. (For example: All boys like baseball. John is a boy. Therefore, John likes baseball.) Second, he provided a theory of proof (demonstration) with links to what became Euclidian geometry. This theory was part of the foundation for the notion of a medieval science *(scientia)*, and it was influential through the early seventeenth centuries. Third, Aristotle provided a way of asking fundamental philosophical questions. Fourth, he presented a revolutionary theory of mind that seemed to be set in opposition to Platonism and to be somewhat distinct from the materialism of Stoicism. In this view the human being was a unity in which mind and body could not be separated without loss of that unity. Thus, the human being was not a "Ghost [spirit] inhabiting a machine," but rather a body-soul unity in which the rational-intellectual soul was seen as that part of the human being that might be unchangeable. This view was strongly resisted by medieval Neoplatonists, who thought that it compromised the spirituality, immateriality, and immortality of the soul. Aristotle had seen his teaching on the soul as the culmination of his natural philosophy. Above all, he placed human knowledge in the context of being in the world and set the foundation for thinking about the

human being as one substance, not as two joined together. Fifth, Aristotle provided an influential treatment of the moral virtues in his *Nicomachean Ethics*. By 1249 Robert Grosseteste had translated this major work of western ethics into Latin, and it became the ethics schoolbook for western students. His *Politics*, translated in about 1260, became the textbook on ancient political theory. Aristotle's ethics and politics favored the sort of mixed government of kingship, aristocracy, and democracy that emerged in the later Middle Ages, providing an alternative to the various forms of Christian Neoplatonic political theory that were used to justify medieval kingship.

Augustine versus Aristotle. It would be an oversimplification to define the basic conflict in later medieval philosophy as one between Aristotle and Augustine. In fact, Neo-Augustinians such as John Peckham and Peter John Olivi, who opposed some of Aristotle's teachings, made use of his philosophy in other areas. For Aristotle moral virtues were closely tied to the use of reason, which deliberates and determines one's actions. There was no need for an additional faculty called the will to perform this operation. This view gives primacy to an intellectual—rather than emotional—basis for virtuous activity. This school of thought came to be associated with the Dominican scholars Albertus Magnus and Thomas Aquinas. Some medieval Neo-Augustinians, specifically Franciscans such as Bonaventure, William of Baglione, John Peckham, and especially Peter John Olivi, argued that Aristotle, "the accursed pagan," should be subordinated to the Christian philosopher Augustine. For these thinkers, Augustine's emphasis on the primacy of free will, in which will was a power related to but different from reason, had moved the debate about moral action beyond Aristotle's purely rational considerations. Concerned with the human propensity to sin and evil, these thinkers thought that Augustine's analysis of moral decisions explored psychological depths not perceived by Aristotle. That is, a person could know the good that they should do, but by a perverse act of the will he or she could end up doing the exact opposite. These Neo-Augustinians, then, wanted to speak about the "virtues of the will" as distinct from purely intellectual virtues. The adherents of these two positions, the Dominicans and Franciscans, tended to become hardened in their commitment to their positions, which have lasted into modern philosophical debates.

Natural Philosophy. The influence of Aristotle and other rediscovered ancient texts in medieval science, then called natural philosophy, may be seen in the career of one of the early chancellors of Oxford University, Robert Grosseteste (circa 1168–1253), who went on to become bishop of Lincoln. His major commentary on Aristotle's theory of demonstrative proof (completed by the late 1220s) in the *Posterior Analytics* raised the notions of argument and proof to a high analytic level and it showed that Aristotle could not be understood without a thorough knowledge of Euclidian geometry. He also composed notes on the *Physics* of Aristotle and wrote

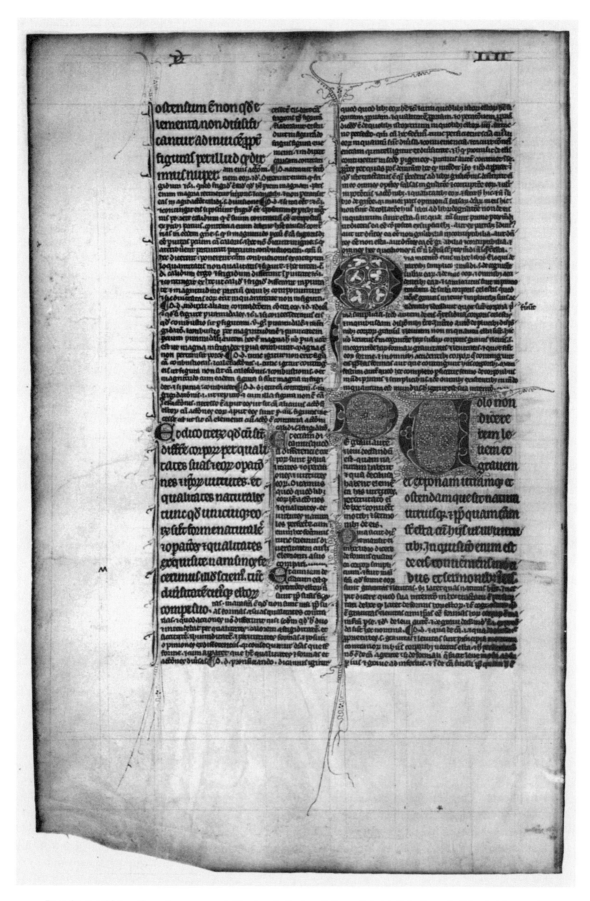

Page from a thirteenth-century manuscript for two Latin translations of Aristotle's *De caelo* (On the Heavens), one from a Greek text (in the largest script) and one from an Arabic text (in a slightly smaller script), with a Latin translation (in smallest script) of Averröes' commentary on Aristotle's work (Bibliothèque Nationale, Paris)

The list of 219 propositions that the bishop of Paris condemned as heretical in 1277 included the following notions:

That there is no more excellent state in life than the study of philosophy. (40)

That the only wise people in the world are the philosophers. (154)

That in order to have some certitude about any conclusion, one must base oneself on self-evident principles. (151)

That one should not believe anything unless it is self-evident or can be shown from self-evident principles. (37)

That one should not be content with authority to have certitude about any question. (150)

That nothing can be known about God except that He is, or his existence. (215).

That God does not know things other than himself. (3)

That God cannot know changeable contingent things immediately except through their particular and proximate causes. (56)

That the first cause cannot make more than one world. (34)

That all separated substances (angels) are co-eternal with the first substance. (5)

That God could not move the heavens in a straight line, the reason being that he would then leave a vacuum. (49)

That the First Principle cannot be the cause of diverse products here below without the mediation of other causes . . . . (43)

That the World is Eternal because that which has a nature by which it is able to exist for the whole future has a nature by which it was able to exist in the whole past. (98)

That the World is Eternal as regards all species contained in it, and that time, motion, matter, agent, and receiver are eternal . . . . (87)

That no agent is in potency to one or the other of two outcomes; on the contrary, it is determined or necessitated. (160)

That nothing happens by chance, but everything comes about by necessity. . . . (21)

That the differences of condition among humans, both as regards spiritual powers and temporal goods are traced back to the diverse signs of the heavens (the Zodiac). (143)

That God cannot make numerically different souls. (27)

That a human is human independent of the rational soul. (11)

That the Intellect is numerically one for all. . . . (32)

That the intellect is not the form of (the structuring principle of) the body, except in the manner in which a helmsman is the form of a ship, and the intellect is not an essential perfection of man. (7)

That the Intellect which is the human's ultimate perfection is completely separated. (121)

That the Will and the Intellect are not moved to act by themselves but by an external cause, namely, the heavenly bodies. (133)

That the Good which is possible for humans consists in the intellectual virtues. (144)

That happiness is had in this life and not in another. (176)

That after death man loses every good. (15)

That religious visions and mystical vision are the result of natural causes. (33)

That the natural moral law forbids the killing of irrational animals, although not only of these. (20)

That the Christian Law impedes Learning. (175)

That there are Fables and Falsehoods in the Christian Law just as in others [that is, Jewish and Islamic Laws]. (174)

That the teachings of Theologians are based on Fables. (152)

That Creation is not possible, even though the contrary must be held according to the Faith. (184)

That one should not pray. (180)

That simple fornication, namely, that of an unmarried man with an unmarried woman, is not a sin. (183)

That a sin against nature, such as abuse in intercourse, is not against the nature of the individual, although it is against the nature of the species. (166)

That pleasure in sexual acts does not impede the act or use of the intellect. (172)

That continence is not essentially a virtue. (168)

That humility in the degree to which one . . . deprecates or lowers himself is not a virtue. (171)

That the philosopher must not concede the Resurrection of the Body because it cannot be investigated by reason. (18)

---

significant scientific treatises such as *De Luce* (On Light), *De sphera* (On the Sphere), and *De iride* (On the Rainbow). For these works Grosseteste drew not only on Aristotle but also on optical knowledge from recently translated works by Euclid and Ptolemy.

Aristotle at the University of Paris. While scholars welcomed the influx of works by Aristotle and other ancient Greeks, as well as the writings of Arabic philosophers, some Church leaders were concerned about challenges to religious orthodoxy that might arise from students of these "pagan" works. In 1210 Church officials in France banned the teaching of Aristotle's *Physics* and *Metaphysics* at the University of Paris and renewed the ban in 1215 and 1228. It also condemned two scholars in philosophy posthumously for expressing heretical views. But despite such condemnations, the university got a charter through the influence of papal legate Robert of Courçon, and interest in philosophy and theology grew. One major figure who emerged during this period was William of Auvergne, who went on to become bishop of Paris and chancellor of the university. After the condemnation of Aristotle's *Physics* and *Metaphysics,* he observed the ban while attempting to integrate other aspects of Aristotle's thought, as well as aspects of the philosophies of other Greek and Islamic thinkers into Augustinian Christian philosophy. Like Grosseteste, he was impressed by the philosophical power of the works of Avicenna and read Aristotle in the light of Avicenna's commentaries.

The Influence of Paris. In 1230 Pope Gregory IX, while continuing the ban on Aristotle's *Physics* and *Metaphysics,* issued a papal bull that led to a serious reorganization of the university that prevented unnecessary theological interference with the faculty of arts. At the same time Emperor Frederick II, who was attempting to control European universities, sent his adviser Michael Scot, to Paris with his new translations of Aristotle's *On Generation* and *Corruption and On the Heavens,* and commentaries by Averroës. These works and other commentaries by Averroës were fundamental to the teaching of philosophy from 1230 until the mid seventeenth century. During the 1230s and 1240s two English philosophers, Richard Rufus of Cornwall and Roger Bacon, lectured on Aristotle at Paris with the help of Averroës' commentaries. The German Dominican friar, Albertus Magnus (Albert of Lauingen), who taught at Paris in the late 1240s, set out around 1250 to paraphrase all the works of Aristotle for students. This paraphrase started out to explain Aristotle but ended up as a critical reading of Aristotle and a discussion of Aristotle's theories in relation to other ancient theories such as those of the Platonists and the Stoics. This project, which he worked at until 1269, established Albertus as a great teacher (*Magister magnus).*

Aquinas and Aristotle. Thomas Aquinas studied under Albertus Magnus in Cologne from 1248 until 1252, when he went to the University of Paris, where he studied and taught until returning to Italy in 1259. (One of his fellow students was Bonaventure, who also graduated in 1256, joined the Franciscan Order, and wrote important philosophical-theological works of his own.) During the next decade Aquinas began his own commentaries and questions on Aristotle and also started work on his great synthetic works, *Summa de veritate Catholicae fidei contra gentiles* (Comprehensive Truth of the Catholic Faith against the Gentiles), which provides an examination of the nature and existence of God and a careful examination of themes from Platonic, Aristotelian, and Stoic philosophies, and *Summa theologiae* (Comprehensive Theology), his great synthesis of Aristotelianism and Christianity.

Crisis at Paris. Aquinas completed both these works after returning to Paris in 1268 or 1269. When he arrived, the university community was in turmoil, charged with polemic about the suitability of Aristotelian philosophy in a Christian context. The issue had reached a crisis point in about 1266, after scholars there had been lecturing on Aristotle for about thirty years and after the curriculum for the English and northern European students at the university had mandated the works of Aristotle as teaching and examination materials for the B.A. and M.A. since 1255. The crisis occurred because some new, young teachers of philosophy, especially Siger of Brabant and Boethius of Dacia, argued that by "necessary reasons" some of Aristotle's basic positions were true; yet, the opposite position was advocated by Christian faith, and therefore one must believe it as well. This argument set up the problem of a double truth, a contradictory relation between the propositions of philosophy and those of the Christian faith. There were three central opposing positions. First, the Aristotelian notion that there was no temporal beginning to the world contradicts the Judaeo-Christian-Islamic notion of the Creation. Second, Averroës imputed to Aristotle a belief that there was one "Possible Intellect" for the whole human race (that is, John Smith or Mary Jones does not actually think, rather all thought is the product of one anonymous universal mind) and a notion that all things on earth including human actions are necessarily determined by the laws that govern the heavens; these ideas contradict the Christian belief in individual free will. Finally, some of these teachers, such as Siger of Brabant and Boethius of Dacia, held that the highest perfection on earth for a thinking human being is the happiness provided by the philosophical life, and, of course, some theologians saw this view as a denial of the primacy of the religious life.

Bonaventure's Response. During the late 1260s and early 1270s, Bonaventure delivered a series of speeches at the Franciscan house of studies at the university, questioning the "orthodoxy" (correct teaching) of these young teachers, making official the claims of his colleagues Roger Bacon and William of Baglioni. In fact, drawing on other ancient philosophical traditions, especially Platonism, Bonaventure led a major challenge to the authority of Aristotle, arguing that while Aristotle had much to offer in logic and natural philosophy, he was deficient in metaphysics. For Bonaventure, Plato, Cicero, and Macrobius were greater philosophers than Aristotle. With Roger Bacon, John Peckham, and other Franciscans, Bonaventure advocated "Augustinianism" over the Averroist Aristotelians, often called Latin Averroists, and their theological partners in dialogue, such as Thomas Aquinas.

Aquinas's Response. Indeed, rather than issuing condemnations, Aquinas had entered into philosophical dialogue with the young masters, especially Siger of Brabant. In 1269, in the polemical treatise *De unitate intellectus contra Averroistas* (On the Unity of the Intellect against the Averroists), he outlined the main reasons why he thought Siger had misunderstood Aristotle on the nature of mind. Avoiding simple-minded appeals to authority, Aquinas set out to prove that both Averroës and Siger had interpreted Aristotle in a way that was neither historically nor conceptually correct. Siger replied in a series of books, but by about 1276 he had come near to agreeing with several of Aquinas's positions.

Aquinas and the Neo-Augustinians. At the same time he was attempting to show the Latin Averroists the errors in their thinking, Aquinas was coming under attack for his own Aristotelian views, not only from Bonaventure but also from his students. In his doctoral defense John Peckham viciously attacked the position of Aquinas, who was present. When Aquinas's friends chided him for not taking Peckham to task, he said that the young man should be allowed to enjoy his great day.

Condemned Propositions. In 1270 Church officials in Paris condemned the Averroists' propositions. Then, matters at the university got increasingly serious, and a papal legate had to intervene. Eventually, in 1277, Pope John XXI asked the bishop of Paris, Stephen Tempier, to examine the matter and report to him. The bishop assembled a theological commission that recommended the condemnation of 219 propositions. Without first reporting to the Pope, the bishop issued the condemned propositions for the diocese of Paris, and the archbishop of Canterbury, Robert Kilwardby, issued his own list at Oxford. These propositions included ideas attributed to Siger of Brabant, Boethius of Dacia, and Thomas Aquinas, among others. Even though it was only a local condemnation, it had far-reaching consequences. Yet, by the end of the century, eminent Parisian scholars such as Godfrey of Fountains were publicly criticizing the list. Some modern scholars, including Edward Grant, believe that the condemnations had a positive effect on the development of the sciences. Since the Church encouraged scholars to explore non-Aristotelian positions, specifically in physics, fourteenth-century scientists such as the Parisians Nicholas Oresme and Jean Buridan asked questions and tried approaches that might not otherwise have arisen.

The Augustinian-Aristotelian Synthesis. Though the Franciscan Neo-Augustinians condemned Aristotle as just another accursed pagan and held that Augustine alone provided the best authority and model for a Christian philosophy and theology, a synthesis of Augustinian and Aristotelean thought did take place in the thirteenth century. In fact, most philosophers of that century attempted some kind of synthesis between Aristotle and Augustine. The Franciscans at Paris followed Augustine's theory of knowledge by illumination, his doctrine of the will, and his views on creation. Yet, their major teachings synthesized Augustine's positions with ideas from the Jewish philosopher Solomon Ibn Gebirol and Avicenna. In fact, Avicenna's influence was so central to the thought of these Neo-Augustinians that the twentieth-century historian of medieval philosophy Etienne Gilson has called them "Augustinian Avicennians." In the 1270s Henry of Ghent emerged as a leader of this group and the influence of his writings—which synthesize ideas from Aristotle and Averroës, as well as Augustine, Plato, and Avicenna—extended to major philosophers of the early fourteenth century, including Duns Scotus and William of Ockham.

The Aftermath. The crisis over teaching Aristotle created antagonism among the clergy. Reasonably open and flexible positions hardened into the "theses" or positions. Religious

orders chose their own "official" philosophers: Albertus Magnus and, much later, Thomas Aquinas for the Dominicans, Bonaventure and Walter de la Mare for the Franciscans (who had to read Thomas Aquinas with a list of "corrections" by Walter de la Mare), and Giles of Rome for the Augustinians. As the orders argued, their struggle was overlaid with the question of the appropriateness of religious orders to own property when Jesus Christ and his Apostles had practiced evangelical poverty and had no property.

Sources:

H. A. Davidson, *Alfarabi, Avicenna and Averroës on Intellect: Their Cosmologies, Theories of the Active Intellect, and Theories of Human Intellect* (New York: Oxford University Press, 1992).

Bernard G. Dod, "Aristoteles latinus," in *The Cambridge History of Later Medieval Philosophy*, edited by Norman Kretzmann, Anthony Kenny, Jan Pinborg, and Elenore Stump (Cambridge: Cambridge University Press, 1982), pp. 43–79.

Oliver Leaman, *Introduction to Medieval Islamic Philosophy* (Cambridge & New York: Cambridge University Press, 1990).

Jacques Le Goff, *Intellectuals in the Middle Ages,* translated by Teresa Lavender Fagan (Cambridge, Mass. & Oxford, U.K.: Blackwell, 1993).

Alain de Libera, *La philosophie medievale* (Paris: Presses Universitaire de France, 1993).

C. H. Lohr, "The Medieval Interpretation of Aristotle," in *The Cambridge History of Later Medieval Philosophy*, pp. 80–98.

David Luscombe, *Medieval Thought* (Oxford: Oxford University Press, 1997).

John Marenbon, *Later Medieval Philosophy (1150–1350)* (London: Routledge, 1987).

Armand A. Maurer, *Medieval Philosophy*, revised edition (Toronto: Pontifical Institute of Medieval Studies, 1982).

Fernand van Steenberghen, *Thomas Aquinas and Radical Aristotelianism* (Washington, D.C.: Catholic University of America Press, 1980).

Jacques Verger, *Men of Learning in Europe at the End of the Middle Ages*, translated by Lisa Neal and Steven Rendall (Notre Dame, Ind.: University of Notre Dame Press, 2000).

John F. Wippel, "The Condemnations of 1270 and 1277 at Paris," *Journal of Medieval and Renaissance Studies*, 7 (1977): 169–201.

Wippel, *Medieval Reactions in the Encounter Between Faith and Reason* (Milwaukee: Marquette University Press, 1995).

REVISING PHILOSOPHY: SCHOLASTICISM

The Scholastic Method. In the Roman Empire, philosophy became a part of the liberal arts taught in the Roman schools. This tradition of teaching and debating philosophy continued in the Latin West. Scholasticism is the name given to the "School Philosophy" of the Middle Ages. It is not the name for a particular doctrine. The Scholastics—philosophers such as Peter Abelard, Robert Grosseteste, Roger Bacon, Thomas Aquinas, Henry of Ghent, John Duns Scotus, and William of Ockham—did not hold the same philosophical or theological views. They exhibited great originality in constructing their positions, and they were not afraid to disagree with one another. What they did share was a method of examining a variety of doctrinal positions in a thorough, logical manner. In fact, the word *Scholasticism* denotes a common style of "doing philosophy and theology." Peter Abelard helped to develop this new methodology in his *Sic et Non* (Yes and No, written circa 1112–1128), a collection of opposing or conflicting statements that set out a method by which opposing claims can be harmonized or correctly synthesized. It also provided the student with much material for logical exercises. This scholastic method of "pro and contra" (question and answer) had great strength in uncovering logical ambiguities in arguments. Hence, for the Scholastics the logical form of an argument, as distinct from its grammatical form, was all important.

Scholastic Style. In general the works that grew out of these practices tend to be stylistically impersonal, with only infrequent personal remarks and references. Comments such as "Some say" or "Others state" indicate that these thinkers were more interested in getting at the "content" or the "theses" of the respective thinkers than engaging in an ad hominem argument (an attack on an opponent's character rather than his ideas). This style had its rhetorical peculiarities: the vocabulary was limited; abstract formulas were abundant; and the structures of arguments tended to be rigid. Scholastic discourse also relied heavily, but not exclusively, on syllogistic argument. In the writings of the Church Fathers, who preceded the Scholastics, and the Renaissance Humanists, who came after, one finds a greater variety of styles, less-rigid formats, and more diverse rhetoric than in the works of these medieval scholars.

Scholasticism and Teaching. The scholastic style was also greatly influenced by the methodology of university teaching. The format consisted mostly of lecture, disputation, and "collation" (conference). The lecture (*lectio,* or reading) consisted of the reading of prescribed texts. This reading was often helped by reference to an official commentator; for example, Aristotle's texts were read with the aid of Averroës' commentary. The master, as the teacher was called, was also expected to go beyond ordinary explication of the text and provide interpretation through his own commentary. The "scholastic method" of pro and contra was applied to all fields, including theology, philosophy, medicine, and law. In each field the teacher started from an "authoritative" text, for example, the Bible with *Sententiarum libri IV (Four Books of Sentences* (written 1148–1151), Peter Lombard's collection of scriptural texts and commentary by the Church Fathers and medieval masters in theology, and Aristotle with Averroës' commentary in philosophy.

Disputation. Masters were expected to engage in regular disputations (*disputatio*). The medieval format for disputation was twofold: first, the regular or ordinary disputation held throughout the school year; second, the solemn disputation usually held before Christmas or Easter. In the latter, called the "Quadlibetal" (Free-for-All) disputation, the master was expected to discuss any issues or questions asked by the audience. Part of the training of a scholastic master consisted in the teaching of debating skills. Young students were expected to prove their verbal-conceptual skills by taking positive and negative sides on important issues. The master served as "debate master" and was expected to sum up the debates and give a resolution. The examination for mastership (like a modern doctorate) provided a format in which a would-be master publicly exhibited his skills in formal debate.

The Quaestio. Perhaps, the most important invention of the Scholastics was the form known as the *quaestio* (question). This form is broader than the modern usage of the word *question.* In the *quaestio* one usually set out the strongest objections to the position that one intended to defend. One then proceeded to give a formal presentation of the main arguments for

one's own position and concluded by answering the initial objections. This format is still preferred in many modern philosophy journals, indicating the continuity of the scholastic method in contemporary practice. A *questio* could develop into a lengthy account. For example, Thomas Aquinas's *Questio Disputatae de Anima* (Disputed Questions on the Soul, written 1269) consists of quite lengthy quaestios.

Commentary and Summa. The other important scholastic literary forms were the commentary and *summa.* The commentary might be a literal reading of a difficult text, such as Thomas Aquinas's *In Libros De Anima* (written 1265–1273), a major commentary on Aristotle's *De anima* (On the Soul). The aim of the work was to enable the student to read and understand fully the text of Aristotle. Initially, in the twelfth century the word *summa* meant a completed selection or gathering of theological and philosophical sentences, but by the thirteenth century it meant a literary work that gives a concise presentation of a whole field of study in a synthetic manner suitable for teaching students.

Sources:

Frederick C. Copleston, *Medieval Philosophy* (London: Methuen, 1952).

Norman Kretzmann, Anthony Kenny, Jan Pinborg, and Eleonore Stump, eds., *The Cambridge History of Later Medieval Philosophy* (Cambridge, U.K. & New York: Cambridge University Press, 1982).

Armand A. Maurer, *Medieval Philosophy,* revised edition (Toronto: Pontifical Institute of Medieval Studies, 1982).

REVISING PHILOSOPHY: THE LATE MIDDLE AGES

Representative Philosophers. With the advent of the fourteenth century came a deepening of philosophical acumen. Three representative figures stand out: John Duns Scotus (circa 1266 – 1308), William of Ockham (circa 1285 – 1347), and Meister Eckhart (circa 1260 – 1328). All were members of religious orders and influenced philosophical thought well beyond the Middle Ages.

Duns Scotus. The American founder of modern Pragmatism, Charles Sanders Peirce, formed the belief that Duns Scotus was one of the most accomplished of all philosophical thinkers, and the modern German philosopher Martin Heidegger wrote part of his doctoral dissertation on him. Duns Scotus placed great importance on the notion of the human will. He believed that the human ability to make decisions is not compromised by factors such as one's temperament, one's environment, or one's genes. Thus, he was a strong advocate of the notion of freedom of choice, which in the ethical realm coincides with the use of reason. He held that it is a mistake to think that choice is based on some kind of blind drive or unconscious urge. Perhaps, the most fundamental change that Duns Scotus brought about was in the way people think of reality. Prior to Duns Scotus, philosophers saw the whole world as a finely differentiated hierarchy of structures: mineral, vegetable, animal, human, angel, and God. Each had a higher degree of being (reality). A human was more real than those structures below him or her in the hierarchy and less real than those above. For Duns Scotus being had one and the same meaning wherever it was found, whether in vegetable, animal, human, angel, or God. There were no different kinds of being.

William of Ockham; illumination from a manuscript for his *Summa Logicae,* written in 1322
(Gonville and Caius College, Cambridge)

There is just being, the opposite of which is nothing. To say that something is, that it has being, is to name a predicate that can be attached to any subject whatsoever. For Duns Scotus the most innate and fundamental concept is that of "what is," being. Without this primary, or primitive, notion, one would not be able to distinguish reality from illusion, what is real from what does not exist. What Duns Scotus meant is that all humans have an innate grasp of *being as being.* Because of this position, Duns Scotus was not able to formulate a proof for God's existence that proceeds from the sensible world to the necessity of a first cause of motion. In his view, such a move would lead only to a first worldly cause. Rather, he built his proof for God's existence on the basis of the innate notion of finite and infinite being, arguing that infinite being (God) is a necessary condition for the existence of a finite world.

William of Ockham. A logician of the first rank, William of Ockham was an intelligent critic of Duns Scotus and all other earlier philosophers. Ockham had reservations about Scotus's new notion of being, and argued that being is not some common nature in things. Rather, it is a name predicated, or spoken of, real individual things. Thus, Ockham rejected Duns Scotus's conceptual argument for God's existence. Ockham held that humans are finite, limited beings; by experience they can grasp the fact that there is some causality at work in the world, but they cannot go on to prove that this causality is either finite or infinite. On the issue of existence and essence, he followed Duns Scotus, but he emphasized that the Latin words *esse* (to be, being), a verb, and *essentia* (essence), a noun, signify the same thing. Neither word names some kind of super being. Given these assumptions, it is not surprising that Ockham had distinctive views on the nature of knowledge, essences, and universals. As he said, "No universal exists outside the mind of the knower." Ockham's theory of signs is important. A word is a sign of (refers to) an actual individual thing; it does not refer to a nature or essence. The universal, form, or essence is simply a mental construct by means of which one can classify the actually existing individual things. Like Duns Scotus, Ockham emphasized the notion of freedom of choice. Ockham distinguished between God's absolute power (say, to create multiple worlds) and God's ordained power (the fact that he created this world). Ockham also dealt with the problem Boethius posed of how humans can have free will if God has foreknowledge of all future events.

Heresy Charges. In 1324 John Lutterell, chancellor of Oxford, accused Ockham of heresy in his theological teaching. Ockham later fulminated with words such as: "against the errors of this pseudo-pope 'I have set my face like the hard rock,' so that neither lies nor slurs nor persecution of whatever sort . . . nor the multitude, however great, of those who believe or favor or even defend him will ever at any time be able to prevent me from attacking and refuting his errors as long as I have hand, paper, pen and ink." What Ockham was claiming was a common teaching among medieval theologians: the task of defining Christian truth was not just the job of pope and bishops alone; the masters of the schools, especially the theologians, had a necessary role in this task. Heresy was a serious charge that could have led to imprisonment or even death. As was the custom, Ockham took his case to the highest court in Christendom, the papal court at Avignon, in the south of France. For four years, he led a scholarly life there and waited while theological and legal experts debated his case, but in May 1328 he and his colleagues decided it was best to leave Avignon by night. Later that year he was excommunicated. Still professing himself a devout Catholic he spent the last seventeen years of his life in the Franciscan friary at Munich.

Nominalism. Ockham had a major impact on the philosophy of the later Middle Ages, as well as the Renaissance and Reformation era. His philosophy was one of the bases for a movement known as the Modern Way (*Via moderna*) to distinguish it from the older way of Aquinas, Duns Scotus, and others. Though he provoked major debates among his contemporaries, Ockham succeeded in forcing philosophers to be more rigorous in their methods and use of language. His name came to be associated with the movement known as Nominalism, based on the premise that names do not designate universal structures; they simply refer directly to individual things. The opposite to Nominalism is Realism—based on the idea that there are objective, universal structures in nature. The debate between the Nominalists and the Realists was the major philosophical issue of the later Middle Ages. Indeed, Duns Scotus and Ockham were part of a larger debate in the universities. Ockham's positions were rejected by Walter Chatton, Adam Wodeham, and Robert Holcot. Duns Scotus's were supported by Henry of Harclay and William of Alnwick. Among the philosophers who contributed to the emergence of Nominalism is Jean Buridan, who taught at Paris in the first half of the fourteenth century and was a professional teacher of philosophy rather than a theologian (like Duns Scotus and Ockham). His ideas gained currency in the late Middle Ages through his students Albert of Saxony and Marsilius of Inghen.

Meister Eckhart. Eckhart is a good example of a university-trained philosopher who ended his career as a preacher and teacher. A member of the Dominican order, he lectured at Paris in 1294–1298, and in 1302–1303, contemporary with Duns Scotus, he held the Dominican chair at Paris. Later, he taught at both Strasbourg and Cologne. Eckhart was unusual in his time because he wrote his university lectures in the technical Latin of university schools, but he wrote his speeches, sermons, and informal talks in Middle High German. He displayed his creative genius in transforming the technical terminology of philosophy in Latin into a new technical terminology of a vernacular language. Since philosophy continued to be written in Latin until Immanuel Kant in the eighteenth century, Eckhart was certainly ahead of his time. In his philosophy Eckhart united Aristotelianism and Neoplatonism while also drawing on such diverse sources as Thomas Aquinas, Albertus Magnus, Bonaventure, and Moses Maimonides. One of Eckhart's concerns was whether God was primarily being or intellect, and he concluded that in God, thought had priority over being. Another of his questions raised the issue of whether being and understanding were the same in God, and he decided that God is pure understanding, not being or existence. Eckhart limited being to creatures, and treated God's knowledge as the cause of being. In this idea one finds the seeds of German Idealism, and indeed, nineteenth-century German Idealists such as Georg Wilhelm Friedrich Hegel proudly referred to Eckhart as a predecessor.

Interpreting the Bible and Preaching. Eckhart is particularly important for his philosophical interpretation of important books of scripture: Exodus, The Book of Wisdom, The Gospel of John. He was also a master rhetorician, and his sermons are notable for his ability to communicate complex philosophy and theology to a popular audience. In stressing the freedom of the children of God, following St. Paul, Eckhart was interpreted by the heretical Free Spirit movement as preaching a message of "do whatever you are inclined to do, since after all the just person is God." It was such teaching which led to his being accused of heresy in 1325–1326. He attempted to defend himself in public debate, and then went before the papal court in Avignon, and at the same time William of Ockham was also defending himself against the charge of heresy. Selections of Eckhart's works were posthumously condemned by the Pope in 1328, but Eckhart had claimed that his statements were capable of orthodox interpretation. Modern scholars have concluded that the papal commission's random selection of Eckhart's statements took them out of context and led to serious misunderstanding of his complex philosophical and theological positions. Eckhart's works were considered dangerous for centuries. In the fifteenth century even a sympathetic reader, Nicholas of Cusa, wrote "Reader Beware" in the margin of an Eckhart text.

The End of an Era. Like many other institutions, medieval philosophy was deeply affected by the advent of the Black Death in 1347. Ockham may have been a victim of this disease, and many other scholars died as well. After the plague abated, new intellectual fashions appeared. One of these was Italian Humanism, which came to dominate thought in the Renaissance. It opposed the medieval emphasis on logic and by the sixteenth century had elevated grammar, history, and poetry in the university curriculum. Yet, the methods of medieval philosophy continued into the Renaissance, and even as late as the eighteenth century Scholastic methods dominated German universities. The Logical Analysis movement of the twentieth century looked to Scotus and Ockham as models, while the continental European philosophers looked to Eckhart and other medieval thinkers for models of how to formulate philosophical questions.

Sources:

Marilyn McCord Adams, *William Ockham*, 2 volumes (Notre Dame: University of Notre Dame Press, 1989).

E. P. Bos, ed., *John Duns Scotus: Renewal of Philosophy*, Amsterdam & Atlanta: Rodolpi, 1998);

Edmund Colledge and Bernard McGinn, trans., *Meister Eckhart: The Essential Sermons, Commentaries, Treatises, and Defense* (New York: Paulist Press, 1981).

Richard Cross, *Duns Scotus* (New York: Oxford University Press, 1999).

Amy Hollywood, *The Soul as Virgin Bride: Mechthild of Magdeburg, Marguerite Porete and Meister Eckhart* (Notre Dame, Ind.: University of Notre Dame Press, 1995).

Alain de Libera, *Le Probleme de l'etre chez Maitre Eckhart* (Geneva: Revue de theologie et de philosophie, 1980).

Armand A. Maurer, *The Philosophy of William of Ockham in the Light of Its Principles* (Toronto: Pontifical Institute of Mediaeval Studies, 1999).

Bernard McGinn, *Meister Eckhart* (New York: Continuum Press, 2001).

McGinn, Frank Tobin, and Elvira Borgstadt, eds., *Meister Eckhart, Teacher and Preacher* (New York: Paulist Press, 1986).

Paul Vincent Spade, ed., *The Cambridge Companion to Ockham* (New York: Cambridge University Press, 1999).

Allan B. Wolter, *The Philosophical Theology of John Duns Scotus*, edited by Marilyn McCord Adams (Ithaca, N.Y.: Cornell University Press, 1990).

Emilie Zum Brunn and Alain de Libera, *Maitre Eckhart: Metaphysique du verbe et theologie negative* (Paris: Beauchesne, 1984).

SIGNIFICANT PEOPLE

PETER ABELARD

CIRCA 1079 - 1142
PHILOSOPHER AND THEOLOGIAN

Abelard and the Rise of the Schools. Peter Abelard, the most skilled logician of his day, was a major figure in the twelfth-century rise of Scholasticism in Paris. His chief influence lay in his work on the subject of universals and his contributions toward defining the Scholastic methodology, which consisted in the systematic application of reason to questions of philosophy and theology. Possessed of an ambitious and even "entrepreneurial" spirit, Abelard lived variously in Melun, Corbeil, and Paris, traveling wherever he thought he could best further his career as a teacher. His lectures were always well attended, and among his later students were Arnold of Brescia and John of Salisbury. Abelard was an important forerunner of the thirteenth-century university schoolmen, though personal scandal and clerical opposition were to mar his own career.

Early Career. A native of Le Palais, Brittany and the first-born son of a knight, Abelard moved to Paris to study philosophy. He quickly established a reputation as a master of dialectic. Indeed, Paul Vignaux refers to Abelard as "The Knight of Dialectics," in that he gave up his birthright as a knight of the sword to become instead a "Knight of the Schools." In Paris he studied first under William of Champeaux at the cloister school of Notre Dame. Before long he felt dissatisfied with his teacher and began to debate him publicly. A similar situation arose when he went to study theology with Anselm of Laon. Finding Anselm's method of scriptural exegesis insufficiently rigorous, Abelard openly challenged him and began to offer lectures of his own. In this way he quickly established himself as a teacher, but in proportion to his academic success he met with envy. As a kind of Socratic figure, he aroused the resentment of fellow teachers, many of whom did not hesitate to conspire against him.

Abelard and Heloise. His career was also threatened for personal reasons. According to a commonly held medieval ideal, the philosopher was supposed to be an ascetic, completely detached from worldly pursuits. Abelard, however, became involved in a love affair with Heloise, a private student of his who was at the time living with her uncle, the canon Fulbert. The affair was not only a scandal on account of Abelard's refusing the normal constraints of the scholarly life, but also because it marked a betrayal of his agreement with Fulbert. The resulting castration of Abelard by Fulbert's servants and the marriage and exile of Abelard and Heloise have inspired many literary treatments of the couple's ill-fated love. Heloise concluded her life as an abbess and Abelard as a humbled monk and theologian, though the affair did not bring an end to Abelard's days as a teacher.

Charges of Heresy. His academic career upset, Abelard had sought refuge at the Abbey of St. Denis. After a quarrel with the brothers there, he went in exile to Nogent-sur-Seine and started a school known as Le Paraclet (The Comforter). Later he served as abbot of St. Gildas in Brittany, but he found the behavior of the monks to be unruly and ill suited to study. Abelard returned to Paris and lectured at St. Genevieve, during which time he became involved in intense theological debate with Bernard of Clairvaux and other major clerics. Several of his writings, including *Sic et Non* (Yes and No, circa 1117–1128) and *Theologia Christiana* (Christian Theology, circa 1134–1138) led to a confrontation with conservative factions who feared what they perceived to be Abelard's overly rational approach to theology. Abelard believed the issues could be settled by means of public debate, of which he was a master. Bernard of Clairvaux had other ideas about the matter: he sought by secret political means to have the full force of ecclesiastical condemnation used against Abelard. When Abelard arrived at Sens for the "debate" on 3 June 1140, he discovered that Bernard had already prejudiced the ecclesiastical authorities against him. Rather than accept their judgment, Abelard departed and made his way to Rome to plead his case. He went to the Monastery of Cluny on the invitation of the abbot, Peter the Venerable, and there he composed *Apologia contra Bernardum* (Defense against Bernard). Bernard, however, was able through his connections to secure a papal condemnation of Abelard as a heretic. Abelard's sentence would have meant his excommunication, confinement to a monastery, and the destruction of his books, had it not been for the diplomacy of Peter the Venerable, who managed to reconcile Abelard and Bernard. Abelard was allowed to reside at Cluny, and the ban of excommunication was lifted. He moved to another Cluniac house at St. Marcel-sur-Saone, where he died peacefully on 21 April 1142.

Logical and Philosophical Works. Abelard's writings reflect above all his mastery of the trivium: grammar, logic, and rhetoric. In addition to commentaries on Aristotle's *Categories* and *On Interpretation*, Porphyry's *Isagoge*, and Boethius's *De differentiis topicis*, Abelard wrote tracts on logic in *Introductiones Parvulorum* (The Lesser Glosses on Logic, believed to have been written circa 1105) and *Logica Ingredientibus* (The Greater Glosses on Logic, circa 1112–1130). He also wrote *Dialectica* (Dialectic, circa 1130–1140), a treatise dealing with propositions, syllogisms, and logical consequences. Perhaps the most influential of all Abelard's logical works was his *Sic et Non*, in which a series of questions are posed, together with conflicting answers from patristic authorities. Though Abelard contented himself with merely collating the relevant passages from the Church Fathers, in his preface he set forth guidelines for comparison, logical scrutiny, and synthesis. The objective and rigorously dialectical methodology modeled in this work became a hallmark of Scholasticism.

Ethical and Theological Works. It would be a mistake to see Abelard as only a logician. His work in ethics, the *Scito te ipsum* (Know Thyself, circa 1138–1142) is an important contribution to the development of moral philosophy. Abelard placed primary emphasis on the role of intention in human deliberative moral action. In particular, he gave a nuanced account of the role of intention in moral decisions. Later in life Abelard applied his dialectical skills to theology. Here he met with great opposition from traditional theologians, who accused him of substituting reason for faith. Some in power viewed him as such a threat to the Christian faith that he was forced to burn one of his earliest works, a treatise on the trinity titled *Theologia Summi Boni* (Theology of the Highest Good, circa 1118–1120). His later theological works include *Commentary on Romans* (circa 1125–1131) and his *Theologia Christiana*. Peter Abelard, one could claim, helped lay the foundation for the world of university theology as distinct from that of monastic *lectio divina* (divine reading of scripture). His aim was not simply to meditate at length on the text of scripture, but to examine the text rationally in terms of its grammatical, logical, and rhetorical possibilities. *Argumentum*, or rational argument in the service of faith, had replaced non-argumentative meditative thought. Henceforth, a person's public ability was measured by the dialectical skill of the debater and not by appeals to the authority of a learned person or a book.

Other Works. Abelard's literary output was not confined to scholarly works. He also wrote Latin and vernacular poetry, including many religious hymns. Perhaps his best-known nonphilosophical work is his correspondence with Heloise. His elegant use of the epistolary form helped to establish the letter as a significant mode of philosophical and theological expression. Abelard also made use of the letter as a frame for his *Historia Calamitatum* (circa 1132–1133), an autobiographical account of his life and troubles. Including biographical detail rare for a figure of the Middle Ages, the work provides a frank description of his career as a gifted but highly controversial scholar.

Sources:
M. T. Clanchy, *Abelard* (Oxford: Blackwell, 1997).

John Marenbon, *Early Medieval Philosophy* (London: Routledge, 1983).

Paul Vignaux, *Philosophy in the Middle Ages: An Introduction* (New York: Meridian, 1959).

THOMAS AQUINAS

CIRCA 1225 - 1274
PHILOSOPHER AND THEOLOGIAN

The Synthesis of Philosophy and Theology. The two defining influences on the great medieval philosopher-theologian Thomas Aquinas were Scholasticism and Aristotelianism. At the time of Thomas's birth, the dominant approach to theology was that of the university Schoolmen (or Scholastics), who considered reason a necessary complement of faith and emphasized the use of logic and the importance of rational inquiry. One of the greatest aids to their task of systematizing Christian doctrine along philosophical lines was the rediscovery, in the late twelfth century, of certain major writings of Aristotle. Thomas was, therefore, born at a time when Scholasticism was reaching its height and the intellectual weight of Aristotelianism was just beginning to be felt. His great contribution to theology was his effort to synthesize Christianity and Aristotelianism, which resulted in one of the most comprehensive philosophical systems in history and the crowning achievement of Scholasticism.

Education. Thomas was born at Roccasecca, a family castle near Naples, Italy, to the noble house of Aquilo. He received his early schooling at the Benedictine monastery of Monte Cassino, where he demonstrated a precocious intelligence and piety. In 1240 he went to Naples to continue his studies at the recently established university, where he was probably introduced to Aristotle, whose *Physics* and *Metaphysics* had recently reached western Europe through Latin translations of Arabic texts preserved by the Muslim world and its philosophers. At Naples, Thomas also came into contact with the Dominicans, a relatively new monastic order with a mission of preaching and instruction and an emphasis on the education of its members. In 1244 Thomas took Dominican vows against the wishes of his family, which even abducted Thomas and held him at various family strongholds during 1244–1245. When Thomas was released the Dominicans sent him to the University of Paris, where he studied under Albertus Magnus, one of the pre-eminent Scholastics and an admirer of Aristotle. When Albertus was sent to Cologne, Thomas went with his teacher and continued to study with him for the next four years, absorbing much of his mentor's Aristotelianism.

Teaching and Writing. In 1252 Thomas returned to Paris and began his career as a teacher, lecturing on the *Libri Quatuor Sententiarum* (Four Books of Sentences, written 1148–1151) of Peter Lombard. About four years later he received the title master of theology. In 1259 he left Paris for Italy, where he taught at Rome and several other cities for a decade before returning to Paris. There he disputed the extreme Aristotelianism of Siger of Brabant and other young scholars. Although Thomas's own thought relied heavily on Aristotle's teachings, he remained loyal to the Christian doctrine of revelation, departing from Artistotle whenever his teachings disagreed with those of the Church. He attested to this loyalty again on his deathbed, when concerning his writings he pronounced, "I submit all to the judgement and correction of the Holy Roman Church, in whose obedience I now pass from this life." Thomas moved a final time in 1272, to establish a Dominican school at Naples. He died two years later, on 7 March 1274, on his way to attend the Council of Lyons.

The *Summa Theologiae*. The number of Thomas's writings is remarkable given the relatively brief span of his life. In fewer than fifty years he wrote scores of commentaries, tracts, and treatises covering a broad range of spiritual and philosophical topics; some of his early biographers mentioned that he had several scribes working for him at once. Among his most influential works are his commentaries on Aristotle and on the Bible, and his *Summa de Veritate Catholicae Fidei contra Gentiles* (Comprehensive Truth of the Catholic Faith against the Gentiles, written 1259–1262). His greatest work is his *Summa Theologiae* (Comprehensive Theology, written 1265-1273), a systematic and thorough treatment of all the major (and many minor) questions of Christian theology. The work is presented in the form of a series of articles, each posing a specific question. Among the more than three thousand questions answered are whether it can be demonstrated that God exists, whether the human soul is incorruptible, whether God is the cause of evil, and whether created goods can bring man happiness. Thomas addressed each question in the Scholastic form prevalent in the lecture halls of his day, first listing every reasonable objection to his proposed answer, then citing an authority to support him, explaining his solution, and finally replying to each of the objections initially raised.

"The Angelic Doctor." The *Summa Theologiae* was left unfinished when Aquinas gave up writing in 1273, not long before his death. According to his medieval biographers, Thomas was often given to mystical ecstasies, and after an especially profound experience at a mass on 6 December he had abandoned his work on the *Summa Theologiae.* When a companion urged him to finish it, Thomas replied, "I cannot . . . in comparison with what I have seen in prayer all that I have written seems to me as if it were straw." His fellow Dominicans seem to have held a loftier view of his written work; in 1278, just four years after his death, his works were made the official doctrinal basis of the order. Despite initial resistance by the Franciscans, the influence of Thomas's works and teaching spread, eventually becoming a cornerstone of Roman Catholic theology. Even theologians who disagreed with Thomas were forced to take some account of his work. Thomas Aquinas was canonized by Pope John XXII in 1323, and in 1567 he was declared a Doctor of the Church.

Sources:

G. K. Chesterton, *St. Thomas Aquinas: The Dumb Ox* (London: Hodder & Stoughton, 1933).

Frederick C. Copleston, *Aquinas* (Harmondsworth, U.K.: Penguin, 1955).

Arthur Cushman McGiffert, "Thomas Aquinas," in *A History of Christian Thought,* 2 volumes (New York & London: Scribners, 1933), II: 257–294.

James A. Weisheipl, *Friar Thomas Aquinas* (Garden City, N.Y.: Doubleday, 1974).

JOHN SCOTTUS ERIUGENA

CIRCA 810 - CIRCA 877
PHILOSOPHER AND THEOLOGIAN

The First Medieval Latin Philosopher. John Scottus Eriugena stands out as the most original thinker of the ninth century and the first systematic philosopher of the Middle Ages. He was born in Ireland but moved to France, perhaps because of the turbulence caused by Viking raids. France was still in the midst of the so-called renaissance of Charlemagne, who one generation earlier had welcomed foreign scholars such as Alcuin of York and Theodulf of Orleans. In this favorable climate Eriugena flourished. His keen mind and breadth of knowledge soon earned him a reputation as one of the finest scholars in Europe. He became a friend of Charlemagne's grandson, King Charles the Bald, and served at his court as a poet, philosopher, theologian, and translator.

Major Works. Eriugena's philosophical works may be divided into two categories. The first includes those works written prior to 860, which bear the influence of traditional Latin sources, notably the writings of Augustine. Among these earlier works are Eriugena's *Glossae Divinae Historiae* (Biblical Glosses, circa 845–850), *De Divinae Praedestinatione Liber* (Book on Divine Predestination, circa 850–851), and *Annotationes in Marcianum* (Annotations on

Martianus Capella, circa 859–860). The year 860 marks a shift in influence from the Latin Fathers to the Greek Fathers, who were at the time relatively unknown in the West. With his Latin translations of Pseudo-Dionysius and Maximus the Confessor, Eriugena began to assimilate Neoplatonic ideas into his own philosophical system. An emended version of one of his translations served as the standard edition of Pseudo-Dionysius for the next three hundred years. The most important result of the synthesis of Greek and Latin philosophy in his own writings was his *Periphyseon* (On Nature, circa 864–866), the most comprehensive and subtle work of philosophical speculation composed between the times of Augustine and Aquinas.

Eriugena's Legacy. As seen in his works on the Bible and on the pagan author Martianus Capella, Eriugena gave reason its rightful place in the interpretation of myth, story, and belief. In his homily on the Prologue of John's Gospel, *Vox Spiritualis Aquilae* (The Voice of the Spiritual Eagle, circa 870–872), Eriugena gave John, a symbol of intelligence, primacy over Peter, a symbol of faith. Reason is no mere slave of the passions, he believed, but an autonomous and necessary compliment of humanity. Reason is capable of resolving the ambiguities of difficult texts and discovering the possible meanings of myths and the human meaningfulness of religious mystery. Eriugena presented an anthropology in which the human being is no mere passive observer of abstract events. Rather, as the workshop of nature, human creativity allows for the restoration and re-visioning of nature. The major figures of German Idealism later found this vision of man congenial to their thought. In terms of the application of technical philosophical vocabulary, Eriugena made skillful use of Aristotle's *Categories,* specifically in regard to language about the world, the human being, and God. Eriugena's use of reason ranged from comprehensive synthesis to acute analysis, and in this regard he stands unrivaled among the philosophers of his day.

Charges of Heresy. Though Eriugena had a following among his contemporaries and in the century that followed his death, narrow-minded thinkers at Paris in the thirteenth century linked his works to the heretical views of David of Dinant. In 1210 Eriugena's *Periphyseon* was burned. Nonetheless, his magnificant rhetorical and poetic achievement, *Vox Spiritualis Aquilae,* circulated throughout the Middle Ages pseudonymously, with various attributions of authorship to Origen, John Chrysostom, and Robert Grosseteste. Eriugena's work was read and admired by Meister Eckhart and Nicholas of Cusa. His thought was rediscovered by the German Idealists during the first part of the nineteenth century. In the late twentieth century Eriugenian studies were revived considerably, with new editions, comments, studies, and translations.

Sources:

Werner Beierwaltes, *Eriugena* (Frankfurt am Main: Klostermann, 1994).

Mary Brennan, *A Guide to Eriugenian Studies (1930–1987),* Vestigia 5 (Freibourg, Switzerland: Editions universitaires / Paris: Editions du Cerf, 1989).

Edouard Jeauneau, *Etudes Eriugéniennes* (Paris: Etudes Augustiniennes, 1987).

Dermot Moran, *The Philosophy of John Scottus Eriugena: a Study of Idealism in the Middle Ages* (Cambridge & New York: Cambridge University Press, 1989).

John J. O'Meara, *Eriugena* (Oxford: Clarendon Press, 1988).

FRANCIS OF ASSISI

1181 - 1226
FRIAR AND PREACHER

His Conversion. One of the most striking embodiments of evangelical revival in the Middle Ages is Francis of Assisi. In his youth, Francis experienced a radical upheaval in his values and assumptions about life. In his *Testament* (1226), he attributes this change to his attitude toward lepers: "When I was still in the world, it was too bitter for me to see lepers; after the Lord granted me to show mercy to lepers, that which had first seemed bitter to me now changed into sweetness of the soul and of the body and a little while later I went out of the world." The reason for Francis's conversion, then, was not so much poverty, for love of which he later became famous, as the awareness of human suffering and its importance as a means of union between the Christian and Christ. With this discovery Francis acquired a new sense of what it meant to live a Christian life.

Love of Poverty. Francis's renunciation of the world reached its height when his father brought him before an ecclesiastical court, suing for the return of goods Francis had sold without his permission and seeking to cut off his son's inheritance. This episode has been connected to Francis's discovery that poverty was a liberating experience that releases one from all servitude and connects one to the great mass of the poor. Francis did not preach rebellion to the poor, nor did he attack the lifestyle of the clergy; he spoke exclusively of the need to imitate Christ. He soon found a large number of followers who wished to join in the task of living out the Gospel joyfully, without property or stable institutions, relying on begging and occasional work for their support.

The Franciscan Order. With papal approval, Francis and his followers began to preach in a manner that was not primarily theological, but exhortative and penitential. Francis's preaching was not intended to educate people. His hearers were frequently fascinated by him and decided to join his order. From Francis's own lifetime, the Franciscan experience was also open to women, even if they were not able, in the social conditions of the time, to enjoy the same freedom to roam about as the friars. Inspired by Francis, Clare of Assisi founded a group of women who lived the religious life and came to be known as the Poor Clares, and took up the work of relieving human suffering by assistance to the poor and the sick. In Francis's time, the Franciscans also became associated with groups of pious laypeople interested in imitating their life. These laypeople, who soon acquired a formal connection with the order, became members of hundreds of Franciscan confraternities throughout Europe, which assisted the practical existence of the order and served as important centers of Franciscan piety and devotion. The success of these confraternities was not always well received by the secular clergy, who saw their reputation weakened by the new orders, as it had been in earlier centuries by popular admiration for monks and other ascetics. Despite this degree of clerical opposition, the new orders were phenomenally successful, responding as they did to the restlessness of urban society and its search for a more intimate and sustaining spirituality. These same needs made for the success of other mendicant orders founded after the Franciscans and Dominicans, such as the Carmelites and the Friar-Hermits of St. Augustine.

The Canticle of the Sun. Francis's last years were afflicted by illness as well as by misunderstandings and difficulties with his brethren within the order. In the midst of these difficulties, however, Francis's joy, which later generations would see as his trademark, emerged. His poverty and renunciation of all that might ease his suffering never stopped him from feeling that life was a precious good because it was the manifestation and gift of the supreme goodness of God. This goodness, he believed, did not touch humankind alone, but was expressed in the beauty of nature, through which God makes himself known to men. For this reason, in the midst of his last sufferings Francis produced his *Canticle of the Sun* (1225). The poem, which was composed in the vernacular, served lay brothers in the order as his Latin *Testament* served for the clerical members; his unlettered brothers and those who had heard and seen him preach throughout Italy found in this poem the exaltation of God through his creatures. In the conclusion of the poem, Francis wrote of the two supreme goods of men,

peace of the heart and holiness before God. The canticle is a message that, beginning with the universe, concludes with man as the only being who can appreciate God's work in the universe and in man's own heart; most dramatically, God's work is seen even in death, which according to Francis ought to cause fear and trembling only in those who, although endowed with eyes, have not been able to see God and who, having allowed themselves to be fascinated by deceitful appearances, are unable to elevate themselves to the eternal beauty of the Creator in his creation.

Stigmata and Canonization. Francis's ideals had a powerful influence among all those who met and heard him. The most striking revelation took place at his death, when his body is said to have manifested the stigmata (wounds of Christ in the hands, feet, and side). Immediately after this miracle, the view of Francis as a second Christ and a renewer of Christ on earth became fixed among believers. Only two years after his death, in 1228, Gregory IX, who had been protector of the Franciscan order and a friend to Francis, proclaimed him a saint.

His Legacy. Francis left to his order the mission to live and work among the masses. The forms of piety developed and fostered by Francis reflect this mission. For example, he is said to be the inventor of the Christmas manger, an expedient intended to reveal to the simple faithful the human reality of Christ. Likewise, it was under the influence of Francis and his order that the sufferings of the crucified Christ began to be depicted much more realistically. The Franciscans have always been present among the poor, not merely to provide pastoral care for them, but also to share their poverty. This witness to poverty made the Franciscans one of the most lively forces in the Church of the later Middle Ages.

Sources:

Rosalind B. Brooke, *The Coming of the Friars* (New York: Barnes & Noble, 1975).

Francis of Assisi and Clare of Assisi, *Francis and Clare: The Complete Works*, translated by Regis Armstrong and Ignatius Brady (New York: Paulist Press, 1982).

DOCUMENTARY SOURCES

Peter Abelard, *Dialogus inter Philosophum, Iudaeum, et Christianorum* (Dialogue of a Philosopher with a Jew and a Christian, circa 1138–1142)—A most important attempt to set out the distinct positions of ancient pagan philosophy, Jewish thinking, and Christian theology.

Peter Abelard, *Ethica seu Scito Teipsum* (Ethics; or, Know Thyself, circa 1138–1142)—A great contribution to the discussion of moral action with its stress on the role of intention.

Peter Abelard, *Historia Calamitatum* (History of My Misfortunes, circa 1132–1133)—The author's autobiography.

Peter Abelard, *Logica Ingredientibus* (The Greater Glosses on Logic, circa 1112–1130)—Commentaries on Porphyry's *Isagoge* and Aristotle's *Categories* and *De interpretatione*.

Adelard of Bath, *De eodem et diverso* (On the Same and the Different, circa 1150)—Work on metaphysics based on Neo-Platonism.

Adelard of Bath, *Questiones naturales* (Questions on Natural Philosophy, circa 1150)—Important work on topics in natural philosophy.

Albertus Magnus, *Summa theologia* (Comprehensive Theology, 1263–1274)—Comprehensive review of the issues in theology.

Albertus Magnus, *Super Dionysium de divinis nominibus* (Commentary on Dionysius on the Divine Names, circa 1250)—Commentaries on Pseudo-Dionysius that had an important influence on Renaissance thought.

Albertus Magnus, *Super Ethica, Commentum et Questiones* (Commentary and Questions on Aristotle's Ethics, circa 1250–1252)—The author wrote "paraphrases" on all of Aristotle's works.

Albertus Magnus, *Super sententiarum* (Commentary on Peter Lombard's *Sentences,* circa 1246–1249)—The commentary was roughly similar to a modern doctoral dissertation; every medieval doctor of theology had to compose one.

Anslem of Canterbury, *Proslogion* (An Address of the Mind to God 1077–1078)—Meditative work on the knowledge of God. It is famous for its so-called ontological proof for God's existence.

Thomas Aquinas, *In decem libros Ethicorum Aristotelis ad Nicomachum expositio* (Ten Ethical Books, 1265–1273)—Commentary on Aristotle's *Nicomachaen Ethics.*

Thomas Aquinas, *Summa de veritate catholicae fidei contra gentiles* (Comprehensive Truth of the Catholic Faith against the Gentiles, 1261–1264)—A comprehensive discussion of many Greek, Roman, Islamic, and Jewish philosophical issues.

Thomas Aquinas, *Summa theologiae* (Comprehensive Theology, 1266–1273)—His major work and a significant theological synthesis.

Averröes, *Commentarium Magnum in Aristotelis De Anima Libros* (circa 1190)—An example of a major commentary on Aristotle. It became an essential tool for reading Aristotle in the Middle Ages.

Avicenna, *Metaphysica, De Anima* (The Healing, circa 1020–1027)—Perhaps the most important contribution to medieval metaphysics and philosophy.

Roger Bacon, *Opus Maius* (Major Work, circa 1267)—An encyclopedic work on the relation of language study and the sciences to theology.

Roger Bacon, *Quaestiones* (Questions on Aristotle, 1240s)—One of the early Latin studies on the texts of Aristotle.

Boethius of Dacia (Boethius or Boetius of Sweden), *Opuscula: De Aeternitate Mundi, De Summo Bono, De Somniis* (Opuscula: On the Eternity of the World, On the Supreme Good, On Dreams, circa 1270–1274)—Together with his important works on the philosophy of language and on Aristotle, they are primary texts for our understanding of the Condemnations of 1277.

Bonaventure (Giovanni di Fidanza), *Collationes in Hexaëmeron sive Illuminationes Ecclesiae* (Collations on the Six Days of Creation; or, Enlightenment of the Church, 1273)—Important lectures at the Franciscan House of Studies, Paris, during the crisis on Averroism.

Bonaventure (Giovanni di Fidanza), *De Reductione Artium ad Theologiam* (On the Reduction of the Arts to Theology, circa 1255–1257 or circa 1273)—An important work showing how the liberal arts and philosophy relate to theology.

John Duns Scotus, *Opus Oxoniense* (Oxford Commentary on the Sentences, circa 1300)—A skillful interpretation of Peter Lombard.

John Duns Scotus, *Quæstiones Quodlibetales* (Quodlibet Questions, 1306–1307)—A complex interpretation of Aristotle. His interpretation of the *Metaphysics* and the *De anima* are of great importance.

John Duns Scotus, *Reportata Parisiensia* (Parisian Commentary on the Sentences, circa 1302–1304)—A new set of interpretations of Peter Lombard's *Sentences*.

Meister Eckhart, *Opus Tripartitum* (Work in Three Parts, 1311–1326)—A major theological work, containing more than one thousand theses that are explained and then proved.

Meister Eckhart, *Quaestiones Parisiensis*, 1–3 (Parisian Questions, 1302–1303)—Eckhart's Latin lectures at the University of Paris.

Meister Eckhart, *Sermones* (Sermons, Latin and German, 1316–1327)—A collection of the German mystic's sermons.

Meister Eckhart, *Von Abgeschiedenheit* (On Detachment, circa 1325)—An important work of spiritual instruction.

John Scottus Eriugena, *Periphyseon* (About Nature, circa 864–866)—This philosophical-theological synthesis unites Greek philosophical traditions coming from Proclus and Damascius through Pseudo-Dionysius, Gregory of Nyssa, and Maximus Confessor with the Latin tradition of Augustine and Boethius.

Robert Grosseteste, *Commentarius in Posterium Analyticorum Libros* (Commentary on [Aristotle's] Posterior Analytics, circa 1214–1235)—The first Latin commentary on the logic of proof in Aristotle, one of the most significant contributions to medieval philosophy.

Robert Grosseteste, *De Iride* (On the Rainbow, circa 1214–1235)—An application of optics to natural phenomena.

Robert Grosseteste, *De Luce* (On Light, circa 1225–1241)—A description of the material world.

Robert Grosseteste, *Hexaëmeron* (Commentary on Genesis, circa 1214–1235)—Complex interpretation of the first book of the Bible.

Moses Maimonides (Rabbi Moshe ben Maimon; acronym: Rambam), *Dux neutrorum* or *Dalalat al-Ha'irin/Moreh Nevukhim* (The Guide for the Perplexed, 1204)—This work is an introduction for students on how to read the scriptures philosophically; it is a study of the limits and powers of reason in dealing with the divine.

William of Ockham (Guillelmus de Ockham), *Dialogus de Potestate Papae I–III* (Dialogue on the Power of the Pope, volumes I–III, 1335–1346)—An important polemical work written at Munich against extreme papal claims to temporal authority.

William of Ockham (Guillelmus de Ockham), *Scriptum in Librum Sententiarum Ordinatio* (Commentary on the book of the *Sentences*, Ordinatio, circa 1319–1321)—A treatise on Peter Lombard's work.

William of Ockham (Guillelmus de Ockham), *Summa Logicae* (Comprehensive Logic, circa 1322)—A major summary of the common medieval teaching on the nature of logic.

John Peckham, *Perspectiva communis* (The Common Account of Perspectiva [Optics], circa 1269–1279)—This work became a most important contribution to a philosophical study of the eye and vision.

John Peckham, *Quodlibeta Quatuor* (Four Quodlibetal [Open/Free for Discussion] Questions, circa 1270–1275)—An important example of the contribution of this major English Franciscan thinker to the debates in Paris.

Siger of Brabant, *De Aeternitate Mundi* (On the Eternity of the World, circa 1271–1272)—An important primary source for the debates at the University of Paris from circa 1265-1277.

Siger of Brabant, *Quaestiones in Tertium De Anima* (Questions on the Third Book of [Aristotle's] On the Soul, 1269–1270)—Another primary source for the debates at the University of Paris from circa 1265-1277.

An ivory panel carved in the 830s or 840s and set into an eleventh-century book cover (Bibliothèque Nationale, Paris)

SCIENCE, TECHNOLOGY, AND HEALTH

by STEVEN A. WALTON and BERT S. HALL

CONTENTS

Sidebars and tables are listed in italics.

814*
- Western Europe is in a period of climate improvement that began circa 700 and continues until about 1200. As a result, agriculture flourishes.

834
- The use of a crank to turn a rotary grindstone is documented in Europe for the first time.

900*
- Over the next century the three-field system of crop rotation begins to appear in Europe, as more and more land comes under cultivation; Europeans begin to use hops to flavor and preserve beer.

1075*
- Europeans invent the crossbow, perhaps from the example of the much older Chinese crossbow.

1096
- Pope Urban II calls for the first of eight crusades to the Holy Land, which continue sporadically until 1291. Returning crusaders employ Arab technology in castle building.

1100*
- Over the next century the first horizontal loom appears in Europe; tidal mills come into use; paper appears in Europe from the Islamic world; Europeans begin to distill oils and alcohol; and scholastic thought, based on the first translations of Aristotle's works into Latin, influences scientific investigation.

1122
- Theophilus Presbyter writes *On Divers Arts*, a textbook of artistic crafts with instructions for mixing paint pigments, making gold amalgams, and casting metal.

1126
- The first documented artesian well is dug in Europe, and percussion drilling is practiced.
- Major efforts begin to ensure the water supplies of major monasteries and cities.
- Adelard of Bath introduces Euclid's *Elements*, his treatise on geometry, into Europe.

1140
- European scholars begin to study magnets and magnetism.

1144
- The monastery of St. Denis in Paris begins a rebuilding program in the "Gothic" style, employing building forms borrowed from the Arabs.

1145
- Robert of Chester translates al-Khwarizmi's *Algebra* into Latin.

***DENOTES CIRCA DATE**

1160* • Europeans begin to use the magnetic compass.

1180 • Over the next decade windmills appear in Europe, and the use of glazed mirrors is recorded for the first time.

1200* • Over the next 150 years universities grow, and education spreads. Commerce flourishes, and interest in science increases.

1202 • Leonardo Fibonacci discusses Arabic numerals, including zero, which later become commonplace and replace Roman numerals, which do not include zero. Fibonacci also describes what is now known as a "Fibonacci Series" (1, 2, 3, 5, 8, 13, 21, 34, . . .), in which each number is the sum of the previous two. The series is eventually employed to describe biological systems. He also uses negative numbers.

1214 • Between this date and his death in 1253 Robert Grosseteste, English intellectual and scientist, translates works by Aristotle and develops ideas in mathematics, optics, and astronomy.

1266 • The Borgogoni brothers recommend narcotic sponges for surgical patients and stitching wounds after they are cleaned with wine.

1267 • Roger Bacon describes gunpowder, marking its introduction to Europe from China.

1269 • Peter of Maricourt (Peter the Pilgrim) describes magnetic polarity and other experiments with a "lodestone."

1285 • Spectacles for reading are invented in Italy and become popular among intellectuals and merchants.

1300* • The Royal Bethlehem Hospital (later known as "Bedlam") is founded in London specifically for mental patients.

• Over the next century water-powered bellows make it possible to smelt iron in blast furnaces and to make iron castings; also, distilled wine ("brandy-wine," or "brandy") becomes common, and the Scots and the Irish use fermented barley to distill whiskey.

• Over the next two hundred years Europe goes through periods of economic difficulties and frequent plagues that reduce the population.

* DENOTES CIRCA DATE

1300
- Over the next seven years Arnald of Villanova writes a series of influential *Regimens of Health* for powerful patrons; these works are widely imitated in later decades.

1305
- Theodoric of Freiberg explains the refraction of light in lenses and raindrops, showing how rainbows are formed.

1315
- The climate of Europe begins to worsen, with crop failures across much of the continent; famine becomes frequent, and croplands shrink in size.

1316
- Mondino da Luzzi publishes *Anatomia*, based on public dissections of human corpses.

1326
- Gunpowder cannons are mentioned for the first time in European records.

1333*
- Richard of Wallingford describes his astronomical clock at the monastery of St. Albans. It shows the movement of stars, the sun, and planets, as well as striking hours on a bell.

1347
- Bubonic plague (Black Death), which has been spreading eastward from China for nearly two decades, reaches Europe. Sweeping through much of the continent it returns roughly every twenty years for several centuries. This first appearance reduces the European population by as much as 65 percent and makes a major impact on social and economic life. (Later occurrences are somewhat less deadly.)

* DENOTES CIRCA DATE

OVERVIEW

The Middle Ages. The thoughts, beliefs, and values of medieval Europeans were dramatically different from those of modern people. Europeans living in postmedieval periods such as the Renaissance and the Enlightenment—as the names of those eras suggest—self-consciously tried to portray themselves as somehow overthrowing the formal structures and restrictions of an earlier age, and in the process they managed to denigrate and misrepresent the life and thought of an entire millennium. The Middle Ages were born in the still-mysterious process that caused the disintegration of the Roman Empire, and the whole of medieval culture was affected by a widespread attempt to regain the glories of classical civilization. Yet, in the midst of this apparent attempt to re-create the past, medieval Europeans moved forward as well. There were many important intellectual advances during the Middle Ages, including the beginnings of almost every modern vernacular European language and the written scripts to record them, the origins of such fundamental institutions as parliamentary government and the university, and a host of everyday inventions from eyeglasses to wheelbarrows to gunpowder. During the nineteenth and twentieth centuries scholars have greatly increased their knowledge about the Middle Ages, gaining respect for the genuine accomplishments of this vital and productive period.

The Dark Ages. The accomplishments of Greco-Roman culture were documented in two languages, Greek and Latin, but much of the scientific and medical knowledge of the classical period was recorded only in Greek. As most educated Romans were fluent in Greek, there was no reason to translate the philosophical and scientific works of antiquity into Latin. The decline of the Roman Empire in the fourth and fifth centuries left the Latin-speaking West largely bereft of the intellectual heritage of the Greek-speaking East, even as the economic collapse of the Roman Empire left the West depopulated and impoverished. The political fragmentation of the Roman Empire into petty kingdoms ruled by Germanic warlords completed the process of cultural decline. Only the Roman Church retained some concept of the old order and its cultural possibilities, and as the most devout individuals clustered in monasteries and nunneries to escape the increasingly ignorant and unstable world outside, these ecclesiastical institutions became the

centers where the fragments of ancient learning were preserved. Meanwhile, as the new Islamic religion arose in Arabia during the 600s and spread vigorously across North Africa and the Middle East, much of Greek learning was translated into Arabic, rather than Latin, and an unprecedented Arab intellectual culture flourished as its Western counterpart declined.

European Revivals. All endings represent opportunities to begin anew, and the intellectual life of medieval Europe began to renew itself as early as 768, when Charlemagne (Charles the Great) succeeded to the throne of France and launched what was later called the Carolingian Renaissance. The director of that "renaissance," the Anglo-Saxon Benedictine monk Alcuin, set up schools, promoted the copying of classical Latin texts, and developed a new handwriting, the direct ancestor of modern lettering. Most classical texts survive owing to this effort. The Holy Roman Empire, Charlemagne's political effort to reinstate a form of the Roman Empire, was less successful, especially as his successors fought among themselves for pre-eminence, foreshadowing the later rivalry between France and Germany. During the later part of the ninth century and most of the tenth, Europe was again on the defensive against "barbarian" invaders, this time the Vikings, Avars, and Magyars (Hungarians). Still, throughout this period the climate steadily improved, and agricultural technology grew more productive, paving the way for genuine economic and demographic growth in the new millennium. The Church found itself struggling for its institutional independence, leading to renewed emphasis on monasteries as exemplars of Christian virtue, which included culture and learning.

High Medieval Culture. By the late eleventh century Christian Europe was prepared to counterattack Islam, which Europeans unfortunately saw as a sworn enemy in possession of Christian patrimony: Jerusalem and the Holy Land. With the First Crusade (1096–1099), a long series of bloody wars between Muslims and Christians began. Even as the West attacked Islam, however, Catholic monks and scholars began the task of translating Greco-Roman philosophical and scientific works from their Arabic intermediaries into Latin, triggering an entirely new medieval revival, which centered on towns and cathedral schools and ultimately gave rise to universities and what is called Scholastic philosophy. Unlike the Carolingian Renaissance, the intellectual flourishing of the twelfth and thirteenth centuries was devoted not merely to saving the best of the past but to integrating the richness and sophistication of ancient culture with the demands of the Christian faith. The result was a virtual explosion of knowledge in a new and useful form. Medieval European civilization reached its height during this time: towns grew into cities; cathedrals reached toward the sky; and new kingdoms took shape.

Medieval Borrowing. Unlike many other civilizations, medieval Europe was always willing to absorb elements from other cultures and to remake them in its own image. The extent of this borrowing is one of the main things that modern scholars have learned about the medieval period, and it occurred in many areas of medieval life. Examples include the "Gothic" arch and instruments such as water clocks and astrolabes from the Arabs, silks and brocades from the Chinese, the principles of philosophy (adapted to a Christianized intellectual context) from the ancient Greeks, and the beaded "rosary" and the palms-together gesture of prayer from Islam. This "syncretic" quality is especially important in technology, where many individual items were borrowed and adapted from the Near East, Asia, and even Africa. Stirrups, cranks, the magnetic compass, the fiddle or violin bow, windmills, crossbows, distilled alcohol, and gunpowder are all borrowings from the East that were adapted by medieval culture and often improved. The history of technology is frequently about creative borrowing, as contrasted with allegedly "original" invention. Medieval Europe excelled at borrowing.

The Persistence of the Middle Ages. Medieval European culture is extraordinary in its persistence and its pervasive influence on the modern world. Modern students are often less than flattered to think of themselves as repositories of medieval material objects and intellectual constructs, but they are. Without denim and jeans—named for the medieval cities of Nimes and Genoa—their wardrobes would be markedly different; lacking eyeglasses, many could not see; rock music is still notated on the staff invented in the Middle Ages and played on modern versions of medieval instruments—the guitar and the keyboard. The most popular computer card game is solitaire, played with cards, a medieval invention. Popular movies feature medieval objects such as firearms, medieval literary conventions such as romantic love, and plotlines that go back to the medieval troubadours. A complete list of such holdovers for the Middle Ages would be much longer.

The End of the Middle Ages. The persistence of medieval culture in the modern period demonstrates the artificial nature of the line dividing "medieval" from "modern." The end of the Middle Ages is much more difficult to establish than the "fall of Rome" that signaled the collapse of classical civilization in the fifth century. Medieval European civilization did not collapse. The advent of bubonic plague in the mid fourteenth century, however, helped to trigger a serious decline in population over most of Europe, and the plague was a recurrent scourge for many centuries.

This process was abetted by a serious worsening of the climate, which made some land unsuitable for crops and restricted agricultural output. (Much more land was plowed and farmed in medieval Europe than has ever been cultivated there since.) Some historians think similar conditions led to population decline and the collapse of ancient civilizations, but if so, medieval civilization proved more resilient than its predecessors. Depressed economic conditions stimulated religious and political movements, some of them quite extreme, but the overall effect was to strengthen nascent institutions such as the modern nation-states of France and England, while keeping intact the economic and social framework of late medieval Europe. When Europeans set out to explore new routes to "The Indies," for better or for worse they wound up carrying European culture to the far corners of the earth. The flood of new wealth and knowledge that came back to Europe did not mark an end to the Middle Ages. The changes this influx sparked were more analogous to growing up than to the cultural destruction that accompanied the end of Rome. All postmedieval cultures are the children of the Middle Ages. To acknowledge this ongoing debt to that period is to begin to understand modern history.

Science, Technology, and Health. In many ways, however, the Middle Ages were unlike the modern world, especially in science, technology, and health. Science was distinctly separate from technology and healing. Sciences were studied and debated in universities, and although scholars might take notice of the "mechanical arts," as technology was called, they regarded this field as a separate and distinct area of investigation. Medicine, as distinct from healing, was a science taught in the universities, and it did not deal directly with sick people. The practical arts of technology and healing were considered subordinate and therefore inferior to theoretical science and medicine. The goal of science was not useful applications, but a better and more perfect understanding of God's creation. Indeed, medieval science is intimately associated with theological concerns of perfection and providence.

A Link to the Ancient World. Medieval science stands as a stepping stone between ancient Greek knowledge of the world and the modern conception of it, which is generally understood to have arisen in the sixteenth and seventeenth centuries, during the so-called Scientific Revolution. While it may seem foreign to the modern understanding of the world, medieval science does make a certain amount of "sense." Many of its explanations of things or processes were formulated, not with reference to observable facts, but to extend or corroborate the overarching religious or philosophical beliefs of the time. The same thing could be said of the ancient worldview as well. Where the medieval world broke free of the ancient mythological understanding of the world was in the belief that it was fundamentally explainable. Medieval scholars asserted that, since God made the world, its laws, and its inhabitants, he must have given humanity the power and intellect to investigate and explain this Christian cosmos. An understanding of the natural world would then lead to a greater understanding of its creator as well—a belief also common among the scientists of the Scientific Revolution. As medieval scientists studied various aspects of the world and its denizens, they formed the foundations for the methods by which modern scientists investigate the world.

Technology. Historians used to believe that, after the fall of Rome, a "Dark Age" settled over Europe and was not lifted until that glorious "rebirth" called the Renaissance. In technology, as in many other areas of medieval studies, this view has been resoundingly disproved as more and more evidence has come to light from archaeological digs and newly discovered or re-examined documentary sources. Scholars now know that people of the Middle Ages were extremely interested in using technology to create wealth, comfort, and change in a society that had lost a central cultural influence with the end of the Roman Empire. In fact, the Middle Ages was the period in which the Western predilection for doing things with machines was born. Pulling themselves from the wreckage of the Roman Empire and aspiring to re-create Roman glories as they understood them, medieval Europeans instead created the foundations of the modern world. From simple "machines" such as the gear and the pulley, they made complex machinery to stamp, grind, pump, jack, throw, pull, and lift. With the simple straightedge and compass, they transformed basic geometry into complex patterns and then erected these patterns in stone, developing in the process new ways to enclose space. In their wars, they sought new mechanical and architectural solutions to the perennial problems of attack and defense. With new understandings of how the elements in a technological system could be manipulated, they reorganized their methods of work and increased productivity manyfold.

Power Sources. For proof of how favorably Europeans looked on machinery, one may examine the technology they employed to harness power. All societies are fundamentally defined by the power sources they have at their disposal. Although medieval Europe had only one source that the Romans did not have (windmills), exploitation of those power sources in the Middle Ages was vastly more impressive than the Romans' use of the same technology. With the harnessing of animals, flowing water, and the winds, medieval Europeans changed the world: they tilled the soil and increased crop production many times over; they pumped and hammered and sawed with a new ease that would have amazed non-Europeans of their time; and they milled enough grain to feed an ever-expanding population. They became skilled at manipulating gears, pulleys, levers, beams, cords, and wheels to make machines do amazing things. They had learned how to harness nonhuman power to perform tasks that had been done by humans before. This fundamental shift in energy sources liberated humanity's potential to alter how that energy was given back to them as useful work. In virtually all ways, the history of medieval technology shows people at their most creative.

Health. Today the concept of medieval "health" might seem a contradiction in terms, for many still agree with the seventeenth-century philosopher Thomas Hobbes, who asserted that life in the Middle Ages was "nasty, brutish, and short." In fact, although average life expectancy was short, a person who survived childhood and adolescence (and especially childbirth) had a good chance of living into his or her sixties, if not longer. At the same time, however, war and plague were ever present, and to many people the specter of death (and final judgment) seemed not far off. In addition, famine and starvation in years of crop failure were a constant threat, and in many parts of Europe, soil, climate, and isolation from trade routes resulted in unhealthy diets for the poor people of those regions. In some areas of Europe the Black Death of the fourteenth century killed an estimated one-third to one-half of the populations of some towns.

Health Care. Nonetheless, medieval people developed many effective strategies to maintain and restore health. Their theoretical understanding has been wholly supplanted, and their success was not as high as that of modern medicine; yet, their methods were not wholly ineffectual. By modifying their behaviors and diets and using various medicines, extracts, herbs, and compounds—derived from a body of works known collectively as the *materia medica* (medical matters)—they dealt quite effectively with many pathogens and ailments. Within the framework of their understanding of the human body and natural conditions, medieval healers and doctors saved and prolonged lives.

Treatment and Prevention of Disease. In the Middle Ages medical information from doctors was often restricted or unavailable, so people frequently turned to herbals—manuscript collections of remedies made from plants to prevent or cure diseases, or ease their symptoms—to help them live in as much comfort and with as little pain as possible. Many of the practices medieval people followed are no longer commonplace, but some are still followed by millions of people. Although medical science once discounted the herbs and natural medicines that medieval people favored, recent research has found value in many of them, and some are still prescribed by doctors around the world. The idea of a balanced regimen of healthy living is another medieval concept that continues to influence modern people. The discovery of how medieval Europeans tried to maintain their health and vitality has discredited the notion that the Middle Ages had little to offer in the field of health. The period was in fact a fertile time for the growth of practical, rather than theoretical, knowledge about getting and staying healthy.

TOPICS IN SCIENCE, TECHNOLOGY, AND HEALTH

ARISTOTLE'S LEGACY

Natural Philosophy. The body of knowledge now called science was known to the Middle Ages as natural philosophy. It encompassed all the ways that one could reason about the world and come to a better understanding of it. From the twelfth century onward the most important medieval scientists tended to be associated with royal households or universities (which were initially offshoots from cathedrals in cities such as Paris, Oxford, and Padua). Before that time monks studied nature in their monasteries. In either case, these scientists divided their time between scientific studies and either teaching or church duties.

Ancient Roots. Roman science was never as developed as Roman technology, and the Romans generally depended on and preserved earlier Greek learning in astronomy, mathematics, medicine, and philosophy. When the administrative structures of Rome crumbled in the fourth and fifth centuries, Europe was left largely without centers of higher learning or repositories of knowledge. Monasteries held some ancient manuscripts, but—as far as historians have been able to tell—virtually no one looked at these sources for many centuries. In the twelfth century, however, European scholars traveled to southern centers of learning, notably Spain and Sicily, as well as to Greece and Constantinople, to translate Greek, Arabic, and Hebrew copies of ancient Greek manuscripts. Some manuscripts were sent to England, France, and Italy to be copied and translated as well. Two of the most important translators of Greek texts were Robert Grosseteste and William of Moerbeke, while Michael Scot, William of Luna, and Hermann the German were notable translators of Arabic manuscripts of Aristotle's works. These Latin translations made nearly the entire body of Aristotle's works accessible to Europeans, whereas only a limited number of works and some fragments had been available before. They also gave Europeans access to the writings of many other Greek thinkers, as well as Arabic and Hebrew "commentaries" on Aristotle. These commentaries were much more than explanations and interpretations of Aristotle's thought, however. Especially in the areas of medicine and optics, Arabic commentaries provided Europeans with knowledge far beyond that available in the Greek sources alone. This so-called twelfth-century renaissance stands as a profound dividing line between the early and high Middle Ages, and the science of the early medieval period remains shrouded in mystery. By the thirteenth and fourteenth centuries, however, scholars at Paris and Oxford began re-examining

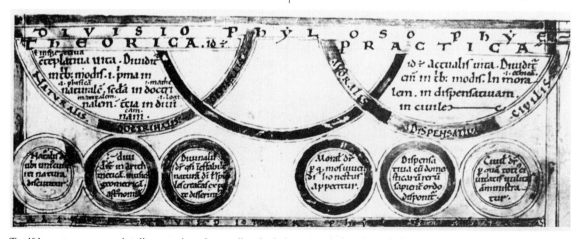

Twelfth-century manuscript diagramming what medieval scholars regarded as the main branches of knowledge recognized by Aristotle: theoretical on the left and practical on the right (St. John's College, Oxford)

the world around them and recasting it in the framework that forms the basis of modern scientific method.

Plato. The works of Plato were not as well known in the Middle Ages as those of his student Aristotle, but as early as the eleventh century, and especially from the thirteenth century onward through the translations of scholars such as William of Moerbeke and Aristippus, Platonic ideas began to appear in medieval philosophers' works as alternatives or complements to those of Aristotle. For scientists in the Middle Ages the most relevant of Plato's works was the *Timaeus,* which includes his ideas about elements. It was known to medieval scholars mainly through the works of the third-century C.E. writers Plotinus and Porphyry, who are known as Neoplatonists. Indirect knowledge of Platonic ideas was also accessible to medieval intellectuals through classical Roman authors, mainly Cicero and Seneca, as well as St. Augustine, who might be regarded as the greatest Christian Platonist. The main seat of medieval Platonism was Chartres in northern France. By the end of the Middle Ages, scholars were associating Plato with the outlook that there were perfect forms in the world and that what people experience is an imperfect reflection of those perfect forms. Practically, this viewpoint meant that there were true, perfect expressions capable of describing nature and that mathematics was the language in which those expressions—or laws—could be described. In particular, medieval thinkers tended to consider geometrical ideas of motion and quantities to be Platonic or Neoplatonic, whether they knew the ideas of Plato directly, indirectly, or at all. This mathematical outlook on nature became predominant in the Scientific Revolution of the sixteenth and seventeenth centuries.

Aristotle. Throughout the Middle Ages, including the early medieval period, the main sources for natural philosophy were the Bible and Aristotle. In fact, medieval science was in many ways an attempt to reconcile Aristotle's ideas and teachings with those of the Bible. Aristotle, the fourth-century B.C.E. teacher of Alexander the Great, left many works to posterity, including *Physics* and *On the Heavens,* as well as many on the subjects now considered biology and botany, including *History of Animals, Parts of Animals, The Motion of Animals, On the Generation of Animals,* and *On Plants.* Aristotle's name was so revered that many other works, such as *Mechanical Problems* (on levers and pulleys) and *On Stones,* came to be associated with him, even though scholars are now quite sure he did not write them. In some areas, Aristotle's ideas seem strange to the modern mind, but in others no one improved on his knowledge for many centuries. Several of his basic ideas are important for understanding medieval concepts of science.

Terrestrial and Celestial Regions. Aristotle taught that the universe is divided into the terrestrial region and the celestial region. The changeable terrestrial region includes the earth, its oceans, and its atmosphere up to and including the close side of the moon. The unchanging celestial region includes everything else: the stars, the heavens, and the dark side of the moon. This way of understanding the universe did not change until the fifteenth century. One of the features of the celestial and terrestrial regions that was much debated and interpreted by medieval Europeans was Aristotle's notion of how motion occurs in different and complimentary ways in each region.

Terrestrial Motion. Aristotle divided motion into "natural" motion and "violent," or unnatural, motion. In the terrestrial region the natural motion is in a straight line toward the center of the earth. For example, a rock falls in a straight line to reach its natural position, that is, at rest in the lowest position possible. Any motion in the terrestrial region that is not in a straight line, or in a straight line but not toward the center of the earth, is violent motion, and can occur only through the force of some outside agent. According to Aristotle, violent motion is eventually spent and natural motion takes over. For example, when a soldier shoots an arrow from his bow, it leaves the bow in a straight line, but horizontally or in an upward arc, not vertically. It therefore starts out with entirely violent motion, but as it flies, it begins to arc more and more downward until it falls more or less vertically, unless it hits a solid target first.

Celestial Motion. In the heavens, or the celestial region, the situation is different. There natural motion takes the form of circles centered on the middle of the earth. Any straight-line motion in the celestial region would be violent, but since humans could not reach the celestial region, there is nothing to cause violent motion there. Thus, in the Aristotelian worldview all motion in the heavens is circular. Anything in the sky that is moving in a straight line—such as a comet or meteor—must actually be below the moon and, therefore, in the terrestrial region. This theory is supported by the related Aristotelian idea that the natural state of motion in the terrestrial region is rest, while in the celestial region, the natural state of motion is perpetual, perfect circular motion.

Elements, Qualities, and Humors. The second important explanation of the natural world that Aristotle gave to the Middle Ages was the ideas of the four elements, the four qualities, and the four humors. Aristotle and many other ancient philosophers considered the physical world to be made of combinations of four elements: earth, water, air, and fire. There is also a fifth element, called the ether or the quintessence (which is the Latin word for the "fifth essence"), which exists only in the celestial region. The four qualities—hot, cold, moist, and dry—are independent entities that are directly related to the four elements. Each quality is opposed to one of the others—moist to dry and hot to cold—and a combination of two nonopposed qualities characterizes each element: fire is hot and dry; air is hot and moist; water is cold and moist; and earth is cold and dry. The four humors—blood, phlegm, black bile, and yellow bile—are the substances that make up the human body and are also related to the four elements and thus to pairs of

poraries were ever explicit about the proportions of earth, air, fire, and water in specific substances, but they believed that in theory those proportions could be determined.

The Motions of the Elements. Aristotle also passed on to the medieval world the notion that each of the elements in the progression earth, water, air, and fire was lighter than one before it and that the weight of an element accounted for its natural motion in the terrestrial region. It is the nature of fire, as the lightest element, to move upward, away from the center of the earth, as is obvious in the way that it carries the sparks and smoke upward from any burning object. Air, the next lightest element, desires to move upward but not as much as fire, which accounts for the swirling of the smoke as the element fire races past the air in its ascent toward the heavens. Water and earth are heavy and move naturally toward the center of the earth. Since stones sink in water, earth is obviously heavier than water, but there are some abnormalities: for example, wood floats. Since it is solid and heavy, wood must be made mostly of the element earth; yet, it must be on average lighter than water. The solution for the ancients and medievals was to consider wood a mixture of earth, air, and water (it contains sap, after all) in such unspecified proportions as to make its overall "heaviness" (*gravitas* in Latin) less than that of water. Also, of course, they reminded themselves that terrestrial water might be mainly the element water, but it also has some of the element earth in it too, which increases its heaviness. By such reasoning, medieval scientists used the Aristotelian system of elements, regions, and motions to explain the mysteries of the natural world.

Sources:

Alistair Cameron Crombie, *Augustine to Galileo: The History of Science A.D. 400–1650,* second edition, revised and enlarged (Cambridge, Mass.: Harvard University Press, 1961).

Richard C. Dales, *The Scientific Achievement of the Middle Ages* (Philadelphia: University of Pennsylvania Press, 1973).

Edward Grant, *The Foundations of Modern Science in the Middle Ages: Their Religious, Institutional, and Intellectual Contexts* (Cambridge: Cambridge University Press, 1996).

Grant, *Physical Science in the Middle Ages* (Cambridge & New York: Cambridge University Press, 1977).

Husain Kassim, *Aristotle and Aristotelianism in Medieval Muslim, Jewish, and Christian Philosophy* (Lanham: Austin & Winfield, 2000).

Claudia Kren, *Medieval Science and Technology: A Selected, Annotated Bibliography* (New York: Garland, 1985).

Helen S. Lang, *Aristotle's Physics and Its Medieval Varieties* (Albany: State University of New York Press, 1992).

David C. Lindberg, *The Beginnings of Western Science: The European Scientific Tradition in Philosophical, Religious, and Institutional Context, 600 B.C. to A.D. 1450* (Chicago: University of Chicago Press, 1992).

R. P. McKeon, "Aristotle and The Origins of Science in the West" in *Science and Civilization,* edited by Robert C. Stauffer (Madison: University of Wisconsin Press, 1949).

Fernand van Steenberghen, *Aristotle in the West: The Origins of Latin Aristotelianism,* translated by Leonard Johnston (Louvain: Nauwelaerts, 1955).

BEDE'S CONTRIBUTIONS

The Venerable Bede. After the fall of Rome and the retreat of learning into the monasteries, Europe produced

A medieval depiction of Aristotle teaching Alexander the Great; carving on an ivory box made circa 1310–1330 (The Cloisters Collection, New York)

nonopposing qualities. Blood (or sanguin), like air, is hot and moist, and a person in whom blood is the dominant humor has a sanguine (happy and confident) disposition. Yellow bile (or choler), like fire, is hot and dry and creates a choleric (hot-tempered) disposition. Black bile (melancholer), like earth, is dry and cold and creates a melancholic (sad) disposition. Phlegm, like water, is wet and cold and creates a phlegmatic (stolid) disposition. Medieval physicians believed that the humors should be kept in balance, so, for example, if a patient was melancholy, they would deduce that he had too much black bile, making him too dry and cold, and prescribe a hot and wet medicament.

Pure versus Earthly Elements. The four pure elements are not necessarily the same as the earthly entities with the same names. Real earth, or dirt, obviously has a preponderance of the element earth in it, just as real water (H_2O) is mostly the element water. In all other things two, three, or all four of the pure elements combine to make terrestrial substances. Just as mud is a mixture of the elements earth and water, a granite rock is a mixture of the elements earth, fire (because granite is found in mountainous and volcanic regions), and perhaps air or water. Sandstone, because it is lighter and softer than granite, has a higher proportion of either water or air in it. Neither Aristotle nor his contem-

few notable scholars who can truly be called scientists until about the twelfth century. One exception was Bede (circa 673–735), who became known among medieval scholars as the Venerable Bede for his great learning and piety. He entered the monastery of St. Peter in Wearmouth, on the rocky northeast coast of England, at the age of seven, and two years later he moved to the nearby abbey of Jarrow, where he spent the remainder of his life. There he wrote important ecclesiastical histories, world chronologies, and commentaries on scripture, grammar, and music—as well as three long works on what now would be considered natural science. *De natura rerum* (On the nature of things, written circa 703) is an encyclopedic treatise on all manner of natural phenomena. Unlike other early encyclopedias, Bede's work is not just a catalogue. He tried to explain why things were as they were and was the first scholar to show an interest in cause and effect.

Works about Time. Bede's other two scientific treatises, *De temporibus* (On time, written in 703) and *De temporum ratione* (On the reckoning of time, written in 725), are about calendars and chronology and set out astronomical rules for determining the date of Easter, an issue of great importance in the early eighth century. The various medieval methods of dating could result in calendars that varied by as much as two weeks, leading to situations in which some of the devout were still in abstinence for Lent while others were celebrating Easter. This confusion arose because it was necessary to use both

Portrait of Bede in a late-twelfth-century manuscript for his *Vita sancti Cuthberti metrica,* a biography of St. Cuthbert, written circa 706–707 (British Library, London)

BEDE ON THE PHASES OF THE MOON

In his *On the Reckoning of Time* Bede was the first northern scholar to explain how to predict the phases of the moon and its position in relation to the constellations in the zodiac.

Should someone rather less skilled in calculation . . . be curious about the course of the Moon, we have also for his sake devised a formula adapted to the capacity of his intelligence, so that he might find what he seeks. Thus we have marked out each day of the twelve-month annual circuit in the calendar by means of alphabets, so that the first and second alphabetical sequences each comprise 27 days, while the third sequence has one day more, namely the day which accrues from three repetitions of the eight superfluous hours. . . .

So if you wish to know what sign or what part of the month the Moon is in on any given day of the any year, open the calendar-codex, and note the letter prefixed to that day. Then, turning to the Table of Regulars . . . you will discover what region, month and sign the moon is in. . . . And reader, whether you are learned or unschooled, you will rejoice to have tracked down what you were looking for, right before your eyes.

Source: Bede, *The Reckoning of Time,* edited and translated by Faith Wallis (Liverpool: Liverpool University Press, 1999), pp. 63–64.

the Roman calendar, based on the solar year, and the Hebrew calendar, based on the lunar month, to determine the exact dates of Easter and other religious holidays. Because there are no common factors for 365 (the approximate number of days in a solar year) and 29 (roughly the number of days in a lunar month), there is no simple way to determine the day of the year in the Julian calendar, the form of solar-year calendar then in use, on which Easter (computed from lunar cycles) falls. Added to this difficulty was the pragmatic way in which individual congregations marked time from one feast to the next through cycles of specific texts and Psalms. Over decades and centuries, these cycles had become badly out of sync with the proper dates as determined by the heavens and as required by Church law. By the third century C.E. an entire discipline had been founded to calculate those dates and came to be called *computus* after the lengthy computations necessary to predict the motions of the moon and the sun throughout the year. For more than eight hundred years, Bede's *De temporum ratione* was the standard textbook for performing these calculations. In it he treats the motions of the sun, the moon, the stars, and even the tides, trying to set down the general laws that govern all these phenomena. For practical purposes, he included tables and formulae for calculation and calendars, as well as mnemonic devices to remind his brethren how to calculate time.

A New Dating System. Bede was the first historian to publicize the modern idea of anno domini (A.D.)—that is, the method of dating events from the birth of Christ. Although he did not intend to cause controversy, this new system led to speculation on the "end of the world" or the second coming of Christ. Bede was unfairly accused of fostering this sort of thinking, and he felt obliged to disavow this rampant speculation in language uncharacteristically strong for such a gentle and scholarly monk: "I am as much grieved as I can be, I confess, or else greatly annoyed, whenever upstarts ask me how many of the last thousand years remain [until the Second Coming]. And I am equally annoyed when they ask me, 'How do you know that the last thousand years are in progress?' The Lord does not state in the Gospels whether the time of His Advent is near or far-distant. . . . If anyone should say to me, 'Lo, here is the Christ!' Or 'Lo, there!' I would not listen to him or follow him."

Sources:

Bede, *The Reckoning of Time*, edited and translated by Faith Wallis (Liverpool: Liverpool University Press, 1999).

Alistair Cameron Crombie, *Augustine to Galileo: The History of Science A.D. 400–1650*, second edition, revised and enlarged (Cambridge, Mass.: Harvard University Press, 1961).

Richard C. Dales, *The Scientific Achievement of the Middle Ages* (Philadelphia: University of Pennsylvania Press, 1973).

Edward Grant, *The Foundations of Modern Science in the Middle Ages: Their Religious, Institutional, and Intellectual Contexts* (Cambridge: Cambridge University Press, 1996).

Grant, *Physical Science in The Middle Ages* (Cambridge & New York: Cambridge University Press, 1977).

Charles W. Jones, *Bede, the Schools and the "Computus,"* edited by Wesley M. Stevens (Aldershot: Variorum, 1994).

Claudia Kren, *Medieval Science and Technology: A Selected, Annotated Bibliography* (New York: Garland, 1985).

David C. Lindberg, *The Beginnings of Western Science: The European Scientific Tradition in Philosophical, Religious, and Institutional Context, 600 B.C. to A.D. 1450* (Chicago: University of Chicago Press, 1992).

Wesley M. Stevens, "Bede's Scientific Achievement" in *Bede and His World: The Jarrow Lectures, 1958–1993* (Aldershot: Variorum, 1994), pp. 645–688.

THE CELESTIAL SPHERES

The Queen of the Sciences. The desire to find general laws that governed the universe provided the rationale for the wide development of one side of medieval science. In the Middle Ages, as well as during the Renaissance, scholars believed that God revealed his handiwork in nature, so its laws were divine truths and understanding them would lead to a greater understanding of God. Believing that God is located in the heavens, medieval scholars placed greater importance on astronomy and Christian astrology than on other sciences. From the eleventh century on, many Churchmen thought and wrote about the workings of the heavens, making astronomy the Queen of the Sciences.

The Celestial Spheres. Medieval astronomy differed little from its ancient predecessor. Based on the concept of an earth-centered universe that had been most clearly enunciated by Alexandrine astronomer Claudius Ptolemy in the first century C.E., the medieval model of the heavens served one purpose alone: to explain God's creation. But, as in all medieval science, they had to reconcile their Christian view of the universe with Aristotle's ideas about it. The Ptolemaic and Aristotelian cosmologies are complementary in many ways, but they approach astronomy differently, and neither is a perfect reflection of what people see in the heavens.

Aristotle's universe. The main difference between Aristotelian and Ptolemaic astronomy was that Aristotle devised a physical theory to account for the motion of the planets, and Ptolemy provided a mathematical one. Aristotle's physical theory posited many crystalline spheres, centered on the earth and nested one within another like the layers of an onion. Each sphere contains a specific substance or body and communicates motions to its neighbors. The earth is surrounded by spheres of water, air, and fire; seven spheres for the sun, the moon, and the five known planets (Mercury, Venus, Mars, Jupiter, and Saturn); and one sphere for the fixed stars. The *primum movens* (first mover), the ultimate spirit or intelligence, activates the *primum mobile* (first moved), which in turn sets the outer sphere in motion, and so on through the inner spheres. The idea of a *primum movens*—the Unmoved Mover—was attractive to Christian philosophers because God could easily be placed in that role.

Ptolemy's Universe. Ptolemy's mathematical explanation agreed with Aristotle's ordering of the planets but omitted the spheres of elements around the earth and minimized the need for a *primum movens*. Ptolemy's universe was described by the mathematical relationships of the distances between the planets and their relative rates of motion. Ptolemaic astronomy—as transmitted through Arabic astronomers—had taken on an explanatory power as well. The idea of mathematical causation has an ancient pedigree, going back to the ancient Greek thinkers Plato and Pythagoras, who believed in the ultimate reality of numbers. If they were real, they could cause things. Yet, Ptolemy's system was primarily descriptive and predictive, rather than explanatory, like Aristotle's.

Planetary Motion. From Ptolemy medieval astronomers learned the ideas of the *epicycle* and the *deferent*. These two mathematical concepts were used to explain why—although Ptolemy, like Aristotle, was sure that all motion in the heavens was circular in shape and uniform in velocity—the planets appeared to wander among the stars in decidedly noncircular paths and at nonuniform velocities. In fact, against the backdrop of the fixed stars, some planets, such as Mars, appeared to stop and reverse direction. The epicycle-deferent system solved that apparent problem. The deferent, according to Ptolemy, was a circular path centered on the earth. The epicycle was a smaller circle in which a planet moved at a uniform speed. The center

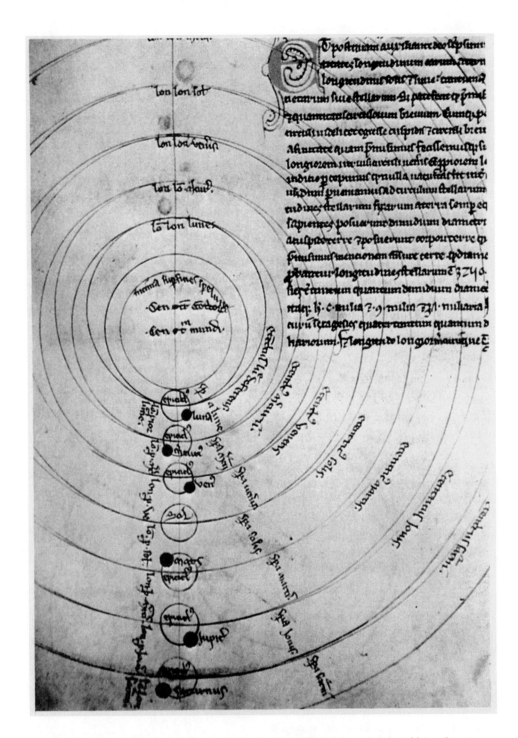

Chart of planetary motions according to the earth-centered Ptolemiac system in a thirteenth-century manuscript for an anonymous *Theorica planetarum* (University Library, Cambridge)

of the epicycle was located on the deferent and proceeded to move around it at a uniform rate. By creating the notion of two separate and uniform circular motions—and in some later refinements even three—the Ptolemaic system provided an accurate way to chart and predict the position of the planets.

Astrology. Medieval astronomers were also astrologers. While the positions of the planets are not of much use for calendar calculations, the known planets, and the stars, nonetheless held great meaning for medieval Europeans, who considered astronomy (the "naming" of the heavens) and astrology (the "laws" of the heavens) as two parts of the

same science. This tradition was also inherited from antiquity; for not only did Ptolemy write his *Almagest* (The Great Mathematical Synthesis, a name acquired from the Arabic versions) on the motions of the planets, he also composed the *Tetrabiblos* (Four Books) of astrology, which set forth the basic rules of what the heavens signified for human activities. His rules about the constellations in which the planets appear to rise and set, as well as the relationships of the planets to each other and the signs of the zodiac, were all set forth in great mathematical detail. So too were the processes to calculate three kinds of horoscopes: "genethliacal" horoscopes that relate to the moment of an individual's birth and fate; "mundane" (worldly) horoscopes that deal with affairs of state; and "electional" horoscopes that deal with determining the correct time for launching any enterprise.

Sources:

Marshall Clagett, *Studies in Medieval Physics and Mathematics* (London: Variorum Reprints, 1979).

Walter Clyde Curry, *Chaucer and the Mediaeval Sciences* (New York & London: Oxford University Press, 1926).

Edward Grant, *Planets, Stars, and Orbs: The Medieval Cosmos, 1200–1687* (Cambridge & New York: Cambridge University Press, 1994).

David C. Lindberg, ed., *Science in the Middle Ages* (Chicago: University of Chicago Press, 1978).

John David North, *Stars, Minds, and Fate: Essays in Ancient and Medieval Cosmology* (London: Hambledon Press, 1989).

Lynn Thorndike, ed. and trans., *The Sphere of Sacrobosco and Its Commentators.* (Chicago: University of Chicago Press, 1949).

THE LAWS OF PHYSICS

The Rules of Nature. One area of science in which the medieval philosophers excelled, discussing important and fundamental concepts of the way nature works, was physics. Because medieval philosophers believed that knowledge of the material world would bring them closer to an understanding of the divine nature of that world, the study of "physica"—the orderly part of nature subject to rules and to cause and effect—was easily accepted in church schools across Europe. The areas most frequently investigated were motion and optics. Studies of both benefited immensely from twelfth-century translations of ancient Greek sources and medieval Arabic commentaries.

Motion. Aristotle taught that all motions are made up of natural motion and violent motion. This theory explains *how* things move, but it did little to explain *why* they moved. (In fact, it was even somewhat unsatisfactory in explaining *how.*) In reading and commenting on Aristotle, medieval Scholastics came to some new and striking insights into the nature of motion. These ideas were passed on to later scientists, including Galileo, and underlie modern physicists' understanding of motion. The realization that Aristotle's explanation of motion was incomplete, or even faulty, came to medieval thinkers as they tried to understand why things kept moving once they no longer had contact with the force that made them move. Aristotle had said that all things that are moving are moved by something. A person can apply a force to make a rock move violently, that is, in a direction (up or side-to-side) in which it would not move on its own. But when the rock leaves a person's hand, as when it is thrown, why does it keep moving in the direction it has been thrown instead of falling straight to the ground? Aristotle said that the air the rock pushes out of the way as it moves rushes around to push the rock from behind, but few medieval scientists were convinced by his explanation. Throughout the thirteenth and fourteenth centuries Scholastics debated the question, and eventually they arrived at a new solution.

Impetus. Jean Buridan, a secular teacher at the University of Paris during the first half of the fourteenth century,

ORESME ON MOMENTUM

Nicole Oresme considered Jean Buridan's idea that impetus is slowly "used up" as objects move, developing a theory that suggests how different motions might be related. In the following passage he compared the swing of a pendulum to the motion of a stone traveling back and forth in a hole through the center of the earth:

I posit that the earth is pierced clear through and that we can see through a great hole farther and farther right up to the other end where the antipodes would be if the whole earth were inhabited; I say, first of all, that if we dropped a stone through the hole, it would pass beyond the center of the earth, going straight on toward the other side for a certain limited distance and that then it would turn back going beyond the center on this side of the earth; afterward it would fall back again, going beyond the center, but not so far as before; it would come and go this way several times, but with a reduction of its reflex motions until finally it would rest at the center of the earth. This is caused by the impetuosity or "momentum" which it acquires by the acceleration of its motion. . . . We can understand this more easily by taking note of something perceptible to the senses: if a heavy object . . . is hung on a long string and pushed forward, it begins to move backward and then forward, making several swings, until it finally rests absolutely perpendicular and as near the center as possible.

Source: Nicole Oresme, *On the Heavens*, II.3.1, in "The Scholastic Pendulum," by Bert S. Hall, *Annals of Science*, 35 (1978): 441–462.

may not have been the first scholar to come up with the idea of *impetus* (motive force), but he is credited with devising the clearest explanation of how it works. Buridan suggested that in throwing a rock, the thrower transfers something to the rock, giving to the rock an impetus that propels it along in its unnatural course until the impetus is gradually used up. The rock then moves according to Aristotle's concept of natural motion: straight to the ground. Buridan also reasoned that if impetus is not opposed by some other force in this case the *gravitas* (weight) of the rock, it will maintain its impetus indefinitely, and hence continue to move. Although he did not think of it in the same way, Buridan's conception of impetus is similar to the modern idea of momentum (the product of mass and velocity). His understanding that motion comes not from an external force, but from some innate or imparted quality of the rock itself, is important because for the first time objects in physics were considered not for their ultimate meaning (the explication of the *primum movens*), but for their particulars. That is, fourteenth-century natural philosophers began to ask how certain things worked rather than considering how those specifics contributed to a wider understanding of God. They became partially liberated from overarching theories that often inhibited the understanding of particulars, such things as the flight of an arrow or the swing of a pendulum. As Buridan and his followers began to pay attention to actual, not hypothetical, examples, the real world began to enter the study of physics.

Quantitative Physics. Other Parisian scholars, including Buridan's student Nicole Oresme, began to quantify impetus and to begin to discuss quantitative understandings of terrestrial physics. Continuing to accept Aristotle's theory that the mechanics controlling objects on earth and the mechanics of the celestial sphere were fundamentally different—an idea contrary to the modern understanding of motion—Oresme nonetheless made significant contributions to the study of mechanics. The use of algebra to create geometric diagrams or graphs was still nearly three centuries away in Europe, so Oresme and his fellow Scholastics related motions, positions, and velocities to each other through ratios. In particular, Oresme was the first scholar to realize that time should be considered as a variable along with position and velocity, and in so doing, he considered acceleration (the rate of change of velocity with respect to time), the most interesting part of motion. Building on Buridan's idea of impetus, he related acceleration to the *gravitas* of the object and proposed uniform acceleration as the consequence of *gravitas*. While his worldview was not as modern as that of Galileo or Sir Isaac Newton, Oresme opened the door for the modern understanding of motion, in which time and acceleration are the fundamental variables.

Optics. Another significant area of investigation in the Middle Ages was the study of the behavior of light rays. The ancient Greeks had investigated how images were altered by lenses and mirrors, and their theories had been reformulated and augmented by the Arabs. Sources from both these traditions came to Europe in the twelfth century and were incorporated into a Christian framework. As one of the foundation elements of Christian theology, light is the instantiation (representation by a physical instance) of God. Just as the cathedrals were built to magnify light (and color), and thus the glory of God, optics was seen as a philosophical way in which to approach God's truths.

Geometrical Optics. Medieval optics was based on Aristotelian foundations, which explained various perceptions as light interacting with different "exhalations" in the air. According to Aristotle the earth gives off moist and dry exhalations, and light traversing regions with more or less of these substances undergoes certain changes. This imprecise explanation was complemented and concretized by the other branch of ancient Greek optics, geometrical optics, which derives from the work of the father of geometry, Euclid, as well as from Ptolemy. Euclidean optics considers two areas: *catoptrics,* the study of the reflection of light from matter, usually metals; and *dioptics,* the study of the transmission of light through crystals, glass, or liquids. Witelo, a thirteenth-century Polish scholar, investigated dioptric relations.

The Arab Contribution. The question of how mankind sees the world was widely discussed in the thirteenth and fourteenth centuries, with scholars basing their investiga-

Diagrams illustrating mixed motion from a fourteenth-century manuscript for Nicole Oresme's *Livre du ceil et du monde* (Book of Heaven and Earth), his commentary on Aristotle's theory of terrestrial and celestial motion (Bibliothèque Nationale, Paris)

tions largely on the work of Arabic physicist and physician Alhazen (Abu 'Ali al-Hasan ibn al-Haytham). His theory of physiological optics suggests that the lens is the sensible element in the eye and responds to rays entering the eye from objects in the field of vision. This explanation runs counter to the Platonic idea that vision occurs when the eye sends out rays to objects. By reversing that belief, Alhazen and others suggested that the world is humankind's to perceive, not to create. From Euclid, Ptolemy, and Alhazen western Europeans formulated the geometry to explain direct vision, reflection, and refraction (the way in which light is bent as it passes from one medium—such as air—to another—such as glass or water).

Sources:

Edward Grant, "Jean Buridan and Nicole Oresme on Natural Knowledge," *Vivarium: Journal for Mediaeval Philosophy and the Intellectual Life of the Middle Ages,* 31 (1993): 84–105.

Grant, *Much Ado about Nothing: Theories of Space and Vacuum from the Middle Ages to the Scientific Revolution* (Cambridge & New York: Cambridge University Press, 1981).

Grant, "Scientific Thought in 14th-Century Paris: Jean Buridan and Nicole Oresme" in *Machaut's World: Science and Art in the 14th Century,* edited by Madeleine Pelner Cosman and Bruce Chandler (New York: New York Academy of Sciences, 1978), pp. 105–124.

David C. Lindberg, *Studies in the History of Medieval Optics* (London: Variorum Reprints, 1983).

Lindberg, *Theories of Vision from al-Kindi to Kepler* (Chicago: University of Chicago Press, 1976).

Anneliese Maier, *On the Threshold of Exact Science: Selected Writings of Anneliese Maier on Late Medieval Natural Philosophy,* translated by Steven D. Sargent (Philadelphia: University of Pennsylvania Press, 1982).

A. George Molland, "Nicole Oresme and Scientific Progress," in *Antiqui und moderni,* edited by Albert Zimmermann (Berlin: de Gruyter, 1974), pp. 206–220.

Nicole Oresme, *Nicole Oresme and the Kinetics of Circular Motion,* edited and translated by Grant (Madison: University of Wisconsin Press, 1971).

John Peckham, *John Pecham and the Science of Optics: Perspectiva Communis,* edited and translated by Lindberg (Madison: University of Wisconsin Press, 1970).

J. M. M. H. Thijssen and Jack Zupko, *The Metaphysics and Natural Philosophy of John Buridan* (Leiden & Boston: Brill, 2001).

James A. Weisheipl, "The Interpretation of Aristotle's Physics and the Science of Motion," in *The Cambridge History of Later Medieval Philosophy: From the Rediscovery of Aristotle to the Disintegration of Scholasticism, 1100–1600,* edited by Norman Kretzmann, Anthony Kenny, Jan Pinborg, and Eleonore Stump (Cambridge & New York: Cambridge University Press, 1982), pp. 521–536.

METEOROLOGY AND ALCHEMY

Meteorology. Although meteorology is now considered a subdivision of the earth sciences, to medieval scientists it was inextricably intertwined with the study of optics. Once again, the connection lies in the Aristotelian view of the world, for in his system both meteorology and optics take place in the sublunary region above the earth. Their natural place was within the spheres of air and fire, which lie above those of earth and water. Thus, the study of rainbows fell under both meteorology and optics, as did investigations of comets, shooting stars, the aurora borealis, and optical "illusions" such as the apparent change in the size of the Moon when it is at the horizon and the change in color of the Sun at dawn and dusk. The medieval scholars Albertus Magnus, Roger Bacon, Witelo, and Theodoric of Freiberg were the first to realize that rainbows were caused by the reflection and refraction of light from individual drops of water in the atmosphere—an advance on the explanation offered by Aristotle, who said rainbows were the result of light rays passing through clouds.

Weather Signs. Meteorology was also intimately tied to the broader field of signs, which also included astrology. Meteorological events such as eclipses, thunderheads, fog, and comets were said to be signs of impending famine, fortune, or failure, but students of meteorology were also concerned about predicting the weather. Although it may seem strange today, medieval weather prediction on the basis of how far the sound of bells carries—part of a seven-year-long investigation in fourteenth-century England—does in fact have validity. Although the scientists who carried out this investigation did not articulate their findings in the same way as a modern meteorologist would, it is true that the distance sound travels is correlated to humidity—that is, the more moisture in the air, the farther sound travels—and is a strong indicator of weather patterns. Since the cornerstone of medieval society was agriculture, the study of weather was important, and—even when interpretations of weather signs were irrelevant—the search for practical meteorological knowledge focused the medieval mind on the concept of cause and effect in the natural world, one of the cornerstones of modern scientific method.

Alchemy. Perhaps the best-known attempt of medieval scientists to discover the underlying principles of the natural world was alchemy. Alchemists sought the deep connections between matter and qualities and heaven and earth, in order to control them. Modern people misunderstand alchemists as irrational magicians trying vainly to turn lead into gold, but they were acting rationally within the medieval belief system. Furthermore, though they failed to transmute lead into gold, they succeeded at teasing apart the threads of the fabric of nature to produce pure forms of elements (in the modern sense of the word) and developed sophisticated laboratory equipment and procedures that were important contributions to later scientific attempts at understanding the natural world.

Non-Aristotelian Roots. Alchemy began in the ancient world and seems to have reappeared when many ancient Greek writings were circulated in the twelfth century. One feature sets alchemy apart from the rest of medieval science: it is not based on Aristotelian doctrine and was thus never studied in the medieval universities. Instead, alchemy is based on mystic ideas from the Near East and India as well as many of the Platonic ideals that Aristotle rejected or modified. Thus, although the Aristotelian theory of the four qualities—hot, cold, moist, and dry—plays a large role in alchemical rationale, as alchemists sought out the connections in the natural world, their explanations differed from those of the Scholastics, or "Schoolmen" (as Aristotelian scholars were called), and hence kept their two worlds apart.

Connecting the Celestial and Terrestrial Realms. While the Scholastics held with Aristotle (and Christianity) that the celestial and terrestrial realms were fundamentally different, alchemists believed that they were connected. The

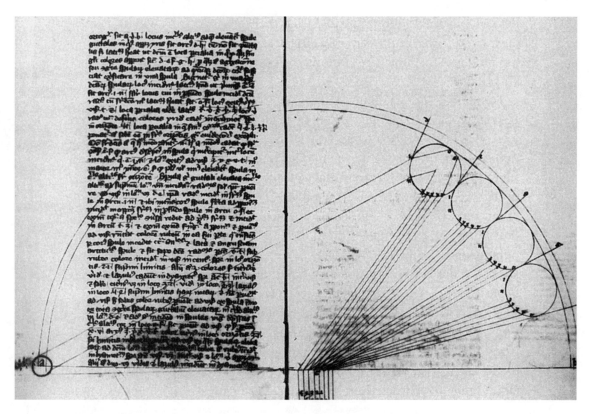

Diagram of Theodoric of Freiberg's theory of the rainbow, showing the sun at lower left, four raindrops at upper right, and the observer at bottom center; illumination from a fourteenth-century manuscript (Offentliche Bibliothek der Universitat, Basel)

motions of the planets interested alchemists, who needed to be well versed in astrology, and, they thought, each planet signifies and controls a primary metal on earth. In alchemical theory the moon controls silver and the sun, gold; Jupiter is linked with tin and Saturn with lead; while Mars controls iron, Venus controls copper, and Mercury, of course, governs mercury. The results of mixing metals were determined not only by the properties of those metals but also by when the experiment was done; that is, where the planets were at the time of the mixture.

The Materia Prima. Alchemists sought control over nature. They hoped to discover a "Philosopher's Stone" that could bring about the transmutation of base substances into fine substances and an "Elixir of Life" that could prolong and even create life. These concepts were based on the Neoplatonic idea that there was some fundamental matter, or *materia prima* (literally, first matter) in nature that was responsible for all change. Linking this idea to the concept of the four qualities, the alchemists attempted to mix substances with either complementary qualities that would reinforce one another or contradictory qualities that would cancel out one another to produce a final substance with the desired balance of hot-cold and wet-dry. Although alchemists worked from these seemingly odd principles, their experiments had some practical results. To perform their experiments they had to produce pure forms of the substances they wanted to combine, and in so doing they advanced medieval knowledge of distillation, smelting, amalgamation, precipitation, and other chemical processes.

At the same time they developed many techniques and pieces of apparatus that were the cornerstone of the modern chemical innovations.

Sources:
Carl B. Boyer, *The Rainbow from Myth to Mathematics* (New York: Yoseloff, 1959).

Lorraine Daston and Katherine Park, *Wonders and the Order of Nature, 1150–1750* (New York: Zone Books, 1998).

Pearl Kibre, *Studies in Medieval Science: Alchemy, Astrology, Mathematics, and Medicine* (London: Hambledon Press, 1984).

David C. Lindberg, *Theories of Vision from al-Kindi to Kepler* (Chicago: University of Chicago Press, 1976).

NATURAL HISTORY

Animals, Plants, and Minerals. An investigation of the medieval study of nature provides an interesting glimpse into how scientists of the period organized their knowledge and why they undertook their study. In some cases their investigations were academic, while in others they were seeking to elaborate and explain scripture, and in still others they had extremely practical goals. To document their studies they produced manuscript herbals, which illustrate plants and their medicinal properties; lapidaries, which show stones and their physical, magical, emblematic, or medicinal qualities; and bestiaries, which depict animals and describe their habits. In all these manuscripts mythical lore, Christian tradition, travelers' tales, workmen's knowledge of their crafts, and direct observations might mingle and intertwine to produce, in some cases, encyclopedic descriptions of the natural world.

Page from a manuscript for Albertus Magnus's *De natura loci* (On the Nature of Places),
written between 1251 and 1253 (Vienna National Library)

Albertus Magnus. One of the most proficient and prolific medieval natural scientists was Albertus Magnus, a thirteenth-century Dominican administrator and teacher in west-central Germany. More than any other medieval scholar, Albertus was responsible for recovering and, most important, legitimizing Aristotle's works on animals and plants, as well as works on those subjects by Arab writers. The teaching of Aristotle's natural science had been condemned by the church in 1210, for these works by a pagan philosopher were considered dangerous, and hence wrong. (The existence of many scientific works by Arab scholars, who were non-Christians as well, also cast suspicion on the study of natural history.) Although the ban was lifted in 1234, most Christian scholars were not immediately favorable to Aristotle or the field of natural science. Albertus almost singlehandedly changed this attitude. Although today many of the natural phenomena that he reported seem odd or ludicrous, even when he claimed that he saw them himself, Albertus insisted that experience and theory must coincide, an idea that seems largely missing from the scientific writings of earlier authors. Among his many and impressive contributions to the physical sciences, his observations in botany, zoology, and geology are particularly notable. He compiled massive treatises listing hundreds, or in some cases thousands, of different plants, animals, or minerals. His remarkably complete descriptive passages are frequently complemented by his perceptive theoretical groupings or explications of causal relationships (as, for example, in the generation or evolution of plants and animals, the ecology of a region, or the uses of stones)—most derived from firsthand observations or reports from sources he trusted, not preconceived overarching theories. In particular, he rejected the ancient idea that fossils were created as they presently existed, accepting instead the idea of Arabic philosopher Avicenna (Abū 'Alī al-Hussayn ibn 'Abd Allāh ibn Sīnā), who said they were petrified animals that had once been living.

Albertus's Limitations. While Albertus's works are masterful, the entries in them often seem fanciful to the modern reader. In many cases his descriptions confuse substances that are now known to be separate entities. Though the descriptive aspects of his works are similar to the entries found in modern guides to animals, plants, or minerals, Albertus's writings are not simply descriptive. To the medieval natural scientist, description was only the first step in interpreting and determining the significance of an object. Entries for plants, animals, or rocks frequently start with where the substance is found and what authorities verify its existence or properties, but then they include information that surely cannot be verified by empirical observation. Like many people of his time, Albertus seems to have accepted that many stones have magical properties. Since institutions such as museums did not exist in the Middle Ages, and travel was difficult and severely limited, Albertus often relied on reports of faraway—and usually exotic—places. He took many things on faith from them, even when descriptions began with comments such as "It is said" or some other qualifying phrase. In many cases Albertus allowed the good reputation of the person who wrote the report to override commonsense skepticism. Still, Albertus and other medieval writers on stones, plants, and animals made a valuable contribution to modern natural science by codifying information from antiquity and adding to from direct or indirect contemporary observations. They bequeathed to later ages a body of "facts" that form the foundation for the modern sciences of geology, botany, and zoology.

Sources:

Albertus Magnus, *The Book of Minerals,* edited and translated by Dorothy Wyckoff (Oxford: Clarendon Press, 1967).

Albertus Magnus, *On Animals,* translated and annotated by Kenneth F. Kitchell Jr. and Irven Michael Resnick (Baltimore: Johns Hopkins University Press, 1999).

James A. Weisheipl, ed., *Albertus Magnus and the Sciences: Commemorative Essays 1980* (Toronto: Pontifical Institute of Mediaeval Studies, 1980).

POWER FOR TECHNOLOGY: ANIMALS

At the outset of the Middle Ages the basic power sources for most tasks were humans and animals. During the Middle Ages the harnessing of animals underwent changes that increased productivity by as much as 200 percent. Farming altered the natural environment to the benefit of humankind. Anything that improves the efficiency or productivity of agriculture benefits the entire civilization. During the medieval period, when 90 to 95 percent of the European population tilled the soil, farmers made the most important advances in agricultural technology of any era before the Industrial and Chemical Revolutions.

These advances were predicated on the more efficient use of animal power.

Oxen versus Horses. The two main draft animals are oxen and horses. Oxen are strong and relatively easy to maintain, while horses are even stronger—and faster—but they are much more expensive to maintain than oxen. Oxen can graze on any grassy plant life, while horses can eat grass fodder, but to remain healthy and strong they also need a substantial proportion of prepared grains, particularly oats, in their diet. Oats were never the standard crop of ancient Europe because they are less prolific than wheat. But during the two centuries preceding the year 1000, changes in agricultural "machinery" and agricultural practice made it possible for European farmers to increase the yield of their crops, including oats. These changes—which seem to have happened almost simultaneously—were simple, but they had profound effects. Furthermore, although any one of them would have been beneficial by itself, as a combined system of agriculture they had a profound effect on Europe in the Middle Ages.

The Moldboard Plow. During the medieval period farmers stopped using light scratch plows and turned to heavier moldboard plows. In the ancient world and even during the medieval period in the Mediterranean region, the scratch plow—basically a pointed stick, or plowshare, dragged behind a beast of burden—was used to break up the topsoil in the fields, and then seeds were scattered across the rough surface. The scratch plow did a sufficiently good job in the light and dry soils of Mediterranean countries, but seed losses to birds could be quite high. Still, that method worked quite well for thousands of years. As ancient civilizations spread north of the Alps, however, they encountered heavier, wetter soils that were hard, or impossible, to break up with scratch plows. The moldboard plow, which came into use in Northern Italy and the Rhine Valley around 700–800, was a response to these new challenges. It retains the vertical pointed stick, or "plowshare," of the scratch plow, but it has two new parts, the "coulter" and the "moldboard." The coulter, a horizontal metal knife attached to the bottom of the plowshare, was added to cut the soil horizontally at the bottom of the slit made by the plowshare. With the coulter, rather than a simple vertical slit in the soil, the moldboard plow made an L-shaped cut. This new plow gets its name from the moldboard—a large, curved piece of wood set behind the share and coulter—which was added to turn the soil up and out of the cut, flopping it over and to the side of the furrow. It created a trench of about 6–12 inches (15–30cm) deep, and with a second pass in the opposite direction, this furrow became a foot or more deep. Instead of breaking up only the top few inches of soil, the moldboard plow churned up deeper soils, bringing more nutrients to the surface than the scratch plow and softening the compacted undersoil—thus giving the crops a better environment in which to grow.

Pulling the Moldboard Plow. Cutting this large amount of heavy soil took more power than one horse or ox could provide, so several animals had to be harnessed together to plow the fields. This need had a twofold consequence. First, since no single peasant was likely to own more than one or two animals, the need for teams of four, six, or eight animals resulted in the development of farming collectives, in which people of the same village shared their animals to everyone's mutual benefit. Second, these large teams were extremely difficult to turn around, so the square fields that had been common in the days of lighter plows gave way to long, narrow strips of land that allowed farmers to minimize the number of times they had to turn their teams while plowing furrows. Determining the length of these long narrow fields resulted in the establishment of the furlong, a unit of measurement equal to 660 feet.

The Padded Horse Collar. With this new plough came a change in the harnessing of draft animals. In the ancient world an animal was harnessed by placing a flat leather strap around its front and up and over its shoulders. This sort of harness was tolerable for oxen, but its breast straps tended to strangle horses. The harder they pulled, the more their windpipes were crushed, which is why during the late Roman Empire edicts were issued limiting the weight of the load a horse could pull. The problem was solved by adapting the ox yoke, which rests on an ox's shoulders. Because a horse's shoulders are not nearly as pronounced as an ox's, the U-shaped ox yoke became an O-shaped padded collar that fits over the horse's head and lies across its chest. The padded horse collar lets horses pull with all their strength and without the danger of strangulation.

Horseshoes. Another seemingly simple development had appeared around 500–600: the humble horseshoe. The Romans seem to have used a form of sandal to protect their horses' hooves, and in the relatively dry climate of the Mediterranean region, these hoof coverings were not regularly needed. In the wetter climate of northern Europe, however, horses' hooves are much more prone to rot, causing crippling damage. Nailing iron horseshoes to horses' hooves not only keeps them a bit above wet ground, keeping them drier, but also provides horses with additional traction, just as modern shoes allow people to walk or run faster and harder than they can barefoot. Taken together, a horse collar and horseshoes increased a horse's pulling capacity up to two or three times.

The Three-Field System. As European farmers began to benefit from using the moldboard plow and more efficiently harnessed horses, the organization of farming underwent a deceptively simple, yet profoundly important, revolution. Some time around 900–1000 farmers moved from what was called the two-field system of crop rotation to a new three-field system. Ancient and early medieval farmers did not usually spread fertilizer over their fields as modern farmers do. For this reason their fields needed time to recover their fertility after bearing a crop. Under the two-field system, a farmer divided his land roughly in half and farmed only one half of it in any given year, leaving the other part fallow (unplanted) to allow the soil to replenish its natural nutrients. For example, in year one a farmer might plant the west side of his property with the

Iluminations from the fourteenth-century Luttrell Psalter depicting two medieval technological innovations: the moldboard plow (top), drawn by oxen wearing U-shaped collars, and the O-shaped horse collar (bottom), worn by a horse pulling a harrow (British Library, London)

standard crop of winter wheat, letting it grow from December until July. The following December, he would plant the eastern half of his property, leaving the west side fallow. The three-field system made the planting cycle a bit more complex. For example, in year one the farmer might plant one third of his land with winter wheat in December, plant another third with a summer crop in April, and let the last third remain fallow. The next year he would rotate, leaving the winter-wheat field of previous year fallow, planting wheat on the field where he had grown a summer crop, and planting his summer crop on the fallow land of the previous year. One more year of planting completed the rotation. Farmers also discovered that whatever crop-rotation system they used, it was worthwhile to plow their fallow fields twice a year to keep weeds down and to till in the manure left there by the animals that they put out to pasture on that land. This practice marked the beginning of regular, large-scale fertilization, which not only increased crop yields but also permitted farmers to keep larger herds of livestock.

Increased Productivity. The use of three-field farming increased crop sizes by 50 to 75 percent, depending on the system of measurement, and actually decreased labor. Consider the same six-hundred-acre farm under the two systems. Under the two-field system the farmer would plow 300 acres for a crop once a year and 300 acres of fallow

twice a year for a total of 900 acres of plowing each year. Under the three-field system, the same farmer would have plowed 200 acres once for the winter crop, 200 acres once for the summer crop, and 200 fallow acres twice, for a total of only 800 acres of plowing each year. While saving himself from 100 acres of plowing, the farmer would also increase the area of his land under cultivation from 300 to 400 acres. Under the three-field system he would plow 800 acres for 400 acres of crops, or 2 plowed acres per acre of yield. With the two-field system he would have plowed 900 acres for 300 acres of crops, or 3 plowed acres per acre of yield. Medieval farmers who used the three-field system, in effect, increased their efficiency by 50 percent.

Increased Use of Crop Lands. At the same time, if a farmer had the time and available labor to plow 900 acres a year, the three-field system allowed him to put another 75 acres under cultivation, plowing 25 acres in the winter, 25 in the spring, and 25 more fallow acres twice during the year. So for the same amount of work he did under the two-field system, he could grow 650 acres of crops for 900 acres of plowing, dropping his plowed-land to crop-yield ratio to 1.38. As yet another benefit of the three-field system, his 900 acres of plowing were spread out more evenly throughout the year. If he had been able to plow 300 acres in one season before, he could still do so under the new system. Now—with the same manpower and available land—he could increase the size of his farm to 900 acres (with 300+300 acres planted in crops and 300 acres fallow). Taken together, the organizational changes in the medieval agricultural system increased productivity by as much as 200 percent.

New Crops. The new spring crops that were added when medieval farmers moved to the three-field system had other benefits as well. While wheat remained the staple crop for winter fields, the spring crops tended to include things such as peas, beans, oats, and rye. Not only did they add variety and nutritional value to the medieval diet, but they were also beneficial to the soil. Peas and beans in particular are called nitrogen-fixing plants. Since nitrogen is an important element for soil fertility, farmers who grew these plants further enhanced the benefits derived from the manure of their pastured livestock. Oats grow better in deeply plowed, well-fertilized lands, so they were grown more widely, providing food for the iron-shod and O-collared horses pulling the new plows, so oats supported that which supported them. Ultimately, all these innovations taken together formed a large, mutual-support system in which the sum of the whole was greater than the sum of the parts. The massive reorganization of the medieval agricultural system resulted in population growth and better health for people and animals. Furthermore, it sparked economic growth: as more crops became available for sale and more land came under cultivation, more taxes went to landlords, who could then use that money for commercial and industrial ventures, which were also supported by the growing population. The story of the Middle Ages in Europe is the story of an upward spiral in wealth, health, and productivity—one that was set back, not stopped, by the Black Death, and one that resulted in the population of Europe spreading out over the entire world.

Sources:

Grenville Astill and John Langdon, eds., *Medieval Farming and Technology: the Impact of Agricultural Change in Northwest Europe* (Leiden & New York: Brill, 1997).

Del Sweeney, ed., *Agriculture in the Middle Ages: Technology, Practice, and Representation* (Philadelphia: University of Pennsylvania Press, 1995).

Lynn White Jr., *Medieval Technology and Social Change* (New York: Oxford University Press, 1962).

POWER FOR TECHNOLOGY: FIRE

Creating Heat. Though historians often think of the Industrial Revolution of the eighteenth century as hinging on the invention of the steam engine and the adoption of coal as the fuel to power it, Europeans of the Middle Ages also used coal—along with prodigious amounts of wood, mainly in the form of charcoal—to power smelters, furnaces, and forges; to cook food and brew beer; and, of course, to heat dwellings.

The Demand for Wood. As the demand for wood by an exploding population grew and grew in the Middle Ages, large sections of Europe were effectively deforested. Kings and the officials of some towns enacted *silvaculture* (or woodland farming) laws to protect the remaining forests and to compel more efficient use of resources. To increase the amount of available wood, woodsmen developed the methods of *coppicing*, felling a tree in such a way as to force the growth of many new saplings from the stump, and *pollarding*, cutting branches back to the trunk to promote dense branch growth on live trees. Trees were sometimes purposefully deformed over their life spans to take on the shapes of needed wooden parts, such as roof beams or hull ribs for ships.

The Use of Coal. Although coal was used in vastly smaller amounts than wood during the Middle Ages, it was an important fuel. As early as the twelfth century, English and French authors wrote about the mining and shipment to London and Paris of "sea-coal" from coal deposits that had been eroded by waves. The impurities in sea-coal made it unsuitable for making iron or glass, but it was commonly used for burning limestone to make quicklime, which was used in cloth finishing and in making mortar or plaster for building construction. By the early fourteenth century, smoke from coal fires had become such a problem in London that attempts were made to ban its use there. By the end of the Middle Ages, as wood and charcoal became scarce, the demand for coal resulted in ever-deeper coal mines and the need for improved pumps to keep these mines from flooding. The end result of these demands was the development of the steam engine at the end of the seventeenth century; by then coal was the dominant industrial fuel.

Sources:

Grenville Astill, *The Countryside of Medieval England* (Oxford: Blackwell, 1988).

William Newman, "Technology and Alchemical Debate in the Late Middle Ages," *Isis*, 80 (1989): 423–445.

Oliver Rackman, *Trees and Woodland in the British landscape* (London: Dent, 1990).

Charles R. Young, "Conservation Policies in the Royal Forests of Medieval England," *Albion*, 10 (1978): 95–103.

Young, *The Royal Forests of Medieval England* (Philadelphia: University of Pennsylvania Press, 1979).

POWER FOR TECHNOLOGY: WATER

Waterwheels. The Romans used waterwheels for various industrial applications, but they were not exploited to their fullest potential until the Middle Ages, when new configurations of the watermill allowed them to do heavy work even when powered by modest streams. A watermill was often the centerpiece of any village in western Europe—and in the European settlements of North America, where, after the church, the first structures built were mills to produce things such as flour, lumber, iron, and mash (for brewing).

Available Water Sources. Waterwheels were especially prevalent in western Europe during the Middle Ages. The reason was geographical. Because that part of Europe receives more rainfall than the Mediterranean basin, it has more rivers and streams that flow swiftly and year round. Mills could be located in more areas than were possible in the Roman Empire, and since rivers flowed all year, it was economically feasible to build

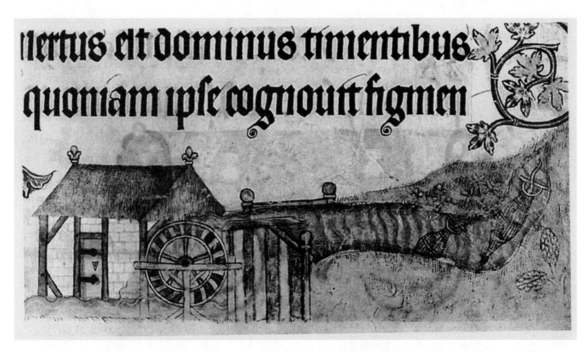

An overshot watermill; illumination from the *Luttrell Psalter* (British Library, London)

them, even though they, like modern factories, were expensive to construct and maintain. If a mill could be used for perhaps only three months during the winter rainy season or if the only usable flowing water were high in the mountains, where it was hard to build a mill and to bring raw materials to it, then there was little incentive to construct one. In the fertile valleys of France, Germany, and England, however, water was plentiful, not only to power the mills but to transport materials to and from the mills. People in those regions could be reasonably confident they could make a living, if not a large profit, from running them. Millers frequently did earn a great deal of money and were often important citizens of their town. The prevalence of the surname Miller today is one result of the importance and prevalence of millers in medieval European society. Because the miller often had a monopoly on a needed service in his town, the miller had the opportunity to overcharge or otherwise cheat his customers, and apparently many did. As Geoffrey Chaucer wrote of his miller in *The Canterbury Tales* (circa 1375–1400), "Well could he steal corn, and charge for it three times over. / And yet he had a thumb of gold, 'tis said."

Replacing Manpower. After the plague swept through Europe during the late Middle Ages, killing up to one-third of the population in some areas, there was not enough manpower left to operate many hand-powered industries, so the automatic power provided by watermills became especially attractive. Although animal power was still available, animals need to eat, and with fewer people to farm the land, crop sizes were reduced, making animal power less feasible. These factors contributed to the widespread use of mills in the fourteenth and fifteenth centu-

ries, but even before that time medieval Europeans were already relying heavily on water power.

Overshot versus Undershot Waterwheels. In ancient times there were two types of waterwheels that could be used to power mills for purposes such as grinding grain, beating rags to make paper, or running hammers to forge iron. The simplest and oldest form is the undershot waterwheel with bottom blades that are set into a swiftly flowing stream. While the undershot waterwheel is effective for fairly slow-moving rivers, in places where there is a large vertical drop, the overshot waterwheel offers more power for the same size wheel and same amount of water. At mills with overshot wheels, water is channeled along an elevated millrace from upstream and falls into buckets on the waterwheel. In this case the weight of the falling water, rather than its flow provides power to the wheel, making the overshot wheel about three times more efficient. Around 1450–1500 (or later), a hybrid model, combining the best features of overshot and undershot wheels, was introduced. At mills with this breast-shot wheel, swiftly flowing water is channeled into buckets on the upstream side of the wheel and the lower part of the wheel is set in the flowing water. Thus, the breast-shot wheel is powered by the weight of the water and its impact.

Grinding Grain. All these waterwheels have limitations. They rotate in a vertical plane with a horizontal axle, like a Ferris wheel. Millstones for grinding grain, however, rotate in a horizontal plane with a vertical axle. So in order to grind grain, far and away the most common and important use of mills in the Middle Ages, the turning horizontal axle of the waterwheel has to be connected to the turning vertical axle of the millstone through a set

Bridge mills under the Grand Pont in Paris; illumination from a fourteenth-century manuscript for *Vie de Saint Denis* (Bibliothèque Nationale, Paris)

of gears. Frequently, additional intermediate gears were added to increase the speed of the millstone. Because of all these gears, some of the power of the waterwheel was lost to friction. This problem motivated medieval people to become adept at the use of gears in mechanisms, developing technology that was later employed in more-complex devices such as clocks.

Norse Mills. There was one other type of waterwheel used throughout Europe and on its northern and western fringes from fairly early in the Middle Ages until well into the modern period. It was called the Norse mill because it was primarily found in Norway, Denmark, and Scandinavian settlements in Ireland—but it seems to have originated in Asia Minor (modern-day Turkey) during the second century B.C.E. The Norse mill used a narrow stream of water directed obliquely against angled or scoop-shaped blades on a horizontal wheel. Since the horizontal wheel had a vertical axle, this same axle could be used as the axle for a millstone, making Norse mills simple to construct. They were not as powerful as mills with overshot wheels. The configuration of the Norse mill was the model for the modern turbine, used in virtually all hydro-electric installations around the world.

Bridge Mills. Because the remains of mills are often easy to find in the landscape, archeologists and historians have been able to ascertain that many cities owe their locations to convenient waterfalls or cataracts on rivers, where it was advantageous to erect mills. Undershot mills were often placed under the arches of bridges over rivers. Because water speeds up to fit through the narrow spaces between bridge piers, a bridge creates a mill race. When a mill wheel was placed under a bridge, however, boats could no longer go through the archway it occupied. Often boat captains and millers both wanted to use the main channels in the river because they provided the deepest water for boats and the swiftest water for mills.

The problem was usually solvable if a bridge had several arches. In some places, however, there were so many mill wheels that they impeded boat traffic up and down a river. In rural areas mill owners often built dams or weirs to improve the efficiency of their mills or to store water to use when the rivers were low. These dams and weirs also impeded boats. Conflicts between millers and boatmen spilled over into manorial, town, and even royal courts, and there was a whole body of laws governing riparian (river) rights.

Wear and Tear. Because of the constant force of the water, waterwheels needed frequent repairs and replacement, and a storm surge could quickly destroy a mill. If possible, a watermill was fed by its own millrace, which allowed it to be sheltered to some extent from the main stream. When its millrace was shut with a sluice gate, a mill often had a good chance of survival.

Limitations of Water Power. Not all medieval Europeans lived near flowing streams and rivers. While northwestern Europe is blessed with more water than the Mediterranean world, by the time rivers reach France and Holland they are wide, meandering waterways that slowly empty into the sea. An undershot wheel needs at least a modest flow, and an overshot or breast wheel needs a significant drop in the elevation of the river. Some parts of European rivers, especially near their mouths, do not have such drops. People living in these areas could not effectively use water to power their mills.

Sources:

Marjorie Nice Boyer, "Water Mills: A Problem for the Bridges and Boats of Medieval France," *History of Technology*, 7 (1982): 1–22.

Frances and Joseph Gies, *Cathedral, Forge and Waterwheel: Technology and Invention in the Middle Ages* (New York: HarperCollins, 1994).

Elizabeth Bradford Smith and Michael Wolfe, eds., *Technology and Resource Use in Medieval Europe: Cathedrals, Mills, and Mines* (Aldershot, U.K. & Brookfield, Vt.: Ashgate, 1997).

Paolo Squatriti, ed., *Working with Water in Medieval Europe: Technology and Resource-Use* (Leiden & Boston: Brill, 2000).

POWER FOR TECHNOLOGY: WIND

Windmills. Medieval Europeans who did not live near rivers or streams capable of turning waterwheels harnessed the wind to power their mills. In the Low Countries, for example, the average elevation is only a few feet above sea level (and many areas where land was reclaimed are actually at mean sea level—that is, below storm-surge levels). While water is plentiful there, it is not suited to powering mills. They do have steady winds coming off the North Sea, however, and the windmill became their principal means of power. Windmills began to appear in Europe during the 1180s, and seem to have come from Asia Minor. The earliest known windmills were horizontal mills used by the mid tenth century in Anatolia, a high, arid region in modern Turkey, which, like the Low Countries, has little water-power potential, but a great deal of wind.

Horizontal Windmills. There are two types of windmills, horizontal and the vertical. The horizontal windmill may have been modeled on the horizontal watermill, for both use a single vertical shaft that is directly connected to the millstone. The horizontal windmill works much like the propeller on top of a child's beanie or a pinwheel turned on its side. Also like a horizontal waterwheel, this kind of windmill tends to be modest in size and power output.

Vertical Windmills. Vertical windmills are much larger and more powerful than horizontal windmills, and they were more common throughout Europe. A vertical windmill has several blades, or sails, mounted on a horizontal shaft and set on a tall tower, where they could turn in the wind. The sails were sometimes made of wood, but frequently they were made of cloth, often in a triangular shape that was efficient at catching the wind. Gearing connected the main axle to the millstone, which was usually placed on the second floor of the tower, so that the ground flour could fall to the lower floor, where it was sifted and bagged.

Catching the Wind. There is a variable in wind power that does not exist in water power. Unlike a river, which always flows in the same direction, the wind can blow in many directions. In many places the wind direction changes from day to day and from season to season. A horizontal windmill can be powered by winds from any direction, but a vertical mill needs to be facing directly, or nearly directly, into the wind. Thus, millwrights need a way to turn vertical windmills into the wind. Moving an entire building was a challenge for medieval Europeans, and their attempts to solve the problem greatly increased their facility with machine design, especially in the areas of gearing and self-regulating, or automated, mechanisms.

Post mills. The earliest solution was the post mill, which was in use by the last third of the twelfth century. A small wooden house that contains the millstone and has the sails attached to the peak of its roof is placed on top of a vertical post that has two crossed timbers attached to its base (much like an old-fashioned Christmas-tree stand) and struts connecting these timbers to the middle of the post. This structure is buried in a small mound to ballast it, and the house sits on a bearing on top of the post. A long tiller can then be used to revolve the whole house on the bearing so it faces the wind. Post mills have several drawbacks. There is a limit to weight a miller can safely perch on the post, and the constant pivoting of the structure creates a large amount of wear, causing frequent breakdowns. They are also cumbersome to operate. Tillers were sometimes thirty, forty, or even fifty feet long, and, to provide enough

A post windmill; illumination from the *Luttrell Psalter* (British Library, London)

leverage to turn the house, millers frequently used horses or oxen to pull the tiller. While the post mill was an effective solution to providing power where watermills were not an option, its drawbacks inspired medieval millwrights to look for a better solution.

Turret Mills. Their solution was the turret mill, which was probably in use by the early fourteenth century. The base of the turret mill is built solidly on the ground, and only the top of its tower turns to face the wind. To operate the turret mill, medieval technicians invented a rotating gear assembly to attach where the sail axle meets the main driving shaft, smooth bearings to allow the turret to turn easily, and self-acting mechanisms to keep the sails facing the wind without any effort on the part of the miller. The technical knowledge necessary for creating the gearing system for the vertical mill came from earlier medieval inventions of gears for things such as clocks, winches, and watermills. Bearings had been one of the great limitations of machinery since ancient times. Placing the turret on wheels arranged in a circle and riding on a wooden track (or one of cut stone if the tower is built of stone) allows it to turn. Then the main difficulty was making sure that the top of the mill did not get blown off in high or even moderate winds. Its weight solves this problem to some extent, as does inclining the sail axle a few degrees to make the thrust from the sails act slightly downward.

Wear and Tear. As with watermills, windmills are subject to wear and tear. The constant force of wind can shred the sails or tear a windmill to pieces in a season or two. Gale-force winds can knock out a mill in a day. Windmills, however, were easier to protect than watermills. If a storm were approaching, the miller could remove the sails from their arms. Post mills were more vulnerable to gales than vertical mills. As millwrights built larger and larger windmills, they often built their towers of stone rather than wood.

Sources:

Richard Holt, *The Mills of Medieval England* (Oxford: Blackwell, 1988).

Edward J. Kealey, *Harvesting the Air: Windmill Pioneers in Twelfth-Century England* (Berkeley: University of California Press, 1987).

John Langdon, "The Birth and Demise of the Medieval Windmill," *History of Technology*, 14 (1992): 54–76.

Elizabeth Bradford Smith and Michael Wolfe, eds., *Technology and Resource Use in Medieval Europe: Cathedrals, Mills, and Mines* (Aldershot, U.K. & Brookfield, Vt.: Ashgate, 1997).

THE TECHNOLOGY OF CONSTRUCTION

New Building Technologies. Two of the most enduring images of the Middle Ages are castles and cathedrals. To construct these magnificent structures medieval building technology advanced to limits the Romans had never approached and used available materials in ways they had never imagined. Medieval builders constructed castles and cathedrals largely from cut stone and used quicklime mortar—sometimes to hold the blocks in place, but more often to fill in gaps. Their solid blocks of stone had to fit together with tolerances of less than a quarter inch (5mm). Though they could use water-powered mills for cutting stone from the quarries into uniform slabs, most of the work was still done by hand with hammer and chisel. By the thirteenth or fourteenth century, the magnificent castles and cathedrals of medieval Europe had begun to revive the "lost glory" of ancient Rome.

Cathedrals. While they were built to exemplify the glory of God, the cathedrals of Europe also stand as monuments to the ingenuity of architects and stonemasons who made them. The adoption of Christianity in the later Roman Empire and its eventual spread throughout Europe provided the motivation for raising big cathedrals and churches. Cathedral building was also intimately tied to the increasing power of cities and the growing influence and wealth of town dwellers, particularly in the twelfth and thirteenth centuries. Europeans inherited an understanding of monumental building from the Romans, but the undertaking of such projects was unusual until the medieval period. In trying to re-create the glory of Rome in the Holy Roman Empire, Charlemagne built an ornate Romanesque palace at Aachen, in eastern Germany, during the eighth century, but it was a lone example.

Romanesque Architecture. Especially in its monasteries, the Church re-created the power and economic force of the Roman Empire. By the ninth and tenth centuries the largely self-sufficient monasteries had become centers of cultural expression. Beyond the society they molded, the art they created, and the literature they preserved and augmented, the building of churches became the centerpiece of their existence. Because they were inspired by the Roman ruins around them and built in conscious imitation of Rome, the solid churches built throughout Europe from the seventh through the twelfth century are known as Romanesque buildings. Their characteristic features are thick walls, small windows, and semicircular arches throughout the building. Although the main central spaces, or naves, reach stunning lengths and heights in some Romanesque churches, they are darker and more somber spaces than the Gothic-style churches that succeeded them.

Barrel Vaults. In Romanesque construction the large open space of the nave was either covered with a flat wooden ceiling supported by large transverse wooden beams, or it was spanned by a stone barrel vault. Used in large-scale Roman buildings, the barrel vault is essentially a round arch extended along the length of the nave. While it covers the nave in a majestic fashion, as the nave to be spanned grows wider, an increasingly thicker vault must be built. As barrel vaults grew thicker and thicker, they also became heavier and heavier, so the walls on which a vault rested had to be made thicker, not only to carry the weight of all that stone but also to resist the tendency of an arched structure to push outward at its base. In architectural terminology this tendency is known as thrust. Initially, Romanesque churches dealt with thrust by building thick, windowless walls, but over time, a desire for some natural light drove builders to put intermittent reinforcing pillars along the outside of the walls.

Romanesque barrel vaulting in the Church of St. Madeleine, Vezelay, France

These pillars, called buttresses, took the load of the vault, while the walls between them could be made slightly thinner and pierced safely for windows. The development of buttresses predicated the Gothic form.

Cluny. The culmination of the Romanesque style was the monastery of Cluny, in Burgundy. Founded in 909 by Benedictine monks, Cluny became the greatest monastery of their order, and it was considered one of the greatest monastic building complexes in Europe until its destruction in 1790 during the French Revolution. A succession of three churches graced the monastery, and the third, built between 1089 and 1132, was the largest church in Christendom until the sixteenth century. A massive Romanesque construction, with a central nave 99 feet (30m) tall and 555 feet (169m) long, the church stood as the centerpiece of a 25-acre (10.1 ha) monastic complex.

Gothic Architecture. By the end of the twelfth century, as the Romanesque style was reaching its height, changes in church construction inaugurated a new style, later disparagingly called "Gothic" during the Renaissance, when it was called barbaric in comparison to the Roman models that influenced the architecture of that period. Today, however, the Gothic style is seen as the pinnacle of medieval architecture. Gothic cathedrals are highly ornate structures. Their sculpture became increasingly naturalistic and expressive. As these impressive churches soared higher and higher, the manner in which they were constructed made them much stronger for their size than Romanesque churches, allowing their stone walls to be interrupted with large expanses of stained glass instead of the small windows that made the interiors of Romanesque structures so dark.

Groin Vaults. Gothic cathedrals were able to achieve great heights through innovations in constructing their vaults and the columns that support them. Architects learned that if they built two intersecting barrel vaults, one running the length of the nave and the other running its width, they could overcome many of the limitations of the single barrel vault. The resulting creased ceiling was called a groin vault. Though this vault can be created with two of the same semicircular arches used in Romanesque architecture, early in the twelfth century European architects discovered that using pointed arches made it possible to make a higher ceiling, and this pointed form made the structure even more rigid. Any structure with creases is more stable than one without them, and can therefore be made thinner. Thus, the pointed Gothic vault used considerably less stone than its Romanesque predecessor. A groin vault generates considerably less thrust than the barrel vault, and a pointed groin vault even less than one with semicircular arches, so a Gothic ceiling could be set atop thinner walls than a Romanesque ceiling of the same size. With arches spanning the length and the width of the nave, the walls no longer needed to be continuous and could be reduced to a series of columns, or piers. The space between them could then be filled with stained-glass windows.

Rib Vaulting. Further refinements were made throughout the Middle Ages. Early Gothic groin vaulting gave way to rib vaulting as early as about 1180, in which the lines of intersection of the vaults were constructed first by creating an arch, or rib, between diagonally opposed piers. With the ribs in place, stone webbing—the minimally structured membranes that fill the space between the ribs—could easily be laid between them to complete the vault. This development allowed the webs to become even thinner, further reducing the weight of the vault and allowing it to be built higher and higher above the church floor. This innovation made possible the construction of soaring cathedrals, but it created new problems for the builders to solve.

Flying Buttresses. Medieval cathedrals with tall, pointed vaults projected high above the landscape, where winds were much stronger than at ground level. Even if the vaults and the roofs did not generate too much thrust, the pressure of the wind hitting the roof broadside did. The solution was to increase the buttressing. Buttresses constructed to support high roofs rose above the tops of the side aisles and became free-standing arcs of stone. These new "flying buttresses" received the thrust of the roof and vault and transferred it to the ground. As time passed, flying buttresses were adorned with elaborate detailing and their own ornate spires. Not only did they complement the artistry of the church, but these pinnacles also added extra weight on the buttresses to provide increased stability in high winds.

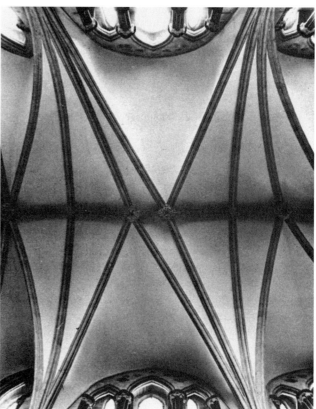

Early Gothic groin vaulting in the crypt at Canterbury Cathedral (circa 1105)
and later Gothic rib vaulting in Le Mans Cathedral (begun in 1218)

Builder's Tools. To create these majestic cathedrals, builders had the straightedge and compass to set out the plan, the simple hammer and chisel to carve stone blocks, and human- or animal-powered tread-wheel hoists to lift the blocks in place. Medieval builders excelled at the geometric construction of cathedrals. There are no known blueprints for complete cathedrals. Instead, scholars have, in a few instances, found templates for the fundamental geometrical constructions that underlie the size, shape, and proportions of a church. Everything, from the overall length and width of the church, down to the curve of the arches and the window mullions, is related through simple geometry to some modulus, or base unit. In a few churches the modulus and base curves for the entire church are inscribed on the floor of the nave. Builders might work out the basic idea on paper, but then they laid out full-scale templates on the building site. Masons would cut stone to fit and work it to a finished or near-finished condition. These blocks would then be hoisted aloft, fitted in place, and possibly given a final fine dressing. Overall, in structures tens of meters tall and hundreds of meters long, medieval architects and builders managed accuracy on the order of centimeters or even of parts of centimeters in many cases.

Rapid Development. Between the mid twelfth and the mid thirteenth centuries medieval architecture advanced through these stages so rapidly that cathedrals begun a mere fifty years apart were vastly different in scale and feeling. The nave of Laon cathedral, begun in 1175 and exhib-

iting all the elements of Gothic architecture, reached a stunning height of 80 feet (24m). Rheims cathedral, begun a mere fifty years later in 1225 and exhibiting mature Gothic elements such as flying buttresses and steeply pointed arches, soared to 125 feet (38m). These buildings and other Gothic cathedrals were stunning places of worship, with painted interiors and vast panels of stained glass. In Christian theology the Holy Spirit is personified in light and light beams, and these soaring houses of worship glorified not only God but their builders as well.

Castles. Castles were raised to the glory of man. In a Europe still far from unified, castle building was stimulated by hostile or potentially hostile relations among neighboring lords. Castles and fortified cities became a common feature throughout Europe, not only in areas such as Germany and Italy, where competing princes and dukes fought for political control, but even in countries that became unified at an early date—notably France and England, where the landscape was dotted with castles that rulers used to maintain their power. In Italy, the Tuscan town of San Gimignano had dozens of fortified tower houses, each built by a different family or faction, not only for protection from invaders, but also from each other. In Germany castles were built along the Rhine River to control and tax river traffic. In some cases, as in Wales under Edward I, castles served to bring or keep a local population under control and to cow local lords into obeisance to a regional lord or king. Fortification allows an individual to establish and maintain power. While it provides security for the

Arundel Castle in West Sussex, England, with a motte (mound) constructed in 1068, a stone-shell keep built atop the motte in the twelfth century, and a barbican (gate tower) added in 1295

inhabitants of a region by providing a refuge in times of crisis, it is also a reminder to them of the certain power of the local lord and the potential power of the ruler of the state. Although the common image of medieval battle is one of chivalrous knights jousting and fighting in full armor, in reality most medieval warfare was conducted through sieges. Because surrounding and attacking a castle or a fortified city occurred much more frequently than infantry battles, good fortifications were much more important than knights. Consequently, fortification technology was remarkably dynamic throughout the Middle Ages.

Early Castles. Fortifications went through several distinct phases from the fall of Rome in the fifth century to the advent of effective gunpowder artillery in the sixteenth. At first, fortifications were simply stout wooden buildings. If they could be built in places that were naturally protected, such as high hills or ocean cliffs, so much the better, but more often than not they were placed where they were most needed, near centers of population. Therefore, castle builders had to make their own defenses, usually by making hills and building castles atop them. The hill—whether natural or artificially constructed—was called a *motte* (the French word for mound or hill). Around the base of the motte, the lord would build housing for his servants and household, creating a village that would attract people such as craftsmen, soldiers, cooks, brewers, and leather workers to settle there as well. Since it was in the lord's interest to

protect these people too, a "palisade," or fence of tall pointed stakes, was built around the motte and these outbuildings. The area between the palisade and the motte was known as the "bailey," so the general term for these early fortifications is motte-and-bailey castle. Motte-and-bailey castles were first built in France, although their precursors, prehistoric hillforts, exist all across Europe. Motte-and-bailey castles spread to England and in a sort of modified form around western Europe.

Castle Walls. As the power of rulers grew, they took many craftsmen and support staff into their households. The wooden palisades were replaced with stone and the separation of motte and bailey shrank. By the thirteenth century, castles were built with a large stone tower, or keep, and an encircling stone wall. This wall enclosed smaller buildings—usually built along its inside—to house the trades originally located in the bailey.

Building for Defense. Castle building for the purpose of defense developed substantially from the eleventh century to the fifteenth century. The simple wall with a gate developed into a set of interlocking defenses designed to keep attackers out for as long as possible. Moats were dug around the outer walls, and were either kept full of water or else built in such a way that they could be flooded in time of crisis. The drawbridges that spanned the moats were retractable to prevent unwanted entry. Huge iron and wood grates called portcullises were placed just behind the draw-

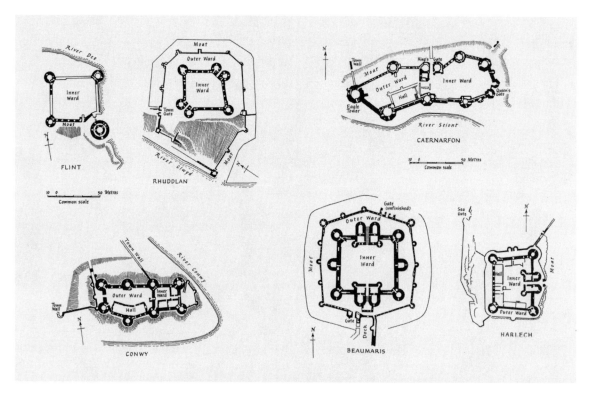

Plans for the castles Edward I began building in Wales during the late thirteenth century (diagrams by Neil Hyslop)

bridge as well as at the far end of the gatehouse, so that if attackers crossed the moat and gained entry, they could be caged between the portcullises, where defenders could attack them from above and through narrow slits in the walls at the sides. These narrow vertical slits (sometimes also augmented by a short horizontal one to make the hole cross shaped) were only a few inches wide on the outside, but were a few feet wide on the defenders' side of the wall. These funnel-shaped openings, known as arrow loops, allowed defenders to shoot arrows through the wall with about a 75-90 degree arc, while presenting a tiny opening for enemy archers. Later, circular holes were carved at the bottom of each arrow loop to accommodate small cannons and handguns. The tops of castle walls were crowned with ramparts, which had regular gaps—called crenellations—for firing arrows—or later guns—at attackers. Some castles were built with multiple sets of walls, so that even if attackers breeched the main wall, they then had to attack another set of walls while vulnerable to defensive fire.

Eastern Influences. There is a great debate among historians over what role Europeans' experiences in the Crusades played in the development of castles. Earlier historians thought that the Crusaders learned many of the building and defensive methods they applied at home directly from Muslim castles, particularly in Syria. More-recent historians have suggested that the Europeans were developing many of these techniques on their own and that the Crusaders' observations in the Holy Land were a catalyst to use these building methods more widely. Still later historians have suggested that the exchange was mutual: Syrians and Europeans learned from each other. In any case, after the Crusaders returned from the Near East dur-

ing the twelfth and thirteenth centuries, increasingly large and complex stone castles were built all across Europe.

Castle Architecture. Medieval castle builders took a different approach to construction from cathedral builders. Cathedrals soared ever higher as their walls became thinner and delicate, but as castles grew larger and larger, their walls became more and more massive. Churches were usually built anew, completely replacing older religious buildings; castles evolved and were expanded over time, absorbing, modifying, and extending defensive structures already in place. The architectural challenges of castles were never as formidable, nor as creatively solved, as those of cathedrals, but throughout the Middle Ages castle building, like cathedral building, was an important opportunity for builders to display their skills through expansive, and expensive, use of stone, labor, and energy.

Castles as Country Houses. By the end of the Middle Ages the castle had begun to lose its military function. One reason was the rise of gunpowder weaponry, which changed how wars were fought. Another was the growth of state power, especially in England and France. Strong castles in the countryside posed a threat to centralized monarchies, so powerful kings discouraged castle destruction and sometimes even destroyed them. As a ruler consolidated his hold over his kingdom, the strategic military importance of castles decreased. Instead, they became mostly centers of provincial administration for lords, both as landholders and as agents of the crown. Castles multiplied to the point that a given lord might make an annual circuit of his castles, and they functioned more like the country houses they became after the Renaissance.

Furnishing Castles and Cathedrals. Once completed, castles and cathedrals needed furnishings and decorations. In the course of fulfilling the demand for such niceties, medieval artists achieved new heights of creative power, and technological innovation kept pace. Contrary to popular opinion, the mechanical processes of artistic creativity involved in decoration of cathedrals and castles were not the sole responsibility of uneducated townsmen. In 1122 the German monk Theophilus Presbyter wrote *On Divers Arts,* in which he explained the creation of artists' pigments and gold amalgams and the art of metal casting. The book is essentially a textbook of medieval artistic craft skills, and as such it is of extraordinary value to historians. Theophilus was a monk, educated in and dedicated to theological learning, but his knowledge of complex techniques and his refined tastes suggest that he was also a goldsmith and painter. Traditionally, the professions of monk and artisan did not go together, but Theophilus provides evidence that in the early twelfth century, this division of labor was breaking down. Slightly later, Hugh of St. Victor, in Paris, wrote his *Didascalicon* (circa 1125–1130), in which he defended the "mechanical arts"—everything from brewing to leatherwork, metalworking, and military technology—as not only useful, but also desirable and honorable. He also provided the first European account of the bell, at just the time that bells were becoming common in the churches that were being built at a prodigious rate throughout Europe.

Sources:

Jean Gimpel, *The Cathedral Builders,* translated by Carl F. Barnes (New York: Grove, 1961); translated again by Teresa Waugh (New York: Grove, 1983).

Theophilus Presbyter, *On Divers Arts: The Treatise of Theophilus,* translated by John G. Hawthorne and Cyril Stanley Smith (Chicago: University of Chicago, 1963); also translated by C. R. Dodwell as *The Various Arts* (London: Nelson, 1961).

Wolfgang F. Schuerl, *Medieval Castles and Cities,* translated by Francisca Garvie (London: Cassell, 1978).

Elizabeth Bradford Smith, and Michael Wolfe, eds. *Technology and Resource Use in Medieval Europe: Cathedrals, Mills, and Mines* (Aldershot, U.K. & Brookfield, Vt.: Ashgate, 1997).

Sidney Toy, *Castles: A Short History from 1600 B.C. to A.D. 1600* (London & Toronto: Macmillan, 1939).

Lynn Townsend White Jr., *Medieval Religion and Technology: Collected Essays* (Berkeley: University of California Press, 1978).

THE TECHNOLOGY OF MACHINERY

Mechanical Marvels. While medieval Europeans professed the desire to emulate Rome (or rather their idealized vision of it), their worldview had changed to such a degree that in striving to achieve their goal, they inadvertently took another, more impressive, course and created a world that in many ways surpassed their model. Not only did they harness animals, wind, and water, and build monumental structures in entirely new forms, but they also created objects that surpassed those of the Romans in their intricacy and subtlety. It has been said that Rome marshaled great masses to provide great forces to create great constructions—for instance, the Coliseum or the Pantheon. Medieval Europeans took a different route: they marshaled

A clepsydra (water clock) believed to have been used at the court of Louis IX of France in the mid thirteenth century (from Robert Delort, *Life in the Middle Ages,* 1973)

mechanical ingenuity to do more with less labor. By the end of the Middle Ages, Europe was filled with mechanical marvels that ancient Romans had never thought possible.

Origins. The genesis of medieval mechanical innovation appears to be the inventions that improved medieval millers' ability to exploit water and wind power. In particular, the shift from horizontal mills to vertical mills required a set of gears to transmit power from the horizontally rotating shaft of the waterwheel or the sails to the vertically rotating shaft of the millstone. These gears allowed rotary motion to be transmitted and used for many purposes, from grinding and polishing to boring and rolling. In addition, medieval engineers learned that a rotating shaft could produce more than just rotational motion. Medieval Europeans were apparently the first society to understand the concept of the—deceptively simple—crank, which is documented in the Utrecht Psalter (820), which includes an illustration of a sword-sharpening grindstone. They soon realized that, not only can a crank be used to turn a wheel, but so too will a rotating wheel turn a crank—and, with the appropriate linkages, that rotating crank can change a rotational motion into a reciprocating (back-and-forth) motion that can be used for such things as sawing wood.

Worm Gears, Cams, and Levers. They next discovered that they could use regular gears with what came to be known as worm gears (wheels whose teeth mesh with the threads of short screws) to magnify greatly the force, or torque, of gear assemblies. They found that, if a pair of gears—each of which had teeth around only one-half of its circumference—is connected to a central main gear (with all its teeth), axles can be made rotate one way and then the other, while the main axle maintains a constant rotation in one direction. They also learned that if a short projection, called a cam, is placed on a rotating shaft, each time the shaft comes around the projection will strike or trip some other machine part. Cams are remarkably powerful, and the combination of a cam and a lever allowed medieval technicians to turn the small motion of the cam into a large motion that could operate a tool such as a hammer head or a stamp, as well as the delicate motion needed to strike a bell. While the crank provided continuous reciprocal motion, the cam allowed intermittent motion. With this development, the door was opened for the invention of all sorts of machines.

Machinery at Work. Once medieval Europeans understood gears, levers, cranks, and cams, they could do much more than using mills to grind grain. Appropriately outfitted mills crushed ore for mining, pumped water for drainage and irrigation, cut wood and stone for construction, pumped bellows for smithies and foundries, hoisted construction materials at building sites, and raised actors through the floors of stages, and above, for dramatic effect. For the first time in human history, a civilization was built first and foremost by machinery, not primarily by human labor (though it still played a significant role).

Clocks. Medieval craftsmen also designed fine machinery to perform precise tasks. From the astrolabe to measure the positions of heavenly bodies as an aid to navigation, to the mechanical clock to mark time, medieval technologists

learned and refined the art of precision engineering. Initially, nearly every society marked time in a different way, but today the standard measures of seconds, minutes, hours, and days are used worldwide. That uniformity is a legacy from medieval Europeans, the first society to develop a reliable mechanical timekeeper, which in turn established the equal hours, minutes, and seconds system.

Variable Time. Each day is, of course, divided into day and night, and from ancient times one way to subdivide day and night was into twelve units each: twelve hours of daylight and twelve hours of darkness. (This same base is the reason there are twelve signs of the zodiac.) The periods of daylight and darkness in a day, however, vary in length: as one travels farther and farther from the equator during summer, daylight lasts longer and longer, while the opposite is true in winter. If one uses a "variable hour" system, marking off twelve hours of light and twelve hours of darkness, a daylight hour in June in London is a great deal longer than a daylight hour in December in the same city. Thus, the amount of time in a variable "hour" changes with the seasons.

Keeping Variable Time. Before and during the Middle Ages the unequal-hour time system worked just fine for most purposes. Though sundials that measure equal hours summer or winter came into use late in the Middle Ages, for most of the period those in use since antiquity divided daylight hours, regardless of their length, into twelve parts. The most common form of timekeeper in antiquity and the early Middle Ages was a water clock, or *clepsydra,* which allows water to drip at a regular rate into a collection vessel. A given amount of water equals a specific amount of time. Water clocks could easily be adjusted to allow for variable hours as the seasons changed. For the majority of society there was no reason to know the time during the night. For agriculture or business, daily tasks were completed as natural light allowed; meetings were scheduled for whenever a certain sun time came around, and life went on as usual.

Telling Time at Night. Astronomers, however, liked to divide the day-night cycle into twenty-four equal parts because it made their calculations easier, and the monastic clergy needed a device that told time during the dark hours as well during daylight. Christian liturgy requires specific prayers to be said in a certain sequence at the "canonical hours"—Matins (midnight), Prime (6:00 A.M.), Terce (9:00 A.M.), Sext (noon), None (3:00 P.M.), Vespers (6:00 P.M.), and Compline, said at nightfall. In monasteries this routine cycles of prayers punctuated the entire twenty-four-hour day, and the first mechanical clocks seem to have been developed as alarms to awaken the brethren for prayers in the night. The name *clock* derives from the German word *Glocke* (bell), and, even before mechanical clocks were developed, there are records of water clocks with mechanisms designed to ring alarm bells. Few of these had dials; apparently they were meant only to sound an alarm.

Mechanical Clocks. The first clocks that dispensed with water or another dripping fluid and used a mechanism made of gears and levers to mark the passage of time

Face and works of a fourteenth-century clock made for Wells Cathedral in England (The Science Museum, London)

appeared in the early fourteenth century. Documents from about that time show clockwork mechanisms with intricate and complex configurations. These clocks divide the day into twenty-four hours, but that function was secondary; their main purpose was to display the motions of the stars and the known planets. Many, though not all, were connected to bell-ringing machinery that could strike bells the appropriate number of times to mark each passing hour. Because the clock was made partly as a sounding device and partly as an aid to astronomers, the counting of the hours was done according to the astronomers' system of twenty-four equal hours per day-night, regardless of the season.

The Clock Mechanism. A simple mechanical clock consists of a weight on a cord that is wrapped around an axle. As the weight is pulled downward by gravity, it turns the axle. The heart of the clock is an ingenious device that slows and regulates the fall of the weight. This "escapement," or timing mechanism, consists of a horizontal bar called a "foliot" turning a vertical shaft called a "verge" (staff or rod) with two "pallets," which are much like the cams used to strike or trip other machine parts in mills. The pallets are pushed one way and then another by the top and bottom teeth of a large saw-toothed gear called the crown wheel. As each tooth catches a pallet, it pushes on it and forces the foliot to swing backward. But this means that the opposing pallet catches the next tooth on the opposite side, reversing the original impulse. The foliot oscillates back and forth, and because reversing direction takes force and therefore time, the verge allows the crown wheel to rotate only in small, even, methodical steps. The driving weight, connected through a series of gears to the crown wheel, "falls" in small increments as the verge and

foliot escapement permits, so slowly one can scarcely see it move. Small weights could be added on the arms of the foliot to regulate the oscillation. The heavier these weights, or the farther out the arms they were placed, the longer it took for each oscillation. The clockwork mechanism was fairly easy to adjust so that it would keep time with the stars and the planets, but it was quite difficult to readjust the foliot on a daily basis to make the clock speed up or slow down as the days grew shorter or longer. The clock, in other words, failed to keep time the way most people had kept time for centuries, and instead made the astronomers' method of telling time the standard for everyone.

Astronomical Clocks. Natural philosophers quickly realized the connection between this worldly signifier of time and the phenomena it was designed to signify: the movements of the heavens. Within a few decades of the first recorded mechanical clocks, two exceedingly complex clocks—one in England and another in Italy—were documented. Richard of Wallingford, an English abbot and philosopher, left a manuscript, dating from roughly 1333, that describes in great detail the construction of an astronomical clockwork mechanism for the monastery of St. Albans. Some thirty years later, Giovanni de'Dondi of Padua also built an astronomical clock and wrote a book describing this "astrarium." Both these machines were amazingly complex: each traced the motions of the sun, the moon, the five known planets, and the so-called fixed stars, as well as displaying the dates of the fixed Church holy days (such as Christmas) and the movable feasts (such as Easter). These clocks were famous far and wide in their day.

Adapting to Clock Time. Equal hours might still have remained an astronomer's special way of time telling, but for the exceptional popularity of the mechanical clock. In less than a century, weight-driven clocks spread to all the cities and most of the important towns of Europe. These new clocks spread because they were easier to build than water clocks and were readily adapted to spaces large and small, high in the church tower or in the houses of the wealthy. Sundials remained in use, but clocks, conspicuously mounted on church and urban towers (where public sundials had been mounted) as a sign of pride, more and more frequently chimed out the equal hours. In fact, sundial makers developed a complex way to make sundial time approximate the equal hours of mechanical clocks.

Hourglasses. Daily life was increasingly regulated by clocks as well. Although clock faces were still not altogether standard or common, and accurate telling of minutes did not come for more than a century, late medieval Europeans told time by the bell (the meaning of "o'clock" in English). One sign of this shift is found in the spread of the common sandglass or hourglass. Sandglasses could have been invented at any time, but none have been found that date before advent the mechanical clock in the fourteenth century. People turned their glasses when the bell sounded the start of an hour and then referred to the state of the sand to give them an approximate indication of the time until the next bell was struck. Sandglasses were made in sets—hour, half hour, and quarter hour—and many regulations limited activities according to the sandglass. Preachers, university lecturers, committees, lawyers arguing cases, and even torturers "examining" their victims were all subject to a new time discipline grounded in the sounding of the clock bell and the slipping of the sand in the hourglass.

Sources:

Gehard Dohrn-van Rossum, *History of the Hour: Clocks and Modern Temporal Orders* (Chicago: University of Chicago Press, 1996).

Giovanni de'Dondi, *Mechanical Universe: The Astrarium of Giovanni de'Dondi*, edited and translated by Silvio Bedini and Francis Maddison, *Transactions of the American Philosophical Society*, new series 56, part 5 (Philadelphia: American Philosophical Society, 1966).

Richard of Wallingford, *Richard of Wallingford: An Edition of His Writings*, 3 volumes, edited and translated by John D. North (Oxford: Oxford University Press 1976).

Lynn Townsend White Jr., *Medieval Religion and Technology: Collected Essays* (Berkeley: University of California Press, 1978).

White, *Medieval Technology and Social Change* (New York: Oxford University Press, 1962).

THE TECHNOLOGY OF MILITARY MACHINES

Waging War. While medieval people used technology to redefine the ways in which they lived every day, they also used it to redefine the ways in which they wrought death and destruction. Warfare at the end of the Middle Ages differed more profoundly from military actions at the beginning of the period than early medieval warfare had differed from battle at any previous time in history. Until fairly late in the Middle Ages, people believed that warfare was predicated on one man attacking another and seeking victory using his own strength. The reality was not that simple. Throughout the Middle Ages, siege warfare, which relied heavily on machinery, was the principle method of waging war. Consequently, military technology was focused on developing and improving methods of laying siege, particularly machines that allowed the invader to attack a fortification from a distance. The first such developments were different sorts of mechanical catapults, but after the knowledge of how to make gunpowder arrived in Europe from China in the mid thirteenth century, guns slowly, but inexorably, became the main focus of technological development.

Catapults. Mechanical artillery dates back at least to the ancient Greeks. The Greeks were not terribly interested in technology for technology's sake, but—as an indispensable element of civic defense—artillery was one of the few machines considered worthy of concerted development and description. The Middle Ages inherited knowledge of ancient catapults, which were simple devices powered by twisted ropes or sinews. By the late Middle Ages—before the cannon became the main siege device in the sixteenth century—medieval engineers perfected a type of catapult known as a *trebuchet*. Originating in China and reaching Europe through Islam, the trebuchet used a long beam of wood with a sling attached to one end to hurl stones and other substances at its target. The beam was mounted on a framework off-center and high above the ground in such a way that, when the short end of the beam was pulled downward, the long end swung upward in a wide arc, sending a projectile violently at a target. The earliest trebuchets, known as traction trebuchets, required a crew of many men—or even women—pulling on ropes attached to the short end to fling a missile. This method was limited by the number of people who could be crowded under the beam and by how much force they could apply.

The Counterweight Trebuchet. Medieval engineers discovered that replacing men with a large box filled with rocks immensely magnified the weight of the missile a trebuchet could launch. This counterweight trebuchet was the single most effective piece of pre-gunpowder artillery ever developed. Counterweight trebuchets with names such as "warwolf" and "wall breaker" appeared in the twelfth century and continued in use until at least the later part of the fifteenth century. They were so powerful that many residents of castles or cities surrendered as soon as they learned they were to be besieged by a trebuchet. These late trebuchets were capable of launching stone balls that weighed hundreds of pounds and could shatter a wall in a single blow. They could also lob disease-infested carcasses or incendiary devices over the walls into the defenders' stronghold. By the late fourteenth century, the odds in siege warfare were for the moment strongly tipped toward the attackers, and the upsurge of castle building in the fourteenth century came in response to these powerful machines.

The Cannon. That the trebuchet continued to be used so late in the Middle Ages is a testament to its strength, as well as an indication of the slow development of the alternative form of siege "engine," the cannon. Gunpowder is a mixture of charcoal, sulfur, and saltpeter (a nitrate salt that

Soldiers besieging a castle with a counterweight trebuchet; illumination from
a fourteenth-century French manuscript (British Library, London)

contributes oxygen and makes the compound burn rapidly). When mixed in ratios of about 1:1:6, gunpowder burns so quickly that, if enclosed in a strong-enough container, it will eject a projectile from the mouth of the container at supersonic speeds. Even though gunpowder was known in the thirteenth century, it was not until the end of the fifteenth that it made any truly appreciable impact on the art of war. Europeans knew how to use artillery and what they could do with cannons in a siege, but one of the key ingredients in gunpowder was rare.

The Search for Saltpeter. When the recipe for gunpowder appeared in Europe, two of its ingredients were readily available throughout most of the region: charcoal was easily prepared from wood, and sulfur deposits were known to form almost anywhere volcanoes or hot springs were active. Saltpeter, on the other hand, first came from Asia with the spice trade. Early reports suggested that saltpeter was mined, and because Europeans knew of no deposits in their region, it was available—if at all—in minute quantities from apothecaries and at high prices. Europeans eventually discovered, however, that the Chinese did not literally "mine" saltpeter. Instead, they learned, saltpeter forms on the deposits of dung, or guano, left by cave-dwelling bats.

The Saltpeter Industry. Saltpeter is a natural byproduct of bacterial decay of organic waste, chiefly animal dung. It took Europeans about a century and a half to learn to collect raw dung in sufficient quantities, store it in a cool, dry place such as a cellar or cave, water it fortnightly with urine, and collect the white salts that grew slowly on the cave or cellar walls. (The name saltpeter comes from the Latin *sal petra,* or salt of the rock.) Once such industries had been developed by the turn of the fifteenth century, the supply of gunpowder increased rapidly and its cost declined greatly. As gunpowder supplies increased, cannons initially became extremely large, in an attempt to hurl the largest stone possible and end a siege quickly. Once again, the technology of offense took the lead, and the technology of defense—castle building—was forced to respond in the sixteenth century. Smaller firearms, such as arquebuses and muskets, were not used in battle until the mid fifteenth century or later. Gunpowder also became more powerful as it was better refined. Initially seen as a complement to archers or crossbowmen, handgunners later became their replacements. As a spin-off of gunpowder artillery, incendiaries and "fireworks" became the mainstay of gunner's training. Such flammable mixtures were useful in war for burning enemy defenses, ships, and towns, which were largely made of wood and often had thatched roofs. In peacetime the gunners were called upon to provide fireworks for fêtes and celebrations such as weddings, coronations, and military victories. By the end of the Middle Ages, the main technologies of warfare had shifted from swords and catapults to firearms, and modern warfare was born.

Sources:

Jim Bradbury, *The Medieval Siege* (Woodbridge: Boydell Press, 1992).

Ivy A. Corfis and Michael Wolfe, *The Medieval City under Siege* (Woodbridge: Boydell Press, 1995).

Kelly DeVries, *Medieval Military Technology* (Peterborough, Ont. & Lewiston, N.Y.: Broadview Press, 1992).

William Hardy McNeill, *The Pursuit of Power: Technology, Armed Force, and Society since A.D. 1000* (Chicago: University of Chicago Press, 1982).

R. Ewart Oakeshott, *The Archaeology of Weapons: Arms and Armour from Prehistory to the Age of Chivalry* (London: Lutterworth Press, 1960).

WELL-BEING: GALEN'S LEGACY

Ancient Roots. As in the rest of science, the medieval world inherited its theories of health from the ancients and based its attempts at remedies on a simplistic and idealized understanding of how the human body works. The most important source of medical knowledge came from a Greek doctor named Galen, who was the personal physician to Emperor Marcus Aurelius in the first century C.E. Galen wrote hundreds of works, and at least 120 of his works on medicine survived to the Middle Ages. Some of his works were available in Latin as early as the fifth century and continued to be translated from the Greek or from Arabic translations from the tenth to the fifteenth centuries. Galen's most important contributions to medieval medicine were the theories of the humors and pneuma (spirit). The idea of humors apparently originated in the fifth century B.C.E. with Hippocrates (whose name lives on in the Hippocratic oath that all doctors still take), and the idea of pneuma was also ancient, but Galen's name is attached to both concepts because he was the best-known writer on the topic.

The Four Humors. In the Galenic system the body is composed of four substances: blood, phlegm, black bile (also known as "choler") and yellow bile (or "melancholer"). Each humor is produced in a different organ of the body: blood in the heart, phlegm in the brain, black bile in the spleen, and yellow bile in the liver. Each humor holds a position analogous to one of the Aristotelian elements and is in fact associated with its corresponding element although they are not one and the same. And, like elements and qualities, the four humors act in opposition to each other according to simple principles. When a person became unhealthy, ancient and medieval people believed that the humors were "out of balance" and designed treatments to restore the natural balance of those humors. The English language still includes phrases that derive from this belief, such as saying that someone is melancholic (too much yellow bile) if sad or phlegmatic (too much phlegm) if listless. A lethargic person was believed to have too much blood, and the doctors called for bloodletting. In mild cases leaches were attached to the patient's arms or abdomen to draw off blood, but in cases a doctor considered acute, the patient might actually be cut and allowed to bleed freely until "sufficient" blood had been drained. Modern medicine does recognize that blood loss stimulates new blood production,

THE HUMORS AND FOOD

Hildegard of Bingen, well known for her knowledge of medicinal plants, related her views on diet to the theory of humors:

If a person eats cold dishes in the summer when he is very hot inside, he easily develops gout [and] builds up phlegm in himself. For that reason, a person should eat moderately hot and cold dishes in the summer, and these will give him good blood and healthy flesh. If a person eats a lot in the summer, when he is very hot within, his blood will become excessively warm because of the great quantity of food; his humours will degenerate, and the flesh of his body will swell up and become unnaturally distended because the air is warm. . . . [When] he is overjoyed, he should eat only moderately, for then his blood is scattered by widening of the blood path. Otherwise the humours release strong fever attacks into his blood if he eats a lot at that time.

Source: Hildegard of Bingen. *Holistic Healing, A Translation of Liber compositae medicinea,* translated by Manfred Pawlik, Patrick Madigan, and John Kulas; edited by Kulas and Mary Palmquist (Collegeville, Minn.: Liturgical Press, 1994), pp. 104-105.

which can help some illnesses, but medieval doctors seem to have believed in the adage "that which does not kill you, makes you stronger."

Pneuma. Galen's theory of pneuma, or spirit, explains how it is that living creatures differ from inanimate lumps of matter, even though they are made of the same four elements. Pneuma is the vital spirit and life force of living creatures, and Galen employed this concept to describe how people breathe in air and eat food. From his work on dissection, he correctly differentiated the cardiovascular system (blood), the respiratory system (air), and the nervous system (brain and spinal cord), and assigned a pneuma to each. While this theoretical understanding permeated the universities, another tradition, deriving from the late Roman tradition, provided the foundation of practical health in the Middle Ages.

Sources:

Donald Edward Henry Campbell, *Arabian Medicine and Its Influence on the Middle Ages* (London: Kegan Paul, Trench, Trübner, 1926).

Benjamin Lee Gordon, *Medieval and Renaissance Medicine* (New York: Philosophical Press, 1959).

Robert Steven Gottfried, *Doctors and Medicine in Medieval England, 1340–1530* (Princeton: Princeton University Press, 1986).

Monica Helen Green, *Women's Healthcare in the Medieval West: Texts and Contexts* (Burlington, Vt.: Ashgate/Variorum, 2000).

Stanley Rubin, *Medieval English Medicine* (Newton Abbot, U.K.: David & Charles, 1974).

Nancy G. Siraisi, *Medieval & Early Renaissance Medicine: An Introduction to Knowledge and Practice* (Chicago: University of Chicago Press, 1990).

WELL-BEING: HEALTH PRACTITIONERS

Preserving Ancient Knowledge. For the first half of the Middle Ages there were no great leaps in medical treatment, but old knowledge was preserved and disseminated by monasteries, where monks copied and recopied works of the ancient authors. They also extracted and epitomized the ideas of these authors in *antidotaria* (collections of antidotes) and *receptaria* (collections of prescriptions) for restorative and preventative health, respectively. In order to preserve and extend this knowledge, a medical school was established in Salerno, south of Rome, in the ninth century. Other medical schools followed at Montpelier (1181) and Padua (1222). There were also medieval faculties at the Universities of Paris, Bologna, and Oxford, founded in 1110, 1113, and 1167, respectively. Beginning in the twelfth century, as more and more ancient knowledge began to enter Europe, a desire to understand and extend the learning of the ancients (and their Arabic commentators) promoted a culture of experimentation at Salerno. As in mathematics and physics, Arabic scholars had preserved Greek knowledge of medicine and added to it Indian and even some Chinese learning. Salerno provided a center for the translation and dissemination of this knowledge.

Medical Treatment. Salernian doctors discoursed on the four-humor theory, but they also inquired into the fabric of the body. Dissections of pigs and other mammals shed light on skeletal structure, organ types and connections, the nervous system, musculature, and ophthalmological questions. Their *antidotaria* not only fixed the standards for preparing drugs (including the old apothecaries' weights of grains, scruples, and drams) but also prescribed how these drugs were to be administered.

The four standard delivery methods were plasters and ointments for absorption through the skin, syrups for imbibing plant extracts, fumigations for the inhalation of medicines, and "electuaries," or powdered remedies, that could be taken internally. Begun as attempts to transmute metals, alchemical investigations also provided many of the skills and experimental procedures that healers needed to create new medicines.

Prevention. In general, people sought help from medical doctors only after the onset of sickness. One area of their expertise, however, was designed to be preventative: astrology. Universities provided astrological training along with medical training, and since both sought to understand and predict future events—such as the right time to conceive or embark on a trip and the restitution of the patient's health—it was natural that they should be used together.

Practitioners. Learned doctors in the Roman period had largely divested themselves of the manual and messy routines of surgery, care, and prescribing medicaments to their patients. They concentrated on higher theory, a trend that continued until the sixteenth century. This division of theory and practice runs parallel to the steadfast separation of science from technology in the Middle Ages. To fill the need for medical practitioners who would care for the sick and injured, barber-surgeons took up the knife; midwives took care of obstetrical needs; apothecaries provided medicines; and nurses prepared healing cuisine for their patients. For traumatic injuries such as wounds in warfare, falls from roofs, or industrial accidents, there was often little doctors could do, but these limitations did not stop practitioners

Medieval doctors advising patients who suffer from vomiting, fainting, toothache, and a hair problem; illumination from a fourteenth-century medical book (British Library, London)

from trying. Dissection of humans and animals was practiced quite widely throughout the Middle Ages, so surgeons were knowledgeable about and quite adept at repairing soft-tissue damage. Damage to the internal organs, however, was more often than not fatal. While the ancient world knew how to perform such delicate operations as eye surgery and while this tradition continued in Islam, medieval European surgeons were not so knowledgeable or able. The Western medieval world made do with amputations and splints, and with trepanation, the process of boring holes in the skull to relieve excess pressure. Anesthetics based on opium, mandragora, or other narcotics made surgery bearable, but postrecovery infections were a serious problem.

Prayer. Linked to all medieval healing strategies was Christianity. Doctors, who were trained at medical schools, were also clerics, and their medical ministries were in no way distinct from their theological ministrations. Even lay medical practitioners used belief as the backbone to their ministrations. Patients with specific ills were given over to the care of individual saints who specialized in those ailments. For example, patients and practitioners prayed to St. Vitus to cure convulsions, to St. Blasius for respiratory and tracheal diseases, and to St. John for difficulties with the legs and feet. The reputation of many a saint was founded on stories of how he or she had brought about miraculous cures. Many ill people undertook pilgrimages to saints' shrines, where they hoped to be cured by seeing, touching, or buying a relic.

Consequently, many churches that housed saints' relics were visited by large numbers of ailing pilgrims and set up infirmaries to treat or at least comfort them. These ecclesiastical infirmaries were often the basis for the formal hospitals that began to appear in the late Middle Ages.

Sources:
Darrel W. Amundsen, *Medicine, Society, and Faith in the Ancient and Medieval Worlds* (Baltimore & London: Johns Hopkins University Press, 1996).

Vern L. Bullough, *The Development of Medicine as a Profession: The Contribution of the Medieval University to Modern Medicine* (New York: Hafner, 1966).

Peter Murray Jones, *Medieval Medicine in Illuminated Manuscripts* (London: British Library, 1998).

Nancy G. Siraisi and Luke Demaitre, eds. *Science, Medicine and the University, 1200–1550: Essays in Honor of Pearl Kibre* (St. Louis: Saint Louis University Library, 1976).

Patricia Skinner, *Health and Medicine in Early Medieval Southern Italy* (Leiden & New York: E. J. Brill, 1997).

WELL-BEING: HEALTH REGIMENS

Theory and Practice Meet. One place at which medieval medical theory and practice came together was in the recommended *regimina sanitatis*, or "regimens of health," that learned physicians drew up for their wealthy patients. The central feature of most of these plans was the list of "six things non-natural" that the wise patient was told to regulate in order to keep in good health. These "non-naturals" were things that would today be called cultural or habitual aspects of daily life—as opposed to "natural" things, such as the pulse, over which one has little control, or wholly "unnatural" things, such as being wounded in battle. In most medical works the non-naturals that a patient should regulate were listed as

Exercise versus Rest
Sleep versus Awake
Fasting versus Feasting
Air (such as Fresh, Foul, or Stagnant)
Food and Drink
Mental States (such as Agitation and Melancholia)

The first three non-naturals were, in good medieval Aristotelian fashion, expressed as pairs of opposites while the remaining three were generic categories. The well-advised patient was told to try to breathe only fresh, pure air, and avoid airs thought to contain "miasmas," or harmful vapors, that might injure the health. If forced to confront foul odor or stagnant air, one might hold to his or her nose a handkerchief scented with peppermint or rosemary to ward off the worst effects. Exercise, usually in the form of walking or horseback riding, was recommended in moderation, along with periods of rest between bouts of activity. Throughout medieval regimens, the emphasis is on moderation: regular periods of sleep were recommended and in sufficient amounts to make being awake both possible and pleasant. Feasting was a highly regarded activity in the Middle Ages, and fasting was a religious duty. Health regimens counseled the reader to avoid extremes in either case.

Psychology. Mental states, or the psychological condition of the patient, was given special emphasis. Medieval doctors knew that depressed ("melancholic") people got sick more easily and healed more slowly than cheerful, optimistic people, and they were familiar with a host of mental illnesses as well. They blamed these conditions, as well as physical illnesses, on imbalances in the four humors, and they prescribed regular, moderate, wholesome activities as the best antidote. Medieval doctors had a humane concern for mental distress and did not employ heroic or barbaric methods to overcome mental illness, even in severe cases. Only after the Middle Ages did "scientific" medicine begin to torment the mentally ill in misguided attempts to "cure" them.

Diet. By far the biggest category among the non-naturals was "Food and Drink." Medieval people—at least those people with enough money to have a regimen composed for them—tried hard to maintain good health by controlling what they ate. Considering things such as whether his patient was male or female, old or young, fat or thin, and melancholic or choleric—a physician took pains to assess the condition of the individual and to prescribe a diet intended to maintain the optimal balance of the four humors of that person. These recommendations usually also included recipes for preparing special foods; certain types of stewed chicken, for example, were held to be especially beneficial to people with weak digestion. Such recipes passed out of the realm of "food for the sick" and became main courses or side dishes for everyday consumption.

The modern diet cookbook, designed to teach people how to "eat better" or "cook healthy," has its origin in these late medieval regimens and their emphasis on food and drink as part of a balanced lifestyle.

Sources:.
Darrel W. Amundsen, *Medicine, Society, and Faith in the Ancient and Medieval Worlds* (Baltimore & London: Johns Hopkins University Press, 1996).

Sheila Campbell, Bert Hall, and David Klausner, eds. *Health, Disease, and Healing in Medieval Culture* (New York: St. Martin's Press, 1992).

Faye Marie Getz, *Healing and Society in Medieval England: A Middle English Translation of the Pharmaceutical Writings of Gilbertus Anglicus* (Madison: University of Wisconsin Press, 1991).

Thomas Francis Graham, *Medieval Minds: Mental Health in The Middle Ages* (London: Allen & Unwin, 1967).

Monica Helen Green, *Women's Healthcare in the Medieval West: Texts and Contexts* (Burlington, Vt.: Ashgate/Variorum, 2000).

Edward J. Kealey, *Medieval Medicus: A Social History of Anglo-Norman Medicine* (Baltimore: Johns Hopkins University Press, 1981).

Simon Kemp, *Medieval Psychology* (New York: Greenwood Press, 1990).

Carole Rawcliffe, *Medicine & Society in Later Medieval England* (Stroud, U.K.: Alan Sutton, 1995).

Rawcliffe, *Sources for the History of Medicine in Late Medieval England* (Kalamazoo, Mich.: Western Michigan University, 1995).

Nancy G. Siraisi, *Medieval & Early Renaissance Medicine: An Introduction to Knowledge and Practice* (Chicago: University of Chicago Press, 1990).

WELL-BEING: HERBALS

Medicinal Plants. For the average person without easy or affordable access to doctors, many cures and preventatives were available through the tradition of the *materia medica* (medical matters), a survival of the late Roman world. This body of works describes hundreds of plants and their medicinal uses, as well as preventative regimens that were believed to lessen the chances of illness. In monasteries, palaces, and in most towns and villages "herbaria," or herb gardens, were kept to grow the vegetables, plants, and herbs used for medical treatments. They were generally laid out in a grid fashion, a trend begun by the influential Benedictine monastery of St. Gall in Switzerland during the ninth century. Many of the plants in the herbaria were ornamental as well as medicinal, and all were practical. Lilies not only look and smell good, but their roots were used to treat skin maladies such as ulcers, warts, and corns. Many flowers produced pigments for dyes, inks, and paints, as well as medicines such as purgatives and soporifics. Hildegard of Bingen (1098–1179), a German mystic and prioress who organized a school for nurses, grew more than forty kinds of medicinal plants and described some more that could be gathered locally in her two books on simple (found in nature) and compound (manufactured) medicines. Combining basic Galenic medical theories with the lore of European folk medicine and remedies, she interpreted both bodies of knowledge in a theological framework but rarely let her medicine become compromised by overriding moral or religious concerns. Her popular writings, which were copied and recopied throughout the Middle Ages, became some of the earliest printed works by a female writer on science and medicine.

Albertus Magnus's description of the daffodil in his *Book of Secrets* is typical of many of his botanical descriptions in its mix of firsthand observations with information from sources of varying reliability.

There be seven herbs that have great virtues, after the mind of Alexander the Emperor, and they have these virtues of the influence of the planets. And therefore, every one of the time taketh their virtue from the higher natural powers.

The first is the herb of the planet Saturn, which is called *Daffodillus*, Daffodilly. The juice of it is good against the pain of the reins [kidneys], and legs; let them that suffer pain of the bladder, eat it, the root of it being a little boiled. And if men possessed with evil spirits, or mad men, bear it in a clean napkin, they be delivered from their disease. And it suffreth not a devil in the house. And if children that breed their teeth, bear it about them, they shall breed them without [teething] pain. And it is good that a man bear with him a root of it in the night for he shall not fear, nor be hurt of other.

Source: Albertus Magnus, *The Book of Secrets*, edited by Michael R. Best and Frank H. Brightman (Oxford: Clarendon Press, 1973).

Entry in a twelfth-century herbal recommending crowsfoot for dog bites and nosebleeds
(British Library, London)

Household Remedies. A type of medieval manuscript created for the management of manors, called a *hausbuch* (house-book) in German, often contained many recipes for herbal medicines and their uses. Some of the advice—such as the suggestion to take purgatives for what is now called food poisoning—is sound. Modern analysis of the many birth-control methods and abortifacients has shown many to be quite effective. Other recipes were of dubious use, but probably of little harm, and were nonetheless widely repeated for the inexorable logic behind them. These recipes often relied on what is known as "sympathetic magic," the belief that the appearance of objects and substances "advertised" their use. Therefore, walnuts were given to cure migraine headaches because the walnut looks like a miniature brain, and turnips were used to treat impotence because of their resemblance to the affected part of the anatomy.

Herbals. The remedies of the *materia medica* were quite effective, but since they derived from the Roman tradition, as this body of work spread northward, many of the recipes became useless because the ingredients in them did not grow north of the Alps. The many new ingredients that did exist in the region, however, inspired an interest in botany, and, incidentally, mineralogy (as in the work of Albertus Magnus), as scholars attempted to understand the properties and uses of all manner of natural substances. The extended manuals they produced became known collectively as medieval herbals, and—from Spain to Scandinavia and Ireland to Austria—they were widely copied and extracted throughout the Middle Ages. As the tradition spread and grew, it also inspired a need for accurate description and illustration, two hallmarks of the inductive scientific method. An herbal is not much use if its readers cannot reliably tell one plant from another, and by the fourteenth century, European artists had begun to strive for a more naturalistic depiction of plant life. By the mid fifteenth century, herbals were extremely common, with more and more accurate illustrations, rivaling and often surpassing their ancient exemplars.

Sources:

Wilfrid Blunt and Sandra Raphael, *The Illustrated Herbal* (Oxford: Oxford University Press, 1979).

Bodley Herbal and Bestiary, Medieval manuscripts in microform, Major treasures in the Bodleian Library, no. 8 (Oxford: Oxford Microform Publications / Toronto: University of Toronto Press, 1978.

Sheila Campbell, Bert Hall, and David Klausner, eds. *Health, Disease, and Healing in Medieval Culture* (New York: St. Martin's Press, 1992).

Minta Collins, *Medieval Herbals: The Illustrative Traditions* (London: British Library / Toronto: University of Toronto Press, 2000).

Margaret Beam Freeman, *Herbs for the Mediaeval Household, for Cooking, Healing and Divers Uses* (New York: Metropolitan Musuem of Art, 1971).

Benjamin Lee Gordon, *Medieval and Renaissance Medicine* (New York: Philosophical Press, 1959).

Monica Helen Green, *Women's Healthcare in the Medieval West: Texts and Contexts* (Burlington, Vt.: Ashgate/Variorum, 2000).

John Hooper Harvey, *Mediaeval Gardens* (Beaverton, Ore.: Timber Press, 1981).

Stanley Rubin, *Medieval English Medicine* (Newton Abbot, U.K.: David & Charles, 1974).

SIGNIFICANT PEOPLE

ALBERTUS MAGNUS

CIRCA 1200 – 1280
NATURAL PHILOSOPHER

The Great Doctor. The patron saint of natural scientists and known in his lifetime as "The Great Doctor," Albertus Magnus (Albert the Great) was one of the most important scientific polymaths of the Middle Ages. In the natural sciences he is known for his clear, accurate observations and his dispelling of erroneous beliefs through careful investigation.

Education and Career. The son of a German knight, Albertus was born near Lauingen in Bavaria and educated at the University of Padua, where he decided in 1223 to join the Dominican order. He undertook further study at the University of Paris in the early 1240s, and after graduating master in theology in 1245 he taught there for several years. He established a school at Cologne in 1248 and served as an administrator in the German Dominican order during the 1250s and as bishop of Regensberg in 1259–1261.

Explaining Aristotle. Albertus's importance as a scientist is based on his efforts to paraphrase and write commentaries on all the works of Aristotle—an ambitious project that he began in 1250 and worked at until 1269. In writing on Aristotle, Albertus commented on mechanics, gravitation, optics, acoustics, thermodynamics, astronomy, zoology, biology, botany, mineralogy, medicine, dentistry, and veterinary science. In cases where Aristotle's work on a particular topic no longer existed (or never had), Albertus filled in what he believed was missing and supplemented it with Arabic writers' works, which in many cases went far beyond those of the ancient writers. In his writings on natural science Albertus demonstrated his keen observational character, supplementing Aristotle's works on animals, plants, and stones with many firsthand observations.

Scientific Method. Albertus firmly established that a scientific principle must correspond to one's observation or it cannot be considered true. Similarly, while he generally supported Aristotelian ideas, he was willing to point out errors in Aristotle and his commentators. Albertus also considered some Platonic and Neoplatonic ideas, but he generally rejected their interpretations of the physical world. He believed that mathematics was essential to the understanding of physics and that metaphysics was essential to the understanding of mathematics; thus, physics and natural things were directly linked to theological speculations. To him mathematics was the language of nature but a subsidiary tool to discover higher truths.

Sainthood. Albertus was beatified in 1622, nearly two and a half centuries after his death, but the canonization process was halted because of charges that he had engaged in sorcery. He was finally canonized in 1931 and declared a saint ten years later.

Sources:

Albertus Magnus, *On Animals: A Medieval Summa Zoologica*, 2 volumes, translated and annotated by Kenneth F. Kitchell Jr. and Irven Michael Resnick (Baltimore: Johns Hopkins University Press, 1999).

Albertus Magnus, *The Book of Minerals*, edited and translated by Dorothy Wycoff (Oxford: Clarendon Press, 1967).

Albertus Magnus, *The Book of Secrets*, edited by Michael R. Best and Frank H. Brightman (Oxford: Clarendon Press, 1973).

B. B. Price, "Albert the Great (Albertus Magnus)," in *Dictionary of Literary Biography*, volume 115: *Medieval Philosophers*, edited by Jeremiah Hackett (Detroit & London: Bruccoli Clark Layman / Gale Research, 1992), pp. 15–23.

James A. Weisheipl, ed., *Albertus Magnus and the Sciences: Commemorative Essays 1980*. (Toronto: Pontifical Institute of Mediaeval Studies, 1980).

ARNALD DE VILLANOVA

CIRCA 1240 - 1311
PHYSICIAN

Health Regimens. Arnald de Villanova is best known for his practical health guides, or regimens, which exerted a strong influence on the Western medical tradition in the later Middle Ages.

Medical Education and Practice. A medical student from Valencia, Arnald was studying at the University of Montpelier in France by about 1260. In 1281 he became the personal physician to Peter III and Alfonso III of Aragon (in modern Spain) and remained there until 1291. He then became a master at Montpelier, where he was fundamental in establishing Scholastic medical studies. Despite his rather unorthodox theological views, Arnald's considerable skills as a physician kept him in good graces with both university authorities and the Vatican. The health regimens he wrote for various royal patrons in the early fourteenth century cover a wide variety of subjects from diet and exercise to childbirth and gallstones, and his advice seems to have rested more on proven experience than on theories or authorities. Arnald also translated Arabic works on the heart, drugs, and health regimens, having easy access to these manuscripts while in residence in Spain. Some of these works were part of the core medical texts used at Montpelier after a papal decree of 1309 that established fifteen Greek and Arab texts as the basis for the curriculum at the school.

Medical Theory. Concerned with both the practical application of medicine and its theoretical underpinnings, Arnald investigated the Western and Eastern works on Galenic medicine and often fused his interpretations with his Christian theological views of humanity and the cosmos. Further, he borrowed mathematical ideas of intensity from the Arabic philosophers al-Kindi and Averroës and suggested that the intensity of a remedy was proportional to the ratio of the Aristotelian qualities of its ingredients (for example, hot/cold or wet/dry). Because he commingled practical operations and theoretical speculation, scholars of the fourteenth and fifteenth centuries associated Arnald with the alchemical tradition; yet, he never considered alchemy a legitimate art.

Sources:
Michael McVaugh, "Arnald de Villanova, in *Dictionary of Scientific Biography,* edited by Charles Coulston Gillispie (New York: Scribner, 1970), I: 289–291.

McVaugh, "Arnald of Villanova and Bradwardine's Law," *Isis,* 58 (1967): 56–64.

Joseph Ziegler, *Medicine and Religion, c. 1300: The Case of Arnau de Vilanova* (Oxford: Clarendon Press; New York: Oxford University Press, 1998).

ROGER BACON

CIRCA 1214/1220 - CIRCA 1292
NATURAL PHILOSOPHER

Experimental Method. An early advocate of employing direct, accurate observation and related mathematical analysis to test the theories of earlier scientists, Roger Bacon also wrote important works on logic, semantics, and semiotics.

Education and Career. Little is known about Bacon's life. Some scholars believe he was born around 1220 while others place his birth date at about 1214. He studied at Oxford University and then began a career as a professor of philosophy at the University of Paris in about 1237. For about a decade he lectured there on Aristotle and pseudo-Aristotelian texts, and on the "new" logic, which was more complex than the old Aristotelian logic. Thirteenth-century scholars employed the new logic to develop a *logica modernorum* (modern logic), which involved some new methods of semantics. In about 1248 Bacon left teaching and for the next nine years devoted his financial resources to the study of languages, experiments, and "books of secrets" (works on subjects such as alchemy, medicine, and statecraft). In 1280 Bacon produced his edition one of the best-known books of secrets, the pseudo-Aristotelian *Secretum Secretorum* (The Secret of Secrets), a work of political education for a prince, which also includes a medical and scientific section.

Scientific Works. After becoming a Franciscan friar in about 1257, Bacon continued his studies, and during the 1260s he published his *Opus maius* (Great Work) and related writings—including *Communia naturalium* (Common Account of Natural Things), his outline for an encyclopedia of the sciences. His *Opus maius* is in seven parts, which cover the academic situation of the time, philosophy and theology, language, applications of mathematics, optics, experimental science, and moral philosophy. The section on optics includes a full physiological description of the eye and the optic nerve and describes a "separate science of vision" through which and without which other sciences cannot be known. That is, he considered optics the key to a universal science because vision allows the scientist to test theory with experience. The section on experimental science again emphasizes the need to test theory with observation. Bacon also applied a practical approach to his ideas on medicine, and he sought to put education on a scientific and experimental basis, hoping the bring about the moral and religious reform of society and church.

Sources:
A. C. Crombie and J. D. North, "Roger Bacon," in *Dictionary of Scientific Biography,* edited by Charles Coulston Gillispie (New York: Scribner, 1970), I: 377–385;

Jeremiah Hackett, "Roger Bacon and Aristotelianism," *Vivarium,* 35, no. 2 (1997): 129–135.

Hackett, ed., *Roger Bacon and the Sciences: Commemorative Essays* (Leiden & New York: E. J. Brill, 1997).

JEAN BURIDAN

CIRCA 1295 - CIRCA 1358
PROFESSOR

Contributions to Science. Probably the most distinguished and influential teacher at the University of Paris during the first half of the fourteenth century, Jean Buridan did little experimental science himself but helped to lay the groundwork for the modern conception of science based on experimentation and observation rather than on "final" causes (that is, the *how* rather than the *why* of phenomena). He did important work in logic, reorganizing the *Summary of Logic* of the thirteenth-century scholar Peter of Spain, and he helped to develop the tradition of Nominalism in the philosophy of language. For the Nominalist individual beings and things alone are real. Ideas and Universals are just names. They are not real entities in nature.

Education and Career. After studying philosophy at the University of Paris, Buridan began teaching there and served as university rector. Before Buridan, most scholars taught for only two years before going on to other careers; Buridan broke with tradition and became the first scholar to pursue a university career in the arts. Like many of his contemporaries, Buridan spent most of his career explaining and extending Aristotelian works of logic, grammar, mathematics (physics), and astronomy. His preferred method was to ask a series of *Questiones* about particular points in Aristotle, present various interpretations and answers, and then pass judgment on these views. In this way he preserved and extended the Aristotelian corpus and other thinkers' ideas as well. During his career Buridan wrote *Questiones* on Aristotle's *Physics, On Heaven and Earth,* and several of his nonscientific works.

Legitimizing Science. Buridan was important for making science (natural philosophy) a legitimate study within the university and for effectively and successfully defining scientific investigation in such a way that it prevented the domination of science by theology. He taught that the behavior of the natural world should be described by a series of observational generalizations (inductive reasoning), rather than from metaphysical (that is, theological) presuppositions (deductive reasoning). Consequently, he argued that supernatural causes should not be admitted as scientific explanations of natural events—though they could, of course, explain miraculous events.

Motion. Buridan's most important specific contribution to medieval science was an inversion of the accepted understanding of motion. Aristotle had proposed that "anything that is moved, is moved by something," thus implying that any projectile could only move as long as another force was pushing it. Buridan suggested instead that a projectile contains a quantity of motive force within itself that has been given to it by the force that initially propelled it. This idea was not new, but Buridan went one step further and proposed that the force does not drain away on its own, but only if there is another, opposing, outside force. He therefore laid the groundwork for the idea perfected by Sir Isaac Newton in the seventeenth century: "Objects in motion tend to remain in motion unless acted upon by an outside force." Buridan also raised questions about whether the earth stood still under rotating heavens or rotated under fixed heavens. He realized that either explanation would produce the same observed effects, but that the idea of a rotating earth was preferable because it put fewer things in motion (one earth versus thousands of stars).

Sources:

Marshall Clagett, *The Science of Mechanics in the Middle Ages* (Madison: University of Wisconsin Press, 1959).

Ernest A. Moody, "Jean Buridan," in *Dictionary of Scientific Biography,* edited by Charles Coulston Gillispie (New York: Scribner, 1970–1980), II: 603–608.

J. M. M. H. Thijssen and Jack Zupko, *The Metaphysics and Natural Philosophy of John Buridan* (Leiden & Boston: E. J. Brill, 2001).

CONSTANTINE THE AFRICAN

FLOURISHED 1065-1085
MEDICAL SCHOLAR

After learning that Italian cities and monasteries had no medical texts, the man known only as Constantine the African took a set of Arabic medical manuscripts to the medical school at Salerno, where he translated them into Latin. Born in Carthage (in present-day Tunisia), where he had been a merchant, Constantine settled at the monastery of Montecassino soon after his arrival in Italy. Becoming a Benedictine monk, he continued to introduce Arabic and classical medical knowledge into Europe. While he did bring works by Hippocrates and Galen, he apparently was primarily interested in passing on Arab medical ideas, which were significantly more advanced than European ones at the time. Many of the translations are so heavily augmented by Constantine's own practical information that he effectively became an important author in his own right. He was concerned with both theory and practice and wrote treatises on specific subjects such as stomach ailments and various surgeries. His writings and the translations of ancient and Arabic authors—as well as those continued by his disciple, Johannes Afflacius—formed the core of the medical curriculum at Salerno for much of the Middle Ages, encouraging medieval physicians to combine and reconcile theoretical and practical medical knowledge.

Sources:

A. G. Chevalier, "Constantinus Africanus and the Influence of the Arabs on Salerno," *Ciba Symposium,* 5 (1944): 1725–1731.

Michael McVaugh, "Constantine the African," in *Dictionary of Scientific Biography,* edited by Charles Coulston Gillispie (New York: Scribner, 1970–1980), III: 393–395.

Mary Frances Wack, *Lovesickness in the Middle Ages: The Viaticum and Its Commentaries* (Philadelphia: University of Pennsylvania Press, 1990).

ROBERT GROSSETESTE

CIRCA 1168 - 1253
CHANCELLOR OF THE UNIVERSITY OF OXFORD AND BISHOP OF LINCOLN

Linking Science and Theology. Robert Grosseteste greatly influenced English scientific thinking by directing the interests of Franciscans there toward natural philosophy and mathematics. Grosseteste (which means "of the large head") wrote some of the first commentaries on Aristotle's physical-science works and composed his own treatises on astronomy, cosmology, comets, motion, sound, heat, light, optics, and the rainbow. He is known for promoting the search for rational and consistent explanations that incorporate natural and divine evidence, and he was also was one of the first scholastic thinkers to try to reconcile the Bible and Church Fathers with the Aristotelian works that were then available in Latin.

Education and Career. By 1190, Grosseteste, who had studied at the University of Oxford, was a member of the household of Bishop William de Vere in Hereford, then a center for scientific and theological knowledge. Sometime after 1198 he began teaching at Oxford, and in 1209 he went to the University of Paris to study theology. Returning to Oxford in 1214, he became chancellor in about 1225. As chancellor, he made the study of languages and the sciences an important part of the curriculum, at a time when the University of Paris placed a heavy emphasis on theology and forbade the study of natural science—especially the "pagan" works of Aristotle and his Arab commentators. He left the university in 1229 but remained in Oxford, where he taught young Franciscan friars until 1235, when he was elected bishop of Lincoln, then the largest diocese in England. As bishop he organized a team of scholars to translate Greek and Hebrew works into Latin.

Studies of Light. For Grosseteste, the fundamental building block of the universe was light, through which God's power was manifested in the world. Consequently, he tried to explain the propagation of light (and sound), colors, reflection and refraction, and even the generation of stars. Although he did not necessarily achieve his goal of advancing a theological understanding of these phenomena, he did develop the medieval science of optics and the related mathematics—the geometry for describing how rays travel and the ratio theory for expressing intensities. He also broadened the concept of *light* to include the general idea of a fundamental, divine "power," which then led him to consider the motion of the tides, sound, and comets. Although his explanations seem farfetched to modern readers, they were groundbreaking in the Middle Ages because they introduced the idea that these things have natural explanations.

Sources:
A. C. Crombie, "Robert Grosseteste," in *Dictionary of Scientific Biography*, edited by Charles Coulston Gillispie (New York: Scribner, 1970–1980), V: 548–554.

Crombie, *Robert Grosseteste and the Origins of Experimental Science, 1100–1700* (Oxford: Clarendon Press, 1953).

Jeremiah Hackett, "Robert Grosseteste," in *Dictionary of Literary Biography*, volume 115: *Medieval Philosophers*, edited by Hackett (Detroit & London: Bruccoli Clark Layman / Gale Research, 1992), pp. 225–235.

NICOLE ORESME

CIRCA 1320 - 1382
NATURAL PHILOSOPHER

Popularizing Science. A scholar of mathematics and natural philosophy (mainly celestial physics), Nicole Oresme devoted a great deal of his time to translating works of natural philosophy from Latin into French for secular audiences, thus popularizing a scientific understanding of the world.

Education and Career. A student of Jean Buridan at Paris and secretary to the household of King John II of France, Oresme divided his time between the University of Paris, where he taught, and the cathedral of Rouen, where he was named canon in 1362 and dean in 1364. In 1377 he was elected bishop of Lisieux and was consecrated the following year.

Scientific Contributions. A vigorous campaigner against astrology, Oresme argued successfully that whether the earth rotated daily while the heavens stood still or the heavens rotated and the earth was still, it would appear the same to people on earth, so there is no necessary reason to assume one or the other. Like other Scholastic thinkers of his day, Oresme spent much time debating Aristotelian ideas and explanations for natural phenomena, but by the mid fourteenth century, European thought had added so many new and different non-Aristotelian explanations for natural behaviors that he also began explore some "modern" concepts. Accepting Buridan's idea of impetus to explain motion, he proposed that the heavens operate like a giant mechanical clock, but his theory also maintained a role for divine action in the heavens. His most fundamental contribution to science was to the understanding of how various forces, velocities, resistances, and other quantities—are related through ratios.

Sources:
Edward Grant, "Jean Buridan and Nicole Oresme on Natural Science," *Vivarium: Journal for Mediaevel Philosophy and the Intellectual Life of the Middle Ages*, 31 (1993): 84–105.

A. George Molland, "Nicole Oresme and Scientific Progress," in *Antiqui und moderni*, edited by Albert Zimmermann (Berlin: deGruyter, 1974), pp. 206–220.

Nicole Oresme, *Nicole Oresme and the Kinematics of Circular Motion: Tractatus de commensurabilitate vel incommensurabilitate motuum celi*, edited and translated by Edward Grant (Madison: University of Wisconsin Press, 1971).

Oresme, *Nicole Oresme and the Medieval Geometry of Qualities and Motions: A Treatise on the Uniformity and Difformity of Intensities Known as Tractatus de configurationibus qualitatum et motuum*, edited and translated by Marshall Clagett (Madison: University of Wisconsin Press, 1968).

PETER OF MARICOURT

FLOURISHED 1260S
ENGINEER

Experimental Method. Also known as Peter Peregrinus (the Pilgrim) of Maricourt, Peter of Maricourt was a French engineer whose *De magnete* (On the Magnet), written on 8 August 1269, is the first major medieval scientific-experimental treatise composed in Western Europe.

Life and Writings. Peter's birth and death dates are unknown, and little is known about his life, except that he wrote his treatise while an engineer in the army of Charles I of Anjou during his siege of Lucerna, Italy. In *De magnete*, written in the form of a letter to a knight named Siger de Foucecourt, Peter castigated reliance on reason alone, stressing experimentation, manual skill, and technique as crucial to science.

Experiments with Magnetism. Peter's work on the magnet, which was used in the Renaissance by William Gilbert in his work *On the Magnet* (1600), describes how to construct a magnet so that the polar north can be found. In Peter's experiment, a needle is placed on the magnet at various points, and each time it comes to rest, a line is drawn. The results demonstrate that the meridians meet at the poles. Another of Peter's experiments shows that a needle placed in a wooden bowl in a large container of water will invariably point north. Peter also discussed the relation of the magnet to iron and the theory of magnetic attraction and repulsion, and he suggested that magnetic instruments could provide new technologies, describing, for example, a perpetual-motion machine and the compass.

Source:

Edward Grant, "Peter Peregrinus," in *Dictionary of Scientific Biography*, edited by Charles Coulston Gillispie (New York: Scribner, 1970–1980), 10: 532–539.

DOCUMENTARY SOURCES

Albertus Magnus, *De Vegetabilibus et Plantis* (On vegetables and plants, circa 1250–1275)—a detailed description of all sorts of plants, including flowers and fruits; their outward appearances; internal structures, including reproduction; and maintenance, including hybridization and grafting; this work is notable for being remarkably free of myth and hearsay and for attempting a synthetic classification scheme not truly supplanted until the eighteenth century.

Albertus Magnus, *De Animalibus* (On animals, circa 1250–1275)—an encyclopedic work that sought to bring together all the known information on the animal kingdom as a companion to the Aristotelian works on that topic; largely following Aristotle's works on the history, parts, and reproduction of animals, the work is supplemented by Albertus's original observations and a paraphrase of other medieval zoological works, integrating Aristotelian frameworks with nature's actualities and experimenting on how animals perceive, reproduce, and are constructed.

Albertus Magnus, *De Mineralibus* (On minerals, circa 1250–1275)—a listing of stones, minerals, and other earthy substances in which Albertus sought to complete his commentaries on Aristotelean topics and filled in a gap where no true Aristotelian source existed; Albertus used some ancient sources, notably Pliny the Elder and Theophrastus, as well as Arabic works and others spuriously attributed to Aristotle, to explain the properties, sources, and medical uses of dozens of stones.

Alhazen (Abu 'Ali al-Hasan ibn al-Haytham), *Kitab f_ al-Manazir* (Optics, circa 1020)—a work investigating optics and perception from first principles, rejecting previous premises and instead proceeding in a experimental, inductive manner; Alhazen cites no authorities but proceeds with the aid of artificial devices ("instruments") to probe how light behaves (especially with respect to vision) rather than the traditional philosophical question of what light "is."

Anonymous, *Mappae Clavicula* (The "little key" [of secrets], circa ninth to twelfth century)—A compilation of compilations of nearly three hundred recipes on various technological subjects including paints, pigments, miscellaneous chemical compositions, dyes, and how to color metals; this work was compiled over a long period, and manuscripts exist from the ninth, tenth, and twelfth centuries, demonstrating that the *Mappae Clavicula* is more of a snapshot of a long tradition of technological recipe books, rather than one single groundbreaking work.

Arnauld de Villanova, *Aphorismi de Gradibus* (Aphorisms on gradations, circa 1300)—a work treating the "complexio" (sensible qualities that characterize health) in a qualitative manner, drawing from Islamic sources, to provide the basis of mathematical pharmacy; Arnauld proposed that the qualitative intensity of a symptom increases arithmetically with a geometric increase in the ratio of the forces that produce that symptom (for example, $(intensity)^2$ = hot/cold), giving the work a strongly theoretical, but hardly practical, tenor.

Roger Bacon, *Opus majus* (The Great Work, by 1266)—a work espousing mathematical explanation and experimentation as the surest path to knowledge, a rejection of popular opinion and custom as well as ancient authority simply on its reputation; Bacon denounced ignorance concealed by arrogance but praises the use of instruments to extend the senses into his four main branches for knowledge creation: mathematics, optics, *scientia experimentalis,* and alchemy; he also mentioned some hypothetical inventions that later became reality: telescopes, microscopes, flying machines, and powered ships.

Bartholomaeus Anglicus, *De proprietatibus rerum* (On the properties of things, circa 1230)—a medieval Latin text that emulated the long Roman poem of the same name by Lucretius and served as an encyclopedia of diverse topics for medieval scholars, but also, according to Bartholomaeus, could be used by the "simple and ignorant" as well, heralding the realization that natural knowledge was not the monopoly of the Church; it was also translated into Middle English by John Trevisa in the fourteenth century.

Bede, *De Temporum ratione* (The reckoning of time, 725)—One of the foundational works on Christian chronology, written to instruct monks on how calendars were composed; it includes calendar calculations based on astronomical events, an explanation of the cycles of feasts and holy days, and a theory of the tides.

Jean Buridan, *Questiones. . .* (Questions [on Aristotle], circa 1330–1350)—a series of commentaries and critiques that asked and attempted to answer questions about what Aristotle wrote in his *Physics, Metaphysics, On the Heavens, Meteorology,* smaller works on nature, and the various books on animals; Buridan integrated ancient Greek ideas with medieval Christian beliefs.

Constantine the African, *Pantechne* or *Pantegni* (All Arts, circa 1075)—A compiled and interpreted version of *Kitab al-Maliki* (The Royal Book) by the eighth-century Arab philosopher Haly Abbas ('Ali ibn al-'Abbas al-Majusi); Constantine's work includes everything a practitioner needed to know about medicine and introduced the theory and practice of Arabic medicine to the West, became the foundation of Western medicine for the next three centuries.

Giovanni de'Dondi, *Planetarium* or *Astrarium* (The Planet-machine, or, The Star-machine, circa 1390)—a book describing the construction of an elaborate clockwork mechanism to track the motion of the planets and stars, and—incidentally—to tell the hours; this book is one of the first to describe complex machinery, with such constructional details as gear ratios, necessary weights, and assembly instructions as well as the theoretical underpinnings for the device.

Robert Grosseteste, *Commentarius in viii libros physicorum Aristotelis* (Commentary on Aristotle's Physics in Eight Books, 1225–1235)—the first commentary on Aristotle's *Physics* in Europe; Grosseteste tried to explain Aristotle's framework within a Christian tradition; although not in itself impressive, this work set the stage for many medieval commentaries and critiques of the ancient Greek conception of motion and substance.

Hildegard of Bingen, *Liber compositae medicinea* (The Book of Medicinal Compositions, circa 1150)—a collection of recipes for treating various ailments, composed in the tradition of rebalancing the humors to restore health; Hildegard also derived much information deriving from folk medicine, astrology, and scriptural tradition.

Hugh of Saint Victor, *Didascalicon: De studio Legendi* ("Didactic Manual,": On Collected Studies, circa 1125–1230)—a work that attempts to define all areas of nature relevant and important for humans to master if they expect to receive divine destiny; Hugh included, for the first time, seven mechanical arts that parallel the seven liberal arts; by including such things as armament, clothing, and agriculture, he legitimated technology as a pursuit not to be despised in the Scholastic universities, elevating it to the status of traditional arts such as logic, rhetoric, and arithmetic.

Robert Kilwardby, *De ortu scientiarum* (On the Origins of the Sciences, circa 1250)—a work that presents the mechanical arts fully developed and integrated into a synthesis of Augustinian, Boethian, and Arabic philosophy; Kilwardby denied the difference between theory and practice, seeing them dependent upon each other in such a way that one could not exist without the other and that all practical arts rely on speculative arts to understand and describe them.

John Peckham (or Pecham), *Perspectiva communis* (Common Optics, 1277–1279)—an elementary book that integrated Roger Bacon's work on optics and that of Alhazen into Western thought; Bacon argued that rays entered our eyes (intromission), rather than being produced by our eyes (extromission), and Alhazen approached the subject by assuming that optics could be explained mathematically and that it was both a physical action and a physiological reaction. Peckham's work was the standard book on optics until the early seventeenth century.

Nicole Oresme, *Le livre du ciel et du monde* (The Book of Heaven and Earth, 1370–1380)—a general description of the workings of the universe that uses the metaphor of heavenly clockwork to describe a world that is set in motion by divine order but does not need continued divine intervention to continue in motion; Oresme attempted to fully integrate Aristotelian physics, Christian theology, and Ptolemaic astonomy into a coherent whole.

Oresme, *Tractatus de commensurabilitate vel incommensurabilitate motuum celi* (Treatise on the Commensurability or Incommensurability of the Celestial Motions, 1370–1380)—a technical treatise on the physics of the celestial sphere in which Oresme attempted to explain aspects of circular motion with mathematical rigor and related velocities through exponential ratios.

Oresme, *Tractatus de configurationibus qualitatum et motuum* (Treatise on the Configuration of Qualities and Motions, 1350s)—a work covering the physics of what is now known as kinematics (a branch of dynamics that deals with aspects of motion apart from considerations of mass and force), Oresme worked out quantitatively the uniformity and difformity of intensities through the used of two-dimensional figures representing different motions, thus taking the first steps toward using graphical figures to calculate unknown quantities.

Peter of Maricourt, *Epistola de Magnete* (Brief letter on the magnet, 1269)—the first concise work on magnetism in Europe; Peter not only praised manual experimentation as the best way to discover knowledge, but also laid out, clearly and concisely, the concept of the poles of a magnet, the laws that govern magnetic forces, and various instruments that used magnets to determine directions.

Richard of Wallingford, *Tractatus horologii astronomici* (The Treatise of Astronomical Hours, 1320–1326)—a large book on the construction of a clock to model the movement of the heavens, showing the motion of the sun, moon, five planets, and the tides on a dial face; written for a monastic community, this work demonstrates the interconnectedness of the Christian liturgy and calendar with daily and annual astronomical events.

Rufinus, *Liber de virtutibus herbarum* (The book of the virtues of herbs, after 1287)—a particularly complete and original attempt to catalogue and classify all cultivated and wild plant matter for their medicinal and digestive properties, providing exacting observation of nearly one thousand vegetables and giving both their Latin and vernacular names so that the readers could more easily identify them.

Richard Swineshead, *Liber calculationum* (Book of Calculations, before 1350)—a book based on the teachings of English mathematician Thomas Bradwardine, which examined the change in velocity of a body when acted upon by a constant outside force; Swineshead began with some dubious premises about the summations of infinite mathematical series but arrived nonetheless at the correct square law of increasing velocity under constant acceleration (force).

Theophilus Presbyter, *De Diversibus Artibus* (On various arts, circa 1100)—a work setting down a series of recipes and instructions for the creation of the fine arts necessary in a monastic setting, such as painting, enameling, bell casting, and fine metalwork; the work is important because for the first time, in a religious context, the manual arts are specifically described and praised as pious and proper ways to praise God; before this time, they had generally either been ignored or actively discouraged as works which distracted the mind from proper intellectual contemplation.

Tacuinum Sanitatis (The Elements of Health, twelfth to fourteenth century)—a book compiling the observations of many authors about the necessities for daily preservation of health: airs, foods, activity, sleep, the balance of humors, and emotions; many variants of this sort of work survive.

Vincent of Beauvais, *Speculum Naturale Majus* (The Great Mirror of Nature, circa 1250)—an encyclopedic work that summarized the state of science in the late thirteenth century and served as a starting point for further investigations on all sorts of natural objects, processes, and occurrences.

William of Conches, *Dragmaticon philosophiae* (Philosophy of the World, before 1150)—a work setting out the principle that God acts regularly through natural processes that could be comprehended by humans; William condemned those who appealed to divine causation to explain phenomena; instead he put the task of understanding directly on human intellect and reason; he was taken to task for denying the first cause of any event (that is, God), but safely maintained belief by arguing that seeking the secondary causes (that is, natural processes) did not deny the existence of an ultimate first cause, thereby marrying natural philosophy and theology.

Cavalrymen and a standard bearer; illumination from the ninth-century *Golden Psalter* (Stiftsbibliothek, Saint Gallen)

GLOSSARY

Abbasids: A dynasty of caliphs who ruled the Islamic empire for more than five hundred years (750–1258); they claimed descent from Abbas, the uncle of Muhammad.

Abolis: Half-penny.

Ad Hominem **Argument:** An attack on an opponent's character rather than his ideas.

Affines: People related through **affinity.**

Affinity: Relationship by marriage rather than blood or descent from a common ancestor.

Agnatic Lineage: *See* **Patrilineal Descent.**

Albigensians: *See* **Cathars.**

Alchemy: A medieval science and philosophy that attempted to achieve the transmutation of base metals into gold, discover a universal cure for disease, and establish a means to prolong life indefinitely.

Apocalypse: The final battle that, in Christian theology, will come at the end of the world.

Apse: A semicircular or polygonal recess, arched or dome roofed, in a building, especially at the end of the choir, aisles, or nave of a church.

Arabs: Semitic people of the Arabian peninsula.

Arians: Followers of Arius, a presbyter of Alexandria in the fourth century who denied that Jesus Christ was consubstantial, or of the same essence or substance with God.

Assart: The process by which serfs would receive their freedom if they agreed to leave their village and clear new lands for the lord to claim as his new territory.

Assize: A judicial inquest (inquiry) and its verdict.

Astrology: The pseudoscience of the laws of the heavens that govern life on earth. Medieval Europeans considered astrology a legitimate part of the same science as astronomy, the "naming" of the heavens.

Auto-de-fe: "Act of Faith." Public events at which the Church sentenced heretics, homosexuals, bigamists, and other individuals who were believed to disturb "God's natural order." After sentencing, the convicted were turned over to the government for punishments that included public burning. The term is commonly used for the public sentencing by the Church as well as the public punishment by the government.

Azymes: Unleavened Communion wafers used in the Western, or Roman, Christian Church.

Barbette: A strap used to secure a medieval woman's veil.

Barbican: A small fortification, located inside a castle and before the gatehouse, through which a visitor had to enter. The passageway through the barbican was built with a ninety-degree turn in it, allowing a defender to ambush an unwelcome visitor.

Beghards: Members of religious communities of men not under vows founded in the Low Countries in the thirteenth century.

Beguines: Members of religious communities of women not under vows founded in the Low Countries in the thirteenth century.

Berbers: Various peoples of North Africa who lived in the area west of present-day Tripoli, Libya.

Bestiary: A medieval manuscript that depicts animals and describes their habits.

Bilateral Descent: Tracing descent through both the maternal and paternal lines of a family.

Black Death: The pandemic of plague (probably **bubonic** and pneumonic) that swept Europe in 1347–1351, killing about one-quarter of the population. Its name comes from the dark buboes, or swellings, that developed in a bubonic plague victim's armpits and groin.

Braies: A medieval man's undergarment, a pair of half trousers that extended to about mid calf.

Bubonic Plague: An illness caused by the bacterium *Yersinia pestis,* which is carried by fleas on household rodents. Another form of bubonic plague, known as pneumonic, is carried by water droplets. (*See also* **Black Death.**)

Burhs: Ramparts made of earth and wood.

Buttress: The architectural term for a projecting mass of masonry used to add strength to a wall. Especially in medieval times, buttresses were used to counteract the **thrust** created by heavy **Romanesque** and **Gothic vault** ceilings. A flying buttress, developed for Gothic churches, is a quarter-circle arch that leans on the building at the point where it needs support and is attached at the other end to a free-standing buttress.

Caliph: Islamic ruler as the temporal and spiritual head of Islam.

Canon Law: Ecclesiastical or Church law codes.

Canonical Hours: The times, roughly at three-hour intervals, at which medieval Christians, particularly monks and clergymen, said specific sets of prayers: Matins (midnight), Lauds (sunrise), Prime (6:00 A.M.), Terce (9:00 A.M.), Sext (noon), None (3:00 P.M.), Vespers (6:00 P.M.), and Compline (nightfall).

Carolingian Dynasty: Frankish rulers dating from circa 613. They ruled France from 751 to 987, Germany from 752 to 911, and Italy from 774 to 961.

Carolingian Miniscule: A clear, readable form of hand-writing developed by scholars and administrators at the court of Charlemagne and his descendants.

Carolingian Renaissance: A renewal of learning and literature that arose at the court of Charlemagne in the 790s and extended into the 860s.

Cathars: Members of various Christian sects of the Late Middle Ages teaching that matter is evil and professing faith in an angelic Christ who did not really undergo human birth or death.

Celestial Region: The medieval term for all the heavens including and beyond the dark side of the moon.

Celestial Spheres: The term Aristotle used in his explanation for the structure of the universe, which he described as a series of crystalline spheres, centered on the earth and nested one within another like the layers of an onion. Thus, Earth is surrounded by spheres of water, air, and fire; seven spheres for the Sun, the Moon, and the five known planets (Mercury, Venus, Mars, Jupiter, and Saturn); and one sphere for the fixed stars. Medieval astronomers employed, and in some cases modified, this model.

Cenobitic Monasticism: The form of monasticism in which monks live with other monks.

Chanson de geste: Literal meaning: song of heroic deeds; a French and West German epic form developed in the eleventh and twelfth centuries.

Chausses: Soldiers' hose made of flexible mail.

Chevauchee: A cavalry raid.

Chivalry: The system, spirit, and customs of medieval knighthood. The ideal qualities of a knight included courteous behavior (especially toward women), generosity, honor, and martial valor.

Churching: A religious ceremony held about one month after childbirth at which the new mother presented herself in public for spiritual cleansing.

Cloister: The monastery buildings, surrounding an enclosed courtyard, where the monks do most of their daily living.

Clerestory: An outside wall of a building that rises above an adjoining roof and contains windows.

Columna: A business contract prevalent in eleventh-century southern Italy. It created a partnership between merchants, sailors, and shipowners whereby a venture's final profits would be shared according to the value of each partner's initial investment.

Commenda: A business contract in which one partner finances a trade venture while the other partner executes it with no financial commitment. At the conclusion of the expedition, both parties share in the profits at agreed upon percentages, with the financial partner alone shouldering any losses.

Commune: A medieval (usually municipal) community.

Concubinage: Cohabitation with a person to whom one is not legally married.

Conjugal Debt: The Christian requirement that husband and wife engage in sexual intercourse.

Consanguinity: Relationship by blood or descent from a common ancestor.

Consorteria: The members of a descent group who owned property in common and make collective decisions about it.

Conversi: An order of lay brothers.

Courtly Literature: A form of love literature, written in the **vernacular,** that arose in noble and royal courts around 1170 and flourished into the fourteenth century.

Cowl: A long, loose, sleeveless, usually wool monk's garment with a deep hood attached.

Crenellation: An embrasure in a battlement.

Cruciform Ground Plan: The basic cross-shaped outline of many medieval churches.

Crusader States: Christian feudal states established in the Holy Land after the First Crusade in 1099.

Crusades: A series of European military expeditions (often counted at eight, although numbering more than that) between 1096 and 1291 to recapture the **Holy Land** from the Muslims.

Dark Ages: *See* **Early Middle Ages.**

Decretal: An official pronouncement of the Church.

Demesne: Manorial land.

Denarius: One penny; the basic silver coin in circulation during the Middle Ages; originally the basic unit of the Imperial Roman monetary system.

Disparagement: The arranged marriage of a nobleman's widow or child to a person of lesser rank as a reward for royal service.

Donatio propter nuptias **(donation on account of marriage):** The Roman term for a substantial marriage gift given to the bride by the groom's family.

Dos: The Roman term for a **dowry.**

Dower: The groom's gift to the bride.

Dowry: The bride's gift to the groom.

Dualism: The doctrine that there are two independent principles, one good and the other evil.

Ducat: A gold coin used in Venice.

Early Middle Ages: The period of European history from 476 to around 1000. Sometimes called the Dark Ages because it was during these centuries that western Europe lost touch with classical (especially Greek) learning and science.

Ecu: French coin.

Eddas: Old Norse epics written down in the tenth century but recited as early as the seventh century.

Emptio: A contract obliging a buyer to pay (usually at a predetermined price) for goods when delivered.

Endogamy: Marriage between cousins. (*See* also **exogamy**.)

Epistemology: The study of the nature and grounds of knowledge especially with reference to its limits and validity.

Erbpachten: A serf's inheritance lease to specific lands.

Ether: The medieval term for a fifth element that occurs only in the **celestial region.** (*See* **four elements**.)

Exogamy: Marriage outside the family group. (*See* also **endogamy**.)

Fabliau: A form of bawdy story that originated in rural France and was popular in the twelfth and thirteenth centuries.

Falcon: Any of several varieties of hawks trained for hunting.

Fealty: The fidelity of a vassal or feudal tenant to his lord.

Feudalism: The economic, political, and social system that prevailed in Europe during the Middle Ages. It was based on the relationship between lords and **vassals**: lords provided vassals with protection and lands, and in return vassals took oaths of **homage** and **fealty.**

Fief: A feudal estate over which a lord had rights and exercised control.

Florin: A gold coin first struck in Florence in 1252.

Four Elements: The medieval term for the substances that combined to make the physical world: earth, water, air, and fire.

Four Humors: The substances that ancient and medieval physicians believed made up the human body and had to be kept in balance to maintain an individual's health. Each humor was thought to be produced in a different organ: blood in the heart, phlegm in the brain, black bile in the spleen, and yellow bile in the liver.

Four Qualities: The medieval term for hot, cold, moist, and dry—independent entities related to the four elements; that is, fire and earth are hot and dry; water and air are cold and moist.

Franks: West Germanic people who settled in Gaul (present-day France and the Netherlands).

Fresco: A technique of wall painting on wet plaster.

Frérèche: The joint ownership of property by all heirs who have a claim to a portion of it.

Gabelle: A tax on salt levied in France.

Genovino: An Italian coin used primarily in Genoa.

General Eyres: Official visitations made by royal judges to English county courts.

Gigliato: A coin used primarily in southern Italy.

Gleaning: Gathering bits of grain left behind after reapers have harvested a field, a privilege often reserved to elderly poor people during the Middle Ages.

Gnostics: Members of various Christian sects that believed matter was evil and that salvation came through gnosis, or the knowledge of spiritual truth.

Goliards: Wandering scholars who supported themselves by reciting satiric verse in Latin and vernacular languages.

Gothic: A style of architecture characterized by high pointed-arch ceilings and large stained-glass windows. Arising in the twelfth century and dominating church architecture into the fourteenth and fifteenth century, it was made possible by the development of the groin vault and buttress, which took the weight of its heavy stone ceilings off its relatively light, window-punctuated walls.

Gros Tournois: A French coin.

Groschen: A coin used in the German kingdoms.

Grosso: An Italian coin used primarily in Florence and Genoa.

Grossus denarius: One groat; an English coin worth several pennies.

Guild: An association of merchants or craftsmen.

Hagiography: Biographies of saints and other venerated people.

Hanse: Trading associations.

Hanseatic League: A commercial confederacy founded by northern European towns in the thirteenth century. Lübeck became the administrative capital in 1358, and other member cities included Bremen, Cologne, Danzig (present-day Gdansk), Hamburg, Lüneburg, Magdeburg, Reval, Riga, and Rostock. The League reached the peak of its power in the late 1300s.

Hauberk: A soldier's tunic made of **mail.**

Herbal: A collection of recipes for remedies made from plants to prevent or cure diseases, or ease their symptoms. Many manuscript herbals existed in the Middle Ages.

Hermitical Monasticism: The form of Monasticism in which each monk lives alone.

High Middle Ages: The period of European history from about 1000 to 1300. It was marked by political expansion and consolidation as well as intellectual ferment.

Holy Land: Present-day Israel and Lebanon.

Holy Roman Empire: The political entity encompassing various lands in western and central Europe ruled over first by Frankish and then German kings from 800 to 1806. Because the empire was established by the papacy, many popes viewed it as the secular arm of the Catholic Church.

Homage: A ceremony by which a man acknowledges himself the vassal of a lord; also the relationship between a vassal and his lord.

Hörigen: German serfs.

Hundred Years' War: A series of intermittent military campaigns (1337–1453) between England and France over control of continental lands claimed by both countries.

Impartible Inheritance: The system by which only one child, usually the eldest living son, inherits his father's entire estate, thus keeping the family's land holdings in a single block. (*See* also **partible inheritance.**)

Indulgence: A remission of temporal and purgatorial punishment that according to the medieval Christian Church was due for sins.

Interdict: A censure of the medieval Christian Church withdrawing most sacraments and Christian burial from a person or a region.

Investiture Controversy: A controversy between secular and papal authorities during the eleventh and twelfth centuries over who had the right to appoint bishops and other Church officials.

Jacquerie: A peasants' rebellion in northeastern France in 1358; it was so named from the nobles' habit of referring to any peasant as Jacques.

Jihad: A holy war waged on behalf of Islam as a religious duty.

Journeyman: A worker who has learned a trade and works for another person usually by the day.

Jus Commune: Common legal procedures and concepts based on Roman law and used throughout Europe by the eleventh century.

Jus Palae: "Spade right"; a serf's rights to a specific plot of land.

Knights Hospitaler: Originally called the Knights of St. John, these knights and priests operated the Benedictine monastery hospital in Jerusalem starting in 1113. Within seven years they supervised a chain of hospices throughout the **Crusader States.** A military order by the end of the twelfth century, the Hospitalers controlled the island of Malta until 1798.

Knights Templar: A military order founded in 1115 in northern France. Originally these knights provided escorts for pilgrims traveling within the Holy Land. They avowed chastity, poverty, and obedience and were sometimes called The Poor Knights. These knights also acted as bankers and money brokers. The order was disbanded in 1307.

Labora: The tasks associated with work.

Labore et ore: The ideal Western monastic lifestyle of work and prayer.

Lapidary: A medieval manuscript depicting various stones and describing their physical, magical, emblematic, or medicinal qualities.

Late Middle Ages: The period of European history from circa 1300 to 1500. It was marked by unprecedented political (**Hundred Years' War,** 1337–1453), social (**Black Death,** 1347–1351), and ecclesiastical (Great Schism, 1378–1417) calamity.

Legerwite: A fine paid by a peasant woman who was caught in fornication or who gave birth to illegitimate children.

Libra: One pound; equivalent to 20 *soldii* or 240 pennies.

Lingua Franca: A common language.

Lingua Romana: Old French.

Lingua Teudisca: Old German.

Mail: Medieval armor made of overlapping steel rings welded (or riveted) together.

Manichaeans: A religious group believing in the release of the spirit from matter through asceticism.

Mappae Mundi: World maps.

Mark: A German silver coin worth 13 *soldii* and four *denarii.*

Marl: A clay soil containing a carbonate of lime, which was spread on fields as a fertilizer.

Maslin: A coarse wheat-rye or barley-rye flour mixture used in the making of bread.

Materia Medica: A body of late Roman works describing the medical uses of hundreds of plants, which medieval Europeans consulted for *measures* to prevent and cure various diseases.

Medieval Period: *See* **Middle Ages.**

Merovingian Dynasty: The first Frankish Dynasty reigning from circa 500 to 751.

Merchet: A fine levied by a feudal lord on a female servant or serf who wanted to marry.

Metaphysics: A division of philosophy that is concerned with the fundamental nature of reality and being. (*See* **epistemology** and **ontology.**)

Middle Ages: The period of European history from about 476 to 1500.

Minnesänger: Wandering poet-musicians of Germany.

Moat: A deep trench surrounding a castle wall, sometimes, but not always, filled with water.

Moldboard Plow: A plow developed in medieval Europe to allow the farmer to plow the soil more deeply than he could with the traditional **scratch plow.** This new plow got its name from the large, curved piece of wood set behind the plowshare to turn the soil up and out of the cut to the side of the furrow.

Mongols: A warlike Asiatic people who originated in Mongolia and invaded eastern Europe in the mid thirteenth century. Also known as the Tatars.

Monism: The belief that all phenomena is reduced to just one principle.

Morgengabe: A gift a husband gives to his bride on the morning after their wedding to acknowledge that his wife came to him as a virgin.

Mortal Sin: According to Thomist theology, a sin such as murder that is deliberately committed and is of such serious consequence that it deprives the soul of sanctifying grace. Compare to **Venial Sin.**

Motte and Bailey: An early medieval form of defensive construction in which a castle was built on a natural or artificially constructed "motte" (French for mound or hill) and surrounded at the base by outbuildings or a village protected by a palisade, a fence made from tall wooden spikes. The area between the motte and the palisade was called the "bailey."

Mystery Plays: Medieval plays on religious subjects; their name may come from the claim that they illustrate the "mysteries" of Christianity, or it may be rooted in a guild's responsibilities for the "mastery" (pronounced *mystery*) of its craft; from there the plays guilds produced became known as mystery plays.

Natural Philosophy: The medieval area of study now known as science.

Nave: The long central section of a **Romanesque** or **Gothic** church.

Ontology: A branch of **metaphysics** concerned with the nature of and relations of being.

Ora: Prayer.

Outremer: "Overseas." The **Crusader States,** consisting of the County of Edessa, Principality of Antioch, County of Tripoli, and the Kingdom of Jerusalem.

Pantheism: The religious and philosophical theory that God and the universe are identical; the doctrine that God is everything and everything is God.

Partible Inheritance: The system by which an estate is divided among some or all of the children in a family.

Patrilineal Descent: Tracing descent through the paternal line of a family.

Penitential: A book containing in codified form the canons of the Church relating to penance.

Pied de Monnaie: A monetary system introduced by French king John II to prevent a financial crisis in his realm. It denoted with one number the intrinsic worth of a coin with respect to its weight and fineness.

Pneuma: An ancient and medieval medical term referring to the vital spirit and life force of living creatures.

Polygamy: Marriage to more than one mate at the same time.

Portcullis: A large, heavy wood and iron gate in a castle wall.

Premise: The first part of a logical argument, which is accepted as true.

Portolan Chart: A navigational aid that was marked with straight lines that intersected. This type of chart was used by mariners to do "plain sailing" in the Mediterranean Sea where the distances covered by ships was not great.

Primogeniture: Inheritance by the eldest son to the exclusion of daughters and younger sons. (*See also* **ultimogeniture.**)

Ptolomaic Universe: The theory advanced by the first century A.D. astronomer Claudius Ptolemy, and accepted by medieval scientists, that the earth lies at the center of the universe with all other celestial bodies revolving around it.

Quadrivium: The four advanced liberal-arts subjects in medieval schools: arithmetic, geometry, astronomy, and music. (*See also* **trivium.**)

Quem quaeritis (**whom do you seek?**) **plays:** Brief plays based on words exchanged by the three Marys at the empty tomb of Jesus; developed in the tenth century and used in Church liturgy, they are one of the earliest examples of medieval theater.

Quintessence: *See* **ether.**

Rampart: A broad embankment raised as a fortification and usually surmounted by a parapet.

Refectory: A monastery dining hall.

Romanesque: A style of architecture characterized by thick walls, small windows, and rounded-arch ceilings; it was widely employed in European churches built from the seventh to the tenth centuries. (*See also* **vault.**)

Rushlights: Lengths of rush, a type of grass, that were dipped in fat and lit to provide light. They were often used by peasants because they were cheaper than candles, but they also provided less light and more smoke than candles.

Sagas: Northern European epics (such as Old Norse, German and English) written in the early Middle Ages.

Saracens: A broad term for Arabs; nomadic people of the deserts between Syria and Arabia.

Scholasticism: A method of study based on logic and dialectic (the art of discovering a truth by finding the contradictions in arguments against it).

Scratch Plow: An ancient form of plow made from a pointed stick, or "plowshare," that is dragged behind a beast of burden and breaks up the uppermost layer of topsoil. (*See* **Moldboard Plow.**)

Scriptorum: The room in a monastery devoted to the copying of manuscripts and housing the monastic library.

Scutage: A tax levied on a knight or a vassal in lieu of military service to his lord.

Seigneur: A feudal lord of a manor.

Serf: A peasant in personal bondage to a feudal lord and his lands.

Syllogism: A logical argument that includes a major premise, a minor premise, and a conclusion. For example: All boys like baseball. John is a boy. Therefore, John likes baseball.

Simony: The buying and selling of Church offices or ecclesiastical seniority.

Solidus: One shilling; equivalent to twelve denarii or pennies.

Spiritual Kinship: A bond formed by the sacraments of baptism or confirmation, such as that between godparents and godchild or priest and the individuals he christens or confirms.

Stem Family: A household structure in which only one child would marry and inherit the family farm while the other children would either remain unmarried and live at home, or marry and start a new household; this complex family unit was desirable in the Middle Ages because it kept the family's land holdings intact.

Strappado: A pulley system used by the Inquisition to torture heretics and other criminals. The person's hands are tied behind his back and then he is lifted off the ground by them, resulting in extreme pain.

Sub pena nubendi **(on pain of marriage):** The condition on which Church courts made unmarried couples who habitually engaged in sex swear to abstain from sexual relations or be forced to marry.

Syncretism: The combining of elements from different cultural or religious practices.

T-O Map: Designed by Isidore of Seville in the late sixth century to early seventh century. This Spanish prelate and scholar envisioned the habitable world as being divided into three continents: Asia, Africa, and Europe. He drew the ocean as a vast *O* that encircled the continents and the Mediterranean Sea and various river networks as a large *T* that divided the land masses.

Tallage: A tax on manorial lands.

Tempura: A technique of wall painting on dry plaster.

Terrestrial Region: The medieval term for the earth, its oceans, and its atmosphere up to and including the side of the moon that faces the earth. (*See also* **Celestial Region.**)

Thatched Roof: A roof made from wild or cultivated grass (such as wheat or rye) woven together atop a wooden frame.

Thrust: The tendency of a heavy arched structure to push outward at the base.

Toft: The rectangular piece of land allotted to an English peasant for a house, garden, and outbuildings.

Transubstantiation: The belief that in Communion the bread and wine become the body and blood of Christ.

Trebuchet: A large medieval siege weapon capable of catapulting heavy rocks or other objects to break down city or castle walls.

Trivium: The three basic liberal-arts subjects in medieval schools: grammar, rhetoric, and dialectics (logic). (*See also* **quadrivium.**)

Troubadours: Wandering poet-musicians of southern France.

Ultimogeniture: Inheritance by the youngest son to the exclusion of daughters and other sons. (*See* also **Primogeniture.**)

Usufruct: "Land-use"; a vassal's legal right of using and enjoying the profits of land belonging to a lord.

Vassal: A person under the protection of a feudal lord to whom he has vowed **homage** and **fealty.**

Vault: A term applied to the construction of roofs by means of a series of arches. The barrel vault used in Romanesque architecture is a series of parallel rounded (or semicircular) arches. The groin vault developed for Gothic buildings was constructed from two vaults at right angles, at first two barrel vaults and later two pointed arches. For rib vaults, which developed from groin vaults, the lines where the vaults intersect are constructed first (forming "ribs"), and then the spaces between the ribs are filled in with stone.

Vellum: Treated animal hide, preferably from sheep, on which medieval documents were written.

Venditio: A sale contract committing a seller to deliver goods (once they become available) at a predetermined price.

Venial Sin: According to Thomist theology, a sin that is relatively slight or that is committed without full reflection or consent and does not deprive the soul of sanctifying grace. Compare with **Mortal Sin.**

Vernacular: Literal meaning: vulgar tongue; the dialects that evolved from Latin and eventually became modern European languages.

Villein: The English term for a **serf.**

Waldenses / Waldensians: The adherents of a religious sect which originated in southern France in the late twelfth century through the preaching of Valdes (also known as Waldo), a rich merchant from Lyons. They were excommunicated in 1184 and eventually became associated with the Protestant Reformation.

Wattle-and-Daub Construction: A method of building walls for a house by interlacing tree branches to form a basic support (wattle) and then coating them with a clay and straw mixture (daub).

Wergild **or** *Wergeld:* Literally "the price of a man." An ancient English custom by which a killer pays his victim's family a certain sum in order to avoid a blood feud.

Wimple: A cloth neck covering that was attached to a medieval woman's veil.

GENERAL REFERENCES

GENERAL

The Avalon Project at the Yale Law School: Documents in Law, History and Diplomacy <http://www.yale.edu/law-web/avalon/avalon.htm>.

Marc Bloch, *Feudal Society* (Chicago: University of Chicago Press, 1961).

Christopher Brooke, *Europe in the Central Middle Ages, 962–1154,* third edition (Harlow, U.K. & New York: Longman, 2000).

Norman F. Cantor, *The Civilization of the Middle Ages* (New York: HarperPerennial, 1993).

Cantor, ed., *The Encyclopedia of the Middle Ages* (New York: Viking, 1999).

The Catholic Encyclopedia, on-line at *New Advent* <www.newadvent.org>.

Albert M. Craig, and others, *The Heritage of World Civilizations,* volume 1, *To 1600,* second edition (New York: Macmillan, 1990).

R. H. C. Davis, *A History of Medieval Europe: From Constantine to Saint Louis* (London & New York: Longmans, Green, 1957).

Encyclopedia Brittanica, on-line at *Britannica.com* <http://www.britannica.com>.

Anthony Esler, *The Human Venture, The Great Enterprise: A World History to 1500,* volume 1, fourth edition (Upper Saddle River, N.J.: Prentice Hall, 2000).

Daniel A. Frankforter, *The Medieval Millennium: An Introduction* (Upper Saddle River, N.J.: Prentice Hall, 1999).

Denys Hay, *Europe in the Fourteenth and Fifteenth Centuries* (London: Longmans, 1966).

Hay, *The Medieval Centuries,* revised edition (New York: Harper & Row, 1964).

C. Warren Hollister, *Medieval Europe: A Short History,* eighth edition (Boston: McGraw-Hill, 1998).

George Holmes, *The Later Middle Ages, 1272–1485* (Edinburgh, U.K.: Nelson, 1962).

Internet Medieval Sourcebook <www.fordham.edu/halsall/sbook.html>.

Angus Konstam, *Atlas of Medieval Europe* (New York: Checkmark Books, 2000).

The Labyrinth: Resources for Medieval Studies <www.georgetown.edu/labyrinth/index.html>.

William L. Langer, ed., *The New Illustrated Encyclopedia of World History,* volume 1 (New York: Abrams, 1975).

ORB: The Online Reference Book for Medieval Studies <http: //orb.rhodes.edu/>.

Karl F. Morrison, *Europe's Middle Ages, 565–1500* (Glenview, Ill.: Scott, Foresman, 1970).

John H. Mundy, *Europe in the High Middle Ages, 1150–1300,* third edition (Harlow, U.K. & New York: Longman, 2000).

NetSERF: The Internet Connection for Medieval Resources, <www.netserf.org>.

Edward Peters, *Europe and the Middle Ages,* second edition (Englewood Cliffs, N.J.: Prentice Hall, 1989).

Kevin Reilly, *The West and the World: A Topical History of Civilization* (New York: Harper & Row, 1980).

Joel T. Rosenthal, *The Borzoi History of England,* volume one, *Angles, Angels, and Conquerors, 400–1154* (New York: Knopf, 1973).

The Rule of Benedict: An Index to Texts On-line and Gateway to RB: Bibliographic Index <http://www.osb.org/rb/>.

Howard Spodek, *The World's History,* volume one, *To 1500* (Upper Saddle River, N.J.: Prentice Hall, 1998).

J. M. Wallace-Hadrill, *The Barbarian West, 400–1000* (London & New York: Hutchinson University Library, 1952).

GEOGRAPHY

Eliyahu Ashtor, *The Levant Trade in the Later Middle Ages* (Princeton, N.J.: Princeton University Press, 1983).

Wolfgang Behringer, "Weather, Hunger and Fear: The Origins of the European Witch Persecution in Climate, Society and Mentality," *German History,* 13 (1995): 1–27.

Mary B. Campbell, *The Witness and the Other World: Exotic European Travel Writing, 400–1600* (Ithaca, N.Y.: Cornell University Press, 1988).

David L. Clawson and James S. Fisher, *World Regional Geography,* sixth edition (Upper Saddle River, N.J.: Prentice Hall, 1998).

Christopher Dawson, ed., *Mission to Asia* (Toronto: University of Toronto Press, 1980).

Bailey W. Diffie, *Prelude to Empire: Portugal Overseas before Henry the Navigator* (Lincoln: University of Nebraska Press, 1960).

Diffie and G. D. Winius, *The Foundations of the Portuguese Empire, 1415–1580* (Minneapolis: University of Minnesota Press, 1977).

Evelyn Edson, *Mapping Time and Space: How Medieval Mapmakers Viewed their World* (London: British Library, 1997).

Brian Fagan, *Floods, Families, and Emperors: El Niño and the Fate of Civilization* (New York: Basic, 1999).

Felipe Fernández-Armesto, *Before Columbus: Exploration and Colonization from the Mediterranean to the Atlantic, 1229–1492* (Philadelphia: University of Pennsylvania Press, 1987).

L. N. Gumilev, *Searches for an Imaginary Kingdom: The Legend of the Kingdom of Prester John* (Cambridge, U.K.: Cambridge University Press, 1987).

Charles J. Halperin, *Russia and the Golden Horde: The Mongol Impact on Medieval Russian History* (Bloomington: Indiana University Press, 1985).

Gwyn Jones, *A History of the Vikings* (New York: Oxford University Press, 1968).

George Herbert Tinley Kimble, *Geography in the Middle Ages* (New York: Russell & Russell, 1968).

Emmanuel Le Roy Ladurie, *Times of Feast, Times of Famine: A History of Climate Since the Year 1000,* translated by Barbara Bray (Garden City, N.Y.: Doubleday, 1971).

Magnus Magnusson and Herman Pálsson, trans., *The Vinland Sagas: The Norse Discovery of America* (Harmondsworth, U.K.: Penguin, 1965).

John Mandeville, *The Travels of Sir John Mandeville,* translated by Charles W. R. D. Moseley (Harmondsworth, U.K.: Penguin, 1983).

Geoffrey Jules Marcus, *The Conquest of the North Atlantic* (Woodbridge, U.K.: Boydell, 1980).

David Morgan, *The Mongols* (Oxford: Blackwell, 1986).

Samuel Eliot Morison, *The European Discovery of America: The Northern Voyages* (New York: Oxford University Press, 1971).

Arthur C. Moule, *Christians in China Before the Year 1550* (New York & Toronto: Macmillan, 1930).

Farley Mowat, *Westviking: The Ancient Norse in Greenland and North America* (Boston: Little, Brown, 1965).

James Muldoon, ed., *The Expansion of Europe: The First Phase* (Philadelphia: University of Pennsylvania Press, 1977).

Arthur P. Newton, *Travel and Travelers of the Middle Ages* (New York: Knopf, 1926).

J. R. S. Phillips, *The Medieval Expansion of Europe* (Oxford: Clarendon Press, 1998).

Frederick J. Pohl, *The Viking Explorers* (New York: Crowell, 1966).

Igor de Rachewiltz, *Papal Envoys to the Great Khans* (London: Faber & Faber, 1971).

P. E. Russell, *Prince Henry the Navigator: The Rise and Fall of a Culture Hero* (Oxford: Oxford University Press, 1984).

John J. Saunders, *The History of the Mongol Conquests* (London: Routledge & Kegan Paul, 1971).

THE ARTS

Jonathan J. G. Alexander, *Medieval Illuminators and Their Methods of Work* (New Haven: Yale University Press, 1993).

T. H. Aston, gen. ed., *The History of the University of Oxford,* volume 1, *The Early Oxford Schools,* edited by J. I. Catto (Oxford & New York: Oxford University Press, 1984).

David Bevington, *Medieval Drama* (Boston: Houghton Mifflin, 1975).

R. Howard Bloch, *Medieval Misogyny and the Invention of Western Romantic Love* (Chicago: University of Chicago Press, 1991).

Robert G. Calkins, *Medieval Architecture in Western Europe: from A.D. 300 to 1500* (New York: Oxford University Press, 1998).

The Camelot Project at the University of Rochester: Arthurian Texts, Images, Bibliographies and Basic Information <http://www.ub.rug.nl/camelot/>.

Michael Camille, *Image on the Edge: The Margins of Medieval Art* (Cambridge, Mass.: Harvard University Press, 1992).

Cantigas de Santa Maria <www.pbm.com/~lindahl/cantigas>.

Mary J. Carruthers, *The Book of Memory: A Study of Memory in Medieval Culture* (Cambridge & New York: Cambridge University Press, 1990).

A.C. Cawley, eds., *Everyman, and Medieval Miracle Plays* (Rutland, Vt.: Tuttle, 1993).

Henry Chadwick, *Boethius: The Consolations of Music, Logic, Theology and Philosophy* (Oxford: Clarendon Press, 1981).

Carol J. Clover, *The Medieval Saga* (Ithaca: Cornell University Press, 1982).

A. B. Cobban, *The Medieval Universities: Their Development and Organization* (London: Methuen, 1975).

Marcia L. Colish, *Medieval Foundations of Western Intellectual Tradition, 400–1400* (New Haven: Yale University Press, 1997).

Richard L. Crocker, *An Introduction to Gregorian Chant* (New Haven & London: Yale University Press, 2000).

Ernst Robert Curtius, *European Literature and the Latin Middle Ages*, translated by Willard R. Trask (Princeton: Princeton University Press, 1990).

Lowrie J. Daly, *The Medieval University, 1200–1400* (New York: Sheed & Ward, 1961).

Peter Dronke, *The Medieval Poet and His World* (Rome: Edizioni di storia e letteratura, 1984).

Virginia W. Egbert, *The Medieval Artist at Work* (Princeton: Princeton University Press, 1967).

Grace Frank, *The Medieval French Drama* (Oxford: Clarendon Press, 1954).

Paul Frankl, *Gothic Architecture*, revised edition (New Haven: Yale University Press, 2000).

Marion E. Gibbs and Sidney M. Johnson, *Medieval German Literature: A Companion* (New York: Garland, 1997).

The Gregorian Chant Home Page <http://silvertone.princeton.edu/chant_html/>.

Barbara A. Hanawalt and Kathryn L. Reyerson, eds. *City and Spectacle in Medieval Europe* (Minneapolis: University of Minnesota Press, 1994).

Richard H. Hoppin, *Medieval Music* (New York: Norton, 1978).

Images of Medieval Art and Architecture <http://www.pitt.edu/~medart/>.

H. W. Janson, *History of Art*, fifth edition, revised (New York: Abrams, 1997).

Hans Erich Kubach, *Romanesque Architecture* (New York: Electa/Rizzoli, 1988).

Jacques Le Goff, *Intellectuals in the Middle Ages*, translated by Teresa Lavender Fagan (Cambridge, Mass. & Oxford, U.K.: Blackwell, 1993).

Luisa Marcucci and Emma Micheletti, *Medieval Painting: A History of European Painting*, translated by H. E. Scott (New York: Viking, 1960).

"Medieval European Drama in Translation" <http://arts-sciences.cua.edu/engl/drama/index.htm>.

"The Middle Ages," in *Artcyclopedia* <http://witcombe.sbc.edu/ARTHmedieval.html>.

Stephen A. Mitchell, *Heroic Sagas and Ballads* (Ithaca, N.Y.: Cornell University Press, 1991).

Armando Petrucci, *Writers and Readers in Medieval Italy: Studies in the History of Written Culture*, edited and translated by Charles M. Radding (New Haven: Yale University Press, 1995).

Suzanne Reynolds, *Medieval Reading: Grammar, Rhetoric, and the Classical Text* (Cambridge & New York: Cambridge University Press, 1996).

Leslie Ross, *Medieval Art: A Topical Dictionary* (Westport, Conn.: Greenwood Press, 1996).

Francesca Canade Sautman, Diana Conchado, and Giuseppe Carlo di Scipio, eds., *Telling Tales: Medieval Narratives and the Folk Tradition* (New York: St. Martin's Press, 1998).

Veronica Sekules, *Medieval Art* (New York: Oxford University Press, 2001).

Otto Von Simson, *The Gothic Cathedral: Origins of Gothic Architecture and the Medieval Concept of Order*, third edition, enlarged (Princeton: Princeton University Press, 1962).

James Snyder, *Medieval Art: Painting, Scupture, Architecture, 4th–14th Century* (New York: Abrams / Upper Saddle River, N.J.: Prentice Hall, 1989).

Gabrielle M. Spiegel, *The Past as Text: The Theory and Practice of Medieval Historiography* (Baltimore: Johns Hopkins University Press, 1997).

Marcelle Thiebaux, ed. and trans., *The Writings of Medieval Women: An Anthology*, second edition (New York: Garland, 1994).

Glyne Wickham, *The Medieval Theater* (London: Weidenfeld & Nicolson, 1974).

COMMUNICATION, TRANSPORTATION, AND EXPLORATION

Charles Burnett, "The Translating Activity in Medieval Spain," in *The Legacy of Muslim Spain*, edited by Salma Khadra Jayyusi (Leiden & New York: E. J. Brill, 1992), pp. 1036–1058.

Carlo M. Cipolla, *Literacy and Development in the West* (Baltimore: Penguin, 1969).

Ross E. Dunn, *The Adventures of Ibn Battuta, a Muslim Traveler of the 14th Century* (Berkeley: University of California Press, 1986).

Lucien Febvre and Henri-Jean Martin, *The Coming of the Book: The Impact of Printing, 1450–1800*, translated by David Gerard (London: N. L. B., 1976).

Francois Garnier, *Le langage de l'Image au Moyen Age*, 2 volumes (Paris: Léopard d'or, 1982–1989).

Marcia Kupfer, "Medieval World Maps: Embedded Images, Interpretative Frames," *Word and Image*, 10 (1994): 262–288.

Margaret Wade Labarge, *Medieval Travellers: The Rich and Restless* (London: Hamilton, 1982).

M. K. Lawson, *Cnut: The Danes in England in the Early Eleventh Century* (London & New York: Longman, 1993).

Arthur Percival Newton, ed., *Travel and Travellers of the Middle Ages* (New York: Barnes & Noble, 1968).

John D. Niles and Mark Amodio, ed., *Anglo-Scandinavian England: Norse-English Relations in the Period before the Conquest* (Lanham, Md.: University Press of America, 1989).

Marco Polo, *The Travels,* translated by Ronald Latham (London: Penguin, 1958).

Marjorie Rowling, *Everyday Life of Medieval Travellers* (London: Batsford, 1971).

Alexander Rumble, ed., *The Reign of Cnut: King of England, Denmark and Norway* (London: Leicester University Press, 1994).

G. V. Scammell, *The World Encompassed: The First European Maritime Empires, c. 800–1650* (Berkeley: University of California Press, 1981).

Kristen A. Seaver, *The Frozen Echo: Greenland and the Exploration of North America ca. AD 1000–1500* (Stanford, Cal.: Stanford University Press, 1996).

Bertold Spuler, *History of the Mongols, Based on Eastern and Western Accounts of the Thirteenth and Fourteenth Centuries,* translated by H. and S. Drummond (London: Routledge, 1972).

SOCIAL CLASS SYSTEM AND THE ECONOMY

John W. Baldwin, *The Medieval Theories of the Just Price* (Philadelphia: American Philosophical Society, 1959).

Robert H. Bautier, *The Economic Development of Medieval Europe* (London: Thames & Hudson, 1971).

Thomas N. Bisson, *Conservation of Coinage: Monetary Exploitation and its Restraint in France, Catalonia, and Aragon, c. A.D. 1000–c. 1225* (Oxford: Clarendon Press, 1979).

Prosper Boissonade, *Life and Work in Medieval Europe* (New York: Harper & Row, 1964).

Christopher Brooke, *The Structure of Medieval Society* (New York: McGraw-Hill, 1971).

G. G. Coulton, *Medieval Village, Manor, and Monastery* (New York: Harper, 1960).

Coulton, comp., *Social Life in Britain from the Conquest to the Reformation* (Cambridge, U.K.: Cambridge University Press, 1918).

Anne Denieul-Cormier, *Wise and Foolish Kings: The First House of Valois, 1328–1498* (Garden City, N.Y.: Doubleday, 1980).

Georges Duby, *The Three Orders: Feudal Society Imagined,* translated by Arthur Goldhammer (Chicago: University of Chicago Press, 1980).

Steven A. Epstein, *Wage Labor and Guilds in Medieval Europe* (Chapel Hill: University of North Carolina Press, 1991).

Patrick J. Geary, ed., *Authors of the Middle Ages: Historical and Religious Writers of the Latin West* (Brookfield, Vt.: Variorum, 1995).

John Bell Henneman, *Royal Taxation in Fourteenth-Century France: The Captivity and Ransom of John II, 1356–1370* (Philadelphia: American Philosophical Society, 1976).

Henneman, *Royal Taxation in Fourteenth-Century France: The Development of War Financing, 1322–1356* (Princeton, N.J.: Princeton University Press, 1971).

John Hicks, *A Theory of Economic History* (Oxford: Oxford University Press, 1969).

R. H. Hilton, *English and French Towns in Feudal Society: A Comparative Study* (Cambridge, U.K. & New York: Oxford University Press, 1992).

Odd Langholm, *Economics in the Medieval Schools. Wealth, Exchange, Value, Money and Usury according to the Paris Theological Tradition, 1200–1350* (Leiden & New York: E. J. Brill, 1992).

Lester K. Little, *Religious Poverty and the Profit Economy in Medieval Europe* (Ithaca, N.Y.: Cornell University Press, 1978).

Robert S. Lopez, *The Commercial Revolution of the Middle Ages, 900–1350* (Englewood Cliffs, N.J.: Prentice-Hall, 1971).

Lopez, *The Shape of Medieval Monetary History* (London: Variorum, 1986).

Lopez and Irving W. Raymond, *Medieval Trade in the Mediterranean World: Illustrative Documents Translated with Introductions and Notes* (New York: Columbia University Press, 1955).

Kate Mertes, *The English Noble Household 1250–1600* (Oxford & New York: Blackwell, 1988).

John H. Mundy and Peter Riesenberg, *The Medieval Town* (Princeton, N.J.: Van Nostrand, 1958).

Henri Pirenne, *Medieval Cities: Their Origins and the Revival of Trade,* translated by Frank D. Halsey (Princeton, N.J.: Princeton University Press, 1969).

M. M. Postan, E. E. Rich, and Edward Miller, eds., *The Cambridge Economic History of Europe* (Cambridge, U.K.: Cambridge University Press, 1965).

Norman J. G. Pounds, *An Economic History of Medieval Europe* (London & New York: Longman, 1974).

Susan Reynolds, *Fiefs and Vassals: The Medieval Evidence Reinterpreted* (New York: Oxford University Press, 1994).

Shulamith Shahar, *The Fourth Estate: A History of Women in the Middle Ages* (London & New York: Methuen, 1983).

George Unwin, *Studies in Economic History* (London: Macmillan, 1927).

Richard Vaughan, *Matthew Paris* (Cambridge, U.K.: Cambridge University Press, 1958).

POLITICS, LAW, AND THE MILITARY

Larry H. Addington, *The Patterns of War Through the Eighteenth Century* (Bloomington & Indianapolis: Indiana University Press, 1990).

Christopher Allmand, *The Hundred Years War: England and France at War c. 1300–c. 1450.* (Cambridge & New York: Cambridge University Press, 1988).

Bernard S. Bachrach, *Early Carolingian Warfare: Prelude to Empire* (Philadelphia: University of Pennsylvania Press, 2001).

Frank Barlow, *The Feudal Kingdom of England, 1042–1216* (London & New York: Longmans, Green, 1955).

Barlow, *William I and the Norman Conquest* (London: English Universities Press, 1965).

John Beeler, *Warfare in Feudal Europe, 730–1200* (Ithaca: Cornell University Press, 1971).

Matthew Bennett, *Agincourt 1415: Triumph Against the Odds* (London: Osprey, 1991).

Jim Bradbury, *The Battle of Hastings* (Stroud, U.K.: Sutton, 1998).

Bradbury, *The Medieval Siege* (Woodbridge, U.K. & Rochester, N.Y.: Boydell Press, 1992).

Bradbury, *Philip Augustus: King of France, 1180–1223* (London & New York: Longman, 1998).

R. Allen Brown, *The Normans and the Norman Conquest,* second edition(Dover, N.H.: Boydell Press, 1985).

James A. Brundage, *Richard, Lion Heart* (New York: Scribners, 1974).

Alfred H. Burne, *The Agincourt War: A Military History of the Latter Part of the Hundred Years War from 1369 to 1453* (London: Eyre & Spottiswoode, 1956).

Burne, *The Crecy War: A Military History of the Hundred Years War from 1337 to the Peace of Bretigny, 1360* (London: Eyre & Spottiswoode, 1955).

James Chambers, *The Devils' Horsemen: The Mongol Invasion of Europe* (London: Weidenfeld & Nicolson, 1979).

Eric Christiansen, *The Northern Crusades* (London & New York: Penguin, 1997).

Philippe Contamine, *War in the Middle Ages,* translated by Michael Jones (Oxford, U.K.: Blackwell, 1984).

H. E. J. Cowdrey, *Popes, Monks, and Crusades* (London: Hambledon, 1984).

Kelly DeVries, *Joan of Arc: A Military Leader* (Stroud, U.K.: Sutton, 1999).

DeVries, *Medieval Military Technology* (Peterborough, Ont. & Lewiston, N.Y.: Broadview Press, 1992).

DeVries, *The Military Campaigns of the Hundred Years War* (Stroud, U.K.: Sutton, 2001).

DeVries, *The Norwegian Invasion of England in 1066* (Woodbridge, U.K. & Rochester, N.Y.: Boydell Press, 1999).

A. E. Dick, *Magna Carta: Text and Commentary* (Charlottesville: University Press of Virginia, 1994).

Joycelyne Gledhill Dickinson, *The Congress of Arras, 1435: A Study in Medieval Diplomacy* (Oxford, U.K.: Clarendon Press, 1955).

David C. Douglas, *William the Conqueror* (Berkeley: University of California Press, 1964).

Katherine Fischer Drew, trans., *The Laws of the Salian Franks* (Philadelphia: University of Pennsylvania Press, 1991).

J. A. S. Evans, *The Age of Justinian: The Circumstances of Imperial Power* (New York: Routledge, 1996).

Heinrich Fichtenau, *The Carolingian Empire: The Age of Charlemagne,* translated by Peter Munz (New York: Barnes & Noble, 1963).

Peter G. Foote and David M. Wilson, *The Viking Achievement: The Society and Culture of Early Medieval Scandinavia* (London: Sidgwick & Jackson, 1970).

Kenneth Fowler, *The Age of the Plantagenet and the Valois: The Struggle for Supremacy, 1328–1498* (London: Elek, 1967; New York: Putnam, 1967).

John France, *Victory in the East: A Military History of the First Crusade* (Cambridge & New York: Cambridge University Press, 1994).

François Louis Ganshof, *Frankish Institutions Under Charlemagne,* translated by Bryce and Mary Lyon (Providence, R.I.: Brown University Press, 1968).

John Gillingham, *Richard the Lionheart* (London: Weidenfeld & Nicolson, 1978).

Leo de Hartog, *Genghis Khan, Conqueror of the World* (New York: St. Martin's, 1989).

Thomas Head and Richard Landes, eds., *The Peace of God: Social Violence and Religious Response in France Around the Year 1000* (Ithaca, N.Y.: Cornell University Press, 1992).

H. J. Hewitt, *The Black Prince's Expedition of 1355–1357* (Manchester, U.K.: Manchester University Press, 1958).

Hewitt, *The Organization of War Under Edward III, 1338–62* (Manchester: Manchester University Press; New York: Barnes & Noble, 1966).

C. Warren Hollister, ed., *The Impact of the Norman Conquest* (New York: Wiley, 1969).

James Clarke Holt, *Magna Carta* (Cambridge: Cambridge University Press, 1965).

P. M. Holt, *The Age of the Crusades: The Near East from the Eleventh Century to 1517* (London & New York: Longman, 1986).

Nicholas Hooper and Matthew Bennett, *The Cambridge Illustrated Atlas of Warfare: The Middle Ages* (New York: Cambridge University Press, 1996).

Norman Housley, *The Later Crusades, 1274–1580: From Lyons to Alcazar* (New York: Oxford University Press, 1992).

David Armine Howarth, *1066: The Year of the Conquest* (London: Collins, 1977).

John Hudson, *The Formation of the English Common Law: Law and Society in England from the Norman Conquest to Magna Carta* (London & New York: Longman, 1996).

William C. Jordan, *Louis IX and the Challenge of the Crusade: A Study in Rulership* (Princeton, N.J.: Princeton University Press, 1979).

Walter E. Kaegi, *Byzantium and the Early Islamic Conquests* (Cambridge & New York: Cambridge University Press, 1992).

Maurice Keen, ed., *Medieval Warfare: A History* (Oxford & New York: Oxford University Press, 1999).

Keen, *Nobles, Knights, and Men-at-Arms in the Middle Ages* (London & Rio Grande, Ohio: Hambledon Press, 1996).

George Williams Keeton, *The Norman Conquest and the Common Law* (London: Benn, 1996; New York: Barnes & Noble, 1996).

F. Donald Logan, *The Vikings in History,* second edition (London & New York: HarperCollins Academic, 1991).

C. A. Macartney, *The Magyars in the Ninth Century* (Cambridge, U.K.: Cambridge University Press, 1968).

Michael Mallett, *Mercenaries and Their Masters: Warfare in Renaissance Italy* (London: Bodley Head, 1974; Totowa, N.J.: Rowman & Littlefield, 1974).

Hans Eberhard Mayer, *The Crusades,* translated by John Gillingham (London: Oxford University Press, 1972).

Rosamund McKitterick, *The Frankish Kingdoms under the Carolingians, 751–987* (London & New York: Longman, 1983).

S. F. C. Milsom, *Historical Foundations of the Common Law* (London: Butterworth, 1969).

Peter Munz, *Frederick Barbarossa: A Study in Medieval Politics* (Ithaca, N.Y.: Cornell University Press, 1969).

Richard Ager Newhall, *The English Conquest of Normandy, 1416–1424: A Study in Fifteenth Century Warfare* (New Haven, Conn.: Yale University Press, 1924).

David C. Nicolle, *Arms and Armour of the Crusading Era, 1050–1350,* 2 volumes (White Plains, N.Y.: Kraus, 1988).

Nicolle, *Medieval Warfare Source Book,* volume one, *Warfare in Western Christendom* (London: Arms & Armour, 1995).

Nicolle, *Medieval Warfare Source Book,* volume two, *Christian Europe and its Neighbors* (London: Arms & Armour, 1995).

Marcel Pacaut, *Frederick Barbarossa* (New York: Scribners, 1970).

Anne Pallister, *Magna Carta: The Heritage of Liberty* (Oxford: Clarendon Press, 1971).

Edouard Perroy, *The Hundred Years War,* translated by W. B. Wells (London: Eyre & Spottiswoode, 1951; New York: Oxford University Press, 1951).

A. J. Pollard, *John Talbot and the War in France* (London: Royal Historical Society, 1983).

Richard A. Preston and others, *Men in Arms: A History of Warfare and Its Interrelationships with Western Society,* fifth edition (Fort Worth: Holt, Rinehart & Winston, 1991).

Michael Prestwich, *Armies and Warfare in the Middle Ages: The English Experience* (New Haven: Yale University Press, 1996).

Geoffrey Regan, *Lionhearts: Saladin, Richard I, and the Era of the Third Crusade* (New York: Walker, 1998).

James Reston, *Warriors of God: Richard the Lionheart and Saladin in the Third Crusade* (New York: Doubleday, 2001).

Jean Richard, *The Crusades, c. 1071–c. 1291,* translated by Jean Birrell (Cambridge & New York: Cambridge University Press, 1999).

Richard, *Saint Louis* (Cambridge & New York: Cambridge University Press, 1992).

Jonathan Riley-Smith, *The Crusades: A Short History* (New Haven: Yale University Press, 1987).

Riley-Smith, ed., *The Oxford Illustrated History of the Crusades* (Oxford & New York: Oxford University Press, 1995).

Theodore John Rivers, trans., *Laws of the Salian and Ripuarian Franks* (New York: AMS Press, 1986).

Steven Runciman, *A History of the Crusades,* three volumes (Cambridge: Cambridge University Press, 1951–1954).

Peter Sawyer, *The Age of the Vikings* (New York: St. Martin's Press, 1962).

Sawyer, *Kings and Vikings: Scandinavia and Europe, A.D. 700–1100* (London & New York: Methuen, 1982).

R. C. Smail, *Crusading Warfare, 1097–1193* (Cambridge: Cambridge University Press, 1956).

Jonathan Sumption, *The Hundred Years War,* two volumes (London: Faber & Faber, 1990).

William Finley Swindler, *Magna Carta: Legend and Legacy* (Indianapolis: Bobbs-Merrill, 1965).

Brian Tierney and Sidney Painter, *Western Europe in the Middle Ages, 300–1475*, sixth edition (Boston: McGraw-Hill, 1998).

Malcolm Vale, *War and Chivalry: Warfare and Aristocratic Culture in England, France, and Burgundy at the End of the Middle Ages* (Athens: University of Georgia Press, 1981; London: Duckworth, 1981).

Richard Vaughan, *Valois Burgundy* (London: Lane, 1975; Hamden, Conn.: Archon, 1975).

J. F. Verbruggen, *The Art of Warfare in Western Europe During the Middle Ages: From the Eighth Century to 1340*, translated by Sumner Willard and R. W. Southern (Woodbridge, U.K. & Rochester, N.Y.: Boydell Press, 1997).

Dorothy Whitelock, and others, *The Norman Conquest: Its Setting and Impact* (London: Eyre & Spottiswoode, 1966).

LEISURE, RECREATION, AND DAILY LIFE

M. W. Barley, *European Towns: Their Archaeology and Early History* (New York: Academic Press, 1977).

Patricia Basing, *Trades and Crafts in Medieval Manuscripts* (London: British Library, 1990).

Judith M. Bennett, ed. *Sisters and Workers in the Middle Ages* (Chicago: University of Chicago Press, 1989).

Maurice Beresford, *New Towns of the Middle Ages* (Wolfboro, N.H.: Sutton, 1988).

Paul Binski, *Medieval Craftsmen: Painters* (Toronto: University of Toronto Press, 1991).

John Blair and Nigel Ramsay, eds. *English Medieval Industries* (London: Hambledon Press, 1991).

Meg Bogin, *The Women Troubadours* (New York: Paddington Press, 1975).

Jean Bony, *French Gothic Architecture of the Twelfth and Thirteenth Centuries* (Berkeley: University of California Press, 1983).

Robert Brentano, *Rome before Avignon: A Social History of Thirteenth Century Rome* (Berkeley: University of California, 1990).

Jean Chapelot and Robert Fossier, *The Village and House in the Middle Ages*, translated by Henry Cleere (London: Batsford, 1985).

John Cherry, *Medieval Craftsmen: Goldsmiths* (Toronto: University of Toronto Press, 1992).

John Clark, ed., *The Medieval Horse and Its Equipment* (London: HMSO, 1995).

Nicola Coldstream, *Medieval Craftsmen: Masons and Sculptors* (Toronto: University of Toronto Press, 1989).

M. P. Cosman, *Fabulous Feasts: Medieval Cookery and Ceremony* (New York: Braziller, 1976).

Sally Crawford, *Childhood in Anglo-Saxon England* (Phoenix Mill, U.K.: Sutton, 1999).

John Cummins, *The Hound and the Hawk: The Art of Medieval Hunting* (New York: St. Martin's Press, 1988).

Q. W. Cunnington and P. Cunnington, *Handbook of English Medieval Costume* (London: Faber & Faber, 1952).

Christopher De Hamel, *A History of Illuminated Manuscripts* (Boston: Godine, 1986).

Georges Duby, ed., *A History of Private Life: Revelations of the Medieval World* (Cambridge, Mass.: Harvard University Press, 1989).

Christopher Dyer, "English Peasant Buildings in the Later Middle Ages (1200–1500)," *Medieval Archaeology*, 20 (1986): 19–45.

Elizabeth Eames, *Medieval Craftsmen: English Tilers* (Toronto: University of Toronto Press, 1992).

Penelope Eames, *Furniture in England, France and the Netherlands from the Twelfth to the Fifteenth Century* (London: Furniture History Society, 1977).

David Edge and John Miles Paddock, *Arms and Armour of the Medieval Knight: An Illustrated History of Weaponry in the Middle Ages* (New York: Defoe, 1988).

John Fitchen, *Building Construction before Mechanization* (Cambridge, Mass.: MIT Press, 1986).

Robert Fossier, *Peasant Life in the Medieval West*, translated by Juliet Vale (Oxford & New York: Blackwell, 1988).

Vito Fumagalli, *Landscapes of Fear: Perceptions of Nature and the City in the Middle Ages*, translated by Shayne Mitchell (Cambridge, U.K.: Polity Press / Cambridge, Mass.: Blackwell, 1994).

Jane S. Gerber, *The Jews of Spain: A History of the Sephardic Experience* (New York: Free Press, 1992).

Frances Gies and Joseph Gies, *Cathedral, Forge, and Waterwheel: Technology and Invention in the Middle Ages* (New York: HarperCollins, 1994).

Gies and Gies, *Life in a Medieval Castle* (New York: Crowell, 1974).

Gies and Gies, *Life in a Medieval City* (New York: Harper & Row, 1981).

Gies and Gies, *Life in a Medieval Village* (New York: Harper & Row, 1990).

Gies and Gies, *Marriage and Family in the Middle Ages* (New York: Harper & Row, 1987).

Hans-Werner Goetz, *Life in the Middle Ages: From the Seventh to the Thirteenth Century*, translated by Albert Wimmer, edited by Steven Rowan (Notre Dame: University of Notre Dame Press, 1993).

Jeremy Goldberg, "Girls Growing Up in Later Medieval England," *History Today*, 45 (June 1995): 25–32.

Lindsay Granshaw and Roy Porter, eds., *The Hospital in History* (London & New York: Routledge, 1989).

H. E. Hallem, *Rural England, 1066–1348* (London: Fontana, 1981).

Barbara Hanawalt, *Growing Up in Medieval London: The Experience of Childhood in History* (New York: Oxford University Press, 1993).

Hanawalt, *The Ties that Bound: Peasant Families in Medieval England* (New York: Oxford University Press, 1986).

Hanawalt and Kathryn L. Reyerson, eds., *City and Spectacle in Medieval Europe* (Minneapolis: University of Minnesota Press, 1994).

Barbara Harvey, *Living and Dying in England, 1100–1500: The Monastic Experience* (New York: Oxford University Press, 1993).

David Herlihy, *Medieval Households* (Cambridge, Mass.: Harvard University Press, 1985.

Herlihy, *Opera Muliebria: Women and Work in Medieval Europe* (New York: McGraw-Hill, 1990).

Cecil Alec Hewett, *English Historic Carpentry* (London: Phillimore, 1980).

David A. Hinton, "'Clothing' and the Later Middle Ages," *Medieval Archaeology,* 43 (1999): 172–182.

Urban Tigner Holmes, *Daily Living in the Twelfth Century, Based on the Observations of Alexander Neckham in London and Paris* (Madison: University of Wisconsin Press, 1952).

George C. Homans, *English Villagers of the Thirteenth Century* (New York: Norton, 1941).

Richard H. Hoppin, *Medieval Music* (New York: Norton, 1978).

Diane Owen Hughes, "Domestic Ideals and Social Behavior: Evidence from Medieval Genoa," in *The Family in History,* edited by Charles E. Rosenberg (Philadelphia: University of Pennsylvania Press, 1975).

John Hunt, *Lordship and the Landscape:* A Documentary and Archaeological Study of the Honor of Dudley c. 1066–1322 (Oxford: BAR, 1997).

Ronald Hutton, *The Stations of the Sun: A History of the Ritual Year in Britain* (New York: Oxford University Press, 1990).

Maurice Keen, *Chivalry* (New Haven: Yale University Press, 1984).

Hugh Kennedy, *Crusader Castles* (Cambridge & New York: Cambridge University Press, 1994).

John R. Kenyon, *Medieval Fortifications,* The Archeology of Medieval Britain (London: Leicester University Press, 1990).

Berenice M. Kerr, *Religious Life for Women, c. 1100–c. 1350: Fontevraud in England* (Oxford: Clarendon Press, 1999).

Rachel Laudan, "Birth of the Modern Diet," *Scientific American,* 243 (August 2000): 76–81.

C. H. Lawrence, *Medieval Monasticism: Forms of Religious Life in Western Europe in the Middle Ages* (London & New York: Longman, 1984).

Jacques LeGoff, *Medieval Callings,* translated by Lydia G. Cochrane (Chicago: University of Chicago Press, 1990).

James Masschaele, *Peasants, Merchants, and Markets: Inland Trade in Medieval England, 1150–1350* (New York: St. Martin's Press, 1997).

Theresa McLean, *The English at Play in the Middle Ages* (Windsor Forest, U.K.: Kensal Press, 1983).

Stephen Mennell, *All Manners of Food: Eating and Taste in England and France from the Middle Ages to the Present* (Oxford: Blackwell, 1985).

Eric Mercer, *Furniture, 700–1700* (New York: Meredith Press, 1969).

Michel Mollat, *The Poor in the Middle Ages: An Essay in Social History,* translated by Arthur Goldhammer (New Haven: Yale University Press, 1986).

Robin S. Oggins, *Castles and Fortresses* (New York: Metrobooks, 1975).

Matthias Pfaffenbichler, *Medieval Craftsmen: Armourers* (Toronto: University of Toronto Press, 1992).

Françoise Piponnier and Perrine Mane, *Dress in the Middle Ages,* translated by Caroline Beamish (New Haven: Yale University Press, 1997).

Norman J. G. Pounds, *Hearth and Home: A History of Material Culture* (Bloomington: Indiana University Press, 1989).

Pierre Riché, *Daily Life in the World of Charlemagne,* translated by Jo Ann McNamara (Philadelphia: University of Pennsylvania Press, 1978).

E. Raymond Role, "The War Games of Medieval Italy," *History Today,* 49 (June 1999), on-line at <http://www.historytoday.com/article/article.cfm?article_id=1428>.

John Schofield, *Medieval London Houses* (New Haven: Yale University Press, 1994).

D. Eleanor Scully and Terence Scully, *Early French Cookery: Sources, History, Original Recipes and Modern Adaptations* (Ann Arbor: University of Michigan Press, 1996).

Jeffrey L. Singman, *Daily Life in Medieval Europe* (Westport, Conn.: Greenwood Press, 1999).

Elizabeth Bradford Smith and Michael Wolfe, eds., *Technology and Resource Use in Medieval Europe: Cathedrals, Mills, and Mines* (Aldershot, U.K. & Brookfield, Vt.: Ashgate, 1997).

Claire Sponsler, "Narrating the Social Order: Medieval Clothing Laws," *Clio,* 21 (1992): 265–283.

Kay Staniland, *Medieval Craftsmen: Embroiderers* (Toronto: University of Toronto Press, 1991).

John Storck and Walter Dorwin Teague, *Flour for Man's Bread: A History of Milling* (Minneapolis: University of Minnesota Press, 1952.

Del Sweeney, ed., *Agriculture in the Middle Ages: Technology, Practice, and Representation* (Philadelphia: University of Pennsylvania Press, 1995).

Naomi Tarrant, *The Development of Costume* (New York: Routledge, 1994).

A. J. Taylor, *Caernarvon Castle and Town Walls* (London: HMSO, 1975).

THE FAMILY AND SOCIAL TRENDS

Danièle Alexandre-Bidon and Didier Lett, *Children in the Middle Ages: Fifth-Fifteenth Centuries,* translated by Jody Gladding (Notre Dame, Ind.: University of Notre Dame Press, 1999).

Philippe Aries, *Centuries of Childhood,* translated by Robert Baldick (London: Cape, 1962).

Clarissa W. Atkinson, *The Oldest Vocation: Christian Motherhood in the Middle Ages* (Ithaca, N.Y.: Cornell University Press, 1991).

Bartholomew of England, *On the Properties of Things: John of Trevisa's Translation of Bartholomaeus Anglicus* De Proprietatibus Rerum: *A Critical Text,* 3 volumes, edited by M. C. Seymour and others (Oxford: Clarendon Press, 1975–1988).

Peter Biller, "Birth-Control in the West in the Thirteenth and Early Fourteenth Centuries," *Past and Present,* 94 (1982): 3–26.

Biller, "Childbirth in the Middle Ages," *History Today,* 36 (August 1986): 42–49.

Jane Bishop, "Bishops as Marital Advisors in the Ninth Century," in *Women of the Medieval World: Essays in Honor of John H. Mundy,* edited by Julius Kirshner and Suzanne F. Wemple (Oxford & New York: Blackwell, 1985), pp. 53–84.

Christopher N. L. Brooke, *The Medieval Idea of Marriage* (Oxford & New York: Oxford University Press, 1989).

James A. Brundage, *Law, Sex, and Christian Society in Medieval Europe* (Chicago: University of Chicago Press, 1987).

Brundage, "Playing by the Rules: Sexual Behaviour and Legal Norms In Medieval Europe," in *Desire and Discipline: Sex and Sexuality in the Premodern West,* edited by Jacqueline Murray and Konrad Eisenbichler (Toronto & Buffalo: University of Toronto Press, 1996), pp. 23–41.

Brundage, "Sexual Equality and Medieval Canon Law," in *Medieval Women and the Sources of Medieval History,* edited by Joel T. Rosenthal (Athens: University of Georgia Press, 1990), pp. 66–79.

Brundage, *Sex, Law and Marriage in the Middle Ages* (Aldershot, Hampshire, U.K. & Brookfield, Vt.: Variorum, 1993).

Elaine Clark, "Some Aspects of Social Security in Medieval England," *Journal of Family History,* 7 (1982): 307–320.

Charles Donahue Jr., "The Canon Law on the Formation of Marriage and Social Practice in the Later Middle Ages," *Journal of Family History,* 8 (1983): 144–158.

Donahue, "The Policy of Alexander III's Consent Theory of Marriage," *Proceedings of the 4th Congress of Medieval Canon Law,* edited by Stephan Kuttner (Vatican City: Biblioteca Apostolica Vaticana, 1976), pp. 251–281.

Georges Duby, *The Knight, the Lady and the Priest: The Making of Modern Marriage in Medieval France,* translated by Barbara Bray (New York: Pantheon, 1983).

Duby, *Medieval Marriage: Two Models from Twelfth-Century France,* translated by Elborg Forster (Baltimore: Johns Hopkins University Press, 1978).

Dyan Elliott, "Bernardino of Siena versus the Marriage Debt," in *Desire and Discipline: Sex and Sexuality in the Premodern West,* edited by Jacqueline Murray and Konrad Eisenbichler (Toronto & Buffalo: University of Toronto Press, 1996), pp. 168–200.

A. J. Finch, "Parental Authority and the Problem of Clandestine Marriage in the Later Middle Ages," *Law and History Review,* 8 (1990): 189–204.

Laurence Fontaine and Jürgen Schlumbohm, *Household Strategies for Survival, 1600–2000* (Cambridge & New York: Cambridge University Press, 2000).

Frances Gies and Joseph Gies, *Marriage and the Family in the Middle Ages* (New York: Harper & Row, 1987).

Guibert of Nogent, *A Monk's Confession: The Memoirs of Guibert of Nogent,* translated by Paul J. Archambault (University Park: Pennsylvania State University Press, 1996).

Barbara A. Hanawalt, *Growing Up in Medieval London: The Experience of Childhood in History* (New York: Oxford University Press, 1993).

Hanawalt, *The Ties That Bound: Peasant Families in Medieval England* (New York: Oxford University Press, 1986).

David Herlihy, "Age, Property, and Career in Medieval Society," *Aging and the Aged in Medieval Europe,* edited by Michael M. Sheehan (Toronto: Pontifical Institute of Mediaeval Studies, 1990), pp. 143–158.

Herlihy, *Medieval Households* (Cambridge, Mass.: Harvard University Press, 1985).

Willy van Hoecke and Andries Welkenhuysen, eds., *Love and Marriage in the Twelfth Century* (Leuven: Leuven University Press, 1981).

Danielle Jacquart and Claude Thomasset, *Sexuality and Medicine in the Middle Ages,* translated by Matthew Adamson (Princeton: Princeton University Press, 1988).

Bernhard Jussen, *Spiritual Kinship as Social Practice: God-parenthood and Adoption in the Early Middle Ages,* translated by Pamela Selwyn, revised edition (Newark: University of Delaware Press, 2000).

Henry Ansgar Kelly, *Love and Marriage in the Age of Chaucer* (Ithaca, N.Y.: Cornell University Press, 1975).

Harald Kleinschmidt, *Understanding the Middle Ages: The Transformation of Ideas and Attitudes in the Medieval World* (Woodbridge, Suffolk, U.K. & Rochester, N.Y.: Boydell Press, 2000).

Emmanuel Le Roy Ladurie, *Montaillou, the Promised Land of Error,* translated by Barbara Bray (New York: Braziller, 1978).

Elizabeth M. Makowski, "The Conjugal Debt and Medieval Canon Law," *Journal of Medieval History,* 3 (1977): 99–114.

James Marchand, "The Frankish Mother: Dhuoda," in *Medieval Women Writers,* edited by Katharina M. Wilson (Athens: University of Georgia Press, 1984), pp. 13–14, 25.

Marie Anne Mayeski, *Dhuoda: Ninth Century Mother and Theologian* (Scranton, Pa.: University of Scranton Press, 1995).

Mary Martin McLaughlin, "Survivors and Surrogates: Children and Parents from the Ninth to the Thirteenth Centuries," in *The History of Childhood,* edited by Lloyd deMause (New York: Psychohistory Press, 1974), pp. 101–182.

Jacqueline Murray, "Individualism and Consensual Marriage: Some Evidence from Medieval England," in *Women, Marriage, and Family in Medieval Christendom: Essays in Memory of Michael M. Sheehan, C.S.B.,* edited by Constance M. Rousseau and Joel T. Rosenthal (Kalamazoo, Mich.: Medieval Institute Publications, 1998), pp. 121–151.

Murray, "Sexuality and Spirituality: The Intersection of Medieval Theology and Medicine," *Fides et Historia,* 23 (1991): 20–36.

John T. Noonan, "Marital Affection in the Canonists," *Studia Gratiana,* 12 (1967): 481–509.

Noonan, "Power to Choose," *Viator,* 4 (1973): 419–434.

Tim North, "Legerwite in the Thirteenth and Fourteenth Centuries," *Past and Present,* 111 (1986): 3–16.

Pierre J. Payer, *The Bridling of Desire: Views of Sex in the Later Middle Ages* (Toronto & Buffalo: University of Toronto Press, 1993).

Frederik Pedersen, "'*Maritalis Affectio*': Marital Affection and Property in Fourteenth-Century York Cause Papers," in *Women, Marriage, and Family in Medieval*

Christendom: Essays in Memory of Michael M. Sheehan, C.S.B., edited by Constance M. Rousseau and Joel T. Rosenthal (Kalamazoo, Mich.: Medieval Institute Publications, 1998), pp. 175–209.

John M. Riddle, *Contraception and Abortion from the Ancient World to the Renaissance* (Cambridge, Mass.: Harvard University Press, 1992).

Richard L. Rudolph, ed., *The European Peasant Family and Society: Historical Studies* (Liverpool: Liverpool University Press, 1995).

Shulamith Shahar, *Childhood in the Middle Ages* (London & New York: Routledge, 1990).

Michael M. Sheehan, "The Bishop of Rome to a Barbarian King on the Rituals of Marriage," *In iure veritas: Studies in Canon Law in Memory of Schafer Williams,* edited by Steven B. Bowman and Blanche E. Cody (Cincinnati: University of Cincinnati, College of Law, 1991), pp. 187–199.

Sheehan, "Choice of Marriage Partner in the Middle Ages: Development and Mode of Application of a Theory of Marriage," *Studies in Medieval and Renaissance History,* 1 (1978): 1–33.

Sheehan, "*Maritalis Affectio* Revisited," in *The Olde Daunce. Love, Friendship, Sex, and Marriage in the Medieval World,* edited by Robert R. Edwards and Stephen Spector (Albany: State University of New York Press, 1991), pp. 32–43.

Fiona Harris Stoertz, "Suffering and Survival in Medieval English Childbirth," *Medieval Family Roles: A Book of Essays,* edited by Cathy Jorgensen Itnyre (New York: Garland, 1996), pp. 101–120.

Jenny Swanson, "Childhood and Child Rearing in *ad status* Sermons by Later Thirteenth Century Friars," *Journal of Medieval History,* 16 (1990): 309–331.

RELIGION AND PHILOSOPHY

Marilyn McCord Adams, *William Ockham,* 2 volumes (Notre Dame: University of Notre Dame Press, 1989).

Malcolm Barber, *The Cathars: Dualist Heretics in Languedoc in the High Middle Ages* (Harlow, U.K. & New York: Longman, 2000).

Werner Beierwaltes, *Eriugena* (Frankfurt am Main: Klostermann, 1994).

Harold J. Berman, *Law and Revolution: The Formation of the Western Legal Tradition* (Cambridge, Mass.: Harvard University Press, 1983).

Jon Irving Bloomberg, *The Jewish World in the Middle Ages* (New York : KTAV Publishing House, 2000).

Uta-Renate Blumenthal, *The Investiture Controversy: Church and Monarchy from the Ninth to the Twelfth Century* (Philadelphia: University of Pennsylvania Press, 1988).

E. P. Bos, ed., *John Duns Scotus: Renewal of Philosophy*, Amsterdam & Atlanta: Rodolpi, 1998).

Adriaan H. Bredero, *Christendom and Christianity in the Middle Ages: The Relations Between Religion, Church, and Society,* translated by Reinder Bruinsma (Grand Rapids, Mich.: Eerdmans, 1994).

Mary Brennan, *A Guide to Eriugenian Studies (1930–1987),* Vestigia 5 (Freibourg, Switzerland: Editions universitaires / Paris: Editions du Cerf, 1989).

Rosalind B. Brooke, *The Coming of the Friars* (New York: Barnes & Noble, 1975).

Peter Brown, *Augustine of Hippo: A Biography* (London: Faber & Faber, 1967).

Brown, *Power and Persuasion in Late Antiquity: Towards a Christian Empire* (Madison: University of Wisconsin Press, 1992).

Brown, *The Rise of Western Christendom: Triumph and Diversity, A.D. 200–1000* (Oxford & Cambridge, Mass.: Blackwell, 1996).

Caroline Walker Bynum, *Jesus as Mother: Studies in the Spirituality of the High Middle Ages* (Berkeley: University of California Press, 1982).

Henry Chadwick, *Boethius: The Consolations of Music, Logic, Theology and Philosophy* (New York: Oxford University Press, 1981).

M. T. Clanchy, *Abelard* (Oxford: Blackwell, 1997).

Norman Cohn, *The Pursuit of the Millennium: Revolutionary Millenarians and Mystical Anarchists of the Middle Ages,* revised edition (New York: Oxford University Press, 1970).

Frederick C. Copleston, *A History of Philosophy,* volume 2, parts 1 and 2: *Mediaeval Philosophy* (Westminster, Md.: Newman Press, 1950).

Copleston, *Mediaeval Philosophy* (London: Methuen, 1952).

H. E. J. Cowdrey, *The Cluniacs and the Gregorian Reform* (Oxford: Clarendon Press, 1970).

Richard Cross, *Duns Scotus* (New York: Oxford University Press, 1999).

Gilbert Dahan, *The Christian Polemic against the Jews in the Middle Ages,* translated by Jody Gladding (Notre Dame, Ind.: University of Notre Dame Press, 1998).

H. A. Davidson, *Alfarabi, Avicenna and Averroës on Intellect: Their Cosmologies, Theories of the Active Intellect, and Theories of Human Intellect* (New York: Oxford University Press, 1992).

Peter Dronke, *A History of Twelfth-Century Philosophy* (Cambridge: Cambridge University Press, 1988).

G. R. Evans, *Bernard of Clairvaux* (New York: Oxford University Press, 2000).

Francis of Assisi and Clare of Assisi, *Francis and Clare: The Complete Works,* translated by Regis Armstrong and Ignatius Brady (New York: Paulist Press, 1982).

Michael Frassetto, ed. *Medieval Purity and Piety: Essays on Medieval Clerical Celibacy and Religious Reform* (New York: Garland, 1998).

Francesco Gabrieli, ed., *Arab Historians of the Crusades,* translated by E. J. Costello (New York: Routledge, 1969).

Stephen E. Gersh, *From Iamblicus to Eriugena* (Leiden: Brill, 1978).

James B. Given, *Inquisition and Medieval Society: Power, Discipline, and Resistance in Languedoc* (Ithaca: Cornell University Press, 1997).

Salomon Grayzel, *The Church and the Jews in the Thirteenth Century,* 2 volumes (New York: Hermon Press, 1989).

Charles Hartshorne, *Anselm's Discovery* (La Salle, Ill.: Open Court, 1965).

Ernest F. Henderson, ed. and trans., *Select Historical Documents of the Middle Ages* (London: Bell, 1910).

Paul Henry, *The De grammatico of St. Anselm* (Notre Dame, Ind.: Notre Dame University Press, 1964).

Henry, *The Logic of St. Anselm* (Oxford: Clarendon Press, 1967).

C. Warren Hollister, *Medieval Europe: A Short History,* eighth edition (New York: McGraw-Hill, 1998).

Amy Hollywood, *The Soul as Virgin Bride: Mechthild of Magdeburg, Marguerite Porete and Meister Eckhart* (Notre Dame, Ind.: University of Notre Dame Press, 1995).

Edouard Jeauneau, *Etudes Eriugéniennes* (Paris: Etudes Augustiniennes, 1987).

Jeauneau, *"Lectio philosophorum," Recherches sur L'Ecole de Chartres* (Amsterdam: Hakkert, 1973).

Hugh N. Kennedy, *Muslim Spain and Portugal: A Political History of Al-Andalus* (London & New York : Longman, 1996).

David Knowles, *Thomas Becket* (Stanford: Stanford University Press, 1971).

Norman Kretzmann, Anthony Kenny, Jan Pinborg, and Elenore Stump, eds. *The Cambridge History of Later Medieval Philosophy* (Cambridge: Cambridge University Press, 1982).

Stephan Kuttner, *Studies in the History of Medieval Canon Law* (Brookfield, Vt.: Variorum, 1990).

Malcolm Lambert, *The Cathars* (Malden, Mass.: Blackwell, 1998).

Lambert, *Medieval Heresy: Popular Movements from the Gregorian Reform to the Reformation,* second edition (Oxford, U.K. & Cambridge, Mass.: Blackwell, 1992).

GENERAL REFERENCES

C. H. Lawrence, *The Friars: The Impact of the Early Mendicant Movement on Western Society* (London & New York: Longman, 1994).

Lawrence, *Medieval Monasticism: Forms of Religious Life in Western Europe in the Middle Ages,* second edition (London & New York: Longman, 1989).

Jacques Le Goff, *Intellectuals in the Middle Ages,* translated by Teresa Lavender Fagan (Cambridge, Mass. & Oxford, U.K.: Blackwell, 1993).

Alain de Libera, *La philosophie medievale* (Paris: Presses Universitaire de France, 1993).

Libera, *Le Probleme de l'etre chez Maitre Eckhart* (Geneva: Revue de theologie et de philosophie, 1980).

F. Donald Logan, ed. *A History of the Medieval Church: An Introduction* (London & New York: Routledge, 1999).

Joseph H. Lynch, *The Medieval Church: A Brief History* (London & New York: Longman, 1992).

Jacob Marcus, *The Jew in the Medieval World: A Sourcebook, 315–1791* (Cincinnati: Union of American Hebrew Congregations, 1938).

John Marenbon, *Early Medieval Philosophy* (London: Routledge, 1983).

Marenbon, *Later Medieval Philosophy (1150–1350)* (London: Routledge, 1987).

Armand A. Maurer, *Medieval Philosophy,* revised edition (Toronto: Pontifical Institute of Medieval Studies, 1982).

Maurer, *The Philosophy of William of Ockham in the Light of Its Principles* (Toronto: Pontifical Institute of Mediaeval Studies, 1999).

Bernard McGinn, *Meister Eckhart* (New York: Continuum Press, 2001).

McGinn, *Visions of the End: Apocalyptic Traditions in the Middle Ages,* expanded edition (New York: Columbia University Press, 1998).

Dermot Moran, *The Philosophy of John Scottus Eriugena: a Study of Idealism in the Middle Ages* (Cambridge & New York: Cambridge University Press, 1989).

Colin Morris, *The Papal Monarchy: The Western Church from 1050 to 1250* (New York: Oxford University Press, 1989).

Karl F. Morrison, *Tradition and Authority in the Western Church, 300–1140* (Princeton: Princeton University Press, 1969).

Francis P. Oakley, *The Western Church in the Later Middle Ages* (Ithaca, N.Y.: Cornell University Press, 1980).

John J. O'Meara, *Eriugena* (Oxford: Clarendon Press, 1988).

Steven Ozment, *The Age of Reform, 1250–1550* (New Haven: Yale University Press, 1980).

Edward Peters, ed., *Heresy and Authority in Medieval Europe* (Philadelphia: University of Pennsylvania Press, 1980).

Alvin Plantinga, ed., *The Ontological Argument* (Garden City, N.Y.: Doubleday, 1965).

Marjorie Reeves, *Joachim of Fiore and the Prophetic Future* (New York: Harper & Row, 1977).

Jonathan Riley-Smith, ed., *The Oxford History of the Crusades* (New York: Oxford University Press, 1999).

Ian S. Robinson, *The Papacy, 1073–1198: Continuity and Innovation* (Cambridge & New York: Cambridge University Press, 1990).

Renee Roques, *L'Univers dionysien: Structures hierarchique du monde selon le pseudo-Denys* (Aubier: Montaigne, 1955).

Steven Runciman, *A History of the Crusades,* 3 volumes (Cambridge: Cambridge University Press, 1951–1954).

Jeffrey Burton Russell, *Lucifer, The Devil in the Middle Ages* (Ithaca: Cornell University Press, 1984).

Jane E. Sayers, *Innocent III: Leader of Europe, 1198–1216* (London & New York: Longman, 1994).

Philip Sherrard, *Church, Papacy, and Schism* (London: SPCK, 1978).

R. W. Southern, *Saint Anselm: A Portrait in a Landscape* (Cambridge & New York: Cambridge University Press, 1990).

Southern, *Scholastic Humanism and the Unification of Europe,* volume 1: *Foundations* (Oxford & Cambridge, Mass.: Blackwell, 1995).

Southern, *Western Society and the Church in the Middle Ages* (Harmondsworth, U.K.: Penguin, 1970).

Paul Vincent Spade, "Medieval Philosophy," in *The Oxford History of Western Philosophy,* edited by Anthony Kenny (Oxford & New York: Oxford University Press, 1994).

Spade, ed., *The Cambridge Companion to Ockham* (New York: Cambridge University Press, 1999).

Fernand van Steenberghen, *Thomas Aquinas and Radical Aristotelianism* (Washington, D.C.: Catholic University of America Press, 1980).

Brian Tierney, *Religion, Law, and the Growth of Constitutional Thought, 1150–1650* (New York: Cambridge University Press, 1982).

Walter Ullmann, *The Growth of Papal Government in the Middle Ages: A Study in the Ideological Relation of Clerical to Lay Power* (London: Methuen, 1955).

Ullmann, *A Short History of the Papacy in the Middle Ages* (London: Methuen, 1972).

André Vauchez, *The Laity in the Middle Ages: Religious Beliefs and Devotional Practices,* edited by Daniel E. Bornstein. translated by Margery J. Schneider (Notre Dame, Ind.: University of Notre Dame Press, 1993).

Jacques Verger, *Men of Learning in Europe at the End of the Middle Ages,* translated by Lisa Neal and Steven Rendall (Notre Dame, Ind.: University of Notre Dame Press, 2000).

Timothy Ware, *The Orthodox Church* (Harmondsworth, U.K.: Penguin, 1997).

Diana Webb, *Pilgrims and Pilgrimage in Medieval Europe* (New York: Tauris, 1999).

Ulrike Wiethaus, ed., *Maps of Flesh and Light: The Religious Experience of Medieval Women Mystics* (Syracuse: Syracuse University Press, 1993).

Garry Wills, *Saint Augustine* (New York: Viking, 1999).

Allan B. Wolter, *The Philosophical Theology of John Duns Scotus,* edited by Marilyn McCord Adams (Ithaca: Cornell University Press, 1990).

Emilie Zum Brunn and Alain de Libera, *Maitre Eckhart: Metaphysique du verbe et theologie negative* (Paris: Beauchesne, 1984).

SCIENCE, TECHNOLOGY, AND HEALTH

Albertus Magnus, *The Book of Minerals,* edited and translated by Dorothy Wycoff (Oxford: Clarendon Press, 1967).

Albertus Magnus, *The Book of Secrets,* edited by Michael R. Best and Frank H. Brightman (Oxford: Clarendon Press, 1973).

Albertus Magnus, *On Animals: A Medieval Summa Zoologica,* 2 volumes, translated and annotated by Kenneth F. Kitchell Jr. and Irven Michael Resnick (Baltimore: Johns Hopkins University Press, 1999).

Darrel W. Amundsen, *Medicine, Society, and Faith in the Ancient and Medieval Worlds* (Baltimore & London: Johns Hopkins University Press, 1996).

Grenville Astill, *The Countryside of Medieval England* (Oxford: Blackwell, 1988).

Astill and John Langdon, eds. *Medieval Farming and Technology: the Impact of Agricultural Change in Northwest Europe* (Leiden & New York: Brill, 1997).

Bartholomaeus Anglicus, *On the Properties of Things: John Trevisa's Translation of Bartholomaeus Anglicus De proprietatibus rerum: A Critical Text.* 3 volumes, edited by M. C. Seymour and others (Oxford: Clarendon Press, 1975–1988).

Bede, *The Reckoning of Time,* edited and translated by Faith Wallis (Liverpool: Liverpool University Press, 1999).

John Blair and Nigel Ramsay, eds., *English Medieval Industries: Craftsmen, Techniques, Products* (London: Hambledon Press, 1991).

Wilfrid Blunt and Sandra Raphael, *The Illustrated Herbal* (Oxford: Oxford University Press, 1979).

Bodley Herbal and Bestiary, Medieval manuscripts in microform, Major Treasures in the Bodleian Library; no. 8 (Oxford: Oxford Microform Publications / Toronto: University of Toronto Press, 1978).

Carl B. Boyer, *The Rainbow from Myth to Mathematics* (New York: Yoseloff, 1959).

Jim Bradbury, *The Medieval Siege* (Woodbridge: Boydell Press, 1992).

Vern L. Bullough, *The Development of Medicine as a Profession: The Contribution of the Medieval University to Modern Medicine* (New York: Hafner, 1966).

Charles Burnett, ed., *Adelard of Bath: an English Scientist and Arabist of the Early Twelfth Century* (London: Warburg Institute, University of London, 1987).

Donald Edward Henry Campbell, *Arabian Medicine and Its Influence on the Middle Ages* (London: Kegan Paul, Trench, Trübner, 1926).

Sheila Campbell, Bert Hall, and David Klausner, eds., *Health, Disease, and Healing in Medieval Culture* (New York: St. Martin's Press, 1992).

Marshall Clagett, *Studies in Medieval Physics and Mathematics* (London: Variorum Reprints, 1979).

Louise Cochrane, *Adelard of Bath: the First English Scientist* (London: British Museum Press, 1994).

Ivy A. Corfis and Michael Wolfe, *The Medieval City under Siege* (Woodbridge: Boydell Press, 1995).

Alistair Cameron Crombie, *Augustine to Galileo: The History of Science A.D. 400–1650,* second edition, revised and enlarged (Cambridge, Mass.: Harvard University Press, 1961).

Crombie, *Robert Grosseteste and the Origins of Experimental Science, 1100–1700* (Oxford: Clarendon Press 1953).

Walter Clyde Curry, *Chaucer and the Mediaeval Sciences* (New York & London: Oxford University Press, 1926).

Richard C. Dales, *The Scientific Achievement of the Middle Ages* (Philadelphia: University of Pennsylvania Press, 1973).

Lorraine Daston and Katherine Park, *Wonders and the Order of Nature, 1150–1750* (New York: Zone Books, 1998).

Giovanni de'Dondi, *Mechanical Universe: The Astrarium of Giovanni de'Dondi,* edited and translated by Silvio Bedini and Francis Maddison. *Transactions of the American Philosophical Society,* new series 56, part 5 (Philadelphia: American Philosophical Society, 1966).

Gerhard Dohrn–van Rossum, *History of the Hour: Clocks and Modern Temporal Orders* (Chicago: University of Chicago Press, 1996).

William Eamon, *Science and the Secrets of Nature: Books of Secrets in Medieval and Early Modern Culture* (Princeton: Princeton University Press, 1994).

Eamon, ed., *Studies on Medieval Fachliteratur: Proceedings of the Special Session on Medieval Fachliteratur of the Sixteenth International Congress on Medieval Studies, Kalam-*

azoo, Michigan (U.S.A.), May 10, 1981 (Brussel: Omirel, UFSAL, 1982).

English Trotula. Medieval Woman's Guide to Health: the First English Gynecological Handbook, translated by Beryl Rowland (Kent, Ohio: Kent State University Press, 1981).

George Gillespie Fox, The Mediaeval Sciences in the Works of John Gower (Princeton: Princeton University Press, 1931).

Roger Kenneth French and Andrew Cunningham, Before Science: the Invention of the Friars' Natural Philosophy (Aldershot, U.K. & Brookfield, Vt.: Scolar Press, 1996).

Ian Friel, The Good Ship: Ships, Shipbuilding and Technology in England, 1200–1520 (Baltimore: Johns Hopkins University Press, 1995).

Faye Marie Getz, Healing and Society in Medieval England: A Middle English Translation of the Pharmaceutical Writings of Gilbertus Anglicus (Madison: University of Wisconsin Press, 1991).

Frances Gies and Joseph Gies, Cathedral, Forge, and Waterwheel: Technology and Invention in the Middle Ages (New York: HarperCollins, 1994).

Gies and Gies, Life in a Medieval Village (New York: Harper & Row, 1990).

Jean Gimpel, The Cathedral Builders, translated by Carl F. Barnes (New York: Grove, 1961). Translated again by Teresa Waugh (New York: Grove, 1983).

Thomas F. Glick, Irrigation and Hydraulic Technology: Medieval Spain and its Legacy (Aldershot, U.K. & Brookfield, Vt.: Variorum, 1996).

Benjamin Lee Gordon, Medieval and Renaissance Medicine (New York: Philosophical Press, 1959).

Anna Götlind, Technology and Religion in Medieval Sweden (Falun: University of Göteborg, 1993).

Robert Steven Gottfried, Doctors and Medicine in Medieval England, 1340–1530 (Princeton: Princeton University Press, 1986).

Thomas Francis Graham, Medieval Minds: Mental Health in The Middle Ages (London: Allen & Unwin, 1967).

Edward Grant, The Foundations of Modern Science in the Middle Ages: Their Religious, Institutional, and Intellectual Contexts (Cambridge & New York: Cambridge University Press, 1996).

Grant, Much Ado about Nothing: Theories of Space and Vacuum from the Middle Ages to the Scientific Revolution (Cambridge & New York: Cambridge University Press, 1981).

Grant, Physical Science in The Middle Ages (Cambridge & New York: Cambridge University Press, 1977).

Grant, Planets, Stars, and Orbs: the Medieval Cosmos, 1200–1687 (Cambridge & New York: Cambridge University Press, 1994).

Grant, "Scientific Thought in 14th-century Paris: Jean Buridan and Nicole Oresme," in Machaut's World: Science and Art in the 14th Century, edited by Madeleine Pelner Cosman and Bruce Chandler (New York: New York Academy of Science, 1978), pp. 105–124.

Grant, Studies in Medieval Science and Natural Philosophy (London: Variorum Reprints, 1981).

Grant, ed., A Source Book in Medieval Science (Cambridge, Mass.: Harvard University Press, 1974).

Edward Green, "Jean Buridan and Nicole Oresme on Natural Science," Vivarium: Journal for Mediaeval Philosophy and the Intellectual Life of the Middle Ages, 31 (1993): 84–105.

Monica Helen Green, Women's Healthcare in the Medieval West: Texts and Contexts (Burlington, Vt.: Ashgate/Variorum, 2000).

Jeremiah Hackett, ed., Roger Bacon and the Sciences: Commemorative Essays (Leiden & New York: Brill, 1997).

Bert S. Hall and Delno C. West, eds., On Pre-Modern Technology and Science; a Volume of Studies in Honor of Lynn White, Jr. (Malibu: Undena Publications, 1976).

John Hooper Harvey, Mediaeval Gardens (Beaverton, Ore.: Timber Press, 1981).

Abdul S. Hassam, Early Muslim Scientists: Their Contributions to Natural Science (New York: Vantage Press, 1978).

Hildegard of Bingen, Holistic Healing, A Translation of Liber compositae medicinea, translated by Manfred Pawlik, Patrick Madigan, and John Kulas; edited by Kulas and Mary Palmquist Collegeville (Minn.: Liturgical Press, 1994).

Ibn Butlân, The Medieval Health Handbook: Tacuinum Sanitatis, edited, with text by Luisa Cogliati Arano, translated by Oscar Ratti and Adele Westbrooke (New York: Braziller, 1976).

Charles W. Jones, Bede, the Schools and the "Computus," edited by Wesley M. Stevens (Aldershot: Variorum, 1994).

Peter Murray Jones, Medieval Medicine in Illuminated Manuscripts, revised edition (London: British Library, 1998).

Husain Kassim, Aristotle and Aristotelianism in Medieval Muslim, Jewish, and Christian Philosophy (Lanham: Austin & Winfield, 2000).

Edward J. Kealey, Harvesting the Air: Windmill Pioneers in Twelfth-Century England (Berkeley: University of California Press, 1987).

Kealey, Medieval Medicus: A Social History of Anglo-Norman Medicine (Baltimore: Johns Hopkins University Press, 1981).

Simon Kemp, Medieval Psychology (New York: Greenwood Press, 1990).

Pearl Kibre, *Studies in Medieval Science: Alchemy, Astrology, Mathematics, and Medicine* (London: Hambledon Press, 1984).

Claudia Kren, *Medieval Science and Technology: a Selected, Annotated Bibliography* (New York: Garland, 1985).

Helen S. Lang, *Aristotle's Physics and Its Medieval Varieties* (Albany: State University of New York Press, 1992).

Y. Tzvi Langermann, *The Jews and the Sciences in the Middle Ages* (Aldershot, U.K. & Brookfield, Vt.: Ashgate, 1999).

David C. Lindberg, *The Beginnings of Western Science: the European Scientific Tradition in Philosophical, Religious, and Institutional Context, 600 B.C. to A.D. 1450* (Chicago: University of Chicago Press, 1992).

Lindberg, *Studies in the History of Medieval Optics* (London: Variorum Reprints, 1983).

Lindberg, *Theories of Vision from al-Kindi to Kepler* (Chicago: University of Chicago Press, 1976).

Lindberg, ed., *Science in the Middle Ages* (Chicago: University of Chicago Press, 1978).

Pamela O. Long, ed., *Science and Technology in Medieval Society* (New York: New York Academy of Sciences, 1985).

Loren Carey MacKinney, *Early Medieval Medicine, with Special Reference to France and Chartres* (Baltimore: Johns Hopkins Press 1937).

Anneliese Maier, *On the Threshold of Exact Science: Selected Writings of Anneliese Maier on Late Medieval Natural Philosophy*, translated by Steven D. Sargent (Philadelphia: University of Pennsylvania Press, 1982).

Mappae Clavicula: A Little Key to the World of Medieval Techniques, edited and translated by Cyril Stanley Smith and John G. Hawthorne. *Transactions of the American Philosophical Society*, new series 64, part 4 (Philadelphia: American Philosophical Society, 1974).

Lister M. Matheson, ed., *Popular and Practical Science of Medieval England* (East Lansing, Mich.: Colleagues Press, 1994).

R. P. McKeon, "Aristotle and The Origins of Science in the West," in *Science and Civilization*, edited by Robert C. Stauffer (Madison: University of Wisconsin Press, 1949).

William Hardy McNeill, *The Pursuit of Power: Technology, Armed Force, and Society since A.D. 1000* (Chicago: University of Chicago Press, 1982).

A. George Molland, "Nicole Oresme and Scientific Progress," in *Antiqui und moderni*, edited by Albert Zimmermann (Berlin: de Gruyter, 1974), pp. 206–220.

Linne R. Mooney, "The Cock and the Clock: Telling Time in the Chaucer's Day," *Studies in the Age of Chaucer*, 15 (1993).

William Newman, "Technology and Alchemical Debate in the Late Middle Ages," *Isis*, 80 (1989): 423–445.

John David North, *Stars, Minds, and Fate: Essays in Ancient and Medieval Cosmology* (London: Hambledon Press, 1989).

R. Ewart Oakeshott, *The Archaeology of Weapons: Arms and Armour from Prehistory to the Age of Chivalry* (London: Lutterworth Press, 1960).

Nicole Oresme, *Nicole Oresme and the Kinematics of Circular Motion: Tractatus de commensurabilitate vel incommensurabilitate motuum celi*, edited and translated by Edward Grant (Madison: University of Wisconsin Press 1971).

Oresme, *Nicole Oresme and the Medieval Geometry of Qualities and Motions: A Treatise on the Uniformity and Difformity of Intensities Known as Tractatus de configurationibus qualitatum et motuum*, edited and translated by Marshall Clagett (Madison: University of Wisconsin Press, 1968).

John Peckham, *John Pecham and The Science of Optics: Perspectiva communis*, edited and translated by David C. Lindberg (Madison: University of Wisconsin Press, 1970).

Platina, *Platina, On Right Pleasure and Good Health: A Critical Edition and Translation of De honesta voluptate et valetudine*, edited and translated by Mary Ella Milham (Tempe, Ariz.: Medieval & Renaissance Texts & Studies, 1998).

Oliver Rackman, *Trees and Woodland in the British Landscape* (London: Dent, 1990).

Carole Rawcliffe, *Medicine & Society in Later Medieval England* (Stroud, U.K.: Alan Sutton, 1995).

Rawcliffe, ed. and trans., *Sources for the History of Medicine in Late Medieval England* (Kalamazoo, Mich.: Medieval Institute Publications, Western Michigan University, 1995).

Richard of Wallingford, *Richard of Wallingford: An Edition of His Writings*, 3 volumes, edited and translated by John D. North (Oxford: Oxford University Press, 1976).

Stanley Rubin, *Medieval English Medicine* (Newton Abbot, U.K.: David & Charles, 1974).

Rufinus, *The Herbal of Rufinus*, edited by Lynn Thorndike, with the assistance of Francis S. Benjamin (Chicago: University of Chicago Press, 1946).

Wolfgang F. Schuerl, *Medieval Castles and Cities*, translated by Francisca Garvie (London: Cassell, 1978).

Joseph Shatzmiller, *Jews, Medicine, and Medieval Society* (Berkeley: University of California Press, 1994).

Nancy G. Siraisi, *Medieval & Early Renaissance Medicine: An Introduction to Knowledge and Practice* (Chicago: University of Chicago Press, 1990).

Siraisi and Luke Demaitre, eds., *Science, Medicine and the University, 1200–1550: Essays in Honor of Pearl Kibre* (St. Louis: Saint Louis University Library, 1976).

Patricia Skinner, *Health and Medicine in Early Medieval Southern Italy* (Leiden & New York: E. J. Brill, 1997).

Elizabeth Bradford Smith and Michael Wolfe, eds., *Technology and Resource Use in Medieval Europe: Cathedrals, Mills, and Mines* (Aldershot, U.K. & Brookfield, Vt.: Ashgate, 1997).

Paolo Squatriti, ed., *Working with Water in Medieval Europe: Technology and Resource-Use* (Leiden & Boston: Brill, 2000).

William Harris Stahl, *Roman Science: Origins, Development, and Influence to the Later Middle Ages* (Madison: University of Wisconsin Press, 1962).

Fernand van Steenberghen, *Aristotle in the West: The Origins of Latin Aristotelianism,* translated by Leonard Johnston (Louvain: Nauwelaerts, 1955).

Stevens, "Bede's Scientific Achievement," in *Bede and His World: The Jarrow Lectures, 1958–1993* (Aldershot: Variorum, 1994), pp. 645–688.

Wesley M. Stevens, *Cycles of Time and Scientific Learning in Medieval Europe* (Aldershot, U.K. & Brookfield, Vt.: Variorum, 1995).

Del Sweeney, ed., *Agriculture in the Middle Ages: Technology, Practice, and Representation* (Philadelphia: University of Pennsylvania Press, 1995).

Edith Sylla and Michael McVaugh, eds., *Texts and Contexts in Ancient and Medieval Science: Studies on the Occasion of John E. Murdoch's Seventieth Birthday* (Leiden & New York: Brill, 1997).

Mariano Taccola, *Mariano Taccola, De ingeneis,* 2 volumes, edited and translated by Gustina Scaglia, Frank D. Prager, and Ulrich Montag (Wiesbaden: L. Reichert, 1984).

Taccola, *Mariano Taccola, De Machinis,* edited and translated by Scaglia (Wiesbaden: L. Reichert, 1971).

Charles H. Talbot, *Medicine in Medieval England* (London: Oldbourne, 1967).

Theophilus Presbyter, *On Divers Arts: The Treatise of Theophilus,* translated by John G. Hawthorne and Cyril Stanley Smith (Chicago: University of Chicago, 1963). Also translated as *The Various Arts,* translated by C. R. Dodwell (London: Nelson, 1961).

J. M. M. H. Thijssen and Jack Zupko, *The Metaphysics and Natural Philosophy of John Buridan* (Leiden & Boston: Brill, 2001).

Lynn Thorndike, ed. and trans., *The Sphere of Sacrobosco and its Commentators* (Chicago: University of Chicago Press, 1949).

Sidney Toy, *Castles, A Short History of Fortifications from 1600 B.C. to A.D. 1600* (London & Toronto: Heinemann, 1939).

Richard W. Unger, *The Art of Medieval Technology: Images of Noah the Shipbuilder* (New Brunswick, N.J.: Rutgers University Press, 1991).

James A. Weisheipl, "The Interpretation of Aristotle's Physics and the Science of Motion," in *The Cambridge History of Later Medieval Philosophy: From the Rediscovery of Aristotle to the Disintegration of Scholasticism, 1100–1600,* edited by Norman Kretzmann, Anthony Kenny, Jan Pinborg, and Eleonore Stump (Cambridge & New York: Cambridge University Press, 1982), pp. 521–536.

Weisheipl, ed., *Albertus Magnus and the Sciences: Commemorative Essays 1980* (Toronto: Pontifical Institute of Mediaeval Studies, 1980).

Lynn Townsend White Jr., *Medieval Religion and Technology: Collected Essays* (Berkeley: University of California Press, 1978).

White, *Medieval Technology and Social Change* (New York: Oxford University Press, 1962).

William of Conches, *A Dialogue on Natural Philosophy = Dragmaticon philosophiae,* translated by Italo Ronca and Matthew Curr (Notre Dame, Ind.: University of Notre Dame Press, 1997).

Charles R. Young, "Conservation Policies in the Royal Forests of Medieval England," *Albion,* 10 (1978): 95–103.

Young, *The Royal Forests of Medieval England* (Philadelphia: University of Pennsylvania Press, 1979).

Contributors

Kelly R. DeVries received his Ph.D. in History from the University of Toronto, and he is currently Associate Professor of History at Loyola College in Baltimore, Maryland. His research interests are medieval and early modern military history and the history of technology. His books include *A Cumulative Bibliography of Medieval Military History and Technology* (2000), *Joan of Arc: A Military History* (1999), *The Norwegian Invasion of England in 1066* (1999), *Infantry Warfare in the Early Fourteenth Century: Discipline, Tactics, and Technology* (1996), and *Medieval Military Technology* (1992).

Kathryn A. Edwards received her Ph.D. from the University of California, Berkeley, and she is currently Assistant Professor of History at the University of South Carolina, Columbia. She specializes in early modern European and sociocultural and intellectual history; her current research is on the social history of religion and regional frontiers and identity. Dr. Edwards edited *Werewolves, Witches, and Wandering Spirits: Folklore and Traditional Belief in Early Modern Europe* (forthcoming), wrote *Families and Frontiers: Recreating Communities and Boundaries in the Early Modern Burgundies* (2001), and contributed articles to several scholarly journals.

Mary Beth Farrell received her M.A. in History from the University of Southern Mississippi. She supervises student teachers for the U.S.M. Department of History and teaches World Civilization courses. She co-edited *Exploring the Sources of World Civilizations, 1650 to the Present* (1997) and wrote *Discovering Mississippi: A Teacher's Guide* (1998).

Jeremiah Hackett received his Ph.D. from the University of Toronto, and he is currently Professor of Medieval and Renaissance Philosophy at the University of South Carolina, Columbia. He edited *Medieval Philosophers, Dictionary of Literary Biography,* volume 115 (1992) and *Roger Bacon and the Sciences: Commemorative Essays* (1997).

Bert S. Hall received his Ph.D. in Medieval History from the University of California, Los Angeles. He is currently Professor of History at the Institute for the History and Philosophy of Science and Technology at the University of Toronto. His research is primarily in the material culture and everyday life of the Middle Ages and the early modern period. He authored *Weapons and Warfare in Renaissance Europe: Gunpowder, Technology, and Tactics* (1997).

Jacqueline Murray received her Ph.D. in Medieval History from the University of Toronto. Her research focuses on ideas and attitudes toward family, sex, and gender. She is currently Dean of Arts and Professor of History at the University of Guelph, Ontario. Her publications include *Love, Marriage, and the Family in the Middle Ages: A Reader* (2001), *Conflicted Identities and Multiple Masculinities: Men in the Medieval West* (1999), and *Desire and Discipline: Sex and Sexuality in the Premodern West* (1996).

Betsey B. Price, Ph.D., is Associate Professor of History and Multidisciplinary Studies at Glendon College, York University, Toronto. Her area of specialty is medieval intellectual history, including economic ideas. She is author of *Medieval Thought: An Introduction* (1992) and co-author of *Verification in Economics and History* (1991). She has also contributed many scholarly articles to books and professional journals.

Giulio Silano, Ph.D., is Associate Professor of Christianity and Culture at St. Michael's College, University of Toronto, and a member of that university's Graduate Department of History. He is also coordinator of the college's Mediaeval Studies Programme. Dr. Silano wrote *Acts of Gubertinus De Nouate, Notary of the Patriarch of Aquileia, 1328–1336* (1990), co-authored *Western Mediterranean Prophecy: The School of Joachim of Fiore and the Fourteenth-Century Breviloquium* (1989) and *The Register* Notule Communium 14 *of the Dioceses of Barcelona, 1345–1348* (1983), and contributed essays to several scholarly works.

Steven A. Walton received his M.S. degree in Engineering from the California Institute of Technology and his Ph.D. in History from the University of Toronto. His specialty is the history of premodern technology and science, particularly their intersection with the military. He is currently a visiting Assistant Professor at Michigan Technological University and has taught at the University of Toronto and York University. He is working on a book about the technology of the military revolution and its cause-and-effect relationship in early modern English society.

Norman J. Wilson is Assistant Professor of History and Coordinator of International Studies at Methodist College in Fayetteville, North Carolina. He received his Ph.D. from the University of California, Los Angeles. He edited *World Eras Vol. 1: European Renaissance and Reformation, 1350–1600* (2001) and wrote *History in Crisis?: Recent Directions in Historiography* (1999). His recent papers and publications focus on Free Imperial Cities in the early modern period.

INDEX OF PHOTOGRAPHS

and a chalice made circa 1240 from sardonyx, other precious stones, and metals for Abbot Suger of the Abbey of Saint-Denis in France (left: Victoria and Albert Museum, London; right: Widener Collection, National Gallery, Washington, D.C.) 282

Caravan moving from Sarai on the Volga River with a destination of Cathay, or China; illumination from the *Catalan Atlas,* circa 1350 (Bibliothèque Nationale, Paris) 105

Carcassonne, France 290

Carolingian light cavalry carrying lances and riding without stirrups; illumination from the *Utrecht Psalter,* 820–830 (Bibliotheek der Rijksuniversiteit, Utrecht) 211

Carolingian miniscule handwriting in the capitularies of Charlemagne, Louis I (the Pious), and Charles II (the Bald), circa 873 (Beinecke Library, Yale University) 69

Cavalrymen and a standard bearer; illumination from the ninth-century *Golden Psalter* (Stiftsbibliothek, Saint Gallen) 478

Chart of planetary motions according to the earth-centered Ptolemiac system in a thirteenth-century manuscript for an anonymous *Theorica planetarum* (University Library, Cambridge) 443

Charter of Canute I, written in Latin and signed by witnesses, granting land to the monk Aefic, circa 1020 (British Library, London) 118

Charter of Richard I for the burgesses of Exeter, granting merchants freedom from tolls in Rouen, 24 March 1190 (Exeter City Archives) 145

Childbirth; illumination from a thirteenth-century manuscript for the Contigas of Alphonse the Wise (Escorial Library, Madrid) 341

Christ and the Apostles sculpted on the tympanum of the church of St. Madeleine at Vézelay, France, after 1120 85

Christ in Majesty, surrounded by a prophet and evangelists; illumination in the large-manuscript Bible executed for Count Vivian, lay ab-

bot of Tours, 844–851 (Bibliothèque Nationale, Paris) 80

A Christian and a Muslim playing chess; illumination, circa 1284 (Escorial Monastery, Madrid) 116

Citadel at Jerusalem 214

A clepsydra (water clock) believed to have been used at the court of Louis IX of France in the mid thirteenth century (from Robert Delort, *Life in the Middle Ages,* 1973) 461

Clock made for Wells Cathedral in England, fourteenth century (The Science Museum, London) 463

A coin die from England, circa 915 (York Archaeological Trust) 146

The "conjugal debt," the only sexual outlet approved by the medieval Church; illumination from a manuscript for Aldobrandino of Siena's *Le Regime de Corps,* circa 1285 (British Library, London) 323

A couple who commit adultery (left) and marry after the birth of their child (right); illumination from a fourteenth-century manuscript for Gratian's *Decretum* (Biblioteca Nazionale Marciana, Venice) 334

Crown of Hungary (1074–1077), a gift to King Geza I from Emperor Michael VII Ducas (Magyar Nemzeti Muzeum, Budapest) 220

A Crusader galley being loaded; illumination from a fourteenth-century manuscript (Bibliothèque Nationale, Paris) 139

Crusaders attacking Constantinople in 1204, during the Fourth Crusade; illumination from a mid-thirteenth-century manuscript for William of Tyre's unfinished history of the Crusades (Bibliothèque Nationale, Paris) 393

King David in bed with concubines; illumination from a fourteenth-century manuscript on canon law (Cambridge University Library) 336

Dictatus Papae (1075), a compilation of twenty-seven dictations written by Pope Gregory VII setting out the authority of the Pope over secular states (Archivio Segreto, Vatican) 222

Doctors advising patients who suffer from vomiting, fainting, toothache, and a hair problem; illumination from a fourteenth-century medical book (British Library, London) 468

Dominican monks in an attitude of contemplation before a bleeding crucifix; illumination from *De Novem Modis Orandi,* Codex Rossianus, circa 1300 (Vatican Library) 144

Dover Castle, built by Henry II of England, circa 1180–1190 262

John Duns Scotus; illumination from a fourteenth-century manuscript (Biblioteca dell'academia dei Concordi, Rovigo, Italy) 412

Edward I's castles built in Wales during the late thirteenth century (diagrams by Neil Hyslop) 460

Edward III's troops sacking Crécy in 1346 (Bibliothèque Nationale, Paris) 226

"Europa Mundi Pars Quarta," a map of Europe from *Liber Floridus,* circa 1120 (University Library, Ghent) 42

An exchange of consent at which a priest is present as a witness but does not perform the marriage ceremony; illumination from a fourteenth-century manuscript for Artus le Restore (Bibliothèque Nationale, Paris) 325

Exchequer tallies (credit instruments) with the amounts payable indicated by the size of the notches on the sticks and the sources of the payments written on them, thirteenth century (Public Record Office, London) 178

The expulsion of the Jews from England, 1290; illumination from an early-fourteenth-century manuscript for *Flores Historiarum* (British Library, London) 398

Family tree showing the descent of the main claimants to the throne of Scotland in the late thirteenth century; the three women are daughters of David, Earl of Huntingdon, a younger son of King David I; illumination from an early-fourteenth-century French verse chronicle by Peter of

INDEX

Page numbers in boldface refer to a topic upon which an essay is based.
Page numbers in italics refer to illustrations, figures, and tables.

A

Abelard, Peter, 356, 412, **423–424**
Abortion, 309, 338–339
Acceleration, 445
Adoubement, 104, 158
Adultery, *331, 334*
Afghanistan village, *29*
Africa, **39–40**
Agriculture
    animal power, **449–452**
    crops, 253–254, 451–452
    feudal system, 140
    food production, 140
    gardening, 254–255
    harvest, 254–255
    horses and, 126
    husbandry, 158
    land reclamation, 253
    Little Ice Age and, 41–43
    moldboard plow, 254, 450, *451*
    padded horse collar, 450, *451*
    peasants, 158
    plowing, 254
    production, 149
    role of climate and geography on, 40
    seasons, 126
    technology, 158
    three-field system, 450–452
    travel and, 126
Al-Kindi, Yaqub Ibn Ishaq, 41
Albertus Magnus, 418, *448,* 449, 470, **471**
Albigensian Crusade, 219, 394–395
Alchemy, **446–447**
Alexander III, Pope, 323–324
The Alexiad (Anna Comnena), 385
Alexius I Comnenus, 214–215, 385
Alfred the Great, 238
Alhazen, 445–446
Alpine Europe, 40–41
Altarpieces, 85
Ancient texts. *See* Books, manuscripts and texts
Andreas Capellanus, 74
Animals, 158, 256, 449–452
    See also Natural science
Anna Comnena, 385
Annulment, 318–319
Anselm of Bec and Canterbury, 390–391
Antioch, 216
Apocalypse, 405
Apothecaries, 296

Apprenticeships
    children and, 310
    contracts, 350
    girls, 350
    social stratification and, 169–170
    training children, **350**
Aquinas, Thomas, 66, 410–413, 418–419, **424–425**
Arabs
    horses and, 123
    language, 119
    literature, 114–115
    optics, 445–446
    scientific contributions, 445–446
    translation of ancient texts, 413, 438
Architecture, **58–62**
    Byzantine, 59–60
    cathedrals, 287–288, 456–458
    churches, 58–59
    Gothic, 61–62, 91, 288, 457–458
    Moorish, 59–60
    Ottonian and Cluniac styles, 60–61
    Romanesque, 58–59, 456–457
    Villard de Honnecourt, 302–303
    See also Art; Sculpture
Arianism, 394
Aristotle, **415–419**
    Aquinas, Thomas, and, 410–411
    Aristotelianism, 387
    astronomy, 442
    branches of knowledge, *438*
    celestial and terrestrial motion, 439
    commentaries by Albertus Magnus, 471
    elements, 440
    humors, 439–440
    influence on medieval science, **438–440**
    motion, 440, 444
Armagnacs, 225
Armor, 209, 274–276
Arnald de Villanova, **471–472**
Art
    cathedrals, 288
    illuminations, 69, 80–81, 283
    marginalia, 81
    overview, **56–57**
    patronage, 57, 288
    See also Architecture; Painting; Sculpture
Arthurian legends, 74–75, 130
Arundel Castle, *459*
Asia
    Catholic missionary efforts in, 28

    contact with, during Late Middle Ages, 28
    expeditions of Marco Polo, 29–31, 106–107, **132–133**
    map of, *32*
    Mongols, **31–34**, 109, **232–233**
    Polo, Marco, 106–107, **132–133**
Astrology, 443–444
Astronomical clocks, 463
Astronomy, 439, 441, **442–444**, 462–463
Augustine, Saint, 317–318, 387–388, 410, 415
Averroës, 114, 401–402, 418–419
Avicenna, 402

B

Bacon, Roger, **38–39**, 76–77, 115, 412–413, **472**
Baileys, 262
Bakers, 295, 296
Banquets, 273
Baptism, 309, **342–343**
Barbarians, 26–27, 207
Barbarossa, Frederick, 202, *218,* 241
Barrel vaults, 456–457
Barter, 174
Bartholomew the Englishman, 344
Battle of Agincourt, 225–226
Battle of Crécy, 223–224, *226*
Battle of Dorylaeum, *215*
Battle of Hastings, 234–235
ibn Battuta, 107–108
Bayeux Tapestry, 105
Beauvais Cathedral, *287*
Becket, Thomas, 379–380
Bedding, 259
Bede, **440–442**
Beer and wine, 255–256
Beghards, 397
Beguines, 397
Benedictine orders, 164–165, 278–280
Benedictine Rule, 402–403
Beowulf, 70, 71, 228, 229
Bernard of Chartres, 63, 391–392, 411
Bernard of Clairvaux, 217, 404
Bertha, **333–334**
Bertolf and Godelieve, **329–330**
Betrothal expenses, **314–315**
Bible, 369–370
Biographies, 67–68
Biology. *See* Natural science
Birth control, 309, **338–339**

Dowry, 105, 314, 315
Drama, 78, **86–88**
Du Guesclin, Bertrand, 225
Duns Scotus, John, *412,* 413, 420–421
Dyes, 257

E

Eastern Church, 392–393
Eastern Europe, 41
Eckhart, Meister, 406, 422
Economics
    barter, 14
    children's work, 150
    Christianity and, 142
    church and artisans, 147–148
    coins, 148, 174, 180, 295
    commercial production, **144–148**
    commodities, 110
    craftsmen, 144–145, 146–148
    Crusades, 155
    currencies, 176
    determinism, 142–143
    feudalism, 142, **152–154,** 154–155, 156
    France and the Valois family, 179–180
    guilds, 141, 147, 152
    journeymen, 145
    land distribution, 140
    lending, 176
    lord-vassal relationship, 154
    marketing, 148–149
    markets, 174–175
    merchant contracts, 176
    merchant economy, 140–141
    methods of exchange, **146–148,** 174–176
    modes of existence, **154–156**
    money, 174, 295
    moneylenders, 148
    occupations and work habits, **148–152,**
      163–168, 176–178
    overview, **140–143**
    partnership in marriage, **316–317**
    patronage, 147
    political limitations, 141
    precious metals, 174
    prices, 147, 295–296
    profit, 178
    revenue raising, 154–155
    scutage, 155–156
    selling services, 147
    serfdom, 154
    social stratification and, 141–142
    trade, 141, 145, 146, **171–178**
    transactions, 141, 146–147
    urban economy, 153
    used-goods dealers, 296
    wages, 148, 150, 295–296
    wealth, 148, 173–174, 177
    women artisans, 150
    workday, 152
Education, **347–349**
    apprenticeship and, 170
    Augustine's contributions to, 387–388
    Carolingian reform, 63
    cathedral and monastic schools, 63
    cathedral schools, 287
    influence of Charlemagne on, 56–57

Latin, 113–114
liberal arts, **62–66**
medical schools, 467
memorization, 65–66
quadrivium, 56
scholasticism, 372, **419–420**
School of Chartres, 391–392
soldiers, 274
student life, 62, 65
translation, 63–64
travel and, 162–163
trivium, 56
universities, 64–65, 168, 371–372, 377,
    413–415
Edward III, 223–225
El Cid. See The Poem of El Cid
Elderly, 310, **352–353**
Eleanor of Aquitaine, **354–356**
Elements, 440
Embroidery, 269
England
    accusatory justice, 229
    Battle of Hastings, 234–235
    church-state conflict, 378–379
    common law, **212–213**
    expulsion of Jews from, 398
    Hundred Years' War, **223–227,** 237
    land division, 250–251
    manors, 251
    prisons, 230–231
    rulers, 221–222
    Tower of London, 230
    Viking attacks on, 237–238
    villages, 250–251
Erik the Red, **47,** 106
Eriksson, Leif, 47–48, 106
Eriugena, John Scottus, 389–390, **425–426**
Etiquette, 104, 270, 273
Eucharist, 104
Euclid, 445
Evil, **410–411**
Exchequer tallies, *178*
Exploration and colonization, **106–117**
    ibn Battuta, 107–108
    Erik the Red, **47,** 106
    Erikson, Leif, 47–48, 106
    Polo, Marco, **29–31,** 106–107, **132–133**
    Vikings, **43–46,** 47–48, 106, 239, 240

F

Fables, 75
Fairs, 175–176, 260, *298*
Falconry, *277*
Family, **338–353**
    affection, 345–346
    baptism, **342–343**
    childcare, 309
    elderly, 310, **352–353**
    familial love, 345
    family tree, *312*
    godparents, 343
    household structures, **310–311**
    illegitimate children, 337–338
    inheritance, **311–314,** 337–338
    lineage, **311–314**
    naming practices, 312

orphans and widows, 310
overview, **308–310**
stepchildren, **346**
surnames, 313–314
widows, **352–353**
    See also Kinship; Marriage
Famine, 249, 250
Farces, 88
Farming. *See* Agriculture
Fashion, 269
Festivals, **86–88, 260–261**
Feudalism
    characteristics of, 153
    defined, 152
    economics, 142, 154–155
    impact of, 140
    marriage and the, 309
    overview of society, **152–154,** 156
    towns, 167
Fire, **452**
Firearms, 465–466
Flatley Book, 48
Florence, 145
Flying buttresses, 457
Folktales, 75
Fontevrault monastery, 182–183
Food and diet
    banquets, 273
    burghers, 293
    controlling diet, 469
    gathering food, 254–255
    humors and, 466
    meals, 255–256, 284–285
    meat, 255, 271
    monasteries, 284
    nobility, 167, 270–272
    peasants, 159, **253–256**
    recipes, 273
    spices, 272
    storage and preservation of food, 255
    wine, 271
Foot soldiers, 126–128
Formularies, 68
Fornication, 337
Fortifications, 289–290
Four humors, 466
Fourth Lateran Council, 376, 383
France
    church-state conflict, 379
    Hundred Years' War, **223–227,** 237
    rulers, 221, 222
    Valois family, 179–180
Francis of Assisi, *381,* 383, **426–427**
Franciscan order, 34–35, 156, 165, 383, 426–427
Franks, 207
Frederick I (Barbarossa), *218,* 220, **241**
Free Spirit movement, 397
Furnishings, 264–265, 292, 461

G

Galen, 336, *414,* **466**
Gambling, 276
Gangs, 298
Gardening, 254–255
Gate of Glory, *60*
Gaunilo of Marmoutier, 391